encyclopedia of
GENOCIDE *and* CRIMES AGAINST HUMANITY

editorial board

encyclopedia of
GENOCIDE *and* CRIMES AGAINST HUMANITY

Dinah L. Shelton [EDITOR IN CHIEF]

[I-S] 2

MACMILLAN REFERENCE USA
An imprint of Thomson Gale, a part of The Thomson Corporation

THOMSON
✳
GALE

Detroit • New York • San Francisco • San Diego • New Haven, Conn. • Waterville, Maine • London • Munich

THOMSON

GALE

Encyclopedia of Genocide and Crimes Against Humanity
Dinah L. Shelton

<u>Library of Congress Cataloging-in-Publication Data</u>

Encyclopedia of genocide and crimes against humanity
Dinah L. Shelton, editor in chief.
    p. cm.
        Includes bibliographical references and index.
        ISBN 0-02-865847-7 (set hardcover : alk. paper)—
        ISBN 0-02-865848-5 (v. 1 : alk. paper)—ISBN 0-02-865849-3
        (v. 2 : alk. paper)—ISBN 0-02-865850-7 (v. 3 : alk. paper)—
        ISBN 0-02-865992-9 (ebook) 1. Genocide—History—
        Encyclopedias. I. Shelton, Dinah.
HV6322.7.E532 2004
304.66303—dc22   2004006587

This title is also available as an ebook.
ISBN 0-02-865992-9
Contact your Gale sales representative for ordering information.

Printed in the United States of America
10 9 8 7 6 5 4 3

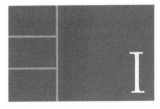

Identification

The defining feature of the crime of genocide is the deliberate destruction of a group. That the term *genocide* denotes group destruction is evident in the term itself: Sensing that no word captured the horror of Nazi atrocities, Polish attorney Raphael Lemkin coined the term from the ancient Greek *genos* (meaning race, nation, or tribe) and the Latin suffix *cide* (meaning "killing") (1947, p. 147). Article II of the 1948 United Nations (UN) Convention on the Prevention and Punishment of the Crime of Genocide (hereinafter referred to as the 1948 UN Genocide Convention) thus describes genocide as the commission of a specified act or acts "with intent to destroy, in whole or in part, a national, ethnical, racial, or religious group, as such." Murder motivated by hatred of one person, as opposed to hatred of the group of which the person is a member, does not comport with this definition. Nor does the deliberate starvation of others, unless the perpetrator deprives victims of food for the purpose of eradicating the group to which the victims belong. There is no doubt that an action perpetrated against an individual can be criminal—in some cases, a crime against humanity. But such an action could not be genocide, the offense often called "the crime of crimes."

The designation of genocide as the supreme crime recognizes the importance of human grouping. Much of human rights law focuses on the autonomy, security, and development of the individual; accordingly, many human rights norms are intended to protect the individual against mistreatment at the hands of those in positions of power. Yet even classical liberals, whose work has provided a philosophical basis for human rights law, consider an individual's assimilation into a society a step toward the realization of individual human dignity. Human beings group together because of shared ideas and interests, and to work for common goals. The intentional destruction of a group—the essence of genocide—warrants the most severe condemnation for the very reason that it thwarts these ends.

Some have argued that all, or perhaps many, human collectivities should be counted as among those groups protected by bans on genocide. The drafters of the 1948 UN Genocide Convention thought otherwise, extending protection only to national, ethnical, racial, and religious groups, and thus excluding other groups, such as political, cultural, or social groups.

Group membership implies a common identity, shared attributes, and a sharing of ideas or beliefs with others. Group members may be linked by a single commonality, such as an affinity for jazz piano, or a passion for the local football team. Groups susceptible to the possibility of genocidal aggression and protected by the ban on genocide typically share unique complexes of traits. *Identification* denotes the process by which one of these complexes of shared attributes—this identity—is recognized. Group nonmembers, as well as members, participate in this process of creating group identity. With regard to genocide, the phenomenon of identification provokes two lines of inquiry: Is it the victim or the perpetrator of genocide who identifies the victim as belonging to a group? Does the subjective understanding of either, or both, suffice to establish group membership? Ad hoc international tribunals established in the 1990s, set up to investigate violations of international criminal law, expressed ambivalence with regard to these questions.

In what was the first international judgment of conviction for the crime of genocide, the International Criminal Tribunal for Rwanda (ICTR) placed emphasis not on subjective perceptions but on objective factors. It thus interpreted the UN proscription against genocide to be applicable only to "'stable' groups, constituted in a permanent fashion," and to groups whose members belong to those groups "automatically, by birth, in a continuous and irremediable manner" (*Prosecutor v. Akayesu*, para. 511). This stable-and-permanent-group formula, as it came to be known, drew criticism. Many social scientists as well as biologists have in recent decades rejected claims that race is fixed and biologically determined; to the contrary, they have concluded that attributions of "race" derive from "social myth," formed in no small part by subjective perceptions (UNESCO Statement, 1950, p. 15). By the mid-1990s Professor Thomas K. Franck had posited a right of individuals "to compose their own identity by constructing the complex of loyalty references that best manifest *who they want to be*" (Franck, 1996, p. 383). Assignment of group status based on a search for constant and unchanging attributes clearly would run counter to this latter view of group identification as a dynamic process of social construction. The Rwanda tribunal's second decision thus underscored the subjective aspects of identity and group membership; in attempting to refine its concept of what constitutes a group, it wrote of "a group which distinguishes itself, as such (self-identification); or, a group identified as such by others, including perpetrators of the crimes (identification by others)" (*Prosecutor v. Kayishema*, para. 98). This new emphasis won praise as "a welcome shift that takes into account the mutable and contingent nature of social perceptions, and does not reinforce perilous claims to authenticity in the field of ethnic and racial identities" (Verdirame, 2000, p. 594).

The 1948 UN Genocide Convention's definition of genocide, it would seem, rested only on the perpetrator's subjective perception. The UN proscription against genocide arose of a desire not just to punish those who succeeded in destroying groups, but more fundamentally to prevent such destruction from occurring in the future. The convention thus prohibits acts executed with the intent to destroy, and permits conviction even if those acts failed to wreak permanent harm on a group. The definition speaks of a group not as an independent and objectively demonstrable element, but rather of one's subjective belief in the existence of a group as a component of the mens rea (the

guilty mind) that one must possess before one's crime qualifies as genocide. The text of the definition could be construed to mean that all that matters is the state of mind of the perpetrator; that is, that the element of the group is met as long as the perpetrator subjectively identified the victim as belonging to a group.

Wholly subjective determinations of group status could lead to absurd results, however. Surely there is a risk of overinclusion. Imagine a serial killer who, aiming to bring an end to the wearing of earrings, chose victims solely on the basis of whether they wore earrings. Earring-wearing could then be viewed as the shared attribute according to which the perpetrator subjectively grouped persons. To identify as composing a group persons who have never grouped themselves—who have never engaged in any of the joint human endeavors that the ban on genocide is supposed to shield—could result in a finding that genocide was "committed against a group that does not have any real objective existence" (Schabas, 2000, p. 110). Conversely, there is also a risk of underinclusion. Imagine a defendant who professed to be unaware of victims' group membership, who maintained that any such membership was coincidental to any violence that might have occurred. If all that mattered were the perpetrator's state of mind, this kind of testimony alone might lead to acquittal, even in the face of objective evidence that victims belonged to an identifiable and protected group. Decision on whether a defendant possessed the requisite malevolent intent, therefore, must entail an examination of more than just the defendant's own perceptions.

Evidence that relates to the subjective understandings of persons who identify with a group is thus key to the resolution of a victim's group status. As in the case of the perpetrator's perceptions, however, this criterion of victim perception ought not to provide the exclusive basis for identification. During the first fifty years that followed World War II, in the absence of any treaty that defined crimes against humanity, groups that had been the objects of certain kinds of violence endeavored to have their sufferings recognized as the aftereffects of genocide; even into the twenty-first century, conventional wisdom reserves its harshest condemnation for persons labeled *génocidaires*. But a desire to establish that victims belonged to a group protected by bans on genocide, and thus that their sufferings constituted a byproduct of genocide, could distort testimony regarding commonalities. In contrast with this risk of overinclusion, there is, again, a risk of underinclusion. Victims unaware that they were targeted because the perpetrator believed that they belonged to a group—victims who may not, in fact, have belonged to any such group—would be unable to establish that they suffered harm on account of the perpetrator's group loathing.

Early tribunal judgments were not oblivious to these concerns; even those that emphasized one type of evidence gave at least passing attention to other types. Group status in the twenty-first century is determined by the comprehensive examination of a particular context. Considerable weight is placed on subjective perceptions. The defendant's understanding, manifested both by the defendant's testimony at trial and by things the defendant has written or told others, receives careful scrutiny. Also receiving careful scrutiny is testimony that victims saw themselves as belonging to a group, or that other group members claimed a victim as one of their own. Contextual inquiry likewise looks to objective indicators. The Rwanda tribunal, for example, recognized Tutsi as a group, in no small part because of the evidence adduced regarding identity cards that the Rwandan government had issued, cards that perpetrators used to confirm cardholders' ethnicity, as a means to select whom to victimize (*Prosecutor v. Akayesu*, paras. 83, 122–123, 170, 702; *Prosecutor v. Kayishema*, paras. 523–526). Similarly, the International Criminal Tribunal for the Former Yugoslavia, even as it refused to look for "scientifically irreproachable criteria," found objective evidence of victims' group status in the Yugoslav Constitution's description of Bosnian Muslims as a "nation" (*Prosecutor v. Krstic*, paras. 70, 559). Both tribunals relied on expert sociohistorical testimony to bolster their conclusions. In short, a combination of case-specific factors—subjective and objective evidence, evidence of self-identification and of other-identification—is relevant to resolution of whether a victim was identified as belonging to a group protected against genocide.

SEE ALSO Ethnic Groups; Racial Groups; Religious Groups

BIBLIOGRAPHY

Amann, Diane Marie (2002). "Group Mentality, Expressivism, and Genocide." *International Criminal Law Review* 2:93–143.

Franck, Thomas M. (1996). "Clan and Superclan: Loyalty, Identity and Community in Law and Practice." *American Journal of International Law* 90:359–383.

Lemkin, Raphael (1947). "Genocide as a Crime under International Law." *American Journal of International Law* 41:145–151.

Prosecutor v. Akayesu. Case No. ICTR-96-4 (September 2, 1998). Trial Chamber I, Judgment, International Criminal Tribunal for Rwanda. Available from http://www.ictr.org.

Prosecutor v. Kayishema. Case No. ICTR-95-1-T (May 21, 1999). Trial Chamber II, Judgment, International Criminal Tribunal for Rwanda. Available from http://www.ictr.org.

Prosecutor v. Krstic. Case No. IT-98-33 (August 2, 2001). Trial Chamber I, Judgment, International Criminal Tribunal for the Former Yugoslavia. Available from http://www.un.org/icty.

Schabas, William A. (2000). *Genocide in International Law: The Crime of Crimes*. Cambridge: Cambridge University Press.

"UNESCO Statement by Experts on Race Problems" (July 18, 1950). In *Statement on Race*, ed. Ashley Montagu. New York: Henry Schuman, 1951.

United Nations (December 9, 1948). Convention on the Prevention and Punishment of the Crime of Genocide. Entered into force January 12, 1951; 78 U.N.T.S.277.

Verdirame, Guglielmo (2000). "The Genocide Definition in the Jurisprudence of the Ad Hoc Tribunals." *International and Comparative Law Quarterly* 49:578–598.

Diane Marie Amann

Immunity

As a general rule of international law, states, some holders of high-ranking office in a state (such as heads of state or heads of government), and diplomatic and consular agents enjoy immunity from civil suits and criminal prosecutions inaugurated in other states (but not those inaugurated in international courts and tribunals). Many treaties, such as the Vienna Convention on Diplomatic Relations (April 18, 1961), the Vienna Convention on Consular Relations (April 24, 1963), and the New York Convention on Special Missions (December 8, 1969), guarantee this immunity. Immunities are meant to allow states and their representatives to engage in international relations as equal and independent entities. Thus, no state can be subject to legal proceedings in another state, as it would imply statuses of inferiority and superiority, or the subordination of one state to another.

A distinction is generally made between functional and personal immunities. Functional immunities cover the activities of any state official carried out in his official capacity—such as issuing passports or negotiating treaties. These activities are attributable to the state, and the individual cannot be held accountable for them, even after he leaves office. Personal immunities attach to the particular status of the holder of these immunities, such as the head of a diplomatic mission. They cover all activities carried out by the holder, but cease to apply when that particular status is concluded (with the exception, obviously, of activities covered by functional immunities).

Recent developments, in particular the establishment of international criminal tribunals and their statutory provisions on immunities, as well as the occurrence of national proceedings against incumbent or former dignitaries, have raised questions about the scope of these traditional immunities. In particular, the applicability of the principle of immunity in the case of genocide, crimes against humanity, or war crimes has been seriously questioned. Some questions have been answered, other have not.

Genocide and Crimes Against Humanity

Article IV of the United Nations (UN) Convention on the Prevention and Punishment of the Crime of Genocide (1948) states: "Persons committing genocide . . . shall be punished, whether they are constitutionally responsible rulers, public officials, or private individuals." Article 7 of the International Law Commission's (ILC's) Draft Code of Crimes Against the Peace and Security of Mankind (1996) states: "The official position of an individual who commits a crime against the peace and security of mankind, even if he acted as head of State or Government, does not relieve him of criminal responsibility or mitigate punishment." These and other authoritative sources clearly indicate that individuals committing crimes against humanity or acts of genocide are individually responsible for them. Even heads of State, when they commit, authorize, attempt, incite, or conspire to commit acts of genocide or crimes against humanity, are personally liable for their actions, their official positions notwithstanding.

But immunity from prosecution is distinct from legal obligation to obey the law, and legal responsibility and immunity are not necessarily irreconcilable. The first question therefore is whether a temporary, procedural bar of immunity applies in the case of international crimes. In its commentary on the abovementioned Draft Code, the ILC stated that Article 7 also aims to prevent an individual from invoking an official position as a circumstance conferring immunity on him, even if that individual claims that the acts constituting the crime were performed in the exercise of his functions.

Second, even if, in principle, the responsibility of dignitaries is accepted, it must be determined which jurisdiction or jurisdictions can prosecute a state or its representative. A judgment of the International Court of Justice (ICJ) of February 14, 2002 (pertaining to *Democratic Republic of the Congo (DRC) v. Belgium*, whereby the DRC launched proceedings against Belgium for issuing an arrest warrant against the DRC's acting minister for foreign affairs, Abdoulaye Yerodia Ndombasi (Mr. Yerodia), for alleged crimes constituting violations of international humanitarian law), distinguishes between international courts and the national jurisdictions of other states.

International Courts

The statutes of the Nuremberg and the Tokyo tribunals that were created in the aftermath of World War II both contained provisions stating that official immunities could not bar prosecution for genocide-related and other crimes in international courts. In its Principles of International Law Recognized in the Charter of the Nuremberg Tribunal and in the Judgment of the Tribunal (the so-called "Nuremberg Principles" of 1950), the ILC stated: "The fact that a person who committed an act which constitutes a crime under international law acted as Head of State or responsible Government official does not relieve him from responsibility under international law" (Principle III). The statutes of the International Criminal Tribunal for the former Yugoslavia (1993), the International Criminal Tribunal for Rwanda (1994), as well as the Special Court for Sierra Leone (2000), contain similar provisions.

The wording in Article 27 of the Rome Statute of the International Criminal Court (ICC, 1998) is even more precise (in rejecting the principle of selective immunity), as it clearly distinguishes between criminal responsibility and immunities, and covers both functional and personal immunities:

> 1. This Statute shall apply equally to all persons without any distinction based on official capacity. In particular, official capacity as a Head of State or Government, a member of a Government or parliament, [or] an elected representative or a government official shall in no case exempt a person from criminal responsibility under this Statute, nor shall it, in and of itself, constitute a ground for reduction of sentence. 2. Immunities or special procedure rules which may attach to the official capacity of a person, whether under national or international law, shall not bar the Court from exercising its jurisdiction over such a person.

One may conclude that there is a *lex specialis*, under customary international law, to the effect that, when charged with the offense of genocide, crimes against humanity, or war crimes by an international jurisdiction, no state official is entitled to functional or personal immunities.

For states parties to the ICC statute—as of early 2004, ninety-two states have ratified or acceded to this statute—Article 27 also has an important effect on national immunities law, even that which is established by constitutional law. Read in conjunction with Article 88 (specifically, that "States Parties shall ensure that there are procedures available under their national law for all of the forms of cooperation which are specified under this Part"), Article 27 imposes an obligation on the states parties to amend national legislation, even constitutionally protected immunities of the head of state, in order to be in a position to comply with ICC orders for arrest or surrender.

In its judgment of February 14, 2002 (*Democratic Republic of the Congo v. Belgium*), the ICJ confirmed the annulment of some immunities before international courts. The court specifically mentions "criminal proceedings before certain international criminal courts, where they have jurisdiction" as one of the circumstances in which the immunity enjoyed under international law by an incumbent or former minister of foreign affairs does not represent a bar to criminal prosecution.

National Jurisdictions

One reading of the ICC statute, favored by Amnesty International and other members of the international coalition of nongovernmental organizations (NGOs) committed to achieving full support for the ICC, holds that the rejection of official immunities with respect to acts of genocide, crimes against humanity, and war crimes applies also to proceedings before national jurisdictions. This is considered to be a consequence of the principle of complementarity that is laid down in the ICC statute (in essence, that the primary role for prosecuting these international crimes remains at the national level), and of the absence of a separate provision in the statute on immunity before national courts.

National proceedings against former Chilean President Augustus Pinochet have also been cited as evidence of the emergence of a new rule of international law denying immunity. Pinochet was arrested in London, on the basis of two arrest warrants issued by U.K. magistrates at the request of Spanish courts for Pinochet's alleged responsibility for the murder of Spanish citizens in Chile, and for conspiracy to commit acts of torture, the taking of hostages, and murder. The alleged crimes were committed while Pinochet held office in Chile as head of state. In its judgment of March 24, 1999, the English House of Lords, which is in effect the country's Supreme Court, held that Pinochet was not entitled to immunity for acts of torture and conspiracy to commit torture, insofar as these acts were committed after the United Kingdom's ratification of the UN Convention Against Torture and Other Cruel, Inhuman or Degrading Treatment or Punishment (1984). As a result, extradition proceedings were allowed to continue. The judgment was welcomed by the international human rights movement as a great step in the international fight against impunity. However, the precedent value of this judgment is subject to various interpretations. The judgment did not cover the issue of personal immunities of incumbent heads of state. Some judges

Former Chilean dictator Augusto Pinochet under house arrest in London, January 16, 1999. National proceedings against Pinochet were cited as evidence of the emergence of a new rule of international law denying individuals immunity for certain crimes. [AP/WIDE WORLD PHOTOS]

expressed the opinion that if Pinochet had still been holding office at the time of his arrest, he would have been entitled to personal immunities and thus protected against arrest and extradition proceedings.

In the abovementioned *Democratic Republic of the Congo v. Belgium* (February 14, 2002), the ICJ ruled, in a thirteen-to-three vote, that the issuance and circulation of the arrest warrant by the Belgian investigating judge against the minister of foreign affairs of the DRC violated international law. The court found that, after a careful examination of state practice, it had been unable to find "any form of exception to the rule according immunity from criminal jurisdiction and inviolability to incumbent ministers for foreign affairs, where they are suspected of having committed war crimes or crimes against humanity." The court also noted that immunities could be invoked in national courts of a foreign state, even when those courts exercise jurisdiction under treaties that deal with the prevention and punishment of certain serious international crimes. The court added that although jurisdictional immunity may bar prosecution for a certain period of time, it does not exonerate the person to whom it applies from criminal responsibility. Emphasizing that immunity does not amount to impunity, the ICJ identified four circumstances under which immunities do not bar criminal prosecution. In the specific context of crimes against humanity, the first two circumstances (criminal prosecution before the domestic legal system or the existence of a waiver of immunity) are highly theoretical. In addition to the abovementioned circumstance of criminal proceedings before certain international criminal courts, the court also referred to the legal standing of former ministers foreign affairs: "[A]fter a person ceases to hold the office of Minister for Foreign Affairs . . . a court of one State may try a former Minister for Foreign Affairs of another State in respect of acts committed prior or subsequent to his or her period of office, as well as in respect of acts committed during that period of office in a private capacity."

Questions That Remain
Despite the illuminations of the ICJ judgment in *Democratic Republic of the Congo v. Belgium*, several issues remain unclear.

First, it is unclear as to which dignitaries enjoy immunity. The court spoke of the immunities that belong to (but not only to) "certain holders of high-ranking office in a State, such as the Head of State, Head of Government, and Minister for Foreign Affairs." In the ICJ judgment, there is no indication as to whether the same immunities apply to, for instance, a minister of defense, or of education, a state secretary of development cooperation, or a senator-for-life charged with international relations. International comity may require analogous treatment of some other dignitaries, but comity is no source of customary law and analogy is a poor basis on which to build legal rules.

Second, the nature and scope of "acts committed in a private capacity" are undetermined. The court seems to be suggesting—without elaboration or specification—that serious international crimes can be committed either in a private capacity or in an official capacity. The postulation of such a distinction is deplorable, and seems untenable within the specific context of international crimes. It would have been preferable for the court to add, as did several judges in a joint separate opinion and as did several members of the House of Lords in deciding the Pinochet case, that serious international crimes can never be regarded as acts committed in an official capacity because they are neither normal state functions nor functions that a state alone (in contrast to an individual) can perform.

Third, it is not clear what type of activities violate the immunities in question. In *Democratic Republic of the Congo v. Belgium*, the ICJ found that the issuance of an arrest warrant and its international circulation "significantly interfered with Mr. Yerodia's diplomatic

activity," and as a result affected the DRC's international relations. In light of the rationale of the immunities, one might agree with those judges who found, to the contrary, that the mere launching of criminal investigations—which may include the hearing of witnesses—does not necessarily negatively affect the carrying out of of a state's international relations and, therefore, does not in itself violate international law on immunities.

Fourth, the ICJ judgment does not address the issue of how this immunities regime applies in the case of criminal prosecutions before criminal tribunals that are located in between the national and international legal orders, such as the Special Court for Sierra Leone.

Finally, the ICJ judgment addresses the immunity of state representatives who have had criminal proceedings brought against them. It does not address the immunity of a state in the instance of civil actions filed against it and its representatives for monetary damages. In the case of *Al-Adsani v. the United Kingdom* (November 21, 2001), heard before the European Court of Human Rights, a Kuwaiti applicant, the victim of acts of torture in Kuwait, was denied the right to initiate civil compensation proceedings against Kuwait before a UK court on the basis of the UK's domestic State Immunity Act. With a majority vote of nine-to-eight, the court found no violation of Article 6, Section 1 (declaring the right of access to court) of the European Convention on Human Rights. The court argued as follows: "Notwithstanding the special character of the prohibition of torture in international law, the Court is unable to discern . . . any firm basis for concluding that, as a matter of international law, a State no longer enjoys immunity from civil suits in the courts of another State where acts of torture are alleged." The eight dissenting judges expressed the view that the prohibition of torture, as a peremptory rule of international law, should prevail over State immunity rules, which do not have the same peremptory character. In their view, the United Kingdom should have allowed the applicant to initiate a civil action against Kuwait.

SEE ALSO Amnesty; Convention on the Prevention and Punishment of Genocide; Conventions Against Torture and Other Cruel, Inhuman and Degrading Treatment; International Court of Justice; International Criminal Court; Pinochet, Augusto; Prosecution; Sierra Leone Special Court; War Crimes

BIBLIOGRAPHY
Bianchi, Andrea (1999). "Immunity versus Human Rights: The *Pinochet* Case." *European Journal of International Law* 10:237–278.

Bröhmer, Jürgen (1997). *State Immunity and the Violation of Human Rights*. The Hague: Nijhoff Publishers.

Bröhmer, Jürgen (2000). "Immunity of a Former Head of State. General Pinochet and the House of Lords: Part Three." *Leiden Journal of International Law* 13:229–238.

Cassese, Antonio (2002). "When May Senior State Officials Be Tried for International Crimes? Some Comments on *The Congo v. Belgium* Case." *European Journal of International Law* 13:853–876.

De Hoogh, Andreas (1996). *Obligations* Erga Omnes *and International Crimes: A Theoretical Inquiry into the Implementation and Enforcement of the International Responsibility of States*. The Hague: Kluwer Law International.

Denza, Eileen (1998). *Diplomatic Law. A Commentary on the Vienna Convention on Diplomatic Relations*, 2nd edition. Oxford, U.K.: Clarendon Press.

Fox, Hazel (2002). *The Law of State Immunity*. Oxford, U.K.: Oxford University Press.

Karagiannakis, Magdalini (1998). "State Immunity and Fundamental Human Rights." *Leiden Journal of International Law* 11:9–43.

Romano, Cesare P. R., and Andre Nollkaemper. "The Arrest Warrant against the Liberian President Charles Taylor." American Society of International Law. Available from http://www.asil.org/insights/insigh110.htm.

Zappala, Salvatore (2001). "Do Heads of State in Office Enjoy Immunity from Jurisdiction for International Crimes? The Ghaddafi Case before the French *Cour de Cassation*." *European Journal of International Law* 12:595–612.

Marc Bossuyt
Stef Vandeginste

Impunity

Generally speaking, *impunity* refers to an offender escaping punishment for an offense that involves a particular form of harm inflicted on an offended party. Such an outcome often is due to the same conditions contributing to the offensive act in the first place. A favorable vantage ground enables a perpetrator not only to commit an offense but also to elude punishment. The related vulnerability of the victim is part of the same equation. However, when transposing this portrayal to the level of intergroup conflicts capable of culminating in crimes against humanity and genocide, a paradigm of impunity becomes discernible. The relationship of the favorable vantage ground of the offender to the vulnerability of the victim yields the principle of disparity in power relations. Within this framework, the offender, seen as relying on his power advantage, seeks and often attains impunity through the artful exercise of power politics. The methods used may include an assortment of tactics of outright denial, blame transfer, trade-offs

through deal-making, intimidation, suppression of evidence, manipulative persuasion, and manipulative dissuasion. Closely related to this practice is the incidence of a culture of general indifference to the offenses at issue that is sustained by growing multitudes of bystanders. Impunity is, accordingly, seen here as intimately connected with the phenomenon of inaction that is being indulged in face of and in the wake of crimes against humanity and genocide. Accordingly, two areas emerge as of paramount importance for the understanding of the consequences of such impunity.

In the area of social psychology these consequences are related first of all to the lingering plight of the victim population and over time to their progeny. At issue is not only the matter of denial of justice that impunity implies, but also problems of residual collective trauma, frustration, bitterness, and even a pathos for revenge. Equally important, however, are the social and psychological effects of impunity bearing on the perpetrator group and those identified with it. Free from the claws of punitive justice and/or the onus of general public condemnation, these people tend to become sufficiently emboldened to twist the facts by redefining at will their offenses. Accordingly, the offenses are suppressed by a variety of methods, rationalized, minimized, or dismissed altogether. The resulting denial complex in extreme cases may also include rebutting the right of others either to question the denial or to condemn it. Inherent in this frame of mind is the tendency to perpetrate in the future similar and perhaps even more grave offenses involving genocidal violence.

The most severe consequences implicit in impunity in this respect are likely to materialize, however, when inaction incrementally becomes part of a political culture in certain areas of international relations and therefore becomes predictable. Historically speaking, this practice of predictable inaction often served as a signal for permissiveness in default. The Sultan Abdul Hamit–era Armenian massacres in the period from 1894 to 1896, their sequel, the 1909 Adana massacre, and the progressive escalation of the tempo and scope of these episodic massacres that culminated in the World War I Armenian genocide epitomize this fundamental fact. Devoid of requisite inhibitions and lacking a weighty sense of remorse, successive Ottoman governments, armed with a legacy of impunity, proceeded to decimate and ultimately destroy the bulk of their subject Armenian population.

Still, acts of genocide rarely manage to eradicate completely the targeted victim group. More often than not the survivors and their progeny remain hostage to the post-genocide incubus of haunting images and memories. The persistent tensions and animosities obtaining between Armenians and Turks, for example, remain fertile soil for the eruption of new cataclysms. Such a possibility is due to the negative reward of impunity accruing to the perpetrators of the Armenian genocide and indirectly to their heirs identified with modern Turkey.

The mitigation, if not elimination altogether, of the problem of impunity through the initiation of institutional remedies involving legal-criminal procedures is therefore of utmost relevance. Of particular concern in this respect are the matters of prevention and punishment of crimes against humanity and of genocide. Impunity as a factor can be reduced to irrelevance when a culture of punishment becomes established and its successful practice functions as a deterrent, thereby paving the ground for prevention. Institutionalized retributive justice is seen here as a principal instrument of remedy against impunity. Yet existing systems of such justice in the past have been handicapped by a whole gamut of problematic subsidiary instruments.

Notable in this respect is the lack of appropriate legislation establishing codes relative to crimes against humanity and genocide; an international criminal court competent to deal with these offenses and administer appropriate justice; operative connectedness between international laws as embedded in certain treaties, and national municipal laws.

These and other inadequacies were cast in stark relief in a series of post–World War I criminal proceedings launched against a whole series of Turkish and German offenders charged with offenses akin to crimes against humanity and genocide. As a result, the national (or domestic) criminal trials in Istanbul (1919–1921) and Leipzig (1921–1922), initiated under the pressure of the victorious Allies bearing down on defeated Turkey and Germany, proved nearly total fiascos. Moreover, rejecting the legal grounds of competence of the courts involved, Holland and Germany refused to extradite Kaiser Wilhelm II and Talaat, respectively, the latter being the architect of the Armenian genocide. The general atmosphere surrounding these legal undertakings became even more clouded when many defendants sought impunity by invoking the principle of immunity. Specifically put forth in this respect were such claims of defense as act of state, superior orders, and sovereign immunity.

Following World War II, these and other technical impediments were gradually cast away through a series of criminal proceedings against offenders charged with not only aggression and war crimes but, above all, crimes against humanity and genocide. By enunciating the Nuremburg doctrine, the Nuremberg International Military Tribunal pioneered in this respect. Its Article

6c codified the new legal precept of "crimes against humanity," which included the companion legal precept of "genocide." This was achieved by adopting and incorporating the May 24, 1915 declaration of the Allies who, for the first time, publicly and formally enunciated that principle of "crimes against humanity" in warning the Ottoman-Turkish authorities in connection with the then unfolding Armenian genocide that after the war they would be prosecuted and punished. The subsequent promulgation of the 1948 UN Genocide Convention further codified these twin legal norms in a new body of international law. Pursuant to this convention, two ad hoc tribunals were instituted to deal with new crimes encompassing, in different combinations, genocide, aggression, war crimes, and crimes against humanity: the ICTY (International Criminal Tribunal for the Former Yugoslavia), in July 1994, and the ICTR (International Criminal Tribunal for Rwanda), in December 1994.

The inauguration in July to October of 1998 of the ICC (International Criminal Court) in Rome marks the apogee of this series of legal endeavors to substitute an international system of retributive justice for the pernicious practice of impunity. When defining crimes against humanity in Article 7, for example, the framers of the statutes of this new court deliberately provided a broad scope for interpreting such crimes. They thereby discarded two major defects in the body both of the Nuremberg Charter and of the UN Convention on Genocide. These defects involved (1) limiting the victim civilian population only to "national, ethnical, or religious" groups; and (2) insisting on the presence of genocidal "intent" in the motivation of perpetrators of genocide. However, the ICC is binding only for those nation-states that are signatories to the international treaty the ICC statutes represent. As of April 2004, 139 states had signed the treaty and there were 92 ratifications. Because only 60 ratifications were required, the treaty came into force as of July 1, 2002.

Unless administered with consistency and optimal results, no criminal justice system, whether domestic or international, can be considered meaningful and functional. Given the vagaries incident to international relations and the sway of a culture of political expediency in the handling of post-conflict situations, there is no certainty that an international criminal court armed with the best available criminal statutes can under all circumstances militate against impunity and deliver appropriate justice. The treatment of the Armenian case in Lausanne in 1923 is illustrative. Through a provision of general amnesty embedded in the respective peace treaty, the first major genocide of the twentieth century was nonchalantly consigned to oblivion.

This was repeated with the amnesty the Truth and Reconciliation Commission in South Africa accorded to "politically motivated" perpetrators in exchange for their willingness to provide "truthful" testimony. It appears that the intrusion of expedient politics in the administration of retributive justice will remain an abiding factor impeding the enforcement mechanisms and thereby handicapping the quest for predictable justice.

SEE ALSO Perpetrators

BIBLIOGRAPHY

Bassiouni, M. Cherif (1997). "From Versailles to Rwanda in Seventy-Five Years: The Need to Establish a Permanent International Criminal Court." *Harvard Human Rights Journal* 10:11–56.

Bassiouni, M. Cherif (1999). *Crimes against Humanity in International Criminal Law*, 2nd revised edition. Boston: Kluwer Law International.

Bassiouni, M. Cherif (2002). *Post-Conflict Justice*. Ardsley, N.Y.: Transnational.

Beigbeder, Yves (2002). *Judging Criminal Leaders: The Slow Erosion of Impunity*. The Hague: Nijhoff.

Burke-White, William W. (2001). "Reframing Impunity: Applying Liberal International Law Theory to an Analysis of Amnesty Legislation." *Harvard International Law Journal* 42:467–533.

The Crowley Program (1999). "Justice on Trial: State Security Courts, Police Impunity, and the Intimidation of Human Rights Defenders of Turkey." *Fordham International Law Journal* 22:2129–2269.

Dadrian, Vahakn, N. (1997). "The Turkish Military Tribunal's Prosecution of the Authors of the Armenian Genocide: Four Major Court-Martial Series." *Holocaust and Genocide Studies* 11:28–59.

Dadrian, Vahakn, N. (1998). "The Historical and Legal Interconnections Between the Armenian Genocide and the Jewish Holocaust: From Impunity to Retributive Justice." *Yale Journal of International Law* 23:503–559.

Dadrian, Vahakn, N. (2003). *History of the Armenian Genocide: Ethnic Conflict from the Balkans to Anatolia to the Caucasus*, 6th revised edition. New York: Berghahn.

Griffin, Mary (2000). "Ending the Impunity of Perpetrators of Human Rights Atrocities: A Major Challenge for International Law in the 21st Century." *International Review of the Red Cross* 82:369–389.

Grigorian, Meher (2003). *The Role of Impunity in Genocide: An Analysis of War Crimes Trials within the Context of International Criminal Law*, ed. C. Tatz. Blackheath, Australia: Brandl and Schlesinger.

McGoldrick, Dominic (1999). "The Permanent International Criminal Court: An End to the Culture of Impunity?" *Criminal Law Review* (August):627–655.

Roht-Arriaza, Naomi (1995). *Impunity and Human Rights in International Law and Practice*. Oxford: Oxford University Press.

Schabas, William A. (2002). *Genocide and International Law* New York: Cambridge University Press.

Sears, Jill M. (2000). "Confronting the 'Culture of Impunity': Immunity of Heads of State from Nuremberg to ex parte Pinochet." *German Yearbook of International Law* 42:125–146.

Vahakn N. Dadrian

Incas

The Incas emerged as a distinct group near present-day Cuzco in approximately 1200 CE. Although their expansion did not begin until 1438 under Pachacuti Inca, by the time the Spanish arrived about 1532 their empire, known as Tawantinsuyu, or the Land of the Four Quarters, extended from Northern Ecuador to Central Chile, a distance of some 3,500 kilometers.

The Incas emerged from conflicts between a number of competing polities in southern Peru and Bolivia. Military success, particularly against the Chanca, helped the Incas to believe that they were under the protection of the sun god, Inti, of whom the emperor was an earthly manifestation. As such, the Incas considered they were on a divine mission to bring civilization to those they conquered. Their expansion was also driven by the development of the royal mummy cult, according to which the lands owned by a dead emperor were needed to support his cult, thereby forcing the new emperor to acquire new lands for himself.

Inca expansion was brought about by military campaigns. Where possible, the Inca used diplomacy by offering gifts to native lords in return for submission to Inca rule. The vast Inca armies, which might have numbered tens of thousands of soldiers, probably intimidated many groups into submission, but others fiercely resisted. This resistance resulted in considerable loss of life. Successful campaigns were concluded by triumphal marches in Cuzco, where the army displayed its trophies and prisoners of war, and subsequently received gifts of gold, cloth, land, or women. Important defeated leaders were executed and their skulls made into trophy cups, and soldiers often used the bones of the enemy for flutes or made the skins of flayed prisoners into drums. Little punishment was exacted on subjugated societies as a whole, except where resistance was fierce or they subsequently rebelled, in which case Inca reprisals were swift and harsh. It has been estimated that between 20,000 and 50,000 and Cayambe and Caranqui were massacred at Yaguarcocha, in northern Ecuador, in revenge for their resistance. To ensure the subjugation of conquered peoples, the Incas established garrisons and undertook massive resettlement schemes that involved the transfer of rebellious groups nearer to the Inca heartland. To further this end, loyal subjects were also moved to regions where Inca control was more tenuous.

Pre-Columbian ruins at Machu Picchu, the center of Inca culture set high in the Andes Mountains of Peru. When the ruins were discovered in 1911, anthropologists found evidence of winding roads, irrigation systems, agricultural storehouses, and landscaped terraces. [ROYALTY FREE/CORBIS]

The emperor or other high-ranking nobles led Inca military campaigns. The professional army comprised the emperor's bodyguard of several thousand soldiers and captains drawn from among the Inca nobility. For military campaigns, local leaders mustered soldiers through a rotational system of labor service called the *mit'a*. Military training began at an early age, and all able-bodied males were required to do military service. Led by their native rulers, these groups of soldiers would link up with campaign armies as they passed through their territories. In this way, armies of tens of thousands of soldiers, and on occasion, in excess of 200,000, were mustered. Storehouses and lodgings strategically placed along the Inca highways facilitated the movement of troops.

Spanish conquest of the Inca Empire was relatively swift, although the last Inca ruler, Tupac Amaru I, was not executed until 1572. The Spanish possessed certain military advantages over the Incas. The Incas knew how to produce bronze, but did not make widespread use of it for weapons, which were largely made of stone. These included stone tipped spears, bows and arrows, clubs, and slings. The Inca also used stone boulders to

ambush enemies in narrow passes. Inca stone weapons made little impression on Spanish steel armor, while their own cotton quilted armor and shields of hide or wood provided little protection against Spanish steel swords. Although the Spanish possessed harquebuses and sometimes cannon, these were unwieldy and only accurate over short distances. More critical were horses, both for the terror they inspired among the Inca, who had never before seen them, and for their speed and maneuverability. They were considered to be worth one hundred men in battle, and they could be used effectively on the Inca highways, facilitating the rapid movement of troops, supplies, and information.

Inca military strategy also proved to have limitations in conflicts with Spaniards. Inca strategy was carefully thought out and was imbued with symbolism and ritual. Hence, Inca attacks were often conducted at the full moon and, in respect for the lunar deity, fighting ceased at the new moon. The Incas were therefore unprepared for Spanish attacks that appeared to follow no ritualized pattern. The Spanish often used surprise tactics effectively, for example, in the capture of the Inca leader Atahualpa at Cajamarca in 1533. Nevertheless the Incas were quick to adapt to the new external threat and often used local geographical knowledge to mount ambushes or to lure the enemy to terrain that was not suitable for the deployment of horses or for open battle, which was favored by the Spanish.

Even though the Spanish may have possessed certain military advantages, most scholars believe that conquest was greatly facilitated by epidemic disease and political conflicts within the Inca Empire that weakened native resistance. In 1525, smallpox arrived in the Andes ahead of the Spanish, probably through native trade networks. This resulted in high mortality, because the Incas lacked immunity to Old World diseases. It was also the cause of the death of the Inca emperor Huayna Capac, which precipitated a dynastic war between his sons, Huascar and Atahualpa. This war was raging when the Spanish arrived.

Spanish rule brought major transformations to native economies and societies. The Spanish sought wealth, primarily from mining gold and silver, and they attempted to convert native Andeans to Christianity. During this process they congregated the Indians into new towns, subjected them to tribute and forced labor, and usurped their lands. Due to epidemic disease, conquest, and changes to native societies, by 1620 the population of Peru alone had fallen from approximately 9 million in 1532 to only about 670,000.

Some people argue that even without the Spanish arrival, the Inca Empire would have collapsed. Its continued expansion depended on a supply of gifts to satisfy subjugated lords and reward those who had taken part in military campaigns. The burden of supplying goods and soldiers increasingly undermined native production and the power of native lords, straining their loyalty to the Inca cause. Indeed, some local groups even became Spanish allies. When the Spanish arrived, the Inca Empire had clearly become overextended.

SEE ALSO Indigenous Peoples; Peru

BIBLIOGRAPHY

D'Altroy, Terence N. (2002) *The Incas*. Oxford: Blackwell Publishers.

Guilmartin, John F., Jr. (1991) "The Cutting Edge: An Analysis of the Spanish Invasion and Overthrow of the Inca Empire, 1532–1539." In *Transatlantic Encounters: Europeans and Andeans in the Sixteenth Century*, ed. Kenneth J. Andrien and Rolena Adorno. Berkeley: University of California Press.

Kendall, Ann (1973) *Everyday Life of the Incas*. New York: Dorset Press.

Rostworowski, María, and Craig Morris (1999). "The Fourfold Domain: Inka Power and Its Social Foundations." In *The Cambridge History of Native Peoples*. Vol. III: *South America*, ed. Frank Salomon and Stuart B. Schwartz. Cambridge: Cambridge University Press.

In July 1533 Francisco Pizarro ordered his Spanish Conquistadors to execute Atahualpa, the last independent Inca king in Peru. Engraving by Alonzo Chappel, eighteenth-century American artist. [BETTMANN/CORBIS]

Linda A. Newson

Incitement

Incitement to commit an offense is an attempt to persuade another person, by whatever means, to commit an offense. There are many ways of doing this. Both rewards and punishments can provide the incentive to commit crimes. Someone can offer a reward for committing genocide, or they can try to blackmail a person. Incitement can be achieved by threats. A person can also try to get others to commit an offense by the use of argument and rhetoric. "Rabble rousing" is a common method of used to convince large groups of people act to in a particular way. Inflammatory speeches in political rallies have been used to prepare the way for genocide, or to whip crowds into states of frenzy in which killings may easily occur. The drafters of the genocide convention knew this all too well, and therefore included incitement to commit genocide as a listed crime in the 1948 Convention.

The Nature of the Crime of Incitement
Direct and public incitement to commit genocide is criminalized in Article III(c) of the 1948 Genocide Convention. A provision akin to Article III(c) can be found in the Rome Statute of the International Criminal Court (Article 25(3)(e)). Incitement is one of a limited group of crimes related to genocide (the others are attempts at genocide and conspiracy to commit genocide) which do not require the commission of one of the genocidal acts set out in Article II of the 1948 Genocide Convention. Incitement, attempt and conspiracy are crimes in themselves. As none of these offenses require an act of genocide to be committed, they are referred to as inchoate (incomplete) crimes. Their incompleteness does not change the fact that they are criminal, as is clear from Article III of the 1948 Convention. However, incitements to commit crimes against humanity or war crimes are not internationally criminal unless they actually lead to the commission of those crimes.

The difference between incitement that does not lead to genocide (or is not proved to have done so) and encouragement that does lead to a crime is an important one. In the case of encouragement leading to an offense, the wrong is in participating in the crime of another by encouraging it. When the incitement does not lead to an offense by another person, the wrong is in the attempt to persuade someone else to commit the crime, as there is no other crime to be complicit in. The difference is not one which has always been respected by courts prosecuting people for acts that amount to incitement. This is probably because there is a considerable overlap between incitement to genocide and complicity in genocide. Therefore incitement can have a dual character, both as an inchoate crime, and, where it leads to others committing genocide, as a form of complicity in crimes of those others.

The History of Incitement to Genocide
The historical background against which Article III(c) of the Genocide Convention was drafted was the trial in the Nuremberg International Military Tribunal of two Nazi propagandists, Julius Streicher and Hans Fritzsche. Streicher was convicted of crimes against humanity by that tribunal, and sentenced to death. Fritzsche was acquitted. Streicher edited the newspaper *Der Stürmer*. *Der Stürmer* was, in both the literal and metaphorical sense, obscene. It mixed vicious anti-Semitism with pornography. Streicher was obsessed with the idea

that the Jewish population represented a threat to the "purity" of the "Aryan race."

Streicher's fantasies were not the basis of his conviction at Nuremberg, however. Instead, it was charged that his writings "infected the German mind with the virus of anti-Semitism" and also advocated participation in the Holocaust. Before the war he was an ardent anti-Semite. In 1939 he continued his campaign of hatred and advocacy of the Holocaust in a leading article in *Der Stürmer*, which read:

> A punitive expedition must come against the Jews in Russia. A punitive expedition which will provide the same fate for them that every criminal and murderer must expect: Death sentence and execution. The Jews in Russia must be killed. They must be exterminated root and branch.

The fact that he made such statements when he knew that the Holocaust was being perpetrated was sufficient for the judges at the Nuremberg International Military Tribunal to sentence him to hang. This was not, strictly speaking, for incitement to genocide. It was prosecuted as complicity in crimes against humanity rather than as an inchoate crime of incitement.

Streicher's conviction has not gone without criticism. Telford Taylor, chief counsel at the later American trials in Nuremberg, did not condone Streicher's actions, but he nonetheless criticized the judges for having allowed their personal disgust for him to lead them to convict him of participating in crimes against humanity without due regard for determining on what principles he was liable. Streicher could easily have been found guilty of inciting genocide, had the offense existed at the time.

Fritzsche was a radio propagandist, best known for his program "Hans Fritzsche speaks," in which he manifested his anti-Semitism. He escaped conviction before the Nuremberg International Military Tribunal because, despite the anti-Semitic thrust of his radio work, he did not advocate the physical destruction of the European Jews. In the words of the Nuremberg International Military Tribunal, Fritzsche's claims that "the war had been caused by Jews and . . . their fate had turned out 'as unpleasant as the Führer had predicted' . . . did not urge persecution or extermination of Jews." The tribunal determined that Fritzsche's broadcasts constituted propaganda for Hitler and the war, rather than direct incitement to participate in the Holocaust. The distinction between the two may not always be clear.

Infamous examples of incitement to genocide occurred in Rwanda, in which mass media, in particular radio, was used to prepare the ground for, then encourage, the genocide against the Tutsi people in 1994. The use of radio was particularly important because a large part of the Rwandan population was illiterate, and therefore earlier attempts to encourage genocide in Rwanda through newspaper editorials failed to reach many people.

The most well-known Rwandan radio station was Radio Télévision Libre Mille-Collines (RTLM). This popular station was known for its informal style and comments such as "the graves are half full, who will help us fill them?" during the genocide. Throughout the genocide in 1994, RTLM broadcast dehumanizing propaganda against Tutsis, gave out information about where Tutsis could be found still alive or hiding, and encouraged people to kill them. In the *Media* trial, the International Criminal Tribunal for Rwanda (ICTR) convicted two of the founders of RTLM, Ferdinand Nahimana and Jean-Bosco Barayagwiza, of incitement to commit genocide in December 2003. They received sentences of life and 35 years imprisonment, respectively. In paragraph 1031 of the judgement, the Trial Chamber described RTLM as "a drumbeat, calling on listeners to take action against the enemy and enemy accomplices," and in paragraph 486 said that through ethnic stereotyping RTLM promoted hatred and contempt for Tutsis. As an illustration of this stereotyping, and its incitement to violence, the Trial Chamber referred to a broadcast of June 4, 1994, in which the announcer said, "just look at his small nose and then break it," referring to an ethnic stereotype of Tutsi physical appearance.

The activities of RTLM also gave rise to controversies about whether or not such stations should be jammed, or prevented from broadcasting by force. Neither happened to RTLM, but when RTS (Radio-Television Serbia) was bombed in the 1999 Kosovo conflict, some justified the bombing on the basis that it was a propaganda organ for the Milosevic regime. The argument proved very controversial, and most commentators seeking to defend the lawfulness of bombing the RTS incorporated the propaganda claim with the charge that RTS was also part of a military information system.

Criminalization of Incitement and the Harm Principle

It is a foundational principle of criminal law that for something to be criminalized there must be some form of relationship between that conduct and harm to others. A conviction for incitement to genocide does not require that anybody who hears, reads, or is exposed to the incitement be offended by it. Indeed, in many incidences of direct and public incitement to commit

Klan member in Reidsville, North Carolina, October 1989, attempting to garner support for the group's participation in a local Adopt-a-Highway program (whereby civic organizations clean roadside litter for official recognition). More inflammatory Klan speeches have urged racial hatred and violence. [JIM MCDONALD/ CORBIS]

genocide, those who are being subject to the incitement agree with the sentiments that are being passed on. Thus, offensiveness alone cannot be a basis for criminalizing incitement. The justification must be found in the harm it causes.

The harm caused by incitement cannot be the harm involved in the actual crime of genocide, however, because the latter crime does not have to be committed for incitement to have occurred. If it did, there would be no appreciable difference between incitement and successful encouragement to commit genocide. Rather, the main type of harm that justifies the criminalization of incitement is that it creates the risk of commission of the final crime of genocide by those incited. Just because the final harm—the actual commission of an act of genocide—has not concretely manifested itself, the criminal law against incitement is not impotent. Subjecting any person (or a group) to an unwarranted risk of harm is, in itself, violating the right of that person or group not to be wrongfully endangered. Although incitement results in a more remote form of harm than that caused by complete acts of genocide, its criminalization is justified on the grounds that it is a form of harm nonetheless.

It can be argued that someone who has tried, but failed, to get a person, a crowd, or even a country, to commit genocide is morally indistinguishable from someone who has successfully encouraged genocide. The only difference between success and failure is the actions of other people, who are responsible for their own actions. Therefore, if the criminal law is to be consistent, it should not criminalize successful incitements and ignore unsuccessful ones.

Criminalizing incitement to commit genocide allows the criminal law to intervene at an earlier stage than the actual attempts to commit the genocidal acts mentioned in Article II of the Genocide Convention. Genocide is an extremely serious, if not the most serious, international crime. It is better to prevent its commission at an early stage than to delay prosecution until after people have been killed. Genocide is usually a crime committed by a number of people at the instigation of smaller number of ringleaders. It usually takes some time to persuade people to commit genocide, with repeated propaganda against the targeted group. Therefore it is a good idea for the law to seek to bring an end to genocidal plans as soon as they have manifested themselves. It is by no means clear that a similar logic should not apply to other serious offenses, namely crimes against humanity and genocide.

Such arguments did not sway the drafters of the Rome Statute, however, so the International Criminal Court has no jurisdiction to prosecute those who directly and publicly, albeit unsuccessfully, incite war crimes or crimes against humanity, but is instead limited to the prosecution of specific incitements to genocide. However, incitement to particular examples of war crimes and crimes against humanity may be as serious as some instances of incitement to genocide. If a sadistic person sought to persuade others to drop a nuclear device on a city which would kill 100,000 people, for motives of personal pleasure or in order to persecute, rather than eliminate, a group, the act he or she seeks to incite would not meet the formal definition of genocide. Yet the act being encouraged is not much less serious than certain examples of genocide. There is perhaps some justification in the idea that genocide, with its eliminationist mental element, is simply different from other crimes, and should thus be treated differently. The question is whether genocide is sufficiently different from war crimes and crimes against humanity to justify that only incitements to genocide are serious enough to be criminalized.

Freedom of Speech and Incitement

There is a countervailing interest to the protection of the right of groups to exist that serves to narrow down the scope of the criminal prohibition of incitement. This interest underlies the limitations that the incitement must be "direct" and "public" and that the mental element required is very high. That interest is encapsulated in the right to freedom of speech. Most national human rights documents include a right of free speech. The first amendment to the U.S. Constitution is an example of such a provision. The right is also protected at the international level, most notably in Article 19 of the 1966 International Covenant on Civil and Political Rights (ICTR). The principle of free speech and the desire to prevent racism and genocide pull in different directions. It is not easy to determine precisely where the line between acceptable and unacceptable abridgments of the right of free speech lies.

The drafters of the Genocide Convention were mindful of this difficulty. The United States, for example, was uncertain about the need for a provision on incitement in the Genocide Convention. United States delegates involved in the drafting of the Genocide Convention pointed to the possibility of using incitement laws to illegitimately stifle the press. Cold War considerations played a role in this debate, for the Soviet Union was a strong advocate of an expansive incitement provision, and the U.S. delegation feared that it would use the provision as an excuse to suppress dissent. A majority of states favored retaining some form of incitement provision, however, and thus a compromise led to Article III(c) being included in the convention.

It does not unduly infringe the right of free speech to criminalize incitement of serious crimes, as the right of free speech, important as it is, has to be balanced with the rights of others. After recognizing the right of free expression, Article 19 of the International Covenant on Civil and Political Rights provides that the right may be limited in certain circumstances, when such limits were necessary to ensure the rights and freedoms of others. Article 20(2) of the International Covenant requires that states must prohibit "any advocacy of national, racial, or religious hatred that constitutes incitement to discrimination, hostility, or violence." Direct and public incitement to genocide is incitement to discrimination, hostility, and violence, and thus it must fall under these exceptions to the right of free speech. Therefore, the criminalization of direct and public incitement to genocide does not violate the right of free speech.

Incitement to genocide is a narrower concept than racist speech. This makes it very unlikely that a domestic statute criminalizing incitement to genocide along the lines of the Genocide Convention definition could fall foul of the International Covenant on Civil and Political Rights. In the *Media* trial, the ICTR engaged in a detailed review of the case-law of the various human rights bodies, and accepted that some balancing of the rights of free speech and the right to freedom from discrimination was necessary. This balancing is done in the Genocide Convention by requiring that incitement be both direct and public for it to qualify as a criminal act.

It is controversial whether or not laws prohibiting Holocaust denial and other hate speech should be part of the law relating to incitement to genocide. They probably do not qualify. The Genocide Convention was not designed to prohibit all hate speech, but to require the prosecution of those who are directly trying to persuade people to kill others with genocidal intent. Hate speech can be the precursor to incitement to genocide. However, such speech, where not accompanied by more direct encouragement to genocide, may be too remote from the harm of genocide to be appropriately included as an aspect of the international prohibition of genocide. Laws against such speech may be justifiable, but they may be better dealt with outside the context of the "crime of crimes," genocide. There is a difference between even ugly propaganda and material that is directly aimed at encouraging people to commit genocide. Nonetheless, the line between the two is not always clear. Manfred Lachs, the Polish delegate to the conference that drafted the Genocide Convention and an international lawyer, noted that creating suspicion around groups by implying that they are responsible for various problems creates an atmosphere in which genocide may occur.

Conduct Amounting to Incitement

Crimes are normally split into two elements: the conduct element (sometimes called *actus reus*) and the mental element (sometimes called *mens rea*). Although the two categories are imperfect, they form a useful basis for discussion of incitement. Unfortunately, Article III(c) of the Genocide Convention does not give much detail about what amounts to incitement. For this, we have to look to the way the concept has been interpreted by courts.

The International Criminal Tribunal for Rwanda has been at the forefront of international interpretation of what amounts to the crime of incitement. The tribunal first attempted to set out examples of incitement in the case of Jean Paul Akayesu, a Rwandan *bourgmestre*

(mayor), who was convicted in 1998 of, among other things, incitement to commit genocide. The basis for these charges was that, in his capacity as a bourgmestre, he had led a gathering over a dead Tutsi and urged those with him to eliminate Tutsis. He then read out lists of names of suspected Tutsis and Tutsi sympathizers, knowing that this would lead to the named individuals being killed. His incitement was successful, and he was prosecuted and convicted of incitement, although it might perhaps have been more appropriate to prosecute him for encouragement of the completed crime of genocide. In the case against Akayesu, the International Criminal Tribunal for Rwanda defined conduct amounting to incitement as follows:

> speeches, shouting, or threats uttered in a public place or at public gatherings, or through sale or dissemination, offer for sale, or display of written or printed material or printed matter in public places or at public gatherings, or through the public display of placards or posters, or through any other means of audiovisual communication.

In the *Media* case mentioned earlier, the ICTR picked up on the specific risks that audio communication poses when compared to newspapers or posters. In paragraph 1031 of its judgment, the Trial Chamber said:

> The nature of radio transmission made RTLM particularly dangerous and harmful, as did the breadth of its reach. Unlike print media, radio is immediately present and active. The power of the human voice . . . adds a quality and dimension beyond words to the message conveyed.

The Chamber also rightly noted that radio transmission added a sense of urgency to the calls for genocide in Rwanda. That is not to say that the Chamber completely discounted the danger of the print media. In the *Media* trial, the editor of the newspaper Kangura was also convicted of incitement to genocide for publishing content that was "a litany of ethnic denigration presenting the Tutsi population as inherently evil and calling for the extermination of the Tutsi as a preventive measure."

The Convention is clear that incitement which is not followed by the commission (by others) of genocidal acts must be public for it to be criminal. Only if incitement in private is consummated with actual acts of genocide is it thought serious enough to be criminal. In this latter case, the criminality arises from complicity in genocide, rather than incitement. In the drafting of the Genocide Convention, some participants proposed that private incitement be included, but these were removed as part of the compromise over the inclusion of the crime of incitement at all.

Karl Wolf raises his arm in a Nazi salute as he marches through the streets of Coeur d'Alene, Idaho, on July 18, 1998. Police in riot gear stand between parading white supremacists and protesters who jeer Aryan Nations marchers. [AP/WIDE WORLD PHOTOS]

The requirement that incitement must be public is a reflection of the need to balance the criminalization of incitement, which often criminalizes speech, against the right of freedom of speech. In the *Akayesu* case, the Rwanda Tribunal interpreted the concept of "public" to include two elements: "the place where the incitement occurred and whether or not assistance was selective or limited."

The Rwanda Tribunal's handling of incitement that is accomplished through the use of audiovisual communication raises interesting issues in relation to electronic communication. There may be no reason in principle for differentiating between someone displaying notices in a street and someone posting messages on an open-access internet page if both incite genocide. It may take more time for people to see a message on an internet page than one that is posted on the street, but this should not matter, because liability for incitement does not require that the actual occurrence of genocide.

Open access internet pages should therefore be considered a public venue for the purpose of the crime of incitement, although there is no judicial authority on this.

E-mail presents a more difficult question. An e-mail to one person would almost certainly not be public, even though it could be read by other people in the same way that a letter sent by the post can be opened by someone other than the addressee. A message inciting genocide sent to a list of recipients, however, presents a more difficult question. If there are numerous subscribers to the list, some may feel that the public requirement is fulfilled. A relevant comparison might be whether a meeting of, for instance, ten people in a village square would be considered public. On the other hand, if the same ten people met in a private house, would this be considered public? If there are 10,000 or 100,000 subscribers to the list, the public criterion would almost certainly be met. Similarly, it would be difficult to claim that an incitement sent as a "spam" e-mail to millions of people around the globe was not public.

To be prosecuted as criminal, the incitement must also be direct. Vague suggestions or hints are not enough. One reason for this limitation is the need to strike a balance between criminalizing incitement and preserving freedom of speech. Another is to reduce the possibility that frivolous claims arising from misinterpretation might be made against those speaking or writing. Such misinterpretations are not unknown. Charles Manson drew inspiration for his (non-genocidal) killings from the song "Helter Skelter" on the Beatles's *White Album*.

The directness problem was understood by the Rwanda Tribunal in Akayesu, which said:

> The direct element of incitement implies that the incitement assume a direct form and specifically provoke another to engage in a criminal act, and that more than mere vague or indirect suggestion goes to constitute direct incitement.

However, what is or is not direct is a matter of interpretation, and where the line is drawn is thus unclear, as the Trial Chamber in Akayesu continued "incitement may be direct and nonetheless implicit."

Matters are made even more complex by the fact that at different times and places, and in different cultural or linguistic contexts, words take on different implications and meanings. For example, it has become known that the word *Endlösung* (final solution), when it appeared in Nazi documents, referred to the Holocaust, and that the word *Sonderbehandlung* (special treatment) meant killing. This was not immediately apparent, however. At least two aspects of the problem of determining directness are worthy of mention. First, in wartime, when many, although not all genocides occur, language mutates very quickly, and in particular, euphemisms frequently gain currency. Many of those euphemisms refer to acts or groups involved the genocide. For example, in Rwanda, *Inyenzi*, which literally translates as "cockroach," was used to refer to Tutsis by proponents of genocide. Second, directness differs with place, language, and culture. The Rwanda Tribunal understood this, averring in its *Akayesu* decision that "a particular speech may be perceived as 'direct' in one country, and not in another." Some languages and cultures are more circuitous than others in modes of expression. In addition, the determination of incitement often relies on translated texts of suspect speeches or written articles, and translation itself adds a degree of ambiguity to the possible meanings of the words being used.

These considerations raise difficulties when the people making decisions on guilt or innocence regarding the crime of incitement are from a different cultural or linguistic background to the person being judged. In this instance, the only way to ensure that decisions on incitement are fair is to get expert cultural and linguistic evidence. This occurred in Canada, in the case of *Mugesera v. Minister of Citizenship and Immigration*.

Leon Mugesera was an academic who became an official in the Rwandan government. In 1992 he made a speech that many believed to have incited the 1994 genocide in Rwanda. He was set to be deported from Canada on the grounds that he had incited genocide in that 1992 speech, but filed an appeal. The Canadian Federal Court of Appeal secured a new translation of Mugesera's 1992 speech, and reversed the original deportation order. The court's strongly worded opinion declared that the initial translation and editing of the speech transcript was seriously misleading. To show this, the Court juxtaposed the version of part of the speech used in proceedings against Mugesera in 1996 and 1998, and the one they had before them in 2003.

The first version read:

> The fatal mistake we made in 1959 . . . was that we let them [the Tutsis] leave [the country]. [Their home] was in Ethiopia, but we are going to find them a shortcut, namely the Nyabarongo river. I would like to emphasize this point. We must react!

The second version read:

> Recently I made these comments to someone who was not ashamed to disclose that he had joined the PL. I told him that the fatal mistake we made in '59, when I was still a boy, was that we let them leave. I asked him if he knew of the Falachas, who had gone back to their home in Israel from Ethiopia, their country of refuge. He told me he did not know about that affair. I replied that he did not know how to listen or read. I went on to explain that his home was in Ethiopia but we were going to find him a shortcut, namely the Nyabarongo River. I would like to emphasize this point. We must react!

The first version omitted parts of the speech that contextualized the statement that the river would be used as a shortcut to return refugees. This implied a stronger link to the later genocide, in which bodies were often thrown into rivers, and suggested that Mugesera was referring to the idea, common in the genocide, that the Tutsis were Ethiopian newcomers to Rwanda. The second translation is considerably less clear on this point. This is not to say that Mugesera's speech could not be interpreted as incitement (many people have interpreted it as such), but the differences in the two translations demonstrate that when euphemistic speech is used, it is not always simple to arrive at a firm understanding of the intended meaning.

These difficulties must not be overstated, however. Sometimes the meaning of a statement is easily determinable. The tone of voice used in the delivery of speeches or transmissions, as well as the context in which the words are used and the reaction of the people who heard them are all relevant clues to meaning. For example, Eliezer Niyitigeka was convicted of incitement to genocide by the Rwanda Tribunal for telling people to "go to work," because it was clear in context that this meant killing Tutsis and was that it was understood as such at the time. RTLM was used during the Rwandan genocide to whip up hatred against Tutsis and tell people where Tutsis could be found and killed. Defendants have tried to take advantage of interpretative difficulties by deconstructing relatively innocuous messages from clear material. In the *Media* trial, Hassan Ngeze attempted to argue that a picture of a machete that appeared on the front page of Kangura to the left of the question "what weapons shall we use to conquer the Inyenzi once and for all?" only represented one alternative. He claimed that another option, democracy, was represented by a photograph of Grégoire Kayibanda, the former president of Rwanda. The Trial Chamber had little problem responding to this argument, noting "that the answer was intended to be the machete is clear both textually and visually".

Mental Element

The other indispensable part of the crime of incitement is the mental element, which is equally fundamental to the definition of genocide. In the *Akayesu* case, the Trial Chamber defined the mental element as follows:

> [The mental element] lies in the intent to directly prompt or provoke another to commit genocide. It implies a desire on the part of the perpetrator to create by his actions a particular state of mind necessary to commit such a crime in the minds of the person(s) he is so engaging. That is to say that the person who is inciting to commit genocide must have himself the specific intent to commit genocide, namely to destroy, in whole or in part, a national, ethnical, racial, or religious group, as such.

Not only must the person intend to persuade others to commit genocide, but he or she must also want the national, ethnical, racial, or religious group to be, at least in part, destroyed. The necessity of finding both these elements remains a subject of debate. Some believe that knowingly persuading another to perpetrate genocide should be enough to qualify an individual for

a charge of incitement, even if the inciter does not personally wish to destroy, in whole or in part, the group against whom the genocide is committed.

The offense of incitement was included in the Genocide Convention in order to prevent acts of genocide before they occurred. Prevention by the timely application of criminal sanctions to those attempting to bring genocide about is preferable to international criminal law only entering the picture when genocide is occurring, when it is already too late. It is arguable, however, that the offense of incitement is too narrowly defined to achieve its intended purpose.

SEE ALSO Complicity; Denial; Genocide; Nuremberg Trials; Propaganda; Radio Télévision Libre Mille-Collines; Streicher, Julius; War Crimes

BIBLIOGRAPHY

Ambos, Kai. (1999). "Article 25." In *Commentary on the The Rome Statute of the International Criminal Court*, ed. O. Triffterer. Baden-Baden: Nomos.

Eser, Albin (2002). "Individual Criminal Responsibility." In *The Rome Statute of the International Criminal Court*, ed A. Cassese, P. Gaeta, and J. R. W. D. Jones. Oxford: Oxford University Press.

Metzl, Jaime Frederc (1997). "Rwandan Genocide and the International Law of Radio Jamming." *American Journal of International Law* 91:628–651.

Schabas, William A. (1999). "Mugesera v. Minister of Citizenship and Immigration." *American Journal of International Law* 93:529–533.

Schabas, William A. (2000). *Genocide in International Law: The Crime of Crimes*. Cambridge, U.K.: Cambridge University Press.

Schabas, William A. (2000). "Hate Speech in Rwanda: The Road to Genocide." *McGill Law Journal* 46:141–170.

Taylor, T. (1992). *The Anatomy of the Nuremberg Trials*. New York: Little, Brown.

Videl-Naquet, Pierre (1993). *Assassins of Memory*. New York: Columbia University Press.

Robert Cryer

India, Ancient and Medieval

For ancient, early medieval, and medieval India, crimes against humanity have to be described against the backdrop of a multi-lingual, multi-religious, and multi-ethnic social complexity. Immediately striking, although not unique to the Indian subcontinent, are those personalities in history associated with perpetrating atrocities against human beings during the course of war and its aftermath. Such crimes most commonly are entwined with the zeal of religious bigotry. On the other hand, the persecution of large segments of the population exclusively in the name of religion or race appears to be rare in the early history of the subcontinent.

Documentary evidence of these ancient crimes exists in different languages of the subcontinent, and present certain limitations for scholars seeking to use them as authoritative sources. For a start, many of them are written according to the conventions of elite literary style, and as such do not represent the perceptions of the lower classes and castes. Most certainly, they do not represent the viewpoint of the victims of the crimes in question. Most, if not all, of these sources were rooted in distinct ideological viewpoints that must be kept in mind while using the texts as historical evidence. It must be understood that, within the temporal and spatial context of these eras of Indian subcontinental history, the descriptions of crimes against humanity, whether committed individually or collectively, are panegyrist and exaggerated. This makes it difficult to apply the word "genocide" in any meaningful way.

Extending our contemporary understanding and usage of this term into the past gives rise to a rather vile and barbaric picture of all these pre-modern and culturally diverse societies. The texts also sometimes incorporate elements of remorse or regret, articulated by the perpetrators of violence, making the use of modern terminology even more problematic. In fact, its use must necessarily hinge on the way ancient and medieval states were defined, the role of religion in defining the character of these polities, and, most importantly, the ethical and moral issues around which the notions of evil and violence were couched.

The Indian subcontinent contains few contemporary sources attesting to the atrocities from the point of view of the victims. This raises a fundamental question: Did large-scale torture and slaughter not occur, or did the sources of the period simply choose to be silent about it? In the latter case, a deeper philosophical understanding of violence and the human action which perpetrates it must be sought within the culture of the times. For instance, the eminent Indiologist Johannes Cornelis Heesterman notes that the ideology of karma views acts of violence, both by agents and recipients, as part of a larger scheme of maintaining or destroying dharma (societal order) and, therefore, the good or bad fruits of these actions would only be witnessed in the next life.

From the early medieval period onwards, inscriptions and contemporary chronicles begin to emerge, and these provide vivid descriptions of the horrors perpetrated, for instance after war. Yet these sources, though rooted in greater historical specificity, are also

Asoka is regarded by many as ancient India's greatest ruler. When Asoka attempted to complete the conquest of the Indian peninsula, he became so disgusted by the cruelty of warfare that he renounced it. Throughout India he ordered the creation of inscriptions, like the one shown here, to convey the peaceful teachings of Buddhism. [ADAM WOOLFIT/CORBIS]

biased. All these descriptions of incidents of violence, killings, persecutions, and torture must be viewed within the context of particular regional situations. They should not be over generalized, nor should our understanding of them be based on the assumption of a monolithic Indian identity or attributed to an overarching religious motivation. In fact, scholarly analysis of these events must recognize the interplay of multiple identities in the society and culture of the time and the region.

Ancient India

Most ancient Indian political theorists glorified war and kings displayed their power through military might. War was central to defining the epic traditions of early India, and it is described in graphic detail in the texts. However, few of the reigning monarchs of the period left records of their thoughts on the nature of human suffering as a result of war. One exception occurred during the period of Mauryan rule (321–185 BCE), which included one of the first attempts at empire-building on the Indian subcontinent. Emperor Ashoka Maurya, who in his edicts is called "Beloved of the Gods" (Devanampiya Piyadassi), invaded a region then called Kalinga in about 260 BCE. In his thirteenth Rock Edict, the emperor admits: "A hundred and fifty thousand people were deported, a hundred thousand were killed and many times that number perished." This record is unique, because the king also expresses remorse for the "slaughter, death and deportation of the people [that was] extremely grievous to the Beloved of the Gods and [had weighed] heavily on his mind. In the same record, Ashoka recognizes that everyone, from the *Brahmins* (priests) and *shramans* (ascetics) down to the ordinary householders, had suffered "violence, murder, and separation from their loved ones" (Thapar, 1997, pp. 255–256).

By way of penance, Ashoka went on to tell his subjects that he had become devoted to the diligent practice and preaching of *dhamma*, a policy of conquest by piety and virtue. He spread this new message through various edicts, and his influence was felt even beyond the frontiers of his own kingdom. It is, however, noteworthy that Ashoka did not announce his remorse immediately after the war. More importantly, the thirteenth Rock Edict was not put up in Kalinga, perhaps because it was considered politically unwise to publicize the King's remorse among the people against whom the war was fought. Thus, the Kalingans of the time did not know the extent of the killing or deportations, nor did they know of the king's repentance on these acts that had inflicted suffering on them.

The post-Mauyan period was marked by a series of foreign invasions. Even so, few descriptions of human slaughter or of conscious attempts to persecute people for their religious beliefs are found in the contemporary sources of the early centuries CE. A typical formulaic description coming from the semi-historical traditions of texts called the *Puranas* the destruction caused in the wake of these invasions. These texts were written in the future tense to depict conditions that would during what was called the Kali Age or the fourth in the stages of general moral decline within a cyclic view of time. An illustrative passage of the *Matsya Purana* reads thus:

> There will be Yavanas (foreigners) here by reason of religious feeling (*dharma*) or ambition or plunder; they will not be kings solemnly anointed, but will follow evil customs by reason of the corruption of the age. Massacring women and children, and killing one another, kings will enjoy the earth at the end of the Kali Age (Parasher, 1991, p. 243).

The use of the future tense may have been intended to suggest a warning of things to come and it may be a response to what has been called a "principled forgetfulness." These early Indian texts gave little importance to recording historical events that were accompanied by violence and this may be a response to what has been called a "principled forgetfulness." The term *Yavana* here refers to the early Greeks, but it became a general label for all outsiders who invaded the subcontinent from the west, and was often employed when traditional ideologues wished to emphasize that normal rules of the social, ethical, and moral order had been upset by people alien to their values.

Throughout much of the ancient world, the Hun armies left death, destruction, and suffering in the wake of their invasions. Although the Huns became a factor in Indian history from the middle of the fifth century CE, the deeds of one their most cruel rulers in India are vividly remembered even six hundred years later in the *Rajatarangini* written by Kalhana during the twelfth century in Kashmir. This text is considered the first systematic history written on the subcontinent. It describes Mihirakula, the Hun, as evil personified; a "man of violent acts and resembling Kala (Death). The notorious and violent acts of Mihirkula's armies did not even spare children, women, and the aged. Kalhana wrote: "He was surrounded day and night by thousands of murdered human beings even in his pleasure-houses."

Textual descriptions of violence often contain exaggerations, but in this case Kalhana's words are supported by the observations and testimony of a Chinese traveler named Hieun Tsiang (629 CE), who wrote an almost contemporary account of Mihirkula's rule. He note that not only did this evil king stir rebellion and kill the royal family in Kashmir and Gandhara, but he also destroyed innumerable Buddhist educational centers and residences. According to Hieun Tsiang, Mihirkula's armies killed thousands of people along the banks of the Indus while looting these religious places. Hieun Tsiang also interestingly noted that when his minister requested he not destroy certain Buddhist establishments, Mihirkula obliged, permitting the monks to return to their estates despite his own religious leanings being otherwise. Kalhana offered a similar observation. After graphically describing Mihirkula's misdeeds, Kalhana stated that the king made a shrine for Lord Shiva, an important god in the Hindu trinity, and that he granted tax-free villages to Brahmins from the Gandhara region, who were supposed to resemble Mihirkula in their habits and deeds.

The Early Medieval Period

Persecution was not the sole prerogative of foreign invaders, nor was it done solely for the protection and glorification of religious beliefs. Kalhana described an earlier willful destruction of Buddhist monasteries by a Shaivite ruler who was a worshipper of Lord Shiva and who later repented and then went on to build a new monastery. In another context he described how temples served as repositories of wealth, and were frequently attacked to satiate the greed of certain kings. One such king, Harshadeva of Kashmir, did not spare a single village, town or city in his attempt to despoil images and carry away the abundant wealth stored in them and even appointed an officer to do so.

One clear example of religious persecution resulting in the killing of members of another faith comes from the Pandyan kingdom of southern India in the eleventh century. This information is attested to by a variety of sources—hagiological literature, inscriptions and architectural evidence—and is best understood within the context of an upsurge in religious fervor and sectarian belief systems based on the idea of devotion (*bhakti*). This conflict is set against the backdrop of the Pandyan king, a Jaina follower, witnessing the debates and tests the Jaina monks had administered to the child Sambhandar, an ardent Shaivite poet and saint of the times. According to the *Periya Pranam*, the king was converted by this saint to Shaivism, a sect based on the sole worship of Lord Shiva and he ordered his minister thus:

> These Jainas, who had made a bet and lost in this test of the respective powers of their religions, had already done undesirable wrong to the Child Saint; Impale them on the lethal sharp stakes and execute the justice due to them.

Scholars put the number of Jainas thus killed at eight thousand. The Jainas having lost the patronage of this king nonetheless remained entrenched in the Tamil territories, but a number of Jaina temples were destroyed or converted into shrines dedicated to the worship of Lord Shiva.

Although the Jainas had a second lease on life in the spread of their faith into the Karnataka and Andhra countries during early medieval times, the Jaina conflict with worshippers of Lord Shiva continued here as well, especially with the rise and spread of a more aggressive form of shaivism called Virashaivism from the twelfth century onwards. A sixteenth century inscription from Srisailam in present-day Andhra Pradesh records the pride taken by Virashaivism chiefs in beheading a sect of Shvetambara Jainas. The Jainas are said to have made pejorative references to Shaivite teachers and sometimes sought protection from the ruling powers when the harassment towards them was severe, as during the Vijayanagar times.

It is well known that before an indigenous Indo-Muslim state was established in India in 1192 CE, there had been several raids by Persianized Turks who looted major cities and temples to support their power bases in Afghanistan. One such raid was in 968 CE by Sabuktigin (r. 977–997 CE), who ravaged the territory of the Hindu Shahi kings between Afghanistan and western Punjab. The *Sharh-I Tarikhi Yamini* of Utbi describes how places inhabited by infidels were burnt down, temples and idols demolished, and Islam established: "The jungles were filled with the carcasses of the infidels, some wounded by the sword, and others fallen dead through fright. It is the order of God respecting those who have passed away, that infidels should be put to death" (Elliot, 1964, p. 22). Writing about the raids of his son Mahmed against king Jaipal, Utbi stated: "The Musulmans had wreaked their vengeance on the infidel enemies of God, killing fifteen thousand of them, spreading them like a carpet over the ground, and making them food for beasts and birds of prey" (Elliot, 1964, p. 26). While noting the religious rhetoric, it has been argued by scholars that Mahmed of Ghazni who raided India seventeen times did so for economic reasons. In fact, he raided and sacked Muslim cities of Iran as well, in an effort to stabilize the Ghaznavid political and economic situation. But the rise of Ghurid power in northwestern Afghanistan from the mid-eleventh century brought the destruction of the city of Ghazni. Sultan Alauddin burned the city to the ground in revenge for the ill-treatment of his brothers by Mahmed Ghazni, and by this act the sultan earned the title of *Jahan-soz* or "the world burner." The Ghurids then came to operate from Ghazni under Shahabuddin Muhammad (1173–1206 CE), known as Muizzuddin Muhammad bin Sam. In the wake of his invasions, Turkish rule was establishment in India, between 1192–1206 CE.

Medieval Period

A major threat to the first Indo-Muslim state with its center at Delhi was the continual threat from the Mongols, who openly used terror as an instrument of war. In 1221 CE the notorious Mongol, Genghis Khan, had reached the Indus River, but the Turkish state at Delhi was yet to witness his full wrath. In fact, Balban (1246–1284 CE) and Alauddin Khilji (1296–1314 CE) effectively held back later Mongol attacks. Many Mongols accepted Islam and were admitted to the nobility or secured royal service. They came to be known as New Muslims but were often a discontented and turbulent lot and a continual source of trouble to the state.

A considerable amount of court intrigue thus developed and one major offshoot of this rivalry was seen when Alauddin Khilji's generals invaded Gujarat. On their return from the invasion, the soldiers rebelled over the share of booty that they were required to turn over to the state. A contemporary chronicle relates the punishments and torture meted out to those who tried to use underhand means to claim their share of booty. In reaction to the inhuman treatment, a large faction of the army, mostly New Muslims, revolted. The chief members of the rebellion escaped, but Alauddin Khilji ordered the rebels' wives and children be imprisoned. In another version, the king dismissed the whole community of New Muslims from his service, believing that the malcontents had hatched a plot to assassinate him. With the discovery of the plot, the king is said to have ordered the massacre of all New Muslims, and all those who killed a New Muslim were promised the right to claim everything their victims had owned. Between twenty and thirty thousand were slaughtered, and the murderers seized their wives, children, and property. A Gujarat campaign veteran, Nusrat Khan, used the decree to avenge the death of his brother, who had died at the hands of the rebels. He is reputed to have thrown the wives of his rebel victims to the scavengers of Delhi, and to have had their children cut into pieces in the presence of their mothers.

Further atrocities occurred as part of the larger Turkish conquest of eastern India during the early thirteenth century. For example, Ikhtiyar-Du-Din conducted raids on the famous Buddhist monasteries of Otandapuri and Vikramshila in Bihar, en route to Bengal, during which he ordered the extensive destruction of human and other resources. The monks there were all killed, and estimates set the death toll for these massacres in the thousands. Writers accompanying this invader are reported to have seen the total destruction of these Buddhist centers of learning. However, Minaju-s-Siraj (1243 CE) informed that they had mistaken them to be fortresses and wrote:

> [M]ost of the inhabitants of the place were Brahmans with shaven heads. They were put to death. Large number of books were found there, and when the Muhammadans saw them, they called for some person to explain their contents, but all the men had been killed. It was discovered that the whole fort and city was a place of study (*madrasas*) (Elliot, 1964, p. 306).

These crimes have to be seen in the larger milieu of intrigue and the need to maintain authoritative control and access to resources during the early days of the Turkish state in India. The relations among the Turkish rulers during times of succession were never peaceful. Controlling the massive local population of Hindus was

equally difficult. Barani narrates a supposed dialogue between Qazi Mughis of Bayana and Sultan Alaudden on an ordinance related to imposing a tax called *jiziya* on the Hindus. The Sultan wanted to lower the prestige and economic power of this population and thus he invoked a Quranic injunction to support his claims:

> Hindus should be forced to pay their revenue in abject humility and extreme submissiveness; for the Prophet Muhammad had ordained that Hindus must either follow the true faith or else be slain or imprisoned and their wealth and property confiscated (Rizvi, 1998, p. 164).

Thus, according to Rizvi, other schools of jurisprudence of the time, except for the law school of Abu Hanifa, ordered for them "either death or Islam."

Timur justified his conquest of India by invoking what he perceived as a willingness of the Muslim rulers of the time to tolerate idolatry—a practice condemned by Islam. He ordered a vicious attack that was unparalleled in the history of the subcontinent. At every stage of his advance beyond the Indus River and especially at places like Talamba and Bhatnair, he massacred people. Subsequently, the cities were plundered and people who failed to escape were enslaved. The most vivid descriptions are those of his crossing the Jamuna River on December 10, 1398. No one was spared. At Loni the Hindu inhabitants were also wiped out. Near Delhi, the local people greeted the news of nearby resistance fighters with joy, but they paid for their indiscretion with their lives. The resisting army, led by Mallu and Mahmed, soon had to retreat, and the city was left to the ruthless invader. Timur initially granted amnesty to the population of Delhi, but an uprising of the people infuriated him. The city was then ransacked for several days, and many thousands of its inhabitants were killed. On January 1, 1399, Timur returned home via Meerut, and on this march, too, great numbers of Hindus were slaughtered.

Raids on peninsular India began around 1295 and continued to the early decades of the fourteenth century, making inroads from Aurangabad as far south as Madurai. After 1323, the Tughluqs sought permanent dominion in the Deccan Peninsula. The first account of the atrocities against the local population and the ruling elites was narrated in the Vilasa Grant of Prolaya Nakaya (1330). Despite the early success of the Kakatiya rulers of Warangal against the Delhi sultans, the invaders were able to overpower the ruling dynasty.

> The cruel wretches subjected the rich to torture for the sake of their wealth. Many of their victims died of terror at the very sight of their vicious countenances . . . the images of gods were overturned and broken; the *Agraharas* of the learned

confiscated; the cultivators were despoiled of the fruits of their labour, and their families were impoverished and ruined. None dared to claim anything, whether it was a piece of property or one's own life. To those despicable wretches wine was the ordinary drink, beef the staple food, and the slaying of the Brahmanas was the favorite pastime. The land of Tilinga, left without a protector, suffered destruction from the Yavanas, like a forest subjected to devastating wild fire.

Literary sources also describe the devastation caused by the barbarians, who were either called Yavanas, Mlecchas, or Turushkas. The *Madhura-Vijaya*, written by Gangadevi in the second half of the fourteenth century, vividly describes Turushka rule over Madurai thus:

> The sweet odour of the sacrificial smoke and the chant of the Vedas have deserted the villages (*Agrahras*) which are now filled with the foul smell of roasted flesh and the fierce noises of the ruffianly Turushkas. The suburban gardens of Madura present a most painful sight; many of their beautiful coconut palms have been cut down; and on every side are seen rows of stakes from which swing strings of human skulls strung together. The Tamraparni is flowing red with the blood of the slaughtered cows. The Veda is forgotten and justice has gone into hiding; there is not left any trace of virtue or nobility in the land and despair is writ large on the faces of the unfortunate Dravias (Chattopadhyaya, 1998, p. 57).

War was common among the various states of the Deccan Peninsula and southern India. Kings professing Islam as their personal faith ruled some of these, whereas rulers of various Hindu sects controlled others. An important point common to both was the utter devastation caused by their armies when they invaded each other's dominions. For instance, the early Bahamani and Vijayanagar rulers struggled for control over the fertile Raichur territory. A contemporary chronicler, Ferishta narrated the various battles between the Bahamani Sultan, Mohammad Shah, and the Vijayanagar ruler Bukka Raya. Ostensibly the sultan insulted the Vijayanagar ruler, who responded with an invasion. He conquered Mudkal and put all its inhabitants—men, women, and children—to the sword. This infuriated Mohammad Shah, who took a solemn oath: "till he should have put to death, 100,000 infidels, as an expiation for the massacre of the faithful, he would never sheathe the sword of holy war, nor refrain from slaughter." The Sultan slaughtered about 70,000 men, women, and children.

The chronicles of Ferishta tell of subsequent and equally ferocious battles between the two. Haji Mull, a maternal relation of the Vijayanagar king, commanded the Brahmins to daily lecture the troops on the merits of slaughtering Mohamedans. During the actual battle, on July 23, 1366, large numbers of people were killed on both sides. Mohammad Shah then ordered a fresh massacre of the unbelievers, during which even pregnant women and children were not spared. According to Ferishta, Mohammad Shah slaughtered 500,000 Hindus, and "so wasted the districts of Carnatic, that for several decades, they did not recover their natural population."

The sources that have come down to us chronicling these crimes against humanity were framed within ideological and political concerns. They should be read as selective representations and thus treated as only partial constructions of the historical reality rooted in the concerns of either the colonial state or the modern nation. The historian must therefore interpret both the primary source and all subsequent interpretations in order to more accurately understand the events that occurred so far in the past.

SEE ALSO Genghis Khan; Historiography, Sources in; Historiography as a Written Form; India, Modern

BIBLIOGRAPHY

Chattopadhyaya, B. D. (1998). *Representing the Other? Sanskrit Sources and the Muslims (Eighth to Fourteenth Century)*. New Delhi: Manohar Publishers.

Eaton, R., ed. (2000). *Essays on Islam and Indian History*. Delhi: Oxford University Press.

Elliot, H. M., and Dowson, J. (1964). *The History of India as Told by Its Own Historians The Muhammadan Period*, vol. II. Allahabad: Kitab Mahal.

Heesterman, J. C. (1985). *The Inner Conflict of Tradition: Essays in Indian Ritual, Kingship, and Society*, South Asia Edition. Delhi: Oxford University Press.

Parasher, A. (1991). *Mlecchas in Early India: A Study in Attitudes towards Outsiders up to AD 600*. Delhi: Munshiram Manoharlal Publishers.

Rizvi, S. A. A. (1998). *The Wonder That Was India*, vol. II. Delhi: Rupa.

Stein, M. A. (1979). *Kalana's Rajatarngini: A Chronicle of the Kings of Kamir*, vol. I. New Delhi: Motilal Banarsidass Publishers.

Suryanarain Row, B. (1998). *A History of Vijayanagar The Never to be Forgotten Empire*. Madras, India: Asian Educational Services.

Thapar, R. (1980). *Ashoka and the Decline of the Mauryas*, 2nd edition. Delhi: Oxford University Press.

Thapar, R. (1987). *Cultural Transaction and Early India: Tradition and Patronage*. Delhi: Oxford University Press.

Wink, A. (1997). *Al Hind: The Making of the Indo-Islamic World*, Vol. 2: *The Slave Kings and the Islamic Conquest, 11th–13th Centuries*. Leiden: E. J. Brill.

Aloka Parasher-Sen

In October 1944 Mohatmas Gandhi and Mohammed Ali Jinnah met in a historic final, and ultimately unsuccessful, attempt to resolve political differences between India's Hindu and Muslim populations. [AP/WIDE WORLD PHOTOS]

India, Modern

The events accompanying the partition of India may be classified as genocidal massacres. While there is no available evidence of the intent to annihilate entire ethnic, national, racial, or religious groups as such, the victims of the mass killings were clearly chosen by their killers on the grounds of their membership in such groups.

No authentic figures are available as to how many people were killed during and after the partition. Radha Kumar, writing on the subject, has estimated that half a million to a million people were killed and over fifteen million were displaced. Genocidal massacre characterized both sides of the divide. While Muslims killed Hindus and raped their women on the Pakistani side, Hindus killed Muslims and raped their women on Indian side.

Muslims made up 25 percent of India's population before partition. They had fought alongside Hindus during the 1857 "mutiny" against the British rulers and also took part in various movements for independence together with Hindus. However, they were divided into various political and religious factions holding differing political opinions and perspectives. Mohammed Ali Jinnah, leader of the Muslim League, was a constitutionalist and, although he shared in the nationalist aspirations, he wanted a foolproof constitutional arrangement with the leaders of Indian National Congress to guarantee that Muslims (essentially the Muslim elite) would have a share in power and to prohibit constitutional changes without Muslim consent.

However, this was not to be. The other Muslim parties and groups, such as the Jami'at-ul-'Ulama-i-Hind the All India Momin conference, and the Ahrar of Punjab, as well as nationalist Muslims within the Indian National Congress, did not agree with Jinnah and his Muslim League. Also, Khan Abdul Ghaffar Khan, a Pathan leader from North West Frontier Province, also known as the Frontier Gandhi as he was close to Mahatma Gandhi and believed in the doctrine of nonviolence, also opposed Jinnah's demands for a separate Muslim homeland.

When no agreement could be reached between Jinnah and the leaders of Indian National Congress on the constitutional arrangements, Jinnah demanded the partition of India, invoking the theory that Muslims and Hindus constituted separate nations. In saying this, he endorsed the Hindu nationalists' stand, which based the idea of nationalism on cultural or religious grounds as opposed to the grounds of territorial unity.

Both sides thus used religious rhetoric to justify separate nationhood. The Hindu Mahasabha and leaders of the Rashtriya Swayamsevak Sang (RSS: National Volunteers Society) like Veer Savarkar, Hedgewar, and Guru Golwalkar also vehemently supported the concept of cultural nationalism. In the Hindu case, however, this nationalism also contained a territorial component, invoking the concept of a Hindu fatherland. Veer Savarkar coined the term *Hindutva* and described India as *pitra bhoomi* and *pavitra bhoomi* ("fatherland" and "sacred land") for the Hindus, and maintained that India could never become a sacred land for the Muslims.

Writing as a member of the Muslim League, an industrialist from Calcutta named Humayun Akhtar enumerated a list of differences between Hindus and Muslims on religious basis. Jinnah also justified his demand for a separate Muslim nation on the basis of religious and cultural differences between Hindus and Muslims. He maintained that the two groups revered different heroes, celebrated different festivals, spoke different languages, ate different foods, and wore different clothing. These claims were not entirely true, but in the heat of the moment were accepted as common knowledge among the educated middle classes of both communities.

Interestingly, however, these ideological battles were being fought primarily among the elites. The lower classes of both communities were untouched by these controversies at first. Nonetheless, when violence erupted, it was the poorer classes on both sides of the ethnic divide that paid the price. In the carnage that followed partition, it was the poor people who were massacred.

The British colonial rulers also bore responsibility for India's partition. If Lord Mountbatten, the last Viceroy had not hurried the declaration of independence, perhaps the history of the Indian subcontinent would have been quite different. The genocidal massacres might have been avoided, half a million to a million lives might not have perished, and millions of people might not have been uprooted.

The Muslims in India suffered the most from partition in every respect. Those Muslims who opted to remain in India came primarily from the poorer classes (the elite and middle class Muslims migrated to Pakistan). Most of them did not support the formation of Pakistan, and yet their blood was shed for that cause and they carried the guilt for dividing the country. Within India they were reduced to small minority—10 percent of the total population, down from approximately 25 percent before partition. As a consequence they lost much of their political influence.

Some leaders of the Indian Congress, such as Mahatma Gandhi, Jawaharlal Nehru, Maulana Abul Kalam Azad, and Babasaheb Ambedkar, were strongly committed to retaining a secular Indian government. In 1953, however, right wing Hindus formed a new party called the Jan Sangh, which rejected the concept of secular India and advocated *Hindu Rashtra* (i.e., Hindu nationhood). They blamed Indian Muslims for partition and seriously doubted their loyalty to India.

Indian Muslims were dubbed as pro-Pakistan, and the Jan Sangh preached hatred against them. The RSS, an extreme Hindu nationalist organization employed thousands of *pracharaks* (preachers) to travel from place to place, spreading hatred against the Muslims. As in the pre-partition period, India's Muslim communities continued to witness carnage year after year. Thousands of people, most of them Muslims, lost their lives in these riots.

The first major post-partition riot took place in Jabalpur, in Central India, during Nehru's lifetime in 1961. Throughout the 1960s, several other major riots of increasing intensity also took place, particularly in

eastern India. In Ahmedabad and other parts of the western Indian state of Gujarat, communal violence broke out on a large scale. More than a thousand people were brutally killed and many women were raped and murdered in 1969. The RSS, the Jan Sangh, and even a congressional faction were involved in organizing and justifying these genocidal massacres.

Another major episode of communal violence broke out in Bhivandi, some 40 kilometers from Mumbai, on May 18, 1970. More than 200 people were killed there. At the same time, in Jalgaon, a marriage party consisting of 40 Muslims (including the bridegroom) were burned alive. The Bhivandi-Jalgaon riots were mainly organized by an extremist Hindu right-wing organization called The Shiv Sena. This was a virulently anti-Muslim organization at the time, although its current leadership appears to have modulated its anti-Muslim virulence in recent years.

In the late 1970s and throughout the 1980s, several additional major communal riots took place. Once again, the main victims of the violence were Muslims. Thousands perished in these riots, which should be characterized as genocidal massacres. In all these riots, the Jan Sangh—renamed the Bhartiya Janata Party (BJP)—raised slogans like *Musalman jao Pakistan* or *Musalman jao qabrastan* ("O Muslims, go to Pakistan," "O Muslims, go to the cemetery"), inciting party followers to killed their Muslim neighbors. Thus did anti-Muslim violence continue in India long after the formal partition of the country in 1947.

The 1980s brought a worsening of the violence. Several major riots took place, some of which were inflamed by the recollection of historical grievances. For instance, controversy broke out over the centuries-old demolition of Hindu temples by medieval Muslim rulers. The BJP launched an aggressive campaign to restore one such temple—of Ramjanambhoomi, in Ayodhya, northern India—by destroying the mosque that had been allegedly constructed in its place by Babar's general, Mir Baqi Khan.

As a consequence of this campaign, several riots broke out throughout India, primarily directed against the Muslim minority. According to one estimate, more than 300 riots, both small- and large-scale broke out across the country. The Ayodhya mosque, Babri Masjid, was demolished on December 6, 1992. The demolition of Babri Masjid triggered further anti-Muslim violence throughout India, particularly in Mumbai, Surat, Ahmedabad, Kanpur, Delhi, and Bhopal. The riots in Mumbai and Surat were the worst. Government estimates for the violence in Mumbai alone suggest that more than a thousand people were killed. Unofficial estimates set the death count significantly higher.

The role of the police in the Mumbai killings was highly questionable. The local police force was openly pro-Hindutva and blatantly anti-Muslim. The Srikrishna Commission, convened to investigate the riots, charged thirty-two police officers with having been involved in killing or abetting the killing of Muslims. The Mumbai riots shocked the whole of India. The Muslims in Mumbai felt intensely insecure, and many of them fled the city. It is estimated that a total of more than 200,000 people—Muslims and Hindus alike—ultimately left Mumbai. The exodus was so huge that the Government had to organize special trains to handle the volume of traffic out of the city.

The riots of Mumbai were followed by similar violence in the western Indian city of Surat. Here, too, large numbers of Muslims were killed, their shops looted and burned, and their businesses completely destroyed. Many Muslim women were mass raped. More than four hudnred Muslims were killed by the right wing Hindu nationalists during the course of the Surat violence.

The worst case of violence in post-independence India was began on February 27, 2002, in the state of Gujarat, in western India. Rioting broke out after a passenger compartment of the Sabarmati Express was set on fire as it travelled from Ayodhya in northern India to Godhra, Gujarat. Fifty-nine Hindus were burned to death, including men, women, and children. Muslims living near the Godhra railway station were suspected to be involved in setting fire to the railway compartment. Some one hundred people were arrested and trials would show whether they were involved in the crime.

Rioting broke out on the morning of February 28, in which more than 1,000 people were massacred in brutal retribution of the Godhra protests. Once again, Muslim women were raped in several Gujarat villages. As a result of the escalating violence, more than 45,000 Muslims were displaced to refugee camps, where they were kept for several months. They were prohibited from returning to their homes, and their businesses were nearly ruined. In the city of Ahmedabad, 100 Muslim residents of a neighborhood known as Narodia Patia were killed (some were burned alive) and many women were raped. The case of Kausar Bano illustrates the violence that was perpetrated during these riots. Eight months pregnant, her womb was ripped opened and her unborn child was extracted and pierced with a sword. In the neighborhood called Gulbarga Society, 40 people, including a member of the Indian Parliament, were burned alive.

The BJP Government in Gujarat, led by Narendra Modi, was allegedly involved in the carnage. Modi jus-tified the violence by saying it was a popular reaction to the Godhra incident. He even invoked the Newtonian law that there is equal reaction to every action, implying that the carnage was a natural, unavoidable occurrence. The genocidal massacre in Gujarat was but the latest in a long history of post-independence violence. Between 1950 and 2002, more than 13,952 outbreaks of local violence took place, 14,686 people have been killed and a further 68,182 have suffered injury.

SEE ALSO Genocide; India, Ancient and Medieval; Massacres

BIBLIOGRAPHY

Engineer, Asghar Ali, ed. (1991). *Communal Riots in Post-Independence India*, 2nd edition. London: Orient Longman.

Engineer, Asghar Ali, ed. (1992). *The Politics of Confrontation: Bahri Masjid–Ramjanambhoomi Controversy Runs Riot*. Delhi: Ajanta Books International.

Engineer, Asghar Ali (2004). *Communal Riots after Independence: A Comprehensive Account*. Delhi: Shipra Publications.

Hasan, Mushirul (1997). *Legacy of a Divided Nation: India's Muslims since Independence*. Oxford: Oxford University Press.

Kumar, Radha (2003). "Settling Partition Hostilities: Lessons Learned, the Options Ahead." In *Divided Countries, Separated Cities*, ed. Gasson Deschaumes and Rada Ivekovic. Oxford: Oxford University Press.

Madon, D. P. (1974). *Report of Inquiry into the Communal Disturbances at Bhivandi, Jalgaon, and Mahad, May 1970* Government of Maharashtra, Mumbai.

Asghar Ali Engineer

Indigeneous Peoples

Indigenous peoples have lived in different part of the globe since time immemorial. In 2003 they number about 350 million, belonging to different nations, communities, and groups, with specific cultures, traditions, customs, languages, and religions. They have survived in spite of the massacres, discrimination, oppression, diseases, poverty, and misery inflicted on them principally by the colonial powers (Spain, Britain, France, the Netherlands, and the United States).

The problems of indigenous peoples exist, to varying degrees, on all continents. Even in countries where the indigenous still constitute a majority, they remain powerless, by and large unheard, misunderstood, or simply ignored by their governments. Their past history is disdained, their way of life scorned, their subjugation unrecognized, their social and economic system unvalued. The belief that indigenous peoples were subhuman and inferior was common among European invaders and colonizers.

Definition

There is not an international consensus on who indigenous peoples are; the term cannot be defined precisely or applied all-inclusively. International debate on the meaning of the term *indigenous* commenced in the late nineteenth century. Among European languages, notably English and Spanish, the term indigenous (*indigena*) shares a common root in the Latin word *indigenae*, which was used to distinguish between persons who were born in a particular place and those who arrived later from elsewhere (*advenae*). The French word *autochtone* has, by comparison, Greek roots and, like the German term *Urspung*, suggests that the group to which it refers was the first to exist in a specific location. Hence, the roots of the terms historically used in modern international law share a single conceptual element: priority in time.

Berlin Conference (1884 and 1885)

A good starting point for the examination of international practice with regard to indigenous peoples is the Berlin Conference of 1884 and 1885. The great powers of the time convened the conference with the aim of agreeing on principles for the recognition and pursuit of their territorial claims in Africa. In Article 6 of the General Act of the Conference, the great powers declared their commitment to "watch over the preservation of the native tribes" of Africa, with the term "native tribes" distinguishing between nationals of the great powers and the peoples of Africa living under the colonial domination of these same nations.

League of Nations

According to Article 22 of the Covenant of the League of Nations, members of the League accepted as a "sacred trust of civilization" the duty of promoting the well being and development of the indigenous population of those colonies and territories remaining under their control. The Covenant specifically used the word "indigenous" to distinguish between the colonial powers and the peoples living under their domination. The Covenant included a second element of qualification, however, characterizing indigenous populations as "peoples not yet able to stand by themselves under the strenuous conditions of the modern world." Both factors, that is, colonial domination and institutional capacity, were to be considered, under Article 22 of the Covenant, in determining the degree of supervision that was appropriate to particular territories and peoples. Another element important to the evolution of the term indigenous appeared in the Covenant. Article 22 also referred to "territories" as places demarcated by internationally recognized borders, in comparison to "peoples," who could be distinguished by sociological, historical, or political factors.

Sami in regional dress, Finmarken, Norway, c. 1885. With forced assimilation, including a ban on their Native language, came the loss of Sami traditions and a fading perception of their history.
[MICHAEL MASLAN HISTORIC PHOTOGRAPHS/CORBIS]

Pan-American Union—Organization of American States (OAS)

The Pan-American Union, the predecessor of the present-day Organization of American States (OAS), began to use the term *indigenous* in a different manner. In its Resolution XI of December 21, 1938, the Eighth International Conference of Americas States declared that "the the indigenous populations, as descendants of the first inhabitants of the lands which today form America, and in order to offset the deficiency in their physical and intellectual development, have a preferential right to the protection of the public authorities."

As a matter of practice in the Americas, the term indigenous was used to identify marginalized or vulnerable ethnic, cultural, linguistic, and racial groups within state borders. The consolidated text of the Draft American Declaration on the Rights of Indigenous Peo-

Sami (or Lapps) are the Native people, primarily farmers and reindeer herders, living in the polar regions of Norway, Sweden, Finland, and Russia. In the 1880s (the time period of this portrait of a rural Sami family), Norway adopted strict policies aimed at assimilating its indigenous population.[MICHAEL MASLAN HISTORIC PHOTOGRAPHS/CORBIS]

ples (being negotiated by the OAS, as of June 2003) refers in its Article 1 to indigenous peoples as those who "descend from a native culture that predates European colonization and who conserve normative systems, usages and customs, artistic expressions, beliefs and social, economic, political and cultural institutions." Negotiations proceed within the OAS in a quest for consensus among states and indigenous peoples of the region on the latter's rights.

International Labor Organization (ILO) Convention
The 1957 International Labor Organization (ILO) Indigenous and Tribal Populations Convention (No. 107) applies to tribal populations that "are regarded as indigenous on account of their descent from the populations which inhabited the country, or a geographical region to which the country belongs, at the time of conquest

or colonization" and who remain socially, economically, and culturally distinct.

The Charter of the United Nations (UN)
The Charter of the United Nations (UN) contains nothing to help reconcile different uses of the term indigenous in international law. Article 73 of the Charter refers merely to "territories whose peoples have not yet attained a full measure of self-government."

In 1987 the UN published *Study of the Problem of Discrimination against Indigenous Populations* by Jose Martinez Cobo that offered the following definition for the term *indigenous*:

Indigenous communities, peoples and nations are those which, having a historical continuity with pre-invasion and pre-colonial societies that developed on their territories, consider themselves distinct from other sectors of the societies now prevailing in those territories, or parts of them. They form at present non-dominant sectors of society and are determined to preserve, develop and transmit to future generations their ancestral territories, and their ethnic identity, as the basis of their continued existence as peoples, in accordance with their own cultural patterns, social institutions and legal systems (p. 379).

This definition combines the element of distinctiveness, which characterizes both indigenous and tribal peoples, with the element of colonialism. In addition, the definition contains the following other essential elements: (1) "non-dominance at present," implying that some form of discrimination or marginalization exists; (2) the relationship with "ancestral land" or territories; (3) culture in general, or in specific manifestations (such as religion, living under a tribal system, membership in an indigenous community; (4) language (whether used as the only language, the mother tongue, the habitual means of communication at home or in the family, or the main, preferred, habitual, general, or normal language); (5) residence in certain parts of the country. This is the definition that has prevailed and is applied by the UN.

The 1989 ILO Indigenous and Tribal Peoples' Convention (No. 169), which revised the earlier 1957 Convention, defines indigenous peoples in terms of their distinctiveness, as well as their descent from the inhabitants of a territory "at the time of conquest or colonization or the establishment of present state boundaries." The only difference between the definition of indigenous and tribal peoples in the Convention relates to the principle of self-identification. A people may be classified as indigenous only if it so chooses by perpetuating its own distinctive institutions and identity. Article 1, paragraph 2, of the Convention provides that self-identification "shall be a fundamental criterion for determining the groups to which the Convention shall apply." Paragraph 3 contains a disclaimer stating, "the use of the term *peoples* in this Convention shall not be construed as having any implications as regards [to] the rights which may attach to the term under international law."

It should be noted in this regard that no accepted legal, sociological, or political definition of the term *a people* exists. General or customary international law does not provide any rules or principles concerning the term indigenous peoples, or its relationship with the wider concept of peoples. Whether a group is a people mainly for the purpose of self-determination depends on the extent to which the members of the group making this claim share ethnic, linguistic, religious, or cultural bonds. There is also a subjective element, which weighs the extent to which members of a group perceive the group's identity as distinct from those of other groups. Indigenous peoples are peoples in every political, legal, social, cultural, and ethnological meaning of this term. They have their own languages, laws, customs, values, and traditions; their own long histories as distinct societies and nations; and a unique religious and spiritual relationship with the land and territories in which they have lived.

Indigenous peoples' right to self-determination should ordinarily be interpreted as their right to freely negotiate their status and representation in the state where they live. This might best be described as a kind of "belated state-building," through which indigenous peoples are able to join with all other peoples making up the state on mutually agreed upon and just terms. It does not mean that indigenous individuals should be assimilated into the dominant culture, but that they should be recognized as distinct peoples and incorporated into the state on that basis. Indigenous peoples have repeatedly expressed their preference for constitutional reform within existing states that would allow this process to take place, as opposed to secession from the state. What most indigenous peoples mean when they speak of self-determination is the freedom to live as they have been taught.

History: West Indies

The Western Hemisphere was densely populated when Europeans began their colonization of the region. In 1492 Christopher Columbus set sail under the flag of King Ferdinand and Queen Isabella of Spain and soon subjugated the West Indies. The so-called Indians lived in a land across the ocean, with their own cultures, civilizations, and languages. The Spaniards waged a series of genocidal campaigns against the Indians of Hispaniola. On horseback, accompanied by infantry and bloodhounds, the conquerors destroyed the hunting and gathering nations of the island, and by 1496 they were in complete control. Besides the subjugation the Europeans also brought their diseases. Smallpox arrived in 1518 and spread to the mainland. By 1540 the Indians in the Caribbean had been virtually exterminated.

Catholic priests accompanying the soldiers would read out in Spanish, on reaching Indian villages the *Requerimiento*, a formal demand that the townspeople adopt Catholicism. If the Indians refused to acknowledge the authority of the king and the pope, the soldiers would kill them. Those who were not slaughtered were seized as slave-laborers for the mines. In 1502 the system known as *encomienda* was introduced, whereby the Crown granted land to Spaniards, usually soldiers, who were also allotted a certain number of Indians to work it. This system of forced labor was known as *repartimiento*.

Subjugation of the Indians was accompanied by hideous acts of cruelty. Representatives sent by Catholic Church authorities began to protest. Spain passed the Laws of Burgos in 1512 in an attempt to control some of the abuses. In 1514 Bartolomé de las Casas, a priest who came to be called the father of human rights in the New World, decided that the Spaniards' treatment of the Indians was unjust and tyrannical, and he tried to intervene with the king to reform the *encomienda* system.

History: North America (Mexico)

After the Spaniards had subjugated the Indians of the West Indies, they invaded the mainland, where they encountered the great empires of the Aztec and Inca. In 1519 Hernando Cortés landed at Veracruz on the eastern shores of Mexico. Reaching the Aztec capital of Tenochtitlan, the Spaniards were astonished to find a beautiful city, the center of an empire of eleven million people. By 1521 Mexico was conquered. The Spaniards brought with them the disease smallpox, which was unknown in Mexico, and Indians died by the hundreds of thousands.

History: South America

By 1532 Francisco Pizarro had conquered Peru, where the Inca ruled over six million Indians. The empire of the Inca, established along the highlands stretching from Ecuador to Bolivia, was an astounding achievement: with winding roads through the mountains, irrigation systems, storehouses, and agricultural terraces. Manco Inca led the revolt of the Inca against the Spaniards. Tupac Amaru, the last Inca king, was captured and brought to Cuzco, where he was beheaded in the central plaza.

As early as 1523, a decade before Pizarro's encounter with Atahualpa, smallpox had begun to depopulate the empire of the Inca. A multitude of plagues, in addition to smallpox, ravaged the Indian population during the sixteenth and seventeen centuries: chickenpox, measles, influenza, pneumonia, scarlet fever; yellow fever, and typhus. Their enormous impact can be best understood by considering population statistics related to both North and South America. In 1519 the Indian population of central Mexico was estimated to be 25 million; by 1523 17 million remained; in 1548 there were only 6 million; and by 1568 a mere 3 million had survived. By the early seventeenth century the number of Indians in central Mexico was scarcely 750,000, that is, 3 percent of the population before the Spanish Conquest began. It is estimated that the Indian population of Peru likewise fell from 9 million before the arrival of Columbus to 1.3 million by 1570.

At the end of a half-century under Spanish rule, the peoples of the Aztec and Inca empires had undergone devastating cultural as well as numerical decimation. Ancient ceremonies of birth, marriage, and death disappeared. Old customs died. A cultural genocide was committed. In the Brazilian rain forest during the twentieth century the epidemics of the earlier Conquest—smallpox and measles—and diseases such as malaria, influenza, tuberculosis, and yellow fever killed thousands of indigenous peoples, in particular, the Yanomami. Depopulation placed terrible stress on the social institutions of indigenous society. From 1900 to 1957, according to Darcy Ribeiro, an anthropologist who sought to help the Urubus-Kaapor in 1950, the Indian population of Brazil dropped from one million to less than two hundred thousand. Seventy-eight Indian communities became extinct. What remains of pre-Colombian civilizations are ruins such as Maccu Picchu, the lost city of the Inca, while the heirs of the conquered peoples sell handicrafts and beg in the streets of Andean cities.

History: North America

In North America the destruction of the Indian population did not necessarily occur at the time of first contact, as was the case in Central and South America. In the sixteenth century a remarkable federal and state structure was established among Indians from the Great Lakes to the Atlantic, and as far south as the Carolinas and inland to Pennsylvania. Known as the Iroquois Confederacy, it incorporated five widely dispersed nations of thousands of agricultural villages. It later included the Tuscarora of the south and refugees from British colonization.

Bordering the Iroquois state to the west were the peoples of the plains and prairies of central North America, from West Texas to the sub-Arctic; in the Canadian prairies, the Cree; in the Dakotas, the Lakota and Dakota (Sioux); and to their west and south the Cheyenne and Arapaho peoples.

Prior to the arrival of the British colonizers with African slaves, the territory was a thriving civilization, with most peripheral areas having been settled by the year 1600. The inhabitants were the Muskogee-speaking Choctaw, Creek, and Chickasaw Nations; the Cherokee, an Algonquin-speaking people just as the Iroquois in the eastern half of the region; and the Natchez Nation to the west, that is, the Mississippi Valley area. The total population of the region is estimated to have been between two to three million. The Natchez

Nation alone, which was totally destroyed by colonization with the remaining population sold into slavery, may have numbered several million.

In the 1890s an American whaling fleet from San Francisco entered the Beaufort Sea and established whaling stations in the western Arctic. Eskimos were hired to gather driftwood to conserve the ships' stocks of coal, and to hunt caribou and musk ox to supply the whalers with fresh meat. The whalers brought syphilis, measles, and other diseases. When the whaling industry collapsed in 1908, of the original population of 2,500, there were only approximately 250 Mackenzie Eskimos left in the region between Barter Island and Bathurst Peninsula.

Alcohol was used by some of the Indians in the Americas. Most indigenous peoples regard the abuse of alcohol as one of the most disruptive forces brought on by colonization and the most serious danger to the future of their communities. There are disturbing contemporary studies of indigenous communities in the Arctic and Sub-Arctic regions that identify a social pathology which threatens to destroy life there: family violence, alcoholism, and a high suicide rate among young people, with most victims being in their teens and early twenties. This is the tragic outcome of the policies pursued by dominant nonindigenous societies for many years. Certain governments and their economic, social, and educational institutions, as well as some missionaries and clergy, have made every effort to destroy indigenous languages, cultures, customs, and traditions. Despite this history, Native peoples remain in the New World.

History: Oceania

With respect to Oceania, there is archaeological evidence that Aborigines have lived in Australia for at least sixty thousand years. On May 13, 1787, a fleet of eleven ships, most carrying convicts, set sail for New South Wales. It arrived on January 26, 1788, giving birth to modern-day Australia. Starting with British occupation, Aboriginal and Torres Strait Islander peoples have been subjected to successive government policies seeking to "protect," "civilize," and "assimilate" them. The policy of assimilation, which often involved removing indigenous children from their families and communities and placing them in nonindigenous communities, government or church institutions, or foster homes, reached its peak between 1910 and 1970. These children, commonly referred to as the Stolen Generations, were not only isolated from their families and traditional lands, but also forbidden to speak their language or practice their culture. Frequently, they never learned of their indigenous origin. This policy and practice may be

Though their numbers declined significantly with the advent of European colonization, Aborigines, whose presence in Australia can be traced back some 60,000 years, still enact their ancestors' rituals. In this 1992 photo, an Aborigine participates in "Dreamtime," a ritual intended to signify the continuity of all life unlimited in space and time. [CHRIS RAINIER/CORBIS]

viewed as a form of genocide on the basis of Article II(e) of the 1948 United Nations (UN) Convention on the Prevention and Punishment of the Crime of Genocide.

History: Asia

In Asia, Japan recognizes the Ainu as a religious and culture minority, but Ainu efforts to celebrate, preserve, and revive their traditions and customs of the past are severely circumscribed. Japan maintains that the Ainu have lost most of their cultural distinctiveness through assimilation. Despite the official position of the Japanese government, the Ainu place strong emphasis on their distinct cultural identity.

Most of the countries in which indigenous peoples live are relatively poor and less developed. Government officials, and the executives of development banks, and other financial institutions and transnational corporations, often have a limited knowledge of indigenous societies and their culture. As a result, the projects these executives conceive, authorize, and fund—dams, roads, and the utilization of natural resources sometimes involving the large-scale relocation of populations—irrevocably affect the peoples who lie in their paths. The land and natural resource issues of indigenous peoples remain critical and unsolved in many states. In North America, Great Britain and later the

United States signed over three hundred treaties with Indian nations that were subsequently broken.

In 1840 the Maori in New Zealand signed the Treaty of Waitangi with Great Britain. According to it, they ceded sovereignty in exchange for exclusive and undisturbed land rights. However, within a few years the British Crown forcibly purchased half of the guaranteed area, some thirty million acres, and by successive acts of Parliament much of the remaining land has also been wrested from the Maori. At the end of the twentieth century they owned only 3 percent of New Zealand territory. Present-day Maori (along with North American Indians, including those residing in Canada) insist on their treaty rights and continue to demand that the treaties they earlier signed be recognized as legitimate international agreements.

In 2002 the indigenous Wanniyala-Aetto in Sri-Lanka; the forest-dwelling Adivasis in India; and the San, Hadzabe, and Ogiek in Africa all faced situations in which they were either denied access to their ancestral lands, or evicted from them in order to make way for commercial hunting or logging interests. Pastoralists suffered hardships in Ethiopia and Tanzania, where land dispossession increasingly threatened their livelihood. Even the Saami reindeer pastoralists of the European Saamiland—considered the most privileged indigenous people in the world—experienced economic setback.

The Torres Strait Islanders are an indigenous Melanesian people of Australia. At present they are slowly working toward a system that will provide both a strong government and relatively autonomous local island councils, together with protection for and political inclusion of the nonindigenous residents of the islands. Such an arrangement will contribute to economic and social improvement for all. In addition the State of Queensland has demonstrated some recognition of Native status since the landmark decision of the high court in *Mabo v. Queensland* (1992), which recognized Native title in the Torres Strait Islands.

Many states regard indigenous peoples as an obstacle to their national development, not as an economic asset. By pursuing such a philosophy and policy, they ignore the potential contribution of a large portion of their national population and condemn them to poverty, despair, and conflict. Ignoring the economic potential of indigenous communities is a waste of resources in the short term, and a source of high social and financial costs in the long term.

In the Andes and Southeast Asia, where the majority of the world's indigenous peoples live, the flow of private foreign investment and expropriation of lands and natural resources continues unabated, without the free consent of indigenous peoples. National parks, biosphere preserves, and the lands set aside for indigenous peoples have been opened to mining and logging. Large-scale development projects, such as hydroelectric dams and transmigration programs have not just displaced many thousand of peoples, they have also leveled rain forests, emptied rivers, and eliminated much of the word's biological diversity. Indigenous peoples have been an integral part of the worldwide environmental movement that led to the 1992 Earth Summit at Rio de Janeiro. Chapter 26 of Earth Summit Agenda 21, Recognizing and Strengthening the Role of Indigenous People and Their Communities, was adopted during this conference.

Indigenous Peoples Movement and Contemporary Global Protection

In 1923 Chief Deskaheh, leader of the Council of the Iroquois Confederacy, traveled to Geneva to inform the League of Nations of the tragic situation of indigenous peoples in Canada and to request the League's intervention in their long-standing conflict with the Canadian government. In spite of Chief Deskaheh's efforts, the League decided not to hear the case, claiming that the issue was an internal Canadian matter.

Since 1921 the ILO has sought to address the plight of Native workers in European colonies. The 1930 Forced Labor Convention (No. 29) was one result. In the period from 1952 to 1972 the Andean Program, a multi-agency effort under the leadership of the ILO, was launched in Argentina, Bolivia, Chile, Colombia, Ecuador, Peru, and Venezuela; its work affects some 250,000 indigenous peoples. The ILO has further adopted two conventions on indigenous peoples (Nos. 107 and 169 on "Indigenous and Tribal Populations" and the "Convention Concerning Indigenous and Tribal Peoples in Independent Countries"). The 1989 convention (No. 169) is an important international standard on the subject.

After the UN was created in 1946, a number of attempts were made to prompt that body to consider the situation of indigenous peoples around the world. From 1960 to 1970 indigenous movements grew in a number of countries to protest the systematic and gross violations of Native human rights, and the discriminatory treatment and policies of assimilation and integration promulgated by various states. In the 1970s indigenous peoples extended their efforts internationally through a series of conferences and appeals to international intergovernmental institutions and nongovernmental organizations (NGOs). Among the hallmark events of the movement was the International NonGovernmental Organization Conference on Discrimination Against Indigenous Populations in the Americas, held in Geneva in 1977. This conference has contributed to forging a transnational indigenous identity that may be subsequently extended to include indigenous peoples from many corners of the world. Of particular interest was the Fourth General Assembly of the World Council of Indigenous Peoples, held in Panama in 1984, which developed a declaration of principles. This declaration is one of the primary papers on which the Draft United Nations Declaration on the Rights of Indigenous Peoples, as of 2003 under debate in the UN Commission on Human Rights, is based.

In 1982 the UN Working Group on Indigenous Populations (WGIP) was created with a twofold mandate: to review developments relating to the promotion and protection of human rights and fundamental freedoms of indigenous peoples, and to elaborate international standards concerning their human rights. The WGIP, under the chairmanship of Erica-Irene Daes, has produced valuable work. Its annual meetings became the official gathering place for more than nine hundred indigenous representatives from all over the world. The principles of openness, freedom of expression, equality and nondiscrimination, the rule of law, transparency, and democracy have been the subject of its debates, and a constructive dialogue between representatives of indigenous peoples, governments, intergovernmental organizations, NGOs, and members of the WGIP have ensued as a result. With the free and active participation of indigenous peoples, it has drafted and unanimously adopted the Draft Declaration on the Rights of Indigenous Peoples.

On the basis of WGIP's recommendation, the UN proclaimed 1993 the historic "International Year of the World's Indigenous Peoples." Then Secretary-General Boutros Boutros-Ghali called on all governments to respect and cooperate with indigenous peoples. The General Assembly then declared 1995 through 2004 "The International Decade of the World's Indigenous People," with the theme of partnership in action. In 1992 the Permanent Forum on Indigenous Issues was established by the UN Economic and Social Council, as a watchdog on behalf of indigenous peoples. Its most important function and role has been to ensure that the operational side of the UN system focuses on the rights of indigenous peoples, including the right to development, and brings indigenous peoples into a real partnership for development with other sectors of international society. As of 2003 the Permanent Forum held two constructive annual sessions (in 2002 and 2003).

Consequently, indigenous peoples are no longer just victims of development, but also contributors to development and the protection of the environment. With their own special talents, deep knowledge, and long expertise, they will gradually contribute to the improvement of their economic situation and to the prosperity of all people throughout the world.

Reconciliation and Recommendations

In the dawn of the new millennium indigenous peoples worldwide, after centuries of inaction and suffering, have become aware of their rights and responsibilities. The injustice, the exploitation, the discriminatory treatment and dark deeds of the past and present require those who have benefited the most to aid those who have endured the greatest injustices during the last five centuries. Governments must recognize the needs of indigenous peoples and then find a path of restitution that leads to reconciliation. No longer can claimed ownership rights of land and natural resources be ignored. No longer can indigenous customary laws, traditions, and culture be disregarded.

There is a need for national constitutional reforms within existing states, as opposed to secession, with the free and active participation of indigenous peoples. Forced assimilation and integration must be prohibited by law. It is imperative that nations worldwide adopt the UN General Assembly's Draft Declaration on the Rights of Indigenous Peoples. The proclamation will serve as the foundation of a new and just relationship between states and indigenous peoples, and contribute to a successful and viable reconciliation. The education of indigenous peoples must be encouraged, and public awareness properly promoted. The World Bank, International Monetary Fund (IMF), and other international and regional financial institutions must take into consideration the culture of indigenous peoples. Making the right to development a reality will need to entail a very effective socioeconomic planning and implementation process. Indigenous peoples in defending their human rights and fundamental freedoms should not be compelled to routinely seek legal recourse in order to achieve these ends. It must be a last resort against oppression; all their human rights, including the rights to self-determination and development, must be recognized and guaranteed by the rule of law.

SEE ALSO Australia; Aztecs; Beothuk; Canada; Cheyenne; Incas; Native Americans; Pequots; Trail of Tears; Wounded Knee

BIBLIOGRAPHY

Aikio, Pekka, and M. Scheinin, eds. (2000). *Operationalizing the Right of Indigenous Peoples to Self-Determination.* Turku/Abô, Finland: Institute for Human Rights.

Alfonso-Martinez, M. (1999). *Study on Treaties, Agreements and Other Constructive Arrangements Between States and Indigenous Populations.* UN Document E/CN.4/Sub.2/1999/20. Geneva: Office of the High Commissioner for Human Rights.

Alfredsson, Gudmundur (1993). "Self-Determination and Indigenous Peoples." In *Modern Law of Self-Determination,* ed. C. Tomuschat. London: Martinus Nijhoff.

Anaya, S. James (1996). *Indigenous Peoples in International Law.* New York: Oxford University Press.

Anaya, S. James, ed. (2003). *International Law and Indigenous Peoples.* Dartmouth: Ashgate.

Barsh, Russel L. (1987). "Evolving Conceptions of Group Rights in International Law." *Transnational Perspectives* 13:1–8.

Barsh, Russell L. (1994). "Indigenous Peoples in the 1990s: From Object to Subject of International Law?" *Harvard Human Rights Journal* 7:33–86.

Battiste, Marie, ed. (2000). *Reclaiming Indigenous Voice and Vision.* Vancouver, B.C.: UBC.

Beckett, Jeremy (1987). *Torres Strait Islanders: Custom and Colonialism.* New York: Cambridge University Press.

Berger, Thomas R. (1985). *Village Journey—The Report of the Alaska Native Review Commission.* New York: Hill and Wang.

Berger, Thomas R. (1991). *A Long and Terrible Shadow.* Vancouver, B.C.: Douglas & McIntyre.

Brown, Dee Alexander (1970). *Bury My Heart at Wounded Knee—An Indian History of the American West.* New York: Henry Holt.

Brysk, Alison (2000). *From Tribal Village to Global Village—Indian Rights and International Relations in Latin America.* Stanford, Calif.: Stanford University Press.

Council for Aboriginal Reconciliation—Constitutional Centenary Foundation (1993). *The Position of Indigenous People in National Constitutions.* Canberra, Australia: Government Publishing Service.

Daes, Erica-Irene A. (1996a). *Standard-Setting Activities: Evolution of Standards Concerning the Rights of Indigenous Peoples.* Working Paper on the Concept of Indigenous People. UN Document E/CN.4/Sub.2/AC,4/1996/2. Geneva: UN Sub-Commission on Prevention and Protection of Minorities.

Daes, Erica-Irene A. (1996b). "Right of Indigenous Peoples to 'Self-Determination' in the Contemporary World Order." In *Self-Determination—International Perspectives,* ed. D. Clark and R. Williamson. London. Macmillan.

Daes, Erica-Irene A. (1997). *Protection of the Heritage of Indigenous People, Study 10.* UN Publication No. E.97.XIV.3.

Daes, Erica-Irene A. (2000). "Protection of the World's Indigenous Peoples and Human Rights." In *Human Rights: Concept and Standards,* ed. J. Symonides. Dartmouth: Ashgate-UNESCO.

Daes, Erica-Irene A. (2001). *Indigenous Peoples and Their Relationship to Land.* Final Working Paper. UN Document E/CN.4/Sub.2/2001/21. Geneva: Economic and Social Council-Commission on Human Rights.

Epstein, R. J. (2002). "The Role of Extinguishment in the Cosmology of Dispossession." In *Justice Pending,* ed. Gudmundur Alfredsson and Maria Stavropoulou. The Hague: Martinus Nijhoff.

Helander, E., and K. Kailo, eds. (1998). *No Beginning, No End—The Sami Speak Up.* Circumpolar Research Series No. 5. Finland: Nordic Sami Institute.

Henriksen, J. B. (2000). "The Right to Self-Determination: Indigenous Peoples versus States and Others." In *Operationalizing the Right of Indigenous Peoples to Self-Determination,* ed. Pekka Aikio and M. Schein. Turku/Abo: Institute for Human Rights-Abo Akademi University.

Jentoft, Skjelfjord, H. Minde, and R. Nilsen (2003). *Indigenous Peoples: Resource Management and Global Rights.* Netherlands: Eburon Delft.

Lam, M. C. (2000). "At the Edge of the State—Indigenous Peoples and Self-Determination." In *Innovation in International Law,* ed. Richard A. Falk. Ardsley, N.Y.: Transnational Publishers.

Lavarch, Michael (1993). *Native Title–Native Title Act 1993.* Canberra, Australia: AGPS Press.

Martinez Cobo, Jose (1987). *Study of the Problem of Discrimination Against Indigenous Populations.* UN Publication No. E.86.XIV.3, Vol. V.

McRae, H., G. Nettheim, and L. Beacroft (1993). "Aboriginal Legal Issues." In *Commentary and Materials,* 2nd edition. Melbourne, Victoria: The Law Book Company.

Moses, T. (2002). "Renewal of the Nation." In *Justice Pending: Indigenous Peoples and Other Good Causes,* ed. G. Alfredsson and M. Stavropoulou. The Hague: Martinus Nijhoff.

O'Conor, Geoffrey (1997). *Amazon Journal—Dispatching from a Vanishing Frontier.* New York: Dutton.

Reynolds, M. (2002). "Stolen Generations." *Australian Report* 4(1):21.

Sanders, D. (1989). "The UN Working Group on Indigenous Populations." *Human Rights Quarterly* 11:406–429.

Sanders, D. (1993). "Self-Determination and Indigenous Peoples." In *Modern Law of Self-Determination,* ed. C. Tomuschat. London: Martinus Nijhoff.

Erica-Irene A. Daes

Indonesia

During about five months, from late October 1965 until March 1966, approximately half a million members of the Indonesian Communist Party (Partai Komunis Indonesia, PKI) were killed by army units and anticommunist militias. At the time of its destruction, the PKI was the largest communist party in the non-communist world and was a major contender for power in Indonesia. President Sukarno's Guided Democracy had maintained an uneasy balance between the PKI and its leftist allies on one hand and a conservative coalition of military, religious, and liberal groups, presided over by Sukarno, on the other. Sukarno was a spellbinding orator and an accomplished ideologist, having woven the Indonesia's principal rival ideologies into an eclectic formula called NASAKOM (nationalism, religion, communism), but he was ailing, and there was a widespread feeling that either the communists or their opponents would soon seize power.

The catalyst for the killings was a coup in Jakarta, undertaken by the September 30 Movement, but actually carried out on October 1, 1965. Although many aspects of the coup remain uncertain, it appears to have been the work of junior army officers and a special bureau of the PKI answering to the party chairman, D. N. Aidit. The aim of the coup was to forestall a predicted military coup planned for Armed Forces Day (October 5) by kidnapping the senior generals believed to be the rival coup plotters. After some of the generals were killed in botched kidnapping attempts, however, and after Sukarno refused to support the September 30 Movement, its leaders went further than previously planned and attempted to seize power. They were unprepared for such a drastic action, however, and the takeover attempt was defeated within twenty-four hours by the senior surviving general, Suharto, who was commander of the Army's Strategic Reserve, KOSTRAD.

There was no clear proof at the time that the coup had been the work of the PKI. Party involvement was suggested by the presence of Aidit at the plotters' headquarters in Halim Airforce Base, just south of Jakarta, and by the involvement of members of the communist-affiliated People's Youth (Pemuda Rakyat) in some of the operations, but the public pronouncements and activities of the September 30 Movement gave it the appearance of being an internal army movement. Nonetheless, for many observers it seemed likely that the party was behind the coup. In 1950 the PKI had explicitly abandoned revolutionary war in favor of a peaceful path to power through parliament and elections. This strategy had been thwarted in 1957, when Sukarno suspended parliamentary rule and began to construct his Guided Democracy, which emphasized balance and cooperation between the diverse ideological streams present in Indonesia.

The PKI, however, had recovered to become a dominant ideological stream. Leftist ideological statements permeated the public rhetoric of Guided Democracy, and the party appeared to be by far the largest and best-organized political movement in the country. Its influence not only encompassed the poor and disadvantaged but also extended well into military and civil-ian elites, which appreciated the party's nationalism and populism, its reputation for incorruptibility, and its potential as a channel of access to power. Yet the party had many enemies. Throughout Indonesia, the PKI had chosen sides in long-standing local conflicts and in so doing had inherited ancient enmities. It was also loathed by many in the army for its involvement in the 1948 Madiun Affair, a revolt against the Indonesian Republic during the war of independence against the Dutch. Although the party had many sympathizers in the armed forces and in the bureaucracy, it controlled no government departments and, more important, had no reliable access to weapons. Thus, although there were observers who believed that the ideological élan of the party and its strong mass base would sweep it peacefully into power after Sukarno, others saw the party as highly vulnerable to army repression. A preemptive strike against the anticommunist high command of the army appeared to be an attractive strategy, and indeed it seems that this was the path chosen by Aidit, who appears to have been acting on his own and without reference to other members of the party leadership.

In fact, the military opponents of the PKI had been hoping for some time that the communists would launch an abortive coup, believing that this would provide a pretext for suppressing the party. The September 30 Movement therefore played into their hands. There is evidence that Suharto knew in advance that a plot was afoot, but there is neither evidence nor a plausible account to support the theory, sometimes aired, that the coup was an intelligence operation by Suharto to eliminate his fellow generals and compromise the PKI. Rather, Suharto and other conservative generals were ready to make the most of the opportunity which Aidit and the September 30 Movement provided.

The army's strategy was to portray the coup as an act of consummate wickedness and as part of a broader PKI plan to seize power. Within days, military propagandists had reshaped the name of the September 30 Movement to construct the acronym GESTAPU, with its connotations of the ruthless evil of the Gestapo. They concocted a story that the kidnapped generals had been tortured and sexually mutilated by communist women before being executed, and they portrayed the killings of October 1 as only a prelude to a planned nationwide purge of anticommunists by PKI members and supporters. In lurid accounts, PKI members were alleged to have dug countless holes so as to be ready to receive the bodies of their enemies. They were also accused of having been trained in the techniques of torture, mutilation, and murder. The engagement of the PKI as an institution in the September 30 Movement

Major General Suharto (in camouflage fatigues) in an October 6, 1965, photograph. Suharto, right-wing dictator and President of Indonesia from 1967 to 1998, ruled through military control and media censorship. When East Timor, a Portuguese colony, declared its independence, on November 28, 1975, Suharto ordered his army to invade and to annex East Timor as an Indonesian province. It is estimated that, during the annexation, one-third of the local population was killed by the Indonesian army. [AP/WIDE WORLD PHOTOS]

was presented as fact rather than conjecture. Not only the party as a whole but also its political allies and affiliated organizations were portrayed as being guilty both of the crimes of the September 30 Movement and of conspiracy to commit further crimes on a far greater scale. At the same time, President Sukarno was portrayed as culpable for having tolerated the PKI within Guided Democracy. His effective powers were gradually circumscribed, and he was finally stripped of the presidency on March 12, 1967. General Suharto took over and installed a military-dominated, development-oriented regime known as the New Order, which survived until 1998.

In this context, the army began a purge of the PKI from Indonesian society. PKI offices were raided, ransacked, and burned. Communists and leftists were purged from government departments and private associations. Leftist organizations and leftist branches of larger organizations dissolved themselves. Within about two weeks of the suppression of the coup, the killing of communists began.

Remarkably few accounts of the killings were written at the time, and the long era of military-dominated government that followed in Indonesia militated against further reporting. The destruction of the PKI was greeted enthusiastically by the West, with *Time* magazine describing it as "The West's best news for years in Asia," and there was no international pressure on the military to halt or limit the killings. After the fall of Suharto in 1998, there was some attempt to begin investigation of the massacres, but these efforts were hampered by continuing official and unofficial anti-communism and by the pressure to investigate more recent human rights abuses. President Abdurrahman Wahid (1999–2001) apologized for the killings on behalf of his orthodox Muslim association, Nahdlatul Ulama, but many Indonesians continued to regard the massacres as warranted. As a result, much remains unknown about the killings.

Many analyses of the massacres have stressed the role of ordinary Indonesians in killing their communist

encyclopedia of GENOCIDE *and* CRIMES AGAINST HUMANITY

neighbors. These accounts have pointed to the fact that anticommunism became a manifestation of older and deeper religious, ethnic, cultural, and class antagonisms. Political hostilities reinforced and were reinforced by more ancient enmities. Particularly in East Java, the initiative for some killing came from local Muslim leaders determined to extirpate an enemy whom they saw as infidel. Also important was the opaque political atmosphere of late Guided Democracy. Indonesia's economy was in serious decline, poverty was widespread, basic necessities were in short supply, semi-political criminal gangs made life insecure in many regions, and political debate was conducted with a bewildering mixture of venom and camaraderie. With official and public news sources entirely unreliable, people depended on rumor, which both sharpened antagonisms and exacerbated uncertainty. In these circumstances, the military's expert labeling of the PKI as the culprit in the events of October 1, and as the planner of still worse crimes, unleashed a wave of mass retaliation against the communists in which the common rhetoric was one of "them or us."

Accounts of the killings that have emerged in recent years, however, have indicated that the military played a key role in the killings in almost all regions. In broad terms, the massacres took place according to two patterns. In Central Java and parts of Flores and West Java, the killings took place as almost pure military operations. Army units, especially those of the elite para-commando regiment RPKAD, commanded by Sarwo Edhie, swept through district after district arresting communists on the basis of information provided by local authorities and executing them on the spot. In Central Java, some villages were wholly PKI and attempted to resist the military, but they were defeated and all or most villagers were massacred. In a few regions—notably Bali and East Java—civilian militias, drawn from religious groups (Muslim in East Java, Hindu in Bali, Christian in some other regions) but armed, trained, and authorized by the army, carried out raids themselves. Rarely did militias carry out massacres without explicit army approval and encouragement.

More common was a pattern in which party members and other leftists were first detained. They were held in police stations, army camps, former schools or factories, and improvised camps. There they were interrogated for information and to obtain confessions before being taken away in batches to be executed, either by soldiers or by civilian militia recruited for the purpose. Most of the victims were killed with machetes or iron bars.

The killings peaked at different times in different regions. The majority of killings in Central Java were over by December 1965, while killings in Bali and in parts of Sumatra took place mainly in early 1966. Although the most intense of the killings were over by mid-March 1966, sporadic executions took place in most regions until at least 1970, and there were major military operations against alleged communist underground movements in West Kalimantan, Purwodadi (Central Java), and South Blitar (East Java) from 1967 to 1969.

It is generally believed that the killings were most intense in Central and East Java, where they were fueled by religious tensions between *santri* (orthodox Muslims) and *abangan* (followers of a syncretic local Islam heavily influenced by pre-Islamic belief and practice). In Bali, class and religious tensions were strong; and in North Sumatra, the military managers of state-owned plantations had a special interest in destroying the power of the communist plantation workers' unions. There were pockets of intense killing, however, in other regions. The total number of victims to the end of 1969 is impossible to estimate reliably, but many scholars accept a figure of about 500,000. The highest estimate is 3,000,000.

Aidit, who went underground immediately after the failure of the coup, was captured and summarily executed, as were several other party leaders. Others, together with the military leaders of the September 30 Movement, were tried in special military tribunals and condemned to death. Most were executed soon afterward, but a few were held for longer periods, and the New Order periodically announced further executions. A few remained in jail in 1998 and were released by Suharto's successor, President B. J. Habibie.

It is important to note that Chinese Indonesians were not, for the most part, a significant group among the victims. Although Chinese have repeatedly been the target of violence in independent Indonesia, and although there are several reports of Chinese shops and houses being looted between 1965 and 1966, the vast majority of Chinese were not politically engaged and were expressly excluded from the massacres of communists in most regions.

Outside the capital, Jakarta, the army used local informants and captured party documents to identify its victims. At the highest level, however, the military also used information provided by United States intelligence sources to identify some thousands of people to be purged. Although the lists provided by the United States have not been released, it is likely that they included both known PKI leaders and others whom the American authorities believed to be agents of commu-

In March 2001 indigenous Dayaks in Indonesia attacked Madurese settlers in the Central Kalimantan town of Sampit, forcing some 50,000 from their homes and killing at least 469. When the government did finally evacuate remaining Madurese—such as the refugees shown disembarking in Surabaya Harbor, East Java, in this March 6 photo—many accused it of ethnic cleansing, in handing the Dayaks a victory in their bid to drive the Madurese from Borneo.[REUTERS/CORBIS]

nist influence but who had no public affiliation with the party.

Alongside the massacres, the army detained leftists on a massive scale. According to official figures, between 600,000 and 750,000 people passed through detention camps for at least short periods after 1965, though some estimates are as high as 1,500,000. These detentions were partly adjunct to the killings—victims were detained prior to execution or were held for years as an alternative to execution—but the detainees were also used as a cheap source of labor for local military authorities. Sexual abuse of female detainees was common, as was the extortion of financial contributions from detainees and their families. Detainees with clear links to the PKI were dispatched to the island of Buru, in eastern Indonesia, where they were used to construct new agricultural settlements. Most detainees were released by 1978, following international pressure.

Even after 1978, the regime continued to discriminate against former detainees and their families. Former detainees commonly had to report to the authorities at fixed intervals (providing opportunities for extortion). A certificate of non-involvement in the 1965 coup was required for government employment or employment in education, entertainment, or strategic industries. From the early 1990s, employees in these categories were required to be "environmentally clean," meaning that even family members of detainees born after 1965 were excluded from many jobs, and their children faced harassment in school. A ban on such people being elected to the legislature was lifted only in 2004. A ban on the teaching of Marxism-Leninism remains in place.

Although the 1948 United Nations Convention on Genocide does not acknowledge political victims as victims of genocide, the Indonesian case indicates that the distinction between victims defined by "national, ethnical, racial, or religious" identity on the one hand and political victims on the other may be hard to sustain. Indonesian national identity is defined politically, rather than by ethnicity or religion, so that the communist victims of 1965 and after, constituting a different political vision of Indonesia from that of their enemies, may be said by some to have constituted a national group.

SEE ALSO East Timor; Kalimantan; West Papua, Indonesia (Irian Jaya)

BIBLIOGRAPHY

Anderson, Ben (1987). "How Did the Generals Die?" *Indonesia* 43:109–134.

Cribb, Robert, ed. (1990). *The Indonesian Killings of 1965–1966: Studies from Java and Bali.* Clayton, Victoria: Monash University Centre of Southeast Asian Studies.

Cribb, Robert (2001). "How Many Deaths? Problems in the Statistics of Massacre in Indonesia (1965–1966) and East Timor (1975–1980)." In *Violence in Indonesia,* ed. Ingrid Wessel and Georgia Wimhöfer. Hamburg: Abera.

Cribb, Robert (2003). "Genocide in the Non-Western World: Implications for Holocaust Studies." In *Genocide: Cases, Comparisons, and Contemporary Debates,* ed. Steven L. B. Jensen. Copenhagen: Danish Center for Holocaust and Genocide Studies.

Crouch, Harold (1978). *The Army and Politics in Indonesia.* Ithaca, N.Y.: Cornell University Press.

Drakeley, Steven (2000). *Lubang Buaya: Myth, Misogyny, and Massacre.* Clayton, Victoria: Monash Asia Institute.

Fealy, Greg (1995). *The Release of Indonesia's Political Prisoners: Domestic versus Foreign Policy, 1975–1979.* Clayton, Victoria: Monash Asia Institute.

Goodfellow, Robert (2002). "Forgetting What It Is to Remember the Indonesian Killings of 1965–1966." In *Historical Injustice and Democratic Transition in Eastern Asia and Northern Europe: Ghosts at the Table of Democracy,* ed. Kenneth Christie and Robert Cribb. London: RoutledgeCurzon.

Hefner, Robert W. (1990). *The Political Economy of Mountain Java: An Interpretive History.* Berkeley, Calif.: University of California Press.

Leclerc, Jacques (1997). "Girls, Girls, Girls, and Crocodiles." In *Outward Appearances: Dressing State and Society in Indonesia,* ed. Henk Schulte Nordholt. Leiden, Netherlands: KITLV.

Robinson, Geoffrey (1995). *The Dark Side of Paradise: Political Violence in Bali.* Ithaca, N.Y.: Cornell University Press.

Vickers, Adrian (1998). "Reopening Old Wounds: Bali and the Indonesian Killings: A Review Article." *Journal of Asian Studies* 57(3):774–785.

Robert Cribb

Inquisition

During the Middle Ages *inquisition* meant an enquiry, undertaken ad hoc by papally appointed inquisitors. While at the time the Latin term *inquisitio* could be applied to enquiries of any kind, historians have come reserve the term to describe the task of detecting, prosecuting, and punishing heretics and their sympathizers by papally appointed judges. This procedure flourished mostly in the thirteenth and fourteenth centuries; in the fifteenth century many aspects of inquisitorial procedure were adopted by bishops to deal with heresy in their dioceses, especially in England and Bohemia.

During the early modern period this office became the basis for the creation of several national institutions, generally dedicated to the prosecution of religious dissent but whose main interests and concerns varied according to local demands. While the medieval and early modern inquisitions share many characteristics, notably of procedure, they should not be confused and shall be discussed here separately.

Inquisition in the Middle Ages

The Christian Church was marked by religious dissent from its very beginning. In the patristic period St. Paul and St. Augustine repeatedly warned about the dangers of heresy. Between the sixth and eleventh centuries the Western Church's concern for heresy waned as it devoted itself to the conversion of Europe. In the eleventh century, however, a spirit of religious reform led to the articulation of a concept of Christian society in which the prospect of salvation was believed to be greatly improved if all Christians reformed their ways. Sometimes called the second wave of conversion, this reform led to a greater concern with individual Christians' beliefs and behavior.

While the origins of medieval heresies remain a complex issue, this climate of religious reform contributed to the creation of heretical movements by those who thought the Church had not gone far enough in its reforms. The spread of popular heresies in Europe during the eleventh and twelfth centuries spurred church officials and lay authorities to action. During the twelfth century, ecclesiastical and lay authorities took steps toward prosecution, the former by making it the duty of bishops to locate and prosecute heresy in their dioceses, and the latter through legislation applying the death penalty or exile to those convicted of heresy. These attempts proved largely ineffective and by the thirteenth century heresy had spread through many parts of southern France, northern Italy, and the Rhineland.

Pope Gregory IX (1227–1241) found a solution to the bishops' ineffectiveness with the appointment, in

1231, of full-time investigators empowered to locate and prosecute heretics. The new inquisitors of heretical depravity followed a Roman law procedure in which the judge was allowed to initiate proceedings ex officio, that is, by virtue of his office, without waiting for an accuser to bring formal charges against a suspect. The judge was also made responsible for every step of the process, from investigation to trial and sentencing. This procedure proved highly effective in dealing with crimes of a public nature and it was not unique to heresy prosecution. In fact, it was adopted by criminal courts through much of Europe at the time.

Inquisitorial tribunals were set up in many areas of present-day France, Germany, Italy, Sicily, and northern Spain. The area most visited by medieval inquisitors was southern France, where they focused especially on the prosecution of Cathars and Waldensians. Different from what is widely assumed, however, there was no single Inquisition coordinated from Rome during the Middle Ages. What is commonly referred to as the medieval Inquisition was in fact not an institution but rather a series of tribunals, following inquisitorial procedure, scattered across Europe and staffed by clergymen and advised by legal experts. Local bishops often had some influence in the workings of a tribunal. Cooperation between the different tribunals depended largely on the initiative of individual inquisitors; there was no official effort in ensuring this cooperation took place.

An inquisition started with the appointment of the inquisitor by the pope to investigate the existence of heresy in a certain locality. The inquisitor was usually drafted from the Dominican or Franciscan order and the area under his jurisdiction varied. Often, as was the case of the tribunals of Carcassone and Toulouse, jurisdiction could extend over the area of several dioceses. Inquisitors' jurisdiction was a priori limited to Christians, but Jews were sometimes prosecuted for returning to Judaism after having converted to Christianity or for protecting those hiding from the inquisitors.

After the area of jurisdiction was determined, the inquisitor then chose a centrally located seat from which to summon suspects from all areas under his purview. At the outset of the investigation, the inquisitor gave a public speech in which he affirmed his authority and established a period of grace (*tempus gratiae*), usually lasting between two weeks and one month, during which anybody who volunteered a full and truthful confession would be spared the harsher punishments allowed by law. From the evidence gathered from confessions, the inquisitor then summoned suspects for interrogation. The many manuals written for inquisitors during the twelfth and thirteenth centu-

ries warned about the need to distinguish between truthful and false abjuration, and inquisitors seem to have paid great attention to accusations based on personal enmity. While the names of witnesses testifying against a suspect were kept secret to avoid retaliation, the accused was allowed to list all of his or her enemies and if any of these were among those who testified against him or her, the name was removed from the roll of witnesses.

If the accused admitted guilt and showed themselves willing to repent, they were usually given a light penance, warning, and absolution. If there was no admission of guilt and sufficient evidence against the accused accumulated, inquisitors were allowed to use torture. The use of torture to exact confessions was not unique to the inquisition—indeed, it was common practice in all ecclesiastical and lay courts of Europe, with the exception of England. Evidence from inquisitorial registers and inquisitors' manuals suggests that the most widely used technique for eliciting confessions was incarceration rather than torture. Separation from family and friends, the mounting cost of imprisonment (for which the accused was held responsible), and the general dreariness of prison life proved more effective than torture in bringing about confessions.

As the aim of the inquisition was to reconcile the accused to the Catholic Church, punishments for heretical crimes were both spiritual and corporal. In theory, a first offender was not supposed to be burned and punishments were calculated to bring about repentance. The harshest penalty for first time offenders was life imprisonment and loss of property. This imprisonment could be either under normal or strict regime; while normal regime was not considered very harsh, strict could mean solitary confinement, little food, and shackles.

Inquisitors were the first judges to use imprisonment as a punishment for crimes. Something akin a parole system was also devised and those who showed contrition and good behavior had their sentences commuted. Life imprisonment, therefore, could mean only a few years of incarceration and the rest of the sentence could be served in freedom pending good behavior or it could be commuted to a lighter punishment. Other forms of punishment included pilgrimages, fasting, wearing penitential garments bearing yellow crosses, and lighter spiritual penances. Burnings were supposed to be a last resort and only unrepentant and relapsed heretics faced relaxation, that is, being handed over to secular authorities for execution.

The ad hoc nature of the process and the lack of centralized control, however, meant that considerable variation existed both regionally and from inquisitor to inquisitor. Conrad of Marburg, a papally appointed inquisitor, created a reign of terror in Germany during his two-year career in the early 1230s. Most inquisitors, however, proved to be conscientious judges and, contrary to popular belief, relatively few heretics were executed. Estimates from thirteenth-century southern France indicate that 1 percent of those convicted by the inquisition received the death penalty and approximately 10 percent were imprisoned. The vast majority received lighter penances.

By the mid-fourteenth century the great heretical movements that constituted the inquisitors' main target, Catharism and Waldensianism, had mostly disappeared. Consequently, the appointment of inquisitors by the papacy waned until the creation of the early modern institutions in the fifteenth and sixteenth centuries.

The Spanish Inquisition

In 1391 a series of pogroms against Jewish communities swept across Castile and the Crown of Aragon, leading to the forced conversion of thousands of Jews. These violent actions created a new group in the Iberian Peninsula, new Christians known as *conversos*. While some truthfully converted, many *conversos* remained practicing Jews. Ferdinand and Isabella, in an effort to ensure their kingdoms were truly Catholic, applied for a license to confront what became known as the *converso* problem.

The creation of the Spanish Inquisition to deal with the *converso* problem took place in stages, beginning with a bull issued by Pope Sixtus IV on November 1, 1478. This bull granted the Spanish monarchs the right to appoint two inquisitors to oversee the eradication of the Judaizing heresy. Four years later, seven more inquisitors were appointed. Initially established only in Castile, the Spanish Inquisition was extended into the Crown of Aragon in 1483 to 1484. For Castile, the imposition of an inquisitorial court was entirely new, as the medieval inquisition had previously existed only in the Crown of Aragon. One crucial difference distinguished the Spanish Inquisition from its predecessor: the former was entirely under the control of the Crown. In 1488, with the creation of the *Consejo de la Suprema y General Inquisicion* (or the *Suprema*), the Inquisition became an organ of the Spanish government.

During the course of its three-hundred year history, the Spanish Inquisition prosecuted many different groups for crimes against Catholic orthodoxy. These included Protestants, *alumbrados* (illuminist mystics), and unruly clergy, as well as the general population for sexual offenses (such as adultery and homosexuality),

blasphemy, and anticlericalism. Their greatest targets, however, were the *conversos* (1478–1530; 1650–1720) and converted Muslims, the *moriscos* (1520–1609, especially in Granada, Valencia, and Aragon). By the end of the seventeenth century, the Spanish Inquisition was largely concerned with enforcing Counter-Reformation ideals of Catholic orthodoxy. The reach of the Inquisition extended throughout the Spanish colonies where indigenous populations also came under its purview.

The Spanish Inquisition was at first itinerant and then established in sixteen urban centers. Structurally, the tribunals consisted of legally and theologically trained inquisitors, prosecutors, and familiars (lay officials who acted within local communities as investigators). All were under the control of the *Suprema* to prevent the abuse of authority by local inquisitors. Centralizing efforts had all sentences submitted to the *Suprema* for review by the mid-seventeenth century, and all prosecutions were initiated by this council in the eighteenth century.

Procedurally, the Spanish Inquisition did not differ from its medieval predecessor. Denunciations by neighbors and voluntary confessions, made after the reading of the Edict of Faith in a community, were thoroughly investigated. Once arrested, suspects had their property confiscated and inventoried. They were then imprisoned until their hearings. Trials consisted of interrogating suspects and witnesses in a series of audiences. One vital difference from the medieval inquisition was the granting of defense counsel to the accused. Judicial torture was licit and, contrary to popular belief, was used by inquisitorial authorities less frequently than in secular courts. Cases were judged by a council of inquisitors and representatives of the local bishop.

In addition to the punishments borrowed from the medieval inquisition, the Spanish inquisitors also imposed flogging and service on the galleys to punish those convicted of heresy. After its initial harsh prosecution of *conversos*, the Spanish Inquisition dealt with those who came before its court with much greater leniency and few of those convicted faced the stake. All sentences were handed out at an *auto de fé,* the public "Act of Faith" designed to act as a deterrent to bad behavior by the rest of the community. By the eighteenth century few prosecutions were initiated, and on July 15, 1834, the Spanish Inquisition was abolished by the acting regent, Queen Maria Cristina.

The Portuguese and Roman Inquisitions

Elsewhere in Catholic Europe, Inquisitions were established on the foundations laid by medieval inquisitors. In Italy, Pope Paul III created the Roman Inquisition in 1542, which centralized the existing office under the authority of Rome. The Italian city-states, however, retained a great degree of influence over its activities. The Roman Inquisition aimed at eradicating Protestantism throughout Italy, although by the end of the sixteenth century, it primarily dealt with crimes of witchcraft, magic, clerical discipline and Judaizing.

Between 1534–1540, King João II of Portugal worked with Rome to bring the Inquisition to his realm. Modeled on the Spanish institution, the Portuguese Inquisition aimed its prosecutions at *conversos*, many of whom had been forcibly converted with the expulsion of the Jews in 1496, but also investigated cases of witchcraft, blasphemy, bigamy, and sodomy. The Portuguese Inquisition had tribunals in Lisbon, Évora, Coimbra, Lamego, and Tomar in Portugal, and in Goa in Portuguese India. It was abolished in 1821.

The Inquisition as Myth

From their creation, the Early Modern Inquisitions were seen as perpetrators of great crimes against humanity, a view that has persisted into the twenty-first century. Associated with indiscriminate arrests, overzealous use of torture, and reliance on false witnesses, all surrounded in a veil of secrecy and leading to certain death, the Inquisition was seen as a great miscarriage of justice. This view is particularly linked with the Spanish Inquisition, which popular legend described as an institution built on fear, terror and violence.

In fact, historical evidence demonstrates that after the initial harsh prosecutions of *conversos* in the late fifteenth and early sixteenth centuries, the Spanish Inquisition was much less vicious than imagined. This is particularly true if it is examined in comparison to other courts of its time. By the beginning of the seventeenth century, when secular courts in areas such as the Holy Roman Empire were burning thousands of suspected witches, the Spanish Inquisition rarely produced a sentence of death and instead handed out relatively mild punishments. Much of the myth surrounding the Spanish Inquisition was created in the seventeenth and eighteenth centuries by European Protestants who used it as an example to demonstrate the evils of Catholicism. Although often accused of horrific crimes, the centralized nature of the early modern Inquisitions worked rather to keep abuses in check, something severely lacking in localized secular courts.

SEE ALSO Cathars

BIBLIOGRAPHY

Arnold, J. H. (2001). *Inquisition and Power: Catharism and the Confessing Subject in Medieval Languedoc.* Philadelphia: University of Pennsylvania Press.

Beinart, H. (1981). *Conversos on Trial: The Inquisition in Ciudad Real.* Jerusalem: Magnes Press.

Bethencourt, F. (1995). *L'Inquisition à l'Époque Moderne: Espagne, Italie, Portugal, Xve–XIXe siècle.* Paris: Fayard.

Edwards, J. (1999). *The Spanish Inquisition.* Charleston, S.C.: Tempus.

Given, J. B. (1997). *Inquisition and Medieval Society: Power, Discipline, and Resistance in Languedoc.* Ithaca, N.Y.: Cornell University Press.

Haliczer, S., ed. (1987). *Inquisition and Society in Early Modern Europe.* London: Croom Helm.

Hamilton, B. (1981). *The Medieval Inquisition.* London: E. Arnold.

Herculano, A. (1972). *History of the Origin and Establishment of the Inquisition in Portugal.* New York: Ktav Publishing House.

Kamen, H. A. F. (1998). *The Spanish Inquisition: A Historical Revision.* New Haven, Conn.: Yale University Press.

Kelly, H. A. (1989). "Inquisition and the Prosecution of Heresy: Misconceptions and Abuses." *Church History* 58:439–451.

Kieckhefer, R. (1995). "The Office of Inquisitor and Medieval Heresy: The Transition from Personal to Institutional Jurisdiction." *Journal of Ecclesiastical History* 46:36–61.

Lambert, M. (2002). *Medieval Heresy: Popular Movements from the Gregorian Reform to the Reformation,* 3rd edition. Oxford: Blackwell.

Moore, R. I. (1987). *The Formation of a Persecuting Society: Power and Deviance in Western Europe, 950–1250.* Oxford: Blackwell.

Netanyahu, B. (2001). *The Origins of the Inquisition in Fifteenth-Century Spain,* 2nd edition. New York: New York: Review Books.

Pegg, M. G. (2001). *The Corruption of Angels: The Great Inquisition of 1245–1246.* Princeton, N.J.: Princeton University Press.

Peters, E. (1988). *Inquisition.* New York: Free Press.

Pullen, B. (1983). *The Jews of Europe and the Inquisition of Venice, 1550–1670.* Oxford: Blackwell.

Tedeschi, J. A. (1993). "Inquisitorial Law and the Witch." In *Early Modern European Witchcraft: Centres and Peripheries,* ed. B. Ankarloo and G. Henningsen. Oxford: Clarendon Press.

Wakefield, W. L. (1974). *Heresy, Crusade, and Inquisition in Southern France, 1100–1250.* Berkeley: University of California Press.

Alexandra Guerson de Oliveira
Dana Wessell

Intent

The anatomies of international crimes tend to include material elements (relevant to conduct), mental elements (relevant to state of mind) and contextual or circumstantial elements (relevant to the context or pattern within which the criminal conduct occurs). Each of these elements must be established beyond a reasonable doubt—within the context of international criminal jurisdictions—if a criminal conviction is to be sustained. In addition, one must establish beyond a reasonable doubt the appropriate mode of liability or form of participation by the accused in the relevant crime, such as individual perpetration, superior responsibility, complicity, or common purpose. Legal definitions of modes of liability have both subjective and objective requirements.

Intent describes a specific state of mind, proof of whose existence is required in the establishment of some of the abovementioned mental elements of crime. The distinction between the scope and degree or quality of requisite intent is valuable in international criminal law in the same way as it is in many national jurisdictions. There is a logical distinction to be made between the intensity of intent (i.e., its degree or quality) and the result, consequence, or other factor that such intent is alleged to have engendered (i.e., its scope). Intent may be described in relative terms, as lesser in degree (at the level of premeditation) or greater in degree (rising to the level of recklessness, or *dolus eventualis*).

This article examines the degree or quality of intent that is requisite to a finding of guilt with regard to the international crime of genocide. The definition of genocide in international law includes specific intent (*dolus specialis*) as a distinctive mental element of the crime; namely, the intent to destroy, in whole or in part, a national, ethnical, racial, or religious group, as such. However, the degree of that specific intent is not articulated explicitly in the relevant international treaties. Thus, a close analysis of case law coming out of the two ad hoc international criminal tribunals—the International Criminal Tribunal for the Former Yugoslavia (ICTY) and the International Criminal Tribunal for Rwanda (ICTR)—is in order. Also relevant are other sources of international criminal law (including the work of the United Nations (UN) International Law Commission), national case law, and commentaries by some publicists in the field. The state of international criminal law is critically appraised, with particular reference made to the Judgment of the ICTY Appeals Chamber in *Prosecutor v. Goran Jelisić* and other related cases.

International Treaty Law on Degree or Quality of Genocidal Intent

International treaty law does not define the degree or quality of intent that is requisite to the international crime of genocide more precisely than is provided by its use of the word *intent*. The 1948 UN Convention on the Prevention and Punishment of the Crime of Genocide (Genocide Convention) simply states that the genocidal conduct must have been committed "with intent to destroy, in whole or in part, a national, ethnical, racial or religious group, as such." This definition is, in the words of the International Law Commission, "widely accepted and generally recognized as the authoritative definition of this crime." The same wording is used in the Statutes of the ICTY, the ICTR, and the International Criminal Court (ICC). The chapeaux of Article 4, paragraph 2, of the ICTY Statute and Article 2, paragraph 2, of the ICTR Statute reiterate a portion of Article II of the Genocide Convention. Article 6 of the ICC does the same. This minimalist formulation of the requisite degree or quality of intent may have been of practical value to the declaratory function of the Genocide Convention and to national counterparts of the Convention, but it has proven to be somewhat vague, to the point where appellate litigation in the ICTY has been needed. *Prosecutor v. Goran Jelisić* provides an appropriate window on the problem.

International Case Law on Degree or Quality of Genocidal Intent
ICTY
The Judgment of the ICTY Appeals Chamber in *Prosecutor v. Goran Jelisić* sets forth the prevailing legal standard on the degree or quality of intent that must accompany the crime of genocide. In this case, the Prosecution appealed the Trial Chamber Judgment on the grounds that it "is ambiguous in terms of the degree or quality of the mens rea required under Article 4 for reasons articulated by the Trial Chamber itself." In its brief for the Appeals Chamber the Prosecution stated that the

> Trial Chamber erred in law to the extent it is proposing that the definition of the requisite mental state for genocide in Article 4 of the Statute only includes the *dolus specialis* standard, and not the broader notion of general intent [. . .].

The expression "to the extent it is proposing" suggests a caution or conditionality in this declaration of the grounds for the appeal; indeed, its written Appeals submission had suggested that the Trial Judgment was far from clear, left open the question of degree of intent, and used inconsistent terminology.

The Appeals Chamber astutely ruled, without any detailed discussion, that in order to convict an accused of the crime of genocide, he or she must have sought to destroy a group entitled to the protections of the Genocide Convention, in whole or in part. The mental state that corresponds to having sought the destruction of a group is referred to as *specific intent*:

The specific intent requires that the perpetrator, by one of the prohibited acts enumerated in Article 4 of the Statute, seeks to achieve the destruction, in whole or in part, of a national, ethnical, racial or religious group, as such.

The Appeals Chamber went beyond setting aside the arguments of the Prosecution. It stated that the Prosecution had based its appeal on a misunderstanding of the Trial Judgment. The Appeals Chamber stated that a "question of interpretation of the Trial Chamber's Judgment is involved," and that

the question with which the Judgment was concerned in referring to dolus specialis was whether destruction of a group was intended. The Appeals Chamber finds that the Trial Chamber only used the Latin phrase to express specific intent as defined above [. . .].

In other words, because the Prosecution was judged to have misunderstood the Trial Chamber's singular use of the term *dolus specialis* in the Trial Judgment, the Appeals Chamber did not consider it necessary to take on the substance of the Prosecution's submissions. Rather, the Appeals Chamber ruled that the term *intent* (as it appears in the definition of genocide that is used in international law) means "specific intent," which again must be understood as an intent to seek the destruction of a group. The Prosecution's attempt to advance a broader interpretation of the term was dismissed as a mere misunderstanding of the Trial Chamber's Judgment.

The Appeals Chamber affirmed that insofar as its preferred term, specific intent, is concerned, it "does not attribute to this term any meaning it might carry in a national jurisdiction." In making this statement the Appeals Chamber could be seen to have characterized comparative analysis of domestic criminal law as having little significance in the development of ad hoc tribunal case law relating to the requisite quality or degree of genocidal intent.

The *Jelisić* Appeals Judgment was rendered on July 5, 2001. Less than five weeks later, in *Prosecutor v. Radislav Krstić*, an ICTY Trial Chamber—in a Judgment dated August 2, 2001—convicted General Krstic of genocide for his participation in genocidal acts following the fall of the "safe area" of Srebrenica in July 1995. The *Krstić* Trial Judgment is in keeping with the *Jelisić* Appeals Judgment with respect to the mental state requirement for the establishment of guilt for the crime of genocide:

For the purpose of this case, the Chamber will therefore adhere to the characterization of genocide which encompasses only acts committed with the goal of destroying all or part of a group.

The Trial Chamber stated that it

is aware that it must interpret the Convention with due regard for the principle of *nullum crimen sine lege*. It therefore recognizes that, despite recent developments, customary international law limits the definition of genocide to those acts *seeking* [italics added] the physical or biological destruction of all or part of the group.

However, the *Krstić* Trial Chamber did not exclude the possibility that the definition of genocide is a portion of the international law on genocide that is evolving. The Judgment provides that "[s]ome legal commentators further contend that genocide embraces those acts whose foreseeable or probable consequence is the total or partial destruction of the group without any necessity of showing that destruction was the goal of the act."

On the whole, in *Prosecutor v. Radislav Krstić*, the Trial Chamber's discussion of genocidal intent was unusually event-dependent. The discussion of the elements of genocide never strayed from the facts of the case. (In this way a Trial Chamber may try to shelter its legal findings and prevent them from being overturned on appeal.) The Trial Judgment did, however, give more space to its finding on the mental state requisite to the crime of genocide than the corresponding (and very brief) discussion in the *Jelisić* Appeals Judgment. The *Krstić* Appeals Chamber held that the Trial Chamber "correctly identified the governing legal principle" and "correctly stated the law," but "erred in applying it."

The *Jelisić* Appeals Chamber standard (with respect to genocidal intent), as reinforced by the *Krstić* Trial Chamber, has been upheld by later decisions of the ad hoc tribunals.

ICTY Trial Chamber III, in *Prosecutor v. Duško Sikirica et al.*, issued a "Judgment on Defense Motions to Acquit" (September 3, 2001), in which it engaged in an elaborate and frank discussion of the law of genocide. The Prosecution's response to the half-time challenges submitted by the Defense, as well as the oral hearing before the *Sikirica* Trial Chamber, predated the *Jelisić* Appeals Judgment. In other words, the Prosecution had not adjusted its statements on the question of intent so as to encompass the *Jelisić* Appeals Judgment. It had, however, formulated these statements so as to be in line with the revised position advanced by the Prosecution during the oral argument in the *Jelisić* appeal.

Hence, the Prosecution proposed that three different mental state standards be part of the mental state requirement of the genocide provision in the ICTY Statute (Article 4):

1. The accused consciously desired the genocidal acts to result in the destruction, in whole or in part, of the group, as such;

2. The accused, having committed his or her genocidal acts consciously and with will to act, knew that the genocidal acts were actually destroying, in whole or in part, the group, as such; or

3. The accused, being an aider and abettor to a manifest, ongoing genocide, knowing that there was such an ongoing genocide and that his or her conduct of aiding and abetting was part of that ongoing genocide, knew that the likely consequence of his or her conduct would be to destroy, in whole or in part, the group, as such.

The Trial Chamber's response to this proposition is, although cursory, unmistakably clear. The Chamber stated that Article 4 of the ICTY Statute, "expressly identifies and explains the intent that is needed to establish the crime of genocide. This approach follows the 1948 Genocide Convention and is also consistent with the ICC Statute. [. . .]." The Chamber also noted that, "[a]n examination of theories of intent is unnecessary in construing the requirement of intent in Article 4(2). What is needed is an empirical assessment of all the evidence to ascertain whether the very specific intent required by Article 4(2) is established."

The Trial Chamber adopted a purely textual approach in its interpretation of genocidal intent, and refused to "indulge in the exercise of choosing one of the three standards identified by the Prosecution"—because, in its opinion, the wording of the ICTY Statute (and hence, the Genocide Convention) expressly provides and explains the applicable standard. The fact that the word *intent* does not reveal the degree of intent that is required suggests that the Trial Chamber wished to defuse the notion of quality or degree of intent (as opposed to its scope) in the context of the international crime of genocide.

The half-time Decision in *Prosecutor v. Milomir Stakić* provides some clarification. It was a Decision pursuant to a Defense challenge to dismiss the Prosecution's case on the grounds that there was insufficient evidence to sustain a conviction prior to the Defense's presentation of its evidence (in accordance with Rule 98*bis* of the ICTY Rules of Procedure and Evidence). The *Stakić* Trial Chamber had observed that genocide is "characterized and distinguished by the aforementioned surplus intent." Genocidal conduct, it held, is only elevated to the crime of genocide

when it is proved that the perpetrator not only wanted to commit those acts but also intended to destroy the targeted group in whole or in part as

a separate and distinct entity. The level of this specific intent is the dolus specialis. The Trial Chamber observes that there seems to be no dispute between the parties on this issue.

At the time of this Decision (October 2002), the ad hoc tribunal Prosecution had for more than one year accepted the mental state requirement as set forth in the *Jelisić* Appeals Judgment and the subsequent *Krstić* Trial Judgment. The emphasis of the *Stakić* Rule 98*bis* Decision was therefore not the quality or degree of genocidal intent, but rather the mental state requirement for accomplices. The *Stakić* Trial Judgment, not surprisingly, confirmed *Jelisić* and *Krstić* and its own half-time Decision. The Trial Chamber observed that the crime of genocide is "characterized and distinguished by a surplus of intent." The perpetrator must not only have "wanted to commit those acts but also intended to destroy the targeted group in whole or in part as a separate and distinct entity. The level of this intent is the *dolus specialis* or *specific intent*—terms that can be used interchangeably."

ICTR

Several decisions of the ICTR in effect confirm that there is a specific intent requirement for the international crime of genocide. In *Prosecutor v. Jean-Paul Akayesu* the Trial Judgment clearly states that a "specific intention" is required, a dolus specialis; however, the Judgment is rather unclear when it attempts to describe what this means. The Judgment suggests that the significance of this "specific intention" is that the perpetrator "clearly seeks to produce the act charged." Accordingly, the object of the seeking is "the act charged," and not the complete or partial destruction of the group, as such. In other words, the ordinary meaning of the formulation used in the Judgment would suggest that the "specific intention" referred to by the *Akayesu* Trial Chamber actually concerns the genocidal conduct or *actus reus,* and not the aim of destruction.

Furthermore, in *Prosecutor v. Clément Kayishema and Obed Ruzindana,* the Trial Judgment states that a "distinguishing aspect of the crime of genocide is the specific intent (dolus specialis) to destroy a group in whole or in part." The Trial Chamber then opined that, "for the crime of genocide to occur, the mens rea must be formed prior to the commission of the genocidal acts. The individual acts themselves, however, do not require premeditation; the only consideration is that the act should be done in furtherance of the genocidal intent."

The expression "done in furtherance of the genocidal intent" is to a certain extent helpful in addressing the relationship between the genocidal conduct and the genocidal intent. The genocidal conduct must be undertaken in the service of the broader intent to destroy a group in whole or in part. The expression suggests the presence of both a cognitive component and volition as part of the mental state. It is difficult to imagine how one can do something to further the realization of an intention without knowing about and wanting the intended result. Doing something in furtherance of a specific intent would seem to imply a conscious desire.

Prosecutor v. Alfred Musema also includes a consideration of genocidal intent. In this case, the Trial Chamber stated that the crime of genocide is distinct from other crimes "because it requires a dolus specialis, a special intent." The Trial Chamber then tried to elucidate what it meant by dolus specialis by positing that the "special intent of a crime is the specific intention which, as an element of the crime, requires that the perpetrator clearly intended the result charged." This language expressly identifies result as the object of the perpetrator's intent or mental state. The specific intent does not refer to the conduct of destroying, but rather the result of at least partial destruction of the group. In this sense, it may be illustrative to use the term *subjective surplus* (of intent).

However, the *Musema* Trial Judgment refers to the result "charged." Identifying the result of destruction as pivotal (in the assignment of guilt), rather than the conduct that contributes to or brings about that destruction, would seem to be based on the assumption that the result of destruction is an integral part of the crime of genocide. Regrettably, paragraph 166 of the *Musema* Trial Judgment reinforces this assumption:

> The dolus specialis is a key element of an intentional offense is characterized by a psychological nexus between the physical result and the mental state of the perpetrator.

The word *nexus* is not particularly descriptive in this context; neither is the reference to physical result. The very notion of subjective surplus presupposes a broader intent that goes beyond the actus reus and includes a further objective result or factor that does not correspond to any objective element of crime. That is why this intent requirement amounts to a "surplus." International case law suggests that there has been no recognition of an objective contextual element (such as actual physical destruction) for genocide in international treaty law. It is certainly difficult to locate such an objective contextual element in the wording of the Genocide Convention.

The Musema decision draws on the earlier *Rutaganda* Trial Judgment (*Prosecutor v. Georges Anderson Nderubumwe Rutaganda*). The latter asserts that the distinguishing feature of the crime of genocide is the re-

quirement of "dolus specialis, a special intent." It also uses the expression "clearly intended the result charged"—as well as "encompass the realization of the ulterior purpose to destroy"—both of which have been discussed in preceding paragraphs.

Finally, the International Court of Justice itself *insisted* (borrowing the word of the *Krstić* Trial Judgment), in its Advisory Opinion on the Legality of the Threat or Use of Nuclear Weapons, that specific intent to destroy is required for the international crime of genocide, and it indicated that "the prohibition of genocide would be pertinent in this case [possession of nuclear weapons] if the recourse to nuclear weapons did indeed entail the element of intent, towards a group as such, required by the provision quoted above." The *Krstić* Trial Chamber noted that some of the dissenting opinions criticized the Advisory Opinion "by holding that an act whose foreseeable result was the destruction of a group as such and which did indeed cause the destruction of the group did constitute genocide."

Other Relevant Sources on the Requisite Quality or Degree of Genocidal Intent
Even if international case law were unequivocal vis-à-vis the question of the requisite quality or degree of genocidal intent, it is also useful to consider additional sources of international law.

International Law Commission
Notably, the International Law Commission stated in its commentary on the 1996 Draft Code of Crimes Against the Peace and Security of Mankind that "the definition of the crime of genocide requires a specific intent which is the distinguishing characteristic of this particular crime under international law." The Commission further observed that

> [a] general intent to commit one of the enumerated acts combined with a general awareness of the probable consequences of such an act with respect to the immediate victim or victims is not sufficient for the crime of genocide. The definition of this crime requires a particular state of mind or a specific intent with respect to the overall consequences of the prohibited act."

Caution should be observed in relying on the *travaux préparatoires* (preparatory work, or works) of the Genocide Convention, insofar as it is often difficult to establish the prevailing thinking of the negotiating states at the time. One can find support for widely differing positions on the same issues in the preparatory work. However, the *Krstić* Trial Judgment invoked the preparatory work for its position, claiming that it "clearly shows that the drafters envisaged genocide as an enterprise whose goal, or objective, was to destroy a human group, in whole or in part." The Chamber continued:

> The draft Convention prepared by the Secretary-General presented genocide as a criminal act which aims to destroy a group, in whole or in part, and specified that this definition excluded certain acts, which may result in the total or partial destruction of a group, but are committed in the absence of an intent to destroy the group.

National Case Law

A few recent cases presented in German courts may be relevant to this discussion (although there is little evidence of other relevant national case-law). The Federal Supreme Court of Germany observed in its review of a 2001 case that genocidal acts "only receive their imprint of particular wrong by their combination with the intent [Absicht] required by section 220a(1) to destroy, in whole or in part, a group protected by this norm as such, keeping in mind that the desired goal, i.e., the complete or partial destruction of this group, does not have to be accomplished." The German term *Absicht* signifies *dolus directus* in the first degree—or, in more familiar terminology, conscious desire. The Court added, with an encouraging degree of precision:

> However, this goal has to be included within the perpetrator's intent as a subjective element of the crime that does not have an objective counterpart in the actus reus. This intent, which really characterizes the crime of genocide and distinguishes it, presupposes that it is the objective of the perpetrator, in the sense of a will directed towards a specific goal, to destroy, in whole or in part, the group protected by section 220a.

In another case that went before the German Federal Supreme Court, the judges provided further elaboration of the same conscious desire standard that was upheld by the *Jelisić* Appeals Chamber:

> The desired result, i.e., the complete or partial destruction of the group as such, does not have to be accomplished; it suffices that this result is comprised within the perpetrators intent [Absicht]. It is through this subjective element that, figuratively speaking, "anticipates" the desired outcome in the subjective sphere, that the crime of genocide [. . .] as such and thus its full wrong is determined.

Commentaries

Antonio Cassese, a widely recognized authority on international criminal law, observes that genocidal intent "amounts to dolus specialis, that is, to an aggravated criminal intention, required in addition to the criminal intent accompanying the underlying offense [. . .]." He states that it "logically follows that other categories of

mental element are excluded: recklessness (or dolus eventualis) and gross negligence." He correctly points out the ad hoc tribunals have contributed greatly to the elucidation of the subjective element of genocide.

William A. Schabas, an expert on the law of genocide, commenting on Article 6 (concerning genocide) of the ICC Statute, mentions "the special or specific intent requirement," "this rigorous definition," and the "very high intent requirement" without describing what the standard set out in the Genocide Convention and the ICC Statute actually is. It would seem that Schabas does not recognize the concept of degree or quality of mental state. He reiterates that the "offender must also be proven to have a 'specific intent' or dolus specialis," but without elaboration of what this phrase or the language of the intent formulation in the Genocide Convention actually means. He does observe that a "specific intent offense requires performance of the actus reus but in association with an intent or purpose that goes beyond the mere performance of the act." He also suggests that the chapeau of Article II of the Genocide Convention actually defines the specific intent via the formulation "with intent to destroy, in whole or in part."

German legal scholar Albin Eser's brief but sophisticated treatment of specific intent in a contribution to Cassese's three-volume commentary on the Rome Statute of the ICC is instructive. He observes that "with special intent particular emphasis is put on the volitional element." Or, more specifically on genocide:

> In a similar way, it would suffice for the general intent of genocidal killing according to Article 6(a) of the ICC Statute that the perpetrator, though not striving for the death of his victim, would approve of this result, whereas his special "intent to destroy" in whole or in part the protected group must want to effect this outcome.

This overview of the positions taken by leading specialists on the issue of degree or quality of genocidal intent shows that there are no significant discrepancies between principal and secondary sources of international law with respect to the requisite degree or quality of intent for the international crime of genocide.

The Nature of the Prosecution's Third Ground of Appeal in *Prosecutor v. Goran Jelisić*

Against the background of such strong and consistent arguments coming out of primary and secondary sources of international criminal law, it is necessary to inquire whether the Prosecution's third ground of appeal (pertaining to genocidal intent) in the *Jelisić* case was completely without merit, and whether it was misinterpreted by the Appeals Chamber.

The essence of the Prosecution's argument was: (1) that the Trial Chamber had erroneously held that the requisite quality or degree of intent for genocide is dolus specialis; (2) that the Trial Chamber had erroneously construed dolus specialis as being confined to consciously desiring complete or partial destruction; and (3) that the Trial Chamber had erred in not including the following two mental states in the scope of the requisite genocidal intent: knowledge that one's acts were destroying, in whole or in part, the group, as such; and that described by the case in which an aider and abettor commits acts knowing that there is an ongoing genocide which his acts form part of, and that the likely consequence of his conduct would be to destroy, in whole or in part, the group as such.

The Appeals Chamber held that the Prosecution's first assertion in the foregoing sequence was wrong and based on a misunderstanding, and that as a consequence it was rejecting the Prosecution's third ground of appeal. The Appeals Chamber proceeded to interpret the word *intent* as requiring that the perpetrator was seeking the result of destruction, which in reality amounts to a requirement of conscious desire. In other words, the Appeals Chamber did not address whether the Trial Chamber had held that the genocide provision of the ICTY Statute requires conscious desire (the Prosecution's second assertion in the foregoing sequence), but the Appeals Chamber itself held that conscious desire in the form of seeking the destruction of the group is required under the Statute. The concern that underlay the Prosecution's third ground of appeal was of course the level of the requisite intent, not whether or not it was called dolus specialis.

The Prosecution had advanced the two additional mental states (described above) that it claimed fell within the scope of the requisite genocidal intent—the first referring to the perpetrator of genocidal conduct, the second referring exclusively to accomplice liability. By insisting that the point of departure of the Prosecution's argument had been based on a misunderstanding, the Appeals Chamber chose not to discuss the merits of the Prosecution's second and third assertions with respect to the Trial Chamber's putative failings. As a consequence, there does not seem to be a recorded consideration by the Appeals Chamber of the possible merit of the Prosecution's material propositions.

This omission is noteworthy, not only against the background of the extensive briefing on this issue by the parties in the *Jelisić* appeal, but also in light of recent case law coming out of the same ad hoc tribunal.

Concluding Considerations

The relevant sources in international criminal law provide a firm legal basis for the conclusion that conscious desire is the special intent requirement for the international crime of genocide.

It would seem that findings by the ICTY *Jelisić* Appeals Chamber and the *Krstić* Trial Chamber of the requisite quality or degree of genocidal intent remain sound. It is difficult to see how one can avoid requiring that the perpetrator of genocide has sought at least partial destruction of the group, or had such destruction as the goal of the genocidal conduct. It is reasonable to assert that the mental state must be composed both of a cognitive and emotive or volitional component. The perpetrator consciously desires the result of destructive action if that is what he or she seeks or harbors as the goal. The idea that one can seek a result with a mind bereft of volition as regards this result seems to be an abstraction not in conformity with practical reality. Consciousness of the result of action undertaken to further the destruction of the group, of the process leading to the destruction of the group, or of how one's conduct is an integral part of this process is not the same as wanting, desiring, or hoping for the destruction to occur. Desiring the destruction itself, with no awareness of a process to bring it about, of one's own contribution to such a process, or of the ability of one's conduct to bring about partial destruction would amount to a mental state that lacks the resolve that characterizes the intent to undertake action with a view to that action's ensuring at least the partial destruction of the targeted group.

It is unlikely that the state of the law will evolve significantly in the milieu of the ad hoc Tribunals, which are expected to be in operation until sometime between 2008 and 2010. The ICTY Appeals Chamber did not leave sufficient room for the Trial Chambers to attempt to expand the scope of the applicable standard for genocidal intent. The *Krstić* Trial Judgment is courageous in this respect, insofar as it suggests that customary international law could have moved on this question but had not done so by 1995.

SEE ALSO Complicity; Convention on the Prevention and Punishment of Genocide; International Criminal Court; International Criminal Tribunal for Rwanda; International Criminal Tribunal for the Former Yugoslavia; Superior (or Command) Responsibility; War Crimes

Morten Bergsmo

International Committee of the Red Cross

The International Committee of the Red Cross (ICRC), the founding agent of the International Red Cross and

Red Crescent Movement, is registered under the laws of Switzerland, where it has its headquarters, as a private association. At the same time, it is recognized in public international law and has signed a headquarters agreement with the Swiss federal authorities as if it were an intergovernmental organization. Although its professional staff has been internationalized since the early 1990s, its top policy-making organ, variously called the Committee or the Assembly, remains all-Swiss. The mandate of the ICRC has always been, and remains, responding to the needs of victims of conflict. The organization started with a focus on wounded combatants in international war, then progressively added a concern for: detained combatants in international war, all persons adversely affected by internal or civil war, those detained by reason of "political" events in domestic troubles and tensions, civilians in international war and occupied territory, and all those adversely affected by indiscriminate or inhumane weapons. The ICRC seeks both to provide services in-country, and to develop legal and moral norms that facilitate its fieldwork.

Historical Overview

In 1859 a Swiss businessman, Henry Dunant, witnessed the Battle of Solferino in present-day northern Italy, then the site of clashing armies from the French and Austro-Hungarian Empires. Dunant was appalled at the lack of attention given to wounded soldiers. At that time European armies provided more veterinarians to care for horses than doctors and nurses to care for soldiers. Dunant not only set about caring for the wounded at Solferino, with the help of mostly female locals, but also returned to Geneva determined to find a more systematic remedy for the problem.

The Original Vision

By 1863 Dunant helped create what has become the ICRC. Originally composed of Dunant and four other male volunteers from the Protestant upper and middle classes of Geneva, the Committee initially adopted a two-track approach to help victims of war. It tried to see that "aid workers" were sent to the field to deal firsthand with primarily medical problems arising from war. It also sought to develop international humanitarian law to guarantee the protection of human dignity despite what states saw as military necessity. An early example of the pragmatic track was the dispatch of observers to the war in Schleswig-Holstein (1864). An early result of the second track was the 1864 Geneva Convention for Victims of War, a treaty that encouraged medical attention to war wounded and neutralized both the wounded and medical personnel. The pragmatic and normative tracks were intended to carve out

a humanitarian space in the midst of conflict, to set limits on military and political necessity in order to preserve as much humanity and human dignity as states would allow. This two-track approach remains, even though the ICRC's scope of action has been expanded in terms of geography covered, conflicts addressed, and victims helped.

At first Dunant and his colleagues on the Committee thought it would be sufficient for them to help organize national aid societies for the pragmatic humanitarian work. They set about promoting, later recognizing, aid societies in various countries. Other dynamic personalities, such as Clara Barton in the United States and Florence Nightingale in the United Kingdom, were also intent on doing something about the human tragedy stemming from war, and they were responsible for the creation of the American and British Red Cross Societies, respectively. These societies, and others, were loosely linked to the ICRC in a growing network that focused first on medical assistance in war.

The Ottoman Empire, the remnant of which is present-day Turkey, was the first Muslim authority to become a party to the 1864 Geneva Convention and create an official aid society primarily for medical assistance in armed conflict. However, Ottoman officials insisted on using the emblem of the Red Crescent rather than the Red Cross. The ICRC, not anticipating subsequent controversies over proliferating emblems and trying to play down the role of religion (Dunant was an evangelical Christian), deferred to this Ottoman fait accompli. In the early twenty-first century there are more than 180 national Red Cross and Red Crescent Societies. They have to be recognized by the ICRC, after meeting a set of conditions, including use of an emblem approved by states when meeting in diplomatic conference. States establish neutral emblems in war through treaty making.

By the 1870s Dunant had retired to the sidelines in the context of failed business ventures carrying the hint of scandal, something not tolerated in Calvinistic Geneva, and his leadership role was taken over by Gustave Moynier. Dunant was later "rehabilitated" and named a cowinner of the first Nobel Peace Prize in 1901. But it was the cautious lawyer Moynier who, with considerable organizational skills, decisively shaped the early ICRC.

A New Vision

The Committee initially overestimated the appeal of international or universal humanitarianism and underestimated the power of nationalism. The Franco-Prussian war of 1870 showed the limits of the original vision, as the French and Prussian aid societies helped only their conationals—and even that was not done very efficiently. Neutral, impartial, and universal humanitarianism, which means tending to victims of conflict without regard to nationality or other characteristics besides human need, was not much in evidence. The emerging Red Cross and Red Crescent movement was in considerable disarray at this time. The various national Red Cross and Red Crescent societies were being nationalized and militarized by their governments.

By World War I the ICRC decided that it must become more of an actor in the field, that Switzerland's permanent neutrality allowed a role for Swiss ICRC personnel that could not be matched by nationals of the fighting parties. If neutral humanitarianism was to survive, the ICRC would have to become more than a mailbox and far-off storage depot. World War I greatly affected the evolution of the organization. For all its brutality the war saw the emergence of the ICRC as a more widely known organization serving the victims of war. It developed a reputation for stellar work not so much in the medical field but as the neutral supervisor of conditions for prisoners of war (POWs).

The ICRC did not, however, play much of a role in the Armenian genocide that occurred in the Ottoman Empire between approximately 1890 and 1922. Historians have yet to establish the precise role of the ICRC in these events, but clearly the American Red Cross played a much more dynamic role in trying to respond to the killings in the 1890s. In 1915 and 1916 the ICRC may have contented itself with discreet overtures to Germany, the ally of the Ottoman Empire, whose personnel sometimes held key positions in the Ottoman military. At this time the ICRC was still defining its exact role as an actor in the field; remained a very small, amateurish, and inconsistent organization; and continued to focus primarily on the sick and wounded and detained combatants rather than civilians. The ICRC was more active on the Western Front, rather than on the Eastern Front and in the Ottoman Empire. To many observers it thus seemed that there was no official war between the empire and the Armenian people.

Despite its limitations the ICRC was awarded its first Nobel Peace Prize as an organization in 1917. Red Cross agencies were mentioned in the League of Nations Covenant, such was their prominence because of World War I. In 1929 the ICRC helped to develop a new Geneva Convention that legally protected prisoners of war, as well as revise the 1864 treaty (which had already been revised once in 1906). A pattern was emerging: first, pragmatic action, then legal codification of that humanitarian effort. This had been true

from 1859 to 1864, and was again the case from 1914 through 1929.

During the years between the two world wars (1919–1939) the ICRC laid the foundations for later important developments. The ICRC was active in the Spanish Civil War of the 1930s, which contributed over time to the further development of international humanitarian law for internal armed conflict, often called civil war. The ICRC was also active in East Africa when Benito Mussolini's Italy invaded Abyssinia, present-day Ethiopia, setting the stage for the ICRC's long involvement in African affairs. In addition, it was involved in Russia's civil war, although the 1917 revolution led to very chilly relations between the new Soviet authorities and the ICRC. The ICRC was not only based in capitalist Switzerland, but also had a leadership hardly sympathetic to communism. The organization also undertook its first visits to political or security prisoners outside situations of war—in Hungary in 1918. The ICRC was much less involved in some other conflicts, for example, in East Asia in the 1930s when Japan invaded China.

Another mark against the ICRC was its failure to speak out when fascist Italy not only bombed clearly marked Red Cross medical vehicles and field hospitals in Abyssinia, but also used poison gas. Being that the ICRC had publicly protested the use of poison gas during World War I, questions arose about double standards and hidden agendas on the part of the organization. Leading ICRC officials like President Gustav Ador were known to have strong anticommunist sentiments. There is speculation that later key ICRC leaders, such as President Max Huber and Carl J. Burkhardt, shared certain views common in Europe at the time—namely, that the fascists, as bad as they might be, were still a barrier against the greater evil of communism. The ICRC's cautious approach toward Mussolini has yet to be definitively explained; other factors might have come into play.

The Revised Vision Debated
During these same interwar years the League of Red Cross Societies was created under the influence of an American Red Cross that had greatly developed during World War I. Once formed, the League (later renamed as the Federation of Red Cross and Red Crescent Societies) often competed with the ICRC for leadership of the international movement. Despite the ICRC's Nobel Peace Prize of 1917, the leadership of the American Red Cross regarded the Committee as too cautious, small, and stodgy to continue to play a central role in international affairs. Moreover, to this group's way of thinking, World War I was supposedly the war to end all wars,

thus removing the need for an ICRC that focused on victims of war, and opening the door to a greater peacetime role for Red Cross actors—like the American Red Cross—that focused on natural disasters and various social programs within the nation. Nevertheless, the ICRC resisted this attempt to minimize or eliminate its role.

The advent of World War II found the ICRC in a very weakened state. The Committee was still very amateurish in its methods and led by individuals who were not always attentive to details or skilled in diplomacy. President Max Huber was in ill health and often away from Geneva. The professional staff was exceedingly small; the Committee relied heavily on the mobilization of volunteers. Despite these problems the ICRC achieved a great deal during World War II, mainly because of a paid staff that was temporarily expanded and the dedicated work of many volunteers. As in World War I, it supervised POW conditions. More so than in the Great War, it provided significant material assistance to devastated civilian populations. For example, working with the Swedish Red Cross and with the cooperation of the British navy, which had established a blockade, it did much for the civilian population in Greece under Nazi occupation. Although its activities were again more developed in the Western theater of military operations than in Asia, it again won a Nobel Peace Prize for its war-time efforts. The ICRC's role in the war, however, was clouded by controversy over whether it had been dynamic enough in responding to the German Holocaust against German Jews and other *untermenchen*, or subhumans, from Berlin's point of view. This controversy merits separate treatment and will be discussed below.

After World War II, as after World War I, there was an effort to transform the ICRC. This time the Swedish Red Cross, rather than the American Red Cross, led the charge. But efforts to internationalize the Committee, and by so doing create greater Swedish influence at the center of the movement, failed to carry the day. Eventually, the dangers of an internationalized but immobilized Committee during the cold war became clear. Moreover, the all-Swiss ICRC demonstrated its capabilities for neutral humanitarianism in places such as Palestine-Israel during the late 1940s and early 1950s, and then in Hungary in 1956 at the time of the Soviet invasion.

The ICRC also played a useful role in developing the four Geneva Conventions of August 12, 1949 for victims of war, still the core of modern international humanitarian law. Again, the pattern was clear: The organization's pragmatic actions from 1939 through 1945

helped shape the further development of international humanitarian law.

The Revised Vision Consolidated

By the 1960s, when the ICRC played a small role in the resolution of the 1962 Cuban Missile Crisis, the Committee had retained its traditional form, and efforts to impose structural reform from the outside eroded. The mono-national makeup of the Committee was seen as providing guarantees of active neutrality in humanitarian work. ICRC statutes, guaranteeing an independent role for the agency, were further reaffirmed by the International Red Cross Conference. (The Conference meets in principle every four years, attended by the ICRC, the Federation, all recognized National Societies, and governments from states that are parties to the Geneva Conventions on the Protection of Victims of War.)

It was the Nigerian civil war (1967–1970) that reopened debates about the effectiveness of the all-Swiss ICRC. In that conflict, covered extensively by the Western communications media, and investigating charges of genocide against the civilian population in secessionist (Biafran) areas, the ICRC seemed to lack strategic vision and defensible policies. In competition with other aid agencies acting to protect civilians in the midst of war, it behaved in ways that, in fact, aided the rebel cause. These policies could not be justified in terms of the rules of the Geneva Conventions. Some of its personnel were insensitive to feelings on the government's side. As a result, a relief plane flying under its aegis was shot down by the federal air force, with loss of life, and the government in Lagos declared its chief delegate persona non grata. The ICRC was, therefore, forced to the sidelines while other humanitarian organizations continued their efforts in that region.

A movement then started to replace neutral Red Cross humanitarianism with a more political kind of humanitarianism that took sides between "good" and "bad" forces. This movement led to the creation of other private aid groups, such as Doctors without Borders and Doctors of the World. For a time they tried to combine work for victims of war with public denunciations of those committing war crimes, crimes against humanity, or genocide. However, in Rwanda in 1994 (discussed below), field-workers from Doctors without Borders had to be absorbed into the ICRC delegation in order to survive. That is, they had to be neutralized. Had they tried to denounce the genocide occurring, they would have been killed by the militant Hutu.

The Nigerian civil war was traumatic for the ICRC, so much so that it set in motion a series of fundamental changes at its headquarters. In the decades that fol-

ICRC compound in Monrovia, Liberia, implores warring factions to avoid civilian casualties. Summer of 2003. [TEUN VOETEN]

lowed the roles of the Committee and its president were reduced, and the role of the professional staff was enhanced. By 2002 the ICRC had a double executive, with the office of director-general, like a prime minister, being responsible for the management of daily affairs. The president became the chief spokesman for the organization to the outside world, although he or she continued to exercise influence on general policy making. The Committee became more like many modern parliaments, mostly reacting to initiatives by the double executive and altering perhaps only 10 percent of what was presented to it. Thus, ICRC policy making and management saw an increased role for professional humanitarians and a diminished role for the mostly "amateur volunteers" serving in the Committee. (Some Committee members were co-opted into that body after retiring from the professional side of the house.) Moreover, from 1990 on the professional staff was internationalized and no longer all-Swiss. Most of this change can be traced back to the amateurish, bumbling performance of the president and Committee during the Nigerian civil war.

Throughout the remaining years of the cold war the ICRC consolidated its position as a major humanitarian actor in conflicts. Starting in 1967 it began a long involvement in the territories taken by Israel in the war of that year, territories which the ICRC regarded as occupied territory under the terms of the Fourth Geneva Convention of 1949. The situation led to various ICRC public statements in keeping with its general policy on public criticism, namely to speak out only when the fate of victims constitutes a major violation of international humanitarian law, the violations are repeated, discreet diplomacy to improve the situation was tried and failed, and any public statement issued is in the interests of victims.

In the 1970s the ICRC played its usual role, developing and then drafting two additional protocols, or additional treaties, to the 1949 Geneva Conventions: the first on international war, the second on internal war. Also noteworthy was the ICRC's extensive work with political or security prisoners, especially in the western hemisphere. Just as the ICRC visited prisoners like Nelson Mandela in South Africa or those incarcerated by the junta ruling Greece from 1967 to 1974, so the ICRC undertook to provide a basic "life insurance policy" to prisoners in South and Central America, even though most of these situations were not regarded by governments as conventional international or internal wars. If a prisoner was considered an "enemy" by detaining authorities, and an adversarial relationship thus existed, the ICRC attempted to play its traditional role through detention visits. Focusing on conditions rather than the causes of detention, and frequently avoiding legal labels and debates, the ICRC tried to counteract "forced disappearances," summary execution, torture, mistreatment, total isolation from family, and other policies devised by mostly military governments in places such as Chile, Argentina, Paraguay, Uruguay, and El Salvador.

Some of these situations, as in Chile under General Augusto Pinochet, may have been characterized by crimes against humanity, namely, a systematic and broad attack on the civilian population through such measures as generalized torture and/or summary execution. The ICRC avoided such legal judgments and focused instead on the pragmatic improvement of detention conditions. The ICRC was not able to secure the cooperation of Cuba for systematic visits in keeping with its policies: that is, access to all prisoners, private visits, follow-up visits, and improvement in general conditions over time. In places like Peru during the era of Alberto Fujimori, the ICRC suspended its visits because of lack of improvement in the treatment of prisoners.

When Poland was under martial law in the 1980s, the ICRC made its first large scale detention visits to security prisoners in a communist country. The ICRC had visited POWs in the border conflict between China and Vietnam in 1979, but had not been able to visit any prisoners held by North Korea from 1950 until 1953, or North Vietnam from 1947 until 1975.

The cold war years also saw the ICRC consolidate its position as a major relief organization, the Nigerian civil war notwithstanding. In places such as Cambodia and the Thai-Cambodian border during 1979 and immediately thereafter, the ICRC was a major actor, along with the United Nations Children's Fund (UNICEF) and the World Food Program (WFP), in providing nutritional and medical relief to a civilian population, including refugees and internally displaced persons, on a major scale. In Cambodia, virtually destroyed by the genocide and crimes against humanity of the Khmer Rouge (radical agrarian communists), the ICRC teamed with UNICEF to provide the primary conduit for international humanitarian assistance. It managed to cooperate with UN agencies while preserving its independence, neutrality, and impartiality—the three key instrumental principles in its global humanitarianism. The ICRC also carried out a major medical relief operation in Pakistan for victims of the fighting in neighboring Afghanistan during the Soviet invasion and occupation (1979–1989).

The Vision in the Twenty-First Century

In the first decade after the cold war, the ICRC found itself center stage in places like Bosnia (1992–1995) and Somalia (1991–1993). In the former, while continuing its work regarding detainees, it ran the second largest relief operation (second only to that of the UN refugee office). Its overall annual budget at this time was in the neighborhood of $600 million. Caught in the midst of genocide, ethnic cleansing, crimes against humanity, and war crimes, it sought to do what it could for both prisoners and civilians. It failed to prevent the massacre of perhaps some seven to eight thousand Bosnian Muslim males at Srebrenica in the summer of 1995 because Bosnian Serb commanders failed to cooperate. However, it actively compiled records of those killed and missing. The ICRC was unable to prevent forced displacement and actually contributed to ethnic cleansing by helping to move civilians out of harm's way, but did prevent considerable death and deprivation. Its chief delegate was killed when his well-marked vehicle was intentionally attacked. (Six Red Cross workers were also intentionally killed in Chechnya.)

In Somalia the ICRC distinguished itself through its dedicated work in coping with massive malnutrition and starvation in that failed state. Staying on the ground when other agencies pulled out, bringing in journalists to dramatize the plight of the civilian population, and dealing creatively with the violent clan structure of that chaotic country, the ICRC finally teamed with the U.S. military, acting under a UN mandate, to break the back of starvation in the winter of 1992 and 1993. It was the first time in the ICRC's history that the organization agreed to work under the military protection of a state, but such was the only way the massive starvation and rampant banditry then in existence could be addressed.

The ICRC did hire its own private protection forces in Somalia, and accepted the military protection of the UN security force in the Balkans, the United Nations Protection Force (UNPROFOR), to guarantee the safe movement of some released prisoners. In places such as Somalia, Chechnya, or Liberia, the ICRC could no longer rely on the Red Cross emblem as a symbol of neutrality that allowed humanitarian efforts in the midst of conflict. Many of the fighting parties in these places had never heard of the Red Cross or the Geneva Conventions.

In Rwanda in 1994, when militant Hutu unleashed genocidal attacks on Tutsi (as well as attacks on moderate Hutu interested in social accommodation and power sharing), the ICRC stayed in-country and provided what aid and shelter it could. It thus helped about 50,000 Tutsi, at the price of not denouncing the genocide that claimed perhaps 800,000 lives. It tried to make known to the outside world what was transpiring in Rwanda, but without using the term "genocide." At this time important outside actors with the ability to intervene, like the United States, chose not to describe the situation in Rwanda as genocide, in order to avoid the legal obligation, as a party to the 1948 Genocide Convention, to take action to stop it. Whether ICRC's public use of the word "genocide" would have affected policy makers in the United States is an interesting question. But as with other aid agencies in Rwanda, the ICRC could not have passed legal judgment on the nature of the conflict and remained operative inside the country. Militant Hutu had made that very clear. Most ICRC personnel were not harmed by those carrying out genocide, with the exception of some Rwandan female nurses working in conjunction with the ICRC.

Although internal or "deconstructed" conflicts like those in Bosnia and Somalia—or Liberia and the Democratic Congo—garnered much of the ICRC's attention after the cold war, it continued to play its traditional roles in international armed conflicts. In Iraq (1991, 2003), Afghanistan (2001–2002), and the Middle East (since 1967), the organization continued with detention visits, relief to the civilian population, efforts to trace missing persons, and attention to weapons that were indiscriminate and/or caused suffering which exceeded military necessity. Even in these more clearly international armed conflicts, its personnel and facilities were sometimes intentionally attacked, sometimes with loss of life. In places like Iraq in 2003, displaying the Red Cross emblem meant providing a target for attack.

The ICRC joined with other groups and governments to develop the Ottawa treaty (the 1997 Convention of the Prohibition, Use, Stockpiling, Production and Transfer of Anti-Personnel Mines and Their Destruction) banning antipersonnel land mines. In places such as Afghanistan, Cambodia, and Angola in particular, the ICRC had seen the devastating effects of indiscriminate land mines, which continued to kill and maim, mainly civilians, long after combat had subsided. The ICRC was also a strong supporter of the International Criminal Court (ICC; negotiated in 1998 and operational as of 2002), especially because the court's jurisdiction included war crimes, as well as genocide and crimes against humanity. However, with the approval of the international community, the ICRC has refused to allow its personnel to provide information to this and other courts, fearing that such information would interfere with its in-country operations. This right not to testify in court was confirmed by the case law of the UN tribunal for the former Yugoslavia and

in the 1998 statute of the International Criminal Court. The ICRC continues to prioritize neutral pragmatic humanitarianism, a form of informal application of the law, while leaving formal legal enforcement to others.

The so-called war on terrorism that the United States began waging after Al Qaeda's terrorist attacks on September 11, 2001, has created special problems for the ICRC. The United States has refused to apply the Geneva Conventions to many prisoners taken in its war on terrorism, which does not always involve a traditional international armed conflict between states. Moreover, the United States has developed a complicated system of detention for such prisoners, holding them without publicity in many places, mostly outside the continental United States and sometimes in foreign countries. Finding these detention centers and securing the cooperation of U.S. authorities have not been easy, especially given the U.S. tendency to hold these prisoners for indefinite duration, in isolation, to extract information from them. On the other side of the conflict, Al Qaeda continues to call for an unlimited, "total" war featuring attacks on civilians and civilian installations, which are violations of international humanitarian law.

Summary: ICRC and Red Cross Humanitarianism
It is therefore clear, even from this brief historical overview, that the ICRC has evolved, from its inception in 1863 to the early twenty-first century, into a major humanitarian actor in world affairs. It has more experience in conducting detention visits with various categories of prisoners than any other worldwide agency. It is one of the four largest relief agencies, the others being the United Nations Refugee Agency (UNHCR), UNICEF, and the WFP. It is a major player in tracing missing persons due to conflict. And it is the "guardian" of international humanitarian law. The latter notion has been expanded to include a focus not just on the legal protection of victims, but also on the legal regulation of means and methods of combat. The ICRC employs about eight hundred workers at its Geneva headquarters and, on average, deploys another twelve hundred people in its field missions, not counting numerous locally recruited staff for administrative and logistical support.

The contemporary ICRC is less amateurish and much more professional than was previously the case. Its scope of action is truly global, as it tries to focus as much attention on victims of conflict in the Democratic Republic of Congo as in Iraq. This is the meaning of impartial humanitarianism toward individuals. The ICRC also attempts to apply the same minimal standards without regard to political ideology. For instance, the humane detention conditions it advocates when dealing with prisoners held by the United States at its detention center in Guantanamo, Cuba, are essentially the same as those the organization has requested for American POWs held captive in North Vietnam or Iraq. This is the meaning of neutrality toward public authorities. The ICRC tries to remain independent from any state, coalition of states, or intergovernmental organization, even though Western liberal democracies provide 85 percent of its budget. (The remaining funds derive from contributions made by national Red Cross and Red Crescent societies, but again mostly in Western nations.)

Controversy over the Holocaust
Still hanging over the head of the ICRC is its record in responding to the Holocaust. Some facts have become clear, although questions remain and the debate continues.

At the outbreak of World War II Swiss federal authorities in Bern wished to ensure that the ICRC in Geneva did not interfere with Swiss national security and other Swiss policies defined in Bern. Swiss authorities therefore established a system of supervision over the ICRC that compromised the organization's independence in major ways. Such supervision was made easy by the fact that at this time it was possible to hold membership in the Committee and also federal office in Bern. The Swiss president in 1942, for example, Philippe Etter, was also a member of the Committee. Moreover, some members of the Committee were sympathetic to whatever Bern might identify as the national interests of the moment. ICRC President Max Huber agreed to supervision by Bern, and influential Committee members such as Carl J. Burckhardt apparently shared many of the views of the governing elite in Bern. Buckhardt was named Swiss Ambassador to France after the war, which showed that he was part of the governing establishment in Bern.

During the early years of World War II it was the policy of Bern to accommodate the Nazis in various ways. (Other European neutrals like Sweden also accommodated the Nazis while German power was ascendant.) Switzerland shared a border with its powerful German neighbor, and some Swiss feared invasion. Moreover, as the war progressed, Switzerland was virtually surrounded by fascist governments. In response it became Germany's banker, converting stolen goods into ready currency. Switzerland also turned back many Jewish refugees, not wanting to draw attention to the Nazi policies responsible for their flight. The Swiss diplomat Paul Ruegger, who became ICRC president after the war, devised the infamous practice of stamping the passports of German Jews with a "J" for

Juden, so they could be identified and turned back at Swiss and other borders.

The ICRC was aware of the German concentration camps from the 1930s. It made overtures, first through the German Red Cross, to gain access to the camps, but never achieved systematic and meaningful access until the very end of the war. The German Red Cross was thoroughly Nazified and functioned as part of the German totalitarian state. The ICRC never de-recognized the German Red Cross, despite its gross violations of Red Cross principles, which included pseudo-medical experiments on camp inmates. It is fair to label ICRC overtures about the camps as excessively cautious. On the other hand, outside of Germany, in places like Hungary, ICRC delegates in the field were creative and dynamic in helping Jews flee Nazi persecution.

By the summer of 1942 the ICRC had reliable information that the concentration camps had become death camps, as the Nazis implemented a policy of genocide after the Wannasee Conference of January 1942, attended by a high number of German officials. In October 1942, the Committee debated whether or not to issue a public statement deploring both unspecified German policies and certain policies adopted by the Allied nations toward German POWs. This relatively innocuous, vague, and balanced draft statement was shelved by the Committee after Swiss President Etter, supported by Burckhardt and a few other Committee members, spoke out against it. Etter had been alerted to pending events by the supervisory system in place, being warned that a majority of Committee members were prepared to vote in favor of issuing the public statement. Etter and his colleagues in Bern feared that such a statement would antagonize Berlin, although at the meeting where the decision to shelve the draft was made, Etter and his Committee supporters urged continued silence so as to avoid a violation of Red Cross neutrality. ICRC President Huber was absent from this meeting. It later became known that he served on the board of directors of his family's Swiss weapons company that used Nazi slave labor in its German subsidiary. Huber's fundamental values and views remain a source of debate. The ICRC thus never publicly condemned the German policy of genocide. The first line of ICRC defense is as follows. The organization was visiting Allied POWs held by Germany as covered by the 1929 Geneva Convention on that subject, and international humanitarian law did not apply to German concentration camp inmates. So the argument runs, the ICRC did not want to risk German non-cooperation on POW matters for the sake of a controversial public statement about German citizens not covered by international law. The second line of defense is that, given the Nazi fixation on eradicating Jews and other "undesirables," a public statement would have done no good. This latter argument is persuasive to some, but not all, given that the Nazis continued to devote time, energy, and resources to operating the gas chambers even when on the brink of defeat.

Later ICRC leaders, particularly President Cornelio Sommaruga (1987–1999), adopted the position that the entire Western world had failed to respond adequately to the Holocaust, and the ICRC was part of that failure. He went on to apologize publicly for any possible mistakes that the ICRC might have made regarding the Holocaust. To some, but not all, this line was an effort to "democratize the blame" and avoid any direct responsibility for mistakes.

The historian Michael Beschloss has written that the administration of President Franklin D. Roosevelt failed to measure up to the gravity of the Holocaust by not responding more decisively to Nazi atrocities, and that its record would have been brighter had it done so. Some observers believe the same could be said of the ICRC. Some of these observers think the real problem lay in how the ICRC came to remain silent. For them, a public statement by the then obscure ICRC could hardly have been expected to change the course of the Holocaust. For them, a public statement by the equally silent Vatican would have carried more weight. For them, the real issue was that the ICRC sacrificed its independent humanitarianism on the altar of Swiss national interests as defined in Bern. Thus, the ICRC's silence damaged its reputation for independent, neutral, and impartial humanitarian work, devoid of any "political" or strategic calculation. Some Committee members made this point in October 1942—before deferring to what Bern wanted.

It is now ICRC policy that one cannot be a member of the Committee and also hold most public offices in Switzerland, at either the federal, state, or local level. A headquarters agreement is in place that makes ICRC premises off-limits to Swiss authorities. Given that Swiss authorities are hardly likely to raid ICRC headquarters, this agreement symbolizes the organization's independence. The most recent ICRC presidents, like Sommaruga and Jacob Kellenberger (1999–), even though former Swiss government officials, seem determined not to allow similar intrusions of Swiss national interests to control the deliberations of the Committee. And presumably, present-day Swiss officials will not seek to project similar political considerations onto ICRC affairs, given the damage done to ICRC independence by the events of the 1940s. The contemporary conventional wisdom is that it is in the Swiss national interest to have an independent and neutral ICRC that reflects well on the Swiss nation.

SEE ALSO Humanitarian Law; Nongovernmental Organizations; Wannsee Conference; War Crimes

BIBLIOGRAPHY

Beschloss, Michael (2003). *The Conquerors: Roosevelt, Truman and the Destruction of Hitler's Germany 1941–1945.* New York: Simon and Schuster.

Best, Geoffrey (1994). *War and Law since 1945.* Oxford: Clarendon Press.

Boissier, Pierre (1978). *History of the International Committee of the Red Cross I: From Solfernio to Tsushima.* Geneva: Henry Dunant Institute.

Bugnion, François (2003). *The International Committee of the Red Cross and the Protection of Victims of War.* Geneva: ICRC.

Coursier, Henri (1962). *La Croix-Rouge Internationale.* Paris: Presses Universitaires de France.

Delorenzi, Simone (1999). *ICRC Policy since the End of the Cold War.* Geneva: ICRC.

Durand, André (1984). *History of the International Committee of the Red Cross II: From Sarajevo to Hiroshima.* Geneva: ICRC.

Durand, André (1981). *The International Committee of the Red Cross.* Geneva: ICRC.

Favez, Jean-Claude (1999). *The Red Cross and the Holocaust.* Cambridge: Cambridge University Press.

Forsythe, David (1977). *Humanitarian Politics: The International Committee of the Red Cross.* Baltimore, Md.: Johns Hopkins University Press.

Forsythe, David (1984). "Humanitarian Mediation by the International Committee of the Red Cross." In *The Theory and Practice of Mediation,* ed. Saadia Touval and I. William Zartman. Boulder, Colo.: Westview Press.

Forsythe, David (1990). "Human Rights and the International Committee of the Red Cross." *Human Rights Quarterly* 12(2):265–289.

Forsythe, David (1993a). "Choices More Ethical Than Legal: The International Committee of the Red Cross and Human Rights." *Ethics and International Affairs* 7:131–151.

Forsythe, David (1993b). "The International Committee of the Red Cross." In *Armed Conflict and the New Law: Effecting Compliance,* ed. Hazel Fox and Michael A. Meyers. London: British Institute of International and Comparative Law.

Forsythe, David (1996). "The ICRC and Humanitarian Assistance: A Policy Analysis." *International Review of the Red Cross* (314):512–531.

Forsythe, David (2001). "Humanitarian Protection: The ICRC and UNHCR." *International Review of the Red Cross* (843):675–698.

Freymond, Jacques (1976). *Guerres, Révolutions, Croix-Rouge: Refléxions sur le rôle du Comité international de la Croix-Rouge.* Geneva: Institut Universitaire de Hautes Etudes Internationales.

Gasser, Hans-Peter (2003). "The International Committee of the Red Cross and Its Development since 1945." In *Swiss Foreign Policy: 1945–2002*, ed. Jurg Martin Gabriel and Thomas Fischer. London: Palgrave.

Hentsch, Thierry (1973). *Face au Blocus: La Croix-Rouge internationale dans le Nigéria en guerre (1967–1970)*. Geneva: Institut Universitaire de Hautes Etudes Internationales.

Hutchinson, John F. (1996). *Champions of Charity: War and the Rise of the Red Cross*. Boulder, Colo.: Westview Press.

Ignatieff, Michael (1999). *The Warrior's Honor: Ethnic War and the Modern Conscience*. New York: Vintage.

Junod, Marcel (1982). *Warrior without Weapons*. Geneva: ICRC.

Lorenzi, Massimo (1998). *Le CICR, le coeur et la raison: entretiens avec Carnelio Sommaruga*. Lausanne, France: Favre.

Minear, Larry and Thomas G. Weiss (1995). *Mercy under Fire: War and the Global Humanitarian Community*. Boulder, Colo.: Westview Press.

Morehead, Caroline (1999). *Dunant's Dream: War, Switzerland and the History of the Red Cross*. New York: HarperCollins.

Moreillon, Jacques (1973). *Le comité international de la Croix-Rouge et la protection des détenus politiques*. Geneva: Institut Henry Dunant.

Willemin, Georges, and Roger Heacock (1984). *The International Committee of the Red Cross*. Boston: Martinus Nijhoff.

Ziegler, Jean (1997). *The Swiss, the Gold, and the Dead: How Swiss Bankers Helped Finance the Nazi War Machine*. London: Penguin.

David P. Forsythe

International Court of Justice

The International Court of Justice (ICJ) is the principal judicial organ of the United Nations (UN), functioning according to its statute, which forms an integral part of the UN Charter. Member states must comply with the decisions of the ICJ, in cases to which they are parties. The ICJ may offer advisory opinions on any legal questions posed by the General Assembly and the Security Council or other organs of the UN and specialized agencies so authorized by the General Assembly on issues arising within the scope of their activities.

Structure and Jurisdiction

The ICJ is composed of fifteen independent members, who posses the qualifications required in their countries for appointment to the highest judicial offices or are jurisconsults of recognized competence in the field of international law. The General Assembly and Security Council elect all members of the ICJ; no two judges

The Palace of Peace in The Hague, 1934. Home of the International Court of Justice; site of international conferences. **[HULTON-DEUTSCH COLLECTION/CORBIS]**

may be nationals of the same state. As a body, they must uphold the main tenets of civilization and represent the principal legal systems. Members of the ICJ are elected for a term of nine years; they may be reelected. If the ICJ bench includes no judge of the nationality of one or both parties to a case, that party (or parties) may choose a legal expert or two as ad hoc judges. Ad hoc judges participate in the decision of the ICJ on complete equality with the court's other members.

Only states may be parties before the ICJ. Its jurisdiction comprises all disputes referred to it by such parties and all matters provided for in treaties and conventions in force. The states who are parties to the present ICJ Statute may recognize as compulsory, and without special agreement in relation to other states accepting the same obligation, the jurisdiction of the ICJ in all legal disputes concerning (1) the interpretation of a treaty; (2) any question of international law; (3) the existence of any fact, which, if established, would constitute a breach of an international obligation; and (4) the nature or extent of the reparation to be made for the breach of that obligation.

The ICJ in deciding international disputes submitted to it applies (1) international conventions, (2) international custom, (3) general principles of law, and (4) the judicial decisions and teachings of the most highly qualified jurists from the states party to such disputes (as subsidiary means for the determination of rules of law). If the parties involved agree, the ICJ can decide a case on the basis of equity. According to Article 41 of the ICJ Statute, the Court may mandate provisional measures to preserve the respective rights of parties to a dispute. A request for such measures takes priority over all other cases.

Decisions of the ICJ on Genocide and Crimes Against Humanity

In November 1950 the General Assembly questioned the ICJ concerning the position of a state that had included reservations in its signature of the Convention on the Prevention and Punishment of the Crime of Genocide, as some signatories of the Convention objected to these reservations. In its advisory opinion of May 28, 1951, the ICJ determined that even if a convention contains no specific rule on reservations, it does not follow that they are automatically prohibited. In the case of the Genocide Convention, the ICJ found that the drafters had two competing concerns: universal acceptance (which could require permitting reservations) and preserving the normative basis of the treaty (which would require rejecting crippling reservations). The ICJ announced reservations could be permitted provided they do not undermine the object and purpose of the Genocide Convention. Every state was free to decide such matters for itself, whether or not the state formulating a reservation was party to the convention. The disadvantages of such a situation could be remedied by inserting in the convention an article on the use of reservation.

In a case concerning the application of the Genocide Convention, Bosnia and Herzegovina asked the ICJ to intervene against the Federal Republic of Yugoslavia (Serbia and Montenegro; FRY) for alleged violations of the Convention. Immediately after filing its application, Bosnia and Herzegovina requested that the ICJ approve provisional measures to preserve its rights. For its part, the FRY asked for provisional measures, too. After establishing that it did, in fact, have valid or sufficient jurisdiction, on April 8, 1993, the ICJ indicated that the FRY could take certain provisional measures. It further ruled that the FRY and Bosnia and Herzegovina should not pursue any action (in fact, they must ensure that no action is taken) that might aggravate or extend the existing dispute.

On July 27, 1993, Bosnia and Herzegovina asked the ICJ to indicate additional provisional measures. The FRY petitioned the Court to reject the application for such provisional measures, claiming that the Court had no jurisdiction to authorize them. In its order dated September 13, the ICJ reaffirmed the provisional measures it had previously indicated, calling for their immediate and effective implementation.

The ICJ suspended the proceeding to address the seven preliminary objections presented by the government of the FRY concerning the admissibility of the application of Bosnia and Herzegovina and the jurisdiction of the Court to entertain the case. The FRY claimed that (1) the events in Bosnia and Herzegovina constituted a civil war and not an international dispute according to the terms of Article IX of the Genocide Convention, (2) the authority for initiating proceedings derived from a violation of the rules of domestic law, (3) Bosnia and Herzegovina was not a party to the Genocide Convention, (4) the FRY did not exercise any jurisdiction within the region of Bosnia and Herzegovina, and (5) the Convention was not operative between the parties prior to December 14, 1995, and certainly not for events that occurred before March 18, 1993. In sum, the Court lacked jurisdiction.

In its judgment rendered on July 11, 1996, the ICJ rejected the preliminary objections of the FRY, holding that all the conditions necessary for its jurisdiction had been fulfilled. The Court also noted that a legal dispute existed between the parties, and none of the provisions of Article I of the Convention limited the acts contemplated by it to those committed within the framework of a particular type of conflict. The Genocide Convention does not contain any clause, the object or effect of which is, to limit the scope of the jurisdiction of the ICJ.

On July 2, 1999, Croatia presented an application against the FRY for having violated the Genocide Convention.

With its status remaining in some respects uncertain, the FRY was admitted on November 1, 2000, to the UN. In an application submitted April 23, 2001, it asked that the ICJ revise its prior judgment, on the grounds that only with the FRY's admission to the UN was a condition laid down in Article 61 of the ICJ Statute now satisfied. Because it was not a member of the UN before November 1, 2000, Yugoslavia argued, it was not party to the Statute and therefore not a state-party to the Genocide Convention.

The ICJ ruled against the arguments of the FRY. It observed that, under the terms of Article 61, paragraph 1 of its Statute, an application for a revised judgment can be made only when it is based on the discovery of a fact unknown at the time the judgment was rendered. According to the ICJ, "A fact which occurs several years after a judgment has been given is not a 'new' fact within the meaning of Article 61." The admission of the FRY to the UN occured well after the ICJ's 1996 judgment. Thus, the ICJ in its decision of February 3, 2003, found the FRY's application for a revision inadmissible.

It follows that the ICJ has jurisdiction to adjudicate on the claims of genocide.

Another important legal issue concerns nuclear weapons: Is their use, or the threat of use, under any circumstances permitted by international law? In its resolution dated December 15, 1994, the General Assembly posed this very question. In its advisory opinion, the ICJ summarized the cardinal principles of humanitarian law and declared with the smallest possible majority the following:

> It follows from the above-mentioned requirements that the threat or use of nuclear weapons would generally be contrary to the rules of international law applicable in armed conflict, and in particular the principles and rules of humanitarian law. However, in view of the current state of international law and of the elements of fact at its disposal, the Court cannot conclude definitively whether the threat or use of nuclear weapons would be lawful or unlawful in an extreme circumstance of self-defense, in which the very survival of a State would be at stake.

All members of the Court made declarations, with some offering separate opinions, and dissenters explaining the principles behind their votes. Such reflects the complexity of the present state of international legislation in this field.

SEE ALSO Hiroshima; International Law

BIBLIOGRAPHY

Fitzmaurice, Gerald (1986). *The Law and Procedure of the International Court of Justice.* Vols. I–II. Cambridge, U.K.: Grotius.

Koroma, A. G. (1995). "Humanitarian Intervention and Contemporary International Law." *Swiss Review of International and European Law* 4.

Oda, Shigeru (1993). *The International Court of Justice Viewed from the Bench (1976–1993).* Recueil des Cours. Vol. 244. Dordrecht: Nijhoff.

Rosenne, S. (1997). *The Law and Practice of the International Court, 1920–1996.* Vols. I–IV. The Hague: Nijhoff.

G. G. Herczegh

International Criminal Court

The establishment of the International Criminal Court (ICC) was arguably one of the most significant achievements of the twentieth century. The ICC Statute was adopted at a Diplomatic Conference held in Rome during June and July of 1998, and entered into effect on July 1, 2002. With ninety-two state parties, and many more signatories, the ICC has received substantial support from the international community and has begun work in its temporary quarters at The Hague. Yet its ultimate success is uncertain, particularly given the strong U.S. opposition to the Court.

Evolution of the International Criminal Court Statute

In 1899 and 1907 Tsar Nicholas II proposed to the governments of the world that they attend two peace conferences in The Hague. The first resulted in the adoption of three conventions; these related to the peaceful settlement of disputes (which established the Permanent Court of Arbitration), the laws and customs of war on land, and maritime warfare. The second conference, during which construction of the Peace Palace began, concluded successfully with the adoption of thirteen Conventions (three of which revised the 1899 Conventions). These included Convention (IV), Respecting the Laws and Customs of War on Land.

The treaties signed at The Hague were silent as to whether or not particular uses of force were lawful (the *jus ad bellum*). They regulated only the means an actor could employ in achieving his military objectives once the decision to use force had already been made (the *jus in bello*). The two Hague Peace Conferences were met with self-congratulation by the parties involved. However, these feelings quickly dissipated, and by the end of World War I, the "world lay breathless and ashamed" by the devastation of a war characterized by bitter savagery and monstrous slaughter.

This led to the idea that some criminal liability might be imposed for acts of war beyond the pale. Over American objections, the Commission on the Responsibility of the Authors of the War and on the Enforcement of Penalties proposed the formation of an international "high tribunal" for the trial of "all enemy persons alleged to have been guilty of offenses against the laws and customs of war and the laws of humanity." After difficult negotiations, Article 227 of the Treaty of Versailles provided for a "special tribunal" that would try the German Emperor, William II of Hohenzollern, for the "supreme offence against international morality and the sanctity of treaties." The trial never occurred, however, as the Netherlands refused to extradite William II.

The idea of an international criminal court was revived after the assassination of King Alexander of Yugoslavia in 1934, and in 1937 a convention was opened for signature on the creation of a court that would try persons accused of offenses established in the Convention for the Prevention and Punishment of Terrorism. Because the proposed court's jurisdiction was so limited and relatively well defined, it avoided many of the objections that earlier proposals had raised. Nevertheless, the convention was signed by only thirteen nations, and never entered into force.

The Nuremberg and Tokyo Trials

The atrocities of World War II rekindled interest in the establishment of a permanent international criminal court. Although a variety of proposals ensued, the model statutes proposed by jurists gave way to the pressure of political events, and the Charters of the Nuremberg and Tokyo tribunals took their place. Much less weight is generally accorded to the decisions of the International Military Tribunal for the Far East than to those of the IMT at Nuremberg for a variety of reasons, including the perception that the Tokyo proceedings were substantially unfair to many of the defendants. Nuremberg, however, was clearly a watershed event both for the ICC and for international law more generally.

Although the criminal procedures employed by the IMT fell considerably short of modern standards, the trials were generally considered to have been conducted in a manner that was fair to the defendants. It is indisputable, however, that the vanquished were tried by judges representing only the nationalities of the victors, and there is little doubt that the Tribunal was influenced by the political and psychological stress of the war.

In issuing its judgment after nine months of trial, the Tribunal addressed many of the defendants' objections to the Tribunal's jurisdiction and the law it was asked to apply. First, the Tribunal rejected the defendants' arguments based on state sovereignty, holding that individuals, including heads of state, and those acting under orders, could be criminally responsible under international law. Second, the Tribunal affirmed the primacy of international law over national law: "[T]he very essence of the Charter is that individuals have international duties which transcend the national obligations of obedience imposed by the individual State." Finally, by holding that individuals may be liable for initiating a war, as well as for the means used in conducting it, the IMT established the wrongfulness of aggression.

The Postwar Period

Nuremberg helped overcome objections to an international criminal court based on sovereignty. But the use of ad hoc or special tribunals raises several problems. First, no matter how "fair" the actual trial proceedings, such tribunals give the impression of arbitrary and selective prosecution. Second, there is the problem of delay. Ad hoc tribunals take time to establish—time during which evidence may be destroyed and additional lives lost. Finally, and perhaps most critically, ad hoc tribunals fail to build the kinds of institutional memory and competence that are the hallmark of a permanent court. Each time prosecutors must be found, staff must be assembled and trained, and judges must be procured who are willing and able to leave their existing commitments, and who may have little or no experience in international criminal law. These problems might not only damage the ad hoc court's ability to conduct an effective prosecution and trial, but could also adversely affect the rights of the accused.

Thus it is not surprising that immediately after World War II, the United Nations considered the establishment of a permanent international criminal court. The subject was raised in connection with the formulation and adoption of the Genocide Convention in 1948. Yet although the Genocide Convention was adopted relatively quickly, efforts to create the international criminal tribunal envisaged in Article VI of the Convention failed. Indeed, the reference to an international penal tribunal found in Article VI had been deleted from earlier drafts, and was restored only after extensive debate.

In a resolution accompanying the adoption of the Genocide Convention, the General Assembly invited the newly established International Law Commission (ILC), along with its work on the codification of international criminal law, to "study the desirability and possibility of establishing an international judicial organ for the trial of persons charged with genocide or other crimes over which jurisdiction will be conferred upon that organ by international conventions." The General Assembly also requested that the Commission consider the possibility that this might be accomplished through the creation of a Criminal Chamber of the International Court of Justice.

Thus instructed, the ILC embarked upon what would prove to be a long and frustrating endeavor. Indeed, it was not until 1989 that the question was actively renewed by the General Assembly, following a Resolution on the subject introduced by a coalition of sixteen Caribbean and Latin American nations led by Trinidad and Tobago.

Adoption of the Rome Statute for the International Criminal Court, July 17, 1998

Following a 1994 report of the International Law Commission on the question of an international court, the General Assembly granted the ILC a mandate to elaborate a draft statute "as a matter of priority." The project gained momentum after the creation of the International Criminal Tribunal for the Former Yugoslavia (ICTY) in 1993 by the Security Council. The adoption of the

ICTY's Statute not only suggested that a permanent court was needed, but that governments, including the United States, might be willing to support its establishment, at least under certain circumstances. The creation of the International Criminal Tribunal for Rwanda (ICTR) shortly thereafter suggested the need for an international institution that could address serious violations of international humanitarian law.

The International Law Commission considered two draft statutes for the ICC before finally adopting a 60-article version in 1994. Aware of the politics involved, and perhaps wary of having its work shelved, the Commission took no position on some of the more difficult questions involved in drafting the Statute (such as the definitions of crimes and financing of the Court), and deferred to state sovereignty on other issues (such as jurisdictional regimes and organizational structure.)

The ILC envisaged a Court with jurisdiction over treaty crimes and violations of international humanitarian law, that would act only when cases were submitted to it, and was, in all instances except for Security Council referrals, completely dependent on state consent for its operation. The basic premise upon which the ILC proceeded was that the court should "complement" national prosecutions, rather than replace them, and that it should try only those accused of the most serious violations of international criminal law, in cases in which national trials would not occur, or would be ineffective.

The ILC sent the Draft Statute to the United Nations' General Assembly for consideration, and the General Assembly then established an ad hoc committee, which met twice in 1995 to review the Commission's report. The ad hoc committee, ably chaired by Adriaan Bos, the legal advisor of the Ministry of Foreign Affairs for the Netherlands, rendered its report in late 1995. This report became the basis for the work of the Preparatory Committee established by the General Assembly to consider the Statute. While the Ad Hoc Committee focused on the general question of whether the establishment of the Court was a viable possibility, the Preparatory Committee turned its attention to the text itself. The Preparatory Committee, open to all members of the United Nations as well as members of specialized agencies, was charged with "preparing a widely acceptable consolidated text of a convention for an international criminal court as a next step towards consideration by a conference of plenipotentiaries." In 1996 and 1997, the Preparatory Committee held six official sessions, each lasting approximately two weeks, and several intersessional sessions. Finally, in April 1998 it issued a consolidated text of a draft Statute for

the consideration of the Diplomatic Conference later that summer.

The Diplomatic Conference to consider the April Draft Statute was held in Rome from June 15 to July 17, 1998. Five weeks of difficult negotiations culminated in a 128-article Statute that reflected nearly a century of work. The Court's Statute was adopted after five intense weeks of negotiations in a vote of 120 to 7, with 21 countries abstaining. The United States voted against the Statute, as did six other countries, although because the vote was unrecorded, their identities are not confirmed.

The Jurisdiction of the Court
Under Article 11 of the Statute, the Court's jurisdiction is limited to crimes committed after the Statute enters into force. This precludes the transfer of cases from the ICTY and ICTR to the Court, an option that had been considered earlier in the Statute's negotiation. The geographic scope of the Court's jurisdiction varies depending on the mechanism by which the case comes to the Court. If the Security Council refers the matter, jurisdiction extends to the territory of every state in the world, whether or not the state in question is a party to the Statute. If the matter is referred by a state party or initiated by the Court's prosecutor, however, the Court's jurisdiction is more restricted. In such instances, jurisdiction requires a state's consent and must concern acts committed in the territory of the consenting state, or an accused who is a national of the consenting state. Only natural persons over eighteen years of age may be accused, thereby excluding organizations or states.

The Rome Statute extends the Court's subject matter jurisdiction to four crimes: genocide, crimes against humanity, war crimes, and aggression. A state may opt out of the war crimes jurisdiction of the Court as regards its nationals or crimes committed on its territory for seven years after the Statute enters into force for that state. Further, the Statute does not define aggression. Article 5(2) provides that the Court can exercise jurisdiction over that crime only after the state's parties have defined it.

The ICC's jurisdiction as ultimately constituted is narrower than the jurisdiction originally contemplated by the ILC Draft Statute, which provided that the Court would also be able to hear cases involving specific crime created by treaties, such as terrorism. Recognizing, however, that treaty crimes present serious problems for the international community, and that some countries felt particularly strongly about their inclusion, Resolution E, which was adopted by the Diplomatic Conference in its Final Act, provides that the issues of terrorism and drug crimes should be taken up at a review conference, with a view to their ultimate inclusion in the jurisdiction of the Court.

Lodging a Complaint with the Court

Under the 1994 ILC Draft Statute, only states and the Security Council could lodge complaints with the Court. The Rome Statute, however, also permits the prosecutor to bring cases before the Court on his own initiative. The ILC Draft originally conceived of four separate jurisdictional hurdles that would be prerequisites to the exercise of the Court's jurisdiction in any particular case, and the combination of these four jurisdictional predicates would have rendered the Court powerless over most international crimes, even those of extreme gravity, unless the Security Council referred a matter to the Court. To many observers, this would have been unsatisfactory, for often the Security Council cannot reach agreement as to the proper disposition of a particular situation, and each of the five permanent members has the right to veto action. Moreover, most states are not members of the Council.

The Rome Statute responds to many of these concerns. The Statute requires all states parties to accept the Court's inherent jurisdiction over all crimes in Article 5, subject to the seven year opt-out for war crimes. It does not permit reservations with respect to the Court's jurisdiction over particular offenses. Moreover, it reduces, but in no way eliminates, the power of the Security Council over ongoing proceedings by permitting the Council to interfere only if it adopts a binding decision requesting the Court not to commence an investigation or prosecution, or to defer any proceeding already in progress. Finally, the ILC requirement of a Security Council determination as to aggression is now uncertain.

The Entry into Force of the ICC Statute

In a Resolution annexed to the Statute for the Court, the Diplomatic Conference established a Preparatory Commission (PrepCom II) to continue work on the development of the Court. Like the Preparatory Committee that had prepared the draft Statute, the Preparatory Commission was composed of representatives from states. Indeed, many of the delegates who had represented their governments during the Preparatory Committee meetings and the Diplomatic Conference continued to attend sessions of the Preparatory Commission, which greatly facilitated the PrepCom's work.

Pursuant to the Final Act of the Diplomatic Conference, the Preparatory Commission was charged with drafting the Rules of Procedure and Evidence (RPE); Elements of Crimes; a relationship agreement between the Court and the United Nations; basic principles of the headquarters agreement; financial regulations and rules; an agreement on the privileges and immunities of the Court; a budget for the first financial year; and the rules of procedure for the Court's Assembly of States Parties (ASP) that would ultimately provide the Court's management and oversight.

A deadline of June 30, 2000, was provided for the completion of the Rules of Procedure and Evidence and the Elements of Crimes, but no specific deadline existed for the other documents to be negotiated. The deadline was imposed to ensure that these two important documents would be finalized quickly, so that negotiation of their texts would not jeopardize either the ratification process or the establishment of the Court itself.

The Preparatory Commission held ten sessions from 1999 to 2002 and completed most of the preliminary work required for the establishment of the Court. The Preparatory Commission, like the Diplomatic Conference, was chaired by Ambassador Phillippe Kirsch, of Canada. During the initial sessions, the focus was on completing the Elements of Crimes, Rules of Procedure of Evidence, and beginning discussions on the crime of aggression. These very technical discussions continued during subsequent sessions of the Preparatory Commission as well as intersessional meetings, and ultimately culminated in the adoption of the Elements of Crimes and Rules of Procedure of Evidence (RPE) by consensus. Having completed the Elements and RPE in a timely fashion, the Preparatory Commission then turned its attention, in its sixth session, to the crime of aggression, to the Relationship Agreement between the Court and the United Nations, the Financial Regulations and Rules of the Court, and the Agreement on Privileges and Immunities of the Court.

By the end of 1998, all fifteen member states of the European Union had added their signatures to the Statute, and by March of 1999, seventy-nine states had signed the Statute and one, Senegal, had ratified it. For many states, the ratification process engendered complications unrelated to their general support for (or opposition to) the Court. Many states were required to amend their constitutions to accommodate a variety of legal obstacles: the imposition of life sentences was unconstitutional in some states, presidential immunity had to be waived for others, and for most states, adoption of the implementing legislation that would be required in order to carry out the Statute's obligations was a lengthy process. Many observers stated both privately and publicly that they expected the process to take ten to twenty years. But pressure to ratify the Statute continued to build, through the work of NGOs, the convening of regional conferences, and the ongoing work of the Preparatory Commission.

By the opening of the seventh session of the Preparatory Commission on February 26, 2001, 139 states had signed the Statute and twenty-nine had ratified it. Thus, although many of PrepCom II's initial agenda items remained, attention began to turn to the practical issues that would soon arise as a result of the Statute's entry into force, including structured contacts with the Netherlands (the host government for the ICC) concerning its preparations for the Court's establishment, and the creation of a "road map" for the coming into force of the Statute.

While the Preparatory Commission continued its work on the ancillary documents, as well as on the ever-present problem of the crime of aggression, NGOs around the world, as well as national and international bar associations, started contemplating the formation of an ICC bar association and attending to the selection of the Court's first judges and prosecutor. The penultimate session of the Preparatory Commission opened on April 8, 2002, with fifty-six states parties to the Statute. To accommodate the wishes of several countries to be considered the 60th state to ratify the Treaty, on April 11, 2002, the United Nations held a ceremony during which ten countries simultaneously deposited instruments of ratification, bringing the total number of state parties to sixty-six, six more than the number required by the Statute for the Treaty's entry into force. The Preparatory Commission also set about finishing its work, so that by the conclusion of its tenth and final session in July 2002, the Assembly of States Parties, which would be assuming the Preparatory Commission's functions, as well as the tasks assigned to it by the ICC Statute, could begin its work. During its first session, the Assembly of States Parties adopted the work of the Preparatory Commission and elected the members of the bureau, including its president, H. R. H. Prince Zeid Ra'ad Zeid Al-Hussein, of Jordan. During its second session, held from February 3 to 7, 2003, the ICC elected its first judges. Candidates from forty-three countries were nominated, and the judges were elected from among those presented. At the end of thirty-three rounds of balloting, eighteen extraordinarily well-qualified judges had been selected, including seven women. A ceremony was held in The Hague during which they were sworn in, pledging to fulfill their duties "honorably, faithfully, impartially, and conscientiously." The judges subsequently elected Canadian Philippe Kirsch as president, and Elizabeth Odio Benito (Costa Rica) and Akua Kuenyehia (Ghana) as vice-presidents.

The selection of the Court's Prosecutor was more problematic, as States endeavored to find a candidate who could be chosen by consensus. Ultimately, a distinguished Argentinian lawyer and law professor was selected, Luis Moreno Ocampo. Moreno Ocampo had established his reputation as a prosecutor during several high profile trials involving leading figures from Argentina's military junta. His nomination was uncontested, and he was installed in The Hague on June 16, 2003.

The United States' Objections to the Court

Although President Clinton and the U.S. Congress expressed general support for the establishment of the ICC, as the opening of the Diplomatic Conference drew near, U.S. negotiators within the administration and other influential political figures and commentators appeared increasingly wary of the Court. Following the Rome Conference, Ambassador David J. Scheffer, head of the U.S. Delegation in Rome, testified before the Senate Foreign Relations Committee and identified several principal objections to the Statute, three of which continued to form the crux of the Bush administration's opposition to the Court. First, Ambassador Scheffer argued "a form of jurisdiction over non-party states was adopted." Second, he complained that the Statute created a prosecutor who could, on his own authority with the consent of two judges, initiate investigations and prosecutions. Finally, he objected that the Statute did not clearly require an affirmative determination by the Security Council prior to bringing a complaint for aggression before the Court.

As a matter of law, the U.S. objections were relatively insubstantial, and most observers felt they could eventually be overcome. On December 31, 2000, the last day the Statute was open for signature, Ambassador Scheffer signed the Rome Statue for the ICC on behalf of the U.S. government. Although President Clinton maintained that his administration still had concerns about "significant flaws" in the treaty, he asserted that the U.S. signed the treaty "to reaffirm our strong support for international accountability," and to "remain engaged in making the ICC International Criminal Court an instrument of impartial and effective justice."

The Clinton policy towards the ICC can be described as an attitude of "cautious engagement," meaning that the United States would stay committed to the Court in principle, but work aggressively to protect American national interests during the negotiating process. The Bush administration, however, rejected this "wait and see" approach to the Treaty in favor of a policy of direct hostility. This reflects the views of Undersecretary John Bolton, an opponent of the Court for

International Criminal Court justices pose with Kofi Annan and Dutch Queen Beatrix in the Hague, Netherlands, in March 2003. The United States was only one of seven nations to vote against the Rome Statute of the International Criminal Court in 1998. [AP/WIDE WORLD PHOTOS]

many years, who has forcefully argued that the Court should be weakened, and ultimately, "wither and collapse, which should be [the U.S.] objective."

This policy led President George W. Bush to sign into law the American Service Members' Protection Act, which, among other things, authorizes the president to use military force to "rescue" any U.S. soldier detained by the ICC at The Hague. The Bush administration has also abandoned all negotiations pertaining to the Court, and has, through the offices of Under Secretary Bolton, written to the secretary-general of the United Nations terminating the effect of U.S. signature of the treaty. The U.S. government has declined to participate in the election of the Court's Judges and Prosecutor, and has negotiated dozens of bilateral immunity (so-called Article 98) agreements with the other countries, requiring them to turn over all U.S. citizens to the United States for prosecution, rather than to the ICC. Finally, the United States has proposed and obtained Security Council Resolutions exempting UN peacekeeping missions from the ICC Statute, despite the strong objections of many allies and the UN secretary-general.

Some observers have suggested that the Bush administration's views may suggest hostility, or at least ambivalence, towards the most fundamental principles of war crimes law. Others opine that the opposition does not stem from any particular feature of the Court or its mission, but from a deep-seated distrust of all international institutions, whatever their mandate. Finally, it may be that the Bush administration's attack on the Court is premised on the belief, expressed in the National Security Strategy Document released by the government in September 2002, that the United States should use its military force preemptively in its own defense, as well as act assertively and militarily to promote U.S. interests in the world. Under this view, it is not only inadvisable for the United States to ratify the Statute, but the Court must be eliminated or disabled to remove it as a potential constraint to the use of U.S. military force.

SEE ALSO Humanitarian Law; International Court of Justice; International Criminal Tribunal for Rwanda; International Criminal Tribunal for the Former Yugoslavia; International Law; Nuremberg Trials; Tokyo Trial; War Crimes

BIBLIOGRAPHY

Cassese, Antonio, Paola Gaeta, and John R. W. D. Jones, eds. (2002). *The Rome Statute of the International Criminal Court,* 2 volumes. Oxford, U.K.: Oxford University Press.

Lee, Roy S., ed. (1999). *The International Criminal Court: The Making of the Rome Statute.* The Hague: Kluwer Law International.

Sadat, Leila Nadya (2002). *The International Criminal Court and the Transformation of International Law: Justice for the New Millennium.* Ardsley, N.Y.: Transnational.

Schabas, William A. (2001). *An Introduction to the International Criminal Court.* Cambridge: Cambridge University Press.

Triffterer, Otto, ed. (1999). *Commentary on the Rome Statute of the International Criminal Court.* Baden-Baden, Germany: Nomos.

Leila Sadat

International Criminal Tribunal for Rwanda

The United Nations (UN) Security Council created the International Criminal Tribunal for Rwanda (ICTR) in November 1994 to investigate and, when an apparent case exists, prosecute a select number of political, military, and civic officials for their involvement in the Rwandan genocide that took place from April to July 1994. An estimated 500,000 Rwandans, overwhelmingly Tutsi, were killed during this period.

The ICTR plays an important, albeit not exclusive, role in promoting accountability for perpetrators of genocide. The Rwandan government, for its part, has incapacitated more than 80,000 suspects and provisionally released another 30,000. It intends to prosecute these individuals through national trials or traditional dispute resolution (*gacaca*). Approximately 6,500 people have thus far been convicted of genocide-related offenses in Rwandan national courts. A handful of perpetrators have been prosecuted in foreign countries, such as Belgium and Switzerland.

The ICTR is a temporary, or ad hoc, institution that will close down once it completes its work. The initial thinking was that the ICTR would complete its investigative and trial work by 2008, to be followed by the resolution of outstanding appeals. It is unclear whether 2008 remains a realistic end-point.

ICTR judgments clarify important aspects of international law regarding genocide and crimes against humanity. In this regard, they establish a strong foundation for the permanent International Criminal Court (ICC), which came into effect in 2002. ICTR experiences have informed and inspired other ad hoc tribunals to involve the international community in the prosecution of systemic human rights abuses, such as the Special Court for Sierra Leone, the hybrid international/national tribunals in East Timor and extraordinary chambers contemplated for Cambodia. Moreover, the ICTR has helped authenticate a historical record of the violence in Rwanda, has decreed that the violence constituted genocide, has educated the international community, and has offered some vindication for victims. That said, the ICTR also has been subject to criticism for its distance—both physically and psychologically—from Rwanda, the length of its proceedings, the small number of accused in its docket, the mistreatment of witnesses in sexual assault cases, and allegations of financial irregularities involving defense counsel and investigators.

Creation of the ICTR

The Security Council, acting under Chapter VII of the UN Charter, created the ICTR by virtue of Resolution 955, adopted on November 8, 1994. Ironically, the only member of the Security Council not to support Resolution 955 was Rwanda, although Rwanda had previously requested that the international community establish a tribunal. Rwanda objected to the limited temporal jurisdiction of the ICTR and the fact the ICTR could not issue the death penalty. On February 22, 1995, the Security Council resolved that the ICTR would be based in Arusha, a city in northern Tanzania. This, too, was of concern to the Rwandan government, as it wished the tribunal to be sited in Rwanda itself.

In Resolution 955 the Security Council recognized reports that "genocide and other systematic, widespread, and flagrant violations of international humanitarian law have been committed in Rwanda." The Security Council determined that this situation rose to the level of a threat to international peace and security. It also affirmed its intention to put an end to these violations and "to take effective measures to bring to justice the persons who are responsible for them."

The ICTR is governed by its statute, which is annexed to Resolution 955. Details regarding the process of ICTR trials and appeals are set out in the ICTR Rules of Procedure and Evidence. These rules were adopted separately by the ICTR judges and have been amended several times since their inception.

Goals

In creating the ICTR, the Security Council affirmed its conviction that the prosecution of persons responsible for serious violations of international humanitarian law in Rwanda would promote a number of goals. The Security Council identified these as: (1) bringing to jus-

The UN Security Council elected not to establish the ICTR in Rwanda, but instead chose the city of Arusha, in neighboring Tanzania. This photo shows the building that houses the tribunal. [LANGEVIN JACQUES/CORBIS SYGMA]

tice those responsible for genocide in Rwanda; (2) contributing to the process of national reconciliation; (3) restoring and maintaining peace in Rwanda and the Great Lakes region of Africa generally; and (4) halting future violations and effectively redressing those violations that have been committed. On a broader level, the Security Council also intended to signal that the international community would not tolerate crimes of genocide—architects of such violence would incur responsibility instead of benefiting from impunity.

In order for the ICTR to fulfill its mandate, the Security Council exhorted that it should receive the assistance of all states. Article 28 of the statute requires states to cooperate with the ICTR in its investigations and prosecutions if a request for assistance or order is issued. Many suspects indicted by the ICTR have been arrested in a variety of African and European countries and been transferred to the ICTR, demonstrating the respect and support foreign national governments exhibit toward the ICTR.

Jurisdiction

Article 1 of the statute provides that the ICTR has the power to prosecute persons responsible for serious violations of international humanitarian law committed in the territory of Rwanda between January 1, 1994, and December 31, 1994, as well as Rwandan citizens responsible for violations committed in the territory of neighboring states. The jurisdiction of the ICTR is thus circumscribed by territory, citizenship, and time.

The ICTR prosecutes three categories of crimes: genocide (Article 2), crimes against humanity (Article 3), and war crimes (Article 4). The ICTR has issued convictions for each of these crimes.

Article 2 defines genocide in standard fashion: as one of a number of acts committed with the intent to destroy, in whole or in part, a national, ethnical, racial, or religious group. According to Article 2(2), the enumerated acts are: (a) killing members of the group; (b) causing serious bodily or mental harm to members of the group; (c) deliberately inflicting on the group conditions of life calculated to bring about its physical destruction in whole or in part; (d) imposing measures intended to prevent births within the group; and (e) forcibly transferring children of the group to another group. The ICTR has jurisdiction to prosecute genocide, conspiracy to commit genocide, direct and public incitement to commit genocide, attempt to commit genocide, and complicity in genocide (Article 2[3]).

Article 3 defines crimes against humanity as certain crimes when committed as part of a widespread or

[PAULINE NYIRAMASUHUKO]

Pauline Nyiramasuhuko (b. 1946) had sometimes been known as a success story and a favorite daughter of Butare. She was a social worker who very quickly became the Minister for Family and Women's Affairs and a powerful member of the Habyarimana government in Kigali. At the start of the genocide, in April 1994, she returned to her hometown to organize and direct the local Interahamwe (right-wing Hutu citizen militias). Night and day for three months, she commanded the anti-Tutsi marauders to commit (among other crimes) the rape and torture of Tutsi women. In July 1994 she fled Rwanda. She lived as a fugitive in Kenya for three years until her arrest in Nairobi by international authorities on July 18, 1997. In recent years she has lived at the UN Detention Facility in Arusha. She and her son are being tried, with four other Hutu leaders from Butare, by the ICTR. All are accused of genocide, crimes against humanity, and war crimes. Nyiramasuhuko's trial began in June 2001 and is expected to continue through the beginning of 2005. **PATTI BRECHT**

systematic attack against any civilian population on national, political, ethnic, racial, or religious grounds. Specified crimes include murder; extermination; enslavement; deportation; imprisonment; torture; rape; and political, racial, or religious persecution.

The ICTR has jurisdiction only over individuals (Article 5). Persons incur criminal responsibility if they planned, instigated, ordered, committed, or otherwise aided and abetted in the planning, preparation, or execution of a crime (Article 6[1]). The statute eliminates official immunity, stipulating that the position of any accused person (even a head of state) does not relieve that person of criminal prosecution or mitigate punishment (Article 6[2]). One of the first convictions issued by the ICTR involved Jean Kambanda, the prime minister of Rwanda at the time of the genocide. The fact that the crime was committed "by a subordinate does not relieve his or her superior of criminal responsibility if he or she knew or had reason to know that the subordinate was about to commit such acts or had done so and the superior failed to take the necessary and reasonable measures to prevent such acts or to punish the perpetrators thereof" (Article 6[3]). If a crime was carried out by a subordinate in the chain of command because that subordinate was so ordered, the subordinate is not relieved of individual criminal responsibility, although

that fact can be considered in mitigation of punishment.

The ICTR shares concurrent jurisdiction with national courts (Article 8[1]). However, the ICTR can exert primacy over the national courts of all states, including those of Rwanda (Article 8[2]), at any stage of the procedure. The primacy of the ICTR also is buttressed by the overall effect of Article 9 of the statute. This provides, on the one hand, that no person shall be tried before a national court for acts for which he or she has already been tried by the ICTR, but, on the other hand, a person who has been tried before a national court for acts constituting serious violations of international humanitarian law may be subsequently tried by the ICTR if one of two conditions applies. These are: (a) the act for which he was tried was characterized as an ordinary crime; or (b) the national court proceedings were not impartial or independent, were designed to shield the accused from international criminal responsibility, or were not diligently prosecuted.

Structure

The ICTR is composed of three units: Judicial Chambers, the Prosecutor's Office, and the Registry. The ICTR has three Trial Chambers and one Appeals Chamber (Article 10). The Trial Chambers handle the actual trials of the accused and pretrial procedural matters. The Appeals Chamber hears appeals from decisions of the Trial Chambers. Appeals may involve judgments (guilt or innocence) or sentence (the punishment imposed on a convicted person). The Office of the Prosecutor is in charge of investigations and prosecutions. The Registry is responsible for providing overall judicial and administrative support to the chambers and the prosecutor.

The structure of the ICTR is intertwined with that of the International Criminal Tribunal for the Former Yugoslavia (ICTY), which was created in 1993 and to some extent served as a precedent for the ICTR. Although both tribunals operate separate Trial Chambers (the ICTY in The Hague [Netherlands], the ICTR in Arusha), they share common judges in their Appeals Chambers (located in The Hague, although these judges sometimes sit in Arusha as well). Until September 2003 the two tribunals also shared a single chief prosecutor, Carla Del Ponte of Switzerland. That changed when the UN Security Council appointed Hassan Jallow from Gambia as ICTR Chief Prosecutor, with Del Ponte remaining as ICTY Chief Prosecutor.

The three Trial Chambers and the Appeals Chamber are composed of judges elected by the UN General Assembly. The Security Council proposes candidates for election based on a list of nominees submitted by member states. Nominations must ensure adequate representation of the principal legal systems of the world. ICTR judges are elected for a term of four years, and are eligible for reelection. Judges "shall be persons of high moral character, impartiality and integrity who possess the qualifications required in their respective countries for appointment to the highest judicial offices" (Article 12). They are to be experienced in criminal law and international law, including international humanitarian law and human rights law.

The full ICTR consists of sixteen permanent judges, no two of whom may be nationals of the same state. This total breaks down as follows: three judges in each of the three Trial Chambers and seven judges in the Appeals Chamber. Five judges of the Appeals Chamber hear each appeal. There also is an option of adding a number of *ad litem* (temporary) judges owing to the workload of the ICTR at any point in time. The permanent judges elect a president from among themselves.

The Office of the Prosecutor acts independently to investigate crimes, prepare charges, and prosecute accused persons. The prosecutor does not receive instructions from any government or from any other source. However, the prosecutor may initiate investigations based on information obtained from governments, UN entities, and both intergovernmental and nongovernmental organizations.

The Registry is responsible for the ICTR's overall administration and management. It is headed by the registrar, who provides judicial and legal support services for the work of the judicial chambers and the prosecution and also serves as the ICTR's channel of communication. The ICTR's working languages are English and French (Article 31).

Trial and Appeal Processes

The trial process begins when the prosecutor investigates allegations against an individual. In this investigative process, the prosecutor has the power to question suspects, victims, and witnesses. The prosecutor may also collect evidence and conduct onsite investigations. If the Prosecutor determines that a prima facie (in other words, apparent) case exists, he or she is to prepare an indictment. It is at this point that a suspect becomes an accused. The indictment contains a concise statement of the facts and the crime(s) alleged against the accused. The indictment then is sent to a judge of the Trial Chamber for review. If this judge is satisfied that a prima facie case has in fact been established by the prosecutor, he shall confirm the indictment (Article 18). If the judge is not satisfied, he is to dismiss the indictment. Once the indictment is confirmed, the judge may, at the request of the prosecutor, "issue such or-

ders and warrants for the arrest, detention, surrender or transfer of persons, and any other orders as may be required for the conduct of the trial" (Article 18[2]).

A person under confirmed indictment can be taken into the custody of the ICTR. That person is then immediately to be informed of the charges. The accused then enters a plea—guilty or not guilty—and, in the event of a not guilty plea, the trial begins thereafter. Details of the trial proceedings are regulated by Rules of Procedure and Evidence.

Hearings are in public unless exceptional circumstances arise, for instance, when witnesses need to be protected. Testifying in a closed session can provide such protection. Of more than eight hundred witnesses who have testified in ICTR proceedings as of 2004, the majority have required protective measures that permit them to testify anonymously and thereby be safeguarded from reprisals. The ICTR also has established a sophisticated witness protection program.

Accused persons are entitled to procedural rights. Some of these—such as the right to counsel—arise as soon as an individual is a suspect. At trial, an accused is presumed innocent until proven guilty. An accused person also is entitled to the rights set out in Article 20(4) of the statute. These include protection against self-incrimination, as well as rights to be tried without undue delay, to be informed of the charges, to examine witnesses, and to an interpreter. Moreover, accused are free to retain counsel of their own choice. If an accused person is unable to afford counsel, the ICTR is to assign counsel to that person. In such a situation, which frequently has arisen at the ICTR, the accused person can choose from a list of qualified counsel. These legal services are without charge to the accused. The ICTR Appeals Chamber, however, has ruled that the right of an indigent person to be represented by a lawyer free of charge does not imply the right to select counsel (*Prosecutor v. Akayesu,* Appeal Judgment, 2001, para. 61).

After the trial has concluded, the Trial Chamber pronounces judgment. The judges are triers of fact and law; there are no juries. At the same time, the judges impose sentences and penalties. This differs from the procedure in a number of national legal systems, such as the United States, where the sentencing stage begins as a separate process following the issuance of a guilty verdict. However, this tracks the process that obtains in many civil law countries. Judgment is by a majority of judges and delivered in public. The majority provides a reasoned written opinion. Dissenting judges may provide their own opinion.

The accused has a right to appeal the judgment and the sentence. The prosecutor also can appeal (this also runs counter to the national practice in some states, e.g., the United States, but reflects national practices in many civil law countries and some common law countries such as Canada). However, the Appeals Chamber is empowered only to hear appeals that stem from an error on a question of law that invalidates the decision, or an error of fact that has occasioned a miscarriage of justice. The Appeals Chamber may affirm, reverse, or revise Trial Chambers decisions.

Article 25 of the statute permits an exceptional measure called a *review proceeding*. This is permitted in instances in which "a new fact has been discovered which was not known at the time of the proceedings before the Trial Chambers or the Appeals Chamber and which could have been a decisive factor in reaching the decision" (Article 25). In such a situation, a convicted person or the prosecutor may submit an application for the judgment to be reviewed.

Article 25 has been successfully invoked by the prosecutor in the case of Jean-Bosco Barayagwiza, the former director of political affairs in the Rwandan Ministry of Foreign Affairs eventually convicted of genocide. Barayagwiza helped set up a radio station whose purpose was to incite anti-Tutsi violence. On November 3, 1999, the Appeals Chamber had quashed the indictment against Barayagwiza and ordered him released owing to the lengthy delays that had occurred during the process of his being brought to justice, which were found to have violated his human rights. One and a half years had elapsed from the time of Barayagwiza's arrest to the time of his actually being charged, and additional delays had subsequently occurred at the pretrial stage. The former prosecutor, Carla Del Ponte, then filed an Article 25 application with the Appeals Chamber for the review of the prior decision to free Barayagwiza. On March 31, 2000, the Appeals Chamber unanimously overturned its previous decision to quash Barayagwiza's indictment (*Prosecutor v. Barayagwiza,* Appeals Chamber, 2000). It found that, although Barayagwiza's rights had been infringed, "new facts" presented to the ICTR for the first time during the request for review diminished the gravity of any rights infringement. For example, it was found that the actual period of pretrial delay was much shorter than previously believed; it was also found that some of the delays faced by Barayagwiza were not the responsibility of the prosecutor. Because of this diminished gravity, the ICTR characterized its previous decision to release Barayagwiza as "disproportionate." Basing itself in "the wholly exceptional circumstances of the case," and the "possible miscarriage of justice" that would arise by releasing Barayagwiza, the ICTR set aside its prior release (*Prosecutor v. Barayagwiza,* Appeals Chamber, 2000, para. 65).

Sentencing

Article 23 limits the punishment that the ICTR can impose to imprisonment. The Trial Chambers do have considerable discretion as to the length of the period of imprisonment. The ICTR has issued a number of life sentences and sentences in the ten to thirty-five–year range. The practice of the ICTR reveals that genocide is sentenced more severely than crimes against humanity or war crimes, even though there is no formalized hierarchy among the various crimes the statute ascribes to the jurisdiction of the ICTR. This comports with the notion, evoked judicially by the ICTR, that genocide is the "crime of crimes" (*Prosecutor v. Serushago,* Sentence, 1999, para. 15; Schabas, 2000, p. 9). Other factors that affect sentencing include the accused's seniority in the command structure, remorse and cooperation, age of the accused and of the victims, and the sheer inhumanity of the crime. In addition to imprisonment, the ICTR "may order the return of any property and proceeds acquired by criminal conduct, including by means of duress, to their rightful owners" (Article 23[3]). In practice, this option has not been utilized.

Convicted persons serve their sentences either in Rwanda or in countries that have made agreements with the ICTR to enforce such sentences. Mali, Benin, and Swaziland have signed such agreements.

Budget and Staff

From 2002 to 2003 the UN General Assembly appropriated $177,739,400 (U.S.) for the ICTR. Approximately 800 individuals representing 80 nationalities work for the ICTR.

History of Prosecutions

The ICTR issued its first indictment in late 1995. By early 2004 it had issued approximately seventy indictments, and more than fifty-five indicted individuals were in the custody of the ICTR, either on trial, awaiting trial, or pending appeal.

As of early 2004, the ICTR had convicted twelve individuals, including a number of very senior members of the Rwandan government, civil society, and clergy. Convicted individuals include Jean Kambanda, the Prime Minister of Rwanda during the genocide; Jean-Paul Akayesu and Juvenal Kajelijeli, both local mayors; Georges Rutaganda, a militia leader; Elizaphan Ntakirutimana, a Seventh-Day Adventist pastor, and Georges Ruggiu, a Belgian-born radio journalist whose broadcasts encouraged the setting up of roadblocks and congratulated those who massacred Tutsi at these roadblocks.

Kambanda is the first head of state to have been convicted of genocide, establishing that international

The International Criminal Tribunal for Rwanda and the International Criminal Tribunal for the Former Yugoslavia operate separately, but the Appeals Chambers of both bodies share a panel of judges. Here, three of the justices confer in The Hague, with a UN flag in the background.[LANGEVIN JACQUES/CORBIS SYGMA]

criminal law could apply to the highest authorities. On October 19, 2000, the Appeals Chamber unanimously dismissed Jean Kambanda's appeal against conviction and sentence (*Prosecutor v. Kambanda*, Appeals Chamber, 2000). Kambanda had previously pleaded guilty to six counts of genocide and crimes against humanity (although he subsequently sought to challenge his own guilty plea and demanded a trial), and had been sentenced to life imprisonment by the Trial Chamber on September 4, 1998. As to conviction, Kambanda had argued that his initial guilty plea should be quashed as he allegedly had not been represented by a lawyer of his own choosing, he had been detained in oppressive conditions, and the Trial Chamber had failed to determine that the guilty plea was voluntary, informed, and unequivocal. The Appeals Chamber rejected all of these arguments. In so doing, it drew heavily from its prior decisions in matters involving appeals from the ICTY Trial Chamber, thereby promoting principles of consistency and precedent. As to sentence, the Appeals Chamber dismissed Kambanda's allegations of excessiveness. Although Kambanda's cooperation with the

prosecutor was found to be a mitigating factor to be taken into consideration, the "intrinsic gravity" of the crimes and the position of authority Kambanda occupied in Rwanda outweighed any considerations of leniency and justified the imposition of a life sentence (*Prosecutor v. Kambanda*, Appeals Chamber, 2000, paras. 119, 126).

Not all prosecuted individuals are convicted. The ICTR issued its first acquittal in the matter of Ignace Bagilishema, the *bourgmestre* (mayor) of the Mabanza commune, who was accused of seven counts of genocide, crimes against humanity, and war crimes related to the murder of thousands of Tutsi in the Kibuye prefecture (*Prosecutor v. Bagilishema*, Appeals Chamber, 2002). The Trial Chamber held that the prosecutor failed to prove beyond a reasonable doubt that Bagilishema had committed the alleged atrocities. It concluded that the testimony of prosecution witnesses was riddled with inconsistencies and contradictions and thereby failed to establish Bagilishema's individual criminal responsibility (*Prosecutor v. Bagilishema*, Trial Chamber, 2001). The *Bagilishema* case demonstrates the ICTR's attentiveness to matters of due process and procedural rights, although the acquittal triggered controversy in Rwanda.

Many ministers of the genocidal regime are in ICTR custody, along with senior military commanders, bureaucrats, corporate leaders, clergy, journalists, popular culture icons, and intellectuals. Many of these individuals are being tried jointly. Joined proceedings involve two or more defendants, among whom there is a nexus justifying their being tried together.

For example, on December 3, 2003 the ICTR Trial Chamber issued convictions in the "media case." The media case explores the role, responsibility, and liability of the media in inciting genocide. This case represents the first time since Julius Streicher, the Nazi publisher of the anti-Semitic weekly *Der Stürmer*, appeared before the Nuremberg Tribunal that a group of leading journalists have been similarly charged. Convicted by the ICTR of inciting genocide through the media are Hassan Ngeze (editor of the extremist *Kangura* newspaper), Ferdinand Nahimana (former director of Radio-Télévision Libre des Mille Collines (RTLM), the national broadcaster), and Jean-Bosco Barayagwiza (politician and board member of the RTLM). Ngeze and Nahimana were sentenced to life imprisonment and Barayagwiza to a term of thirty-five years. In its judgment, the ICTR Trial Chamber underscored that "[t]he power of the media to create and destroy fundamental human values comes with great responsibility. Those who control such media are accountable for its consequences." The media case unpacks the interface between international criminal law and freedom of expression. The defense vigorously argued that the impugned communications constituted speech protected by the international right to freedom of expression. The ICTR disagreed. It distinguished "discussion of ethnic consciousness" from "the promotion of ethnic hatred." While the former is protected speech, the latter is not. On the facts, it was found that the exhortations to incite genocide constituted the promotion of ethnic hatred and, hence, unprotected speech.

The prosecutor is charging political leaders jointly in three separate groups. The "Butare group," which consists of six accused, includes Pauline Nyiramasuhuko, the former Minister for Family and Women's Affairs and the first woman to be indicted by an international criminal tribunal (among the charges she faces is inciting rape). Butare is a city in southern Rwanda and the seat of the national university. The second group, known as the Government I group, involves four ministers from the genocidal government, including Edouard Karemera, former Minister of the Interior, and André Rwamakuba, former Minister of Education.

The third group, Government II, includes four other ministers from the genocidal government. All defendants in the Government I and II groups face charges of genocide and crimes against humanity based on theories of individual criminal responsibility that include conspiracy and direct and public incitement to commit genocide.

The military trial involves Colonel Théoneste Bagosora, the Director of the Cabinet in the Ministry of Defense, and a number of senior military officials. It examines how the genocide allegedly was planned and implemented at the highest levels of the Rwandan army. Bagosora is alleged to be the military mastermind of the genocide.

Former prosecutor Del Ponte had affirmed an interest in investigating allegations of crimes committed by Tutsi armed forces (the RPA). This is a matter of considerable controversy for the Rwandan government. Thus far, no indictments have been issued against the RPA, notwithstanding allegations that it massacred up to thirty thousand Hutu civilians when it wrested control of the Rwandan state from its genocidal government in 1994.

Contribution to Legal and Political Issues Concerning Genocide

The ICTR shows that those responsible for mass violence can face their day in court. In this sense, the ICTR helps promote accountability for human rights abuses and combat the impunity that, historically, often has inured to the benefit of those who perpetrate such abuses.

However, the ICTR—and legal responses to mass violence more generally—cannot create a culture of human rights on its own. Democratization, power-sharing, social equity, and economic opportunity each are central to transitional justice. Moreover, although the law can promote some justice after tragedy has occurred, it is important to devote resources prospectively to prevent genocide in the first place. In this sense, by creating the ICTR the international community only addressed part of the obligation announced by the 1948 UN Genocide Convention, namely the prevention and punishment of genocide.

For many Rwandans, the international community's response to and effort in preventing the genocide is questionable at best. The international community was not willing to meaningfully invest in armed intervention that may have prevented, or at least mitigated, genocide in Rwanda in the first place. Various independent reports and studies have found the UN (as well as many states) responsible for failing to prevent or end the Rwandan genocide.

The ICTR's most significant contribution is to the development of international criminal law. Its decisions build a jurisprudence that informs the work of other international criminal tribunals, such as the ICTY, other temporary institutions, and prospectively the permanent ICC. National courts in a number of countries have also relied on ICTR decisions when these courts have been called on to adjudicate human rights cases.

Several of the ICTR's decisions highlight these contributions. One of these is the Trial Chamber's groundbreaking 1998 judgment in the *Akayesu* case (subsequently affirmed on appeal), which provided judicial notice that the Rwandan violence was organized, planned, ethnically motivated, and undertaken with the intent to wipe out the Tutsi (the latter element being a prerequisite to genocide). The *Akayesu* judgment marked the first time that an international tribunal ruled that rape and other forms of systematic sexual violence could constitute genocide. Moreover, it provided a progressive definition of rape. Another important example is the Trial and Appeals Chamber's conviction of Clément Kayishema, a former local governmental official, and Obed Ruzindana, a businessman, jointly of genocide and crimes against humanity, and its sentencing them to life imprisonment and twenty-five years imprisonment, respectively, clarifying the law regarding the requirement of the "mental element" (proof of malevolent intent) in the establishment of the crime of genocide, and the type of circumstantial evidence that could establish that mental element (*Prosecutor v. Kayishema*, Appeals Chamber, 2001).

Also significantly, the notion of command responsibility was squarely addressed and expanded in the case of Alfred Musema, the director of a tea factory. Along with other convictions for crimes for which he was directly responsible, Musema was held liable for the acts carried out by the employees of his factory over whom he was found to have legal control, an important extension of the doctrine of superior responsibility outside the military context and into the context of a civilian workplace (*Prosecutor v. Musema*, Trial Chamber, 2000, paras. 141–148). In the *Musema* case, the ICTR also provided interpretive guidance as to what sorts of attacks could constitute crimes against humanity.

Contribution to Postgenocide Rwanda

There is cause to be more circumspect regarding the contribution of the ICTR to postgenocide Rwanda. Many Rwandans are poorly informed of the work of the ICTR. Moreover, many of those aware of the work of the ICTR remain skeptical of the process and results. The justice resulting from the operation of the ICTR is distant from the lives of Rwandans and may inure more to the benefit of the international community than to victims, positive kinds of transition, and justice in Rwanda itself. This provides a valuable lesson: In order for international legal institutions to play catalytic roles, it is best if they resonate with lives lived locally. This signals a need for such institutions to work in harmony with local practices. Moreover, there also is reason to suspect that for many afflicted populations justice may mean something quite different than the narrow retributive justice flowing from criminal trials. In this vein, it is important for international legal interventions to adumbrate a multilayered notion of justice that actively contemplates restorative, indigenous, truth-seeking, and reparative methodologies.

There is evidence the international community is moving toward this pluralist direction, both in terms of the work of the ICTR and also the construction of recent justice initiatives that are more polycentric in focus. There is an emphasis on institutional reform that could make the work of the ICTR more relevant to Rwandans. The ICTR has, in conjunction with Rwandan nongovernmental organizations, launched a victim-oriented restitutionary justice program to provide psychological counseling, physical rehabilitation, reintegration assistance, and legal guidance to genocide survivors. There also is a possibility—as of 2004 unrealized—of locating ICTR proceedings in Kigali, where the ICTR has opened an information center. Such a relocation would invest financial resources and infrastructure into Rwanda itself and thereby facilitate one of the unattained goals of Resolution 955, namely to "strengthen the courts and judicial system of Rwanda" (Resolution 955, 1994, Preamble).

SEE ALSO Arbour, Louise; Del Ponte, Carla; Goldstone, Richard; International Criminal Court; International Criminal Tribunal for the Former Yugoslavia; Rwanda; War Crimes

BIBLIOGRAPHY

Alvarez, Jose (1999). "Crimes of State/Crimes of Hate: Lessons from Rwanda." *Yale Journal of International Law* 24:365–484.

Arbour, Louise (2000). "The International Tribunals for Serious Violations of International Humanitarian Law in the Former Yugoslavia and Rwanda." *McGill Law Journal* 46(1):195–201.

Bassiouni, Cherif, ed. (1999). *International Criminal Law*, 2nd edition. New York: Transnational Publishers.

Des Forges, Alison (1999). *Leave None to Tell the Story: Genocide in Rwanda*. New York: Human Rights Watch.

Drumbl, Mark A. (2000). "Punishment, Postgenocide: From Guilt to Shame to Civis in Rwanda." *New York University Law Review* 75(5):1221–1326.

Drumbl, Mark A., and Kenneth S. Gallant (2002). "Sentencing Policies and Practices in the International Criminal Tribunals." *Federal Sentencing Reporter* 15(2):140–144.

International Criminal Tribunal for Rwanda. "ICTR Rules of Procedure and Evidence." Available from http://www.ictr.org/ENGLISH/rules/index.htm.

International Criminal Tribunal for Rwanda. "Statute of the International Criminal Tribunal for Rwanda." Available from http://www.ictr.org/ENGLISH/basicdocs/statute.html.

Morris, Madeline (1997). "The Trials of Concurrent Jurisdiction: The Case of Rwanda." *Duke Journal of Comparative and International Law* 7(2):349–374.

Morris, Virginia, and Michael P. Scharf (1998). *The International Criminal Tribunal for Rwanda.* New York: Transnational Publishers.

Prosecutor v. Akayesu. Case No. ICTR-96-4, Appeals Chamber (2001).

Prosecutor v. Bagilishema. Case No. ICTR-95-1A-T, Trial Chamber (2001); Case No. ICTR-95-1A-A, Appeals Chamber (2002).

Prosecutor v. Barayagwiza. Case No. ICTR-97-19-AR72, Appeals Chamber (2000).

Prosecutor v. Kambanda. Case No. ICTR 97-23-A, Appeals Chamber (2000).

Prosecutor v. Kayishema. Case No. ICTR-95-1-A, Appeals Chamber (2001).

Prosecutor v. Musema. Case No. ICTR-96-13, Trial Chamber (2000).

Prosecutor v. Serushago. Case No. ICTR-98-39-S, Sentence (1999).

Sarkin, Jeremy (2001). "The Tension between Justice and Reconciliation in Rwanda: Politics, Human Rights, Due Process and the Role of the Gacaca Courts in Dealing with the Genocide." *Journal of African Law* 45(2):143–172.

Schabas, William (2002). *Genocide in International Law.* Cambridge: Cambridge University Press.

Schabas, William (2000). "Hate Speech in Rwanda: The Road to Genocide." *McGill Law Journal* 46(1):141–171.

United Nations Security Council (1994). "United Nations Security Council Resolution 955, Adopted by the Security Council at Its 3,453rd Meeting, on November 8, 1994." UN Document S/RES/955.

Uvin, Peter, and Charles Mironko (2003). "Western and Local Approaches to Justice in Rwanda." *Global Governance* 9(2):219–231.

Michelle S. Lyon
Mark A. Drumbl

International Criminal Tribunal for the Former Yugoslavia

The establishment of the International Criminal Tribunal for the Former Yugoslavia (ICTY) by the United Nations Security Council in 1993 is one of the most significant contemporary developments for the prevention and punishment of crimes against humanity and genocide. Born out of the horrors of ethnic cleansing in the former Yugoslavia, the ICTY successfully prosecuted perpetrators irrespective of rank and official status, and became the first tribunal to prosecute a sitting head of state, Slobodan Milosevic. Against a long-standing culture of impunity that countenanced the likes of Pol Pot, Idi Amin, and Mengistu, it represented a revolutionary precedent that led to the acceptance and proliferation of other international and mixed courts, national trials, and other accountability mechanisms. As a central element of post-conflict peace-building in former Yugoslavia, it also challenged the conventional wisdom of political "realists," who held that accountability and peace are incompatible. Furthermore, ICTY jurisprudence made significant contributions to the law of crimes against humanity and genocide.

Creation of the ICTY

The unfolding of the atrocities in former Yugoslavia coincided with the end of the cold war and the consequent transformation of international relations. In the new political dispensation, the Soviet-era paralysis of the United Nations was increasingly replaced by cooperation between the five permanent members of the UN Security Council and unprecedented recourse to enforcement measures under Chapter VII of the UN Charter, especially in response to Iraq's invasion of Kuwait in 1990. Equally important was the rapid emergence of democratic governments in Eastern Europe, Latin America, and elsewhere in the world, giving human rights an unprecedented prominence.

In 1992 the Security Council took the unprecedented step of creating a Commission of Experts to investigate humanitarian law violations in the former Yugoslavia. On May 25, 1993, the Council unanimously adopted Resolution 827, pursuant to which it established the ICTY. The Tribunal was created under Chapter VII, which authorizes the Security Council to take enforcement measures binding on all member states of the UN. This was an unprecedented use of Chapter VII enforcement powers, and it directly linked accountability for humanitarian law violations with the maintenance of peace and security. This approach was necessary because Yugoslavia was unwilling to consent to an international criminal jurisdiction, because a treaty mechanism was too time-consuming in view of the need for expeditious action, and because the primary objective of the armed conflict was ethnic cleansing and other atrocities committed against civilians.

The ICTY Statute is a relatively complex instrument that had to express developments in contempo-

Bosnian Serbs sit behind their defense lawyers prior to a session at the International Criminal Tribunal for the Former Yugoslavia in The Hague, May 11, 1998. [AP/WIDE WORLD PHOTOS]

rary international humanitarian law that had evolved over the half-century since the Nuremberg trials. It also had to elaborate the composition and powers of a unique independent judicial organ created by the Security Council. Under the statute, the subject-matter jurisdiction of the ICTY is based on norms that had been fully established as a part of customary international law. Articles 2 and 3 of the statute define war crimes, including violations of the 1949 Geneva Conventions and the 1907 Hague Regulations respectively. Article 4 reproduces the definition of genocide as contained in the 1948 Genocide Convention, and Article 5 defines crimes against humanity based on the Charter of the International Military Tribunal at Nuremberg. Article 7(1) defines the basis for the attribution of individual criminal responsibility, encompassing persons who "planned, instigated, ordered, committed or otherwise aided and abetted in the planning, preparation or execution of a crime" recognized under the statute. Article 7(2) expressly rejects any form of immunity for international crimes, stipulating that "[t]he official position of any accused person, whether as Head of State

or Government or as a responsible Government official, shall not relieve such person of criminal responsibility nor mitigate punishment." Furthermore, Article 7(3) codifies the doctrine of command responsibility, providing that crimes committed by subordinates may be attributed to their superior "if he knew or had reason to know that the subordinate was about to commit such acts or had done so and the superior failed to take the necessary and reasonable measures to prevent such acts or to punish the perpetrators thereof." Conversely, Article 7(4) provides that superior orders shall not relieve a subordinate of criminal responsibility, though it may be considered in mitigation of punishment.

Article 8 restricts the jurisdiction of the ICTY to the territory of the former Yugoslavia, and limits the ICTY to consideration of crimes beginning on January 1, 1991, coinciding with the early stages of Yugoslavia's disintegration. There is however, no outer temporal limit to jurisdiction. Article 9 provides that the ICTY and national courts enjoy concurrent jurisdiction, but that the ICTY shall have primacy, it can request national courts to defer investigations and prosecutions to the

ICTY. Article 10 provides, however, that the principle of double jeopardy must also be respected, which means that a person may not be tried before the ICTY for crimes already tried before a national court, unless the earlier proceedings were not impartial or independent, or were designed to shield the accused from criminal responsibility, or otherwise not diligently prosecuted.

The ICTY was initially composed of a prosecutor, the registry, three trial chambers with three judges each, and an appeals chamber with five judges that also serves the International Criminal Tribunal for Rwanda (ICTR). Since its early days, additional judges have been added to the tribunal. Unlike the Nuremberg Tribunal, the ICTY cannot rely on an army of occupation to conduct the investigation or to apprehend accused persons. Thus, Article 29 provides that UN member states are under an obligation to render judicial cooperation to the ICTY. Specifically, they are obliged to "comply without undue delay with any request for assistance or an order issued by a Trial Chamber" in matters such as the identification and location of persons, the taking of testimony and the production of evidence, the service of documents, the arrest or detention of persons, and the surrender or the transfer of an accused to the ICTY. Such extensive powers derive from the binding character of Chapter VII enforcement measures, and are unprecedented in the history of international tribunals.

The ICTY was created by the Security Council, which also prepared a list of potential judges. The judges were then elected by the UN General Assembly. Furthermore, the General Assembly is responsible for reviewing and approving the ICTY's budget. Although the ICTY is a subsidiary judicial organ of the Security Council, the Council has no power to interfere in judicial matters such as prosecutorial decisions or trials. The ICTY Statute and its rules of procedure and evidence contain numerous procedural safeguards to ensure the independence and impartiality of the tribunal, and to guarantee the rights of the accused to a fair trial.

The first chief prosecutor, South African Constitutional Court judge Richard Goldstone, was appointed in July 1994. In the early days, the Office of the Prosecutor (OTP) was understaffed and inexperienced; investigators and prosecutors who were familiar only with domestic law enforcement wasted scarce resources investigating low-ranking perpetrators for the direct commission of crimes such as murder, rather than focusing on leadership targets.

During Judge Goldstone's tenure, the ICTY's prospects for arrest were meager because the war was still raging, and even after the conclusion of a peace agreement, the prosecutor had to rely on reluctant peacekeeping forces or local police to arrest and surrender indictees. In contrast with the Nazi leaders who were put on trial at Nuremberg, the first defendant before the ICTY was a low-ranking Bosnian Serb, Dusko Tadić, who was captured haphazardly while visiting relations in Germany. He was accused of torturing and killing civilians at detention camps in Bosnia's Prijedor region. Although he was a relatively low-profile defendant, his trial created the image of a court in action.

In 1996 Judge Goldstone stepped down and a Canadian appellate judge, Louise Arbour, was appointed as the new ICTY prosecutor. Her emphasis was on increasing the overall professional standards and effectiveness of the prosecutor's office. Her major accomplishment was in enhancing international cooperation in obtaining intelligence and executing arrest warrants, particularly with NATO countries. Although peacekeeping forces in the former Yugoslavia were initially reluctant to make arrests, it soon became clear that the leaders responsible for inciting ethnic hatred and violence were an impediment to post-conflict peace- and nation-building. UN peacekeepers began arresting indictees, and the ICTY's fortunes were dramatically changed. The first such arrest was that of Slavko Dokmanović, the mayor of Vukovar during the war, and it was affected by Polish peacekeepers belonging to the UN Transitional Authority in Eastern Slavonia, a Serb-controlled region of Croatia. With the arrest of more and more defendants, Arbour streamlined the work of the prosecutor's office, dropped several indictments against low-ranking perpetrators, and increasingly focused on the "big fish."

The pressure to indict the biggest "fish" of all, Slobodan Milosevic, became particularly intense, and on May 27, 1999, Arbour made public the indictment of Milosevic and four other senior officials for crimes against humanity and war crimes in Kosovo, both in relation to mass expulsions and massacres in certain locales. This move was initially controversial. Some viewed the indictment as an obstacle to a deal with Milosevic, while others criticized the appearance that the ICTY was unduly influenced by NATO countries.

Following intense international pressure, the Serbian government arrested Milosevic and surrendered him to the ICTY in June 2000. In October 2000, Milosevic was indicted for atrocities committed in Bosnia and Croatia. His historic trial began in 2002, consummating the ICTY's remarkable emergence from obscurity. Arbour resigned as prosecutor in 1999, to be replaced by Carla Del Ponte, a Swiss prosecutor renowned at home for prosecuting mobsters. Del Ponte focused heavily on the Milosevic case and on securing the arrest of other indicted leaders, from both Serbia and Croatia.

By 2003, the final wave of indictments was issued for atrocities committed in the Kosovo conflict. Many were against Serb military officers, but some were also issued against high-ranking members of the Kosovo Liberation Army for atrocities committed against ethnic Serbs in Kosovo. With the success of the ICTY and the mounting costs of time-consuming international trials, the Security Council called upon the prosecutor to complete all investigations by the end of 2004 and for the ICTY to complete trials by the end of 2008. The Council also approved the establishment of war crimes trial chambers in Bosnia and Herzegovina for the prosecution of lower-ranking defendants, in order to alleviate the ICTY's burden. As of early 2004, the ICTY prosecutor was not only responsible for trials of crimes committed in the former Yugoslavia, but also for the International Criminal Tribunal for Rwanda. In August 2003, the Security Council decided that the two spheres of responsibility should be split, and appointed a separate prosecutor for the ICTR.

Jurisprudence and Legal Developments

The jurisprudence of the ICTY has made significant contributions to international law, particularly in honing the definition of crimes against humanity and genocide. In an effort to effectively use its limited resources, ICTY trials were focused on the most serious crimes and on those most responsible for committing them. In practice, this focus was on crimes committed in execution of the ethnic cleansing campaign that amounted to crimes against humanity and, in certain important aspects, genocide. In order to ensure an appearance of impartiality, there were indictments not only against ethnic Serbs, but also against ethnic Croats, Muslims, and Kosovar Albanians. Furthermore, while focusing on those in leadership positions, certain prosecutions focused on issues of particular importance, such as the systematic use of rape as a weapon of war, and the destruction of cultural property. This prosecutorial strategy influenced and shaped the jurisprudence of the ICTY.

Jurisdiction

The first ICTY trial was the case of *Prosecutor v. Dusko Tadić*. This trial involved significant pronouncements on international humanitarian law, but the case is best known for its jurisprudence on the jurisdiction of the ICTY. Tadić challenged the legality of the ICTY's establishment, both on the grounds that it was beyond the powers of the UN Security Council, and because it was not a court established by law, insofar as the Council was not a legislative body. Appeals chamber president

Antonio Cassese heard these arguments, and held that the establishment of a judicial organ was a valid exercise of the powers of the Security Council, in accordance with Chapter VII of the Charter of the United Nations. He also found that the ICTY was duly established by law in the international context because its standards conformed with the rule of law, there being no analogue to a legislature in the UN system. The appeals chamber also rejected challenges to the primacy of ICTY over national courts, based on the overriding interest of the international community in the repression of serious humanitarian law violations.

Enforcement Powers

The leading case dealing with the ICTY's enforcement powers and the corresponding obligation of states to render judicial assistance is *Prosecutor v. Blaškić*. The case revolves around the refusal of the Croatian government to comply with orders for the production of evidence issued by an ICTY Trial Chamber. The Appeals Chamber held that Article 29 of the ICTY Statute obliged states to comply with ICTY orders, and that Chapter VII of the UN Charter was sufficient to assert the authority of ICTY to issue such orders. The Appeals Chamber also held that the failure of a state to comply with orders of the court could result in a charge of noncompliance against the state (or its agent), which could then be turned over to the UN Security Council for further action.

Arrest Powers

The arrest powers of the ICTY are found in Articles 19, 20, and 29 of the tribunal's statute, and in Rules 54 through 59 of the rules of procedure and evidence. Rule 55 obligates states to execute arrest warrants. The most significant cases on arrest powers were *Prosecutor v. Slavko Dokmanović* and *Prosecutor v. Dragan Nikolić*, respectively. In both cases, the defendants alleged that they had been arrested through either abduction or duplicity (in legal terms, the charge is called "irregular rendition"). The defendants argued that the nature of their arrests should preclude the ICTY from exercising jurisdiction over them.

At least one of the arrests had, in fact, involved subterfuge. In Dokmanović's case, he was arrested after having been tricked getting into a vehicle that he thought was going to take him to a meeting. In this case, the trial chamber made a distinction between "luring" and "forcible abduction," and held that the former (which is what was done to Dokmanović) was acceptable, whereas the latter might provide grounds for a dismissal in future cases. Dokmanović was not permitted to appeal this decision. (Dokmanović's trial was later terminated because the defendant committed suicide).

Nikolić, whose motion was heard six years after Dokmanović's, was subject to a much more straightforward abduction by "persons unknown" from the territory of the Federal Republic of Yugoslavia, and subsequently turned over to the ICTY. He based his appeal against his arrest on the grounds that the sovereignty of the Federal Republic of Yugoslavia was violated by his abduction, and that his rights were violated in a manner sufficiently serious to warrant discontinuance of proceedings. The Appeals Chamber held that state sovereignty does not generally outweigh the interests of bringing to justice a person accused of a universally condemned crime, especially when the state itself does not protest. Moreover, it found that, given the exceptional gravity of the crimes for which Nikolić was accused, a human rights violation perpetrated during his arrest must be very serious to justify discontinuance of proceedings.

Crimes Against Humanity
The definition of crimes against humanity found in Article 5 of the ICTY Statute is based on the Nuremberg Charter, but it incorporates enumerated acts such as imprisonment, torture, and rape, which were not included in the charter. Furthermore, while the Charter required that crimes against humanity be linked to an international armed conflict, the ICTY Statute also includes internal armed conflicts. This issue came up in the *Tadić* case. The defendant maintained that prosecution of crimes against humanity in the former Yugoslavia deviated from customary international law because the conflict was not international in character, as required by the Nuremberg Charter. Being that there was no existing law extending jurisdiction to the ICTY, the defense argued, there could be no legitimate charge of criminal action. The Appeals Chamber rejected this submission, however, commenting that customary law had evolved in the years since Nuremberg, and stating that the need for a connection to international armed conflict was no longer required. In fact, it argued that customary law might recognize crimes against humanity in the absence of any conflict at all.

This precedent helped persuade the drafters of the Rome Statute of the International Criminal Court to omit a requirement of a connection with armed conflict in the definition of crimes against humanity under its Article 7. Thus, under contemporary international law, atrocities committed outside the context of armed conflict also qualify as crimes against humanity, and this has resulted in a significant expansion of the protection afforded by this norm.

According to the ICTY, a crime against humanity is committed when an enumerated offence is committed as part of a widespread or systematic attack directed against a civilian population. ICTY jurisprudence has elaborated upon what is meant by a "widespread or systematic" attack. In *Tadić*, the Trial Chamber held that this requirement is inferred from the term "population," which indicates a significantly numerous victim group. While it does not necessitate that the entire population of a given state must be targeted, it does refer to collective crimes rather than single or isolated acts.

A finding either that the acts were committed on a large scale (widespread), or were repeatedly carried out pursuant to a pattern or plan (systematic), is sufficient to meet the requirement that they be committed against a population. It is the large number of victims, the exceptional gravity of the acts, and their commission as part of a deliberate attack against a civilian population, which elevate the acts from ordinary domestic crimes such as murder to crimes against humanity, and thus a matter of collective international concern. ICTY jurisprudence has also expanded the definition of potential victim groups vulnerable to crimes against humanity. This is done through its interpretation of the requirement that attacks must be "directed against any civilian population." In the Vukovar Kupreškić cases, the ICTY held that the definition of "civilian" is sufficiently broad to include prisoners of war or other noncombatants.

ICTY jurisprudence has also affirmed that crimes against humanity may be committed by people who are not agents of any state, thus broadening the ambit of possible perpetrators to include insurgents and terrorists. This definition was adopted in Article 7 of the Rome Statute, which requires that an attack be "pursuant to or in furtherance of a State or organizational policy."

Crimes against humanity also require a so-called mental element, which has to do with the intent of the perpetrators. For an act to be termed a crime against humanity, the perpetrator must not only meet the requisite criminal intent of the offence, but he must also have knowledge, constructive or actual, of the widespread or systematic attack on a civilian population. This requirement ensures that the crime is committed as part of a mass atrocity, and not a random crime that is unconnected to the policy of attacking civilians. ICTY jurisprudence has held that this requirement does not necessitate that the accused know all the precise details of the policy or even be identified with the principle perpetrators, but merely that he be aware of the risk that his act forms part of the attack.

ICTY jurisprudence has also developed definitions of the enumerated offences included under the rubric of crimes against humanity. These include extermination, enslavement, forced deportation, arbitrary imprisonment, torture, rape, persecution on political, racial, or religious grounds, and other inhumane acts. In addition, it has further sharpened the definition of genocide itself.

The definition of the crime of extermination was developed in the *Krstić* case, wherein the Trial Chamber noted that extermination was a crime very similar to genocide because it involves mass killings. Unlike genocide, however, extermination "may be retained when the crime is directed against an entire group of individuals even though no discriminatory intent nor intention to destroy the group as such on national, ethnical, racial or religious grounds" is present. Nonetheless, the crime had to be directed against a particular, targeted population, and there must have been a calculated intent to destroy a significant number of that targeted group's members. In one of the Foča rape cases, *Prosecutor v. Kunarac et al*, the Trial Chamber similarly contributed to the definition of the elements that make up the crime of enslavement. It held, that the criminal act consisted of assuming the right of ownership over another human being, and that the mental element of the crime consisted of intentionally exercising the powers of ownership. This included restricting the victim's autonomy, curtailing his freedom of choice and movement. The victim is not permitted consent or the exercise of free will. This curtailment of the victim's autonomy can be achieved in many ways. Threats, captivity, physical coercion, and deception, are but four such ways. Even psychological pressure is recognized as a means of enslavement. Enslavement also entails exploitation, sometimes (but not necessarily always) involving financial or other types of gain for the perpetrator. Forced labor is an element of enslavement, even if the victim is nominally remunerated for his or her efforts. Important to note is that simple imprisonment, without exploitation, can not constitute enslavement.

The ICTY Statute lists deportation as a crime against humanity, but goes on to specify that such deportation must be achieved under coercion. According to the statute, deportation is the "forced displacement of the persons concerned by expulsion or other coercive acts from the area in which they are lawfully present, without grounds permitted under international law." In the *Krstić* case, deportation was distinguished from forcible transfer. Deportation requires a population transfer beyond state borders, whereas forcible transfer involves internal population displacements. Both types of forced population movements were none-

theless recognized as crimes against humanity under customary law. The Trial Chamber in *Krstić* found that deportations or forcible transfers must be compulsory. In other words, they must be driven by force or threats or coercion which go beyond a fear of discrimination, and that there be no lawful reason for ordering the transfer, such as for the protection of the population from hostilities.

An ICTY Trial Chamber first defined imprisonment as a crime against humanity in *Prosecutor v. Dario Kordić* and in *Prosecutor v. Mario Čerkez*. However, such imprisonment must be arbitrary, without the due process of law. Further, it must be directed at a civilian population, and the imprisonment must be part of a larger, systematic attack on that population. ICTY jurisprudence also redressed a long-standing omission in humanitarian law, because prior to its rulings, a clear, explicit definition of torture had yet to be formulated. The leading ICTY case on torture is *Prosecutor v. Anto Furundžija*, as elaborated by *Prosecutor v. Kunarac et al.* In the *Furundžija* case, the Trial Chamber borrowed legal concepts from the human rights law of torture. Ultimately, the Trial Chamber determined that torture:

(i) consists of the infliction, by act or omission, of severe pain or suffering, whether physical or mental; in addition

(ii) this act or omission must be intentional;

(iii) it must aim at obtaining information or a confession, or at punishing, intimidating, humiliating or coercing the victim or a third person, or at discriminating, on any ground, against the victim or a third person;

(iv) it must be linked to an armed conflict;

(v) at least one of the persons involved in the torture process must be a public official or must at any rate act in a non-private capacity, e.g. as a de facto organ of a state or any other authority-wielding entity.

When the ICTY was established, there was also no clear definition for rape under humanitarian or indeed, customary international law. Thus, the ICTY was required to define it more precisely when difficult cases came up. Borrowing from legal systems around the world, the Trial Chamber in *Furundžija* held that rape is the coerced sexual penetration of a victim (vaginally or anally), whether by the perpetrator's penis or by some other object, or the penetration of the victim's mouth by the perpetrator's penis. Coercion could involve force or the threat of force, and the coercion might be imposed on the victim or on a third party. The Trial Chamber added that

[I]nternational criminal rules punish not only rape but also any serious sexual assault falling

After the NATO-led liberation of Kosovo, FBI forensics teams descend upon Kosovo to collect evidence of war crimes committed by Serbian forces against Kosovars. The evidence will be used in the International Criminal Tribunal for the Former Yugoslavia. [TEUN VOETEN]

short of actual penetration. It would seem that the prohibition embraces all serious abuses of a sexual nature inflicted upon the physical and moral integrity of a person by means of coercion, threat of force or intimidation in a way that is degrading and humiliating for the victim's dignity. As both these categories of acts are criminalised in international law, the distinction between them is one that is primarily material for the purposes of sentencing.

In a later case, *Prosecutor v. Kunarac et al.*, an ICTY Trial Chamber expanded the second element of the crime to encompass situations in which the threshold of force may not be met, but where consent is not freely given as a result of the complainant's free will. In *Prosecutor v. Kupreškić*, the ICTY drew on Nuremberg jurisprudence to clarify the definition of persecution, and set out its conclusions in the *Prosecutor v. Tadić* judgment. It defined persecution as a form of discrimination on the grounds of race, religion, or political opinion that is intended to be, and results in, an infringement of an individual's fundamental rights. In *Prosecutor v. Kupreskić,* the court determined what actions or omis-

sions could amount to persecution. Drawing on various human rights instruments, the Trial Chamber defined persecution as

[T]he gross or blatant denial, on discriminatory grounds, of a fundamental right, laid down in international customary or treaty law, reaching the same level of gravity as the other acts prohibited in Article 5. In determining whether particular acts constitute persecution, the Trial Chamber wishes to reiterate that acts of persecution must be evaluated not in isolation but in context, by looking at their cumulative effect. Although individual acts may not be inhumane, their overall consequences must offend humanity in such a way that they may be termed "inhumane". This delimitation also suffices to satisfy the principle of legality, as inhumane acts are clearly proscribed by the Statute. . . . In sum, a charge of persecution must contain the following elements:

(a) those elements required for all crimes against humanity under the Statute;

(b) a gross or blatant denial of a fundamental right reaching the same level of gravity as the other acts prohibited under Article 5;

(c) discriminatory grounds.

Room for Further Evolution

The ICTY included a non-specific category of offenses, styled "other inhumane acts" as residual provision that allows for the inclusion by analogy of inhumane acts not enumerated. This was done to ensure that acts of similar gravity do not go unpunished simply because they are not expressly contemplated. This however, raises problems of legal principle. The concept of *nullem crimen sine lege* requires that there can be no crime if no law exists prohibiting an act. This, in turn, requires that crimes be exhaustively defined in order to be prosecutable. The Trial Chamber in *Prosecutor v. Kupreskic* discussed this problem and noted that, by drawing on various provisions of international human rights law, such as the Universal Declaration of Human Rights and the two UN Covenants for Human Rights,

it is possible to identify a set of basic rights appertaining to human beings, the infringement of which may amount, depending on the accompanying circumstances, to a crime against humanity. Thus, for example, serious forms of cruel or degrading treatment of persons belonging to a particular ethnic, religious, political or racial group, or serious widespread or systematic manifestations of cruel or humiliating or degrading treatment with a discriminatory or persecutory intent no doubt amount to crimes against humanity.

Once the legal parameters for determining the content of the category of "inhumane acts" are identified, the trial chamber held, resort may be had to comparing their similarity to other crimes against humanity to determine if they are of comparable gravity.

Genocide

The definition of *genocide* in the ICTY Statute is identical to that in the Genocide Convention. Of great significance in determining that an act of genocide has been committed is the mental element of the crime. This requires a finding of a special intent, in which the perpetrator desires to bring about the outcome of destroying, in whole or in part. a national, ethnical, racial or religious group, in addition to the criminal intent required by the enumerated offence. ICTY jurisprudence has elaborated on the threshold of the special intent that must be demonstrated in a charge of genocide. Two particularly noteworthy cases are the *Prosecutor v. Goran Jelisić* case and *Prosecutor v. Radislav* appeal. Goran Jelisić was a detention camp leader who styled

himself a "Serbian Adolf" and who had "gone to Brčko to kill Muslims." Despite compelling evidence of genocidal intent, the Trial Chamber acquitted Jelisić of genocide on the grounds that

the acts of Goran Jelisić are not the physical expression of an affirmed resolve to destroy in whole or in part a group as such. All things considered, the Prosecutor has not established beyond all reasonable doubt that genocide was committed in Brcko during the period covered by the indictment. Furthermore, the behavior of the accused appears to indicate that, although he obviously singled out Muslims, he killed arbitrarily rather than with the clear intention to destroy a group.

The Trial Chamber seemed to create an extremely high threshold for an individual committing genocide, because it is not satisfied even if the defendant was clearly driven to kill and did kill large numbers of a particular religious group. However, the Appeals Chamber held that the Trial Chamber had erred in terminating the trial on the genocide count, and that a reasonable trier of fact may have found Jelisić guilty of genocide on the evidence presented. It noted that occasional displays of randomness in the killings are not sufficient to negate the inference of intent evidenced by a relentless campaign to destroy the group. Notwithstanding this conclusion, the Appeals Chamber declined to remand the matter back to trial for a proper hearing on the genocide count, on the ground of public interest. Jelisić had pleaded guilty to crimes against humanity and war crimes for the same murders and was already sentenced to forty years' imprisonment, a probable life sentence. Judge Wald's partial dissent suggested that the decision may have reflected the view that convicting such a low level offender of genocide would diminish this "crime of crimes" and create a problematic precedent.

The Krstić appeal also explored the evidentiary threshold for the special intent of genocide, along with elaborating on the definition of aiding and abetting genocide. Major-General Krstić was charged with genocide for his part in the perpetration of the Srebrenica massacre, in which about seven thousand Bosnian Muslim men from the Srebrenica enclave were systematically separated from the rest of the population, transported to remote areas, and executed over the course of several days. The Appeals Chamber overturned the verdict and substituted a conviction of aiding and abetting genocide, an offence not taken from the genocide provisions of the Statute, but rather from the article providing individual criminal responsibility for persons participating in the commission of crimes under the Statute. The genocide conviction of Krstić, the chamber noted, rested on circumstantial evidence that could only demonstrate that the accused had knowledge of the killings and was aware of the intent of others to commit genocide. The Appeals Chamber held that this evidence could not be used to infer that Krstić possessed a genocidal intent, and thus he should not have been convicted as a principal perpetrator. Nonetheless, the Chamber held that his knowledge of the killings, and his allowing the use of personnel under his command, did meet the threshold of aiding and abetting genocide, a lesser offense.

The elements of genocide require that a national, ethnical, racial or religious group be targeted for destruction. The Trial Chamber in *Krstić* considered the definition of *group,* and found that what constitutes a group is a subjective and contextual determination, one criterion being the stigmatization of the group by the perpetrators. The *Krstić* trial judgement, supplemented by the Appeals Chamber, also considered the definition of *part of a group* in the requisite intention "to destroy in whole or in part." It held that genocide could be perpetrated against a highly localized *part of a group,* as exemplified by the Muslim population of Srebrenica, which formed part of the protected group of all Bosnian Muslims. On this question, the Chamber held,

> the killing of all members of the part of a group located within a small geographical area, although resulting in a lesser number of victims, would qualify as genocide if carried out with the intent to destroy the part of the group as such located in this small geographical area.

The Appeals Chamber affirmed that the "part" must be "substantial," as "[t]he aim of the Genocide Convention is to prevent the intentional destruction of entire human groups, [thus] the part targeted must be significant enough to have an impact on the group as a whole." But beyond considerations of numeric importance, if a specific part of a group were essential to the survival of the group, the Chamber held that such a part could be found to be substantial, and thus meet the definition of *part of a group.* The Appeals Chamber noted that the population of the Bosnian Muslims of Srebrenica was crucial to their continued presence in the region, and indeed, their fate would be "emblematic of that of all Bosnian Muslims."

The case against Krstić also considered whether the killing of only the men of Srebrenica could be held to manifest an intention to destroy a part of the protected group, the Muslims of Bosnia. The Trial Chamber noted that the massacre of the men of Srebrenica was being perpetrated at the same time that the remainder of the Muslim population was being ethnically cleansed out of Srebrenica. It concluded that the community's physical survival was jeopardized by these atrocities

and, therefore, these acts together could properly be held to constitute the intent to destroy part of group:

> The Bosnian Serb forces could not have failed to know, by the time they decided to kill all the men, that this selective destruction of the group would have a lasting impact upon the entire group. Their death precluded any effective attempt by the Bosnian Muslims to recapture the territory. Furthermore, the Bosnian Serb forces had to be aware of the catastrophic impact that the disappearance of two or three generations of men would have on the survival of a traditionally patriarchal society, an impact the Chamber has previously described in detail. The Bosnian Serb forces knew, by the time they decided to kill all of the military aged men, that the combination of those killings with the forcible transfer of the women, children and elderly would inevitably result in the physical disappearance of the Bosnian Muslim population at Srebrenica.

The material element of genocide requires that one or more acts be committed which are enumerated in the definition, namely, killing members of the group; causing serious bodily or mental harm to members of the group; deliberately inflicting on the group conditions of life calculated to bring about its physical destruction in whole or in part; imposing measures intended to prevent births within the group; or forcibly transferring children of the group to another group. On several occasions, the ICTY has considered whether ethnic cleansing alone—that is, the forcible expulsion of the members of a protected group—meets the material threshold of genocide. The appeal in the *Krstić* case confirmed that forcible transfer in and of itself does not constitute a genocidal act. However, it may be relied upon, with evidence of enumerated acts targeting the group, to infer a genocidal intent.

According to the findings of the ICTY, for a charge of genocide to be apt, the killing or causing of serious bodily or mental harm to members of a group must be intentional, but they need not be premeditated. The ICTY has also held that, with regard to causing bodily or mental harm, the harm need not be permanent and irremediable harm, but it must result in a "grave and long-term disadvantage to a person's ability to lead a normal and constructive life." Such acts could include cruel treatment, torture, rape, and deportation, or, for example, the agony suffered by individuals who survive mass executions.

From its modest beginnings, the ICTY has become an essential element of post-conflict peace-building in the former Yugoslavia. The link between prosecution of leaders responsible for incitement to ethnic hatred and violence, and the emergence of democratic multiethnic institutions that can secure a lasting peace has become increasingly apparent. Beyond abstract human rights considerations, international criminal justice has become an element of enlightened realpolitik. The initially haphazard ICTY precedent was an important catalyst for the resumption of efforts after the Nuremberg Judgement to establish an international criminal justice system. It prepared the path for the ICTR, the Special Court of Sierra Leone and other hybrid tribunals, and encouraged national courts to prosecute international crimes. Most significantly, it expedited and informed the deliberations leading to the adoption of the Rome Statute for the ICC in 1998. Thus, beyond the former Yugoslavia, the ICTY has introduced an accountability paradigm into the mainstream of international relations, challenged a hitherto entrenched culture of impunity, and helped alter the boundaries of power and legitimacy.

SEE ALSO Arbour, Louise; Del Ponte, Carla; Goldstone, Richard; International Criminal Court; International Criminal Tribunal for Rwanda; Milosevic, Slobodan; Yugoslavia; War Crimes

BIBLIOGRAPHY

Akhavan, Payam (2001). "Beyond Impunity: Can International Criminal Justice Prevent Future Atrocities?" *American Journal of International Law* 95:7.

Arbour, Louise (1999). "The Prosecution of International Crimes: Prospects and Pitfalls." *Washington University Journal of Law and Policy* 1:13–25.

Askin, Kelly D. (1999). "Sexual Violence in Decisions and Indictments of the Yugoslav and Rwandan Tribunals: Current Status." *American Journal of International Law* 93:97.

Boas, Gideon (2003). *International Criminal Law Developments in the Case Law of the ICTY.* The Hague: Martinus Nijhoff Publishers.

Burg, Steven L., and Paul S. Schrop (1999). *The War in Bosnia and Herzegovina.* Armonk, N.Y.: M. E. Sharpe.

Hagan, John (2002). *Justice in the Balkans.* Chicago: University of Chicago Press.

Ignatieff, Michael (1994). *Blood and Belonging: Journeys into the New Nationalism.* New York: Penguin Books.

Kalinauskas, Mikas (2002). "The Use of International Military Force in Arresting War Criminals: The Lessons of the International Criminal Tribunal for the Former Yugoslavia." *Kansas Law Review* 50(383).

Kerr, Rachel (2004). *The International Criminal Tribunal for the Former Yugoslavia: An Exercise in Law, Politics, and Diplomacy.* Oxford: Oxford University Press.

Lamb, Susan (1999). "The Powers of Arrest of the International Criminal Tribunal for the Former Yugoslavia." *The British Yearbook of International Law* 70(165).

McDonald, Gabrielle Kirk, ed. (2001). *Essays on ICTY Procedure and Evidence in Honour of Gabrielle Kirk McDonald.* The Hague: Kluwer Law International.

Mettraux, Guenael (2002). "Crimes Against Humanity in the Jurisprudence of the International Criminal Tribunals for the Former Yugoslavia and for Rwanda." *Harvard International Law Journal* 43(237).

Morris, Virginia, and Michael P. Scharf (1995). *Insider's Guide to the International Criminal Tribunal for the Former Yugoslavia.* Irvington-on-Hudson, N.Y.: Transnational Publishers.

Ramet, Sabrina P. (2002). *Balkan Babel*, 4th edition. Boulder, Colo.: Westview Press.

Schabas, William A. (2003). "Mens Rea and the International Criminal Tribunal for the Former Yugoslavia." *New England Law Review* 37(1015).

Wald, Patricia (2001). "The International Criminal Tribunal for the Former Yugoslavia Comes of Age: Some Observations on Day-To-Day Dilemmas of an International Court." *Washington University Journal of Law and Policy* 5(87).

Williams, Paul R., and Michael P. Scharf (2002). *Peace with Justice? War Crimes and Accountability in the Former Yugoslavia.* Lanham, Md.: Rowman & Littlefield.

Zimmerman, Warren (1996). *Origins of a Catastrophe.* Toronto: Random House.

Payam Akhavan
Mora Johnson

International Law

International law is the law governing states and other participants in the international community. It is formed largely by agreement among the participants, especially states, to create rules applicable to their affairs and is born out of the necessity to coexist and cooperate.

History

In early human history, large families and tribes exchanged food, concluded alliances, and fought each other often according to a code of conduct. The creation of organized political entities in the eastern part of the Mediterranean Sea, such as Egypt and Babylon, but also on a smaller scale, Greek city-states, resulted in a comparable system, in more organized forms. In the absence of a central authority, rules governing such relations had a contractual nature, developing a real legal system based on treaties. In ancient India and in China, during certain periods, political units also created and applied law governing their mutual relations.

The Roman Empire was born of treaties between Rome and cities in the neighboring area and then developed into a network of legal relations with other peoples. Later, however, Rome affirmed the ambition to govern the other states that it no longer considered as its equals. It also developed the idea of a *jus gentium,* a body of law designed to govern the treatment of aliens subject to Roman rule and the relations between Roman citizens and aliens, thus a legal system that was based on its domination.

Approximately three hundred years after the fall of the Roman Empire, distinct kingdoms emerged in Europe in the eighth century. Relations between private persons became progressively more frequent and needed the creation of norms to ensure personal security. This evolution led to the development of generally accepted rules between state entities that affirmed their exclusive power over the territory they dominated. In other words they proclaimed their sovereignty. Scholars of the sixteenth and seventeenth centuries, especially Spanish precursors and later the Dutch jurist Hugo Grotius, systematized the generally applied rules and elaborated a broad theory of law to govern the relations between states in times of peace and war. In 1648 the Peace Treaties of Westphalia (1648) ending the Thirty Year's War, which devastated the center of Europe, established a real international system that was progressively reinforced. Indeed, citizens of different countries cooperated in a growing number of fields, and states recognized their needs by exercising protection over them. In the nineteenth century, after the Napoleonic wars, the Final Act of the Congress of Vienna in 1815 reorganized Europe, establishing rules for diplomatic relations and recognizing that sovereign states had common concerns in matters such as navigation on international rivers.

This essentially European system expanded progressively to the Americas and to other parts of the world. Colonial expansion that provoked competition between European powers also involved the application of international legal rules to other parts of the world, even if it was mainly within the context of relations between colonial powers. By the end of the nineteenth century international law applied to the entire world.

Technological developments in fields such as transportation and communication helped the evolution of international law. World War I was a first step toward globalization and at its end states created the first international political organization in order to maintain peace, the League of Nations. With World War II came the failure of that order that generated hostilities in almost every part of the world. In 1945 the United Nations (UN) Charter created a new organization recognizing the primacy of fundamental values of humanity, such as safeguarding peace and protecting human rights. It also created an elaborate machinery

for solving disputes among nations. In the following half-century the UN contributed considerably to the development of international law in different fields, such as the international protection of human rights, the law governing the seas, environmental protection, and the economic development of poor countries.

Definition and Scope
International law is mainly composed of rules adopted by states in the form of treaties, but it also contains customary rules resulting from state practice generally accepted by states and recognized as having a binding character. In addition, general principles of law are considered applicable in the relations between states.

Although international law originally only concerned relations between states as sovereign entities, recently other entities have emerged and been recognized as having a role to play in the international system: international intergovernmental organizations, nongovernmental organizations, businesses, and even individual stakeholders.

Sources of International Law
Traditionally, international law identifies its sources in Article 38(1) of the Statute of the International Court of Justice. Although applying only to the court, Article 38 represents the authoritative listing of processes that are deemed capable of creating rules binding on states. It sets out, in order, general or specialized international conventions (i.e. treaties), international custom as evidence of a general practice accepted as law, general principles of law recognized by civilized nations, and, as subsidiary means, international judicial decisions and doctrine. This enumeration is the accepted minimum, but many scholars contend that it does not reflect either the current international practice or the diverse activities that can contribute to the development of a new rule of law. In particular, it omits all texts, other than treaties, that are adopted by international organizations, although they play more than a nominal role in the formation of international law in general and especially in human rights law and humanitarian law.

Treaty Law
According to the Vienna Convention on the Law of Treaties of May 23, 1969, generally accepted as the expression of international law related to treaties, a treaty is an international agreement concluded between states in written form and governed by international law, whether embodied in a single text or in two or more related texts and whatever its particular designation. The last words reflect the variety of terms used for designating a treaty: convention, charter, agreement, covenant, protocol, general act, exchange of letters or notes.

The essential criterion of a treaty, whatever its title, is the will of the states to commit themselves. Thus, the often used term the *contracting parties* designates the states that intend to be bound by a specific treaty. Every state possesses the capacity to conclude treaties.

The consent of a state to be bound by a treaty is expressed by the signature of its duly authorized representative or by the exchange of the text(s) constituting a treaty. As a general rule, treaties that have a major impact on the domestic legislation of the contracting parties are submitted for the approval or ratification of national authorities such as the heads of state of the contracting parties, or of their legislative organ, or both. When the treaty provides for it, states that did not sign the original agreement can become parties by accession.

Unless the treaty prohibits it, contracting parties may make reservations. A reservation is a unilateral statement made by a state, when signing, ratifying, accepting, approving, or acceding to a treaty, whereby it purports to exclude or to modify the legal effect of certain provisions of the treaty, in their application to that state. Nevertheless, as stated by the International Court of Justice in its advisory opinion related to the Reservations to the Convention on the Prevention and Punishment of the Crime of Genocide (May 28, 1951), the object and purpose of a convention can limit the freedom of a state to make reservations. The intention of the treaty's authors to have as many states as possible participate must be balanced by ensuring that the very objective of the treaty is not undermined or destroyed.

One of the fundamental principles of international law is that every treaty in force is binding on the parties to it and must be performed by them in good faith. A party may not invoke the provisions of its internal law as justification for its failure to perform a treaty. In principle, a treaty has no retroactive effects, unless a different intention surfaces from it or is otherwise established. It shall be interpreted in good faith in accordance with the ordinary meaning given to its terms and in light of its objective and purpose. A treaty generally does not create either obligations or rights for states that are not parties to it without their consent; however, rules of customary international law in a treaty will have independent force of law.

A treaty may be amended by agreement between its parties. The termination of a treaty or the withdrawal of a party may take place in conformity with the provisions of the treaty concerning its termination or by consent of all parties. If the treaty contains no provision regarding its termination and does not allow for denunciation or withdrawal, it in principle cannot be denounced.

International law contains various rules that may invalidate certain agreements, making their provisions have no legal force. Treaties, for instance, can be invalidated if an error led to a state's consent to be bound by it or the state has been induced by fraud to conclude a treaty. An additional factor that can result in the invalidity of a treaty is the corruption or coercion of a representative of a state. A much discussed principle is that of *jus cogens*, according to which a treaty is void if at the time of its conclusion it conflicts with a peremptory norm of general international law. Such a norm of general international law must be accepted and recognized by the international community of states as a norm from which no deviation is permitted. Although no treaty has identified any norm as one of *jus cogens*, there is general agreement that the prohibition of genocide is such a norm. This means that any treaty to commit genocide would be void.

Treaties can be bilateral if only two states conclude them, or multilateral. The number of the contracting parties to multilateral agreements may be very high. Several conventions with a worldwide scope, such as the Convention on Biological Diversity of 1992, are binding on almost all the 189 member states of the UN. The Convention on the Rights of the Child has been accepted by all but two states (the United States and Somalia). The Convention against Genocide has 133 parties as of September 2003.

Treaties may include different parts. Their text generally starts with a list of the contracting parties followed by a preamble that in itself has no binding character but explains the reasons why contracting states accept the obligations imposed by the treaty. The main part of the treaty is divided into articles that sometimes constitute chapters. The technical provisions frequently form one or several annexes to the treaty. They have the same binding character as the main text, but often they can be more easily modified.

A growing proportion of treaties only establish the principles of cooperation between contracting parties and are instead completed at the time of their adoption with additional treaties, generally called additional protocols or simply protocols. The European Convention on Human Rights has thirteen protocols, adopted between 1952 and 2003. Despite the links protocols generally have with the main treaty, legally they are independent from it and the whole of such texts can be considered as a treaty system creating a special regime.

During the last half of the twentieth century a fundamental characteristic of treaties was modified. In conformity with the traditional contracts approach originating with Roman law, treaties were as a rule based on reciprocity. This means the contracting states had to offer advantages equivalent to those that they received from the other contracting parties. The emergence and universal recognition of values common to humanity, such as maintaining peace, protecting human rights, and safeguarding the environment, promoted the drafting and adoption of treaties that include no reciprocity. Thus by virtue of such treaties, the contracting states accept obligations without any direct and immediate counterpart. Such obligations include respecting fundamental rights and freedoms of all persons under the treaty's jurisdiction, protecting biological diversity, and respecting international norms prohibiting the production and use of certain substances or weapons. International conventions prohibiting and punishing genocide and crimes against humanity fall into this category.

Other sources of international law

A large number and wide variety of international legal rules are generated by means other than the explicit consent of states expressed in treaties. Customary law was for centuries the main source of international laws, but essential parts of it, such as the rules governing international treaties themselves, the rules of diplomatic and consular relations, the law of the sea, and a portion of the rules related to international watercourses, have been transformed into treaty rules by the codification process that is much encouraged by the UN. At the same time rules repeated in a significant number of treaties, such as the principle of prevention and the precautionary approach in treaties related to environmental protection, may be considered as having become rules of customary law with a scope much larger than the treaties that include them. A good example is the Martens Clause, repeated or referred to in most treaties related to armed conflicts. According to it, in cases not covered by international agreements, civilians and combatants remain under the protection and authority of the principles of international law derived from established custom, from the principles of humanity and from the dictates of public conscience.

In addition, resolutions and recommendations adopted by international institutions or conferences, which formally are not binding on the states that participated in their elaboration, the so-called soft law, can be considered in certain cases as creating customary law when state practice supports it.

Other sources of international law that are not based on the consent of states also play a certain role in interstate relations. When they decide disputes involving states, judicial institutions—whether national or international—cannot avoid applying general principles of law, such as good faith, the prohibition of abuse

of rights, rules concerning evidence, and other procedural rules. In addition, equity may inspire such decisions, but most often reference to equity needs the consent of the states who are parties to a dispute.

States

Until the middle of the twentieth century it was generally held that only states could have rights and duties in international law. They were thus the only subjects of international law who could create the rules of international law (see above) and have official relations with others on equal footing. As persons of international law, they had to possess a defined territory, a permanent population, and an effective government.

Exclusive control over a territory, or sovereignty, is the essence of a state. It means that the state may adopt and enforce laws within that territory and prohibit foreign governments from exercising any authority in its area. Such exclusive jurisdiction has as its corollary the obligation to protect within the territory the rights of other states and to apply the rules of international law. The territory of a state is defined by borders that separate it from other areas. Within the territory, which includes the air space above the land and the earth beneath it, the state is united under a common legal system. Territory also includes a part of the sea adjacent to the coast up to twelve miles out. A state exercises territorial jurisdiction over all people present on its territory, even if they are not its citizens.

A state also requires a permanent population, the human basis of the existence of a state. Who belongs to the state's population is determined by the rules on nationality that the state itself promulgates, in its discretion. The most common ways in which nationality is conferred on a person are by birth, marriage, adoption or legitimization, and naturalization. When a territory is transferred from one state to another, the population of the transferred territory normally acquires the nationality of the annexing state. There are no legal requirements regarding the ethnic, linguistic, historical, cultural, or religious homogeneity of the population of a state. Issues related to lack of homogeneity of the population, such as the rights of minorities and indigenous peoples, are not relevant as criteria to determine the existence of a state. The size of the population and its territory may be very small: Micro-states with areas less than 500 square miles and populations under 100,000, such as Andorra, Grenada, Liechtenstein, Monaco, Antigua, and Barbuda, are considered states. A state exercises personal jurisdiction over its nationals, as well as over the ships and aircraft flying its flag when abroad.

A government's effective control of territory and population is the third core element that brings together the other two into a state. Internally, the existence of a government implies the capacity to establish and maintain a legal order, including respect for international law. Externally, it means the ability to act autonomously on the international level in relations with other states and to become a member of international organizations. The requirement of effective control over territory is, however, not always strictly applied. A state does not cease to exist when it cannot temporarily exercise its authority because its territory is occupied by foreign armed forces or when it is temporarily deprived of an effective government as a result of civil war or similar upheavals. In any case, in principle, international law is indifferent to the internal political structure of a state. A government must only establish itself in fact; the choice of government is a domestic matter to be determined by individual states. International law does not generally delve into the question of whether the population recognizes the legitimacy of the government in power, although this has been changing in recent years with an increasing emphasis on fair elections and democratic institutions.

The notion of effective government is linked with the idea of independence, often termed *state sovereignty*. Indeed, a government is considered a real one in international law if it is free of direct orders from and control by other governments. International law however, does not investigate the possibility that a state may exist under the direction of another state, as long as a state appears to perform the functions that independent states normally do.

International intergovernmental organizations

The first international organization was created in 1815 for ensuring the freedom of navigation on the river Rhine. Since 1865 with the establishment of the International Telegraphic (present-day Telecommunications) Union and 1874 with the founding of the Universal Postal Union, international organizations have proliferated. After World War I the League of Nations, the first universal institution with a political character, had the task of maintaining peace and intergovernmental cooperation. Since the end of World War II the UN has sought to ensure a more developed form of collective security. Its Charter attempted to provide it with means of action, including the power to discuss any question having an impact on international relations and to act when peace is at stake. States also created independent but related specialized agencies for ensuring cooperation between governments in a number of fields, such as food and agriculture, health, science, education and culture, meteorology, and civil aviation.

During the period following the adoption of the UN Charter states of different regions created organiza-

tions with a more limited territorial scope but broad aims, functions and powers: the Organization of American States, Council of Europe, and Organization of African Unity. These three regional organizations also established special systems for the protection of human rights in their respective areas. In addition, specialized organizations for regional cooperation have been instituted for specific purposes, such as defense (the North Atlantic Treaty Organization, otherwise known as NATO) or the economy (the OECD or European Free Trade Association). Altogether there are approximately five hundred international organizations created by states. Most of them are of a traditional nature; they are in essence based on intergovernmental cooperation. Their institutions generally include an assembly with deliberating power, one or more restricted branches for acting in the name of the organization, and a secretariat. Only rarely do states give an organ or organization power to adopt decisions that legally bind their members. The UN Security Council is an example of an international organ that does have such power.

A new type of international organization created a higher level of cooperation, and the term *integration* is often used to designate it. It implies the transfer of sovereignty from member states to the regional level. The European Union is the most developed model for such organizations. It includes branches composed of persons who are not government representatives, and it can make binding decisions that have a direct legal effect on individuals and companies. Decisions may be taken by a majority vote and the compliance of member states in meeting their obligations is subject to judicial review.

Whatever their legal status might be, it is recognized that intergovernmental organizations have a legal presence in international law, at least as far as their functions require such a status. This means that they can conclude international treaties among themselves or with states, receive and send diplomatic representatives, and enjoy immunities granted to states and state representatives.

Nongovernmental Organizations

Private international organizations, such as Amnesty International, the Human Rights Watch, or Doctors without Borders, play an active role in international affairs. They are generally called nongovernmental organizations (NGOs) because they are not established by a government or by an agreement between states. Instead their members are private citizens and they are usually created as non-profit corporations under the law of a particular state, such as England for Amnesty International. International NGOs have proliferated considerably during the past few decades and are engaged in a broad variety of different areas, ranging from the legal and judicial field, the social and economic domain, human rights and humanitarian relief, women's and children's rights, education, and environmental protection. In the field of international business important NGOs include the International Chamber of Commerce (ICC), the International Air Transport Association (IATA), and international federations of trade unions and employers. All are incorporated under the law of a particular state, with the possibility of creating substructures in other states. There are no standards governing the establishment and status of international NGOs, and this may cause problems because national laws differ from one country to another.

Intergovernmental organizations may agree to grant NGOs a certain consulting or observer status and thereby a limited international standing, but this does not make them directly governed by international law.

The role of NGOs in the international legal system is an informal one, although their representatives may be included in national delegations that participate in international conferences or meetings of intergovernmental bodies. In practice NGOs have four categories of function. They can propose to governments initiatives related to international cooperation. They can participate in law making, by providing the information and expertise intergovernmental bodies need to draft treaties or resolutions. In some cases NGOs attend meetings of contracting states that discuss compliance with multilateral treaties. Finally, they can inform the public of state or interstate activities and of their results or failures, if necessary by organizing campaigns, and thus exercise in this way an influence on governmental policy. Thereby, if NGOs are not subjects of international law, they can be in some situations very effective, especially those recognized as having a high moral standing.

Individuals and companies

Early international law encompassed individuals in three basic ways. First, states had the right to protect their nationals abroad against the misconduct of foreign authorities, invoking the international responsibility of the territorial state, provided such authorities were acting on behalf of the state. Protecting states could and did ask for remedies. That procedure is called *diplomatic protection*. It may be exercised only by states, under conditions established by international law. Both international responsibility and reparation belong to the sphere of interstate relations. Second, international law also recognized the immunity and privileges of certain categories of individuals representing

a foreign state: heads of state, diplomats, and special envoys on mission in a foreign country. Finally, in times of armed conflict prisoners of war, the wounded, and the sick as well as civilian populations were protected by the rules of international humanitarian law. As a result, doctrine generally held that states were the direct participants (subjects) in the international legal system and they could regulate or protect individuals who were not direct participants but could be the object of state regulation or action.

Modern international law first directly recognized individuals when certain acts were deemed criminal as attacks on international society. Initially, piracy and then slave-trading were outlawed. After World War I those responsible for breaches of international obligations related to armed conflicts were personally accused of war crimes; some of the accused were even condemned to death. After the war the creation of the International Labour Organization called for the implicit recognition of certain rights later called economic and social rights. The UN Charter and Universal Declaration of Human Rights proclaimed in 1948 recognized the fundamental rights of individuals. Conventions with a general scope as well as in specific fields, both at a worldwide level and within regional frameworks, further developed such norms. Recent evolution further developed norms concerning the direct criminal responsibility of individuals under international law.

Present international law thus directly recognizes the rights to individuals and imposes certain duties on them. In terms of rights some of the conventions protecting human rights allow individuals and victims of violations of protected rights to submit their case to specific international jurisdictions. Different nonjudicial systems were also developed to remedy such violations, especially within the framework of the UN. In terms of duties, following the example of the Nuremberg and Tokyo tribunals that judged and condemned the German and Japanese perpetrators of crimes against humanity committed during World War II, international criminal jurisdictions have multiplied. First, they were created for crimes committed in specific areas, such as the former Yugoslavia and Rwanda. Finally, a convention adopted in Rome on July 17, 1998, established a permanent International Criminal Court.

Companies and especially multinational ones may hold more economic and political power than many states, especially within the context of economic globalization. Still, states do not accept them on legally equal footing. As such, they generally do not benefit from the protection of human rights and as a rule they are not criminally responsible before international tribunals. States and international bodies have tried to find a compromise by establishing partnerships with corporations and by formulating codes of conduct of a recommended nature.

In summary, states do not recognize individuals, NGOs, and companies as equal subjects of international law or even as having, like intergovernmental organizations, a specific international legal status corresponding to their functions. Nonetheless, they exercise a real influence on the behavior of states in areas such as economy and policy, especially within the context of sustainable development and globalization. Referred to as the *international civil society*, they are, however, progressively accepted as important players in international relations.

Some historians and observers take a further step and, given the growing number and expanding complexity of economic and other relations, use the term stakeholders to include all those who are concerned with a particular legal situation. If no one has so far suggested that international law should recognize the new category in legal terms, states as well as international bodies increasingly accept their existence and potential role in the international field.

Ethnic Minorities and Indigenous Peoples
The status and protection of ethnic, linguistic, or cultural minorities in international law emerged in Europe after World War I. After World War II certain rights were granted to such groups, but states were reluctant to take steps that might increase the danger of claims to independence and secession. Owing to efforts made by international bodies such as the UN General Assembly and the Council of Europe, progress was made toward the better protection of minority rights. Such rights are most often conceived of as a category of human rights, to be exercised by the individual belonging to a minority, rather than as rights attributed to a collective entity or group.

Indigenous peoples were virtually unmentioned in international law several decades ago. Although historically important differences may exist between such groups and minorities, from a legal perspective the distinction is not easy to make. International conferences and institutions, however, progressively proclaim and recognize the rights of indigenous and local communities. The question of the international legal standing of indigenous groups is, in fact, a question of the specific rights attributed to them by states. They are not subjects of international law, but actors contributing to the formation of international rules of law.

In conclusion, it may be stated that international law is undergoing a transformation, progressively recognizing the role and place of nonstate actors and the

need to implement norms protecting fundamental values, such as peace, human rights, and the environment.

SEE ALSO Crimes Against Humanity; Humanitarian Intervention; Humanitarian Law; Human Rights; International Court of Justice; United Nations; War Crimes

BIBLIOGRAPHY
Amerasinghe, C. F. (1996). *Principles of the International Law of International Organizations.* Cambridge, U.K.: Cambridge University Press.

Aust, A. (2000). *Modern Treaty Law and Practice.* Cambridge, U.K.: Cambridge University Press.

Daillier, P., and A. Pellet (1999). *Droit international public,* 6th edition. Paris: Librairie générale de droit et de jurisprudence.

Degan, V. D. (1997). *Sources of International Law.* The Hague: Nijhoff.

Elias, A. O., and C. L. Slim (1998). *The Paradox of Consensualism in International Law.* The Hague: Kluwer.

Evans, Malcolm, ed. (2003). *International Law.* New York: Oxford University Press.

Gelber, H. G. (1997). *Sovereignty through Independence.* The Hague: Kluwer.

Macdonald, R. St. John, and D. M. Johnston, eds. (1983). *The Structure and Process of International Law.* The Hague: Nijhoff.

Malanczuk, P. (1997). *Akehurst's Modern Introduction to International Law,* 7th edition. London: Routledge.

McNair, Lord (1961). *The Law of Treaties.* Oxford, U.K.: Oxford University Press.

Schachter, O., and C. Joyner, eds. (1995). *U.N. Legal Order.* Cambridge, U.K.: Cambridge University Press.

Schermers, H. J., and M. M. Blokker (1995). *International Institutional Law, Unity within Diversity.* The Hague: Nijhoff.

Tatsuzawa, K., ed. (1997). *The Law of International Relations.* Kujike, Abiko, Japan: Chuogakuin University.

Tomuschat, C., ed. (1995). *The United Nations at Age Fifty. A Legal Perspective.* The Hague: Kluwer.

Wolfrum, R., ed. (1995). *United Nations Law, Policies and Practice.* Dordrecht, Netherlands: Nijhoff.

Wolfze, K. (1993). *Custom in Present International Law.* The Hague: Kluwer.

Alexandre Kiss

International Law Commission

The International Law Commission (ILC) is a specialized body of experts that is subordinate to the General Assembly of the United Nations. Its mandate is to codify and progressively develop international law. The international law concerning genocide and crimes against humanity has benefited from the commission's attention. Since its creation, the ILC has been responsible for the preparation of several important documents, including the Draft Statute of the International Criminal Court, the Code of Crimes Against the Peace and Security of Mankind, the formulation of principles recognized in the Charter of the Nuremberg Tribunal, and the Articles on State Responsibility.

The ILC was established by the UN General Assembly in 1947, in accordance with its authority under Article 13(1) of the Charter of the United Nations. There was no direct ancestor of the ILC in the League of Nations system, although attempts had been made to convene expert meetings with a view to codifying international law. The ILC held its first session in 1949, and since then has met annually for several weeks. It is composed of thirty-four experts with recognized competence in international law. The experts are distinguished academics or diplomats, for the most part, rather than delegates from specific countries. Each expert acts in his individual capacity.

Over the years, the ILC's program of work, which is established in consultation with the General Assembly, has included a wide range of international law issues. Among the topics it has addressed are the treatment of aliens, the law of the high seas, diplomatic and consular immunities, and the law governing international treaties including the issue of reservations. At its very first session, the ILC decided not to consider the codification of the laws and customs of war. The Swiss Government and the International Committee of the Red Cross had taken the lead in organizing activity that, in August 1949, resulted in the adoption of the Geneva Conventions on the protection of persons in armed conflict. Several ILC members considered it inappropriate that a United Nations body study the laws of war, given the commitment in the Charter of the United Nations to prohibit the use of force.

One of the first topics assigned by the General Assembly to the ILC was the formulation of the principles of international law recognized in the Charter of the Nuremberg Tribunal. The Trial of the Major War Criminals, held in Nuremberg in 1945 and 1946, had been set up by the four Allied powers (France, the United States, the United Kingdom, and the USSR) in accordance with a treaty adopted at London in August 1945 known as the London Charter or the Charter of the Nuremberg Tribunal. The ILC considered that the principles recognized by the Charter of the Nuremberg Tribunal, and by the final judgment of the Tribunal of September 30 to October 1, 1946, were already recognized as properly forming a part of international law, given their endorsement in December 1946 by General

Assembly Resolution 95(I). In 1950 the ILC adopted its formulation of seven principles. These included individual criminal responsibility for crimes under international law, with liability attaching to heads of state or government and to accomplices; a rejection of the defense based on following a superior's orders; the right to a fair trial; and an acknowledgment of the definitions of three categories of international crime, including crimes against humanity.

A year later, in 1948, the ILC was given responsibility for a study of the desirability and possibility of establishing an international criminal court. The issue arose in the context of drafting the Convention for the Prevention and Punishment of the Crime of Genocide. The countries involved in drafting the Genocide Convention rejected the concept of universal jurisdiction out of concern for politically motivated prosecutions in the context of the emerging cold war. Instead, Article VI of the Convention said that the crime of genocide would be prosecuted by the courts of the state where the crime took place—an unlikely scenario—or by "such international penal tribunal as may have jurisdiction with respect to those Contracting Parties which shall have accepted its jurisdiction."

The ILC gave the matter of an international court some preliminary consideration in 1949. Then the General Assembly set up a specialized committee, which prepared a draft statute. In 1954 the General Assembly decided to postpone further work on the concept of an international criminal court until a satisfactory definition of the crime of aggression had been agree to. That activity was to take two decades until, in 1974, the General Assembly adopted a resolution providing a definition of aggression. The effect, for the ILC, was to suspend work on the subject of an international criminal court.

The ILC did not resume its study of the international criminal court until 1990, following yet another resolution of the General Assembly. The ILC worked quickly, setting up a working group in 1992 and assigning James Crawford as its special rapporteur on the subject. A proposed draft statute was considered by the ILC at its 1993 session. It was circulated to governments for their comments. A revised version, taking into account this consultation, was adopted by the ILC in 1994 and promptly submitted to the General Assembly. The important work of the ILC provided the General Assembly with a framework for discussions, and much of the text proposed by the ILC survived in the final version of the Rome Statute of the International Criminal Court (ICC), which was adopted in July 1998.

Another major contribution by the ILC is its Code of Crimes Against the Peace and Security of Mankind. This idea was originally conceived in 1947 and was related to the mandate of formulating the Nuremberg Principles. The great interest in international criminal law generated by the post–World War II prosecutions evolved into an effort at codifying the international crimes. Lack of an accepted definition prior to the Nuremberg prosecutions had vexed those who had established the tribunal and provided arguments to the defendants, who claimed they were victims of ex post facto criminal legislation. This brought into sharp relief the importance of codifying this emerging area of law by an authoritative body, and the International Law Commission was the logical choice.

The ILC completed its first draft of the Code of Crimes in 1951. It did not follow the Nuremberg definitions exactly. It agreed to confine the scope of the code to offences with a political element that endangered international peace and security. Accordingly, it did not address such issues as piracy, trafficking in persons and in dangerous drugs, slavery, counterfeiting, and damage to submarine cables, although in the past these had fallen within the ambit of international criminal prosecution. The 1951 draft was submitted to governments for comments and then revised in 1954, when it was submitted to the General Assembly. As it had done with the international criminal court project, the General Assembly decided to suspend work on the codes, pending elaboration of a definition of aggression.

Work only resumed on the code in the late 1970s. Over the next decade and a half, the ILC gave detailed consideration to the definitions of the crimes of genocide and crimes against humanity. It also examined issues of substantive criminal law related to the prosecution of these crimes, including the nature of complicity and other forms of criminal participation, and the admissibility of defences such as superior orders and various immunities. This detailed work resulted, in 1991, in a draft of the code, which was submitted to governments for their comments. A few years later, the ILC returned again to the code, adopting its definitive version in 1996.

When the International Criminal Tribunal for the Former Yugoslavia (ICTY) began its activities, it drew on the work of the ILC in international criminal law for guidance. A judgment of the International Criminal Tribunal for the Former Yugoslavia described the code in the following terms:

[A]n authoritative international instrument which, depending upon the specific question at issue, may (i) constitute evidence of customary law, or (ii) shed light on customary rules which are of uncertain contents or are in the process of formation, or, at the very least, (iii) be indicative of the legal views of eminently qualified publicists representing the major legal systems of the world.

In another case, the ICTY referred to the work of the commission in order to distinguish between the crime of genocide and that of extermination, which is a punishable act falling within the rubric of crimes against humanity.

Similarly, the ILC materials on the code provided theoretical guidance for debates at the Rome Conference at which the Statute of the International Criminal Court was adopted. There was a major conceptual difference, however, in the version of the Statute of the International Criminal Court adopted at Rome and the 1994 draft of the ILC. The commission had viewed the proposed court as an organ that fit neatly within the system of the United Nations Charter, especially as concerned the Security Council. The ILC's proposal was for a court subordinate to the Security Council, essentially similar to the ad hoc tribunal that the Council had established in 1993 for the former Yugoslavia. In the course of political debate about the nature of the court that took place under the auspices of the General Assembly between 1994 and 1998, the court became progressively detached from the domination and control of the Security Council. The Rome Statute authorizes the International Criminal Court to prosecute cases at the initiation of an independent prosecutor, an idea rejected by the ILC. Furthermore, it subjects any decision by the Security Council to suspend prosecution to much more rigorous process than had been imagined by the ILC.

The ILC has also addressed issues related to genocide and crimes against humanity in other contexts, notably in the course of its preparation of the draft Articles on State Responsibility. The Genocide Convention of 1948 appears to contemplate genocide as both an individual crime, capable of being committed by physical persons, and as a breach of international law, committed by states. In fact, on several occasions, one state has sued another before the International Court of Justice for violations of the Genocide Convention, although a final judgment has yet to be rendered in any of these cases. In its draft Articles, adopted in 2000, the ILC agreed to treat genocide and related crimes as "internationally wrongful acts" rather than as "state crimes," which was a controversial concept on which it could reach no consensus.

The various draft instruments adopted by the ILC, the reports of its rapporteurs, and the debates and proceedings of its annual meetings provide students of international crimes with a rich resource. These materials have been widely drawn upon by lawyers and judges at the international courts, as well as by academic lawyers. The contribution of the ILC to the codification and development of international law relating to the repression of genocide and crimes against humanity is both immense and invaluable.

SEE ALSO Code of Crimes against the Peace and Security of Mankind; International Criminal Tribunal for Rwanda; International Criminal Tribunal for the Former Yugoslavia; International Law; Nuremberg Laws; Responsibility, State

BIBLIOGRAPHY

Crawford, James (1994). "The ILC's Draft Statute for an International Criminal Tribunal." *American Journal of International Law* 88:140.

Crawford, James (1995). "The ILC Adopts a Statute for an International Criminal Court." *American Journal of International Law* 89:404.

Crawford, James (2002). *The International Law Commission's Articles on State Responsibility.* Cambridge: Cambridge University Press.

Morton, Jeffrey S. (2000). *The International Law Commission of the United Nations.* Columbia: University of South Carolina Press.

Ramcharan, B. G. (1977). *The International Law Commission, Its Approach to the Codification and Progressive Development of International Law.* The Hague, Netherlands: Martinus Nijhoff.

United Nations (1996). *The Work of the International Law Commission,* 5th edition. New York: United Nations.

United Nations (1997). *Analytical Guide to the Work of the International Law Commission 1949–1997.* New York: United Nations.

Watts, Arthur (1999). *The International Law Commission 1949–1998.* Oxford: Oxford University Press.

William A. Schabas

Investigation

Telford Taylor, a Nuremberg proceedings prosecutor, observed in his Final Report that the issue of genocide and crimes against humanity and their investigation "was far bigger and far more difficult of solution than anyone had anticipated." The experience of more recent cases, and particularly the UN ad hoc tribunals, has confirmed that investigating crimes of this kind is far more complex a duty than the public opinion and the policymakers may think when the call for justice is made. The investigation of these crimes raises hard questions of method at different levels, from epistemol-

Photographers watch as International War Crimes Tribunal investigators gather evidence at a mass grave site near Srebrenica, on April 3, 1996.[AP/WIDE WORLD PHOTOS]

ogy and cognitive psychology, to forensic sciences and resource management. The hardest investigative challenges are not related to the criminal act as such, which is often a blatant and notorious phenomenon, but to the questions on specific intent and individual responsibility, particularly for those suspects at higher levels of authority.

Early precedents of investigations date back to the sixteenth century with Bartolomé de Las Casas, who documented crimes committed by the Spanish conquerors on the American population. He based these writings on his field research, as well as on numerous affidavits and documentary evidence. De las Casas invoked "the congregation of the faithful" to stop these offenses, much in the way that contemporary human rights reports conclude with appeals to the "international community." Historical chronicles and accounts from the victimized communities show different forms of investigation carried out between the seventeenth and the twentieth centuries, for example, in the cases of mass violence against the Jewish and Moors from Spain, and against Christian subjects in Japan.

The work of the International Commission to Inquire into the Causes and Conduct of the Balkan Wars did pioneering work in the twentieth century. In 1914 they published a thorough investigative report comprising numerous interviews, pictures and detailed maps, and reached the conclusion that the Balkan leaders and not the peoples were "the real culprits in this long list of executions, assassinations, drownings, burnings massacres and atrocities furnished by our report."

World War I also gave rise to a number of investigative initiatives in the form of official commissions of enquiry, criminal investigations and research literature. Most significantly, in 1918, the Ottoman authorities established two commissions to investigate the massacres of Armenians, one parliamentary and another one administrative. The latter had powers to search and seize documents, interview witnesses and arrest suspects. After two months of work this commission recommended criminal prosecutions and forwarded the evidence to the judicial authorities. This led to an indictment by the Ottoman Procuror General against the Ittihad leaders for "the massacre and destruction of the Armenians," and to their subsequent conviction.

The crimes committed in World War II led to far greater developments on both national and international, judicial and academic investigations of international crimes, which in turn inspired renewed interest on this matter beginning in the early 1990s. A definite methodology of investigations does not seem plausible because of the variety of criminal offences and scenarios, but review of the investigative experiences does suggest the following ten key areas.

Opportunity Structure
The success of the investigations depends on a structure of opportunity determined by a range of social, political and operational factors. While international crimes are typically the result of a complex web of organizations and complicities, to investigate and prosecute them requires a complex array of contributions; in other words, where international crimes are concerned, it takes a network to fight a network.

Taylor observed how the initial support for the Nuremberg proceedings had declined sharply by 1948 as a result of the "waning interest on the part of the general public and the shift in the focus of public attention resulting from international events and circumstances." For this reason, the courts were obliged to accelerate the proceedings and reduce the number of cases. The UN ad hoc tribunals have faced very similar

problems fifty years later, having to adjust their schedule to varying levels of political and financial support. The scope of attention and support of the societies and institutions that sponsor the investigations is always limited, and dependent on changing trends and priorities. A thorough assessment of the resulting opportunity structures is essential for the success of the investigations.

Inquisitorial Temptation
A certain tendency to downgrade the presumption of innocence of the accused is common to the investigations of international crimes, due to the gravity of the crime and the expectations created by the proceedings. In an atmosphere of public outcry the temptation may arise to assume that, as was suggested in the Demjanjuk case, "the cost of allowing the real Ivan to go free by far outweighs the cost of convicting an innocent man" (Wagenaar, 1988). Demjanjuk was actually wrongly accused and convicted of being "Ivan the Terrible," the officer in charge of the gas chamber of Treblinka. He is a paramount example of investigative and judicial mistake concerning a case of genocide.

Such an approach would amount to a return to the classic doctrine that justified lowering the standards of proof in cases of atrocious crimes, by the maxim *in attrocissimis leviores coniecturae sufficiunt et licet iudice iura transgredi* ("in very atrocious crimes light assumptions suffice and it is licit for the judge to transgrede the law"). This approach was already dismissed by C. Beccaria in the eighteenth century as a "cruel imbecility," and contrary to the modern principles of due process.

Deviations from investigative objectivity may emerge in the following aspects of a case: selective choice of the matter by extrajudicial criteria; prejudice suspect-driven (as oppose to offence-driven); investigation design followed by a bias of corroboration (as opposed to objective testing of allegations by both corroboration and falsification); speculative focus on the intentions rather than the actions of the suspect; emphasis on the suffering of the victims while overlooking the individual responsibility of the suspect; and use of vague charges and liability concepts.

Feelings of outrage and demands for swift action provoked by mass violence are understandable among victims as well as among the general public. However, investigators need to rise above such a pressing atmosphere and conduct their work with strict objectivity and respect for the guarantees of the accused, beginning with the presumption of innocence. As it was observed of the miscarriage of the Demjanjuk case: "the fact that the charge involves the murder of 850,000 innocent people does not justify a reduction of the standards of meticulousness that in other circumstances would be accepted as a normal requirement" (Wagenaar, 1988). To the contrary, the gravity of the case only increases the responsibility of the investigating officer and demands the highest standards of objectivity.

A Multidisciplinary Approach

Investigations of international crimes require an approach that can integrate various fields of knowledge, from forensics to social sciences and information technology. Conventional investigative techniques are not sufficient because of the distinctive features of the matter, which make it essentially different from the investigation of common crime. This contradiction surfaced in the investigations for the Tokyo trials, when FBI agents were assigned to the prosecution in the belief that their expertise would meet the challenges of the investigation. However, these agents lacked background knowledge on Japanese society and institutions, and thus were unable to understand the role of the suspects, and ended up asking them for basic information.

The Office of Special Investigations (OSI) of the U.S. Department of Justice (focused on Holocaust investigations) initially relied on police officers, only to replace them progressively with historians through the 1980s. Similarly, the National Investigations Team for War Crimes of the Netherlands abandoned the original plan of 1998 to have a staff of police officers, after realizing that experts with advanced training and proper contextual knowledge were indispensable. Nevertheless, important contributions have originated in the domain of domestic investigations the fields of forensic sciences and criminal analysis, providing key physical evidence and mastering large volumes of data with advanced technological tools.

Mutual support between criminal proceedings and social research has been the rule in every major investigation of international crimes. The Armenian genocide had among its initial reporters historian A. J. Toynbee, whereas subsequent historiography on the issue has relied substantially on judicial records. The first historiographic wave on the Holocaust in the 1950s and 1960s (Ritlinger, Hilberg, Poliakov and others) used the evidence and findings of the Nuremberg trials. Those authors in turn were utilized by the interrogators of Eichmann and contributed themselves as witnesses for a number of trials. This tradition of cooperation has continued with different national commissions, as well as in the United Nations ad hoc tribunals, who utilized a number of historians and social scientists in their investigation teams. Descriptive statistics, based on medical records or victim statements, have been utilized to measure the volume and profiles of victimization, since the Crimean War (1854–1855) and World War I, up to the Guatemala and Peru Truth Commissions, ICTY (International Criminal Tribunal for the Former Yugoslavia) and the victimization of children in Uganda.

Concerning nonjudicial reporting, there is a whole field of research comprising reports by human rights organizations, Ombudsman offices, state supervision organs, immigration agencies, and parliamentary or truth commissions. The works of these bodies of enquiry may anticipate and enable criminal investigations, as happened in the cases of the Armenian genocide, Nuremberg (preceded by the UN War Crimes Commission), the Argentinean juntas trial (CONADEP, National Commission on the Disappearance of Person), ICTY (UN Commission of Experts), Guatemala (UN Commission for Historical Clarification and Commission for the Recovery of Historical Memory), and East Timor (Commission of Inquiry and International Committee of Inquiry). The contributions of nongovernmental organizations are particularly important, as they often pioneer the investigative effort and manage to achieve remarkable results with limited resources.

Intelligence agencies have also made investigative contributions, when appropriately instructed to this effect. Antecedents are known since the reports of British military intelligence on the massacres of Armenians. A case in point is the contribution to the Nuremberg proceedings of the Research and Analysis Branch of the U.S. Office of Strategic Studies. The investigations related to the former Yugoslavia have also been assisted by a number of intelligence agencies, such as the Bosnian Agency for Information and Documentation.

Last but not least, local expertise is indispensable in interpreting the relevant information in its authentic social context. In the Nuremberg investigations this expertise was integrated through a number of analysts familiar with the German society and institutions (notably F. Neuman, Chief of Analysis). International tribunals have taken different approaches on this matter; while the prosecutor of the ICTY was reluctant to integrate local officers for reasons of impartiality and security, the prosecutor of the SCSL (Special Court Sierra Leone) has relied on national investigators acquainted with the relevant society and conflict.

Disregard Simplistic Explanations

The easiest and most impressionistic explanations of international crimes need to be discarded: the criminal usually is not a psychopath, command structures are never perfect, and the crimes are not the mere result of ideology or a flawlessly planned course of action. Un-

A Canadian forensics expert brushes off a bone found at a mass grave site in Vlastica, Kosovo, on June 30, 1999. Thirteen victims, killed in the end of April during the NATO bombing campaign, were found in this bulldozed house.[AP/WIDE WORLD PHOTOS]

fortunately for the investigating officer, the events are usually much more difficult to explain and prove than in other cases. The criminals, particularly at the leadership level, tend to be "terribly and terrifyingly normal" (as Hannah Arendt said of Eichmann). Ideology may be one of the criminogenic factors, but it is rarely a decisive one. Command structures are fluid phenomena with frequent anomalies that "cannot be understood in isolation" (in the words of M. van Creveld), which obliges one to employ a complex contextual analysis of their de facto functioning. And no matter how much prosecutors like reductionist conspiracy theories, waves of violence over extended periods of time are most often the result of complex decision-making processes, conflicting interests, and unexpected factors. For investigative success, it is best to discard simplistic conceptions, and to face the complexity of these phenomena with the appropriate human and material resources.

The Centrality of Analysis

The tension between operations (collecting evidence) and analysis (evaluating and integrating it) is inherent to any criminal investigation and evolves around the basic question of "do we have enough evidence?" which can only be addressed through systematic analysis of what has been collected. This then typically prompts the question "Do we use our limited time and resources to analyze or to collect?"

The imagination of the lay audience may be captured by the picture of an investigation led by an operational strike force moving hurriedly to the scene of the crime to seize the evidence and deliver a "tough" and prompt response. In reality, an operations-led model tends to cause lack of focus and a certain evidentiary hypertrophy, a situation where there is more information than is manageable, of lower quality than is needed. The alternative is an analysis-led model, where the purpose of analysis is not just to support field operations, but rather to design and guide a focused collection process.

Experience indicates that systematic analysis must be central for a successful and cost-efficient investigative cycle. Some surveys of agencies investigating non-organized crime suggests an average ratio of one analyst to twelve investigators, while the Office of the Prosecutor of the ICTY reached a ratio close to one analyst to two investigators, and the relative weight of analysis is intended to be even greater for the ICC investigations.

Focus on Specific Intent and Contextual Elements

The legal definitions of genocide and crimes against humanity include elements that operate as qualifiers of gravity and restrictors to limit international jurisdictional intervention to extraordinarily offensive crimes. These are mainly the specific intent (for genocide) and the requirement of widespread or systematic commission and civilian condition of the victims (for crimes against humanity). Such elements are the hallmark of these international crimes, and usually the most difficult ones to investigate and to prove.

The specific intent of genocide is rarely manifested explicitly, and international jurisprudence has acknowledged that it can be inferred from the material events and circumstantial indicia. Concerning the elements specific to crimes against humanity, systematicity refers to aspects of organization and modus operandi, as well as to the functionality of the crime vis-à-vis predetermined objectives. The widespread requirement is essentially a matter of scale, for which there is no clear quantitative threshold; however some parameters can be inferred from international jurisprudence.

There is an ontological issue in proving the widespread scale, in that it requires ascertaining if a series of events do in fact constitute a single coherent entity, or if they are instead multiple autonomous entities. Objective answers to these aspects draw on crime pattern analysis, which is the set of analytical techniques utilized to identify significant correlations among large series of events (including systematic categorizations and statistics).

Documentary Evidence

Reasons of probative value (quality and reliability of the evidence) procedural economy (easier and faster to handle) and security (to reduce the exposure of witnesses) advise prioritizing documentary evidence. In cases of criminal orders and related records, documents may be the *corpus delicti* itself, the instrument that materialized the crime and ultimate proof of its commission (as Vahakn N. Dadrian has observed regarding the documentary records of the Armenian genocide).

In Nuremberg, prosecutor Robert Jackson planned from the beginning to rest his case on documentary evidence and gave instructions to gather "documents such as military or political orders, instructions, or declarations of policy which may serve to connect high personalities with the actual commission of crimes." The Nuremberg judgment stated explicitly the importance of documentary evidence and quoted a whole range of original Nazi documents, from Hitler's *Mein Kampf* to different orders for the killing of prisoners and civilians. Compared to Nuremberg, in the Tokyo Trials documentary evidence was less significant because Japanese forces were more successful in the destruction of their documents. Similarly, documentary evidence was remarkably more relevant to ICTY than to ICTR (International Criminal Tribunal for Rwanda).

At the litigation stage the authenticity of the documents is often an issue in contest. The U.S. OSI in the 1980s systematically used Nazi archival records from various states. When confronted with evidence originating from the USSR, the accused often alleged that documents had been manipulated by the KGB and made necessary the use of different forensic methods to test their authenticity (generally with positive results). Similar allegations have been made in the hearings of the ICTY regarding documents tendered by the prosecutor, who most often has succeeded at proving their authenticity through testimony of the analysts who collected them and through evidence of their internal and contextual consistency.

Witnesses and Evidence Sampling

Witnesses are the soul of the proceedings. Without them the human suffering that originated the whole ju-

dicial effort could not be appreciated. Nevertheless, difficult decisions need to be made to limit and select the number of witnesses that can be considered, for pragmatic reasons related to limited court-time and resources, security, and the problems of secondary victimization and witness fatigue. It is best to anticipate these constraints from the beginning of the investigation, in order to optimize the choice of witnesses, and to focus on the most significant ones.

Such selection calls for careful design, in a way similar to the techniques of sampling in social empirical research, so that a subset of evidence can provide a valid representation of the whole universe to be proved. In the case of the Argentinean junta trials, prosecutor L. Moreno (who was in charge of investigations in 1984 and in 2003 was appointed the first ICC prosecutor) choose 700 individual cases from the National Commission on the Disappeared (CONADEP) data with the aim of representing a scope of several thousands of victims of "all armies, of all periods, and the whole country." Typically, at the litigation stage the defense will try to challenge the validity of the sample, arguing that the evidence in question is not representative, but rather anomalous or exceptional, which highlights the need for strict methodology and objectivity in the process of choosing the witnesses.

The Importance of Insider and International Witnesses

Experience indicates that insiders and internationals are among the most valuable witnesses. The former are important because of their ability to establish the intimate de facto functioning of the criminal apparatus, and the latter because of the panoramic knowledge of criminal patterns and their enhanced credibility (particularly before international judges).

Insiders were already considered in the Ottoman investigations. There was, for example, General Vehib, who gave testimony on the assassination of some two thousand Armenians and his knowledge about a broader scheme of extermination. International witnesses have been used in many cases, from the missionaries that testified in Tokyo about "the rape of Shanghai," to numerous similar witnesses that have appeared before the chambers of the ICTY and ICTR (including field workers of NGOs and international organizations, journalists and peacekeepers). Often the testimony of these witnesses is supported by the reports that they produced at the relevant time (a technique already utilized in the Tokyo Trials and greatly exploited before the ad hoc tribunals). However, some organizations are reluctant to authorize the testimony of their officers for reasons of confidentiality and security.

Interviewing an insider or a suspect is a particularly difficult task, and often one with controversial results. In Nuremberg Nazi officers were initially interrogated with a highly formal and confrontational approach, conducted by attorneys through interpreters. This was soon replaced with a friendly and informal approach trusted to a team of native speakers who interacted with the interviewees in German, which proved more effective. In the case of R. Hoss (the Auschwitz commander), the officers that conducted his first interrogation in Poland were convinced of his sincerity, while subsequent research proved that they had failed to distance themselves sufficiently from the interviewee, and Hoss had been fairly truthful concerning the crime as such, but had lied systematically concerning his own role.

The interrogation of Eichmann was conducted by a German-born person, who communicated with the accused in German and was assisted by a team of officers from all the different countries relevant to the case. Initially they encountered a very common problem in this type of interviews, which was that the interviewee was more well-versed in the subject than they were, and hence was in a position to control the exchange.

Some historians have observed that the interrogators imposed some preconceptions on the Nazi organizations, through a series of leading questions that prevented more objective findings. In the case of General M. Carmel, his denial of any responsibility concerning massacres and mass expulsion of Palestinians in 1948 was disproved years later when the researcher who interviewed him (Benny Morris) could gain access to the relevant documentary evidence.

The cases above exemplify the problems of cognitive control, leading questions, and language issues, as well as the untrustworthy behavior of the suspects, that are all too common in every investigation and the international tribunals have faced in numerous occasions. The solutions typically result from a measure of teamwork to master the broad and complex issues at stake. In this way, investigators can establish a distance from the interviewee, and prevent any bias caused by empathy, confronting the interviewee as much as possible with documentary evidence, and keeping a literal record of the statement, to assure utmost accuracy and to be able to confront the source.

Security Needs

Most often international crimes are caused by powerful organizations that may remain active and will have an interest in sabotaging the investigations through means of intimidation or outright attack. For this reason, the requirements of security for the witnesses, the investigating personnel and the evidence need to be anticipated and duly handled. Witnesses are likely to ask for protective measures as a pre-condition to collaborate, in which case the investigating officer has to first of all not promise or create unrealistic expectations beyond the available means, and then assess carefully the merits of such request, because protection measures are always subject to constraints of procedure and resources.

Witness protection programs have developed since the 1980s, most typically for insiders in cases of organized crime, in Italy (for the mafia "pentiti"), the United States, and other countries. Similar programs have been established by the UN ad hoc tribunals, also focused often on insiders or particularly vulnerable witnesses. In Colombia the national witness protection program devotes much of its work to cases related to armed groups. In one notorious case in 2001, a former member of a paramilitary group was located and killed in spite of being under the strictest level of protection granted by the national prosecutor. Measures to protect the identity of the witnesses during proceedings have been used frequently, among others, by the ad hoc tribunals, and war crimes cases in Colombia but, as a matter of due process, they will need to be reconciled with the rights of the accused to know the identity of the accusing witnesses.

SEE ALSO Evidence; Forensics; International Criminal Court; International Criminal Tribunal for Rwanda; International Criminal Tribunal for the Former Yugoslavia; Mass Graves; Nongovernmental Organizations; War Crimes; World War I Peace Treaties

BIBLIOGRAPHY

Agirre, Xabier (1997). *Yugoslavia y los Ejércitos. La legitimidad militar en tiempos de genocidio.* Madrid, Spain: Ediciones de La Catarata.

Dadrian, Vahakn (1995). *The History of the Armenian Genocide.* Oxford, U.K.: Bergham Books

de las Casas, Bartolomé (1552). *Brevísima relación de la destruición de las Indias.* Puerto Rico: Universidad Central de Bayamón, 2001.

Hilberg, R. (2001). *Sources of Holocaust Research. An Analysis.* Chicago: Ivan R. Dee

International Commission to Inquire into the Causes and Conduct of the Balkan Wars (1914). *Report of the International Commission to Inquire into the Causes and Conduct of the Balkan Wars.* Washington, D.C.: The Carnegie Endowment.

Moreno Ocampo, L. (1996). *Cuando el Poder Perdió el Juicio.* Buenos Aires, Argentina: Planeta.

Morris, Benny (2004). *The Birth of the Palestinian Refugee Problem Revisited.* Cambridge: Cambridge University Press.

Neumann, F. (1944). *Behemoth: The Structure and Practice of National Socialism 1933–1944*. Oxford: Oxford University Press.

Shiroyama, S. (1997). *War Criminal: The Life and Death of Hirota Koki*. Tokyo: Kodansha International.

Taylor, T. (1949). *Final Report to the Secretary of the Army on the Nuernberg War Crimes Trials under Control Council Law No 10*. Washington, D.C.

Van Creveld, M. (1985). *Command in War*. Cambridge, Ma.: Harvard University Press

Wagenaar, W. A. (1988). *Identifying Ivan. A Case Study in Legal Psychology*. New York: Harvester.

Xabier Agirre Aranburu
The author contributed in his personal capacity. The views expressed in this article are based on public information and do not represent those of the ICTY nor the ICC.

Iran

The turbulent history of modern Iran begins with the fall the Qajar dynasty's traditional polity in 1925, followed by the westernizing policies of Reza Shah and Muhammad Reza Shah, who ruled until the Islamic revolution in 1979. The revolution introduced a new ruler, Ayatollah Khomeini, who created an Islamic republic that was a hybrid of tradition and modernity.

The Qajar Shahs had ruled autocratically in a traditional Iran where due process of law was unknown and punishment was swift, involving physical torment and at times violent death. Hardly anyone was sentenced to prison. Torture was a part of the process by which the guilt of the accused was established. With the arrival of European-style "modernity," the Pahlavi dynasty adopted new policies. Reza Shah, who ruled from 1926 to 1941, created a centralized administration, a standing army, a police force for cities, and a gendarmerie for the countryside. In the absence of legal safeguards, however, these paraphernalia of a modern state were abusive of the rights of citizens.

The state built prisons and created the category of political prisoners. The new elite who employed Western-designed instruments of power without much hesitation, were much more distrustful of Western-style safeguards such as constitutional limits of authority, representative assemblies, individual liberties, and due process of law. The Shah felt comfortable with adopting Western instruments of power for he did not see them as a cultural imposition much different from what was known in the past. Their safeguards, however, were rejected as Western cultural intrusions. The same selective borrowings in the interests of those who wield power have continued under the Ayatollahs into the twenty-first century.

Under Reza Shah, the number of political prisoners was small, although a few men were murdered for po-

litical reasons. However, political and economic abuses of the modernizing elite generated resentment among the country's relatively small, modern middle class. Thus emerged a counter elite of nationalistic and populist persuasions. The ensuing political confrontations did not create an evolutionary process toward a more democratic state. Instead, they increasingly engendered political violence. As the severity of the challenge increased, so did the use of torture and execution. At the beginning of this process under Reza Shah, the confrontations lacked the intensity that they later assumed under his son, Mohammad Reza Shah. The latter's rule, in turn, appears far less violent when compared with what awaited the people under the Ayatollahs. There seems to be a correlation between the increasing commitment to conflicting ideologies and the escalating level of violence.

Faced with the state's forceful modernization of educational norms and the Westernization of the public space (e.g., the removal of the veil), traditionalist Shiite clerics offered some resistance. This was put down with little killing and a relatively minimal use of torture. When a group of Marxists arose in 1938 to present a secular challenge, the state charged them with anti-state sedition. None of them was executed, and after the initial harsh interrogations, accompanied by the use of physical pressure, the prisoners settled into routine, monotonous prison life. Iranian prisons lacked the brutalities that were associated with military dictatorships throughout the Third World in the second half of the twentieth century. The regime did not torture its imprisoned opponents. In the words of historian Ervand Abrahamian, the regime "was more interested in keeping subjects passive and outwardly obedient than in mobilizing them and boring holes into their minds. Reza Shah had created a military monarchy—not an ideologically charged autocracy" (1999, p. 41).

After Reza Shah's abdication in 1941, the country experienced a period of political openness, during which the influential leftist Tudeh Party ("Masses" party) was formed. The CIA induced a coup in 1953 that brought the almost-deposed Mohammad Reza Shah back to Iran, but which also ended the period of openness, forfeiting the possibility of a gradual democratic process. The leftists were prosecuted without due process of law and were subjected to torture. Overall, whatever mistreatments and physical abuses the nationalists and leftists experienced from 1953 to 1958, these proved to be only a dress rehearsal for the array of state-sanctioned tortures that were imposed in the 1970s.

Both Mohammad Reza Shah and his opponents became increasingly ideological. The Shah's new doctri-

In Washington, D.C., in the fall of 1978, demonstrators oppose the U.S. government's backing of Mohammed Reza Pahlavi, Shah of Iran. The hoods conceal their identities from SAVAK, the Iranian intelligence agency that had strong ties to the CIA. [OWEN FRANKEN/ CORBIS]

naire drive to recreate the greatness of ancient Persia moved him far away from the liberal tendencies of modernization theory and into the intolerant impulses of single-party authoritarianism. Across the deepening ideological divide of the 1970s, the apparently overconfident Shah faced a new generation of leftist activists whose political leanings were enmeshed in the rising tide of revolutionary movements throughout the Third World. Young and inexperienced, these activists announced their arrival on the political scene with a marked militancy in the mid-1970s, when the Shah's administration was being hailed as a model of progress by his conservative backers in Washington. Nevertheless, the number of dissidents and the range of their activities remained relatively small, compared with what was being seen in some Latin American countries at the time. By the time that the country was going through the seismic political changes that led to the Islamic Republic in 1979, some 400 guerrillas had lost their lives, and hundreds of others were imprisoned and tortured.

The Shah's political police, known by the acronym SAVAK, was designed to strike fear in the hearts of the regime's young opponents. A new generation of tortur-

ers creatively honed their craft. It appeared as if SAVAK was deliberately flaunting its brutality. Tehran's Evin Prison symbolized SAVAK's merciless image. It is not clear how much of SAVAK's brutality actually occurred and how much was the result of the deliberately cultivated image of SAVAK violence or the creative allegations of political opponents. In the end, the brutality and the reputation of SAVAK fed upon each other.

Torture was used to extract confessions and recantations. More significantly, torture began to cast a dark shadow over the lives of the leading activists. The torture-induced confessions, broadcast nationally, were meant to break the resolve of the activists and dissuade university students from entering the forbidden political arena. In many cases, however, it had the opposite effect. In this convoluted world, which would outlast the dynasty and continue into the Islamic Republic, having been tortured—and not any independent act of bravery or a prolonged service to political causes—became the arbiter of who would rise as heroes and who would fall into infamy. Dying under torture created real martyrs.

Martyrs' photos adorned the revolutionary banners of the organizations that helped to overthrow the Shah in 1979. In this time of confession and recantation, Evin Prison linked the Shah's regime with that of the Ayatollah's. Interestingly, the man who shaped the prison life under the Ayatollah's regime had been himself a prisoner in Evin during the Shah's rule. When the monarchy was overturned, the prison was quickly emptied of the Shah's opponents and packed instead with high officials who had previously served the monarchy.

The Ayatollah presented his revolutionary state as Islamic and thus unlike any other in modern history. However, in the early years of the consolidation of the Islamic Republic, many of human rights violations had very little to do with Islam, or even with the politicized clerics' reading of it. The politically shrewd mullahs moved aggressively to eliminate any real or imagined challenges to the legitimacy of the newly established state. Their actions corresponded with the revolutionary patterns that had been created by totalitarian states elsewhere in the world. The mullahs merely added their own Islamic terminology to rationalize actions whose motivations lay in the realities of the contemporary nation–state in the context of an illiberal political culture. For political prisoners who crowded the prisons in the 1980s, the judiciary was characterized by the absence of justice, Islamic or otherwise.

Summary executions are the signature of all revolutionary states, as are torture-induced confessions and repentance. The tactics used by the Ayatollah's mullahs to extract information and to break the resolve of political prisoners were thus almost identical to those used by other revolutionary states, from the Stalinist Soviet Union, to the U.S.–supported juntas in Latin American countries during the cold war. The Islamic Republic's ideological fervor, however, was matched by an unprecedented intensification of executions and torture, and in their wake, many came to absolve the Shah of his own unsavory record, which paled in comparison.

The young activists who opposed Ayatollah Khomeini were ill-prepared for what awaited them in prison. They based their expectations on their own experiences in the Shah's prisons, or on what they had heard from previous generations of political prisoners. The Shah's tactics of repression offered no realistic measure of what followed with the rise of Ayatollah Khomeini to power, however. By 1985, approximately thirteen thousand individuals who politically opposed the Ayatollah had been executed.

In a creative interpretation of medieval Islamic laws, the clerics found a way to justify torture as Islamic *Ta'zir* ("discretionary punishment" in Shi'ite jurisprudence). A prisoner who "lied" to interrogators could receive *Ta'zir* of as many as seventy-four lashes until the "truth" was extracted. Many well-known individuals of all ideological persuasions were displayed on national television giving "voluntary interviews": confessing, recanting, denouncing their past political associations, and praising the Ayatollah as the "Leader of the Islamic Revolution." In these broadcasts, the mullahs far out-performed the showmanship of the Shah's SAVAK. By extracting formal recantations, the clerics intended to show that God was on their side, and that history, with its teleological direction and ultimate destiny, had vindicated them. Captives were forced to deliver a version of history that rendered them, prior to their repentance and return to Islam, as the essence of all evils, ancient and modern.

Thousands of rank and file activists whose "interviews" had no additional propaganda value, were nonetheless subjected to a crude combination of physical torture, psychological pressure, Islamic "teachings," and public confession, all aimed at remolding their thoughts and conscience. The Islamic Republic added a new term with clear religious undertones to Iran's prison lexicon: *Tawaban* (singular *tawab*) were prisoners who had recanted. In fact, the clerics wished to turn the entire secular population of Iran into *tawaban*. The result was a severe violation of the right of political prisoners to freedom of thought, conscience, and religion, as well as the freedom to hold opinions without interference.

Prior to his death, Ayatollah Khomeini's crowning achievement was the prison massacre of 1988, unique in the annals of the country's brutalities. For reasons not entirely clear, the Ayatollah decided to dissolve the category of "political prisoners" by dispatching them to death or setting them free. The political prisoners faced an inquisition that had no proper judicial task other than inquiring about their thoughts on Islam and the central institution of the Islamic Republic. No consideration was given to the prisoners' alleged crimes or to the sentences under which they had been serving since the early 1980s. Instead, the inquisitors passed judgment on the prisoners' apostasy. Each prisoner was asked, "Are you Muslim, and do you perform your daily prayers." The prisoners understood the true meaning of the question: "Will you renounce your conscience and live?" Many held fast to their beliefs, and were hung the same day.

In the prisons, the prosecutors asked those who had confirmed their faith in Islam to prove it by performing the required daily prayers. If they refused, they would receive twenty lashes for each of the daily five sets of prayers—a total of one hundred lashes every twenty-four hours. Both male and female prisoners were subject to this daily regimen of whippings. One judge told the prisoners that the punishment for a female infidel was death under prolonged whipping. In fact, however, the clerics treated women differently from men. Men were considered responsible for their apostasy and had to be killed. Women, on the other hand, were not believed to be competent enough to take total responsibility for their actions, so the clerics would punish them with imprisonment until they repented. Thus, one misogynist rule saved many women's lives. Female members of the Mojahedin—an anti-clerical Islamic organization—were not so fortunate. They were executed for continuing to support their exiled leaders.

In contrast to the early years of the Ayatollah's regime, the executioners stopped publishing the body counts for their daily activities in 1988. An official veil of secrecy shrouded the ongoing massacre, and the rulers denied that mass killings continued to take place inside the prisons. Many scholars accept the estimate of 4,500 to 5,000 dead for the entire country that year, although some have alleged that the figure was much higher—as many as 10,000 to 12,000. Opposition publications abroad, however, claimed a national death toll of 30,000.

Like human rights violators in other ideological states, the Islamic rulers of Iran engaged in extrajudicial activities. Scores of intellectuals and journalists were killed in this fashion. From 1990 onward, these crimes were committed by members of the shadowy groups who either worked for or were loosely associated with the Intelligence Ministry. These extrajudicial actions made a mockery of the due process of law, even when considered in terms of purely Islamic, or *shari'ah*, law. Because of this, the Intelligence Ministry tried very hard to conceal its murderous, extra-judicial actions from the public. Even the reformist president, Khatami, elected in 1997, was unable to put an end to these activities, although the intelligence officials became more circumspect.

Although there were similarities between the Islamic Republic and more secular authoritarian regimes in their use of violence and repression, there were also major differences that created new patterns of human rights violations. These differences originated from the invocation of *shari'ah*, or rather from the much larger and loosely structured cultural habits and norms derivative of the *shari'ah* paradigm. One major new category of human rights violations resulted from the re-imposition of Islamic punishments such as flogging, amputation, and stoning to death of adulterers and common criminals.

The Ayatollah's revolution was Islamic, and the majority of its victims were Muslim Iranians, but non-Muslim Iranians suffered repression and persecution unlike any in modern Iranian history. Iran's Islamic tradition recognizes followers of three monotheistic religions—Zoroastrianism, Judaism, and Christianity (Armenians, Assyrians, and Chaldeans)—as people of the book. The Islamic Constitution recognizes them, as "the only religious minorities who, within the limits of the law, are free to perform their religious rites and ceremonies and to act according to their own canon in matters of personal affairs and religious education." To put it differently, they are free to perform their religious rites and ceremonies, but only within the limits of Islamic *shari'ah*. Nonetheless, discrimination against non-Muslim people of the book became blatant. A majority of each community saw no future for themselves in Iran and left.

The largest religious community in Iran was not named in the constitution, however. This was the Bahā'ī, whose faith was never recognized in Iran, its troubled birthplace. Because Bahā'ī were assumed to have been Muslims before accepting their "false" revelation, the Iranian Bahā'īs were considered to be apostates. By omitting them from constitutional recognition, the clerics' hoped to destroy the conditions needed for their survival as a community with a distinct religious identity. They attacked Bahā'īs on all possible grounds and in all spheres of public life, from elementary education to professional occupations, from marriage ceremonies to cemeteries. More than 200 of their leaders were murdered. Although many fled the country, the community endured and survived the harshest years of the 1980s.

By the beginning of the twenty-first century, Iran had already defeated Islamic fundamentalism. A majority of the people were patiently waiting for a nonviolent institutional and legal transformation that would allow the young population to experience personal freedoms and a measure of democracy. The regime lost its Islamic mooring and its institutions completed with each other. The land of ancient Persia had lost the imperial, monarchic facade that was once a source of national pride.

SEE ALSO Bahā'ī; Kurds

BIBLIOGRAPHY

Abrahamian, Ervand (1999). *Tortured Confessions: Prisons and Public Recantation in Modern Iran*. Berkeley: University of California Press.

Afshari, Reza (2001). *Human Rights in Iran: Abuse of Cultural Relativism*. Philadelphia: University of Pennsylvania Press.

Rejali, Darius (1994). *Torture and Modernity: Self, Society, and State in Modern Iran.* Boulder, Colo.: Westview Press.

Schirazi, Asghar (1997). *The Constitution of Iran: Politics and State in the Islamic Republic.* London: Tauris Press
Reza Afshari

Iraq

Iraq has experienced a turbulent history during the twentieth and early twenty-first centuries, during which the country has witnessed invasions, military occupations, independence, violent regime changes, war, genocide, and gross human rights violations. Iraq's record on human rights abuses, war crimes, crimes against humanity, and genocide during this period has been among the most abysmal throughout the Arab world and the regions of southwest Asia. This was true especially after the seizure of power by the Ba'th Party in 1968, and the subsequent totalitarian regime of Saddam Hussein from 1979 to 2003. The significance of this fact looms large not only for Middle Eastern history but for global history as well.

Ba'th Party Rule

Most of the gross violations of human rights and dignity committed in modern Iraq were perpetrated when the Arab Socialist Renaissance (Arabic: Ba'th) Party was in power. The Ba'th was a pan-Arab nationalist party founded in Syria in the mid-1940s, whose message soon spread to other Arab countries in the Fertile Crescent, including Iraq. Its slogans were "Unity, Freedom, Socialism" and "One Arab Motherland, with an Eternal Mission." Ba'thism was dedicated to effecting Arab unity, fighting imperialism and Zionism, and achieving domestic social justice. Its vision of a non-Marxist, "Arab" type of socialism, national unity, and ethnic destiny represented a type of Middle Eastern fascism, something certainly magnified by the leadership cults established in the two repressive regimes it eventually established: in Syria since 1963, and in Iraq briefly in 1963 and thereafter from 1968 to 2003. These two Ba'thist regimes—ironically, considering their advocacy of pan-Arab unity, bitter rivals—pursued a highly nationalistic pan-Arab ideology in countries that, although largely Arab, contained significant numbers of non-Arabs.

Iraq has long been the abode of a number of ethnic and religious groups. The southern half of the country has been home to Arabs who practice the Shi'ite branch of Islam. Although Shi'ites are a small minority in the wider Islamic world, they constituted 60 percent of the population of Iraq by the end of the twentieth century. Central Iraq hosts Arabs practicing the Sunni branch of Islam, approximately 20 percent of the population. Although fewer in number than the Shi'ite Arabs, regimes based in Baghdad that have held political sway in the region for centuries have always been led by Sunnis. Northern Iraq has long had a particularly heterogeneous population. In addition to Sunni Arabs, the mountainous northern regions feature a large number of Kurds. Between 15 and 20 percent of the population, Kurds are Sunni Muslims who are ethnically and linguistically distinct from Arabs. Other religious and ethnic groups in the north include small numbers of Kurdish Shi'ites and Yezidis, Assyrian Christians, and Turkoman. Iraq also counts among its residents small populations of Chaldean Christians (Assyrian Catholics), Sabeans, and Armenian Christians. Iraq was home to an ancient Jewish community for millennia as well, although the vast majority emigrated from 1950 to 1951.

Saddam Hussein (1937–) was the main figure behind the 1968 Ba'thist coup in Iraq, and formally added the presidency to his party leadership portfolio in July 1979. He immediately gave an indication of his brutal methods of maintaining his absolute rule by purging and executing a number of leading Ba'thists whom he considered rivals. For the next two decades Saddam reduced the Ba'th Party to an instrument of his personal rule and used the myriad intelligence forces he oversaw to intimidate and eliminate rivals and anyone else he deemed a threat, including entire categories of people. Thousands were arrested, executed, or simply disappeared from 1979 to 2003. Beyond this, Saddam's regime practiced ethnic genocide against the Kurds, tried to "Arabize" the northern region around Kirkuk, and directed whole-scale oppression against Shi'ite Arabs. Estimates as high as 300,000 have been proposed for the number of persons killed by Saddam's regime. Beyond that, Saddam exported his brutality when Iraqi forces committed war crimes and/or crimes against humanity during the Iran–Iraq war of 1980 to 1988, and the occupation of Kuwait of 1990 to 1991.

The Kurdish Genocide

No one specific group suffered more under Saddam's rule than the Kurds. The Iraqi state began armed action against Kurdish nationalists in 1961, before the Ba'th came to power. The bulk of the fighting against the insurrection, which lasted until 1975 and flared up again thereafter, however, came while the Ba'th was in power. In July 1983, the regime arrested 8,000 males from the Barzani family, which has produced the leading figures in the Kurdish national movement over the decades. They were deported to southern Iraq and presumably murdered. In the spring of 1987, as Iraqi fortunes were improving in the long Iran–Iraq war of 1980 to 1988,

Halabja, 1988. Kurd victims of Iraq gas attack. [AP/WIDE WORLD PHOTOS]

Iraqi forces launched a renewed offensive against the Kurds, who had been supported by Iran at various periods during the insurrection. The government created "forbidden areas" in the north to deny sanctuary to Kurdish *peshmergas* (fighters; literally, "those who face death"). Large-scale deportations removed thousands of villagers. At least 700 villages were demolished. Any human or animal remaining in the "forbidden areas" was subject to death. It was during this campaign that the first documented Iraqi uses of chemical weapons inside Iraq occurred. The first incident was an attack on a Kurdish political party headquarters in Zewa Shkan on April 15, 1987, followed the next day by chemical strikes in the villages of Balisan and Shaykh Wasan.

Yet it was the Ba'thist regime's 1988 Anfal campaign against the Kurds that rose to the level of genocide according to international observers. Taking its name from a chapter entitled "Anfal" (Arabic: "spoils") in the Koran, Anfal was a massive counterinsurgency campaign following up on the similar efforts of 1987. It once again sought to deny large portions of Kurdistan to the *peshmergas* by deporting and/or killing the areas' inhabitants and destroying their villages. Anfal consisted of eight military offensives launched between February 23 and September 6, 1988 as the Iran–Iraq war was concluding. Although it was dependent on state institutions for its execution, the campaign was a Ba'th Party operation. The person responsible for supervising the genocide, below Saddam Hussein himself, was his cousin and party stalwart, Ali Hasan al-Majid (1941–). Decree No. 160 of March 29, 1987 placed all state and party apparatuses in the north under al-Majid, secretary of the Ba'th Party's Northern Bureau Command, for the purpose of carrying out the Anfal campaign. This included the military, military intelligence, general intelligence, Popular Army, and pro-regime Kurdish *jahsh* militia. Most of the Anfal campaigns were undertaken by army units subsumed under al-Majid's command: the Iraqi army's First Corps, based at Kirkuk, commanded by Lieutenant General Sultan

encyclopedia of GENOCIDE *and* CRIMES AGAINST HUMANITY

Hashim Ahmad al-Jabburi Ta'i (1944?–), and the Fifth Corps based at Irbil, commanded by Brigadier General Yunis Muhammad al-Zarib. When the fifth Anfal that began in May stalled, the Office of the President ordered operations renewed—indicating Saddam's personal involvement in the execution of the campaign. According to Human Rights Watch, a total of 115 Iraqis may have had criminal responsibility for the genocide.

The ethnic dimensions of the Anfal campaign were clear. It was preceded by a national census held on October 17, 1987. All persons in Iraq were required to register themselves according to ethnicity, either "Arab" or "Kurd." Those refusing to "return to the national ranks" and be counted, which in effect meant those Kurds living in areas under *peshmerga* control who did not participate, were classified as "deserters." Thereafter, entire areas deemed outside the "national ranks" and containing "deserters" were designated "forbidden areas" and subject to "collective measures." These measures included military sweeps through the areas, followed by mass deportations and the demolition of villages. Any person or animal thereafter found in a "forbidden area" was to be killed. Many Kurdish males rounded up in the operations were later taken away, shot, and buried in mass graves by uniformed execution squads. It is surmised that these squads were made up of party members, among others.

By September 6, 1988, when the government declared an amnesty, an estimated 2,000 Kurdish villages had been depopulated and destroyed, although some figures are higher. Conservative estimates place the death toll at 50,000, but most put the count higher, in the range of 100,000 to 182,000. Ali Hasan al-Majid himself later suggested that "no more" than 100,000 Kurds were killed. Mines were sown in many destroyed localities to prevent reinhabitation. Middle East Watch also has determined that Iraqi forces attacked at least sixty villages with chemical weapons during Anfal. The worst and most famous massacre occurred in a town, not a village: the March 16, 1988 chemical attack on Halabja. Somewhere between 3,200 and 5,000 Kurds were killed there with mustard gas (a blistering agent) and Sarin (a nerve agent).

The memory of Anfal prompted the flight of hundreds of thousands of Kurds into the mountains after the failed Kurdish uprising of March 1991, and drew calls for global action. UN Security Council Resolution 688 condemned the "repression" of the Kurds and other Iraqis on April 5, 1991. On April 10 the United States created a "no fly zone" north of the 36th parallel, forbidding Iraqi military aircraft from operating there. The "safe haven" for the Kurds announced by the United States seven days later eventually turned into what was called the Kurdish Autonomous Zone, protected by United States and other troops, in which a Kurdish Regional Government began functioning in July 1992.

Persecution of the Shi'ites and Marsh Arabs
Although ostensibly a secular party, the Ba'th Party in Iraq long drew its support from, and based its rule on, the country's Sunni Arab population, just as had previous regimes in the country. The Shi'ite community was subject to persecution. In July 1974, the regime arrested dozens of Shi'ite clerics and executed five of them. The oppression worsened during Iraq's long war with Shi'ite Iran. The government expelled between 350,000 and 500,000 Shi'ites to Iran in the 1980s because of their alleged Iranian origin; approximately 50,000 other men were arrested, many of whom simply disappeared. The Shi'ite uprising of March 1991 was brutally suppressed and led to even more extreme measures. Mosques and seminaries were closed. Leading Shi'ite clerics like Ayatullah Muhammad Sadiq al-Sadr (1933–1999), Ayatullah Murtada al-Burujerdi (1931–1998), and Ayatullah Mirza Ali al-Gharawi (1930–1998) were later assassinated as well, almost certainly by Ba'thist agents. Security Council Resolution 688 of 1991 condemned the attacks on the Shi'ites as well as those against the Kurds. The United States, Britain, and France later began enforcing another "no fly zone" over Iraq south of the 32nd parallel (later expanded to the area south of the 33rd parallel.

In addition, the government moved against the Shi'ite Marsh Arabs and the unique ecosystem where they lived in south-central Iraq. These Arabs, called the Ma'dan, numbered some 250,000 in 1991. They lived in the marshlands between the Tigris and Euphrates rivers, the Middle East's largest wetlands area. In addition to forced imprisonment, killings, and disappearances, the Ma'dan faced forced deportations from the marshlands into government-built settlements. Only 40,000 remained in their ancestral lands by the late 1990s.

The government also initiated a massive program to drain the marshes. A document later captured entitled "Plan of Action for the Marshes," dated January 30, 1989, refers to an earlier 1987 plan approved by Saddam himself—another indication of the dictator's personal involvement in these crimes. While claiming it was implementing earlier plans to reclaim land that dated to 1953, the government undoubtedly was trying to deny shelter to antiregime Shi'ite guerrillas and army deserters that the marshes had provided. The UN Environmental Program has estimated that 90 percent of the marshes had been destroyed by the late 1990s, constituting a major international ecological disaster.

War Crimes in the Iran–Iraq War and in Kuwait

Saddam ordered the Iraqi army to attack Iran in September 1980, precipitating the twentieth century's longest conventional war. Iraq used chemical weapons against the numerically stronger Iranian forces throughout the war, in violation of the 1899 Hague Declaration IV, 1907 Hague Convention IV, and 1925 Geneva Protocol. (Iran responded with its own chemical attacks, but on a smaller scale than Iraq.) The United Nations launched an investigation, and the Security Council condemned the use of chemical weapons in the fighting, without specifying by whom, in March 1984, and again in September 1988.

Iraqi forces carried out a number of war crimes against Kuwaitis during their occupation of Kuwait from August 1990 to March 1991, including torture, rape, killings, looting, theft of cultural property, executions, and disappearances. An estimated 1,000 Kuwaitis were killed during the occupation, and an additional 600 remain unaccounted for after having been taken away by retreating Iraqi forces. A 1992 U.S. Defense Department study found Iraq guilty of sixteen violations of the laws of war during the occupation of Kuwait and the subsequent Gulf War. The Kuwaiti government also compiled extensive documentation on Iraqi war crimes.

Prosecution

United States and British forces invaded Iraq in March 2003 and Saddam's rule in Baghdad quickly collapsed. United States forces began rounding up high-ranking Iraqis suspected of war crimes, genocide, and crimes against humanity. They captured Ali Hasan al-Majid on August 19, 2003. Saddam himself evaded arrest until December 14, 2003. Saddam and eleven others, including al-Majid, former Deputy Prime Minister Tariq Aziz (1936–), and former Vice President Taha Yasin Ramadan al-Jazrawi (1938–), were arraigned before an investigative judge of the Iraqi Special Tribunal for Crimes Against Humanity on July 1, 2004. Lieutenant General and former Defense Minister Sultan Hashim Ahmad al-Jabburi Ta'i, commander of the army's First Corps during Anfal, were also captured by coalition forces and could stand trial in the future.

Conclusion

Iraq under Saddam Hussein and the Ba'th represented the most brutal and totalitarian regime anywhere in the Middle East during the last decades of the twentieth century, as well as one of the worst such regimes anywhere on earth. The scope and scale of the human rights abuses, war crimes, crimes against humanity, and genocide committed by the Ba'thist regime were rivaled only by the fastidious bureaucratic measures and records used to execute and document them, as well as by the megalomaniacal ego of Saddam Hussein himself. His downfall not only opened a new chapter in Iraq's history but paved the way for what likely will be the most sensational human rights trial of the early twenty-first century.

SEE ALSO Gas; Kurds; Saddam Hussein; Safe Zones

BIBLIOGRAPHY

Batatu, Hanna (2004). *The Old Social Classes and the Revolutionary Movements of Iraq,* 3rd edition. London: Saqi Books.

Bulloch, John, and Harvey Morris (1992). *No Friends but the Mountains: The Tragic History of the Kurds.* Oxford: Oxford University Press.

Darwish, Alexander (1991). *Unholy Babylon: The Secret History of Saddam's War.* New York: Diane Publishing.

Hiro, Dilip (2001). *The Longest War: The Iraq-Iran Military Conflict.* New York: Routledge.

Hiro, Dilip (2004). *Secrets and Lies: Operation "Iraqi Freedom" and After: A Prelude to the Fall of U.S. Power in the Middle East?* New York: Nation Books.

Human Rights Watch (1994). *Iraq's Crime of Genocide: The Anfal Campaign against the Kurds.* New Haven, Conn.: Yale University Press.

Karsh, Efraim, and Lawrence Freedman (1992). *The Gulf Conflict 1990–1991: Diplomacy and War in the New World Order.* Princeton, N.J.: Princeton University Press.

Makiya, Kanan (1998). *The Republic of Fear: The Politics of Modern Iraq,* updated edition. Berkeley: University of California Press.

Nakash, Yitzhak (2002). *The Shi'is of Iraq.* Princeton, N.J.: Princeton University Press.

Tripp, Charles (2002). *A History of Iraq,* 2nd edition. Cambridge: Cambridge University Press.

Michael R. Fischbach

Irian Jaya see West Papua, Indonesia (Irian Jaya).

Irving, David, Libel Trial of

On January 11, 2000, a libel trial opened in the British High Court. The plaintiff was David Irving, a British author of more than twenty books on World War II and Nazi Germany and its leadership. The defendants were the American academic Deborah Lipstadt and her publisher, Penguin Books. In *Denying the Holocaust* (1993), Lipstadt provides a comprehensive overview of the multifaceted phenomenon of Holocaust denial, the attempt to deny that the Nazis planned and carried out the systematic murder of six million Jews and others. She identifies Irving as "one of the most dangerous spokesman for Holocaust denial" (1993, p. 181). She further charges that "familiar with historical evidence, he bends it until it conforms with his ideological leanings and political agenda" (1993, p. 181). In 1996 Lipstadt was one of many who successfully lobbied against the publication of Irving's biography of Joseph Goebbels, the Nazi minister of propaganda. The publisher, St. Martin's Press, ended up pulping all printed copies of the book. Irving was enraged and decided to take revenge by bringing suit against Lipstadt, claiming not only that her description of Irving had been libelous, but also that she was pursuing a "sustained, malicious, vigorous, well-funded and reckless world-wide campaign of personal defamation" (van Pelt, 2002, p. 64).

Irving's involvement with Holocaust deniers came in the wake of the publication of *Hitler's War* (1977), in which he argues that although the Holocaust, as generally understood, occurred, Hitler had neither real or direct responsibility for what happened nor knowledge about it. This thesis attracted the attention of hard-core deniers such as Robert Faurisson in France and Ernst Zündel, a German residing in Canada. Both recognized that the denial of the Holocaust, or *revisionism* as they called it, suffered from the fact that no historian had ever endorsed its position. They saw an opportunity to bring the well-known Irving to their cause. In 1988 they succeeded.

That same year Zündel went on trial in Toronto for publishing material that, among other issues, denied the existence of gas chambers at Auschwitz to murder human beings. In defense of this charge, Zündel recruited on the advice of Faurisson, a consultant on the design of execution facilities in the United States, Fred Leuchter. He was subsequently dispatched to Auschwitz, where he took some samples from various parts of the architectural remains of Auschwitz and analyzed them for the presence of residual cyanide. Leuchter then authored a report in which he stated that there had never been any gas chambers at Auschwitz.

The judge in the Zündel trial declared the report inadmissible, citing Leuchter's lack of relevant expertise, but Irving, who had been asked to testify on Zündel's behalf, endorsed Leuchter's conclusions in court. In fact, he was so enthusiastic about the report that he became its publisher in the United Kingdom, describing it in his foreword as unchallengeable.

Irving became a Holocaust denier, conducting as he called it a "one-man intifada" (van Pelt, 2002, p. 64) against the official history of the Holocaust. The essence of his campaign was that the Holocaust, symbolized by Auschwitz, is a lie deployed by Jews to blackmail the German people into paying vast sums in reparations to supposed victims of the Holocaust. In a

revised edition of *Hitler's War* (1991), all traces of the Holocaust disappeared. Whereas in the 1977 edition Irving had characterized Auschwitz as a monstrous killing machine, according to the 1991 edition it was a mere slave labor camp. Irving commented that readers would "not find one line on the Holocaust. Why dignify something with even one footnote that has not happened?" (van Pelt, 2002, p. 54). In a lecture given that same year he stated, "I don't see any reason to be tasteful about Auschwitz. It's baloney. It's a legend. . . .I say quite tastelessly in fact that more people died on the back seat of Edward Kennedy's car in Chappaquiddick than ever died in a gas chamber in Auschwitz" (van Pelt, 2002, p. 1f). The once respected author became a rabble-rousing speaker at gatherings of the extreme right. Accused and convicted in both German and French courts, Irving turned into a pariah of the historical community.

Through his libel action, Irving hoped to regain his standing and provide Holocaust denial respectability as a revisionist view of the past. British law made this seem possible, as the burden of proof was on the defendants, and not him. The defense, led by Anthony Julius and Richard Rampton, focused on exposing Irving as a falsifier of the truth who had used invention, misquotation, suppression, distortion, manipulation, and mistranslation to achieve his objective. Irving's historiography, and not the existence of the Holocaust, was central. The defendants therefore engaged four historians (Richard Evans, Christopher Browning, Peter Longerich, and Robert Jan van Pelt) to issue reports on the case's central issues. Evans considered Irving's historiography in general, and Browning the evidence of mass killings by the Nazi mobile killing groups (Einsatzgruppen), which Irving claimed had not operated under Berlin's direct control. Longerich examined the decision-making process, showing that Hitler in fact played a central role, and van Pelt the evidence at Auschwitz, and the scientific and historical absurdity of the arguments advanced by Faurisson, Leuchter, and others.

The defense also engaged a political scientist, Hajo Funke, who traced Irving's connections with neofascist and neo-Nazi groups, white supremacist organizations, and Holocaust deniers. By revealing his deep involvement with the extreme right and his profound anti-Semitism, the defense hoped to show Irving's motivation in resorting to lies, distortions, misrepresentations, and deceptions in pursuit of his exoneration of Hitler and his denial of the Holocaust.

Irving decided not to engage a barrister, and represented himself in person. This undoubtedly increased the excitement of the proceedings. Deliberately choosing to cast himself in the role of the lone David against the seemingly mighty "Golipstadt," represented by a phalanx of lawyers and experts, Irving only engaged one expert witness—an evolutionary psychologist named Kevin MacDonald who has theorized that Jews are to be blamed for anti-Semitism. As Lipstadt's lawyers considered MacDonald's theories as irrelevant to the case, they decided not to cross-examine him, correctly assuming that the judge would ignore whatever MacDonald would have to say during his evidence-in-chief.

The libel trial lasted some thirty-three days, and involved many heated exchanges between Irving and Rampton, and Irving's long cross-examinations of the defense's expert witnesses. Many visitors attended the trial; it was also widely covered by the British and international press. The impact of such media attention were the mistaken impressions that the Holocaust was on trial—a clear distortion of the fact that Lipstadt and Penguin were the defendants—or that Irving himself was on trial—a reflection of the effective defense strategy that had transformed the de jure plaintiff Irving into the de facto defendant.

On April 12, 2000, Justice Charles Gray ruled for the defendants in pronouncing Irving a falsifier of history, a right-wing pro-Nazi polemicist, an anti-Semite, and a racist. He also ordered Irving to pay the defendants' legal costs, which exceeded 2 million pounds. Many who had feared that a victory for Irving would give Holocaust denial certain legitimacy were relieved. Israel's Prime Minister Barak declared the outcome of the trial to be a "victory of the free world against the dark forces seeking to obliterate the memory of the lowest point humanity ever reached." In its lead article, *The Independent* noted that "the cogency of the testimony presented by the defense" had vindicated "the great liberal principle, enunciated by John Stuart Mill, of the marketplace of ideas in which false coin is tested and replaced by true." *The Guardian* agreed: "Other jurisdictions make denying the Holocaust a crime. After this case, we can rely on empiricism and the sheer weight of evidence" (van Pelt, 2002, p. xf).

SEE ALSO Auschwitz; Denial

BIBLIOGRAPHY

Evans, R. J. (2001). *Lying about Hitler: History, Holocaust, and the David Irving Trial.* New York: Basic Books.

Gray, Charles (2000). *The Irving Judgment: David Irving v. Penguin Books and Professor Deborah Lipstadt.* Harmondsworth, U.K.: Penguin Books.

Guttenplan, D. D. (2001). *The Holocaust on Trial.* New York: W. W. Norton.

Irving, David (1977). *Hitler's War.* New York: Viking.

Leuchter, F. A. (1989). *Auschwitz: The End of the Line. The Leuchter Report: The First Forensic Examination of Auschwitz.* London: Focal Point.

Lipstadt, Deborah (1993). *Denying the Holocaust: The Growing Assault on Truth and Memory.* New York: Free Press.

Longerich, Peter (2001). *The Unwritten Order: Hitler's Role in the Final Solution.* Stroud, U.K.: Tempus.

van Pelt, Robert Jan (2002). *The Case for Auschwitz: Evidence from the Irving Trial.* Bloomington: Indiana University Press.

Robert Jan van Pelt

Izetbegović, Alija

[AUGUST 8, 1925–OCTOBER 19, 2003]
Bosnian Muslim and political leader in the post-independence Bosnia and Herzegovinian government

Alija Izetbegović was a Bosnian Muslim born on August 8, 1925 in Bosanski Šamac, a town in northern Bosnia, in what was then the Kingdom of Serbs, Croats and Slovenes. He died on October 19, 2003, in an independent Bosnia and Herzegovina (Bosnia), a state whose creation and survival he did as much as anybody to bring about. However, the Bosnia in which he died was so divided that he would have had extreme difficulty returning to his birthplace, had he so wished. The town of his birth is located in the so-called Republika Srpska, one of two entities into which the country is split, and which is dominated by Serbs.

Izetbegović was jailed twice in communist Yugoslavia for subversion, for three years in the 1940s and five years in the 1980s. His 1980s imprisonment resulted from the publication of his main political statement, the *Islamic Declaration* originally published in 1970. The government found his viewpoint extremist and dangerous, as in declarations such as: "There can be no peace or co-existence between the Islamic faith and non-Islamic institutions. . . . Islamic renewal cannot be . . . successfully continued and concluded without a political revolution." In 1990 Izetbegović helped create and subsequently led the *Stranka demokratske akcije* (Party of Democratic Action) or SDA, a political party that exclusively represented the narrow ethnic interests of Bosnia's Muslims and whose candidates campaigned behind the slogan "In our land with our faith."

As first Yugoslavia and then Bosnia disintegrated, Izetbegović found himself in an increasingly difficult situation and feared for the very survival of Bosnia's Muslims. Together with Macedonia's President Kiro Gligorov, he tabled eleventh-hour proposals in June 1991 to head off Slovene and Croatian independence declarations and worked to keep Yugoslavia together. Memorably, he compared the choice between Franjo

Tudjman's Croatia and Slobodan Milosevic's Serbia to one between a brain tumor and leukemia. As conflict loomed, he became increasingly unsure of himself and seemingly was unable to prepare for war.

The defense of Sarajevo after the outbreak of fighting in April 1992 was initially organized by the city's criminal gangs. In 1998, six years after the events, the Sarajevo investigative weekly *Dani* published details of crimes allegedly committed by one of the gang leaders, Mušan Topalović-Caco, whom Izetbegović personally knew from prison and who was who was killed in October 1993. The report charged that "Caco" had eliminated Serbs from parts of Sarajevo, revelations which incurred Izetbegović's enduring wrath.

Izetbegović became president of Bosnia at the end of 1990, while Bosnia was still a republic of the Socialist Federal Republic of Yugoslavia. This was an office that he should have shared in rotation with other members of the Bosnian presidency, but because war erupted in Bosnia in April 1992, he became the first sole president of an independent Bosnia and is remembered as the country's beleaguered wartime leader. He was elected chairman of Bosnia's presidency in the first postwar elections in 1996, stepping down before the second postwar elections two years later. He retired from politics in 2001.

In the immediate aftermath of his death, Izetbegović was hailed internationally as a statesman for his efforts to keep Bosnia and Herzegovina together. He was also deeply loved and respected by Bosnian Muslims, who called him "dedo" ("grandpa"). By contrast, the Croats and Serbs of Bosnia and Herzegovina generally despised him. The International Criminal Tribunal for the Former Yugoslavia (ICTY) in The Hague revealed that it had been investigating him for war crimes. The investigation was aborted with his premature death.

Izetbegović's detractors accused him of bearing responsibility for the deaths of Serbs in Sarajevo at the hands of criminal gangs; of bearing responsibility for atrocities committed by Bosnian Muslims against Croats and Serbs in detention camps such as that at Čelebići; and of bearing responsibility for atrocities committed by the Bosnian Army against Croats and Serbs, especially during its advance in summer and autumn 1995. He was even accused of shelling his own people to generate maximum media sympathy for their plight in order to encourage international intervention.

In the absence of a thorough ICTY investigation, no definitive judgment can be made about the allegations against Izetbegović, although his relationship with Mušan Topalović-Caco is a matter of record. Given the logistical difficulties that Izetbegović faced simply in communicating with his lieutenants around Bosnia during the war, it would be almost impossible to link him personally to any individual atrocity committed against Croats and Serbs. Nonetheless, he failed to make any public effort to curb the actions of overzealous Bosnian Muslims. He also failed to take international concerns about Muslim excesses seriously, justifying them by the scale of the atrocities that were committed against Bosnian Muslims by Serbs and to a lesser extent by Croats.

The charge that Izetbegović shelled his own people, came from both his enemies and various UN officials. Lewis MacKenzie, the first UN general from Canada to arrive in Sarajevo in 1992, and Michael Rose, the British general who commanded UN operations in Bosnia in 1994, went on record with the accusation both at the time and later. At the time, the international presence in Sarajevo was unable to determine what happened during the so-called "bread queue massacre" in 1992 (one instance where Izetbegović was alleged to have shelled his own people). Moreover, UN investigations of the "marketplace massacres" of 1994 and 1995 were inconclusive. Most analysts, however, give Izetbegović the benefit of the doubt and assume that, given the great number of shells being fired into Sarajevo by the Bosnian Serbs, some were bound to have killed large numbers of civilians.

The Western countries that belatedly intervened militarily in Bosnia in August 1995 wished to see Izetbegović as a moderate who stood for the preservation of a multi-ethnic state, being that they effectively intervened on his side. However, all that can be said for sure is that Izetbegović was a complex individual and a devout Muslim whose primary concern in the run-up to and during the war was the preservation of his own people.

SEE ALSO Bosnia and Herzegovina; Croatia, Independent State of; Ethnic Cleansing; Rape

BIBLIOGRAPHY

Burg, Steven L., and Paul S. Shoup (1999). *The War in Bosnia and Herzegovina: Ethnic Conflict and International Intervention.* Armonk, N.Y.: M. E. Sharpe.

Chris Bennett

Jackson, Robert

[FEBRUARY 13, 1892–OCTOBER 9, 1954]
United States Chief Prosecutor at the Nuremberg Trial

Robert H. Jackson was born on a small farm in Pennsylvania. Although his legal education consisted of only one year at Albany Law School in upstate New York, Jackson's legal career included key positions in President Franklin D. Roosevelt's administration. In 1934 he was nominated as general counsel of the Bureau of International Revenue. In 1936 he became assistant attorney general in charge of tax matters and in 1938 solicitor general; in 1940 he was promoted to attorney general. In 1941 Jackson was appointed to the United States Supreme Court.

On May 2, 1945, President Harry S. Truman named Jackson as the Chief of Counsel for the United States in prosecuting the principal Axis war criminals. Jackson's primary views on the charges to be leveled against the defendants were presented to Truman in a report that the White House released on June 6, 1945. They were essentially based on a plan the War Department had prepared in the fall of 1944. Jackson outlined the following three categories of crimes that the defendants would be asked to account for:

- Atrocities and offenses against persons or property constituting violations of international law, including the laws, rules, and customs of land and naval warfare;

- Atrocities and offenses, including atrocities and persecutions on racial or religious grounds, committed since 1933;

- Invasions of other countries and initiation of wars of aggression in violation of international law or treaties. (The Nuremberg Case, 1971, 13)

The latter charge Jackson regarded as central to the entire conception of the trial. "It is high time," he wrote to the president, "that we act on the juridical principle that aggressive war-making is illegal and criminal" (The Nuremberg Case, 1971, p. 15). Jackson also insisted on proving that the Nazis had planned to conquer all of Europe and to dominate the world. "Our case against the major defendants is concerned with the Nazi master plan, not with individual barbarities and perversions which occurred independently of any central plan." Jackson also stressed the need "to establish the criminal character of several voluntary organizations which have played a cruel and controlling part in subjugating first the German people and then their neighbors." If in the main trial an organization was found to be criminal, he continued, "the second stage will be to identify and try before military tribunals individual members not already personally convicted in the principal case." Jackson knew that this plan introduced some far-reaching legal innovations, but he believed that "we must not permit it to be complicated or obscured by sterile legalisms developed in the age of imperialism to make war respectable." Jackson's first challenge, however, was to convince British, Soviet, and French jurists who met shortly after the end of the war in London for the International Conference on Military Trials, to accept the U.S. plan. Formulating a joint Allied policy was a complicated undertaking because of the need to overcome differences between the common law (in the United States and United Kingdom) and the

U.S. Chief Prosecutor Robert Jackson opposing a defense motion to sever the case against Gustav Krupp von Bohlen from the 1945 Nuremberg Tribunal. Although Krupp, a German industrialist and weapons manufacturer, had benefited from slave labor provided by the Nazis, he never stood trial due to failing health.[BETTMANN/CORBIS]

continental legal systems (in France and the Soviet Union). The negotiations began on June 26, 1945, and dragged on for almost six weeks; they were characterized by tension and distrust, especially between Jackson and his Soviet counterpart, Major General Ion T. Nikitchenko.

Jackson, who had no experience in negotiating with the Soviets, wrongly believed that the prospects for a quick agreement on protocol were good. Instead, he had to face attacks on the central pillars of the U.S. plan. Annoyed by the prolonged nature of the negotiations, Jackson did not regard cooperation with the Soviets as imperative, and even contemplated the option that each nation would try its own prisoners by its own procedures, applying the international agreement as to definition of crimes. However, he was compelled to regard such a course as only a last resort as he was well aware of the importance Washington attributed at the time to cooperation with the Soviets in general.

The most controversial aspect of the U.S. proposal was the issue of prosecuting conspiracy. Although the British sided on this innovation with the Americans,

the Soviets and French firmly attacked it, arguing that the focus should be on the criminal acts themselves. Jackson, however, was a strong supporter of the conspiracy theory, which he saw as designed to tie the whole trial together. Both the Soviets and French also had difficulties with the U.S. concept of indicting several principal Nazi organizations. While regarding them as criminal groups, they believed that organizations could not be tried. They were further concerned about convicting individuals only by association. Soviet and French jurists also challenged Jackson's insistence on indicting aggressive war as a crime. A different kind of dispute arose over the site of the trial when the Soviets insisted on Berlin, situated in the Soviet zone of occupation. The agreement that was eventually signed on August 8, 1945, by the heads of the four delegations "for the prosecution and punishment of the major war criminals of the European Axis" and outlining the Charter of the International Military Tribunal may be regarded as a success for Jackson, not only because it created a legal framework for the trial and defined international crimes, but also because it had the U.S. plan at its core and the trial was to be conducted at Nuremberg, in the American zone of occupation.

The process of preparing the American team for the trial exposed some of Jackson's weaknesses, especially that of being a poor administrator. However, when he rose on November 21, 1945, to deliver the opening statement for the prosecution, Jackson's rhetorical skills as well as his passion, determination, and vision gave his speech the legal, public, moral, and historical importance the event required. A large part of his speech was devoted to proving the conspiracy charge. He stated,

> It is my purpose to open the case, particularly under Count One of the Indictment, and to deal with the Common Plan or conspiracy to achieve ends possible only by resort to Crimes against Peace, War Crimes, and Crimes against Humanity. My emphasis will not be on individual barbarities and perversions which may have occurred independently of any central plan. . . .Nor will I now dwell on the activity of individual defendants except as it may contribute to exposition of the common plan (The Nuremberg Case, 1971, p. 37).

Well aware of the historical importance of the trial, Jackson predicted that "the record on which we judge these defendants today is the record on which history will judge us tomorrow." Recognizing possible criticism that the trial could be described as "victor's justice," Jackson explained:

> Unfortunately, the nature of these crimes is such that both prosecution and judgment must be by victor nations over vanquished foes. The worldwide scope of the aggressions carried out by these men has left but few real neutrals. Either the victors must judge the vanquished or we must leave the defeated to judge themselves.

The defendants, Jackson stressed, "do have a fair opportunity to defend themselves—a favor which these men, when in power, rarely extended to their fellow countrymen."

Jackson expected the Nuremberg Trial to serve as a landmark in future international relations and international law, particularly as a deterrent force on statesmen. He was realistic enough to recognize the weakness of juridical action to prevent future wars, but still believed that "the ultimate step in avoiding periodic wars, which are inevitable in a system of international lawlessness, is to make statesmen responsible to law." The trial, Jackson told the judges, "is part of the great effort to make the peace more secure." His concern with the future no less than with the conviction of the twenty-two defendants and his expectation that

Robert Jackson, Chief Prosecutor for the United States at the Nuremberg Trials. From Jackson's famous closing statement: "Having sneaked through the portals of power, the Nazis slammed the gate in the face of all others who might also aspire to enter. Since the law was what the Nazis said it was, every form of opposition was rooted out, and every dissenting voice throttled."

the trial would be a milestone for coming generations also came to the fore in his closing address on July 26, 1946: "If we cannot eliminate the causes and prevent the repetition of these barbaric events, it is not an irresponsible prophecy to say that this twentieth century may yet succeed in bringing the doom of civilization."

As the chief architect of the Nuremberg Trial, Jackson was pleased with the results, even though not all of his and his colleagues' legal arguments had been accepted at the prosecutorial level and were reflected in the formal charges. The tribunal had declared, he wrote with much satisfaction in his final report to the president on October, 7, 1946, that

> To prepare, incite, or wage a war of aggression, or to conspire with others to do so, is a crime against international society, and that to persecute, oppress, or do violence to individuals or minorities on political, racial, or religious grounds in connection with such a war, or to exterminate, enslave, or deport civilian populations, is an international crime, and that for the commission of such crimes individuals are responsible (The Nuremberg Case, 1971, XV).

Jackson, who regarded the Nuremberg Trial as the most important and interesting experience of his life and expected its outcome to guide and influence future international law, would have undoubtedly viewed with much satisfaction not only the verdicts but also the 1948 United Nations (UN) Convention on Genocide and Universal Declaration of Human Rights, as well as, some forty-eight years after his death, the establishment of the International Criminal Court (ICC) in 2002. All may be seen as direct descendants of the Nuremberg Charter and Trial.

SEE ALSO Göring, Hermann; Lemkin, Raphael; London Charter; Morgenthau, Henry; Nuremberg Trials; United Nations War Crimes Commission; War Crimes

BIBLIOGRAPHY

Jackson, Robert H. (1971). *The Nüremberg Case*. New York: Cooper Square Publishers.

Kochavi, Arieh J. (1998). *Prelude to Nuremberg: Allied War Crimes Policy and the Question of Punishment*. Chapel Hill, N.C.: University of North Carolina Press.

Taylor, Telford (1992). *The Anatomy of the Nuremberg Trials: A Personal Memoir*. New York: Knopf.

Tusa, Ann, and John Tusa (1983). *The Nuremberg Trial*. London: Papermack.

Arieh J. Kochavi

Japan

It is well known that Japan committed atrocities during World War II. In the 1990s, however, these crimes and related prewar and wartime policies began to be viewed in a new light, as forms of genocide. This characterization of Japan's behavior was controversial, and was challenged for specific historical, political, and conceptual reasons.

For decades, Japan had been virtually absent from postwar discourses on genocide, which gave primacy to the Nazi holocaust as a phenomenon of modernity centered in Europe. This changed in the 1990s, with the rise of new global concerns with restitution and the negotiation of historical injustices. Asian citizens and their governments, in particular China, began to demand official apologies and compensation for Japanese war crimes committed against them. At the end of the twentieth century, the creation of historical knowledge about Japanese genocide and crimes against humanity engaged previously silent or silenced witnesses, changing political constituents in Asia, as well as feminist and postmodern paradigm shifts both in academic and popular discourse. Japanese people asserted themselves not only as perpetrators, but more clearly as victims of

crimes against humanity, including the indiscriminate firebombing of Japanese cities by the United States in the spring of 1945, and especially the August 1945 atomic bombings of Hiroshima and Nagasaki, which claimed hundreds of thousands of civilian lives. Meanwhile, many Koreans asserted multiple sources of victimization, first by Japanese colonial policies, and then by U.S. bombing campaigns, and even by the Allied war crimes tribunal, which convicted Korean and Taiwanese guards of prisoners-of-war camps as Japanese war criminals.

These multiple claims for public recognition and justice rendered previous attempts to define and punish Japan's crimes against peace and humanity inadequate, and ended the enduring silences that they inaugurated. The Tokyo War Crimes Trial (1946–1948), Japan's counterpart to the Nuremberg Trials in Germany, left controversial legacies that became embedded in the cold war structures of international and domestic political relations. The failure of this trial to pursue Emperor Hirohito's war responsibility, the tacit cover-up of Japan's large-scale biological warfare experiments, and the neglect of crimes committed against women in war came to light. This, in turn, led to the public investigation of these issues, albeit belatedly, at a time when the right of individuals (rather than nation-states) to hold states liable for crimes committed against them could no longer be ignored.

For decades after the war, the South Korean, Chinese, Southeast Asian, and Pacific victims of Japanese war atrocities were recognized neither by the Japanese nor by their home governments. The need for newly formed nation-states to find their own niches within the harsh divisions of the cold war world called not for honest reconciliation, but for the ability to move on. In the 1990s, however, an emerging Asian regionalism conferred upon China the ability to wield considerable economic muscle, raised the possibility of a reunified Korea, and led to Japan's expected—yet feared—political leadership in the region.

The 1990s brought shifting international relations, combined with changes in public culture, which acquired an unprecedented global reach through new forms of non-governmental and cross-national organizing. In addition, communications advances enabled the political viability of diasporas and contributed to a widely shared sensibility for the need to address not only contemporary but historical injustices. In Asia, the combination of unresolved and overlapping legacies of Western imperialism, Asian modern nation-building, Japanese colonialism, and World War II inspired people to address larger questions concerning the global history of genocide and crimes against humanity. A

Chinese prisoners being buried alive by their Japanese captors outside the city of Nanking, during the infamous "Rape of Nanking."

survey of Japan's early modern history reveals instances of religious persecution, forced ethnic assimilation, and protracted crimes against humanity committed by military forces as well as bureaucracies, but few qualify as genocide in the strict sense of premeditated and systematic annihilation of a defined population.

Early Modern Eradication of Religious Institutions

Japan has historically accommodated different religious traditions, with few instances of faith-based persecutions. Attempted genocide of religious groups, when it occurred, was limited to specific military, economic, and social policies in the course of political unification between 1570 and 1640. Oda Nobunaga (1834–1582) emerged as Japan's first unifier at the end of the civil war period. His success was due, in part, to eradicating the Ishiyama Honganji and Enryakuji Buddhist establishments at Mt. Hiei in the 1570s, whose huge land-

holdings, economic independence, and substantial military power stood in the way of political unification. Between September 30 and October 8, 1571, Nobunaga burned the entire Enryakuji complex and its hundreds of subtemples on Mt. Hiei to the ground. His troops went on to kill the temple community to the last man, woman, and child—an estimated 3,000–4,000 priests and laity. The destruction of the Honganji, in contrast, took ten years (1570–1580) and claimed more than 40,000 lives, in part because the considerable power of the Honganji rested on the control of local populations rather than on territory. Although Nobunaga clearly targeted selected religious establishments, his rationale for eliminating the temples had little to do with faith-based religious intolerance.

The notorious persecution of Christian missionaries and Japanese converts under Nobunaga's successors, Toyotomi Hideyoshi (1534 to 1582), Tokugawa Ieyasu (1543–1616) and Tokugawa Iemitsu (1604–1651), must also be understood primarily in political and economic rather than religious terms. Jesuit missionaries were initially not only tolerated, but even welcomed by local rulers in Kyushu, who benefited from the lucrative Portuguese trade in Chinese silk in the 1570s and 1580s. Hideyoshi, Japan's second unifier, abruptly turned against the Jesuits for two reasons: domestic political competition from converted Christian *daimyō* (local lords), and the importation of international power struggles to Japan with the arrival of Spanish friars as well as Dutch and English traders, all of whom competed with one another and with the Portuguese Jesuits. Beginning in July 1587, Hideyoshi and his successors issued periodic decrees expelling all missionaries from Japan. These decrees were at first lightly enforced. Later, more vicious means were used to secure compliance. The first crucifixion took the lives of of twenty-six Christians, nine foreign missionaries, and seventeen Japanese laymen. This took place in Nagasaki in 1597, at the peak of Christianity's expansion, which had achieved an estimated 300,000 converts. Between 1622 and 1633, Tokugawa Iemitsu ordered 131 Christians to be executed in public spectacles witnessed by tens of thousands, in conjunction with elaborate torture methods and rituals of recantation to force public apostasy. By 1637, the shogun's genocidal policies against the Christian community became intertwined with the last substantial mobilization of military forces in the Tokugawa era (1603–1868). This action was taken in order to put down a peasant rebellion against taxation in Shimabara, near Nagasaki, which had taken on Christian overtones. In April 1638 37,000 peasants and unemployed samurai, some of them Christian converts, were massacred in the final battle. This marks the official end of the Christian community in Japan and the inauguration of the Tokugawa shogunate's "policy of seclusion," under which all foreign relations were tightly controlled. With the regime change in 1868, an estimated 30,000 "hidden Christians" came forth to revive the church in Japan.

Aggressive Assimilation of Ethnic Groups under Meiji Nation-Building

Japanese employed different discriminatory policies towards its ethnic minorities, who were located at the country's geographical margins (Hokkaido in the north and Okinawa in the south). Once again, domestic and international political pressures converged, this time in the context of establishing a modern nation-state. The Ainu, who comprised the indigenous population of northeastern Honshu, Hokkaido, and the adjacent islands (the Kurils and southern Sakhalin), began to be

recognized as a distinct ethnic group only in the sixteenth century. At that time, the Tokugawa shogunate designated Hokkaido a buffer zone vis-à-vis Northeast Asian areas with which the Ainu had once formed an autonomous trading region. This was accomplished by the gradual conversion of much of the Ainu hunting and gathering economy into forced dependency on Japanese contract-fishing. An unintended outcome of this policy was the introduction of new diseases such as smallpox, which reached epidemic proportions in the eighteenth and nineteenth centuries. Yet it was the Meiji state's perceived need to secure Hokkaido as Japanese territory against Russian interests that underlay its aggressive policy of assimilation through deculturation. Begun in 1871, and institutionalized by the Hokkaido Former Natives Protection Act of 1899, the Meiji colonization project systematically eliminated the Ainu language, religion, customs (i.e., tattooing and wearing earrings), and lifestyles. Land redistribution, often accompanied by forced relocation, made Ainu into impoverished agriculturists indentured to Japanese immigrant landowners. The Ainu were classified as imperial subjects, whose decreasing numbers distinguished them in public discourse as a "dying race." From approximately 80,000 in the early eighteenth century, the Ainu population had decreased to 16,000 by 1873, accounting for 14.63 percent of the total population in Hokkaido. By 1939, they constituted only 0.54 percent of Hokkaido's population, even though the actual number of Ainu, now heavily intermarried with Japanese, remained about the same. In the later decades of the twentieth century, an Ainu ethnopolitical movement began to address this historical treatment. The adoption of the Ainu New Law in 1984 marks the viability of the movement, which recognizes the genocidal quality of Japanese policy towards the Ainu and forges links with a worldwide indigenous peoples' movement.

Okinawa was likewise coercively assimilated into the Meiji state, beginning in the 1870s, in an effort to remove any territorial ambiguity with China. The last Okinawan king, Sho Tai, was forced into exile in Tokyo in 1879, leaving the people deeply divided in their response to Japanese assimilationist policies. Initial efforts to suppress Okinawan cultural and religious practices and simultaneously to impose language standardization and public reverence to the Japanese emperor were only moderately successful. After Japan's victory against China in 1895, however, Okinawans themselves decided to voluntarily assimilate with Japan. Thereafter, Okinawans struggled to be recognized as full Japanese citizens, rather than as a colonized ethnic group. Unlike heavily developed Hokkaido, Okinawa was to remain an economic backwater, useful for exploitation through over-taxation but other-

The violent and widespread destruction of Nanking, China—often referred to as the "Rape of Nanking"—followed the city's capture on December 29, 1937, by forces of the Japanese Imperial Army. [AP/WIDE WORLD PHOTOS]

wise expendable. In the first decades of the twentieth century, poverty and discrimination drove tens of thousands of Okinawans to emigrate to Hawaii, South America, and the Philippines. Another 32,000 found work in the factories of mainland Japan's cities. At the end of World War II, in the Battle of Okinawa, the deadliest conflict of the Pacific Theater, an estimated 130,000–140,000 Okinawan civilians (more than one-fourth of the population) perished at the hands of both American and Japanese soldiers. After the war, the United States occupied Okinawa for twenty years longer than it did mainland Japan. Okinawa hosts three quarters of the United States' military bases in Japan, even though it comprises one percent of the Japanese landmass.

Crimes against Humanity Committed under Colonialism and War

Japan modernized its first colonies, Taiwan (1895–1945) and Korea (1910–1945) in order to exploit them for its own imperialist purposes. As the price for main-

taining the empire rose, and as local resistance against the colonizers sharpened, Japanese rule became increasingly more oppressive and genocidal, especially in Korea after 1939. The classification of Japanese crimes against the civilian Korean population is complicated by the fact that the Japanese colonizers used existing social divisions in Korea to turn the people against one another. Between forty and fifty percent of the National Military Police, which enforced Japanese colonial policies and punished resistance, were Korean. Japan's colonial policy vested exclusive authority over the military, judiciary, legislature, and civil administration in the Government-General of Korea, which was directly responsible to the Japanese emperor. All political organizations, the media, and the education system were suppressed and replaced by organs of the colonial government, although a lively—albeit heavily censored—Korean public sphere did develop in the 1920s and 1930s.

Organized resistance against Japanese colonial rule in Taiwan, Korea, and Manchuria was met by violent crackdowns and claimed thousands of lives. The Korean Independence Movement, which began on March 1, 1919, left between 553 (Japanese official count) and 7,500 (Korean nationalist sources) dead. Japanese forces employed such methods as locking protesters into a church and burning it down. In Tokyo, after the 1923 Great Kanto Earthquake, more than 6,000 resident Koreans were killed by local authorities and mobs because they were suspected of having set fires. Resistance was fiercest in Korea, and stood in some reciprocal relation to the particular harshness with which the Japanese enforced their assimilation policies. After 1939, when Japan mobilized for total war in Asia and the Pacific, the use of the Korean language was prohibited and all Koreans were forced to adopt Japanese names and worship regularly at Shinto shrines.

The colonies' economic exploitation took on criminal if not exactly genocidal dimensions. In the 1910s and 1920s, the Korean economy was restructured in order to meet Japan's rice shortages. This caused huge social dislocations, as large landholders profited from land reallocations and small farmers were forced into tenancy or emigration to Manchuria or Japan. By 1931, 57 percent of Korea's total rice production was exported to Japan. Concurrently, the Korean emigrant population in Manchuria swelled from a few hundred to 700,000, and to 270,000 in Japan. After 1939, all imperial subjects, Japanese and colonized alike, became subject to the National General Mobilization Law. For 1.2 million Koreans, this meant performing forced labor in Japan and, later, forced military service. By the end of the war, Koreans constituted one-third of Japan's industrial labor force, of which 136,000 worked in mines under abominable conditions. Recruitment took place through labor mobilization offices located in local Korean police stations. These were usually staffed by Koreans, and targeted mostly the poor and disadvantaged. After the beginning of war with China in 1937, at least 41,000 Chinese forced laborers were brought to Japan. Many of these were confined to camps run by Japanese business firms. One such company was Kajima Construction, in Hanaoka in northern Honshu, where an abortive uprising in June 1945 resulted in a massacre of hundreds of Chinese.

The Japanese state also organized the sexual exploitation of young women and girls after 1932, in the so-called military comfort women system. This policy resulted in their multiple victimization as women, colonial subjects, Asians, and objects of sexual conquest for Japanese soldiers throughout the protracted and increasingly vicious war. About eighty percent of an estimated 80,000 to 100,000 military comfort women were Koreans, recruited from poverty-stricken rural areas recruited by labor brokers who employed deception, intimidation, violence, and outright kidnapping as procurement methods. Japan's Ministries of Home Affairs, Foreign Affairs, and War were all involved in creating and administering this system by ordering the establishment of hundreds of comfort stations, first in China and later in conquered areas of Southeast Asia and the Pacific Islands. Senior staff officers of each army oversaw the movement of women, expanded their recruitment to local women, including 300 Dutch women in Indonesia, and issued strict hygiene and venereal disease–control laws. The use of these stations by Japanese soldiers, however, was voluntary. Officially designed to prevent large-scale rape of local populations, the comfort stations were themselves places of constant rape, with or without minimal pay, and left tens of thousands of women either dead or physically and mentally scarred for life.

In part, the comfort women system was instituted as a response to the extreme brutality exhibited by Japanese forces on the Chinese mainland. The most atrocious example of this occurred in the weeks after the fall of the Chinese nationalist capital Nanking in December 1937. Between 40,000 and 300,000 Chinese men, women, and children died in the so-called Nanking Massacre. They were raped, mutilated, burned alive, drowned, or otherwise slaughtered by Japanese troops on an indiscriminate killing and looting rampage. The international media reported on the killings at the time, and Matsui Iwane, the general in charge of the Japanese troops, was convicted as a Class A war criminal in Tokyo and hanged in December 1948. Nonetheless, the massacre was not thoroughly investigated, either in court or by historians, until the 1990s. Since then, it has been used as a central tool in the politics of memory both within Japan and between Japan, China, and the Chinese-American community.

In contrast, Japan's secret biological and chemical warfare research program, led by Shiro Ishii of Unit 731, was deliberately covered up both by the Japanese and, later, by the U.S. occupation forces. The Japanese troops burned all of Unit 731's facilities to the ground in the last days of the war. The United States, eager to acquire the Unit's research data for American military use, continued the cover-up by refusing to prosecute the facility's personnel.

General Ishii, who has been compared to the Nazi Doctor Mengele, officially directed the Guandong Army's Anti-Epidemic Water Supply Unit from his facility in Pingfan near the Manchurian city of Harbin, but he also secretly masterminded Japan's efforts to become the world's leader in the production of biological weapons. Under his direction, thousands of Chinese,

General Tomoyuki Yamashita was the commanding general of the Japanese Imperial Army in the Philippine Islands during the unsuccessful defense of the islands against the invading Allies under Douglas MacArthur. He was the Japanese Military Governor of the islands from October 9, 1944, until his surrender to the Allies on September 3, 1945. Forces under Yamashita's command and control allegedly committed atrocities (including murder, torture, rape, and arson) against the civilian population of the islands (and others), resulting in the deaths of tens of thousands of people.

Following his surrender, Yamashita was tried for war crimes by the American Military Commission in the Far East, starting on October 29, 1945. Specifically, Yamashita was charged with culpability in connection with 123 counts of war crimes, including the murder and brutal mistreatment of more than 36,500 Filipino civilians and U.S. prisoners of war, hundreds of rapes, and the arbitrary destruction of private property. During the course of the trial, the military commission, consisting of five U.S. officers having the rank of general, heard 286 witnesses and saw 423 documents that were admitted into evidence. The prosecution argued that Yamashita had to have known that these high crimes were being committed, and it was adduced that the large number and widespread occurrence of the crimes suggested that they were planned and deliberate, and were carried out under a central command. Yamashita denied any knowledge of these crimes, and argued that his tactical situation at the time (which included a shutdown in his communications with his subordinate field commanders) and the fact that his army was retreating from the advancing Allied forces precluded his knowledge of the crimes taking place.

Although the military commission found that, although it concurred that Yamashita had experienced real communications difficulties owing to geographic and military contingencies, these difficulties were not the barriers to awareness of what was going on that General Yamashita contended they were. Moreover, the commission concluded that, due to the scope and scale of the crimes his forces had committed, the accused had to have known of the crimes. Consequently, on December 7, 1945, the military commission found Yamashita guilty of war crimes and sentenced him to death by hanging.

In the several decades that have followed, legal and historical analysts have often misunderstood and misstated the findings of the military commission. Many analysts have advanced the notion that the military commission in the Yamashita case imposed the legal doctrine of strict liability on military commanders—that is, military superiors may be found guilty if it can be established that they must have known that crimes against civilian (or prisoner of war) populations were being committed and failed to either halt such crimes or punish the perpetrators. This is not an accurate interpretation. Rather, the case stands for the proposition that commanders have an affirmative duty to take such measures as are within the commanders' powers, and appropriate in the circumstances, to wage war within the boundaries prescribed by international humanitarian law. These measures require commanders to exercise control over subordinates and to obtain the information that enables them to determine what is occurring in their areas of responsibility. The commander who disregards these duties has committed a violation of the law of war.

On appeal, the Yamashita case was argued before the U.S. Supreme Court, on January 7, 1946, and on February 4, 1946, the Supreme Court upheld the military commission's trial decision. (See *In re Yamashita,* 327 U.S. 1 [1946].) General MacArthur approved the findings of the military commission on February 7, 1946, and Yamashita was executed on February 23, 1946. **DARYL MUNDIS**

Korean, and Russian prisoners-of-war, along with local civilians (including women and children) were infected with a wide range of diseases such as plague, typhoid, smallpox, and frostbite, and some were even dissected alive. By the end of the war, at least ten such "death factories" existed from Manchuria to Singapore. Although the use of biological weapons in combat did not become common practice, germ warfare was directed against civilian populations in China's Zhejiang province in 1940, and an estimated 36,000 civilians died from the plague and other diseases in Manchuria in the aftermath of Japan's defeat, after retreating troops released scores of infected animals into the countryside.

At the end of World War II, there was overwhelming evidence of Japanese crimes against humanity committed against Asian populations conquered under the pretense of liberating Asia from Western imperialists. Nevertheless, the Allied war crimes trials paid more heed to the maltreatment of Allied prisoners of war, which had captured the public imagination since the 1942 Bataan Death March in the Philippines. In defiance of war conventions, the Japanese mobilized Asian and Allied prisoners as forced laborers for war-related projects—as many as 60,000 alone died building the Burma-Thailand railroad—and often refused to grant them adequate food and shelter. The average percentage of deaths in prisoner of war camps was thus staggeringly high compared to camps in the European theater. By recent calculations, out of about one million captives, well over one-third died. In the 1990s, a number of forced-labor survivors filed lawsuits in Japanese and American courts against Japanese companies such as Mitsui, Mitsubishi, Kajima, and Nippon Steel to demand compensation for their wartime labor. Others, including former comfort women and victims of biological warfare research, filed suits directly against the Japanese government. Between 1977 and 2002, seventy compensation cases were brought to court, many of them still unresolved.

SEE ALSO China; Death March; Ethnocide; Medical Experimentation; Nuclear Weapons; Rape; Tokyo Trial; Women, Violence against

BIBLIOGRAPHY

Christy, Alan S. (1993). "The Making of Imperial Subjects in Okinawa." *Positions: East Asia Cultures Critique* 1(3)(Winter):607–639.

Elison, George (1973). *Deus Destroyed: The Image of Christianity in Early Modern Japan.* Cambridge, Mass.: Harvard University Press.

Harris, Sheldon H. (1994). *Factories of Death: Japanese Biological Warfare, 1932–45, and the American Cover-Up.* London: Routledge.

Hein, Laura (2003). "War Compensation: Claims against the Japanese Government and Japanese Corporations for War Crimes." In *Politics of the Past: On Repairing Historical Injustices,* ed. J. Torpey. Lanham, Md.: Rowman & Littlefield Publishers.

Li, Fei Fei, Robert Sabella, and David Liu, eds. (2002). *Nanking 1937: Memory and Healing.* Armonk, N.Y.: M.E. Sharpe.

McMullin, Neil (1984). *Buddhism and the State in Sixteenth-Century Japan.* Princeton, N.J.: Princeton University Press.

Shin, Gi-Wook, and Michael Robinson, eds. (1999). *Colonial Modernity in Korea.* Cambridge, Mass.: Harvard University Asia Center.

Siddle, Richard (1996). *Race, Resistance, and the Ainu of Japan.* London: Routledge.

Tanaka, Yuki (2002). *Japan's Comfort Women: Sexual Slavery and Prostitution During World War II and the US Occupation.* London: Routledge.

Utsumi, Aiko (2004). "Japanese Racism, War, and the POW Experience." In *War and State Terrorism: The United States, Japan, and the Asia-Pacific in the Long Twentieth Century,* ed. M. Selden and A. Y. So. Lanham, Md.: Rowman & Littlefield Publishers.

Waterford, Van (1994). *Prisoners of the Japanese in World War II.* Jefferson, N.C.: McFarland & Company.

Franziska Seraphim

Jehovah's Witnesses

The Jehovah's Witness movement was founded in the United States in the late nineteenth century. From there the movement spread to Europe, and in Germany it came face to face with the demands of the Third Reich for total allegiance to National Socialism. The result was a bitter and heroic conflict as Witnesses refused to yield to a regime they perceived as evil.

Jehovah's Witnesses believe that humans are living in the last days of a world where Satan rules, and that at the end they will join with the forces of good to defeat Satan and his troops. God, whom the Witnesses address as Jehovah, will then establish his kingdom of peace and plenty on earth. In the meantime, Jehovah's Witnesses spread knowledge of Jehovah and his plans through door-to-door missionary work.

With a strong belief in family and personal ethics, Witnesses see themselves as citizen of God's kingdom and soldiers in his army. Thus, they will not bear arms, vote, belong to a political party, or swear on oath. They are therefore not able to offer allegiance to a state or regime that demands total obedience and loyalty from its citizens.

In democracies Witnesses are generally tolerated, but in repressive regimes they are not. Under the Third Reich the Witnesses stood out from the two hundred other minority Christian groups that the Gestapo investigated as posing a special danger to National Socialism. Their survival as a group and as individuals could have been negotiated in return for total, public obedience, but Witnesses, because of their religious beliefs, chose not to compromise.

As a result, members were rounded up and imprisoned. Jehovah's Witnesses were among the first groups to be transported to concentration camps and later death camps throughout the Reich. They were the special focus of torture and ridicule by prison and camp guards. Witnesses lost their civil rights, families were separated, and some of their children were taken away to be brought up in Nazi homes. Nevertheless, their public meetings and door-to-door missionary work continued.

Witnesses could buy their freedom from prison or a camp by signing a paper denying their faith. Very few opted to do this. The majority continued to preach and pray, and cling to their convictions within the confines of prisons and camps. Many survivors of the Holocaust recounted stories of Witnesses' courage, their willingness to share meager rations, and their ability to support each other.

Deaths from torture and disease, and a great deal of suffering, occurred among Witnesses in the camps, but their suicide rate was low. Their beliefs afforded them a framework by which they might understand the reasons for the seemingly mindless horror of the camps. To their way of thinking, the Holocaust was Satan's work and the role of Witnesses was clear: to bear witness to Jehovah in the midst of so much destruction. Witnesses not only kept their faith, but also made converts. When the camps were liberated at the end of World War II, there were more Jehovah's Witnesses freed than had entered them.

Jehovah's Witnesses have continued to face persecution in a number of totalitarian regimes around the world, for example, in Malawi where the religion was banned in 1967, and its members suffered the destruction of their property and brutal physical attacks. The atrocities and ban persisted until international pressure forced the government to restore human rights. In 1993 the ban was lifted, and by 1995 the Witnesses were fully and openly operating once again in Malawi.

Nonetheless, Witnesses continue to be harassed and imprisoned in a number of nation-states.

SEE ALSO Persecution; Religious Groups

BIBLIOGRAPHY

Berenbaum, Michael (1993). *The World Must Know: A History of the Holocaust as Told in the United States Holocaust Memorial Museum.* Boston: Little, Brown and Company.

King, Christine E. (1990). "Jehovah's Witnesses under Nazism." In *A Mosaic of Victims: Non-Jews Persecuted and Murdered by the Nazis,* ed. M. Berenbaum. New York: New York University Press.

King, Christine E. (2000). "Responses Outside the Mainstream Catholic and Protestant Traditions." In *The Holocaust and the Christian World,* ed. C. Rittner, S. D. Smith, and I. Steinfeldt. London: Kuperard.

Reynaud, M and S. Graffard (2001). *Jehovah's Witnesses and the Nazis—Persecution, Deportation and Murder 1933–1945.* New York: Cooper Square Press.

Christine E. King

Kalimantan

Instances of mass murder and gross human rights violations in Kalimantan, Indonesia and the processes underlying them are multiple and complex. Government authorities have always placed a greater value on the island's vast natural resources than on its sparse population, whose exceedingly diverse indigenous peoples have been reduced to the collective label Dayak. State-building on the island by central government authorities predates the New Order regime (1966–1998). But it was not until 1966, when General Suharto assumed the presidency, that a government based in Jakarta and backed by Western allies acquired sufficient financial and governmental capacities to penetrate the island systematically. In late 1967, such state intrusion into the province of West Kalimantan instigated horrific bloodshed. Suharto's military officers, in an effort to wipe out a local communist rebellion, used indigenous "warrior" Dayaks to expunge ethnic Chinese from the region's heartland. Thousands were killed, and tens of thousands were forced to relocate to coastal urban locales where they could be controlled, monitored, and governed.

On the heels of this counterinsurgency campaign, New Order authorities enacted a series of policies with ethnocidal implications for Dayak peoples. Foremost was land dispossession, which was facilitated by the rapacious extraction of natural resources. The mega-scale forestry concessions held by foreign and Jakarta-based companies ran roughshod over traditionally held, indigenous lands. Soon thereafter vast tracts of land, for which Dayaks were given little to no compensation,

were converted into palm oil plantations. These land-clearing practices significantly contributed to the island's massive forest fires during the period 1982 to 1993 and in 1997. Experts have calculated the consequent economic ruin, let alone the social costs, to total hundreds of millions of dollars. Meanwhile, the denuding of hills due to deforestation has silted rivers and killed once abundant fish supplies, thereby further threatening rural livelihoods.

State authorities also forced "backward" and "primitive" Dayaks, whose beliefs were belittled as mere superstitions, to convert to Islam or Christianity. Putatively, this was done to insulate these communities from communist influences. Meanwhile, to inculcate feelings of loyalty to the Indonesian Republic and to assimilate Dayaks into mainstream society, compulsory state education prohibited the teaching of local languages and histories.

Similarly destructive to Dayak cultural identity and welfare was the transfer by Suharto's regime of hundreds of thousands of families from overcrowded Java (951 people per sq. km. according to a 1999 estimate) to a number of sparsely populated outer islands, including Kalimantan (21 people per sq. km.). Known as transmigration, this program precipitated significant demographic changes—for instance, the increased Islamization of the island.

Abundantly funded by the World Bank and other international donors, transmigration has contributed to the general marginalization and attendant frustrations of Dayaks. They justifiably fear becoming minorities in their homeland. Despite the transmigration program's many ills, however, it cannot be held exclusively to blame for Kalimantan's infamous anti-migrant riots of the late 1990s.

The origins of this form of communal violence anticipate the arrival of transmigrants under the New Order, although the international community and media did not take notice of the bloodletting until the massive episodes of 1997 and 1999. In West Kalimantan, Dayaks and migrant Madurese (from East Java) first came to blows in late 1967 and early 1968 over lands from which the Chinese had been expelled. Minor, intermittent riots continued in this same area. Authorities, however, did not earmark the province as an official transmigrant destination until 1973. Madurese also rarely participated in such government-sponsored programs. Instead, they have migrated in large part on their own, a phenomenon known as spontaneous migration. Furthermore, early resettlement sites were located in areas unaffected by this periodic bloodletting. Finally, the dynamics of transmigration can hardly explain the first major Dayak-Madurese clash in the neighboring province of Central Kalimantan in early 2001. This riot led to the thorough expulsion of tens of thousands of Madurese from the province.

More informed accounts for the violence point to local political reasons. Here, attempts of local Dayak elites to capture lucrative gains from Indonesia's decentralization program were pivotal. Enacted in the post-Suharto state, decentralization transfers substantial financial and administrative authority to the regional governments. It thus represents a treasure trove for the elites who control local bureaucracies and legal and illegal economic networks and activities. Fortunately, South and East Kalimantan provinces, areas also home to transmigration sites, have remained free of similar instances of collective violence.

SEE ALSO Indigenous Peoples; Indonesia

BIBLIOGRAPHY

Davidson, Jamie (2003). "The Politics of Violence on an Indonesian Periphery." *South East Asian Research* 11, (1):59–89.

Van Klinken, G. (2002). "Indonesia's New Ethnic Elites." In *Indonesia: In Search of Transition*, eds. Henk Schulte Nordholt and Irwan Abdullah. Yogyakarta, Indonesia: Pustaka Pelajar.

Jamie S. Davidson

Kalmyks

The Kalmyks, traditionally Mahayana Buddhist pastoral nomads, originated as an offshoot of the Mongols.

They moved into the southern Volga Steppe region in the 1660s. Strong under Khan Aiuka (1669–1724), they allied with Peter the Great who used them as a buffer against possible Persian invasion.

Subsequently, the tsarist government "divided and ruled," and a continuing influx of peasants severely hampered the Kalmyk pastoral-nomadic life. Despairing and desperate, in 1771 they attempted a coordinated flight back to their ancestral home, Dzungaria. Weather prevented the Kalmyks on the western bank from leaving, but both groups residing on the eastern bank fled eastward. It was at this point that the first genocide occurred. The harsh winter killed many, but Bashir units sent by the tsarist government massacred many more. Perhaps only a quarter of the fleeing Kalmyks reached Dzungaria. There the Ching government annihilated large numbers and forcibly dispersed the remainder into cultural oblivion among other pastoral nomadic groups.

In the nineteenth-century the poverty and demographic decline of the Kalmyks began to worry the Russian government. These circumstances threatened the Kalmyks' continued ability to provide a significant share of the cavalry mount for the Russian army. Also, low population density would leave the Kalmyk region of the northwest Caspian littoral open to Turkish invasion from the south. In the 1880s and 1890s the tsarist government improved education and health conditions, and the Kalmyk population started to recover.

The eventual Russian revolution impacted the Kalmyks. Some fought with the White Army and then fled to Serbia. The communists established the Kalmyk Autonomous Oblast in 1920; it became the Kalmyk Autonomous Soviet Socialist Republic (ASSR) in 1935, with its capital at Elista. A devastating blow, a de facto second genocide, came with Joseph Stalin's enforced collectivization during the 1920s; violence and starvation killed many.

In World War II numerous Kalmyk soldiers fought in the Red Army; some received the highest military decorations. However, in the summer of 1942, when the Nazis occupied Kalmykia, some local Kalmyks, and others from Nazi-occupied Serbia, sided with the Nazis as a way to throw off the communist yoke. The Soviets reconquered the Kalmyk ASSR in December 1942. Stalin declared all Kalmyks Nazi collaborators and ordered them deported. In December 1943 boxcars carried the total population of the Kalmyk ASSR, including communists and Komsomols, to prison camps in Siberia and Central Asia. This was the third great Kalmyk genocide—about half survived.

In his Secret Speech to the Communist Party in February 1956, Soviet Premier Nikita Khrushchev denounced this forcible exile of the Kalmyks and that of the Karachai, Chechen, Ingush, and Balkhars from elsewhere. However, only after international pressure were some Kalmyks finally allowed to return home in 1957. Although traumatized by their forced exile into Gulag, the returnees started over in their reconstituted homeland.

After the Soviet Union broke up in 1991, the Republic of Kalmykia became federated within Russia. Twenty-first-century Kalmyks realize that, while the genocide perpetrated from 1944 through 1957 failed, much cultural destruction occurred, and economic globalization and other pressures could lead to ethnocide. Therefore, both in Kalmykia and within overseas communities of Kalmyks, including several in New Jersey, leaders seek to preserve and revitalize the Kalmyk language and key parts of the culture.

SEE ALSO Cossacks; Union of Soviet Socialist Republics

BIBLIOGRAPHY

Khrushchev, Nikita S. (1956). *Crimes of the Stalin Era, Special Report to the 20th Congress of the Communist Party of the Soviet Union.* New York: New Leader.

Nekrich, Alexander M. (1978). *The Punished Peoples: The Deportation and Fate of Soviet Minorities at the End of the Second World War,* tran. George Saunders. New York: Norton.

Linda Kimball

Karadzic, Radovan

[JUNE 19, 1945–]
Leader of the Serbian Democratic Party (SDS); became first president of the Republika Srpska in 1992 but was forced to flee office after being charged with genocide, crimes against humanity, and violations of the laws of war for his involvement in ethnic cleansing against non-Serbs during the years 1990 to 1995

Radovan Karadzic was born to Vuk and Jovanka Karadzic on June 19, 1945, in the village of Petnjica, in Montenegro. In 1960 Karadzic moved to Sarajevo to study medicine. During the 1960s, Karadzic married his Ljiljana Zelen, and became involved in politics. In 1971, he received a medical degree in psychiatry from the University of Sarajevo. From the 1970s to the late 1980s, Karadzic worked as a psychiatrist in Kosevo Hospital in Sarajevo, as a team psychiatrist for the Sarajevo and Red Star soccer teams, and at the Vozdovac Health Center in Belgrade.

Rise to Political Power

In 1990, in the Socialist Republic of Bosnia and Herzegovina, Karadzic cofounded the party of the Bosnian

Serbs, Srpska Demokratska Stranka (SDS), and became its first president. The SDS was formed to challenge nationalist Muslim and Croat parties in the November 1990 multi-party elections, and won 72 of the 240 Assembly seats. The mission of the SDS was to form a unified Serbian state, or Greater Serbia, by linking Serb-occupied parts of Bosnia and Herzegovina and Croatia with Serbia. Karadzic declared a large portion of the territory of Bosnia and Herzegovina as exclusively Serbian. However, large numbers of Bosnian Muslims and Croats already resided in these territories. The SDS mission, therefore, included a policy of ethnic cleansing to eliminate non-Serb populations in these areas. In order to implement such a policy, the SDS needed to convince the Bosnian Serb population that preemptive action against non-Serbs was critical for self-preservation.

In 1990, Karadzic and the SDS began saturating the Bosnian Serb population with nationalist propaganda. Karadzic, following the lead of Serbian President Slobodan Milosevic, gained control over airwaves and publications. SDS-influenced media sources manipulated and falsified news reports, creating the perception of intense and ancient hatreds between the Serbs, Croats, and Muslims. Bosnian Serbs became fearful of oppression and extinction at the hands of Bosnian Muslims and Croats. This ethnic fear and hatred set the stage for the SDS to finalize plans for ethnic cleansing. In late 1991, the SDS worked with the Yugoslav National Army (JNA) to arm civilian Bosnian Serbs.

On March 27, 1992, Bosnian Serb leaders approved a Constitution for the Serbian Republic of Bosnia and Herzegovina, later known as the Republika Srpska. On April 6, 1992, the European Community officially recognized the Serbian Republic. On May 12, 1992, the Bosnian Serb Assembly created the Bosnian Serb Army (BSA), comprised of JNA forces that were citizens of Bosnia and Herzegovina. On the same day, Karadzic became the President of the three-member Presidency of Republika Srpska, and Supreme Commander of the BSA. General Ratko Mladic became Commander of the BSA, directly subordinate to President Karadzic. On December 17, 1992, Karadzic was elected sole President of Republika Srpska.

The Ethnic Cleansing Program

In late March 1992, while the politicians were drafting the new constitution, Bosnian Serb forces seized control of municipalities in eastern and northwestern Bosnia by committing executions, sexual violence, torture, and destruction of property. Thousands of Bosnian Muslims and Croats were transported to SDS-established detention facilities where many were tortured, raped, and killed. The systematic terror provoked thousands of Bosnian Muslims to flee to the Srebrenica region, where the United Nations had established a safe zone. On July 6, 1995, Bosnian Serb forces, acting on orders from Karadzic, shelled the safe area. Between July 11 and July 18, 1995, Bosnian Serb forces entered the zone and executed thousands of Bosnian Muslims. From April 5, 1992, to November 30, 1995, Bosnian Serb forces also engaged in a prolonged attack on Sarajevo. Forty-four months of daily shelling and sniping by Bosnian Serb forces wounded and killed thousands of citizens. Following NATO air strikes in late May 1995, Bosnian Serb forces detained over two hundred United Nations peacekeepers and observers as hostages in Pale and Sarajevo to prevent further air strikes.

On July 25, 1995, the International Criminal Tribunal for the Former Yugoslavia (ICTY) indicted Karadzic and Mladic for crimes of genocide, crimes against humanity, and violations of the laws or customs of war. An amended indictment against Karadzic, confirmed on May 31, 2000, charged him, on the basis of individual and superior criminal responsibility, for crimes committed in connection with ethnic cleansing, the attacks on Sarajevo and Srebrenica, and the taking of hostages. Karadzic was charged with two counts of genocide, five counts of crimes against humanity, three counts of violations against the laws or customs of war, and one count of grave breaches of the Geneva Convention. On July 19, 1996, Karadzic resigned as president of Republika Srpska and as president of the SDS. He went into hiding and remains a fugitive.

SEE ALSO Bosnia and Herzegovina; Croatia, Independent State of; Ethnic Cleansing; Humanitarian Intervention; Incitement; Massacres; Mass Graves; Memorials and Monuments; Memory; Mladic, Ratko; Nationalism; Peacekeeping; Propaganda; Refugees; Safe Zones; Srebrenica; Superior (or Command) Responsibility; Yugoslavia

BIBLIOGRAPHY

Bassiouni, M. Cherif, and Peter Manikas (1996). *The Law of the International Criminal Tribunal for the Former Yugoslavia.* New York: Transnational Publishers, Inc.

Cigar, Norman, and Paul Williams (2002). *Indictment at The Hague.* New York: New York University Press.

Oberschall, Anthony (2000). "The Manipulation of Ethnicity: From Ethnic Cooperation to Violence and War in Yugoslavia." *Ethnic and Racial Studies* 23(6):982–1002.

United Nations International Criminal Tribunal for the Former Yugoslavia (2000). "The Prosecutor of the

Tribunal Against Radovan Karadzic Amended Indictment." Available from http://www.un.org/icty/indictment/english/kar-ai000428e.htm.

WGBH/Frontline (1998). "Frontline: The World's Most Wanted Man." Available from http://www.pbs.org/wgbh/frontline/shows/karadzic/etc/synopsis.html.

Zimmerman, Warren (1995). "The Last Ambassador: A Memoir of the Collapse of Yugoslavia." *Foreign Affairs* 74(2):1–20.

Laura E. Bishop

Katyn

The mass execution of twenty thousand Polish POWs by the Soviet security police (the NKVD) is one of the most notorious atrocities of World War II. Stalin and the politburo authorized the executions on March 5, 1940, following their receipt of a memorandum from Lavrenti Beria, the head of the NKVD. Beria reported that NKVD prisons held a large number of Polish army, police, and intelligence officers who were unremittingly hostile to the Soviet system, engaged in anti-Soviet agitation within the camps, and eager to escape and to participate in counterrevolutionary activities. Because these prisoners were all "hardened and uncompromising enemies of Soviet authority," Beria recommended they should all be indicted by a special tribunal of the NKVD, and then shot.

According to NKVD records there were 21,857 such executions during March and April of 1940. Most of the victims were Polish officer POWs who had been captured by the Soviets when the Red Army invaded Eastern Poland in September 1939. The executions took place at a number of locations in Russia and the Ukraine; most famously in the Katyn Forest near Smolensk.

By the standards of Stalin's Russia, these executions were not a particularly large-scale affair. Indeed, they formed part of a much larger process of political and ethnic cleansing occurring in Western Belorussia and Western Ukraine from 1939 to 1941. These territories had been lost to Poland as a result of the Soviet-Polish war (1920–1921). Following their reconquest by the Red Army, however, these disputed territories, were brutally and bloodily incorporated into the Soviet system. In the process, hundreds of thousands of people were persecuted, uprooted, dispossessed, deported, imprisoned, and/or executed. Among the many victims were the families of the Polish POWs who were executed at Katyn and elsewhere. These families were rounded up by the NKVD and deported to Kazakhstan, in Soviet Central Asia.

The Polish officers who were held as POWs, together with other "bourgeois" elements among Polish captives, were incarcerated in special NKVD camps that were designed to isolate them from the imprisoned rank and file of Poland's armed forces. Initially, the aim was to educate them into being passive, if not good, citizens of the new Soviet order in Eastern Poland. The prisoners were bombarded with propaganda for many months and forced to take part in lectures, discussions, and other events extolling the virtues of the Soviet system. It was the pathetic failure of the NKVD's indoctrination program that led Beria to propose execution as the solution to the problem of what to do with these POWs.

The timing of the executions was probably prompted by a number of circumstances connected to the Soviet-Finnish war (winter, 1939–1940). The Soviets feared that an Anglo-French intervention in that conflict would encourage resistance activities in the POW camps and might even forge links with escaping prisoners. It is possible, too, that Beria wanted to clear the way for an anticipated batch of Finnish POWs. But most important was the fact that Beria's proposal to Stalin in March 1940 was fully in accord with the established Stalinist practice of physically eliminating those who were considered to be the worst class and ideological enemies of the Soviet regime.

In the 1930s Stalin had presided over the imprisonment, deportation and execution of millions of Soviet citizens, so it is unlikely that he dwelt long on this particular decision. But the murder of the Polish POWs turned out to be by far the most troublesome and embarrassing of Stalin's atrocities.

The problem was that after the German invasion of Russia in June 1941, Stalin found himself in alliance with his erstwhile Polish enemies. In July 1941, a treaty of alliance was signed with the Polish government in exile in London, and Stalin subsequently agreed to an amnesty for all Polish detainees in the Soviet Union. Hundreds of thousands of Poles were released from Soviet prison camps during 1941 and 1942, many of whom joined a Polish army that later fought in North Africa and Italy. It soon became apparent to the Polish authorities that a large number of officers and officials remained missing—in particular from three camps: Kozelsk in the Smolensk region; Starobelsk in Eastern Ukraine, and Ostashkov in northern Russia. Stalin was personally pressed on a number of occasions to explain the whereabouts of these disappeared POWs. He feigned ignorance and suggested they had somehow left the country.

The truth finally began to emerge in April 1943, when the Germans, who occupied the Smolensk area, announced the discovery of a mass grave of Polish POWs at Katyn. Moscow immediately denied all re-

February 8, 1952—Katyn Forest, Poland: Mass grave of some of Polish soldiers with some of the investigators looking over bodies.
[BETTMANN/CORBIS]

sponsibility and blamed the Germans for the massacre. The Polish government in exile, however, had long been convinced of Soviet culpability, and it supported calls for an independent inquiry into the murders. The Soviets retaliated by severing diplomatic relations with the London-based, exiled government. Later in the war Stalin established his own Polish provisional government.

When Smolensk was recaptured by the Red Army in January 1944, the Soviets established a special commission to conduct a forensic examination of the Katyn massacre site. The commission, headed by Academician N. N. Burdenko, chief surgeon of the Red Army, concluded that the POW camps had been overrun by the Germans and that the shootings had been carried out in the autumn of 1941. In light of the record of German atrocities on the Eastern Front, this was not an implausible scenario. The commission's verdict was largely accepted by Allied public opinion.

Given the wartime grand alliance between Britain, the United States, and the Soviet Union, it was highly expedient for the Western governments to blame the Germans too, notwithstanding suspicions that the Soviets were the guilty party. But after the war, doubts grew about the authenticity of the medical evidence and about witness testimony presented by the Soviet commission of enquiry. Polish émigré organizations, in particular, waged a long campaign to expose the truth about the crime of Katyn. In 1952 a U.S. congressional committee concluded that the NKVD had conducted the massacre. This was very much a cold war verdict, but most independent observers also agreed that the Soviets were responsible for the murders. Questions remained, however, about the precise circumstances in which the massacre took place. Were the killings a panic measure in the face of German invasion in 1941? Was this a local action by the NKVD, acting on its own initiative rather than on orders from Moscow? How much did Stalin and the Soviet leadership know about the murders?

It was Mikhail Gorbachev's campaign for *glasnost* (openness) in the Soviet Union that led to the final resolution of these questions. The reforming Soviet leader was committed to the view that there should be no blank spots in Soviet history, and in October 1990, Gorbachev handed a over number of archival documents to the Polish government. These demonstrated beyond any doubt that the NKVD had carried out the killings. Gorbachev's initiative was partly the result of the discovery in June 1990 of the mass graves of the executed POWs from the Ostashkov and Starobelsk camps. Gorbachev had not, however, made public any of the politburo documents detailing the role of Stalin and the Soviet leadership in the decision-making process leading to the murders at Katyn and elsewhere. That task was carried out by Russian President Boris Yeltsin in October 1992. These revelations led to an extensive discussion in post-Soviet Russia of the Katyn affair.

SEE ALSO Massacres; Stalin, Joseph

BIBLIOGRAPHY

Polish Cultural Foundation (1965). *The Crime of Katyn: Facts and Documents.* London: Polish Cultural Foundation.

Katyn': Plenniki Neob'yavlennoi Voiny (Katyn: Prisoners of an Undeclared War) (1997). Moscow: Mezhdunarodhyi Fond "Demokratiya."

FCO Historians (2003). *Katyn: British Reactions to the Katyn Massacre, 1943-2003.* London: Foreign and Commonwealth Office.

"Stalin's Order to Shoot the Polish POWs in 1940." Available at http://www.katyn.org.au/beria.html.

U.S. Congress (1952). *The Katyn Forest Massacre: Final Report of the Select Committee to Conduct an Investigation and Study of the Facts, Evidence and Circumstances of the Katyn Forest Massacre.* Union Calendar No.792, House Report No.2505. Washington, D.C.: United States Government Printing Office.

Geoffrey Roberts

Khmel'nyts'kyi, Bohdan see
Chmielnicki, Bogdan.

Khmer Rouge

Cambodia's Prince Norodom Sihanouk coined the term *Khmer Rouge* in the 1960s to describe his country's then heterogeneous, communist-led dissidents, with whom he allied after his 1970 overthrow. More precisely, he called them *Khmers rouges* in French, *khmaer krahom* in Khmer, both meaning "Khmer Reds." In 1975, the Khmer Rouge leadership, secretly headed by Pol Pot, took power, pushed the Prince aside, and established the Democratic Kampuchea regime (DK).

Origins

Cambodian communism first emerged in 1930 as part of a multinational anti-French independence movement, the Indochina Communist Party (ICP), which extended throughout what was then French Indochina. In 1951, the Vietnamese communist leader, Ho Chi Minh, separated the ICP into national branches. In Cambodia, the ICP set up the Khmer People's Revolutionary Party (KPRP). Its members, especially former Buddhist monks, led the nationwide Khmer Issarak ("independence") movement. They adopted for its flag a silhouette of the medieval temple of Angkor Wat: five towers on a red background. A faction of the movement made early use of the name "Democratic Kampuchea." An anti-KPRP group flew a flag with a three-towered Angkor motif which would later become the emblem of the DK regime. Members of another anti-communist splinter group perpetrated portentous racial massacres, targeting minority Vietnamese residents in 1949 and Cham Muslims in 1952. A Cambodian student in Paris named Saloth Sar, then calling himself the "Original Khmer," returned home in 1953 and served briefly in the communist-led Issarak ranks. He later assumed the *nom de guerre* "Pol Pot."

The First Indochina War ended with the 1954 Vietnamese victory over the French at Dien Bien Phu. The Geneva settlement brought Cambodia full independence under Prince Sihanouk, who soon adopted a foreign policy of cold war neutrality. That was, in part, an accommodation to the communists' internal challenge, implicitly acknowledging both the their role in the independence war and their potential to disrupt a

Cambodian troops dispassionately carry off the bodies of the dead. It has been estimated the Khmer Rouge annihilated some two million victims in their Killing Fields between 1975 and 1979. [AP/WIDE WORLD PHOTOS]

more pro–United States regime. Neutrality also served an international strategy to keep Cambodia out of the escalating conflict in neighboring Vietnam.

The Changing of the Vanguard

Radicals of both the left and the right, dissatisfied with Sihanouk's domestic and foreign policies, had to bide their time, head for the hills, or leave for Vietnam or Thailand. Half of Cambodia's Issarak veterans took up exile in Hanoi. Most of the remaining grassroots leftists were either mollified by Sihanouk's neutrality, jailed by his police, or disappeared, like the underground Cambodian communist leader, Tou Samouth, who was mysteriously killed in 1962. At that point a group of younger, Paris-educated militants headed by Saloth Sar, Ieng Sary, and Son Sen quickly assumed top leadership positions within the debilitated KPRP. Of these, only Sar had previously been a member of the three-person Standing Committee of the party's Central Committee; in 1960 he had been named No. 3, ranking third in that three-person body. Now, however, Saloth Sar and Ieng Sary ranked first and third in an expanded Standing Committee of five members. Former students occupied

the first, third, fifth, sixth, and eleventh ranks in the Central Committee of twelve.

With the support of ICP veteran Nuon Chea, who became Sar's second in command, the younger cohort now dominated both the Standing Committee and the Central Committee, referring to themselves as the "Party Center" (mocchim paks). Technically this was a codeword for the Central Committee, but henceforth, the latter rarely if ever met. Quietly abandoning their teaching jobs in the capital for rural redoubts, the party's new leadership launched it onto the offensive, changing its name to the Communist Party of Kampuchea (CPK) in 1966.

The veteran party leaders had been from rural and Buddhist backgrounds, and were pro-Vietnamese though relatively moderate. However, they were mostly replaced by younger, urban, French-educated, anti-Vietnamese extremists headed by "the Original Khmer," Pol Pot. Ieng Sary and Son Sen were both Khmer Krom, natives of Vietnam's Mekong Delta, and were resentful of the Vietnamese majority there. From the jungles of Cambodia's remote northeast, these new

CPK leaders planned an armed rebellion against Si-hanouk's independent regime, ignoring his neutral nationalism and labeling him a U.S. puppet. Sihanouk sensed the threat and cracked down on all leftists, driving above-ground moderates into the arms of the younger militants who were leading the CPK. Sihanouk began denouncing other "Khmers Rouges," especially three prominent elected politicians: Khieu Samphan, Hou Yuon, and Hu Nim. In 1967, they too joined the rural underground.

Accompanying them into clandestine opposition came a new generation of disgruntled youth who had benefited from Sihanouk's rapid post-independence expansion of educational opportunities, but had failed to secure commensurate employment in a fragile economy that grew in the period spanning 1963 to 1965 and remained plagued by corruption. Young rural schoolteachers and students soon comprised the bulk of "Khmer Rouge" cadres.

War, 1967–1975

In 1967, the CPK Center launched a limited insurgency, which provoked repression by the Cambodian Army. Sihanouk's regime was also unable to handle the Vietnam War's impacts on Cambodia, from plunging national revenues to the politically explosive presence of Vietnamese communist troop sanctuaries. General Lon Nol overthrew Prince Sihanouk on March 18, 1970, and allied Cambodia with the United States. From his exile in Beijing, the Sihanouk quickly joined forces with the Khmer Rouge insurgents, led by Pol Pot's shadowy CPK Center. Lon Nol's army massacred thousands of the country's ethnic Vietnamese residents, driving 300,000 more to flee to Vietnam. This set a precedent for later "ethnic cleansing" by the CPK Center, which began attacking its Vietnamese-communist military allies in September 1970.

Both sides in the Vietnam conflict treated Cambodia as a theater of their ground and air war. United States aerial bombardments of Cambodia's border areas, begun in March 1969, escalated across the country until August 1973. American aircraft dropped over half a million tons of bombs on rural Cambodia, killing over 100,000 peasants and driving many survivors into the insurgent ranks.

This triggered a second wave of Khmer Rouge rural recruitment. On May 2, l973, the Directorate of Operations of the U.S. Central Intelligence Agency reported the results of its investigations in Kandal province:

1. Khmer Insurgent (KI [Khmer Rouge]) cadre have begun an intensified proselyting [sic] campaign among ethnic Cambodian residents in the area of Chrouy Snao, Kaoh Thom district, Kandal prov-

ince, Cambodia, in an effort to recruit young men and women for KI military organizations. They are using damage caused by B-52 strikes as the main theme of their propaganda. The cadre tell the people that the Government of Lon Nol has requested the airstrikes and is responsible for the damage and the "suffering of innocent villagers" in order to keep himself in power. The only way to stop "the massive destruction of the country" is to remove Lon Nol and return Prince Sihanouk to power. The proselyting [sic] cadres tell the people that the quickest way to accomplish this is to strengthen KI forces so they will be able to defeat Lon Nol and stop the bombing.

2. This approach has resulted in the successful recruitment of a number of young men for KI forces. Residents around Chrouy Snao say that the propaganda campaign has been effective with refugees and in areas of Kaoh Thom and Leuk Dek districts which have been subject to B-52 strikes.

CPK internecine purges also accelerated during the U.S. bombardment. Portending the genocide to come, and while secretly, systematically killing off nearly all one thousand Khmer Issarak communist returnees from Hanoi, in 1973 and 1974 the Center stepped up CPK violence against ethnic Vietnamese civilians. It also purged and killed ethnic Thai and other minority members of the CPK's Western and Northeast Zone committees, banned an allied group of ethnic Cham Muslim revolutionaries in the East, and instigated severe repression of Muslim communities. Other victims of the Center included its former Sihanoukist allies, moderate local communists, and more independent Marxists such as Hou Yuon, a popular Paris-educated intellectual who had differed with Pol Pot. Yuon was marginalized, then murdered in 1975. The Center sponsored the CPK Southwest and Northern Zone military commanders, Chhit Choeun (alias "Mok") and Ke Pauk, in their purges of suspected rivals and opponents there. CPK moderates were concentrated in the Eastern Zone, where regional differences remained evident as late as 1977.

The U.S. Congress ended the American bombardment on August 15, 1973. The opposing Cambodian armies fought out the last two years of the war, with continuing large-scale U.S. military assistance to Lon Nol's Republican forces based in the cities, and sporadic Vietnamese aid to the Khmer Rouge dominating the rural areas, which the CPK termed its "bases" (*moultanh*).

Victory

On April 17, 1975, Khmer Rouge armies entered Phnom Penh. The new state was formally re-named

Democratic Kampuchea (DK) the following January. CPK Secretary-General Pol Pot headed the regime as DK's Prime Minister. He and the other members of the CPK Center who moved into the capital comprised the regime's effective national leadership. They included the CPK Standing Committee members Nuon Chea (Deputy CPK Secretary), Vorn Vet, Ieng Sary, and Son Sen (hierarchically ranked three, five, and eight, respectively) who served as Deputy Prime Ministers for the Economy, Foreign Affairs, and Defense. Also among the leadership was Khieu Samphan, who ranked number nine and served as DK's head of state. In the rural Zones, in concert with the Center, Southwest, and Northern military chiefs Mok (who ranked seventh in the Standing Committee hierarchy) and Ke Pauk (ranking thirteenth still outside the Standing Committee, but a member of the CPK Central Committee) gained increasing power as they consolidated the CPK's victory, executed its enemies, and purged its regional administrations. Mok and Pauk later became National Chief and Deputy Chief of the army's General Staff. Two other CPK Standing Committee members, So Phim and Moul Sambath (numbers four and six in the hierarchy), ran the Eastern and Northwest Zones, but held no comparable national posts.

Immediately upon victory, the CPK labeled the two million conquered urban dwellers "new people" (*neak thmei*), driving them in all directions from the capital and other cities. It forcibly settled townspeople among the rural "base people" (*neak moultanh*) who had lived in the countryside during the 1970–1975 war, and put them to work in agricultural labor camps without wages, rights, or free time. Before the rice harvest of late 1975, the CPK Center again rounded up 800,000 of these urban deportees from various regions and dispatched them to the Northwest Zone, doubling its population. Tens of thousands died of starvation there during 1976, while the regime began exporting rice. Meanwhile, the CPK hunted down, rounded up, and killed thousands of Lon Nol's defeated Khmer Republic officials, army officers, and increasingly, soldiers, schoolteachers, and alleged "pacification agents" (*sant-ec sampoan*) who, in most cases, had merely protested the repression or just the rigorous living conditions imposed on them. By early 1979, approximately 650,000 people, or one quarter of the "new" Khmer, died from execution, starvation, overwork, disease, and denial of medical care.

The Khmer Rouge revolution had won initial support among the peasant "base people," but they, too, were rewarded with a life of unpaid collective labor. The CPK regime prohibited rights to land, freedom of religion, and family life. Meals were served in planta-tion-style communal mess halls. Couples were separated, and youths were drafted into the workforce, army, or militia. Many peasant children were trained to spy on their parents, and to kill suspected "enemies" such as former city dwellers, "CIA" and "KGB agents," recalcitrants, and alleged malingerers. In 1976 and 1977, the CPK Center and its security apparatus, the *Santebal*, supported by Mok's and Pauk's divisions, conducted massive new purges of the Northwest and Northern Zone CPK administrations, arresting and killing tens of thousands of peasants who were related to the purged local officials. Starvation and repression escalated nationwide in 1977 and especially in 1978. By early 1979, 675,000 Khmer "base people" (15% of the *neak moultanh*) had perished from execution or other causes like starvation, for which CPK policies were responsible.

Pol Pot claimed to be "four to ten years ahead" of other Asian communist states, adding: "We have no model in building up our new society." This disguised the Maoism in the CPK's call for a "Super Great Leap Forward," the influence of Stalinism, and even that of the French revolution, which DK copied by introducing a ten-day working week (with one-day weekends). The CPK exported agricultural and forest products, including rare tropical fauna, to China in return for its massive military assistance program. In all, imposing these policies by force caused the deaths of 1.7 million Cambodians.

The Center charged that local and national veteran communists, who were more moderate and favored "a system of plenty" over the DK regime's policies, with being corrupted by "a little prosperity," neglectful of ideology, and "taken to pieces" by material things. Its Santebal purged and killed prominent national-level communists like Keo Meas in 1976, Hu Nim in 1977, and So Phim, Moul Sambath, and even Vorn Vet in 1978, all the while asserting increasingly tight control of Zone and Region committees. By 1978 the Santebal had executed over half the members of the CPK Central Committee, accusing most of involvement in fantastic plots hatched by a hostile new troika: "the CIA, the KGB, and the Vietnamese." Deuch, the commandant of the Santebal's central prison, "S-21" or Tuol Sleng, incarcerated and executed 14,000 Khmer Rouge members and others, leaving only seven survivors.

Genocide

The Center's severe repression of the majority Khmer rural population and its Stalin-like massive purge of the party were accompanied by intensified violence against ethnic minorities, even among the "base people," escalating the patterns of 1973–1975. In mid-1975, the new CPK regime expelled from Cambodia more than

A Khmer Rouge soldier waves his pistol and yells orders in Phnom Penh, Cambodia, on April 17, 1975, as the capital fell to communist forces. [AP/WIDE WORLD PHOTOS]

100,000 Vietnamese residents. In the next four years, more than half of the nation's ethnic Chinese, 250,000 people, perished in the Cambodian countryside, the greatest tragedy ever to befall Southeast Asia's Chinese diaspora. In late 1975, the CPK ferociously repressed a Cham Muslim rebellion along the Mekong River. Pol Pot then ordered the deportation of 150,000 Chams living on the east bank of the Mekong, and their forced dispersal throughout the Northern and Northwest Zones. In November 1975, a Khmer Rouge official in the Eastern Zone complained to Pol Pot of his inability to implement "the dispersal strategy according to the decision that you, Brother, had discussed with us." Officials in the Northern Zone, he complained, "absolutely refused to accept Islamic people," preferring "only pure Khmer people." Santebal communications, available through the Documentation Center of Cambodia, show that Northern Zone leader Ke Pauk sent a message to Pol Pot two months later, in which he listed "enemies" such as "Islamic people." Deportations of Chams began again in 1976, and by early 1979, approximately 100,000 of the country's 1975 Cham population of 250,000 had been killed or worked to death.

The 10,000 ethnic Vietnamese remaining in the country were all hunted down and murdered in 1977 and 1978. Oral evidence suggests that the ethnic Thai and Lao minorities were also subjected to genocidal persecution.

Meanwhile the Khmer Buddhist monks were decimated in a nationwide CPK campaign to repress "reactionary religion," banned by DK's 1976 Constitution. A Center document stated in September 1975: "Monks have disappeared from 90 to 95 percent . . . Monasteries . . . are largely abandoned . . . the cultural base must be uprooted." Of a total of 2,680 monks in a sample of 8 of Cambodia's 3,000 monasteries in 1975, only 70 monks were found to have survived to 1979. If this toll could be extrapolated to the other monasteries, as few as 2,000 of the country's 70,000 Buddhist monks may have survived. That constitutes a prima facie case of genocide of a religious group.

Rebellion and Vietnamese Intervention

Most of the CPK's victims came from the majority Khmer population, and the major resistance it faced was in the East. From late 1976, accelerating the purges of regional administrations, the Santebal and Center army units subjected all five regions of the Eastern Zone to concerted waves of arrests and massacres of local CPK officials and soldiers. These reached a crescendo on May 10, 1978, when Phnom Penh Radio broadcast a call not only to "exterminate the 50 million Vietnamese" but also to "purify the masses of the people" of Cambodia. Khmer Rouge officers in the Eastern Zone mutinied two weeks later. Pol Pot's divisions were unable to crush them quickly. One and one-half million easterners were now branded as "Khmer bodies with Vietnamese minds" (*kbal yuon khluon khmaer*). Center forces massacred between 100,000 and 250,000 people in six months. Of the 1.7 million dead in less than four years of CPK rule, more than 500,000 had been deliberately murdered.

The Eastern Zone rebels, led by Heng Samrin and Chea Sim, fought back for several months before retreating across the Vietnamese border, where they requested aid and joined earlier Khmer Rouge rebels and defectors like Hun Sen. Hanoi was ready to intervene. Beginning in early 1977, Phnom Penh had mounted brutal cross-border attacks on Thailand, Laos, and especially Vietnam, slaughtering thousands of both Vietnamese and Khmer Krom there. On December 25, 1978, 150,000 Vietnamese troops launched a multipronged assault and took the Cambodian capital on January 7, 1979. They drove the CPK forces, including Pol Pot and most Center leaders, to the Thai border.

The dissident Khmer Rouge commanders established a new communist-led regime in Phnom Penh. Former regimental officer Hun Sen, who had defected to Vietnam in mid-1977, became Foreign Minister. Promoted to Prime Minister in 1985, he began a limited liberalization which accelerated in 1989. After UN-organized elections in 1993, Hun Sen became Second Prime Minister in a coalition with Sihanoukist party leader Prince Norodom Ranariddh. But Pol Pot's 10,000-strong rump Khmer Rouge army, revived during the 1980s by international assistance and enjoying sanctuary in Thailand, posed a continuing threat on the northwestern border.

The Khmer Rouge movement finally began to unravel in August 1996. First, in return for a "pardon," Ieng Sary defected to the Cambodian government with the military units under his command. Other Khmer Rouge leaders sought similar treatment from Phnom Penh. In June 1997, fearing further betrayal, Pol Pot murdered Son Sen. In the jungle of northern Cambodia, as the last military forces loyal to Pol Pot evacuated their headquarters, they drove their trucks over the bodies of Son Sen, his wife Yun Yat—the former DK minister of culture—and a dozen family members.

Mok turned in pursuit, arrested Pol Pot, and subjected him to a show trial in the jungle. But in March 1998, Pauk led a new mutiny against Mok and defected to the government. Pol Pot died the next month. Then, in December 1998, Nuon Chea and Khieu Samphan abandoned Mok and surrendered to the Cambodian government. They said they were now "sorry" for the crimes they had perpetrated. In 1999, the Cambodian army captured Mok and arrested the former Center security chief, Deuch. As of May 2004, they remained in jail awaiting trial.

SEE ALSO Cambodia; Ethnic Cleansing; Khmer Rouge Prisons and Mass Graves; Khmer Rouge Victim Numbers, Estimating; Pol Pot

BIBLIOGRAPHY
Central Intelligence Agency (1973). "Efforts of Khmer Insurgents to Exploit for Propaganda Purposes Damage Done by Airstrikes in Kandal Province," Intelligence Information Cable, May 2, l973, Directorate of Operations, declassified February 19, 1987.

Chandler, David P., and Ben Kiernan, eds. (1983). *Revolution and Its Aftermath in Kampuchea: Eight Essays.* New Haven, Conn.: Yale Council on Southeast Asia Studies.

Kiernan, Ben (1985). *How Pol Pot Came to Power: Colonialism, Nationalism, and Communism in Cambodia,* 1930-1975, 2nd edition. New Haven, Conn: Yale University Press, 2004.

Kiernan, Ben (1989). "The American Bombardment of Kampuchea, 1969–1973." *Vietnam Generation* 1:1 (Winter):4–41.

Kiernan, Ben, ed. (1993). *Genocide and Democracy in Cambodia: The Khmer Rouge, the United Nations, and the International Community.* New Haven, Conn.: Yale Council on Southeast Asia Studies.

Kiernan, Ben (1996). *The Pol Pot Regime: Race, Power and Genocide in Cambodia under the Khmer Rouge,* 1975–1979, 2nd edition. New Haven, Conn.: Yale University Press, 2002.

Peschoux, Christophe (1992). *Les "nouveaux" Khmers rouges: enquête, 1979–1990: reconstruction du mouvement et reconquête des villages.* Paris: Éditions L'Harmattan.

Vickery, Michael (1984). *Cambodia 1975-1982.* Boston: South End.

Ben Kiernan

Khmer Rouge Prisons and Mass Graves

"They say that dead men tell no tales," but in fact they do. Many stories have been told by investigators unearthing mass graves in the Balkans, Central America, and elsewhere. Information gathered from mass graves can help resolve disputes about the nature of communal or international conflict, and shed light on historical facts. With modern forensic science, mass graves yield evidence that can be used to prosecute war crimes and other violations of international humanitarian law. Mass graves may even help to relieve the anguish of families whose loved ones disappeared in a time of war. In Cambodia mass graves dating to Cambodia's 1975 to 1979 revolution have told all these tales, and more.

The Communist Party of Kampuchea, popularly known as the Khmer Rouge, led Cambodia's revolution. It was one of the most violent revolutions of the twentieth century. Demographers estimate that two million or more lives were lost in the four years that the Khmer Rouge ruled Cambodia, from a population of around seven million before the uprising. This scale of violence earned Cambodia a dubious title, the Killing Fields.

Between 1995 and 2003 researchers from the Documentation Center of Cambodia identified 19,471 mass graves at 348 sites located throughout the country. Investigators believe that these mass graves contained the remains of more than 1.1 million victims of execution. Virtually all these mass graves were located within 2 kilometers of what the Khmer Rouge euphemistically called security offices, but which might more accurately be labeled extermination centers. More than 185 such extermination centers have been discovered. At most of these sites witnesses have testified that the mass graves were created during the years the Khmer Rouge held power, and that the victims were detained in the so-called security offices prior to their execution. Although the Documentation Center's figures are only estimates, it is clear that whatever the actual numbers may be, they are large.

Senior Khmer Rouge officials have attempted to explain the existence of the mass graves by asserting that they were created by Vietnamese spies who had infiltrated the revolution. However, the uniform distribution of the mass graves throughout populated areas of the country casts doubt on this claim. More tellingly, senior Khmer Rouge officials are contradicted by many lower-level Khmer Rouge cadre who have testified that they carried out the executions at the mass grave sites on the orders of senior officials within the Khmer Rouge organization.

The vast number of mass graves in Cambodia, along with their uniform distribution, are in and of themselves legally probative facts. In order for acts such as murder to qualify as a crime against humanity, the acts must be mass and systematic. Some twenty thousand mass graves distributed relatively evenly across Cambodia clearly meet these criteria.

Forensic work at the Documentation Center of Cambodia has demonstrated that the individuals interred in the mass graves were not merely soldiers killed in combat nor victims of nonviolent causes of death such as disease or starvation. Many of the remains—bones of men, women, and children—exhibit evidence of trauma, including blunt force trauma, sharp force trauma, and gunshot wounds. This physical evidence confirms the testimony of former Khmer Rouge who have described in detail the methods they used to execute their victims.

The Cambodian People's Party (CPP) has ruled Cambodia since the 1979 overthrow of the Khmer Rouge regime. The CPP has systematically exploited the mass graves as a mechanism to aggregate political support ever since they came to power. Memorials created at many mass grave sites are the locations for annual national observances: the Day of Liberation on January 7th, marking the ouster of the Khmer Rouge regime, and the Day of Hatred on May 20th, intended to remind the population of their suffering under the Khmer Rouge, as well as the ruling party's claim that it delivered Cambodia's people from that suffering.

Many ordinary Cambodians have come to view the mass graves not as a focus of political activity, but rather as a locus for ancestor veneration. With some two million people missing and presumed dead after the Khmer Rouge regime, Cambodian traditions of ancestor veneration were severely challenged. Cambodians consequently adapted traditional ceremonies for paying respect to their dead, and commonly perform these rituals with the remains of anonymous victims at genocide memorials serving as a proxy for missing relatives.

In one variation of this practice, at Wat Skoun in Kampong Cham Province, a genocide memorial now contains only femurs and tibia exhumed from nearby mass graves. The crania were gradually consumed as religious officials permitted bereaved families to claim one exhumed skull for each missing relative. Those skulls were then used to represent lost loved ones, allowing families to perform ritual cremation and thereby possess symbolic remains with which they can conduct Buddhist ceremonies for their dead.

Although Cambodia's thousands of mass graves are thus seen by the country's ruling elite as rich in political symbolism, and by the country's ordinary citizens as rich in religious symbolism, the mass graves also convey historical facts crucial for any process of legal accountability. Whether or not the Killing Fields will be found to constitute genocide or crimes against humanity in a court of law depends in significant measure on how that court understands the origin and nature of Cambodia's mass graves.

SEE ALSO Anthropology, Cultural; Archaeology; Cambodia; Forensics; Khmer Rouge; Statistical Analysis

BIBLIOGRAPHY

Etcheson, Craig (2000). *"The Number"—Quantifying Crimes against Humanity in Cambodia.* Phnom Penh: Documentation Center of Cambodia.

Heuveline, Patrick (2001). "The Demographic Analysis of Mortality in Cambodia." In *Forced Migration and Mortality*, ed. Holly E. Reed and Charles B. Keely. Washington, D.C.: National Academy Press.

Pollanen, Michael S. (2002). "Forensic Survey of Three Memorial Sites Containing Human Skeletal Remains in the Kingdom of Cambodia." Mission Report to the Coalition for International Justice, Washington, D.C.

Sliwinski, Marek (1995). *Le Génocide Khmer Rouge: une analyse démographique.* Paris: Éditions L'Harmattan.

Craig Etcheson

Khmer Rouge Victim Numbers, Estimating

There are at least four possible approaches to determining the number of people killed in a given instance of genocide or other crimes against humanity. The best estimate of such fatalities is possible if the perpetrators have kept accurate records, but this seems rare. A second approach requires the investigation of mass graves, either by taking an actual count of exhumed bodies, or making an estimate based on the number and the sizes of the graves. A third approach is the demographic analysis of census data or other population data. A fourth approach involves interviewing survivors of the violence about fatalities in their families, followed, in most cases, by a statistical extrapolation from the results of the interviews. The advantages and disadvantages of each approach can be understood by reference to the case of Cambodia, where all of these methods have been applied.

One of the first attempts to gauge the magnitude of the Cambodian genocide was a project undertaken by the People's Republic of Kampuchea, which took control of the country when the Khmer Rouge fell from power. In a four-year project, the "Research Committee on Pol Pot's Genocidal Regime" conducted survivor interviews, along with mass grave exhumation and analysis, to come up with the figure of 3.316 million dead during the Khmer Rouge period (1975–1979). Later analysts have questioned the methodology used in making this estimate, arguing that its results were likely inflated by the double counting of some victims—for example, a victim reported as killed by a family member may have been counted again when the body was exhumed from a mass grave—along with an underestimate of net migration.

Another early effort at estimating the magnitude of the Khmer Rouge genocide was published in 1980 by the U.S. Central Intelligence Agency (CIA), which employed demographic analysis. The CIA began with Cambodia's 1962 census, then used subjective reports to estimate trends in fertility, mortality, and migration through 1979. The agency calculated that Cambodia's population had declined by somewhere between 1.2 and 1.8 million during the Khmer Rouge regime. Numerous assumptions underlying this analysis have been criticized, particularly its conclusion that the number of rural dwellers increased marginally between 1975 and 1979. Later analysts determined that there was significant excess mortality among the peasant population, and by implication, a relatively higher overall death toll.

More recent demographic analyses have taken advantage of post-genocide population data to refine the CIA's estimate. Based on data collected through a Cambodian administrative census conducted in 1980, Judith Bannister and Paige Johnson calculated a population loss between 1975 and 1979 of 1.8 million. In their 1993 report, they concluded that 1.05 million of these deaths were excess mortality. Patrick Heuveline employed birth cohort data derived from the 1993 electoral register to determine that the most likely figure for excess mortality during the Khmer Rouge regime was 2.2 million, also concluding that about half of these deaths, or 1.1 million, were from violent causes, primarily execution. All of the well-understood weaknesses of census and other population data are imported into such analyses, particularly with methodologically unsound censuses such as the 1980 count. This inherent propensity for error is further magnified by the assumptions made to compensate for missing data, such as fertility rates.

Interview and survey data have also been used to construct estimates of the death toll during the Khmer Rouge genocide. Ben Kiernan launched one of the first such efforts, interviewing some 500 subjects in 1979 and 1980, and extrapolating his findings to the national population for an estimate of 1.5 million deaths. He later refined his estimate to 1.671 million. Similarly, Steve Heder surveyed more than 1,000 Cambodian subjects, concluding that there were approximately 1.7 million deaths under the Khmer Rouge, with a death rate of 33 percent among urban Cambodians, 25 percent among rural Cambodians, and 50 percent among Sino-Khmer. A more systematic interview project was conducted by Marek Sliwinski between 1989 and 1991, with some 1,300 respondents. His data yielded an esti-

A Cambodian man observes skulls of Khmer Rouge victims on display at the Toul Sleng genocide museum, a former Khmer Rouge prison center in Phnom Penh. [AP/WIDE WORLD PHOTOS]

mate of 1.84 to 1.87 million excess deaths during the Khmer Rouge regime. It is notable that these three interview approaches yielded very similar results, ranging from 1.5 to about 1.9 million. Nonetheless, this method entails numerous potential sources of error. It is difficult to construct a representative and random sample of subjects. Moreover, this method also depends on estimates of pre- and post-genocide populations, which are typically unreliable. This method does, however, have the advantage that it can be carried out by a single investigator, relatively soon after the genocide has been halted.

A hard count of victim remains is yet another potential approach. Such a project has been underway at the Documentation Center of Cambodia since 1995. The effort involves mapping mass graves and estimating of the number of victims contained therein. As of May 2003, the Documentation Center had identified 19,471 mass graves, which were believed to contain the remains of an estimated 1.1 million victims of Khmer Rouge execution. Interestingly, this matches Heuveline's estimate of the number of deaths from violent causes, even though Heuveline reached his figure by a very different method. An advantage of the hard count

method is that it is primarily empirical, and does not rely on overall population estimates. Nonetheless, error can be introduced from several sources, such as the method used to estimate the contents of graves. The possibility of faulty witness testimony regarding the origin of mass graves is also a problem. Finally, the hard count method cannot necessarily distinguish between excess mortality due to execution and deaths due to other causes, such as starvation, disease, and exhaustion.

The use of perpetrator records to determine the magnitude of a genocide has rarely, if ever, been implemented, because of the problem of gaps in record-keeping. For example, at most of the 167 Khmer Rouge extermination sites identified in Cambodia, no contemporaneous records appear to have survived, if indeed they were maintained in the first place. Even at the most meticulously documented Khmer Rouge extermination center, Tuol Sleng Prison, gaps in the records have resulted in death toll estimates ranging from a low of 15,000 to a high of more than 20,000, quite a high degree of uncertainty. Obvious questions about the integrity of data produced by perpetrators also increases doubts about the reliability of this method.

The challenges apparent in all these varying approaches to estimating the magnitude of genocide or crimes against humanity suggest that analysts should approach this task with a certain degree of humility. Public records such as birth and death registers are typically among the first casualties during instances of extreme socio-political upheaval. This problem is often compounded by unreliable population data prior to and in the immediate aftermath of the crisis. Humans are notoriously unreliable as witnesses, and plumbing the depths of mass graves is a labor intensive, uncertain undertaking. The optimal approach may be to pursue all these methods—hard count, demographic analysis, and interview data—and, mindful of the pitfalls of each, triangulate the results into a range of estimates. In the Cambodian case, this range is from 1.7 million to 2.2 million, with the more recent and methodologically sophisticated efforts tending to produce results in the upper end of that range.

SEE ALSO Cambodia; Khmer Rouge; Khmer Rouge Prisons and Mass Graves; Pol Pot; Statistical Analysis

BIBLIOGRAPHY

Banister, Judith, and Paige Johnson (1993). "After the Nightmare: The Population of Cambodia." In *Genocide and Democracy in Cambodia: The Khmer Rouge, the United Nations and the International Community*, ed. Ben Kiernan. New Haven, Conn.: Yale University Southeast Asia Studies.

Central Intelligence Agency (1980). *Kampuchea: A Demographic Catastrophe*. Washington, D.C.: Author.

Documentation Center of Cambodia (May 2003). *Master Genocide Site Data*. Phnom Penh: Author.

Etcheson, Craig (2000). *'The Number': Quantifying Crimes Against Humanity in Cambodia*. Phnom Penh: Documentation Center of Cambodia.

Heuveline, Patrick (1998). "'Between One and Three Million': Towards the Demographic Reconstruction of a Decade of Cambodian History (1970–1979)." *Population Studies* 52(1):49–65.

Heuveline, Patrick (2001). "The Demographic Analysis of Mortality in Cambodia." In *Forced Migration and Mortality*, eds. Holly E. Reed and Charles B. Keely. Washington, D.C.: National Academy Press.

Kiernan, Ben (1996). *The Pol Pot Regime: Race, Power, and Genocide in Cambodia under the Khmer Rouge, 1975–1979*. New Haven, Conn.: Yale University Press.

People's Republic of Kampuchea, Research Committee on Pol Pot's Genocidal Regime (1983). *Report of the Research Committee on Pol Pot's Genocidal Regime*. Phnom Penh: People's Republic of Kampuchea.

Sliwinski, Marek (1995). *Le Génocide Khmer Rouge: un analyse démographique*. Paris: Editions L'Harmattan.

Craig Etcheson

King Leopold II and the Congo

The European colonization of Africa was one of the greatest and swiftest conquests in human history. In 1870 roughly 80 percent of Africa south of the Sahara Desert was governed by indigenous kings, chiefs, and other rulers. By 1910 nearly this entire huge expanse had become European colonies or land, like South Africa, controlled by white settlers. The bloodiest single episode in Africa's colonization took place in the center of the continent in the large territory, known as the Congo.

For centuries African slave dealers had raided parts of this area, selling their captives to American and European captains who sailed Africa's west coast, and to traders who took slaves to the Arab world from the continent's east coast. But heat, tropical diseases, and the huge rapids near the mouth of the Congo River on the Atlantic had long kept the Congo's interior a mystery to Europeans. From 1874 through 1877 the British explorer and journalist Henry Morton Stanley (1841–1904) crossed Africa from east to west. For much of the journey he floated down the river, mapping its course for the first time and noting the many tributaries that, it turned out, comprised a network of navigable waterways more than 7,000 miles long.

Although Stanley is best known as the man who found Livingstone, his trip across the Congo basin was the greater feat of exploration and had far more impact on history. As he headed back to England, Stanley was assiduously courted by King Leopold II of Belgium. Leopold (1835–1909) had ascended to the throne in 1865. A man of great charm, intelligence, ruthlessness, and greed, he was openly frustrated with inheriting the throne of such a small country, and in doing so at a time in history when European kings were rapidly losing power to elected parliaments. He had long wanted a colonial empire, and in Stanley he saw someone who could secure it for him. The Belgian cabinet of the day was not interested in colonies. But for Leopold this posed no problem; he would acquire his own.

In 1879 Stanley returned to the Congo as Leopold's agent. He built outposts and a road around the river's rapids and, using small steamboats, he traveled up and down the great river and its tributaries. Combining gift-giving with a show of military force, he persuaded hundreds of illiterate African chiefs, most of whom had little idea of the terms of the agreement to which they were ostensibly acceding, to sign away their land to the king.

Stanley made his way back to Europe with a sheaf of signed treaties in 1884. Meanwhile, Leopold had already begun the job of persuading first the United

Nsala, of the district of Wala, looking at the severed hand and foot of his five-year-old daughter, a victim of the Anglo-Belgian India Rubber Company (A.B.I.R.) militia. [ANTI-SLAVERY INTERNATIONAL]

States and then all the major nations of Europe to recognize his claim. A master of public relations who portrayed himself as a great philanthropist, the king orchestrated successful lobbying campaigns in one country after another. He made further progress toward realizing his objective at a diplomatic conference in Berlin in 1884 and 1885 that the major European powers attended. In 1885 he proclaimed the existence of the misnamed *État Indépendant du Congo,* or, as it was known in English, the Congo Free State, with himself the King-Sovereign. In later years he sometimes referred to himself as the Congo's proprietor. It was the world's only major colony owned by one man.

Equipped with repeating rifles, cannons, and machine guns and fighting against Africans with only spears or antiquated muskets, King Leopold's 19,000-man army (black conscripts under white officers) gradually took control of the vast territory. From the start

the regime was founded on forced labor. Hundreds of thousands of Africans were put to work as porters to carry the white men's goods, as cutters of the wood needed to fire steamboat boilers, and as laborers of all kinds. In the early years the main commodity Leopold sought was ivory. Joseph Conrad, who spent six months in the Congo in 1890, draws a memorable portrait of this rapacious trade in his novel *Heart of Darkness.*

The Rubber Boom

In the early 1890s, however, a larger source of wealth suddenly loomed. The invention of the inflatable bicycle tire, followed soon by that of the automobile tire, triggered an enormous boom in rubber. Throughout the world's tropics people rushed to establish rubber plantations. But new rubber trees often require fifteen years of growth before they can be tapped. During that window of time those who profited were the people

King Leopold II's rule over the Congo met fierce resistance. In the far south, for example, a chief named Mulume Niama led warriors of the Sanga people in a rebellion that killed one of the king's officers. State troops pursued them, trapping Mulume Niama and his soldiers in a large cave. They refused to surrender, and when troops finally entered the cave three months later, they found 178 bodies. Nzansu, a chief in the region near the great Congo River rapids, led rebels who killed a hated colonial official and pillaged several state posts, although they carefully spared the homes of nearby Swedish missionaries. Nzansu's men fought on sporadically for five years more, and no record of his fate exists.

In addition, Leopold's regime faced resistance from within his own conscript army, whose soldiers sometimes found a common cause with the rebel groups they were supposed to pursue. The largest mutiny involved three thousand troops and an equal number of auxiliaries and porters, and continued for three years. "The rebels displayed a courage worthy of a better cause," (Flament et al., 1952, p. 417) acknowledged the army's official history—which, remarkably, devoted fully one-quarter of its pages to the various campaigns against mutineers within the army's own ranks.

The king also faced enemies of another sort. To curry diplomatic favor, he allowed several hundred Protestant missionaries into the Congo. Most made no protest, but some were outraged at the brutal forced labor system. In articles in church magazines and in speeches throughout the United States and Europe on visits home, they described what they saw: Africans whipped to death, rivers full of corpses, and piles of severed hands—a detail that quickly seared itself on the world's imagination.

Army officers often demanded of their men a severed hand from each rebel killed in battle.

E. V. Sjöblom of Sweden was one of the first and most outspoken missionaries in the Congo. Alice Harris, a British Baptist, took photographs of the atrocities she witnessed. William Morrison, a white man, and William Sheppard, the first black missionary in the Congo, were Presbyterians from Virginia whose acts of witness so infuriated Congo colonial authorities that they put the men on trial for libel.

Leopold's most formidable enemy surfaced in Europe. A British shipping company had the monopoly on all cargo traffic between the Congo and Belgium, and every few weeks it sent to the port of Antwerp a young junior official, Edmund Dene Morel, to supervise the unloading of a ship arriving from Africa. Morel, in his mid-twenties at the time, noticed that when his company's ships arrived from the Congo, they were filled to the hatch with enormously valuable cargoes of rubber and ivory. When the ships turned around and steamed back to Africa, however, they carried no merchandise in exchange. Nothing was being sent to the Congo to pay for the goods flowing to Europe. Instead, the ships carried soldiers, and large quantities of firearms and ammunition. Standing on the dock, Morel realized that he had uncovered irrefutable proof that a forced labor system was in operation 4,000 miles away.

Morel soon quit his job and in short order turned himself into the greatest British investigative journalist of his time. For a dozen years, from 1901 to 1913, working sometimes fourteen to sixteen hours a day, he devoted his formidable energy and skill to putting the story of forced labor in King Leopold's Congo on the world's front pages. In Britain he founded the Congo Reform Association, and affiliated groups sprang up in the United States and other countries. He wrote three books on the Congo, several dozen pamphlets, and hundreds of newspaper articles, making much use of eyewitness testimony from the missionaries. He traveled throughout Britain speaking to large audiences and was adept at recruiting bishops, well-known writers, and other luminaries to join him on the lecture platform. More than one thousand mass meetings to protest slave labor in the Congo were held, mostly in Britain and the United States, but also in Europe and as far away as Australia and New Zealand.

After Morel orchestrated a protest resolution by the British Parliament, the government, in response, asked its representative in the Congo to investigate his charges. The British consul, an Irishman named Roger Casement, later famous as an Irish patriot, took the assignment seriously. Renting a missionary steamboat, he spent more than three months traveling in the interior. He produced an excoriating, detailed report, complete with sworn testimony from witnesses, which is in many ways a model for the reports produced by contemporary organizations like Amnesty International or Human Rights Watch.

who owned land where rubber grew wild. No one owned more land like this than King Leopold II, for equatorial rain forest, dotted with wild rubber vines, comprised half of his Congo state.

The king's colonial officials quickly set up a brutal but effective system for harvesting wild rubber. A detachment of soldiers would march into an African village and seize the women as hostages. To secure their wives' release, the men would have to disperse into the rain forest to collect the sap of wild rubber vines. As the vines near a village were often drained dry, the men would sometimes have to walk for days to find areas where they could gather their monthly quota of rubber. As rubber prices soared, so did the quotas. Discipline was harsh; reluctant military conscripts, disobedient porters, and villagers who failed to gather enough rubber all fell victim to the notorious *chicotte,* a whip made of sun-dried hippopotamus hide with razor-sharp edges. A hundred lashes of the chicotte, a not infrequent punishment, could be fatal. Army officers and colonial officials earned bonuses based on the amount of rubber collected in areas under their control. These were an incentive for ruthless, devastating plunder.

Many women hostages were raped and a significant number starved to death. Male rubber gatherers often died from exhaustion. And under such circumstances people tended to stop having children, so the birthrate plummeted as a result. With most able-bodied adults prisoners or forced laborers for several weeks out of each month, villages had few people who could plant and harvest food, or go hunting or fishing, and famine soon spread. Furthermore, huge, uncounted numbers of Congolese fled the forced labor regime, but the only refuge to which they could escape was the depths of the rain forest, where there was little food and no shelter; travelers would discover their bones years later. Tens, possibly hundreds, of thousands of Africans also died in two decades' worth of unsuccessful uprisings against the king's regime.

An even greater toll was taken by disease: various lung and intestinal diseases, tuberculosis, smallpox, and, above all, sleeping sickness. The great population movements caused by the colonial regime brought these illnesses into areas where people had not built up an immunity to them, and many would have died even under a government far less brutal than Leopold's. However, disease of any kind always takes a far greater toll on a traumatized, half-starving population, with many people already in flight as refugees.

In two ways the Congo's rubber boom had lasting impact beyond the territory itself. First, the system of exploitation established there became a model for colonial rule in other parts of central Africa. Many of the surrounding colonies also had rain forests rich in wild rubber—Portuguese-controlled northern Angola, the Cameroons under the Germans, and the French Congo, part of French Equatorial Africa, across the Congo River. Seeing what profits Leopold was reaping from forced labor, officials in these colonies soon adopted exactly the same system—including women hostages,

forced male labor, and the chicotte—with equally fatal consequences.

The events in King Leopold's Congo also rippled beyond its borders in a more positive way: They gave birth to the twentieth century's first great international human rights movement (see sidebar). The movement, in fact, eventually forced Leopold to relinquish his private ownership of the Congo to the Belgian state in 1908. By that point he had made a huge profit from the territory, conservatively estimated as the equivalent of more than $1.1 billion in early twenty-first century terms.

The Toll

In the newly christened Belgian Congo, however, the forced labor system did not immediately end. It was too lucrative, for the price of rubber was still high. Eventually, the price fell and wild rubber supplies began to run out, but by that time World War I had begun, and large numbers of Africans were forced to become porters, carrying supplies for Belgian military campaigns against Germany's African colonies. Forced labor remained a major part of the Congo's economy for many years after the war. Starting in the early 1920s, however, the system became considerably less draconian, mainly because colonial officials realized that otherwise they would soon have no labor force left.

"We run the risk of someday seeing our native population collapse and disappear," declared the permanent committee of the National Colonial Congress of Belgium in 1924, "so that we will find ourselves confronted with a kind of desert" (Hoornaert and Louwers, 1924, p. 101).

Between the time that Leopold started to assume control of the Congo (around 1880) and when the forced labor system became less severe (after 1920), what happened could not, by strict definition, be called genocide, for there was no deliberate attempt to wipe out all members of one particular ethnic group. But the slashing of the territory's population—through a combination of disease, famine, slave labor, suppression of rebellions, and diminished birthrate—indisputably occurred on a genocidal scale.

In estimating situations without the benefit of complete census data, demographers are more confident speaking of percentages than absolute numbers. Using a wide variety of local and church sources, Jan Vansina, professor emeritus of history and anthropology at the University of Wisconsin and the leading ethnographer of Congo basin peoples, calculates that the Congo's population dropped by some 50 percent during this period, an estimate with which other modern scholars concur. Interestingly, a longtime high colonial

[GEORGE WASHINGTON WILLIAMS]

Virtually no information about the true nature of King Leopold's Congo reached the outside world until the arrival there, in 1890, of an enterprising visitor named George Washington Williams. He was a veteran of the American Civil War, a historian, a Baptist minister, a lawyer, and the first black member of the Ohio state legislature. Wearing one of his many hats, that of a journalist, Williams expected to see the paradise of enlightened rule that Leopold had described to him in Brussels. Instead, he found what he called "the Siberia of the African Continent." Almost the only early visitor to interview Africans about their experience of the regime, he took extensive notes, and, a thousand miles up the Congo River, wrote one of the greatest documents in human rights literature, an open letter to King Leopold that is one of the important landmarks in human rights literature. Published in many American and European newspapers, it was the first comprehensive, detailed indictment of the regime and its slave labor system. Sadly, Williams, only forty-one years old, died of tuberculosis on his way home from Africa, but not before writing several additional denunciations of what he had seen in the Congo. In one of them, a letter to the U.S. Secretary of State, he used a phrase that was not commonly heard again until the Nuremberg trials more than fifty years later. Leopold II, Williams declared, was guilty of "crimes against humanity."

ADAM HOCHSCHILD

1920, pp. 657, 660, 662). Writing in the same year, R. P. Van Wing, a Belgian Jesuit missionary, estimated that the population of the Bakongo people, one of the territory's largest ethnic groups, had been reduced by two-thirds.

Obtaining more precise statistics is difficult, for in 1908 King Leopold ordered the archives of his Congo state burned. But numerous surviving records from the rubber-bearing land in the adjoining French Congo, which closely followed the model of the Leopoldian forced labor system, also suggest a population loss there of around 50 percent. If the estimates from varied sources of a 50 percent toll in King Leopold's Congo are correct, how many people does this mean? In 1924 the first territory-wide census, when adjusted for undercounting, placed the number of colony inhabitants at some ten million. If that figure is accurate and it represents 50 percent of what the population had been in 1880, this would suggest a loss of 10 million people.

Some writers, almost entirely in Belgium, claim that such estimates are exaggerated. But other scholars use even higher numbers. Although neither figure is well-documented, Hannah Arendt's seminal *The Origins of Totalitarianism* cites an estimated minimum population loss of 11.5 million, and a Congolese historian writing in 1998, Isidore Ndaywel è Nziem, estimates the loss at roughly 13 million. Humankind will never know even the approximate toll with any certainty, but beyond any doubt what happened in the Congo was one of the great catastrophes of modern times.

SEE ALSO Slavery, Historical

BIBLIOGRAPHY

Ascherson, Neal (1963). *The King Incorporated: Leopold II in the Age of Trusts*. London: George Allen & Unwin.

Benedetto, Robert, ed. (1996). *Presbyterian Reformers in Central Africa: A Documentary Account of the American Presbyterian Congo Mission and the Human Rights Struggle in the Congo, 1890–1918*. Leiden, Netherlands: E.J. Brill.

Bierman, John (1990). *Dark Safari: The Life behind the Legend of Henry Morton Stanley*. New York: Alfred A. Knopf.

Bulletin Officiel du Congo Belge (1920). 13(May 15).

Flament, F., et al. (1952). *La Force publique de sa naissance à 1914: Participation des militaires à l'histoire des premières années du Congo*. Brussels: Institut Royal Colonial Belge.

Franklin, John Hope (1985). *George Washington Williams: A Biography*. Chicago: University of Chicago Press.

Hochschild, Adam (1998). *King Leopold's Ghost: A Story of Greed, Terror and Heroism in Colonial Africa*. Boston: Houghton Mifflin.

official, Major Charles C. Liebrechts, made the same estimate in 1920. Shocked by recent local census statistics that showed less than one child per woman, the official *Commission Institueé pour la Protection des Indigènes* made a similar reckoning in 1919. Its report that year to the Belgian king mostly focused on disease, but stressed that forced labor for rubber and other products "subjects the natives to conditions of life which are an obstacle to their increase" and warned that this situation, plus "a lack of concern about devastating plagues ancient and modern, an absolute ignorance of people's normal lives [and] a license and immorality detrimental to the development of the race," had reached "the point of threatening even the existence of certain Congolese peoples" and could completely depopulate the entire region (Bulletin Officiel,

Hoornaert, André and O. Louwers (1924). *La question sociale au Congo: Rapport au comité du congrès colonial national*. Brussels: Goemaere.

Marchal, Jules (1996). *E. D. Morel contre Léopold II: L'histoire du Congo 1900–1910*. 2 volumes. Paris: Editions L'Harmattan.

Marchal, Jules (1996). *L'état libre du Congo: Paradis perdu. L'histoire du Congo 1876–1900*. 2 volumes. Borgloon, Belgium: Editions Paula Bellings.

Morel, E. D. (1904). *King Leopold's Rule in Africa*. London: Heinemann.

Morel, E. D. (1919). *Red Rubber: The Story of the Rubber Slave Trade Which Flourished on the Congo for Twenty Years, 1890–1910. New and revised edition*. Manchester, U.K.: National Labour Press.

Morel, E. D. (1968). *Morel's History of the Congo Reform Movement*. Ed. William Roger Louis and Jean Stengers. Oxford, U.K.: Clarendon Press.

Pakenham, Thomas (1991). *The Scramble for Africa: The White Man's Conquest of the Dark Continent from 1876 to 1912*. New York: Random House.

Shaloff, Stanley (1970). *Reform in Leopold's Congo*. Richmond, Va.: John Knox Press.

Vangroenweghe, Daniel (1986). *Du sang sur les lianes*. Brussels: Didier Hatier.

Adam Hochschild

Kosovo

Kosovo was ineluctably tied to Serbia at the Battle of Kosovo Polje in 1389, wherein the victorious Muslim Turks left the dead for blackbirds to scavenge, according to Serbian folklore. Kosovo was then etched in Serbian ethno-religious consciousness as a place of Serbian torment and sacrifice, ushering in five hundred years of Turkish domination. The Battle of Kosovo marked the end of the Serbian empire. The Turks conquered Albania by 1468, but although most Albanians converted to Islam, they maintained their separate ethnic identity.

Ottoman rule was ending by 1878. Serbia, Montenegro, Greece, and Bulgaria amassed troops and finally succeeded in driving out the Ottoman forces in the Balkan Wars (1912–1913). The geographical extent of Albania was reduced at the behest of France and Russia, leaving more than half of the total Albanian population outside the borders of the diminished state, and placing the area of Kosovo within Serbia. The Serbian victors massacred entire Albanian villages, looting and burning anything that remained. European press reports estimated that Serbs killed 25,000 Albanians.

From the end of the Balkan Wars to World War II, Albanians lived under Serb domination. Their language was suppressed, their land confiscated, and their

mosques were turned into stables, all part of an overt Serb policy designed to pressure Muslim Albanians to leave Kosovo. The cycle of revanchism (revenge-based conflict) continued when a part of Kosovo was united with Albania by Italian fascists during World War II and Albanian Nazi collaborators expelled an estimated forty thousand Serbs.

A postwar Constitution, adopted in 1946, defined Yugoslavia as a federal state of six sovereign republics. Kosovo was granted autonomy, allowing it to have representatives in the federal legislature yet keeping its internal affairs under Serbian control. In 1948, Yugoslavia broke away from Stalin's Russia, a move that pitted the Albanian Kosovars against the country of Albania, which was staunchly pro-Russian. Yugoslav and Albanian border guards clashed along the Albanian border, and the Yugoslav secret police intensified its persecution of ethnic Albanians in Kosovo. As Serbs persecuted Albanian-Kosovars, the Kosovars harassed Serbs in turn.

Demographic studies from 1979 show that Albanian Kosovars had the highest population growth rate in Europe, especially in rural areas. Increasing numbers of young ethnic Albanians were under the age of 25 and unemployed, fueling dissent. When the President of Yugoslavia, Croat-born Marshall Tito, allowed an Albanian-language university to be established in Kosovo, it became the center of Albanian national identity. Following Tito's death in 1980, students demonstrated for better living conditions in 1981, inspiring construction and factory workers to take to the streets in protest throughout Kosovo.

Retribution was immediate and harsh. The Yugoslav army was sent to Kosovo, killing Albanians and arresting people for "verbal crimes," for which substantial prison sentences were imposed. The press, local governments, and schools were purged of the Albanians who held such jobs (most such employees were Serbs). At the same time, approximately 30,000 Serbs left Kosovo (according to Yugoslav government estimates), ostensibly because of Albanian retaliation. Critics, however, have suggested that the Serbs left for economic reasons. The Yugoslav government economic policy toward Kosovo was one of resource extraction. Wealth, in the form of minerals, was siphoned out of Kosovo for the benefit of the other republics, with very little ever coming back to the impoverished area.

In the mid-1980s Serb-Kosovars complained to the Yugoslav government that the escalating ethnic Albanian birthrate constituted a willful plot against the Serbs. Ethnic Albanian women stopped going to government-run hospitals to have babies, fearing that Serb doctors would kill their babies to reduce the birthrate. In 1987,

Djakovica, Kosovo, 1999. Caskets and portraits of the dead. Both Serbs and Albanians had for centuries regarded Kosovo as their own historical space. The predictable result was that the two sides embarked on cycles of violent attacks, followed by cycles of violent reprisals. Here, Kosovar Albanians mourn friends and loved ones killed by Serb forces. [TEUN VOETEN]

Slobodan Milosevic attended a meeting in Kosovo during which a raucous crowd of Serbs tried to push their way in. Milosevic commanded the police to let "his" Serbs through, establishing himself as the savior of Serbs outside the borders of Serbia. Critics allege that the event was arranged in advance. After Milosevic was elected President of Serbia in 1990, Albanian police officers in Kosovo were suspended from their jobs and replaced with 2,500 Serb policemen imported from Belgrade.

In the spring of 1990, thousands of Albanian schoolchildren became sick and were hospitalized, and it was rumored that Serbs had poisoned them. When Albanian parents attacked Serb property in response, Milosevic immediately transferred another 25,000 police to the area. Serb police were allowed to keep Albanians in jail for three days without charges, and to imprison anyone for up to two months if they had been charged with insulting the "patriotic feelings" of Serbs. The conflict in Kosovo and the Serb annexation of the province in 1987 led to concerns in the other republics that Serbia was intending to transform Yugoslavia into "Greater Serbia." However, the pattern of revanchism

in response to the mounting human rights abuses was broken when Albanians turned to passive resistance, following the model of non-violence espoused by Mahatma Gandhi.

The Serb war against Bosnia from 1992 to 1995 worsened the situation for Albanians in Kosovo. This time, Albanians suffered from the anti-Muslim fervor of Serbs and the hardships resulting from the economic sanctions imposed by the United Nations in response to the war. The Bosnian war ended with the negotiation of the Dayton Accords in 1995, but Kosovo was left out of the discussion. Disappointed Kosovars watched Western diplomats congratulate Milosevic on his peacemaking efforts. Albanian Kosovars continued their practice of passive resistance until 1997, when the country of Albania collapsed into chaos and Kosovo was flooded with weapons from across the border. The ethnic majority, Albanian Kosovars, now had access to weapons, a serious concern for the Serbs. Suspected members of the newly formed Kosovo Liberation Army were arrested and charged with "hostile association," a charge that was never denied.

Some observers compared the bombing of Kosovo with the earlier Russian onslaught against Grozny, depicted here. The latter was an exercise in ethnic cleansing, far from any attempt to come to the aid of a brutalized people. [TEUN VOETEN]

A Serb policeman was murdered in 1998, prompting a police attack on a village in which one hundred Albanians were killed. Further massacres of Albanians continued to fuel the mobilization of the Kosovo Liberation Army. As Muslim refugees streamed into Albania, Serbs lined the borders with landmines. An estimated 270,000 Albanians fled to the hills of Kosovo. In the fall of 1998, NATO authorized air strikes against Serb military targets and Milosevic agreed to withdraw his troops. By the winter of 1998, however, the United States was proclaiming that Serbs were committing "crimes against humanity" in Kosovo.

Negotiations to offset the looming humanitarian disaster and end the alleged Serb crimes were fashioned in Rambouillet, France, in early 1999. The peace plan proposed by the United Nations was rejected by both Serbs and Albanian Kosovars. The political blueprint called for NATO troops to be placed in Kosovo to oversee peace and protect the combatants from each other, but Serbia rejected the presence of foreign troops on its soil. A United Nations force, similar to the peacekeepers in Bosnia might have been accepted, but the West insisted on a NATO force. The ostensible reason for this insistence was that the West wanted to

avoid a replay situation that occurred in Bosnia. There, the peacekeepers were forced to stand by idly and watch Bosnian women and children be killed. For their part, the Kosovo Liberation Army (KLA) refused to comply with the Rambouillet mandate that they disarm. There had been too many instances in Bosnia, they argued, where Muslims disarmed and put themselves under the protection of the United Nations, only to be murdered by Serbs. This had occurred in Srebenica in 1995, when approximately seven thousand boys and old men were murdered by Serbs while in a United Nations designated safe-haven.

With the negotiations stalled, Serbia sent 40,000 troops to the border of Kosovo, exploiting the break in diplomacy to further what appeared to be preparations for an all-out occupation of Kosovo. Fearing a blood bath, knowing the far superior military strength of the Serb army, and with knowledge of the atrocities committed in Bosnia, the Albanians agreed to the stipulations of the Rambouillet treaty. Hundreds of thousands of ethnic Albanians were hiding in the winter hills, thousands more were displaced, and over 2,000 civilians had been killed. The KLA signed the treaty. NATO threatened Serbia with bombing if it refused to sign, but

---

NATO had made such threats before, and the powers in Belgrade had no reason to believe action would be taken against them this time. Despite the NATO rhetoric, they refused.

NATO began bombing strategic targets in Kosovo on March 24, 1999, in response to Serbia's "Operation Horseshoe." Fanning out into the region in a pattern that took on the shape of a horseshoe, Serb soldiers went village-to-village, killing and burning, forcing those who could to run for their lives. To many, it looked as if the NATO bombings caused the extraordinary events that followed. Within three days of the bombing, 25,000 Albanian Kosovars were fleeing in terror. Within weeks 800,000 were fleeing. Serbian border guards took their identification papers and money, destroying any proof they ever existed.

Televised satellite technology yielded pictures of mass graves. Serbs then moved the remains and burned their victims, leaving the victims' families with no way of knowing what had happened to their missing relatives. A common means of disposal was to throw bodies into a well or water supply, rendering the water undrinkable. Cultural monuments and Islamic religious sites were destroyed. Reports estimated that up to 20,000 rapes and sexual assaults were committed against Albanian women. Albanian residents in Mitrovica were expelled, their houses and mosques burned, and women were sexually assaulted during attacks beginning on March 25, 1999. Albanians in other areas, most notably Pristine, were also expelled or killed, and women here, too, were sexually assaulted.

By May 20, 1999, one-third of the Albanian population had been expelled from Kosovo. The refugee crisis overwhelmed Macedonia and Albania, threatening to undermine the weak economies of both countries and flood the rest of Europe with refugees and asylum seekers from Kosovo. The International Criminal Tribunal for the Former Yugoslavia, convened to prosecute war crimes in Bosnia, indicted Milosevic for crimes against humanity in Kosovo on May 27, 1999, and NATO escalated its air strikes. With questionable legality, NATO bombed the capital of Serbia, Belgrade, accidentally including in its targets a maternity hospital and the Chinese embassy. On June 2, 1999, Milosevic capitulated to the terms of NATO, and within ten days, Serb troops began pulling out of Kosovo. Between mid-June, when the NATO troops were deployed, and mid-August, 1999, more than 755,000 Kosovars returned to Kosovo.

The situation was reversed for the Serbs. There were an estimated 20,000 Serbs in Pristina, Kosovo, before the NATO bombing. By mid-August, the United Nations High Commission of Refugees reported only 2,000 Serbs left in the capital city, and increasingly violent attacks on the Serb population by Albanian Kosovars were on the rise. Albanian Kosovars used the same tactics that Serbs had used against them, forcing Serbs to sign over their property and possessions and leave. Nearly 200,000 Serb refugees from Kosovo fled into Serbia and Montenegro as the Albanian-Kosovars returned. Again, the departure was abrupt and fearful. The United Nations and NATO asserted their presence in the area, providing the appearance of protection for the now targeted Serbs. Nonetheless, tensions between ethnic Serbs and Albanian erupted into violent conflict again in Kosovo in March 2004. Albanian violence against Serbs was especially pronounced in areas where the International Criminal Tribunal for the Former Yugoslavia had documented atrocities committed against Albanians, especially around the areas of Mitrovica and Pristina, Kosovo. The violence in March 2004 left nineteen dead. Serbian Orthodox monasteries were demolished, and Serb houses and property were burned and destroyed. Intense debate regarding the partition of Kosovo from Serbia and Serbs from Albanian Kosovars was given new immediacy, but all sides were entrenched in their oppositional positions.

The trial of Milosevic by the International Criminal Tribunal for the Former Yugoslavia commenced on October 29, 2001, in which he was charged with genocide, crimes against humanity, murder, and persecution (including command responsibility for the sexual assaults on Kosovo Albanian women and the wanton destruction of religious sites) in Kosovo. The prosecution rested its case in February 2004, with the United Nations allowing the defense, judgment, and appeals processes to extend through 2010. The legacy of ethnic cleansing touched everyone throughout the former Yugoslavia. Thousands of Roma (Gypsy) who lived in Kosovo and the surrounding areas remained homeless and have been overlooked by the judicial process. For the Kosovars—both Albanian and Serb—history and experience have provided no solid template for establishing peace.

SEE ALSO Ethnic Cleansing; International Criminal Tribunal for the Former Yugoslavia; Milosevic, Slobodan; Nationalism; Peacekeeping; Prevention; Rape; Reconciliation; Safe Zones

BIBLIOGRAPHY

Anzulovic, Branimir (1999). *Heavenly Serbia.* New York: New York University Press.

International Criminal Tribunal for the former Yugoslavia. "Kosovo Indictment. Slobodan Milosevic: IT-02-54." Available from http://www.un.org/icty/glance/index.htm.

Judah, Tim (1997). *The Serbs.* New Haven, Conn.: Yale University Press.

Malcolm, Noel (1998). *Kosovo: A Short History*. New York: New York University Press.

Vickers, Miranda (1998). *Between Serb and Albanian: A History of Kosovo*. New York: Columbia University Press.

Vucinich, Wayne S., and T. Emmert (1991). *Kosovo: Legacy of a Medieval Battle*. Minneapolis: University of Minnesota Press.

Young, Kathleen (2001). "Kosovo." In *Europe: Struggles to Survive and Thrive*, ed. Jean S. Forward. Westport, Conn.: Greenwood Press.

Kathleen Z. Young

Kristallnacht

According to a 1938 report published by the organization called Reíchsueriretung der Juden, Kristallnacht, the action launched against the Jews within the Reich (then consisting of Germany and Austria), was a historical turning point. "Crystal Night" refers to the tons of shattered window glass after Jewish-owned businesses and homes were destroyed. A document issued by Joachim von Ribbentrop's Foreign Ministry on January 25, 1939 to all German diplomatic and consular services, provided the justification for the Kristallnacht action. Under the title, "The Jewish Question, a Factor in Our Foreign Policy," it stated

> It is not by chance that 1938, the year of our destiny, saw the realization of our plan for Greater Germany as well as a major step towards the solution of the Jewish problem. . . . This disease in the body of our people had to be eradicated first before the Great German Reich could assemble its forces to overcome the will of the world.

Months earlier, in November 1937, Adolf Hitler had told his followers that "the determination to secure the safety and the expansion of the racial community implied such risks" as the use of force and of war if necessary. Since Hitler's rise to power in January 1933, he had successfully crushed his opponents at home, excluded and isolated the Jews of Germany and Austria, rearmed and proceeded with the military occupation of the Rhineland despite the provisions of the Versailles Treaty of 1919.

The unwillingness of Germany's neighbors (notably France and the United Kingdom), to challenge Hitler all but guaranteed his success. Hitler also supported Franco's military putsch against the Spanish Republic, and annexed neighboring Austria. These actions created a flood of Jewish refugees seeking safety in other European nations and in the United States. In July 1938, U.S. President Franklin Delano Roosevelt convened an international summit to urge the delegates from thirty-two attending nations to open their borders to the refu-

gees. This meeting, known as the Evian Conference, failed dismally. Instead, Polish and Hungarian observers requested that they, too, be relieved of their Jews.

When France and Britain signed the Munich Agreements in September 1938 and abandoned their Czech ally to Hitler's advance, they gave free rein to Hitler's territorial demands. With this, the situation in Europe passed what Berthold Brecht called Hitler's "resistable ascent." Hitler continued in his aggressive policies, including his treatment of the Jews. He was encouraged further when France's Premier Edouard Daladier, representing the Evian Intergovernment Committee, declared in a memorandum to the Ribbentrop ministry that "none of the States (members of the Committee) would dispute the absolute right of the German government to take with regard to certain of its citizens such measures as are within its own sovereign powers."

Such was the context in which the Jews were terrorized into emigrating. In October 1938 they were driven out of the recently annexed Sudetenland and on the nights of October 29 approximately 17,000 Jews were expelled from Germany to the Polish border. Berlin did this in anticipation of Warsaw's decision to revoke Polish passports if their bearers had lived abroad for more than five years. On November 3, 1938, Herschel Grynszpân, a young Polish Jewish refugee living in hiding at his uncle's home in Paris, received a postcard from his sister informing him that his family, settled in Hanover since 1911, had been expelled and were now confined, penniless, in the Polish border village of Zbazsyn. The next day the Yiddish newspaper, *Pariser Haint,* published a detailed account of the inhumane conditions of this act of massive deportation.

After forty-eight hours of feverish agitation, Grynszpân came to a decision. On Monday morning, November 7, 1938, he purchased a gun and went to the German Embassy in Paris. He gained entry by saying he had to deliver an important document, but once inside he fired five shots at the Third Secretary, Ernst vom Rath, the only diplomat then present. Badly hurt, vom Rath was taken to a neighboring clinic. The embassy porters handed Grynszpân over to the French police. He offered no resistance. Hitler heard of the attempt against vom Rath that same evening, and dispatched his personal physician to the embassy official's bedside. A few days later, on November 9, Hitler learned that vom Rath had died of his wounds. In response, he gave his chief propagandist, Joseph Goebbels, permission to launch a pogrom against the Jews of the Third Reich.

Grynszpân's attempt against the life of a representative of the Third Reich was by no means the first one.

On the "Night of Broken Glass" in November 1938, Nazi-orchestrated riots erupted in Germany and Austria. Angry mobs vandalized and ransacked some 7,500 Jewish businesses and an incalculable number of homes. [BETTMANN/CORBIS]

In February 1936, a young Jewish student named David Frankfurter had shot down the leader of Swiss Nazis, Wilhelm Gustloff, in Davos, Switzerland. At the time Hitler had vetoed reprisals against Jews, for fear of international reactions that might compromise his military plan (the reoccupation of the Rhineland) or disqualify Berlin as the host site for the Olympic games to be held in July of that year. By then, however, Hitler was far more confident. His goal now was to make Germany *Judenrein* ("Free of Jews").

Although the pogrom that Goebbels set in motion on the night of November 9, 1938 was later hailed as a "spontaneous wave of righteous indignation," the *Sturm Abteilung* (SA, "storm trooper unit") and the *Schutzstaffel* (SS, "protective corps") were actually in charge of the violent action. Their mission was explicit: preserve Aryan property, isolate the main Jewish institutions and seize their archives before they were de-

stroyed, and arrest approximately 30,000 Jewish men (later to be herded into concentration camps); such were the duties of the SA and the SS, according to the instructions issued by Goebbels, Reinhard Heydrich, Obergruppenfuehrer of the SS, and the chief of the Gestapo in Berlin.

The reports of Nazi leaders, diplomats, journalists stationed in the Reich, and victims who succeeded in emigrating before October 1941 give only approximate results of the Kristallnacht pogrom: dozens of suicides—among them a young couple in Stuttgart and their two little boys (one two-year-old and another who was only a few months old). A report from the Chief Judge of the Nazi Party's Supreme Court mentioned 91 dead and 36 injured, and went on to condemn those Nazi participants who raped Jews during Kristallnacht—for "defiling the race." No less than 267 synagogues and places of worship as well as 7,500 shops not yet "Aryanized" (taken over from Jewish owners) and hundreds of dwellings were looted and smashed.

In the evening of November 10, Goebbels officially called a halt to the pogrom. Reichsmarschall Hermann Wilhelm Göring, who was in charge of making decisions for the whole Reich, now enacted new laws intended, he claimed, "to harmonize the solution of the Jewish problem to its logical outcome." He chaired a meeting November 12, 1938 at the Air Ministry for senior ministers, the chiefs of police and security, and other influential Nazis and announced his new policies. Jews were now required to pay a million mark fine; their property (already registered according to a 1938 law) was to be confiscated, and their assets exchanged for government bonds. Compensation for property losses paid to them by insurance companies was also confiscated by the State.

Beginning on January 1, 1939, Jews were barred from conducting business or visiting public places except those designated for them. A Reich Central Office for Jewish Emigration was created in Germany modeled on one that Adolf Eichmann had established in Austria. Jewish associations were ordered to disband and their property was transferred to the Central Organization of German Jews, which was now under the authority of the Reichssicherheitshauptamt (RSHA; Nazi Department of Security). The issue of forcing Jews to wear special identifying insignia and herding them into ghettos was discussed, but the idea was shelved for the moment, because Göring believed that ghettoization would be achieved naturally as the Jews grew increasingly destitute.

Despite the international indignation aroused by the scope and the violence of Kristallnacht, democratic countries were not inclined to open their borders to the victims. On November 11, 1938, Switzerland signed an agreement with Germany, promising to prohibit German Jews from entering Swiss territory. The countries of Scandinavia suggested settling the Jews outside Europe. British Prime Minister Neville Chamberlain agreed under pressure to allow 500 Jewish refugees per week into Britain, but he also blocked their entry into Palestine.

The French Premier, Daladier, was on delicate ground, because he had reached an accommodation with Germany and was set to sign a treaty of friendship and cooperation on December 6, of 1938. Complaining that France had already admitted many Jews (at that time, approximately 30,000), he offered to take in a few more as long as doing so would not jeopardize France's rapprochement with Germany. In front of more than 200 journalists, U.S. President Roosevelt recalled his ambassador to Germany "for consultation." This, however, was a hollow gesture, for Roosevelt had no intention of taking retaliatory measures against Hitler. American Jewish organizations suggested that he authorize an increase in the immigration quotas for European Jews—even if only temporarily—but he declined to do so.

A few days later, on November 23, the *New York Times* published the translation of an article that had appeared in *Das Schwarze Korps,* an SS publication known for its extreme anti-Jewish policy: "At this stage of development we must therefore face the hard necessity of exterminating the Jewish underworld in the same manner in which in this state of order we exterminate criminals generally: by fire and by the sword."

Grynszpân, whose act of anger and grief against the German embassy in France provided the excuse for Kristallnacht, disappeared from history after being handed over by Vichy government to the Germans. The pogrom that ensued, however, was indeed a turning point in the official Nazi policy on Jews. Unfortunately, the Third Reich's threat to exterminate all Jews, openly declared by the SS on November 23, 1938, was ignored by France, England, and the United States, as was Hitler's own threat, two months later, to exterminate all the Jews of Europe.

SEE ALSO Goebbels, Joseph; Göring, Hermann; Heydrich, Reinhard; Himmler, Heinrich; Hitler, Adolf; Holocaust

BIBLIOGRAPHY

Barkai, A. (1989). *From Boycott to Annihilation: The Economic Struggle of German Jews 1933–1945.* Hanover, N.H.: Brandeis University Press.

Bauer, Yehuda (1994). *Jews for Sale? Nazi-Jewish Negotiations 1933–1945.* New Haven, Conn.: Yale University Press.

Ben Elissar, E. (1969). *La Diplomatie du IIIè Reich et les Juifs 1933–1939.* Paris: Julliard.

Kaplan, M. A. (1998). *Between Dignity and Despair: Jewish Life in Nazi Germany.* New York: Oxford University Press.

Morse, A. D. (1968). *While Six Million Died: A Chronicle of American Apathy.* New York: Longman.

Roizen, R. (1986). "Herschel Grynszpân: The Fate of a Forgotten Assassin." *Holocaust and Genocide Studies* 1(2):217–228.

Thalmann, Rita, and Emmanuel Feinermann (1974). *Crystal Night, 9–10 November 1938.* New York: Coward, McCann & Gheogegan.

Rita Thalmann

Kulaks

Kulak, in Russian, means a "fist." When used for rich peasants, it alludes to their alleged fist-like hold on their poorer brethren. Vladimir Lenin saw the kulak as a "village bourgeoisie" that would be crushed by a socialist revolution. This was achieved during Joseph Stalin's "revolution from the top" that mandated collectivization and dekulakization.

When the Bolsheviks assumed power, peasants made up 85 percent of Russia's population. Peasants were tied to village communes that practiced the joint ownership of land with periodical redistribution for individual exploitation. The 1906 Stolypin reforms encouraged peasants to establish separate farms, but eleven years later communes were still the norm in Russia. Only in Ukraine and other non-Russian regions did individual farming prevail. Most peasants remained poor, but many made a decent living and some even became wealthy. The kulaks were rich enough to hire farm help and lease out agricultural machinery. Less than a tenth of the peasant population belonged to this group. There were significantly more middle peasants whose holdings made them economically self-sufficient. More numerous than the other two groups combined were the poor peasants. They could not support their families with the earnings from their meager farms, and often they had to supplement their income with outside employment.

During the Russian civil war, the reconquest of break-away non-Russian republics, and the struggle with interventionist forces, kulaks became a target for the Bolshevik policy of "war communism" or the requisitioning of foodstuffs for and by the armies and urban population. Meanwhile, incited by socialist agitators, poor peasants began to seize land and farm implements from their richer neighbors. Some kulaks were killed, others fled, and still others lost some or all of their holdings. Their numbers dwindled to less than half of what they had been before the revolution. The poor peasants improved their situation by appropriating land and other property from large landowners. Eventually, the middle peasants outnumbered the other two groups combined. Their numbers and economic importance assured them a certain tolerance on the part of the Soviet state. However, the position of the middle peasant remained ambiguous: While not an enemy like the kulak, he or she was also not a fellow proletarian like the poor peasant. The middle peasant could only be an "ally" and a temporary one at that.

The New Economic Policy adopted in 1921 put socialized agriculture on hold and encouraged private farming. In 1925 the leading spokesman for the right, Nikolai Bukharin, urged the Russian Communist Party to adopt a pro-peasant policy with an "enrich yourselves" slogan. The kulaks won a temporary reprieve, but in ideological terms they remained class enemies.

The revival of Soviet agriculture after the famine of 1921 through 1923 benefited the peasants although it did little for Stalin's ambitions. Peasants now consumed more of what they grew and this left little for export, the main source of capital for industrialization. Stalin intended to reorganize all of agriculture into large estates, the so-called state farms (sovkhozy) and collective farms (kolkhozy). All peasants would eventually be included in these two systems, particularly the second one. Collectivization would achieve the regime's ideological, economic, political, and social goals: socialized agriculture, direct access to cereals for export, the elimination of the village bourgeoisie, and Party control over the peasantry. Collectivization meant the destruction of the kulaks as a class and thus the elimination of peasant elites that could oppose the regime.

The difficulties in grain procurement experienced in 1927 prompted the government to return to a policy of requisitions. Facing exorbitant taxes and other repressive measures, many well-off farmers sold inventory and livestock, liquidated their land, and moved to industrial centers. This was called "self-dekulakization." Stalin announced an all-out, state-enforced policy of dekulakization on December 27, 1929. The following month the Party and state machinery was set in motion, under the watchful eyes of Viacheslav Molotov and other Party leaders, to prepare plans for full-scale dekulakization and deportation. Quotas were worked out for each region, and it was stipulated that the number of kulak households was not to exceed 3 to 5 percent in grain-producing areas and 2 to 3 percent in non-grain-producing areas. In regions selected for wholesale collectivization, kulak property was to be confiscated and its owners driven out.

Kulaks were divided into three categories. The OGPU (political police) drew up lists of the most dangerous counterrevolutionary activists for inclusion in the first category. The heads of these households were to be arrested and executed or sent to a concentration camp, and the rest of the family would be deported outside the region. The second category, picked by local authorities, included large-scale exploiters and the active opponents of collectivization. These enemies of the state would also be exiled outside the region, but together with their families. The least anti-Soviet kulaks formed the third category; they would be resettled in their own region, but given land of inferior quality and not allowed to join the collective farms.

Two waves of dekulakization—the first during the winter and spring of 1930, and the second a year later—netted about 1,800,000 individuals; over the course of the next two years another 400,000 were added. Two-thirds of these kulaks were deported to

Northern Russia, Siberia, the Urals, and Kazakhstan; the rest were resettled in their own regions. Between 30 and 40 percent were children, and there were also significant numbers of the elderly. Each family of deportees (on average, five members) was allowed to take a thousand pounds of property, including a two-month supply of food, and 500 rubles. In reality most families lacked adequate food and proper winter clothing. Mortality was high, especially among children and the elderly, in the convoys and places of resettlement.

After the first year of state-run dekulakization, kulaks no longer played a role in the economy. However, class criteria were not rigorously applied to determine who was a kulak. Quotas for dekulakization established by higher authorities were often met at the local level by including middle and even poor peasants. The latter could also be dekulakized for having a kulak mentality, betrayed by their opposition to collectivization. "Kulak" thus became a catch-word for all those whom Stalin's regime considered alien and hostile to the new socialist order: It came to include village priests, village intelligentsia, former members of the Russian White Army, and the anti-Russian national armies. Abuse was widespread, and even families of Red Army personnel and industrial workers were swept up in the fray.

Stalin's dekulakization program had a national dimension. The 400,000 peasants deported from Ukraine were among the most dynamic and nationally minded peoples in the Ukrainian countryside. Their loss to Ukraine had dire consequences. Simultaneously, deportees from Russia were transported to Ukraine (3,500 families arrived in 1930–1931 from Soviet Asia). This policy continued during and after the famine of 1932 and 1933. As a result, the number of ethnic Ukrainians in the peasant population of the Ukrainian republic dropped from 89 percent in 1926 to 71 percent in 1939.

The reaction of the Soviet population toward dekulakization was not uniform. It was mainly positive among the urban and rural proletariat. Some 25,000 so-called activists, mostly Russian city workers, were mobilized and sent to the countryside, where they were joined by the village poor, to help the state and party functionaries carry out collectivization and dekulakization. The kulak property confiscated up to July 1, 1930, and transferred to the collectives was enormous. Its value, taking into account the entire Soviet Union, has been calculated at 175,000,000 rubles, but some historians believe that the more accurate value was two or three times greater. A poor peasant might profit as well from the kulak's misery: take a family's house and farm tools, and join the collective enriched by them. Many poor peasants were enticed by these possibilities, or

other more noble if misguided convictions, and gave their support to the authorities in helping to eliminate the kulaks.

Nonetheless, many middle and even poor peasants, especially those who did not want to join the collectives themselves, joined their richer neighbors in opposing dekulakization, seen as part and parcel of collectivization. There were village demonstrations, often organized and led by women. In some cases uprisings arose with hundreds of participants. Such rebellions sometimes lasted for weeks until they were crushed by the army. Historians have calculated that over seven thousand such mass disturbances occurred in 1930 alone. Poorly armed and deprived of any qualified leadership, these uprisings could not succeed; repression inevitably followed. Ringleaders were shot or sent to concentration camps, and the rest of the "rebels" joined the kulaks in those locales where the latter had been deported.

SEE ALSO Lenin, Vladimir; Stalin, Joseph; Ukraine (Famine); Union of Soviet Socialist Republics

BIBLIOGRAPHY
Conquest, Robert (1986). *The Harvest of Sorrow: Soviet Collectivization and the Terror-Famine.* Edmonton, Canada: Candian Institute of Ukrainian Studies.
Graziosi, Andrea (1966). *The Great Soviet Peasant War: Bolsheviks and Peasants, 1917–1933.* Cambridge, Mass.: Ukrainian Research Institute, Harvard University.
Ivnitskii, N. A. (1996). *Kollektivizatsiia i raskulachivanie (nachalo 30-kh godov).* Moscow: Izdatel'stvo Magistr.
Lewin, Moshe (1975). *Russian Peasants and Soviet Power: A Study of Collectivization.* New York: Norton Library.
Viola, Lynne (1996). *Peasant Rebels under Stalin: Collectivization and the Culture of Peasant Resistance.* New York: Oxford University Press.

Roman Serbyn

Kuper, Leo
[NOVEMBER 24, 1908–MAY 23, 1994]
Genocide scholar and activist

Leo Kuper's concern with the prevention of genocide was that of an academic and an activist. His pioneering scholarship influenced the development of a distinctive interdisciplinary field of genocide studies. He also worked to create public awareness on the nature of genocide that would lead to very early warnings and action to prevent, suppress, or punish it.

Kuper was born in Johannesburg, South Africa. He received his B.A. and L.L.B. from Witwatersrand University, graduating in 1931. Kuper then practiced law until 1940, defending human rights victims and representing one of the first interracial trade unions. During World War II he served as an intelligence officer in the Eighth Army.

In 1947 Kuper completed his M.A. in sociology at the University of North Carolina and soon thereafter became a lecturer at the University of Birmingham in England, where he earned a doctorate in sociology. He returned to South Africa in 1952, serving as a professor of sociology at the University of Natal, and remained there until 1961. At the 1960 World Congress of Sociology, Kuper presented a paper that outlined hypothetically a sociologist's recommendations on how best to increase racial tension in South Africa, and went on to show that the policies of the National Party government could be regarded as their very implementation. This exercise of the sociological imagination engendered considerable interest in his work.

Two of Kuper's studies on South African society, *Passive Resistance in South Africa* (1957) and *An African Bourgeoisie* (1965), were banned by the government. When racial tests were imposed on universities, Kuper wrote a satire on the newly segregated universities, *College Brew* (1960), and reluctantly decided to leave his country. In 1961 he accepted an appointment as a professor of sociology at the University of California at Los Angeles, where he remained until his retirement in 1976.

In California, Kuper developed a sustained interest in genocide. Given his background, it is no surprise that Kuper's interest was both academic and practical, and his writing both analytical and prescriptive. Concerned with the international community's approach to genocide, Kuper attended sessions of the United Nations (UN) Commission on Human Rights as a delegate of the accredited human rights organization, the Minority Rights Group (MRG). This experience provided an exposure to member states that informed his later thinking on genocide.

Kuper published three works on genocide in the early 1980s: *Genocide: Its Political Use in the Twentieth Century* (1981), regarded as his most important work; *International Action against Genocide* (1982); and *The Prevention of Genocide* (1985). Kuper's academic work on genocide returned him to his legal roots and thrust him into the arena of international relations, as he described how states pursued their own interests, even when supposedly acting on behalf of humankind. His comments on the drafting of the 1948 UN Genocide Convention, based on a reading of the negotiations leading to it, are particularly telling. He concluded that diplomats negotiated a treaty that was ambiguous,

weak, and lacking a guardian that might preserve its integrity within the UN system.

Kuper also studied genocides that occurred before and after the Genocide Convention's entry into force, analyzing risk factors and preventive measures. He concluded that "the sovereign territorial state claims, as an integral part of its sovereignty, the right to commit genocide, or engage in genocidal massacres, against peoples under its rule, and that the United Nations, for all practical purposes, defends this right" (1982, p. 161). Kuper recognized the UN Secretary-General's role in making intercessions and the humanitarian relief that the UN provided for refugees from genocide. However, he also demonstrated how the UN often stood by, acceding to states' claims to territorial integrity or to the enforcement of law and order, while genocide unfolded beneath its gaze.

Kuper made a number of suggestions for preventing genocide. He suggested that the UN devise an early warning system, drawing on the impartial observations of potential genocides linked with procedures to raise the alarm that could monitor situations and undertake initial preventive measures. Nongovernmental organizations (NGOs) could enlist sympathetic states to press the UN and delinquent governments. Informed public opinion could develop emergency campaigns to avert the genocide. Should the genocide escalate, then all possible means should be employed to suppress it. This would include the normal range of bilateral and intergovernmental measures, including UN Security Council sanctions. In addition, Kuper advocated a resort to forceful humanitarian intervention by states together or alone in extreme circumstances.

His study of genocide completed, Kuper sought to apply his findings to its prevention. In 1985, with the help of fellow sociologist Lord Young of Dartington, he established International Alert in Los Angeles and London to alert decision makers and public opinion to the advent of genocide. He was also a founding member of the International Council of the Institute on the Holocaust and Genocide, which had similar aims.

Kuper died on May 23, 1994. His final weeks saw South Africa's peaceful transition to democracy, a vision Kuper had maintained throughout apartheid's worst hours. Those weeks also witnessed the start of the genocide in Rwanda, a tragic vindication of all that Kuper had argued for in the field of genocide prevention.

SEE ALSO Holocaust

BIBLIOGRAPHY

Kuper, Leo (1982). *Genocide: Its Political Use in the Twentieth Century*. New Haven, Conn.: Yale University Press.

Kuper, Leo (1984). *International Action against Genocide*. London: Minority Rights Group.

Kuper, Leo (1985). *The Prevention of Genocide*. New Haven, Conn.: Yale University Press.

Bernard F. Hamilton

Kurds

The Kurds are often referred to as the world's largest non-state nation. The population is estimated at between 25 to 35 million, which makes them the fourth-largest ethnic group in the Middle East, outnumbered only by Arabs, Turks, and Persians. The majority live in Kurdistan, a borderless homeland whose territory is divided among the neighboring countries of Turkey, Iran, Iraq, and Syria. Some Kurdish populations are scattered throughout western and central Asia and, since the 1960s, can also be found in Europe, North America, Australia, New Zealand, and other countries.

The territory's rich natural resources have supported nomadic populations practicing animal husbandry, as well as rural and urban economies rooted in agriculture, long-distance trade, and regional markets. According to historical and archeological evidence, the region was the site of the world's earliest agrarian societies, cities, and states, all of which coexisted uneasily in a web of antagonisms that were rooted in cleavages based on class, empire, ethnicity, religion, race, and gender.

Although the Kurds appear to be an indigenous people of Western Asia, living largely astride the Zagros Mountains, their territory was home to numerous other civilizations and peoples, as well. Most of these (except for Assyrians, Armenians, and Jews) are now extinct or have been assimilated into the Kurdish population. The landscape is full of relics of monumental construction projects ranging from ancient irrigation networks to bridges and citadels, side by side with evidence of the ongoing destruction of life and property through conquest, wars, massacres, and forced population movements.

Pre-Modern States

We have more knowledge about the Kurds in the years following the conquest of the region by Islamic armies in the seventh century. Kurdistan lay very close to Baghdad, the capital of the Islamic caliphate. It was the site of incessant wars among the armies of the caliphs, as well as governors, Kurdish rulers, and conquerors coming from as far as the Roman empire in the west and Mongolia in the east. Although the conflicts were primary over land, taxes, and the recruitment of military service from the population, ethnic and religious differences also provided justifications for conquest and subjugation. Unrestrained violence, including atrocities against both civilians and combatants was widespread, and was aimed, in part, at intimidating the adversary and the population into submission. To give one example, the army of Adhud al-Dawla, ruler of the Buwayhid dynasty centered in Baghdad, besieged the Hakkari Kurds in 980, forced them into surrender on a promise of sparing their lives, but then crucified them and left their bodies hanging along 15 miles of roadside near Mosul.

Several factors helped to reshape the ethnic composition of Western Asia. For one, the Oghuz Turks arrived in the region from the Asian steppes in the eleventh century. Also important was the formation of the Seljuk dynasty (11th through 13th centuries) and Turkoman dynasties (Aq Qoyunlu and Qara Qoyunlu), which were followed by the fall of the caliphate in 1258 in the wake of the Mongol invasion. According to historian Vladimir Minorsky, "the Kurdish element was exhausting itself" in these unceasing wars. It is during this period, however, that the Kurds emerge as a distinct people, their territory becomes identified by outsiders as Kurdistan, and Kurdish statehood emerges in the form of mini-states and principalities.

Some of the indigenous populations of Kurdistan include the Armenians, Assyrians (Christians), and Kurds (mostly Muslims). There are also other goups, such as the Yezidis, who are followers of minority religions, as well as scattered minorities such as the Jews. These peoples survived the intensive colonization of the region by Turkic (Oghuz, Turkoman, Ottoman) and Mongol nomadic and tribal peoples from central Asia. The homogenizing force of centuries of conversion, forcible population movements, and massacres was offset by the inability of feudal states to centralize power and therefore assimilate their conquered peoples of the region into the language, culture and religion of the conquerors. Equally important in preventing the total annihilation of the indigenous populations was the labor-intensive nature of feudal agrarian production. Without a sizeable productive labor force, the fertile lands of Armenia, Azerbaijan, Kurdistan, and Mesopotamia could not sustain elaborate state structures. Although some Kurdish territories were Turkicized due to conquest and the violent elimination of Kurdish ruling families (especially by the Aq Qoyunlu dynasty, 1378–1508), as well as by massacres and deportations, some Kurdish mini-states were, nonetheless, gaining ground.

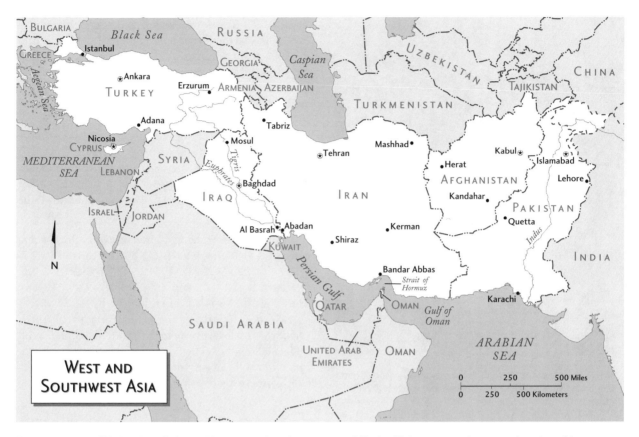

Present-day map of Turkey, Iran, Syria, and Iraq—countries where oppressed Kurds with long ancestral roots continue to reside. [XNR PRODUCTIONS, INC. BERKSHIRE PUBLISHING GROUP]

By the early sixteenth century, Western Asia was under the rule of two rival Turkish dynasties, the Ottomans and Safavids, which in 1639 drew their borders along the Zagros mountain range. Armenia and Kurdistan were thus divided, and the region experienced intermittent wars. The two empires pursued a policy of administrative centralization by removing hereditary Kurdish principalities. However, the Kurdish ministates benefitted from the rivalry between the dynasties, and some survived until the mid-nineteenth century. Shah Abbas I (1588–1626), was suspicious of the loyalty of the Kurdish rulers of principalities of Biradost and Mukriyan. He supervised and personally participated in the massacres of the rulers and their subjects (1610–1611), and resettled Turkish tribes in their territory. He deported another 15,000 Kurds from another region of Kurdistan to northeastern Iran. An eyewitness to the mass killings, the Shah's official chronicler Eskandar Monshi Torkman, whose *History of Shah Abbas the Great* was translated into English in 1971, detailed with pride the "general massacre" of the Mukri Kurds and noted that the shah's "fury and wrath" could not be allayed "but by shedding the blood of those unfortunate ones" and that the "slicing of men" and the "en-

slavement of women and girls . . . had been inscribed on the annals of time by destination." He labeled the Kurds as "base-born," "human beings of savage disposition," and "impious."

The Modern Nation-State

In the mid-nineteenth century, Ottoman Turkey and Iran began adopting a more European style of administrative and military centralization. The two states used their armies to overthrow the six remaining Kurdish principalities, and extended their direct rule over all parts of Kurdistan. With the emergence of modern style nation-states in Iran (after the Constitutional Revolution of 1906 to 1911) and Ottoman Turkey (especially after the 1908 Young Turk revolution), the Kurds were incorporated into the state as citizens rather than a distinct people enjoying the right to self-rule. Feudal and tribal relations continued to prevail in the predominantly rural society of Kurdistan, but Kurdish nationalist ideas began to appear in the poetry and journalism of the last decade of the nineteenth century.

World War I turned Kurdistan into a battlefield between the Ottomans, Russians, Iranians, and British. The Ottoman government committed genocide against

Kurdish women work fertile fields in the Azerbaijan region of Iran, 1968. Iran's recent Islamic governments have continued the "Persianization" policies of earlier regimes, seeking to eliminate the Kurdish language and culture. [ROGER WOOD/CORBIS]

Armenians and Assyrians in 1915, and forcibly transferred some 700,000 Kurds to Western Turkey in 1917. At the same time, the tsarist Russian army conducted massacres of the Kurds in Sauj Bulagh in 1915 (now Mahabad, Iran), Rawandiz (Iraq), Khanaqin (Iran) and throughout the eastern parts of Kurdistan. As in previous wars, both armies committed crimes against humanity, including enslavement, murder, extermination, rape, sexual slavery, sexual violence, persecution. They also engaged in such war crimes as willful killing, inhuman treatment, unlawful deportation and transfer, attacking civilians, pillaging, and cruel treatment. The Russian army also committed gendercide—the killing of adolescent and adult males—in the massacre of Sauj Bulagh, and carried away some 400 women and girls for abuse. Armenian and Assyrian militias participated in the Russian massacres, and some Kurdish tribal, feudal, and religious leaders acted as accomplices in the genocide of Armenians and Assyrians. At the same time, many Kurds sheltered Armenian victims, and Assyrians helped starving Kurds.

The dismantling of the Ottoman empire in World War I led to the division of its Kurdish region and the incorporation of that territory into the newly created states of Iraq (under British occupation and mandate, 1918–1932), Syria (under French occupation and mandate, 1918–1946), and Turkey (Republic of Turkey

since 1923). The formation of these modern nation-states entailed the forced assimilation of the Kurds into the official or dominant national languages and cultures: Turkish (Turkey), Persian (Iran), and Arabic (Syria, and, in a more limited scope, Iraq). In Turkey and Iran, in particular, the political power of religious, tribal, and feudal leaders was uprooted. State violence was the principal means of integration and assimilation. According to historian Mark Levene, (Ottoman) Turkey had turned Eastern Anatolia, which includes Armenia and Kurdistan, into a "zone of genocide" from 1878 to 1923. This "zone" has persisted into the twenty-first century.

Kurdish resistance to assimilation was diverse and extensive, including a series of armed revolts in Turkey (1921, 1925, 1927–1931, 1937–1938), Iran (1920–early 1930s), and Iraq (early 1920s, 1940s). These revolts were led, often jointly, by heads of religious orders (sheikhs) and feudal and tribal chiefs (aghast) as well as an emerging group of nationalist intelligentsia, political activists, and deserting army officers, who were mostly urban and secular. The repression of these revolts was most brutal in Turkey and Iran.

The region was not a theater of war in World War II, except for the northern part of Iranian Kurdistan, which was occupied by the Soviet Union from 1941 to 1946. After the war the four countries acceded or ratified the 1949 Geneva Conventions (Turkey, 1954; Iran, 1957; Iraq, 1956; Syria, 1953) and its 1977 Additional Protocols.

Turkey

The intent to commit genocide is inscribed, explicitly, in Turkey's Law No. 2510 of 1934, which stipulated the transfer of non-Turks to Turkish speaking regions, where they would not be allowed to form more than 5 percent of the population. This law provided for the depopulation of non-Turkish villages and towns, resettlement of Turks in non-Turkish areas, and other assimilationist projects, such as the establishing of boarding schools, which were intended to turn non-Turkish children into monolingual Turkish speakers. The law was applied a year later in the wake of Law No. 2884, which decreed the systematic turkification of the Dersim region, renamed as Tunceli, through military control, boarding schools, the banning of the Kurdish language and culture, changing place names, and deportation.

This forced turkification project led to the Dersim uprising, which the army and the air force brutally suppressed from 1937 to 1938, and the repression of which some researchers consider to be an act of genocide. The

Turkish Republic considered popular uprisings to be reactionary and religious opposition to the civilizing and westernizing policies of the Turkish nation-state. The Kurds were branded as tribal, uncivilized, illiterate, primitive, backward, dirty, and ignorant. Any expression of Kurdish identity was treated as a crime against the "indivisibility of the Turkish nation" and "territorial integrity" of Turkey.

Dersim was the last uprising until the armed resistance of 1984–1999, led by Kurdistan Workers Party (PKK, in Kurdish acronyms). Nonetheless, various governments continued Turkification through the deliberate elimination of Kurdish as a spoken and written language, and through ethnocide—eliminating Kurdish culture and ethnic identity. The use of the Kurdish language, music, dance, dress, personal and geographic names, and even listening to broadcasting and recorded music were all criminalized by the Turkish state.

Because of Turkey's aspirations to full membership in the European Union, the parliament acceded to pressure and legalized the private use of spoken Kurdish in 1991. A decade later the parliament removed some of the constitutional and legal restrictions on the language. However, linguistic genocide continues to be the official state policy.

During its repression of the PKK, which it labeled counterinsurgency operations, Turkey declared a state of emergency in parts of its southeastern (Kurdish) territory. According to the Human Rights Watch Turkey committed "gross violation of its international commitments to respect the laws of war" (1995, p. 7). This included forced displacements, indiscriminate shootings, summary executions, and disguising the identity of perpetrators, as well as violations of international law, including summary execution, torture, forcible displacement of civilians, pillage, destruction of villages, failure to care for civilians displaced by government forces, injury of civilians, destruction of civilian property, inhumane and degrading treatment, kidnaping of civilians to act as porters and as human shields against attack, disappearances, life-threatening conditions of detention and inadequate medical attention leading to death. The Human Rights Watch also noted that the United States, Turkey's close ally and its major weapons supplier, was deeply implicated, and, much like NATO, chose to "downplay Turkish violations for strategic reasons" (1995, p. 13). It also charged that the PKK, which was not party to the Geneva Protocols, also engaged in "substantial violations of the laws of war," including "summary executions, indiscriminate fire and the intentional targeting of non-combatants" (1995, pp. 12–13).

Kurdish homestead, Lake Rezaiyeh, Azerbaijan region of Iran.
[ROGER WOOD/CORBIS]

During the operations, according to a Turkish parliamentary commission, the armed forces displaced 378,335 villagers while destroying or evacuating 3,428 rural settlements (905 villages and 2,523 hamlets) from the mid-1980s to 1997. These figures are generally treated as underestimations. The Turkish security forces further destroyed the infrastructure of rural life in the Kurdish region, and thus threatened the survival of the Kurds as a distinct people. Other crimes included systematic sexual violence against women in custody.

Iran

Especially under Reza Shah Pahlavi (1925–1941), Iran undertook a policy of forcible Persianization of the Kurds through linguicide and ethnocide as well as war, killing, jail, and deportations. As early as 1923, speaking Kurdish had been banned in schools and other state institutions, and by the mid-1930s, a total ban on the language and culture was imposed. Under the Pahlavi dynasty (1925–1979), crimes against humanity and war crimes were committed in military operations against the Kurds. The Islamic regime that followed the Shahs continued the persianization policy, although on a more limited scale. During its suppression of Kurdish autonomists, which began once it came to power, the government committed crimes against humanity including murder, extermination, imprisonment, and torture, and war crimes such as wilful killing, inhuman treatment, appropriation of property, denying a fair trial, unlawful deportation and transfer, attacking civilians, execution without due process, and attacking undefended places.

Iraq

Iraq was the only country, other than the Soviet Union, where the existence of the Kurds was recognized and the Kurdish language was allowed limited use in primary education, local administration, and the mass media. However, Iraq did institute a policy of containing Kurdish nationalism through arabization. The government committed crimes against humanity and war crimes during the long conflict with Kurdish autonomists, which raged intermittently from 1961 to the 1990s. During the first Ba'ath regime's offensive against the Kurds in 1963, the Mongolian People's Republic asked the UN General Assembly to discuss "the policy of genocide carried out by the government of the Republic of Iraq against the Kurdish people," and the Soviet Union referred the case to the Economic and Social Council. Mongolia later withdrew the request, and the Economic and Social Security Council refused to consider the Soviet request.

The second Ba'ath regime (1968–2003) constructed a cordon sanitaire along its northern borders with Iran and Turkey by destroying hundreds of Kurdish villages soon after the defeat of the Kurdish armed resistance in 1975. In 1983 it killed all the adolescent and adult males of Barzani Kurds, numbering about 8,000. In addition, during its war with Iran (1980–1988), in violation of the 1925 Geneva Protocol, the regime used chemical weapons against both the Iranians and Iraqi Kurds who lived in a number of settlements, including the town of Halabja (March 16, 1988). Moreover, the oil-rich Kirkuk region was arabized by forcibly uprooting Kurds from the city and villages. The 1988 campaign of mass murder, code-named Operation *Anfal* ("spoils" of war, also the title of a chapter in the Koran), is widely considered a genocide. According to a 1993 report by the Human Rights Watch, it entailed the killing of more than 100,000 Kurds, the disappearance of tens of thousands of noncombatants, the destruction of 4,006 villages (according to Kurdistan Regional Government), the forced displacement of hundreds of thousands of villagers, the arbitrary arrest and jailing of thousands of women, children, and the elderly under conditions of extreme deprivation, and the destruction of rural life.

Syria

Although the Kurds of Syria have not engaged in armed conflict with the state, they were targeted for ethnic cleansing beginning in the early 1960s. Some 120,000 Kurds were stripped of Syrian citizenship. According to a 1991 report by the Middle East Watch, the Syrian

government planned for the depopulation of Kurdish regions by creating an "Arab belt" along the Turkish border, evicting peasants from 332 villages, and replacing them with Arab settlers.

Soviet Union and Caucasia

Although the Kurdish communities of Soviet Caucasia and Turkmenistan enjoyed cultural and linguistic rights, thousands of Caucasian Kurds were subjected to two waves of forced deportation to the Central Asian republics of Kazakhstan, Kirgizia, and Uzbekistan in 1937 and 1944. During the disintegration of the Soviet Union, the Muslim Kurdish populations of Armenia and Nagorny-Karabakh were largely displaced in the course of the war between Armenia and Azerbaijan between 1990 and 1994, when, according to the Human Rights Watch, both countries "systematically violated the most basic rule of international humanitarian law."

Prevention, Education, and Political-Judicial Reform

Since ancient times, mass killing and related crimes have been a permanent feature of life in the region. Modern genocide in Kurdistan is distinguished from earlier crimes by its rootedness in the nation–state and its nationalist ideology, which safeguards the territorial integrity of the homeland.

While there is little progress in reversing state politics, citizens, both Kurds and non-Kurds, have taken significant steps toward recognizing, documenting, and resisting genocide in literary words, academic research, conferences, film, and journalism. Much remains to be done, however, toward legal-political reform, promoting genocide education, and monitoring early warning signs of impending crimes.

SEE ALSO Ethnocide; Gas; Iran; Iraq; Linguistic Genocide

BIBLIOGRAPHY

Andrews, Peter A. (1989). *Ethnic Groups in the Republic of Turkey*. Wiesbaden, Germany: Ludwig Reichert Verlag.

Baran, Ute (1989). "Deportations: Tunceli Kanunlari." In *Documentation of the International Conference on Human Rights in Kurdistan*. Bremen, Germany: Initiative for Human Rights in Kurdistan.

Besikçi, Ismail (1991). *Kürtlerin Mecburi İskâni*. Ankara: Yurt Kitab-Yayin.

Besikçi, Ismail (1992). *Tunceli Kanunu (1935) ve Dersim Jenosidi*. Ankara: Yurt.

Bruinessen, Martin (2000). *Kurdish Ethno-Nationalism versus Nation-Building States. Collected Articles*. Istanbul: The ISIS Press.

Fernandes, Desmond (1999). "The Kurdish Genocide in Turkey, 1924–1998." *Armenian Forum* 1:57–107.

Fossum, Ludvig Olsen (1918). "The War-Stricken Kurds." *The Kurdistan Missionary* 10(1):5–6.

Hassanpour, Amir (2000). "The Politics of A-Political Linguistics: Linguists and Linguicide." In *Rights to Language: Equity, Power, and Education*, ed. Robert Phillipson. Mahwah, N.J.: Lawrence Erlbaum Associates.

Hiltermann, Joost (2000). "Elusive Justice: Trying to Try Saddam." *Middle East Report* 215(Summer):32–35.

Human Rights Association (2003). *House Demolitions and Forced Evictions Perpetrated by the Turkish Security Forces: A Form of Cruel, Inhuman or Degrading Treatment or Punishment Against the Kurdish Population.* Available from http://www.ihd.org.tr.

Ismael, Jacqueline, and Shereen Ismael (2000). "Gender and State in Iraq." In *Gender and Citizenship in the Middle East*, ed. Joseph Suad. Syracuse, N.Y.: Syracuse University Press.

Jwaideh, Wadie (1960). "The Kurdish Nationalist Movement: Its Origins and Development." Ph.D diss. Syracuse, N.Y.: Syracuse University.

Kuper, Leo (1981). *Genocide: Its Practical Use in the Twentieth Century.* New Haven, Conn.: Yale University Press.

Kurdish Human Rights Project (2001). *State Violence against Women in Turkey and attacks on Human Rights Defenders of Victims of Sexual Violence in Custody.* London: Kurdish Human Rights Project.

Kurdish Human Rights Project (2002). *Denial of a Language: Kurdish Language Rights in Turkey—KHRP Fact-Finding Mission Report.* London: Kurdish Human Rights Project.

Levene, Mark (1998). "Creating a Modern 'Zone of Genocide': The Impact of Nation and State Formation on Eastern Anatolia, 1878–1923." *Holocaust and Genocide Studies* 12(3):393–433.

Levene, Mark (1999). "A Moving Target, the Usual Suspects and (Maybe) a Smoking Gun: The Problem of Pinning Blame in Modern Genocide." *Patterns of Prejudice* 33(4):3–24

McDowall, David (2000). *A Modern History of the Kurds.* London: I.B. Tauris.

Middle East Watch (1991). *Syria Unmasked: The Suppression of Human Rights by the Asad Regime.* New Haven, Conn.: Yale University Press.

Mojab, Shhahrzad (2003). "Kurdish Women in the Zone of Genocide and Gendercide" *Al-Raida* 21(103):20–25.

Müller, Daniel (2000). The Kurds of Soviet Azerbaijan, 1920–1991. *Central Asian Survey* 19(1):41–77.

Power, S. (2003). *"A Problem from Hell": America and the Age of Genocide.* New York: Perennial Books.

Torkman, Eskandar Beg Monshi (1978). *History of Shah Abbas the Great*, vol. 2, tran. Roger Savory. Boulder, Colo.: Westview Press.

Ussher, Clarence (1917). *An American Physician in Turkey: A Narrative of Adventure in Peace and War.* Boston: Houghton Mifflin Company.

Amir Hassanpour

Labor Camps, Nazi

Most people can conjure up a particular set of images when they think of labor camps under the Third Reich; usually, they picture emaciated prisoners in striped uniforms, performing heavy manual labor and subject to frequent beatings from sadistic SS guards. There is an essential truth to those images, in that they accurately reflect the experiences of many thousands of people. At the same time, however, the term *labor camp* can be deceptive. On the one hand, the Germans classified a great many places of detention as forced labor camps (*Zwangsarbeitslager*), but the term tells us little about conditions, which often differed radically from camp to camp. On the other hand, forced labor was a central part of life in most camps and ghettos, with or without the label. In fact, by the last years of the war, forced labor was ubiquitous in Germany, and some knowledge of the system is essential to an understanding of the Third Reich.

The National Socialists used forced labor from the very start of their rule, in the so-called wild camps that local authorities and party members established throughout the country in the first months of 1933. Later the Schutzstaffel (SS) gained control of such places and established a more rigidly controlled system of concentration camps (*Konzentrationslager*), which they modeled on their first camp at Dachau. Here, too, labor was at the center of the prisoners' existence. The Nazis saw work as having two complementary functions: as punishment and—for those whom the Nazis deemed suitable to exist in German society, either as citizens or so-called inferior foreign laborers—as a means of instilling proper discipline and socially acceptable behavior. Eventually, the SS would establish over twenty main concentration camps at places such as Buchenwald, Sachsenhausen, Flossenbürg, and Mauthausen. At Auschwitz, another such site, they eventually combined a work camp with an industrialized killing center. Moreover, especially in the last two years of the war, the main camps spawned nearly one thousand subcamps (*Aussenlager* or *Nebenlager*), each of which provided labor for some local work site. By this time the SS had in mind not just punishment and socialization, but also financial gain for the organization and cheap labor for its construction and resettlement programs, as well as a simultaneous benefit for Germany's war effort in many instances.

Concentration camp prisoners were, however, usually the last choice when German labor managers sought workers. Some time before such purportedly criminal elements came into use, the Germans began importing foreign labor from territories they had occupied. In some cases, especially in western Europe and (before September 1939) in Poland, the initial drive was to recruit volunteers who would go to Germany and work under relatively normal conditions. But in other cases, especially in the east after the war began, racism and perceived military necessity eventually led the German authorities to simply round up civilians, ship them back to the homeland, and parcel them out to forced labor camps. No one has yet determined the number of such camps with any accuracy, but the best available estimate is that there were at least three thousand. They operated under the control of many different agencies, ranging from private firms and local labor

In the 1930s the Nazis primarily used forced labor camps for punishment, and as a means of instilling discipline and "socially acceptable" behavior. Here, German political prisoners await transport to a nearby labor camp in Land Niedersachsen (West Saxony). [CORBIS]

boards to state work organizations such as the *Deutsche Arbeitsfront*, the *Organisation Todt*, and the *Generalbevollmächtigten für den Arbeitseinsatz*.

Along with the prisoners in the concentration camps, their subcamps, and the forced labor camps, inmates in many other kinds of detention facilities also had to work. The German armed forces allowed prisoners of war to be used in war production, in violation of the Geneva Convention. The military also turned tens of thousands of Soviet prisoners over to the SS, which worked many of them to death. The SS ran its own forced labor facilities, outside its system of concentration camps, where it put Jews and other undesirables to work on specific projects, such as building major roads in the occupied east. The inhabitants of ghettos often found themselves called up for forced labor of one kind or another; in fact, the Germans eventually reclassified many ghettos as forced labor camps. Prisoners in civilian police detention camps, troubled German youths, and even ethnic Germans waiting for resettlement in conquered territory had to work. The numbers of all these facilities ran into the thousands. And finally,

the SS even operated nearly two hundred so-called *Arbeitserziehungslager*, work education camps, where they sent both German and foreign laborers who had violated work rules in their regular jobs or forced labor assignments. A little hard work under SS supervision, it was thought, would teach them a lesson—and if the laborers failed in their eight-week stints there, they often went on to concentration camps.

Forced laborers' experiences varied tremendously within and between camps, because of differences in the kinds of labor they performed, in their individual status, and in the camps' administrative systems. These variables literally meant the difference between life and death for thousands of people.

The Germans employed prisoners in nearly every imaginable kind of work. Some did hard manual labor, much of it dangerous. Prisoners worked in mines and quarries, where the backbreaking nature of the work, plus factors such as stone dust, accidents, and other hardships of life in the camps quickly destroyed their health. Others worked in construction, demolition,

Prisoners in a German Labor Camp. [CORBIS]

rubble clearance, or even bomb disposal, which entailed similar hazards. Some did agricultural work, which, although hard, offered opportunities to steal (or organize, as the prisoners put it) extra food. Some worked inside at manufacturing jobs, where the work was somewhat less physically exhausting. There were also prisoners working in a wide variety of small businesses, governmental offices, and even church facilities. The fortunate ones worked in offices, laundries, laboratories, or other places requiring skilled labor, where they could conserve their strength and sometimes organize items to trade for additional food or protection.

The prisoners' experiences also differed because of their status, in at least three respects. The most important factor was the basic category to which a prisoner belonged. Prisoners of war (POWs) from the United States and Great Britain were perhaps the most fortunate, in general, partly because the Germans treated them better than most other prisoners, and partly because they often received Red Cross food parcels that

kept them from starving. Soviet POWs, on the other hand, were near the bottom of the Germans' hierarchy of perceived worth. They received some of the hardest jobs, the worst shelter, and the least amount of food; millions of them died. Likewise, among the foreign forced laborers, those from western nations did better than those from the east. The concentration camp inmates were among the worst off, but even in this instance, there was a definite hierarchy, with career criminals or political prisoners at the top, often holding camp offices, and Jews at the bottom. The second factor revolved around each prisoner's skills set; someone who knew chemistry, or who could type or repair complex machinery, might be assigned a relatively easy job. And the third factor concerned connections. Prisoners of particular nationalities or common political persuasions often stuck together and helped one another. Individuals, meanwhile, especially if they were good at organizing, could curry favor with prison leaders and guards. Corruption was rampant, and it worked in favor of some prisoners and to the detriment of others.

The camp administration was important because it directly controlled the conditions under which the prisoners lived and worked. The amount and kind of food, the quality of the clothing, opportunities to bathe, the type and pace of the work, and the attitudes of individual guards could all vary significantly. In some camps one authority would control the camp itself, while another, usually a business, controlled the working conditions. There are examples of workplaces in which the civilian foremen let their charges get some extra sleep, or in which civilian coworkers would smuggle in extra food. In other places a business's overseers could be every bit as cruel as any SS guard. Similarly, prisoner accommodations could consist of anything from a hole in the ground, to a stable or workshop with straw on the floor for bedding, to (albeit rarely) a relatively clean, warm barracks with individual cots and blankets.

Whatever the degrees of difference, however, most prisoners shared some common experiences. On the most basic level they lost their freedom; to their employers they were usually a resource to be used more or less efficiently, not people whose welfare or wishes were at all important for their own sake. Work shifts typically lasted twelve hours per day, six or seven days per week. Discipline was often arbitrary and brutal. The food decreased in both quality and quantity as the war went on; many prisoners existed at or below subsistence level. Clothing was usually inadequate in cold weather, and the prisoners often lacked the wherewithal to wash either themselves or their clothes. All in all, their existence was a miserable one, until death or advancing Allied armies released them.

SEE ALSO Compensation; Gulag; Historical Injusticies; Holocaust; Stalin, Joseph

BIBLIOGRAPHY
Dieckmann, Christoph, Ulrich Herbert, and Karin Orth, eds. (1998). *Die nationalsozialistischen Konzentrationslager: Entwicklung und Struktur.* Göttingen: Wallstein.

Gutman, Israel, and Avital Saf, eds. (1984). *The Nazi Concentration Camps: Structure and Aims, The Image of the Prisoner, The Jews in the Camps: Proceedings of the 4th Yad Vashem International Historical Conference, Jerusalem, January 1980.* Jerusalem: Yad Vashem.

Herbert, Ulrich (1997). *Hitler's Foreign Workers: Enforced Foreign Labor in Germany under the Third Reich,* tran. William Templer. New York: Cambridge University Press.

Hirschfeld, Gerhard (1986). *The Policies of Genocide: Jews and Soviet Prisoners of War in Nazi Germany.* Boston: Allan & Unwin.

Homze, E. (1967). *Foreign Labor in Nazi Germany.* Princeton, N.J.: Princeton University Press.

Jaskot, Paul B. (2000). *The Architecture of Oppression: The SS, Forced Labor and the Nazi Monumental Building Economy.* New York: Routledge.

Kogon, Eugen (1980). *The Theory and Practice of Hell: The German Concentration Camps and the System behind Them (SS Staat).* New York: Berkley, 1984.

Orth, Karin (1999). *Das System der nationalsozialistischen Konzentrationslager. Eine politische Organisationsgeschichte.* Hamburg: Hamburger Edition.

Schwarz, Gudrun (1990). *Die nationalsozialistischen Lager.* Frankfurt: Campus.

Geoffrey P. Megargee

Language

Practices of genocide and crimes against humanity emerge from and depend upon a language of genocide and crimes against humanity. Language itself is inseparable from power, and language can facilitate the most violent exercise of power against a people. Linguistic violence directed against a people leads to physical violence against a people. In genocide, such linguistic violence is institutionally sanctioned, and the ensuing physical violence is lethal and aims to be total.

The meanings of terms within semiological systems are based upon the oppositions among the signs. A non-linguistic example is the use of red, yellow, and green lights in traffic signals. In relation to classifications of peoples, many social groups use binary oppositions of an "us-them" type, such as Greeks and barbarians, freedom fighters and terrorists, and culture bearers and culture destroyers. The last example enters the realm of the language of genocide. In a 1988 article, "Language and Genocide," Berel Lang has shown the close connection between this language and the slaughter of millions in the Holocaust. Practices of genocide and crimes against humanity begin with a classification that divides people into two groups, one viewed positively and the other as subhuman or unworthy of existence. The use of condemnatory terms prepares a social group to practice atrocities and is used to perpetuate these atrocities throughout their duration.

Since the 1960s, Anglo-American theory has been strongly influenced by the work of John Austin, particularly his 1962 book, *How to Do Things with Words.* This approach often describes one set of language statements in terms of speech acts. A speech-act of language, for example, can be used to distinguish peoples who speak different languages. Such a speech-act can go beyond merely differentiating to also judging, such as designating Tutsis as "*inyenzi*" (a slang epithet meaning cockroaches) in the years preceding the 1994 genocide in Rwanda. A similar effect is achieved by Nazi references to Jews as "bacillus," and even by neo-

Nazi calls to "kill faggots" beyond the million "queers" massacred by Hitler until all homosexual "scum" are "wiped out." Raphael Lemkin's coinage of the term *genocide* in 1943 can also be considered a speech act when it carries a condemnatory tone against and a branding of perpetrators of a practice that aims to kill an entire people. Lemkin suggested *ethnocide* as another term with the same meaning. Language, however, often relies on euphemisms that mask the reality of persecution, such as using "ethnic cleansing," instead of "ethnocide," to describe slaughters and forcible relocation like the ones that occurred in Bosnia in the 1990s.

Since the 1920s, continental theory, following the lead of Ferdinand de Saussure's 1916 Course in General Linguistics, distinguishes between the established sign system (*la langue*) and speaking (*la parole*). The established sign system reigns (synchronic immutability), but over time speaking alters that system (diachronic change). Persons with political power can speak in distinctive ways that become part of the official language, which shapes how citizens think and behave.

Beyond primarily referring to killing of an entire people, genocide is used in at least two other colloquial senses, namely, in reference to linguistic genocide and genocidal weapons. The usage differs from the strictly legal meaning of genocide. By suppressing or even eliminating the language of a people, linguistic genocide destroys a culture but it does not necessarily lead to the slaughter of a people. By contrast, "genocidal" weapons, such as strategic nuclear weapons targeted against cities, are intended to achieve the large-scale or even total killing of a people, although this slaughter could occur within an entire nation rather than being directed against a specific type of people. In principle, although not yet in fact, beyond nuclear weapons, some other weapons of mass destruction, especially biological ones, could be genocidal. However, one characteristic of such weapons is the prospect that their use may not be controllable and could therefore inflict death on the perpetrator along with the intended victims.

In showing the connection of language and power, Friedrich Nietzsche went so far as to say, in his 1887 *Genealogy of Morals,* that the "right of bestowing names" is a fundamental expression of political power. Governments that seek absolute power over the groups they control use language as a principal support, because they believe that by changing terminology and definitions they can alter the ways individuals and groups think and act. In 1991, in his book *Totalitarian Language: Orwell's Newspeak and Its Nazi and Communist Antecedents,* John Wesley Young reports that even in the extremes of totalitarian language found in Nazi concentration camps and the Soviet gulags, significant

numbers of individuals avoided being fully brainwashed by constructing alternative words and discourses that eluded the understanding of their oppressors. Nevertheless, the one who controls the politics of definition controls the political agenda, and the step from the linguistic dehumanization of a people to their slaughter is rather small. So one important step in the prevention of genocide is the elimination of the names that are used in the perpetration of genocide. However, writing in 1999 on "The Language of War and Peace," William Gay has noted that the elimination of such names may be necessary, but it is not sufficient to achieve the desired results, and may result in a situation that is more like negative peace (the mere absence of war) than positive peace (the presence of justice as well). In this case the difference is between a temporary suspension of name-calling that does not remove the prejudicial attitudes that lie behind it and a permanent removal of any intent or desire to eradicate a people and the achievement of a genuine embracing of the appropriate diversity among peoples.

SEE ALSO Hate Speech; Lemkin, Raphael; Linguistic Genocide; Propaganda

BIBLIOGRAPHY
Gay, William (1999). "The Language of War and Peace." In *Encyclopedia of Violence, Conflict and Peace,* vol. 2, ed. Lester Kurtz. San Diego, Calif.: Academic Press.

Lang, Berel (1988). "Language and Genocide." In *Echoes from the Holocaust: Philosophical Reflections on a Dark Time,* ed. Alan Rosenberg and Gerald E. Myers. Philadelphia: Temple University Press.

Young, John Wesley (1991). *Totalitarian Language: Orwell's Newspeak and Its Nazi and Communist Antecedents.* Charlottesville: University Press of Virginia.

William Gay

Lemkin, Raphael

[JUNE 24, 1900–AUGUST 28, 1959]
Leader of efforts to make genocide an international crime

His gravestone, at Mount Hebron Cemetery in New York City, declares Raphael Lemkin to be the "Father of the Genocide Treaty" although in his unpublished autobiography Lemkin characterized himself as a "totally unofficial man." In fact, whether as a member of an official delegation or as a private individual, Lemkin single-mindedly pursued a lifelong agenda to establish international protection for minorities. He coined the word *genocide.* He worked on the Nuremberg indictments and prevailed until genocide was added to the charge sheet. He analyzed the regulations of the Nazi occupiers and in *Axis Rule in Occupied Europe* (1944) concluded that they were aimed at the destruction of the essential foundations of minority groups. He then lobbied successfully for the adoption and entry into force of the 1948 United Nations (UN) Convention on the Prevention and Punishment of the Crime of Genocide. In short, Lemkin demonstrated how an individual could bring about profound changes in human rights.

Lemkin was born to Jewish parents in Bezwodene, Poland. His parents were tenant farmers and, until the age of thirteen, he was educated by his mother and tutors. A brilliant linguist, Lemkin initially studied philology at the University of Lwow, but in 1921 switched to law following the trial of the assassin of Talaat Pasha, an Ottoman minister regarded as responsible for the extermination of over a million Armenians in World War I. Lemkin felt passionately about the massacres and argued with his law professor that such actions should be viewed as crimes against international law. The professor asserted that no law could interfere with the actions of a sovereign state, but Lemkin insisted that state sovereignty encompassed activities directed toward the well-being of its citizens and did not extend to their mass killing. Resolving this question was to become Lemkin's lifelong vocation.

After his graduation Lemkin was appointed deputy prosecutor at Warsaw District Court. In 1933, still concerned with international law, he submitted a paper on criminal law to a conference sponsored by the League of Nations in Madrid; the paper called for "the destruction of national, religious and racial groups" to be regarded as "an international crime alongside of piracy, slavery and drug smuggling." Lemkin proposed two new international crimes: *barbarism*, which he referred to as the extermination of human collectivities, and *vandalism*, which he defined as the malicious destruction of works of art and culture. Two German jurists walked out of the conference and his proposals were shelved. His own government, which was seeking a policy of conciliation toward Hitler, opposed him. Lemkin left public service for private practice and continued to attend conferences on international criminal law, once engaging in a heated debate with delegates from Nazi Germany.

Following the invasion of Poland by Soviet and German armies, Lemkin escaped to Sweden, where he lectured at Stockholm University. There, he persuaded associates to collect the decrees associated with German occupation. From these documents he deduced that Hitler's *Neu Ordnung* (New Order) was nothing less than the coordinated extermination of nations and ethnic groups, either by destroying them or assimilating their identity by Germanizing groups perceived to be related by blood to Germans. Variations among the protein rations in Nazi-dominated territory illustrate this. Germans received 97 percent, the Dutch 95 percent, the French 71 percent, the Greeks 38 percent, and the Jews 20 percent.

As a lawyer, Lemkin recognized the significance of official documents for an understanding of policy, but it was his extensive knowledge of the oppression of minorities that enabled him to believe the unbelievable and reach the conclusion he did. The results of his work were published in *Axis Rule in Occupied Europe,* three years after his arrival with other refugees in the United States, in 1941. The term *genocide* first appeared in that book; it is derived from the Greek *genos* (species) and the Latin *cide* (killing). Lemkin devised it because he wanted to use a word that, unlike the terms barbarity and vandalism, which he employed in 1933, had no other meaning. He defined genocide as "a coordinated plan of different actions aiming at the destruction of essential foundations of the life of national groups, with the aim of annihilating the groups themselves" (1944, p. 79).

Soon after arriving in the United States to lecture at Duke University, Lemkin got in touch with the Judge Advocate General's office at the War Department. He became a consultant at the Board of Economic Warfare and in 1945 was appointed legal advisor to the United States Chief Prosecutor at the Nuremberg trials, Robert Jackson. In September 1945 Lemkin traveled to London, and on October 18 he witnessed the first use of the term genocide in an official document, when he succeeded in having the charge of genocide added as Count 3 of the indictment against the twenty-four Nazi leaders on trial. Lemkin was disappointed by the Nuremberg judgments, which, although making an indirect reference to genocide, failed to convict anyone of the crime.

Dissatisfied with the limited precedent set by the Nuremberg verdict, Lemkin turned his attention to the newly established UN. He persuaded delegates from Cuba, India, and Panama to propose a resolution declaring genocide a crime under international law. No longer in good health and saddened by the news that of his many relatives, only his brother's family had survived the Holocaust, Lemkin lobbied tirelessly. He used his linguistic skills to research and draft supportive statements for thirty different ambassadors. The resolution was adopted unanimously in 1946. Lemkin argued in the *American Journal of International Law* (1947) that, by asserting that genocide was an international crime and a matter of international concern, the 1946 declaration had established "the right of intervention on behalf of minorities slated for destruction" (p. 146).

Then UN Secretary-General Trygve Lie asked Lemkin to help prepare a draft of the Genocide Convention. The drafting was completed by Lemkin, Henri Donnedieu de Vabres, and Vespasian V. Pella during April and May 1947. Lemkin sought to exclude political groups from the draft, fearing that international disagreement on this would imperil the treaty. Having resigned his consultancy at the War Department to concentrate on the task, Lemkin set about lobbying for the treaty, scraping together funds to attend the General Assembly session in Paris. There, Lemkin experienced further setbacks. He encountered considerable objections to the draft article on cultural genocide. Lemkin saw cultural patterns, such as language, traditions, and monuments, as the shrine of a nation, and had tried to protect them in 1933 with his proposed international crime of vandalism. Rather than jeopardize the treaty, he accepted defeat. Lemkin had also assumed that states would accept the need for an international criminal tribunal with compulsory jurisdiction when a nation failed to investigate or prosecute genocide. He was surprised to find states agreeing that such a tribunal would only be binding on those states which accepted its jurisdiction.

Lemkin was additionally alarmed by other measures his opponents had inserted in the text of the treaty, so-called Trojan horses. He viewed Article XIV, which limited the duration of the Convention to ten years from its entering into force and then successive periods of five years, as one such measure. Another was Article XVI, which permitted a state to request a treaty revision at any time and empowered the UN General Assembly to determine the response to such a request. Despite these concerns, Lemkin took pleasure in seeing the Convention adopted by fifty-five votes, with none opposing, on December 9, 1948. Journalists discovered him hours after the meeting had adjourned still seated in the chamber, with tears flowing down his cheeks. Lemkin called the treaty an epitaph on his mother's grave.

Lemkin was repeatedly nominated for the Nobel Peace Prize during the 1950s. He went on to teach at Yale and Rutgers, and continued to lobby states to ratify the Genocide Convention. By October 1950 the Convention had twenty-four ratifications, four more than the twenty required for it to come into force. At the time of his death, in August 1959 following a heart attack, the treaty had some sixty signatories.

SEE ALSO Convention on the Prevention and Punishment of Genocide; Genocide; Language; Nuremberg Trials

BIBLIOGRAPHY

Hamilton, Bernard (2001). "The Passionate Adovocate Who Coined the Term Genocide." *Jewish Chronicle* 6875:30.

Jacobs, Steven Leonard and Samuel Totten, eds. (2002). "Totally Unofficial Man." In *Pioneers of Genocide Studies.* New York: Transaction Publishers.

Lemkin, Raphael (1944). *Axis Rule in Occupied Europe: Laws of Occupation, Analysis of Government, Proposals for Redress.* Washington, D.C.: Carnegie Endowment for International Peace, Division of International Law.

Lemkin, Raphael (1947). "Genocide as a Crime in International Law." *American Journal of International Law* 41(1):145–151.

Schabas, William A. (2000). *Genocide in International Law.* Cambridge, U.K.: Cambridge University Press.

Bernard F. Hamilton

Lenin, Vladimir
[APRIL 10, 1870–JANUARY 21, 1924]
Russian revolutionary, leader of the Bolshevik (later Communist) Party, and first ruler of the Union of Soviet Socialist Republics.

Vladimir Lenin was born Vladimir Ilich Ulianov and assumed the pseudonym of Lenin in 1900. His father was a school inspector in the central Russian town of Simbirsk, where Lenin was born on April 10, 1870. His older brother, Alexander, was executed in 1887 for his involvement in a failed assassination attempt on the life of Tsar Alexander the Third. Lenin's initial involvement in politics reflected his loyalty to the memory of his dead brother and his devotion to the ideals of equality and justice.

Lenin studied and then briefly practiced law before devoting himself to the revolutionary socialist doctrine of Marxism, beginning in 1893. Lenin married a fellow revolutionary, Nadezhda Krupskaia, after being sentenced in 1895 to his first period of internal exile. On the run from tsarist authorities, Lenin played little part in the unsuccessful 1905 revolution, and from 1907 to 1917 he lived outside of Russia. In 1903 Lenin assumed the leadership of the Bolsheviks, initially one of two factions of the Russian Social Democratic Labor Party, which was founded in 1898 (the other faction was called the Mensheviks, of which Leon Trotsky was an important leader). Lenin devoted his time to party organization duties and writing in an effort to win control over and give direction to the splintered left-wing opposition to the tsar.

Lenin was so appalled when Europe's socialists supported their countries' participation in World War I that he rejected the label of social democracy and adopted the term *communist,* in its place. The new name was a reference to the failed revolutionary government of the Paris Commune of 1871.

A victorious Lenin greets his supporters. After the Bolshevik Revolution of 1917, and during the ensuing war and famine, Lenin demonstrated a chilling disregard for the sufferings of his fellow countrymen. [GETTY IMAGES]

In 1917 Lenin was living in exile in Switzerland. He was as surprised as nearly everyone else by the sudden and total collapse of the tsarist government in March of that year, but quickly made plans to return home. The German government, seeing an opportunity to add to the chaos in Russia, allowed Lenin to travel on its railway back to Russia, and Lenin arrived there in April 1917. In that month he published his April Thesis, which virtually declared war on the Russian Provisional Government, the liberal but unelected ruling body that had taken over from the tsar. Lenin's genius lay in riding a wave of mounting discontent directed at this provisional government, which foolishly launched a new military offensive, failed to hold elections, and delayed crucial land reform.

At the fall of the tsarist government, the Russian population numbered more than 150 million people, but Lenin's Bolshevik Party boasted only twenty thousand members. Within six months of his return from exile, however, Lenin had greatly expanded his base of support and was in a position to bid for power. With the aid of the former Menshevik, Leon Trotsky, the Bolsheviks won control of the Petrograd garrison and on October 25, 1917, Lenin seized power from the enfeebled Provisional Government.

Lenin shrewdly justified his violent seizure of power as merely a transfer of authority to the soviets, the popular councils elected by workers and soldiers that sprang up everywhere after the fall of the tsar. Lenin declared the formation of a Soviet government, withdrew Russia from World War I, and invited the peasants to take charge of the land that had formerly belonged to the nobles, state, and church. At the same time, Lenin's government quickly moved to shut down opposition political parties and to censor the press, introduced conscription for the Red Army, and requisitioned grain from the peasants in order to fight the bloody Russian Civil War of 1918–1920. In January 1918, Lenin closed down the Constituent Assembly after the Bolsheviks won only 24 percent of the popular vote. In 1918, Lenin renamed the Bolshevik Party as the Communist Party.

The Cheka, the Russian acronym for the Extraordinary Commission for the Struggle against Counter-Revolution and Sabotage, was established on December 7, 1917, as the government's instrument of terror in its fight against political enemies. When Lenin was badly injured in a failed assassination attempt on August 30, 1918, his government quickly responded with the September 5, 1918, announcement of a policy of Red Terror that would take the form of arrests, imprisonments, and murders, triggering a civil war. Historian Richard Pipes has estimated that the Russian Civil War claimed two million combat deaths, two million deaths from epidemics, and five million deaths from famine. Another two million or more, mostly drawn from the better-educated classes, fled in the face of the violence. Their departure drained the country of its already small pool of experienced leaders, managers, and entrepreneurs. The final death toll of the Russian Civil War exceeded the eight million deaths of World War I.

Lenin believed that socialism was irreversible, and he admired the revolutionary spirit of the Russian working class, but he despaired of its economic and cultural backwardness. Karl Marx had predicted that socialism would triumph first in an advanced capitalist country like Britain or Germany, but Lenin hoped to lead the way and believed that the establishment of a Soviet government in Russia would inspire similar revolutions elsewhere in Europe. In August 1920, Lenin urged the Red Army to move rapidly to occupy Poland as a first stage in an attack upon the postwar settlement established by the Treaty of Versailles. For Lenin Russia was no more and no less than a staging post on the road to world revolution.

When the Red Army proved unable to defeat Poland and Communism failed to inspire a successful revolution in Germany, Lenin, retreated to a more cautious set of policies. In 1921 he initiated the New Economic Policy (NEP). Peasants were subjected to minimum taxation and allowed to trade their surpluses, whereas the government maintained its control of large industry and foreign trade. In December 1922, Lenin renamed his revolutionary state as the Union of Soviet Socialist Republics. Meanwhile, working-class protestors who demanded greater democracy, such as the Kronstadt mutineers in 1921, were brutally suppressed. The same fate awaited dissident factions within the Bolshevik Party, which were banned at the Tenth Party Congress of 1921. Before Lenin's death in 1924, the Soviet Union's first labor camps were set up on the remote Solovetsky Islands, and by the following year the population of these camps reached 6,000 prisoners. Under Stalin, these camps would evolve into the notorious Gulag, through which more than 20 million forced laborers would pass. During Lenin's rule compulsory collective farms never became policy, but he created the system of repression that, under Stalin, would lead not only to collectivization but also the extermination of kulaks (wealthy landholders).

Lenin suffered his first stroke on May 26, 1922, and died of a cerebral hemorrhage on January 21, 1924. Unlike Stalin, Lenin had never encouraged a personality cult. Nevertheless, after his death his body was embalmed and put on public display in Red Square. A cult celebrating the "living Lenin" was encouraged and pressed into service by his successors to add legitimacy to their rule. For sixty years, Russians read a sanitized version of Lenin's life. Documents that portrayed him in an unfavorable light were banned until after the Gorbachev era (1985–1991). For more than sixty years, Russian readers did not know that Lenin was happy to accept money from the German government in 1917 or that he probably ordered the murder of the tsar and the entire royal family in Ekaterinburg on July 16, 1918.

Both during his life and after his death, critical views of Lenin circulated. Bertrand Russell visited the Russian leader in 1920, and came away disturbed by Lenin's seeming indifference to the human suffering and loss that had taken place during the Russian Civil War. Other critics characterized him as an intelligent but humorless and intolerant fanatic. Since the fall of communism, archival documents dating from his rule tend to confirm previously existing impressions of the man and his rule. Nevertheless, historians are still divided over Lenin and his legacy. John Gooding, Roy Medvedev and Neil Harding consider Lenin to have pursued worthy ideals that were grotesquely distorted by the subsequent dictatorship of Stalin. Martin Malia, on the other hand, has argued that it was Lenin's championing of a wildly impractical strain of Marxism that

condemned Russia to its failed communist experiment. Pipes has described Lenin as embodying the hubris of Russia's *intelligentsia*, who were willing to sacrifice millions of lives for the sake of their utopian fantasies. According to Pipes, Lenin's system of government was the model whose features were copied not only by Stalin, but also by Benito Mussolini, Adolph Hitler and Mao Tse Tung.

Lenin was a prolific writer. His first essay appeared in 1894 and his collected works amounted to fifty-five volumes. In *What Is To Be Done*, Lenin argued for a strongly centralised party of professional revolutionaries. Critics have found in *What is to be Done* the germ of the idea for a one-party state. *Imperialism the Highest Stage of Capitalism* (1916) argued that finance capital had reached its final irrational phase and a new wave of revolutions was to be expected. *State and Revolution* (1917) is the most utopian of Lenin's writings, in that it hints at the Marxist vision of the good life after capitalism. His last pamphlets, including *Better Fewer But Better* (1923) suggest a less radical Lenin who is ready to accept a more evolutionary political path for the Soviet Union.

Lenin's fanatical commitment to his ideals in the face of immense human suffering must be viewed within the context of the repressive tsarist political system that preceded him and the pointless slaughter that took place throughout Europe during World War I. These events confirmed for Lenin that parliamentary democracy was a sham concealing the horror of war and repression. Abandoning all democratic constraints upon the activities of his revolutionary government, Lenin moved Europe and the world further along the road towards the mass killings of the later twentieth century.

SEE ALSO Gulag; Kulaks; Stalin, Joseph; Union of Soviet Socialist Republics

BIBLIOGRAPHY

Gooding, John (2002). *Socialism in Russia. Lenin and his Legacy, 1890-1991*. Basingstoke, U.K.: Palgrave.

Harding, Neil (1977). *Lenin's Political Thought*. London: Macmillan.

Malia, Martin (1994). *The Soviet Tragedy: A History of Socialism in Russia, 1917–1991*. New York: Free Press.

Pipes, Richard (1994). *Russia under the Bolshevik Regime, 1919–1924*. London: Harvill.

White, James D. (2001). *Lenin: The Practice and Theory of Revolution*. Basingstoke, U.K.: Palgrave.

Stephen Brown

Lepsius, Johannes

[DECEMBER 15, 1858–FEBRUARY 3, 1926]
German pastor, historical archivist

Johannes Lepsius is widely recognized as one of the most important opponents of the Turkish genocide of Armenians and as an early campaigner for modern concepts of human rights. Lepsius's work among Armenians during World War I, more so than that of any other individual, helped to document genocide and place it on the public agenda.

As a young man, Lepsius trained as a German evangelical church (Lutheran) pastor and became a missionary in Turkey during the mid-1890s. He came to public attention when he traveled in disguise to gather evidence on the Turkish massacres of tens of thousands of Armenians. Lepsius's report on the pogroms, *Armenien und Europa* (1896, 1897), stirred considerable controversy and significantly affected international relations with the Turkish sultanate. He also helped found the Deutsche Orient Mission to operate orphanages and schools for Armenian children.

New massacres of Armenians began in late 1914 and early 1915. The Young Turk military junta moved secretly and with extraordinary violence to exterminate Armenians. Protestant missionaries deep inside Turkey were among the few outsiders who witnessed the first months of the unfolding genocide. Lepsius compiled eyewitness accounts of the killings and deportations and, at some risk to his life, formally appealed to Turkish authorities to end the deadly deportations of Armenian women and children. The Young Turk war minister, Enver Pasha, refused this request.

Lepsius turned to publicity in an effort to bring pressure on the German government and, though it, the Young Turks. To avoid wartime censorship, in 1916 he privately published and distributed a report on the killings. Lepsius secretly collaborated with then U.S. Ambassador to Turkey, Henry Morgenthau, to document the Armenian genocide for English-speaking audiences.

Later, Lepsius also testified for the defense in the trial of Soghomon Tehlirian, the assassin of Turkish Interior Minister Tal'aat Pasha. Tehlirian was acquitted.

In the first months following the defeat of Germany and Turkey in World War I, the German foreign ministry perpetrated a deception on Lepsius that went undiscovered for the next seventy years. The post-war Turkish government rightly accused Germany of helping to mastermind the Armenian massacres. Germany was already facing allegations of committing atrocities in Europe and sought to avoid responsibility for crimes inside Turkey. For his part, Lepsius was committed to unearthing the most comprehensive record possible of the genocide of Armenians. Thus, he readily agreed to the foreign ministry's offer to let him prepare a series of books based on formerly secret German diplomatic records, beginning with a volume documenting German activities in Turkey and Armenia between 1914 and 1918.

German officials claimed that they were releasing a copy of the complete record to Lepsius, but they actually supplied him with censored versions of dozens of documents in order to conceal German complicity in the killings. In the end, Lepsius's published collection presented unusually frank and detailed evidence of the Young Turks's campaign of genocide, but tended to absolve Germany of any responsibility for those acts. The foreign ministry then used Lepsius's account in publicity and in international negotiations concerning German reparations for war crimes.

Lepsius went on to help prepare further volumes of previously secret German records concerning German-Turkish-Armenian relations. It was not until the 1990s that the ministry's true tactics were clearly documented, when scholars compared the published records with those captured after the fall of Nazi Germany in 1945 and with edited copies discovered in Lepsius's personal archives.

SEE ALSO Armenians in Ottoman Turkey and the Armenian Genocide; Germany; Morgenthau, Henry

BIBLIOGRAPHY

Alexander, Edward (1986). "The Lepsius Symposium: A Report in Summary." *Armenian Review* 39(4):95–99.

Dadrian, Vahakn (1995). *The History of the Armenian Genocide*. New York: Berghan Books.

Gust, Wolfgang, and Sigrid Gust, eds. (2003). *Armenian Genocide during the First World War: Documents from German State Archives, Revised and Extended Collection of Diplomatic Documents published by Johannes Lepsius in 1919 under the title, "Germany and Armenia."* Available from http://www.armenocide.net.

Christopher Simpson

Liberia

The beginnings of Liberia as a modern state are rooted in American circumstances that led to a back-to-Africa movement among a relatively small number of African-Americans, and which was supported by white American sponsors. With multiple motives, some far from charitable, the American Colonization Society launched the Liberian experiment in the early years of the nineteenth century. Liberia's initial purpose was to serve as a beachhead for the redemption of Africa from its perceived state of degradation. The agencies of this redeeming work were to be, in order of importance, the white man, the westernized black man, and then at the bottom of the heap, the non-westernized African peoples. Much of what became public policy in early Liberia rested on this hierarchical vision of human civilization. Liberia labored under this vision through the rest of the nineteenth century and into the early decades of the twentieth century.

The Rise of President Doe

A paradigm shift occurred at the end of World War II, when Liberia's supporters and its citizens moved from a commitment to their founding mission of civilizing and Christianizing the peoples of Africa and adopted in its place a philosophy of natural rights and its offshoot of democratic governance and respect for fundamental human rights. In a real sense Liberia was in the throes of this shift when the coup d'état of 1980 occurred.

Immediately prior to the coup, during the administration of President William R. Tolbert (1971–1980), a national reform movement was initiated. Tolbert had clear reformist proclivities, but he was not a strong political leader. Challenging Tolbert were several politically progressive groups, notably the Progressive Alliance of Liberia (PAL) and the Movement for Justice in Africa (MOJA). They were perceived as legitimate alternatives to the regime then in power.

There were many confrontations between advocates of change and those who wished to preserve the status quo before the fateful challenge occurred. Then the government announced the possibility of an increase in the price of rice, the country's staple food. The PAL demanded that the price of rice be left unchanged and signaled that, unless the government acceded to its demands, it would call for a mass rally to press its case. When the government replied that the price increase was only under discussion, and refused to grant PAL the necessary demonstration permit, PAL defiantly called for the rally anyway.

An unprecedented clash ensued between a throng of demonstrators and the government's security forces on April 14, 1979. Many of the demonstrators were killed, scores were maimed, and millions of dollars worth of property was destroyed or damaged. The demonstrators were expressing widespread disgust and anger with the entire political system, and voiced their dissatisfaction with the president, who symbolized that system.

The government attempted to put down the dissidents, but its efforts failed because the society was per-

Liberia map, 1998. [MARYLAND CARTOGRAPHICS]

ilously divided, especially within the nation's security forces. The police were prepared to carry out government orders, but military personnel refused to fire into the demonstrators, pointing out that their own children and kinsmen might be in the crowd. Abandoned and insecure, the Tolbert administration sought and received military assistance from President Sekou Touré of Guinea. When Guinean military forces arrived in Liberia, the Liberian military and a great many Liberian civilians were deeply offended.

On April 12, 1980, seventeen enlisted men in the Liberian Army led an attack on the President's mansion under the leadership of Master Sergeant Samuel K. Doe. They assassinated President Tolbert and overthrew his government, creating a new governing body, the People's Redemption Council (PRC), and Doe assumed the interim presidency.

The coupmakers' declaration of intent upon seizing power convinced most observers that the new government would implement progressive policies. They released all political prisoners and invited key figures in the opposition to help them form a new government. A progressive political agenda was announced, and it appeared that Doe and his followers were about to impose significant changes on the country by fiat. Accompanying the expression of intent, however, was a pattern of behavior that belied the stated progressive aims. Military personnel and other regime figures quickly adopted opulent lifestyles, lording it over their subordinates. More ominous still, the new regime began singling out individuals and families that they deemed associates of the deposed Tolbert administration. This development became clearer when, in the weeks following the coup, the PRC suddenly and publicly executed thirteen senior officials of the old regime. The executions touched off an international chorus of outrage and condemnation for this gross violation of rights, as did the apparent targeting of dissident Liberians for execution or persecution.

Regardless of internal and international outcries, these persecutions and secret executions continued. Soon, deadly conflicts sprang up within the PRC itself, as personality differences led to political purges. Several senior PRC members were executed on President Doe's orders. Eventually, Doe found himself in conflict with Commanding General Thomas Quiwonkpa, a popular soldier and a senior member of the PRC. After several bloody encounters between the Doe and Quiwonkpa factions, Quiwonkpa was forced to flee the country.

Fall of the Doe Regime

In 1985 two major events transpired. The first was a purported democratic election. When the people voted against Doe's military regime, the government illegally intervened in the process and reversed the outcome, declaring Doe the winner. The second event was Quiwonkpa's reappearence in Monrovia on November 12, 1985. Upon his return to Liberia, he attempted to lead a coup against Doe and install the candidate who was popularly believed to have won the election. Quiwonkpa's coup attempt failed. Incensed, President Doe carried out a rash of retaliatory killings. Estimates as to the number executed during this period range from 500 to as many as 3,000. The victims were largely drawn from the police, military, and security personnel of Nimba county, which was the home region of Quiwonkpa. The many who were killed were buried in mass graves in Nimba.

The Western media soon created a shorthand for understanding the gathering conflict, blaming the violence as arising from an ethnicity-based conflict between the Krahn (Doe's people) and his Mandingo supporters versus the Dhan and Mano peoples of Nimba County. This was only partially true, however. Doe was in fact lashing out at all opponents, real and imagined, regardless of their ethnic background. As a result, his presidency devolved into a reign of terror.

Doe was inaugurated President of Liberia in January 1986. He soon found it difficult to rule, however. The violence that followed the elections, coupled, in a curious way, with the events that immediately followed his own coup of 1980, engendered covert protest that eventually became open acts of rebellion. By the start of 1989, Liberia became increasingly unsafe.

A fallout in Africa at the end of the cold war was the emergence of the warlord insurgencies threatening to destabilize national governments. On Christmas Eve of 1989, the insurgent leader, Charles Taylor, announced to the Liberian and international media that he was heading an insurgency under the banner of the National Patriotic Front of Liberia (NPFL). His goal was to bring down the Doe regime and end the reign of terror. He set himself the goal of completing the unfinished work of Thomas Quiwonkpa.

Taylor's rebels advanced from the border between Liberia and neighboring Ivory Coast. As they penetrated Nimba County, Doe responded by initiating a scorched earth policy, sending his soldiers to raze whole villages and kill everything that moved. This tactic quickly galvanized the people, first in Nimba County, then in the nation as a whole. As the insurgency gathered momentum, the brutality on both sides was unparalleled in the history of Liberia. The violence was not limited to a clash between armies; tens of thousands of civilians died, and countless others were maimed or otherwise injured by the war.

The extreme violence early in the civil war was a consequence of problems at three levels. First was the inter-ethnic hostility that existed between Doe's Krahn and Mandingo supporters and the remnants of Quiwonkpa's Dahn and Mano followers, who now rallied behind Charles Taylor. Second, the Liberian population was, and is, comprised of a great many other ethnicities, distinguished by language and culture, so no true sense of shared national identity could be called upon to mitigate the violence. Finally, Liberia suffered from international neglect after the Cold War ended and Africa ceased to be viewed as strategically important to the United States, its traditional ally. The result for the Liberian people was that more than 200,000 of Liberia's 2.6 million people were killed, another 800,000 became internally displaced persons, and more than 700,000 fled abroad to live as refugees.

As the rebel groups approached Monrovia in early 1990 and engaged Doe's Armed Forces of Liberia (AFL), the slaughter increased. Some 2,000 Dhan and Mano, mostly women and children, sought refuge at the International Red Cross station in the main Lutheran Church compound in Monrovia. Although the Red Cross insignia were clearly visible, AFL death squads invaded the refuge on the night of July 29, 1990, and massacred the more than 600 people who sheltered there. In the days that followed, the death squads roamed the streets of Monrovia and its environs, attacking any civilians suspected of being sympathetic to the rebels or lukewarm toward Doe's regime.

By mid-1990 Doe's control of the country was limited to the area around the presidential palace. Prince Johnson, leader of the breakaway Independent National Patriotic Front of Liberia (INPF), risked a meeting with Doe at the Barclay Training Center (a military barracks) in Monrovia on August 18, 1990. Doe suggested that Johnson join him in a "native solidarity" alliance against Taylor, who was accused of representing "settler" interests (meaning the interests of descendents of the African Americans who came to the region in the nineteenth century). Johnson declined the offer of alliance and returned to his base on the outskirts of Monrovia.

A few days after this meeting, Doe led a foray into territory held by Johnson's forces in order to visit the leaders of the Economic Community Monitoring Group (ECOMOG), a peacekeeping force that the economic community of West African states (ECOWAS) has created in an effort to help resolve African conflicts. During this foray, however, Doe's entourage was attacked, most were killed, and Doe himself was captured. Badly injured and bleeding from serious leg wounds, he was taken to Prince Johnson's compound. There he was tortured and then left to bleed to death, the whole gruesome episode captured by Johnson's video camera. On September 10, 1990, he died and his naked body was placed on public display.

Taylor's Rise to Power

With Doe's death, the struggle for power intensified. The rival factions headed by Taylor and Johnson now faced a third challenger: a civilian Interim Government of National Unity (IGNU). This entity was the creation of an ECOWAS-sponsored summit meeting held in the Gambia, where the leaders of Liberia's neighbors in West Africa sought ways to end the conflict. Professor Amos Sawyer, a Liberian national, was chosen the head of the IGNU by a representative body of Liberian political and civil leaders.

Two years later, the conflict still raged on. Taylor attempted to seize Monrovia, in October 1992. His self-styled "Operation Octopus" was a bloody military showdown in which he pitted an army of children (their ages ranged from 8 to 15) against the professional soldiers of ECOMOG. Thousands were slain, including five American nuns serving homeless Liberian children. Taylor's coup attempt failed.

By 1996 a coalition government composed of former rebel leaders and civilians had been put in place, but endemic distrust led to a second showdown in Monrovia. Three members of the ruling Council of State, Charles Taylor of the NPFL, Alhaji Kromah of the United Liberation Movement of Liberia, and Wilton Sankawolo, the civilian chair of the Council, attempted to arrest another government minister, Roosevelt Johnson, for allegations of murder. Seven weeks of fighting ensued and, once again, thousands of Liberians—mostly civilians—were killed. This phase of the civil war ended when regional and international peace facilitators decided to hold new elections, in which warlords were permitted to participate. Taylor, according to some observers, won the vote, but other election observers have suggested that many who voted for him did so only out of fear. Taylor promised peace, but he was unable to establish legitimacy for his presidency at either the domestic or international level.

In fact, just as Liberia appeared to be settling down, neighboring Sierra Leone erupted into war, with the May 25, 1997, overthrow of that country's elected government. Taylor had undergone guerilla insurgency training in Libya in the late 1980s alongside Foday Sankoh and other West African dissidents. An informal pact was made between Taylor and Sankoh that they would remain in solidarity as they embarked upon violently changing the political order in the subregion. Sankoh fought with Taylor's NPFL, and when in 1991 Sankoh's RUF appeared on the Sierra Leone scene, a close relationship characterized their leaders. Thus, when the 1997 coup brought Sankoh's Revolutionary United Front (RUF) into power, however briefly, Taylor was prepared to recognize Sankoh's claim to legitimacy and assist his Sierra Leonian ally.

The destabilizing effects of Taylor's support of the RUF were not only felt in Sierra Leone, but throughout much of West Africa. This led the United Nations to order an investigation. The resulting UN Security Council Panel of Experts Report implicated the President of Liberia in the exploitation of Sierra Leone's diamond mines through his ties with the RUF, and of using a portion of the proceeds to keep the RUF supplied with arms. The charges were clearly documented, but Taylor stoutly denied them. Despite his denials, in May 2001 the UN Security Council imposed punitive sanctions on Liberia.

A United Nations peacekeeper from Gambia welcomes a battalion of Bangladesh peacekeepers upon their arrival at Roberts International Airport in Liberia in 2003. [AP/WIDE WORLD PHOTOS]

The End of Taylor's Regime

In 2002 the war in Sierra Leone was largely contained, due to massive international intervention, and democratic elections were held. Sankoh's RUF, now transformed into the Revolutionary United Party (RUP), was roundly defeated. For his part in supporting the RUF, Taylor's government in Liberia was now internationally viewed as a pariah regime. Taylor's troubles, however, had begun three years earlier, when a group of Liberians formed a rebel group called Liberians United For Reconciliation and Democracy (LURD). LURD's stated objective was Taylor's removal from power because of his atrocious human rights record and the impunity that generally characterized his leadership.

LURD stepped up its attacks in early 2003, and a new rebel group, the Movement for Democracy in Liberia (MODEL), made its appearance in March. MODEL quickly gained ascendancy in the southern part of the country, whereas LURD's power was concentrated in the north. In March, LURD's forces opened several fronts, advancing to within a few miles of Monrovia. Tens of thousands of civilians were displaced during

the fighting. On June 4 of the same year, Taylor was indicted by the UN sponsored Special Court in Sierra Leone for his complicity in war crimes and crimes against humanity arising from his activities in that country. U.S. President George W. Bush publicly called on Taylor to resign and leave the country, thus increasing the pressure on Taylor's regime.

On July 17, a LURD offensive into the capital resulted in hundreds more killed and displaced persons. International intervention finally produced a respite, as international facilitators set up peace talks in Ghana. Taylor bowed to the pressures on August 11, when he handed power over to his vice president and accepted exile in Nigeria. The peace talks concluded on August 18, and on August 21 a new leader, Gyude Bryant, was chosen to chair an interim government. To maintain the peace, the UN Security Council sent 15,000 peacekeeping troops and set up a rescue operation to help deal with the aftermath of two decades of bloody civil wars.

SEE ALSO Peacekeeping; Sierra Leone

BIBLIOGRAPHY

Adebajo, Adekeye (2002). *Building Peace In West Africa: Liberia, Sierra Leone, and Guinea-Bissau.* Boulder, Colo.: Lynne Rienner Publishers.

Adebajo, Adekeye (2002). *Liberia's Civil War, Nigeria, ECOMOG, and Regional Security in West Africa.* Boulder, Colo.: Lynne Rienner Publishers.

Dunn, D. Elwood (1999). "The Civil War in Liberia." In *Civil Wars In Africa: Roots and Resolution,* ed. A. Taisier and R. Matthews. Montreal: McGill-Queen's University Press.

International Crisis Group (2003). "Tackling Liberia: The Eye of the Regional Storm." *Africa Report* (April 30) 62: p. 49.

Lawyers Committee for Human Rights (1986). *Liberia, A Promise Betrayed: A Report on Human Rights.* New York: The Lawyers Committee.

Reno, William (2001). *Warlord Politics and African States.* Boulder, Colo.: Lynne Rienner Publishers.

Daniel Elwood Dunn

Linguistic Genocide

When the United Nations (UN) undertook preparatory work for what became the 1948 International Convention for the Prevention and Punishment of the Crime of Genocide, linguistic genocide as a central aspect of cultural genocide was discussed along with physical genocide as a serious crime against humanity. The ad hoc committee that prepared the Convention specified the following types of acts as examples of cultural genocide in Article III:

> Any deliberate act committed with intent to destroy the language, religion or culture of a national, racial or religious group on grounds of national or racial origin or religious belief, such as (1) Prohibiting the use of the language of the group in daily intercourse or in schools, or the printing and circulation of publications in the language of the group; and (2) Destroying or preventing the use of libraries, museums, schools, historical monuments, places of worship or other cultural institutions and objects of the group.

When the UN General Assembly finally approved the Convention, sixteen member nations voted against Article III covering linguistic and cultural genocide (*Official Records of the General Assembly,* Third Session, Part I, Sixth Committee, 83rd meeting). Among those who "opposed the prohibition of cultural genocide" were Denmark, the United States, and Great Britain. Britain wanted the Convention to be restricted "to the physical extermination of human groups" (Freedman, 1992, p. 89; McKean, 1983, pp. 105–112).

The use of a group's language can be prohibited directly or indirectly. Books in prohibited languages have been burned. Earlier, the use of indigenous and minority groups' languages was often prohibited by physically punishing people, especially children, who used them. Many children, all over the world, have been beaten, left without food, locked in dark places, and forced to drag stones or wear other heavy objects around their necks just for uttering a few words in their own languages in schools. Shame is the tool most frequently used: Schoolchildren speaking a banned language have been made to stand in corners or in front of the class, carry objects showing that they have broken the rules, write a sentence such as "I am an idiot" countless times on a blackboard, or pay fines. In other instances, they have been transformed into traitors and spies, escaping punishment or receiving some small reward if they reveal to their teachers the identity of other children using the forbidden language.

Emphasis on the assimilation of immigrants into the United States led to state laws at the end of the nineteenth and beginning of the twentieth century, such as the 1873 Minnesota law requiring that only English be spoken in the classroom. Nebraska prohibited all teaching of modern foreign languages. During and after World War I other states, including Louisiana, Ohio, and Indiana, prohibited the teaching of German. Bans on teaching foreign languages were successfully challenged in the U.S. Supreme Court in *Meyer v. Nebraska* (262 U.S. 390 [1923]). In the early twenty-first century physical punishment is resorted to less frequently to repress the use of a language. Instead, structural arrangements within a country and economic punishment and rewards are utilized. If the children's own language has no place in the curriculum, if it is not the main language of teaching, and if there are no teachers in daycare centers or schools who are legally allowed to use the children's language, its use in "daily intercourse or in schools" becomes de facto prohibited, and the children are forced to assimilate to a dominant majority or foreign language. Most of this prohibition is more sophisticated than the earlier physical punishment for speaking the mother tongue (Skutnabb-Kangas, 2000).

In addition to the specific definition of linguistic genocide presented above, two of the five definitions of genocide from the present UN Convention (Articles II[b] and II[e]) apply to the contemporary education of most indigenous and minority peoples:

- forcibly transferring children of the group to another group (from Article II[e])

- causing serious bodily or mental harm to members of the group (emphases added) (from Article II[b])

Assimilationist submersion education, in which indigenous and minority children are forced to accept teaching through the medium of dominant languages, also causes mental harm and often leads its students to using the dominant language with their own children later on. Over a generation or two, the children are linguistically and in other ways forcibly transferred to a dominant group. This happens to millions of speakers of threatened languages all over the world. There are no schools or classes teaching children through the medium of the threatened indigenous or minority languages. The transfer to the majority language-speaking group is thus not voluntary: Alternatives do not exist, and parents do not have enough reliable information about the long-term consequences of the various choices available to them. As a consequence, this is not an issue of "language suicide," even though it might at first seem as if the speakers are themselves abandoning their languages.

It is in a child's best interest to learn the official language of his or her country. But learning new languages, including the dominant languages, should not happen subtractively, but additively, that is, in addition to their own languages. Formal education that is subtractive, that is, education that teaches children something of a dominant language at the cost of their first language, is genocidal. This dominant language often is an old colonial language, spoken only by a small but powerful numerical minority (such has been the case, for example, in many African countries). An educational philosophy claiming that minority children learn the dominant language best if they receive most of their education through it is mistaken; minority children educated mainly through the medium of their own language learn the dominant language better than if they are educated only or primarily in the dominant language.

Though some argue that the absence of any deliberate intention in such acts means that these acts are not in contravention of the Convention, a contrary position suggests that if a state organizes minority education contrary to massive research evidence, so that this education results in serious mental harm and forcible transfer of minority children to a dominant group, such acts must be seen as intentional on the part of the state in the same way as any failure to take into account obvious evidence of harm is culpable.

State policies leading to diminishing numbers of languages may be based on the false premise that monolingualism is normal and natural (even though most countries are multilingual), or more desirable, or, at the very least, more efficient and economical even if such policies waste the talents of its citizens and decrease democratic participation. Others believe the extinction of minority languages is inevitable: Moderniza-

tion leads to linguistic homogenization and only romantics regret it. However, linguistic diversity and multilingualism enhance creativity and are necessary in knowledge-driven societies where diversity is highly valued. Furthermore, some states regard linguistic human rights as divisive on the rationale that minorities will reproduce themselves, and even demand cultural autonomy, economic autonomy, and, in the end, political autonomy or even their own state, thus ultimately leading to the disintegration of nation-states. These erroneous beliefs are an important causal factor behind the death of languages. The prognosis of the United Nations Educational, Scientific, and Cultural Organization (UNESCO) is that only 5 to 10 percent of the approximately seven thousand spoken languages in modern times may still be used by the year 2100.

SEE ALSO Genocide; Language

BIBLIOGRAPHY

Capotorti, Francesco (1979). *Study on the Rights of Persons Belonging to Ethnic, Religious and Linguistic Minorities.* UN Document E/CN.4/Sub.2/384/Rev.1 1991.

Freedman, Warren (1992). *Genocide: A People's Will to Live.* Buffalo, N.Y.: William S. Hein.

McKean, Warwick (1983). *Equality and Discrimination under International Law.* Oxford: Oxford University Press.

Skutnabb-Kangas, Tove (2000). *Linguistic Genocide in Education—Or Worldwide Diversity and Human Rights?* Mahwah, N.J.: Lawrence Erlbaum.

Whitaker, Ben (1985). *Study of the Question of the Prevention and Punishment of the Crime of Genocide.* Revised. UN Document E/CN.4/Sub.2/1985/6.

Tove Skutnabb-Kangas

London Charter

The London Charter was part of an agreement concluded August 8, 1945, by the World War II allies to prosecute the "major war criminals of the European Axis." Several Allies had considered the possibility of summarily executing Nazi leaders. The United States then pressed for trials, and the other Allies agreed. Parties to the agreement were France, the United Kingdom, the USSR, and the United States. The Charter provided for the creation of a court, the International Military Tribunal (IMT), composed of four judges, one from each signatory state. The Charter gave the Tribunal jurisdiction over three categories of offense: crimes against peace, war crimes, and crimes against humanity.

At the conclusion of World War I, the Treaty of Versailles had called for trial of the German Kaiser "for a supreme offense against international morality and the sanctity of treaties," but that trial was never held. The London Charter represented the first successful attempt to carry through with trials, at the supra-national level, of major figures accused of responsibility for an aggressive war and for particular atrocities perpetrated during that war.

The category of war crimes included offenses found in established principles of customary international law, which had previously been applied by courts of individual countries to prosecute military personnel. War crimes were defined in the Charter to include "murder, ill treatment, or deportation to slave labor, murder or ill treatment of prisoners of war, and wanton destruction of cities, towns, or villages."

The category of crimes against humanity was less well grounded in customary international law. The Charter defined it as "murder, extermination, enslavement, deportation, and other inhumane acts committed against any civilian population before or during the war or persecutions on political, racial, or religious grounds in execution of or in connection with any crime within the jurisdiction of the Tribunal, whether or not in violation of the domestic law of the country where perpetrated."

The category of crimes against peace included the "planning, preparation, initiation or waging of a war of aggression." This category was only weakly grounded in customary international law. War among states was first prohibited by treaty in the 1920s, and even if war was wrongful on the part of a state, as legal experts of the time argued, it was not clear that it was wrongful as a penal offense for which an individual could be held responsible.

Importantly, the London Charter stipulated that the official position of an accused individual provided no immunity from prosecution, and that superior orders were not a defense, although they might be taken into account to mitigate punishment.

The London Charter provided that if an accused acted as a member of a group, the Tribunal could declare the group a "criminal organization." The effect of such a declaration was that in subsequent trials to be held in the four zones of occupation of Germany, the court of an occupying power would be authorized to try persons for membership in such an organization.

The prosecution team as stipulated by the Charter was composed of a chief prosecutor from each of the four signatory states. Rights of defendants were specified, including receipt of a particularized indictment, the opportunity to present evidence and cross-examine witnesses, translation of proceedings into a language the accused would understand, and the right to be represented by counsel or to represent oneself.

The London Charter had a major impact on the subsequent development of internationally defined crimes. The category of crimes against humanity served as the basis for conceptualizing the category of genocide, which was defined and criminalized in the UN Convention on the Prevention and Punishment of the crime of genocide, adopted in 1948.

The United Nations (UN) General Assembly tasked its International Law Commission with drafting a code of offenses based on the London Charter, with the idea that it might be adopted as a treaty. Although this effort eventually came to naught, the categories of be international crime outlined in the London Charter were used, with modifications, in the crime definitions written into the charters of the two tribunals that the UN Security Council formed in the 1990s to address atrocities committed in Yugoslavia and Rwanda. These categories also served as the model for the crime definitions in the Statute of the International Criminal Court (ICC), which came into force in 2002.

The London Charter was also a precursor to the concept of human rights law that emerged in international society after World War II. Whereas the London Charter placed responsibility on leaders, human rights law ascribed it to states, establishing an elaborate network of mechanisms to ensure that states would not mistreat individuals.

SEE ALSO Control Council Law No. 10; Crimes Against Humanity; Germany; Nuremberg Trials; War Crimes

BIBLIOGRAPHY
International Military Tribunal (1947). *Trial of the Major War Criminals before the International Military Tribunal.* 42 vols. Nuremberg: International Military Tribunal.
Office of Chief Counsel for the Prosecution of Axis Criminality. *Nazi Conspiracy and Aggression.* 8 volumes. Washington, D.C.: U.S. Government Printing Office.
John Quigley

Mandela, Nelson

[JULY 18, 1918–]
Anti-apartheid peace activist; former president of South
Africa

Nelson Rolihlahla Mandela was born in 1918 in Quno,
a village near Umtata in the province of Transkei on the
southeastern coast of South Africa, near the Indian
Ocean. A scion of the Madiba tribal clan, he belonged
to the Thembu people, his great-grandfather having
been a Thembu king. Nelson's father, Gadla Henry
Mphakayiswa Mandela, was chief counselor to the paramount chief of Thembuland. He had four wives and
thirteen children, but died in 1927. Young Mandela
then became the ward of the chief and was groomed for
the chieftainship. An African teacher at the local primary school gave the young Mandela the English name
Nelson, but he was affectionately known as Madiba by
his friends. He attended Healdtown Methodist Boarding School and matriculated for a bachelor's degree at
Fort Hare University, where he completed two years
before leaving for Johannesburg in 1940. He received
his degree, completed articles of clerkship, and met
Walter Sisulo, who introduced him to the law firm Wit-
kin, Sidelsky, and Eidelman. He attended the University of Witwatersrand and became a lawyer.

Struggle against Apartheid

In 1943 Mandela joined the African National Congress
(ANC). Founded in 1912, the goal of the ANC was to
end white domination and create a multiracial South
Africa. At this time he made friends with the leaders of
the Indian community, who were protesting against

new legislation restricting their right to purchase land.
Mandela observed their practice of peaceful resistance
and learned about the philosophy of nonviolent disobedience advocated by the Indian lawyer Mohandas Gandhi. Gandhi spent twenty-one years in South Africa
helping the Hindu population defend their human
rights.

In 1944 Mandela, together with Oliver Tambo and
Walter Sisulu, formed the Youth League of the African
National Congress. The Youth League was impatient
with the slow pace of progress and was determined to
make the ANC an activist organization. Also in 1944
Mandela married Evelyn Mase, a nursing student who
had grown up in Thembuland. He had three children
with Mase. They divorced in 1957 and a year later he
married Winnie Madikiyela, a social worker from Pon-
doland. She bore him two daughters, Zenani and
Zindzi.

In 1948 the white National Party came to power
under Daniel Malan, whose platform was called apartheid, or "apartness." Although racial laws and land dispossession had already been known during the colonial
period, the National Party enacted new laws providing
for racial segregation, including the Separate Representation of Voters Act and the Prohibition of Mixed Marriages Act.

In 1949 the ANC Youth League drafted a program
of action calling for mass strikes, boycotts, and passive
resistance. As a response, the National Party passed the
Suppression of Communism Act, the Population and
Registration Act, and the Group Areas Act, aimed at en-

A triumphant Nelson Mandela, leader of the African National Congress' struggle against apartheid. [AP/WIDE WORLD PHOTOS]

forcing apartheid policies and crushing any mass resistance movement.

As a member of the ANC executive committee from 1949, Mandela organized the Defiance Campaign in 1952, a nonviolent mass resistance movement against apartheid laws. Also in 1952 Mandela and Tambo opened a law firm in downtown Johannesburg, the first black law firm in South Africa, specializing in defending black South Africans from the injustices associated with apartheid laws, particularly the so-called pass laws that restricted freedom of residence and movement.

White rule in South Africa meant that some 5 million whites governed over a population of 25 million blacks, Indians, and other ethnicities. As an alternative to apartheid, Mandela offered a plan for a multiracial society, in which majority black rule would guarantee the welfare of all South Africans, black and white alike. As early as June 1955 he drafted an idealistic program, the "Freedom Charter," containing principles of coexistence and reconciliation.

Mandela also struggled against the so-called Bantustan policy launched by the government of prime minister Hendrik Verwoerd in 1959, a program that aimed at forcibly resettling parts of the black population into larger reservations or ghettos, called "homelands," frequently separating the work force from their families. This partly implemented policy of resettlement constituted a crime against humanity according to the Nuremberg judgment, which condemned Nazi demographic manipulations, including mass deportations, population transfers, and internal displacements carried out during World War II. These acts of war affected nearly one million Poles, who were expelled from the Warthegau into eastern Poland, and more than 100,000 French Alsatians expelled into Vichy, France.

Conflict and Imprisonment

While the African National Congress vigorously condemned the 1959 Promotion of Bantu Self-Government Act, which fragmented the black African population into eight separate black homelands, some tribal leaders accepted the policy and cooperated with the apartheid government. Mandela's vocal opposition to the Bantustan policy exacerbated tensions with the government, and he was repeatedly arrested and harassed, ultimately being charged with high treason and subjected to the treason trial, which dragged on for several years.

In a climate of escalating violence, demonstrations in March 1960 culminated in a massacre at Sharpeville, a town southwest of Johannesburg, in which sixty-nine protesters were killed by the white police. The government declared a state of emergency and banned the ANC. Mandela was again arrested and kept for five months at the prison center known as Pretoria Local. Quite unexpectedly, when the treason trial ended in March 1961, he was found not guilty.

Facing the reality that peaceful overtures were met with force, in the summer of 1961 Mandela endorsed the necessity of armed struggle and formed the *Umkhonto we Sizwe* ("the Spear of the Nation") or MK, the military wing of the ANC, which mainly targeted government offices, economic installations, and symbols of apartheid.

Early in 1962 Mandela illegally left South Africa for a period of six months, to canvas in London and elsewhere for financial support for the armed struggle. He took military training in Ethiopia and addressed the Conference of the Pan African Freedom Movement of East and Central Africa in Addis Ababa. Upon his return to South Africa in August 1962 he was arrested, charged with illegal exit and incitement to strike, tried, and sentenced to five years' imprisonment. He was first held in Pretoria and then transferred to the maximum security prison at Robben Island, some four miles off the coast of Cape Town. Although already imprisoned, he was newly indicted on charges of sabotage and attempting to overthrow the government by violence. Mandela's statements from the dock at his trial in Rivonia, a suburb of Johannesburg, constitute classics in the history of resistance movements:

> During my lifetime I have dedicated myself to this struggle of the African people. I have fought against white domination, and I have fought against black domination. I have cherished the ideal of a democratic and free society in which all persons live together in harmony and with equal opportunities. It is an ideal which I hope to live for and to achieve. But if needs be, it is an ideal for which I am prepared to die (Meredith, 1998, p. 268).

Mandela escaped capital punishment, but was sentenced to life imprisonment. In all, he spent twenty-seven years in prison, including eighteen at Robben Island as prisoner number 466/64, where he worked in a lime quarry until he was transferred in March 1982 to Pollsmoor Prison in Cape Town. In December 1988 he was transferred to the Victor Verster Prison near Paarl, from which he was released on February 11, 1990.

Peacemaker and Renowned Leader

Decades of international condemnation of apartheid, accompanied by severe economic sanctions, denial of bank loans, widespread disinvestment in South Africa, and international ostracism, including exclusion from the United Nations General Assembly and from participation in the work of international organizations, persuaded the South African government that the price of maintaining the apartheid system was too high, even for the white South African population. Thus, in February 1990 president Frederik Willem de Klerk lifted the ban on the ANC and paved the way for a nonviolent departure from apartheid.

In 1991, at the first national conference of the ANC held inside South Africa, Mandela was elected president of the ANC. In 1992 president de Klerk and Mandela signed a Record of Understanding and established an elected constitutional assembly to develop a new democratic constitution for South Africa. Later they developed the idea of "truth commissions" aimed at reconciliation of white and black in the post-apartheid period.

In 1992 Mandela separated from Winnie, who had become a controversial figure in South Africa. They divorced in March 1996 and on his eightieth birthday, in 1998, Mandela married Graca Machel, the widow of the former president of neighboring Mozanbique.

Mandela was awarded the Nobel Peace Price in 1993, together with de Klerk. Mandela was the second opponent of apartheid to win the prize; in 1984 archbishop Desmond Tutu had been honored for his efforts to end apartheid in South Africa.

From April 26 to April 29, 1994, the first all-races election took place in South Africa on the basis of the one-man/one-vote principle. Mandela was elected president, the ANC won 252 of the 400 seats in the national assembly, and de Klerk became deputy president.

On May 10, 1994, Mandela took office as the first democratically elected president of South Africa and served one term until June 1999. His generosity of spirit and unwillingness to take revenge won him the respect of his white South African adversaries. Mandela's legacy is a new South Africa that enjoys greater racial harmony than ever before and a quality of reconciliation that remains an example for other conflict-ridden societies.

SEE ALSO Apartheid; South Africa

BIBLIOGRAPHY

Benson, Mary (1986). *Nelson Mandela: The Man and the Movement.* New York: W.W. Norton.

de Klerk, Willem (1991). *F. W. de Klerk: The Man in His Time.* Johannesburg, South Africa: Jonathan Ball.

Holland, Heidi (1989). *The Struggle: A History of the African National Congress.* London: Grafton.

Mandela, Nelson (1993). *Nelson Mandela Speaks: Forging a Democratic, Non-Racial South Africa.* New York: Pathfinder.

Mandela, Nelson (1994). *Long Walk to Freedom: The Autobiography of Nelson Mandela.* Boston: Little, Brown.

Mandela, Winnie (1985). *Part of My Soul* (1985). Harmondsworth, U.K.: Penguin.

Meredith, Martin (1998). *Nelson Mandela: A Biography.* New York: St. Martin's Press.

Sampson, Anthony (1999). *Mandela: The Authorized Biography* New York: Knopf.

Alfred de Zayas

Mao Zedong

[DECEMBER 26, 1893–SEPTEMBER 9, 1976]
Communist leader of People's Republic of China

Born in Shaoshan (Hunan), Mao Zedong was the son of a moderately wealthy peasant. After a checkered classical primary education and training at the Hunan Teacher's College, the young Mao gathered like-minded anarchists in his bookstore in Changsha. In 1921 he cofounded the Chinese Communist Party (CCP). After the collapse of the united front with the

After the communist victory in the long Chinese civil war, Chairman Mao prepares to deliver a public proclamation. Tiananmen Square, 1949. [BETTMANN/CORBIS]

Chinese population in a nuclear war so long as this would help bring about the downfall of world capitalism.

Mao's desire at Yan'an to cement his leadership of the CCP met opposition from two directions. First, pro-Soviet communists returned from Moscow to work for the Bolshevization of the party. Second, urban intellectuals who had been attracted by the utopia Yan'an seemed to promise in an otherwise corrupt China demanded greater freedoms once they recognized the repressive nature of the CCP regime. Benefiting from his disputed but, as it eventually turned out, correct decisions with regard to conduct of the civil war, Mao in the early 1940s pushed for a party purge, with the goal of installing his version of communism. A small number of dissidents were driven to commit suicide or killed. Although Mao in 1945 apologized publicly for the brutality of the campaign, it nevertheless set a precedent for future campaigns against dissidents, real or imagined.

The Korean War (1950–1953) against the "imperialist" United States provided the backdrop for class warfare against so-called capitalist elements, designed to rectify abuses tenant farmers and workers had endured in the past. Incomplete evidence from China's countryside suggests that it often served as a pretext for the continuation of local clan conflict by other means. According to Mao ("On the Correct Handling of Contradictions among the People," February 27, 1957), 800,000 counterrevolutionaries were killed (in 1952 China's population was 575 million).

In the wake of Nikita Khruschev's Secret Speech (February 1956), in which the Soviet leader charged his predecessor Joseph Stalin with criminal and arbitrary rule, and the resulting Hungarian uprising against Soviet occupation (October 1956), Mao tried to preempt the outburst of pent-up dissatisfaction by allowing criticism under highly controlled conditions (the Hundred Flowers Campaign that occurred during the spring of 1957). Despite all the precautions taken to avoid this, party members and intellectuals called for greater freedoms. In the resulting antirightist campaigns in subsequent years, critics, including leaders of national minorities (particularly in Xinjiang and after 1959 also in Tibet), were persecuted, lost their positions, and were sent to reeducation camps. An unspecified, but probably large, number of victims died or suffered permanent damage to their health from forced labor, abuse, and malnutrition in the camps.

By far the greatest loss of life during Mao's regime stemmed from the deadly spring famines (1959–1961) of the Great Leap Forward. Unlike the Ukrainian famines in the early 1930s, which Stalin had planned to

Nationalist Party in 1927, the two former allies fought a civil war until 1949. At its beginning the CCP found itself in rural areas trying to stem rapid decline. Forced from its largest base in Jiangxi in 1934, the party commenced its famous, yearlong Long March to Yan'an (Shaanxi), during which Mao rose to a preeminent leadership position. Only after continued internal struggle did Mao emerge in 1945 as the "chairman" of the CCP—a position he retained until his death in 1976 in Beijing. In 1949, after victory in the civil war, the CCP founded the People's Republic of China, with Mao serving as the chairman (or president) of the new country until 1959.

Given the merciless nature of political conflict in Republican China (1911–1949) and the extraordinary brutality of the Japanese occupation (1931–1945), it is no surprise that Mao concluded that a "revolution is not a dinner party" (*Investigation of the Peasant Movement in Hunan*, 1927). His astonishing disregard for individual human lives in later years, however, cannot be explained solely by the brutalizing experiences of his early career. Starting in the mid-1950s, Mao repeatedly affirmed his willingness to sacrifice up to a third of the crush as anti-Russian nationalism, the famine of 1959 resulted from the misguided economic policies of the Great Leap Forward. However, once it became clear that the Great Leap Forward had not only failed to produce the promised economic miracles but also led to serious economic disruptions, Chairman Mao refused to change course because he feared a loss of face, if not his preeminent position. The acrimonious debates about economic reform in 1959 convinced Mao that alleged rightists in the party wanted to replace him. After crushing his supposed enemies, Mao relaunched the Great Leap Forward in late 1959; it collapsed on its own a year later. Due to lack of direct evidence, the number of famine victims can only be calculated on the basis of incomplete demographic data. Most historians agree that excess deaths (the difference between projected and actual demographic data) total at least 20 million (with more than two-thirds of these deaths occurring in 1960 alone); high estimates stand at 65 million (in 1957 China's population was 646 million).

Although still poorly understood, the Cultural Revolution (1966–1976) was, in many respects, Mao's most far-reaching attempt to rid China of his supposed opponents. Unlike Stalin, who remained in firm control of the Soviet party from the 1920s, Mao never had complete command over the CCP. Many of the campaigns from 1957 onward were attempts to increase his political control over the party. However, once Mao realized by the mid-1960s that his quest for undisputed leadership had been stymied, he turned to forces outside the CCP to attack what he considered a reticent party unwilling to implement his erratic policies. The Cultural Revolution was a mixture of party purge and class warfare, during which radicalized students persecuted, humiliated, tortured, and even murdered alleged rightists or counterrevolutionaries. The exact number of those who were killed, committed suicide, or died in camps is not known; nonetheless, it is clear that most of the victims came from the educated strata, had party backgrounds, or were from minorities.

SEE ALSO China; Famine

BIBLIOGRAPHY

Becker, Jasper (1996). *Hungry Ghosts: China's Secret Famine.* London: John Murray.

Lee, Hong Yung (1978). *The Politics of the Chinese Cultural Revolution: A Case Study.* Berkeley, Calif.: University of California Press.

Mao Zedong. "On the Correct Handling of Contradictions among the People," February 27, 1957, Harold C. Hinton, ed. (1980). *The People's Republic of China, 1949–1979: A Documentary Survey.* Volume I, 1949–1957. Wilmington: Scholarly Resources, 534–551.

Mao Zedong. "Investigation of the Peasant Movement in Hunan, March 1927." Mao Zedong (1965). *Selected Works of Mao Zedong.* Volume 1. Beijing: Foreign Languages Press, 23–59.

Short, Philip (1999). *Mao: A Life.* New York: Henry Holt.

Teiwes, Frederick C. (1979). *Politics and Purges in China: Rectification and the Decline of Party Norms, 1950–1965.* White Plains, N.Y.: M.E. Sharpe.

Lorenz M. Lüthi

Massacres

The term *massacre* can be defined as a form of action, usually collective, aimed at the elimination of civilians or non-combatants including men, women, children or elderly people unable to defend themselves. The definition may also include the killing of soldiers who have been disarmed. One of the most notorious European examples of the latter was when Soviet troops massacred Polish officers in Katyn in February 1940. There are various definitional problems inherent in the notion of "massacre." For instance, there are divergent interpretations between adversaries, such as can be seen in the Israeli-Palestinian dispute over the tragic events at Jenin in April 2002. The Palestinians labeled the event a massacre, a charge that Israel denied. The Palestinian charge was further undercut by a report from the Secretary General of the United Nations, which challenged the Palestinian claim of hundreds of dead, substituting instead the much lower estimate of about fifty-five. This brings up an additional problem regarding the determination of a massacre based on victim tallies. After the Guatemalan Civil War, a UN commission conducting an inquiry on human rights violations stated that a massacre implies at least three murders, while certain experts consider this number to be "very low."

Debates Surrounding the Notion

Another debate surrounds the practices attached to the term *massacre.* Etymologically, the word derives from the popular Latin *matteuca,* meaning "bludgeon." The word contains the sense of butchery, designating both the abattoir and the butcher's shop. In Europe from the eleventh century on, *massacre* became synonymous with the putting to death both of animals and human beings. Massacre has historically presupposed a situation where the perpetrator and his victim are face-to-face, since it is based on the practice of slitting the throat—the technique used to slaughter animals for market. This technique was used in massacres such as the civil wars fought in Algeria or Greece. However, if the concept of massacre implies a type of one-on-one interaction, must we conclude that technologies of murder exercised from a distance cannot be considered

In July 1992 after the Serbs were defeated in Mostar (the main city of Herzegovina), the Croats proclaimed their own state in the area. In this photo, from September 1992, Serbian prisoners-of-war dig up bodily remains from a mass grave in the area around Mostar as Croatian soldiers look on. [TEUN VOETEN]

massacres? What then of the modern technique of air bombing? If we retain such a limited definition, we ignore the evolution of the technologies of war and the political motivation of the practice. Military forces that employ air strikes to create a climate of terror in order to force a town or country to surrender exemplify this phenomenon. In that regard, it makes sense to distinguish between local massacres (face-to-face encounters) and long-distance massacres (aerial bombings).

The connection between war and massacres poses another problem, because it is easy to assume that massacres only happen within the context of war. However various historical examples show that massacres can be perpetrated in relatively peaceful times. For instance, in Nazi Germany the Crystal Night (*Kristallnacht*) pogrom against the Jewish community took place on November 9, 1938), and in Indonesia, an even larger massacre was directed against all suspected communist partisans from October 1965 to June 1966. It is also possible to consider famine as a type of slow, "soft" massacre. If we do, we can cite the Ukraine famine that was essentially willed by Stalin from 1932 to 1933.

Nevertheless, the context of war can without a doubt generate various practices of massacre, since war provokes a radical social polarization into the dialectic pair "friend vs. foe."

A massacre can then be one of several types. It can be integrated into the act of war when it is an extension of war. Such was the case of the massacre at Oradour-sur-Glane in France by a division of the SS on June 10, 1944. In this massacre, the military killed the whole population of this village just to intimidate the so-called terrorists in the area. Alternatively, a massacre can be deeply associated with the objectives of a war. Thus, for example, when a nationalistic power wants to force a given population to flee, one of the most efficient means is to massacre this population. As a result, the flow of refugees generated by this killing is not the consequence of the war but is, rather, its very goal. This was the case in the ethnic cleansing operations within the former Yugoslavia during the 1990s. Finally, a massacre may be quasi-autonomous with regard to war. This happens when practices of massacre tend to be detached from the battlefield and grow on their own. One such case is the genocide of European Jews during the Holocaust. The logic of war seemed to contrast with the logic of massacre in this instance. Indeed, soldiers or trains were employed to destroy civilian populations instead of being deployed on the front, where they could be more useful from a military standpoint.

This leads to another problem: how can we differentiate between the notions of massacre and genocide? Some authors do not make any distinction between the two, and even go so far as to include within the concepts such industrial catastrophes as the Chernobyl nuclear disaster in 1986. Other experts consider it crucial to distinguish between the notions of massacre and genocide. These experts believe the term *massacre* refers to the deliberate but unsustained killing of unarmed human beings within a relatively short period of time and in a relatively small geographic area. According to this definition, neither the Saint Bartholomew massacre in France (August 24, 1572) that was perpetrated by Catholics against important members of the Protestant community; the Kishinev pogrom in Russia (April 19–20, 1903), when Moldavian Christians killed dozens of Jews in the city; nor the Amristar massacre in Punjab (April 13, 1919), perpetrated by British general Reginald Dyer against Indian demonstrators, can be considered genocides. Nevertheless, sometimes a variety of massacres tend to evolve in a genocidal process, in which case certain authors use the expression "genocidal massacre." One of the key issues in genocide studies is to explain why and how this particular framework of violence can pass—slowly or suddenly—from massacre to genocide. The answer to this question presupposes developing our understanding of the logics of massacre operations.

Delusional Rationality

When a massacre is committed and is made known by the press, journalists are inclined to stress its apparent irrationality. Why attack children, women, and the elderly? Details of atrocities are also given in such reports. The appalling aspects of massacres must not, however, prevent us from examining the question of the perpetrators' rationale, their operating techniques, their objectives, and their perceptions of the enemy. Beyond the horror, it must be acknowledged that they are pursuing very specific aims, which may include amassing wealth, controlling territory, gaining power, destabilizing a political system, or other goals.

Envisaging the notion of massacre thus means attempting to understand both its rationality and its irrationality. This means taking into account the human capacity for both cold calculation and folly, in sum, for delusional rationality. The term *delusional* relates to

two mental phenomena. The first is psychosis. In this context, the psychotic element of the aggressor's behavior toward the victim or victims stems from the belief that the victim can and must be destroyed. The aggressor in effect denies the humanity of the victims, perceiving them as "other," as "barbarians."

However, *delusional* can also signify a paranoid image of this "other" (the victim) who is perceived as constituting a threat or even as the embodiment of evil. The particularity and dangerousness of a paranoid syndrome and the conviction that one is dealing with an evildoer are so strong that they create the risk of acting out against the perceived enemy. In a massacre, the "good vs. evil" and "friend vs. foe" binary polarization is at its peak, as is also true in war. Massacre is therefore always compatible with war and, if there is no actual war, it is experienced as an act of war.

Hence massacres are not irrational in the eyes of those who perpetrate them, because they are part of one or more dynamics of war. In this respect, those who commit massacres attribute specific political or strategic aims to them. These aims can, however, change with the course of the action, the international context, the victims' reactions, or other variables. The diversity of historical situations in which massacres occur leads us to distinguish between at least two fundamental types of objectives linked to the processes of partial and even total destruction of a community: its subjugation and its eradication.

Destruction in Order to Subjugate

The aim here is to bring about the death of civilians with a view to partially destroying a community in order to subjugate what remains of it. The destruction process is partial by definition, but it is intended to have an impact on the total community because those responsible for the deed rely on the effect of terror in order to impose their political domination on the survivors. The act of massacre is particularly suited to such a strategy. The slaughter need not be wholesale; it only has to become widely known so that its terrorizing effect spreads throughout the population.

Since the dawn of time, this form of massacre has been associated with warfare. The civilian destruction-and-subjugation dynamic can in fact be fully incorporated within a military operation to precipitate an adversary's surrender, speed up the conquest of its territory, and facilitate the subjugation of its people. Massacres can be found in most wars, both ancient to modern, and not merely as excesses of war but as part of its actual dimensions. However, such types of destruction sometimes turn "mad." This occurred during the Japanese invasion of China, when Japanese soldiers, apparently free to pursue their will, raped, slaughtered, and pillaged the Chinese people of Nanking for six weeks from December 1937 to January 1938. What could have been justified as an awful but rational practice of war by some realist strategists became completely irrational in this case, particularly due to the impunity of the invading soldiers.

Such destruction-and-subjugation methods can also be found in contemporary civil warfare, where the distinction is no longer made between combatants and non-combatants. Even if the women and children of a village are unarmed, they can be suspected of supporting enemy forces by furnishing them with supplies. They therefore become potential targets that must be destroyed. Many examples of this phenomenon can be found in certain past conflicts (e.g., Lebanon, Vietnam, Guatemala, and Sierra Leone) or in ongoing conflicts (e.g., Colombia and Algeria).

These destruction-and-subjugation practices can also extend to the ways in which people are governed. A war of conquest, which may have been conducted by massacre, might give way to the economic exploitation of the conquered population, with further recourse to the murder of some of its members if necessary. That was the essential attitude of the Conquistadors toward Native Americans, whom they perceived as worthless beings existing to do their (Spanish) masters' bidding. History offers other political variants of the shift of the destruction-and-subjugation strategy from a means of warfare to a tool of governance. In this instance, Clausewitz's formula ("War is the continuation of politics by other means") could be reversed. Instead, politics becomes the means of pursuing war against civilians.

Those who win a civil war are logically drawn into this power-building dynamic, as illustrated to some extent by the example of revolutionary France. There, the "Colones infernales" slaughtered large segments of the Vendean population in 1793. The Bolsheviks in Lenin's Russia after 1917 and the Khmers Rouges in Pol Pot's Cambodia (1975–1978) illustrate this phenomenon even more radically than the case of the French Revolution. The perpetration of extreme violence that builds up in the course of a civil war tends to be transferred to a power-building phase.

Whether in the case of civil wars or not, this process dates back a long time. Torture and killing to "set an example" constitute one of the standard techniques of the tyrant seeking to quash an internal rebellion. A more recent example was the tactic of hostage execution employed in Europe by the Nazis, who executed one hundred civilians for every German killed in a bid to overcome armed resistance groups. Sometimes dictatorial powers do not hesitate to kill nonviolent demon-

strators, as the racist South African regime did in Sharpeville on March 21, 1960 against black opponents. In this case the massacre was committed in order to deter any kind of resistance. Other regimes developed more sophisticated techniques, such as the "disappearance" method implemented by various Latin American dictatorships in the 1970s.

Destroy in Order to Eradicate
The destruction-and-eradication dynamic is quite different. Its aim is not the actual subjugation of a populace, but rather the utter elimination of a fairly extensive community. This involves "cleansing" or "purifying" the area where the targeted group (which is deemed undesirable or dangerous) is present. The concept of *eradication* is particularly relevant here, because the word's etymology conveys the idea of "severing roots" or "removing from the earth," in short "uprooting," as one would root out a harmful weed.

This identity-based process of destruction and eradication can also be connected with wars of conquest. The massacre process, combined with rape and pillage, is the means by which one group makes its intentions clear and consequently hastens the departure of another group, either because that group is deemed undesirable or because it occupies territory that the attacking group wants for its own use. The partial destruction of the victimized group and the resulting terror bring about and accelerate such departure. This was the practice employed by European settlers in North America against Native American peoples, who were driven further and further west, beyond the Mississippi River. In the Balkans, the forced movement of populations from a territory has been termed *ethnic cleansing,* in particular to describe the operations conducted mainly by Serbia and Croatia in the early 1990s. However the methods used (e.g., slaughtering people, burning villages, and destroying religious buildings) can be linked to earlier practices in that region. Since at least the nineteenth century, similar practices occurred in the context of the rise of nationalism and the decline of the Ottoman Empire.

These practices of massacre aimed at chasing away undesirable populations are genuinely universal. Regimes often used militias to do their work. These militias could usually rely on the support of conventional armed forces, however, even though the latter might prefer to remain in the background. One example of this situation is the Sabra and Shatila massacre in Lebanon (September 18, 1982), in which more than 1,000 Palestinians were killed by the Christian Lebanese militia with the support of the Israeli army. The goal was to terrorize the Palestinians and chase them out of Lebanon. This episode can be related to massacres that were perpetrated in 1948 by Israel in an attempt to chase Palestinians out of the territory claimed by the newly formed Israeli state. Numerous other such examples can also be found dating to the eighteenth century, when state building began to imply a homogeneous population. Achieving this homogeneity entailed the forced departure of populations that did not share in the same cultural, ethnic, or religious heritage. If war makes the State to the same extent as the State makes war, as historian Charles Tilly put it, the same could be said of massacres.

Once again, the processes at work in warfare can be reemployed in terms of the internal governance of a destroyed people. This is the case across the spectrum of ethnic and religious nationalistic conflicts, which include the riots between Muslims and Hindus in India since at least the late 1940s. Generally speaking, these types of conflicts involve the instrumental use of ethnic or religious criteria for the purposes of a group's political domination over an entire community. Recourse to killing is justified by the appeal to homogeneity in order to resolve a seemingly insoluble problem.

This process can, however, take on an even more radical form, such as the total elimination of a targeted community whose members are not even given the chance to flee. In such circumstances, the aim is to capture all of the individuals belonging to the targeted community, with the goal of eradicating them. The notion of a territory to be cleansed becomes secondary to the idea of actual extermination. Some colonial massacres were probably perpetrated with this in mind, such as the slaughter of the Herero population in 1904 by the German colonial army in Namibia. We still know far too little about colonial massacres, including those perpetrated by England, France, and Belgium in their conquest of African territories in the nineteenth and early twentieth centuries.

The leaders of Nazi Germany went further than any others in the planned total destruction of a community. Their systematic extermination of European Jews between 1941 and 1945, which followed the partial elimination of mentally sick Germans, is the prototypical example of this eradication process taken to the extreme. In very different historical contexts, the same can be said of the extermination of the Armenians within the Ottoman Empire in 1915 and 1916, and that of the Rwandan Tutsis in 1994. In each of these cases, the objective was not to scatter a people across other territories, but rather, in the words of Hannah Arendt, "to cause it to disappear not just from *its* own land, but from *the* land."

It is at this final stage of the eradication process that the concept of genocide can be introduced as a notion in social science. In general, the public at large sees genocide as a form of large-scale massacre. In the popular view, whenever the death toll reaches several hundred thousand, it becomes possible to refer to a genocide. This kind of intuitive criteria, based on a large number of victims, is not, however, adequate to describe genocidal behavior. Moreover, no expert could effectively set a minimum number of deaths as the necessary criterion for declaring that genocide has occurred. A qualitative criterion *combined* with a quantitative criterion, however, could offer a more reliable definition of genocide. For instance, most experts would agree that widespread killing combined with the implicit or express desire for the total eradication of a community qualifies for the label of "genocide."

Genocide thus fits within the same destructivity continuum as ethnic cleansing, but is essentially distinguishable from it. Their respective dynamics are both aimed at eradication; however, in the case of ethnic cleansing the departure or flight of the targeted population is still possible, whereas in the case of genocide, escape is futile or impossible. In this regard, genocide can be defined as the process of specific civilian destruction directed at the total eradication of a community, for which the perpetrator determines the criteria.

However, such reasoning is necessarily further complicated by the fact that the destruction-and-subjugation and destruction-for-eradication processes can coexist and even overlap within the same historical situation by targeting different groups. In general, one is the dominant process and the other is secondary. In 1994, Rwanda saw the attempted eradication of the Tutsi population (which can therefore be classified as a genocide) occurring simultaneously with the killing of Hutu opponents of the government (which constitutes a destruction-and-subjugation process. Conversely, the mass killing in Cambodia clearly constituted a destruction-and-subjugation process because Pol Pot never sought to destroy all the Khmers, but that process included certain eradication offensives directed at specific groups, particularly the Cham Muslim minority. Identifying these different dynamics of violence is often a very complex task, because they may not only overlap, but also change over time, shifting, for example, from subjugation to eradication.

SEE ALSO Algeria; Armenians in Ottoman Turkey and the Armenian Genocide; Bosnia and Herzegovina; Comparative Genocide; Developmental Genocide; Ethnic Cleansing; Genocide; Katyn; National Prosecutions; Rwanda; Sabra and Shatila; Utilitarian Genocide

BIBLIOGRAPHY

Horowitz, Donald (2000). *Deadly Ethnic Riots*. Berkeley: University of California Press.

Levene, Mark, and Penny Proberts (1999). *The Massacre in History*. New York: Bargain Books.

Semelin, Jacques (2003). "Towards a Vocabulary of Massacre and Genocide." *Journal of Genocide Research* 5(2):193–210.

Jacques Semelin

Mass Graves

Several definitions of mass graves have been offered. From a scientific perspective, a mass grave contains two or more bodies that are in contact with each other. More legally precise is the definition offered by one United Nations (UN) special rapporteur, who interpreted a mass grave as a location where three or more bodies are buried, victims of extrajudicial, summary, or arbitrary executions, not having died in combat or armed confrontations (ICTY, 1996). Mass graves are an expedient method of disposing of large numbers of human remains. However, not all mass graves result from criminal actions; some contain legally buried combatants or victims of natural disasters.

Mass graves are investigated to collect and document physical evidence for accountability purposes and/or to identify the dead for return to their families. Forensic exhumations provide evidence to establish accountability and bring those responsible to justice. The process of investigation and documentation creates a historical record. From a humanitarian perspective, families may finally know the fate of their loved ones and be able to give them a proper burial. Finally, forensic exhumations reconfirm the dignity of the victims and of human life (Haglund, 2002; Stover and Ryan, 2001).

It is important to note that for the purpose of successful prosecution of crimes such as genocide and crimes against humanity, personal identification of victims may not be required. Identification at the categorical level of national, religious, ethnic, or racial group may suffice. This said, in the course of examinations, experts are ethically bound to collect information that may further the personal identification process.

Investigation of mass graves requires a multidisciplinary effort, and for large ones completion may involve days, weeks, or even months. Prominent among experts involved are forensic archeologists, anthropologists, pathologists, and evidence technicians. First, a detailed documentation of surface features and potential evidence is conducted. Once the grave boundaries have been defined, the overburden (deposits of soil or other materials that cover the remains) is removed. This too is inspected for evidence. As excavation progresses, graves yield evidence bearing on circumstances of burial, as indicated by marks from tools or machines that may have been used to dig them. Sometimes, it is possible to ascertain whether or not victims were killed at the site or somewhere else. Once human remains are reached, each individual remains are carefully exposed and recovered. Postmortem examinations of the victims reveal information concerning cause of death, as well as information supportive of their identification, such as sex, age, stature, and trauma during life. Throughout the exhumation process written narratives, maps, and photographs document the findings and observations.

Forensic investigations of mass graves date to World War II. In 1943 forensic specialists of the Axis powers carried out the exhumation and study of victims from graves in the Katyn Forest, located in the modern-day region of Russia named Smolensk. When the Nazis took over the area, rumors circulated that previously occupying Soviet forces had systematically executed and buried approximately 11,000 Polish prisoners of war in 1940. The Germans, on occupying the Katyn, immediately organized investigations, prompted by the anticipation of accusations of Nazi culpability for the deaths. Findings based on the examination of 4,143 victims appeared in an April 1943 report. The majority had been shot in the head, and 5 percent were found with their hands tied behind their backs with ropes. On the basis of recovered personal artifacts and documents, 2,914 bodies were identified (Fitzgibbon, 1977). The report went on to comment that the absence of insects, as well as the presence of documents, correspondence, diaries, and newspapers, in the grave indicated that the deaths occurred from March through May of 1940.

A footnote on the Katyn mass massacres occurred during the Nuremberg trials. At the insistence of the Soviets and over the reluctance of the French, British, and American prosecutors, the Soviets successfully advocated that allegations of the massacres be included in count three of the indictment against the Nazis. Although the falsehood of these allegations was strongly suspected, they were allowed to stand, but were not mentioned in the tribunal's final verdict (Davidson, 1997; Taylor, 1992).

Other World War II–era mass grave exhumations were carried out after the war, notably in Saipan (Russell and Flemming, 1991) and Ukraine (Bevan, 1994). The Australians conducted the Ukraine investigation, with the cooperation of the Soviets, into the case of Nazi Officer Ivan Polyukhovich, who was indicted for

Mass grave of unidentified victims discovered west of Baghdad, April 17, 2003. [TEUN VOETEN]

his involvement in a massacre of Polish Jews outside the town of Serniki in the fall of 1942. Limited examinations of 533 selected crania confirmed that 410 of the men, women, and children exhumed had been shot in the head. Polyukhovich died before the prosecution was completed.

In May 2001 an aborted attempt was made to investigate the 1941 execution and burial site of an alleged 1,600 Polish Jews on the outskirts of the hamlet of Jadwabne, Poland. Addressing Jadwabne was an effort on the part of the Polish government to set the record straight on whether the killers had been occupying Nazis or fellow Polish neighbors of the victims. Strict Jewish orthodox interpretation of religious objections to the disturbance of graves was successful in closing down the exhumation efforts (Gross, 2001; Polak, 2001).

Except for the investigation of World War II graves, a four-decade hiatus passed before the momentum for a second and continuing era of mass grave investigations gathered. In 1984, prompted by a request from newly elected Argentine President Raúl Alfonsín, the American Association for the Advancement of Science's Committee on Scientific Freedom and Responsi-

bility assembled a group of forensic experts. They were asked to investigate the fate of the thousands of disappeared, those who went missing, during Argentina's military rule from 1976 to 1983. This historic plea led to the development of Latin American forensic teams and exhumations throughout Central and South America, with major mass burial sites investigated in Guatemala, El Salvador, Chile, and Peru.

A virtual explosion in the export of forensic experts to investigate mass graves occurred in 1996. The ad hoc International Criminal Tribunals for the Former Yugoslavia (ICTY) and Rwanda (ICTR) provided the impetus. Throughout 1996 multidisciplinary teams staffed by forensic experts made available by the nongovernmental organization (NGO) Physicians for Human Rights (PHR) exhumed and examined the remains of nearly 1,200 individuals in Rwanda, Croatia, and Bosnia and Herzegovina. The first exhumation was of 496 victims at the Kibuye Roman Catholic Church. Seventy percent of the victims were women and children, 74 percent died of blunt and/or sharp force trauma, and 25 percent were children 10 years of age or younger. These findings were presented in the trial of

Two men wearing masks have transported the bodies of victims of the Rwandan genocide to the site of a mass grave. One man hurls a body into the pit. [TEUN VOETEN]

Clement Kiashima, a pediatrician and former Prefect of Kibuye, who was convicted of crimes against humanity.

The 1996 exhumations continued in the former Yugoslavia. The initial focus was on graves believed to contain the seven thousand men and boys who had disappeared in July 1995, immediately after the fall of Srebrenica. In relation to these deaths, Radislav Krstic became the first person to be convicted by the ICTY of genocide and was sentenced to forty-six years of imprisonment (ICTY, 2001). As presented in the Krstic trial, these and other graves exhumed in subsequent seasons showed that many graves had been robbed in an attempt to destroy evidence. Deaths resulted primarily from gunshot wounds, with many of the victims blindfolded or bound.

The fieldwork in 1996 concluded with exhumation of the Ovcara grave in eastern Croatia. This grave held the remains of patients and staff taken from the Vukovar hospital after the fall of that city in September 1991. Although the grave had been discovered that same year, occupying Serb military prevented the first exhumation

attempt in 1993. Fifty-five percent of the victims, whose ages ranged from 17 to 66 years old, demonstrated evidence of medical attention or recent hospitalization. Of the two hundred victims, the majority died of gunshot wounds. DNA identifications have confirmed the identity of over 90 percent of the victims. It is the unfortunate fate of many families that the graves containing their relatives may never be found. For example, of the estimated 28,500 people missing from Bosnia during the Yugoslav conflict, as of 2004 the remains of nearly 16,500 have been found and of those about 11,500 identified.

Initial hurdles to mass grave exhumations are lack of will or authority to investigate. Until regimes change or international will forces the issue, atrocities hidden in mass graves are not addressed. In order for investigations to proceed and accountability to take place, a forum such as a tribunal, special court, or truth commission needs to be established. Even when these criteria have been met, access to sites may be blocked for lack of security.

Once authority is granted and security insured, the focus shifts to support of the project: its funding, resources, staffing, and logistics. Limitations of time, funding, and support may impact the approach to the examinations. If not considered beforehand, religious, cultural, or other community concerns may prove to be impediments to the investigation. For all mass graves, there are deep concerns revolving around what will be the fate of remains in relation to their identity and return to families. In the end, accountability is ever at the mercy of societal will and a legitimate judicial forum.

As a phenomenon, mass graves are, unfortunately, all-too-common features in the landscape of genocide and crimes against humanity. Alarm at the atrocities of World War II was, in small part, hastened by evidence of mass graves. The mass grave investigations of the ICTR and ICTY have, in large part, triggered expectations for similar exhumations from far-flung regions of the globe. In the early twenty-first century requests for the investigation of mass graves came from a host of countries, including Afghanistan, Bangladesh, Cambodia, Congo, East Timor, Indonesia, Iraq, Nepal, Sierra Leone, and Sri Lanka. Even when forensic investigations of mass graves are undertaken, accountability and punishment of perpetrators may not follow.

SEE ALSO Babi Yar; Forensics; Katyn; Srebrenica

BIBLIOGRAPHY

Bevan, D. (1994). *A Case to Answer: The Story of Australia's First European War Crimes Prosecution.* Kent Town, South Australia: Wakefield Printing.

Davidson, E. (1997). *The Trial of the Germans: An Account of the Twenty-Two Defendants before the International Military Tribunal at Nuremberg.* Columbia: University of Missouri Press.

Fitzgibbon, L. (1977). *Katyn Massacre.* London: Corgi Books.

Gross, J. T. (2001). *Neighbors: The Destruction of the Jewish Community in Jadwabne, Poland.* Princeton, N.J.: Princeton University Press.

Haglund W. D. (2002). "Recent Mass Graves, an Introduction." In *Method, Theory, and Archaeological Perspectives,* ed. W. D. Haglund and M. H. Sorg. Boca Raton, Fla.: CRC Press.

International Criminal Tribunal for the Former Yugoslavia Bulletin (1996). *Twin Tribunals ICTY 9/10,* 14-VIII-1996.

International Criminal Tribunal for the Former Yugoslavia. *Judgment and Sentence, Defendant Radislav Krstic.* Case No. ICTY-98-33 (May 29, 2000).

International Criminal Tribunal for the Former Yugoslavia (2001). "Radislav Kristic Becomes the First Person to Be Convicted of Genocide at the ICTY and Is Sentenced to 46 Years Imprisonment." Press Release 609e.

International Criminal Tribunal for Rwanda. *Judgment and Sentence, Defendants Clement Kayishema and Obed Ruzindana.* Case No. ICTR-95-1 (May 21, 1999).

Mant, A. K. (1987). "Knowledge Acquired from Post-War Exhumations." In *Death, Decay and Reconstruction: Approaches to Archaeology and Forensic Science,* ed. A. Boddington, A. N. Garland, and R. C. Janaway. Manchester, U.K.: Manchester University Press.

Polak, J. A. (2001). "Exhuming Their Neighbors." *Tradition: A Journal of Orthodox Jewish Thought* 35(Winter):23–43.

Russell, S., and M. A. Flemming (1991). "A Bulwark in the Pacific: An Example of World War II Archaeology on Saipan." In *Archaeology Studies of World War II,* ed. W. R. Wood. Columbia: University of Missouri.

Snow, Clyde C., Lowell Levine, Leslie Lukash, et al. (1984). "The Investigation of the Human Remains of the 'Disappeared' in Argentina." *The American Journal of Forensic Medicine and Pathology* 5(4):297–299.

Stover, Eric (1985). "Scientists Aid Search for Argentina's 'Desaparecidos.'" *Science* 230:56–57.

Stover, E., and G. Peress (1998). *The Graves: Srebrenica and Vukovar.* New York: Scalo Press.

Stover, E., and M. Ryan (2001). "Breaking Bread with the Dead." *Historical Archaeology* 35(1):7–25.

Taylor, T. (1992). *The Anatomy of the Nuremberg Trials.* New York: Alfred A. Knopf.

William D. Haglund

Medical Experimentation

The use of experimentation on human subjects is a necessary method of advancing medical and public health knowledge. However, it has been abused extensively in the context of genocide and crimes against humanity, especially by the Axis Powers during World War II. Experimentation was part of the state-sanction behavior of Nazi doctors within the broader program of extermination of races considered inferior or of targeted political groups. The medical and health personnel involved were charged with having committed war crimes and crimes against humanity during World War II, and many were convicted by a U.S. tribunal set up in tandem with the International Military Tribunal sitting in Nuremberg.

Medical experimentation refers to the testing and evaluation of a new drug or procedure on a human person in order gain generalizable knowledge that can be used for various purposes. In its accepted form, such experimentation is conducted on willing human subjects for the purpose of advancing the curative or preventive role of medicine. In its prohibited form—done in connection with genocide or crimes against humanity—it is conducted without the consent of the individ-

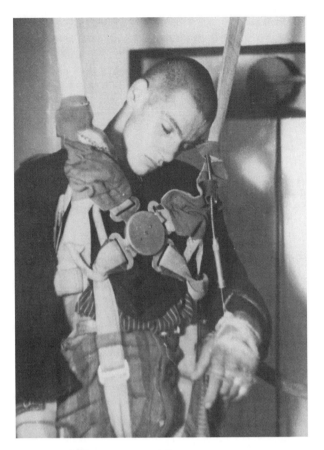

To better understand the effects of high altitudes on German pilots (in particular, pilots needing to eject from damaged aircraft), physicians of the German Experimental Institute for Aviation subjected concentration camp prisoners at Dachau, such as this man, to simulated high-altitude conditions. Many of the subjects died during the experiments. [USHMM]

uals tested and for purposes that may purport to have positive value for medical science, such as finding a vaccine against smallpox, or for the misuse of medicine, such as learning how to keep a prisoner from dying under torture, in order to continue the acts of torture.

Medical Experimentation in History

The trial of the Nazi doctors was in many ways the defining moment of standard setting regarding medial experimentation. The practice is, however, an ancient one, found among physicians in ancient Greece and Rome, the Arab and Ottoman Empires, and especially in European medical practice during the eighteenth and nineteenth centuries. Among the best-known examples of medical advances made thanks to medical experimentation are Edward Jenner's inoculation of an eight-year-old boy with cowpox against smallpox, Sir James Young Simpson's use of chloroform for anesthesia, and Louis Pasteur's testing an antidote to rabies. Al-

though these advances have proved important, the experimentation sometimes took place without adequate attention to aquiring informed consent or reference to previous scientific studies, and testing usually took advantage of vulnerable groups, such as children, orphans, prisoners, and mental patients.

One of the first efforts to establish ethical standards for medical experimentation was made by the English physician, Thomas Percival, in 1803. He wrote that doctors performing "new methods of chirurgical treatment . . . should be scrupulously and conscientiously governed by sound reason, just analogy, or well-authenticated facts . . . and no such trials should be instituted without a previous consultation of the physicians or surgeons." More directly to the point of human experimentation was the code drafted by an American, William Beaumont, in 1833, requiring voluntary consent of the subject and cessation of the experiment when it causes distress to the subject or when the subject is dissatisfied with it. The French physician Claude Bernard, writing in the middle of the nineteenth century, defined the basic principle of "never performing on man an experiment which might be harmful to him to any extent, even though the result might be highly advantageous to science, i.e., to the health of others."

The principle of informed consent evolved as a result of several well-known experiments. During World War I, Walter Reed experimented with mosquitoes as a vector of yellow fever, first on servicemen and then on Spanish workers. His test subjects signed a contract by which they accepted the risk of yellow fever in exchange for $100 in gold, twice that amount was paid if they contracted the disease. The ethical problem with Reed's experiment was that prospective test subjects were recruited on the basis of false information. The certainty of non-participants in the experiment contracting yellow fever was exaggerated, and the possible fatal consequences of the experiment were understated.

In the early twentieth century, a collaborator of Reed, George Sternberg, experimented on children in an orphan asylum, as well as on mental patients and prisoners. Although criticized for it, Hideyo Nogushi and his colleagues tested a drug (luetin) to diagnose syphilis on uninformed mental patients, patients in public hospitals, and orphans. These examples raised problems of medical ethics, and this concern contributed to the rethinking of rules governing medical experimentation in the mid-twentieth century.

During World War II, the Committee on Medical Research of the Office of Scientific Research and Development—the precursor to the National Institutes of Health—conducted major experimental research using human subjects on diseases such as dysentery, influenza, and especially malaria. Again, mental patients and prisoners were infected to determine their response to antimalarial therapies and flu vaccines. The subjects were usually considered volunteers, but little attention was paid to the nature of their consent. For instance, prisoners were often promised early release, but no one stopped to think of how that promise might induce a prisoner to give consent to the experimentation. The overriding concern was for results, because the tests would directly effect the health of soldiers engaged in the war effort. Hepatitis testing on mentally retarded children at Willowbrook, and cancer research, using live cancer cells, on unsuspecting patients at the Brooklyn Jewish Chronic Disease Hospital were also conducted without adequate attention to the consent of the subjects and the ethics of the use of live cancer cells.

Perhaps the most notorious example in the United States of failure to apply standards of informed consent was the Tuskegee study, which the U.S. government ran from 1932 to 1972. The test subjects were African Americans with secondary syphilis and were not conscripted during the war and in order to allow the scientific team to continue studying the progression of the disease, were not given penicillin even after its efficacy against the disease was discovered. It was not until Henry Beecher published his groundbreaking article, "Ethics and Clinical Research," in 1966 that the laxity of standards for experimentation in medical schools, hospitals, and government institutions was considered urgent enough for clear rules and monitoring procedures to be established.

By far the most significant precedent for the dangers of unrestricted and barbaric medical experimentation was that set by the Nazi and Japanese doctors before and during World War II. Japanese physicians conduced germ warfare experiments in the early 1930s under the direction of Lieutenant-General Shiro Ishii. Some 20,000 Japanese professionals were involved in experiments on humans and participated in massive germ warfare attacks against Chinese and Korean civilians and U.S. prisoners of war. An estimated 400,000 Chinese died of cholera as a result of these attacks, and the final death toll of Japan's medical-biological war crimes has been estimated at 580,000. Unit 731, the most notorious secret military medical unit of the Imperial Japanese Army, was a facility of 150 buildings on six square kilometers. There, a number of experiments were carried out on human subjects, including vivisections, grenade tests, frostbite experiments, and a bacilli bomb developed for use as a defoliant. The U.S. government did not prosecute the Japanese perpetrators for these acts as they did in the case of the Nazi doctors. Instead, the crimes were left unprosecuted, in exchange for access to test results and documents.

Experiments Carried Out by Nazi Physicians during World War II

At the end of World War II, twelve experiments were singled out for prosecution as war crimes. Extensive evidence was presented for each of them during the trial of the Nazi physicians.

High-Altitude (or Low Pressure) Experiments
Inmates of the Dachau concentration camp in 1942 were locked in an airtight pressure chamber and the pressure was altered to simulate atmospheric conditions at very high altitude without oxygen. In the words of the official report on this experiment, performed on a 37-year-old Jew:

> After 4 minutes the experimental subject began to perspire, and wiggle his head; after five minutes cramps occurred; between 6 and 10 minutes breathing increased in speed and the experimental subject became unconscious; from 11 to 30 minutes breathing slowed down to three breathes per minutes, finally stopping altogether. Severest cyanosis developed in between and foam appeared at the mouth. About one-half hour after breathing had stopped, dissection was started.

The report then provides a detailed description of the autopsy.

Freezing Experiments
In experiments conducted in Dachau in 1942 and 1943 to learn how to rewarm German pilots downed in the North Sea, victims were forced to stand naked in freezing weather for nine to fourteen hours, or in a tank of ice water for three hours. The official Nazi report notes, "the experimental subjects died invariably, despite all attempts at resuscitation." In October 1942, one of the defendants presented a paper, "Warming Up after Freezing to the Danger Point," based on these experiments to a conference held in Nuremberg on the prevention and treatment of freezing.

Malaria Experiments
Over 1,200 Dachau inmates were infected by mosquitoes or injected from the glands of mosquitoes and then treated with various drugs. As a consequence, thirty inmates died from malaria, and 300 to 400 more died from complications and overdoses of some of the drugs.

Mustard Gas Experiments
Victims in Sachsenhausen, Natzweiller, and other camps were deliberately inflicted with wounds. These were subsequently infected by mustard gas, or were injected with the gas, or were forced to ingest it by inhaling or drinking. Nazi reports of these experiments in 1939 describe the swelling and intense pain the victims suffered.

Experiments with Drugs, Muscle and Nerve Regeneration, and Bone Transplantation

Chief Prosecutor Telford Taylor described these experiments as "perhaps the most barbaric of all." They were performed primarily on women in Ravensbrück, and consisted in inflicting wounds to simulate battle injuries, into which a gangrene-producing culture was introduced to cause severe infections. Some victims were then treated with sulfanilamide, others with nothing. Bone transplantation was performed on other subjects. In Buchanwald, victims—usually Polish Catholic priests—were injured and then treated with polygal or sulfanilamide. Many died from these tests or from untreated blood poisoning and other infections.

Seawater Experiment

Conducted in Dachau in 1944, these experiments involved feeding the victims shipwreck rations. Some were given no water, others received ordinary seawater, or seawater in which the salty taste was concealed, or seawater that had been treated to remove the salt. The tests were performed primarily on Roma (Gypsies). The test subjects suffered deliriums and convulsions, and some died.

Epidemic Jaundice Experiments

Eight Jews of the Polish resistance were selected for this experiment in Sachsenhauser and Natzweiler camps. The experiment began in an effort to find an inoculation against epidemic jaundice and resulted in the torture and death of the subjects.

Sterilization Experiments

These experiments, conducted on victims in Auschwitz, Ravensbrìck, and other camps, were part of Nazi planning for genocide by the most efficient, scientific, and least conspicuous methods. The aim was to eliminate Russians, Poles, Gypsies, Jews, and other undesirable populations by using medicinal rather than surgical sterilization, primarily through injection of caladium sequinum and other substances. In addition, gland transplantation was performed on fourteen inmates of Buchanwald, two of whom died. Others were subjected to sterilization by X-rays and castration. The aim was to prevent reproduction among Jews who were preserved from extermination in order to perform labor.

Typhus and Other Virus Experiments

For nearly five years, until the end of the war, medical experiments were performed on inmates of Buchanwald and Natzweiler to test vaccines for typhus, yellow fever, smallpox, paratyphoid A and B, cholera, and diphtheria. For the typhus experiments, hundreds of prisoners were infected with typhus. Some of these had received an antityphus vaccine to be tested, the others were used as the control group or simply infected to provide a supply of the virus for further testing.

Poison Experiments

Russian inmates of Buchanwald were injected with poisons, sometimes administered through poison bullets. The tests were designed to permit the Nazi doctors to observe the victims' reactions to the poison up to the point of death.

Incendiary Bomb Experiments

These experiments took place in Buchanwald in 1943. Five inmates were burned with phosphorous material taken from an English bomb and were severely injured as a result.

Anthropology Experiments

Two of the defendants in the Doctors' Trial were obsessed with racial theories and had collected skulls representative of "all races and peoples," but lacked those of the "Jewish race." In order to complete the collection, they had requested that Jewish victims be photographed and that "anthropological measurements" of their skulls be taken while they still lived. The victims were then killed and beheaded, and their heads were brought to the laboratory in a sealed tin filled with conserving fluid. In requesting this service from the Wehrmacht, one of the defendants had explained that he wanted skulls to "represent the prototype of the repulsive but characteristic subhuman." Prosecutor Taylor called these experiments "perhaps the most utterly repulsive charges in the entire indictment."

The Trial of the Nazi Doctors

The trial of the Nazi doctors, known as the *United States of America vs. Karl Brandt et al*, the Medical Case, or the Nazi Doctors Case, was based on the Agreement for the Prosecution and Punishment of the Major War Criminals of the European Axis, signed in London on August 8, 1945 by the United States, the United Kingdom, France, and the Soviet Union, which created the International Military Tribunal (IMT). The Nazi doctors were not tried by the IMT, but rather by a U.S. tribunal acting pursuant to Control Council Law No. 10, signed on 20 December 1945.

The trial of the Nazi doctors was officially Case No. 1 of Military Tribunal I, constituted on October 25, 1945, and consisting of Walter Beals, Harold Sebring, Johnson Crawford, and Victor Swearingen. Telford Taylor served as chief of counsel for the prosecution, and James McHaney was chief prosecutor. Taylor charged the defendants with "murder, tortures, and other atrocities committed in the name of medical science." There were four counts in his indictments:

(1) Conspiracy to commit war crimes against humanity: The ordering, planning, and organization of the war crimes and crimes against humanity charged in counts two and three. Although all the defendants were charged on this count, the tribunal decided not to convict.

(2) War crimes: The tribunal found fifteen defendants guilty on this charge and acquitted eight.

(3) Crimes against humanity: Charged against all defendants. Fifteen were found guilty, eight were acquitted.

(4) Membership in a criminal organization: Ten defendants were charged with membership in the SS. All were found guilty.

The trial began on December 9, 1946. The judgment was returned on August 19, 1947, and sentencing was pronounced on the following day. The tribunal met 139 times, heard 85 witnesses, and examined 1,471 documents. There were twenty-three defendants, seven of whom were found guilty of war crimes and crimes against humanity and sentenced to death. Four of these were physicians. Five other defendants were sentenced to life imprisonment. Seven were found not guilty and one was found guilty of the charge of belonging to the SS but not of crimes relating to medical experimentation. Thirty-one lesser officials were put on trial and found guilty, of whom twenty-two were sentenced to death.

Taylor gave the opening statement for the prosecution, noting that "most of [the defendants] are trained physicians, and some of them are distinguished scientists." He set aside from the medical trial the charges of "euthanasia" and slaughter of tubercular Poles because they did not relate to actual medical experiments. The charges retained against the defendants related to experiments that constituted war crimes or crimes against humanity, and murder for so-called anthropological purposes. Some of these experiments were aimed at assisting the German Wehrmacht in coping with battlefield problems and diseases encountered in occupied territories. However, others, in Taylor's words, were not aimed at determining "how to rescue or to cure, but how to destroy and kill." Among the latter, he listed the sterilization experiments and shooting of poison bullets at prisoners in Buchanwald to see how quickly they died. He called these crimes "thanatology," or the science of producing death.

The Nuremberg Code

The judgment of the tribunal included a section on "permissible medical experiments," in which the judges enumerated ten principles that "must be observed in order to satisfy moral, ethical, and legal concepts." Through these principles, the judges intended to identify "requirements which are purely legal in nature" and not to venture into the field of medicine, which they deemed a "field that would be beyond our sphere of competence." Nonetheless, the principles have come to be known as the "Nuremberg Code," and have had far-reaching significance for bioethics.

The Nuremberg Code begins with that core principle that "the voluntary consent of the human subject is absolutely essential." The other requirements are that any experiment on a human subject should be for the good of society; it should build on the results of animal experimentation and scientific knowledge, it should "avoid all unnecessary physical and mental suffering and injury;" there should be no "a priori reason to believe that death or disabling injury will occur" (with the possible exception of the experimental physicians serving as subject); the degree of risk should be proportionate to the humanitarian gain; adequate precautions should be taken "to protect the experimental subject against even remote possibilities of injury, disability, or death;" only scientifically qualified persons should conduct the experiment; the subjects should be able to halt the experiment "if he has reached the physical or mental state where continuation of the experiments seems to him to be impossible;" and the lead scientist should be prepared to end the experiment at any stage "if he has probable cause to believe, in the exercise of the good faith, superior skill, and careful judgment required of him, that a continuation of the experiment is likely to result in injury, disability, or death to the experimental subject."

The Nuremberg Code sets a very high standard, for which it has sometimes been criticized, especially in relation to the absolute character of voluntary consent. It should be noted that it only deals with adult consent in the context of the Nazi experiments, and was not intended to cover all situations. The tribunal drew heavily on two expert witnesses, Andrew Ivy and Leo Alexander, who compiled historical precedents and proposed most of the points that were eventually incorporated into the judgment. Michael Grodin, an expert on the Nuremberg Code, has called it "the cornerstone of modern human experimentation ethics."

Since the tribunal's judgment, standard-setting regarding medical experimentation has followed two major trends. The first is the development of detailed ethical codes and procedures for protecting human subjects involved in experimentation. This has been accomplished primarily through the World Medical Association's Helsinki Declaration and the Council for International Organizations of Medical Sciences

(CIOMS)'s Ethical Guidelines for Biomedical Research Involving Human Subjects. These standards are implemented primarily through national legislation and institutional review boards. The second is through the incorporation of provisions that ban impermissible medical experimentation in international humanitarian and human rights treaties.

International Humanitarian and Human Rights Law

As a result of the Nazi medical trial, the issue of medical experimentation and other biological experiments was a preoccupation of the drafters of the principal post–World War II instruments of international humanitarian and human rights law. Under the First and Second Geneva Conventions, the wounded, sick, and shipwrecked armed forces "shall not be. . .subjected to torture or to biological experiments" (Article 12 of each convention). Article 13 of the Third Geneva Convention, regarding the treatment of prisoners of war stipulates: "In particular, no prisoner of war may be subjected to physical mutilation or to medical or scientific experiments of any kind which are not justified by the medical, dental, or hospital treatment of the prisoner concerned and carried out in his interest." In the Fourth Geneva Convention, regarding the protection of civilians in time of war, Article 32 bans "mutilation and medical or scientific experiments not necessitated by the medical treatment of a protected person." Protocol I, relating to the protection of victims of international armed conflicts (Article 11) states the following:

> [I]t is prohibited to subject the persons described in this Article to any medical procedure which is not indicated by the state of health of the person concerned and which is not consistent with generally accepted medical standards which would be applied under similar medical circumstances to persons who are nationals of the Party conducting the procedure and who are in no way deprived of liberty.

It further prohibits carrying out "on such persons, even with their consent: (a) Physical mutilations; (b) Medical or scientific experiments; (c) Removal of tissue or organs for transplantation." As for Protocol II, which deals with the protection of victims of non-international armed conflicts, it is similarly "prohibited to subject the persons described in this Article to any medical procedure which is not indicated by the state of health of the person concerned, and which is not consistent with the generally accepted medical standards applied to free persons under similar medical circumstances." This prohibition appears in Article 5.2, concerning internment or detention. All four Geneva Conventions of 1949 list among the grave violations, which all parties are required to punish, "willful killing, torture or inhuman treatment, including biological experiments."

The 1998 Rome Statute of the International Criminal Court continues this trend in international law. It defines "war crimes" in Article 2 as:

> Grave breaches of the Geneva Conventions of 12 August 1949, namely, any of the following acts against persons or property protected under the provisions of the relevant Geneva Convention: . . . Torture or inhuman treatment, including biological experiments; [and] Willfully causing great suffering, or serious injury to body or health.

In addition, Article 2(b) lists the following as serious violations of the laws and customs applicable in international armed conflict:

> Subjecting persons who are in the power of an adverse party to physical mutilation or to medical or scientific experiments of any kind which are neither justified by the medical, dental, or hospital treatment of the person concerned, nor carried out in his or her interest, and which cause death to or seriously endanger the health of such person or persons.

Although the Genocide Convention does not specifically mention medical experimentation, the 1992 International Covenant on Civil and Political Rights stipulates, in Article 7, "No one shall be subjected to torture or to cruel, inhuman or degrading treatment or punishment. In particular, no one shall be subjected without his free consent to medical or scientific experimentation." In its General Comment 7 on this article, the Human Rights Committee took special note, as follows:

> [T]he reports of States parties have generally given little or no information on this point. It takes the view that at least in countries where science and medicine are highly developed, and even for peoples and areas outside their borders if affected by their experiments, more attention should be given to the possible need and means to ensure the observance of this provision. Special protection in regard to such experiments is necessary in the case of persons not capable of giving their consent.

The issue of experimentation was also included in principles for the protection of persons with mental illness and the improvement of mental health care, adopted by the UN General Assembly in 1991. Principle 11 stipulates the following:

> Clinical trials and experimental treatment shall never be carried out on any patient without in-

formed consent, except that a patient who is unable to give informed consent may be admitted to a clinical trial or given experimental treatment, but only with the approval of a competent, independent review body specifically constituted for this purpose.

Finally, in the Draft Comprehensive and Integral International Convention on the Protection and Promotion of the Rights and Dignity of Persons with Disabilities, it is provided that "States Parties shall prohibit, and protect persons with disabilities from, medical or scientific experimentation without the free and informed consent of the person concerned, and shall protect persons with disabilities from forced interventions or forced institutionalization aimed at correcting, improving, or alleviating any actual or perceived impairment."

Through these normative developments since the trial of the Nazi doctors, the medical profession and authors of international treaties on human rights and humanitarian law have sought to draw lessons from the atrocities and wonton misuse of science during World War II and the disregard for welfare of human subjects involved in biological and medical experimentation in democratic societies in peacetime. Medical experimentation continues to be a critical step in improving human health but must come under strict limitations and control in accordance with the Kantian imperative (in his *Metaphysical Foundations of Morals*) to "act so as to treat man . . . always as an end, never merely as a means."

SEE ALSO Auschwitz; Eugenics; Euthanasia; Japan; Mengele, Josef; Physicians

BIBLIOGRAPHY

Annas, George J., and Michael A. Grodin (1992). *The Nazi Doctors and the Nuremberg Code: Human Rights in Human Experimentation.* New York: Oxford University Press.

Barenblatt, Daniel (2004). *A Plague upon Humanity: The Secret Genocide of Axis Japan's Germ Warfare Operation.* New York: HarperCollins.

Beecher, Henry K. (1966). "Ethical and Clinical Research" *New England Journal of Medicine* 274(24):1354–1360.

Bernard, Claude (1927). *An Introduction to the Study of Experimental Medicine*, tran. Henry Coply Green. New York: Macmillan.

Council for International Organizations of Medical Sciences (CIOMS) in collaboration with the World Health Organization (1993). *International Ethical Guidelines for Biomedical Research Involving Human Subjects.* Geneva: CIOMS.

Gold, Hal (1996). *Unit 731 Testimony: Japan's Wartime Human Experimentation and the Post-War Cover-Up.* Tokyo: Yenbooks.

Howard-Jones, Norman. (1982) "Human Experimentation in Historical and Ethical Perspective" *Social Science Medicine* 16(15):1429–1448.

Kater, Michael H. (1989). *Doctors under Hitler.* Chapel Hill: University of North Carolina Press.

Katz, Jay, Alexander M. Capron, and Eleanor Swift Glass (1972). *Experimentation with Human Beings.* New York: Russell Sage Foundation.

Lifton, Robert J. (1986). *The Nazi Doctors: Medical Killing and the Pathology of Genocide.* New York: Basic Books.

McNeil, Paul M. (1993). *The Ethics and Politics of Human Experimentation.* Cambridge: Cambridge University Press.

National Commission for the Protection of Human Subjects of Biomedical and Behavioral Research (1979). *The Belmont Report: Ethical Principles and Guidelines for the Protection of Human Subjects of Research.* Washington, D.C.: U.S. Government Printing Office.

Proctor, Robert M. (1988). *Racial Hygiene: Medicine under the Nazis.* Cambridge, Mass.: Harvard University Press.

Rothman, David J. (2004). "Research, Human: Historical Aspects." In *Encyclopedia of Bioethics,* 3rd edition, ed. Stephen G. Post. New York: Macmillan Reference.

Trials of the War Criminals before the Military Tribunals under Control Order No. 10, Military Tribunal I, Case 1, vol. II. U. S. Government Printing Office, 1949.

World Medical Association (1964). *Declaration of Helsinki: Ethnical Principles for Medical Research Involving Human Subjects.* France: Ferney Voltaire. Available from http://www.wma.net/e/policy/b3.htm.

Stephen P. Marks

Memoirs of Perpetrators

Perpetrator behavior shakes one's sense of humanity and provokes a desire to be separate from such cruel barbarism, often achieved by characterizing perpetrators as demonic or psychologically deformed. The historical record and insights of scholars are used to confirm this judgment. But most contemporary work on this subject supports the recent conclusion of social psychologist James Waller who argues, "that it is ordinary individuals, like you and me, who commit extraordinary evil. Perpetrators of extraordinary evil are extraordinary only by what they have done, not by who they are" (2002, p. 18).

Judgments about perpetrators are often made without their own accounts. Facing condemnation and punishment, perpetrators are unlikely to record their experiences in memoir form. Thus, while survivor memoirs, especially of the Holocaust, multiply, those of perpetrators are rare, even when supplemented by the writings of those who examined perpetrators. Among perpetrator memoirs are those of the Commandant of Auschwitz, Rudolf Höss, written while he awaited trial in Poland for crimes for which he was executed in 1947, and of Djemal Pasha, who as Minister of the Marine in the Young Turks government of the Ottoman Empire and Commander of the Fourth Army in Syria was one of three key architects of the Armenian genocide of 1915. Among studies of perpetrators are those of Nazi leaders tried at Nuremberg that were authored by American psychologists Douglas Kelley and Gustave Gilbert, and that of Franz Stangl, Commandant of Treblinka, by the journalist Gita Sereny, based on her extensive interviews with him following the 1970 trial for his role in genocide.

Given an extremely thin resource base, what claims can be made about the historical value of perpetrator memoirs? These texts are, after all, suspect, and readers must approach them with critical skepticism. Perpetrators have obvious reasons to diminish their responsibility for or role in murderous actions. Djemal, for example, stated that when World War I began in 1914, he left Constantinople and thus had no input in the momentous 1915 decision to deport Armenians from the Ottoman Empire. He claimed that he took "the necessary measures to protect the Armenians against any attack while passing through my command . . . [and] did everything possible during the whole period of their deportation to give help to the Armenians" (1922, pp. 277–278). Scholars of the Armenian genocide paint a radically different picture of Djemal's involvement and actions.

Although both Höss and Stangl acknowledged and often accurately detailed their roles in the Holocaust, the reader must be cautious in accepting their accounts. Like most perpetrators, they developed an extensive set of rationalizations for their actions and these permeate their narratives. Both Höss and Stangl portrayed themselves as initially ignorant of the true nature of their assignments as commandants of their respective death camps, as administrators who devoted their energies solely to building and maintaining efficient camps in fulfillment of their duty, and as men who did not personally hate Jews or indulge in deliberate cruelty toward prisoners. By separating themselves from the actual killing process, not personally brutalizing the victims, and highlighting their roles as good fathers and husbands, they attempted to defuse their own responsibility and affirm their decency. Arguing that serious threats to his safety and that of his family trapped him in his perpetrator role, Stangl stated, "It was a matter of survival—always of survival. What I had to do, while I continued my efforts to get out, was to limit my own actions to what I—in my own conscience—could answer for" (Sereny, 1974, p. 164). No matter that he commanded two death camps with ener-

gy and dedication; as long as he personally did not pull the trigger or start the engines for the gas chambers, he was not guilty in his own mind.

Armed with the knowledge of perpetrator evasions and justifications, the reader can profitably use such materials to better understand: (1) how rather normal persons could become part of genocidal projects; (2) the various perpetrator roles, including killers, bureaucrats, and policy makers; (3) their motives for becoming involved; (4) the costs they paid for their involvement; and (5) the fact that perpetrators were essentially ordinary men.

If contemporary readers can gain significant insights from reading these memoirs, did their writing have any therapeutic value for the authors? If the memoir was the product of a genuine effort at self-understanding, including a willingness to accept responsibility for one's actions, then it could have such a value. Djemal's memoir, however, takes a very different tact as he essentially blames others, primarily the Russians, and unfortunate circumstances for the Armenian deaths and, thus, does not see himself in need of therapy or forgiveness. With death the likely outcome of his impending trial, Höss had an incentive to engage in such a therapeutic exercise. He begins his autobiography promisingly, "In the following pages I want to try and tell the story of my innermost being. . .and of the psychological heights and depths through which I have passed" (1959, p. 20). But the end result is so full of rationalizations, self-justifications, and evasions, that one questions whether it did have genuine therapeutic benefit. At the end of his extensive and probing interviews with Sereny, Stangl haltingly, painfully offered a kind of confession: "But I was there. So yes, in reality I share the guilt. Because my guilt . . . my guilt . . . only now in these talks . . . now that I have talked about it all for the first time. [pause] My guilt is that I am still here" (Sereny, 1974, p. 364). Nineteen hours later Stangl died of heart failure, perhaps more at peace with himself than he had been in many years.

SEE ALSO Diaries; Memoirs of Survivors

BIBLIOGRAPHY

Broad, Pery (1991). "Reminiscences of Pery Broad." In *KL Auschwitz Seen by the SS*, ed. Kazimierz Smoen et al. Warsaw: Interpress Publishers.

Djemal (also Cemal), Pasha (1922). *Memories of a Turkish Statesman, 1913–1919*. New York: Doran.

Gilbert, G. M. (1947). *Nuremberg Diary*. New York: Farrar, Straus.

Gilbert, G. M. (1950). *The Psychology of Dictatorship: Based on an Examination of the Leaders of Nazi Germany*. New York: Ronald Press.

Höss, Rudolf (1959). *Commandant of Auschwitz*. New York: Popular Library.

Kelley, Douglas M. (1947). *22 Cells in Nuremberg*. New York: MacFadden.

Sereny, Gita (1974). *Into That Darkness: An Examination of Conscience*. New York: Random House.

Waller, James (2002). *Becoming Evil: How Ordinary People Commit Genocide and Mass Killing*. New York: Oxford University Press.

Donald G. Schilling

Memoirs of Survivors

Genocides destroy human communities, physically and culturally. Unimaginable acts of cruelty characterize genocide, and the horrific becomes commonplace. For those who manage to survive the maelstrom, the tasks of reconstructing broken lives, often in new settings; of making sense of the nonsensical; and of piecing together the fragments of memory represent new and daunting challenges. The temptation to repress the past and live only for the present and future is powerful, yet without confronting the past, healing is impossible. Some survivors almost immediately record their experiences, bearing witness to an indifferent humanity of the crimes they endured; others take decades before they can examine their shattered pasts in this manner; and still others can only come forward as the end of life approaches. An outpouring of oral and video testimonies and of written memoirs has accumulated, especially from survivors of the Holocaust and, to a lesser extent, from those of the Armenian Genocide. For many other twentieth century genocides, however, survivor memoirs are rare. This may be because these survivors were not literate, or lacked the resources to create their memoirs, or perhaps they had to continue to live among or under the perpetrators of the genocide.

Survivors write for multiple reasons. For many, the commitment to bear witness—and thus deny the perpetrators one more victory—is motivation enough. Primo Levi, a survivor of Auschwitz, published a powerful survivor's memoir, *Se Questo è un uomo* (1947; published in English as *Survival in Auschwitz*; 1986). In the introduction to a second English-language publication of the book, issued in 1993, he explained his reasons for writing:

> Its origins go back . . . as an idea, an intention, to the days of the Lager concentration camp. The need to tell our story to 'the rest', to make 'the rest' participate in it, had taken on for us, before our liberation and after, the character of an immediate and violent impulse, to the point of competing with our other elementary needs.

To speak for the silenced and to commemorate their lives and communities, to reinforce the identity of their people, to instruct one's children, to sound a warning for the future, and to make meaningful and coherent their own inchoate memories are among the other reasons survivors assume the burden of writing. Elise Hagopian Taft, who wrote of her experiences during the Armenian genocide, observes, "I did it for my three sons so they would know something of their roots, the mass deportations, the atrocities perpetrated by the Turkish government in 1915 and thereafter," and she admonishes, "May the world get to know through these pages the true meaning of Genocide and what it does the human spirit, and resolve never to let the Holocaust happen again to any people on earth" (1981, pp. vii–viii).

In writing, survivors might find some relief from their wounds. This was true for Isabella Leitner, a Hungarian Jew, who wrote:

> America . . . put its healing arms around me. Still the pain would not go away. To get some relief, I needed to talk. But to whom? . . . Auschwitz was—and is—unfathomable. Naïve questions only increased my frustration. Yet I had to talk. . . . I began to "speak" on little scraps of paper in my native tongue, Hungarian, using a pencil (1994, p. 15).

Those little scraps became a part of her first book, *Isabella: From Auschwitz to Freedom*. Similarly, as Gerda Weissmann Klein finished her celebrated memoir, *All But My Life*, she felt "at peace, at last. I have discharged my burden, and paid a debt to many nameless heroes. . . . For I am haunted by the thought that I might be the only one left to tell their story" (1995, p. 1). To be sure "there are pains that will not go away, adding their burden over extended periods of time" (1995, p. 252), but even in surveying the desolate landscape of genocide, survivors often find some therapeutic value.

If survivors' memoirs serve a critical function for their creators, they are of inestimable worth for those spared such trauma. Despite the inadequacies of language to render the unimaginable, powerful survivor memoirs can draw readers into the depths of genocide, touching hearts and heightening understanding. Were historical narratives solely dependent on the sanitized records of the perpetrators, or on the more distanced descriptions of bystanders, they would be impoverished. The concrete, personal narratives of survivors can break through numbing impersonal statistics and cultivate empathy, arouse compassion, and fuel anger at injustice. As survivors of the genocides of the first half of the twentieth century pass away, their memoirs become an enduring legacy to educate the inquiring and confound the denier.

To be sure, memoirs should not be treated as sacred texts. Like all written work they reflect the conventions of the memoirist's genre. The author benefits from hindsight and thus can impose a degree of coherence on a fragmented past. While the memoir derives its authenticity and power from lived experience, it can also be enriched by historical research—to check the vagaries of memory and expand its reach—and by the reconstruction of scenes and conversations unlikely to have been preserved intact in memory, but which capture the essential truth of the event. Survivor memoirs present an interpretation informed by strategies of historical and literary reconstruction, and must be subject to critical evaluation, just as any other source. For example, in his best selling memoir, *Man's Search for Meaning*, Viktor Frankl "wanted simply to convey to the reader by way of a concrete example that life holds a potential meaning under any conditions, even the most miserable ones" (1985, p. 16). However, in carrying out this purpose, his critics argue that Frankl made himself the hero of the story and created a myth of heroic survival that belied the devastating reality of Auschwitz. Critical judgment also needs to be applied when reading Abraham Hartunian's moving memoir of the Armenian catastrophe, *Neither to Laugh nor to Weep* (1968). Hartunian, an evangelical Christian pastor, understands his survival and that of his family in the face of numerous encounters with death as a result of God's providential mercy. He cannot, however, ask why that mercy was withheld from all those who perished in misery.

Although they shared certain experiences, survivors and their memoirs reflect considerable diversity, depending upon the genocide about which the survivor writes and upon the particular aspects of the genocide experienced: the ghetto, labor camp, concentration camp, death camp, death march, forced relocation, hiding, passing, or fighting in a partisan band. Further, the survivor's age, gender, class, and location can all produce important variations in the survivor's story. Such diversity reminds us of how critical survivor memoirs are as sources for reconstructing the complex histories of modern genocides and of our need for caution in generalizing about such diverse materials.

SEE ALSO Diaries; Memoirs of Perpetrators; Memorials and Monuments; Memory

BIBLIOGRAPHY

Arad, Yitzhak (1979). *The Partisan: From the Valley of Death to Mt. Zion.* New York: Holocaust Library.

Delbo, Charlotte (1995). *Auschwitz and After.* New Haven, Conn.: Yale University Press.

Dolot, Miron (pseud.) (1985). *Execution by Hunger: The Hidden Holocaust.* New York: W.W. Norton.

Donat, Alexander (1978). *The Holocaust Kingdom: A Memoir.* New York: Holocaust Library.

Frankl, Viktor (1985). *Man's Search for Meaning.* New York: Washington Square Press.

Hartunian, Abraham (1968). *Neither to Laugh nor to Weep: A Memoir of the Armenian Genocide.* Boston: Beacon Press.

Klein, Gerda Weissmann (1995). *All But My Life.* New York: Hill and Wang.

Leitner, Isabella and Irving Leitner (1994). *Isabella: From Auschwitz to Freedom.* New York: Anchor Books.

Levi, Primo (1993). *Survival in Auschwitz: The Nazi Assault on Humanity.* New York: Collier Books.

May, Someth (1986). *Cambodian Witness: The Autobiography of Someth May.* Boston: Faber and Faber.

Ngor, Haing, and Warner, Roger (1988). *Haing Ngor: A Cambodian Odyssey.* New York: Macmillan Publishing Co.

Ramati, Alexander (1986). *And the Violins Stopped Playing: A Story of the Gypsy Holocaust.* New York: Franklin Watts.

Taft, Elise Hagopian (1981). *Rebirth.* Plandome, N.Y.: New Age Publishers.

Totten, Samuel (1991). *First-Person Accounts of Genocidal Acts Committed in the Twentieth Century: An Annotated Bibliography.* New York: Greenwood Press.

Donald G. Schilling

Memorials and Monuments

What should memorials of mass murder or genocide accomplish? Are they intended to honor the dead, even if, all too often, there are too many to name? Are they meant to provide a place for people to gather, mourn, and find solace? Or is their role to document the events and perpetrators of the crime and contextualize the crime in history? Is their ultimate goal to shift the focus from mass murder to future peace? For many faced with the grim task of building such memorials and monuments, the answer seems to be some or all of the above. And it is often the case that what is omitted from the memorial may be more telling than what is included.

Naming the dead is a time-honored way of acknowledging their sacrifice, because in a sense any mass memorial is also, in part, a cemetery. An important precedent was set by Sir Edwin Lutyens's World War I memorial, Thiepval Arch in the Somme, which contains the engraved names of soldiers lost during that war, listed by military unit on the interior of the memorial's massive arches. Maya Lin followed this practice, listing the names of dead or missing soldiers in order of their death or disappearance on the Vietnam Veterans Memorial in Washington, D.C. People re-

In the rear courtyard of Budapest's Great Synagogue, a memorial honors the many thousands of Hungarian Jews who perished in Nazi concentration camps. Created by Imra Varga, this metal sculpture in the shape of a giant weeping willow bears the following inscription: "Whose agony is greater than mine." [DAVE BARTRUFF/CORBIS]

spond to this display by touching the names and leaving objects at the base of the memorial walls. This has led later memorial and monument designers to incorporate provisions for public response. Thus, listing the names of the dead is a major component of the 9/11 memorial project in New York.

Without names, and sometimes even with them, relics of the dead are considered powerful memorials. In Rwanda, where over 800,000 Tutsi and moderate Hutus were murdered in April 1994, skeletons were stored for a time in schools and churches as grim reminders of what occurred. The Roman Catholic Church in Ntarama has become a memorial, for it contains the remains of people who died there during the killings. At Hiroshima, where the United States dropped its first nuclear bomb in 1945, ashes of the deceased are incorporated into in a central mound in the Memorial Peace Park. For the 9/11 memorial in New York, an underground chamber has been designated to hold cremated remains of those who perished, as well as portions of the physical structure of the World Trade Center Towers, known as the slurry wall. Relics of

structures, such as A-Bomb Dome (previously the Industrial Promotional Hall) in Hiroshima, prove to be lastingly evocative structures, providing physical evidence of past destruction in a radically altered present.

Without physical evidence, the deceased, like the six million Jews who perished in the Holocaust, are often honored by eternal flames. Sometimes a single such flame stands for many or even all of the victims. Alternatively, the Hall of Remembrance at Yad Vashem, the Holocaust memorial complex in Jerusalem, has the names of the 22 largest Nazi concentration camps inscribed on the ground, and the name of each camp serves to stand for the victims who were murdered therein. In an attempt to encapsulate memory in a variety of expressive forms, Yad Vashem also includes a history and an art museum, a hall of names (a constantly updated record of those who died in World War II), a separate Children's Memorial, a synagogue, a Memorial Cave, and an archival library.

The desire for green places to mourn the dead and soothe the living, an essential aspect of established cemetery practice, is incorporated into many genocide memorials as well. Hiroshima's memorial complex is also a park. Jerusalem's Yad Vashem has many outdoor spaces and paths for walking from one structure to the next. The above-ground portion of New York's 9/11 memorial will include a landscaped park or garden.

Museums have taken on a critical function for remembering and contextualizing genocide. Holocaust Museums in many cities are frequently intended to serve also as memorials, such as the United States Holocaust Memorial Museum in Washington D.C. Serving as a national institution for the documentation, study, and interpretation of Holocaust history, it also is considered a national memorial to the millions murdered during the Holocaust. It combines its scholarly function with collections of artifacts (including a very moving collection of victims' shoes), films, photos, and oral histories.

Memorial museums and memorial complexes try to encapsulate the horror of genocide in a variety of ways, but sometimes it is the single symbolic structure or the individual work of art that resonates most. In a residential section of Berlin, removed from the memorial building activity of the center, an apparently innocuous bronze sculpture of a table and two chairs stands in the middle of the Koppenplatz, in a quarter where Eastern European immigrants once lived and where Jewish institutions co-existed with their Christian counterparts. This is Karl Biedermann's sculpture, called *The Abandoned Room* (*Der verlassene Raum*), and in it one senses rather than sees its underlying strangeness. The chair and table are just slightly larger than life, and there is a second, overturned chair lying on the ground. Nearby there is an inscription written by the Holocaust poet Nellie Sachs. Like Baroque still-life paintings with their abruptly overturned crystal goblets and pewter bowls, these simple pieces of furniture, as well as their location in an otherwise normal residential site, suggest a life suddenly interrupted. Part of the first large East German Holocaust memorial project, commissioned in 1988 but realized only in 1996, the sculpture and accompanying inscription commemorate the fiftieth anniversary of Kristallnacht and recalls the Jewish citizens of Berlin prior to World War II. It is an effective memento mori sculpture, evoking not only thoughts of the fragility of earthly life, but also the eerie sense of individuals who have apparently vanished without a trace.

Even more profoundly disturbing is Israeli sculptor Micha Ullman's *Library* (1994–1995), situated in the Bebelplatz in Berlin. This work marks the site of the infamous Nazi book burning of May 1933. A bronze plaque on the ground quotes the German poet Heinrich Heine: "Where they burn books/At the end they also burn people." Immediately adjacent, flush to the ground, is a glass-covered view into a subterranean but glaringly lit room with floor-to-ceiling walls of empty shelves painted a stark white. During the day the now scratched viewer's portal is often fogged, rendering the empty library all but invisible, and many people stroll past without noticing, or even walk right over it. At night, however, people are drawn to the light that emanates from the sculpture. Thus, the very ground of Berlin, like the unconscious mind, seems to suppress trauma during the day, only to release it, hauntingly transformed into the night.

SEE ALSO Architecture; Memory of Survivors

BIBLIOGRAPHY

Foote, Kenneth E. (1997). *Shadowed Ground: America's Landscapes of Violence and Tragedy*. Austin: University of Texas Press.

Hogan, Michael J., ed. (1996). *Hiroshima in History and Memory*. Cambridge, U.K.: Cambridge University Press.

Senie, Harriet F. (1999). "In Pursuit of Memory: Berlin, Bamberg, and the Specter of History." *Sculpture* (April):46–51.

Yoneyama, Lisa (1999). *Hiroshima Traces: Time, Space, and the Dialectics of Memory*. Berkeley: University of California Press.

Young, James E. (1993). *The Texture of Memory: Holocaust Memorials and Meaning*. New Haven, Conn.: Yale University Press.

Young, James E., ed. (1994). *The Art of Memory: Holocaust Memorials in History*. Munich: Prestel-Verlag.

Harriet F. Senie

Memory

A useful way to situate memory within the context of modern genocide is to consider the Holocaust of the Jews by Nazi Germany. First, the Holocaust represents what may be called open memory that has become part of popular culture in Western societies. The relatively high level of literacy among the victims plus the traditions within the Jewish religion about memory gave birth very quickly to survivors' written accounts called Memorial Books, composed from memory and testimonies, makeshift memorials in places of destruction, and ultimately, published memoirs, films, and art. Second, and in contrast, the Romani and Sinti (gypsies), also victims of genocide by the Nazis, did not tell their story because of reverse literacy issues and traditions within the culture that prohibited talking about the dead. The creation of the State of Israel in 1948 became a repository for the memory of the Holocaust as well as the counterimage of the new Israeli Jew in his or her own nation-state.

With other genocides issues regarding memory are more complex and often politicized because of denial by the perpetrators, or descendants of the perpetrators. Thus, the main issue of the Armenian genocide is the search by Armenians around the world for confirmation of the event as "genocide" by the Turkish Republic. The Armenian diaspora population, although it has constructed memorials, overseen the writing of memoirs, and directed video and oral history projects among survivors, still views the need for Turkish official recognition of the events of 1915 through 1922 as genocide as critical to the well-being of the community. Turkish denial of the genocide, and even the creation of reverse history whereby accusations of Armenian genocide against the Turks have been made, has created a counterproblem in Turkey, where Turks are uncertain about their own modern history. Therefore, the Armenian case might be characterized by deliberately suppressed memory.

In sites of genocide and crimes against humanity during the 1990s, conflicting stories have emerged about those responsible for atrocities and as a result of the intersection of age-old antagonisms in recent political, economic, and national issues that the victims as well as the perpetrators may not have been cognizant about. Thus, the Yugoslavian War of 1992 and beyond produced contradictory memory about oppressor and victim among Croats, Bosnians, and Serbs. In the Kosovo War of 1998 mutual recriminations existed between Serbs and Kosovar Albanians. Even if the war crimes tribunals addressing these conflicts convict leaders of crimes against humanity or genocide, it is doubtful that a standard narrative explaining clearly who is the victim and who is the perpetrator will emerge. Oral histories, however, in addition to art forms, poetry, and folk idioms, will undoubtedly be significant in creating and maintaining memory.

Memories of the Rwandan genocide are wrapped up in the completion of trials for those accused of genocide, as well as the difficult issue of creating a common memory that allows both perpetrators and victims to live together in the same society in the aftermath of genocide.

As time passes, memory fades. Influenced by contemporary events, films, and historical writing, survivors of genocide who write their memoirs a long time after liberation or rescue may have flawed memories that would be deemed inadmissible in court proceedings. Children of survivors often receive the memory of their parents' tragedies in fragmented ways; this produces trauma in what is called the "second generation." Actual memories of events, however, are reserved for those who unfortunately experienced them, whereas the second generation receives the story as a kind of fable.

The collective memory of genocide has been formed in many different ways. For Jewish memory there remains the traditional *Yizkor* service of remembrance of the dead on Yom Kippur, the Day of Atonement in the Jewish calendar. *Yom HaShoah* (Day of Holocaust Remembrance) has been added to this same calendar; it is commemorated in both Israel and the Jewish diaspora on the 27th of the Hebrew month of Nissan, usually late April on the Gregorian calendar. Because it appears only in the Hebrew calendar, *Yom HaShoah* is reserved for Jewish memory, not that of other victims. European secular memory of the Holocaust, however, suggests some contradictions, as its commemoration annually occurs on January 27th, the day the Soviet army liberated Auschwitz. For a survivor who was in another concentration camp until the end of World War II on May 8, 1945, the European commemorative date may be meaningless. For other genocides often the date of their onset has become the date of commemoration. Thus, April 7 is usually the date the Rwandan genocide is commemorated, and April 15 marks the commemoration of the Armenian genocide.

Art and monuments can play an important role in creating memory, especially if such manifestations of culture evoke memories at unexpected moments. Various generations of artistic memory may be found in every genocide. The most visceral images are generally uncovered in children's art. Survivors often create works of art as a form of witnessing or grieving. The second generation and those not touched by the event itself nevertheless often attempt to deal with the subject as part of an informal discourse about collective memory. The result may be representations in the plastic arts, memorials, film, and plays that may create problems over issues such as historical accuracy and the ability to represent what many describe as "unrepresentable." The only case of a perpetrator nation creating significant memorials to its victims is Germany. In most other cases it is the nation of the victims that has developed memorials to genocide, in its own country, such as Armenia, or among diasporas. The unwillingness to address genocide through historical writing, official apologies, commemorative dates, compensation, or memorialization is perhaps an indication that genocide, for some regimes, remains an unfinished project.

SEE ALSO Art as Representation; Diaries; Historiography as a Written Form; Memoirs of Perpetrators; Memoirs of Survivors; Memorials and Monuments

BIBLIOGRAPHY

Adorno, Theodore W. (1984). *Aesthetic Theory*, tran. C. Lenhardt. New York: Routledge and Kegan Paul.

Friedlander, Saul (1993). *Memory, History and the Extermination of the Jews of Europe.* Bloomington: Indiana University Press.

Hoffman, Eva (2004). *After Such Knowledge: Memory, History and the Aftermath of the Holocaust.* New York: HarperCollins.

Kugelmass, Jack and Jonathan Boyarin, eds. (1983). *From a Ruined Garden: The Memorial Books of Polish Jewry.* New York: Schocken.

Sicher, Efraim, ed. *Broken Crystal.* Urbana: University of Illinois Press.

Young, James E. (2000). *At Memory's Edge.* New Haven, Conn.: Yale University Press.

Stephen C. Feinstein

Mengele, Josef

[MARCH 16, 1911–1979]
Notorious Nazi war criminal known as the "Angel of Death."

Born March 16, 1911, to Karl and Walburga Mengele, Josef Mengele grew up in Gunzburg Germany. His father, an engineer, owned a foundry and manufactured farm equipment for milling, wood sawing, and straw cutting. These enterprises formed the base of the Mengele family fortune that ultimately supported Mengele when he became a fugitive. Josef was raised in a devout Catholic home, passed his high school exams in April 1930 and by October had enrolled at Munich University as a student of philosophy and medicine, with a focus in anthropology and human genetics.

In Munich, Mengele became enamored with the Nazi Party and joined the military. At the rank of *Unstersturmfuhrer* (sub lieutenant), he was first posted to the Ukraine. His next military assignment was to the Geological Section of the Race and Resettlement Office. This was a program involved with classifying and eliminating non-Germans from annexed territories, including orphans and persons falsely claiming German blood. As a captain, in May 1943, Mengele was posted to Auschwitz. He served there from May 1943 through January 1945.

For many prisoners disembarking at the concentration camp railhead, one of the last things they would ever see was Mengele, the immaculate, well-mannered SS officer who greeted them. With a flick of his cane, the "Angel of Death" directed newly arrived prisoners to the right or to the left. This was the selection process employed to separate those fit to work from those destined for the gas chambers. Mengele was later charged with more than simply selecting victims. It was alleged that he used electricity to test women's endurance of pain; subjected patients to massive, burn-producing doses of radiation; and conducted bone marrow transplant experiments on healthy inmates. Most notorious of all were his abhorrent experiments on twins.

Mengele departed Auschwitz on the evening of January 17, 1945, with a ten-day head start on the advancing Russian Amy. Thus began a flight that successfully eluded his pursuers six years beyond his death. Mengele's first destination was Gross Rosen Concentration Camp, infamous for its biological warfare experiments using Soviet prisoners. On February 16 he fled again, this time into the no-man's land between the Russian and Allied Armies. He was captured in a sweep by American troops and detained for two months, but was then released. Part of the time during his detention, as often during the rest of his life, Mengele used his correct name. Nonetheless, his captors did not recognize him, even though his name had been placed on lists of wanted war criminals, including the list published by the U.S. Judge Advocates General and the First Central Registry of War Criminals and Security Suspects. The oversight has been attributed to Allied administrative failure.

Upon release he took the name Fritz Hollman, and found work on a farm, milking cows and growing potatoes near Mangolding, in an agricultural area in southern Germany. He remained there for four years, during which the Nuremberg Trials were underway. Among the prosecutions, the Doctors Trials most likely provided Mengele with an incentive to depart from Europe. In mid-July 1949, he sailed for Buenos Aires, Argentina. In subsequent years, Mengele successively took up residence in Paraguay and Brazil. There he apparently suffered a fatal heart attack while swimming. A death certificate, issued in the name of his then-alias, Wolgang Gerhard, attributed the cause of death due to drowning. The body was buried in Brazil in 1979. Six years later authorities tracked down the grave's location.

In June 1985, a team of forensic experts from the United States, West Germany, and Israel released a controversial identification of Mengele's skeletal remains. In the absence of ante mortem dental records or medical X-rays, U.S. experts refused to definitively confirm the identification. Their cautious opinion was limited to a statement that the remains were those of Josef Mengele "within reasonable scientific certainty." Subsequent DNA analysis has provided strong independent evidence that the remains were indeed those of Josef Mengele.

WANTED

Dr. Josef Mengele
For his crimes against humanity

Josef Mengele was responsible for the death of 400,000 persons at Auschwitz Concentration Camp. He tortured children and made their parents suffer. He brutalized people with horrible medical experiments.

Mengele is 74. Height 1.7 m (5'10"). Eyes, greenish brown. He became a citizen of Argentina in 1954, a citizen of Paraguay in 1959.

Rewards worldwide total more than U.S. $2.375 million for information leading to the arrest and extradition of Dr. Josef Mengele. **Contact: Martin Mendelsohn, P.O. Box 33126, Washington, D.C. 20033, or call Simon Wiesenthal Center, (213) 553-9036. All information will be held confidential.**

Dr. Mengele in his mid 40's.

An artist conception of what Mengele would look like today at age 74.

REWARDS—U.S. $2,375,000

Wanted poster for the Nazi "Angel of Death," infamous for the cruelty he exhibited at Auschwitz in selecting victims for the gas chamber and conducting medical experiments on those who survived. [**GETTY IMAGES**]

SEE ALSO Auschwitz; Medical Experimentation; Physicians

BIBLIOGRAPHY

Jeffreys, A. J., M. J. Allen, E. Hagelberg, and A. Sonnberg (1992). "Identification of the Skeletal Remains of Josef Mengele by DNA Analysis." *Forensic Science International* (September) 56(1):65–76.

Posner, G. L., and J. Ware (1986). *Mengele: The Complete Story*. New York: Dell Publishing.

Stover, Joyce C., and E. Stover (1991). *Witnesses from the Grave: The Stories Bones Tell*. Boston: Little Brown.

William D. Haglund

Mercenaries

The general definition of *mercenaries* focuses on the following two elements: the foreign nature of the military service provided and the primarily financial motivation in providing combat service. Mercenarism refers to the hiring of foreign individuals or groups of individuals by a state or entity to serve in a combat role for private gain. In 1987 the United Nations Commission on Human Rights appointed Special Rapporteur Enrique Bernales Ballesteros of Peru to analyze, monitor, and report on all forms of mercenarism. Despite growing condemnation, mercenaries continue to exist in many different forms and are involved in diverse activities.

Historical Overview

Mercenarism dates back to antiquity, a time during which armies were predominantly comprised of foreign professional soldiers seeking personal gain. The first account of mercenarism was recorded by Xenophon in *Anabasis*; there he noted Cyrus's use of ten thousand mercenaries against his brother Artaxexers in a bid for the Persian throne in 401 BCE. A large number of these foreign soldiers were Arcadians, Achaeans, and Peloponnesians who had endured economic instability following the Peloponnesian War. In 334 BCE the Persians used Greek mercenaries to fight against Alexander the Great, who in turn brought more than 44,000 mercenaries to Asia Minor. His Macedonian successors also used highly trained mercenary armies to wage war, as did Greek city-states in the fourth century BCE. The First Punic War between Rome and Carthage (264–261 BCE) originated in mercenary activity, and in the second century German mercenaries played a pivotal role in defending the Roman Empire. For more than one thousand years mercenaries were the backbone of the army of the Eastern Roman Empire. The rulers of Byzantium and Carthage also relied on the military expertise of foreign soldiers in defending their respective empires.

Throughout the Middle Ages the phenomenon of mercenaries persisted and their recruitment increased. In the twelfth century mercenaries were mostly used for colonial expansion and for maintaining foreign domination in colonized countries. The Crusades gave rise to a more anarchic form of mercenarism, including postconflict exploits following the emergence of mercenary groups. The formation of coalitions in response to these groups eventually led to their temporary defeat in the twelfth and thirteen centuries. Comprised of a variety of nationalities, including English, French, Flemish, German, Italian, and Catalan fighters, these groups reappeared as *Grandes Compagnies* during the One Hundred Years War (1337–1453) and were finally disbanded in 1453. Between the thirteenth and sixteenth centuries the *condottieri*, freelance commanders of Catalan, English, German, and Hungarian troops, were hired in Italy to recruit and arm men and to conduct hostilities within the Italian republics. The rise of the absolute monarchy in the fifteenth and sixteenth centuries led to an enhancement in the status of mercenaries, whom rulers relied on to fight wars and to maintain order within their kingdoms. Mercenarism was thus relatively institutionalized during the feudal period; kings and lords had at their disposal a collection of individuals willing to fight for pay.

Both the progressive extinction of privatized war and the consolidation of the nation-state eventually gave rise to a new form of mercenarism. Traditionally, the mercenary had sold his services to a foreign state or entity. However, in the fifteenth and sixteenth centuries a prescribed number of soldiers were temporarily rented out by one state to another foreign sovereign. This procurement of foreign troops was extensive during the Renaissance and differs from the undisciplined mercenary companies of the Middle Ages. Swiss and German troops were leased regularly between the fifteenth and nineteenth centuries, and played an important role in the religious wars during this period. For

example, the Swiss Guard, founded in the sixteenth century, continues to serve the Vatican. Widespread state practice gave mercenaries an international legal status and legitimacy until the eighteenth century, during which the rise of nationalism and the adoption of the standing army to defend the state led to a decline in mercenarism. The development of the law of neutrality in the nineteenth century, which generally prohibited the enlistment of a state's citizens in foreign armies, also prompted a regression of mercenary activities. This evolution was most notable in Europe, for colonial powers continued to rely on the use of local mercenaries in the Americas, Indies, and Africa.

In the twentieth century the practice of mercenarism evolved and reappeared in a different form. Mercenarism intensified within the context of decolonization in the 1960s and the recognition of the right to self-determination. These independent mercenaries, often referred to as "soldiers of fortune," "wild geese," or *les affreux* (the dreaded/horrible ones), surfaced in postcolonial Africa and were used to destabilize newly independent governments. By the 1960s, however, mercenaries were no longer accepted as an integral component of armed forces. The use of mercenaries nevertheless continued in the following decades, including their active participation in the civil wars in the Congo (1960–1963; 1964–1967), Nigeria (1968–1969), the Sudan (1970), Angola (1975), and Latin America in the 1980s. Also commonly referred to as traditional mercenaries—many of whom came from former colonial armies, including the French Foreign Legion and Belgian army—they threatened weak, newly independent nation-states, often influencing intrastate conflict on the African continent. During this time mercenary activities tended to be disorganized and undisciplined and were comprised of a relatively small number of individuals. Vital economic interests were often at stake and mercenarism involved activities such as insurgencies and counterinsurgencies, regime change, and civil conflicts.

International Law

Recently, the legal framework to prohibit mercenaries has been envisaged through norms regulating the general use of force between states. Of particular relevance to the question of mercenaries is Article 4 of the 1907 Hague Convention Respecting the Rights and Duties of Neutral Powers and Persons in Case of War on Land (Convention V), which stipulates that "(c)orps of combatants cannot be formed nor recruiting agencies opened on the territory of a neutral Power to assist the belligerents." States that have chosen to remain neutral during an armed conflict are obliged under Article 4 to prevent the formation of mercenary groups on their territory for the purpose of intervention in the armed conflict. However, international humanitarian law (the law of armed conflict) made no formal distinction between mercenaries and other combatants prior to the adoption of the protocol additional to the Geneva Conventions of 12 August 1949, and relating to the Protection of Victims of International Armed Conflicts, 8 June 1977. Before that time mercenaries were regarded as respectable professionals and usually accorded prisoner-of-war status when captured, thus benefiting from protection under the Third Geneva Convention relative to prisoners of war, provided that they met the conditions of Article 4.

According to Article 47 of Additional Protocol I, mercenaries are not entitled to prisoner-of-war status, although a state may grant them equivalent treatment if it so desires. Under Article 45 any captured combatant is presumed to be a prisoner of war until his or her status has been determined by a competent tribunal. If a mercenary is not granted combatant or prisoner-of-war status, he or she must be treated as a civilian having unlawfully participated in armed conflict. In qualifying as a civilian, protection is afforded by Article 4 of Convention (IV) relative to the protection of civilians in times of war (Geneva, August 12, 1949), subject to certain conditions enumerated in Article 5. Furthermore, all parties to a conflict must observe the fundamental treatment and judicial guarantees afforded to persons affected by armed conflict and who find themselves in the hands of a party to the conflict (Article 75).

International humanitarian law does not address the issue of the legality of mercenary activities or prohibit the use of mercenaries by states or other entities. The law of armed conflict simply defines the status of mercenaries and the implications in the event of capture. According to the definition contained in Article 47 of Additional Protocol I, a mercenary is any person who:

(a) is specially recruited locally or abroad in order to fight in an armed conflict;

(b) does, in fact, take a direct part in the hostilities;

(c) is motivated to take part in the hostilities essentially by the desire for private gain and, in fact, is promised, by or on behalf of a Party to the conflict, material compensation substantially in excess of that promised or paid to combatants of similar ranks and functions in the armed forces of that Party;

(d) is neither a national or a Party to the conflict nor a resident of territory controlled by a Party to the conflict;

(e) is not a member of the armed forces of a Party to the conflict; and

(f) has not been sent by a State which is not a Party to the conflict on official duty as a member of its armed forces.

These requirements are cumulative in that they must all be applicable for an individual to be categorized as a mercenary. The narrow scope of this definition reflects a fundamental tenet of international humanitarian law, which is to ensure that the loss of special safeguards only occurs in very limited circumstances.

The law of armed conflict does not envisage protection in internal armed conflict (civil wars) for persons who would otherwise qualify as mercenaries in international armed conflict, because the status of combatant does not exist in situations of internal conflict. In an international armed conflict a prisoner of war cannot be convicted for having fought in a conflict, whereas in a civil war, no such immunity exists. Nevertheless, civil war mercenaries are entitled, at a minimum, to certain fundamental guarantees such as humane treatment and nondiscrimination (Common Article 3 of the Geneva Conventions). Out of battle mercenaries are also protected by applicable international human rights law and other applicable humanitarian law, especially Articles 4 and 5 of Protocol Additional to the Geneva Conventions of 12 August 1949, and Relating to the Protection of Victims of Non-International Armed Conflicts. Mercenaries in situations of internal armed conflict are also subject to the laws of the territory in which the conflict takes place.

In contrast to Additional Protocol I, the Convention for the Elimination of Mercenaries in Africa prohibits both mercenaries and mercenarism, which is considered a crime against peace and security in Africa regardless of whether committed by an individual, a group, an association, a state, or a state representative. Adopted by the Organization of African Unity (OAU) in 1977, the Convention, which came into force in 1985, defines the crime of mercenarism as "the attempt by an individual to enroll, or his enlistment or enrollment as a mercenary; the employment or support of mercenaries in any way; and when a State allows mercenary activities to be carried out within its territory or in any place under its control while intending to overthrow or undermine the constitutional order or territorial integrity of another State." Substantively, the definition of a mercenary contained in the OAU Convention differs little from that of Article 47 of Additional Protocol I. The OAU Convention is significant in that it creates a specific offense of mercenarism and contains a series of corresponding obligations, including the adoption of measures to eradicate mercenary activities, and the prosecution or extradition of those committing an offense under the Convention. Additionally, state representatives may be punished if a state accused of involvement in mercenary activities is brought before any competent OAU or international tribunal and is found to have breached the Convention. Whereas Additional Protocol I is internationally recognized, the OAU Convention is regional in scope, as it is only applicable to states in the African region that have completed the ratification process.

The International Convention Against the Recruitment, Use, Financing and Training of Mercenaries was adopted in 1989 and came into force on October 20, 2001. Its international scope is similar to that of Additional Protocol I, but the International Convention expands the definition of mercenary to cover situations other than armed conflict by including situations in which individuals are recruited to participate in a concerted act of violence for the purpose of overthrowing a government or undermining the constitutional order of a state, or infringing on the territorial integrity of a state. The International Convention identifies specific offenses, including the recruitment, use, financing, or training of mercenaries, or the attempt to do so. It also criminalizes the accomplice of any person who either commits or attempts to commit an offense cited in the Convention, regardless of whether the mercenaries in question have taken part in the concerted act of violence. States are obliged to refrain from taking part in any of the activities designated in the Convention and to prevent such activities by others through the adoption of appropriate measures. The prosecution of offenders at the national level is also set out within a framework established by the Convention. Although the International Convention is a binding instrument of international law, it lacks widespread ratification.

Generally, efforts to deal with the mercenary phenomenon, whether regionally or internationally, have met with little success. The various instruments lend themselves to different and sometimes contradictory interpretations, and a number of legal inadequacies and gaps make it difficult to accurately classify the act of mercenarism and identify those who commit it. According to United Nations (UN) Special Rapporteur Enrique Bernales Ballesteros, questions to which there are no definitive answers include the following: What is the status of foreigners who, following their entry into a country, acquires its nationality in order to cover up the fact that they are mercenaries in the service of either a third state or the other side in an armed conflict? What is the status of a nonresident national paid by a third state to undertake criminal activities against his or her own country of origin? What is the status of those with dual nationalities—one of them being that

of the state against which they are carrying out criminal activities—who are paid either by the state of their other nationality or a third party? What are the limits of *jus sanguinis,* a right by which nationality or citizenship may be conferred to any person born to a parent who is a national or citizen of that state? In particular, what are the limits of jus sanguinis in armed conflict when those paid and sent to fight in the country of their ancestors invoke this right in either a domestic or international armed conflict? The definition of a mercenary contained in Article 47, although failing to address these questions, is almost literally repeated in the definitions adopted in both the OAU and International Conventions. According to the Special Rapporteur, "The relevant international legal instruments are but imperfect tools for dealing with the issue of mercenaries." Furthermore, these definitions fail to address recent changes that have taken place in mercenary activities.

The New Mercenaries
International restructuring and transition following the end of the cold war have revealed the need for alternative security measures in the absence of superpower support. This security vacuum includes, for example, the resurgence of extreme nationalism and separatism and ethnic and religious intolerance, and the inability of smaller states to contain internal security threats. The post–cold war period has thus witnessed the emergence of new categories of mercenaries and mercenary activities. Mercenary activities have increased and diversified in both theory and practice, and are no longer predominantly confined to the African continent. For example, mercenaries were used in wars that took place within the territory of the former Yugoslavia and in wars that affected some states having emerged from the former Union of Soviet Socialist Republics. They were also used in long-term conflicts, such as that in Colombia, and in attempts to destabilize political regimes, including Fidel Castro's communist government in Cuba. The modernization of mercenary activities has significantly altered mercenary practice, which has taken on complex and multifaceted forms in a variety of situations and contexts.

In the 1990s private security companies specializing in military services supplemented the use of traditional mercenaries. Groups of professionals have partially replaced the relatively small number of individuals that dominated the mercenary scene between the 1960s and 1980s. Such companies existed prior to the end of the cold war, including the *condottieri* and *Grandes Compagnies* of the Middle Ages and Renaissance period. Similar to their predecessors, private security companies contract their soldiers out to

The hiring of foreigners to wage aggressive war is not a contemporary phenomenon. The drawing reproduced here shows hessians (German mercenaries) about to depart for the American Revolution in the service of Great Britain. [BETTMANN/CORBIS]

foreign entities, but have adapted to the needs and structure of the post–cold war world. Operational methods now include the offer of security services and military advice and assistance on the international market in return for money, as well as mining and energy concessions. The Special Rapporteur notes that private companies offering military, consultancy, and security services are now established on all five continents, and that some of these companies have recently obtained contracts worth tens of millions of United States dollars. Unlike traditional mercenaries, who are mostly covert in nature, private security companies are registered corporate companies. According to the Special Rapporteur, they are generally part of corporate holding companies and subsidiaries and take part in various services through other companies, including transport, communications, economic and financial consultancy, and health and sanitation services. In addition to sovereign governments and government entities, clients range from international organizations, foreign embassies, and nongovernmental organizations (NGOs) to multinational corporations that are usually involved in oil and exploration and mineral prospecting. The Spe-

cial Rapporteur also notes that some of these private security companies provide training to combat forces or pilots for troop transport, offer specialized technical services, and on occasion actively participate in combat situations.

Some of the most important private security companies include Executive Outcomes (now disbanded), Military Professional Resource Institute, Defense Systems Ltd., and Sandline International. In April 1995 Executive Outcomes was hired by the government of Sierra Leone to confront the threat from a rebel army, the Revolutionary United Front (RUF). Executive Outcomes prompted the RUF to negotiate a peace settlement in November 1996, after having destroyed the rebels' headquarters in the southeastern part of the country. The success of Executive Outcomes in Sierra Leone, however, may be contrasted with the fact that it provided a temporary, short-term solution to the conflict. Once the company had withdrawn from this West African country in January 1997, the peace agreement disintegrated and violence erupted once again. According to the Special Rapporteur, the right to life, security, and peace, including the preservation of both the rule of law and democracy, are not matters that can be entrusted to private security companies. One of the most controversial aspects of this issue includes the claim that security companies operate legally because they sign their contracts with legitimate governments. However, according to the Special Rapporteur, responsibility for the internal order and security of a sovereign state lies with the state itself; it can neither transfer nor renounce these responsibilities. Despite the fact that in recent years security has been partially privatized and the state now shares this function, a number of limits should not be exceeded. According to the Special Rapporteur, companies should not actively participate in armed conflicts or recruit and hire mercenaries. Additionally, the state should retain the right to protect external borders or maintain public order. In short, companies should not attempt to replace the state in defending national sovereignty.

Moreover, the premise underlying the claim that security companies fill a critical void in offering an alternative security model cannot be confused with the effectiveness of the services offered and the nature of the acts that they carry out, according to the Special Rapporteur. For example, some activities conducted by mercenaries and the hiring of this type of professional services extend to other illicit activities, including arms trafficking, drug trafficking, terrorism, attempts to destabilize legitimate governments, and acts to take forcible control of valuable natural resources. According to the Special Rapporteur, the involvement of mercenaries in other criminal activities has also led to their participation in the commission of serious violations of human rights and of international humanitarian law. The concern thus lies with companies offering military security services on the international market that recruit, hire, and use mercenaries and the instances when these companies become involved in armed conflict.

The restrictive approach adopted by the UN in linking mercenaries with concerted acts of violence aimed at violating the right of peoples to self-determination and undermining the constitutional order of a state or its territorial integrity, while seeking substantial personal gain and material compensation, is such that private security companies, as presently constituted, do not fall within this definition. Although they do have some mercenary traits, the personnel that work for private military, advisory, training, and security companies, and the contracts concluded between such companies and states, cannot be described as completely mercenary, according to the Special Rapporteur. Loopholes encountered in the definition of mercenaries led the General Assembly to request, in December 1999, that the United Nations High Com-

missioner for Human Rights convene several expert meetings to study the current forms of mercenary activities and to propose recommendations for an updated legal definition that would provide a more effective prevention mechanism for and punishment of mercenary activities. This the Office of the High Commissioner did at two meetings where amendments to the 1989 International Convention were proposed.

Experts from various regions attending the first meeting in 2001 recommended that the review of the legal definition include the elements of motive, purpose, payment, type of action, and nationality, with particular attention given to the purpose for which a mercenary is hired. In relation to private security and military companies, the group of experts recommended that states introduce specific laws and regulations prohibiting these companies from participating in armed conflicts, creating private armies, engaging in illicit arms trafficking, recruiting mercenaries, and partaking in the illegal extraction of natural resources. Efficient firms offering a widespread range of services do exist, according to the experts. Opposition to such firms offering their services on the international market lies in their participation in armed conflicts through mercenary groups forming private armies, rather than in their operation per se or the private nature of such companies.

At the second meeting held in 2002, the experts analyzed issues concerning recent events related to mercenary activities, the mandate of the Special Rapporteur, the criminalization or penalization of mercenary activities, the definition of mercenary, state responsibility for mercenary activities, the relationship between terrorism and mercenary activities, and the regulation of private security companies that offer military assistance and consultancy services. In particular, analysis focused on the definition of mercenary, including aspects related to the legal framework within which the question arises and the difficulties in taking into consideration the various forms of mercenary activities. The experts did not, however, reach a consensus regarding the legal definition of mercenary, most notably with regard to the constituent elements, international treatment of the mercenary question, and identifying the nature of mercenary activity that required criminalization from activities which already constitute crimes under international law.

The Special Rapporteur has considered these elements in his own formulation of a new legal definition for a mercenary in his report to the United Nations General Assembly in its fifty-eighth session. In its resolution on the use of mercenaries as a means of violating human rights and impending the exercise of the right of peoples to self-determination, the General Assembly noted with appreciation the proposal of a legal definition of mercenaries by the Special Rapporteur, and requested that the Secretary-General seek member states' comments to include them in the report of the Special Rapporteur to the General Assembly. It also requested that the Special Rapporteur include specific recommendations to the General Assembly in its fifty-ninth session.

In his final report submitted to the United Nations Commission on Human Rights, the Special Rapporteur recommends that the Commission support the decision to circulate among states his new proposal, which consists of amendments to the first three articles of the 1989 Convention Against the Recruitment, Use, Financing, and Training of Mercenaries. The alternative definition covers unlawful acts, including the following: trafficking in persons, arms, and drug trafficking and other illicit trafficking, terrorism, transnational organized crime, actions to destabilize legitimate governments, and actions aimed at taking forcible control of valuable national resources. It also considers that mercenaries who directly participate in the commission of the crime be criminally responsible, and extends criminal liability to those who recruit, finance, employ, or train mercenaries to participate in criminal activities. Rather than limiting itself to the mercenary as an individual agent, the proposed definition includes *mercenarism* as a concept related to the responsibility of the state and to other organizations and individuals. The alternative definition also considers the participation of mercenaries in international and internal armed conflict, as well as concerted acts of violence. Given both that the definition of mercenary contained in Article 1 of the 1989 International Convention is difficult to apply in practice, and the consensus that a new definition should be established, the Special Rapporteur believes that the definition must be modified by amending the International Convention if mercenary activities are to be prevented, eradicated, and punished.

According to the Special Rapporteur, the amendment should be debated and approved within the existing text of the International Convention, without prejudice to Article 47 of Additional Protocol I to the 1949 Geneva Conventions. He also makes a number of suggestions, including the fact that domestic and international law must clearly differentiate between military consultancy services on the international market from participation in armed conflict, and from activities that could be conceived as intervention in matters of public order and security that are the exclusive responsibility of the state. Such companies should be regulated and placed under international supervision, according to the Special Rapporteur. He also suggests the refining of legal instruments that allow the effective legal prosecution of both the mercenary and the company that hires and employs him. The various United Nations bodies and regional organizations that combat the presence and use of mercenaries must also be strengthened, and should include the link between mercenaries and terrorism, and their participation in organized crime and illegal trafficking.

The Special Rapporteur also states in his formulation of a proposal that mercenary activity must be considered a crime in and of itself and must therefore be internationally prosecutable. According to the Special Rapporteur, states are not authorized to recruit and employ mercenaries, and must be punished if they use mercenaries to attack another state or to commit unlawful acts against persons. A factor that should also be taken into account is that existing norms of international law and customary international law referring to mercenaries and their activities condemn mercenary acts in the general sense of paid military services that often lead to the commission of war crimes and human rights violations, because such services are not subject to humanitarian norms applicable in armed conflict. The Special Rapporteur also states that the foreign nationality requirement be reviewed in order for the definition to rest primarily on the nature and purpose of the illicit act with which an agent is connected by means of monetary gain.

SEE ALSO Humanitarian Law; Sierra Leone

BIBLIOGRAPHY

Major, M.-F. (1992). "Mercenaries and International Law." *Georgia Journal of International and Comparative Law* 22:103–150.

Musah, A.-F., and J. K. Fayemi, eds. (2000). *Mercenaries: An African Security Dilemma.* London: Pluto Press.

Nossal, K. R. (1998). "Roland Goes Corporate: Mercenaries and Transnational Security Corporations in the Post–Cold War Era." *Civil Wars* 1:16–35.

Peter, C. M. (1984). "Mercenaries and International Humanitarian Law." *Indian Journal of International Law* 24:373–392.

Zarate, J. C. (1998). "The Emergence of a New Dog of War: Private International Security Companies, International Law, and the New World Disorder." *Stanford Journal of International Law* 34:75–162.

ORGANIZATION PUBLICATIONS

Gaultier, L., et al. (2001). *The Mercenary Issue at the UN Commission on Human Rights: The Need for a New Approach.* London: International Alert.

United Nations Commission on Human Rights (2002). *The Impact of Mercenary Activities on the Right of Peoples to Self-Determination.* Fact Sheet No. 28. New York: United Nations.

INTERNATIONAL INSTRUMENTS

Convention Relative to the Protection of Civilian Persons in Time of War (August 12, 1949). 6 UST 3516, 75 UNTS 287.

Convention Relative to the Treatment of Prisoners of War (August 12, 1949). 6 UST 3316, 75 UNTS 135.

Convention Respecting the Rights and Duties of Neutral Powers and Persons in Case of War on Land (1910). Hague Convention No. V, Regulations Concerning the Laws and Customs of Land War, 3 Martens (3rd) 461, 2 AJIL Supplement 20 TS 9.

International Convention Against the Recruitment, Use, Financing and Training of Mercenaries (1989). ATSD 3714.

Protocol Relating to the Protection of Victims of International Armed Conflicts (Protocol I) (1977). 1125 UNTS 3, reprinted in 16 ILM at 1391.

Protocol Relating to the Protection of Victims of Non-International Armed Conflicts (Protocol II) (1977). 1125 UNTS 606, reprinted in 16 ILM at 1142.

REGIONAL INSTRUMENT

OAU Convention for the Elimination of Mercenaries in Africa (1972). OAU Document CM/433/Rev.L, Annex 1.

REPORTS OF THE SPECIAL RAPPORTEUR

Bernales Ballesteros, Enrique (February 20, 1997). *Report on the Question of the Use of Mercenaries as a Means of Violating Human Rights and Impeding the Exercise of the Rights of Peoples to Self-Determination.* UN Document E/CN.4/1997/24.

Bernales Ballesteros, Enrique (October 16, 1997). *Report on the Question of the Use of Mercenaries as a Means of Violating Human Rights and Impeding the Exercise of the Rights of Peoples to Self-Determination.* UN Document A/52/495.

Bernales Ballesteros, Enrique (January 13, 1999). *Report on the Question of the Use of Mercenaries as a Means of Violating Human Rights and Impeding the Exercise of the Rights of Peoples to Self-Determination.* UN Document E/CN.4/1999/11.

Bernales Ballesteros, Enrique (August 30, 2000). *Report on the Question of the Use of Mercenaries as a Means of Violating Human Rights and Impeding the Exercise of the Rights of Peoples to Self-Determination.* UN Document A/55/334.

Bernales Ballesteros, Enrique (January 11, 2001). *Report on the Question of the Use of Mercenaries as a Means of Violating Human Rights and Impeding the Exercise of the Rights of Peoples to Self-Determination.* UN Document E/CN.4/2001/19.

Bernales Ballesteros, Enrique (February 14, 2001). *Report on the Question of the Use of Mercenaries as a Means of Violating Human Rights and Impeding the Exercise of the Rights of Peoples to Self-Determination.* UN Document E/CN.4/2001/18.

Bernales Ballesteros, Enrique (July 27, 2001). *Report on the Question of the Use of Mercenaries as a Means of Violating Human Rights and Impeding the Exercise of the Rights of Peoples to Self-Determination.* UN Document A/56/224.

Bernales Ballesteros, Enrique (January 10, 2002). *Report on the Question of the Use of Mercenaries as a Means of Violating Human Rights and Impeding the Exercise of the Rights of Peoples to Self-Determination.* UN Document E/CN.4/2002/20.

Bernales Ballesteros, Enrique (November 29, 2002). *Report on the Question of the Use of Mercenaries as a Means of Violating Human Rights and Impeding the Exercise of the Rights of Peoples to Self-Determination.* UN Document E/CN.4/2003/16.

Bernales Ballesteros, Enrique (July 2, 2003). *Report on the Question of the Use of Mercenaries as a Means of Violating Human Rights and Impeding the Exercise of the Rights of Peoples to Self-Determination.* UN Document A/58/115.

Natalie Wagner

Milosevic, Slobodan

[AUGUST 20, 1941–]
Serb nationalist and Yugoslav leader

Slobodan Milosevic, who presided over Yugoslavia's disintegration in the 1990s, was born in Pozarevac, Serbia, the largest of the six Yugoslav republics. (Yugoslavia then included Bosnia and Herzegovina, Croatia, Macedonia, Montenegro, Slovenia, and the autonomous regions of Kosovo and Vojvodina as well.) During an unhappy childhood, Milosevic was abandoned by his father, an orthodox priest, and later survived the suicides of both his father and schoolteacher mother. In high school Milosevic met his future wife Mirjana Markovic, daughter of a leading communist family.

In 1964, following his legal studies at the University of Belgrade, Milosevic embarked on a career as a communist technocrat, serving in a variety of government and industry positions. In 1984 he was appointed to lead the Belgrade Communist Party and two years later became head of the Serbian Communist Party.

Milosevic rose to national prominence in April 1987. A rioting Serb crowd had surrounded the town hall in Kosovo Polje, claiming mistreatment by Kosovo's ethnic Albanian majority. Milosevic quieted the crowd, assuring them, "No one should dare to beat you!" As word of this event spread, Milosevic's popularity grew dramatically throughout Serbia, solidifying his reputation as an ardent Serb nationalist. In 1989 Milosevic became President of Serbia.

Pursuing his dream of an ethnically pure "greater Serbia," Milosevic purged the Yugoslav Army of non-Serbs and fomented unrest in areas outside Serbia with sizable minority Serb populations. The multiethnic Yugoslav state quickly disintegrated. In 1991 Croatia, Slovenia, and Macedonia declared their independence. Milosevic encouraged Serbs in Croatia to take up arms

A defiant Slobodan Milosevic (center) faces trial at the International Criminal Tribunal for the Former Yugoslavia, accused of wreaking "medieval savagery and a calculated cruelty" on the Balkans. [REUTERS/CORBIS]

and, assisted by the Yugoslav Army, seized control of large portions of Croatia.

In 1992 Bosnia and Herzegovina seceded. Bosnian Serbs, supported by Milosevic's military and paramilitary forces, rebelled, beginning a brutal struggle to "purify" Bosnia of its Muslim inhabitants. During the ensuing conflict, hundreds of thousands in Bosnia were killed, raped, and confined in concentration camps. Despite the dispatch of United Nations (UN) peacekeeping troops, the international community was unable to halt the genocide. The war finally ended in 1994 when a North Atlantic Treaty Organization (NATO) ultimatum forced a Serb ceasefire. In December 1995 a permanent peace agreement was signed in Dayton, Ohio, by Milosevic and the presidents of Bosnia and Herzegovina and Croatia.

In July 1997, after serving the maximum two terms as President of Serbia, the Federal Parliament appointed Milosevic as president of the rump Yugoslav state, which consisted only of Serbia (including Kosovo and Vojvodina) and Montenegro.

In 1998, in response to an ethnic Albanian uprising in Kosovo, Milosevic sent in his military. Within weeks hundreds of thousands of ethnic Albanian refugees were forced to flee to neighboring countries. Fearing a repeat of the ethnic cleansing that had occurred in Bosnia, NATO delivered an ultimatum to Milosevic to halt the offensive. When its warnings were ignored, NATO began a bombing campaign against Yugoslavia on March 24, 1999. After over two months of continuous air strikes Milosevic agreed to a plan for Serb withdrawal, the return of refugees, and UN administration of Kosovo.

In May 1999 the UN's International Criminal Tribunal for the Former Yugoslavia (ICTY) indicted Milosevic and four subordinates for crimes against humanity and violations of the laws and customs of war during the Kosovo conflict. Milosevic, however, remained Yugoslav president and beyond the reach of the Court.

On September 24, 2000, Yugoslavs went to the polls for the first-ever direct presidential elections. Although it initially appeared that Milosevic's challenger, Vojislav Kostunica, had won the election, the Milosevic-controlled election commission announced that Kostunica had failed to gain an absolute majority, mandating a runoff. Angry Kostunica supporters took to the streets, prompting strikes and protests that swept the country. On October 5 a massive anti-Milosevic mob rampaged through Belgrade and seized Parliament. Milosevic conceded defeat, and on October 7 Kostunica was sworn in as the new President of Yugoslavia.

On April 1, 2001, Milosevic was arrested at his Belgrade villa. He was handed over to the UN tribunal on June 28 and taken to The Hague to stand trial. In addition to the Kosovo charges, Milosevic was indicted on charges related to the wars in Croatia and Bosnia and Herzegovina, including violations of the laws and customs of war, crimes against humanity, grave breaches of the 1949 Geneva Conventions, complicity in genocide, and genocide.

In his first court appearance on July 3, Milosevic refused to enter a plea, accusing the tribunal of being an "illegal" body established by his enemies in the West. The Court entered a plea of not guilty on his behalf. On February 12, 2002, Milosevic's trial began, with Milosevic acting as his own attorney. In 2003 Milosevic ran for a seat in the Serbian Parliament from his prison cell and won, highlighting the resurgence of Serb nationalism since his departure.

Milosevic's trial has suffered significant delays due to his fragile health and the resignation of the presiding judge. In February 2004 the prosecution rested its case after presenting over 200 witnesses and 29,000 pages of evidence. Milosevic began his defense by submitting a list of 1,631 intended witnesses, including British prime minister Tony Blair and former U.S. president Bill Clinton.

SEE ALSO Bosnia and Herzegovina; International Criminal Tribunal for the Former Yugoslavia; Immunity; Kosovo; Yugoslavia

BIBLIOGRAPHY

Doder, Dusko, and Louise Branson (1999). *Milosevic: Portrait of a Tyrant.* New York: Free Press.

Ramet, Sabrina Petra (1999). *Balkan Babel: The Disintegration of Yugoslavia from the Death of Tito to the War for Kosovo.* Boulder, Colo.: Westview Press.

Scharf, Michael P., and Willam A. Schabas (2002). *Slobodan Milosevic on Trial.* New York: Continuum Books.

Sell, Louis (2002). *Slobodan Milosevic and the Destruction of Yugoslavia.* Durham, N.C.: Duke University Press.

Silber, Laura, and Allan Little (1996). *Yugoslavia: Death of a Nation.* New York: Penguin USA.

Daniel L. Nadel

Minorities

Who can be considered as a person belonging to a minority? Is the definition of minority essential to a regime protecting a minority?

On the one hand, the more precisely the target group is defined, the more effective the international rules on protection and promotion may be. On the other, an overall definition of minority is not only impossible but it would also lead to a deadlock: No precise rules could be internationally developed because of the differences in situations, needs, traditions, economies, and so on.

Several scholars (e.g., Francesco Capotorti, the United Nations [UN] rapporteur on the topic in the 1970s) have attempted to propose a definition for the term *minorities* (at least for the purpose of formulating an international legal instrument). Here is Capotorti's definition:

> A minority is a group numerically inferior to the rest of the population of the State, in a non-dominant position, whose members—being nationals of the State—possess ethnic, religious or linguistic characteristics differing from those of the rest of the population and show, if only implicitly, a sense of solidarity, directed towards preserving their culture, traditions, religion or language (1979, p. 96).

Nonetheless, it seems impossible at a universal or even a regional level to arrive at a definition that is operative for and at the same time acceptable to all member states. As a consequence, the related instruments in this field have been adopted without international organizations advancing any precise definition of minorities.

It is clear, however, that for theoretical and practical reasons it would be useful to make a distinction between linguistic, national, or religious minorities on one side, and sexual, political, and social minorities on the other. Even if the principle of nondiscrimination and tolerance should equally apply to both groups, the concrete needs of each (e.g., in case of the first group, the use of a special language in different private and public settings, and the exercise of belief) are motivated and satisfied in a different manner with different financial consequences for the states involved.

For the same reasons it is easier to formulate separate regulations for "traditional/historical minorities" (who often become minorities because of historical retribution, border changes, etc.) and "immigrant workers, refugees, and other new minorities" (whose status in a given state is a result of their personal choice). The attitude vis-à-vis assimilation or the use of language in public varies between these two groups.

In the same way facilities for the physically challenged are regulated separately according to both national and international laws. Even if nondiscrimination is equally applied, concrete rules and needs are promoted in a manner that is partly similar, partly different.

All this does not suggest that such overlap is unimaginable or erroneous. This can be proved, for example, by the complexity of the Romani problem facing contemporary Europe, in which a real mixture of historically rooted ethnic, linguistic, and especially social handicaps exists.

Historical Birth of Minority Issues: Interdependence with the Nation-State

Even if almost all states are composed of different linguistic communities throughout their history, a minority issue (as a legal and political problem) is closely linked to a definite historical period. In the early twenty-first century the basic problem underlying most minority issues is that for various reasons, partly resulting from intolerance but also from the insensitive policies of governments, persons belonging to a minority (and generally their whole community as such) are linguistically, socially, and politically disadvantaged. This has not always been the case during the history of humankind. One can link modern minority problems to the nation-state concept due to its reductionist tendencies and the temptation it creates to perpetuate linguistic and cultural hegemony. When Central and Eastern Europe embraced the concept and applied it on a broad scale, more tensions than existed in Western Europe soon developed, and border changes and the establishment of new states incited local politicians to take revenge on history by establishing nation-state structures favoring their own linguistic community over others. This particularly occurred following the breakup of empires.

The Lessons of the League of Nations

When U.S. president Woodrow Wilson advanced his ideas about the reconstruction of the world after World War I, he was full of idealism. It was his belief that "open diplomacy" and a golf-club-like international organization could prevent the outbreak of such conflicts that had earlier transformed an act of retaliation against a form of state-sponsored international terrorism (e.g., the murder of Austro-Hungarian archduke and heir Francis Ferdinand in Sarajevo in 1914) into a genuine world war. Wilson also realized that his ideas about the self-determination of peoples were not actually the deeply held beliefs of political interest groups who had spoken a similar message in their attempts to dissolve a particular government structure, for instance, the Austro-Hungarian monarchy and Ottoman Empire. During the final delineation of state boundaries after those events, strategic, economic, and alleged historical factors were taken into account much more seriously

than the given ethnic data of the annexed territories. Wilson's ideas about true international cooperation were maintained, however, in the minority protection system of the League of Nations, the first international organization to claim general (and not only sectorial) competencies in this area.

The League of Nations (the de facto predecessor of the UN) was charged with a supervisory role in implementing international commitments for the protection of minorities in defeated states and territorially enlarged or newly created (recreated) states. The commitments outlined in conventions (or in the case of the Baltic states, Albania, and Iraq in unilateral statements) enjoyed constitutional value in national laws and could not be altered without the approval of the Council of the League of Nations. Violations could be deferred by states to the Council, but individuals were also entitled to directly submit petitions to the League of Nations. If these survived several filters (including the so-called committee of three procedure), they could be placed on the Council's agenda. The Permanent Court of International Justice (the predecessor of the International Court of Justice) also had the right to intervene in any such matters, providing advisory opinions at the request of bodies such as the League of Nations (in fact the Council) or judgments in interstate disputes when both states previously fell under the jurisdiction of the Hague World Court—this occurred quite often, contrary to twenty-first-century tendencies. The complex of rules and international proceedings was referred to as procedural or formal minority law.

Material law was embodied in the abovementioned conventions or unilateral declarations. Most of the rules were virtually identical (prohibition of discrimination, free use of language in private intercourse, adequate facilities for the use of minority languages before tribunals or other authorities, and some guarantees for teaching the minority language, mainly in private schools). Despite such unified rules, it is interesting to note that some regions were put under international control, for instance, in the case of the territorial autonomy of the Swedish-speaking Aaland Islands (belonging to Finland) and Ruthenia (belonging to Czechoslovakia at that time), or the personal autonomy of certain subgroups of the Hungarian- or German-speaking minorities of Romania.

In the end no one was satisfied with the League of Nations' mechanisms. Minorities complained about the lengthy nature of the uncertain, endless process, whereby in contrast to governments party to a complaint, their claims were not made in person but only through submitted documents. Respondent governments decried the assymmetry of minority protection:

The League of Nations' commitment mostly applied to Central and Eastern European states but not Western European nations. Modern scholars laud some landmark statements of the Permanent Court of International Justice (e.g., those pertaining to the merits of so-called positive discrimination, or *affirmative action* to use the American term) and some technical details of rulings and procedures that can be construed as precursors of modern international human rights systems (the admissibility criteria of petitions and, in particular, the exhaustion of local remedies, polite and deferential language, etc.). Nevertheless, the system became paralyzed in the mid-1930s when more and more states failed to reply to petitions after Germany's withdrawal from the League. Even though Germany officially departed from the League after Adolf Hitler's rise to power, the collective memory of several states (unjust it may be countered) is that the League of Nations' system was more or less supportive of Nazi subversive or revisionist policy. Despite its merits, the minority protection system of the League of Nations disappeared along with the organization itself, and after World War II the UN chose not to continue on the same path.

The UN and the Protection of Minorities

The UN has presented decidedly different attitudes vis-à-vis the protection of minorities. The first period of activity may be associated with Eleanor Roosevelt, the widow of president Franklin D. Roosevelt and the first U.S. ambassador to the UN. She played a very active role in the negotiations on the text of the Universal Declaration of Human Rights in the UN General Assembly, and an important part in formulating the UN's human rights concept as such. It stated that the promotion of traditional civil and political rights, with the prohibition of genocide and a strict nondiscrimination policy, is in itself sufficient and neither special social or cultural rights or a group-oriented approach is required, the latter being either useless or even dangerous.

This reductionist approach, combining the American melting-pot concept with the lessons learned from the crimes committed by Nazis and their collaborators, was not adequate for genuinely multicultural countries in which the presence of different ethnicities could be traced not to voluntary immigration but historical phenomena, namely changes in borders. The harrassment of certain ethnic groups because of their difference, the residual role of their language in public life and schooling, not to mention political and legal condemnation on the basis of collective culpability for alleged collaboration with the Nazis, all contributed to the recreation of well-known tensions. Often, legislative acts directed against some minorities may be regarded as being based

on purely racial considerations (see, e.g., the Benes' decrees adopted in Czechoslovakia against Germans and Hungarians or the deportation of the Volga German, Chechen, Ingush, and Crimean Tatar population in the Soviet Union by Joseph Stalin).

During its first decade of existence the UN did not insist on the inclusion of clauses protecting minorities in the peace treaties of former Axis powers. Moreover, the UN Secretary-General, when pressed about the legal validity of the League of Nations' rules protecting minorities, concluded that they should be extinct for several legal reasons, most linked to the principle of *rebus sic stantibus* (i.e., a fundamental change in circumstances). (See the UN's 1950 *Study on the Legal Validity of Undertakings Concerning Minorities.*)

It is true, nonetheless, that the most evident assault on minorities was codified as a crime against humanity when the 1948 UN Convention on the Prevention and Punishment of the Crime of Genocide was adopted. The Convention is based on the five main categories of indictment, as outlined by the Nuremberg International Tribunal in its well-known statute, the 1945 London Agreement:

> [K]illing members of the group; causing serious bodily or mental harm to members of the group; deliberately inflicting on the group conditions of life calculated to bring about its physical destruction in whole or in part; imposing measures intended to prevent births within the group; forcibly transferring children of the group to another group (Article 2).

The General Assembly rejected proposals (submitted by Denmark) that attempted to add to the Universal Declaration a minority clause, or to the Genocide Convention the category of so-called cultural genocide. The former Soviet Union backed the proposals as they perfectly complemented its ideological campaign during the cold war. In 1948 politicians apparently considered the clauses of the Genocide Convention as being qualitatively different from "minor" violations of minorities' interests. The end of the 1990s, however, saw the tragedy of the Balkans and that of Rwanda, and examples of ethnic cleansing as a method of warfare surfaced, the cruelty of which its perpetrators tried to justify in terms of their own harassment and humiliation as a former minority. The international community then witnessed the proper codification and punishment of these horrifying acts by different international tribunals, such as the International Criminal Tribunal for the Former Yugoslavia, the International Criminal Tribunal for Rwanda, the International Criminal Court, and so on.

In the 1950s, nevertheless, the UN took steps toward the adoption of some specific rules to protect minorities. Beside the nondiscrimination conventions in general, and its efforts in the area of global education, the UN adopted a special clause for minorities in the 1966 International Covenant on Civil and Political Rights (CCPR). Its Article 27 stipulates: "In those States in which ethnic, religious or linguistic minorities exist, persons belonging to such minorities shall not be denied the right, in community with the other members of their group, to enjoy their own culture, to profess and practise their own religion or to use their own language."

Moreover, since the 1970s (and on a Yugoslav initiative, however strange that may seem after the southeast European tragedy of the 1990s), efforts have been made within the UN General Assembly to pass a comprehensive resolution on the inherent rights of minorities. These efforts have generally met with hostility, not only on the part of some influential European states but also many newly independent countries, former colonies. The number of member nations opposing an international measure of protection for minorities has only increased. Because the boundaries of these countries as inherited from the colonial period did not take ethnic configuration into consideration and as the divide-and-conquer policy of the former administrative power often favored the minority population in terms of the makeup of the local administration, police, and army, the new tribal majority frequently harassed, punished, and intimidated this minority, and only because of the past, national pride, and shortsightedness. Africa's modern history, for the most part, may be tragically linked to ethnically colored pogroms and bloody civil wars. The governments of these countries emphasized economic and social rights and the so-called right to development over civil and political rights. If they were not in favor of comprehensive control, they were even less supportive of adopting new rights. Within the context of American-Soviet rivalry characterizing the world before the 1990s, nepotism and tribal corruption were also forgiven by these close allies.

The collapse of the Soviet empire, the recognition of the United States' unquestionable military omnipotence, and the ethnic tensions and bloody civil wars of the 1990s in the former Soviet territories and Yugoslavia all contributed to the UN General Assembly's adoption of the Declaration on the Rights of Persons Belonging to National or Ethnic, Religious and Linguistic Minorities (Resolution GA 47/135).

This document, conceived by several high-ranking politicians as an example of the *prevention vs. cure* policy, unfortunately could not prevent the tragedy of the Balkans, although it is a worthwhile reflection of the collective opinion of early-twenty-first-century's inter-

national community about the importance of a legally guaranteed place for minorities and their languages. It is the greatest achievement of the otherwise not too successful Sub-Commission on Prevention of Discrimination and Protection of Minorities that formulated it.

Even if the General Assembly's declaration focuses mostly on classic political and civil rights tailored slightly to serve the needs of minorities, it is worth emphasizing the political and pedagogical importance of the multiple refererences to the use of minority language in worship and administration, as well as the effective participation of minorities in public and economic life. The UN also took a historic step when referring to affirmative actions in its Article 8: "Measures taken by States to ensure the effective enjoyment of the rights set forth in the present Declaration shall not prima facie be considered contrary to the principle of equality contained in the Universal Declaration of Human Rights." This reference is slightly more generous than that of the UN Convention on the Elimination of All Forms of Racial Discrimination.

The real merit of the Declaration on the Rights of Persons Belonging to National or Ethnic, Religious and Linguistic Minorities may be observed in the impact it has had on otherwise inactive UN organizations, inspiring them to play a more assertive role. The Human Rights Committee on Civil and Political Rights (the monitoring organ of the 1966 Covenant) suddenly realized in 1994 that the previously cited Article 27 of the Covenant stipulates not only passive but also active obligations. In addition, it emphasized at the time that the article's scope of application concerns persons belonging to a minority irrespective of their citizenship and does not depend on an earlier recognition of minorities by the state. (See CCPR General Comment No. 23.) The Human Rights Committee has also contributed to the evolution of the concept of minority protection in its examination of some individual applications. Most of them have concerned, however, indigenous problems, for example, the claims of Native Americans (see the *Lovelace*, *Ominayak*, and *Connors* cases), Samis (see the *Kitok*, *Sara*, and *Länsman* cases), and Maoris (see the *Mahuika* case).

The applications made to the Human Rights Committee have generally dealt with the alleged negative impact of some major industrial or agricultural interventions on the fishing and hunting rights of indigenous peoples. The complaints have been rejected if the governments in question could offer a sufficient amount of water, land, or forest to the aggrieved parties. The *Lovelace* v. *Canada* case was particularly interesting in the sense that the state was condemned because it had failed to grant adequate protection to a

Native-American woman against the actions of her own tribe. (The case was linked to the fact that marriage outside one's tribe could deprive a woman of her tribal membership, and that a return to tribal territory after the end of such a marriage did not automatically confer on that woman the right to renewal of tribal membership.)

The Committee on the Elimination of Racial Discrimination (CERD), the UN organization monitoring the 1965 Convention on the Elimination of All Forms of Racial Discrimination, also wrote several comprehensive reports, including one on some aspects of reporting minorities and another on the right of self-determination. (See CERD's General Recommendations No. 8 and 21.)

In addition, the specialized institutions of the UN formulated some related instruments of treaty law. The United Nations Educational, Scientific, and Cultural Organization (UNESCO) adopted the 1960 Convention on Discrimination in Education, applied in the area of education, and the International Labor Organization (ILO) elaborated Conventions 107 (1957) and 169 (1989), both addressing the rights of indigenous laborers and obligations of governments and employers. Article 30 of the 1989 Convention on the Rights of the Child is in its language almost identical to the already cited Article 27 of the 1966 Covenant, and it also promotes the use of minority language in the media and education.

It is a well known that making international law is hostage to the smallest common denominator principle. In the case of the nearly two hundred member states of the UN, reaching an acceptable but at the same time serious and truly comprehensive treaty law is manifestly impossible. Is the situation any better in regional terms?

International Minority Protection: European Results

The nondiscrimination principle is embodied in the three main regional conventions, namely the European Convention on Human Rights, the Inter-American Convention on Human Rights, and the African Charter on Human and Peoples' Rights.

The basic international treaty of the Council of Europe, an organization established on the initiative of Great Britain's Prime Minister Winston Churchill to promote international cooperation based on the rule of law, the European Convention of Human Rights is considered to be the most widely used and effective mechanism for protecting human rights. As of 2003 the European Court of Human Rights had reviewed and pronounced judgment on approximately 3,800 cases.

Few of them were related to classic national or linguistic minority issues. Scholars mainly attribute this fact to the formulation of Article 14 that—contrary to the UN approach (manifested in Article 26 of the International Covenant on Civil and Political Rights)—may not be applied by itself but only in conjuction with another article of the Convention. (The same can be said about the nature of nondiscrimination clauses in the Inter-American Convention and the African Charter.)

Because the other articles of the European Convention of Human Rights do not in fact address the traditional needs of minorities (e.g., the use of languages in schooling or before an administration), minorities have had practically no chance of submitting a succesful claim on the basis of a current or future discrimination.

Political efforts and endeavors to supplement the European Convention with an additional protocol covering minority rights were consequently rejected in the 1960s and 1970s. Only in 1999 did the Council of Europe adopt a twelfth additional protocol putting nondiscrimination in a larger perspective, prohibiting discrimination as a right secured by "law."

The same development may be observed in the jurisprudence of the European Court of Human Rights, whereby the Court's hesitation to tackle minority problems during the second half of the twentieth century (see the judgment in the Belgian linguistic case in which the Court recognized the admissibility of affirmative action; see also *Mathieu-Mohin & Clerfayt v. Belgium, Tyrer v. United Kingdom*, and *Gillow v. United Kingdom* concerning legislation and the practice of some special territorial autonomies) was followed by a deeper desire to address these issues at the start of the twenty-first century.

Still in this new phase, the European Court of Human Rights seems poised to examine the problems of minorities within the interrelated context of religious freedom or the right to the integrity of family life. When the freedom of religion of ethnic or linguistic minorities was involved in recent cases (see *Serif v. Greece, Hassan & Chaush v. Bulgaria*, and *Orthodox Metropolitan Church of Bessarabia v. Moldova*), the Court decided in favor of the applicants. In 2001 a minority organization won a case linked to freedom of association (see *Stankov and Ilinden United Macedonian Organization v. Bulgaria*).

On the other hand, the applications submitted by Romani were unsuccesful either because of lack of evidence (*Assenov v. Bulgaria*) or because of the Court's limited authority over governments in regulating a nomadic way of life and squatting (unlawful settlement) (*Buckley v. United Kingdom, Chapman v. United Kingdom*).

The most important theoretical breakthrough occurred, however, in a legal dictum delievered by an ad hoc tribunal, the Arbitration Commission of the International Conference on ex-Yugoslavia. This organ, also known as the Badinter Arbitration Commission (named after its chairman, Robert Badinter, the president of the French Constitutional Court), pronounced several advisory opinions in 1992 emphasizing that the protection of minorities falls within the peremptory norms of international law (*jus cogens*).

The decision on whether or not to supplement the European Convention on Human Rights was not only a political issue but also a legal one. Opponents of an additional protocol generally based their arguments on solid legal grounds, namely the fact that the Convention's control mechanism is based on the existence of an individual victim whose precise right has been violated. Such a philosophy works well when contemplating classic civil and political rights, that is, individual rights. However, mostly everything that is important for minorities is of a collective nature (or at least requires a collective approach), and in these cases, some states are apparently not ready to accept precise norms. As these obligations cannot be deferred to a court, there is no need to envisage such a procedure of complaint.

Within the Council of Europe, the repeated rejection of proposals aiming to complement the European Convention on Human Rights with an additional protocol resulted in a change of attitude among those who were open to a minority breakthrough. Their view was that if the adequate protection of minorities was not possible through traditional human rights safeguards, a fresh approach must be chosen. Defining the obligations of states instead of the rights of minorities became the new watchword.

The Council of Europe benefited from this new approach when drawing up two international treaties, namely the European Charter for Regional or Minority Languages and the Framework Convention for the Protection of National Minorities. The aim was to prepare an adequate and effective, but—and this is always the big challenge for those codifying international law—widely acceptable instrument of treaty law.

In the 1992 case of European Charter for Regional or Minority Languages, the novelty consisted of an optional (à la carte) system of commitments operating in harmony with the real needs of minority languages. The assumption was that by allowing sovereign states to choose from different commitments according to the real situation surrounding minority or regional languages spoken in their territory, and according to the specific uses of those languages (in schooling, administration, the judiciary, economic and social life, the media, culture, and transboundary cooperation), they would demonstrate more willingness to accept them. These options vary from the lowest to the highest level (e.g., teaching all subjects in a minority language, teaching a substantial part of the curriculum in a minority language, or teaching the minority language as such). States, the contracting parties to the Charter, are not obliged to apply these options to all the languages spoken in their territory, only those that are chosen explicitly in the instrument of ratification. For the other languages, general principles enumerated in the Charter are to be applied. Even if the title of the Charter itself seems slightly redundant, according to the original drafters, the wording allows states that do not recognize "minorities" as a distinct category of public law in their constitution to accept it. The Charter was drafted before the admission of Central and Eastern European "new democracies"—but it was approved in their presence and with the active participation of Hungary and Poland.

The 1995 Framework Convention for the Protection of National Minorities is the fruit of the second wave of minority codification in the 1990s. This convention addresses not only language issues, but also other aspects of day-to-day minority life. The hot button of minority codification, that is, how the convention or statute might reflect collective interests when several states who must be party to it oppose the recognition of collective rights for minorities, was mollified in three ways: (1) Some classic individual rights were formulated in a minority-friendly style (as also occurred in the UN Declaration on the Rights of Persons Belonging to National or Ethnic, Religious and Linguistic Minorities). (2) Instead of the rights of persons or groups, the Convention refers to obligations of states. (3) General legal premises and programmatic norms were formulated.

In this complicated and sometimes very obscure way, the Framework Convention contains rules concerning the use of a minority language in education, the judiciary, and administration; the prohibition of gerrymandering; the protection of minority identity; the promotion of minority culture; and the effective participation of minorities in the decision making of public authorities. It is worth noting that affirmative action is proclaimed here, too, moreover not only as an eventual possibility but as a rule whose application may even be mandatory in certain cases.

The control mechanism of both the European Charter and the Framework Convention is based on periodic reports submitted by states. Even if no possibility of submitting individual or collective applications exists, the independent experts' committees can organize hearings where not only governments but also minority representatives may have their say. In addition, experts can visit the countries concerned: Apparently, governments invite such individuals quite often, on their own initiative. The reports prepared by these expert committees are used to formulate recommendations and resolutions by the Committee of Ministers, composed of ministers of foreign affairs for the member states of the Council of Europe. Despite the genuinely intergovernmental character of this organ, its resolutions closely follow the criticisms developed by the expert committee. Even if such a process concludes without any binding decision, these soft-law-type resolutions enjoy considerable moral and political authority.

It is worthwhile to note the identity and number of contracting parties in an international treaty. More than half the member states of the Council of Europe are contracting parties to the Framework Convention for the Protection of National Minorities and a good dozen are bound by the European Charter for Regional or Minority Languages.

The Organization for Security and Co-operation in Europe (OSCE) was created within the context of the so-called Helsinki process, the series of follow-up conferences since the 1975 summit meeting in Helsinki on security and cooperation in Europe. A landmark of 1970s détente policy, the ad hoc 1975 summit conference of East and West became progressively institutionalized, and the end of bipolar rivalry resulted in a new impetus for this process, composed of followup conferences. From the so-called three baskets (with the first basket signifying disarmament and confidence-building measures; the second basket a reduction in the number of obstacles to commerce between capitalist and Marxist economies; and the third basket an emphasis on "human dimensions," a euphemism for human rights), the third was used to establish a code of conduct for the trans-Atlantic protection of minorities. The 1990 Charter of Paris for a New Europe and especially the Final Act of the 1990 Copenhagen Conference are considered basic documents. Even if the documents do not enjoy a legal value, they repeat legal norms already stipulated elsewhere or proclaim political commitments. This is especially true of the Copenhagen Document, which contains a long list of principles supporting the rights minorities.

The Office of the OSCE High Commissioner on National Minorities was established after the 1992 OSCE Conference in Stockholm. Its original mandate concerns fact-finding and early warnings vis-à-vis minority-related tensions (with the exception of international terrorism). In reality the High Commissioner

generally mediated between states or states and minorities. With a very small staff but backed by the international scientific community, the Office of the High Commissioner launched an interesting standard-setting activity: Instead of creating new rules, it attempted to compile existing international documents (on both treaty law and soft law). The documents issued are mostly recommendations of a commendable nature, but to a certain extent they also merely reflect the existing customs in the areas of education, use of language, and effective participation (see the Hague, Lund, and Oslo Recommendations).

In the 1990s the OSCE adopted important instruments such as the 1992 Stockholm Convention on Conciliation and Arbitration and the 1995 Pact on Stability in Europe, whose aim was to settle interstate disputes related among other issues to minority protection.

Bilateralism and Unilateralism in Minority Protection

Multilateral instruments on minority protection may be complemented by bilateral agreements. These are generally more comprehensive than multilateral treaties, which nonetheless often encourage states to enter into complementary bilateral treaties.

When regulating minority issues, national law may simply be implementing an already contracted commitment, but it need not be based exclusively on international law. It can be generous beyond that obligation, even also within itself, without any interstate commitment. Besides a nondiscrimination clause and some requirements concerning language, which are specified in the constitution of most European states, certain countries have gone as far as regionalization (Spain) or the recognition of the autonomy of local authorities, as happened recently within the context of devolution in the United Kingdom.

In Central and Eastern Europe, one may observe how the links between kin-state and kin-minority have greatly multiplied. States are offering educational or social opportunities to persons belonging to a minority living in another state but speaking their language. As the European Commission for Democracy through Law (the Venice Commission's *Report on the Preferential Treatment of National Minorities by Their Kin-States*) put it, these legally institutionalized contacts may be matched by current international law when they are restricted to items closely linked to national and cultural identity. The observance of the nondiscrimination rule, reciprocity, and cooperation with one's state of citizenship are, however, important in avoiding interstate conflicts (see the European Commission's *Report on the*

Preferential Treatment of National Minorities by Their Kin-States).

Conclusion

The basic principles of minority protection in the modern world may be summarized as follows: Respect for and the protection of the identity of persons belonging to a minority presuppose the free choice of identity, that is, despite any alleged outside characteristics, one cannot be considered as legally belonging to a group against one's will. International law (in its universal, regional, and bilateral forms) and national law are getting closer to not only sanctioning diversity but also promoting the concrete expression of the most important aspects of minority life, often by affirmative actions necessary for genuine equality. Minority participation in decision making is emphasized in a wide range of legal documents, especially within national legal systems where one can find different forms of self-government or a home rule system, based on territorial or personal approaches. The legal systems of states vary greatly, and the adaptability and tangible expression of the aforementioned legal principles are very different as a result.

It is thus evident that with tolerance of and respect for another's identity, language, religion, and culture and by providing the opportunity for all individuals to have a good life in the contemporary world, countries draw closer to eliminating the animosity, suspicion, and national arrogance that characterized a certain period of history.

SEE ALSO Disabilities, People with; Economic Groups; Ethnic Groups; Political Theory; Racial Groups; Religious Groups

BIBLIOGRAPHY

MINORITY ISSUES AS DELIBERATED WITHIN THE UNITED NATIONS

Capotorti, Francesco (1979). *Study on the Rights of Persons Belonging to National, Ethnic, Religious and Linguistic Minorities*. New York: United Nations. Document E/CN/4/Sub.2/384/Rev.1.

Committee on the Elimination of Racial Discrimination (March 15, 1996). *Right to Self-Determination*. General Recommendation no. 21. New York: United Nations.

Committee on the Elimination of Racial Discrimination (August 24, 1999). *Reporting of Persons Belonging to Different Races, National, Ethnic Groups or Indigenous Peoples*. General Recommendation no. 8. New York: United Nations.

European Commission for Democracy through Law (2001). "Report on the Preferential Treatment of National Minorities by Their Kin-States." Document CDL-INF(2001)19. Available from http://www.venice.coe.int/docs.

Human Rights Committee on Civil and Political Rights (April 8, 1994). *The Rights of Minorities*. Comment no. 23. New York: United Nations.

Trygve Lie (1950). *Study on the Legal Validity of Undertakings Concerning Minorities*. New York: United Nations. Document E/CN/4/367.

MINORITY ISSUES AS ADJUDICATED BY THE HUMAN RIGHTS COMMITTEE ON CIVIL AND POLITICAL RIGHTS

Apirana Mahuika v. New Zealand. Application 547/1993 (November 16, 2000). Available from http://www.unchr.ch.

Ilmari Länsman v. Finland. Application 511/1992 (October 26, 1994). Available from http://www.unchr.ch.

Ivan Kitok v. Sweden. Application 197/1985 (March 24, 1994). Available from http://www.unchr.ch.

Jouni E. Länsman & cons. v. Finland. Application 671/1995 (November 22, 1996). Available from http://www.unchr.ch.

Lovelace v. Canada. Application 27/1977 (July 30, 1982). Available from http://www.unchr.ch.

Ominayak and Lubicon Lake Tribe v. Canada. Application 167/1984 (March 26, 1990). Available from http://www.unchr.ch.

O. Sara v. Finland. Application 431/1990 (October 26, 1994). Available from http://www.unchr.ch.

RL & Connors v. Canada. Application 358/1989 (November 5, 1991). Available from http://www.unchr.ch.

MINORITY ISSUES AS ADJUDICATED WITHIN THE COUNCIL OF EUROPE

Assenov v. Bulgaria. Application 24760/94 European Court on Human Rights (October 28, 1998). Available from http://www.echr.coe.int/Eng/Judgments.htm.

Beard v. United Kingdom. Application 24882/94 European Court on Human Rights (January 18, 2001). Available from http://www.echr.coe.int/Eng/Judgments.htm.

Buckley v. United Kingdom. Application 20348/92 European Court on Human Rights (September 25, 1996). Available from http://www.echr.coe.int/Eng/Judgments.htm.

Chapman v. United Kingdom. Application 27238/95 European Court on Human Rights (January 18, 2001). Available from http://www.echr.coe.int/Eng/Judgments.htm.

Gillow v. United Kingdom. Application 9063/80 European Court on Human Rights (November 24, 1986). Available from http://www.echr.coe.int/Eng/Judgments.htm.

Hassan & Chaush v. Bulgaria. Application 30985/96 European Court on Human Rights (October 26, 2000). Available from http://www.echr.coe.int/Eng/Judgments.htm.

Lee v. United Kingdom. Application 25289/94 European Court on Human Rights (January 18, 2001). Available from http://www.echr.coe.int/Eng/Judgments.htm.

Mathieu-Mohin & Clerfayt v. Belgium. Application 9267/81 European Court on Human Rights (March 2, 1987).

Available from http://www.echr.coe.int/Eng/Judgments.htm.

Orthodox Metropolitan Church of Bessarabia v. Moldova. Application 45701/99 European Court on Human Rights (December 13, 2001). Available from http://www.echr.coe.int/Eng/Judgments.htm.

Serif v. Greece. Application 38178/97 European Court on Human Rights (December 14, 1999). Available from http://www.echr.coe.int/Eng/Judgments.htm.

Stankov and Ilinden United Macedonian Organization v. Bulgaria. Applications 29221/95 and 29225/95 European Court on Human Rights (October 2, 2001). Available from http://www.echr.coe.int/Eng/Judgments.htm.

Tyrer v. United Kingdom. Application 5856/72 European Court on Human Rights (April 25, 1978). Available from http://www.echr.coe.int/Eng/Judgments.htm.

MINORITY ISSUES AS DELIBERATED WITHIN THE ORGANIZATION FOR SECURITY AND CO-OPERATION IN EUROPE

Hague Recommendations Regarding the Education Rights of National Minorities & Explanatory Note (October 1996). The Hague: Foundation on Inter-Ethnic Relations.

Lund Recommendations on the Effective Participation of National Minorities in Public Life & Explanatory Note (June 1999). The Hague: Foundation on Inter-Ethnic Relations.

Oslo Recommendations Regarding the Linguistic Rights of National Minorities & Explanatory Note (October 1998). The Hague: Foundation on Inter-Ethnic Relations.

MINORITY ISSUES AS DISCUSSED WITHIN OTHER EUROPEAN ORGANIZATIONS

Arbitration Commission of the International Conference on ex-Yugoslavia (1992). *Opinions on Questions Arising from the Dissolution of Yugoslavia, 31 International Legal Materials* 111448, 1500 (1992).

Péter Kovács

Mladic, Ratko

[MARCH 12, 1942–]
Commander of the Bosnian Serb Army

Fueled by a deep-seated animosity hearkening from the days of the Ottoman Empire's control of Bosnia and Herzegovina (BiH) and the Croatian alliance with Nazi Germany, General Ratko Mladic rose through the ranks of the Bosnian Serb Army by appealing to Serbian nationalism. As Commander, Mladic left in his wake at least ten thousand dead and several hundred thousand forcibly transferred or internally displaced.

Born in Kalinovik, a small town in southern Bosnia, Mladic spent his early years training at the military academy in Belgrade for the Yugoslav People's Army (JNA), in which he later served as an officer. Between the summers of 1991 and 1992 Mladic's military au-

thority and popularity increased exponentially. In June 1991 he was appointed Commander of the 9th Corps of the JNA, and within a year he was promoted to General Lieutenant and Chief of Staff of the Second Military District Headquarters of the JNA in Sarajevo. When the Bosnian Serb Assembly voted to create the army of the Serbian Republic of the BiH (VRS) in May 1992, Mladic was also appointed Commander of the Main Staff of the VRS, where he remained until December 1996. As commander of the military, he exclusively followed the directives of political leaders Radovan Karadzic and Slobodan Milosevic.

Some of the most egregious charges leveled against Mladic by the International Criminal Tribunal for the former Yugoslavia (ICTY) stem from his campaign, as VRS Commander, to "ethnically cleanse" BiH of Bosnian Muslims and other non-Serbs. The fifteen-count indictment includes charges of genocide or the complicity to commit genocide against Bosnian Muslims; various crimes against humanity—such as persecution, extermination, murder, deportation, and inhumane acts—against Bosnian Muslims, Bosnian Croats, and other non-Serbs; and the taking of United Nations (UN) hostages.

Although Mladic may not have physically committed the crimes with which he was charged, he remains responsible as commander of the army under the 1949 Geneva Conventions on the laws of war and the statute of the ICTY. Moreover, UN Security Council resolutions repeatedly warned that those who perpetrated or ordered the commission of war crimes would be held accountable. While Mladic denies the allegations, several of his subordinates have insisted that they were following Mladic's orders—most notably his most immediate subordinate, Radislav Krstic.

From 1992 to 1996 Mladic and Karadzic unleashed a brutal campaign of ethnic cleansing to eradicate all non-Serbs from BiH. During this period continuous reports detailed the killings, rapes, forcible expulsion, imprisonment, cruel and inhumane treatment, and forced labor of non-Serbs. Numerous concentration camps were discovered along the Croatian border, reminiscent of camps the Nazis had established during the Holocaust. Private property and places of religious worship were common targets for misappropriation and destruction throughout BiH. The exactitude and similarity of the crimes repeated in both northwestern and eastern Bosnia strongly suggest that they were part and parcel of a widespread, systemic operation.

In July 1995 Mladic ignored Security Council Resolution 819 declaring Srebrenica and surrounding regions "safe areas." He not only commanded his troops to capture Srebrenica, but also enlisted the assistance

Genocide under General Mladic in Bosnia and Herzegovina. [MAP BY XNR PRODUCTIONS/THE GALE GROUP]

of several Serbian paramilitary groups, ostensibly to distance himself from any wrongdoing. Thousands of Muslim men were rounded up and executed in the ten-day fall of Srebrenica, under the pretext of capturing Muslim soldiers and "suspects of war crimes." More than twenty thousand Muslim women, children, and the elderly were forcibly expelled. The mass graves later exhumed in the farms and rural villages surrounding Srebrenica indicate that the killings were part of a well-rehearsed and organized plan. Individual acts of revenge could not have resulted in thousands of deaths, nor would the manner of death have been so eerily similar—a single gunshot wound to the head.

Despite the UN's warnings, the ICTY's indictment, and his alleged complicity in the atrocities Krstic com-

mitted from 1992 to 1996, Mladic has never seen the inside of a courtroom. Initially he lived openly in BiH—an affront to the tribunal's authority—but after the arrest of Milosevic in 2001 Mladic fled into hiding. Without increased international political pressure mounted against his staunch allies, Mladic is unlikely to face prosecution either at home or through extradition to the ICTY, and will live with impunity.

SEE ALSO Bosnia and Herzegovina; Ethnic Cleansing; Humanitarian Intervention; Incitement; Karadzic, Radovan; Massacres; Mass Graves; Nationalism; Peacekeeping; Safe Zones; Superior (or Command) Responsibility; Yugoslavia

BIBLIOGRAPHY

Ball, Howard (1999). *Prosecuting War Crimes and Genocide.* Lawrence: University Press of Kansas.

BBC News (August 2, 2001). "General Guilty of Bosnia Genocide." Available from http://news.bbc.co.uk/1/hi/world/europe/1469896.stm.

Honig, Jan Willemand, Norbert Both (1996). *Srebrenica, Record of a War Crime.* New York: Penguin Books.

The International Criminal Tribunal for the Former Yugoslavia (2002). "Amended Indictment of Ratko Mladic." Available from http://www.un.org/icty/indictment/english/mla-ai021010e.htm.

Statute of the International Criminal Tribunal for the Former Yugoslavia (2003). Available from http://www.un.org/icty/legaldoc/index.htm.

Stover, Eric, and Gilles Peress (1998). *The Graves.* New York: Scalo.

United Nations (1992). Security Council Resolution 771. Available from http://ods-dds-ny.un.org.

United Nations (1993). Security Council Resolution 819. Available from http://ods-dds-ny.un.org.

Jaspreet K. Saini

Mongol Conquests

In many parts of the world, in particular, the Arab Middle East, Europe, and the Americas, the Mongols have become synonymous with murder, massacre, and marauding mayhem. Their advent is portrayed as a bloody "bolt from the blue" that left little but destruction, death, and horrified grief in its wake. A medieval Russian chronicle from Novgorod vividly describes their impact on the region:

> No one exactly knows who they are, nor whence they came out, nor what their language is, nor of what race they are, nor what their faith is . . . God alone knows (Mitchell and Forbes, p. 64).

A thirteenth-century Persian eyewitness succinctly summarized their initial impact in Iran: "They came, they sapped, they burnt, they slew, they plundered and they departed" (Juwayni, 1916/1997, p. 107). The Arab chronicler ibn al-Athir, although not an eyewitness, described his emotions on hearing of the Mongols' rise in words that have echoed down through history and colored half the world's perception of the Eurasian hordes:

> O would that my mother had never borne me, that I had died before and that I were forgotten [so] tremendous disaster such as had never happened before, and which struck all the world, though the Muslims above all . . . *Dadjdjal* [Muslim Anti-Christ] will at least spare those who adhere to him, and will only destroy his adversaries. These [Mongols], however, spared none. They killed women, men, children, ripped open the bodies of the pregnant and slaughtered the unborn (Spuler, 1972, pp. 29–30).

The reasons for such negative impressions are not hard to discern. Genghis Khan (1167–1227) even described himself as "the punishment of God" and was pleased that others perceived him to play this role. The Mongol period is not only noted for its supposed barbarity, but also for the plethora of historians and chronicles it produced. These many scribes, both within the Mongol camp and without, were happy to pander to the Mongols' desire for notoriety and a reputation for barbarism and cruelty. Primary sources in a wealth of languages have survived the so-called Mongol mayhem. Critical analysis and comparison of these various sources yield a more balanced and less sensationalist picture of what actually occurred during the thirteenth and fourteenth centuries than the lurid portrait that myths and legends have conjured up. Since Bernard Lewis questioned the basis of the Mongols' tainted reputation in 1995, scholarly opinion has grown more sympathetic toward the legacy of Genghis Khan.

Turco-Mongol Unity

By 1206 the Turco-Mongol clans of the steppe were united under the charismatic rule of Genghis Khan. It was the size and unity of this force and its endurance that distinguished it from previous steppe armies. Prior to Genghis the tribes had often been manipulated by the Chinese and other settled peoples, and often the nomads' predatory raids had occurred at the behest of a hidden hand. Genghis raided for the prestige he accrued on which to build his power, and for the booty with which to placate his rivals, satisfy his followers, and outwit any reckless challenger to his rule. The initial raids into northern China during the early decades of the thirteenth century were characterized by the barbarity for which the name of Genghis Khan and the Mongols have become inextricably identified. However, Mongol rule subsequent to this, during the reigns of Genghis Khan's grandsons, Hülegü in Iran (ruled 1256–1265) and Qubilai Qa'an in China (ruled 1260–1294), stands in sharp contrast to this earlier violent eruption. The "storm from the East" arose from anger, a spirit of vengeance, and the need to assert power.

Genghis Khan, the leader of the "people of the felt-walled tents" and the "the peoples of the Nine Tongues" (Onon, 1993, p. 102), was born Temüjin and had endured a brutal and merciless childhood. His father was murdered when he was still young, and his mother and her offspring were abandoned by their clan to survive in a very harsh and unforgiving environment. Compassion was not a virtue valued on the steppe. This was a society of submit or be challenged, fight or be beaten, and often kill or be killed.

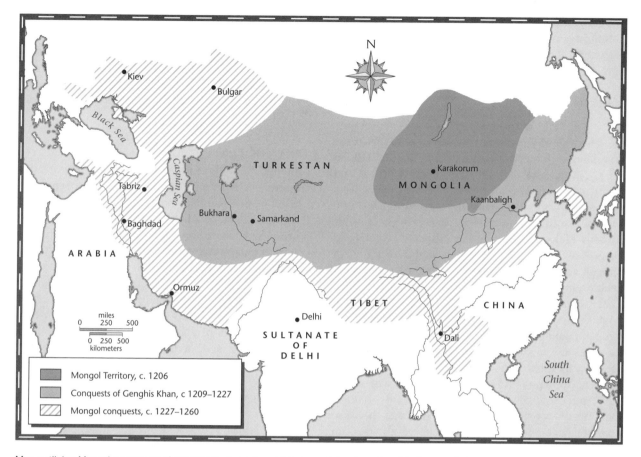

Map outlining Mongol conquests of the thirteenth century. Historians of the time chronicled many of these campaigns as barbarous massacres. [MAP BY XNR PRODUCTIONS. THE GALE GROUP.]

Force of personality, military and physical might, and tribal alliances were the means through which tribal leaders of the steppe clans rose to power. They maintained power only by delivering on promises of wealth and plenty. If the promise did not materialize, the leader fell, or was forced to join an alliance with another leader who could meet the aspirations of the tribe. Steppe life was brutal, and knowing nothing else, the steppe tribes initially exported this ethos.

The Mongols themselves were few in number, but from the outset Genghis absorbed other Turkish tribes and later any conquered troops into his armies. He used traditional steppe military tactics, with light cavalry, feigned retreats, and skillful archery to conduct what were initially raids of pillage and plunder from bases in the steppe into the agriculturally developed and settled lands as opposed to the steppe grasslands, home to the nomads. Terror, real and imagined, was an important element in the success of these raids. In 1211 the Mongols invaded the independent Chin of northern China, helped by renegade seminomadic Khitans, in a struggle that continued, after Genghis's death, until 1234. It was the defeat of the Chin capital, Zhangdu (the site of

modern Beijing), that gave rise to one of the most notorious stories of Mongol atrocities:

> [An envoy from the Khwarazmshah] saw a white hill and in answer to his query was told by the guide that it consisted of bones of the massacred inhabitants. At another place the earth was, for a long stretch of the road, greasy from human fat and the air was so polluted that several members of the mission became ill and some died. This was the place, they were told, where on the day that the city was stormed 60,000 virgins threw themselves to death from the fortifications in order to escape capture by the Mongols (Raverty, 1995, p. 965).

The World-Conqueror

Genghis then turned his attention westward in campaigns against the ethnically Chinese Qara Khitai, whose Muslim merchants and administrators would form the backbone of his emerging empire, and reluctantly against Khwarazm (corresponding to present-day Turkmenistan and Uzbekistan), the first Muslim state to experience the full fury of the Mongol onslaught. This apocalyptic invasion occurred in retaliation for the murder of a commercial and political trade delegation composed of Mongols, Chinese, and Muslims. As the self-proclaimed "punishment of God," Genghis Khan unleashed the bloody raids and merciless devastation on the Islamic west that has made his name synonymous with barbaric mass slaughter.

The trail of blood and massacre that followed the crumbling of the Khwarazmshah's empire in 1220 led from Central Asia through Iran to the Caucasus and north into the plains of Russia. The chronicles have told us that 1,600,000 or possibly as many as 2,400,000 were put to the sword in Herat (a city in present-day western Afghanistan), while in Nishapur, the city of Omar Khayyám, 1,747,000 were slaughtered. The two Mongol *noyans* (generals) Jebe and Sübedei led an expedition in pursuit of the fleeing Khwarazmshah (died 1221), demanding submission to, and assistance and human shields for their advancing armies, or death, destruction, and slavery. These were the two options for the cities and towns in their path. Outside every town they reached, the Mongols would deliver a chilling message: "Submit! And if ye do otherwise, what know we? God knoweth" (Juwayni, 1916, p. 26). In fact, there were few who did not fully understand their fate upon the conquerors' arrival. This epic cavalry mission was perhaps the greatest reconnaissance trip of all time, including not only intelligence gathering but also the conquest, massacre, and defeat of all lands neighboring the Caspian Sea and beyond. Jebe and Sübedei's expedition of pursuit, terror, and reconnaissance represents the Mongols at their destructive peak; thereafter their armies became for those who fell under the shadow of their approach both the invincible wrath of God and the emissaries of the biblical Gog and Magog (Revelations 20). The Mongols wore their notoriety like a *khil'at* (a robe of honor).

Khorasan in particular suffered grievously for the sins of its deluded leader, the Khwarazmshah. Although the massacres and ensuing destruction were widespread, there was method in the Mongols' madness. Artisans and craftsmen, with their families, were often spared the Great Khan's fury. Separated from their less fortunate fellow citizens, they were often forcibly transported east to practice their crafts in other parts of the empire. It is said that in Khwarazm (Kiva) in 1221, each of the 50,000 Mongol troops was assigned the task of slaughtering 24 Muslims before being able to loot and pillage. However, it is also reported that Genghis Khan personally implored the famed Sufi master and founder of the Kubrawiya order, Najm al-Din Kubra, to accept safe passage out of the condemned city. The saint refused to flee, but allowed his disciples to do so. Even at this early stage the "barbarian" Tatars demonstrated a respect for and knowledge of scholars and learning. (Although previously they had been a Turco-Mongol tribe rivaling Genghis, the Tatars came to be a generic term for the Genghisids in Europe and western Asia. *Tartarus* in Greek mythology was Hades or Hell.)

The World Ruler

Although Genghis died in 1227, unlike other steppe empires, his survived through his progeny who succeeded in maintaining and extending his power and territories. Genghis Khan rode out of the steppe as a nomadic ruler intent on rapine, pillage, and booty, and combining these traditional steppe practices with dexterous political and military skills, he proved unstoppable. The devastation he inflicted differed only in its scale from the raids of other nomadic rulers before him. Cities were razed, walls were consistently demolished, the *qanat* system of underground irrigation was damaged physically and, perhaps more serious, allowed to fall into disrepair through neglect. However, Genghis was astute enough to recognize that continued pillage and killing would be counterproductive and eventually succeed in destroying the source of the Mongols' wealth. He had wreaked horror and destruction on an unprecedented scale and achieved legendary status within his own lifetime, but it was only as long as he could deliver the prosperity to sate his hungry followers that he and his progeny would reign unchallenged.

Genghis was a man of vision. The blood and destruction, the plunder and the terror had been in the tradition of the age-old conflict between the steppe and the sown. Although the steppe had won, Genghis knew that its future depended on the sown. The mean tents of his childhood had been transformed into the lavish pavilions of his kingdom. The ragged camps of old had been replaced by mobile cities of wealth, splendor, and sophistication. The infamy he now enjoyed served as his security. In fact, the death tolls recorded and descriptions of the desolation his armies had caused were beyond credibility. The province of Herat, let alone the city, could not have sustained a population of two million, and the logistics involved in actually murdering this number of people within a matter of days are inconceivable. The already mentioned chronicler ibn al-Athir did much to perpetuate the mythology of the Mongol rule of terror. He recounts that so great was people's fear that a single Mongol could leisurely slaughter a whole queue of quaking villagers too afraid to resist, or that a docile victim would quietly wait, head outstretched, while his executioner fetched a forgotten sword (Browne, 1997, p. 430).

These apocryphal tales and the exaggerated accounts of massacres and mayhem were believed as literal truth. This vision of the Tatars as a visitation from Hell was readily accepted by religious zealots, both Christian and Muslim, who were able to shift responsibility for the carnage to their faithful followers.

Successors

Before his death Genghis Khan had appointed his second son Ögödei as his successor and divided his empire among the others. By 1241 Batu, his grandson, had overrun the principalities of Russia, subdued eastern Europe, and reached the coastline of Croatia. The year 1258 witnessed the fall of Baghdad and another grandson, Hülegü, firmly established in western Asia. Qubilai Qa'an was able to proclaim himself not only Great Khan (Qa'an means "Khan of Khans"), but also in 1279 the emperor of a united China. War and conquest had continued, but the nature of the conquerors and rulers had changed.

Qubilai Qa'an is quoted in contemporary Chinese sources as declaring that "having seized the body, hold the soul, if you hold the soul, where could the body go?" to explain his support and cultivation of Tibetan Buddhism (Bira, 1999, p. 242). The new generation of Mongols were essentially settled nomads, living in semipermanent urban camps, educated, sophisticated, and appreciative of life's fineries and luxuries. Qubilai Qa'an has been described as "the greatest cosmopolitan ruler that has ever been known in history" (Bira, 1999, p. 241). His brother Hülegü and the Ilkhans in Iran received other praises for their rule: justice, farsightedness, and statesmanship.

Once in power, the Mongol princes sought to rule their subjects, avowedly, with justice and tolerance, and for the prosperity of all. They ruled by the standards of the time, and their contemporaries differentiated between the "barbarian" nomads of the past and their masters residing in fabulous imperial courts. The ragged remains of the Khwarazmshah's army, led by the bandit king Jalal al-Din Mangkaburti, inspired far more fear and loathing than the disciplined Mongol troops. The Mongols had never targeted specific groups for persecution on religious, nationalistic, or ethnic grounds. When Baghdad was attacked, it was with the advice of Muslim advisers such as Nasir al-Din Tusi, and the supporting Muslim armies were led by Muslim rulers. Co-option was the desired result of conquest or the threat of attack. Top administrators in all parts of the empire were Mongol, Chinese, Persian, Uighur, Armenian, European, or Turkish. Loyalty and ability were prized above ethnicity or religion. A center of learning was established around 1260 in Iran's first Mongol capital, Maragheh. It attracted scholars from around the world who flocked, in particular, to see the observatory built for the court favorite, Tusi. The Syriac cleric Bar Hebraeus used the libraries, stocked from the ruins of Baghdad, Alamut, and other conquered cultural centers, to research his own acclaimed studies and historical accounts. The nation of archers had changed its priorities.

Most of what is now known of the Mongols comes from non-Mongol sources, among them Persian, Arabic, Armenian, European, and Chinese observers and commentators. While recognizing the might of the Mongols, these sources often betrayed a degree of anti-Mongol bias. Even in the writings of their most loyal proponents, servants, such as the Persian Muslim Juvaini (died 1282), there is a sense of distain and condescension for these *arriviste*. In many ways the Mongols became victims of their own propaganda and success. The horrors they perpetrated were the crown by which they managed to rise so high. Their impact was of such might that their achievements have been drowned in that initial sea of blood.

SEE ALSO Genghis Khan

BIBLIOGRAPHY

Allsen, Thomas T. (2001). *Culture and Conquest in Mongol Eurasia.* Cambridge, U.K.: Cambridge University Press.

Bar Hebraeus (2003). *The Chronography of Gregory Abu'l Faraj, Bar Hebraeus,* vol. 1, tran. Ernest Wallis Budge. Piscataway, N.J.: Gorgias Press.

Bira, Sh (1999). "Qubilai Qa'an and Phags-pa Bla-ma." In *The Mongol Empire and Its Legacy,* ed. Reuven Amitai-Preis and David O. Morgan. London: Brill.

Browne, E. G. (1997). *Literary History of Persia,* vol. 2. New Delhi: Munshiram Manoharlal Publishers.

Juwayni (1916). *Tarikh-i Jahan Gusha,* tran. J. Boyle, ed. M. Qazwini. Manchester, U.K.: Manchester University Press, 1997.

Komparoff, Linda, and Stefano Carboni (2002). *The Legacy of Genghis Khan.* New York: Metropolitan Museum of Art.

Lane, George (2003). *Early Mongol Rule in 13th Century Iran: A Persian Renaissance.* London: Routledge.

Lewis, Bernard (1993). "The Mongols, Turks, and the Muslim Polity." In *Islam in History.* Chicago: Open Court.

Mitchell, R., and N. Forbes, tran. (1914). *The Chronicle of Novgorod.* London: The Camden Society.

Onan, Urgunge, tran. (1993). *The Golden History of the Mongols: The Secret History.* London: The Folio Society.

Raverty, Major H. G., tran. (1995). *Tabakat-i-Nasiri,* vol. 2. Calcutta, India: The Asiatic Society.

Spuler, Bertold (1972). *History of the Mongols,* tran. H. and S. Drummond. London: Routledge & Kegan.

George Lane

Henry Morgenthau, Jr., played a major role in the creation of a wartime refugee policy during World War II when he persuaded President Franklin D. Roosevelt to establish an independent refugee agency—the War Refugee Board. It helped save the lives of as many as 200,000 European Jews. [LIBRARY OF CONGRESS]

Morgenthau, Henry

[MAY 11, 1891–FEBRUARY 6, 1967]
Author of a plan to rebuild post–World War II Europe

Henry Morgenthau served as secretary of the treasury in Franklin D. Roosevelt's administration from January 1, 1934, until July 22, 1945. Born in New York City into a German Jewish family, Morgenthau was a friend and a neighbor of Roosevelt in Hyde Park, New York. During the final months of the war, Morgenthau became a catalyst for the U.S. plan on punishing German war criminals that—although very different from what he had envisioned—was to become the core of the Nuremberg Charter.

Morgenthau's involvement in the question of punishing war criminals was a by-product of his deep interest in the overall question of the treatment of Germany after the war. Disturbed by the U.S. Army's *Handbook for Military Government in Germany* and other policy papers on the issue, Morgenthau succeeded in winning the president's support for a comprehensive memorandum, entitled Program to Prevent Germany from Starting a World War III, which he presented to Roosevelt

on September 5, 1944. The Morgenthau Plan, as it became known, had two major themes: the complete demilitarization and deindustrialization of Germany, and the severe punishment of all Germans involved in perpetrating war crimes. Morgenthau did not try to hide his prime motive—to eliminate once and for all Germany's threat to world peace, and to take revenge for the atrocities Germany committed during World War II.

Morgenthau's stand on punishing suspected war criminals corresponded with his overall view favoring the harsh treatment of Germans. The treasury secretary suggested the preparation of a list of arch-criminals whose guilt had generally been recognized by the United Nations (UN). Anyone on the list who was apprehended and identified by military authorities would be executed by firing squads made up by United Nations soldiers. Morgenthau also suggested establishing military commissions to deal with crimes that had been committed "against civilization during this war." In this category he included the killing of hostages and execution of victims because of their nationality, race, creed, color, or political conviction. Morgenthau advocated that any person convicted by such a military commission "be sentenced to death, unless the military commissions, in exceptional cases, determine that there are extenuating circumstances, in which case other punishment may be meted out, including deportation to a penal colony outside of Germany. Upon conviction, the sentence shall be carried out immediately." In this respect, Morgenthau's Plan much resembled the suggestions Britain's Prime Minister Winston Churchill had made to the British War Cabinet in late 1943 in anticipation of the war's end.

Fearing that Allied military authorities would be unable to tackle the enormous number of cases of war criminals, Morgenthau called for the detention, until the extent of their guilt had been determined, of all surviving members of the SS and Gestapo; high-ranking officials of the police, SA, and other security organizations; high-ranking government and Nazi Party officials; and all leading public figures closely identified with Nazism.

Morgenthau's Plan was vehemently opposed by U.S. Secretary of War Henry L. Stimson, who argued that in the long run it would prevent the achievement of world peace. Stimson also strongly disapproved of Morgenthau's proposals about the treatment of war criminals for their failure to include at least the rudimentary aspects of the Bill of Rights, namely, notifying the accused of the charge, giving them the right to be heard, and within reasonable limits allowing them to call witnesses in their defense. Instead, Stimson envisaged an international tribunal to try the chief Nazi officials on the charge of committing offenses against the laws and rules of war, whereas those who had committed war crimes in Nazi-subjugated territories would be tried by military commissions of the countries involved.

The Stimson-Morgenthau collision over the question of the treatment of postwar Germany formed a watershed in Washington's handling of the war criminals problem. In spite of the fact that Morgenthau enjoyed the president's support as well as Churchill's in principle, Stimson won out by taking advantage of Roosevelt's political weakness prior to the elections of November 1944 and the press criticism of the Morgenthau Plan. The president was compelled to withdraw his backing for the summary execution of major criminals.

Morgenthau's involvement in the war criminals issue, however, did produce important achievements: First, it prompted the administration to finally take the problem seriously, and second, it led the United States to include within the rubric of "war crime" the notion of crimes the enemy had committed against its own nationals from 1933 on. The prevailing stand in Washington had been not to view as a war crime any massacre of Axis nationals. As late as September 1944 Stimson drew an analogy to lynching in a letter to Roosevelt, arguing that Allied courts would be in the same predicament that foreign courts would be if they attempted to prosecute lynching in the United States.

Stimson's eventual decision to include crimes against nationals of Axis countries in the War Department's plan to punish war criminals, which became the essence of the final U.S. plan, was more the result of political calculation rather than moral or legal considerations on his part, that is, to appease Morgenthau and to dispel accusations that he supported the soft treatment of Germany. In effect, Stimson was convinced that Morgenthau's position derived from the fact that he was Jewish. As of mid-1943 Morgenthau had demonstrated growing concern for the fate of Europe's Jews, and in early 1944 he played a significant role in galvanizing Roosevelt to seek a halt to the Nazis' ongoing extermination of the Jews. Roosevelt's executive order of January 22, 1944, establishing the War Refugee Board, which was mandated to take all measures within its power to rescue and assist the victims of enemy oppression, was the administration's main operative action on behalf of the Jews during World War II. After Roosevelt's death on April 12, 1945, Morgenthau's influence within the White House significantly diminished, and he resigned from President Harry S. Truman's administration in July 1945.

SEE ALSO Jackson, Robert; London Charter; Nuremberg Trials; United Nations War Crimes Commission; War Crimes

BIBLIOGRAPHY

Blum, John Morton (1970). *Roosevelt and Morgenthau: A Revision and Condensation of Morgenthau's Diaries.* Boston: Houghton Mifflin.

Kimball, Warren F. (1976). *Swords or Ploughshares? The Morgenthau Plan for Defeated Nazi Germany, 1943–1946.* Philadelphia: Lippincott.

Kochavi, Arieh J. (1998). *Prelude to Nuremberg: Allied War Crimes Policy and the Question of Punishment.* Chapel Hill: Univeristy of North Carolina Press.

Morgenthau, Henry, Jr. (1945). *Germany Is Our Problem.* New York: Harper.

Arieh Kochavi

Moriscos

The term *Moriscos* is used to refer to those Spanish Muslims who were, under various degrees of duress, converted to Christianity at the beginning of the sixteenth century, and continued to live in Spain until the general expulsion of the Moors that occurred from 1609 to 1614. Muslims had been a minority in Christian Spain during the Middle Ages, at which time time they enjoyed a legal status that allowed them to practice Islam, retain their own communal authorities, and be ruled by Islamic Law. This minority was known as the Mudejar. In Castile, the Mudejar population was small, predominantly urban, and highly acculturated. In Aragon and Valencia, the Mudejar population was much more numerous and mainly rural. For the most part, they lived on the estates of large landowners, to whom they owed labor and who protected them from the interference of Church and State. The Mudejars of Valencia spoke Arabic, whereas the Muslims of Castile and Aragon produced a literature known as *Aljamía*, which combined Castilian or Aragonese vernacular with an Arabic script.

In 1469 King Ferdinand of Aragon and Queen Isabella of Castile had wed, uniting their two formerly independent kingdoms. Together they launched measures aimed at the creation of an homogeneous country ruled under a single body of law and loyal to a single religion. Spain became a territorial nation, with new social classes and new institutions. Among these institutions was Inquisition, established in 1478 for the purpose of creating an all-Catholic nation. Jews were the first victims of the homogenizing policies of this new state, for in 1492 they were obliged to choose between conversion to Catholicism and exile. The majority chose exile. In that same year, Castile conquered the

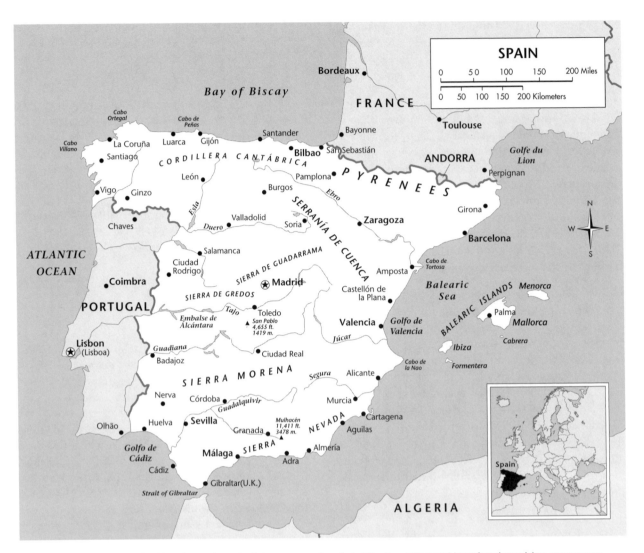

Spain, where the Moriscos (or Moors) experienced religious persecution during the Inquisition and later faced expulsion. [EASTWORD PUBLICATIONS DEVELOPMENT. GALE GROUP.]

Kingdom of Granada, which was the last region in the Iberian Peninsula to be ruled by a Muslim political power. This had enormous consequences for minorities in the whole of Spain.

In capitulating to the Spanish Christian forces, the Moorish population of the Kingdom of Granada was guaranteed certain rights which gave them a status similar to that of the Mudejar. Nevertheless, the upper classes quickly emigrated to North Africa, The Crown encouraged this emigration during the first two years after Granada fell by paying the costs of transport across the Straits of Gibraltar for all those who wished to go, and by permitting the émigrés to take their movable property with them.

The situation deteriorated rapidly after the end of the fifteenth century, however, when new Christian settlers arrived in Granada. In a country in which the

state tended to intervene in every aspect of its subjects' lives, society was becoming increasingly intolerant of difference. In February 1502, the Muslims of the Kingdom of Castile (which now included Granada) were offered the choice between conversion or emigration by a decree very similar to the one previously applied to Jews. This time, however, conditions were added which made emigration practically impossible. In 1512 the Castilan decree was extended to Navarre, whose Mudejar communities fled to Aragon (including Valencia), where the practice of Islam remained, for a time, legal. During the Germanías rebellion against landlords and crown (1521–1522), the rebels turned against the Mudejar vassals who supported their lords and subjected them to forced baptism. The validity of these baptisms was contested by theologians, but in 1526 the general conversion of all Muslims in the lands of Ara-

encyclopedia of GENOCIDE *and* CRIMES AGAINST HUMANITY

gon and Valencia was decreed. From 1526 on, therefore, no Muslim could legally be a subject of the kings of Spain.

Only their legal status separated Mudejars, who were permitted to practice Islam, from Moriscos, who were forcibly converted to Christianity. Of course, most of the new converts, in spite of missionary efforts, continued to practice Islam in secret. If they were caught they were persecuted by the Inquisition as apostates or as heretics, for, after all, they had been baptized, however unwillingly. Inquisitorial persecution of Moriscos was particulaly intense in the 1550s and 1560s. Inquisition documents reflect the pressure that Christian society exerted upon the Moriscos communities, and its efforts to eradicate all cultural, social, and religious differences. The Crown, in the person of Philippe II, took new and radical repressive measures. In 1567 a law was passed forbidding the spoken or written use of Arabic, the publication or possession of Arabic books, the use of Arabic names, the wearing of Arabic clothing, and the patronage of Arabic bathhouses.

This decree, together with other factors such as the crisis in the silk industry, which employed many Granadan Moriscos, ignited a Morisco rebellion in the mountains of Granada, known as War of the Alpujarras (1568–1570). This was a long and cruel war, with all the atrocities which are inherent to civil wars. The outcome was a difficult and costly Christian victory and the deportation, in the winter of 1569 and 1570, of the entire Morisco population of Granada to the territories of northern Castile. There the Moriscos were settled in small, scattered groups. Many of these impoverished and uprooted Granadan exiles turned to outlawry, and tension between Moriscos and Christians, hitherto unknown in those territories, grew considerably.

The Spanish government grew to fear the prospect that Moriscos might seek to ally themselves with North African pirates, with Morocco, or with the Ottoman Empire. This concern led to a ban on Moriscos residing near the coasts. From 1582 onward, the expulsion of Moriscos was an idea that grew increasingly attractive to the Spanish government. When the final decision to expel all Moriscos was reached in 1609, it was mainly justified on grounds of national security. Moriscos were considered unrepentant Muslims, regardless of their conversion status, and were thought likely to conspire with foreign powers—mainly Muslim, but also with French Protestants. Some Moriscos were Muslims, of course, but by this time many had fully assimilated to Christian society and were sincere Christians. The authorities did not trouble to make such fine distinctions.

Between 1609 and 1614, about 320,000 Moriscos were expelled in phases. The first to be obliged to leave were the Moriscos of Valencia, considered the most dangerous. The last to go were those of Castile. Some communities were directly transported to North Africa via the harbors in the south and east of Spain. Others crossed to France, from where they went (sometimes via Italy) to the Ottoman Empire and Egypt. The majority of Morisco exiles to North Africa settled in Morocco and Tunisia, but some settled in Algiers. In their new countries they had a distinct personality, which was manifest during the first century after their arrival. Most of these first generation of exiles did not speak Arabic, and their knowledge of Islam was scant. Their integration into the societies of North Africa was generally difficult. Only in Tunisia did they find an easy entry, for the Tunisian *Dey* (governor), Uthman, applied a generous settlement policy to these newcomers.

In their new countries, Moriscos tended to settle in small, ethnically homogeneous enclaves near the coasts. Many turned to the sea for their livelihoods, and considerably increased the ranks of the corsairs and pirates that plied the shipping lanes. In the Moroccan port of Sale, a group of Moriscos founded a pirate republic, which maintained its independence for a time. Other Moriscos settled in the agricultural plains of North Africa, where they introduced the irrigational techniques that they had used in spain. They also introduced new crops, some of which had only recently come to Spain from the Americas. Moriscos also settled in the capital cities, near the courts, where their knowledge of Spanish and of European ways helped some of them to become secretaries, interpreters, translators, and ambassadors. Before the end of the seventeenth century, the Moriscos were totally assimilated to North African societies. By the early twenty-first century, only a few family names and some fragments of folklore remained of their once distinctive culture.

SEE ALSO Catholic Church; Ethnic Cleansing; Inquisition; Nationalism

BIBLIOGRAPHY

Benítez Sánchez-Blanco, Rafael (2001). *Heróicas decisiones. La Monarquía Católica y los Moriscos valencianos.* Valencia: Institut Alfons el Magnanim.

Cardaillac, Louis, ed. (1990). *Les Morisques et l'Inquisition,* Paris: Publisud.

Domínguez Ortíz, Antonio, and Bernard Vincent (1997). *Historia de los Moriscos. Vida y tragedia de una minoría.* Madrid: Alianza.

García-Arenal, Mercedes (1996). *Los moriscos.* Granada: Universidad.

Lea, Henry Charles (1931). *The Moriscos of Spain: Their Conversion and Expulsion.* Philadelphia: University of Pennsylvania Press.

Wiegers, G. A. (1994). *Islamic Literature in Spanish and Aljamiado: Iça de Segovia (d. 1450) His Antecedents and Successors.* Leiden: E. J. Brill.

Mercedes García-Arenal

Music, Holocaust Hidden and Protest

Nazi cultural policies toward the arts were foreshadowed in Weimar Germany, where party spokesmen denounced jazz, the musical avant-garde, and any work by a Jewish composer, regardless of category. With the advent of the Third Reich in January 1933, institutionalized harassment of Jews and antifascists began in earnest. A great many Jewish and politically dissident musicians fled Germany at this time, while those who remained were quickly forced from the public sphere. Facing unemployment and social isolation, a group of Berlin-area musicians, artists, and entertainers led by Dr. Kurt Singer established the *Kulturbund deutscher Juden* (Culture League of German Jews), an all-Jewish performance society, in the spring of 1933. With approval from the authorities (who reasoned the organization would serve to further separate Jews from the cultural mainstream), Kulturbund branches soon thrived in many Germany localities. The Kulturbund at its peak in the mid-1930s supported four orchestras, two opera companies, and several large choirs, each offering a busy schedule of concert events. In the wake of escalating state terror, these programs—in time restricted to Jewish-themed fare—provided respite and spiritual renewal for audience and performers alike. Immigration, deportations, and the onset of war significantly curtailed Kulturbund activities well before the Gestapo shut down the organization in 1941.

Concentration Camps

Songs of resistance from the first Nazi concentration camps (built to imprison Hitler's political opponents) often reflected the inmates' socialist and communist sympathies. The best known of these songs, "Die Moorsoldaten" (The peat bog soldiers), written in August 1933 at the Börgermoor camp by political prisoners Johann Esser, Wolfgang Langhoff, and Rudi Goguel, is emblematic of the repertoire. With lyrics hinting at the Nazis' downfall and a march melody symbolically shifting between the minor and major modes, the song became a model for later resistance songs such as "Dachau-Lied" (Dachau song, 1938), written by two Austrian Jewish political prisoners, and "Fest Steht" (Stand fast, 1942), sung by Jehovah's Witnesses imprisoned for their religious beliefs. Disseminated outside Germany by refugees, "Die Moorsoldaten" became an international symbol of spiritual opposition to Nazi barbarism.

Prisoners' performance ensembles had been established at many camps both before and after the outbreak of war in 1939. Official orchestras at Sachsenhausen, Buchenwald, Auschwitz, and elsewhere accompanied the inmates' forced march to labor and provided entertainment for the camp command. Orchestra members, while compelled to oblige, were often spared the worst hazards of camp life. Music making also took place in secret, with popular, patriotic, and satirical songs offering a measure of diversion and psychological release to prisoners. Such activity, particularly among non-Jewish inmates not prioritized for extermination, may have been fairly widespread: The archive of former Polish prisoner Aleksander Kulisiewicz lists approximately five hundred topical songs and numerous instrumental works originating in thirty-six different camps for the period from 1939 to 1945. This kind of activity was also dangerous. Kulisiewicz, himself the author of many anti-Nazi songs, noted that those caught performing such music risked torture and execution at the hands of the authorities.

Of the Nazi camps, Theresienstadt (Terezín), near Prague, was an exception, a "model camp" where for propaganda purposes the Germans allowed inmates a relatively open and varied cultural life. Drawing on a deep well of Jewish talent from throughout occupied Europe, the camp administration scheduled a full calendar of programs that included opera, operetta, symphony, chamber, and choral concerts. In addition, many gifted artists—among them the cabaret writer Karel Ávenck and composers Viktor Ullmann, Hans Krása, Pavel Haas, and Gideon Klein—produced original works for performance at the camp. Ullmann, whose allegorical anti-Nazi opera *Der Kaiser von Atlantis* (Emperor of Atlantis) was rehearsed but never staged at Theresienstadt, spoke for his colleagues and himself when he proclaimed "our endeavor with respect to the arts was commensurate with our will to live" (Bloch, 1989).

Ghettos

The larger ghettos of German-occupied eastern Europe were scenes of a flourishing if precarious cultural life. Jews crowded into ghettos in Warsaw, Lodz, Vilna, and Kovno could attend concerts by orchestras and choirs of a professional caliber, and recitals by famous singers and instrumentalists, and enjoy cabaret-style entertainment in local cafés. Although archival sources and survivor memoirs indicate that original classical compositions were created and performed in the ghettos, few such works remain extant. However, hundreds of Yiddish songs from dozens of ghettos survive to bear witness to events and personalities that would otherwise be lost. Renowned troubadors such as Jankiel Herszkowicz of Lodz and Mordecai Gebirtig of Kraków, and legions of lesser known and nameless scribes, chronicled ghetto life in songs that addressed the subjects of hunger, smuggling, ghetto "elites," hidden children, deportations, death, and remembrance. Often based on popular prewar melodies, these songs were easily memorized and circulated widely. The documentary value of this repertoire was recognized early on, and published collections began to appear within a month of the Allied victory in Europe. Of these, the anthology *Lider fun di getos un lagern* (Songs of the ghettos and camps), compiled in 1948 by Shmerke Kaczerginski, remains the most comprehensive, with 233 song texts (not all with musical notation).

In the aftermath of World War II the ghetto song assumed a new function as memorial music. Performed at the gatherings of Holocaust survivors and commemoration ceremonies worldwide, the mainstays of this repertoire include "Vu ahin zol ikh geyn" (Where shall I go), with lyrics by the Warsaw writer Y. Korntayer; "Ani Ma'amin" (I believe), a text by Maimonides sung by Hasidic Jews en route to execution; and the partisans' anthem "Zog nit keynmol az du geyst dem letstn veg" (Never say that you have reached the final road), with lyrics by the Vilna poet and underground fighter Hirsh Glik.

SEE ALSO Architecture; Ghetto; Memorials and Monuments; Music and Musicians Persecuted during the Holocaust; Music at Theresienstadt; Music of the Holocaust

BIBLIOGRAPHY

Eisler, Ejal Jakob, Rainer Lotz, et al. (2001). *Vorbei: Beyond Recall. A Record of Jewish Musical Life in Nazi Berlin 1933–1938*. Hambergen: Bear Family Records.

Fackler, Guido (2000). *"Des Lagers Stimme" Musik im KZ*. Bremen: Edition Temmen.

Geisel, Eike, and Henryk Broder, eds. (1992). *Premiere und Pogrom: der Jüdische Kulturbund 1933–1941*. Berlin: Siedler.

Kaczerginski, Shmerke (1948). *Lider fun di getos un lagern*. New York: Congress for Jewish Culture.

Karas, Joza (1985). *Music in Terezín 1941–1945*. New York: Beaufort Books.

Lammel, Inge, and Günther Hofmeyer, eds. (1962). *Lieder aus den faschistischen Konzentrationslagern*. Leipzig: Friedrich Hofmeister.

Levi, Erik (1994). *Music in the Third Reich*. New York: St. Martin's Press.

Mlotek, Eleanor, and Malke Gottlieb, eds. (1983) *We Are Here: Songs of the Holocaust*. New York: Workmen's Circle.

Bret Werb

Music and Musicians Persecuted during the Holocaust

On November 15, 1936, three years after Adolf Hitler came to power, the *New York Times* reported that the statue of Felix Mendelssohn in Leipzig had been destroyed. This violent action clearly signaled that music by composers of the Jewish faith or tradition would no longer be performed in opera houses and concert halls. The great compositions of Salomon Sulzer, Jaques Offenbach, Erich Korngold, Gustav Mahler, Arnold Schönberg, Mendelssohn, and many others were also silenced throughout the Third Reich and Nazi-occupied Europe.

Prior to the destruction of the Mendelssohn statue, Jewish musicians were systematically expelled from concert halls and opera houses throughout German-controlled Europe. In early March 1933, Bruno Walter, one of Germany's most beloved and renowned conductors, had just returned to Berlin after a successful concert tour in the United States. Walter was informed of "certain difficulties" should he decide to follow through with a previously scheduled guest appearance in Leipzig. The management of the concert hall, however, decided to go ahead with Walter's appearance. A few hours before the doors opened, however, the performance was banned. A week later, Walter was to conduct a concert in Berlin's Philharmonic Hall. Again, he was advised to cancel the performance in order to avoid "unpleasant occurrences." What the Nazis meant by that became clear on April 1, 1933, when Nazis boycotted Jewish stores, defaced the storefronts of Jewish-owned businesses, and publicly blackmailed those who continued to shop in stores owned by Germans of the Jewish faith.

From that point on, every week brought further governmental decrees that robbed Jews of their livelihood and their right to German citizenship. Between 1933 and 1939, more than 2,000 conductors, soloists, concert masters, singers, members of orchestras, and musicologists were banned or expelled from stages and teaching positions throughout Germany, Austria, and Poland because they were Jewish.

Many musicians left Europe for the United States. The ramifications of this forced migration were enormous. Europe lost thousands of its best artistic and intellectual minds. For the United States, however, the arrival of European artists meant tremendous enrichment. The distinguished cultural elite made a decisive mark on American institutions of higher learning, and redefined these schools in terms of research, teaching, and performance styles.

Although this process was of decisive benefit to the United States as a whole, the individual émigré, being outside Europe, often endured a marked decline in social status and a loss of identity. The difficulties émigré musicians faced in finding employment is poignantly expressed in a letter by Arnold Schönberg, the most prominent composer of modern tonality. On February 26, 1940, he wrote from his new home in Los Angeles to Adolf Rebner, who was himself trying to eke out a living in Cincinnati: "Dear friend, . . . I am happy that you could escape hell. . . . But it has become rather difficult to procure positions. There are so many gifted people here, though few of your reputation and ability." Even Schönberg's work was considered too obscure in the United States, and he lacked the appropriate contacts to help his former students and associates.

Nazi Germany not only expelled its Jewish artists and intellectuals; it also poisoned the intellectual intimacy of people who had once been professional associates. In 1932, the composer Richard Strauss had asked Stefan Zweig, a poet and novelist of Jewish heritage, to write the libretto for his new opera, *The Silent Woman*. The ensuing relationship between the two men was, according to Zweig, most cordial and harmonious at first. Then Zweig learned that Strauss had assumed the position of president of the official Nazi *Reich Music Chamber*. Zweig later wrote: "To have the most famous musician of Germany align himself with them at so embarrassing a moment [constituted an] immeasurable gain to Goebbels and Hitler." Zweig reproached Strauss for the self-serving "art-egotism" that permitted him to serve such evil masters.

One of the most exceptional and painful aspects of this dark period is the fact that Jewish musicians were forced to perform in concentration camps and for the German SS. Auschwitz is reported to have had six orchestras. One of the musicians was Alma Maria Rosé, Gustav Mahler's niece. A student of her father, Arnold Rosé, she was a renowned violinist. After the annexation of Austria in 1938, she escaped to France. There she was captured, interned, and eventually she was deported to Auschwitz. The orchestra of young female musicians that she founded in Auschwitz is memorialized in *Playing for Time*, a book written by her surviving assistant conductor, the singer Fania Fénelon. We also know of the musicians Henry and Poldek Rosner through their mention in the movie *Schindler's List*. The Rosners were forced to perform for Amon Göth, the commander of the Plaszow concentration camp.

There was also a vibrant cultural life in the camp of Terezin (Theresienstadt). In his book *The Terezin Requiem*, Josef Bor tells of the performance in camp of Verdi's *Requiem*, conducted by Rafael Schächter.

Schächter was deported to Auschwitz shortly after the performance. Another important event was the performance of the opera for children, *Brundibar*, by Hans Krasà. Both the Czech composer and the entire cast of children were deported to Auschwitz. Victor Ullmann composed his opera *The Emperor of Atlantis* while incarcerated in Terezin. Ullmann was a student of Arnold Schönberg and was murdered in Auschwitz. The opera had its premiere in New York in 1977.

Also banned were many of the composers and performers of Klezmer music, a popular musical form that originated in the Jewish *stetls* and ghettoes of eastern Europe and celebrated traditional aspects of Jewish life. Similarly, the composers and performers of partisan songs and songs of resistance were murdered as well. Mordecai Gebirtig was one of the most popular balladeers in Poland. He was deported to the Krakow ghetto and killed there in 1942. His song "Our Town Is Burning," written in 1938, became one of the most popular anthems in ghettos and concentration camps.

The number of musicians and composers who perished in the Nazi-run camps will never be known with certainty. However, among them are: the baritone and cantor Erhard E. Wechselmann, murdered in Auschwitz; the contralto Magda Spiegel, murdered in Auschwitz; Richard Breitenfeld, a member of the Frankfurt opera ensemble, murdered in Theresienstadt; James Simon, a student of Max Bruch, murdered in Auschwitz; the Czech composers Pavel Haas and Viktor Ullmann, murdered in Auschwitz; the jazz pianist Martin Roman and the cabaret singer and songwriter Kurt Gerron, murdered in Auschwitz as well.

The creative products of those banned as "Jewish" or "degenerate" belong among the early twenty-first century's most cherished expressions of popular and high culture. Their legacy has generated and intensely personal post-Holocaust oeuvre that continues to enhance our understanding of the infamous years of the Nazi era. Among the composers represented in this body of work are: Krzysztof Penderecki, composer of *Dies Irae* (1967), a memorial to the victims of Auschwitz; Demitri Shostakovich, whose symphony *Babi Yar* (1962) commemorates the victims of the massacre near the city of Kiev; Arnold Schönberg, who wrote *A Survivor from Warsaw* (1947); Francis Schwartz, who created the electronic music piece *Caligula* (1975) with human voices chanting, howling, and groaning; and Charles Davidson, whose *I Never Saw Another Butterfly* (1968) is based on the collection of poetry written by children of the Terezin camp.

SEE ALSO Art, Banned; Music at Theriesienstadt; Music of the Holocaust

BIBLIOGRAPHY

Baaske, Andrea (1991). *Musik in Konzentrationslagern.* Freiburg, Germany: Projektgruppe.

Brinkmann, Reinhold, and Christoph Wolff, eds. (1999). *Driven into Paradise. The musical Migration from Nazi Germany to the United States.* Berkeley: University of California Press.

Kurz, Jan (1995). *"Swinging Democracy": Jugendprotest im 3. Reich.* Münster, Germany: Literature.

Potter, Pamela Maxine (1998). *Most German of the Arts: Musicology and Society from the Weimar Republic to the End of the Hitler's Reich.* New Haven, Conn.: Yale University Press.

Priesberg, Fred K. (2000). *Musik im Dritten Reich.* Cologne, Germany: Dittrich.

Weissweiler, Eva (1999). *Ausgemerzt! Das Lexikon der Juden in der Musik und seine mörderischen Folgen.* Cologne, Germany: Dittrich.

Viktoria Hertling

Music at Theresienstadt

During the Third Reich music played significant roles for Nazi oppressors and their victims. The history of both the Nazi *Entartete Musik* policy and musical activities in the concentration camps is a compelling mixture of terror, inspiration, irony, and surrealism. Ultimately, it was the inspiring determination of artists, particularly those incarcerated in Theresienstadt, which left an enduring musical and social legacy for future generations.

Entartete Musik

The Nazi regime used music, as well as other arts, as a political tool to unify and indoctrinate the German *Volk* (the public). *Entartete Musik* was the name given by the Nazis to a wide variety of composers and musical genres as part of their propaganda machine. *Entartete* (degenerate, a term connoting psychologically abnormal behavior) signified something aberrant about the art, thus perceived as a threat to German society. In addition to educating people about the dangers of degenerate music, the public was also "protected" from cultural pollution by a ban on the performance, recording, and publication of this music. This policy was initially introduced at an exhibit of visual arts, *Entartete Kunst* (degenerate art), displayed in Munich in 1937. The following year in Dusseldorf, music received similar attention in the *Entartete Musik* exhibition.

The *Entartete* program became a policy of censorship that supported the ethnic and political cleansing of German society. The music targeted was enormously varied, as were the lives and backgrounds of the composers. What the Nazis identified in common for all were either elements of jazz, atonal music, or, most insidiously and specifically, any music written by Jewish composers. Simply put, jazz was deemed "Negro" music and atonality bore the subversive influences of the "Jew" and Bolshevism. Racial considerations aside, the compositions of many German composers experimenting with such new musical forms were also targeted. According to this twisted formula, such music was symptomatic of a cancer infecting German culture. The Nazi Propaganda Ministry was determined to "educate" the public about the danger of this music, and to revitalize the concept of a pure German music as exemplified by the work of Richard Wagner and Anton Bruckner.

Some targeted musicians, such as Arnold Schoenberg, Franz Waxman, Berthold Goldschmidt, and Bruno Walter, fled to the United States and United Kingdom to start anew. Others were not so fortunate; many exceptionally gifted artists were imprisoned and eventually murdered.

Theresienstadt

A number of artists who were among the intelligentsia of Western Europe were sent to the Theresienstadt (Terezín in Czech) concentration camp in Czechoslovakia. Theresienstadt functioned not only as a transit camp to the Nazi death camps, but also as a propaganda vehicle designed to deceive the world community about the true nature of the Final Solution. Originally a garrison town of approximately six thousand, Theresienstadt was converted into a concentration camp, growing to a prison population almost ten times that number.

The overcrowding, inadequate medical care, and starvation in Theresienstadt made for intolerable living conditions. Around 120,000 people passed through Theresienstadt; 33,000 would die there. Remarkably, in the midst of horrid living conditions, musical instruments were smuggled in as early as the second transport. At first concerts were held secretly in the attics and basements of the barracks. The performances increased with the mounting number of amateur and professional artists arriving with each transport. This active cultural community included many of Europe's most gifted artists, musicians, and literary figures. On eventually discovering these secret performances, the Nazis realized the great importance of culture to the prisoners, and believed that in allowing such cultural activities, they could more easily contain the Theresienstadt prisoners.

The *Freizeitgestaltung* (Administration for Free Time Activities) was instituted by the Nazi SS command. This Jewish-run organization was responsible for a wide range of cultural activities for prisoners, including lectures, theater, opera, jazz, cabaret, and chamber music. Amateur and professional musicians formed a variety of ensembles. Egon Ledec, former associate concertmaster of the Czech Philharmonic, established the Ledec Quartet, one of several string quartets and ensembles in Theresienstadt. Kurt Gerron, who was the original "Tiger Brown" in Kurt Weill's *Three Penny Opera* and costarred with actress Marlene Dietrich in *Der blaue Engel* (The Blue Angel), produced cabaret productions. In the realm of jazz and popular music, Martin Roman led the Ghetto Swingers. Czech choirmaster Raphael Schächter directed productions of operas by Wolfgang Amadeus Mozart, Bedrich Smetana, and Georges Bizet. Schächter's most inspiring act of musical resistance was exemplified by his determination to perform Giuseppe Verdi's *Requiem*. Between 1943 and 1944 he and over 150 fellow prisoners rehearsed and performed the requiem 15 times for inmates, and ultimately the Nazi elite. Twice the chorus was decimated by transports to Auschwitz.

Four classical composers emerged among the central creative forces in this extraordinarily rich cultural community: Gideon Klein, Pavel Haas, Hans Krása, and Viktor Ullmann. Before their incarceration these men were active participants in the principal trends of European culture, and were among the gifted students and musical successors of Arnold Schoenberg, Alois Haba, and Leos Janáček. Their works were performed under the direction of such notable conductors as Leopold Stokowski, William Steinberg, George Szell, and Serge Koussevitzky. Deported to Theresienstadt within four months of each other, they were important figures in the *Freizeitgestaltung*.

In one of many of the twisted and surrealistic aspects of Theresienstadt, the imprisoned artists and audience members experienced a cultural freedom impossible in Germany and Nazi-occupied countries. Programs were rarely censored, especially with consideration to the racial criteria of the degenerate policy.

The Nazis attempted to portray Theresienstadt as a *paradeis ghetto* (paradise ghetto) to the outside world. This was highlighted in the summer of 1944 with the carefully orchestrated inspection by the International Committee of the Red Cross (ICRC) and the production of a propaganda film entitled *Der Fuehrer schenkt den Juden eine Stadt* (The Führer Gives the Jews a City). Theresienstadt was superficially beautified with an outdoor concert pavilion and fake storefronts. During the staged Red Cross visit, Krása's children's opera *Brundibár* was performed, and a scene from the opera was shot for the Nazi propaganda film. Theresienstadt's prisoners—children and adults alike—were forced to produce

and participate in the film, which was directed by Gerron. The film also included a sham performance of Haas's *Study for String Orchestra*, (with the narrator asserting: "Musical performances are happily attended by all. The work of a Jewish composer in Theresienstadt is performed"). Shooting of the film ended in September 1944. Within a month most of Theresienstadt's cultural establishment, including Gerron and Haas, were deported to the gas chambers of Auschwitz.

For almost half a century the music and history of these artists, whose careers and lives were cut short by Nazi policies, have been absent from concert halls and mainstream musical consciousness. The reemergence of these composers represents a significant addition to humankind's understanding and appreciation of twentieth-century classical music. In the face of the Final Solution the history of these artists is poignant testimony to their determination and creative legacy.

SEE ALSO Music, Holocaust Hidden and Protest; Music and Musicians Persecuted during the Holocaust; Music of Reconciliation; Music of the Holocaust

BIBLIOGRAPHY

Adler, H. G. (1960). *Theresienstadt 1941–1945. Das Anlitz einer Zwangagemeinschaft*, 2nd edition. Tuebingen: JCB Mohr.

Barron, Stephanie (1991). *"Degenerate Art," the Fate of the Avant-Garde in Nazi Germany*. Los Angeles: Los Angeles County Museum of Art.

Bondy, Ruth (1989). *"Elder of the Jews": Jakob Edelstein of Theresienstadt*. New York: Grove Press.

Goldstein, Phyllis, and Mark Ludwig (2000). *Finding a Voice: Musicians in Terezín*. Boston: Terezín Chamber Music Foundation and Facing History and Ourselves.

Lederer, Zdenek (1983). *Ghetto Theresienstadt*. New York: Howard Fertig.

Redlich, Gonda (1992). *The Diary of Gonda Redlich*. Lexington, Ky.: The University Press of Kentucky.

Mark D. Ludwig

Music Based on the Armenian Genocide

The Armenian genocide (1915–1923) reportedly took the lives of over 1.5 million Armenians and is considered by many to be the first genocide of the twentieth century. Despite the Turkish government's general denial of the event, for the Armenians this period in history is an omnipresent source of pain and historical consciousness that finds itself expressed through literature, art, and music. Three overarching areas of Armenian music have been infused by the genocide: (1) Armenian music history and the work of Armenian musicologist Komitas Vardapet; (2) the style and content of some Armenian songs that validate the experience of the Armenian genocide; and (3) religious ritual performances for the preservation of Armenian identity in the diaspora.

Komitas Vardapet and the Armenian Genocide

In terms of Armenian musical history, the genocide profoundly affected musicologist Komitas Vardapet, who is regarded as the father of Armenian national music. Born Sogomon Soghomonian in 1869, Komitas, renaming himself after a seventh-century writer of hymns, studied music in Berlin and transcribed Armenian folk songs during the reign of the Ottoman Empire. As a participant in the International Musical Society Congress in Paris (May–June 1914), he introduced the music of Armenia to the Western world. On orders from the Ottoman government, he and other Armenian scholars were deported to the interior of the country. Komitas suffered a breakdown, and from 1919 until his death he lived in a mental hospital in Paris. As a result, much of his groundbreaking work was lost. Despite this the Arts Institute of the Armenian Academy of Sciences has published six volumes of his musicological works. His *Armenian Sacred and Folk Music* (1998) includes eight original essays, and has provided much of what is known about Armenian music in general.

Songs as Oral History

Historical validity is often conferred by written texts or other visual means, that is, newspapers and photographs. Oral history can also be an exceedingly important source of historical evidence and allow for truthful descriptions of general conditions. Jan Vansina states in his *Oral Tradition As History* that "the expression 'oral tradition' applies both to a process and to its product. . . . The process is the transmission of such messages by word of mouth over time until the disappearance of the message" (Vansina, 1985, p. 3). By passing down songs, the Armenian people have, in fact, cemented the Armenian genocide's place in history.

The most significant work linking the genocide directly to music is Verjine Svazlian's *The Armenian Genocide in the Memoirs and Turkish Language Songs of Eye-Witness Survivors* (1999). In the 1950s Svazlian began transcribing and recording the memoirs and interviews of survivors of witnesses to the Armenian genocide. She characterized these songs as follows:

1. Created under the immediate impression of specific historical events on the western segment of the Armenian people, these songs are saturated with historicity.

2. Similar songs have been simultaneously created, in different variants and modifications.

3. Although the songs have been created in the Turkish language, they are, however, of Armenian origin (Svazlian 1999, p. 10).

For example, the testimonies of Serpoohi Makarian (b. 1903) and Mikael Keshishian from Adana (b. 1904) recall the horror of the events:

Hey, cedars, cedars, variegated cedars,

The resin drips every time the sun strikes,

Alas! Adana River is full of corpses and blood,

Behold! I've come to see you, slaughtered Adana,

Alas! I've seen you, massacred children (Svazlian, 1999, p. 11).

This song depicts the beginning of the genocide, "when young Turks feverishly prepared the total extermination of the Armenian people waiting for a propitious occasion" (Svazlian, 1999, p. 11). Later in the same work Svazlian provides songs characterizing the experiences of those who were pressed to walk the "death road":

Green grass did not grow in the desert of Deyr-el-Zor,

Fifty thousand persons were shot down,

The people's teeth fell down from affliction,

Armenians dying for the sake of faith!
(1999, p. 20)

Here the Christian faith becomes a shining badge of "Armenianness." Having embraced Christianity in the fourth century CE, Armenia is regarded by many as the first Christian nation. In the very name of faith, Svazlian reports that the following song recounts the torture inflicted on Armenians in the town of Marash:

Marash is called Marash, alas!

Marash, how do they call you Marash?

When they burn a church in Marash,

And they burn Armenians in the church.
(1999, p. 33)

These are but a sample from the vast collection of ethnographic songs that Svazlian assembled. The songs are memorials to the many who perished—in the writer's own words, "the Armenian folk memoirs and the Turkish-language songs entrusted to the generations, become owing to their historico-cognitive value, testimonies, artistic, yet reliable, objective and evidential documents illustrating, in a simple popular language, the historic events and the Armenian Genocide" (1999, p. 36).

Sacred Music: Preserving Armenian Identity in the Diaspora

Armenians have maintained much of their history through the ritual performance of their Christian faith throughout the diaspora. The Armenian liturgy and its music comprise the *Badarak* (Mass) and the *sharagan* (hymns) sung at the services, also called offices, and the *sharagan* sung for the sacraments. Sung in the classical Armenian language of *Graber,* the music lends spiritual meaning to the text of the *Soorp Badarak* (Divine Liturgy) or Holy Sacrifice. With the participants gathering for the liturgy, their performance becomes an active expression of communal identity, evoking their worldview, which is a direct reflection of their religious belief system as well as the event that brought many of them to the diaspora—the Armenian genocide. If music is then considered in ritual contexts, one can look at it not only as an integral part of the liturgical performance, but also as a way of maintaining historical identity.

If music is a sign of a people, then without a doubt Armenian music may be regarded as a referential idiom—embodying meaning that extends the purely musical to that of memory, history, and identity.

SEE ALSO Armenians in Ottoman Turkey and the Armenian Genocide

BIBLIOGRAPHY

Komitas, Vardapet (1950). *Chants of the Divine Liturgy of the Armenian Apostolic Orthodox Church*, adapt. Wardan Sarxian. New York: Delphic Press.

Komitas, Vardapet (1998). *Armenian Sacred and Folk Music*, tran. Edward Gulbekian. Richmond, Surrey, U.K.: Curzon.

McCollum, Jonathan (2004). "Music, Ritual, and Diasporic Identity: A Case Study of the Armenian Apostolic Church." Ph.D. diss., University of Maryland, College Park, Md.

McCollum, Jonathan, and Andy Nercessian (2004). *Armenian Music: A Comprehensive Bibliography and Discography*. Lanham, Md.: Scarecrow Press.

Nersessian, Vrej, ed. (1978). *Essays on Armenian Music*. London: Kahn and Averill.

Poladian, Sirvat (1942). *Armenian Folk Songs*. Berkeley: University of California Press.

Poladian, Sirvat (1978). "Komitas Vartabed and His Contribution to Ethnomusicology: Komitas the Pioneer." In *Essays on Armenian Music*, ed. Vrej Nersessian. London: Kahn and Averill.

Svazlian, Verjine (1995). *Genocide: Oral Evidences of the Western Armenians*. Yerevan: Gitutiun.

Svazlian, Verjine (1999). *The Armenian Genocide in the Memoirs and Turkish Language Songs of Eye-Witness Survivors*, ed. Sarkis Harutyunian. Yerevan: Museum-Institute of the Armenian Genocide of the National Academy of Sciences of the Republic of Armenia.

Yekmalian, Makar (1919). *Chants of the Divine Liturgy of the Armenian Apostolic Church*. Boston: Azk Press.

Jonathan McCollum

Music of Reconciliation

In Rwandan history and society, music has always played a very important role. In this society, where history has been kept through spoken rather than written words, music has been one essential tool of keeping memory alive. However, music has been used in both a negative and positive way. During the 1994 genocide, music was used to initiate hatred and terror against the Tutsi minority and Tutsi-friendly Hutus. The rhythm of hate speech was broadcast daily on Radio Television Mille Collines (RTMC), a popular, nationalist-oriented but unofficial Hutu radio station based in Rwanda's capital city, Kigali. RTMC offered music that was not allowed to be played on official radio, including extremist nationalist folk music by Hutu singers. Lyrics dealt with the superiority of the Hutu race and encouraged people to kill their Tutsi neighbors. A single extremist song might be played ten or fifteen times a day, so people could learn its lyrics by heart. During the 1994 genocide, the role of music used in this manner had been to incite hatred and separation within communities.

The sound of music, its lyrics and rhythms, is used in to achieve the opposite goal—to bring together communities that had once been driven apart. For instance, in 2002, Rwanda's government, under President Paul Kagame, established traditional courts to hear the trials of genocide suspects. In support of this effort, the radio aired a folksong with lyrics such as, "Now, here they are: the *Gacaca* tribunals. The tribunals, which should help to strengthen reconciliation and unity." The song explains the idea of the popular courts and their procedures to listeners, and exhorts the people to cooperate: "My dear fellow countryman, witness of the tragedy without name. Tell the truth. Tell who is innocent and who is guilty." Most such songs are broadcast on national radio, Radio Rwanda, as part of a campaign to sensitize the population of the upcoming court procedures.

During the actual court hearings, music has been used by the suspects to ask the audience for merciful treatment. Usually, the prisoners, dressed in rose-colored prison uniforms, start to dance and sing together before the start of the hearing. They sing about what they have done and ask the survivors and families of the victims for forgiveness. In other cases, prisoners sing about being wrongly arrested and they plead their innocence. When the singing ends, the actual court proceeding starts. Singing and dancing is here seen as one way of building a bridge between perpetrators and victims.

Another way that music is used in reconciling the communities torn apart by genocide is found in the government-sponsored reintegration or solidarity camps. Under the supervision of the Rwanda Demobilization and Reintegration Commission and the National Unity and Reconciliation Commission, these camps were installed to prepare surrendered or captured combatants from armed groups for their return to civil society. These former members of the Forces Armées Rwandaises and Interahamwe militias carried out most of the 1994 Rwandan genocide and fled to neighboring countries after the fall of the regime. On their return to Rwanda they are required to stay in a solidarity camp for several weeks, during which time they receive counseling, medical screening, and psychological treatment. They are also taught—and are required to sing—songs with lyrics like: "We are no Hutus, we are no Tutsis. We are all Rwandese now." Most of the camp songs are about peace, unity, and how to live together. Through these songs, former soldiers are asked to learn the new framework of the state: a reunited, reconciled Rwanda.

The benefit of using music in order to overcome a difficult past is especially important while reaching out to young people. The youth of Rwanda have suffered greatly from the genocide. Many youngsters, especially those from a poor background, were recruited by the militias at the time of the genocide. According to World Bank figures, there were more than three thousand former child-combatants who had to be reintegrated into society. Most of them had to learn how to live as children again. They were sent to special camps and schools, where they were undergoing sensitization and counseling activities.

Singing and dancing have been used with good effect to help these children to cope with their difficult past. In 2004 many of them, as well as the thousands of children who lost their families to the slaughter, still live in orphanage centers throughout the country. Music projects involving modern dance or hip hop music have been set up to give young people their own voices and to help them overcome the traumas of their past. All forms of artistic expression—theatre plays, music bands, dancing—have been integrated into projects by various non-governmental organizations working in Rwanda as well. The Kimisagara Youth Centre on the outskirts of Kigali, for instance, offers children and teenagers singing and dancing classes in which they can talk about their past and their future.

Music can strengthen unity and reconciliation, but it has to be seen as only one aspect within a wider framework of understanding and overcoming the legacy of the Rwandan genocide. It is not by singing, "We are all Rwandese now" that the history of the genocide can be properly commemorated. Critics of the government's reconciliation strategies have already made this point by demanding that the lessons of recent history must be learned in order for all of Rwanda's citizens to learn to live together again. However, music can contribute to opening the hearts and minds of the people: it can play a role in reaching out to victims, survivors, and perpetrators, and it can help to keep the memory of the past and the hope of a better future alive.

SEE ALSO Hate Speech; Music, Holocaust Hidden and Protest; Music and Musicians Persecuted during the Holocaust; Music of the Holocaust; Propaganda; Radio Television Mille-Collines; Reconciliation; Rwanda

Tania Krämer

Music of the Holocaust

From 1933 to 1945 Nazi ideologues devised and implemented schemes whereby music could be used to further their goals. Their propaganda promoted the idea of German superiority in the art of composition and the inferiority of any music touched by Jews.

For centuries many German non-Jews had considered Jews to be culturally inferior. In his article "Das Judenthum in der Musik" (Judaism in Music), the composer Richard Wagner wrote, "The Jew speaks the modern European languages merely as learned, and not as mother tongues. This must necessarily prevent him from any capability of therein expressing himself idiomatically, independently and comfortably to his nature. Our entire European art and civilization have remained a foreign tongue to the Jew" (1850/1995, p. 84). Wagner also decried the influence of Jewish conductors and music critics: "The Jew . . . has been able to reach the rulership of public taste in the widest spread of modern art forms, especially in music" (1850/1995, p. 87).

Eighty years later Adolf Hitler wrote, "I have the most intimate familiarity with Wagner's mental processes. At every stage of my life I come back to him" (Rose, 1992, p. 182). Indeed, the Nazis carried out Wagner's theories in a way that had never been done before. In 1933 the *Reichsmusikkammer* (National Ministry of Music) introduced a succession of policies aimed at protecting Aryan culture. All Jewish music teachers, performers, composers, and musicologists were expelled from their posts. Music composed or performed by Jews was banned from concert programs and broadcasts; their recordings and sheet music were removed from stores; textbooks were revised to remove offending references to their accomplishments. In 1938 Hans Ziegler organized an exhibit of degenerate music (*Entartete Musik*) in Düsseldorf. Visitors to the exhibit could see and hear examples of what Ziegler called "the artistic aspects of Cultural Bolshevism . . . and the triumph of Jewish impudence" (Levi, 1994, p. 96).

The Nazis also used music to control prisoners in concentration camps. An orchestra of Jewish inmates was created to play joyous music to distract new arrivals as they disembarked from trains and awaited selection, and to perform rousing marches to energize prisoners as they marched off to forced labor. The performers were rewarded with extra rations of food, better clothing, and more humane living conditions; they were temporarily spared from the murderous work details and the crematorium itself.

In one camp the Nazis organized extensive musical activities. In November 1941 the Nazis evacuated Theresienstadt (in Czech Terezín) and transformed that ancient walled city into a huge holding pen for the Jews of Czechoslovakia until they could be shipped to death camps. At first the Nazis organized cultural activities to promote calm among ghetto residents and to distract them from their fate. However, a year later they decided to use Theresienstadt as a "model camp," a facade to hide the truth of the extermination of European Jewry. There were choirs, chamber ensembles, orchestras, opera companies, a cabaret, and a jazz band called the Ghetto Swingers. The Nazis allowed inspectors from the International Committee of the Red Cross (ICRC) to visit Theresienstadt, where they were shown gardens, schools, concerts, and cafés. The prisoners' performances were even featured in a Nazi propaganda film. But, in fact, of the 140,000 men, women, and children who were sent to Theresienstadt, only 11,000 survived.

Composition and performance thrived at Theresienstadt, not merely because it was enforced, but because it provided spiritual uplift. Ghetto residents eagerly participated in various activities, led by some of Europe's most prominent composers and performers, including Karel Ancerl, Karel Berman, Pavel Haas, Gideon Klein, Paul Kling, Hans Krása, Rafael Schächter, Zikmund Schul, and Viktor Ullmann. Ullmann declared, "Terezin served to enhance, not to impede, my musical activities. By no means did we sit weeping on the banks of the waters of Babylon. Our endeavor with respect to Art was commensurate with our will to live" (Bloch, 1979, p. 162).

Jews also used music as a means of protest, satire, and warning. At Theresienstadt Ullmann and Peter Kien collaborated on *Der Kaiser von Atlantis* (The Emperor of Atlantis), an opera that satirized Hitler and the Nazi death machinery. A pogrom in the village of Przytik inspired the Polish singer Mordecai Gebirtig to compose "Es Brent" (It's Burning), a song that warns of the dangers of passivity in the face of oppression. In the Sachsenhausen concentration camp, Martin Rosenberg wrote "Jüdischer Todessang" (Jewish Death-Song) for his clandestine chorus of twenty-five prisoners when they were about to be sent to the Auschwitz death camp. Rosenberg hoped that his song would survive and thus inform the free world of this horror.

For others music served as a means of expressing unbearable sadness. Mothers sang lullabies to their children not only to soothe the youngsters' spirits, but also to be unburdened of their own anguish. In songs such as "Shtiller Shtiller" (Quiet, quiet) or "Nit Keyn Rozhinkes" (No more raisins), a disturbing mixture of comfort (addressed to a baby) and despair (spoken to oneself) exists.

Those who wished to maintain their faith and hope developed their own songs, too. Even in the face of death, some Jews sang of their ultimate faith in God and the goodness of humankind with "Ani Ma'amin" (I believe) and "Zol Shoyn Kumen Di Ge'uleh" (Let our redemption come soon). And throughout Europe Jews found courage in the words of Hirsh Glick's partisan anthem "Zog Nit Keyn Mol" (Never say this is the end).

Music also served as an antidote to the dehumanizing tactics to which the Jews were subjected. While Nazis were branding them as subhuman, Jews used music to affirm their humanity. When they were barred from attending public concerts, they formed their own orchestras. When they were prohibited from leaving their homes at night, they organized clandestine concerts there. In the Vilna (Vilnius) ghetto Jewish musicians, artists, writers, and poets formed the Literary Artistic Circle, which met nearly every week throughout the war for lectures, discussions, and concerts. They declared, "Our bodies may be enslaved, but our souls are not." Music allowed the condemned to cling to life. As Theresienstadt survivor Greta Hofmeister stated so eloquently, "Music! Music was life!" (Karas, 1985, p. 197).

SEE ALSO Music, Holocaust Hidden and Protest; Music and Musicians Persecuted during the Holocaust; Music of Reconciliation

BIBLIOGRAPHY
Basart, Ann (1986). "Music and the Holocaust: A Selective Bibliography." *Cum notis variorum* 101:1–30.
Bergmeier, Hort, Ejal Jakob Eisler, and Rainer Lotz (2001). *Vorbei: Beyond Recall. A Record of Jewish Musical Life in*

Nazi Berlin 1933–1938. Hambergen: Bear Family Records.

Bloch, Max (1979). "Viktor Ullmann: A Brief Biography and Appreciation." *Journal of the Arnold Schoenberg Institute* 3(2):150–177.

Jacobson, Joshua (1995). "Music in the Holocaust." *The Choral Journal* 36(5):9–21.

Jacobson, Joshua (2000). "Tsen Brider: A Jewish Requiem." *The Musical Quarterly* 84(3):452–474.

Kalisch, Shoshana (1985). *Yes, We Sang.* New York: Harper and Row.

Karas, Joza (1985). *Music in Terezín.* New York: Beaufort Books.

Newman, Richard, with Karen Kirtley (2000). *Alma Rosé: Vienna to Auschwitz.* Portland, Ore.: Amadeus Press.

Rose, Paul Lawrence (1992). *Wagner: Race and Revolution.* New Haven, Conn.: Yale University Press.

Wagner, Richard (1995). *Judaism in Music and Other Essays,* tran. William Ashton Ellis. Lincoln: University of Nebraska Press.

RECORDINGS

Hear Our Voices: Songs from the Ghettos and the Camps. HaZamir HZ-009. Music from Theresienstadt, Vilna, Vishnetz, Sachsenhausen, and Pryztik.

Krása, Hans. *Brundibar: A Children's Opera in Two Acts.* Arabesque Recordings Z6680.

Kulisiewicz, Aleksander. *Songs from the Depths of Hell.* Folkways FSS 37700.

Ullmann, Viktor. *Der Kaiser von Atlantis.* London 440 854-2.

VIDEO

The Führer Gives a City to the Jews (1944). Produced by the Ministry of Propaganda of the Third Reich. Available from the National Center for Jewish Film.

Joshua Jacobson

Namibia (German South West Africa and South West Africa)

Prior to the establishment of German South West Africa in 1884, a number of African states and peoples, including the Herero and Ovambo, had established themselves within the territory that would eventually become the Republic of Namibia in 1990. By the early 1840s Oorlam raiders, who had originated on the Cape's colonial frontier in what is presently South Africa, governed a string of small but highly centralized multiethnic polities in southern and central Namibia. In so doing, they conquered and incorporated the Khoisan-speaking Nama communities that had existed there before.

In the late 1860s, as Oorlam hegemony in central and southern Namibia crumbled, disenfranchised Basters (the term used to refer to the descendents of Africans and Europeans) from the Cape Colony trekked into central Namibia and established an independent Trekker republic centered in Rehoboth on the southern fringes of Hereroland. Alarmed by the establishment of this republic, Herero chieftains appealed for the establishment of a British protectorate over central Namibia. In 1876, anxious not to incur any excessive costs, Britain declared a protectorate over the immediate environs of Walvis Bay.

The late 1870s and early 1880s saw the reemergence of Nama polities in southern and eastern central Namibia. In southern Namibia, Hendrik Witbooi, the son of the chieftain of Gibeon, claimed to have received a vision from God, which instructed him

to trek north with his followers to a promised land. As Witbooi trekked north, he and his followers were ambushed and driven off by Herero. As a result of this attack, Witbooi unleashed an unrelenting guerrilla war on the Herero. At the same time a German entrepreneur, Adolf Luderitz, sought to acquire land rights along the Namibian coast. In early 1884 the imperial German government granted protectorate status to lands acquired by Luderitz by means which it knew to be fraudulent. Shortly thereafter Germany annexed the Namibian coast, with the exception of Walvis Bay, from the Orange River in the south to the Cunene in the north. To fulfill the conditions agreed to at the Berlin conference in 1884, German officials were sent to central Namibia in 1885 to sign protection treaties with Namibian leaders. In the immediate aftermath of an attack by Witbooi forces, Maharero Tjamuaha, the most powerful of the Herero chiefs, agreed to sign a protection treaty with the Germans. Although the treaty proved to be ineffective in terms of protection, and the Herero annulled it and expelled the German officials from their territory in 1888, it proved to be the basis for further German involvement in Namibia.

In 1889 German troops landed at Walvis Bay and seized control of the trade routes leading from the coast into the interior. Thus cut off from arms and under continual attack from Witbooi's forces, the majority of Herero withdrew from central Namibia. In 1890 Tjamuaha died. In the ensuing succession dispute his son, Samuel Maharero, was able to mobilize German support against his Herero rivals, as well as the forces of Witbooi. In 1894 the future German governor, Theo-

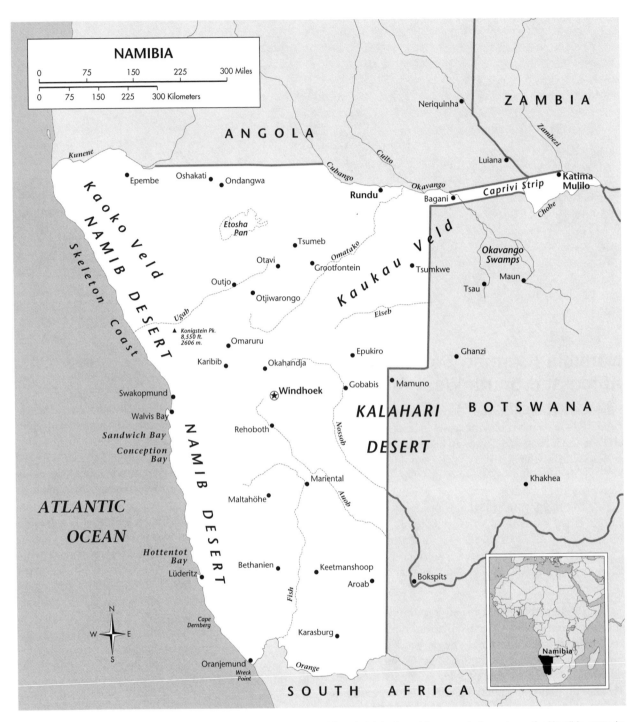

Map of Namibia. It was not until 1988 that South Africa agreed to end its administration of the area. Independence for Namibia came in 1990 following multiparty elections. [EASTWORD PUBLICATIONS DEVELOPMENT]

dor Leutwein, arrived in the territory. Through a mixed policy of divide and rule, and cooperation with a number of local chiefs at the expense of others, Leutwein was able to expand German control over the territory to the south of the Etosha pan. The rinderpest epidemic and ensuing drought and famine of 1897 and 1898 shattered the pastoral and pastro-forager economies of the indigenous communities of Namibia. Chiefs, who in the past had already sold large tracts of land to European settlers, were forced to sell more of their land and supply a greater number of their subjects as laborers to the new colonial economy.

In early 1904, following a series of misunderstandings, war broke out. Under the command of General Lothar von Trotha, the German army waged a genocidal war against the Herero. An estimated 80 percent of the Herero died as they were summarily hung or shot, driven to die of thirst in the *Omaheke* region of the Kalahari desert, or incarcerated in concentration camps. At the same time that a *Vernichtungsbefehl* (extermination order) against the Herero was issued in October 1904, the Nama chieftains in southern Namibia, under the command of Witbooi, waged war against the Germans. Nama survivors were also driven into concentration camps, deported to Togo and Cameroon, and forced to work as laborers under harsh conditions. An estimated 75 percent of the Nama were killed, and though some Nama leaders continued a guerilla war until 1908, the Nama, too, were defeated. After the war all Nama and Herero above the age of eight had to wear numbered metal tags, were prohibited from owning cattle or land, and were constrained within a web of inhumane labor laws.

Independent African chiefs and chieftains ceased to exist in German South West Africa. Bureaucrats euphemistically referred to the destruction of Nama and Herero societies as having been dissolved (*aufgelöst*). German civilian administrators, in view of labor needs within the colonial economy, opposed the wholesale extermination of African societies, but were overruled by the military and the German emperor, Kaiser Wilhelm II.

German administrators attempted to establish a single amorphous African working class bereft of, and indeed prohibited from having, an ethnic and cultural identity beyond that deemed acceptable to the colonial state. Lands cleared of African occupants were allocated as ranch lands to German settlers, many of whom had served as soldiers in the Herero and Nama wars. In 1908 diamonds were discovered in southern Namibia, and along with the already established copper and zinc mines in northern Namibia, this led to a blossoming of the Namibian colonial economy. An extreme shortage of labor in the colony due to the wars resulted in the recruitment of a large labor force from the northern territory of Ovamboland. There a rising population, declining hunting and export opportunities, as well as frequent battles with the Portuguese colonial armies in southern Angola, had led to economic hardship and impoverishment.

In the context of World War I, troops from the Union of South Africa invaded Namibia in 1915 and defeated the German troops. With the end of German rule in the territory, thousands of Herero and Nama left their sites of employment and migrated back to their ancestral homes. Ovambo, fleeing south in the face of extreme drought in Ovamboland, replaced them as the labor force. Anxious to extend their control over Ovamboland, something that Germany had not done, Union forces defeated and killed Mandume, the Kwanyama king in 1917.

By 1918 Nama and Herero had reacquired substantial herds of cattle and were able to pressure the new South African administration into assigning reserves to them. Following the Treaty of Versailles, Namibia was granted to South Africa as a class C mandate; while legally separate, in reality it became a fifth province of the Union of South Africa.

Throughout the 1920s South Africa sought to strengthen its hold over Namibia, in part through the resettlement of Afrikaner families on newly created farms in central Namibia. African resistance to the continued dominance of German missionaries in their churches led the majority of the Herero and Nama to establish independent Ethiopian churches. Dissatisfaction with the new South African administration meant that organizations such as the Universal Negro Improvement Association (UNIA), as well as the Industrial and Commercial Workers Union of South Africa, were able to quickly and extensively mobilize in the territory. However, airplanes and brute force crushed all serious opposition, such as the Bondelswarts revolt in southern Namibia in 1922, the Rehoboth rebellion in central Namibia in 1924, and the Ukuambi revolt under Ipumbu in northern Namibia in 1935.

Although Namibian soldiers had died fighting fascism in World War II, this did not prevent the election of the Nationalist Party in the 1948 South African elections. Intent on acquiring Namibia as a fifth province, the South African government sought to convince the outside world that Namibia's population had agreed to their formal incorporation into the Union of South Africa. Hosea Komombumbi Kutako was able to successfully mobilize opposition to the intended annexation of Namibia. In one of its first acts after being created, the United Nations (UN) rejected South Africa's claim, but South Africa prohibited a UN commission from visiting the territory and prevented Herero delegates from presenting the Nambian case to the General Assembly.

In the 1940s the African Improvement Society, a direct descendent of the UNIA, was founded primarily among Herero intellectuals. It was partly from these same ranks that in 1959 the South West African National Union (SWANU) evolved. In Cape Town Ovambo migrant laborers, inspired by the Congress movement in South Africa, formed the Ovambo People's Congress. In 1958 OPC leader Andimba Toivo Ja Toivo was deported to Namibia, where in 1959 he founded the Ovamboland Peoples Organisation, which later became the South West African Peoples Organisation (SWAPO).

In keeping with apartheid legislation, the South African administration set about clearing so-called black spots; Africans were cleared off lands and deported to new so-called homelands and locations. In December 1959 more than ten people protesting their forced removal from the capital city of Windhoek were shot. In the ensuing crackdown many SWANU and SWAPO members fled the country. Undaunted, the South African administration continued its apartheid policies and established the Odendaal Commission, which recommended "further extending apartheid throughout the Territory and to make it the basic political, economic and social principle of South Africa." In 1966 SWAPO guerrillas entered northern Namibia and an armed struggle against South African rule began. In 1971 and 1972 wildcat strikes in the mining industry marked a turning point in the territory itself.

In 1973 some one hundred member states of the UN, with the notable exception of a few European states and the United States, adopted the International Convention on the Suppression and Punishment of the Crime of Apartheid. With the independence of Angola in 1975, SWAPO forces became more effective. This, coupled with the continued petitioning activities of SWAPO at the UN, forced the colonial administration into reaching an internal settlement advantageous to South Africa.

The South African administration organized the Turnhalle Conference beginning in 1975. Namibians appointed by the South African powers to serve as representatives of administration-defined ethnic communities were expected to form the local authorities within the constraints of apartheid. Petty apartheid laws, such as the mixed marriages act were abolished, yet legislation continued to be applied on the basis of race. Control and ultimate power remained in the hands of the newly appointed South African administrator general.

In 1977 all Namibian men above the age of seventeen became eligible for conscription in the South West African Territorial Force, formed as a South African proxy force in the territory. By 1980 there were an estimated 80,000 men bearing arms in the service of the South African government in a territory populated by little more than a million people. An estimated 100,000 Namibians fled to neighboring states. Operating out of northern Namibia, South Africa sought to eliminate SWAPO bases in southern Angola and became directly involved in the Angolan civil war. Northern Namibia was transformed into a war zone in which all forms of

civil government and administration were ended and made subservient to the South African military.

In the war both sides committed numerous human rights abuses. South African forces, which ranged from regular conscripted soldiers, to shadowy para-militaries and officially sanctioned death squads, freely roamed northern Namibia and southern Angola. In cross-border raids South African forces targeted refugee camps and killed thousands of civilians. Within the war zone thousands of people were detained without formal charge and were tortured. Thousands more were forced to move from their homes. In this manner the whole of the northern strip of Caprivi was cleared of its civilian population. No less than 10 percent of the Namibian population fled into exile, and thousands of people disappeared without a trace. During the course of South Africa's Truth and Reconciliation Commission meetings, it was revealed that many people captured and detained without charge or trial in Namibia and southern Angola had been thrown out of aircraft into the Atlantic Ocean. In addition, many others had been summarily executed and left in the bush, or buried in unmarked graves.

The People's Liberation Army of Namibia (PLAN), the military wing of SWAPO, also committed human rights abuses in its operations from bases in Angola and Zambia. In internal feuds and spy-scares, hundreds of SWAPO members were detained, tortured, and killed. In the interests of propaganda hundreds of young recruits were sent to their certain death on military operations doomed to failure. Within the organization all forms of dissent were prohibited and silenced. As with the thousands of missing attributed to South Africa, many hundreds of Namibians who were detained by SWAPO are still unaccounted for.

Between 1977 and 1989 the Namibian economy went into decline, and the country's gross domestic product, an estimated $1 billion, barely covered the annual military expenditure. At the same time the South African economy continued to decline, in part because of international boycotts and sanctions. Social expenditure was equally high; in 1986 an estimated 2,500 white South African soldiers lost their lives—this coupled with continued urban unrest in South Africa served to bring about less and less support for government policies from the white electorate. In 1988 Angolan government forces, supported by Cuban forces and SWAPO guerrillas, were able to turn the tide and inflict a heavy defeat on South African forces at Cuito Cuanavale in southern Angola.

In April 1989, on the basis of UN Security Council Resolution 435, the United Nations Transition Assistance Group (UNTAG), operating in conjunction with the South African administrator general, took over the administration of Namibia. A UN-supervised ceasefire got off to a shaky start as UNTAG forces were unable to confine South African forces to base and prevent them from attacking SWAPO guerrillas seeking to report to UNTAG forces. Subsequently, elections under UN monitoring took place. SWAPO won 57 percent of the vote and representatives were chosen for an assembly authorized to draft and adopt a constitution guaranteeing minority, property, civil, human, and religious rights. South African troops were withdrawn, and on March 21, 1990, Namibia gained its independence as the South African flag was lowered and the new Namibian flag raised in the national stadium.

Independent Namibia has been largely peaceful and able to establish good relations with its neighbors. Walvis Bay, Namibia's sole deep-water harbor, was handed over to Namibia shortly after independence and is being developed as a free trade zone. Following independence, tourism expanded with an average annual growth of 30 percent. Together with relative industrial stability and continued investor confidence, this ensured the Namibian economy showing an average growth of 2 percent in the first five years of independence. Unfortunately, since the elections in 1995, the rule of law in Namibia has come under increasing threat. In 1996, without parliament's approval, soldiers of the Namibian Defence Force (NDF) were deployed in the war in the Democratic Republic of Congo. That same year the Special Field Force (SFF), a Namibian para-military force of demobilized PLAN fighters, started operating in northern Namibia and southern Angola. More often than not, SFF operated beyond the rule of law, with numerous documented cases of murder, torture, rape, and detention without trial. In 1996 the Namibian government entered into a dispute with Botswana regarding the delineation of their common border. In 1998 the regional government of Liambezi (formerly Caprivi) sought refugee status in Botswana, and in 1999 a political uprising in Liambezi was brutally suppressed by NDF and SFF forces. Human rights organizations have reported the reestablishment of detention centers, and there are numerous reports of detentions without trial. Another major problem is land distribution—over 85 percent of arable land remains in the hands of white settlers or their descendants, creating hardship and resentment.

The territories and peoples incorporated within the republic of Namibia, formerly known as South West Africa, have a long and troubled history of human rights abuse and ethnic conflict. As of 2004 Namibia stands at a historical juncture: It may descend even further into a spiral of even more blatant human rights abuses,

or return to the stability and rule of law that were attained with independence in 1990.

SEE ALSO Apartheid; Herero; Historical Injustices; Slavery, Historical; South Africa

BIBLIOGRAPHY

Dierks, Klaus (1999). *Chronology of Namibian History: From Pre-Historical Times to Independent Nambia.* Windhoek: Namibia Scientific Society.

Emmett, Tony (1999). *Popular Resistance and the Roots of Nationalism in Namibia, 1915–1966.* Basel, Switzerland: Schlettwein Publishing.

Gewald, Jan-Bart (1999). *Herero Heroes: A Socio-Political History of the Herero of Namibia 1890–1923.* Athens: Ohio University Press.

Henning, Melber, ed. (2003). *Re-Examining Liberation in Namibia: Political Culture since Independence.* Uppsala, Sweden: Nordic Africa Institute.

Saul, John, and Colin Leys, eds. (1995). *Namibia's Liberation Struggle: The Two-Edged Sword.* Athens: Ohio University Press.

Serfontein, J. H. P. (1976). *Namibia.* Randburg, South Africa: Suid Publishers.

Siegfried, Groth (1995). *Namibia the Wall of Silence: The Dark Days of the Liberation Struggle.* Wuppertal, Germany: Peter Hammer Verlag.

Silvester, Jeremy, and Jan-Bart Gewald, eds. (2003). *Words Cannot Be Found: German Colonial Rule in Namibia, an Annotated Reprint of the 1918 Blue Book.* Boston: Brill.

Jan-Bart Gewald

National Groups see Ethnic Groups; Minorities.

Nationalism

The twentieth century has been defined as the century of nationalism and genocide. How intense is the relationship between the two, given the fact they so often tend to occur simultaneously? Nationalism is the doctrine that "the rulers should belong to the same ethnic (that is, national) group as the ruled" (Gellner, 1983, p. 1). The doctrine assumes that a ruler belonging to an alien nationality or ethnic group is not fully legitimate. However, the inverse formula is a sure recipe for ethnic cleansing, mass deportation, and genocide: to claim that the inhabitants of a specific constituency must share the same ethnic lineage as its leaders is effectively to give full legitimacy to the mass expulsion of different ethnicity and the drastic redrawing of boundaries to suit the group's pedigree. Nationalism also holds that "nation and political power should be congruent" (Gellner, 1983, p. 1). This longing for congruence, or ethnopolitical purity, is the historical hall-mark of most nationalist attempts to erase ethnic distinctiveness by homogenizing entire populations.

Nationalism is a modern Western phenomenon that has mutated and adapted its chameleonic shape according to geography and history. Industrialization, accompanied or preceded by state militarism, changed the shape of the world forever. Nationalism in the post-industrializing era was most often accompanied by assimilationism and the elimination of minorities. The very assimilationist (hence intolerant) nature of the modern state has created the preconditions for turning its unprecedented powers against hapless minorities. Thus, the modern itinerary of genocide follows the spread of nationalism and modernity.

However, nationalism in itself cannot account for the worst episodes of genocide. Nationalism can only become fully lethal if it is infused with the power of the modern state. It is ultimately state power, with its repressive, bureaucratic, media, and military machine, that can account for the most tragic occurrences of genocide. Among other things, state institutions can define the criteria of citizenship. If the state's definition of citizenship is based on ethnicity, it can provide the basis for inciting intolerance, crimes against humanity, and even genocide.

The connection between Westernization, modernity, war, and genocide has become well established in academia. All of these terms are strictly related to both state formation and nationalism. Many Holocaust scholars describe genocide as an entirely modern phenomenon, with its unprecedented systematic technological dimension. Leon Poliakov, in his 1974 volume, *The Aryan Myth*, argued that the Nazis envisaged the Holocaust as a triumph of Western civilization, the latter being conceived in terms of racial superiority against spurious Oriental, non-Western influences. Genocide is therefore intensively related to European state expansion and interstate rivalry, including the state's intrusion into the private realm via the consolidation of central power. Patriotism and nationalism provided the state with its ideological glue and emotional underpinning.

The earliest avatar of this tragic trend was probably the Armenian genocide. Systematic pogroms had already occurred between 1894 and 1896, when Westernizing nationalism emerged as an influential force among Turkish elites. But the mass extermination campaigns that took place between 1914 and 1916 were unprecedented by any standard, and were the direct consequences of rapidly modernizing state structures emulating Western models in the wake of the Ottoman Empire's collapse. Young Turk army officials fought against victorious nationalist uprisings in the Balkans and ended up imitating them, while forging links with German and other nationalisms. In addition, the Young Turks' nationalist movement was inspired by, and mimicked, its post-1789 Western archetypes. Paradoxically, the main victim's of Turkey's secular and anti-Islamic nationalism were non-Muslim minorities that had previously enjoyed protection and prosperity under the more liberal consociational laws of the Ottoman Empire.

Historically, genocide occurred in the wake of both imperial expansion and its disintegration. Even before the conquest of the Americas, the fate of the indigenous Guanches of the Fortunate Islands (present-day Canaries) anticipated a pattern of European expansion leading to cultural destruction, environmental collapse, and physical extermination. Downsizing semi-authoritarian states or contracting autocratic empires, such as the French in Algeria during the 1950s or the Ottoman Empire in its death throes, also occasionally display genocidal behavior.

Typically, genocides have been carried out by modern totalitarian regimes (the Nazis, the Soviet Union, Saddam Hussein in Iraq, the Khmer Rouge in Cambodia) and authoritarian states (post-Ottoman Turkey, Slobodan Milosevic's Serbia, and Vladimir Putin's Russia). Most of these have used a patriotic defense of national security to justify the extermination of minorities. Dehumanization and demonization of the ethnically defined "other" are recurring harbingers and symptoms of genocide: "seeing or treating the other as a threat is . . . an intrinsic part of the process of genocide" (Rummel, 1994, p. 40). In the nationalist *Weltanschauung*, the main internal threat comes from the ethnically different, whether assimilated or not. Moreover, nationalist history typically attempts to erase all evidence that implies complicity in genocide, while exaggerating the pain that the ethnic in-group has had to undergo in one's own nation. Revisionism, denial, and a general temptation to forget inconvenient historical facts are therefore in-built into nationalist historiography.

Modern genocides and inter-ethnic wars are rarely, if ever, directed against wholly differentiated groups. With the exception of the Roma and several indigenous victims of imperial expansion, most nationalist-led mass murders are directed against minorities that are fully integrated and assimilated into the mainstream culture. Therefore, cultural factors are never in themselves a cause of genocide, nor any other form of political murder. Instead, the target victims are most frequently similar looking groups, often sharing the same language, outlook, and customs as their persecutors.

The Tutsis in Rwanda, the Croats and Muslims in Bosnia and the Jews in Nazi Germany were fully integrated into their societies and assimilated into the mainstream culture of their time. A possible counter-argument to this view may be the case of the *Porajmos* (the Gypsy Holocaust): The Roma were typically seen as a stateless people, and hence as incompatible with the nationalist project of an homogeneous nation-state. They have therefore often been targeted by nationalist regimes and ultra-nationalist groups.

The relationship between genocide and nationalism or patriotism is among the most powerful ones. The three terms have common roots (*genos*, from *gens*, meaning lineage; nation from the Latin *nasci*, meaning to be born; *patria* from the Latin *pater*, meaning father). They all relate to the idea of shared descent and of belonging into a single extended family. The exaltation by the state of a dominant nation as superior to all others inevitably leads to a series of discriminatory acts against competing stateless nations, ranging from assimilation and marginalization to genocide. The role of central governments and the military appears to be of key importance in most instances of genocide, in tandem with media censorship and popular misinformation. Globalization provides a third, still unexplored, item in a triangular relationship that includes nationalism and genocide. Like nationalism, globalization destroys whole communities and lifestyles, exerting unprecedented homogenizing pressures.

SEE ALSO Ethnic Cleansing; Ethnicity

BIBLIOGRAPHY

Bauman, Zygmunt (1989). *Modernity and the Holocaust.* Ithaca, N.Y.: Cornell University Press/Polity Press.

Cigar, Norman L. (1995). *Genocide in Bosnia: The Policy of "Ethnic Cleansing".* College Station: Texas A&M University Press.

Cohen, Stan (2000). *States of Denial: Knowing about Atrocities and Suffering.* Cambridge, U.K.: Polity.

Connor, Walker (2004). "Nationalism and Political Illegitimacy." In *Ethnonationalism in the Contemporary World*, ed. Daniele Conversi. London: Routledge.

Conversi, Daniele (1999). "Nationalism, Boundaries, and Violence." *Millennium: Journal of International Studies* 28(3):553–584.

Crosby, Alfred W. (1986). "The Fortunate Isles." In *Ecological Imperialism: The Biological Expansion of Europe, 900–1900.* Cambridge, U.K.: Cambridge University Press.

Cushman, Tom, and Stipe Mestrovic, eds. (1996). *This Time We Knew. Western Responses to the War in Bosnia.* New York: New York University Press.

Melson, Robert (1996). "The Armenian Genocide as Precursor and Prototype of Twentieth Century

Genocide." In *Is the Holocaust Unique?* ed. Alan S. Rosenbaum. Boulder, Colo.: Westview Press.

Poliakov, Leon (1974). *The Aryan Myth: A History of Racist and Nationalist Ideas in Europe.* London: Chatto & Windus Heinemann for Sussex University Press.

Rummel, R. J. (1994). *Death by Government.* New Brunswick, N.J.: Transactions Publishers.

Shaw, Martin (2003). *War and Genocide. Organized Killing in Modern Society.* Cambridge, U.K.: Polity Press.

Smith, Anthony D. (1998). *Nationalism and Modernism: A Critical Survey of Recent Theories of Nations and Nationalism.* London: Routledge.

Van den Berghe, Pierre, ed. (1990). *State, Violence, and Ethnicity.* Niwot, Colo.: University Press of Colorado.

Daniele Conversi

National Laws

Genocide, crimes against humanity, and war crimes are considered the core international crimes. The definition and penalization of these offenses date back to post–World War II instruments such as the Charter of the Nuremberg Tribunal, the 1948 Convention on the Prevention and Punishment of the Crime of Genocide, and the 1949 Geneva Conventions Relating to the Protection of Victims of Armed Conflict. Their legal origin is thus clearly international and relatively recent. In practice, genocide, the crime of crimes according to William Schabas, and crimes against humanity may encompass war crimes (see, e.g., the decisions of the International Criminal Tribunal for Rwanda [ICTR]). When genocide or crimes against humanity committed within the context of an armed conflict are involved, therefore, national war crimes legislation may apply as well.

Core International Crimes and National Law

States parties to the Genocide Convention undertake "to prevent and to punish" genocide (Article I) and "to enact . . . the necessary legislation to give effect to the provisions of the Convention and, in particular, to provide effective penalties for persons guilty of genocide . . ." (Article V). Article VI of the Convention provides that "[p]ersons charged with genocide . . . shall be tried by a competent tribunal of the State in the territory of which the act was committed, or by such international penal tribunal as may have jurisdiction with respect to those Contracting Parties which shall have accepted its jurisdiction." The international court envisaged in 1948 was established on July 1, 2002, when the Statute of the International Criminal Court (ICC) entered into force.

For war crimes the Geneva Conventions require adhering States "to enact any legislation necessary to provide effective penal sanctions for persons committing . . . any of the grave breaches of the present Convention. . . ." *Grave breaches*, the term used in the treaties, is understood to mean war crimes. States are also required to search for persons alleged to have committed, or to have ordered war crimes, and bring such persons, regardless of their nationality, before their own courts (Articles 49, 50, 129, and 146 of the four respective Geneva Conventions). Similar obligations exist for states who are parties to the Convention against Torture and Other Cruel, Inhuman or Degrading Treatment or Punishment (Articles 4, 5, 6, and 8).

Crimes against humanity, in contrast, are not the subject of a specific convention. A treaty obligation "to prevent and to punish'" therefore does not exist, but resolutions by intergovernmental bodies, such as the United Nations (UN) General Assembly, have called on states to do so.

International law thus traditionally has allowed but not consistently required states to prosecute and punish international crimes. This has led to piecemeal domestic legislation. However, the creation of the ICC, which is "complementary to national jurisdictions" (ICC Statute, Article 1) has been an impetus for states to review and consolidate their relevant laws.

National Laws and Decisions

The countries discussed below are examples of states that have rendered related legal decisions and enacted related legislation. These landmark judicial cases include:

> *Public Prosecutor v. Cvjetkovic.* (Austria.) Trial judgment, Landesgericht Salzburg (May 31, 1995); Appeals judgment, Oberste Gerichtshof (July 13, 1994).
>
> *Public Prosecutor v. the "Butare Four."* (Belgium.) Trial judgment, Assize Court of Brussels (June 8, 2001).
>
> *Regina v. Finta.* Trial judgment, 69 O.R.2d 557 (H.C. 1989), Ontario Court of Appeal (73 Canadian Criminal Case 3d 65; Ont. C.A.1992), Supreme Court of Canada [1994] 1 SCR 701 (March 24, 1994).
>
> *Sivakumar v. Canada.* Minister of Employment and Immigration, Federal Court of Canada, Court of Appeal, 1 F.C. 433, 163 N.R. 197, 44 A.C.W.S (3d) 563 (November 4, 1993).
>
> *Mugesera v. Minister of Citizenship and Immigration.* Immigration and Refugee Board, Adjudication Division, File No. QML-95-00171 (July 11, 1996).
>
> *Mugesera v. Canada.* Immigration and Refugee Board, Appeal Division, Case No's. M96-10465 and

M96-10466, Reasons and Order (November 6, 1998).

> *Mugesera et al. v. Canada.* Minister of Citizenship and Immigration, 4 FC 421 (TD) (2001).
>
> *Public Prosecutor v. Barbie.* (France.) Trial judgment, Assize Court of Rhône (July 4, 1987).
>
> *Public Prosecutor v. Touvier.* (France.) Trial judgment, Assize Court of Yvelines (April 20, 1994).
>
> *Public Prosecutor v. Papon.* (France.) Trial judgment, Assize Court of Gironde (April 2, 1998).
>
> *Attorney General of Israel v. Eichmann.* Trial judgment, District Court of Jerusalem (December 12, 1961); Appeals judgment, Supreme Court of Israel (May 29, 1962).
>
> *Attorney General of Israel v. Demjanjuk.* Trial judgment, District Court of Jerusalem (April 18, 1988); Appeals judgment, Supreme Court of Israel (July 29, 1993).
>
> *Unión Progresista de Fiscales de España et al. v. Pinochet.* (Spain.) Central Investigating Tribunal No. 5, Audiencia Nacional (October 16 and 18, November 3, 1998); Criminal Division, Plenary Session, Audiencia Nacional (November 5, 1998).
>
> *Menchú Tum et al. v. Montt et al.* (Guatemala.) Criminal Division, Plenary Session, Audiencia Nacional (December 13, 2000); Criminal Division, Supreme Court (February 25, 2003).
>
> *Military Prosecutor v. Niyonteze.* (Switzerland.) Trial judgment, Military Tribunal, Division 2, Lausanne (April 30, 1999); Appeals judgment, Appeals Military Court 1A, Geneva (May 26, 2000); Cassation judgment, Military Court of Cassation (April 27, 2001).

Austria

One of the first trials for genocide anywhere in the world was held in Austria. *Public Prosecutor v Cvjetkovic* arose out of the war and ethnic violence in the former Yugoslavia that occurred during the first half of the 1990s, which caused an influx of thousands of refugees, including Cvjetkovic, into Austria. According to the indictment, the accused, as military commander, was responsible for the ethnic cleansing of the Muslim section of the village of Kucice. He was charged with genocide and complicity in genocide. A jury acquitted him.

The genocide charges were brought under Sections 321 and 65(1), subparagraph 2, of the Austrian penal code. The former makes genocide a criminal offense; the latter provides that offenses committed abroad shall be punished in Austria "if the offender, though he was a foreigner at the time when he committed the offense, was found in this country and if, due to reasons different from the nature and characteristics of the offense, is not extradited to a foreign State." The foreign authorities were notified but did not respond, and the International Criminal Tribunal for the Former Yugoslavia (ICTY) declined to take over the proceedings.

Belgium

After years of controversy Belgium repealed in 2003 its Act Concerning Grave Breaches of International Humanitarian Law, which made the core international crimes punishable in Belgium, even when the offense had no direct connection to Belgium. In other words, formal prosecutions were possible even though the crime was committed outside of Belgium by someone of another nationality, none of the victims were Belgian, and the accused did not reside in Belgium. Application of this law to the actions of foreign officials led to several serious diplomatic incidents and litigation before the International Court of Justice (ICJ) (e.g., *Democratic Republic of the Congo v. Belgium*, April 2000, holding that an incumbent minister of foreign affairs is immune from criminal jurisdiction of other states).

The repeal of the act does not mean, however, that the core crimes, even when committed abroad, can no longer be prosecuted in Belgium. Indeed, while repealing the law, the legislator simultaneously introduced most of the act's substantive provisions into the criminal code (Article 136, *bis–octies*), while amendments to the code of criminal procedure establish the extraterritorial jurisdiction of Belgian courts, provided there is some connection with Belgium.

One successful prosecution occurred under the repealed act. *Public Prosecutor v. the "Butare Four"* arose out of the genocide against the Tutsi and the massacres of moderate Hutu in Rwanda during the armed conflict between government armed forces and a rebel army in 1994. The accused were among hundreds of Rwandans from both sides of the conflict who fled to Belgium. They were charged with war crimes, not crimes against humanity or genocide, most likely to avoid a possibly controversial retroactive application of the Act Concerning Grave Breaches of International Humanitarian Law, which back in 1994 did not include these offenses.

Canada

Canada was among the first countries to consolidate and harmonize its legislation regarding the core international crimes following ratification of the ICC Statute. Prosecutions in the early 1990s of alleged foreign war criminals (under repealed legislation) had all failed (e.g., *Regina v. Finta*). The Canadian government then proceeded with administrative procedures, especially denaturalization and deportation. Among the most well-known deportation cases are *Sivakumar v. Canada* (involving crimes against humanity committed by the Liberation Tigers of Tamil Eelam in Sri Lanka) and *Mugesera v. Minister of Citizenship and Immigration* (involving genocide against the Tutsi in Rwanda).

The 2000 Crimes against Humanity and War Crimes Act incorporates the provisions of the ICC Statute into Canadian legislation. Its twofold objective is to allow full cooperation with the ICC in matters of investigation and prosecution, and to increase national capacity and punish alleged perpetrators of genocide, crimes against humanity, and war crimes. Prosecution of extraterritorial offenses under the act always requires a link with Canada.

East Timor and Indonesia

After the people of East Timor voted in a UN-administered referendum for independence from Indonesia, the Indonesian National Army and Timorese militias launched a campaign of murder, arson, and forced expulsion (in September 1999). A UN commission of inquiry called for the establishment of an international tribunal.

Indonesia successfully staved off such a tribunal by promising to prosecute those responsible for the atrocities. To this end it created an ad hoc court with jurisdiction over genocide and crimes against humanity (Law No. 26/2000 on the Human Rights Court and Presidential Decree No. 53/2001). As of 2003, seventeen individuals, mostly senior civilian, police, and military officials, have been tried meanwhile in Jakarta for crimes against humanity. Twelve defendants were acquitted; five received prison sentences between three and ten years.

In East Timor a procedure was also created to prosecute Indonesians and Timorese responsible for the 1999 violence. The UN Transitional Administration in East Timor (UNTAET) created the Serious Crimes Investigative Unit, with an international staff, to investigate and prosecute crimes against humanity and other serious offenses before Special Panels for Serious Crimes of the newly created Dili District Court (UNTAET Regulation No. 15/2000). The trials before the Special Panels, which are composed of both Timorese and international judges, were still ongoing in late 2003. Dozens have been sentenced to prison terms ranging from eleven months to thirty-three years. Indonesia has refused to extradite any Indonesian for trial in East Timor.

Ethiopia

Ethiopia took part in the negotiations that led to the adoption of the Genocide Convention in 1948; it was the first nation to ratify the Convention on July 1, 1949. Its penal code of 1957 incorporates genocide and crimes against humanity in Article 281. However, in addition to the groups named in the Genocide Convention—national, ethnic, racial, or religious groups—Article 281 includes political groups.

These provisions have been the basis for the prosecution of the Dergue regime (1974–1991), infamous for its campaign of "Red Terror." After the overthrow of the Dergue, a Special Prosecutor's Office was established to investigate Dergue crimes and prosecute those responsible. Thousands were arrested and charged with genocide and war crimes.

Trials began in 1994. By mid-2004 only a fraction of the accused have been tried. Just over 1,500 decisions have been handed down, with 1,017 convictions. Some 6,000 defendants are still awaiting trial. Colonel Mengistu Haile Mariam, the Dergue leader, is being tried in absentia. He lives in exile in Zimbabwe.

France

Before March 1, 1994, crimes against humanity were incorporated in the French legal system by reference to the Nuremberg Principles (December 26, 1964). However, French case law restricted crimes against humanity to crimes committed within the context of World War II by or on behalf of the Axis powers, thus excluding possible French crimes during World War II, the Algerian War, and French operations in Indochina. In 1987 French courts convicted Klaus Barbie, the head of Gestapo in Lyon during the wartime occupation of France, as well as Vichy collaborators Paul Touvier (in 1994) and Maurice Papon (in 1998), of crimes against humanity for their activities during Word War II.

The penal code in force since March 1, 1994, includes crimes against humanity (Article 212-1) and genocide (Article 211-1). French courts are vested with extraterritorial jurisdiction, provided either the perpetrator or victim is a French national.

Following the establishment of the ICTY and ICTR, the French parliament adopted special cooperation laws that provide for French jurisdiction over all offenses falling within the competence of both tribunals, if the perpetrators are found in France. Despite credible information regarding the presence of Rwandan *génocidaires* in France, no prosecution of these individuals has so far taken place.

Germany

Germany is another country that has consolidated and harmonized its legislation regarding the core interna-

tional crimes following ratification of the ICC Statute. To align domestic law with the ICC Statute, Germany has opted for a unique solution: a national Code of Crimes Against International Law (*Völkerstrafgesetzbuch*) that makes the core ICC crimes offenses under domestic law, "even when the offense was committed abroad and bears no relation to Germany" (Article 1).

Prior to the Code of Crimes Against International Law's enactment, genocide was an offense under Section 6(1) of the ordinary penal code, regardless of the place of commission. On the basis of the repealed provision, four Bosnian Serbs (all at some point German residents) have been tried in Germany for their role in the ethnic cleansing that characterized the armed conflict in the former Yugoslavia during the first half of the 1990s. One of the defendants was acquitted of genocide because it was found that he lacked the necessary mens rea (or intent).

Iraq

After the overthrow of the Baathist regime by the United States and its allies, the Iraqi Governing Council established the Iraqi Special Tribunal for Crimes Against Humanity in December 2003. The tribunal has jurisdiction over Iraqi nationals or residents accused of genocide, crimes against humanity, war crimes, and violations of certain Iraqi laws, committed between July 1968 and May 2003, in Iraq or elsewhere. The tribunal's statute specifies its jurisdiction over crimes committed against the people of Iraq, "including its Arabs, Kurds, Turcomans, Assyrians and other ethnic groups, and its Shi'ites and Sunnis, whether or not committed in armed conflict" (Article 1b).

It is expected that the some of the captured Baath Party leaders, including former President Saddam Hussein, will be tried before the Special Tribunal.

Israel

As the new homeland of many Holocaust survivors, Israel was one of the first countries to enact legislation criminalizing serious violations of international humanitarian law. The Nazi and Nazi Collaborators (Punishment) Law of 1950 applies retroactively to certain offenses committed "in an enemy country" during the period of the Nazi regime or World War II. The principal offenses under the law are "crimes against the Jewish people", crimes against humanity, and war crimes (Article 1). The Crime of Genocide (Prevention and Punishment) Law of 1950 implements the Genocide Convention, granting universal jurisdiction to Israeli courts (Article 5).

Two foreigners as well as some Israeli citizens (former Jewish collaborators or *Kapos*) have been prosecuted under the Nazi and Nazi Collaborators (Punishment) Law for their role in the Holocaust. The most famous trials were those of Adolf Eichmann (in 1961) and John Demjanjuk (in 1987). Eichmann, the director of the Office of Jewish Affairs and Evacuation Affairs in the Third Reich, was abducted from Argentina by members of the Israel Secret Service. He was tried and sentenced to death for coordinating the Final Solution. Demjanjuk was accused of being Ivan the Terrible, the individual responsible for operating the gas chambers at the Treblinka death camp in Poland. His conviction was later overturned by the Israeli Supreme Court.

Rwanda

More than 100,000 individuals have been arrested on charges of participation in the 1994 genocide and massacres in the African nation of Rwanda. A special retroactive statute, Organic Law 8196 (Loi organique No. 8196 du 30/8/96 sur l'organisation des poursuites des infractions constitutives du crime de génocide ou de crimes contre l'humanité, commises à partir du 1er Octobre 1990) is the basis for their prosecution. The law classifies the perpetrators into four groups based on their degree of participation. For the first category of offenders (planners, organizers, instigators, supervisors, and zealots), the law mandates the death penalty. Note that the ICTR, which has primary jurisdiction, cannot impose the death penalty.

By 2001 fewer then five thousand suspects had been tried. To increase trial capacity, the government decided to resort to a customary institution, the *gacaca*. This system of participatory justice brings together all protagonists at the actual location of the crime, that is, the survivors, witnesses, and presumed perpetrators. All are asked to participate in a discussion of what happened in order to establish the truth, draw up a list of victims, and identify the guilty. These "debates" are chaired by nonprofessional judges elected from the men of the community who are deemed to have the most integrity. Suspects falling under the first category (estimated to be between three and ten thousand in number) will continue to be judged by the ordinary courts. For all other cases, the government has created approximately eleven thousand *gacaca* courts. They began their deliberations in 2002.

Spain

Genocide is an offense under Article 607 of the Spanish criminal code. Article 23.4(a) of the Organic Law of the Judicial Power (Ley Orgánica del Poder Judicial) provides that "Spanish courts have jurisdiction over acts [of genocide] committed abroad by Spaniards and foreigners." These provisions were the bases for criminal proceedings in Spain against former Chilean president Augustus Pinochet and former Guatemalan ruler General Efraín Ríos Montt. The characterization of the Pinochet regime's brutal repression of political opponents as genocide is questionable. The charges against Ríos Montt included acts of genocide committed against groups of Maya between 1981 and 1983 by Guatemalan state agents.

Neither of these cases ever went to trial. Pinochet, after his arrested in the United Kingdom at the request of Spain, was allowed to return to Chile on medical grounds. The proceedings against Ríos Montt came to an end when the Spanish Supreme Court held that "no particular State is in the position to unilaterally establish order, through resort to criminal law, against anyone and in the entire world, without their being some point of connection that renders legitimate the extension of extraterritorial jurisdiction."

Switzerland

To implement the Genocide Convention and take the "first step in the adaptation of Swiss law to the ICC Statute," Switzerland added Title 12*bis* to its penal code. As of 2003 Title 12bis only addresses genocide (Article 264), but it is expected that in a second phase the Swiss legislature will introduce the notion of crimes against humanity and possibly also revise the existing war crimes legislation.

In 1999 a Swiss tribunal successfully tried and convicted a Rwandan refugee for war crimes (*Military Prosecutor v. Niyonteze*). The prosecution also had charged the same defendant, the former mayor of Mushubati, with genocide and crimes against humanity for his role in the genocide against the Tutsi and massacres of moderate Hutu in Rwanda in 1994. For these counts the prosecution relied on customary international law, but the tribunal held that the notions of genocide and crimes against humanity under customary international law were not directly applicable in the Swiss legal system.

Former Yugoslavia

The conflicts in the former Yugoslavia in the 1990s will forever be associated with the practice of ethnic cleansing. However, few prosecutions for genocide have occurred in the various entities that comprised the former Yugoslavia, and this despite the fact that there were no legal hurdles, given that the crime of genocide had been defined and a punishment established pursuant to Article 141 of Yugoslavia's Criminal Law, which was in force when the conflict began (Schabas, 2003). As it turns out, more trials have taken place in third-party states (see the above sections on Austria and Germany) than in the former Yugoslavia.

The District Military Court of Bosnia and Herzego-vina, sitting in Sarajevo in 1993, convicted two defendants of genocide. A second trial reportedly took place in 1997 before the Osijek District Court in Cro-atia. The defendant there was sentenced to five years imprisonment for genocide pursuant to Article 119 of the Basic Criminal Law of the Republic of Croatia. In 2001 the Supreme Court of Kosovo reversed a genocide conviction by the District Court of Mitrovica on the grounds that

> The exactions committed by the Milosevic's [sic] regime in 1999 cannot be qualified as criminal acts of genocide, since their purpose was not the destruction of the Albanian ethnic group in whole or in part, but its forceful departure from Kosovo as a result of [sic] systematic campaign of terror including murders, rapes, arsons and se-vere maltreatments (Schabas, 2003, p. 56).

Conclusion

World War II–related cases aside, domestic prosecu-tions of the core international crimes are a recent phe-nomenon. In the wake of the creation of the ICTR, ICTY, and ICC, and spurred by a powerful internation-al human rights movement, national authorities have started to take the issue more seriously by considering measures such as the adoption or review of relevant laws, the training of law enforcement officials, and the establishment of special investigative units or tribunals. The list of countries and cases is likely to grow in the years to come.

SEE ALSO Barbie, Klaus; Bosnia and Herzegovina; Demjanjuk Trial; East Timor; Eichmann Trials; Ethiopia; Geneva Conventions on the Protection of Victims of War; Immunity; National Prosecutions; Pinochet, Augusto; Punishment; Ríos Montt, Efraín; Rwanda; Truth Commissions; Universal Jurisdiction

BIBLIOGRAPHY

Ambos, Kai, and S. Wirth (2001). "Genocide and War Crimes in the Former Yugoslavia before German Criminal Courts." In *International and National Prosecutions of Crimes under International Law. Current Developments*, ed. Horst Fischer, Claus Kress, and Sascha Rolf Lüder. Berlin: Berlin Verlag Arno Spitz.

Ambos, Kai, and S. Wirth (2002). "The Current Law of Crimes against Humanity. An Analysis of UNTAET Regulation 15/2000." *Criminal Law Forum* 13:1–90.

American University Washington College of Law, War Crimes Research Office. "Status Report for the Special Panels for Serious Crimes in East Timor." Available from http://www.wcl.american.edu/warcrimes/easttimor_status.cfm.

Amnesty International (2001). "Comments on the Law on Human Rights Courts (Law No. 26/2000) (Indonesia)."

AI Index No. ASA 21/005/2001. http://news.amnesty.org/library/index/engasa210052001

Brody, R., and M. Ratner, eds. (2000). *The Pinochet Papers. The Case of Augusto Pinochet in Spain and Britain*. The Hague: Kluwer Law International.

Cottier, M. (2001). "What Relationship between the Exercise of Universal Jurisdiction and Territorial Jurisdiction? The Decision of 13 December 2000 of the Spanish National Court Shelving the Proceedings against Guatemalan Nationals Accused of Genocide." In *International and National Prosecutions of Crimes under International Law. Current Developments*, ed. Horst Fischer, Claus Kress, and Sascha Rolf Lüder. Berlin: Berlin Verlag Arno Spitz.

Engelschiøn, T. S. (1994). "Prosecution of War Crimes and Violations of Human Rights in Ethiopia." *Yearbook of African Law* 8:41–56.

Human Rights Watch. "Justice Denied for East Timor. Indonesia's Sham Prosecutions, the Need to Strengthen the Trial Process in East Timor, and the Imperative of UN Action." Available from http://www.hrw.org/backgrounder/asia/timor/etimor1202bg.htm.

Mayfield, J. V. (1995). "The Prosecution of War Crimes and Respect for Human Rights: Ethiopia's Balancing Act." *Emory International Law Review* 9:553–593.

Reydams, Luc (2002). "Niyonteze v Public Prosecutor." *American Journal of International Law* 96:231–236.

Reydams, Luc (2003a). "Belgium Reneges on Universality: The 5 August 2003 Act on Grave Breaches of International Humanitarian Law." *Journal of International Criminal Justice* 1:679–689.

Reydams, Luc (2003b). "Belgium's First Judicial Application of Universal Jurisdiction: The Butare Four Case." *Journal of International Criminal Justice* 1:428–436.

Reydams, Luc (2003c). *Universal Jurisdiction: International and Municipal Legal Perspectives*. Oxford: Oxford University Press.

Sadat Wexler, L. (1994). "The Interpretation of the Nuremberg Principles by the French Court of Cassation: From Touvier to Barbie and Back Again." *Columbia Journal of Transnational Law* 32:288–380.

Schabas, W. A. (2000). "Canadian Implementing Legislation for the Rome Statute." *Yearbook of International Humanitarian* 3:337–346.

Schabas, W. A. (2003). "National Courts Finally Begin to Prosecute Genocide, the 'Crime of Crimes.'" *Journal of International Criminal Justice* 1:39–63.

Wenig, J. M. (1997). "Enforcing the Lessons of History: Israel Judges the Holocaust." In *The Law of War Crimes. National and International Approaches*, ed. T. L. H. McCormack and G. J. Simpson. The Hague: Kluwer Law International.

Luc Reydams

National Prosecutions

States exercise domestic criminal jurisdiction over indi-viduals for the commission of genocide, war crimes, and crimes against humanity (hereinafter "the major crimes") committed within their own territory or by nationals of the state. In addition to prosecutions in domestic criminal courts, states have tried perpetrators of major crimes before military tribunals; conducted special inquiries, generally of a non-criminal nature; held truth and reconciliation commissions; and granted limited or general amnesties. Other venues for prosecuting alleged breaches of these offences include ad hoc international criminal tribunals, the International Criminal Court (ICC), and criminal courts of other states prosecuting perpetrators pursuant to some form of extraterritorial jurisdiction.

Domestic Criminal Jurisdiction

The purpose of prosecution is to punish the perpetrator and provide the victim with a measure of satisfaction, thus reducing the victim's desire to seek revenge. Prosecution ensures that a state's laws, and the value system underlying them, are respected, and demonstrates the state's, and (by extension) the people's, abhorrence for the offence. The consistent prosecution of offences also informs other people within the state that they will be punished for similar actions.

One of the most important aspects of a state's sovereignty is its right to create and enforce criminal laws. The territorial principle, whereby jurisdiction is determined by reference to the site of the crime, forms the bedrock of most domestic criminal justice systems. It is the state that determines whether a particular act committed within its territory is or is not a crime. That state normally has the greatest interest in seeing that the perpetrator is tried, as it is the state itself, inhabitants of the state, or property located within that state which has been victimized by the crime. From a more practical perspective, the territorial state generally has the greatest and most immediate access to evidence of the offence, the crime scene, and any witnesses to the offence. Usually, there are investigation and prosecution organizations in place. It is also likely that the state would have custody of the alleged perpetrator.

The second basis for jurisdiction, the nationality principle, is used by a state whose national commits an offence on the territory of another state. The exercise of jurisdiction on this basis is usually reserved for specific crimes that the perpetrator's state feels should be singled out as being particularly nefarious, such as torture or hostage-taking, or for crimes committed by individuals who are or may be taken as representing the state, such as military personnel or members of the state's diplomatic corps. By prosecuting its national, the state effectively distances itself from the crime.

The universality principle, on the other hand, is triggered in response to a treaty, international conven-tion or customary international law-based obligation. It requires a state to take into custody an alleged perpetrator who has fled to that state after committing certain offences elsewhere. The custodial state is obliged to either extradite the perpetrator to a state willing to conduct a territorial or nationality-based prosecution or to prosecute the alleged perpetrator itself.

Post–World War I Turkish Prosecutions for Crimes against the Armenians

On October 29, 1914, the Ittihadist government in the Turkish-dominated Ottoman Empire brought that state into World War I as an ally of Germany. During the course of the war, and particularly during mobilization and deportation actions in 1915, hundreds of thousands of Turkish citizens of Armenian descent were killed, allegedly by Turkish military personnel at the instigation of the Turkish government, in what some have referred to as genocide.

The Treaty of Peace between the Allied Powers and Turkey (the Treaty of Sèvres) was signed on August 10, 1920. Article 230 of that treaty recognized the right of the Allied Powers to establish military tribunals to prosecute Turkish nationals alleged to have committed violations of the laws and customs of war. However, the Treaty of Sèvres was never ratified. Instead, it was replaced by the Treaty of Lausanne of July 24, 1923. This treaty included a declaration of amnesty for crimes connected with political events committed during the war. One of the bases for this reversal was the lack of valid law criminalizing these actions.

Following an investigation conducted by a commission of inquiry, Turkey itself formed a special court martial to try some of the alleged perpetrators, relying entirely on the Ottoman penal code. Despite the fact that a number of the highest-level perpetrators had escaped custody, a series of courts martial were held. Common to all of the trials was the question of whether the mobilization and deportation of the Armenians was an aspect of a central plan for the destruction of the Armenian population in Turkey. A number of the senior perpetrators were sentenced to death in absentia. Some lower-level perpetrators were sentenced to imprisonment. Many others were acquitted.

Nearly all of the accused senior Ittihadists party members escaped before having to stand trial. Many of those middle level perpetrators who were sentenced later escaped or were set free. With a change in government, and the finalization of the declaration of amnesty attached to the Lausanne Treaty, Turkish efforts to prosecute the many remaining perpetrators ended.

Post–World War I German Prosecutions

World War I formally ended with the signing of the Treaty of Versailles. A Commission on the Responsibility of the Authors of the War and on Enforcement of Penalties was established, and a list of approximately 895 people accused of war-related atrocities was drawn up, with a recommendation that they be tried before an international tribunal. However, Kaiser Wilhelm II of Hohenzollrn, the former emperor of Germany, had fled to the Netherlands following Germany's defeat. When it became clear that the Dutch government would not surrender him for prosecution, international interest in conducting trials dissipated. As efforts to prosecute lagged at the international level, diplomatic pressure applied by the German government resulted in its being given the responsibility of prosecuting the alleged war criminals.

Nationalistic fervor was running high in Germany, and the government was not eager to conduct criminal proceedings against its own nationals for their wartime conduct. Although trials were held before the German Supreme Court sitting in Leipzig, of the approximately 895 people named on the Commission's list, only twelve were prosecuted, and only six were convicted. The most famous case dealt with the sinking of the *Llandovery Castle*, a hospital ship, and the subsequent firing upon survivors in lifeboats by two naval lieutenants. The two lieutenants were given the longest sentences imposed by the Leipzig court: four years imprisonment. A number of the convicted escaped before serving their full sentences.

The post–WWI Turkish and German prosecutions represent one of the first times in history that a state used its domestic law to try its own nationals for the commission of what are now internationally recognized as the major crimes. The sad legacy of the failed efforts to conduct these prosecutions effectively and punish the perpetrators is that there remained an air of impunity surrounding the commission of these offences. By permitting perpetrators to escape before trial or after conviction; by not prosecuting known perpetrators; and by allowing political interests, both domestic and international, to trump the rule of law, the Turkish and German governments, and the international community, announced that the purposes of criminal prosecution were of insufficient importance in these circumstances to warrant prosecution. The Turkish government still maintains that the Armenian deaths were a result of intensive fighting, and not genocide.

Within a generation, the world was engaged in an even more horrific war. The air of impunity engendered by the failure to prosecute perpetrators following World War I undoubtedly underlay Adolf Hitler's chilling announcement, on August 22, 1939, of the first step toward the Final Solution, which was the Nazi regime's concentrated effort to destroy the Jewish people. He said: "I have given orders to my Death Units to exterminate without mercy or pity men, women, and children belonging to the Polish-speaking race. After all, who remembers today the extermination of the Armenians?"

World War II–Related Domestic Prosecutions

Following World War II, the allied powers prosecuted major Nazi war criminals pursuant to the London Agreement for the Trial and Punishment of the Major War Criminals of the European Axis Countries and the annexed Charter of the International Military Tribunal (August 8, 1945). Similar efforts were undertaken to prosecute Japanese perpetrators, pursuant to the Charter of the International Military Tribunal for the Far East (January 19, 1946, as amended by General McArthur's General Order No. 20, April 26, 1946).

Prosecutions within the Occupied Zones

On December 20, 1945, the Control Council for Germany enacted Control Council Law No. 10 (CCL 10), ostensibly to provide a uniform, domestic legal basis for the prosecution of alleged perpetrators of the major crimes, other than those prosecuted by the International Military Tribunal. However, instead of relying on CCL 10, each occupying power utilized its own, in many cases specially enacted, law and conducted trials using its own court martial procedures.

The Canadian government, under provisions of the War Crimes Regulations of August 30, 1945 and later the Canadian War Crimes Act of 1946, held courts martial for former Nazi officers and soldiers who murdered Canadian prisoners of war. The British military courts conducted trials pursuant to the Royal Warrant of June 14, 1946. The United States, pursuant to Military Government Ordinance No. 7 of October 18, 1946, appointed commissions composed of civilian judges— the only country to do so. The French conducted trials pursuant to ordinances dated November 25, 1945, and March 8, 1946. And in the British Zone of Control, Special Ordinance No. 47 provided German courts with jurisdiction to prosecute German nationals for crimes committed against German citizens or stateless people.

By October 31, 1946, CCL 10 trials had resulted in 413 death sentences, 704 prison sentences, and 262 acquittals. Despite this impressive start, however, the number of investigations and trials conducted by the Allied Powers in the West soon began to decrease, and by 1955, proceedings had ceased. In 1958, under a general amnesty, most convicted perpetrators still in prison were released.

The exception to this was the prosecution of major crime perpetrators by Germany. By mid-2004, the Federal Republic of Germany had investigated more than 100,000 people for crimes committed during World War II, resulting in 6,456 convictions. These include the 1958 prosecution of Brigadier General Fischer-Schweder, who, as police chief in Tilsit, Lithuania, participated in the mass execution of Jews. He was sentenced to twelve years in prison. Nine officers and administrators from the Maidenak concentration camp in Poland were also prosecuted. One of the accused, Hermine Ryan-Braunsteiner, was found to be directly responsible for the deaths of over 1,000 people and complicit in the deaths of 700 others. He was sentenced to life imprisonment.

Twenty-one major trials took place in Germany between 1960 and 1965. Following an amendment to the statute of limitations for murder, from 1965 through 1969, 361 people were tried, resulting in 223 convictions. Sixty-three of the convicted were sentenced to life imprisonment. From 1970 through 1979, 219 accused were tried in 119 prosecutions, resulting in 137 convictions.

The German government also obtained the extradition of a number of individuals from countries around the world. In 1982, the United States extradited Hans Lipschis to stand trial in Germany for his participation in the deaths of tens of thousands of prisoners in Auschwitz and Birkenau. Canada extradited Helmut Rauca for his role as an officer in a concentration camp near Kaunas, in Lithuania, where Rauca was responsible for the deaths of more than eleven thousand people. Rauca died in prison while awaiting trail. Josef Schwammberger, extradited from Argentina, faced charges of participating in the murder of over 3,500 prisoners of the Przemysl and Razwadow concentration camps. He was sentenced to life imprisonment.

Some of Germany's most important trials took place between 1960 and 1980, well after the conclusion of the war. The German infrastructure had been rebuilt with international assistance. The country had become a stable political entity. A new generation of Germans, freed from the tensions of the conflict period, were able to effectively apply criminal law against fellow nationals who had been perpetrators of the century's worst crimes.

Prosecutions Outside of the Occupied Zones

Outside of the occupied area, formerly occupied states enacted domestic legislation enabling the investigation and prosecution of perpetrators of the major crimes committed on their territory or by their own nationals. France conducted three of the most famous postwar

prosecutions outside of the Occupied Zones, namely of Klaus Barbie, Paul Touvier, and Maurice Papon. Barbie was accused of committing 340 crimes against French citizens. The Cour de Cassation determined that the concept of crimes against humanity, as set out in the London Charter, was applicable in French domestic law, and covered seventeen of the charges against Barbie. Included in the list of crimes was Barbie's participation in the deportation of forty Jewish children to Auschwitz and over 650 French citizens to German concentration camps in the last deportation action undertaken in France. On July 4, 1987, Barbie was convicted of crimes against humanity and sentenced to life imprisonment.

Paul Touvier was originally charged with numerous offences, including torture and deportation, allegedly committed while he was a Nazi collaborator and assistant to Barbie. After years of legal arguments, trials, and appeals, on April 20, 1994, Touvier was convicted of complicity to commit crimes against humanity in the murder of seven Jews at Rillieux-la-Pape and was sentenced to life imprisonment.

Maurice Papon had a postwar career which included positions as a high-level civil servant, the prefect of police for Paris, and France's budget minister. In the early 1980s, however, documentary evidence was uncovered linking Papon to the deportation of almost 1,700 Jews to German concentration camps during 1942. Despite overwhelming evidence, after a lengthy trial, Papon was convicted of complicity with respect to the arrest and imprisonment of some of the victims, but was acquitted of all murder charges. On April 2, 1998, he was sentenced to ten years imprisonment, but released in 2002 because of bad health.

Other Western European countries conducted similar trials, in greater or lesser numbers. In most cases, these trials elicited strong political debate concerning the role of nationals in the commission of gross offences against their own people. Politics and the political and social implications of the prosecutions overshadowed most of the trials. In Eastern Europe, the Soviet Union conducted thousands of trials for war-related crimes. However, the alleged widespread use of torture to elicit confessions or obtain evidence casts doubt over the validity of these trials.

The broad acceptance of a state's power to prosecute its own nationals for major crimes using domestic law was a tremendous development in efforts to address the problem of impunity. However, the prosecutions suffered from a number of flaws that reduced their overall impact. There were not enough prosecutions, in many cases as a result of a real or imagined lack of proper domestic legislation. The prosecutions that did occur were often politically motivated, or the courts were influenced by political considerations. Sentencing procedures were nonexistent or not followed. Once again, the message conveyed by these failures was that the states concerned, and the international community, felt that the purposes of criminal prosecution were of insufficient importance in these circumstances to warrant more effective efforts.

Modern Domestic Prosecutions

With respect to modern prosecutions of the major crimes, most of the attention has been paid to the International Criminal Tribunals for the Former Yugoslavia and Rwanda (ICTY, ICTR), combined national and international tribunals such as the Special Court for Sierra Leone, and the International Criminal Court (ICC). In addition, there are third-party states that use universal jurisdiction principles to prosecute perpetrators found within their territory following the commission of the offences. Some states, attempting to balance political realities with legal obligations, conduct Commissions of Inquiry into alleged major crimes in an effort to uncover the truth outside of the more threatening arena of a criminal court. Territorial and nationality-based major crime prosecutions remain the exception rather than the rule, however.

My Lai

On March 26, 1968, American soldiers and officers assaulted My Lai village in Vietnam. During the operation, described as a "command-directed killing spree," 567 unarmed civilians were murdered. Four officers and nine enlisted men were charged with war crimes, including rape and murder. Twelve other officers were charged for their participation in cover-up activities. All were tried before military courts martial. Only First Lieutenant William Calley was convicted. He was sentenced to life imprisonment. The Secretary of the Army reduced the sentenced to 10 years. Calley served only three years under house arrest.

Israel's Commission of Inquiry

In 1982, Israeli military forces invaded Southern Lebanon in an effort to end Palestinian Liberation Organization–instigated terrorist attacks emanating from that area. Trained and equipped by Israel, and under Israeli control, was the largely Christian Lebanese Phalange faction. Israeli forces moved into West Beirut, and ordered the Phalengists to enter Sabra and Shatila refugee camps, ostensibly to search for terrorists. Between 300 and 1,000 Palestinian civilians were murdered by the Phalengists during the 48 hours of occupation.

Israel established the Commission of Inquiry into the Events at the Refugee Camps in Beirut, which pro-

duced a startlingly candid report. However, while the commission recognized the command-and-control failures of senior members of the Israeli government and military, and particularly noted the personal responsibility of then Defence Minister Ariel Sharon, it concluded that the determination of responsibility for most senior political and military offenders was sufficient penalty. It did recommend that the Prime Minister consider removing Sharon from office.

Canadian Commission of Inquiry

During the first six months of 1993, members of the Canadian Armed Forces (CF) occupied the area in and around Belet Huen, Somalia, as part of a U.S.-led peace-making operation. During that time, CF members committed a number of war crimes, including the beating death of a Somali teenager and the shooting of two unarmed Somalis in the back as they fled one of the compounds. One victim died.

A Commission of Inquiry was established to investigate events surrounding the CF deployment. After two years of investigations and public hearings, and the issuance of an Order-in-Council terminating the inquiry, a report was released which addressed all pre-deployment and in-theater aspects of the mission. The CF conducted courts martial. Master Corporal Matchee, the primary culprit in the beating death, was found unfit to stand trial following an apparent suicide attempt. Private Brown was sentenced to five years imprisonment for manslaughter and torture. Another private, Brocklebank, was acquitted. Captain Sox and Major Seward were convicted of negligent performance of duty and given minor sentences. One charge was laid against Captain Rainville, who led the reconnaissance platoon involved in the shootings. He was acquitted. Lieutenant Colonel Mathieu, the on-site commanding officer, was acquitted of negligent performance of duty.

Amnesties in Latin America

In many post-conflict states, transitional governments grant or uphold amnesties for crimes committed by the former rulers. Proponents of amnesties argue that they are the price of peace. Victims-rights groups argue that amnesties conflict with internationally imposed obligations to extradite or prosecute perpetrators of the major crimes, and are in reality a tool for permitting perpetrators of the world's worst crimes to continue to operate with impunity. Often, both positions share in the truth. The use of amnesties became custom in Latin America during the 1980s and 1990s to reduce or eliminate criminal liability for some or all offences committed by prior regimes.

Chile's Amnesty Law

In September 1973, a military junta led by General Augusto Pinochet overthrew the government of President Salvador Allende in Chile. Within three months, approximately 1,500 suspected leftist party members and sympathizers had been murdered or "disappeared." By August 1977, a further 600 had been murdered. In 1978, Pinochet issued an unconditional amnesty for most criminal offences committed between September 1973 and March 1977. The exceptions included armed robbery and rape, but not murder, kidnapping, and assault, which were the most common forms of terror used by Pinochet's military. In 1990, a new government, led by Patricio Aylwin, was elected. However, General Pinochet retained strong support in the army and Congress, and Aylwin's tentative efforts to revoke the amnesty met with considerable opposition. A Truth and Reconciliation Commission was nonetheless tasked to identify the victims of human rights violations and to recommend reparation measures. Any evidence of criminal activity was to be directed to the Supreme Court.

In 1998, while in England, General Pinochet was arrested pursuant to an international warrant issued by Spain. The British House of Lords determined that General Pinochet could be extradited to Spain to stand trial for major crimes. Although General Pinochet was returned to Chile as a result of his ill health, the publicity surrounding the British extradition hearings resulted in the Chilean Supreme Court annulling the 1978 amnesty law, some twenty years after its proclamation.

Despite the amnesty, some successful prosecutions have taken place, including the prosecution and conviction of the head of the secret police, General Manuel Contreras, and his second-in-command, Brigadier Pedro Espinoza, for the murder of Orlando Letelier, the Chilean Minister of Foreign Affairs. Letelier was murdered in Washington, D.C. Pressure exerted by the United States resulted in his prosecution in the face of the amnesty. Contreras was subsequently convicted for the abduction of a member of the Movement of the Revolutionary Left and the disappearance of journalist Diana Aaron in 1974.

Other Latin American Amnesties

Other Latin American governments have issued unconditional or partial amnesties, ostensibly to help stabilize the post-conflict state. Immediately prior to the 1983 Argentine elections, then-President Leopoldo Fortunato Galtieri enacted the Law of National Pacification, which granted amnesties to individuals within both his and former President Juan Peron's governments, for acts of state terrorism committed during the "dirty war"

period from 1976 to 1983. Despite initial efforts by the newly elected President, Raoul Alfonsin, to repeal the amnesty law, and the creation of the National Commission on the Disappeared, political pressure from within the country resulted in a series of retrenchments, culminating in the granting of unconditional amnesties and pardons to known perpetrators on the basis that it was time to put aside the divisions within the country. Finally, in August 2003, following the issuance of international arrest warrants for forty-five former Argentine military officers by a Spanish judge, both houses in the Argentine Congress voted to repeal the amnesty laws and reopen trials of former military officers.

In 1993, broad, unconditional amnesties for political crimes were granted in El Salvador, following a report by a UN-sponsored Truth Commission which recommended that, given the close ties between the judiciary and the government, prosecutions would likely be biased and lead to further instability. The amnesties covered decades of civil strife, during which more than 70,000 people were murdered or disappeared, and countless more were tortured.

Full or partial amnesties have also been granted in Guatemala, where an estimated 140,000 to 200,000 people were "disappeared" or murdered in an ongoing civil war that ended in 1996; in Honduras, where an estimated 179 people were "disappeared" by the armed forces between 1980 and 1993; and in Peru, where, in 1995, an unconditional amnesty was granted to Peruvian military, police, and civilians involved in brutal anti-terrorist activities between 1980 and 1995. In a number of these cases, truth commissions were established to investigate alleged abuses and advise their respective transitional governments. While these commissions arguably made contributions to the protection and promotion of justice and the preservation of evidence, the lack of criminal sanctions against the perpetrators has encouraged the sense of impunity surrounding the commission of major crimes.

Domestic Prosecutions in the Former Yugoslavia

Domestic prosecutions of the major crimes in Bosnia and Herzegovina are governed by the Rules of the Road, adopted in 1996 by Presidents Izetbegovic of Bosnia and Herzegovina, Franjo Tudjman of Croatia, and Slobodan Milosevic of Yugoslavia as a follow up to the Dayton Peace Accords. Under the rules, potential major crime cases are forwarded to the International Criminal Tribunal for the Former Yugoslavia (ICTY) for a decision as to whether there is sufficient evidence, under an international standard, to conduct a prosecution. As of January 2004, the ICTY has referred back to Bosnia and Herzegovina approximately 550 cases determined to have sufficient evidence to prosecute. Of these, approximately 10 percent have reached trial stage in Bosnia and Herzegovina, primarily at the cantonal court level.

The greatest advantage of this process, and of the work of the international community in Bosnia and Herzegovina, is that the justice system is being brought into line with international standards. The criminal legal system has undergone reform with the enactment of new procedural codes, court restructuring, and the creation of the High Judicial and Prosecutorial Council. Judicial and prosecutorial training programs are being implemented. Prison reform initiatives are underway. An Implementation Task Force is working towards the establishment of a War Crimes Chamber within the State Court, which should be ready to accept the transfer of cases from the ICTY by the end of 2004. While there remains room for improvement, particularly with witness protection programs and the elimination of prosecutorial and judicial bias, continued support by the international community will ensure that Bosnia and Herzegovina will be able to assume increasingly greater responsibility for domestic prosecution of the major crimes.

Croatian prosecutions have experienced problems similar to those in Bosnia and Herzegovina. Hundreds of trials have come before national courts, but the vast majority have been against Croatian Serbs, and many of these have been conducted without the accused being present. Only a handful have been commenced against Croats for crimes perpetrated against Serbs, and these have been tainted by allegations of witness intimidation and judicial bias. The worst example is the Lora Prison case in Split County Court in 2002. Eight Croatian military officers were accused of torturing and killing Serbian and Montenegrin prisoners in 1992. Evidence of the offences had been reported by local and international nongovernmental organizations (NGOs). Witness intimidation was rampant. Witnesses refused to testify, retracted their statements on the stand, or went into hiding. All accused were acquitted. While the Croatian government appears to be increasingly committed to conducting domestic trials of the major crimes, enhanced witness protection programs and the elimination of prosecutorial and judicial bias are essential.

In Serbia-Montenegro, following the transfer of former president Milosevic and other former Serb political and military leaders to the ICTY, legal reform has resulted in the commencement of prosecutions of Serbs for atrocities committed against non-Serbs. In July 2002, Ivan Nikolic, a former Yugoslav army reservist, was sentenced to eight years for the murder of two Ko-

sovar Albanians in 1999. In September 2002, Nebojsa Ranisavljevic, a Bosnian Serb Army volunteer, was sentenced to fifteen years for the murder of nineteen Yugoslav Muslims abducted from a train near the border town of Strpci in February 1993. In October 2002, a military court convicted two Yugoslav army officers and two privates for the killing of two ethnic Albanians during the Kosovo crisis. Finally, the trial of Sasa Cvjetan, a member of a Serbian police anti-terrorist unit, was commenced in October 2002. He is accused of the murder of nineteen Kosovar Albanians in March 1999. These prosecutions of ethnic Serbs in their own state demonstrates a limited but growing acceptance of the government's responsibility to exercise territorial and nationality-based jurisdiction over the major crimes. However, prosecutions of more senior military and non-military leaders are necessary to demonstrate a full commitment to justice.

Domestic Prosecutions in Rwanda

Following the 1993 genocide, the Rwandan government found itself faced with the daunting task of prosecuting the perpetrators of the atrocities. Organic Law 8/96 of September 1996 divided offenders into four categories, based on their level of participation in the atrocities. Confessions and the provision of information concerning other accused were to be rewarded with a significant reduction in sentence. However, by 1998, the number of prisoners being held in jails throughout the country amounted to almost 130,000, and comparatively very few trials had taken place. Frustrated by the massive numbers of accused and the lack of proper infrastructure and evidence, and recognizing the need for both justice and reconciliation, the government began to experiment with the traditional form of judicial process, called *gacaca*.

The original gacaca was a semi-formal judicial process designed to deal with local issues. The community met in the open and participated in the process, with local respected figures elected to serve as judges. The Gacaca Law on the Creation of Gacaca Jurisdictions, approved by the Constitutional Court on 26 January 2001, adapted traditional gacaca law to meet the demands imposed by the number and magnitude of the crimes committed during the genocide. The new law incorporated the provisions of Organic Law 8/96 concerning the classification of perpetrators and the confession/sentence reduction program. The "gacaca jurisdictions" are empowered to try anyone accused of involvement in the atrocities, except for those who held positions of power within Rwandan society and used that power to organize and carry out the genocide. These senior perpetrators are to be tried before normal criminal courts.

An early experiment with the new *gacaca* process was undertaken when 544 prisoners being held in Kibuye prison on little or no evidence participated in gacaca trials. Over a period of six weeks, the prisoners were presented one-by-one to the local population. Individuals who attended the trials were permitted to speak for or against each prisoner, and then to determine his guilt or innocence. By the end of the process, 256 of the prisoners had been released.

Victims rights groups have protested that the gacaca trials do not meet internationally recognized criminal process requirements, and fail to adequately punish offenders or to address victims' concerns, including the right to compensation. However, using the traditional process has significant advantages. Local people recognize and are comfortable with the procedures. They witness justice being done. The decision-making power rests with the community, tempered by the elected judges. The intent of the gacaca process is to discover the truth and to bring the offender back into the community after admission of the offence; a rehabilitation process fully in accord with the purposes of criminal prosecution. While the actual punishment imposed by the gacaca process might be lenient by international standards, it may be that it is the only available option for the Rwandan government, given the massive number of alleged perpetrators waiting for justice in horribly overcrowded jails.

Conclusion

History demonstrates that leaving states to prosecute their own nationals for major offences is rarely effective. Social and political tensions (post–World War I; Latin America), inadequate infrastructure (Rwanda), or simple disregard for justice when addressing major crimes committed by nationals against civilians in foreign countries (the United States in My Lai; Israel in Southern Lebanon; Canada and Somalia) have all played their part in undermining prosecutorial efforts. On the other hand, international institutions, operating on their own, are incapable of dealing with the large number of perpetrators normally involved in these offences, and the state concerned loses the cathartic benefits of the investigative process.

The most effective way to address impunity for major crimes is through a two-step process. The international community must intervene and conduct prosecutions of the most senior offenders at the earliest possible moment. This allows for the creation of a record of the offences and the removal from the transitional society of powerful elements potentially willing to reignite the conflict if threatened with domestic prosecution. Additionally, assistance must be provided to the transitional government for the rebuilding of infrastructure and the maintenance of political stability. As conflict-related tensions within the community begin to ease, the new government can commence domestic prosecutions of middle- and lower-ranking offenders, using domestic practices and laws amended to address these extraordinary offences.

SEE ALSO Argentina; Chile; Eichmann Trials; El Salvador; Guatemala; Immunity; Impunity; National Laws; Nuremberg Trials; Prosecution; Rehabilitation; Rwanda; Sierra Leone Special Court; Universal Jurisdiction; War Crimes; World War I Peace Treaties

BIBLIOGRAPHY

Assicott, Jeffrey, and William Hudson (1993). "The Twenty-Fifth Anniversary of My Lai: A Time to Inculcate the Lessons." *Military Law Review* 139:153.

Bassiouni, M. Cherif (2003). *Introduction to International Criminal Law.* New York: Transnational Publishers.

Browning, Christopher (1992). *Ordinary Men: Reserve Police Battalion 101 and the Final Solution in Poland.* New York: Harper Perennial.

Dadrian, Vahakn N (1989). "Genocide as a Problem of National and International Law: The World War I Armenian Case and Its Contemporary Legal Ramifications." *Yale Journal of International Law* 14:221.

Daly, Erin (2001–2002). "Between Punitive and Reconstructive Justice: The Gacaca Courts in Rwanda." *New York University Journal of International Law & Policy* 34:355.

Davanzo, Jeannine (1999). "An Absence of Accountability for the My Lai Massacre." *Hofstra Law and Policy Symposium* 3:287.

De Than, Claire, and Edwin Shorts (2003). *International Criminal Law and Human Rights.* London: Sweet & Maxwell.

Fairchild, Erika, and Harry Dammer (2001). *Comparative Criminal Justice Systems.* Belmont, Ca.: Wadsworth.

Margolian, Howard (1998). *Conduct Unbecoming: The Story of the Murder of Canadian Prisoners of War in Normandy.* Toronto: University of Toronto Press.

Marschik, Axel (1997). "The Politics of Prosecution: European National Approaches to War Crimes" in *The Law of War Crimes: National and International Approaches*, ed. Timothy McCormack and Gerry Simpson. The Hague: Kluwer Law International.

Matas, David, (1989). "Prosecuting Crimes Against Humanity: The Lessons of World War I." *Fordham International Law Journal* 13:86.

McManus, John (2004). "A New Era of Accountability through Domestic Enforcement of International Law." In *La voie vers la Cour pénale internationale: tous les chemins mènent à Rome (The Highway to the International Criminal Court: All Roads Lead to Rome)*, ed. Hélène Dumont and Anne-Marie Boisvert. Montreal: Éditions Thémis.

Neuner, Matthias, ed. (2003). *National Legislation Incorporating International Crimes: Approaches of Civil and Common Law Countries.* Berlin: Wissenschafts-Verlag.

Sadat-Wexler, Leila (1999). "National Prosecutions for International Crimes: The French Experience." In *International Criminal Law,* 2nd edition, ed. M. Cherif Bassioiuni. New York: Transnational Publishers.

Schabas, William A. (1999). "International Sentencing: From Leipzig (1923) to Arusha (1996)." In *International Criminal Law,* 2nd edition, ed. M. Cherif Bassioiuni. New York: Transnational Publishers.

Schabas, William A. (2004). "Addressing Impunity in Developing Countries: Lessons from Rwanda and Sierra Leone." In *La voie vers la Cour pénale internationale: tous les chemins mènent à Rome (The Highway to the International Criminal Court: All Roads Lead to Rome),* ed. Hélène Dumont and Anne-Marie Boisvert. Montreal: Éditions Thémis.

Schwelb, E. (1946). "Crimes Against Humanity." *British Yearbook of International Law* 178.

Tully, L. Danielle (2003). "Human Rights Compliance and the Gacaca Jurisdictions in Rwanda." *British Columbia International & Comparative Law Report* 26:385.

Viout, Jean-Olivier (1999). "The Klaus Barbie Trial and Crimes Against Humanity." *Hofstra Law & Policy Symposium* 3:155. New York: Hofstra University Press.

Weinschenk, Fritz, (1999). "The Murders among Them—German Justice and the Nazis." *Hofstra Law & Policy Symposium* 3:137.

John McManus
Matthew McManus
The views herein expressed are those of the author, and
do not necessarily reflect the views of the Canadian
Department of Justice or the Government of Canada.

Native Americans

The international community has not legally admonished the United States for genocidal acts against Native Americans, yet it is clear that examples of genocidal acts and crimes against humanity are a well-cited page in U.S. history. Notorious incidents, such as the Trail of Tears, the Sand Creek Massacre, and the massacre of the Yuki of northern California are covered in depth in separate entries in this encyclopedia. More controversial, however, is whether the colonies and the United States participated in genocidal acts as an overall policy toward Native Americans. The Native-American population decrease since the arrival of Spanish explorer Christopher Columbus alone signals the toll colonization and U.S. settlement took on the native population. Scholars estimate that approximately 10 million pre-Columbian Native Americans resided in the present-day United States. That number has since fallen to approximately 2.4 million. While this population de-

crease cannot be attributed solely to the actions of the U.S. government, they certainly played a key role. In addition to population decrease, Native Americans have also experienced significant cultural and proprietary losses as a result of U.S. governmental actions. The total effect has posed a serious threat to the sustainability of the Native-American people and culture.

Ideological Motivations

Two conflicting yet equally harmful ideologies significantly influenced U.S. dealings with Native Americans. The first sprang from the Enlightenment and, more specifically, John Locke's *Second Treatise of Government.* Locke proposed that the individual had an exclusive claim to one's person. The fruits of one's labor, as an extension of the individual, then, become the laborer's property. Thus, individuals acquire property rights by removing things from the state of nature through the investment of their labor. This particular theory of property helped justify the many harmful policies against Native Americans throughout United States history. European settlers falsely saw the Americas as a vast and empty wasteland that the Native Americans had failed to cultivate and, therefore, had no worthy claim to. Euro-Americans saw themselves as the torchbearers of civilization and therefore thought they were uniquely situated to acquire the vast wilderness and develop it (this later developed into the idea of Manifest Destiny). To the Euro-American mind, that the Native Americans must yield to European settlement was inevitable. This line of reasoning went so far as to result in a common nineteenth-century belief that the extinction of Native Americans was also inevitable.

The second ideological motivation behind U.S. treatment of Native Americans was the policy of assimilation. Its origins are manifested in president Thomas Jefferson's idea of the yeoman farmer. Jefferson envisioned a land populated by industrious and autonomous yeoman farmers. Native Americans stood in the way of this vision by their communal occupation of vast quantities of land. The best solution, then, would be for Native Americans to assimilate to Euro-American ways. Thus, the Native Americans would require less land and the remainder would be available to white settlers. Under this ideological view of Native Americans' role in the new world, there was no place for Native-American culture as it existed before colonization. It was a useless stump in fertile land that had to be extracted. Assimilation of Native Americans and the intentional destruction of Native-American culture remained overt policies into modern times and were often tied to many religious groups' interactions with Native Americans.

Colonies and States

One of the lesser known facts in U.S. history is that the Virginia and Carolina colonies were heavily engaged in the slave trade of Native Americans. In the Carolinas, the proprietors of the colonies favored cultivating Native-American ties for the lucrative fur trade. Settlers, some from Barbados where slavery was already established, however, raided Native-American tribes and exploited long-standing native rivalries in order to capture and sell Native Americans on the slave market. Historian Thomas R. Berger notes that a South Carolinian, James Moore, abducted and enslaved 325 Native Americans in the Florida region in 1704 and also launched a lucrative attack against the North Carolinian Tuscarora tribe in 1713, killing 200 and capturing 392. The end result of such campaigns was to displace many of the eastern seaboard tribes. The majority of Native Americans in this region were enslaved domestically, sold abroad, or forced to flee into the interior. Such displacement necessarily also destroyed these tribes' cultural unity. These acts of intentional enslavement and displacement would qualify as genocidal acts under the United Nations (UN) definition of genocide. While slavery is not specifically mentioned in the UN Genocide Convention's definition of genocide, it fits the spirit of the convention. These acts deliberately caused bodily and mental harm and imposed conditions on the eastern tribes that made life near the colonized settlements precarious to the point of becoming impossible.

Relations between the northeastern tribes and colonists were also precarious and often hinged on perceived threat, land conflicts, and trade relations. The Puritans of New England recognized native land title only if the land was being cultivated and had a persistent practice of enslaving Native Americans. What harmony existed was often disturbed by conflicts over new settlements and further encroachment on native land. The Pequot War of 1637 illustrates this tension. The Pequot had faired the influx of Western disease better than other tribes and had the strength to resist settlements rather than acquiesce to them. When settlers moved into the Connecticut Valley, the Pequot did just that. In response, a group of settlers launched an attack against the Pequot stronghold at night, surrounding and setting fire to it. The result was the killing of more than five hundre Pequot and the enslavement of the survivors. The desire to eliminate a threat also motivated a similar policy of extermination in Virginia following the Indian massacres of 1622 and 1644.

The western states did not fair much better with their relations with Native Americans. The Sand Creek Massacre in Colorado (1864) and the massacre of the

A mass burial in the aftermath of the Wounded Knee massacre, 1890.[CORBIS]

Yuki of northern California (1856–1860) demonstrate that the competition for land and other resources was not fixed in time, but enduring throughout the United States' westward expansion. Both the desire to eliminate a threat and competition for resources, usually land, led many colonies and states to actions that would probably be considered war crimes or crimes against humanity under the Rome Statute.

Federal Government

Much of the federal government's dealings with Native Americans were fueled by states' and individuals' desire for land. After the French and Indian War (1754–1763), the English strongly opposed encroachment on native lands for fear that it would provoke native retaliation and the destruction of beneficial military and trade alliances. King George's Proclamation of 1763 forbade settlement beyond the eastern mountain ranges and granted the Crown the exclusive right to purchase Native-American land. This law frustrated many colonists and land speculators, including Virginia statesman George Washington, who wished to purchase native lands. Under the Proclamation, native lands could be acquired from the Crown, but at a much higher price. The restriction on settlement of certain portions of land also greatly hindered the expansion that many colonists saw as desirable and inevitable. The Crown's interference with settlers' desire for cheap, arable land contributed to many colonists' support and justification for the Revolutionary War. This property system, whereby Native Americans had occupancy rights but because the Europeans "discovered" the continent the Crown had exclusive purchasing rights, was later absorbed into U.S. federal law in the seminal case

Map showing location of Native-American tribes throughout the United States prior to their annihilation and forced relocation westward in the nineteenth century.

Johnson v. McIntosh in 1823. Despite this paternalistic relationship between the federal government and the native tribes in the post-revolutionary United States, settlers continued to attempt to acquire native lands through direct purchase and coercion. The promise of economic gain at Native Americans' expense by taking native land was a cornerstone of the voting Euro-American population's interaction with Native Americans and heavily influenced U.S. Native-American policy.

The War of 1812 marked a turning point from the policy of Native-American assimilation and partial retention of native land to the policy of outright removal of native tribes to the West of the Mississippi. The forced removal or tribes also resulted in a total relinquishment of traditional native land. After many largely unsuccessful attempts to convince the five relatively prosperous and assimilated tribes of the Southeast (Cherokee, Choctaw, Chickasaw, Seminole, and Creek) to voluntarily move westward, the federal government acquiesced to state pressure and passed the Indian Removal Act of 1830. It offered a trade of land in the East for land in the West. The particularly coercive aspect of the act was that those who refused the exchange would no longer be protected under federal law and would be subject to hostile state regulation. The removal policies of the federal government resulted in the humanitarian disaster referred to by the Cherokee as the Trail of Tears.

Approximately four thousand Cherokee perished on this forced walk to western lands. Removal, however, was a larger policy than this one famed act. It occurred both before and after 1830 and represented the belief that American Indians were not capable of existing with nor desired to coexist with white settlers. There were conflicting motivations behind the policy. For some, it was a thinly veiled method of evicting Native Americans from land that was desired by white settlers. For others, it was based on the belief that Native Americans were members of an inferior civilization that could not survive in the civilized world and therefore needed to be removed for their own sake. Either way, some scholars reference the federal removal policy as a genocidal act due to the death and proprietary loss incurred to Native Americans as well as the destruction of their traditional way of life.

A second and particularly destructive policy was that of assimilation. Behind assimilation policies lies the desire to remove all that is "Indian" from the Native Americans. A particularly poignant historical example of how this policy was also tied to the continued desire for more land is the General Allotment Act of 1887 (the Dawes Act). This act terminated communal land holdings on the reservations and redistributed land to individual Native Americans by a trust system. After twenty-five years, they would own the land individually and become U.S. citizens. Any "surplus" land would be taken for sale to settlers. It was an attempt to assimilate Native-American traditions of communal land holdings to the Euro-American system of private ownership. Thereby, it was thought, Native Americans would join mainstream society and, at the same time, require less land. This act had disastrous effects on traditional Na-

tive-American life and reduced their land holdings by two-thirds.

Yet another assimilation policy was the forced removal of Native-American children from their parental homes to boarding schools for "civilized" education. The Northwest Ordinance of 1787 established an involuntary boarding-school system where children were typically forbidden to speak their native language and were stripped of all outward native characteristics. The Carlisle Indian Industrial School was one of these schools and incorporated an "outing system" whereby children were placed with white families in order to learn American customs and values. While having the good intention to provide education to Native-American children, this system of indoctrination was also aimed at "killing the Indian and saving the man" (Glauner, 2002, p. 10) as Richard Pratt of the Carlisle School said. In the twenty-first century, this policy would be considered both a potential violation of the UN Genocide Convention's prohibition on transferring children from one group to another, and a blatant intention to cleanse the Indian population of their native language and cultural values through the re-education of their children.

A clearer example of a federal genocidal act against Native Americans was the involuntary sterilization of approximately seventy thousand Native-American women. The federally funded Indian Health Services carried out these sterilizations between 1930 and the mid-1970s. They were often done without informed consent, covertly, or under a fraudulent diagnosis of medical necessity. This directly contravenes the UN Genocide Convention. Destroying a group's ability to reproduce is an obvious and crude method of ensuring the inability of the group's survival.

Whether government actions such as the Trail of Tears and assimilation policies qualify as genocidal acts or as crimes against humanity continues to be a subject of much disagreement and debate. The UN Genocide Convention requires that a state actor have "intent to destroy" a group to satisfy the definition of genocide. As previously outlined, many of the actions taken by the federal, state, and colonial governments fell short of actual intent to destroy the Native Americans. Scholars Frank Chalk and Kurt Jonassohn maintain that the closest cases are the massacres at Sand Creek and of the Yuki of Round Valley (a modern example would be the sterilization programs). In both instances, government officials played key roles in facilitating the purposeful killing of Native Americans. The circumstances under which the United States committed genocide against Native Americans tended to be when other methods failed to clear a path to settlement, or other notions of progress. "Ethnocide was the principal United States policy toward American Indians in the nineteenth century . . . the federal government stood ready to engage in genocide as a means of coercing tribes when they resisted ethnocide or resorted to armed resistance" (Chalk and Jonassohn, 1990, p. 203).

The U.S. government was more often guilty of acts of "advertent omission" (that is, without intent to commit genocide, failing to act to prevent private acts that have genocidal effects or failing to perform obligations that prevent genocidal effects). There is a debate as to whether such acts should be incorporated into the definition of genocide, although they currently are not a part of the UN definition. Continually turning a blind eye to aggressive settlers' illegal consumption of native land and to other private acts of intimidation are examples. On the plains, the U.S. government did not prevent the destruction of tribes' primary food source and government officials often spoke in approval of it. From 1883 to 1910, the buffalo, upon which tribes in that area were dependent, were killed in such great quantities that the number fell from 60 million to 10 buffalo. Without their traditional food source and with the pressure exerted by settlers mounting, the plains Indians experienced famine or were forced to relocate to reservations. Further, the United States often failed to uphold treaty obligations to provide protection, food, and blankets to Native Americans. The failure of the U.S. government to protect Native Americans and, in some cases, to follow through on its own obligations, left Native Americans with few options and contributed to their destruction.

The third possibility is to categorize U.S. actions as crimes against humanity under Section 7 of the Rome Statute of the International Criminal Court. Murder, extermination, and deportation or forcible transfer of population fall under this statute when done "as part of a widespread or systematic attack directed against any civilian population. . . ." Because many of the acts of removal were coercive, they could qualify as crimes against humanity.

Conclusions

The aforementioned allegations of genocidal acts against American Indians occurred before the United States ratified the UN Genocide Convention in 1948 (as of 2004, the United States has not ratified the Rome Statutes). Most treaties in international law are not retroactive. Legal reprisal under the UN Genocide Convention, then, is not likely. An argument may be made, however, that the involuntary sterilization of Native-American women occurred after the United States signed the UN Genocide Convention (although before ratification) and that the United States violated its obligation not to act against the object and purpose of the treaty.

Perhaps more important than formal legal sanctions, however, is the recognition of the colonies', the United States', and individuals' role in the devastation of Native-American population and culture. As the description of state policies and actions attest, the destruction of Native-American communities and culture was neither by chance nor mandated by fate. It was directly connected to government policies and actions.

SEE ALSO Cheyenne; Forcible Transfer; Indigenous Peoples; Pequots; Racism; Sand Creek Massacre; Trail of Tears; Wounded Knee; Yuki of Northern California

BIBLIOGRAPHY

Axtell, James (1981). *The European and the Indian: Essays in the Ethnohistory of Colonial North America.* New York: Oxford University Press.

Berger, Thomas R. (1999). *A Long and Terrible Shadow: White Values, Native Rights in the Americas since 1492.* Seattle: University of Washington Press.

Berkhofer, Robert F., Jr. (1965). *Salvation and the Savage: An Analysis of Protestant Missions and American Indian Response, 1787–1862.* Lexington: University of Kentucky Press.

Chalk, Frank, and Kurt Jonassohn (1990). *The History and Sociology of Genocide: Analyses and Case Studies.* New Haven, Conn.: Yale University Press.

Churchill, Ward (1997). *A Little Matter of Genocide: Holocaust and Denial in the Americas, 1492 to the Present.* San Francisco: City Lights Books.

Dippie, Brian W. (1982). *The Vanishing American: White Attitudes and U.S. Indian Policy.* Middletown, Conn.: Wesleyan University Press.

Glauner, Lindsay (2002). "Comment: The Need for Accountability and Reparation: 1830–1976 The United States Government's Role in the Promotion, Implementation, and Execution of the Crime of Genocide Against Native Americans." *DePaul Law Review* 51:911.

Hagan, William T. (1979). *American Indians.* Chicago: University of Chicago Press.

Horsman, Reginald (1970). *The Origins of Indian Removal 1815–1824.* East Lansing: Michigan State University Press.

Lynden, Fremont J., and Lyman H. Legters, eds. (1992). *Native Americans and Public Policy.* Pittsburgh: University of Pittsburgh Press.

Sheehan, Bernard W. (1973). *Seeds of Extinction: Jeffersonian Philanthropy and the American Indian.* New York: W.W. Norton.

Wilkins, David E. (2002). *American Indian Politics and the American Political System.* New York: Rowman & Littlefield.

The secretary general of Amnesty International, Pierre Sane (second from right), discusses the organization's 1996 China campaign, March 15, 1996. [AP/WIDE WORLD PHOTOS]

Williams, Robert A. Jr. (1990). *The American Indian in Western Legal Thought: The Discourses of Conquest.* New York: Oxford University Press.

Stacie E. Martin

Nongovernmental Organizations

There is a vast diversity among nongovernmental organizations (NGOs) in respect to composition, methods of working, membership, and purpose. If there is a common denominator to be found, it is less in what NGOs are but rather in what they are not. As Deborah Spar and James Dail have noted, NGOs are not "states or firms; not elected or appointed" (2002, p. 173). Some have argued that this creates a "democratic deficit," meaning NGOs are self-appointed representative agencies that may not be accountable to those they represent. NGOs differ in size, focus, wealth, and working methods, as do their clientele and target groups. NGOs may be local (working within a single state), regional (working across national borders), or international. They range from one-person operations to organizations with large numbers of workers and with offices

in numerous countries. Some, like Amnesty International, are membership-driven and supported largely by donations from its constituent members. Others, such as Human Rights Watch, rely primarily on foundations or single donors for the funds needed to pay operating costs. The degree to which an organization's membership base is drawn from civil society provides some clue as to what extent the organization suffers from the "democratic deficit" attributed to these "unelected" bodies.

Definitions

Given the rather fluid nature of the composition of the NGO community, it can be difficult to provide a precise definition of this type of organization. The *Encyclopedia of Public International Law* defines NGOs as:

> private organizations (associations, federations, unions, institutes, groups) not established by a government or by an international agreement, which are capable of playing a role in international affairs by virtue of their activities, and whose members enjoy independent voting

encyclopedia of GENOCIDE *and* CRIMES AGAINST HUMANITY

rights. The members of an NGO may be individuals (private citizens) or bodies cooperate. Where the organization's membership or activity is limited to a specific state, one speaks of a national NGO and where they go beyond, of an international NGO.

In contrast, the *Oxford Dictionary of Law* defines an NGO as:

> A private international organization that acts as a mechanism for cooperation among private national groups in both municipal and international affairs, particularly in economic, social, cultural, humanitarian, and technical fields. Under Article 71 of the United Nations Charter, the Economic and Social Council is empowered to make suitable arrangements for consultation with NGOs on matters within its competence.

This more limiting definition reasserts the notion that NGOs are international in character and serve to facilitate national organizations.

The World Bank has defined NGOs more narrowly yet, as "private organizations that pursue activities to relieve suffering, promote the interests of the poor, protect the environment, provide basic social services, or undertake community development" (Operational Directive 14.70). This definition is specific to developmental NGOs, the partner community of the World Bank.

What characterizes NGOs and makes them distinct is their nongovernmental character. They may operate within a target state or across state boundaries, or indeed internationally, but they are independent from states, and ostensibly, from state influence.

Categories of NGOs

The World Bank places NGOs into three primary groupings. There are community-based organizations (CBOs), which serve a specific population in a narrow geographic area; national organizations, which operate in individual developing countries; and international organizations, which are typically headquartered in developed countries and carry out operations in more than one developing country.

Such distinctions are useful, but each of the categories subsume a rather disparate group of NGOs. To further identify the various strands of the NGO community, Spar and Dail offer a useful typology of NGOs. They divide the NGO community along ten focus topics: health services, infrastructural services, development assistance, education, commercial services, refugee assistance, basic needs, social development, the environment, and human rights. Undoubtedly, these topics and subtopics could be expanded or subdivided fur-

ther, but the typology's usefulness is twofold. First, the diversity of groups and topical areas of interest highlights just how expansive the umbrella under which NGO groups are housed actually is. Second, the typology helps to categorize NGOs by function and, flowing from this, facilitates assessment of how well they fulfill their functions.

As well as their specific focus, NGOs may also be categorized according to their modus operandi. NGOs can be divided into two groups—those that are primarily advocacy oriented and whose work is to promote a particular cause or position, and operational NGOs, mainly found in the development field, whose primary purpose is to design and implement projects. Advocacy orientated groups use lobbying or public campaigns and education to influence policies and promote action. Development organizations, which include such groups as CARE, Oxfam, and Habitat for Humanity undertake projects, such as building housing for the poor, designing and implementing well systems for clean drinking water, and building irrigation systems for crop development, to name but a few.

Role of NGOs among Global Institutions

The significance, whether global or regional, of NGOs in shaping discourse at the international level and in the development of international law is undeniable. Often nonpolitical and unencumbered by the influence of governments, NGOs have become both the conscience and the voice of international civil society. Nongovernmental organizations, whether domestic or international, figure prominently in both the creation and implementation of international law. Accordingly, the development and increasing influence of NGOs somewhat mirrors the development and influence of the international legal regime. Historically, the rise of NGO activities parallels the growth in intergovernmental organizations starting at the end of the nineteenth century and especially after World War II.

Article 71 of the UN Charter expressly acknowledges the role of NGOs in international law and development:

> The Economic and Social Council [hereafter referred to as ECOSOC] may make suitable arrangements for consultation with nongovernmental organizations, which are concerned with matters within its competence. Such arrangements may be made with international organizations and, where appropriate, with national organizations after consultation with the Member of the United Nations concerned.

The impact of this measure is twofold. First, it recognized the formalized consultative relationship that

NGOs had assumed with national and international bodies, both inside and outside the League of Nations, during the period 1919 to 1934. Second, and more confining, are two conditions set forth under Article 71 that, in contrast to the previous and non-formalized period of engagement, actually place limits on NGO participation. The provisions of Article 71 confine the consultation areas to those that fall within the mandate of ECOSOC. As stipulated, the relationship between NGOs and the UN is limited to one of consultation.

> This distinction, [of consultative status] deliberately made in the Charter, is fundamental and the arrangements for consultation should not be such as to accord to non-governmental organizations the same rights of participation as are accorded to States not members of the Council and to the specialized agencies brought into relationship with the United Nations.

Thus, the position of NGOs and their representatives is in marked contrast to that of representatives of UN agencies, for the latter are able to "participate without vote" in ECOSOC deliberations. It is also worth noting that Article 71 specifies that engagement with national NGOs is to be made only on an exceptional basis.

The initial arrangements for consultation with NGOs were set out in ECOSOC Resolution 1296 (XLIV) on May 27, 1968. Resolution 1296 reaffirmed the international requirement of consultative status for NGOs, and noted that this status could be waived for national NGOs only when the participation of the national NGO was necessary to reflect a "balanced and effective representation of NGOs," or where that NGO had specific or "special" experience or expertise useful to the Council. ECOSOC Resolution 1996/31 subsequently amended resolution 1296 on July 25, 1996, enumerating the requirements for obtaining consultative status, as well as delineating the duties and responsibilities of NGOs in consultative status. Of note, the organization must demonstrate:

- Its activities are relevant to the work of ECOSOC;
- It has a democratic decision-making mechanism;
- Is of recognized standing within the particular field of its competence or of a representative character;
- It has been in existence (officially registered with the appropriate government authorities as an NGO or non-profit agency) for at least two years; and
- Its basic resources are derived primarily from contributions of the national affiliates, individual members, or other non-governmental components.

Significantly, Resolution 1996/31 appears to lower the bar for national NGOs to obtain consultative status,

because the key requirement for the status is that the organization "is not established by a governmental entity or intergovernmental agreement." However, as noted above, the organization must still be of "recognized standing," which may serve to exclude national NGOs that fail to meet that criterion. Currently there are 2,350 NGOs in consultative status with ECOSOC, and some 400 NGOs accredited to the Commission on Sustainable Development (CSD), a subsidiary body of ECOSOC.

Status within International Law

There is some debate regarding the legal personality of NGOs. An entity possesses an international legal personality when it bears rights and duties under international law. Traditionally, the notion of bearing rights and responsibilities has rested primarily within the domain of states. The question is whether international law has evolved enough to recognize the role of non-state actors. The answer may well be both yes and no. Clearly states remain the primary rights-and-duty holders in international law. Nonetheless, the evolution of international law, combined with the increasing role of NGOs in the international playing field, suggests that NGOs have obtained some form of legal personality. This would most certainly apply to the International Committee of the Red Cross, whose position is recognized in international humanitarian law treaties.

NGO Effectiveness

Spar and Dail reasonably posit that the categorization of NGO functions goes some way in assessing an individual NGO's effectiveness. For example, it is possible to audit NGOs that are largely operational, in that they provide a particular service to a particular community, as is true of many development-oriented NGOs. It then becomes possible to assess how well that service has been provided, and how many in the target community are served. Such an audit may calculate how many planned projects were successfully executed and, further, what mechanisms were used for follow-up (e.g., was there training of local staff).

Measuring the effectiveness of advocacy-oriented groups, however, is a much more difficult task. Certainly, such groups might be assessed according to their success of changing a piece of legislation or government policy. Alternatively, effectiveness might be measured by an NGO's success in providing expertise and effective lobbying that culminates in a new treaty or undertaking, or a change in legislation, as happened in the Landmines Campaign (which led to the Landmines Treaty), the creation of a permanent International Criminal Court (ICC), and the worldwide move toward abolition of the death penalty. However, the tangibles are often harder to codify when assessing the effectiveness of human rights NGOs. Worldwide campaigns to stop the use of child soldiers, to stop torture and extra judicial killings, to establish transitional justice processes that demand accountability for gross violations of human rights (including genocide and crimes against humanity), to free political prisoners and to secure socio-economic and cultural rights often operate on the principle of "one step forward and sometimes two steps back."

Limitations

Although NGOs have increased in both numbers and professionalism, and have assumed a significant role as players within the international arena, they still are limited in a number of areas. They can only engage on the international legal level when invited to do so by states, or when allowed by provisions within an international treaty. Some international instruments and regional instruments do allow for third party interventions before courts, which allow NGOs to directly participate in the proceedings. In their work, international, and indeed some national human rights, NGOs principally draw upon the so-called International Bill of Rights, comprised of the Universal Declaration of Human Rights, the International Covenant on Civil and Political Rights, and the International Covenant on Social, Economic and Cultural Rights. These primary human-rights instruments are supplemented by thematic mechanisms—such as treaties that specifically focus on the rights of women or children, or on specific forms of violations, such as torture or discrimination—and other instruments of international law to serve as guiding mechanisms for human rights NGOs. Although international human rights NGOs and some national NGOs rely on international law and are active in more than one country, the term has also been applied to national NGOs that may work only in one country and may rely on a domestic, rather than international legal framework.

Despite the rather broad sense in which the term has been applied, there are fundamental criteria that human rights organizations must meet in order to qualify for NGO status:

- It must not be established by a government or have officers or board members appointed by a government;

- It must not be funded by one government, and if the organization accepts donations from states, the donor countries must not have an influence on the decision making of the organization;

- It must be a not-for-profit organization; and

- It must have the promotion and protection of human rights as its fundamental objective.

Beyond these essential criteria, the operations, support, advocacy, research methodology, funding, and structure can differ profoundly. There are many established and respected international human-rights NGOs that merit some specific mention in the campaign against impunity.

Amnesty International

Amnesty International (AI, at www.amnesty.org) was founded in 1961 by Peter Benenson, a lawyer and activist from the United Kingdom. The organization's mission has evolved from its initial focus on specific issues within the civil and political rights arena to a broader scope, which now encompasses social, economic, and cultural rights. Although it still "concentrates on ending grave abuses of the rights to physical and mental integrity, freedom of conscience and expression, and freedom from discrimination," its mandate has been expanded to include investigating abuses by non-state actors, addressing issues that arise from conflict, and striving for accountability for human rights violations "in the home or community where governments have been complicit or have failed to take effective action."

The organization states that it currently has over 1.5 million members from more than 150 countries. AI's 2002 report describes its operation and structure as follows:

> Its nerve center is the International Secretariat in London, with more than 410 staff members and over 120 volunteers from more than 50 countries around the world. The AI movement consists of more than 7,800 local, youth, specialist, and professional groups in over 100 countries and territories. There are nationally organized sections in 58 countries, and pre-section coordinating structures in another 22 countries and territories worldwide.

> Amnesty International is a democratic movement, self-governed by a nine-member International Executive Committee (IEC) whose members are elected every two years by an International Council representing sections.

The organization distinguishes itself from other international human rights NGOs in that it is membership-based and membership-driven. During 2002 and 2003, its international budget was listed as £23,728,000 ($43,809,006 in U.S. dollars), which comes from membership fees as well as donations from trusts, private individuals, foundations, and corporations. Amnesty International does not accept money from governments.

Lawyers Committee for Human Rights

The Lawyers Committee for Human Rights (LCHR, at www.lchr.org) was established in 1978. According to its mission statement, the organization works

> in the U.S. and abroad to create a secure and humane world by advancing justice, human dignity, and respect for the rule of law. We support human rights activists who fight for basic freedoms and peaceful change at the local level; protect refugees in flight from persecution and repression; promote fair economic practices by creating safeguards for workers' rights; and help build a strong international system of justice and accountability for the worst human rights crimes.

The LCHR, now known as Human Rights First, has offices in both New York City and Washington, D.C. The organization is funded exclusively by private donations and does not accept government funding. Its 2001 annual budget was listed as $6.1 million. The organization is strongly supported through pro-bono work done by the legal community, which, according to their annual report was valued at $15 million in 2001.

Human Rights Watch

Human Rights Watch (HRW, at www.hrw.org) is the largest United States–based international human rights organization. Its organizational headquarters is in New York City and it has thirteen other offices worldwide. As of 2002, the organization employed 189 staff members as well as short-term members and fellows. In the past, HRW has distinguished itself from Amnesty International in that it had a broader mission statement. Its work includes

> not only prisoner-related concerns but also many abuses that do not involve custody, such as discrimination, censorship, and other restrictions on civil society, issues of democratisation and the rule of law, and a wide array of war-related abuses, from the indiscriminate shelling of cities to the use of landmines. Human Rights Watch prides itself on aggressively expanding the categories of victims who can seek protection from our movement. Since the late 1980s, we have gradually added special programs devoted to the rights of women, children, workers, common prisoners, refugees, migrants, academics, gays and lesbians, and people living with HIV/AIDS.

Amnesty International's refocus on thematic rather than country specific issues, and the broadening of its work to include more civil and political as well as social, economic, and cultural rights, has blurred the distinction between AI and HRW, at least with regard to their individual missions. In terms of function and membership, however, HRW is very different from Amnesty International. HRW does not have a mass-membership base, whereas such a base serves as the core of Amnesty's advocacy work. For HRW, a smaller membership base, together with staff and consultants, undertakes the organization's "principal advocacy strategy." HRW's total operating revenues during 2001 and 2002 have been noted to be $21,715,000. Like its counterparts, HRW does not accept government contributions.

All Groups Not Equal?

As the sheer number of NGOs have grown, so too has their level of professionalism, earning them a role as influential actors in an increasingly globalized international community. However, the broad universe of human rights NGOs has also come to include organizations that do not fit some of the basic NGO criteria. This has prompted some within the human rights field to note, "not all human rights groups are equal." In a letter to the *New York Times*, Aryeh Neier, the former Executive Director of Human Rights Watch argued that there has been a "proliferation of groups claiming to speak in the name of the human rights cause, but actually engaged in efforts to promote one or another side in a civil conflict" (Steiner and Alston, 2000, p. 945). Neier's concerns are not without merit. The credibility and effectiveness of the human rights movement rests on its ability to work impartially—in fact as well as in appearance.

Neier suggests that, in addition to the criteria previously outlined, the work of groups claiming to be human rights focused should be scrutinized to ensure that both their methodology and advocacy are of a consistently high standard. Fieldwork must be systematic and carried out in as transparent and impartial a manner as possible. When abuses occur, the organization must be willing to apply legal standards to critique and hold actors accountable for all violations—whether these arise from state or non-state actors. Language used to describe the violation must have legal determinacy and must accurately reflect the level and extent of abuse. Finally, when opposing or contradictory evidence or statements are documented and are found to be credible, they should be noted.

Working against Impunity

International human rights NGOs are primarily advocacy organizations, although some national human rights groups may also have caseworkers or operate clinics that provide legal support in the domestic courts systems. Both domestic and international human rights organizations produce reports or memoranda which detail the organizations' concerns regarding an issue or practice in one or more countries. Reports are often supplemented by updates or alerts on specific countries or issues. Amnesty International, for example, produces *Urgent Actions*, which are bulletins used to mobilize its membership on cases that require immediate attention. Members are requested to lobby their local representatives on these issues and to engage in letter-writing campaigns to the relevant government or international actor.

Although human rights NGOs may differ slightly in their methods of collecting and disseminating information, there are some standard research procedures that can be noted. Organizations such as Amnesty International and Human Rights Watch will routinely send staff into individual countries to investigate human rights conditions there. These field missions are normally undertaken by a specific researcher from the country or region being investigated. The reasearcher may be accompanied by independent consultants who offer specific expertise in either the region or in a specific field (e.g., forensic pathology, military, or munitions experts). Field work may involve site visitations where violations have been alleged to have occurred, interviews with witnesses and victims, collection of medical or forensic evidence (where appropriate), photo or video documentation, interviews with both state and non-state actors (where violations are said to have been undertaken by state military or opposition groups), and interviews with all appropriate other parties.

The duration of the field visitations vary significantly, and depend on the scale of the work and the breadth of topics that are to be covered. Collection and dissemination of materials to a wider audience are a large part of the advocacy work undertaken by human rights groups. As these groups do not comprise political actors and are nongovernmental, the emphasis is on the use of documentation collected as part of its public education and advocacy missions. HRW stresses that a large part of its work focuses on lobbying and its "principal advocacy strategy is to shame offenders by generating press attention and to exert diplomatic and economic pressure on them by enlisting influential governments and institutions." These claims are true for other international human rights NGOs as well. Amnesty International, on the other hand, uses its membership base as an effective means of disseminating reports and fieldwork findings and mobilizes its members to lobby.

Additionally, most international human-rights NGOs use their materials for human rights education, providing online databases of their reports and summaries for use by locally based NGOs as well as others in the field and the general public. One important aspect of the work of international human rights NGOs is the use of mass media. Although organizations approach the question of media contact differently, with some groups putting large resources toward its media work, virtually all human rights groups at local or international levels depend on the media to assist in disseminating its findings and not just as a means to further public education on a given issue. Through the use of the media, these groups reach an audience that would fall outside of the human rights advocacy networks but might be motivated to apply pressure to governments to answer questions and create the impetus for appropriate action.

Human rights NGOs are increasingly becoming players at the international level. They are no longer limited to monitoring and advocating for the respect of international law and legal mechanisms, but are now active participants in the formulation of legislation. One recent example has been NGO involvement in the United Nations Diplomatic Conference of Plenipotentiaries on the Establishment of an International Criminal Court, which was held in Rome, Italy between June 15 and July 17, 1998. Amnesty International, Human Rights Watch, and the Lawyers Committee for Human Rights were among the hundreds of international and national NGOs in attendance. NGO contributions ranged from the technical and prescriptive to the aspirational. This conference was the result of General Assembly Resolution 52/160 of December 15, 1997, which authorised the participation of selected NGOs in the preparatory work for the establishment of the International Criminal Court.

As part of its work, the Preparatory Committee for the International Criminal Court, which included a significant number of NGOs, established a Victims' Trust Fund. Article 75, paragraph 2 of the Rome Statute allows the ICC to direct a convicted person to pay compensation to a victim. NGO participation in the drafting of the guidelines for the Victims' Trust Fund ensured that it would operate independently of the court and would be the body to distribute financial awards. The Victims' Trust Fund is supported by a Victims' Trust Fund Campaign, based in the United States and coordinated by an organization called Citizens for Global Solutions. The Victims' Trust Fund Campaign has a number of United States–based participating organizations, including a number of national and international human rights NGOs. The conference, together with NGO participation in the preparatory work of the ICC, highlights a trend toward increased NGO participation at an almost quasi-state level.

Investigating War Crimes, Crimes against Humanity and Genocide

International human rights legislation and humanitarian law remain the primary framework of human rights organizations when investigating and reporting on allegations of violations. Investigations undertaken by local and international human rights organizations into allegations of genocide in Rwanda and Bosnia and Herzegovina, and crimes against humanity and war crimes in Israel and the Occupied Territories (to name but a few) have provided critical and independent sources of information. Moreover, these organizations have often played central fact-finding roles that the international community was unable to fulfill.

In cases where the UN has been slow to react to gross human rights violations or has been seen to be ineffective, particularly in the case of Rwanda, international human rights NGOs have spearheaded the research and public dissemination of information, and in calling to hold alleged perpetrators accountable. The work of international NGOs, such as Amnesty International and Human Rights Watch, in documenting the genocide in Rwanda and Bosnia and Herzegovina not only provided a historical record of the events, but moved the campaign against impunity further by pressing for the establishment of the ad hoc International Criminal Tribunals for Rwanda and the Former Yugoslavia. A brief look at a 2002 investigation by international human rights organizations in Israel and the Occupied Territories serves to highlight the sometimes pivotal role of human rights NGOs.

Israel and the Occupied Territories

There have been a number of reports issued by international as well as locally based human rights organization that have alleged grave violations of human rights in the Occupied Territories. However, one particular series of events merits review. In March 2002, the Israeli Defence Forces (IDF) launched a new offensive, Operation Defensive Shield, in Palestinian residential areas. An Amnesty International report stated that this offensive

> followed a spate of killings of Israeli civilians by Palestinian armed groups during March. According to the IDF, the purpose of the offensive—like the incursions into refugee camps, which preceded it in March and the occupation of the West Bank, which followed in June—was to eradicate the infrastructure of "terrorism."

Enormous speculation and concern was raised with regard to the Jenin refugee camp (although this concern was not to the exclusion of other areas in the West Bank). Both the city of Jenin and the camp of the

same name had been designated controlled military areas, and those who had fled the fighting that followed the IDF's incursion into the camp were suggesting that the situation within the camp was quite grave. On April 5, 2002, the UN Commission on Human Rights ordered a UN fact-finding mission be undertaken in the Occupied Territories. However, the mission was not allowed to enter Israel and was therefore disbanded. A high-level fact-finding mission that had been agreed upon by Foreign Minister Shimon Peres and UN Secretary-General Kofi Annan and which had been authorized by the unanimous vote of the UN Security Council was also barred from entering Israel and was forced to disband after weeks of negotiations.

Amnesty International and Human Rights Watch, as well as several locally based human rights NGOs dispatched teams of investigators to the West Bank. Because the UN investigating team was not allowed into the areas of concern, the burden fell upon the international and locally based human rights organizations to undertake research and make public their findings on events surrounding the IDF operation. Human rights NGOs in the areas most affected provided critical information regarding the conditions within the camp and in Jenin, as well in other parts of the West Bank that were under Israeli military control. Moreover, using international legal instruments to guide their research and public comment, groups such as AI and HRW, were able to make preliminary assessments as to whether the IDF had operated within the laws of war and the applicable human rights framework.

Two significant reports were published as a result of these investigations. HRW released a report in May 2002, focused solely on Jenin, shortly after the IDF withdrew from the Jenin refugee camp. The report alleged grave breaches of Article 147 of the Fourth Geneva Convention, and suggested that a prima facie case existed for the charge that war crimes were committed. HRW listed several recommendations calling for investigations and accountability, and specifically called upon the Government of Israel to undertake a full investigation into these allegations. Further, HRW recommended that, should Israel fail in this undertaking, the international community should hold accountable those found to have violated human rights.

Amnesty International's report followed in November of that same year, and included a section on the West Bank city of Nablus. For the most part, AI's conclusions and recommendations mirrored those of HRW, but the AI report posited their findings in the wider context of its work in Israel and the Occupied Territories. Amnesty International concluded that some of the reports findings revealed part of a pattern in which many of the violations

> have been committed in a widespread and systematic manner, and in pursuit of government policy (some, such as targeted killings or deportations, were carried out in pursuit of a publicly declared policy). Such violations meet the definition of crimes against humanity under international law.

These reports, together with findings from locally based human rights organizations, remain the only independently researched historical record of these events.

NGO Work-Product

International human-rights organizations use existing international legal frameworks as an important guide when evaluating and presenting their research findings. Additionally, some local as well as international human-rights groups have begun to use different mediums for presenting their research findings. For example, *Witness*, previously a project component of the Lawyers Committee for Human Rights, uses videography as its primary campaigning medium. Nonetheless, the main substantive tool for research dissemination for most human rights organizations remains a written report or informational booklets, which are often preceded by report summaries and press alerts. For international human rights organizations, there is a general format to these reports.

In a 1996 article, Stanley Cohen noted that the standard report format employed by human-rights organizations contains seven fixed elements. According to him, these include expressing concern, stating the problem, setting the context, enumerating the sources and methodology employed, detailing the allegations, citing relevant international and domestic law; and calling for the required action. This outline does, in fact, capture the layout of most international human-rights organizations reports. Neither the format nor the methodology used in compiling such reports differ significantly among the larger international human rights NGOs. However, there is a great deal of variance among national and thematic international human-rights organizations regarding the quality of research and the degree to which international legal frameworks play a role in determining findings.

The Challenges Ahead

The challenges that face human rights NGOs in large part mirrors the broader challenges facing internal human-rights and humanitarian legal mechanisms. The attempt to sideline, ignore, or challenge the relevance

of human rights and humanitarian law, under the guise of state security and the need to combat the global threat of terrorism has gathered momentum. The adversarial relationship between the protection of human rights and the question of state sovereignty, traditionally fought between human rights NGOs and repressive state regimes, has now been extended to democratic or quasi-democratic states, which view the interference of international legal regimes as an impediment to state security and the fight against terrorism. The very public unpacking and demoting of international legal protections is particularly evident, although not unique to, the events that followed September 11, 2001.

SEE ALSO Documentation; Evidence; Humanitarian Intervention; Human Rights; International Committee of the Red Cross; United Nations

BIBLIOGRAPHY

Aall, Pamela R. (2000). *Guide to IGOs, NGOs, and the Military in Peace and Relief Operations*. Washington, D.C.: United States Institute of Peace Press.

Beigbeder, Yves (1991). *The Role and Status of International Humanitarian Volunteers and Organizations: The Right and Duty to Humanitarian Assistance*. Boston: M. Nijhoff.

Carey, Henry F., and Oliver P. Richmond, eds. (2003). *Mitigating Conflict: The Role of NGOs*. London: F. Cass.

Charnovitz, Steve (1997). "Two Centuries of Participation: NGOs and International Governance." *Michigan Journal of International Law* 18:183.

Diller, Janelle M. (1997). *Handbook on Human Rights in Situations of Conflict*. Minneapolis: Minnesota Advocates for Human Rights.

Edwards, Michael (2000). *NGO Rights and Responsibilities: A New Deal for Global Governance*. London: The Foreign Policy Centre.

Gidron, Benjamin, Stanley N. Katz, and Yeheskel Hasenfeld (2002). *Mobilizing for Peace: Conflict Resolution in Northern Ireland, Israel/Palestine, and South Africa*. Oxford: Oxford University Press.

Hudock, Ann (1999). *NGOs and Civil Society: Democracy by Proxy?* Malden, Mass.: Polity Press.

Iriye, Akira (2002). *Global Community: The Role of International Organizations in the Making of the Contemporary World*. Berkeley: University of California Press.

Kamata, Ng'wanza (1999). *Coalition-Building and NGOs Politics: Some Lessons from Experience*. Dar es Salaam, Tanzania: University of Dar es Salaam.

Korten, David C. (1990). *Getting to the 21st Century: Voluntary Action and the Global Agenda*. West Hartford, Conn.: Kumarian Press.

Lawyers Committee for Human Rights (1998). *NGO Action Alert on the International Criminal Court*. New York: Author.

Mahony, Liam (1997). *Unarmed Bodyguards: International Accompaniment for the Protection of Human Rights*. West Hartford, Conn.: Kumarian Press.

Mertus, Julie (2000). "Considering Nonstate Actors in the New Millennium: Toward Expanded Participation in Norm Generation and Norm Application." *Journal of International Law and Politics* 32:537

Olz, Martin (1997). "Non-Governmental Organizations in Regional Human Rights Systems." *Columbia Human Rights Law Review* 28:307.

Rotberg, Robert I., ed. (1996). *Vigilance and Vengeance: NGOs Preventing Ethnic Conflict in Divided Societies.* Washington, D.C.: Brooking Institution Press.

Steiner, Henry J. (1991). *Diverse Partners: Non-Governmental Organizations in the Human Rights Movement.* Cambridge, Mass.: Harvard Law School Human Rights Program.

United Nations (1987). *The United Nations and Non-Governmental Organization Activities on the Question of Palestine.* New York: United Nations.

Weiss, Thomas G., ed. (1998) *Beyond UN Subcontracting: Task-Sharing with Regional Security Arrangements and Service-Providing NGOs.* New York: St. Martin's Press.

Weissbrodt, David, and James McCarthy (1981–1982). "Fact-Finding by International Nongovermental Human Rights Organizations." *Virginia Journal of International Law* 22:1.

Welch, Claude E., Jr., ed. (2001). *NGOs and Human Rights: Promise and Performance.* Philadelphia: University of Pennsylvania Press.

West, Katarina (2001). *Agents of Altruism: The Expansion of Humanitarian NGOs in Rwanda and Afghanistan.* Burlington, Vt.: Ashgate.

Willetts, Peter, ed. (1996). *"The Conscience of the World": The Influence of Non-Governmental Organisations in the UN System.* Washington, D.C.: Brookings Institution.

Kathleen Cavanaugh

Nuclear Weapons

Genocide and crimes against humanity can be carried out with machetes. They can be carried out with nuclear weapons. It appears, however, that in the current state of international law, using a nuclear weapon on people may not, in itself, be genocide, a crime against humanity, or otherwise absolutely forbidden.

The Nuclear Age arrived in the desert near Los Alamos, New Mexico, on July 16, 1945, with the first nuclear test detonation. That same year, the bombs were dropped from U.S. planes on the Japanese cities of Hiroshima, on August 6, and Nagasaki, three days later. Hiroshima and Nagasaki have been the only uses of nuclear weapons in armed conflict.

Subsequently, the Soviet Union, the United Kingdom, France, and China became avowed members of the Nuclear Club. The United States and the Soviet Union tested hydrogen devices of ever more awesome power. Israel is widely believed to have nuclear weapons. South Africa probably had the capability but forswore development after the demise of apartheid. India and Pakistan tested devices in 1998. North Korea apparently has the capability, and Iran, Iraq, Libya, and Brazil have been suspected of developing it. Iraq's nuclear potential was a significant factor in the efforts by the United Nations and the International Atomic Energy Agency (IAEA) to control that country's development of weapons of mass destruction following the Gulf War of 1991. (The IAEA is an intergovernmental organization associated with the United Nations that is devoted to encouraging peaceful uses of nuclear energy.) Nuclear potential figured prominently in the rationale articulated by the United States for its pre-emptive invasion of Iraq in 2003.

Nuclear weapons are explosive devices whose energy comes from fusion or fission of the atom. Their explosion releases vast amounts of heat and energy as well as immediate and long-term radiation. Radiation, unique to nuclear weapons, can cause nearly immediate death and long-term sickness, as well as genetic defects and illness in future generations. Nuclear weapons can have dramatically greater explosive effect than conventional weapons. The bomb dropped on Hiroshima from the airplane named *Enola Gay* was the explosive equivalent of approximately three thousand B29 bombers carrying conventional bombs. The "Bravo" hydrogen test at Bikini Atoll in 1954 had one thousand times the power of the Hiroshima blast.

The Case of Hiroshima and Nagasaki

What might international law say of such forces? The first legal assessment came as a protest from the Japanese Imperial Government through the Government of Switzerland, four days after the bombing of Hiroshima. Referring to Articles 22 and 23 (e) of the Regulations respecting the Laws and Customs of War on Land annexed to the Hague Convention of 1907, the Japanese government emphasized the inability of a nuclear bomb to distinguish between combatants and belligerents, and the cruel nature of its effects, which it compared to poison and other inhumane methods of warfare. Article 22 of the Hague Regulations provides: "The right of belligerents to adopt means of injuring the enemy is not unlimited." Article 23 (e) provides that ". . . it is especially forbidden . . . (e) To employ arms, projectiles, or material calculated to cause unnecessary suffering." The Japanese protest decried "a new offence against the civilization of mankind." Its adversary, however, emphasized how the use of the bomb had quickly brought the war to finality, with millions of lives saved by avoiding a sea and land assault on the Japanese mainland.

The Japanese protest appears as Exhibit III in *Shimoda v. State*, a case brought in the Tokyo District Court in 1963. The plaintiffs sought damages for injuries suffered in Hiroshima and Nagasaki. The plaintiffs argued the illegality of the use of nuclear weapons, founded on an expanded version of the 1945 protest. Damages were claimed from the Japanese government on the theory that it had, in the Peace Treaty, waived the rights of victims to obtain redress from the United States without supplying an alternative source of compensation. The court agreed that the bombings were illegal, but held there was no right to press a claim for damages against the Japanese government.

The concepts of genocide and crimes against humanity were not yet in wide usage when the Japanese government made its August 1945 protest. If the events had occurred a little later, after the concepts gained currency, the government might have added references to those concepts in its protest. Given the international conflict with the United States, however, it was natural to rely on the law of the Hague.

The general principles of the laws of armed conflict have been a major recurring theme in the efforts to rein in nuclear weaponry through international law. This strategy emphasizes banning the use (but not necessarily possession) of such weapons. Other means have included: the quest for partial or total nuclear disarmament (including efforts at non-proliferation and strategic arms limitation); attempts by treaty, resolutions in international organizations, and litigation to stop the testing of such devices; limitations on the development of delivery systems (and defenses thereto); and the creation of Nuclear Free Zones, such as Antarctica, the moon, the South Pacific, and Latin America.

From June 30, 1946, to August 18, 1958, the United States conducted sixty-seven nuclear tests near the Marshall Islands in the South Pacific Ocean. In the first experiment, Able, which is shown here, a B-29 bomber released 23 kilotons of atomic energy into the atmosphere. Compensation claims for the effects of radiation suffered as a result have continued into the twenty-first century. [CORBIS]

Australia/New Zealand Law Suits

New Zealand incurred the wrath of its traditional allies in the 1980s by instituting a total ban from its ports of nuclear-armed and nuclear-powered vessels. In 1973 Australia and New Zealand endeavored to obtain a ruling from the International Court of Justice on the legality of French nuclear tests in the Pacific. Their arguments relied primarily on environmental law and the law of the sea. A majority of the court in effect held the case moot, without reaching a finding on the merits. France had, until the time of the proceedings, been testing in the atmosphere. It now announced that its future tests would be underground. The court held that this announcement was legally binding on the government, which meant that the object sought by Australia and New Zealand had been achieved.

The court, in vague language, left open the possibility of revisiting the case "if the basis of this Judgment were to be effected." New Zealand believed that its case dealt not only with tests in the atmosphere, but also tests that resulted in the entry of radioactive material into the marine environment, even if the testing took place below the ground. Receiving indications that radioactive material was escaping from underground, New Zealand tried to resurrect its case in 1995. A majority of the court refused to reopen the case, taking a narrow view of the earlier proceedings and insisting that, like Australia's somewhat differently worded case, only atmospheric testing had been at issue.

International Court of Justice Advisory Opinion

A further significant effort to draw the various legal strands together occurred in the mid-1990s with efforts at the World Health Organization (WHO) and the United Nations General Assembly to seek an advisory opinion from the International Court of Justice on the legality of the use, or threat of use, of nuclear weapons. Ultimately, a majority of the court held that the WHO's efforts went beyond its constituted powers.

The court, however, had few qualms about trying to answer the concerns of the General Assembly, because the United Nation held much wider competence on questions regarding peace and security. The Assembly asked: Is the threat or use of nuclear weapons in any circumstance permitted under international law? The court rendered its opinion on July 8, 1996. States opposed to nuclear weapons argued that the use, or threat of use, of nuclear weapons is illegal in itself, any time and anywhere. Three of the fourteen judges on the court agreed. Seven more said that it would "generally" be contrary to the laws of war to use or threaten to use nuclear weapons. The seven added that they were not sure whether such a use "would be lawful or unlawful in an extreme circumstance of self-defence, in which the very survival of a State would be at stake." Four judges, Stephen Schwebel (United States), Sheru Oda (Japan), Gilbert Guillaume (France), and Rosalyn Higgins (United Kingdom), disagreed with both of these positions: They believed that each individual case had to be considered against the relevant standards and that no general rule was possible.

The arguments primarily drew upon the law of armed conflict (humanitarian law); environmental law; human rights law (especially the right to life and the law relating to genocide); and the constitutional documents of the UN and the WHO—the UN Charter and the WHO Constitution. Opponents of nuclear weapons argued that these bodies of law pointed, individually or cumulatively, in the direction of the illegality of nuclear weapons. Instruments such as the Partial Test Ban Treaty (PTBT) of 1963 and the Non-Proliferation Treaty (NPT) of 1968 were said to provide further indications of the aversion of international law to nuclear weaponry. The 1963 treaty bans nuclear weapons tests in the atmosphere, in outer space, and under water. The NPT recognizes that the original five nuclear powers—the United States, Russia, The United Kingdom, France and China—already have the weapons, but it nonetheless tries to keep others from developing them.

The essence of the argument by the nuclear powers was that none of these bodies of law expressly addresses the use of nuclear weapons and that, consequently, there was nothing to prohibit their use, or the threat of their use. Moreover, the NPT, they contended, legitimized the possession and thus potential use of nuclear weapons. The benevolent intentions of the nuclear powers were said to be supported by the "negative security guarantees" given in 1995 by the United States, Russia, the United Kingdom, and France. Essentially, they promised not to use nuclear weapons on a non-nuclear state, unless that state carried out an attack in association or alliance with a nuclear-weapon state.

(China made a similar promise, without the exception.) Many developing countries, on the other hand, saw the NPT as discriminatory.

After initial discussion of the court's jurisdiction and of the question itself, the court addressed the arguments that were based on human rights and environmental law. It suggested that human rights arguments are inconclusive where nuclear weapons are concerned because they ultimately send the enquiry to the laws of armed conflict. The court then held that the laws of armed conflict amount to a *lex specialis* in the present context. In other words, the provisions of the laws of armed conflict would prevail over the more general precepts of human-rights law. The same was true of the environmental arguments. "Respect for the environment is one of the elements that go to assessing whether an action is in conformity with the principles of necessity and proportionality [in the laws of armed conflict]." Similarly, the provisions of the UN Charter on when force is, or is not, lawful do not get to the ultimate conclusion. They have to be read subject to the laws of war—even lawful self defense is subject to the constraints of those rules.

Of particular interest is the discussion of genocide. Some nations had contended that the prohibition contained in the 1948 Convention was a relevant rule of customary law that the court must apply to nuclear weapons. Article I of the Genocide Convention confirms that it applies "in time of peace or in time of war." The court summarized the arguments as follows:

> It was maintained before the Court that the number of deaths occasioned by the use of nuclear weapons would be enormous; that the victims could, in certain cases, include persons of a particular national, ethnic, racial, or religious group; that the intention to destroy such groups could be inferred from the fact that the user of the nuclear weapon would have omitted to take account of the well-known effects of the use of such weapons.

According to the court, however, this might sometimes be the case; sometimes not:

> The Court would point out in that regard that the prohibition of genocide would be pertinent in this case if the recourse to nuclear weapons did indeed entail the element of intent, towards a group as such, required by the provision quoted above. In the view of the Court, it would only be possible to arrive at such a conclusion after having taken due account of the circumstances specific to each case.

While the Court did not specifically address it, the logic of its argument on genocide must apply also to the

A hazardous warning sign marks Frenchman's Flat, the Atomic Energy Commission's former nuclear proving ground near Mercury, Nevada. The site of numerous tests for four decades starting in the late 1940s, it is not far from the increasingly populated Las Vegas area.[TED STRESHINSKY/CORBIS]

invocation of crimes against humanity in the attempt to ban the use of nuclear weapons. Unless the thresholds for a crime against humanity can be shown—an attack on a civilian population, and knowledge of that attack—there is no crime against humanity. Use of a nuclear weapon may, in some ill-defined circumstances, be justified or excused. In others it may be the engine of a crime against humanity. The court saw itself as concerned with international conflict. It could be argued that the most likely kind of case where it would be necessary to concentrate, for purposes of legal analysis, on genocide and crimes against humanity following the use of a nuclear weapon will be in the case of an internal conflict. In that context, the laws of armed conflict are still developing, and there the victims are not in a position to engage in the kind of armed resistance that would bring those laws into play. Thus the court arrived at what it regarded the nub of the debate: the laws of armed conflict.

Opponents of nuclear weapons argued that existing treaty provisions and customary law were broad enough to proscribe nuclear weapons, even though the laws do not say so explicitly and for the most part had been written before nuclear weapons were invented. The laws' relevance could be found, for example, by interpreting treaties (and customary law) that ban the use in armed conflict of items such as poison or asphyxiating substances as also including nuclear weapons. Alternatively, one could look to international customary law (anchored mainly in a series of General Assembly resolutions) specifically proscribing nuclear weapons. Another way to achieve the same end would be to acknowledge that it is impossible to use nuclear and other weapons of mass destruction without contravening the prohibitions of unnecessary suffering, indiscriminate attacks which include civilians as targets, and breaches of the neutrality of non-participants in the conflict. Eleven members of the court thought otherwise, however, stating, "There is in neither customary nor conventional international law any comprehensive and universal prohibition of the threat or use of nuclear weapons as such."

Views of the Court

So far as treaty language banning specific weapons goes, these eleven members did not regard what nuclear weapons do to people as bringing them within prohibitions relating to asphyxiating gases or poisons. Apparently, what radiation does is just incidental to the prime effect of nuclear energy, namely, to blow people to smithereens or to incinerate them. That is different from poisoning or asphyxiating and thus acceptable, or at least not illegal by virtue of the ban on poisons or gases. Moreover, the various treaties on nuclear-free areas and the NPT do not create a general prohibition on the use of nuclear weapons.

Nor did the eleven regard numerous nuclear-specific General Assembly resolutions as sufficient. The series of General Assembly resolutions in question begin with Resolution 1653 of November 24, 1961: the Declaration on the Prohibition of the Use of Nuclear and Thermo-Nuclear Weapons. Adopted by a majority of 55 to 20, with 26 abstentions, it asserted, "Any State using nuclear and thermo-nuclear weapons is to be considered as violating the Charter of the United Nations, as acting contrary to the laws of humanity, and as committing a crime against mankind and civilization." The reference to the laws of humanity evokes the Martens Clause in the preamble to the Fourth Hague Convention of 1907. This clause asserts that, until a more complete code has been attained for the laws of war, "the inhabitants and the belligerents remain under the protection and the rule of the principles of the law of nations, as they result from the usages established among civilized peoples, from the laws of humanity, and the dictates of the public conscience." In the 1981 Declaration on the Prevention of Nuclear Catastrophe, also adopted by a large majority, the Assembly declared, "States and statesmen that resort first to the use of nuclear weapons will be committing the gravest crime against humanity." There is a close historical connection between the Martens Clause and the development of the concept of a crime against humanity, of which genocide is one branch.

Scholars usually assert that customary international law has two elements: consistent practice and a sense of obligation (or *opinio juris*) concerning that practice. The court acknowledged that although the General Assembly has no general law-making power, its resolutions may have a role in ascertaining customary law:

General Assembly resolutions, even if they are not binding, may sometimes have normative value. They can, in certain circumstances, provide evidence important for establishing the existence of a rule or the emergence of an *opinio juris*. To establish whether this is true of a given Gen-eral Assembly resolution, it is necessary to look at its content and the conditions of its adoption; it is also necessary to see whether an *opinio juris* exists as to its normative character. Or a series of resolutions may show the gradual evolution of the *opinio juris* required for the establishment of a new rule.

The eleven did not see the failure to use nuclear weapons since 1945 and the practice represented by the line of GA resolutions as enough:

[S]everal of the resolutions under consideration have been adopted with substantial numbers of negative votes and abstentions; thus, although those resolutions are a clear sign of deep concern regarding the problem of nuclear weapons, they still fall short of establishing the existence of an *opinio juris* on the illegality of the use of such weapons.

The opinion then turns to principles of the law of war, such as unnecessary suffering, indiscriminate targeting, and breaches of neutrality, which the court locates in an overlapping mixture of customary and treaty law. All fourteen judges agreed that these principles apply to nuclear weapons. The opinion even cites statements by the nuclear powers to this effect in the oral pleadings. It is the implication of these principles, which leads to a sharp divergence. "The Court" (in fact seven of the judges, with the tie broken by the unusual rule of the court that gives the President the right to cast a tie-breaking vote in addition to his normal one) offers some cryptic remarks on the topic, summarized at paragraph 105 (2) E of the opinion:

It follows from the above-mentioned requirements that the threat or use of nuclear weapons would generally be contrary to the rules of international law applicable in armed conflict, and in particular the principles and rules of humanitarian law;

However, in view of the current state of international law, and the elements of fact at its disposal, the Court cannot conclude definitively whether the threat or use of nuclear weapons would be lawful or unlawful in an extreme circumstance of self-defense, in which the very survival of a State would be at stake.

The individual opinions of the seven in the "majority" covered a broad spectrum, particularly on the second sub-paragraph of Paragraph E, which dealt with the possible exceptional case—self-defense—when the use of nuclear weapons would not be contrary to international law regarding armed conflict. At one end, some seemed to have doubts about even the validity of the ultimate self-defense exception. At the other, some seemed to accept that there was an in extremis self defense exception.

The seven person dissent comprised two diametrically opposite groups. Judges Christopher Weeramantry, Abdul Koroma, and Mohamed Shahabuddeen voted against the majority finding because they felt that the opinion did not go far enough; Judges Stephen Schwebel, Sheru Oda, Gilbert Guillaume, and Rosalyn Higgins voted against it because they felt the opinion went too far. For Weeramantry, Koroma, and Shahabuddeen, the rules of armed conflict, the specific and the general, proscribe nuclear weapons in all circumstances. No conceivable use of nuclear weapons could comply with the rules. For Schwebel, Oda, Guillaume, and Higgins, the laws of armed conflict apply, but each individual use or threat of use must be considered on its own merits, as would be true of any other weapon that is lawful in itself.

One other inquiry, which the court addressed only inconclusively, related to the nuclear powers' doctrine of deterrence, the argument that the possession of nuclear weapons deterred their use and intimidated non-nuclear nations who might otherwise be tempted to engage in aggression or to use nuclear or other weapons of mass destruction. During the cold war period, it was widely argued that the doctrine of Mutually Assured Destruction (MAD) meant that no leader would dare risk starting a nuclear war in which all might perish. While the court opined that it could not ignore the doctrine, it did not offer a legal characterization of it. Judge Schwebel, in his dissenting opinion, however, seemed to regard the doctrine as supportive of the nuclear powers' position on customary law.

Having split three ways on the crucial issue, the court spoke unanimously regarding a certain matter that was not directly responsive to the question asked. It nonetheless points in the only possible direction now open regarding the issue of nuclear weapons. The presence of this matter in the court reflected widespread frustration that, after nearly thirty years, the promise of Article VI of the 1968 Non-Proliferation Treaty (NPT) had not been fulfilled. Article VI provides that:

> Each of the Parties to the Treaty undertakes to pursue negotiations in good faith on effective measures relating to cessation of the nuclear arms race at an early date and to nuclear disarmament, and on a treaty on general and complete disarmament under strict and effective international control.

At the time that the Advisory Opinion was written, 182 countries were parties to the non-proliferation treaty. By the end of 2003, there were 188, but one had claimed to withdraw. The opinion reiterates the Article VI obligation in various ways, hinting that it applies (as customary law) to parties and (the few) non-parties to the treaty alike. There is an obligation both to negotiate in good faith and to achieve a particular result—total nuclear disarmament—as well as to reach the broader goal of general and complete disarmament.

The whole object of the case had been to delegitimize the nuclear bomb. No one doubted that ultimately it would still be necessary to complete the disarmament negotiations. Even total success in the case would not have magically eliminated existing stockpiles. The success of the case in chipping away at the acceptability of nuclear weapons should have made it a little more likely that those negotiations would be completed sooner rather than later.

Nuclear Nonproliferation

The NPT envisaged that conferences would be held at five-year intervals in order to review the operation of the treaty. Concluded in 1968 and in force in 1970, it was initially effective for a period of twenty-five years. In 1995, while the advisory proceedings were pending, the parties agreed that it would continue in force indefinitely. At the review in 2000, a group known as the "New Agenda Coalition" (Brazil, Egypt, Ireland, Mexico, New Zealand, South Africa, and Sweden) spearheaded the effort that resulted in an "unequivocal undertaking by the nuclear-weapons States to accomplish the total elimination of their nuclear arsenals leading to nuclear disarmament to which all States are committed under Article VI."

It is hard to see this vision being realized. In 1997 Costa Rica submitted a Model Nuclear Weapons Convention to the United Nations. Its title says it all: "Convention on the Prohibition of the Development, Testing, Production, Stockpiling, Transfer, Use, and Threat of use of Nuclear Weapons and on Their Elimination." It would lead to progressive prohibition and stringent inspections to ensure compliance. The model has been increasingly refined by nongovernmental groups, such as the Lawyers Committee on Nuclear Policy, but has not captured the imagination of governments. Negotiations proceed glacially in various forums, including the First Committee of the United Nations General Assembly, the sixty-six nation Conference on Disarmament which meets in Geneva and the Assembly's Commission on Disarmament.

Although they have worked toward reducing their arsenals, the nuclear powers seem determined to rely on them in some circumstances, and even to continue research and development. Albeit observing a moratorium on testing, the United States, for example, seeks to develop a "mini-nuke" capable of going after deeply buried weapons of mass destruction. In December 2001, President Bush announced the United States' withdrawal from the 1972 agreement with Russia on the limitation of anti-ballistic missile systems. That agreement complemented the two super-powers' policy of Mutually Assured Destruction (MAD) and was a basic element of their search for deterrence. The 1972 treaty prohibited the parties from putting into place systems capable of defending their entire territories from intercontinental ballistic missiles and from developing, testing, or deploying sea-, air-, space-, or mobile land-based antiballistic missile systems.

Those in favor of withdrawing saw the treaty as an obstacle to developing a comprehensive defense against weapons of mass destruction. Those opposed feared the U.S. government would now embark on an incredibly expensive technological effort, which had no guarantee of success. At the same time, they argued, ending the treaty could result in a new arms race with Russia and even China. Meanwhile, a more pressing danger was posed by terrorists and rogue states with delivery systems other than intercontinental missiles. A relatively small "dirty bomb" or radiological instrument in the hands of terrorists might present a greater danger than a developed bomb, and resources might be better spent in dealing with such dangers.

In December of 2002, the United States issued a new "National Strategy to Combat Weapons of Mass Destruction" which asserts that the United States "reserves the right to respond with overwhelming force—including through resort to all of our options—to the use of WMD against the United States, our forces abroad, friends, and allies." The phrase, "all of our options," clearly includes both conventional and nuclear responses, even in "appropriate cases through preemptive measures." This is perhaps even clearer than a similar statement made earlier in the year in a Nuclear Posture Review. Serious questions have been raised about the compatibility of these moves with the United Nations Charter and with the International Court of Justice's opinion.

Three nations (India, Israel, and Pakistan) have remained resolutely outside the NPT. Another, North Korea, has purported to withdraw. It claims the right under a treaty provision (similar to that the United States invoked in withdrawing from the ABM treaty) that a party "shall in exercising its national sovereignty have the right to withdraw from the Treaty if it decides that extraordinary events, related to the subject matter of this Treaty, have jeopardized the supreme interests of its country." North Korea asserted its security was jeopardized by the United States, which North Korea claimed was threatening a pre-emptive nuclear strike, other military action, and a blockade. North Korea's right to withdraw is hotly debated.

Divisions and Debate

More positive have been developments involving the IAEA's inspection regime. Under the NPT, the IAEA enters into safeguard agreements with non-nuclear weapons states to maintain controls over nuclear material for peaceful activities. Efforts to strengthen that system have been undertaken since 1992, with the discovery of the extent of Iraq's weapons program, notwithstanding the safeguards. These efforts entailed the development of more intrusive reporting and inspection. States are encouraged to accept this by becoming party to an optional protocol, a model of which was developed by the Agency in 1997. Late in 2003, Iran agreed to such a protocol and Libya was about to. The IAEA inspections regime could provide a precedent, along with that developed by the Organization for the Prevention of Chemical Weapons, for a more comprehensive nuclear abolition treaty, along the lines of the model introduced by Costa Rica. Meanwhile, efforts continue to put greater international control over fissile material adaptable to bomb-making.

Shortly after the International Court of Justice rendered its opinion, in September 1996, the United Nations approved the Comprehensive Nuclear Test Ban Treaty (CTBT). Its rationale is expressed succinctly in a preambular paragraph:

> The cessation of all nuclear weapon test explosions and all other nuclear explosions, by constraining the development and qualitative improvement of nuclear weapons and ending the development of advanced new types of nuclear weapons, constitutes an effective measure of nuclear disarmament and non-proliferation in all its aspects.

Parties undertake not to carry out any nuclear weapon test explosion or any other nuclear explosion, and to prevent any such nuclear explosion at any place under their control. At the end of 2003, the treaty was not yet in force. While it had over one hundred signatories, by its own terms it cannot come into effect until ratified by forty-four named States that possess nuclear reactors. About three-quarters of them had done so by 2004, including France, the Russian Federation, and the United Kingdom. There were notable holdouts, such as China, the United States (where the treaty was rejected in the Senate), India, Pakistan and North Korea.

An effort to include the use of nuclear weapons as a war crime in the Rome Statute of the International Criminal Court failed in 1998. In a negotiation based on finding consensus, a majority supported it but it was adamantly opposed by the Nuclear Club, and thus failed. The way was left open for re-examination in the future.

Perversely perhaps, the laws of armed conflict regulate the ethics and modalities of killing. They place an absolute ban on certain kinds of weapons, such as exploding bullets below a certain size, dum-dum (expanding) bullets, poison, asphyxiating gases, and bacteriological substances. Use of such weapons is always a war crime, no matter how good the cause. Judge Weeramantry, dissenting in the Nuclear Weapons Case, raised the fundamental question how such modalities can be proscribed, yet permit nuclear weapons to remain lawful:

> At least, it would seem passing strange that the expansion within a single soldier of a single bullet is an excessive cruelty which international law has been unable to tolerate since 1899, and that the incineration in one second of a hundred thousand civilians is not. This astonishment would be compounded when that weapon has the capability, through multiple use, of endangering the entire human species and all civilization with it.

One might equally ask whether it is "passing strange" that use of a nuclear weapon is not yet genocide or a crime against humanity as a matter of law. But genocide, as defined in the Genocide Convention, requires a specific mental element, the "intent to destroy, in whole or in part, a national, ethnical, racial, or religious group, as such." It will often be possible to infer such an intent from use of nuclear weapons, but apparently not always. A crime against humanity requires knowledge that what is being done is part of an attack on a civilian population. Again, inferences may be drawn, but some think that may not always be so.

SEE ALSO Hiroshima; Humanitarian Law; International Court of Justice; Weapons of Mass Destruction

BIBLIOGRAPHY
Boisson de Chazournes, Laurence, and Philippe Sands, ed. (1999). *International Law, the International Court of Justice and Nuclear Weapons.* Cambridge: Cambridge University Press.

Burroughs, John (1997). *The Legality of the Threat or Use of Nuclear Weapons: A Guide to the Historic Opinion of the International Court of Justice.* Muenster: Lit Verlag.

Clark, Roger S., and Madeleine Sann (1996). *The Case against the Bomb: Marshall Islands, Samoa and the Solomon Islands before the International Court of Justice in Advisory Proceedings on the Legality of the Threat or Use of Nuclear Weapons.* Camden, N.J.: Rutgers University School of Law.

Criminal Law Forum: An International Journal 7, no. 2 (1996). Contains written submissions to the International Court of Justice, pro and con the legality of Nuclear Weapons, by the United States and Solomon Islands.

International Review of the Red Cross (January–February 1997). No. 316. Special issue on the "Advisory Opinion of the International Court of Justice on the Legality of Nuclear Weapons and International Humanitarian Law."

Lifton, Robert Jay (1990). *The Genocidal Mentality: Nazi Holocaust and Nuclear Threat.* New York: Basic Books.

Matheson, Michael J. (1997). "The Opinions of the International Court of Justice on the Threat or Use of Nuclear Weapons." *American Journal of International Law* 91(417).

Moxley, Charles J., Jr. (2000). *Nuclear Weapons and International Law in the Post Cold War World.* Lanham, Md.: Austin & Winfield.

Nagan, Winston P. (1999). "Nuclear Arsenals, International Lawyers, and the Challenge of the Millenium" *Yale Journal of International Law* 24(484).

Nanda, Ved, and David Krieger (1998). *Nuclear Weapons and the World Court.* Ardsley, N.Y.: Transnational Publishers.

Roff, Sue Rabbit (1995). *Hotspots: The Legacy of Hiroshima and Nagasaki.* New York: Cassell.

Sagan, Carl A. (1990). *A Path Where No Man Thought: Nuclear Winter and the End of the Arms Race.* New York: Random House.

Schwartz, Stephen I., ed. (1998). *Atomic Audit: The Costs and Consequences of U.S. Nuclear Weapons Since 1940.* Washington, D.C.: Brookings Institution Press.

Ware, Alyn (2003). "Rule of Force or Rule of Law: Legal Responses to Nuclear Threats from Terrorism, Proliferation, and War" *Seattle Journal for Social Justice* 2(243).

LEGAL CASES
Australia v. France. International Court of Justice, Nuclear Tests Case, Judgment of 20 December 1974, 1974 I.C.J. Reports 253.

International Court of Justice. *The Legality of the Threat or Use of Nuclear Weapons, Advisory Opinion of 8 July 1996,* 1996 I.C.J. Reports 226.

New Zealand v. France. International Court of Justice, Nuclear Tests Case, Judgment of 20 December 1974, 1974 I.C.J. Reports 457.

New Zealand v. France. International Court of Justice, Request for an Examination of the Situation in Accordance with Paragraph 63 of the Court's Judgment of 20 December 1974 in the Nuclear Tests Case, Order of 22 September 1995, 1995 I.C.J. Reports 288.

"Shimoda v. State." *Japanese Annual of International Law* 8, no. 212 (1964).

Roger S. Clark

Nuremberg Laws

In August 1935 Adolf Hitler spoke of the need to codify provisions of the Nazi Party's program with a law that would define the status of Germany's Jews. In accor-

The Nuremberg Laws led to a September 1, 1941, decree requiring all German Jews above the age of six to wear a prominent star of David when in public. [BETTMANN/CORBIS]

The Reich Citizenship Law excluded Jews as full Reich citizens: "A citizen of the Reich is only that subject who is of German or kindred blood, and, who through his conduct, shows that he is both desirous and fit to serve faithfully the German people and Reich." The legal and administrative machinery necessary to enforce the law fell under the jurisdiction of Reich Minister of the Interior William Frick, who expanded the law's reach to "members of other races whose blood is not related to German blood, as, for example, Gypsies and Negroes."

German Jews soon found themselves excluded from the positions in government, society, and cultural, educational, and financial institutions that they had acquired after their emancipation in the nineteenth century. Jews now forced into the position of second-class citizens lost critical human and civil rights. Disenfranchised from German society, they faced mounting political, economic, and cultural barriers. Tenured Jewish civil servants, who had been protected by their status as war veterans, were dismissed from the public sector. Jewish professors, physicians, and teachers were banned from the civil service; many Jews lost their pension rights. Insurmountable professional and legal obstacles were placed on physicians, pharmacists, and lawyers. In 1938 Jewish professionals were banned from practicing their professions within German society. Social exclusion accompanied professional exclusion; that same year Jews were forbidden to attend the theater, concerts, the cinema, and art exhibitions; they were also banned from restaurants, hotels, and resort areas. And starting in early 1939 Jews were compelled to use a first name of Sara or Israel.

Unresolved in the initial September 15th legislation was the biological definition of a Jew; in subsequent weeks, this issue generated considerable debate. The first of thirteen supplementary decrees, all designating the composition of Jewish blood, was published on November 14, 1935, and defined a Jew in terms of lineage. Thus, a "full Jew" was one with three or four Jewish grandparents; those with two Jewish grandparents and two Aryan grandparents were considered "half-Jews." Such half-Jews had to meet certain conditions in order to be regarded as full Jews and therefore subject to the provisions of the new law. Half-Jews were to be considered full Jews if they practiced Judaism as a religious faith, or if they had married a Jew or were the legitimate or illegitimate children of Jewish and Aryan parents. The practical effect of these distinctions was that people with two Jewish grandparents, but who did not practice Judaism or who had been baptized, were not considered Jews. This group was referred to as *Mischlinge,* but even their fate generated consider-

dance with his wishes a Nazi conference in Nuremberg, September 1935, drafted two pieces of legislation to legally sanction a set of psychological and cultural attitudes toward Jews. The intent was to permanently segregate the Jewish presence within German society. The Nuremberg Laws—the Reich Citizenship Law and Blood Protection Law—legislated by the Reich Party Congress soon thereafter covered critical areas of human life: rights of citizenship under German law and the regulation of sexual relations between Jews and other Germans. The Blood Protection Law referred only to Jews, but a supplemental decree issued in November 1935 expanded the law to include additional groups, specifically Romani and Negroes, that constituted a so-called threat to German blood. The interpretation of "racially alien blood" was further expanded in subsequent decrees, which included special categories for Germans with mental and genetic deformities, and other biological embarrassments to the master race.

encyclopedia of GENOCIDE *and* CRIMES AGAINST HUMANITY

able debate at the infamous Wannsee Conference in January 1942 that initiated planning for the Final Solution, the annihilation of all European Jewry. Germans married to Jews were encouraged to divorce their spouses. The regime relied primarily on church records to determine the ancestry of racial Jews who had been living as "non-Aryan" Christians.

The Supreme Court of the Reich subsequently became quite involved in litigation interpreting the Blood Protection Law in terms of miscegenation. It and other courts were asked to decide on the types of sexual contact considered to be criminal: what constituted sexual intercourse; did criminal behavior include sexual contact that led to intercourse; how much touching was to be defined as sexual? In 1939 a Jewish man was sentenced to one month in jail for the crime of having looked at a fifteen-year-old Aryan girl.

The Blood Protection Law prescribed severe penalties for Jews engaging in sexual relations with Germans. Jewish men and women convicted of sexual crimes could be imprisoned or executed. Two additional provisions of the law prohibited the employment of any female Aryan servants under the age of forty-five in Jewish households, and Jews from holding or hoisting the German flag.

The Nuremberg Laws were a defining legislative moment in the history of the Third Reich. They codified what for several years had been a growing psuedo-scientific and medical set of perceptions regarding so-called healthy Aryan traits, genes, and blood. The laws provided additional statutory justification for the euthanasia program that began in 1938, whereby German citizens, including Jewish and German children, suffering from congenital illness, alcoholism, and feeble-mindedness, or anyone deemed otherwise mentally or genetically deficient, could be killed by the state. After 1938 major mental hospitals became killing centers for individuals designated as "life unworthy of life."

The major impact of the Nuremberg Laws was to isolate the Jewish and Romani populations; to deprive them of rights of citizenship; and to effectively bar marriages between Jews and other racially "unfit" groups, and Germans. To marry in Germany, a couple was required to demonstrate the purity of their genetic heritage. In disputed or questionable cases local commissions or courts determined if the amount of Jewish blood in a family's history was sufficient to deny a marriage license. Furthermore, the Nuremberg Laws had the practical effect of legitimizing concentration and death camps such as Auschwitz, Sobibor, Treblinka, and Maidanek.

The Nuremberg Laws also led to a decree issued on September 1, 1941, requiring all Jews above the age of

English translation of the original Nazi decree curtailing the rights of Jews. [CORBIS SYGMA]

six to wear a Jewish star when in public. In Germany alone more than 166,000 Jews were forced to wear the badge, although over 17,000 Jews of mixed marriages remained exempt from this regulation. In Poland the chief sanitation inspector (the head of medical affairs in the Nazi-controlled government) decreed that even medication bottles issued by Jewish pharmacists must be identified with a Jewish star. German officials feared that if Germans or Poles touched one of these bottles, they might become infected with a "Jewish disease." As early as November 1939 the German head of Poland's general government, Hans Frank, ordered all Jews above the age of ten to wear a star of David on their right arm; he also forced Jewish businesses to display a similar sign in their windows.

The denial of fundamental human rights to Jews, Romani, and the psychologically disabled elicited little reaction from the German public. No mass protests were organized, and German citizens appeared undisturbed by the racist and medical assumptions of the Nazi regime. Indeed, the majority of prosecutions that involved "race pollution" arising from the Nuremberg Laws were initiated by ordinary citizens. The regime never forced its citizens to denounce Jews to the authorities for acts of miscegenation. The Gestapo on occasion pursued cases involving violations of the Blood Protection Law.

The Nuremberg Laws were enormously popular with ordinary German citizens; they accepted the underlying pseudo-scientific and medical theories that viewed the Jew as a race pollutant and a danger to the purity of Aryan genes. *National therapy* (a term coined by Carl Schneider, a psychiatrist active in defining and elaborating the psychological assumptions of Nazi ideology and science) meant ethnic cleansing: ridding the populace of genetic and blood contaminants threatening the psychological and physical health of the German/Aryan population. The Nuremberg Laws, rather than creating a state of mind, confirmed already existing psychological prejudices and phobias against Jews, and fantasies regarding their power to poison and degrade society, and pervert physiological and biological reality.

SEE ALSO Anti-Semitism; Auschwitz; Einsatzgruppen; Euthanasia; Extermination Centers; Gas; Gestapo; Ghetto; Goebbels, Joseph; Göring, Hermann; Heydrich, Reinhard; Himmler, Heinrich; Hitler, Adolf; Holocaust; Intent; Kristallnacht; Labor Camps, Nazi; Nuremberg Trials; SS; Streicher, Julius; Wannsee Conference

BIBLIOGRAPHY

Aly, Gotz, and Susanne Heim (2002). *Architects of Annihilation*. Trans. A. G. Blunden. Princeton, N.J.: Princeton University Press.

Burleigh, Michael, and Wolfgang Wipperman (1991). *The Racial State: Germany, 1933–1945*. Cambridge, U.K.: Cambridge University Press.

Friedlander, Henry (1995). *The Origins of Nazi Genocide: From Euthanasia to the Final Solution*. Chapel Hill: University of North Carolina Press.

Glass, James M. (1997). *"Life Unworthy of Life": Racial Phobia and Mass Murder in Hitler's Germany*. New York: Basic Books.

Weindling, Paul (1989). *Health, Race and German Politics between National Unification and Nazism 1870–1945*. Cambridge: Cambridge University Press.

James M. Glass

Nuremberg Trials

On November 20, 1945, six months after the surrender of Nazi Germany to allied forces, twenty-one military, political, media, and business leaders of the Third Reich filed into the dock of the Palace of Justice in the devastated and occupied German city of Nuremberg. There they stood trial for the most heinous crimes known to humankind, which were committed during World War II. Over the course of the next eleven months, unprecedented trials that profoundly influenced the development of international law and how governments must treat civilian populations unfolded. There were moments of lofty rhetoric and high drama, but often there was also the tedium that has characterized most criminal trials throughout history.

The four major victorious allied powers in the European theater of World War II—the United States, the United Kingdom, France, and the Soviet Union—met in London during the summer of 1945. On August 8 these nations entered into an international agreement, known as the London Charter, that created a special court called the International Military Tribunal (IMT). The IMT consisted of an organizing charter and constitution "for the just and prompt trial and punishment of the major war criminals of the European Axis." The aggressive military assaults of the German army, the criminal Nazi occupation policies in numerous conquered lands, and the Nazi-inspired extermination of millions of Jews and other victims seemed at the time to provide ample justification for establishing the IMT.

During the height of armed combat, on November 1, 1943, the Foreign Ministers of the United States, United Kingdom, and the Soviet Union declared in Moscow that their war efforts would not prejudice "the case of the major criminals whose offenses would have no particular location and who will be punished by a joint decision of the Governments of the Allies." They thus established a distinction between major war criminals in leadership positions and the many thousands who committed crimes in the field. This differentiation set the stage for the Nuremberg trials of prominent leaders in 1945 and 1946, followed by thousands of trials of war criminals of lesser stature in the courts of the four occupying powers of Germany.

Alternatives to Nuremberg

During World War II, there were many competing ideas about how best to deal with the war criminals of the Third Reich, and the IMT's creation was by no means a certainty until the very end of the war. There always was an expectation that soldiers charged with conventional war crimes would be prosecuted. However, enemy leaders responsible for the atrocities of the Third Reich might have faced an entirely different fate, consistent with the Moscow Declaration. For instance, British officials, aware of a vengeful British public, advocated summary execution of the fifty to one hundred top Nazi leaders. British Prime Minister Winston Churchill wrote to Soviet leader Josef Stalin in September 1944, arguing that such leaders should be executed as "outlaws" within six hours of capture, and that "the question of their fate is a political and not a judicial one." Such plans were kept secret, however, so as to avoid German reprisals against British prisoners of war. In late 1943, Stalin recommended to Churchill and President Franklin D. Roosevelt that 50,000 to 100,000 of the German Commanding Staff "must be physically liquidated."

Within the U.S. government, there were strong advocates for summary execution. Treasury Secretary Hans Morgenthau, who had distinguished himself early in the war as a fierce opponent of the Nazis' anti-Jewish atrocities, was opposed to war crimes trials. In November 1944 he submitted a summary execution plan that initially targeted five million Nazi Party members but settled on 2,500 members. Roosevelt was prepared to adopt Morgenthau's plan, but Secretary of War Henry Stimson argued vigorously for war crimes trials with basic rights of due process drawn from the U.S. Bill of Rights. He believed that such trials would establish individual responsibility for the crimes of the Nazi leadership and uphold democratic notions of justice. Stimson warned, "Remember this punishment is for the purpose of prevention and not for vengeance." The tide turned in Stimson's favor with Roosevelt's endorsement of war crimes trials on January 3, 1945. This was followed by the strong backing of Roosevelt's successor, President Harry Truman. The Soviet Union based its own belated support on their own experience with show trials in the 1930s, believing that war-crimes trial verdicts would result in the public (and popular) execution of the German war criminals.

Victor's Justice?

The IMT can be viewed as symbolic of "victor's justice" and its associated charge of hypocrisy, meaning that the victors in World War II judged the vanquished. The inference of such a view is that the trials might be tainted by the lack of investigation and prosecution of any war crimes that the allied powers might have committed during the global conflict. It was no accident that aerial bombing was excluded as a war crime in the London Charter for the IMT. Including it would make prosecution of German aerial bombings (e.g., of London) appear as victor's vengeance, unless parallel investigations of American and British bombings of German cities (including the fire-bombings of Hamburg and Dresden) were also undertaken.

The German people accepted the reality of reprisals, but they deeply resented the failure at Nuremberg to hold accountable those who inflicted so much horror upon them. German historian and journalist Jorg Friedrich has noted that 700,000 German soldiers and civilians lost their lives in the last three months of the war. During one June 1943 British bombing raid of Hamburg, 43,000 residents died, 8,000 of them young children. Of the aftermath of Allied bombing missions, Friedrich has written:

> Nearly all large and medium-sized German cities lay in ruins, charred and exploded into rubble by aerial warfare. In February 1945, in the Baltic port of Swinemunde, a hospital city, more than 20,000 sick, exhausted refugees from eastern Pomerania had been killed in bombings. German settlements in and beyond the eastern and southeastern borders had been purged, in the course of which 1.5 million people perished. In Yugoslavia, 98,000 ethnic Germans were killed or starved to death, one in five members of the population. Two million women were raped by the invading [Soviet] Red Army.

The Soviet government had no interest in being judged for its conduct during the war, including the Soviet Army's role in massacring the Polish officer corps (in the Belorussian forests of Katyn and elsewhere). It also wished to avoid being held responsible for the Nazi-Soviet Pact of 1939 carving up Poland, the Soviet attack on Finland in 1940, and the concentration camps in Soviet-occupied regions during the war. In those camps, Soviets inflicted extreme mistreatment on civilian and military detainees, often in cooperation with German SS and Gestapo officials, and caused the deaths of tens of thousands of German prisoners of war.

During his trial, defendant Admiral Karl Doenitz (Supreme Commander of the German navy) effectively used in his defense an interrogatory from Admiral Chester W. Nimitz, the Commander in Chief of the American Naval Forces in the Pacific Ocean during the war. His lawyer used Admiral Nimitz's testimony to confirm that it was American policy to interpret the London Submarine Agreement of 1936 "in exactly the same way as the German Admiralty," supporting his claim "that the German sea war was perfectly legal." German submarine surprise attacks against British and other merchant ships, which doomed to the ocean's depths the lives of passengers and crew, mirrored what the U.S. Navy had done to sink Japanese merchant ships. Doenitz escaped conviction on the charge of having breached the international law of submarine warfare, although he was convicted on other charges.

The Nuremberg trials would not have taken place if there had been a requirement for reciprocal justice, because the allied powers could not have agreed to the intensive self-examination that such a criminal investigation would demand. However deep this apparent flaw in the process was at the time, there remains great value in what was accomplished to establish individual criminal responsibility for the atrocity crimes of senior Nazi leaders. Summary executions were avoided and crimes of great magnitude and horrific character were publicly identified with their perpetrators, who were brought to justice relatively speedily. The manner in which the Nuremberg trials were conducted achieved a lasting credibility for its attention to due process rights. Further, the lessons of Nuremberg and the justice rendered there upon German leaders probably had a positive influence on later generations of Germans, who have been less affected by what their ancestors endured during World War II than they otherwise might have been. Probably as a result of the Nuremberg legacy, Germany has become a strong supporters of human rights, the non-use of force, international justice, and the work of the permanent International Criminal Court.

Composition of the Tribunal

The composition of the IMT reflected the multinational character of the victorious Allied powers. The United States, United Kingdom, France, and the Soviet Union were represented by four sitting judges and four alternate judges, one from each allied nation. All but the Soviet judge and alternate were drawn from non-military legal professions at the time of the trials. The prosecution counsel numbered fifty-two lawyers, again drawn from each of the four allied powers. The U.S. prosecution team was led by Justice Robert H. Jackson, on leave from the U.S. Supreme Court. Two of his American military prosecutors, Lieutenant Commander Whitney Harris and Brigadier General Telford Taylor, later wrote highly acclaimed, comprehensive histories of the Nuremberg trials. Twenty-eight German lawyers served as counsel for the individual defendants, and eleven German lawyers defended the six organizations that were charged with criminal conduct.

The London Charter required a fair trial for all of the defendants, and set forth fundamental rules for that purpose. These rules included the right to counsel and the right to cross-examine any witness. As the trials got underway, however, defense lawyers often found it difficult to obtain documents sought for the defense of their clients, and delays in the translation of key documents created difficulties for both the prosecution and defense.

Selection of Defendants

The selection of whom to indict and prosecute at Nuremberg bedeviled the four allied powers during the summer of 1945. For practical reasons, the total number of individuals who could stand trial before the IMT had to be extremely limited. Non-German Axis leaders were soon removed from the working list of targets for prosecution. Key Nazi leaders like Adolf Hitler, Joseph Goebbels, and Heinrich Himmler were already dead. The allies had to understand how power was exercised in Nazi Germany, and had to discover who wielded the most authority, and thus responsibility, for perpetrating the crimes described in the London Charter. Since first-hand information and actionable evidence about the crimes of the Holocaust had only begun to emerge, some of the obvious candidates for prosecution for the extermination of the Jews and others were not pursued. Among these were Gestapo chief Heinrich Muller and his deputy, Adolf Eichmann. In the end, notable and some far less notorious figures were selected.

The final list of twenty-four German defendants arose from political compromises and the intent of the allied powers to arrange the defendant pool to indict several branches of the Nazi leadership: military, political, propaganda, finance, and forced labor. The military defendants were Admiral Doenitz, Hermann Goering (Chief of the Air Force), Alfred Jodl (Chief of Army Operations), Wilhelm Keitel (Chief of Staff of the High Command of the Armed Forces), and Erich Raeder (Grand Admiral of the Navy). The political defendants were Hans Frank (Minister of Interior and Governor-General of occupied Poland), Wilhelm Frick (Minister of Interior), Rudolf Hess (Deputy to Hitler), Ernst Kaltenbrunner (Chief of the Reich's Main Security Office. under which the Gestapo and SS operated), Alfred Rosenberg (Minister of the Occupied Eastern Territories), Arthur Seyss-Inquart (Commissar of the Netherlands), Albert Speer (Minister of Armaments and War Production), Constantin von Neurath (Minister of Foreign Affairs and Protector of Bohemia and Moravia), Franz von Papen (former Chancellor of Germany), Joachim von Ribbentrop (Minister of Foreign Affairs), Baldur von Schirach (Reich youth leader), and Martin Bormann (Chief of the Nazi Party Chancery). Bormann was tried and convicted in absentia, meaning he was never located for arrest and thus did not physically appear for trial. The finance defendants were Walter Funk (President of the Reichsbank), Hjalmar Schacht (Minister of Economics prior to the war and President of the Reichsbank), and the industrialist Gustav Krupp von Bohlen und Halbach (the aging former president of the German munitions company, Friedrich Krupp A.G.). Gustav Krupp's prosecution was postponed indefinitely due to his poor health. He died in 1950, having never stood trial. The forced-labor defendants were Fritz Sauckel (Plenipotentiary General for the Utilization of Labor) and Robert Ley (former leader of the German Labor Front). Ley, however, committed suicide upon being indicted and thus never stood trial. The propaganda defendants were Hans Fritzsche (Ministerial Director and head of the radio division in the Propaganda Ministry) and Julius Streicher (editor of the newspaper *Der Stürmer* and Director of the Central Committee for the Defense against Jewish Atrocity and Boycott Propaganda).

Criminal Organizations

In addition to these individual defendants, the Allied prosecutors, strongly encouraged by Jackson, were determined to prosecute certain organizations in Nazi Germany, alleging that they were illegal criminal enterprises. The prosecutors believed that individual defendants could be prosecuted and convicted by virtue of their membership in such organizations. Such a finding also would make it much easier to prosecute thousands of other defendants in subsequent trials simply by identifying an individual as a member of any such criminal organization. "Guilt by association" thus became the guiding principle of the prosecution strategy for these later trials. The London Charter empowered the IMT to define as criminal any group or organization to which any defendant appearing before the IMT belonged. Once such a finding was reached, the national, military, and occupation courts of the Charter signatories could bring individual members of those organizations to trial for years thereafter, with the criminal nature of such groups or organizations already considered proven. Such defendants would be permitted only limited defense arguments, for example that they joined the organization in question under duress. This represented the first of several legal innovations in the Nuremberg trials. Never before had national organizations been prosecuted, particularly by an international tribunal, for criminal conduct. Their alleged criminal character was determined by the IMT only after the war, thus raising concerns about retroactive justice.

Nevertheless, the IMT declared three of six organizations named in the indictment as criminal in character. The Gestapo, paired with the SD (*Sicherbeitsdienst*), was declared criminal for its role in "the persecution and extermination of the Jews, brutalities and killings in concentration camps, excesses in the administration of occupied territories, the administration of the slave labor program, and the mistreatment and murder of prisoners of war." The Leadership Corps of the [Nazi] Party, which included Hitler, his top staff officers, and an estimated 600,000 members, was declared criminal for "the Germanization of incorporated territory, the persecution of the Jews, the administration of the slave labor program, and mistreatment of prisoners of war." The IMT declared the SS (*Schutzstaffeln*), which ran the concentration camps and cleared Jews and others out of the ghettos, criminal for conducting the same activities as the Gestapo.

The Indictment

The indictment, issued on October 19, 1945, included four charges drawn from the London Charter: a common conspiracy to wage aggressive war, crimes against peace, war crimes, and crimes against humanity. The second category, crimes against peace, had no pre-existing definition in international law. It was defined in the London Charter as the "planning, preparation, initiation, or waging of a war of aggression, or a war in violation of international treaties, agreements, or assurances, or participation in a common plan or conspiracy for the accomplishment of any of [war crimes or crimes against humanity]."

The third category, war crimes, was a well-established concept in international law. It was defined in the London Charter as follows:

> violations of the laws or customs of war. Such violations shall include, but not be limited to, murder, ill-treatment or deportation to slave labor or for any other purpose of civilian population of or in occupied territory, murder or ill-treatment of prisoners of war or persons on the seas, killing of hostages, plunder of public or private property, wanton destruction of cities, towns or villages, or devastation not justified by military necessity.

The fourth category, crimes against humanity, had at best a very problematic foundation in international law. Such crimes were defined as follows:

> murder, extermination, enslavement, deportation, and other inhumane acts committed against any civilian population, before or during the war; or persecutions on political, racial or religious grounds in execution of or in connection with any crime within the jurisdiction of the Tribunal, whether or not in violation of the domestic law of the country where perpetrated.

War of Aggression

Despite the apparent injustice of the aggressive assaults by the German Army in World War II, there was no codified or even customary rule of international law in 1945 that explicitly outlawed a war of aggression. Yet Justice Jackson was determined to make "aggression" or "crimes against peace" the dominant allegation of the Nuremberg trials, and the American prosecution team assumed full responsibility for prosecuting the crime. In the aftermath of World War I, there had been a number of initiatives to outlaw wars of aggression, giving Jackson something to work with in legislating a new legal principle in the London Charter. Article 227 of the Versailles Treaty (1919), attempted to establish individual criminal responsibility for Germany's aggression in World War I by requiring the prosecution of the German Kaiser for "a supreme offense against international morality and the sanctity of treaties." The viability of this provision, however, was never put to the test, for the Kaiser enjoyed sanctuary from prosecution in The Netherlands, which refused to surrender him for trial.

The Kellogg-Briand Pact of 1928 was sponsored by the United States as manifesting "the outlawry of war" and signed by sixty-five nations, including such World War II aggressor nations as Germany, Italy, and Japan. This agreement expressed the intent to renounce war as a means of settling disputes. Various other pronouncements prior to World War II declared aggression to be an international crime, but no law had yet been written that prohibited a war of aggression. Justice Jackson faced opposition from legal scholars and other allied prosecutors, who challenged his effort to establish a new crime of aggression.

Justice Jackson prevailed with a bold strategic move. He argued that there had been a conspiracy to wage an aggressive war that swept within its reach war crimes and crimes against humanity (the two other major categories of crimes). He went on to assert that the entire indictment of the Nuremberg defendants would be premised on the allegation of this "master plan" that had been implemented through a conspiracy stretching back to 1933, when the Nazi Party came to power in Germany. He noted that war crimes had a relatively solid basis in existing international conventions that already required a connection with warfare. Therefore, he argued, doubts about the legality of any particular charge of aggression or crime against humanity (along with many other kinds of criminal conduct) should be overcome by implicating such crimes within the overall conspiracy to wage aggressive war. The conspiracy theory, in which all participants can be held equally responsible for criminal conduct, was established in Article 6 of the London Charter and underpinned the first count in the Nuremberg indictment:

> Leaders, organizers, instigators and accomplices participating in the formulation or execution of a common plan or conspiracy to commit any of the foregoing crimes are responsible for all acts performed by any persons in execution of such plan.

Conspiracy charges were a based on a legal concept that was peculiarly rooted in common law as understood in Britain and the United States. The French, Soviet, and German legal systems had no legal tradition for framing conspiracy charges. They preferred charging defendants for direct participation in specific crimes. The Soviets were extremely worried that Jackson's formula could be used to implicate them for their own suspicious conduct during the war and embarrass them as essentially unindicted co-conspirators in many of the crimes.

Wartime Crimes against Humanity

The operational compromise that emerged in the course of the trials meant that the IMT judges would entertain the charge of conspiracy only for acts of aggression by the Axis powers, and not for the commission of war crimes or crimes against humanity. The crime of conspiracy was further limited to actions closely related to the commencement of armed conflict and to those leaders who met together to plan specific acts of aggression. However, the nexus-to-war that originally drove Justice Jackson's conspiracy theory remained as a key practical requirement for the prosecution of crimes against humanity, primarily because these were crimes that had not been previously codified in international law and remained highly contentious as an example of retroactive justice by the IMT. By limiting the charges to crimes against humanity committed during wartime, the IMT could amplify the illegality of the acts within the context of the overall aggressive war. This would serve to blunt at least some of the arguments that defense counsel could raise about the legality of the charges, particularly those pertaining to the period from 1933 to 1939, even though the London Charter permitted investigation of all but one type (persecutions) of pre-war crimes against humanity.

The perspective of American prosecutor Whitney Harris reflects the general view that guided the IMT's approach at the time. He wrote:

> [The limitation to wartime crimes against humanity] was a proper one in view of the status of the Tribunal as an international military body, charged with determining responsibility for war and crimes related thereto. If the Tribunal had assumed jurisdiction to try persons under international law for crimes committed by them which were not related to war it would have wholly disregarded the concept of sovereignty and subjected to criminal prosecution under international law individuals whose conduct was lawful under controlling municipal law in times of peace. Such jurisdiction should never be assumed by an ad hoc military tribunal established to adjudicate crimes of war.

The requisite nexus-to-war required by the IMT created a precedent for examining crimes against humanity that influenced, and arguably retarded, the development of the law for decades thereafter, until it was definitively broken in the 1990s in the Statute of the International Criminal Tribunal for Rwanda.

The conspiracy theory, particularly as it applied to crimes against humanity, had its doubters. Shortly before he committed suicide, Nuremberg defendant Robert Ley wrote: "Where is this plan? Show it to me. Where is the protocol or the fact that only those here accused met and said a single word about what the indictment refers to so monstrously? Not a thing of it is true." Ley's charges have received support from more recent scholarship on the subject. In 2003, historian Richard Overy of King's College, London, wrote:

> Subsequent historical research has confirmed that no such thing as a concerted conspiracy existed, though a mass of additional evidence on the atrocities of the regime and the widespread complicity of many officials, judges, and soldiers in these crimes has confirmed that, despite all the drawbacks of the trial and of its legal foundation, the conviction that this was a criminal system was in no sense misplaced.

The Nuremberg prosecutors nonetheless presented much evidence to support the conspiracy theory during the trials. The fact that three defendants were acquitted on all four counts, including the conspiracy charge, does not diminish the fact that some defendants were found to be participants in a conspiracy to wage a war of aggression.

Retroactive Justice
There is a general principle of law which states that individuals must not be held criminally responsible for conduct that was not illegal at the time it occurred (*nullum crimen sine lege,* also called the retroactivity rule). This principle was a very powerful presence at Nuremberg. Concerns about the credibility of the IMT arose with respect to defendants' arguments that they were only complying with German national law in the performance of their duties. Although German law under the Nazi regime became a vehicle of extreme discrimination and persecution of the Jews and other minorities, the invocation of national law as a defense, particularly regarding crimes against humanity, proved almost entirely unpersuasive to the IMT judges, who had a mandate to apply international law to the proceedings. The drafters of the London Charter struggled with these defenses; and defense counsel frequently offered them as mitigation for their clients' wartime actions.

Prosecutors and judges at the IMT found the legal basis for crimes relating to aggression and for crimes against humanity in the deep well of human experience and morality. For instance, Lieutenant Commander Harris drew upon how international law had over time criminalized acts of piracy on the high seas. He wrote:

> the Nuremberg judges declared against aggressive war and related acts which they considered

to have been morally condemned by the majority of nations. In the Tribunal's view these acts, like piracy, could no longer be tolerated in a civilized world, and the Tribunal concluded that the responsible individuals could be punished for their actions, just as earlier courts had resolved upon the punishment of men for acts of piracy.

The IMT took a judicial leap by assuming that international law had been fairly rapidly evolving toward the view that aggression and crimes against humanity should be outlawed, and that individual criminal responsibility for such crimes had become legally enforceable. In a very real sense, the IMT took the initiative to declare and act upon what it regarded as international law at a momentous period in world history, when clarity of interpretation and action was being sought. The extreme violence of World War II elicited such an exercise of discovery. Justice Jackson wrote to President Truman in June 1945 with disarming understatement:

> Unless we are prepared to abandon every principle of growth for International Law, we cannot deny that our own day has its right to institute customs and to conclude agreements that will themselves become sources of a new and strengthened International Law.

The retroactivity rule challenged the IMT's jurisdiction over the crimes against humanity set forth in the London Charter. The overlap of many of these crimes with established war crimes presented little problem to the prosecutors. However, international legal principles of sovereignty and of non-interference in the internal affairs of other nations meant that the German assaults on their own civilian population, particularly the Jewish population, and the persecution inflicted on so many civilians might have been shielded from international criminal prosecution. To forestall this possibility, the IMT determined that its own self-made authority required freshly conceived jurisdiction over such "internal" crimes. Again, the IMT found strength of reason in the requirement that such crimes be committed in connection with an on-going war and another crime "within the jurisdiction of the Tribunal." In other words, the context of aggressive war and/or a war crime was required to trigger individual criminal responsibility under international law. Having taken this leap of logic, the IMT prosecutors and judges acted prudentially in the trials to enforce a newly defined law on crimes against humanity.

Defense of Superior Orders
The London Charter addressed one of the most common defenses for defendants who claimed they were only acting, and had to act, pursuant to orders from su-

perior officers and officials: "The fact that the Defendants acted pursuant to order of his Government or of a superior shall not free him from responsibility, but may be considered in mitigation of punishment if the Tribunal determines that justice so requires." The Nuremberg defendants' high rank and their direct role in formulating the policies of the Third Reich (including for some of them the plotting of a war of aggression) left them with little opportunity to credibly claim that they were acting on the orders of superiors. They usually were the superiors who drafted many of the orders; they often played a political role in decision-making; and the orders they responded to came from leaders, such as Hitler, who issued commands of obvious criminal character, particularly to men of the stature in the Nazi regime as those in the dock at Nuremberg. Their individual accountability could not be extinguished by claiming obligation to follow a superior's orders. If the orders of superiors were unchallengeable when weighed against the crimes they sought to unleash, then the entire foundation for the Nuremberg trials, the laws and customs of war, and the legal principles that defined crimes against peace and crimes against humanity would crumble. The IMT pronounced that, "[t]he true test, which is found in varying degrees in the criminal law of most nations, is not the existence of the order, but whether moral choice was in fact possible."

Defendant Wilhelm Keitel sought to explain to the IMT how the traditional training and concept of duty of the German officers "taught unquestioned obedience to superiors who bore responsibility" and "caused them to shrink from rebelling against these orders and these methods even when they recognized their illegality and inwardly refuted them." Keitel also testified that the decision to wage a war of aggression is solely political, and that the military soldier must obey orders relating to it. The IMT rejected the credibility of these arguments for an officer of Keitel's exceptionally high rank—a senior officer who knew what was at stake, played a role in the decision-making, and yet remained indifferent to the legal issues. American prosecutor Telford Taylor wrote of Keitel, "His attitude was not far from that of Goering, who was not moved by 'considerations of international law.'" Although Keitel may have criticized some of the orders he received, he enforced them.

Judgment

During the Nuremberg trials, ninety percent of the prosecution's evidence consisted of the Third Reich's own governmental files, which had been seized by Allied forces. Prosecutors had access to 100,000 German documents, millions of feet of video film, and 25,000

still photographs, including some taken by Hitler's personal photographer. Court stenographers prepared 17,000 transcript pages recording the testimony and proceedings of the trials. Active and often lengthy defenses were raised, frustrating the prosecution but also strengthening the fairness of the trials. It took twenty-eight sessions to hear the defenses of just the first four accused. Defense counsel took sixteen days to make their closing arguments.

The IMT judges delivered their opinions regarding the twenty-two individual defendants and six organizations on September 30 and October 1, 1946. They did not convict all defendants on all counts of the indictment for which they had been charged. Instead, the judges found that the evidence fell short of the requirement that guilt be proven "beyond a reasonable doubt" with respect to some of the charges against the defendants.

The IMT fully acquitted three defendants of all charges: Schacht, Papen, and Fritzsche. Of the remaining nineteen defendants, all but two of them were convicted on multiple charges, and six were convicted on all four counts of the indictment. Eight defendants were convicted on the first count, charging conspiracy to wage aggressive war. Twelve defendants were convicted on the second count, crimes against peace. Sixteen defendants were convicted on the third count, war crimes. Sixteen defendants also were convicted on the fourth count, crimes against humanity. The IMT sentenced twelve defendants (including the absent Bormann) to die by hanging, and sentenced the remaining seven defendants to prison terms ranging from ten years to life. Goering committed suicide before he could be hanged. The Soviet judge dissented on each of the acquittals and on the life imprisonment (rather than hanging) sentence for Hess.

Witnesses at the Nuremberg trials confirmed the Nazi regime's own death count of the Jewish population and others in the extermination (also known as concentration) camps and during killing operations in the field. One witness, an SS reporter who knew Adolf Eichmann, confirmed that in mid-1944 Eichmann reported to Himmler that the latter's orders for extermination of the European Jewry were being implemented. (Although he remained at-large and unindicted at Nuremberg, Eichmann was later found in Argentina, abducted, and brought to trial in Israel. He was convicted in 1961 and sentenced to death.) The witness testified that Eichmann wrote, "Approximately four million Jews had been killed in the various extermination camps while an additional two million met death in other ways, the major part of which were shot by operational squads of the Security Police during the campaign against Russia." Although the prosecution had initiated the Nuremberg trials with a strong focus on charging the defendants with conspiracy to wage a war of aggression and with violations of "crimes against peace," in the end the trials also established the horrific truth of the Holocaust, namely the genocide against the Jewish population of Europe. It is that truth and the criminality arising from the charges of Nazi crimes against humanity that became the most prominent legacies of justice at Nuremberg.

Influence of Nuremberg Trials

The Nuremberg trials of 1945 and 1946 influenced later developments of international law and the courts that enforce it. It underpinned the work of the Tokyo War Crimes Trials (1946–1948) and subsequent trials under Control Council Law No. 10 in occupied Germany. They also firmly established the basis for attributing individual criminal responsibility for atrocity crimes such as genocide, serious war crimes, and crimes against humanity that would constitute the core jurisdiction of international criminal tribunals at the end of the twentieth century and beyond. The trials accelerated the further development of the principles of international criminal law and international humanitarian law, as reflected in the Genocide Convention of 1948, the Geneva Conventions of 1949, the Geneva Protocols of 1977, the Statutes of the International Criminal Tribunals for the Former Yugoslavia and for Rwanda, and the 1998 Rome Statute of the International Criminal Court.

The UN General Assembly affirmed in Resolution 95(I) of December 11, 1946, the "Principles of International Law Recognized by the Charter of the Nuremberg Tribunal." The illegality of aggression was further elaborated in a 1974 UN General Assembly resolution defining aggression with regard to state responsibility, and in the Draft Code of Crimes Against the Peace and Security of Mankind, which was adopted by the International Law Commission. Deeply influenced by the record of the Nuremberg trials, the states that are party to the Rome Statute of the International Criminal Court continue to negotiate how to activate the crime of aggression which, for purposes of individual criminal responsibility, is included in the new court's jurisdiction. In Justice Jackson's opening statement at the Nuremberg trials, he summed up what they were all about:

> The wrongs which we seek to condemn and punish have been so calculated, so malignant, and so devastating, that civilization cannot tolerate their being ignored, because it cannot survive their being repeated. That four great nations, flushed with victory and stung with injury, stay the hand of vengeance and voluntarily submit their captive enemies to the judgment of the law is one of

the most significant tributes that Power has ever paid to reason.

SEE ALSO Göring, Hermann; Jackson, Robert; London Charter; Morgenthau, Henry; Nuremberg Trials, Subsequent; Tokyo Trial; War Crimes

BIBLIOGRAPHY

Bass, Gary Jonathan (2000). *Stay the Hand of Vengeance.* Princeton, N.J.: Princeton University Press.

Benton, Wilbour, and George Grimm, eds. (1955). *German Views of the War Trials.* Dallas, Tex.: Southern Methodist University Press.

Best, Geoffrey (1994). *War and Law Since 1945.* New York: Oxford University Press.

Bosch, William J. (1970). *Judgment on Nuremberg.* Chapel Hill, N.C.: University of North Carolina Press.

Calvocoressi, Peter (1948). *Nuremberg.* New York: Macmillan.

Conot, Robert E. (1983). *Justice at Nuremberg.* New York: Harper & Row.

Cooper, Belinda, ed. (1999). *War Crimes: The Legacy of Nuremberg.* New York: TV Books.

Gerhart, Eugene C. (1958). *Robert H. Jackson, America's Advocate.* New York: Bobbs-Merrill.

Harris, Whitney R. (1999). *Tyranny on Trial*, Revised edition. Dallas, Tex: Southern Methodist University Press.

International Military Tribunal (1947). *Trial of the Major War Criminals.* 42 volumes Nuremberg, Germany.

Jackson, Robert H. (1947). *The Nürnberg Case.* New York: Alfred A. Knopf.

Maser, Werner (1977). *Nuremberg: A Nation on Trial.* New York: Charles Scribner's Sons.

Neave. Airey (1978). *On Trial at Nuremberg.* Boston: Little, Brown.

Sands, Philippe, ed. (2003). *From Nuremberg to The Hague.* Cambridge: Cambridge University Press.

Smith, Bradley F. (1982). *Reaching Judgment at Nuremberg.* New York: Basic Books.

Stimson, Henry L., and McGeorge Bundy (1947) *On Active Service in Peace and War.* New York: Harper & Brothers.

Taylor, Telford (1949). *Final Report to the Secretary of the Army.* Washington, D.C.: U.S. Government Printing Office.

Taylor, Telford (1949). *Nuremberg Trials: War Crimes and International Law.* New York: Carnegie Endowment for International Peace.

Taylor, Telford (1992). *The Anatomy of the Nuremberg Trials.* New York: Alfred A. Knopf.

Thompson, H. K., Jr., and Henry Strutz, eds. (1976). *Doenitz at Nuremberg: A Reappraisal.* New York: Amber Publishing.

Tusa, Ann, and John (1983). *The Nuremberg Trial.* New York: Atheneum.

Zawodny, J. K. (1962). *Death in the Forest: The Story of the Katyn Forest Massacre.* Notre Dame, Ind.: University of Notre Dame Press.

David J. Scheffer

Nuremberg Trials, Subsequent

On November 1, 1943, as the tides of World War II began to turn, leaders of the United Kingdom, the United States, and the Soviet Union convened in Moscow. Germany had been put on notice in 1941 and 1942 that perpetrators of war crimes would be held to personal account "through the channel of organized justice." The earlier warnings were renewed as President Franklin D. Roosevelt, Prime Minister Winston Churchill, and Soviet Marshal Joseph Stalin issued a solemn Declaration on German Atrocities. On behalf of thirty-two Allied powers, they proclaimed that Germans responsible for war crimes committed in territories overrun by Hitler's forces would be sent back to be judged by the people they had outraged. Major criminals, whose offenses had no particular geographic location, would be punished by joint decision of the Allies.

U.S. Army War Crimes Trials at Dachau

The war ended with Germany's unconditional surrender in May 1945. Captured German records disclosed that millions of Germans had been avid supporters of the Nazi Party and policies. Allied trials for such large numbers were logistically and politically impossible. They could be dealt with later in German "denazification" procedures. The U.S. Army lost no time in bringing to justice suspected war criminals who were already in custody. U.S. military commissions were convened to try Germans accused of murdering downed flyers or prisoners of war as well as perpetrators or accomplices responsible for atrocities committed in concentration camps freed by U.S. forces. Ironically, these little-known U.S. Army trials were held in the liberated camp at Dachau, near Munich.

The prosecutors, defense counsel, and judges were all U.S. army officers. Defendants were grouped according to the camps where they were captured. The summary proceedings generally followed rules for court martials. Between June 1944 and July 1948, when the trials unceremoniously ended, over 1,600 defendants had been tried. Almost all were convicted and over 400 were sentenced to death. After military reviews, fewer than 300 of the death sentences were confirmed. The guilty were confined in War Crimes Prison No. 1, formerly renowned as the Bavarian jail at Landsberg, where Adolf Hitler, after his failed coup in 1923, had written *Mein Kampf.*

Chief Prosecutor for the United States, Benjamin Ferencz, as he launches the "biggest murder trial in history," the case against twenty-four Einsatzgruppen, members of the SS killing unit that slaughtered over a million helpless civilians as Germany advanced into Poland and Russia. On the strength of their own meticulous records, all were convicted. [USHMM, COURTESY OF BENJAMIN FERENCZ.]

The First International Military Trial at Nuremberg

The trials in Dachau were overshadowed when the spotlight shifted to a new International Military Tribunal (IMT) established in Nuremberg, where Hitler's deputy, Hermann Göring and other prominent Nazi accomplices held center stage. The four victorious powers—the United States, the Soviet Union, the United Kingdom, and France—in their capacity as the sole acting government of Germany, signed an agreement in London on August 8, 1945, that provided for the establishment of an International Military Tribunal "for the just and prompt trial and punishment of the major war criminals of the European Axis."

The IMT Charter, which was annexed to the London Agreement, became the foundation stone for the IMT trial and for twelve lesser-known Nuremberg trials that soon followed.

The IMT prosecution began on November 30, 1945. After a trial that was generally considered to be eminently fair, the judgment against the twenty-four defendants was handed down on October 1, 1946. The Presiding Judge, Lord Geoffrey Lawrence of Great Britain, read the sentences. Three of the defendants were acquitted. Twelve others were sentenced to death for having planned and participated in aggressive war, which the tribunal condemned as "the supreme international crime," as well as for crimes against humanity and violations of the laws of war. After the Allied Control Council confirmed their sentences, those condemned to die were hanged. Göring committed suicide and Martin Bormann, Hitler's deputy, who was tried in absentia, was never found. Those sentenced to imprisonment were confined in Spandau Prison in Berlin, where they remained under strict quadripartite supervision until their sentences were fully served.

Trials under Allied Control Council Law

Defeated Germany was divided into four zones. Each zone was occupied and administered by one of the four victorious powers. Berlin was occupied jointly. The governing body was the quadripartite Control Council. Because the London Charter anticipated the possibility of more than one trial, the Control Council enacted Law 10, on December 20, 1945, to provide a uniform legal basis for any subsequent trials and to add some needed clarifications. The most important change was to make clear that crimes against humanity could be punishable even if committed in peacetime against one's own nationals. Invasions as well as wars were specifically made punishable, and rape was added as a specific example of a crime against humanity. These articulations would play an important role in the evolution of international criminal and humanitarian law.

The single trial by the IMT against two dozen culprits could not adequately portray the full extent of Nazi criminality. The Allies all agreed that additional speedy trials would be desirable to hold accountable those mid-level policy makers and accomplices without whose assistance Hitler's overwhelming reign of terror would not have been possible. Where and how such trials would be held posed a problem. The leading architect of the Nuremberg trial, Justice Robert M. Jackson, on temporary leave from the U.S. Supreme Court to serve as Chief Prosecutor for the United States, noted that quadripartite trials in four languages were both costly and time-consuming. With the Allies failing to reach an accord on another international trial, it was finally decided that each of the occupying powers could handle future war crimes prosecutions in its own zones of occupation as each might see fit.

In time the French conducted a few trials in their zone and the British did the same under rules prescribed by traditional royal warrants for military procedures. What the Soviets did in areas they occupied remains obscure, but millions of German prisoners of war were kept in Soviet custody for many years. The United States decided that justice would best be served by additional trials against a wide array of high-level Germans suspected of being the powers behind the Nazi hierarchy of crime. United States Zone Ordinance No. 7, adopted on October 18, 1946 (amended by Ordinance 11 on February 17, 1947), laid down rules for implementing Control Council Law No. 10 to guarantee a fair and speedy trial for all accused. Although the later proceedings were conducted in the name of the United States and the prosecutors and judges were U.S. citizens, the trials, based on the London Charter, had characteristics of international law rather than national law. The courts were created and the trials conducted pursuant to the quadripartite Control Council decrees and ordinances. They were bound to respect the legal findings of the IMT.

Nuremberg, ravaged by war, was in the U.S. zone. The old German courthouse had been refurbished for the IMT and would be available as soon as the international trial was completed. Telford Taylor, a Harvard law graduate who had served on the staff of Justice Jackson, was charged with responsibility for organizing and directing any subsequent proceedings. Taylor, promoted to Brigadier General, was designated Jackson's deputy and named Chief of Counsel for further trials. Nazi leaders who were not tried by the IMT as well as their principal agents and accessories, and members of Nazi groups found by the IMT to be criminal organizations, were potential targets for the new war crimes courts.

The evidence before the IMT had only outlined the broad sweep of Nazi criminality. Crimes of such magnitude could not have been committed without help from many sectors. German doctors, for example, had performed brutal medical experiments on victims considered racially undesirable or subhuman. German judges and lawyers had used the law as a tool for persecuting presumed enemies. High-ranking military officers directed or assisted massive war crimes in violation of the laws of war. The Nazi Party had been financed by banks and industrialists who were fully aware of Hitler's plans and programs. German companies had seized foreign assets and helped build concentration camps where helpless inmates were worked to death. German diplomats and ministers had planned and aided Hitler's repeated aggressions. To follow up on the IMT, a sample of such wrongdoers would be called to account for their actions in courts of law set up in Nuremberg by the United States.

The challenge was daunting. Evidence had to be assembled quickly to prove beyond reasonable doubt that the suspects knowingly committed crimes within the jurisdiction of the court. The alleged perpetrators would have to be in custody and in mental and physical condition to stand trial. New staff had to be recruited and trained; bilingual researchers, investigators, and translators had to be hired. Qualified and available judges had to be recruited in the United States. Witnesses had to be located, housed, and safeguarded. Budgets were limited. Most important of all, it was imperative that any subsequent trial(s), be absolutely fair in fulfilling humanity's aspirations to do justice.

The Twelve Subsequent Trials at Nuremberg

Doctors and Lawyers on Trial

The lead defendant in Case No. 1, the so-called Medical Case, was Karl Brandt. Like many other Nazi leaders, he was given high rank in the SS (Security Services) and reported directly to Hitler. Dr. Brandt, together with twenty-two others, was indicted on December 9, 1946, for experiments on helpless concentration camp inmates and prisoners of war. The unwilling "guinea pigs" were deliberately infected with diseases and subjected to wounds designed to test the limits of human endurance. Euthanasia and sterilization programs had been organized against the aged, incurably ill, and others characterized as "useless eaters." The defendants all denied personal culpability, arguing that they were acting under "superior orders" and that such experiments were carried on legally elsewhere.

The U.S. judges, who came from superior courts in Oklahoma, Florida, and Washington, found there was unquestionable proof that war crimes and crimes against humanity had been committed. Individual responsibility had to be established beyond a reasonable doubt. Seven defendants were acquitted. The others were convicted on July 19, 1947, and sentenced to long prison terms. Five were condemned to hang and in due course were executed in Landsberg Prison. The tribunal laid down ten basic principles that had to be observed to satisfy ethical and legal standards for medical experiments. These guidelines became important signposts for the medical profession throughout the world.

Nazi lawyers and judges did not escape scrutiny. In the "Justice Case" that opened on January 4, 1947, fourteen leading officials of the judicial system of the Third Reich were accused of crimes against humanity by distorting the legal process to justify and support Hitler's programs of persecution and extermination. The trial judges came from benches in Ohio, Oregon,

and Texas. They found that the dagger of the assassin was concealed beneath the robe of the jurist. The proceedings, which lasted less than a year, reinforced principles established by the IMT and became the subject of a popular Hollywood film, *Judgment at Nuremberg*.

The American judges denied that they were imposing ex post facto or retroactive law. International law, in contrast to national law, was described as an evolving process that relies on broad principles of justice and fair play, which underlie all civilized concepts of law and procedure. No one was convicted without proof that he knew or should have known that in matters of international concern he was guilty of participating in a nationally organized system of injustice and persecution shocking to the moral sense of mankind. The fairness of the trial was evidenced by the fact that four of the accused were acquitted. The six remaining were sentenced to life imprisonment or lesser terms.

Nazi Administrators and Executioners

Three subsequent trials were directed against leaders of different Nazi offices. The Pohl Case indicted Oswald Pohl, Chief of the Economic and Administrative Departments, and seventeen of his highest-ranking associates. They were accused of kidnapping and enslavement of millions of civilians, and the construction and administration of concentration camps, where forced laborers toiled under conditions that made work and death almost synonymous. Defendants argued that during the war food was scarce for everyone and hard work was mandatory, not unlawful. The judgment in November 1947 held that there is no such thing as benevolent slavery; compulsory, uncompensated labor under the most inhumane conditions was a crime. The trial lasted approximately six months and resulted in death sentences for Pohl and three of his cohorts. Three others were acquitted, while the rest received prison terms.

The second case against Nazi officials indicted fourteen leaders of the Main Race and Resettlement Office (RuSHA) whose assignment was to safeguard the purity of German blood by eliminating ethnic "inferiors," such as Jews, Romani (Gypsies), and Poles. Other non-Aryans were to be resettled or "Germanized." The trial lasted about four months and ended on March 10, 1948. The lead defendant, Ulrich Greifelt, was sentenced to life imprisonment. The one female defendant in all of the Nuremberg trials was acquitted. Others received prison sentences and those convicted only of membership in criminal organizations were allowed to go free for time already served.

Of special interest was the case against the special extermination squads known as SS Einsatzgruppen. Twenty-four high-ranking officers, including six generals, were accused of slaughtering more than a million Jews, Romani, and other men, women, and children as part of the Nazi Final Solution to eradicate perceived opposition to Hitler's Reich. The defendants were commanders of units, totaling about three thousand men, who followed behind the German advance into Poland and the Soviet Union, where they rounded up helpless civilian victims for execution in ditches or gas vans. Their daily reports to higher headquarters and ministries tabulated the number of victims "eliminated," and the location and identity of the units and commanders in charge. Unfortunately for them, these official records, from about June 1941 to mid-1942, fell into the hands of U.S. war crimes investigators.

Relying on the defendant's own reports, the prosecution rested its case two days after delivering its opening statement on September 29, 1947. The defense took 136 trial days. They challenged the authenticity of the documents, and offered alibis, denials, excuses, and purported justifications, including the standard plea of superior orders. Presiding Judge Michael Musmanno, of Pennsylvania, allowed the defendants the opportunity to introduce any evidence they felt might save them. But they could not escape the damaging impact of the overwhelming proof against them. The judgment was comprehensive and devastating. On April 10, 1948, all defendants were convicted and fourteen sentenced to death. Executions were stayed pending appeals. The trial was widely publicized as "the biggest murder trial in history."

The defendants were well-educated men. Eight of them were lawyers and most others had advanced degrees. The lead defendant and an intellectual, SS General Otto Ohlendorf freely admitted that his unit had killed about ninety thousand Jews. He testified that he would do it again to answer his country's call. Even after Ohlendorf was sentenced to death, he showed not the slightest remorse. The trial offered new insights into the mentality of fanatics who are so convinced of the righteousness of their cause that they remain willing to kill or be killed for their own ideals.

The victims were killed because they did not share the race, religion, or creed of their executioners. The prosecution emphasized that no penalty could balance the enormity of the genocidal crime. The goal of the trial was not vengeance or merely justified retribution. It was a plea of humanity to law—that all people should have a legal right to live in peace and dignity regardless of their race or creed. The Opinion of the three U.S. judges confirmed that genocide and crimes against humanity were crimes that could never be tolerated. The trial and judgment set significant landmarks to advance the evolution of international criminal and humanitarian law.

Industrialists Called to Account

Three more trials focused on industrial leaders and financiers who backed the Hitler regime. The Farben, Krupp, and Flick cases also reflected the mentality of persons who aided and abetted the Nazi reign of terror without any regret or subsequent remorse. They were accused of profiteering from the slave labor programs of the Third Reich and from confiscation of properties plundered in occupied countries. Many of the defendants argued that loyalty to the regime made it necessary to go along with the Nazi government.

In the trial against Friedrich Flick and five of his associates, the defendants were charged with seizing properties as well as exploiting camp inmates under the most atrocious conditions. It was shown that Flick took the initiative for economic plunder and was a big contributor to Nazi entities. German defense lawyers argued that their clients had done no more than others would have done in defense of home and country. The arguments of economic and military necessity persuaded the American judges to acquit three of the accused. On December 22, 1947, Flick was sentenced to five years imprisonment and the two remaining defendants received lesser terms. With time off for good behavior, they would all soon be released.

Alfried Krupp was the sole owner and director of Hitler's major arms producer. (His father Gustav had been dropped as a defendant in the IMT trial when it was found that he was senile.) Alfried and eleven other key members of the company were indicted on a variety of charges. The court acquitted all of having been accessories to crimes against peace. The judges were not convinced that the defendants had sufficient knowledge of Hitler's aggressive intentions to be found guilty. Judge Hu C Anderson, from Tennessee, believed that liability for planning aggressive war should be limited to the leaders who did the planning and not include civilians who were not policy makers.

On other counts of the indictment the defendants did not fare as well. The judgment covered 122 printed pages. Eleven of the accused were found guilty beyond a reasonable doubt of plunder and violating laws of war by mistreatment of prisoners and camp inmates who slaved in their plants. The arguments that they acted under superior orders and feared they might otherwise be penalized were rejected. It was shown that the industrialists shared the goals of the Nazi regime and were in no way coerced. Any disadvantage that might have befallen them was trivial when compared to the suffering of the inmates they abused. Krupp was sentenced to twelve years in prison plus forfeiture of all his property. His colleagues received lesser sentences. In the spring of 1949 they were transported to War Crimes Prison No. 1, where they began plans to obtain their release. It would not be long in coming.

The most difficult and complicated industrial trial was against the directors of the IG Farben chemical cartel. The "Farben Case" indicted twenty defendants, including Farben's Chairman of the Board, Hermann Schmitz. The charges were essentially the same as those leveled against Krupp. Farben had assisted Hitler in attaining power. Farben directors had worked closely with the military in restoring German might. Farben had financed the building of the concentration camp at Auschwitz. Farben was one of the heaviest users of slave labor in the camps. Farben had planned the unlawful acquisition of foreign companies to strengthen Germany's potential to wage war.

The tribunal's judgment in July 1948 acquitted all defendants of conspiracy and the crime of aggression. Two of the three judges were not persuaded that the accused were aware of Hitler's plans to start an aggressive war. Judge Paul Hebert, Dean of the Louisiana Law School, was not convinced that justice had been served. He dissented on some of the acquittals. Of the twenty-three defendants, ten were acquitted of all charges. Thirteen were found guilty of plunder or slave labor abuses. Those convicted received light sentences, of eight years or less—much to the disappointment of the young U.S. prosecutors.

Generals Face the Court

German field marshals and generals were among the high-ranking military leaders called to account in the Hostages Case for the murder of prisoners of war and civilian hostages in occupied territories. The trial lasted about six months and ended in February 1948. The judgment, led by Charles Wennerstrum of Iowa, helped to clarify the law regarding the status and rights of partisans and other belligerents as well as the limits of "command responsibility" and "military necessity." Superior orders were considered in mitigation. No death sentences were imposed and some generals were acquitted. Fourteen of the convicted men were sentenced to prison terms.

The second military trial had only one defendant. In the Milch case, Field Marshal Erhard Milch, deputy to Göring, was sentenced to life imprisonment in April 1947 for his deep involvement in slave labor programs. In another such trial in the summer of 1948, all fourteen defendants in the "High Command" case were acquitted of planning or waging aggressive war since they were not found to be the policy makers. Most of the thirteen other defendants were sentenced to prison terms for abuse of forced laborers and other war crimes.

Ministers and Diplomats on Trial

The last and longest of the subsequent Nuremberg trials was the "Ministries" case that began in January 1948 with twenty-one defendants and spanned some fifteen months. High officials of Germany's Foreign Office and other government ministries were charged with responsibility for crimes against peace, crimes against humanity, and a large variety of war crimes and atrocities. Five defendants, including Ernst von Weizsaecker, a career diplomat who was State Secretary in the Foreign Office, were convicted of "crimes against peace." Following IMT reasoning, the court held that those leaders clearly responsible for initiating or cooperating in waging unlawful war, knowing that it was aggression, must be held accountable. They noted particularly that the principles laid down in the judgment were not binding merely on Germans but were applicable to all nations. Those found guilty were sentenced to prison terms ranging from four to fifteen years.

Clemency for War Criminals

The twelve Nuremberg trials had indicted 185 persons and convicted 142. The convicts joined more than a thousand prisoners sentenced by the Dachau military commissions to confinement in War Crimes Prison No. 1. Life in the Landsberg jail was relatively comfortable, but the prisoners lost no time in trying to win their freedom.

As the passions of war cooled and the political climate in Germany changed, the attitude toward the convicts in Landsberg also changed. The Soviet Union, which had been a wartime partner, soon came to be regarded as an enemy by the United States. West Germany, a wartime enemy, was seen as a potential ally in opposing communist expansion. German veteran's organizations, Nazi sympathizers, influential friends of the prisoners, as well as church and humanitarian groups, joined respected German politicians who beseeched the Americans to release the prisoners in Landsberg. They were not without friends in the U.S. Congress, where senator Joseph McCarthy and others argued that the real enemy was not Germany but the communists. German militarists made plain that they could not be expected to join Allied forces as long as their revered wartime commanders were imprisoned as criminals.

General Lucius Clay, as U.S. Military Governor, had personally reviewed both the Dachau and subsequent Nuremberg trials in 1948. He had affirmed practically all the verdicts, including hundreds of death sentences. As part of the movement away from military occupation, he was replaced in 1949 by a civilian high commissioner, John J. McCloy, a prominent New York lawyer who had served as Assistant Secretary of War. McCloy was left with the unenviable task of signing death warrants that would trigger the hanging of fifteen prisoners who had been convicted at Nuremberg but whose execution had been postponed pending appeals.

In July 1950 McCloy appointed an Advisory Board for Clemency for War Criminals to advise him. The board was instructed not to challenge any of the findings of law or fact reached by Nuremberg judges. Its sole purpose was to consider discrepancies in sentences for the same offense as well as personal hardships of health or family. It was not an appellate review and no Nuremberg prosecutors were consulted. On January 31, 1951, after all legal appeals had been exhausted, including petitions to the U.S. Supreme Court, which refused to accept jurisdiction, McCloy announced his final decisions. Thirty-one of the Nuremberg defendants, including the nine industrialists who had been sentenced to prison in the Krupp case, all had their terms reduced to "time served." On February 5, 1951, Krupp walked out of prison a free and happy man. High Commissioner McCloy ordered the return of the enormous Krupp fortune to him.

Taking account of every consideration in favor of the prisoners, McCloy commuted ten of the fifteen death sentences to life imprisonment. He could find no grounds for clemency for four Einsatzgruppen commanders (Paul Blobel, Werner Braune, Erich Naumann, and Ohlendorf) or for Pohl, who had been responsible for mass murders in concentration camps. Aware that Germany had abolished the death penalty, McCloy nevertheless confirmed that those five genocidal killers should be executed.

At the same time the commander of the U.S. Army in Europe, General Thomas Handy, who was responsible for the prisoners convicted in the army trials at Dachau, reduced sentences for about four hundred of those under his charge who were still detained in the war crimes prison. He commuted eleven death sentences that remained pending, but directed that two others face the gallows. The five Nuremberg defendants on death row plus the two convicted at Dachau were hanged in Landsberg Prison on June 7, 1951.

In December 1951 many of the war criminals convicted at Dachau or Nuremberg were granted their freedom as a "Christmas amnesty." Attempts to secure the release of the remaining Landsberg prisoners were unrelenting. The sympathetic U.S. authorities were increasingly creative in quietly finding ways to reduce sentences or grant paroles to remaining prisoners. Sim-

ilarly, the British, eager to have German forces join in the defense of Europe, found reasons to release Hitler's leading commanders, Field Marshals Albert Kesselring and Fritz Erich Von Manstein, in 1952 and 1953. By the end of 1958 all war criminals convicted at any of the twelve subsequent trials at Nuremberg were free.

Significance of the Nuremberg Trials

The thirteen judicial proceedings at Nuremberg were designed to protect the fundamental rights of all human beings to live in peace and dignity regardless of their race or creed. In careful and well-reasoned judgments, the law was clarified and affirmed. Bringing at least a handful of Nazi leaders before the bar of justice helped to diminish some of the anger and pain of survivors of persecution and encouraged hope for a more humane world in which perpetrators of such crimes would never be immune from punishment. The number of convictions was not as important as the confirmation of the principles emerging to guide future international behavior of nations and individuals.

The details presented in open court at Nuremberg made plain how an entire nation could be led astray by a ruthless tyrant. Revulsion against the horrors encouraged acceptance of the Charter of the United Nations (UN) and the slow awakening of the human conscience. The Convention on the Prevention and Punishment of the Crime of Genocide, adopted on December 9, 1948; the Universal Declaration of Human Rights, adopted on December 10, 1948; and a growing host of other international agreements gave birth to new disciplines focused on humanitarian law and the protection of human rights everywhere.

The impulse of Nuremberg spread internationally. Trials of Japanese war criminals were based on the IMT Charter. Countries that had been occupied by Nazi Germany also held war crimes trials following similar principles. German courts conducted postwar trials against concentration camp personnel. A central office in Germany directed investigations of war criminals throughout the land. Suspected war criminals who fled abroad were seized and called to account for their prior actions. An ad hoc tribunal was set up by the United Nations Security Council in 1993 to deal with crimes against humanity and war crimes committed in Yugoslavia. A similar tribunal was created in 1994 to cope with genocide in Rwanda. Their decisions built upon the law laid down at Nuremberg. Several new national or international criminal courts are being planned to cope with terrorism and other atrocities in other parts of the world. They all bear the mark of Nuremberg. After many years of difficult negotiation, a permanent international criminal court, widely recognized as "the missing link in the world's legal order," was sworn into office in the Hague on March 11, 2003.

The many legal fruits that have grown from the seeds planted at Nuremberg reflect the enduring hopes of humankind. But, as seen from the clemency shown to criminals convicted at Nuremberg, the progress of the law does not proceed upward in a straight line or in a political vacuum. The creation of new judicial institutions with universally binding authority on matters of vital concern to many nations is not something that can be achieved quickly or easily.

There have always been those who oppose enforceable international rules as an infringement on national sovereignty. They prefer to rely on their own economic or military might rather than trust any untried new legal tribunals. Without looking for solutions, they point to shortcomings, even though some problems must be expected in every new institution. Opposition to the new international criminal court is, in effect, a repudiation of the principles and goals enunciated at Nuremberg. The historical record shows, however, that despite hesitation and vacillation, the Nuremberg principles live on. A peaceful and humane world requires an improved and enforceable rule of law that applies equally to everyone. The universal acceptance of that principle will be the enduring legacy of the Nuremberg trials.

SEE ALSO Jackson, Robert; Nuremberg Trials; Superior (or Command) Responsibility

BIBLIOGRAPHY
Bloxbam, D. (2001). *Genocide on Trial*. New York: Oxford University Press.

Cooper, B., ed. (1999). *War Crimes—The Legacy of Nuremberg*. New York: TV Books.

Greene, J. M. (2003). *Justice at Dachau*. New York: Broadway Books.

Ferencz, Benjamin B. (1979). *Less Than Slaves*. Bloomington: Indiana University Press.

Ferencz, Benjamin B. (1980). *An International Criminal Court*. 2 volumes. New York: Oceana Publications.

Maguire, Peter (1993). *Law and War—An American Story*. New York: Columbia University Press.

Sadat, L. N. (2002). *The International Criminal Court and the Transformation of International Law*. Ardsley, N.Y.: Transnational Publishers.

Taylor, T. (1949). "Nuremberg Trials—War Crimes Law and International Law." In *International Conciliation*, New York: Carnegie Endowment (450)April:241–371.

Taylor, T. (1992). *The Anatomy of the Nuremberg Trials*. New York: Knopf.

Trial of War Criminals before the Nuremberg Military Tribunals under Control Council Law No. 10 (1946–1949). 15 volumes. Washington, D.C.: U.S. Government Printing Office.

Benjamin B. Ferencz

Organization for Security and Cooperation in Europe

The first Conference on Security and Cooperation in Europe (CSCE) ended with the Helsinki Final Act, signed on August 1, 1975, by the leaders of the thirty-five participating states. Those states included Canada, the United States, the Western European democracies, and the Soviet Union and its Eastern European satellites, as well as a few neutral and nonaligned countries. For Moscow, the main objective of the Final Act was to confirm the postwar status quo, and to achieve political recognition of the territorial conquest of the Red Army and the ideological supremacy of communism. For the members of the Atlantic Alliance, the objective was to ease the political situation in Europe, especially between the two German states, and to underline the principles of the UN Charter.

Evolution from CSCE to OSCE
Long and difficult negotiations from 1973 to 1975 focused on three set of issues, the three "baskets" of the Final Act. The first basket addressed security issues in Europe, the second sought to establish economic, scientific, and technological cooperation, and the last attempted to create a cooperative approach to humanitarian and related issues. The three baskets of issues were diplomatically linked, and compromises were required before general agreement was reached between the countries of the western and eastern blocs. In itself, the Final Act is not a legally binding treaty; rather it is a set of political commitments, adopted by consensus and in a spirit of peaceful coexistence. These political commitments involve a high level of dedication to the universal principles of the UN Charter, including sovereign equality of states and the inviolability of national borders, as well as "respect for human rights and fundamental freedoms."

The rule of consensus and the linkage between the three baskets of the CSCE imposed certain limits to progress in the field of human rights during the first ten years, from 1975 until 1986. The turning point was reached through the leadership of Russian Premier Mikhail Gorbachev, who experimented with domestic reform (*perestroika*) and a new diplomatic openness (*glasnost*). The Conference in Vienna, from 1986 to 1989 made the best of this opportunity by adopting a substantial document on human rights issues, the Vienna Document of 1989. This marked the start of a new and far-reaching agenda that focused on the human dimension of international relations.

The 1990 Summit of Heads of State and Government was organized in Paris to give visible recognition of the new reality in international relations inaugurated by the end of the cold war, freedom for Eastern democracies, and the political triumph of Western values. The CSCE incorporated democratic principles in the Charter of Paris for a New Europe, which was signed on November 21, 1990. The Paris Charter was lauded as the starting-point of "a new era of democracy, peace and unity in Europe." The participatiing states pledged "to build, consolidate, and strengthen democracy as the only system of government of our nations." The Paris Charter created the Office for Free Elections in Warsaw. This was the first standing institution of the CSCE, now called the Office for Democratic Institutions and Human Rights. It also created a number of decision-making bodies. The Charter called for a summit to be held every other year, with annual meetings of the CSCE Council, consisting of foreign affairs ministers, and regular meetings of senior diplomats as well as "implementation meetings of the human dimension committments" each year in Warsaw. The Warsaw meetings reviewed the record of the CSCE member states' commitments in the field of human rights, democracy, and the rule of law.

The scope of CSCE broadened rapidly after the break up of the Soviet Union and of Yugoslavia. In 2004 there were fifty-five participating states, drawn from a geographical area that stretches from Vancouver eastward to Vladivostok. Its political nature has also changed, with greater emphasis being given to the commitment to democracy, human rights, and rule of law, and mechanisms have been developed for the prevention and settlement of disputes. Its legal status has remained unchanged, but there has been a degree of creeping institutionalization. At the Budapest Summit of 1994, the CSCE underwent a symbolic name change, becoming the Organization for Security and Cooperation in Europe (OSCE, effective January 1, 1995). That summit also saw an organizational innovation, creating the position of Chairman in Office (CIO). The holder of this office is selected from among the foreign ministers of the participating states, serves a one-year term, presides over official meetings, and exercizes personal diplomacy on behalf of the OSCE.

The OSCE is not based on a binding treaty, but on political committments. It requires good faith and the good will of participating states, and as such is hindered from action by its continued reliance on the rule of consensus. Once, in 1992 during the crisis in Yugoslavia, the organization invoked a principle of "consensus minus one" in order to suspend the participation of a member state, the Federal Republic of Yugoslavia, on the eve of the Helsinski Summit. The Russian Federation did not attend the biennial summit meetings held after the Istanbul Summit of 1999, due to its disagreement with the Western democracies over the Chechnya crisis, and its foreign minister strongly disputed the conclusions of the Ministerial Councils in Vienna (2000) and Maastricht (2003), which were issued as statements of the CIO. To achieve consensus, the OSCE's official statements are, of necessity, watered down and legally non-binding. However, the OSCE's assertion of the link between security and human-rights issues, embodied in the concepts of cooperative security, can be an asset to the organization, as is its flexible legal framework, which allows it to adapt and react quickly to new challenges in the international community.

Evolving Commitments

The CSCE arose to promote the goal of peaceful coexistence among the states of Europe, and this orientation explains the absence of any reference to humanitarian law or criminal law in the early years. At the most, the Helsinki Declaration makes a general reference to international law, as follows:

> The participating State will fulfill in good faith their obligations under international law, both those obligations arising from the generally recognised principles and rules of international law and those obligations arising from treaties or other agreements, in conformity with international law, to which they are parties.

Any specific reference to international humanitarian law was precluded, however. Principle I of the Declaration stressed, "refraining from the threat or use of force." On the other hand, Principle VII invokes "the respect for human rights and fundamental freedoms," and specifically mentions national minorities in this regard:

> The Participating States on whose territory national minorities exist will respect the right of persons belonging to such minorities to equality before the law, will afford them the full opportunity for the actual enjoyment of human rights and fundamental freedoms and will, in this manner, protect their legitimate interests in this sphere.

The CSCE's concern with humanitarian concerns was very narrowly defined, with no mention of humanitarian law as such. In deference to the matters of the Soviet Union and its allies, the word *humanitarian* was used euphemistically, which wanted to avoid employing the vocabulary of "human rights."

The Concluding Document of the Vienna Conference of 1989 put a new emphasis on humanitarian issues, dealing explicitly with commitments "concerning respect for all human rights and fundamental freedoms, human contacts, and other issues of a related humanitarian character." At the Copenhagen Meeting of the Conference on the Human Dimension of the CSCE (June 1990) a set of national minority rights was developed for the first time, and greater attention was paid to the rise of racism and aggressive nationalism:

> The participating States clearly and unequivocally condemn totalitarianism, racial and ethnic hatred, anti-Semitism, xenophobia and discrimination against anyone as well as persecution on religious and ideological grounds. In this context they also recognize the particular problems of Roma [gypsies].

The states declared their firm, individual intention to combat these phenomena by a number of measures, including the passage of laws designed "to provide protection against any act that constitutes incitement to violence against persons or groups based on national, racial, ethnic or religious discrimination, hostility or hatred, including anti-Semitism." They further committed themselves to promote understanding and tolerance in the fields of education, culture, and information.

The Paris Charter summed up this political will: "We express our determination to combat all forms of racial and ethnic hatred, anti-Semitism, xenophobia and discrimination against anyone as well as persecution on religious and ideological grounds." The communist old-guard putsch of August 1991 against Mikhail Gorbachev, which led to the end of the Soviet Union, had a sobering effect on the October 1991 Moscow Meeting of the Conference on the Human Dimension of the CSCE. In the closing document of that session, the member states "deplored acts of discrimination, hostility, and violence against persons or groups on national, ethnic, or religious grounds."

The sense of emergency within the CSCE was even more evident at the Helsinki Summit of 1992, which addressed the Yugoslavia crisis. On July 10, 1992, the organization released its Summit Declaration, which stated, in part:

> This is a time of promise but also a time of instability and insecurity. Economic decline, social tension, aggressive nationalism, intolerance, xenophobia and ethnic conflicts threaten stability in the CSCE area. Gross violations of the CSCE commitments in the field of human rights and fundamental freedoms, including those related to national minorities, pose a special threat to the peaceful development of society, in particular in new democracies.

The allegation of gross violations deliberately invoked the strong vocabulary of international law. There was no direct accusation against specific perpetrators, but the reference to "aggressive nationalism" was a clear indication of the CSCE's intent.

The Helsinki Summit was the first time that the CSCE made explicit reference to international humanitarian law. The decisions reached at that meeting called for the establishment of a High Commissioner on National Minorities; enhanced the role of the Office for Democratic Institutions and Human Rights (ODIHR), which was in charge of the annual implementation meetings; and reaffirmed the whole range of humanitarian commitments undertaken by member states. A special caveat was added with regard to national minorities, directing the participating states to "refrain from resettling and condemn all attempts, by the threat or use of force, to resettle persons with the aim of changing the ethnic composition of areas within their territories."

After dealing with refugees and displaced persons, the Helsinki Document stressed the importance of international humanitarian law in a number of further provisions. The participating States:

(47) Recall that international humanitarian law is based upon the inherent dignity of the human person;

(48) Will in all circumstances respect and ensure respect for international humanitarian law including the protection of the civilian population;

(49) Recall that those who violate international humanitarian law are held personally accountable;

(50) Acknowledge the essential role of the International Committee of the Red Cross in promoting the implementation and development of international humanitarian law, including the Geneva Conventions and their relevant protocols;

(51) Reaffirm their commitment to extend full support to the International Committee of the Red Cross as well as to the Red Cross and Red Crescent Societies, and to the United Nations organizations, particularly in times of armed conflict, respect their protective emblems, prevent the misuse of these emblems and, as appropriate, exert all efforts to ensure access to the areas concerned;

(52) Commit themselves to fulfilling their obligation to teach and disseminate information about their obligations under international humanitarian law.

The Moscow Mechanism

The Yugoslavia crisis was the first challenge to the consistency of the CSCE's commitments and to the efficiency of its mechanisms and structures. According to the Moscow Mechanism, participating states could establish fact-finding missions involving a team of CSCE (now OSCE) rapporteurs. This emergency process calls for ten participating states to request such a mission can be formed, if possible with the cooperation of the requested participating state. After convening such a mission, the rules require that an emergency report be prepared and presented in three weeks.

On August 5, 1992, the United Kingdom gained the support of nine other participating states in order to invoke the Moscow Mechanism with respect to Bosnia and Herzegovina and Croatia. The United Kingdom appointed Ambassador Hans Corell (Sweden) to the mission. Bosnia and Croatia appointed Ambassador Helmut Turk (Austria) as rapporteur. A third member of the mission was Gro Hillestad Thune, a member of the European Commission of Human Rights (Norway). The first mandate of the mission was to investigate reports of attacks on unarmed civilians in Bosnia and Herzegovina, especially in Sarajevo and Goradze, and in Croatia. On September 28, 1992, the mandate was redrafted and broadened to visit, if feasible, areas that may be under the threat of ethnic cleansing.

From September 30 to October 5, the OSCE mission focused specifically on Croatia, working with high level contacts in Zagreb and making onsite visits to United Nations Protected Areas (UNPAs), such as Knin and Vukovar. It presented its report on October 7, 1992, (CSCE communication no. 342). The main conclusion was that atrocities against unarmed civilians and ethnic cleansing were indeed committed in the Republic of Croatia. It attributed these crimes to both sides of the conflict, but singled out the Yugoslavian Peoples Army (JNA), Serbian paramilitary groups and the police forces at Knin as having committed the most serious offenses. The report detailed the means employed for the creation of ethnically pure areas, alleging mass murder and forced deportation, as well as confiscation of property, arbitrary firings from employment, torture, random killings, and incarceration in overcrowded detention camps that lacked adequate food, sanitation, and access to medical care. The effect of these policies, according to the mission's report, was to create "a climate of fear [that] eventually force[d] people to leave their towns and villages."

The fact-finding mission stopped short of any legal qualification of specific "atrocities," instead using the vague wording of its mandate. Although it did specifically allege that the perpetrators were following a "systematic policy" (which is a substantial component of the crime of genocide), it did not go so far as to use the term *genocide*. Instead, it concluded that

> it is beyond any doubt that gross violations of human rights and norms of international humanitarian law, including war crimes and crimes against humanity, have been committed in connection with the armed conflict in the former Yugoslavia. It is also common knowledge that every day atrocities continue to be committed. The evidence is overwhelming and undeniable.

The report took note of Yugoslavia's ratification of the Genocide Convention of 1948 and stressed that "serious crimes such as war crimes and crimes against humanity" are punishable based on the continuing applicability of the Criminal Code of the former Yugoslavia,

but the rapporteurs saw no real possibility for an effective prosecution of these crimes at the national level, and concluded that it would be necessary to establish an international ad hoc tribunal to prosecute these crimes.

The mission report called for the formation of an expert committee, with experts drawn from interested OSCE member nations, that would be empowered to draft a treaty to establish a tribunal to try the crimes that the mission had discovered. As stressed in the concluding remarks of the report:

> the international community shares a common responsibility to bring to justice those who have committed crimes in connection with the armed conflict in the former Yugoslavia. The rules enshrined in the relevant international legal instruments should be enforced in order to punish those responsible and to demonstrate the determination of the international community to take action now and in the future.

These concerns were taken up during the third meeting of the CSCE Council—a meeting at the level of Foreign Ministers—in Stockholm, in December 1992. The ministers called upon an organ of the CSCE—the Committee of Senior Officials and the High Commissioner on National Minorities—to address the grave violations ongoing in the former Yugoslavia. This call for greater CSCE involvement in countering the ethnic cleansing and other human rights violations provided the opportunity to stress the responsibility of states and of individuals in regard to international humanitarian law, and to affirm the accountability of governments and individuals for the commission of war crimes and crimes against humanity.

Although the team of rapporteurs was encouraged to continue its work, it was unable to visit Bosnia-Herzegovina. On February 9, 1993, it did, however, transmit an additional report on this country, with a new proposal for an International War Crimes Tribunal for the Former Yugoslavia. In the meanwhile, several other international missions were investigating the gross violations of human rights in former Yugoslavia. During an extraordinary session, the Commission on Human Rights designated its own special rapporteur, Tadeusz Mazowiecki. In addition, UN Security Council Resolution 780 (1992) established a commission of experts, chaired by Frits Kalshoven. Cooperation among these teams of experts helped to build a strong legal case, and the triggering of the Moscow Mechanism was thus instrumental in the ultimate adoption of UN Security Council Resolution 827 on April 25, 1993, instituting the International Criminal Tribunal for Former Yugoslavia (ICTY).

Follow-up to the Yugoslavian Crisis

One year later, December 1993, at the fourth meeting of the OSCE Council in Rome, the same alarm was evident. This time, the organization made a much more direct reference to criminal law, adopting the Declaration on Aggressive Nationalism, Racism, Chauvinism Xenophobia, and Anti-Semitism. Noting the strong relationship between these phenomena and violence, the ministers participating in the meeting

> focused attention on the need for urgent action to enforce the strict observance of the norms of international humanitarian law, including the prosecution and punishment of those guilty of war crimes and other crimes against humanity. The Ministers agreed that the CSCE must play an important role in these efforts. The clear standards of behaviour reflected in CSCE commitments include active support for all individuals in accordance with international law and for the protection of national minorities.

At the Budapest Summit of 1994, the participating states issued a condemnation of the practice of ethnic cleansing and all acts related thereto. They also affirmed their support of the ICTY. Furthermore, the meeting's Summit Declaration addressed the issue of international humanitarian law standards:

> The participating States deeply deplore the series of flagrant violations of international humanitarian law that occurred in the CSCE region in recent years and reaffirm their commitment to respect and ensure respect for general international humanitarian law and in particular for their obligations under the relevant international instruments, including the 1949 Geneva Conventions and their additional protocols, to which they are a party. . . .
>
> They emphasize the potential significance of a declaration on minimum humanitarian standards applicable in all situations and declare their willingness to actively participate in its preparation in the framework of the United Nations. They commit themselves to ensure adequate information and training within their military services with regard to the provisions of international humanitarian law and consider that relevant information should be made available.

During the Lisbon Summit of 1996, the OSCE member states reiterated their condemnation of continuing human-rights violations in the former Yugoslavia. A similar stance was taken in the OSCE's Istanbul Charter for European Security. Russia, embroiled in wars in Chechnya, opposed more specific invocation of international humanitarian law, out of concern that it would itself become vulnerable to prosecution. This, again, demonstrated the inherent limits to action that

derive from the OSCE's reliance on consensus and the risk that member states faced of being accused of imposing double standards.

At the annual Implementation Meeting organized in Warsaw by the ODIHR, attendees dealt with the issues of migration, refugees, and displaced persons, as well as problems relating to migrant workers and the treatment of citizens of other participating states. They also discussed the development of international humanitarian law at the very end of the working session. According to the ODIHR agenda, which was prepared in advance for the 2002 Implementation Meeting:

> The presence of internal armed conflicts within the OSCE region (as well as a legacy of international armed conflict) highlights the importance of the implementation of humanitarian law by member states, especially as concerns the protection of civilians and the respect for fundamental non-derogable rights. It is to be stressed that provisions such as article 3 common to the Geneva Conventions and article 4 of Additional Protocol II contain minimum requirements of humane treatment that cannot be derogated from.

In addition, the ODIHR mentioned establishment of the International Criminal Court and the issue of the co-operation with the International Criminal Tribunals for the former Yugoslavia and for Rwanda as topics that might be addressed during the meeting.

New Trends

In fact, the OSCE mechanisms are mainly oriented toward prevention. For instance, the mandate for the High Commissioner on National Minorities, established by the Helsinki Summit in 1992, was described as follows:

> The High Commissioner will provide "early warning" and, as appropriate, "early action" at the earliest possible stage in regard to tensions involving national minority issues which have not yet developed beyond an early warning stage, but, in the judgement of the High Commissioner, have the potential to develop into a conflict within the CSCE area, affecting peace, stability, or relations between participating States, requiring the attention of and action by the Council.

According to this mandate, the high commissioner is specifically charged with taking before a political crisis or civil strife can mature into full-scale conflict, with promoting dialogue, and with gaining the confidence and cooperation of the parties to the crisis or strife. The successes of the first high commissioner, former Dutch Foreign Minister Max van der Stoel, can be measured by the fact that his goodwill and quiet diplomacy helped to avoid the breakout of further conflict among the newly independent states of Eastern Europe. However, the High Commissioner is expressly prohibited from becoming involved in ongoing, open crisis situations, such as occurred in the former Yugoslavia or in Caucasia. Van der Stoël's successor, Rolf Ekeus, has shown a marked reluctance to take any actions that could antagonize participating states, preferring to rely on personal diplomacy to achieve his goals.

Participating states generally do not use the full range of OSCE mechanisms and institutions to deal with challenge about national minorities. They only invoked the Moscow mechanism in 2002, ten years after it was first developed, after the attempted assassination of President Niyazov of Turkmenistan. The rapporteur assigned to the case was given the specific mandate to deal with the massive repression that followed the attempt. The resulting report stressed the risk of forced resettlement of national minorities, and made a transparent reference to the 1948 Genocide Convention, but as an emergency mechanism, the rapporteur could not assure any practical follow-up of the situation. Nonetheless, the work produced by the OSCE has galvanized the Commission on Human Rights and the UN General Assembly to finally adopt resolutions on the human rights situation in Turkmenistan in 2003, and to order a follow-up study of the situation in 2004.

SEE ALSO United Nations; United Nations Sub-Commission on Human Rights; Yugoslavia

BIBLIOGRAPHY

Bloed, Arie, ed. (1993). *The Conference on Security and Co-operation in Europe, Analysis and Basic Documents, 1972–1993.* Dordrecht: Kluwer Academic Publishers.

Bothe, Michael, Natalino Ronzitti, and Allan Rosas, ed. (1997). *The OSCE in the Maintenance of peace and Security, Conflicts Prevention, Crisis Management and Peaceful Settlement of Disputes.* The Hague: Kluwer Law International.

Decaux, Emmanuel (1992). *Sécurité et coopération en Europe, les textes officiels du processus d'Helsinki, 1973–1992.* Paris: Documentation Française.

Decaux, Emmanuel, and Linos-Alexandre Sicilianos, eds. (1993). *La CSCE : Dimension humaine et règlement des différends.* Paris: Montchrestien.

Ghebali, Victor-Yves (1996). *L'OSCE dans l'Europe post-communiste, 1990–1996.* Brussels: Bruylant.

Organization for Security and Cooperation in Europe (2000). *OSCE Handbook,* 4th edition. Prague: Author.

Organization for Security and Cooperation in Europe (2001). *OSCE Human Dimension Commitments: A Reference Book.* Prague: Author.

OSCE On-line. Available from http://www.osce.org.

Emmanuel Decaux

Peacekeeping

Peacekeeping is a process that involves military operations aiming to provide a buffer between warring parties. The principal objective of a peacekeeping mission is to halt armed conflict or prevent its reoccurrence. This is achieved by peacekeepers acting as a physical barrier between hostile parties and monitoring their military movements. Peacekeeping techniques are applied to both interstate and internal conflicts.

The Nature of Peacekeeping

Peacekeeping is based on the principle that an impartial presence of foreign troops on the ground can ease tensions and allow the achievement of a negotiated solution to a conflict. A critical first step before peacekeepers are deployed is for the United Nations (UN) or another intergovernmental body to obtain an end to fighting and to gain the consent of both parties in the dispute.

The term *peacekeeping* does not appear in the UN Charter. Former Secretary-General Dag Hammarskjold described peacekeeping as falling within "Chapter Six and a Half" of the charter. That is, it falls between traditional methods of resolving disputes peacefully (such as conciliation, mediation, and fact-finding) outlined in Chapter VI and resort to more forceful action (such as economic coercion and military intervention) authorized in Chapter VII.

Peacekeeping is distinctive. It resembles neither traditional means of dispute settlement nor the model of collective security. Peacekeeping compares with collective security only insofar as each technique involves the deployment of military forces. The objective is not to defeat an aggressor, but to prevent fighting, act as a buffer, preserve order, or maintain a cease-fire. Peacekeeping troops are usually instructed to use their weapons only in self-defense. Their role is more closely akin to that of policemen than combat soldiers. To be effective, peacekeeping forces must maintain attitudes of neutrality and impartiality toward the adversaries. Each peacekeeping operation has its particular mandated tasks, but common aims as well—to minimize human suffering and improve conditions for a self-sustaining peace. Thus, although peacekeeping operations have as their core an armed military component, they also employ various civilians, among them police officers, electoral experts, de-miners, human rights monitors, civil affairs specialists, and public information experts. UN peacekeepers normally coordinate efforts closely with field staffs of other UN agencies, especially the Office of the UN High Commissioner for Refugees, the World Food Programme, the UN Children's Fund, and the Office of the UN High Commissioner for Human Rights.

Certain factors contribute to the prospects for a peacekeeping operation's success. One is financing. Peacekeeping is expensive, and it is critical to adequately fund the supplies, equipment, salaries, and administrative costs of an operation. A second consideration is geography. More successful operations occur on flat, desert terrain in sparsely populated areas, where it is easier to observe military movements. Mountainous, jungle, or urban environments greatly complicate the monitoring mission of peacekeepers. Third, mandates for peacekeeping operations must be

United Nations peacekeepers from Portugal patrol the only mosque in Dili, the capital of East Timor, on May 25, 2000, following a series of attacks on the Muslim community. [AP/WIDE WORLD PHOTOS]

clear, and rules of engagement must be realistic relative to the situation. Fourth, peacekeeping forces need a centralized command and control system to facilitate efficient, effective policies. Finally, the peacekeeping forces must be neutral and not work to the benefit of either party in a dispute. Drawing forces from non-aligned countries works toward this end. In all cases the disputants' desire to peacefully solve their differences is critical to the success of any peacekeeping operation.

UN Peacekeeping and Genocide

Since the establishment of the UN in 1945, the Security Council has authorized 56 peacekeeping missions employing more than 800,000 military and police personnel from 118 countries. Of those forty-three UN peacekeeping operations were created by the Security Council after 1988. Fifteen missions remained ongoing in 2004. Since its creation in 2002 the Department of

Peacekeeping Operations has shouldered responsibility for providing political and administrative directions for missions in the field.

UN peacekeeping operations between 1945 and 1988 mainly involved the positioning of forces between former belligerents, with their consent, to monitor ceasefire agreements. The close of the cold war in 1989 witnessed the emergence of more multidimensional peace operations, as the Security Council authorized ambitious missions to reduce armed tensions, implement peace accords, and prevent widespread genocidal atrocities within states ravaged by ethnic strife and civil war. Among these multidimensional missions were several UN interventions motivated by humanitarian concerns, including those in Somalia (1992–1995), Bosnia and Herzegovina (1992–1994), Rwanda (1994), Sierra Leone (1997–1999), Kosovo (1996–1998), Liberia (1999–2003), and the Congo (1998–present). Even so, the record of international peacekeeping enjoys only mixed success because ethnic wars often degenerate into massive genocidal atrocities that severely challenge peacekeeping efforts.

In 1992 a U.S., and later UN-led, peacekeeping operation intervened in Somalia to protect international food aid personnel working to save local populations from famine and prevent the collapse of civil governance. When Somali warlords killed eighteen American soldiers in October 1993, the incident prompted the United States to withdraw its forces in early 1994, precipitating the collapse of the entire UN mission. Likewise in Bosnia, the Security Council deployed the UN Protection Force (UNPROFOR) in 1993 to end the bloody civil war between Serbs and Muslims that eventually resulted in the death of some 250,000 persons, mostly Muslims. However, the inability of UN peacekeepers to halt the slaughter of civilians, especially in Sarajevo and Srebrenica, led to their disengagement in 1995 and replacement by NATO troops—the first time a UN force was replaced by a regional organization's troops. The most tragic failure in peacekeeping occurred in Rwanda between April and June of 1994, when the world watched marauding Hutus murder thousands of their own countrymen, mostly Tutsis. The Security Council did not act, and when it did, it was too little, too late. A French-led UN peacekeeping force arrived in late June, as the genocidal massacres ended. In the interim 800,000 victims perished.

UN peacekeeping efforts since 1997 have focused on African intrastate wars, both to limit armed conflict and promote peaceful settlement. In Sierra Leone internal violence broke out in 1997. The UN established the UN Observer Mission in Sierra Leone in July 1998 to disarm the combatants, and although fighting continued, UN diplomacy facilitated negotiation of the Lomé Peace Agreement that officially ended hostilities in 1999. To implement this agreement and monitor the protection of human rights, UN forces were then increased to six thousand troops.

The deployment of a UN peacekeeping mission to Liberia in 1997 facilitated resolution of a civil war that had been ongoing since 1989, claimed the lives of 150,000 people—mostly civilians—and displaced some 850,000 refugees throughout neighboring countries. Civil turmoil erupted again in Liberia in July 2003, as fighting between government forces and warring factions intensified. In the face of a humanitarian tragedy, a peace treaty was signed in August that halted the violence. This agreement requested that the UN deploy a force to Liberia to support the government's transition and assist in implementing the terms of peace. In September 2003 the Security Council authorized the transport of fifteen thousand UN military personnel to assist in the maintenance of law and order throughout Liberia.

More tragic is the case of the Democratic Republic of the Congo. In 1998 fighting broke out between the Lendu and Hema tribes. The conflict erupted into a brutal civil war that became complicated when local militias were backed by Uganda, Rwanda, Angola, and Zimbabwe, who all sought control over mineral resources and diamonds in the Congo's eastern provinces. In November 1999 the UN dispatched 6,500 peacekeepers to control the violence, with only partial success. Widespread fighting diminished after 2001, but by then more than 3.5 million people had perished, mostly displaced civilians who had starved to death.

Regional Peacekeeping Missions

Some peacekeeping efforts are undertaken by regional organizations. For example, in response to pressure from the United States, in 1994 the North Atlantic Treaty Organization (NATO) authorized air strikes in Bosnia against Serbs who were attacking Muslims. These strikes led to the cessation of hostilities and negotiation of the Dayton Peace Accords in November 1995. During 1995 and 1996 a NATO-led international peacekeeping force (IFOR) of sixty thousand troops served in Bosnia to implement and monitor the military aspects of the agreement. IFOR was succeeded by a smaller, NATO-led Stabilization Force (SFOR) whose mission is to deter renewed hostilities. SFOR remains in place, although troop levels were reduced to approximately twelve thousand by late 2002.

Violence broke out in February 1998 between indigenous Serbs and Albanians in Kosovo. Over the next year 800,000 Kosovar Albanians fled to neighboring countries to escape ethnic cleansing. The refusal of the Serbs to negotiate, coupled with the likelihood of genocidal atrocities, prompted the United States through NATO to launch in March 1999 an intense bombing campaign against local Serbian militias. These air strikes lasted until June, when Serb forces withdrew from Kosovo and the United States, Great Britain, Italy, France, and Germany deployed a combined peacekeeping force of forty thousand peacekeepers to maintain peace and political stability.

The Economic Community of West African States (ECOWAS), supported by the UN, sought to end the 1989 civil war in Liberia. Fighting continued though 1997, when an ECOWAS-brokered peace agreement ended the conflict and established a democratically elected government. Likewise in 1997 the Security Council authorized the ECOWAS Military Observer Group (ECOMOG) to intervene in Sierra Leone's civil war to restore order, followed later that year by a special UN peacekeeping force. By January 1999 twenty thousand peacekeepers were stationed in Sierra Leone and peace had been restored.

Pervasive violence in the Balkans region and in Africa during the 1990s demonstrated the limits of peacekeeping where there is no peace to be kept, as well as the serious political complications for peacekeeping when armed force must be used against local citizens. Nonetheless, peacekeeping can work to preserve order if the parties to a dispute are willing to let it happen. And importantly, UN peacekeeping enjoys the advantages of universality and greater legitimacy compared to similar efforts undertaken by national or regional interests. In the long term, though, deploying peacekeeping operations to stop genocidal violence is not enough. Efforts at peacekeeping must have genuine political, financial, and military support from the major powers, and peace-building efforts must be made to develop stable political institutions, justice systems, and police forces that can maintain civil order and contribute to the creation of a civil society.

SEE ALSO Bosnia and Herzegovina; Humanitarian Intervention; Kosovo; Prevention; Rwanda; Somalia, Intervention in; United Nations Security Council

BIBLIOGRAPHY

Boutros-Gali, B. (1995). *An Agenda for Peace,* 2nd edition. New York: United Nations.

Diehl, P. F. (1993). *International Peacekeeping.* Baltimore, Md.: Johns Hopkins University Press.

Durch, W. J. (1996). *UN Peacekeeping, American Policy, and the Uncivil Wars of the 1990s.* New York: St. Martin's Press.

Ratner, S. R. (1996). *The New UN Peacekeeping: Building Peace in Lands of Conflict after the Cold War.* New York: St. Martin's Press.

UN Department of Public Information (1996). *The Blue Helmets: A Review of United Nations Peace-Keeping,* 3rd edition. New York: United Nations.

Weiss, T. G., ed. (1993). *Collective Security in a Changing World.* Boulder, Colo.: Lynne Rienner.

UN Peacekeepzing website. Available from http://www.un.org/Depts/dpko/dpko/home.shtml.

Christopher C. Joyner

Pequots

On May 26, 1637, an English military force, supported by Native allies, attacked a Pequot settlement on the Mystic River in Connecticut, and set it on fire. Almost all the Pequots who escaped the flames were killed by the troops surrounding the village. Six to seven hundred Pequots died. Many Pequots who were not in the village at the time were killed later, and others were enslaved. In 1638 the Pequots were forced to sign a treaty officially dissolving their nation. The English forbade the use of the Pequot name.

Whether this incident was a case of genocide has been the subject of much dispute. Frank Chalk and Kurt Jonassohn include it in their history of genocide. Steven Katz has argued that it was not genocide. Michael Freeman has challenged his argument. The dispute turns mainly on the question of whether the English intent was genocidal. This is difficult to determine, but most of the facts of what is usually called the Pequot War are uncontroversial.

Early contacts between Europeans and Native Americans were sometimes friendly and at other times hostile. The origins of their conflicts are often obscure, but probably include cultural misunderstandings and the escalation of minor offenses. Europeans despised Natives as heathens, and feared them as savages and agents of Satan. European attitudes were not uniformly hostile, however, and some thought that the Natives could become good Christians and trading partners. Puritan attitudes were not very different from those of other English settlers, but their conception of themselves as God's elect only intensified their distrust of Native Americans. Native-American attitudes toward Europeans were generally friendly, unless provoked. The English immigrated to America to settle, trade, and/or bring their religion to the heathen. These motives were not inherently genocidal, but they did contain the potential for violence, because many English believed that Natives who obstructed these goals should justly be punished. Some saw English colonists as new Israelites entering the promised land of Canaan, given to them by God, and inhabited by devil-worshippers. This belief had genocidal potential.

The first Puritan colony in New England was established at Plymouth in 1620. In 1630 a new colony was established in Boston Harbor; it rapidly grew during the 1630s. The local Natives welcomed the Boston settlers. Puritan attitudes toward the Natives were ambivalent. On the one hand, they were motivated by both Christian goodwill and the desire to trade. On the other hand, they feared the Natives as wild and untrustworthy savages.

The Pequot War

At the time of their first contact with Europeans, the Pequots occupied the coastal area between the Niantic River in Connecticut and the Wecapaug River in western Rhode Island. In 1622 the Dutch became the first Europeans to trade with them. This trade enabled the Pequots to dominate the other Natives of the Connecticut Valley. In 1633 the Dutch established a trading post on the Connecticut River. They concluded an agreement with the Pequots, according to which the Pequots would allow all Natives access to the trading post. Almost immediately the Pequots broke this agreement by killing some Natives bound for the post. When the Pequot principal *sachem* (chief), Tatobem, boarded a Dutch vessel to trade, he was held for ransom. The Pequots sent the Dutch the ransom. The Dutch sent the Pequots Tatobem's corpse. In response the Pequots killed the captain and crew of a European ship anchored in the Connecticut River.

The Pequots' victims were, however, not Dutch, but English. The captain was John Stone, a smuggler and privateer. In 1632 he had attempted to steal a ship of the Plymouth colony. He went to Boston, from which he was expelled for unbecoming conduct. When news of his death became known, neither Plymouth nor Boston showed any inclination to avenge him. In 1634 the Pequots sent an envoy to the Massachusetts Bay Colony, seeking the friendship of the English. Colony authorities made the surrender of Stone's killers a condition of friendship with the Pequots. The Pequot *sachems* did not accept these conditions, but instead made a payment to Boston for Stone's murder.

Shortage of good land in Massachusetts led to increasing English settlement in Connecticut. In June 1636 a Plymouth trader, Jonathan Brewster, reported that the Pequots were planning an attack. On July 4 the Massachusetts Bay Colony demanded that the Pequots honor the supposed agreement of 1634 that they surrender Stone's killers and pay compensation for his murder. Later that month Captain John Gallop found

When this photo of a young Pequot boy was snapped in 1938, fewer than twenty members of the once rich and powerful tribe survived on two small reservations in northern Connecticut. By 2004, a community of approximately 1,000 Pequots were attempting to rebuild, and reestablish some of its traditions, in the same Mashantucket region of the state. [BETTMANN/CORBIS]

the ship of John Oldham abandoned near Block Island. Onboard he discovered Oldham's dead body. The probable killers were the Narragansetts and the Block Islanders, who were tributaries of the Narragansetts. The Narragansetts returned Oldham's two sons and his possessions to Massachusetts, and made a reprisal raid on Block Island. The Bay Colony nevertheless decided to seek revenge on the Block Islanders and the Pequots. On August 25 a punitive expedition set sail from Boston to take revenge on the Block Islanders and to demand from the Pequots the surrender of Captain Stone's killers and compensation for his death. The expedition found few Native men on Block Island, destroyed various Native possessions, and then set off in pursuit of the Pequots. They were, however, unable to engage them, and, after killing one Pequot, they returned to Boston. In revenge the Pequots attacked English settlers in Connecticut during the winter of 1636

and 1637. A dispute with settlers at Wethersfield led to a Pequot attack in April 1637 resulting in the deaths of nine settlers. A week later the General Court of Connecticut declared war against the Pequots.

Connecticut mobilized a troop of ninety Englishmen under Captain John Mason and about seventy Natives hostile to the Pequots. The troop marched to Narragansett Bay, and then with Narragansett guides headed toward the Pequot settlement on the Mystic River. Mason later wrote that his plan was to destroy the Pequots. The English attacked the settlement, and the systematic massacre of its inhabitants ensued. Pequots who were not in the settlement at the time were rounded up and killed or sent into slavery. The English officially annihilated the Pequot nation as such. English apologists employed Old Testament justifications for their actions, comparing the Pequots to the Amalekites, whose name was supposed to be eliminated from the world.

The Puritan destruction of the Pequots has been explained as a preemptive strike motivated by fear of Pequot attack. The Pequot threat was, however, exaggerated, and the Puritans' inconsistent attitude about Stone's murder suggests that they had another agenda. The basis of the conflict lay in the complex, competitive relations among various Native groups and Europeans generated by European colonization and trade. The tensions these produced were aggravated by religious and cultural differences. The increasing Puritan demand for land might have brought conflict in the absence of these factors.

The Puritans sought to punish the Pequots severely and succeeded in destroying them in the process. Whether their intent was genocidal is not clear.

SEE ALSO Genocide; Massacres; Racism

BIBLIOGRAPHY

Cave, Alfred A. (1996). *The Pequot War.* Amherst: University of Massachusetts Press.

Chalk, Frank, and Kurt Jonassohn (1990). *The History and Sociology of Genocide: Analyses and Case Studies.* New Haven, Conn.: Yale University Press.

Freeman, Michael (1995). "Puritans and Pequots: The Question of Genocide." *New England Quarterly* 68:278–293.

Katz, Steven T. (1991). "The Pequot War Reconsidered." *New England Quarterly* 64:206–224.

Katz, Steven T. (1995). "Pequots and the Question of Genocide: A Reply to Michael Freeman." *New England Quarterly* 68:641–649.

Vaughan, Alden T. (1979). *New England Frontier: Puritans and Indians, 1620–1675,* revised edition. New York: W. W. Norton.

Michael Freeman

Perpetrators

Perpetrators are those who initiate, facilitate, or carry out acts of genocide or crimes against humanity. Genocide and crimes against humanity involve many of the same acts; the distinction between them is primarily that of intent. For genocide, the goal is the elimination of a group in whole or substantial part, whereas for other crimes against humanity, the goal is primarily to render a group powerless. The motivations of the perpetrators in other respects are the same. In what follows, the focus will be on perpetrators of genocide in its various forms, because the study of perpetrators in that context is most advanced.

The Variable Characteristics of Perpetrators

Genocide may involve the forcible transfer of children from the victim group to that of the perpetrators, or systematic rape that is intended to contribute to the disintegration of the group. Perpetrators also inflict on members of the victimized group conditions of life calculated to bring about its complete or partial physical destruction, such as the inducement of famine, deportations into deserts, or sealing victims into disease-ridden ghettos. Although it can be argued that all perpetrators of genocide intend the elimination of a definable human group, it is important to recognize that individual perpetrators may play different roles and bear different degrees of responsibility within the overall genocidal project. Various scholars have dealt with this by contrasting the roles of decision-makers and direct perpetrators, "desk murderers" and "shooters," and ideologues and technicians. Similarly, courts have assigned punishment, not on the basis of a convicted perpetrator's proximity to violence, but rather in accordance to his or her degree of responsibility for it. There are also those who design and manufacture the implements of death, use slave labor, drive the vehicles used to transport victims to their death, or propagandize in order to incite violence, as in Rwanda, where radio broadcasts were used to tell the Hutu that "the graves of the Tutsi are only half-full."

The concept of perpetrator is complicated further by its blurred edges. Numerous Holocaust memoirs mention that the first blows struck against the Jews at Auschwitz were delivered by fellow prisoners. These accounts are filled with descriptions of the brutalities committed by the *kapos* (prisoner-functionaries who helped run the camps). Were these kapos perpetrators? Or, is another term necessary, such as *victim-perpetrator*? Similarly, bystanders might not generally be considered perpetrators, but what if they supplied the weapons, chemicals, or tools used to commit genocide? In an even grayer area, does an individual's inaction qualify him as a perpetrator if that inaction facilitates genocide?

A commonly held view of the perpetrator is that only those who are mad, bestial, evil, or primitive commit genocide. While it is true that madmen and sadists are found among those who commit genocide, it is unlikely that the thousands, and sometimes hundreds of thousands, of perpetrators necessary to carry out genocide are insane. Likewise, if the perpetrators of genocide were invariably mad, no one could be held responsible for the commission of this, the worst crime that can befall a people. The charge that those who commit genocide must be bestial in nature is equally false, for the perpetration of the crime of genocide requires distinctly human capacities, such as abstraction, symbolization, and organization, in order to envision and carry out the destruction of entire human groups. Humans are the only animals that commit genocide.

The charge that the commission of genocide is something that is done only by primitive peoples is equally untenable. The crime has, in fact, been committed by peoples well-versed in science, technology, medicine, and the arts. Not only that, but in many instances, those who actually initiate and manage the destruction in such societies are often highly educated: professors, doctors, lawyers, skilled technicians. Finally, evil people for the most part are not the source of genocide, but the result: prolonged involvement in killing tends to dehumanize the perpetrator and removes from them any pity for the suffering of the victims. In rare cases, however, hardened criminals are recruited to augment the forces available for killing and rape. This was the case most notably in the Armenian genocide.

The view that perpetrators of genocide and other massive crimes against humanity are utterly different from average folk derives from the human desire to believe that this is a just and orderly world, composed mainly of persons who would harm others only in self-defense. In fact, however, genocide is committed by ordinary persons, more or less normal, more or less moral, who are caught up in a particular set of circumstances.

Contexts and Justifications
Genocide is not inevitable; it occurs because those in power choose to resolve political and social issues by eliminating the groups that are said to constitute the problem. Nor is genocide a discrete act. Rather, it is a process, typically initiated by the state, legitimated by tradition or ideology, carried out through a variety of organizations, and requiring the cooperation of individuals, some of whom may be bystanders, others perpetrators. It most often occurs when the state and society have been weakened by defeat in war, economic collapse, the breakdown of old ideologies, or demands by minority groups for autonomy or independence. Nationalism, new ideologies, demands for security, and the increasing dehumanization of the "other"—usually a subgroup who can be blamed for the current social ills—come to the fore. War is another natural context for genocide: the centralization of power, absence of restraints on the use of violence, a heightened sense of fear, and the pre-existence of organizations dedicated to killing, provide a cover for and justification of the elimination of the targeted group.

Those who initiate genocide do so for a variety of reasons: conquest, revenge, economic gain, monopoli-

zation of power, and, where a utopian ideology is involved, as in Nazi Germany and Cambodia, the purification of society leading to salvation for the nation. For individuals who become perpetrators, the motives are also varied and usually mixed. These depend in part on the mode of participation in genocide and the perpetrator's location with regard to the commission of genocidal acts. Some perpetrators act in obedience to orders; others become involved because of peer pressure, fear, careerism, and opportunities for material benefits, ideology, or dedication to a "higher cause." Some are drawn into committing acts that they would otherwise condemn because the circumstances provide them with permission to do so, others are encouraged through role playing, and some "learn by doing," starting with small acts of cruelty that lead to acts of increasing brutality until atrocity begins to seem normal because it has become routine. But whether they are conscripted into their roles or, more commonly, assume them voluntarily, individuals who become perpetrators enter into a continuum of destruction, in which their very behavior transforms their values and beliefs. Moreover, perpetrators operate not as isolated individuals, but as members of groups. Groups provide a shared view of the world and rewards for conformity, both of which facilitate the shedding of inhibitions.

The Role of Authority
The types of groups and organizations most often involved in genocide are authoritarian in structure, provide strong incentives for obedience, and encourage perpetrators to develop a psychological distancing from the victims through an emphasis on bureaucratic routines and the dehumanization of the group under attack. For example, bureaucracy was crucial in the Holocaust, and in less developed forms, it has been important in all of the genocides of the twentieth century. Perpetrators can sit at their desks and impersonally issue orders that send millions to their death. Logistics, communications, and technology used in the commission of genocide or other massive crimes against humanity must all pass through the hands of bureaucrats, who are culpable for their roles in the crimes but remain far from the killing fields or the routes of deportation.

Military and paramilitary organizations are also common institutional structures used to facilitate the perpetration of genocide or crimes against humanity. Such organizations enforce obedience, encourage conformity, provide training in violence, desensitize their members' responses to killing, and provide absolution. In some cases, pre-existing military organizations are used, but new ones may be created specifically for the commission of genocidal acts. Such was the case for the

SS of Nazi Germany, and the creation of the "Special Organization" in Turkey in 1915, whose sole purpose was the destruction of the Armenians.

This latter group was a secret Young Turk organization that controlled elements of the army, police, and local officials, and brought into the killing process thousands of Kurds and Turkish peasants. Most notably, however, it released some 30,000 criminals from jail, placed them under the control of the Special Organization, and gave them permission to murder, rape, and kidnap Armenians. Neither the peasants nor the criminals were under strict control. Rather, they were given permission to work their will on helpless people, with those in charge of the Special Organization knowing full well what that would mean. In contrast, militias and paramilitary groups, along with regular army troops, have played major roles in the perpetration of genocide in East Timor, Bosnia, and Rwanda. In East Timor and Rwanda, many of those in the militia were teenagers; in Bosnia, many were also young, recruited from soccer club hooligans, and some of the leaders were criminals. In each case, members of the militias were trained and armed by the military and had governmental support, but could be officially disavowed, fending off any international criticism.

Numbers of Perpetrators Needed

Genocide of any magnitude requires a sizable number of participants, but the extent to which this is true varies from case to case. The number required is partly determined by the technology that is employed—some forms of genocide are labor-intensive, others less so—and whether or not the victims are concentrated in one area or over a large territory. A further determining factor is the extent to which the victims are able to resist. In addition, some regimes, such as that of Ugandan President Idi Amin, restrict genocidal acts to an elite killing force. Others, such as Ottoman Turkey, Indonesia, and Rwanda, involve the participation of large segments of the population.

The decision to utilize a large number of perpetrators may also be influenced by certain political objectives. Those who initiate genocide may seek to gain support for their actions by allowing elements of society to satisfy their passions and greed at the expense of the victims. Alternatively, by plunging large numbers of the population into murder, the forces encouraging genocide may more tightly bind the perpetrators to the regime. In other cases, such as that of Nazi Germany, the intended magnitude of destruction is so great, and the victims so scattered, that most social and political institutions must be harnessed to the overriding aim of taking life.

Gender and Genocide

During the three thousand years for which genocidal acts have been documented or inferred, perpetrators have been predominantly males. For the most part, women have been involved in subordinate roles, but in rare cases female rulers, such as the first-century Celtic queen Boadicea, have also initiated genocide. One explanation for the relative absence of women from direct participation in genocide is the claim that women are naturally less aggressive and more compassionate. However, twentieth-century women have committed atrocities in Nazi Germany, Cambodia, and Rwanda. It is therefore more likely that women's lesser participation in genocide, historically speaking, is because they have been excluded by males from active involvement in the crimes. This exclusion derives from basic tenets of patriarchal society: women are weak and dependent, and their sexual and reproductive capacities too valuable to risk in war and genocide. In this view, the function of women is to produce life, whereas the function of men (at times) is to take life. Women are viewed as resources and, particularly in societies with small populations, were therefore far too valuable to risk in battle.

In the twentieth century, however, there were three major examples of women directly participating in genocide: in Nazi Germany, Cambodia, and Rwanda. There were some three thousand female SS who supervised the numerous Nazi concentration and extermination camps for women from 1939 to 1945. Most were labor conscripts and few were members of the party. They came from all social classes and occupations, and most appeared normal. Nonetheless, they learned quickly to whip and club their female prisoners, to work them to the point of exhaustion, and to assist in the selection process that sent many victims to their deaths. For the most part, it was the more sadistic women who rose to the top of the women's SS, but there were also female *kapos* who carried out much of the administration of the camps and made beatings and brutality of every sort a part of the inmate's daily existence.

Women were also deeply involved as perpetrators of genocide in Cambodia from 1975 to 1979, but the contrast with female perpetrators in Nazi Germany is striking. First, the Cambodian genocide was directly controlled by the Khmer Rouge, and the entire country functioned as a labor camp. Second, the scale of participation was greater: instead of the approximately three thousand (primarily conscripted) female prison guards in Germany, tens of thousands of Cambodian women served as leaders and guards, and the roots of their participation and commitment were much more varied.

Perhaps the greatest motivator for female (as well as male) Cambodian perpetrators was the need to establish a more secure identity in the face of ongoing warfare. Participation also provided a means of dealing with bewildering changes in government. A further motivation arose from the widely shared fear that Khmer culture was being destroyed by both Vietnamese and Western influence. Cambodian women were involved in the whole process of destruction: enforcing the killing pace of work, maintaining close surveillance over individuals and families, using violence to whip people into line, and direct killing. Moreover, Cambodia presents one of the few modern examples of a woman (Ieng Thirith) being one of the initiators of genocide.

Rwanda's political leaders attempted to involve as much of the nation's Hutu population in the genocide of Tutsi (and Tutsi sympathizers) as possible. Among the initiators of this genocide were at least three women—the wife of the assassinated President and two cabinet members—but many thousands of others joined in the killing, incited the militias to attack, betrayed the hunted, looted the dead, and encouraged men to rape Tutsi women. Some women were coerced into killing, but many joined in enthusiastically. Rwanda is a largely male-dominated society, however, and few women were members of the main organizations that carried out the genocide: the army, police, and militias. But, the women who did participate in the genocide were a cross-section of the country: peasants, teachers, nurses and doctors, nuns, journalists, school girls, local administrators, and even staff members of international aid organizations.

Enlisting the Children

If genocide's perpetrators include women, they also include children. In Cambodia, a large number of those who carried out the genocide were male and female children between the ages of twelve and seventeen. The pervasive role of children in the Khmer Rouge stemmed in part from their availability (the young generally comprise a large part of guerilla movements, worldwide). There was also a strong ideological dimension. In their quest to inaugurate an entirely different kind of society, the Khmer Rouge eliminated distinctions between adults and children.

In Rwanda, on the other hand, young men and, to a lesser extent, teenage girls, were involved in the killing. This was, again, partly a matter of availability—more than half the population was under twenty, and many young people were unemployed, without prospects for the future. Where extreme deprivation exists, material rewards may be all that are needed to bring the

young into the killing process. However, in Rwanda it was also a matter of how the genocide was organized. Political parties had formed youth groups to attack opposing political groups, and these groups were later converted into local militias to carry out the genocide.

Whether in Cambodia, Rwanda, or some other place, it has not been difficult for adult perpetrators to recruit children to help with the dirty work. There are a variety of techniques that can be used to turn child members of the perpetrators' group into killers. Some may simply need encouragement, others may be forced into doing brutal acts, sometimes beginning with killing, but always ending there. Children learn by doing, but they also learn by seeing the acts of others. When children commit brutal acts that are sanctioned by authority, and when, over time, such acts become routine; they learn to define morality strictly in terms of loyalty to the group. These children can be seen as victims, but they also are perpetrators. How they are to be legally judged is problematic.

Aftermath for Perpetrators

Few survivors of genocide ever free themselves from the horrors they have experienced. Most perpetrators, however, seem able to distance themselves from the acts they committed and go on with their lives. Nor is there evidence that many suffer from a guilty conscience. Those involved in direct killing are brutalized by the very process, becoming desensitized to the sufferings of others. In addition, many perpetrators of genocide participate in the killing from a distance. These, too, frequently show no remorse. Both the individuals directly, physically involved in the killing and those who participate bureaucratically may overcome remorse through individual psychological mechanisms, such as denial and repression. Further, they can attempt to find excuses for their actions, the main varieties being: "I knew nothing," and "I was only obeying orders." More powerful, however, are techniques of neutralization that combine both excuses and justifications. These include the denial of responsibility (an inability to control the situation, self-defense), denial of the humanity of the victim, transforming the victim into the perpetrator and condemning the condemners, (by asserting that they—victim or condemner—have done worse deeds), and appealing to a higher loyalty—to race, class, God's will, the good society—as the motivation for the violence. All cultures encourage responsibility, but also provide escape routes (excuses, distancing, justification) for offenses both minor and grave. Perpetrators seize upon the cues society provides for neutralizing responsibility, magnifying them to a self-serving extreme. Paradoxically, while many survivors feel guilt for being alive, those who perpetrate genocide more frequently are able to look back upon their actions with consciences at rest.

Understanding Why

There are many approaches to understanding the behavior of perpetrators and why humans resort to genocide. Psychologists once focused on the "authoritarian personality," but later started focusing on a combination of social identity, culture, and historical context. Political scientists tend to focus on the policy process, institutions, leadership, and international relations. Social science offers three overlapping approaches that help to explain specific portions of the behavior of perpetrators. Structuralism explores how the social environment shapes choices: structures of authority, group dynamics, and bureaucracy. Functionalism, in contrast, is concerned with how particular structures perform various functions. Applied to the study of genocide, it can illuminate the role of various organizations in the process of destruction. Perhaps more important, however, a functional approach can help to illuminate the many purposes that genocide actually serves: physical, material, political, and psychological. For instance, rape may be encouraged to reward the perpetrators while simultaneously terrorizing and shaming the victim group, making resistance to genocide or ethnic cleansing more difficult. It poses a series of questions: Why do perpetrators so often engage in acts of cruelty or perform rituals of degradation? What do these acts mean to the perpetrator? Symbolic interaction theory can also help explain the formation of social identity, the growth of stereotypes, and dehumanization of those who will fall victim to genocide.

All of these approaches and disciplines have their uses, but none is adequate in itself. Moreover, much investigation of perpetrators requires a moral theory that allows distinction between different kinds of responsibility (criminal, moral, political) and acknowledgement of different degrees of responsibility. To arrive at such a moral theory, philosophers must grapple with the fundamental question of the nature of "good" and "evil."

SEE ALSO Collaboration; Memoirs of Perpetrators; Psychology of Perpetrators; Sociology of Perpetrators

BIBLIOGRAPHY

Alvarez, Alex (2001). *Governments, Citizens and Genocide: A Comparative and Interdisciplinary Approach.* Bloomington: Indiana University Press.

Browder, George C. (2003). "Perpetrator Character and Motivation: An Emerging Consensus?" *Holocaust and Genocide Studies* 17:480–497.

Browning, Christopher R. (1992). *Ordinary Men: Reserve Police Battalion 101 and the Final Solution in Poland.* New York: HarperCollins.

Jones, David H. (1999). *Moral Responsibility in the Holocaust: A Study in the Ethics of Character.* Lanham, Md.: Rowman & Littlefield.

Hirsch, Herbert (1995). *Genocide and the Politics of Memory: Studying Death to Preserve Life.* Chapel Hill: University of North Carolina Press.

Kelman, Herbert (1973). "Violence without Moral Restraint: Reflections on the Dehumanization of Victims and Victimizers." *Journal of Social Issues* 29:25–61.

Kuper, Leo (1982). *Genocide: Its Political Use in the Twentieth Century.* New Haven, Conn.: Yale University Press.

Milgram, Stanley (1974). *Obedience to Authority.* New York: Harper and Row.

Smith, Roger W. (1987). "Human Destructiveness and Politics: The Twentieth Century as an Age of Genocide." In *Genocide and the Modern Age*, ed. I. Wallimann and M. Dobkowski. Westport, Conn.: Greenwood Press.

Smith, Roger W. (1994). "Women and Genocide: Notes on an Unwritten History." *Holocaust and Genocide Studies* 8:315–334.

Staub, Ervin (1989). *The Roots of Evil: The Origins of Genocide and Other Group Violence.* Cambridge: Cambridge University Press.

Weitz, Eric D. (2003). *A Century of Genocide: Utopias of Race and Nation.* Princeton, N.J.: Princeton University Press.

Roger W. Smith

Persecution

In colloquial usage the term *persecution* can refer to any identity-related maltreatment, either of a group or an individual. However, its historical and legal meanings, although still subject to a degree of ambiguity, are more precisely delineated.

Historical Meaning

Throughout history myriad groups have been maltreated because of their identity, with distinctions drawn on such grounds as religion, race, gender, culture, national origin, ethnicity, politics, or socioeconomic status. Persecuted groups have been identified through both positive and negative criteria. At certain junctures people were persecuted because they belonged to a particular group. At others people were persecuted because they did not belong to a particular group, usually that of the persecutor.

A range of different measures, in terms of both type and degree, have been referred to as persecution. This maltreatment has taken a variety of forms—corporeal punishment, material deprivation, psychological trauma, segregation, and other forms of discrimination.

Legal Meaning

Prior to World War II states protested one another's acts of persecution, especially when the victims were a minority group that shared a bond (e.g., religion, ethnicity, or national origin) with the protesting state. In some instances bilateral treaties were concluded between such states to regulate the treatment of a minority population. At times persecution led to, or was at least cited as a justification for, military intervention.

In the early twenty-first century persecution is clearly prohibited by international law. It constitutes a violation of international criminal law as well as human rights law. Although most violations of public international law involve only state responsibility, the commission of persecution, as a crime under international law, gives rise to the notion of individual criminal responsibility. In a legal context the international crime of persecution falls within the broader category of crimes known as crimes against humanity.

International Criminal Law

In 1998 the drafters of the Rome Statute of the International Criminal Court (ICC) reached agreement on a definition of persecution. According to Article 7(2)(g) of the Rome Statute, persecution means "the intentional and severe deprivation of fundamental rights contrary to international law by reason of the identity of the group or collectivity." However, for much of the twentieth century, despite its prevalence in fact, persecution as a crime under international law escaped precise definition.

Prior to World War II the principle of nonintervention, whereby states were prohibited from intervening in matters essentially within another state's domestic jurisdiction, was thought to pose an insurmountable obstacle to the international criminalization of such conduct.

Persecution first emerged as a specific crime under international law in the charter (the so-called London Charter) of the International Military Tribunal (IMT) at Nuremberg. Article 6(c) of the London Charter empowered the tribunal to prosecute:

> Crimes against Humanity: namely, murder, extermination, enslavement, deportation, and other inhumane acts committed against any civilian population, before or during the war, or persecutions on political, racial or religious grounds in execution of or in connection with any crime within the jurisdiction of the Tribunal, whether or not in violation of the domestic law of the country where perpetrated.

The inclusion of crimes against humanity within the jurisdiction of the IMT was a watershed event in international law because it made punishable conduct that could be perpetrated by state authorities against their own nationals.

However, the cautious drafters were not prepared to depart entirely from the primarily interstate structure of classical international law. Under Article 6(c) of the Charter, persecution would constitute a crime against humanity punishable under the Charter only if it was committed in connection with another crime within the jurisdiction of the IMT (i.e., crimes against peace or war crimes), all of which would have had an international (i.e., interstate) dimension. In practice this meant that the IMT could not punish as such wrongful acts committed prior to the start of World War II.

Although the London Charter failed to provide a definition of persecution, the IMT made clear that the complete exclusion of Jews from German life prior to the start of World War II amounted to persecution. In so doing, it cited the adoption of discriminatory laws, the espousal of hatred toward Jews, discriminatory arrest and detention, the looting of Jewish businesses, the arrest of prominent Jewish businessmen, the confiscation of assets, the burning and demolition of synagogues, the creation of ghettos, restriction of freedom of movement, the imposition of a collective fine, and the organization of pogroms. Nonetheless, the IMT did not enter a conviction for any solely pre–World War II conduct, finding that it was prevented from doing so by the nexus requirement mentioned above.

A significant post–World War II development aimed at preventing persecution was the 1948 adoption of the Convention on the Prevention and Punishment of the Crime of Genocide. Although the Genocide Convention does not define persecution, it criminalizes a particularly severe form of it. Genocide is defined as the commission of certain inhumane acts with the intention of destroying, in whole or in part, a national, ethnical, racial, or religious group.

Extensive nondiscrimination provisions were also included in each of the four Geneva Conventions of 1949, which regulate the treatment of victims of armed conflict. The Fourth Geneva Convention, devoted to the protection of civilians in time of war, provides specific protection against persecution. Article 45 states, "In no circumstances shall a protected person be transferred to a country where he or she may have reason to fear persecution for his or her political opinions or religious beliefs."

The end of the cold war witnessed the rejuvenation of international criminal law and, with it, further elaboration of the criminal prohibition of persecution. The

United Nations (UN) Security Council's creation of the International Criminal Tribunals for the Former Yugoslavia (ICTY) and Rwanda (ICTR) in 1993 and 1994 spurred the rapid development of this area of international law.

Both tribunals were empowered to prosecute genocide, war crimes, and crimes against humanity. Persecution was mentioned in the statutes of both tribunals as a form of crime against humanity. Although neither statute contains a definition for the crime of persecution, both provide more elaborate definitions of crimes against humanity than was advanced in the London Charter.

Although the definitions for crimes against humanity in the two statutes are not identical, their broad outlines are similar: They both make a distinction between enumerated inhumane acts and contextual elements. The list of inhumane acts is identical—namely, murder; extermination; enslavement; deportation; imprisonment; torture; rape; persecutions on political, racial, and religious grounds; and other inhumane acts. Notably, persecution is the only enumerated act committed on discriminatory grounds. Both statutes require, as a contextual element, that such an act (or acts) be committed as part of an attack against a civilian population.

There are significant differences in the contextual elements of the definition in each statute. Although both definitions require that the enumerated acts be committed as part of an attack against a civilian population, the ICTY statute also requires that the acts be committed during armed conflict. While the ICTR definition of crimes against humanity has no such armed conflict requirement, it does mention discrimination, something absent from the ICTY definition. Under the ICTR definition of crimes against humanity, the attack of which the inhumane act is a part must be discriminatory in nature. Thus, for the crime of persecution to have occurred, it must be shown that the act was persecutory and that the overall attack of which it was a part was also discriminatory. However, although the persecutory act must have been discriminatory on political, racial, or religious grounds, the possible grounds of discrimination for the broader attack also include nationality and ethnicity.

A number of significant advances of particular relevance to the issue of persecution have evolved though the practice of the tribunals. First, the jurisprudence of the tribunals has made clear that the contextual element of armed conflict in the ICTY statute and the contextual element of discrimination in the ICTR statute are merely jurisdictional in nature and do not form part of the definition of crimes against humanity under customary international law. Second, the tribunals have also found that crimes against humanity need not be supported by some larger government policy. Third, in interpreting their respective statutes, both tribunals have elaborated a definition for persecution—essentially, an intentional and severe deprivation of fundamental rights on discriminatory grounds. Fourth, the ICTY has suggested that a single individual can be the victim of persecution, as long as the contextual elements for crimes against humanity have otherwise been met.

As for the range of persecutory maltreatment, the ICTR and ICTY have found that each of the acts enumerated within their statutes' provisions for crimes against humanity may qualify as persecution. In addition, the ICTY has established a "same level of gravity" test for acts not listed within the crimes against humanity provision of its statute. Only acts of comparable gravity constitute persecution. However, under such a test, acts are examined cumulatively; thus, the cumulative effect of even noncriminal acts may be sufficient to reach the same level of gravity as the enumerated acts. In general, crimes involving property are not considered to be of sufficient gravity to constitute persecution, unless they threaten the livelihood of the victim population. Nonetheless, several ICTY judgments have found that the destruction of property can amount to persecution when committed in conjunction with other inhumane acts.

Many of these developments are reflected in the Rome Statute's definition of persecution as constituting a crime against humanity. In line with the findings of the tribunals as to the content of customary law, the contextual elements for crimes against humanity in the Rome Statute include neither a requirement for armed conflict nor one for discriminatory animus. As noted above, persecution is defined as "the intentional and severe deprivation of fundamental rights contrary to international law by reason of the identity of the group or collectivity." According to Article 7(h) of the statute, the ICC has jurisdiction to prosecute "[p]ersecution against any identifiable group or collectivity on political, racial, national, ethnic, cultural, religious, gender . . . , or other grounds that are universally recognized as impermissible under international law." However, persecution alone is not a crime within the jurisdiction of the ICC, even when the contextual elements for crimes against humanity are met. Recalling the nexus requirement set forth in the London Charter for all crimes against humanity, the drafters of the Rome Statute chose to limit the prosecution of persecution to situations in which persecutory acts are committed "in connection with any act referred to in this paragraph or any crime within the jurisdiction of the Court."

Refugee Law

The Universal Declaration of Human Rights, adopted by the UN General Assembly in 1948, declares in Article 14 that "[e]veryone has the right to seek and to enjoy in other countries asylum from persecution." The 1951 Convention Relating to the Status of Refugees (the so-called Refugee Convention), together with its 1967 Protocol, provides for the implementation of this right by requiring contracting states to afford a range of rights to any individual who

> [o]wing to well-founded fear of being persecuted for reasons of race, religion, nationality, membership of a particular social group or political opinion, is outside the country of his nationality and is unable, or owing to such fear, is unwilling to avail himself of the protection of that country; or who, not having a nationality and being outside the country of his former habitual residence as a result of such events, is unable or, owing to such fear, is unwilling to return to it.

Further, contracting states must refrain from expelling or returning a refugee "in any manner whatsoever to the frontiers of territories where his life or freedom would be threatened on account of his race, religion, nationality, membership of a particular social group or political opinion." However, as with earlier instruments, the Refugee Convention failed to define persecution.

To alleviate the suffering of groups fleeing persecution, the UN General Assembly established in 1950 the Office of the UN High Commissioner for Refugees. According to its statute, the UN High Commissioner for Refugees is charged with providing international protection, under the auspices of the UN, to refugees and with seeking permanent solutions to the problem of refugees by assisting governments and nongovernmental organizations (NGOs) to facilitate their voluntary repatriation or assimilation within new national communities. This protection takes various forms, including monitoring the treatment of refugees and striving to provide a minimum level of humanitarian relief to such individuals.

Discriminatory Grounds

As is apparent from the provisions cited above, a degree of variation exists among the types of discrimination required to constitute persecution as recognized under current legal instruments. While persecution under the ICTY and ICTR statutes must be committed on political, racial, or religious grounds, the Refugee Convention recognizes persecution on the grounds of race, religion, nationality, membership in a particular social group, or political opinion. The practice of some national courts has included other grounds, such as gender, within the category of "social group."

The statute of the ICC has the most extensive list of grounds, including "political, racial, national, ethnic, cultural, religious, gender as defined in paragraph 3, or other grounds that are universally recognized as impermissible under international law." The wording at the end of this provision will enable the list of categories to expand as the international community reaches consensus on additional grounds. The mention of gender makes clear that gender refers only to the "two sexes, male and female, within the context of society." The inclusion of this qualifying phrase appears to represent an attempt by the drafters to prevent the ICC from interpreting gender to include sexual orientation, as a number of other human rights mechanisms have done in considering discrimination based on sexual orientation to constitute a form of sex discrimination.

International Human Rights Law

Although the major human rights treaties, including the International Covenant on Civil and Political Rights, the International Covenant on Economic, Social and Cultural Rights, and their regional counterparts, do not expressly refer to persecution, these instruments provide broad protection from discrimination in general.

Even more extensive protection is provided under the International Convention on the Elimination of All Forms of Racial Discrimination, the Convention on the Elimination of All Forms of Discrimination Against Women, and related regional human rights treaties. These conventions provide far-reaching protections encompassing economic and social rights as well as civil and political rights, and penetrating both the public and private spheres. In addition to a guarantee of equality of treatment, these conventions require states to take positive steps toward ensuring that groups experience substantive equality.

Furthermore, human rights treaties provide protection specifically for minority groups. For example, the International Covenant on Civil and Political Rights states that persons belonging to minority groups "shall not be denied the right, in community with the other members of their group, to enjoy their own culture, to profess and practice their own religion, or to use their own language."

Nonstate Actors as Agents of Persecution

Although international criminal law, international human rights law, and refugee law are all distinct areas of public international law, there is a dynamic interplay among them. One development that cuts across all three fields is the increasing recognition of nonstate agents of persecution, and attempts to assign accountability for their conduct and to provide redress for their victims.

Traditionally, public international law governs relations among states. Notwithstanding the persistence of the classical interstate structure of the international legal system, over the course of the twentieth century international law evolved significantly in its relation to individual human beings. Two phenomena in particular led to astonishingly rapid developments in the substance of international law, and even the very structure of the international legal system. The first is the universal recognition that the protection of human dignity is a proper concern of international law, and the second is the accumulation and exercise of power by nonstate actors. As a result, the expanding lens of public international law has increasingly examined the conduct of nonstate actors.

Although it was unclear whether the London Charter's definition of crimes against humanity could apply to persecution by nonstate actors, the practice of the ICTY and ICTR has made clear that persecution may be committed by nonstate actors, with the ICTY in particular convicting a number of nonstate actors for crimes against humanity. While the Rome Statute requires a policy as a contextual element for all crimes against humanity, such a policy may be a "State or organizational policy," clearly indicating that persecution may be committed by individuals with no connection to the state.

Similarly, national courts have interpreted persecution within the context of refugee law as including inhumane treatment by nonstate actors, particularly when the state has acquiesced to such treatment. Further, various human rights instruments elaborated in the second half of the twentieth century have all been interpreted to encompass, albeit to varying degrees, conduct committed by nonstate actors.

Remedies
A variety of remedies under domestic and international law are available, depending on the jurisdiction in which the persecution occurs whether or not the state involved is a party to any of the above-mentioned treaties.

As for remedies within the municipal sphere, most states have some form of nondiscrimination legislation that may be invoked in domestic courts. Such legislation could include protection from discrimination in a range of fields, from employment and education, to health care and participation in public life. Some states also have hate crimes laws, which provide increased penalties for crimes committed on discriminatory grounds. As most countries are parties to the Refugee

Convention, most domestic legal systems also allow for the possibility of asylum for victims of persecution.

On the international level, remedies exist in both international criminal law and human rights law. An increasing number of international criminal justice mechanisms exist, most notably, the ICC. The ICC has potentially worldwide jurisdiction as long as the perpetrator is the national of a state party, or if the persecutory act was committed on the territory of a state party. The ICC is empowered not only to prosecute the perpetrator, but also to provide reparations to victims.

The various human rights regimes discussed here have established monitoring mechanisms that are capable of providing varying degrees of redress to victims. The focus of such mechanisms is the responsibility of the state and its obligation to make reparations for human rights violations suffered by victims. Such reparations may encompass a range of measures, including amendment of domestic law, alteration of existing practices, prosecution of perpetrators, and rehabilitation and compensation of victims.

SEE ALSO Cathars; Catholic Church; Huguenots; Inquisition; International Court of Justice; Jehovah's Witnesses

BIBLIOGRAPHY
"Charter of the International Military Tribunal." Agreement for the Prosecution and Punishment of the Major War Criminals of the European Axis, August 8, 1945, art. 6, 82 U.N.T.S. 279. Available from http://www.yale.edu/lawweb/avalon/imt/proc/imtconst.htm

Preparatory Committee on the Establishment of an International Criminal Court, Working Group on Definition of Crimes (1997). *Draft Consolidated Text, Crimes Against Humanity*. UN Document A/AC.249/1997/WG.1/CRP.5.

Prosecutor v. Milomir Stakic. Case No. IT-97-24, Judgment, ICTY Trial Chamber II (July 31, 2003).

Rome Statute of the International Criminal Court (1998). Available from http://www.un.org/law/icc/statute/romefra.htm.

John Cerone

Peru

The year 2000 ushered in more than just a new millennium in Peru. It witnessed a return to democracy after years of internal armed conflict and authoritarian rule. It also signaled the beginning of the country's efforts to come to terms with a long legacy of widespread and systematic human rights abuses. Peru's political transition, triggered by the fall of President Alberto Fujimori in 2000, revolved in significant part around how to respond to the terrible crimes against humanity committed between 1980 and 2000 by Peruvian security forces and their principal nemesis, a guerrilla group known as *Sendero Luminoso* (the Shining Path). The ultimate success of Peru's return to peace, democracy, and the rule of law depends in no small measure on whether the perpetrators of the worst crimes can be held accountable.

Peru's civil conflict was a vicious struggle for power between rebel forces, primarily the Shining Path, and Peruvian security forces. According to the Peruvian Truth and Reconciliation Commission, which was established in 2001 to investigate the widespread violations of human rights that had occurred, nearly seventy thousand people were unlawfully killed or forcibly disappeared during the war, virtually all of them civilians. The Truth Commission found that nearly 54 percent of these deaths or disappearances were attributable to the Shining Path guerrillas. Peru's state security apparatus composed of the armed forces, the police, and local "self-defense" committees organized and armed by the state was responsible for 37 percent of the violations. In addition, the victims of Peru's political violence were subjected to the systematic practice of torture by the Peruvian armed forces and national police; the Shining Path also resorted to torture on a regular basis, although not nearly to the same extent. Similarly, state agents were by far the most active perpetrators of sexual violence against women, especially rape, as a method of torture.

Caught between the warring parties, the civilian population bore the brunt of these abuses. It is estimated that of the approximately seventy thousand people killed or disappeared, over 80 percent lived in the most destitute regions of the country. The population most affected was primarily the poor, rural, and predominantly indigenous communities of Peru's Andes region. In fact, three out of every four victims were from this region. These marginalized communities have historically suffered from extreme political, economic, and social exclusion. Peruvian society's biases were clearly reflected in the war's disproportionate impact on its most vulnerable sectors: The Truth Commission found that the vast majority of all victims were lower-class *campesinos* (farm laborers), as well as Andean and Amazonian Indians whose Native language was either Quechua or Ashaninka, not Spanish.

Few dispute that responsibility for initiating the war rests squarely with the Shining Path guerrillas, one of the most savage insurgent movements ever. As part of its Maoist strategy to overthrow the established order, this group systematically targeted local authorities, as well as community leaders and activists, for ex-

termination, often through massacres. Using these brutal tactics, the Shining Path was responsible for more than half of the estimated seventy thousand killings and disappearances tabulated by the Truth Commission, and nearly a quarter of all torture. Its leaders, especially the group's founder, Abimael Guzmán, a former university professor captured by police in 1992, undoubtedly bear the bulk of responsibility for the crimes against humanity committed by this insurgent organization. The only other guerrilla movement in the country, the comparatively small Tupac Amaru Revolutionary Movement, was ultimately responsible for less than 2 percent of all human rights violations occurring during the conflict, primarily the kidnapping of civilians and taking of hostages.

Even so, it is arguable that the cure may have been worse than the disease: The increasingly authoritarian responses of successive civilian administrations caused the military conflict to deepen, leading to serious human rights violations on a massive scale. The Peruvian government under President Fernando Belaunde Terry (1980–1985) was unprepared to counter organized insurgency in the countryside. This led to the declaration of a state of emergency in those provinces most affected by the violence, principally in Ayacucho, and the militarization of counterinsurgency operations in 1982. Significant human rights violations ensued. Nearly a third of all deaths and disappearances during the twenty-year conflict occurred from 1983 to 1984. The Truth Commission determined that the inept government of President Belaunde failed to prevent, investigate, or punish the rampant abuses which transpired during his tenure, adding that this failure was a product of discrimination against Peru's indigenous population and other marginalized sectors.

Belaunde's elected successor as president, Alan García (1985–1990), attempted at first to regain civilian control over the security forces. Simultaneously he adopted policies aimed at undermining the guerrillas' social and political base, not least by preaching official respect for human rights. The worst excesses on both sides diminished. However, several events conspired to plunge Peru back into a spiral of escalating violence. In June 1986 an uprising by political prisoners at El Frontón prison was crushed by the armed forces, resulting in the death and disappearance of hundreds of inmates. This set off a new wave of guerrilla attacks and military successes, which for the first time began to reach beyond the rural regions of the country's interior to include targets in Lima, the capital city.

By bringing terror to urban Peru's doorstep and creating a climate of insecurity throughout the country, the guerrillas succeeded in undermining the civilian

Alberto Fujimori claims he was born on Peruvian Independence Day, July 28, 1938, in Lima, Peru (some commentators dispute this). His parents emigrated from Japan in 1934. Fujimori studied agricultural engineering at the prestigious *La Molina* National Agrarian University, graduating at the top of his class in 1961. He subsequently earned a masters degree in mathematics from the University of Wisconsin on a scholarship. He was first a professor and then rector of *La Molina*. In 1987 he was elected president of the National Association of University Rectors, an experience that introduced Fujimori to the rough and tumble world of Peruvian politics.

Before launching his underdog bid for the presidency in 1990, Fujimori made a name for himself as the host of a television talk show dedicated to political analysis. In 1989, he founded "Change 90," a new political party with a grassroots approach and populist appeal. In the election run-off against the aristocratic Mario Vargas Llosa, a famous author, the modest Fujimori won a record-setting 60 percent of the vote. In the face of a deepening social and political crisis, President Fujimori seized control of the Peruvian state on April 5, 1992. He suspended the Constitution, dissolved Congress, fired top government officials and judges unsympathetic to him, arrested political opponents, and censored the press. Despite these undemocratic actions, Fujimori's popularity was bolstered by the capture of Abimael Guzm·n, leader of the Shining Path, in September of 1992, and he was eventually reelected in 1995. From 1995 until late 2000, when his government finally collapsed, Fujimori and his closest associates were the object of numerous scandals involving grave human rights violations, corruption, and electoral fraud.

Fujimori's reign ended in November 2000, when he faxed his resignation from Japan where he had been attending a trade conference. The Peruvian Congress rejected the resignation and instead voted to remove him from office for being morally unfit. In September 2001 a judge ordered Fujimori's arrest for murder, serious injury, and forced disappearance in relation to the massacres of La Cantuta and Barrios Altos, which had been carried out by the Grupo Colina, a notorious death squad attached to the National Intelligence Service. Interpol subsequently issued an international warrant for his arrest in connection with these crimes. Fujimori was also indicted in Peru on charges of embezzlement. In 2003 the Truth and Reconciliation Commission found that Fujimori was personally responsible for crimes against humanity committed with his knowledge by the Grupo Colina. It also held him and his government politically responsible for the torture, disappearances, and extra-judicial executions that took place during his ten-year presidency.

It is unlikely that Fujimori will be brought to justice. Japan refused a request by the government of President Alejandro Toledo to extradite him to Peru to face the charges against him. Fujimori became a Japanese citizen, and there is no extradition treaty between the two countries. As of 2004, Fujimori remained in exile in Japan, where he continued to opine on Peruvian politics via his personal website (www.fujimorialberto.com). **ARTURO CARRILLO**

government's authority and reinforcing that of the Peruvian military. By the end of President Garcia's term in 1990, nearly half the national population and a third of its territory were under a state of emergency and subject to the direct control of the armed forces. Restrictions had been placed on civil liberties, institutional democracy, and the independence of the judiciary. These measures, in turn, had fueled a new surge in the number of killings, disappearances, and other grave human rights violations. The Truth Commission established that the government of President García had further contributed to the human rights crisis by attempting to cover up many of the rampant abuses carried out by state agents during this period.

Alberto Fujimori, a political upstart whose populist platform played well with Peru's marginalized masses (see sidebar), was the surprising victor in the landmark 1990 election. President Fujimori further ex-

tended military control over the government through a series of draconian legislative and executive initiatives that exacerbated an already dire human rights situation. One of the most controversial measures authorized military courts to try civilians accused of "terrorism," which led to the arbitrary detention and unjust conviction of hundreds of innocent people. Fujimori effectively placed the Peruvian state's security apparatus under the direction of the National Intelligence Service led by Vladimiro Montesinos, his closest advisor. This consolidation of authority allowed Fujimori to carry out in April 1992 the infamous *autogolpe* (self-coup), whereby he directly seized power by suspending the constitution and suppressing all opposition.

Fujimori's autocratic control over the levers of power and the media, coupled with public successes such as capturing the guerrillas' main leaders, allowed him to remain in power until rampant corruption toppled his government in 2000. His decade in power was characterized by a progressive deterioration of the rule of law as the regime became more brazen in its abuse of power. A good example is the adoption in 1995 of amnesty laws that shielded all police and military agents from prosecution for any human rights violations committed since 1980 (the law was later annulled). It is no coincidence that the Fujimori government was at the time under intense scrutiny due to several high-profile scandals involving grave human rights violations attributed to government agents. In particular, the government was under national and international pressure to account for two cold-blooded massacres, La Cantuta and Barrios Altos, in which dozens of victims were either assassinated or disappeared by a death squad. It was later revealed that the death squad was a clandestine creation of the intelligence network run by Montesinos on Fujimori's behalf. The Truth Commission held both men individually responsible for these crimes against humanity.

The transition back to democracy after Fujimori's abrupt resignation was initiated by the interim government of Valentín Paniagua, a congressman selected to be the caretaker president. He began by dismantling much of his predecessor's corrupt and oppressive security apparatus. In one of his first official acts, Paniagua established the Truth and Reconciliation Commission with a broad mandate to report on the abuses of the past and make recommendations on how to address them. The Truth Commission was subsequently ratified by President Alejandro Toledo, who was elected in April 2001. In August 2003 the Truth Commission issued its final report, which identified many of the groups and individuals responsible for the worst human rights violations. It was but the first step toward overcoming the impunity that has long benefited the perpetrators of crimes against humanity in Peru.

SEE ALSO Amazon Region; Incas

BIBLIOGRAPHY

Bowen, Sally (2000). *The Fujimori File: Peru and Its President, 1990–2000*. Lima: Peru Monitor.

Human Rights Watch (1992). *Peru under Fire: Human Rights since the Return to Democracy*. New Haven, Conn.: Yale University Press.

Human Rights Watch (1997). *Torture and Political Persecution in Peru*. New York: Human Rights Watch.

Inter-American Commission on Human Rights. Organization of American States. General Secretariat (1993). "Report on the Situation of Human Rights in Peru." Available from http://www.cidh.oas.org/countryrep/Peru93eng/toc.htm.

Inter-American Commission on Human Rights. Organization of American States. General Secretariat

(2000). "2nd Report on the Situation of Human Rights in Peru." Available from http://www.cidh.oas.org/countryrep/Peru2000en/TOC.htm.

McClintock, Cynthia (1998). *Revolutionary Movements in Latin America: El Salvador's FMLN & Peru's Shining Path*. Washington, D.C.: United States Institute of Peace Press.

Peruvian Truth and Reconciliation Commission (2004). "Comisión de la Verdad y Reconciliación: Informe Final." Available from http://www.cverdad.org.pe.

U.S. State Department. "Country Reports on Human Rights Practices: Peru 1993–2002." Available from http://www.state.gov/g/drl/hr/c1470.htm.

Youngers, Coletta (2000). *Deconstructing Democracy: Peru under President Alberto Fujimori*. Washington, D.C.: Washington Office on Latin America.

Arturo Carrillo

Philosophy

Having survived the Holocaust, Nazi Germany's genocide against the Jews, the philosopher Jean Améry concluded that the Nazis "hated the word humanity" (Amery, 1980, p. 31). They wanted to destroy the idea that all men, women, and children possess shared and perhaps even divinely created origins, which imply basic equality and obligations to respect human life. Instead, Adolf Hitler called for racial purity that would be Aryan or German, and not merely human. According to this ideology, allegedly inferior forms of life—Jewish life first and foremost—threatened German superiority. Genocide eventually became the Final Solution for the Nazis' Jewish question.

Although philosophy often highlights characteristics shared by all persons, its history contains theories that have negatively emphasized differences—religious, cultural, national, and racial. Such theories have encouraged senses of hierarchy, superiority, and "us versus them" thinking in which genocidal policies may assert themselves, especially in times of economic and political stress. If philosophy itself is divided between views upholding that all people are equal members of humanity and others stressing differences between groups as fundamental, how can philosophy contribute to stopping or mitigating genocide?

Philosophy is critical inquiry about reality, knowledge, and ethics. It explores what is, what can be known, and what ought to be. Germany has produced some of the world's greatest philosophers, including Immanuel Kant, G. W. F. Hegel, Friedrich Nietzsche, and Martin Heidegger (1889–1976). Regrettably, neither in Germany nor elsewhere have philosophers done all that they could to protest genocide and crimes against humanity. On the contrary, as Heidegger's case reveals, philosophy can expedite genocide.

Hitler rose to power on January 30, 1933. Three months later Heidegger joined the Nazi Party. On May 27, 1933, he was inaugurated as rector of Freiburg University. Although Nazi book burnings and the dismissal of many non-Aryan academics had taken place a few weeks earlier, Heidegger's inaugural address advocated stepping-into-line with the times, which was at least an implicit embrace of Nazi anti-Semitism. He also stressed that the Führer's leadership was crucial for Germany's future. In February 1934 Heidegger resigned his rectorship, but he never became an obstacle to the Third Reich's genocidal policies.

Living for more than thirty years after Hitler's defeat in 1945, Heidegger neither explicitly repudiated National Socialism nor said much about the Holocaust. Debate continues about his philosophy as well as the man himself. In *Being and Time* (1927) and other major works, Heidegger analyzed human existence, its significance within Being itself, and the need for people to take responsibility within their particular times and places. Arguably, his philosophy includes a fundamental flaw: The abstract, even obscure, quality of its reflection on Being and "authentic" action precludes a clear ethic that speaks explicitly against racism, anti-Semitism, genocide, and crimes against humanity.

If support for genocide has philosophical roots at times, resistance to genocide is also deeply grounded in philosophy. For example, philosophy's history includes defenses of human rights, and genocide is morally condemned because it violates rights, especially the right to life. An important chapter in the development of the philosophical conception of genocide involves Raphael Lemkin (1900–1959), who coined the term *genocide* and spearheaded the drive that led to the United Nations (UN) Convention on the Prevention and Punishment of the Crime of Genocide (1948). That document sought to define "acts committed with intent to destroy, in whole or in part, a national, ethnical, racial, or religious group, as such."

Unfortunately, the UN's definition does not make it simple to identify genocide, particularly in its early stages when intervention could stop genocide before it is too late. Identifying genocide depends on determining intent, which can be a complex philosophical issue. If intent is not included in the meaning of words such as genocide or *genocidal*, it would be hard to understand how one might account for the very thing that genocide turns out to be: namely, the conscious targeting for destruction, in whole or in part, of some specific group of people. Nothing, however, makes the concept of genocide more ambiguous than the emphasis on intent that seems unavoidably to be built into it.

Although no perfect definition of genocide or intention is likely to be found, genocide's reality has alerted numerous post-Holocaust philosophers—Emmanuel Levinas and Hannah Arendt, to name only two of the most important—to claim that philosophy's integrity depends on its ability to help bring genocide to an end. Philosophy's best contributions to genocide prevention appear to be in criticisms against racism, anti-Semitism, religious dogmatism, and tyranny and in defenses of shared human rights.

SEE ALSO Genocide

BIBLIOGRAPHY
Amery, Jean (1980). *At the Mind's Limits: Contemplations by a Survivor on Auschwitz and its Realities.* Translated by Sidney Rosenfeld and Stella P. Rosenfeld. Bloomington: Indiana University Press.
Glover, Jonathan (2000). *Humanity: A Moral History of the Twentieth Century.* New Haven, Conn.: Yale University Press.
Lindqvist, Sven (1996). *Exterminate All the Brutes.* Trans. Joan Tate. New York: New Press.
Rittner, Carol, John K. Roth, and James M. Smith, eds. (2002). *Will Genocide Ever End?* St. Paul, Minn.: Paragon House.
Sluga, Hans (1993). *Heidegger's Crisis: Philosophy and Politics in Nazi Germany.* Cambridge, Mass.: Harvard University Press.

John K. Roth

Photography of Victims

Photography is a powerful tool for documenting the fate of victims of crimes against humanity. Contrary to verbal testimony, which may have inadvertently changed over time or been deliberately manipulated, and which is subject to personal interpretation, a photograph is a direct registration of reality or, to be more exact, a slice of reality.

Of course, a photograph is never totally objective, subjected as it is to the choices and interpretations its creator decided to make. But it connects with a past reality in a way that verbal or textual testimony never does. For all the written testimonies about Nazi cruelties in World War II, the photographs taken of the concentration camps after their liberation have a historical directness that is impossible to convey verbally.

It was only with the introduction of fast and portable 35-mm cameras in the 1930s that photojournalists could travel with light and practical equipment to document events throughout the world. Photos of victims of crimes against humanity hardly existed before this period.

Photographs of victims are taken with a few purposes in mind. Strictly, they are made to document the results of crimes against humanity. In this sense they are objective registrations and testimony. At a later stage they can be used as forensic evidence in future war tribunals or criminal investigations.

Second, but more important, they are taken to arouse indignation about situations perceived by the photographer as being unjust and inhumane. The primary objective is to shed light on hidden abuses and to influence and alter public opinion so policy changes will take place. Most photographers go to great lengths and endure physical risks to take such pictures, and undeniably an ethical drive is present in the photographer. This drive emerges from a basic engagement with the less fortunate and victimized people in the world and a strong sense of what is right and wrong.

By choosing to photograph victims, photographers face a moral dilemma: They sometimes feel as if they are preying on the most vulnerable. Elements of voyeurism and sensationalism can creep into their images. Critics often accuse photographers along this line of reasoning. These issues are very subjective, and it is usually the photographer's personal values and taste that decide how they are addressed.

Most photographers and journalists agree that is the photographer's task to portray victims with dignity. A main aim of photos is to arouse not only indignation, but also sympathy and identification. The public is unable to identify with victims who are portrayed as utterly hopeless human beings. The same holds true for photos of a graphic nature. A close-up image of tangled, bloody body parts or decayed corpses can shock viewers to such an extent that they will block the image from their minds. However, the photographer can choose a different point of view and capture an image of a man crying over or a young girl looking stunned at the same graphic scene; such a photo might be taken out of focus or in the distance to be less explicit and shocking. In this way the atrociousness of a crime is not explicitly depicted, but suggested in a manner that is often more powerful. Viewers tend to absorb these kinds of powerful images more easily.

An important obstacle many photographers face is the fact that it is very difficult to document perpetrators at work. From the two largest episodes of genocide in the last decade, those occurring in Rwanda and Bosnia, there exist hardly any images of the perpetrators of those crimes. Only photographer Ron Haviv managed to travel in 1992 with a Serbian death squad (Arkan's Tigers) and document their mission of killing Bosnian Muslims in the town of Bjelina. When these photographs were published internationally and subsequently caused a public fury, the warlord Arkan added

Haviv's name to a death list and the photographer was declared persona non grata by the Serbian government.

Sometimes, perpetrators photograph their own acts, for fun, or as grizzly souvenirs, to document their military campaigns. These images are not meant for external publication; mostly they are amateurish in quality. However, when they reach the general public, they are even more shocking.

There are, for instance, gruesome images of Nazis executing rows of prisoners. These were not taken by intrepid reporters, but by Nazi forces themselves. Also worth mentioning are the images captured of executions and cruelties committed by the Revolutionary United Front (RUF) rebel movement in Sierra Leone. The RUF had employed their own photographer to document their actions. A prisoner managed to obtain the original negatives and smuggle them out of the country. They are currently being used as evidence in the Sierra Leone War Tribunal. On a less dramatic scale are the photos taken by Belgian paratroopers in Somalia (1993) and British soldiers in Iraq (2003) maltreating civilians. They were meant as private snapshots, but somehow found their way into the public sphere.

Some images manage to reach iconic status. Of course, it is impossible to say in hindsight that a certain photo changed world history; however, it is undeniable that when contemplating the Vietnam War, the image of a crying girl, on fire, running down the road after a napalm strike by U.S. forces, often comes to mind. In recalling the war in the former Yugoslavia, one is likely to remember the image of starving camp inmates behind barbed wire. For a photographer, it is the greatest honor to not only have taken images that influenced the way world events unfolded, but to also see these same images reprinted over and over again in history books. It is hoped that future generations will learn something from them.

SEE ALSO Films, Holocaust Documentary

BIBLIOGRAPHY

Sontag, Susan (2003). *Regarding the Pain of Others.* New York: Farrar, Strauss and Giroux.

Voeten, Teun (1999). "Neo-Vulturism in Contemporary Documentary Photography." In *A Ticket To. . . .* Leiden, Netherlands: Veenman.

Voeten, Teun (2002). *How de Body? One Man's Terrifying Journey through an African Country.* New York: St. Martins Press.

Teun Voeten

Physicians

Usually, physicians are regarded as the guardians of health and lives, but what happens when healing con-

Erika Flocken, medical doctor, at a labor camp in Germany in 1940. Flocken's job was to decide which inmates were fit to work and which were not, with the latter being exterminated. Flocken has put on a facsimile of the armband of the International Red Cross. [CORBIS]

flicts with larger state aims? How do physicians reconcile their Hippocratic oath with a mandate of genocide? Like many other professional groups, doctors are simultaneously members of the social elite and public servants. As such, ruling authorities sometimes use them as agents to provide a legitimizing framework for actions taken by the state. At the same time, doctors are human beings, and as members of a particular society, they are equally susceptible to that society's prevailing social mores and climate. When a state adopts an exclusionary policy of hyper-nationalism, all of its citizens, doctors included, can find themselves on both sides of the divide. Whether as willing participants or as reluctant accomplices, physicians have become involved in the planning and implementation of mass murder in numerous countries.

In 1915 Ottoman Turk physicians conducted medical experiments, participated in mass deportations, and promoted a genocidal ideology that led to the widespread death of the Armenian population. Less than two decades later physicians in Nazi Germany perpetrated similar atrocities in a system that culminated in the Holocaust. Carnage also occurred when Hutu doctors turned against Tutsi patients during the Rwandan genocide. Similarly, an international tribunal charged Serbian doctors with war crimes for their role in ethnic cleansing in Bosnia and Kosovo. Even in situations not necessarily intended as full-scale genocides, doctors have lent their medical expertise in an effort to remove or restrict "undesirable" elements of the population. Medical personnel in Argentina, Bolivia, Chile, Iraq, and elsewhere participated in the torture and death of dissidents and enemies of the state. Additionally, in Britain, the United States, Norway, and Sweden physicians helped to carry out involuntary sterilizations as part of their country's eugenic policies.

Four theories offer differing perspectives to explain how physicians could come to endorse programs so seemingly at odds with their role as healers. The first theory argues that doctors do not abandon medical ethics to follow eugenic or genocidal policies; rather, they reinterpret those ethics to coincide with the dominant and prevailing agenda. Generally, this involves placing the health of the collective ahead of that of the individual. Doctors then become charged with cutting out so-called cancerous elements of the population the same way they would remove cancerous tumors from a sick individual. Physicians are often aided in their actions by state-sponsored propaganda campaigns. The Nazis were particularly effective in promoting this approach through films for public consumption, such as *Victims of the Past* (1937) and *Existence without Life* (1940–1941). These films were designed to convince the population that the elimination of mentally and physically disabled people was not only in their collective best interest, but actually merciful, and furthermore, as in the case of the film *I Accuse* (1941), often the desire of the patients themselves.

The second theory promotes the idea of participation via the "slippery slope," whereby transgressions of the medical, ethical, and societal moral codes begin on a small scale, gradually build on themselves, and eventually spiral out of control. For example, doctors do not start out by killing individuals for the purpose of medical experimentation. Rather, by first defining certain people as inferior and then subhuman, it eventually becomes acceptable to use them as scientific specimens without regard for their rights as human beings.

A third theory argues that physicians participate because they cannot find a way to excuse themselves from such activities without suffering grievous personal, professional, or bodily harm. Their actions are motivated by a fear of losing their license, profession, social standing, or even life. For example, according to one source, Iraqi doctors under Saddam Hussein's regime

encyclopedia of GENOCIDE *and* CRIMES AGAINST HUMANITY

were ordered to cut the ears off torture victims or suffer the same fate themselves. In another case, doctors during the Third Reich often faced internment in a concentration camp if they failed to comply with state rules. This theory raises questions about individual agency and choice. Why, when faced with identical situations, do some physicians find a way to circumvent such rules, while others, seemingly, cannot?

Whereas the first three theories are predicated on the idea that (some) physicians accept, or at least do not actively resist, involvement in such programs, a final theory argues that other doctors aggressively seek to participate in genocidal or eugenic programs. Their motivations range from an opportunistic desire for personal or professional gain to an entrenched belief in the advocated exterminationist ideology. Such was the case with National Socialist physician Leonardo Conti. His early membership in the Nazi Party (he joined the SA in 1923) qualified him as a member of the Old Guard. Conti rose through the system to eventually become the senior ranking medical officer in the Third Reich. Additional Nazi physicians who found scientific opportunity in the suffering of others included: Karl Brandt, who, along with Phillip Bouhler, headed the euthanasia program known as T-4; Gerhard Kujath, whose film *A 4½-Year-Old Patient with Microcephaly* (1936–1937) was a product of the regime's euthanasia program for children; Josef Mengele, best known for his infamous twin experiments; Sigmund Rascher, who conducted hypothermia and cold-water testing in Dachau; Heinrich Berning, who starved numerous Soviet prisoners of war in the name of famine experimentation; Carl Clausberg, known for his sterilization and castration experiments; and Kurt Gutzeit, who injected Jewish children at Auschwitz with hepatitis.

SEE ALSO Eugenics

BIBLIOGRAPHY

Dadrian, Vahakan (1986). "The Role of Turkish Physicians in the World War One Genocide of Ottoman Armenians." *Holocaust and Genocide Studies* 2:169–192.

Kater, Michael H. (1989). *Doctors under Hitler*. Chapel Hill: University of North Carolina Press.

Proctor, Robert (1988). *Racial Hygiene: Medicine under the Nazis*. Cambridge, Mass.: Harvard University Press.

Schmidt, Ulf (2002). *Medical Films, Ethics and Euthanasia in Nazi Germany: The History of Medical Research and Teaching Films of the Reich Office for Educational Films/ Reich Institute for Films in Science and Education, 1933–1945*. Husum, Germany: Matthiesen Verlag.

Sirkin, Susannah (2003). "Accountability for Crimes against Humanity in Iraq." Published in "Human Rights Violations under Saddam Hussein: Victims Speak Out,"

Proceedings of Hearing Before the House Committee on International Relations' Subcommittee on the Middle East and Central Asia. Available from http://www.phrusa.org/research/iraq/testimony_112003.html.

Lynne Fallwell

Pinochet, Augusto
[NOVEMBER 25, 1915–]
Chilean dictator from 1973 to 1990

Recognized as one of the most ruthless and violent strongmen in the history of Latin America, General Augusto Pinochet's name became synonymous with human rights atrocities during the last quarter of the twentieth century. During his seventeen-year military regime in Chile, his security forces were responsible for the murders of 3,197 Chilean citizens. Of those, 1,100 were "disappeared"—abused to death and buried in still-secret graves, or thrown from military helicopters into the Pacific Ocean. An estimated 30,000 Chileans survived imprisonment and severe torture by agents of Pinochet's secret police—electric shock, beatings, near-drowning, and rape in secret detention facilities. In the mid-1970s, the Pinochet regime also organized a network of secret police agencies (given the code name Operation Condor) that coordinated the repression of groups and individuals who had been identified as opponents of the military governments of the Southern Cone (Argentina, Brazil, Chile, Paraguay, and Uruguay). Condor's methods included secret surveillance, kidnapping, interrogation, torture, and terrorist attacks. International efforts to hold General Pinochet legally accountable for human rights atrocities in Chile and acts of terrorism abroad led to his arrest for crimes against humanity in London in 1998.

Officials of Scotland Yard detained Pinochet on October 16, 1998, while he was recovering from back surgery at a private London hospital. He was served with an arrest warrant filed through Interpol by Spanish judges seeking to extradite him to Madrid to stand trial for "crimes of genocide and terrorism." For more than five hundred days, Pinochet was kept under house arrest in England; legal proceedings against him became a cause célèbre around the world. His detention became a leading symbol of the globalization of justice, and elevated and transformed the principle of universal jurisdiction—the ability of the international community to pursue the prosecution of dictators, torturers, and mass murderers beyond the borders of their home nations—into a precedent for future legal efforts against perpetrators of human rights crimes.

General Augusto Pinochet took power on September 11, 1973, during a U.S.–supported bloody military

General Augusto Pinochet. On May 28, 2004, the Chilean Court of Appeals voted to annul a judgment (by a lower court) that Pinochet suffered from dementia—stripping Pinochet of his immunity from prosecution. The judges found that a television interview was proof the former Chilean president was both lucid and mentally competent to stand trial.[AP/WIDE WORLD PHOTOS]

coup that overthrew the democratically elected Popular Unity government of Salvador Allende. In a country that had a long tradition of civility and constitutional rule, the military takeover was brutal and violent. In the six weeks that followed the coup approximately 1,500 civilians were killed, including some 320 to 360 who were summarily executed, according to U.S. intelligence reports. More than 13,500 Chilean citizens and several thousand foreigners were detained through mass arrests and sent to detention camps. Many of those were brought to Chile's National Stadium, which was transformed from a sports arena into a center for interrogation, torture, and execution. Two U.S. citizens, Charles Horman and Frank Teruggi, were among the hundreds who were killed there.

Born on November 25, 1915, Pinochet entered the military academy in Santiago at age seventeen and rose steadily through the ranks of the Chilean army over the forty years that followed. In late August 1973, he succeeded General Carlos Prats as Commander-in-Chief of the Army. In the months leading up to the coup Prats opposed the overthrow of the elected government; his forced resignation and his replacement by Pinochet enabled coup-plotting to accelerate.

As head of the powerful Chilean army, Pinochet outmaneuvered other commanders of the Chilean Armed Forces who had expected to govern Chile after the coup by way of a rotating leadership within the military junta. In June 1974 Pinochet pressured the other members of the junta to name him "Supreme Chief of the Nation." On December 18, 1974, he decreed himself "President of the Republic"—a title he kept until early 1990, when he was forced to yield power to a new civilian government.

During his seventeen-year rule Chile became a pariah state, internationally condemned for ongoing, systematic violations of human rights. Pinochet played a leadership role in initiating and overseeing many of these atrocities. One month after the coup, he authorized a death squad, led by his close associate General Sergio Arellano, to "expedite justice" in relation to civic leaders of the former Allende government—police chiefs, mayors, local union officials—who had been arrested in the northern provinces after the coup. Using a Puma helicopter, a five-member military team led by General Arellano flew to various northern cities and, at each stop, selected prisoners and shot or bayoneted them in the middle of the night. Over a period of four days, sixty-eight civilians were killed, having committed no crime other than serving in local community leadership roles under the elected Allende government. This series of atrocities became known as "the Caravan of Death."

Members of the caravan team were subsequently integrated into a new secret police force known as the Directorate of National Intelligence (DINA). Pinochet handpicked Colonel Manuel Contreras, a close friend of his in the Chilean military with no background in intelligence, to be director of DINA. United States intelligence reports described Contreras as a "strong character, with intense loyalty to President Pinochet. . . . [H]e will advance only with the personal support of President Pinochet" (Kornbluh, 2003, pp. 160–161). Between 1974 and 1977 DINA expanded into a massive, institutionalized force of repression in Chile, terrorizing Chilean society at every level. DINA agents conducted clandestine raids and arrests; it forced prisoners through a network of clandestine interrogation centers to extract information from them. Many DINA prisoners were tortured to death and then "disappeared." The U.S. military reported from Santiago that DINA was "becoming a modern day Gestapo" (Kornbluh, 2003, p. 160). One informant announced to U.S. officials, "There are three sources of power in Chile: Pinochet, God, and DINA" (Kornbluh, 2003, p. 153).

DINA served as the central pillar of Pinochet's power. It actively eliminated all leftist opposition to his regime in Chile, and Contreras assigned agents to spy on other military commanders and intimidate anyone who challenged Pinochet's authority. Through executive decrees Pinochet bestowed on DINA the authority to establish a virtual monopoly over repression in Chile. Officially, DINA fell under the jurisdiction of the military junta. In reality, Contreras reported only to—and only took orders from—General Pinochet. Contreras met with Pinochet every morning, at 7:30 AM, to brief him on DINA operations. United States intelligence agents reported: "The President issues instructions on DINA; is aware of its activities; and, in fact, heads it" (Kornbluh, 2003, p. 166).

Pinochet's secret police not only carried out vicious acts of repression at home, but also sought to dispose of opponents of his regime abroad. In September 1974 DINA agents, using a car bomb, assassinated General Prats (Pinochet's predecessor as Commander-in-Chief of the army) who was living in exile in Buenos Aires, Argentina. The bomb also killed Prats's wife. A year later, DINA agents orchestrated the shooting of a leader of the Chilean Christian Democratic Party and his wife in Rome, Italy. In November 1975 Colonel Contreras decided to coordinate efforts with the military regimes of other Southern Cone countries to track down and eliminate dissidents in exile; he invited intelligence officials from Argentina, Paraguay, Uruguay, and Bolivia to come to Santiago and establish what he called an "Interpol against subversion in Latin America." This network of military intelligence services (the aforementioned Operation Condor) carried out violent, clandestine acts of terror in the region and throughout the world for more than five years.

Operation Condor quickly became the most sinister state-sponsored terrorist network in the Western Hemisphere, if not the world. In coordination with neighboring military governments, the Pinochet regime implemented surveillance, kidnappings, brutal interrogations, and the secret detention of political opponents in the Southern Cone, Europe, and even the United States. United States intelligence agencies eventually learned that "a third and reportedly very secret phase of 'Operation Condor' involves the formation of special teams from member countries who are to carry out operations to include assassinations" (Kornbluh, 2003, p. 324). In September 1976, with the assistance of Paraguay, agents of DINA traveled to the United States to undertake what has become the best known Condor plot: the car-bombing assassination of Pinochet's leading critic-in-exile, former Chilean Ambassador Orlando Letelier. That September 21, 1976, car bombing in downtown Washington, D.C., also took the life of Letelier's colleague, 25-year-old Ronni Karpen Moffitt, and

was considered at the time to be the most egregious act of international terrorism to ever have taken place in the U.S. capital. Within a week of the assassination, the FBI reported that it had probably been the work of Operation Condor.

In the spring of 1978, when the U.S. Justice Department presented the Chilean military government with clear evidence of DINA's role in the car bombing, General Pinochet personally took the lead in covering up the crime and obstructing U.S. efforts to bring those guilty to justice. The CIA learned that Pinochet was pursuing a multifaceted plan to derail the investigation, which included protecting DINA director Manuel Contreras from prosecution; stalling on U.S. requests for evidence; tampering with witnesses—Pinochet ordered one member of the assassination team who wanted to turn himself over to the FBI to "stay at his post"; and intervening with the Chilean Supreme Court to assure that neither Contreras nor his subordinates would be extradited to Washington. Pinochet, the CIA reported, "has manipulated the Supreme Court judges and now is satisfied that the court will reject extradition of any Chileans indicted" (Kornbluh, 2003, p. 401).

Up to the point of the Letelier-Moffitt assassination, General Pinochet had enjoyed positive relations with the United States. In a private meeting in June 1976, Secretary of State Henry Kissinger said to Pinochet: "[I]n the United States, as you know, we are sympathetic with what you are trying to do here. . . . We want to help, not undermine, you" (Kornbluh, 2003, p. 201). After the assassination, however, President Jimmy Carter held Pinochet at arms length and openly pressed the regime to improve its human rights record. Initially, the Reagan administration supported General Pinochet as a forceful anticommunist ally and a kindred spirit in the furtherance of free-market economic policies. But by the mid-1980s, when the Chilean economy suffered a severe recession and the left wing of that nation began to reemerge as a significant political force despite continuing repression, the United States moved to support what the State Department called a "real and orderly transition to democracy."

In an effort to extend his dictatorship through to the end of the twentieth century, Pinochet called a plebiscite for October 1988. If a majority of Chileans voted "No" (to Pinochet), new elections would be held in 1989 and the military would turn over power to a civilian president. Although Pinochet expected to win, he developed a contingency plan that would go into effect if it appeared that he was losing. "Close supporters of President Pinochet are said to have contingency plans to derail the plebiscite by encouraging and staging acts of violence," one top-secret U.S. intelligence re-

[THE CORRUPT DICTATOR]

For much of his career General Pinochet maintained the image of the incorruptible, if ruthlessly violent, Prussian-style officer. But in July 2004, a financial scandal shattered his carefully honed image as an austere, modest, professional soldier—a reputation that had distinguished Pinochet's career from other Latin American strongmen who were known as much for their greed as their repression.

A U.S. Senate Committee, investigating money laundering and foreign corruption at the Washington D.C.-based Riggs National Bank, uncovered detailed documentation on secret bank accounts Pinochet maintained outside of Chile after he was forced from power in 1990. The Senate investigation revealed that Riggs had opened multiple accounts for Pinochet and "deliberately assisted him in the concealment and movement of his funds while he was under investigation [in London] and the subject of a worldwide court order freezing his assets."

Pinochet's Chilean tax returns record an official income of $90,000 a year. But between 1994 and 2002, he deposited up to $8 million into three personal and three shell corporation accounts created by Riggs officials to hide his wealth. During his long detention under house arrest in London, he drew on these funds even as Spanish authorities seeking his extradition obtained a court order that his assets be frozen. After his return to Chile, Riggs officials arranged for $1.9 million in cashiers checks to be secretly couriered from the United States. At the same time as the Chilean courts declared him mentally incompetent to stand trial on human rights crimes, Pinochet was repeatedly conferring with Riggs officials on the surrepticious transfer of his monies, and personally cashing some thirty-eight checks—each one for the sum of $50,000—at different banks in Santiago.

Revelations of Pinochet's unexplained and hidden wealth, known in Chile as the "Pinocheques" scandal, cost Pinochet his legacy even among those who had benefited from his regime. His supporters in the military, the rightwing media, and Chilean economic elite, all who had backed the general against accusations of murder, disappearances, torture and terrorism, now abandoned him. The Chilean government initiated no less than three official criminal investigations—to identify the source of Pinochet's illicit funds, as well as to determine whether he was guilty of tax evasion.

port stated (Kornbluh, 2003, p. 424). Pinochet would then institute a state of emergency and declare the election "invalid." When his own commanders failed to implement that plan on the day of the plebiscite, Pinochet attempted to get the rest of the junta to authorize the use of the armed forces to seize the capital and nullify the election. The junta refused. The campaign of "No" won.

General Pinochet turned over the presidency to a civilian leader, Patricio Aylwin, on March 11, 1990. Yet, he retained his powerful position as commander of the Chilean armed forces, a post from which he commanded the new civilian government not to pursue any prosecution of the human rights crimes that had been committed under his regime. "The day they touch one of my men the state of law ends," he warned (Constable and Valenzuela, 1991, p. 317). When Pinochet finally stepped down from the military command, in March 1998, he assumed the title of *Senador Vitalica* (Senator for Life), providing himself with additional legal immunity from prosecution inside Chile.

Early judicial cases filed against Pinochet by the families of his victims failed to overcome the legal obstacles his regime had imposed on the Chilean court system. Internationally, however, other avenues were being explored. In 1996, in Madrid, Joan Garcés, a Spanish lawyer and former aide to Salvador Allende, filed a criminal case with a special branch of the Spanish judiciary called the *Audiencia Nacional*, which accepted the principle of universal jurisdiction for offenses such as genocide, terrorism, and other crimes against humanity. For two years, however, Spanish authorities had no way of physically securing the target of their investigation. After Pinochet traveled to London on September 21, 1998, however, Garcés arranged for Judge Baltazar Garzón to send a detention request to Scotland Yard, under the European Anti-Terrorism Convention. A British magistrate signed an arrest warrant for Pinochet on October 16; late that evening, Scotland Yard detectives secured his room at the private London clinic where he was recuperating from back surgery, disarmed his bodyguards, and served him with a "priority red warrant" for crimes against humanity.

The saga of Pinochet's arrest in London lasted sixteen months and caught the attention of the world community. His case was unprecedented: a former head of state detained outside his homeland for extradition to a third country. Already a recognized symbol of human rights atrocities, Pinochet became the leading symbol of the globalization of justice for perpetrators of such crimes. His arrest fostered hopes for many of his victims and their families that they might finally face him in a court of law. And the international effort to bring him to justice paved a legal path for similar prosecutions against other former dictators and military commanders accused of human rights crimes.

Pinochet lost all legal battles in Britain to prevent his extradition to Madrid. But behind-the-scenes political lobbying by the Chilean government, which found itself under intense pressure from the military to obtain Pinochet's release, and the resistance of José Aznar, the conservative Spanish prime minister who opposed Judge Garzón's effort to prosecute Pinochet in Madrid, appeared to convince British authorities to let Pinochet go. On March 2, 2000, British Home Secretary Jack Straw ruled that Pinochet had suffered a stroke that had resulted in mild dementia and therefore would be released on humanitarian grounds.

Pinochet returned to Chile the next day, believing himself to be finally free of legal threats. Within three days of his return, however, Chilean Judge Juan Guzman filed a legal request to have Pinochet's immunity lifted so that he could be prosecuted for disappearances associated with the Caravan of Death atrocities. On May 23, 2000, Chile's Court of Appeals surprised Chileans and the international community by voting to strip Pinochet of his immunity; the Chilean Supreme Court upheld that decision on June 5. In December, Judge Guzman indicted Pinochet as the "intellectual author" of the Caravan of Death; and in early 2001, for the first time, Pinochet was actually interrogated about his knowledge of and role in those crimes.

But, just as the British had released Pinochet on health grounds, eventually the Chilean courts yielded to the arguments of Pinochet's lawyers that he was "mentally unfit due to dementia" and therefore unable to stand trial for the murders and disappearances in the Caravan case. Pinochet then issued a statement that he was retiring from political life. "I have a clean conscience," he said. "The work of my government will be judged by history" (Kornbluh, 2003, p. 482).

At age eighty-eight, Pinochet did not retire quietly. In November 2003 he gave an interview to the Spanish language television network *Telemundo*, in which he described himself "as a good angel" who should be thanked for his contributions to Chile. Citing Pinochet's lucidity during the interview, Judge Guzman again petitioned the courts to strip Pinochet of his immunity—this time to prosecute him for murders relating to Operation Condor. On May 28, 2004, a Chilean

court ruled that Pinochet could indeed stand trial for these crimes against humanity. While it remained likely that Pinochet would still escape justice through a decision of the Chilean Supreme Court to block his prosecution, the Condor case assured that he would not evade the verdict of history.

SEE ALSO Amnesty; Chile; Crimes Against Humanity; Disappearances; Immunity; Universal Jurisdiction

BIBLIOGRAPHY

Burbach, Roger (2004). *The Pinochet Affair*. London: ZED Books.

Constable, Pamela, and Arturo Valenzuela (1991). *A Nation of Enemies: Chile under Pinochet*. New York: W. W. Norton.

Dinges, John (2004). *The Condor Years*. New York: The New Press.

Ensalaco, Mark (2000). *Chile under Pinochet: Recovering the Truth*. Philadelphia: University of Pennsylvania Press.

Kornbluh, Peter (2003). *The Pinochet File: A Declassified Dossier on Atrocity and Accountability*. New York: The New Press

O'Shaughnessy, Hugh (2000). *Pinochet: The Politics of Torture*. New York: New York University Press.

Peter Kornbluh

Pius XII, Pope
[b. EUGENIO PACELLI, MARCH 2, 1876–OCTOBER 11, 1958]
Italian Pontiff of the Roman Catholic Church, 1939 to 1958

The controversy over Pope Pius XII's alleged silence on the Holocaust is one of the most heated in modern history. Although he was praised by Jewish leaders after World War II and following his death in 1958, Rolf Hochhuth in his play *The Deputy* (1963) accused the pontiff of indifference to the plight of Jews. Hochhuth contended that had Pius XII spoken out in protest against the Holocaust, countless Jews would have been saved. The activities of Vatican-supported individuals and institutions in the postwar rescue of former Nazi officials only added to the criticism. The controversy that ensued pitted papal detractors against papal supporters and has continued unabated into the twenty-first century.

Pius XII's detractors claim that as papal secretary of state (1930–1939) before he became pope, Pacelli's negotiation of a concordat or treaty with Hitler's Germany in 1933 gave prestige to the Nazi regime and destroyed whatever power the Catholic Center Party of Germany still held. In response, the pope's supporters

Named pontiff of the Roman Catholic Church on the eve of World War II, Pius XII remains a controversial historical figure. Many question the Vatican's silence while Europe's Jews perished.
[HULTON-DEUTSCH COLLECTION/CORBIS]

nication of Hitler (a born Catholic) would have had a significant impact on Catholics in German-occupied Europe. Supporters insist that the excommunication of Hitler would have had no effect on the leader's manic obsession with exterminating Jews, and they question how word of any excommunication might have been able to travel beyond Nazi censors.

Pius XII's reputation has suffered even more blame for his weak response to the Nazi roundup of Rome's Jews in October 1943 when the city was under German occupation. Detractors insist that he should have gone to the Jews' place of imprisonment and demanded their release. Supporters point out that he instructed his secretary of state to threaten a public protest if the roundup continued, even though he feared such a protest would give the Germans a reason to invade neutral Vatican buildings in their search for Jewish refugees.

Detractors and supporters of the pope each cite specific rationales for Pius XII's behavior during the course of World War II. Detractors claim that the pope was an anti-Semite; that he feared a protest would provoke the Germans to destroy Rome; that he favored the Germans over the Allies because of his long residence there as papal nuncio in the 1920s; that he did not want to force German Catholics into a crisis of conscience by making them choose between their church and their state; and that he was so fearful of Soviet Communism that he favored German Nazism as a bulwark against Russian expansion.

Against these specific charges, papal supporters argue that Pius XII did, in fact, try to help Jews by instructing the clergy on how to make their religious houses places of refuge (and that even if no specific document detailing such a policy can be found, the action could hardly have occurred without papal approval), and that no evidence of anti-Semitism on the part of the pope exists. As for the pontiff's alleged fears about the destruction of Rome, the possibility of this event only developed after the German occupation in 1943, which took place more than a year after news of the death camps reached the pope, and thus it cannot have been a motivating factor for his public silence.

Supporters counter the claim that Pope Pius XII favored Germany by pointing to numerous Nazi officials' comments to the contrary, both before and during the war. They call attention to the fact that the pontiff actually agreed to be a conduit between Germans opposed to Hitler and the British government to arrange a compromise peace early in the war. As for the charge that the pope did not want to create a crisis of conscience for German Catholics, papal supporters insist that German Catholics would simply have ignored a papal statement which, in any event, Nazi propagandists

observe that Pacelli negotiated the concordat to protect German Catholics against the dictatorial regime, and that the Center Party was already doomed to extinction.

After Pacelli became Pope Pius XII on the eve of the outbreak of war in 1939, and up to the end of the war in 1945, papal detractors argue that he never spoke out in public against the Nazi regime, and even though he knew by mid-1942 that the Germans were operating death camps and killing Jews on a massive scale, he did not publicly protest the Holocaust. Supporters of the pontiff point out that early in the war he condemned atrocities against noncombatants as "actions that call for vengeance in the sight of God." They also direct critics' attention to his address of June 1943 in which he stated, "every one of our public utterances has had to be weighted and pondered . . . in the very interest of those who are suffering, so as not to render their position even more difficult and unbearable than before." Detractors claim that these words were not specific or harsh enough, and that the church's formal excommu-

encyclopedia of GENOCIDE *and* CRIMES AGAINST HUMANITY

might have transformed into a message of support for the regime.

Against the claim that the pope preferred German Nazism to Soviet communism, his supporters respond that although Pius XII undoubtedly feared the communization of Europe, he viewed the wartime Western alliance with Soviet Russia as necessary to defeat Nazism. Thus, he steadfastly refused German requests to characterize its invasion of the Soviet Union in 1941 as a Christian crusade, and he furthermore counseled American Catholics to support the wartime alliance with Soviet Russia.

The pontiff's supporters offer two reasons for Pius XII's behavior. They proffer that he wanted to serve as a mediator between the warring sides and therefore could not condemn either. Thus, his criticism of the Nazi regime was implicit in order to preserve his neutrality. Papal critics counter that the mediation of the war was unrealistic, given the Allied statement of unconditional surrender and Hitler's unwillingness to compromise.

Supporters point to Pope Pius XII's own recorded statement that a public protest would have made the conflict worse as proof of his main rationale. Detractors, citing the enormity of the Holocaust, ask how the situation could have been worse. Supporters insist that no one outside of its Nazi planners, not even Jews themselves, ever imagined the immensity of the Holocaust, and that Pius XII, thrust into the most difficult position of any pope in modern history, felt a primary obligation to preserve the safety of Catholics in German-occupied Europe.

SEE ALSO Catholic Church; Religion

BIBLIOGRAPHY

Chadwick, Owen (1986). *Britain and the Vatican during the Second World War*. Cambridge: Cambridge University Press.

Conway, John (1994). "The Vatican, Germany and the Holocaust." In *Papal Diplomacy in the Modern Age*, ed. Peter Kent and John Pollard. Westport, Conn.: Praeger.

Cornwell, John (1999). *Hitler's Pope: The Secret History of Pius XII*. New York: Viking.

Phayer, Michael (2000). *The Catholic Church and the Holocaust, 1930–1965*. Bloomington: Indiana University Press.

Rychlak, Ronald (2000). *Hitler, the War, and the Pope*. Columbus, Miss.: Genesis Press.

Sánchez, José M. (2002). *Pius XII and the Holocaust: Understanding the Controversy*. Washington, D.C.: Catholic University of America Press.

José M. Sánchez

Poetry

The Armenian genocide and the Holocaust produced some important and critically acclaimed poets. These poets bore witness to genocide and wrote about exile, grief, and moral outrage.

Poetry of the Armenian Genocide

Siamanto (Adom Yarjanian) was born in 1878 in Akn, Ottoman Empire (present-day Kemaliye, Turkey). He wrote a cycle of poems in *Bloody News from My Friend* (1909) that depict the atrocities of the 1909 massacre of the Armenians when converging Turkish political coalitions and local Turkish citizens killed about thirty thousand Armenians living in Adana province; this was a prologue to the Armenian Genocide of 1915. "The Dance," "Grief," "The Mulberry Tree," and "The Dagger" are graphic, realistic depictions of massacre, torture, and rape. Scholars consider Siamanto a groundbreaking poet because he preceded the British trench poets of World War I and refused to be ornamental, generic, or metaphysical in his writings. During the Armenian genocide, he was one of the 250 intellectuals and cultural leaders arrested in Constantinople on April 24, 1915, and later executed by the Ottoman government.

Along with Siamanto, Daniel Varoujan (1884–1915), was a leading voice of the new generation of western Armenian writers (Armenians of the Ottoman Empire). His early poems embody the recovery of Armenian myths, legends, and folklore that characterized the cultural revival of Armenians in the Ottoman Empire at the turn of the twentieth century. He was arrested by the Ottoman government on April 24, 1915, and later tortured and murdered on August 19. While he was in prison he wrote poems about Armenian agrarian life and a longing for the land. His poem "The Red Soil" depicts the culture of massacre Armenians were subjected to from the time of Sultan Abdul Hamid's massacres of the Armenians in the 1890s through the eve of the Armenian genocide.

Eghishe Charents (1897–1937) was born in Kars, then Russian Armenia (in present-day Turkey). His epiclike poem "Dantesque Legend" deals with his experience of the Armenian genocide during his participation in a resistance movement that took him into northeastern Turkey in order to rescue Armenians. Many other Charents poems deal with the trauma of the genocide.

Vahan Tekeyan (1878–1948), born in Constantinople, was in Cairo, Egypt, when the genocide commenced, and so escaped execution. His selected poems, *Sacred Wrath* (1983), include a number of finely controlled and often elliptically transformed poems of loss, exile, and grief: "On a Sonata by Beethoven" is a meditation on music and exile. "We Shall Say to God," "We Shall Forget," "There Are Boys," "To God," and "Scutari" are highly acclaimed poems about trauma and the meaning of suffering in the wake of genocide.

Poetry of the Holocaust
In the aftermath of the Holocaust, Jewish poets produced a range of important poems that bore direct witness to atrocity, to the aftermath of trauma, and to the metaphysical meaning of suffering. Nelly Sachs (1891–1970) was born into a wealthy family in Berlin. When the Nazis came to power, she barely escaped arrest, and fled to Sweden, where she lived for the rest of her life, writing and translating Swedish poetry. Her career as a poet flowered when she was in her fifties. *In the House of Death* (1947) deals with the suffering of the Jews and the overarching suffering of humanity. *Eclipse of Stars* (1949), *And No One Knows Where to Go* (1957), and *Metamorphosis* (1959) explore suffering, persecution, and exile. She was awarded the Nobel Prize in literature in 1966.

Miklos Radnoti (1909–1944), a Hungarian Jew, was an avant-garde poet and editor before being deported and sent to labor camps in Yugoslavia. On a forced march back to Hungary with some three thousand men, he was shot. When his body was exhumed from a mass grave in 1946, his widow found a notebook full of poems in his pockets that included some of the most powerful poems written about the Holocaust: "Forced March," "Letter to My Wife," "Peace, Horror," "Picture Postcards," and "Seventh Ecologue."

Primo Levi (1919–1987) was born in Turin, Italy, and fought with the partisans in Italy until he was captured in 1944 and sent to the Bunz-Monowitz concentration camp. His professional training as a chemist helped him survive until the Russians liberated his camp in 1945. Although he is most well known for his works *Survival in Auschwitz* (1947) and *The Drowned and the Saved* (1986), Levi was also a poet. His poems bear an austerity and plain style that addresses the concentration camp experience with a unique rhetorical power that does not betray poetic texture. Levi's *Collected Poems* (1984) include "Shema," "For Adolf Eichmann in Jerusalem," "Buna," and "Annunciation," among others. Levi, never able to overcome the psychological burden of his experiences, committed suicide in 1987.

Paul Celan (1920–1970) was born Paul Antschel in Bukovina, a German enclave of Romania, which was occupied by Romanian Fascists and Nazis in the early 1940s. His parents died in a concentration camp, but

Celan—who was sent into forced labor—escaped to Paris in 1944 where he settled and continued to write poetry in German. His poems are written with an inventive dissonance that bears his tortured relationship to the perpetrator's language, thus defining him as a major and experimental poet. "Death Fugue," a poem that deals with concentration camp life, may be the most famous poem of the Holocaust. He committed suicide by drowning himself in the Seine in 1970. Selections from his nine books of poems appear in *Poems of Paul Celan* (1970). Other important poets of the Holocaust include Tadeusz Borowski (1922–1951), Dan Pagis (1930–1986), Abraham Sutzkever (1913–), and Gertrud Kolmar (1894–1943).

SEE ALSO Fiction

BIBLIOGRAPHY
Der Hovanessian, Diana, and Marzbed Margossian, eds. and trans. (1978). *Anthology of Armenian Poetry*. New York: Columbia University Press.
Der Hovanessian, Diana, and Marzbed Margossian, eds. and trans. (1986). *Land of Fire: Selected Poems of Eghishe Charents*. Ann Arbor, Mich.: Ardis.
Forché, Carolyn, ed. (1993). *Against Forgetting: Twentieth-Century Poetry of Witness*. New York: W.W. Norton.
Peter Balakian

Pogroms see Cossacks; Ghetto; Persecution; Pogroms, Pre-Soviet Russia; Union of Soviet Socialist Republics.

Pogroms, Pre-Soviet Russia

Communal riots between rival religious and ethnic groups were not unknown in the modern Russian Empire. However, only in 1881 did they resemble a mass movement, with the widespread outbreak of anti-Jewish riots throughout the southwestern provinces of the empire. The name applied to the riots—*pogroms*—came into widespread usage in Russia and abroad, and evolved into a generic term for any attack on an ethnic or religious minority.

The pogroms of 1881 and 1882 are widely regarded as the major turning point in modern Jewish history. Among Jews the pogroms prompted disillusionment with a solution to the Jewish question based on civic emancipation and social integration. They inspired new forms of Jewish politics of a nationalist form, such as Zionism and socialist organizations aimed at Jewish proletarians. The Russian state, in turn, moved away from policies designed to promote Jewish acculturation and integration.

These same pogroms also gave rise to a host of assumptions that became firmly established in the histor-

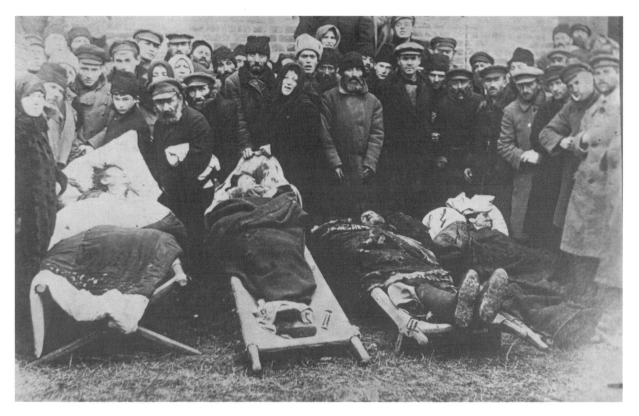

Survivors of a pogrom at Proskurov, in the Podovia region of Ukraine. On February 15, 1919, Ataman Semosenko commanded a brigade of Cossacks and regiment of Gaidamaks (local band of lawless plunderers) to murder the town's Jews. Barely three hours later approximately 1,500 people lay dead. [BETTMANN/CORBIS]

ical literature: (1) that the pogroms were instigated, tolerated, or welcomed by Russian officials, on either the national, provincial, or local level; (2) that the pogroms were invariably accompanied by atrocities, including rape and murder; (3) that Jews were always passive, unresisting victims, at least until Jewish socialists organized armed self-defense in the early twentieth century; (4) that, especially in the twentieth century, pogroms were an officially inspired effort to divert popular discontent against the Jews, "to drown the Russian revolution in Jewish blood"; (5) that the great wave of Jewish out-migration from the Russian Empire in the quarter-century before the Great War was prompted by pogroms and restrictive legislation. Recent scholarship has questioned all these assumptions.

Pogroms before 1881

Interethnic riots involving Jews in the southwestern port city of Odessa (in the province of Kherson) occurred in 1821, 1848, 1856, and 1871. The first pogroms involved attacks on Jews by Greek commercial rivals; subsequent pogroms were carried out, in the main, by Russian mobs, the so-called barefoot brigade. The Odessa pogrom of 1871 inspired some Russian Jewish intellectuals to question the prospects for Jewish

integration and emancipation. There was also a poorly documented pogrom against the Jews of Akkerman (in the province of Bessarabia) in 1865. These attacks entailed vandalism and looting, with only a handful of fatalities.

The Pogroms of 1881 and 1882

On March 1, 1881, Alexander II, the Tsar-Liberator, was assassinated by terrorists from the group Narodnaia Volia (The People's Will). A period of great uncertainty followed and an avalanche of rumors swept over the country. On April 15, 1881, a riot broke out between Christians and Muslims in the provincial town of Baku, on the Caspian Sea. On the same day a tavern brawl in the city of Elisavetgrad (in the province of Kherson) escalated into a serious riot, during which Jewish shops and homes were attacked and looted. News of the anti-Jewish disorders traveled along railroad lines, rivers, and other routes of communication, provoking additional, but less violent, attacks in the countryside and small towns. On April 26 a major riot erupted in Kiev, which lasted for three days and prompted copycat violence all over Kiev Province. A third wave of pogroms began in Pereislav (in the province of Poltava) on June 30.

The outbreak of violence on such a wide scale, in what was seen as a police state, as well as the apparent unwillingness or inability of the authorities to suppress the pogroms, inspired contemporaries to claim that the pogroms had been instigated and organized. Suspicion initially fell on the revolutionaries who had assassinated Emperor Alexander II on March 1, 1881. Although some revolutionary publicists welcomed the pogroms as the beginning of a potential social revolution, for the most part the revolutionaries were ambivalent about the outbreak, which they had neither instigated nor manipulated. Accusations of having instigated the pogroms later fell on such varied culprits as the central government, especially N. P. Ignatiev, the Minister of Internal Affairs; on "Pan-Slav publicists in Moscow" in the pay of the Jews' commercial rivals; or on local satraps, such as the governor-general of Kiev, Podolia, and Volynia Provinces, A. R. Drentel'n, a well-known Judeophobe.

Published and unpublished archival sources reveal that the government took extensive measures to anticipate, prevent, and repress anti-Jewish riots in 1881 and 1882. These efforts failed because of the scarcity and ineptitude of the police, and difficulties attending the use of the army to suppress urban disorders. There is no contemporary evidence for the significant presence of agitators or provocateurs. A number of officials were removed from office because they were judged to have been derelict in suppressing pogroms. Over a thousand *pogromshchiki* suffered some form of punishment for their activities. Despite contemporary claims no evidence exists of a sustained campaign in the press encouraging attacks on Jews because "the Yids have killed the Tsar." Nonetheless, there were widespread rumors among urban mobs to this effect, accompanied by the belief that a special *ukaz* (decree) authorized the crowds "to beat the Jews."

There were approximately 250 pogroms, varying greatly in length and severity. They produced about 50 fatalities, of whom half were *pogromshchiki* killed during the suppression of the riots. There were a number of rapes during the pogroms, but not in the massive numbers claimed by contemporary publicists.

Both Russian officialdom and society depicted the pogroms as a popular protest against "Jewish exploitation" in the countryside. This assumption inspired legislative efforts (the so-called May Laws of 1882) to segregate peasants and Jews by driving the latter out of the countryside. These measures did not prevent additional pogroms in 1882, most notably in Balta (in the province of Podolia), on May 29 and 30. There was also a large pogrom in Warsaw, Kingdom of Poland, on December 25, 1881.

There were serious but one-time pogroms in Ekaterinoslav (1883) and Nizhnyi Novgorod (1884). Labor disturbances in Iuzovka and settlements in the so-called Dnieper Bend occasionally included the looting of Jewish shops.

The Kishinev Pogrom

Kishinev, capital of Bessarabia Province, with a mixed ethnic population of Slavs, Moldavians, and Jews, had a history of minor clashes between Christians and Jews, but nothing to match the scale of the pogrom that broke out during Easter week of 1903, claiming forty-nine victims. Kishinev gained greater notoriety than virtually any other pogrom. The provincial authorities were seen as openly complicit. They failed to censor a local Jew-baiting newspaper, *Bessarabets*, edited by P. A. Krushevan, when it disseminated false reports of a ritual murder carried out by Jews. They took insufficient precautions to prevent or repress holiday violence, despite warnings of potential disorders. They failed to act decisively against the pogrom, allowing it to run for three days. There was a measure of truth to all these charges.

The Kishinev pogrom was also accompanied by claims that the central government had sent agents to the city to organize the pogrom, and that the Minister of Internal Affairs, V. K. Pleve, specifically instructed the local authorities not to use physical force to suppress the anticipated pogrom. No reliable evidence exists to support these claims.

The Kishinev pogrom discredited Russia abroad, scandalized moderate and leftist opinion within the empire, and reenergized all forms of Jewish political activity. Jewish bodies of self-defense were organized and enjoyed some success in a subsequent pogrom in Gomel (in the province of Mogilev), beginning on August 29, 1903.

The pogrom inspired a classic work of poetry by Chaim Nachman Bialik, *The City of Slaughter,* written in Hebrew and Yiddish versions, which did much to enshrine the legends of the Kishinev pogrom, especially the claim that the Jews were passive, nonresisting victims.

The Revolution of 1905

The Revolution of 1905 witnessed the breakdown of legal order all over the Russian Empire, together with the widespread claim in right-wing circles that the Jews were major participants in revolutionary disorders. Consequently, counterrevolutionary or loyalist manifestations often degenerated into spontaneous anti-Jewish violence, as in Odessa (October 19–22) and Kiev (October 19–20), that claimed hundreds of Jewish victims and resulted in massive property damage. After the Imperial Manifesto of October 1905, right-wing parties, such as the Union of the Russian People, were founded that utilized anti-Semitism as a mobilizing device. Although such groups, the so-called Black Hundreds, carried out small-scale attacks on Jews and assassinated several Jewish political leaders, they were incapable of organizing pogroms on a massive scale. A rogue operation in the Department of Police printed pogrom-mongering proclamations during this period, but such activity, when discovered, was suppressed by S. I. Witte, the chairman of the Council of Ministers. Emperor Nicholas II, while not specifically approving pogroms, viewed them as an expression of support for the regime. Subsequent serious pogroms, such as one in Bialystok (in the Kingdom of Poland) in 1906, arose from local social and political conditions.

The Russian Civil War (1919–1921)

The February and October Revolutions of 1917, the Russian withdrawal from World War I, and the collapse of the imperial government culminated in the Russian Civil War of 1919 through 1921, in the midst of which the fledgling communist government also fought a war with the newly independent Poland (1920–1921). Participants in the Civil War included a broad variety of political, social, and national groups. In the southern and western provinces of the empire extensive hostilities took place in the former Pale of Settlement, where the Jewish population was concentrated. The Civil War was accompanied by levels of anti-Jewish violence never before witnessed in the Russian Empire and unequaled before the Holocaust. The historiography of this period is sharply divided over the causes of and responsibility for the pogroms.

Virtually all armed forces in the conflict carried out pogroms, but only the Red Army punished them in any meaningful way. Forces comprising the anticommunist Whites and anti-Russian nationalists gained an unsavory reputation for pogrom-mongering. The chief White Army in the area, General A. I. Denikin's Volunteer Army, was a major perpetrator of pogroms, despite half-hearted efforts on the part of the central command to maintain discipline. Forces loyal to the Directory, the executive of the Ukrainian National Republic, were especially active in carrying out pogroms. Officially, the Directory, led by S. V. Petliura, condemned pogroms, but had little control over the ill-disciplined, irregular forces that fought in its name. Nor did the Directory have much to gain by forcibly repressing pogrom activity among its troops. These forces, often led by self-styled Cossack commanders or Atamans, carried out numerous, well-documented atrocities against the Jewish population. Despite claims that these outrages were ideologically motivated, designed to punish Jewish support for the Bolsheviks, or a reflection of "traditional Ukrainian anti-Semitism," they appear to have been largely motivated by the desire for plunder. Jews were also victimized by the numerous anarchist bands that roamed Ukraine, including those nominally loyal to Nestor Makhno. The debate over the culpability of Petliura grew sharply after his assassination in Paris in 1926 by Sholem Schwartzbard, who claimed to be avenging the pogroms. Schwartzbard was subsequently acquitted by a French court. The total number of Jewish fatalities during civil war pogroms is disputed, but certainly exceeded 500,000. Immense property damage also resulted.

SEE ALSO Anti-Semitism; Cossacks

BIBLIOGRAPHY

Abramson, Henry (1999). *A Prayer for the Government: Ukrainians and Jews in Revolutionary Times, 1917–1920.* Cambridge, Mass.: Harvard University Press.

Aronson, I. Michael (1990). *Troubled Waters: The Origins of the 1881 Anti-Jewish Pogroms in Russia.* Pittsburgh: University of Pittsburgh Press.

Dubnow, S. M. (1916–1920). *History of the Jews in Russia and Poland.* 3 vols. Philadelphia: Jewish Publication Society of America.

Frankel, Jonathan (1981). *Prophecy and Politics: Socialism, Nationalism, and the Russian Jews, 1862–1917.* Cambridge, U.K.: Cambridge University Press.

Gergel, N. (1951). "The Pogroms in the Ukraine in 1918–21." *YIVO Annual of Jewish Social Science* VI:237–252.

Hamm, Michael F. (1993). *Kiev: A Portrait, 1800–1917.* Princeton, N.J.: Princeton University Press.

Hunczak, Taras (1969). "A Reappraisal of Symon Petliura and Jewish-Ukrainian Relations, 1917–1921." *Jewish Social Studies* XXXI:163–183.

Judge, Edward H. (1992). *Easter in Kishinev: Anatomy of a Pogrom.* New York: New York University Press.

Klier, John D., and Shlomo Lambroza, eds. (1992). *Pogroms: Anti-Jewish Violence in Modern Russian History.* Cambridge: Cambridge University Press.

Rogger, Hans (1986). *Jewish Policies and Right-Wing Politics in Imperial Russia.* London: Macmillan.

Weinberg, Robert (1993). *The Revolution of 1905 in Odessa: Blood on the Steps.* Bloomington: Indiana University Press.

John Klier

Political Groups

A political group exists when people assemble together in order to promote a common ideology and achieve particular objectives in the public, governmental sphere. Political parties and trade unions are political groups. These days the existence of an opposition party is usually regarded as the characteristic of a democracy itself, as the strength of democracy is to allow political dissent.

Governing elites are likely to use political repression for several reasons. It is often the case that political repression and lack of democratic representation are linked. Government officials use political repression against opponents—real or potential—in order to weaken their capacity to question or offer alternatives to official government policy.

In some situations governing elites view certain political groups as inherently suspect, because the ideology advocated by the group, or its methods, threaten democracy itself. This is the case with respect to fascist movements or terrorist groups. The difficulty here is that categorizing a political group as "antidemocratic" because of the ideology it promotes is very subjective. For example, during the apartheid regime in South Africa, the African National Congress (ANC, the movement of black resistance against racial separatism) was considered a terrorist organization and thus banned. The head of the ANC, Nelson Mandela, spent twenty-seven years in jail for so-called terrorist activities. He was released in 1990 and in 1993 he received the Nobel Peace Prize with the then president of South Africa, F. W. de Klerk. Mandela was subsequently elected president of South Africa in 1994.

The effectiveness of political repression is controversial. Repression can decrease opposition activity, for example, when it limits the ability of opposition groups to mobilize resources and supporters. Conversely, repression can increase opposition activity and harm the popular legitimacy of the political elite. Actors that previously were neutral may decide to engage in opposition, by reaction against repression. Experience has shown that when the level of repression is high, there are fewer activist opponents, but they become more radical: Violent opposition increases, while nonviolent opposition decreases.

The persecution of political groups may lead to the violation of several human rights recognized in the 1966 International Covenant on Civil and Political Rights. These include the right to self-determination; freedom of expression and the right to hold opinions without interference; the right to peaceful assembly; the right to freedom of association, for instance, the right to form and join trade unions; and the right of equality before the law.

When the persecution of political groups reaches a certain threshold—that is, it becomes widespread or

systematic, and purposely targets a civilian population—it may qualify as a crime against humanity. Qualifying the persecution of political groups as genocide is more problematic. According to the 1948 International Convention on the Prevention and Punishment of the Crime of Genocide, a crime (such as murder) may constitute genocide only when the person persecuted is targeted because he or she belongs to a "national, ethnical, racial or religious group." This list is limitative, and it is notable that political groups are not included; such an approach was also confirmed by the definition adopted in the Rome Statute of the International Criminal Court (ICC).

Consequently, according to these international conventions, the persecution of people because they belong to a particular political group may not qualify as genocide. Hence, numerous scholars have determined that the massacres perpetrated by the Khmer Rouge in Cambodia from 1975 through 1978, in which about one-fifth of the population was exterminated, cannot be categorized as "genocide" according to the 1948 Convention. It nonetheless certainly qualifies as one of the most horrific crimes against humanity. However, some national laws adopt a broader definition of genocide and include political groups (e.g., Article 211-1 of the French Penal Code, and Article 281 of the Ethiopian Penal Code).

In addition, it remains possible that members of a political party may also share an ethnic, religious, or national identity. For example, in Northern Ireland the Sinn Fein Party assembles mainly members of the Catholic community, while the Ulster Unionist Party is mostly composed of Protestants. In Rwanda the Front Patriotique Rwandais (FPR) is principally composed of Tutsi.

Political groups' oppressors may be prosecuted if their actions qualify as a violation of fundamental human rights, such as the right to freedom of expression. If political persecutions are widespread or systematic, and target civilian population, alleged offenders may face charges for crimes against humanity. In some countries their crimes may also amount to genocide.

In any case, when asylum seekers are likely to be persecuted in their country because of their political opinions, they may benefit from refugee status (Convention Relating to the Status of Refugees Adopted by the United Nations on 28 July 1951).

SEE ALSO Minorities

BIBLIOGRAPHY

Harris, Peter, and Ben Reilly, eds. (1998). *Democracy and Deep-Rooted Conflict: Options for Negotiators*. Stockholm:

International Institute for Democracy and Electoral Assistance (International IDEA).

Mandela, Nelson (1994). *Long Walk to Freedom*. London: Little, Brown and Company.

Ramaga, Philip (1992). "The Bases of Minority Identity." *Human Rights Quarterly* 14:409–428.

Rodley Nigel, Sir (1995). "Conceptual Problems in the Protection of Minorities: International Legal Developments." *Human Rights Quarterly* 17(1):48–71.

Schabas, William A. (2000). *Genocide in International Law*. Cambridge: Cambridge University Press.

Clémentine Olivier

Political Theory

Political theory can help explain elements of gross human rights violations, especially genocide. Liberalism, for example, is helpful in suggesting that liberal democracies typically do not engage in mass murder, nor do they wage war on each other. Genocides and other massive human rights violations generally have occurred during time of war. In its emphasis on the self-defeating character of war and the need for limitations on its conduct, Grotian international legal theory also is helpful. Common gains for the world's communities as the result of liberal international cooperation suggest the constitution of international regimes that would implicitly or even explicitly prohibit mass murder. International legal frameworks for such cooperation typically do just that. The European Union as a prototypical example has increasingly emphasized democracy and the protection of human rights as a condition of state membership. Utilitarianism, especially in John Stuart Mill's (2002) advocacy of governmental noninterference in individual behavior that does not harm others, indicates a strong ethical basis for the prohibition of mass murder.

Theoretical approaches of this type help in establishing conditions that prevent the occurrence of genocide. However, they do not provide an account of the dynamics through which genocide is effected. Among the many varieties of political theory, realism comes closest and is preeminent for its explanatory power in understanding the etiology of genocide. Most important, realism as a theory of international politics sensitizes us to the presence of Realpolitik as state-centered policy in which "success is the ultimate test of policy, and success is defined as preserving and strengthening the state" (Waltz, 1979, p. 117). It is the state-centric aspect of both realism and Realpolitik that helps explain the onset of genocide. The deadliest genocides of the past century have been initiated by the administrative departments of a state.

Three twentieth-century cases of genocide illustrate the importance of Realpolitik: the Armenian genocide of 1915 and 1916, the Holocaust of 1941 through 1945, and the massacre of the Tutsi of Rwanda in 1994. Two variants of Realpolitik are considered. The first is that of brute force in which state officials initiate and direct genocide; all three of the genocides examined were characterized by such behavior. In the second type, referred to as cynical Realpolitik, the interests of another state or international actor, not the perpetrator, are satisfied by the genocide. Effectively, the bystander abets the genocide because of the unique perception of its own interests. This article will emphasize the latter type.

The Armenian Genocide

Germany was a bystander during the Armenian genocide and the most important superpower influencing Ottoman policy. Already during the period of the 1894 and 1896 massacres, the outlines of German policy concerning the Armenians were decisively formed. In November 1898 a policy brief was put forward by the German foreign ministry that became the basis not only for German official reaction to the massacres, but also for the later genocide. Essentially, it stated that the Armenians were crafty and seditious and had provoked the Ottoman authorities. Further, Germany had little, if any, reason to intervene on behalf of the Armenians, especially given the business interests of many German firms in the Ottoman Empire that might be endangered by German intervention. Very early in the day, Realpolitik had become the basis of German policy on the Armenian Question. Only two years after the end of the 1896 massacres, with great pomp and circumstance, Kaiser Wilhelm II visited Turkey, was greeted lavishly by Sultan Abdulhamit II, and the upward trajectory of Turko-German collaboration was firmly established.

Yet this open expression of support by the Kaiser came after the massacres had occurred. How could the Ottomans think that they could massacre 200,000 people, often in the most brutal fashion, without repercussions from interested superpowers such as Great Britain and France? The answer to the question of Ottoman impunity is found in the emerging German presence in Turkey prior to the massacres. Militarily, between 1885 and 1888, huge Krupp cannon were put into place to guard the Dardanelles Straits and the Üatalca defense line north of Constantinople. Upon request, Helmuth von Moltke, the Chief of the German General Staff, sent some of his best officers to reform the army, including General Colmar von der Goltz of later fame as commander of the Ottoman forces in Arabia during World War I.

When the Ottoman government entered World War I on the side of Germany and Austria-Hungary,

Germany became virtually the official protector of the Ottomans. German military leaders like von der Goltz actively encouraged the development of a religiously, if not ethnically, homogenous Ottoman state. German military officers, in fact, participated in the planning and implementation of the 1915 and 1916 deportations, especially of Armenians working on the Berlin-Baghdad railway under German supervision.

The Holocaust

It has been suggested by contemporary historians that the abetting or permitting agent in the case of the Holocaust was the Vatican. There were several elements to the Realpolitik of Eugenio Pacelli, papal nuncio in Munich between 1917 and 1930, Cardinal Secretary of State between 1930 and 1939, and Pope Pius XII thereafter until his death in 1958. Most important was a virulent anti-communism that demanded the subordination even of national Catholic interests for purposes of defeating the larger threat of Soviet-inspired communism.

As Cardinal Secretary of State, Pacelli had the opportunity to formulate Vatican foreign policy. According to commentators, in that position he was decisive in silencing the German Catholic Center Party that could have provided the only coherent opposition to the Nazi Party. The Nazis were seen by Pacelli as the only effective bulwark against the western expansion of communism from its Soviet base.

Left to its own devices, the Center Party likely would have remained committed to a pluralist democracy, as it had committed itself at the beginning of the Weimar Republic. The last functioning chancellor of the Republic, Heinrich Brüning, a leader of the party and a devout Catholic, was thoroughly committed to parliamentary democracy and utterly opposed to concordats with totalitarian regimes. As chancellor, he also had been opposed to Pacelli's notion of a concordat that had centralized papal ecclesiastical authority at the core of German Catholic decision-making instead of local needs and desires. After Hitler's accession to power, Brüning desperately argued against the concordat that would have depoliticized German Catholicism. His opponent had become the leader of the Center Party, Ludwig Kaas, a Jesuit priest and an intimate of Pacelli, increasingly under his influence. Kaas argued that a concordat with Hitler would better serve the German Catholic Church than its continuance as a political minority opposed to Nazism.

With a simple stroke on July 20, 1933, the Reich concordat was signed, the Center Party was disbanded for good, and Hitler expressed the chilling opinion that the concordat would be "especially significant in the urgent struggle against international Jewry" (Scholder, 1987, p. 404). For the sake of erecting a central European bulwark against communism, Pacelli effectively silenced the only potential large-scale opposition to Hitler's violently anti-Semitic program. Additionally, during the Holocaust the Vatican was almost entirely silent in its public statements on the mass murder of the Jews. In December 1942, at the end of a long Christmas radio message, Pacelli, by then Pope Pius XII, did refer briefly to the need to restore a just society, partly because of the deaths of large numbers of people as a result of their nationality or descent. Not mentioned were anti-Semitism, the genocide of the Jews, or the identity of the perpetrators. After the roundups and deportations of Italian Jews in the autumn of 1943, many Catholic institutions in Italy opened their doors to Jews seeking to evade the Nazis. But had the Pope openly condemned the Nazi genocide, many more Christians might have been encouraged to help Jews in distress throughout occupied Europe, Jews might have been more likely to go into hiding because of the assumed veracity of the papal source, and many more lives could have been saved.

The Genocide of the Tutsi

Finally, in the case of Rwanda, France, another European superpower, was the principal agent in establishing a permissive context. In accordance with the Realpolitik model, Rwanda, precisely because of its francophone status and widespread Roman Catholicism, was in the process of inclusion in the French-dominated African community. It would be the first such country not to have experienced French colonial rule. On the negative side, there was potential opposition stemming from anglophone African states, especially Uganda, home base of the Rwandese Patriotic Front (RPF), a Tutsi rebel organization that invaded Rwanda in 1990. According to Gérard Prunier (1995), the French were reacting to the so-called Anglo-Saxon threat. The confrontation between the heirs of "les Anglais" and the French in Africa has been dubbed the "Fashoda syndrome" by Prunier, after the 1898 confrontation between English and French troops in southern Sudan. He asserts that this syndrome is the main reason why France intervened so quickly and so deeply in the Rwandan crisis.

Equally, if not more important, for understanding the genocide in Rwanda is the amount of French military aid and troop training supplied to the Rwandan army. Arms and ammunition had been continually supplied, but beginning in early 1993 as many as twenty tons of material per day were sent. According to both French and Tanzanian military intelligence sources, the RPF offensive stopped short of the Rwandan capital, Kigali, in February 1993, only because of the presence of French troops in the vicinity.

Officials in France, Belgium, the United States, and the United Nations (UN) were well aware of the possibility of mass killing, yet did little if anything to stop it. France was in the best position to intervene, but did not. Indeed, when President Francois Mitterrand, the intimate of President Juvenal Habyarimana and architect of France's Realpolitik policy in Central Africa, was asked by a journalist about the genocide, he answered: "The genocide or the genocides? I don't know what one should say!" (Prunier, 1995, p. 339), as if there existed a symmetry between Hutu and Tutsi behaviors during that period. One might just as well have argued that the German mass murder of Jews was occasioned by the Jewish mass murder of Germans.

Conclusion

The cynical variant of Realpolitik identified here is a necessary adjunct to the brute force variety. By establishing a permissive context for the genocide, opposition groups both within the targeted state and without are weakened in their resolve to oppose the perpetrators. At the same time the perpetrators are strongly encouraged to wreak their destruction, as was Hitler after the concordat with the Center Party. Agents with either moral or political authority, or both, can be extremely influential in this regard. The theory of realism with its policy adjunct, Realpolitik, sensitizes us to the potential cynicism of international actors having their own state-centric interests.

SEE ALSO Explanation

BIBLIOGRAPHY

Dadrian, Vahakn (1997). *The History of the Armenian Genocide: Ethnic Conflict from the Balkans to Anatolia to the Caucasus.* Providence, R.I.: Berghahn.

Des Forges, Alison (1999). *"Leave None to Tell the Story":* *Genocide in Rwanda.* New York: Human Rights Watch.

Kaiser, Hilmar (1999). "The Baghdad Railway and the Armenian Genocide, 1915–1916: A Case Study in German Resistance and Complicity." In *Remembrance and Denial: The Case of the Armenian Genocide,* ed. Richard G. Hovannisian. Detroit, Mich.: Wayne State University Press.

Lewy, Guenter (1964). *The Catholic Church and Nazi Germany.* New York: McGraw-Hill.

Midlarsky, Manus I. ed. (2000). "Identity and International Conflict." In *Handbook of War Studies II.* Ann Arbor: University of Michigan Press.

Mill, John Stuart (2002). *The Basic Writings of John Stuart Mill: On Liberty, the Subjection of Women, and Utilitarianism.* New York: Modern Library.

Phayer, Michael (2000). *The Catholic Church and the Holocaust, 1930–1965.* Bloomington: Indiana University Press.

Prunier, Gérard (1995). *The Rwanda Crisis: History of a Genocide.* New York: Columbia University Press.

Rummel, Rudolph J. (1997). *Power Kills: Democracy as a Method of Nonviolence.* New Brunswick, N.J.: Transaction.

Scholder, Klaus (1987). *The Churches and the Third Reich,* vol 1, trans. John Bowden. London: SCM Press.

Waltz, Kenneth N. (1979). *Theory of International Politics.* New York: Random House.

Zuccotti, Susan (2000). *Under His Very Windows: The Vatican and the Holocaust in Italy.* New Haven, Conn.: Yale University Press.

Manus I. Midlarsky

Pol Pot

[MAY 19, 1925–APRIL 15, 1998]
Cambodian leader of that country's underground communist party, Khmer Rouge, from 1962; became head of the genocidal regime of Democratic Kampuchea (DK) in 1975 and ruled until his overthrow in early 1979

Pol Pot was born Saloth Sar, in Kompong Thom province, on May 19, 1925 (or 1928). His father, Phen Saloth, owned twelve hectares of land, and had connections at Cambodia's court. Sar's sister was a consort of King Monivong. From age six, Sar lived in Phnom Penh with his brother Suong, a palace protocol officer. He spent a year in the royal Buddhist monastery, and six years in an elite Catholic school. Phnom Penh's inhabitants were mostly Chinese traders and Vietnamese workers. Sar's upbringing was strict, and he had little or no contact with Khmer vernacular culture.

In 1948 Sar received a scholarship to study radio-electricity in Paris (at École Française de radio-électricité). There he joined the Cambodian section of the French Communist Party. He also met Khieu Ponnary, the first Cambodian woman to earn a *baccalauréat* degree.

Sar's fellow students in Paris, Khieu Samphan, Ieng Sary, and Son Sen, remained in his circle until 1996. He chose a racial alias, or, nom de plume: the "Original Cambodian" (*khmaer daem*). Having repeatedly failed his course, he went home in January 1953. King Norodom Sihanouk had declared martial law to suppress Cambodia's independence movement, which was radicalized by the French colonial force and Vietnamese communist influence. Sar's brother Saloth Chhay joined the communists and took him along. After independence in 1954, Sar became a teacher, and two years later he married Khieu Ponnary, on July 14, 1956 (Bastille Day). Sar rose secretly within the Khmer communist movement, and in 1962 became Party leader after his predecessor, a former Buddhist monk, was mysteriously killed. Sar soon thereafter went underground, criticizing Sihanouk's neutrality and Hanoi's support of it.

The "Original Khmer" treasured the Cambodian "race," not individuals or "hereditary enemies," especially Vietnamese. He saw a need for war and secrecy as "the basis of the revolution." He trusted few of the more pragmatic, veteran Khmer communists who had been trained by the Vietnamese. Sar adopted the codename "Pol," later "Pol Pot," but never publicly admitted his real name.

After visiting Mao's China between 1964 and 1965, Sar returned home to launch a rural insurgency in 1967. Three years later, the U.S.–backed general, Lon Nol, overthrew Sihanouk. At about this time, the Vietnam War came crashing over the border as well. Khmer Rouge forces defeated Lon Nol in 1975, and Pol Pot became Prime Minister of the new Democratic Kampuchea regime. The DK evacuated Cambodia's cities, launching a series of political and ethnic massacres, and in 1977, raids on Vietnam, Thailand, and Laos.

Running a secretive party, Pol Pot even came to be called "the Organization" (angkar)—a shadowy institution which documents or reported making speeches, or was sometimes "busy working." His wife, Ponnary, went mad. One day in late 1978, a poster bearing Pol Pot's image was put up in a communal mess hall in Kompong Thom. Only upon seeing the poster did his brother, Suong, learn who was running the country. Terrified of being identified as someone who knew too much about his brother, Suong kept quiet about his relationship to the ruler. Two months later, the regime fell to a Vietnamese invasion.

In Thailand in 1988, Pol Pot blamed most of his regime's killings on "Vietnamese agents." However, he acknowledged having massacred the defeated Lon Nol government's leaders and troops, defending his actions by insisting that "[t]his strata of the imperialists had to be totally destroyed." Pol Pot's army continued to wage war from the Thai border until broken by defections and mutinies that occurred from 1996 to 1999. He died in the jungle on April 15, 1998.

Pol Pot never faced trial for his crimes. From 1979 to 1993, the United Nations, at the insistence of China and the United States, legitimized Pol Pot's anti-Vietnamese cause and supported his exiled Khmer Rouge as Cambodia's representatives. In 1999 the UN proposed establishing an international tribunal to judge his surviving accomplices for genocide and crimes against humanity.

SEE ALSO Cambodia; Khmer Rouge

BIBLIOGRAPHY

Chandler, D. P. (1992). *Brother Number One: A Political Biography of Pol Pot*. Boulder, Colo.: Westview.

Kiernan, Ben (1985). *How Pol Pot Came to Power: Colonialism, Nationalism, and Communism in Cambodia, 1930–1975*, 2nd edition. New Haven, Conn.: Yale University Press, 2004.

Kiernan, Ben, ed. (1993). *Genocide and Democracy in Cambodia: The Khmer Rouge, the United Nations, and the International Community*. New Haven, Conn: Yale Council on Southeast Asia Studies.

Kiernan, Ben (1996). *The Pol Pot Regime: Race, Power and Genocide in Cambodia under the Khmer Rouge, 1975–1979*, 2nd edition. New Haven, Conn.: Yale University Press, 2002.

Ben Kiernan

Prevention

Whenever the crime of genocide or crimes against humanity have occurred, the international community and human rights nongovernmental organizations (NGOs) have asked themselves whether the developments that led to the atrocities could have been anticipated and possibly prevented. They question why no attempts had been made by the state involved, its society, or the international community at large to stop the carnage or events leading up to the genocide. Even if the perpetrators are later brought to justice, their sentencing cannot redress the human tragedy associated with the genocidal acts or the suffering of each individual. In most cases of genocide after World War II, the possibility of human tragedy could have been foreseen. Despite this reality, no fully convincing strategy has yet been designed to effectively prevent genocide. In fact, it remains an open question whether such a strategy can be developed given the complex social, economic, cultural, and psychological issues that may lead to genocide.

Existing means of preventing genocide or of preventing serious and widespread human rights violations that may lead to genocidal acts may be grouped, general speaking, into two categories: procedural and substantive ones. The former embrace all of those techniques developed by human rights institutions, which, for example, provide for the monitoring of human rights situations. The latter embrace nonprocedural obligations of states and individuals, such as the prohibition of incitement to racial hatred or the prohibition of racist organizations. Providing for criminal prosecution of acts of genocide, related acts, or acts that may create an environment that is or may become a fertile ground for genocide also has preventive effects. The threat of criminal prosecution not only labels certain human behavior as morally and socially unacceptable but also attempts to establish a psychological barrier that may prevent a potential perpetrator from taking criminal action.

All attempts to develop an effective system for eliminating genocide and crimes against humanity face one significant problem. Despite many attempts, there is no agreement on which factors may lead to such acts. Certain scholars have made reference to human destructiveness leading to instinctual aggression, to humankind's intraspecific warfare, and to human destructiveness developing from the fear of death. These attempts to explain the unthinkable are rather academic. The restructuring of the human psyche is not a workable solution, even if warfare or human destructiveness is assumed to be part of the human character. One has to proceed to a different level of assessment, and attempt to answer the question: What are the social, cultural, religious, political, or economic conditions under which instinctual human aggression may find its expression in genocidal or related acts?

Factors Likely to Induce Genocide

There is no single explanation of why a government and a society pursue a policy of genocide or crimes against humanity. In most cases throughout history, genocide or related acts were not the result of sudden decisions but, as with the Holocaust, the result of ideological and political preparation and indoctrination. Particular groups are identified as inferior or somehow unworthy in a given society. Such identification of a group of people may be initiated by that part of the society or the government preparing for genocide. Alternatively, or additionally, the identification of a particular group or groups within a larger community can be the result of an act of self-identification of that particular group or groups with the view to preserve its cultural, linguistic, religious, or historical particularity.

Such self-identification as a group is protected under international law. Under the ever increasing relevance of human rights, the world has become aware of the fact that states are neither ethnically and culturally homogeneous, nor is there any merit in being so. In fact, attempts to create ethnically homogeneous states in the aftermath of the dissolution of the former Yugoslavia have resulted in the term "ethnic cleansing," an activity related to genocide.

The branding of a particular, targeted group as being inferior or dangerous for another part of the community, or the stability of the respective state, is the first clear indicator of a situation that may lead to genocide. Even the development and fostering of negative feelings or stereotypes within a society against individual members of a group just because they are members of that group should be considered a warning signal. It would be naive, however, to believe that only the dominant group in a given society could stimulate misunderstandings and tension; the later targeted group may contribute to feelings of alienation by excluding itself from the society, by conveying an attitude of superiority, by giving the impression of not being loyal to the state it lives in, or by advocating its secession from the given state. Frequently the attempt is made to rationalize the perceived difference or inferiority of the targeted group or the superiority of the dominant group by developing pseudo-scientific theories. This was particularly true for the German policy leading to the Holocaust. The development of such theories and their publication should also be considered a potential precursor to genocidal or related acts.

What is the mechanism that makes the dominant part of a society take action against a particular group? Several historians offer explanations. Individuals such as Leo Kuper hold that material interests may be an important factor in the development of genocide. This may be true in cases where a particular group is occupying an area that is of significant interest for the economic well being of the region or country. This is a situation indigenous groups have faced and are still facing; for example, the repression of the Native Americans or the Australian aborigines was mostly economically motivated. Expelling indigenous populations or even transferring them to other areas may take the form of or may result in genocide.

However, economic interests may have little or no significance in the genocide against targeted groups that are singled out for purely ideological reasons. Economic factors were irrelevant, for example, in the German genocide against Gypsies, which was motivated by pure malevolence and historical prejudices. In fact, prejudices can exist and may even become quite virulent—even in societies where Jews and Gypsies do not play any significant role in the society or where they do not exist at all. Perhaps it is most appropriate to say that aggressive attitudes toward particular ethnic or religious groups are likely to materialize in times of a society's transition, when it faces an identity crisis, or when it is in the midst of economic crisis.

Factors Likely to Prevent Genocide

Having touched upon situations that are more likely to bring about aggression against a particular group in a given society, it is worthwhile also to touch upon situations that are more immune to such development.

History has shown that the attitude of singling out a particular spectrum of the society develops less in societies that are pluralistic and used to be so. Equally democratic societies are usually less vulnerable to genocide. Given the wave of xenophobic and anti-Semitic attitudes western European countries are facing, it would be credulous to believe that democratic societies are absolutely immune from anti-Semitic, xenophobic, or related attitudes. It is essential that states—apart from their form of organization—are socially and economically stable. All occurrences of genocide in modern times have taken place at times when states underwent significant transitions and thus lost their previous identity, or perceived it as endangered. For example, the progressive disintegration of the Ottoman Empire was one of the causes of the aggression against the Armenian population. Likewise, the destabilization of Germany and Austria after World War I facilitated and fuelled the growth of anti-Semitic feelings.

Genocide only takes place when it is organized by a state, endorsed by state authorities, or approved of by the majority of the dominant members in a society. Therefore, preventive actions either have to strive for the immunization of the society against any attempts to make any group a target for discrimination or suppression, or to provide interventions from the outside if such developments are about to unfold in a given society.

Preventive Measures under the Genocide Convention

The Convention on the Prevention and Punishment of the Crime of Genocide, also referred to as the United Nations' Genocide Convention (1948), refers both to prevention and to the punishment of the crime of genocide, however, the Convention focuses on the second aspect rather than on the first. The concept of prevention is repeated in Article 1 of the Genocide Convention, however, no particular consequences follow. Nevertheless, the punishment of the crime of genocide or even the threat to punish it is meant to have a preventive effect. In that respect the Genocide Convention is not different from national criminal law. Apart from that, some of the acts referred to in Article 3 of the Genocide Convention have a preventive dimension. The prosecution of conspiracy, or of attempts of public incitement to commit genocide, is an attempt to fight future occurrences of genocide. Another preventive element can be found in Article 8. According to that provision, any contracting party may call upon the competent members of the United Nations to take such action

as considered appropriate for the prevention and the repression of acts of genocide.

This rudimentary mechanism is all that remained from a more substantial provision in the draft of the Genocide Convention prepared by the secretariat. According to the scholar Nehemiah Robinson, the secretariat draft contained an elaborated prevention mechanism. Article 12 of that text, which was titled "Action by the United Nations to Prevent or to Stop Genocide," stated that, irrespective of the deterring function of penalizing genocide, contracting parties may have the right to call upon the competent organs of the United Nations to take measures for the suppression and prevention of such crimes. The secretariat obligated states to do everything in their competence and support any actions of the United Nations to prevent or to stop genocide. In particular, the United States had some doubts about these provisions whereas the Soviet Union pushed for an even stronger formulation that would have obliged all states to report genocide to the Security Council. The consequence would have been that measures could have been taken in accordance with Chapter 7 of the United Nations (UN) Charter. In 1973 the provision of Article 8 of the Genocide Convention was included in the Convention against Apartheid.

Scholarly opinions differ as to the relevance of Article 8 of the Genocide Convention. Several writers dismiss its relevance. Others, such as Hans-Heinrich Jescheck, have indicated that Article 8 provides the Security Council with a basis to take action, which, in view of Article 2 of the UN Charter, was necessary to include. This argument was based upon the assumption that the Security Council could only act in cases or situations falling under Article 39 of the UN Charter and that genocide or crimes against humanity could not be qualified as such. However, because the Security Council has developed the practice that significant and widespread human rights violations may be qualified as a threat to international security, Article 8 of the Genocide Convention has lost some of its relevance.

Despite these elements that refer to prevention, the Genocide Convention has shied away from providing a genuine mechanism for the prevention of genocide. The reasons for that are open to speculation. The prevailing reason might be the fear that any attempt to set up the respective mechanism would mean an infringement into the internal affairs of a state and an erosion of Article 2, paragraph 7 of the UN Charter as it was understood in 1948. Only the increasing relevance of international human rights standards—which was initiated with the Universal Declaration on Human Rights and the Genocide Convention—has changed international law in this respect. Meanwhile it is untenable to argue that serious violations of internationally protected human rights are an internal affair of any given state. The international community of states may intervene or may be under an obligation to take action to redress the situation.

Preventive Measures under Different Human Rights Agreements

The Human Rights Committee, the Committee on Economic Social and Cultural Rights, the Committee on the Rights of the Child, and the Committee on the Elimination of Racial Discrimination have adopted procedures on preventive action. These include early warning and urgent procedures as a guide for the committees' future work concerning possible measures to prevent in a more effective way any violation of the respective conventions. This includes actions taken to prevent genocide, and even a situation that may lead to genocide. This approach was taken upon the recommendation of the UN General Assembly in the context of the Agenda for Peace. As far as conceptuality and the implementation of such procedure are concerned, the Committee on the Elimination of Racial Discrimination has developed the most systematic and far-reaching practice. Like the other human rights treaty bodies, the Committee was particularly induced to establish such a procedure by the events in the former Yugoslavia and in the Grand Lakes Region of Central Africa. The members of the Committee felt that the regular monitoring of the human rights situation in these regions had proven to be inadequate to prevent the occurrence or reoccurrence of genocide.

Preventive actions of the Committee on the Elimination of Racial Discrimination include early warning measures to address existing structural problems that might escalate into conflicts. Such a situation calling for early warning is warranted when the national procedures for the implementation of human rights are inadequate or there exists the pattern of escalating racial hatred and violence, racist propaganda, or appeals to racial intolerance by persons, groups, or organizations, notably by elected or other officials. The criterion for initiating an urgent procedure, according to the decision of the Committee, is the presence of a pattern of massive or persistent racial discrimination.

The reaction in its preventive functions and in response to problems requiring immediate attention are similar under all the early warning procedures. The Committee on the Elimination of Racial Discrimination will first exhaust its advisory function vis-à-vis the respective state party. The Committee may address its concern, along with recommendations for action, to all

or any of the following: the state party concerned, the special rapporteur established under a Commission of Human Right Resolution, the Secretary-General of the UN, and all other human rights bodies. The information addressed to the secretary-general may, in the case of urgent procedures, include a recommendation to bring the matter to the attention of the Security Council. In this case the Committee may appoint a special rapporteur.

An important mechanism of a nonprocedural character meant to prevent racial discrimination and genocide is the obligation of states to prohibit hate speech and to ban organizations advocating racial intolerance. The Genocide Convention lacks a provision to address this, although other human rights instruments have addressed issues of hate speech.

Article 7 or the Universal Declaration of Human Rights, adopted the day after the Genocide Convention, contains a rudimentary reference to limitations to the freedom of speech by protecting against the incitement of discrimination. Article 29 of the Universal Declaration further opens the possibility for states to limit the enjoyment of fundamental rights and freedoms, including the freedom of expression, for the purpose of securing due recognition and respect for the rights and freedoms of others and for meeting the just requirements of morality, public order, and the general welfare in a democratic society. This covers limitations on the freedom of speech with the view to eliminate hate speech and hate propaganda as well as a denial of the Holocaust.

A more focused provision obligating states to limit freedom of speech is contained in the Convention on the Elimination of All Forms of Racial Discrimination. The Committee considered this provision to be of prime importance for the implementation of the Convention against racial discrimination. According to the provision, it is mandatory that states not only enact appropriate legislation—which, in fact, means enactment of criminal law—but also ensure that such criminal law is effectively implemented. The said provision equally obliges state parties to the Convention against Racial Discrimination to prohibit organizations with a racist program and make the participation therein a criminal offense. The Committee has frequently emphasized the importance of this provision, although several states have stated that their constitution would not allow them to prohibit and dissolve such organizations. Those state parties that for reasons of their national legal order cannot implement this obligation are called upon to be of particular vigilance. This provision raises particular legal problems in respect to political parties promoting racist ideologies because the dissolution of political parties may be the means to preserve the domination of a ruling regime. Under the conditions of a democratic society, it may be argued that it is preferable to fight racist attitudes and ideologies within the framework and the means of a democratic discourse rather than through repressive means. Past experience, however, proves that in periods of transition and of economic or political instability this may not be effective enough to protect the society from racial tensions or racially motivated violence.

The International Covenant on Civil and Political Rights also contains provisions providing for the limitation of fundamental rights, including the freedom of expression and of association, which may be used to prevent the incitement of racial hatred or violence. The Covenant recognizes that the human right of freedom of expression is subject to special duties and responsibilities. It imposes an obligation upon states to prohibit any adversarial speech of national, racial, or religious hatred that constitutes incitement to discrimination, hostility, or violence. Further, the Covenant provides for restrictions to the freedom of expression by law necessary to respect the rights and reputations of others or for the protection of national security or of public order. This would cover hate speech and hate propaganda as referred to in Article 20 of the Covenant. Although the European Convention on Human Rights does not include an obligation to prevent hate propaganda, it is held that hate propaganda is not protected by Article 10 of the Convention, which includes freedom of expression. In the *Jersild v. Denmark* case in 1994, the European Court of Human Rights agreed that the freedom of expression provision of the European Convention on Human Rights should be interpreted, "to the extent possible, so as to be reconcilable with its obligations" under the International Convention for the Elimination of Racial Discrimination. The freedom of speech provision in the American Convention on Human Rights is broader than in the other international instruments. However, despite its large vision of freedom of expression, the provision also contemplates the case of racist propaganda. Article 13, paragraph 5, of the Convention is more or less identical with Article 20 of the International Covenant on Civil and Political Rights.

Whereas Article 4 of the International Convention on the Elimination of all Forms of Racial Discrimination obliges states to take action against "incitement to, or acts of such [racial] discrimination" the United Nations Educational, Scientific, and Cultural Organization (UNESCO) Declaration on Race and Racial Prejudice addresses the root problem of racial prejudices. It reaffirms that all human beings belong to a single species and are descended from a common stock; they are born equal in dignity and all form an integral part of humanity. The Declaration further emphasizes that all individuals and groups have the right to be different, to consider themselves as different, and to be regarded as such. However, the diversity of lifestyles and the right to be different may not, in any circumstances, serve as a pretext for racial prejudice. Apart from stating these principles and declaring theories on racial superiority or inferiority as being without scientific foundation, the Declaration is moot when it comes to describing actions to be taken by states.

The aforementioned measures discussed are of a "repressive" nature, in as much as they provide for the criminal prosecution of genocide or for the prosecution of preparatory acts as provided for in Article 3 of the Genocide Convention or for the repression of acts that may prepare the political or ideological ground for inter-ethnic strife or intolerance. Less attention has been paid to measures meant to positively influence society, such as education and information.

Positive measures are touched upon in Article 7 of the Convention on the Elimination of all Forms of Racial Discrimination. The Convention does not outline specifically the appropriate actions for states to take. Most social scientists agree the teaching of human rights, in general, and the principles enshrined in the UNESCO Declaration on Race and Racial Prejudice, in particular, should be included into the curriculum of schools at all levels. Many call for curriculum that includes information on the Holocaust and other occurrences of genocide or similar events after World War II. However, it is up to individual states to develop mechanisms that are most suitable for the education of tolerance. The UNESCO Declaration on Fundamental Principles concerning the Contribution of the Mass Media to Strengthening Peace and International Understanding, to the Promotion of Human Rights and to Countering Racialism, Apartheid and Incitement to War (1978) refers to the role mass media may play in stigmatizing genocide.

Conclusion

Democratic societies that perceive themselves as pluralistic and those societies that believe that ethnic or religious pluralism is an enrichment rather than a weakness are less likely to fall under the spell of racist theories. The Genocide Convention is meant not only to prosecute those having committed the crime of genocide but also to prevent the development of genocide. Later international human rights instruments place a heavy emphasis on preventing genocide by providing states with the means to suppress attitudes or ideologies of racial superiority. Historians agree that more emphasis should be placed on educational efforts; for example, helping children strive for a better understanding of the world's different cultures, lifestyles, and religions. Other historians have suggested an effective system for the protection of minorities.

SEE ALSO Denial; Early Warning

BIBLIOGRAPHY

Banton, Michael P. (1996). *International Action against Racial Discrimination.* New York: Oxford University Press.

Banton, Michael P. (2002). *The International Politics of Race.* Malden, Mass.: Blackwell.

Charny, Israel W. (1987). *How Can We Commit the Unthinkable? Genocide: The Human Cancer.* Boulder, Colo.: Westview Press.

Coliver, Sandra, ed. (1992). *Striking a Balance: Hate Speech, Freedom of Expression, and Non-discrimination.* Colchester, U.K.: Human Rights Center, University of Essex.

Fein, Helen (2001). "The Three P's of Genocide: With Application to a Genocide Foretold—Rwanda." In *Protection against Genocide: Mission Impossible?* ed. Neal Riemer. Westport, Conn.: Praeger.

Jescheck Hans-Heinrich. (1995). "Genocide." In *Encyclopedia of Public International Law,* vol. 2, ed. Rudolph Bernhardt. New York: North-Holland.

Koestler, Arthur (1978). *Janus: A Summing Up.* New York: Random House.

Kuper, Leo (1985). *The Prevention of Genocide.* New Haven, Conn.: Yale University Press.

Lieblein, Julius (1987). "The Bottomline: Preventing Future Holocausts." In *Toward the Understanding and Prevention of Genocide: Proceedings of the International Conference on the Holocaust and Genocide,* ed. Israel W. Charny. Boulder, Colo.: Westview Press.

Lorenz, Konrad (1977). *On Aggression.* New York: Harcourt, Brace and World.

O'Flaherty, Michael (1996). *Human Rights and the UN: Practice before the Treaty Bodies.* New York: M. Nijhoff Publishers.

Robinson, Nehemiah (1960). *The Genocide Convention: A Commentary.* New York: Institute of Jewish Affairs.

Schabas, William A. (2000). *Genocide in International Law: The Crimes of Crimes.* New York: Cambridge University Press.

Scherrer, Christian P. (2001). *Preventing Genocide.* Moers, Germany: Venlo.

Zimmer, Anja (2001). *Hate Speech im Völkerrecht, Europäische Hochschulschriften,* vol. 3302. Frankfurt: A. M. Lang.

Rüdiger Wolfrum

Propaganda

Discrimination and its promotion through hate propaganda disturb peace and can pave the way to massive human rights violations such as genocide. Hate propaganda is the public promotion or incitement of hatred against people and identifiable groups and that is likely to result in harm to those targeted. It is directed at persons or groups based on factors such as color, race, religion, nationality, or ethnic origin.

Hate propaganda causes harm to individuals by degrading them, attacking their dignity and sense of self-worth. It also hurts society as a whole, because it destroys social harmony and encourages discrimination and violence, thus creating a hostile environment for the targeted members of that same society. Hate propaganda is defined as a crime in most domestic law systems and in international law.

Propaganda serves to dehumanize the members of the targeted group. It degrades them and stigmatizes them, creating the necessary illusion that the identifiable group is the enemy. Propaganda has more than once contributed to the development of a climate that led to the implementation or toleration of exclusionary behavior, and hate speech has preceded massive physical persecutions. Propaganda is used to trivialize the importance of crimes committed against its targets, it confers a sense of social acceptability and even desirability upon those crimes. This was the case with both the Holocaust and the Rwandan Genocide. Propaganda is the starting point of the progression that leads to genocide. Beginning with limited propaganda directed at an identifiable group, the crime moves to more systematic propaganda, then to state-sponsored hate speech, and finally to the direct incitement to hate, ultimately giving rise to publicly-supported, mass crimes.

The Role of Hate Propaganda in Causing Genocide
Propaganda has a long-term effect. Its repercussions can take years to appear, making it more difficult to regulate than direct acts and overt public incitements to genocide. Propagandist rhetoric dulls the conscience, thus furthering the development of a social psyche willing to tolerate inhumanities. It works to modify people's normal and expected reaction, leading them to accept, rather than condemn, discriminatory behavior. The propagandist uses speech to persuade others to his view, or at least to create a climate in which the oppression he champions is acceptable.

Propaganda legitimizes aggression by conveying the message that something has to be done regarding a targeted group. Genocide requires such a collective agreement among perpetrators and also bystanders. Di-

These two books, from the collection of Hermann Göring, are examples of the anti-Semitic literature that flooded Germany in the 1920s and 1930s. Though his influence had greatly eroded by World War II's end, Göring was one of the earliest participants in the Nazi campaign of propaganda against European Jews. [HULTON-DEUTSCH COLLECTION/CORBIS]

rect incitement to genocide is usually not enough, it generally needs to be based on a pre-established ideology, shared by an indoctrinated population. In a culture already inundated with anti-Semitic or anti-Tutsi propaganda, and in which inter-group tensions are high, innuendos about the killing of members of those groups may be enough to instigate violence, eliminating the need for explicit calls to violence. In a context of economic difficulties, social and political turmoil, or during a war, propaganda becomes even more efficient. In such situations people are often disconnected from certain aspects of society, and thus cannot assess the accuracy of what they are being told, allowing propagandists to create rumors and invent "facts" that suit their goals.

The Nazis raised anti-Semitic propaganda to an unprecedented level by turning it into a state-sponsored

dogma. Nonetheless, the Nazis based their implementation of propaganda on pre-existing linguistic casuistry. They took well-known, popular anti-Jewish sentiment and systemized it, and in so doing they cleared the way for the devestation of the Holocaust. The Holocaust, in other words, required lengthy propaganda preparation to induce the different actors involved—the perpetrators to commit such actions and the population to be numb vis-à-vis such a catastrophe.

Propaganda was the springboard from which the Nazis launched the Holocaust. Anti-Semitism was disseminated by many, including government representatives such as Josef Goebbels and full-time anti-Semitic propagandists and ideologues such as Julius Streicher, the publisher of the notorious anti-Semitic newspaper *Der Stürmer.* Streicher may not have been a murderer himself, but he created the climate for murder. After the war, Streicher was at Nuremberg for his propagandist's role in bringing about the Holocaust. Without the climate Streicher established, the court held, the Holocaust would probably never have taken place, because too many would have rejected the orders to execute Jews. Thus, the court suggested that Streicher may have been even more responsible for the crimes than the other defendants who appeared with him in the dock. The final judgment rendered by the International Military Tribunal does not explicitly note a direct causal link between Streicher's publications and any specific murders, but characterizes his work as a poison "injected into the minds of thousands of Germans which caused them to follow the National Socialists' policy of Jewish persecution and extermination." Streicher was found guilty of crimes against humanity because of his propaganda.

Form, Means, Strategy and Diffusion of Propaganda

Hate propaganda takes many different forms. It can be disseminated in public meetings, through radio, television, movies, books, pamphlets, graffiti, government-sponsored messages, telephone messages, gestures, signs or other visible representations. More recently, the Internet has become a popular medium for the dissemination of hate propaganda.

Propagandists prefer simple and clear arguments and descriptions over complex ones. It targets the emotions of its audience, rather than the intellect, and it seeks to build up a disdain for rational dissenting arguments or explanations. Propagandists are often charismatic orators. They tend to use straightforward, colorful language. They employ images, symbols, and evocative examples. Effective racist propaganda is usually couched in simple terms, and touches citizens emotionally through examples and stories to which they can relate. Streicher, for example, used caricature and cartoons to represent Jews, and argued that the hard times that German's were suffering were all caused by the Jews.

Propaganda themes are repeated frequently, preferably using all forms of the media. Exclusionary speeches, constantly repeated, break down the normal resistance of their audiences, and people soon begin to wonder if what is being said about the targeted group might actually be true. Such speeches are not intended to convert their listeners with genuine arguments; rather, they are aimed at creating a kind of emotional and intellectual numbness. As the message spreads through the various media, the messages become so omipresent that their truth begins to appear self-evident.

Key words are repeated to remain in the listeners' minds. The technique is to hit the same themes over and over again, until the audience internalizes the major points. In the Rwanda genocide, a propagandist named Mugesera constantly repeated the warning that Hutus beware that the *Inyenzi* (cockroaches, an epithet used against the Tutsis of Rwanda) and their accomplices. Listeners were gradually conditioned to associate the Tutsis with the Front Patriotique Rwandais (FPR), a rebel faction that was accused of wanting and trying to overthrow the Hutu lead government. By constantly linking the term *Inkotanyi* (infiltrators, a term for the FPR) with *Inyenzi*, he effectively accused all Tutsis of being infiltrators as well. The intent was to blur the distinction between the rebels and Tutsi civilians in order to justify the widespread killing of Tutsis as a preventive measure.

Der Stürmer worked in much the same way. The publication helped the Nazis persuade as many people as possible that first, there was a problem in regard to the Jewish question, and second, that it was absolutely critical to solve it. The concept, reproduced in many different ways, was that the Jews were responsible for all the evils of the world in general, and for Germany's misfortune in particular, and that the world would therefore be better off if all the Jews were wiped out.

Propagandists use various techniques and media to make their statements more appealing. Sex and horror stories in which Jews were portrayed as evildoers were frequently added to *Der Stürmer*, allowing Streicher to sell more copies and reach an even broader audience. The cinema played a central role in the Nazi's propaganda strategy, as well. It reached a large audience and could add the power of visual imagery to the propaganda message. The Nazis spread propaganda by shooting fictional films and false documentaries such as *Der ewige Jude,* depicting Jews in very unfavorable ways. Goebbels himself ordered the creation of such films. Graphic representations, cartoons, and manipulated photographs of the targeted group are also common in the propagandists' arsenal. *Der Stürmer*, in Nazi Germany, and *Kangura*, the anti-Tutsi newspaper in Rwanda, both employed these media. The "Fips" cartoons, which portrayed Jews in the most exaggerated stereotypes, were a regular feature in *Der Stürmer*. In Rwanda, *Kangura* regularly featured cartoons of Prime Ministers Uwilingiyimana, Twagiramungu, and General Dallaire (who lead the UN peacekeeping force), depicting them in unfavorable situations and employing popular stereotypes.

The use of stereotypes furthers the audience's acceptance of propaganda because the images are so familiar. Stereotypes provide the audience with a common denominator. The Nazis based the identification of the Jews on exaggerated physical attributes. Propagandists added to the stereotypes by describing Jews as cockroaches, vermin, rats, and spiders. In *Der Stürmer*, Jews were described as bent-nosed, fat, and having unpleasant features. It then attempted to establish a link between stereotypical impressions of Jews with current or historical events. For instance, *Der Strürmer* accused Jews of conducting ritual murders during which Christians were killed.

In Rwanda, the Tutsis were stereotyped as inherent liars, thieves, and killers. *Kangura* also depicted the Tutsis as biologically distinct from the Hutus and as being consumed by malice and wickedness. Radio Télévision Libra Mille-Collines (RTLMC), the local media outlet, joined in the propaganda effort, accusing the Tutsis of being plotters and parasites, and using the Tutsis' historical domination of Rwandan politics and society as a propaganda tool: Tutsis were still perceived as "the ones who have all the money," a reference to the fact that a Tutsi royalty once ruled Hutus. Tutsi women were stereotyped as tall and slim with a "beautiful nose," thus very attractive to male Hutus. Tutsi women, because of these alleged attributes, were accused of being enemy agents, used by the *Inyenzi* to deprave Hutu men.

Propaganda seeks to reverse normal allocation of the burden of proof, forcing their targets onto the defense. It also seeks to generate the sense of constant threat, so that its audience is forced to be vigilant vis-à-vis the targeted group. By spreading fear, propagandists gather ever larger groups of supporters. *Kangura* persistently conveyed the message that Tutsis intended to conquer the country in order to restore the Tutsi feudal monarchy, subduing all Hutus. *Kangura* repeated that the enemy was among them, waiting to strike, and that the day would come when Hutus would have to defend themselves. RTLMC also played on the public's fear of an armed Tutsi insurrection. In a speech, Mugesera made repeated references to this fear, not to ease it but to inflame it. Mugesera pleaded, "the one whose neck you don't cut is the one who will cut your neck."

The Role of Propaganda in the Holocaust and the Rwandan Genocide

The Holocaust and the Rwandan genocide are two of the clearest examples of propagandist exploitation of racist beliefs among the broader popularion. In both cases, the propagandist's work paved the way to genocide.

Propaganda in Germany

The Nazis exploited racist ideology and economic hardship to influence a nation to persecute a minority. It offered a scapegoat to a population that had been de-

feated in World War I and was suffering under the burden of a devastated post-war economy. Germany's disastrous situation was portrayed as mono-causal: the Jews were to blame for everything. Anti-Semite propaganda had become common even before Hitler came to power.

The source of much of this early propaganda, the *Protocols of the Elders of Zion*—a famous anti-Semitic document—was widely circulated. It is a work of fiction that allegedly contains the minutes of a meeting held by a shadowy group of Jewish Elders, and sets forth their fictional plan to take over the world. The document employed all the commonly used religious and physical stereotypes associated with the Jews. Judeophobia, inflamed by documents such as *The Protocols*, proved an effective tool for bringing together a broad cross sampling of German society, drawn from religious, intellectual, and political walks of life. That the document was exposed as a fraud in the early 1920s did not stop anti-Semites from referring to it. In fact, it is still used by Holocaust deniers to support their claim that the Holocaust is just another myth created by the world's Jewry to achieve their ultimate goal of global domination.

When the Nazis came to power, propaganda became a government policy, used to create a climate that would support the genocidal plans of Hitler and his followers. Goebbels, serving as the Minister of Information and Propaganda, controlled all of Germany's media outlets and later assumed the same control over media in the occupied territories. Goebbels was the father of propagandist strategies such as the "Big Lie Theory," in which he argued that by repeating lies about the Jews and progressively magnifying these lies, he could increase public acceptance of the lies and mobilize public support for Hitler's policies.

Public boycott campaigns against Jewish businesses were made possible through propaganda. Legislation was passed to isolate and stigmatize all Jews. This was followed by state-sponsored, anti-Semitic propaganda to galvanize the intolerance of the non-Jewish population. This approach led to *Kristallnacht*, an anti-Jewish riot organized by Goebbels. The strategy was extremely successful. Beginning on November 9, 1938, and continuing well into the next day, German citizens who had been exposed to hate propaganda directed at Jews exploded into the streets to burn synagogues, destroy Jewish properties, and kill Jews.

Propaganda in Rwanda

The newspaper, *Kangura*, and the audio-visual media controlled by RTLMC were instrumental in systematically spreading propaganda against the Tutsis. *Kangura* published cartoons and editorials that inflamed Hutu prejudices against Tutsis, and ultimately published the so-called Hutus' Ten Commandments, which comprised a blanket condemnation of all Tutsis on the sole basis of their ethnicity.

Rwanda's high illiteracy rate meant, however, that *Kangura* could reach only a limited audience. For non-readers, the radio played a significant role both before and during the genocide. RTLMC was used to broadcast orders and detailed information on the positions and names of Tutsis to be killed. United States–based NGOs pleaded to have the airwaves jammed during the genocide, but the U.S. government opposed the idea.

After the genocide was ended, the International Criminal Tribunal for Rwanda (ICTR) brought charges against the management of both the RTLMC and *Kangura*. The court held that both media outlets indulged in ethnic stereotyping in a manner that promoted hatred for the Tutsis, and were thus implicated in the genocide.

Leon Mugesera's Speech

On November 22, 1992, Leon Mugesera made a speech that was repeated on Rwandan radio and in which he frequently uttered incitements to hatred for the Tutsis. In January 1993, an international human rights fact-finding mission to Rwanda found the country in a state of turmoil and agitation provoked in part by Mugesera's speech. Mugesera eventually fled Rwanda to take refuge in Canada, but the Canadian authorities tried to deport him for having committed a criminal act before obtaining his permanent residence. The criminal act to which they referred was the speech he had given, back in 1992.

In his speech, Mugesera claimed that FPR rebels were in secret collusion with all of Rwanda's Tutsis. Mugesera's speech was made two years after the Hutus' Ten Commandments had appeared in *Kangura,* at a time when other propaganda outlets were increasingly active in the attempt to isolate all Tutsis. Mugesera's speech was intended to build upon that propaganda effort, to encourage Hutus to seek out and kill Tutsis, civilian or otherwise, because they were all, in his words, infiltrators and traitors to Rwanda.

The Canadian courts failed to recognize the true meaning of Mugesera's speech, and declined to deport him. The court failed to recognize Mugesera's genocidal intent because he couched his incitements to violence in indirect and figurative language, but the incitement he intended was nonetheless clear to Rwanda's Hutus as a call to mobilize against all Tutsis. The court only considered the literal content of the speech, and lacked the understanding of the social context in which

the speech was made. It did not recognize that there was a direct link between the speech and the genocide that ensued eighteen months later. It could not understand that thousands of killers were following orders passed by various means after a propaganda campaign initiated years before. Mugesera was not deported, but the prosecution has filed an appeal to challenge the court's decision.

Legal Issues Facing the Regulation of Hate Propaganda

Measures to eradicate harmful propaganda are controversial. Hate propaganda undermines the humanity of those targeted, but democratic societies are reluctant to pass laws limiting the freedom of expression. Freedom of expression is probably the most universally recognized human right. Most international human rights instruments, as well as numerous national constitutions, contain provisions protecting it. The freedom to express one's opinion constitutes one of the basic conditions for society's progress and for the development of every human being. Unfortunately, such freedom is not always used for the benefit of that society. History, in many circumstances, has demonstrated that harmful propaganda has led to tragic events such as crimes against humanity and genocide. In most cases, propaganda is in fact the prerequisite for such crimes. That is why freedom of speech comes with duties and responsibilities.

Most international human rights instruments and international jurisprudence recognize that language can cause severe social harm, and that the suppression of hate speech is warranted when it is needed to protect other rights, such as equality. Article 19 of the International Covenant on Civil and Political Rights (ICCPR) states that freedom of speech may be subject to restrictions when they are necessary to guarantee respect for the rights of others. Similar to the Convention for the Protection of Human Rights and Fundamental Freedoms (European Convention), the ICCPR contains a provision that nothing in the instrument should be interpreted as granting any person the right to engage in an activity aimed at the destruction of any of the other rights recognised by the ICCPR. International bodies such as the European Court of Human Rights have developed a considerable jurisprudence on the limitation of freedom of expression. When faced with restrictions of that freedom, the court views that it is not faced with two conflicting rights, but with a freedom of expression that is subject to a number of exceptions, which, in turn, need to be interpreted narrowly.

There are two opposing approaches concerning the regulation of hate speech and propaganda. The causationist approach, supported mainly by the United States, requires that a direct causal link be proved to exist between the expression and the harm such expression has allegedly caused. Without that link, there can be no limitation imposed on the freedom of speech. The correlationist approach, supported by a broad international consensus, requires the regulation of hate speech if there is a rational correlation between the expression and the harm that ensues afterward.

Hate Speech Regulation in International Law

The regulation of hate speech revolves around the interplay between and the reconciliation of the freedom of expression and the right of equality. There is an international consensus that hate speech threatens democracy, justice, and equality, which is why so many countries attempt to prohibit it. The Convention on the Prevention and Punishment of the Crime of Genocide declares direct and public incitement to commit genocide is a punishable act, but goes no further, and it omits hate propaganda in its list of crimes. Two subsequent international instruments have gone a step further than simply acknowledging the limits of the freedom of speech by requiring states to penalize hate propaganda.

Article 20 of the International Covenant on Civil and Political Rights states that any propaganda for war and any advocacy of national, racial, or religious hatred that constitutes incitement to discrimination, hostility, or violence shall be prohibited by law. Article 4 of the International Convention on the Elimination of all Forms of Discrimination (CERD) is even more precise. States that are party to the convention must adopt positive measures to eradicate incitement to discrimination, and must declare a punishable offense all dissemination of ideas based on racial superiority or hatred, incitement to racial discrimination, as well as all acts of violence or incitement to such acts against any race or group of persons of another color or ethnic origin. The United States signed the document in 1966, but ratified it only in 1994. Ratification was made with reservations to protect the freedom of speech doctrine developed in the United States, thus making the ratification of that point almost pointless.

International jurisprudence recognizes the possibility, even the obligation, of limiting free speech when faced with expressions of negative value, like hate speech. The ICCPR Committee has affirmed the duty of states to restrict the freedom of expression in order to assure the protection of others rights. In a case involving Holocaust denial, which is viewed by France as a subtle form of anti-Semitic propaganda, the committee expressed the view that the prosecution of the defendant, Faurisson, did not breach his fundamental right of freedom of expression.

The European Convention does not contain any specific provision dealing with hate propaganda. In numerous cases, the European Commission of Human Rights has nonetheless excluded hate propaganda from the protection of Article 10, which otherwise safeguards the freedom of speech. For the commission, hate propaganda is contrary to the text and spirit of the European Convention and contributes to the destruction of the rights and freedoms set forth therein.

In two cases, the European Court of Human Rights has dealt explicitly with hate propaganda and has made it clear that hate speech regulation was compatible with the European Convention. Recognizing the utmost importance of the freedom of speech, the court nonetheless agreed that the convention should be interpreted, whenever possible, in a way reconcilable with the CERD, which explicitly prohibits hate speech. Denial of the Holocaust and the justification of pro-Nazi policies were considered to be a form of hate and racist propaganda that was not protected by the free-expression provisions of Article 10 of the convention.

Hate Speech Regulation in Canada

Canada has a comprehensive legal mechanism with regard to freedom of speech and hate propaganda. Article 2 of the Canadian Charter of Rights and Freedoms protects the freedom of speech. Similar to the limitation clauses found in international instruments, Article 1 of the charter recognizes that fundamental rights such as the freedom of expression are nonetheless subject to limits which need to be reasonable, prescribed by law, and justified in a free and democratic society.

Willful public incitement to hatred for any identifiable groups is a criminal offense in Canada. The Canadian Supreme Court upheld the constitutionality of the findings in the case of *Keegstra,* which involved a teacher who had taught that Jews were "child killers," and "treacherous," and that the Holocaust was a myth. The court found that the defendant had abused his right to freedom of speech and recognized the role of the government in penalizing hate propaganda. The court further held that hate propaganda harmed both the targeted persons and groups—by humiliating and degrading them—and society as a whole. It emphasized the long-term harmful influence of propaganda, recognizing that messages of racial discrimination and hatred can remain in one's mind for a long period of time. In other cases, the Canadian Supreme Court has stated that hate propaganda threatens society by eroding the tolerance and open-mindedness that must flourish in a multicultural society committed to the idea of equality.

Hate Speech Regulation in the United States.
In the United States, only the narrowest and absolutely necessary restrictions of the freedom of expression are justified. The First Amendment states, "Congress shall make no law . . . abridging the freedom of speech, or of the press." It does not provide grounds by which the government may justify limitations of that freedom.

In most instances, jurisprudence in the United States does not recognize the link between propaganda and the harm that may ensue therefrom. It imposes the demonstration of a clear and present danger before a limitation of free speech may be considered constitutional. Under that test, restrictions can be justified only when violence is clearly likely to arise from the expression, that the danger will occur very soon after the expression, and that no other reasonable means of preventing the violence can be used. It is not sufficient to demonstrate that there is a probability that the expression might cause such violence. The Supreme Court does not recognize the long-term effect of propaganda. The First Amendment may allow legislation to prohibit hate speech that advocates the use of force, but only in very narrowly defined circumstances.

Suppression of expression based on content is generally prohibited in U.S. law, and is considered to be unconstitutional. The Supreme Court has extended this prohibition of content-based regulation, rendering the regulation of speech targeting identifiable groups even more difficult to justify. In a case involving the burning of a cross in an African-American family's yard, the law became involved because the act was listed as a misdemeanor under a local St. Paul ordinance. However, the ordinance itself was found to discriminate against expression based on the content of that expression, and so it was found to contravene the First Amendment. The Supreme Court held the view that only a prohibition of all fighting words would be justifiable under the Constitution, whereas the selective prohibition of racist hate speech and anti-Semitic speeches or displays was unconstitutional. This ruling, along with the imminent threat test and the total lack of recognition of the long-term effect of propaganda, makes the prohibition of hate speech in the United States almost impossible.

The United States believes in an idealized free market of ideas, in which all acts of expression should be allowed to compete. Under this approach, it follows that citizens should be exposed to all sorts of expression. The approach basically considers an expression as a commodity, for it puts hate speech and any other expression on an equal basis, and it considers the opposition between hate propaganda and counter-argument as a legitimate debate. This relies on the premise that truth and reason will always prevail over hate propaganda, and that intolerance can be countered by more free expression. This idealism, however, is questionable in the light of history. Even in two of the most recent cases of hate propaganda, it was not reason but military victory that put an end to the hate speech that characterized Nazi propaganda as well as the Rwandan incitements to genocide.

Racist behavior takes time to gain general acceptance. Even when it does not pose an immediate threat to society, propaganda is the first step leading toward extermination policies. It establishes the basis upon which genocide can later be justified, however inappropriately. Propaganda prepares society for the crimes committed in its name by making the messages it is conveying acceptable to those who are systematically exposed to them. The Holocaust and the Rwandan Genocide are but two examples in which propaganda was allowed, tolerated, and supported, ultimately paving the way to tragic events. This contradicts the philosophy underlying the U.S. policy toward freedom of expression. Unfortunately, there is little historical support for the idea that hate propaganda will simply go away by itself or fall to well-reasoned counterarguments. The more society tolerates hate speech, the more frequent it is likely to become accepted, thus increasing the probability of success of the message that is being conveyed.

SEE ALSO Denial; Der Stürmer; Goebbels, Joseph; Incitement; Radio Television Libre Mille-Collines

BIBLIOGRAPHY

Bytwerk, Randall L. (2001). *Julius Streicher: Nazi Editor of the Notorious Anti-Semitic Newspaper, Der Stürmer.* New York: Cooper Square Press.

Guttenplan, D. D. (2001). *The Holocaust on Trial.* New York: W. W. Norton.

Gaudreault-DesBiens, Jean-François (2000). "From Sisyphus's Dilemma to Sisyphus's Duty? A Meditation on the Regulation of Hate Propaganda in Relation to Hate Crimes and Genocide." *McGill Law Journal* 46(121):122.

Schabas, William A. (2000). *Genocide in International Law: The Crime of Crimes.* Cambridge: Cambridge University Press.

Tsesis, Alexander (2002). *Destructive Messages: How Hate Speech Paves the Way to Harmful Social Movements.* New York: New York University Press.

Martin Imbleau

Prosecution

Crimes against the basic principles of humanity are nothing new to the history of mankind. In nearly all historical cases, investigations never took place, and criminal sentences were never passed on the responsible persons. There was only one conviction in a remarkable case, that of Peter von Hagenbach, in 1474. Charles the Bold, Duke of Burgundy, known to his enemies as Charles the Terrible, had placed Landvogt Peter von Hagenbach at the helm of the government of the fortified city of Breisach, which was located at the French-German Rhine border. The governor, overzealous in following his master's instructions, introduced a regime of arbitrariness, brutality and terror in order to reduce the population of Breisach to total submission. When a large coalition put an end to the ambitious goals of the powerful Duke, the siege of Breisach and a revolt by both his German mercenaries and the local citizens led to Hagenbach's defeat. Hagenbach was then brought before a tribunal initiated by the Archduke of Austria and charged with murder, rape, perjury, and other crimes. The tribunal found him guilty and deprived him of his rank and related privileges. Hagenbach was then executed. This trial is often referred to as the first international criminal law or war crimes prosecution. It kept this distinction until the twentieth century, when the first serious efforts were begun to prosecute and punish persons guilty of international crimes.

World War I Prosecutions

When the Allied and Associated Powers convened the 1919 Preliminary Peace Conference, the first international investigative commission was established. At the conference, Germany's surrender was negotiated and the Versailles Peace Treaty was dictated. This Treaty established a new policy of prosecuting war criminals of the vanquished aggressor state after the end of the hostilities. The legal basis of that policy was laid down in the Paris Peace Treaties concluded by the victorious Allies (Britain, France, Russia, Italy, the United States, and Japan) with the defeated Central Powers (Germany, Austria, Bulgaria, Hungary, and Turkey) in 1919. Four groups of offenses were created: crimes against the sanctity of the treaties, crimes against international morality, war crimes (defined in a narrow sense), and violations of the laws of humanity. The first three offenses were integrated in Articles 227 and 228 of the Versailles Treaty. Crimes against the laws of humanity were omitted from the treaty because the United States of America argued that this offense could not be exactly defined and thus was too vague to serve as a basis for prosecutions. The United States also doubted that there was a universal standard for humanity.

The Versailles Treaty was the first international treaty to recognize individual responsibility for crimes committed against international law. It further recognized that such responsibility could not be limited to individuals of a certain rank or position. Thus, the Allies were able to accuse the former German emperor, William II of Hohenzollern, of having committed a supreme offense against international morality and the sanctity of treaties.

Germany, which had previously passed a national law to implement Articles 228 and 229, passed new legislation in order to prosecute German suspects before its own Supreme Court (the *Reichsgericht*), which convened at Leipzig. The German Prosecutor General had the authority to decide which cases would be brought to trial. In fact, only twelve Germans were prosecuted before the German Supreme Court for war crimes. These so-called Leipzig Trials were widely criticized as a failure because the German authorities appeared to lack the will to seriously prosecute their war criminals. Moreover, the government failed to hand over 900 persons whom the Allies wanted to prosecute. Emperor William II found refuge in the Netherlands and was never extradited. In addition to these obvious shortcomings, however, the Leipzig prosecutions lacked impartiality and objectivity because they only dealt with the crimes of the vanquished. Further, the impact of the prosecutions and of the Versailles Treaty in general on internal German policy was counterproductive because it prepared the ground for a revanchist interpretation of the German capitulation (the famous "*Dolchstoβlegende*") and the rise of the Nazi movement.

Turkey entered World War I on December 2, 1914. In April 1915 the organized homicide of 600 intellectuals, doctors, priests, and lawyers in Constantinople was the beginning of the Armenian genocide. The atrocities committed led to a joint declaration by France, Great Britain, and Russia on May 24, 1915, asserting that all members of the Ottoman Government and those of its agents found to be involved in those massacres would be held personally responsible for the crimes. The British High Commissioner suggested that the appropriate punishment for the Armenian massacre would be to split up the Turkish Empire and prosecute its high officials. Although the newly installed Turkish authorities arrested and detained a couple of the previous leaders, many were later released in response to public demonstrations and other internal pressure. Attempts by Turkish jurists to prosecute the crimes before the national courts were slightly more successful. Several ministers of the wartime cabinet and leaders of the Ittihad party were found guilty of "the organization and execution of crime of massacre."

The Treaty of Sèvres, signed on August 10, 1920, was in many aspects similar to the Treaty of Versailles. It differed, however, in that it specified a list of offenses, which later were considered as crimes against humanity. However, the Treaty of Sèvres never took effect. It was replaced by the Treaty of Lausanne of July 24, 1923, which included a declaration of amnesty for all offenses committed by the Turkish government and its agents between August 1, 1914, and November 20, 1922.

World War II: Nuremberg and Tokyo Trials

The first series of trials following World War II took place in Nuremberg under the terms of a charter drafted in London between June and August 1945 by representatives of the United States, the United Kingdom, the USSR, and France. The Nuremberg Charter contained three categories of offenses: crimes against peace, war crimes, and crimes against humanity. Article 7 of the Charter excluded defenses based on official position (i.e., no head-of-state immunity), and Article 8 disallowed defenses claiming non-responsibility because the crimes were committed on orders from a superior.

The Tokyo Trials were based on the Charter for the Far East (the Tokyo Charter), which was proclaimed on January 19, 1946, by the Supreme Commander of the Allied Powers, General Douglas MacArthur. This charter, unlike the London Charter that instigated the Nuremberg Trials, was not part of a treaty or an agreement among the Allies. Representatives of the allied nations that had been involved in the struggle in Asia (the United States, Great Britain, France, the Soviet Union, Australia, Canada, China, the Netherlands, New Zealand, India, and the Philippines) formed the Far Eastern Commission (FEC), whose main tasks were to establish a policy of occupation for Japan and to coordinate the Allied policies in the Far East. Part of this policy was the prosecution of the major war criminals. Thus, the International Military Tribunal for the Far East (IMTFE) was created. It was composed of judges, prosecutors, and other staff from the allied nations. It was to prosecute crimes against peace, as defined in the London Charter; conventional war crimes understood as violations of the laws or customs of war; and crimes against humanity. The definition of crimes against humanity differed from that provided in the IMT charter in two ways: First, the IMTFE charter expanded the list of crimes to include imprisonment, torture, and rape. Second, it eliminated the requirement that crimes against humanity had to be committed before or during war to be actionable in court. As with the IMT charter, the IMTFE also excluded defenses based on official position or superior orders.

The prosecution selected twenty-eight defendants, among them former premiers (Hiranuma, Hirota,

Koiso, and Tojo), foreign ministers (Matsuoka, Shigemitsu, and Togo), and one colonel (Hashimoto). Sixteen of the convicted persons were sentenced to life imprisonment, seven were sentenced to death, one was sentenced to seven years imprisonment, and another to twenty years in prison. All of those sentenced to hanging were convicted of one or both of the major counts of war crimes in the indictment, namely the ordering, authorizing, or permitting of atrocities, or disregard of duty to secure observance and prevent breaches of the law of war. Five defendants were convicted for a crime against humanity: Dohihara, Kimura, Muto, Itagaki and Tojo.

Post-Nuremberg World War II Trials

The Nuremberg and Tokyo trials were followed by a second series of prosecutions of Nazi leaders, pursuant to Control Council Law No. 10 (CCL10). This law formed the basis for Allied prosecutions in their respective zones of occupation. The most famous proceedings were the twelve that were held before the U.S. court in Nuremberg. One of these was the so-called Doctors Trial, in which twenty-three persons were accused of taking part in the Nazi euthanasia program (*U.S. v. Brandt et al.*). Also important were the proceedings against Generalfeldmarschall Milch (*U.S. v. Milch*) and the trial of the Ministry of Justice officials (*U.S. v. Altstoetter et al.*). The remaining nine proceedings conducted by the United States included one against high SS officials (*U.S. v. Pohl et al.*); the proceeding against Friedrich Flick and five of his employees (*U.S. v. Flick et al.*); the proceeding against twenty-three heads of the IG-Farben-Industrie-AG (*U.S. v. Krauch et al.*); the Balkan Generals Trial (*U.S. v. List et al.*); the "Resettlement or Genocidium Trial" (*U.S. v. Greifelt et al.*); the "Einsatzgruppen Trial" (*U.S. v. Ohlendorf et al.*) against twenty-four heads of the task-forces of the *Sicherheitspolizei* (security police) and the *Sicherheitsdienst* (security service); the proceeding against Alfred Krupp von Bohlen and twenty-four heads of the Krupp-company (*U.S. v. Krupp et al.*); the "Wilhelmstraßen-Trial" against twenty-one ministers, permanent secretaries, gauleiters, high-ranked SS leaders, and other leading persons (*U.S. v. von Weizäcker et al.*) and the trial against fourteen high-ranking officers of the German armed forces (*U.S. v. von Leeb et al.*).

Other important cases have been documented by the UN War Crimes Commission (UNWCC). It was established on October 20, 1943, and its task was to investigate war crimes, collect evidence, and identify the responsible parties, and to inform the allied governments about the cases where a sufficient basis for prosecutions existed. In total, the UNWCC has documented eighty-nine war crimes trials. The documentation was published in fifteen volumes from 1947 to 1949, under the title *Law Reports of Trials of War Criminals*. However, there are only very few judgments dealing with crimes against humanity.

Apart from these rather well documented cases, there have been other national prosecutions in the immediate aftermath of World War II, either in the occupation zones or in the territory of the allied countries. There is no complete documentation of these cases. Sometimes this lack of documentation was intentional, to avoid subsequent investigations into the fairness of these proceedings. The proceedings instituted by the occupation powers ended a few years after the end of the war. Step by step, the responsibility for the prosecutions was passed along to German courts, despite the negative experience of the Leipzig trials. However, the legal basis of these proceedings soon changed. During the brief existence of the Supreme Court for the British Zone, which functioned from February 9, 1948, to September 30, 1950, the court applied the CCL10 in half of all its cases. Its successor, the renamed German Supreme Court, successfully refused to apply this disliked law by neglecting all unresolved cases until August 1951, when the CCL10 practically ceased to exist (it was formally abolished on May 30, 1956, with the formal ending of the German occupation). The newly autonomous German criminal justice system did not apply the Nuremberg law, but instead imposed the ordinary penal code. This situation was only remedied with the enactment of the German Code of International Criminal Law on June 26, 2002.

Prosecutions of Nazi war criminals still continued within and outside Germany for years after the end of the war. One case is famous as much for its reliance on the concept of universal jurisdiction as for the crimes of its defendant. This was the trial of Adolf Eichmann. Eichmann had been the head of Section IV B 4 of the *Reichssicherheitshauptamt*, an office that resulted from the merger of the security service of the Nazi party and of the security police of the Nazi state. Eichmann organized and coordinated the deportations of Jews to the concentration camps. In 1960 it was discovered that he was living in Argentina. The Israeli secret service, the Mossad, abducted him and brought him to Israel to stand trial for charges under the Nazis and Nazi Collaborators (Punishment) Law. On December 12, 1961, he was found responsible for the implementation of the so-called Final Solution of the Jewish question, an act that fulfilled the requirements of genocide and crimes against humanity. Eichmann was sentenced to death by the District Court of Jerusalem on December 15 of the same year. The special importance of the Eichmann trial lies in the fact that the state of Israel did not exist at the time that he committed the crimes for which he was found guilty. Thus, Israel's jurisdiction could not be based on the right of a conquering nation to administer punishment.

Another noteworthy trial of the years following World War II is that of Klaus Barbie, which was prosecuted in France. Barbie was head of the Gestapo in Lyon during Germany's occupation of France. The French authorities issued an arrest warrant at the end of the war. Barbie was soon arrested, but he subsequently escaped and then disappeared. He was tried in absentia for war crimes and sentenced to death by the Tribunal Permanent des Forces Armées de Lyons. Barbie was found to have taken refugee in Bolivia, and after a long and complicated procedure involving diplomatic pressure was extradited to France in 1983. Meanwhile, new proceedings relating to crimes against humanity had been instituted against him in Lyons in February 1982. He was sentenced to life imprisonment on July 4, 1987. Other cases dealing with the war crimes of Germany during World War II include that of Paul Touvier in France, who was sentenced to life imprisonment on April 20, 1994, by a Crown Court in Versailles; and that of Imre Finta, who was tried in Canada and finally acquitted by the Supreme Court on March 24, 1994.

Modern Trials on the Basis of International Criminal Law

The long and stable period of peace that followed World War II was broken in 1991 by massive violations of international humanitarian law and human rights in the territory of the former Yugoslavia. In reaction to this situation, the UN established the Commission of Experts Pursuant to Security Council Resolution 780. This commission was charged to report on the situation in the former Yugoslavia, and, on the basis of its first interim report, the UN Security Council decided to establish the ad hoc International Criminal Tribunal for the Former Yugoslavia (ICTY) on May 25, 1993.

According to Articles 2 through 5 of the ICTY Statute, the tribunal exercises jurisdiction over grave breaches of the four Geneva Conventions, violations of the laws or customs of war, genocide, and crimes against humanity. The underlying offenses of crimes against humanity include murder, extermination, enslavement, deportation, imprisonment, torture, rape, persecutions on political, racial and religious grounds, and other inhumane acts.

Another ad hoc tribunal was formed some three years later. This was the International Criminal Tribunal for Rwanda (ICTR), established by UN Security Council Resolution 955 in July 1994. Its establishment was also preceded and initiated by a report filed by a commission of experts, much as was the ICTY. The ICTR also exercises jurisdiction over genocide, crimes against humanity, and crimes committed in the course of internal armed conflict.

The creation of ad hoc tribunals by the UN Security Council is not the only way to deliver international criminal justice. As a result of the growing international tendency toward accountability for international crimes, a permanent International Criminal Court (ICC) was established in Rome in 1998, to which nearly one hundred states have signed on as member parties. The first investigations for genocide and crimes against humanity, both codified in the Rome Statute, were begun in the early years of the twenty-first century. Further, new approaches in the conduct of international criminal justice have emerged, either within the framework of a UN Transitional Administration (e.g., in Kosovo and East Timor), or on the basis of bilateral agreements between the UN and a host state (as has occurred in Sierra Leone and Cambodia). In all these cases, prosecutions for genocide and crimes against humanity have taken or will take place. Interestingly enough, the respective court statutes and regulations are essentially based on the Rome Statute of the ICC, and they copy the provisions contained therein on genocide and crimes against humanity. Even the statute of the Iraqi Special Tribunal, established by the Coalition Provisional Authority in 2004, relies on the ICC statute, although the U.S. administration of the time was fiercely opposed to the ICC.

Modern Trials on the Basis of National Law

The international trend towards accountability has been accompanied by a significant number of prosecutions of genocide and crimes against humanity on the national level. Domestic judicial systems have increasingly recognized that these crimes do not belong to the jurisdiction of the territorial states, but rather that they affect the security and well being of mankind as a whole. Thus, national prosecutions are initiated for extraterritorial crimes on the basis of the principle of universal jurisdiction, or other principles that provide for extraterritorial jurisdiction. Austria, for example, has investigated and prosecuted the case of the Serbian Cvetkovic, who was charged with genocide. The ICTY refused to take over the proceedings, so Austria based its jurisdiction on Section 65(1) of the Austrian Criminal Code, which entitled Austria to punish offenses committed abroad if the offender was found within the country's borders and is not extradited to a foreign state.

Belgium has been involved in four cases invoking universal jurisdiction: One, the trial of a Rwandan named Higaniro, ended with a conviction for genocide. In another case, *Aguilar Diaz et al. v Pinochet*, the question arose whether the notion of crimes against humanity, as defined by international law, was directly applicable in Belgium's domestic law. The examining magistrate held that it did, and the Belgium government requested Pinochet's extradition from Great Britain in order to force him to stand trial. (The request was never granted, because Pinochet was released from prison for medical reasons and returned to Chile). A third important Belgian case of universal jurisdiction is *Abbas Hijazi et al. v. Sharon et al.* This case against Sharon was dismissed on February 12, 2002, after the Court of Cassation held him to be immune from prosecution under international law. However, the court allowed the proceedings against Sharon's co-defendants to go forward, even in absentia. Under pressure from the U.S. government, the Belgian government agreed to stop prosecuting international crimes that relied on universal jurisdiction, and in August 2003 the parliament approved an amendment requiring all plaintiffs to be Belgian nationals. As a result, the cases of Sharon's co-defendants were also dismissed.

In the French case of *Javor et al. v. X*, the defendant was accused of genocide and crimes against humanity committed in a Serbian detention camp in the former Yugoslavia in 1993. However, because these offenses did not exist in the French Penal Code prior to 1994, it was held that the prosecution could not go forward. In Switzerland, a Rwandan citizen named Niyonteze was charged with genocide and crimes against humanity, and the German courts rendered five judgments concerning war crimes and genocide committed in the former Yugoslavia: The first judgment was rendered by one of the superior appeals courts of the State of Nordrhine-Westphalia, on December 26, 1997. The accused, N. Jorgic, was sentenced to life imprisonment for eleven counts of genocide, thirty counts of murder, fifty counts of severe physical injuries, and 355 counts of detaining persons against their will. The judgment was confirmed on March 30, 1999, and by the Constitutional Court on December, 12, 2000. Another Serbian offender, N. Djajic, was convicted for aiding and abetting fourteen war crimes of murder on May 23, 1997, by the highest court in Bavaria, Germany. He was sentenced to five years in prison. A further defendant, M. Sokolovic, was sentenced on November 29, 1999, to nine years of imprisonment for aiding and abetting genocide and for committing war crimes. Finally, D. Kuslic was convicted for genocide and murder on December 15, 1999, and sentenced to life imprisonment. The basic legal findings of both these judgments were confirmed on February, 21, 2001.

Other cases have concerned gross human rights violations, among them the forced disappearance of persons, during the military dictatorships in Argentina, Chile, and Guatemala. In July 1996, the Progressive Union of Prosecutors in Spain lodged a criminal complaint against General Augusto Pinochet and other members of the Chilean military junta. The complaint included the offense of genocide. The examining magistrate in that case, Baltasar Garzón, considered himself competent to investigate charges of genocide, terrorism, and torture regardless of the nationality of the victims, although in this case the victims included Spanish citizens. He issued a warrant of arrest for General Pinochet. During a private visit to London, Pinochet was detained by the British authorities pursuant to the Spanish request. The competent Spanish court first confirmed the Spanish jurisdiction on November 5, 1998, dismissing an appeal that challenged its jurisdiction. In a second decision, the court extended the terms of the arrest warrant for Pinochet, which now included seventy-two charges against the general. Pinochet was never extradited, however, and instead was sent back to Chile.

In another case, initiated by Nobel laureate Rigoberta Menchú Tum in 1999 against the former Guatemalan military junta headed by Ríos Montt, Spain's highest court concluded that Spain could not exercise jurisdiction, and affirmed that the jurisdiction of the territorial state (Guatemala) would prevail. Another case, this time against the Argentine naval officers Adolfo Scilinogo and Miguel Angel Cavallo, was still ongoing in 2004. Both of the accused face charges for their complicity in crimes committed during Argentina's military dictatorship, including crimes against humanity. Last but not least, the Nuremberg judicial authorities have undertaken thorough investigations into the murder of two German students—Klaus Zieschank and Elisabeth Käsemann—who were killed in Argentina during the 1970s. The court has issued arrest warrants against high-ranking members of the former Argentinean junta, among them former Generals Jorge Videla and Emilio Massera. The German authorities demanded the extradition of Videla in March 2004.

Domestic courts of the states of the former Yugoslavia have slowly started prosecuting war crimes. Thus, for example, on June 25, 1997, the Osijek District Court in Croatia convicted a Serbian for genocide, charging that he had participated in acts of ethnic cleansing in the village of Branjina during the war. In Bosnia and Herzegovina, war crimes trials have been paralyzed for years, either because the judicial authorities were reluctant to pick up these controversial cases or because of confusion over jurisdiction since the adoption of the new Bosnia and Herzegovina Criminal Code.

Specific Legal Issues

One of the major achievements of modern international criminal law is the evolution of increasingly exact definitions of international crimes. Articles 6 through 8 of the Rome Statute offer an explicit codification of genocide, crimes against humanity, and war crimes. The definitions may not yet be perfect, but they are a considerable improvement over the definitions upon which the Nuremberg, Tokyo, and The Hague trials were formerly based.

Genocide, for instance, was not understood as a separate crime in the Nuremberg trials, although some defendants were charged with "deliberate and systematic genocide, viz., the extermination of racial and national groups, against the civilian populations of certain occupied territories in order to destroy particular races and classes of people, and national, racial, or religious groups, particularly Jews, Poles and Gypsies." Although the final judgment of the Nuremberg tribunal never used the term explicitly, it described at great length what would later be defined as genocide in the Genocide Convention of 1946. The U.S. Military Tribunals sitting at Nuremberg thus demonstrated the emerging acceptance of the concept. In fact, the indictment and judgment for the Einsatzgruppen trial used the word *genocide* to characterize the activities of the German troops in Poland and the Soviet Union.

The problem with the concept of genocide is that, even though the overt act—the commission of mass killings—is more or less clear, there is a mental requirement that must also exist to qualify the charge of genocide. In other words, the killing or other overt act must be committed in order "to destroy, in whole or in part" a protected group. This entails at least three major problems. First, it turns the offense into a special-intent crime, which necessitates an understanding of the subjective state of the defendant. Second, it is very difficult to prove the specific genocidal intent. For this reason, the Bavarian Supreme Court acquitted Novislav Djajic of charges that he had aided and abetted the commission genocide, because it could not be proven beyond a reasonable doubt that Djajic knew of the main perpetrators' special intent to destroy the group of the Bosnian Muslims who were his victims, nor could it be shown that he himself had such an intent. Finally, it is unclear whether the specific genocidal intent is required of any participant in a genocide, or if it need only be proven for a certain category or group of participants. A perpetrator, whether he or she acted alone and directly, was one of several co-perpetrators, or participated only indirectly, must always act with specific intent. This also applies to the superior who is responsible for ordering the genocidal act. Minor contributors, especially the mere accomplice who lends physical or psychological assistance (an aider and abettor), need not have acted with specific intent, but need only be aware of the genocidal intent of the main participants in order to bear some criminal responsibility for the act.

The definition of crimes against humanity developed from the older concept of war crimes. The term "crimes against the laws of humanity" was first mentioned in the Paris Peace Treaties, which drew on the so-called Martens Clause contained in the Preamble of the 1907 Hague Convention. The underlying rationale for the 1907 convention was the maintenance of basic principles of the law of nations and the establishment of basic rules of humanity, even in armed conflict and in the absence of other specific rules. The Nuremberg tribunal employed the term without providing a clear theoretical and methodological basis of the concept. To avoid a blatant violation of the principle of legality, which holds that a thing cannot be a crime in the absence of a law that makes it one, the Allies interpreted crimes against humanity as a jurisdictional extension of war crimes. While the prohibition of war crimes was intended to protect civilians during armed conflict between states, the concept of "crimes against humanity" extended this protection to civilians within a particular state, provided that there was a link to armed conflict. Thus, such crimes, if they were committed before 1939, that is, before the Nazi aggression, could not be prosecuted.

SEE ALSO Arbour, Louise; Eichmann Trials; International Criminal Court; International Criminal Tribunal for Rwanda; International Criminal Tribunal for the Former Yugoslavia

BIBLIOGRAPHY

Ahlbrecht, Heiko (1999). *Geschichte der völkerrechtlichen Strafgerichtsbarkeit im 20.* Baden-Baden: Nomos Verlagsgesellschaft.

Ambos, Kai (2004). *Der Allgemeine Teil des Völkerstrafrechts*, 2nd edition. Berlin: Duncker und Humboldt.

Ambos, Kai, and Mohammed Othman (2003). *New Approaches in International Criminal Justice: Kosovo, East Timor, Sierra Leone, and Cambodia.* Freiburg: Max Planck Institute for Foreign and International Criminal Law.

Bassiouni, M. Cherif (1997). "From Versailles to Rwanda in Seventy-Five Years: The Need to Establish a Permanent International Criminal Court." *Harvard Human Rights Journal* 10:11–62.

Bassiouni, M. Cherif (1999). *Crimes against Humanity in International Criminal Law*, 2nd edition. The Hague: Kluwer Law International.

Cassese, Antonio, Paola Gaeta, and John R. W. D. Jones (2002). *The Rome Statute of the International Criminal Court Comentary*, 3 volumes. New York: Oxford University Press.

Dinstein, Yoram, and Mola Taboryl (1996). *War Crimes in International Law.* The Hague: Kluwer Law International.

McCormack, Timothy, and Gerry J. Simpson (1997). *The Law of War Crimes: National and International Approaches.* The Hague: Kluwer Law International.

Möller, Christina (2003). *Völkerstrafrecht und Internationaler Strafgerichtshof-kriminologische, straftheoretische und rechtspolitische Aspekte.* Münster: Lit. Verlag Münster.

Paust, Jordan J., Cherif M. Bassiouni, Michael Scharf, Jimmy Gurulé, Leila Sadat, Bruce Zagaris, and Sharon A. Williams (2001). *Human Rights Module.* Durham, N.C.: Carolina Academic Press.

Reydams, Luc (2003). *Universal Jurisdiction.* New York: Oxford University Press.

Rückert, Adalbert (1979). *Die Strafverfolgung von NS-Verbrechen 1949–1975.* Heidelberg: Müller, Juristischer Verlag.

Rückerl, Adalbert (1982). *NS-Verbrechen vor Gericht.* Heidelberg: Juristischer Verlag.

Schabas, William (2000). *Genocide in International Law.* Cambridge, U.K.: Cambridge University Press.

United Nations War Crimes Commission (1947–1949). *Law Reports of Trials of War Criminals*, 15 volumes. London: Majesty's Stationary Office of the UNWCC.

Kai Ambos

Proxmire, William
[NOVEMBER 11, 1915–]
U.S. senator

For nineteen of his thirty-one years as a U.S. senator, William Proxmire made repeated and frequent speeches calling for Senate ratification of the United Nations (UN) Genocide Convention. Representing Wisconsin in the Senate from 1957 to 1989, Senator Proxmire began his prolonged campaign for the Convention in January 1967 at the urging of Milwaukee lawyer Bruno Bitker (1899–1984). Calling the Senate's failure to approve the treaty a "national shame," Proxmire committed himself to "speak day after day in this body to remind the Senate of our failure to act and of the necessity for prompt action" (Power, 2002, p. 79). From this point forward he took a personal responsibility for this issue and persisted for two decades until he prevailed.

As a U.S. senator, William ("Bill") Proxmire was best known for his work on the Senate Banking and Ap-

A beaming William Proxmire, the former Democratic senator from Wisconsin who sponsored the 1986 Genocide Convention Implementation Act that made genocide a criminal act under U.S. federal law. [BETTMANN/CORBIS]

propriations Committees. Over the years he gained a reputation as an outspoken debater with tenacious personal and political commitments. Most of all, Proxmire was known for attacking wasteful and frivolous government spending. Beginning in 1974 he awarded a monthly "golden fleece" award to little-known budget items, which he considered as a "wasteful, ridiculous or ironic use of the taxpayers' money." In his personal life, Proxmire began each day with a four-mile run, and authored a 1973 book on health and fitness. To set an example of frugality, his Capital Hill office regularly returned over one-third of its allotments to the federal budget. Over time the senator's tenacity took the form of never missing Senate votes. He eventually held the record of 10,000 consecutive votes over a 22-year period. This approach to his life and work was needed to win Senate passage of the Genocide Convention.

Treaty ratification requires the votes of two-thirds of senators for approval. Proxmire and his allies Jacob Javits and Claiborne Pell encountered tireless opposi-

tion to ratification from a minority led by Sam Irvin and later Jesse Helms. To keep this issue constantly before the Senate, Proxmire gave 3,211 speeches calling for ratification of the Convention, an average of 168 each year. The speeches were pointed reminders to his colleagues made during the Senate's "Morning Hour" before the chamber began scheduled business. More expert in domestic issues than foreign policy, what motivated Proxmire to persist in this effort was his service during World War II, his disdain for the practice of killing legislation in committee without a vote, and daily headlines from Biafra, Bangladesh, Uganda, Kampuchea, and elsewhere bringing news of atrocities and possible genocide.

Finally, on February 19, 1986, the Senate approved the Convention by a vote of 86 to 11, but only with reservations and understandings that Proxmire reluctantly agreed to accept. The implementing legislation became known as "The Proxmire Act," despite the senator's disapproval of the practice of naming legislation for sponsors. On November 25, 1988, only weeks before the fortieth anniversary of the Convention's 1948 approval by the UN General Assembly, the United States deposited instruments of ratification at the UN headquarters. Soon after this, Proxmire retired from the Senate. He announced his treatment for Alzheimer's disease in 1998.

SEE ALSO Convention on the Prevention and Punishment of Genocide; United States Foreign Policies Toward Genocide and Crimes Against Humanity

BIBLIOGRAPHY

Korey, William (1998). *NGO's and the Universal Declaration of Human Rights: A Curious Grapevine.* New York: St. Martin's Press.

Power, Samantha (2002). *A Problem from Hell: America and the Age of Genocide.* New York: Basic Books.

James T. Fussell

Psychology of Perpetrators

In the years immediately following the Holocaust, studies tended to associate the horrendous genocidal acts with pathological personalities. This was understandable as it reflected a common social need: If one could attribute the Holocaust to specific bad or insane types of people, the future might seem different. All that was then necessary was to screen out the potential killers and prevent them from completing such evil acts, and the world would become a safe place once again. It took a great deal of human insight from philosophers such as Hannah Arendt and research by social psychologists such as Stanley Milgram and Phillip G. Zimbardo to understand the so-called banality of evil: that for the most part normal people, sometimes even well-educated people, carried out the industrialized killing of the Jews, Romani, Jehovah's Witnesses, and mentally ill in Nazi Germany. These findings were especially disturbing, as they suggested the conditions in which genocidal acts sprout and spread need to be controlled. Thus, the viewpoint developed that people are not usually born with genocidal mentalities; such a mentality is developed and created by the architects of genocide and their societies. Although this proposition has been mostly offered within the context of the Holocaust, it could be applied to other genocides as well.

When analyzing the question of genocidal mentalities, one has first to consider the architects who carefully plan the process, and usually these are people with sophisticated, although not necessarily formal, psychological understanding. These architects determine how to turn peaceful citizens into vicious killers. They know that most citizens will resist becoming killers, if presented with a choice. The careful planning and subsequent socialization of people into genocidal roles are therefore essential elements in developing genocidal mentalities. In certain genocidal systems the architects initially seek individuals who have a previous record of criminality or sadistic pathological characteristics. Still, massive genocidal acts require many more killers than the available sadists or criminals in a society. Usually, younger men are the first to be recruited, based on the assumption that it is easier to manipulate and train them as killers because they are more receptive to authority figures. But once there are not enough young men, more mature people will also be recruited to carry out genocide (as happened during the Holocaust and also in Bosnia and Rwanda during the 1990s).

In order to socialize ordinary men (such socialization usually occurs with men, although there are exceptions to this rule) to adopt genocidal mentalities, several factors have to be taken into consideration. Ordinary men are usually part of a social and moral network that helps them maintain their humanity toward others and prevents them from becoming involved in inhuman acts. In order to socialize them into becoming murderers, they have to be insulated from their original social network and an alternative network has to be created for the potential killers, composed of men like themselves, led by a genocidal authority. This is not an easy a task to achieve, and therefore careful attention needs to be given to the process that the potential killers are led through.

To successfully achieve insulation, the architects of genocide have to be equipped with strong mechanisms

for social indoctrination. They have to maintain full control of the reward and punishment system for the men assigned to conduct the killing. The planners of genocide can provide potential killers with food and social advancement, and they can also decide to kill them if they do not comply with orders. They may even promise potential killers entry into paradise, with seventy virgins waiting for them (as was the case with Muslim suicide bombers in the early twenty-first century). The planners must provide potential killers with a convincing rationale for committing genocidal acts. This rationale should include a moral or positive goal achieved by the genocide (e.g., "purity of the race" and "eliminating the cancer of our nation"), combined with monolithic dehumanization and devaluation of the target population (e.g., "They are bad: the bacteria of our society"). There is usually a paradoxical message in this rationale: The target population is seen as being both strong (the threat) and weak (they can be easily killed), but the clear division between the good (us) and the evil (them) is stronger than this paradox. Ethnic differences can easily be used to develop such a rationale, especially when there is a history of ethnic tension, oppression, and exclusion. As already mentioned, the architects of genocide must devise a careful, gradual process that will enable peaceful citizens to slowly adapt to the mode of becoming killers. And, of course, they have to provide the killers with the technical means to effectively carry out the genocidal acts, which are usually culture-bound, such as the use of chemicals (Zyklon B) in Germany and machetes in Rwanda.

Social Conditions That Support Insulation of Mass Murder

How do the architects of genocide succeed in so completely insulating the designated killers from the rest of their society? It is an easier to achieve this insulation and plan genocidal acts when the society involved is in economic, ethnic, cultural, or military crisis and there is ambiguity in regard to its own future. In a society in which many people have lost their jobs, the religious or cultural belief systems are threatened, people exclude an ethnic group, or where killing or humiliation is a daily occurrence, it is easier to instigate the rationale for a genocidal system, based on insulation, because the rationale for a very strong corrective act and monolithic identity seems to be available and widespread. But even when some of these conditions are lacking, talented planners (e.g., Slobodan Milosevic in former Yugoslavia) found in distant history (the fourteenth century) an event that could be manipulated to trigger such strong sentiments of collective injury and humiliation—especially in an ethnically diverse and tense society—thereby providing the necessary strong rationale for developing a genocidal process. The exclusion and scapegoating of the target population may have the character of projective identification. This process is known to arise when addressing internal social tensions or conflicts may seem too frightening to openly address.

In many cases, however, such will still not be enough, because moral or religious convictions, or the belief that they are civilized will not allow people to take part in genocidal acts. Therefore, the architects of genocide have to develop a sophisticated system of disinformation, deceit, and cover-up. This manipulation of language, on one hand, creates the necessary insulation of potential killers from their social network and criticism, and on the other, deceives the target population. This is why the slogan *Arbeit Macht Frei* ("work liberates") welcomed new inmates at the entrance to Auschwitz. The Nazi genocide was referred to as the Final Solution, and Jews were shipped to the East for supposed work and resettlement. When the train transports arrived at the death camps, physicians carried out the selection process as if it were based on some medical logic. The perceived healers were made to perform killing acts.

The reason why society at large does not usually resist or oppose such behavior is associated with the careful planning mentioned above. People are mostly not aware of the planning phases of genocide, that is, the deception and disinformation practiced by the architects, together with the sophisticated methods they have used to develop genocidal mentalities. Most people are not aware of the mechanisms of insulation, gradual socialization, and indoctrination used to socialize the murderers. Perhaps, in addition, there is the general human tendency to keep out of trouble, to turn a blind eye, as it were, especially when living in a regime that manipulates and instigates fear of an enemy to account for current crises.

Can quiet citizens suddenly become perpetrators, without a long socialization process? There are several such known cases, especially when the social atmosphere has already legitimized genocidal acts. For example, in Austria toward the end of World War II, several inmates of the Mauthausen concentration camp succeeded in escaping. The people who lived in the villages around the camp had long been aware of the atrocities taking place near their homes and did not mind; perhaps they even supported them. When the inmates escaped, some villagers took their hunting rifles and working tools and ventured into the woods to hunt for the escapees. These individuals had not been trained to carry out genocide, but could participate in murderous acts willingly, because they had been ex-

posed long enough to the genocidal atmosphere of their society. A society steeped in genocidal acts can become genocidal at large, without the socialization mentioned earlier.

The following question could still be asked: What motivates so many people to actively take part in the massive killing during genocide? Besides the socialization described above, is it indifference, fear, or actual hatred, or is it perhaps a combination of all three? Although most scholars agree about fear, scholars such as Daniel J. Goldhagen tend to emphasize the hatred toward the Jews, its long tradition in Germany and other parts of Europe, and researchers such as Charles Browning prefer to emphasize indifference. The Nazis learned how to both manipulate and create the dehumanization of their victims, turning them into scapegoats for the inner contradictions that the perpetrators themselves could not face.

The Paradoxical Morality of Perpretrators

Do perpetrators see themselves as evil criminals? Not surprisingly, the answer to that question usually is no. Perpetrators invariably see themselves as moral people who simply did their job, completed their mission. A number of Nazi perpetrators, in retrospect, argued that they had participated in the killings of Jews and others against their will; otherwise, they or their families would have been in danger. However, such rationalizations often surface when society has already denounced the atrocities the perpetrators committed. Moreover, supportive evidence for this argument does not exist. Goldhagen investigated one hundred cases involving Nazis who refused to participate in the shooting or gassing of Jews and other victims, and determined that nothing had happened to them: They were simply assigned other tasks within the regime.

How could the Nazi perpetrators of genocide and other atrocities maintain a "moral self-image"? In *The Nazi Doctors: Medical Killing and the Psychology of Genocide*, Robert Jay Lifton (1986) claims that they were able to maintain such a positive self-image through the psychological mechanism of doubling: That is, they succeeded in building a kind of inner wall between what they did at the killing site and how they continued to live their personal lives. There were very few people who collapsed during mass executions. One father, a deeply religious person, broke down after witnessing the execution of his Jewish workers near Para via Novo in Belarus. But he was the exception, which suggests that, as a rule, perpetrators learn to live with their atrocious acts. Some need to consume large quantities of drugs and/or alcohol in order to keep going. Others describe the process of becoming involved in atrocities as breaking through a threshold of sorts. Once they had killed the first person, the next was much easier and later anything was possible.

Interestingly, the Nazis specifically, and genocidal architects in general, paid attention to the potential psychological inhibitions of the executioners. While delivering a speech to the Nazi leadership in Posen in 1943, Heinrich Himmler referred directly to the "psychological hardships" of the executions. He stated that for the executors "This is an unwritten and never-to-be written page of glory in our history" but they would have to keep it secret and steer a middle course between "the task that made us hard" and "cases of human weakness" in relation to their victims (Charny and Rappaport, 1992, pp. 240–241).

After World War II, with the Nazi regime authoritative mental and physical support system gone, how did individual Nazi perpetrators manage to adjust to the postwar democratic government? One might have expected them to become criminals in any postwar society, continuing their former socialization. However, this was usually not the case: The past perpetrators readjusted quite well to the demands of the new social order and tried to conceal their previous participation in genocide. Was that stressful for them? For example, did they return to their religious congregations and confess to their priests about the atrocities they had committed? In one study in which eighty Christian clergy were interviewed, only two perpetrators were identified as having spoken in confession about their experiences during the war. One of these individuals, a former soldier, confessed that after being ordered to do so, he stabbed a six-year-old girl who ran to him from the ruins of the Warsaw ghetto after the Jewish uprising. He admitted that ever since the "brown eyes of this girl never gave him peace" (Bar-On, 1989, p. 196). Perhaps it was not a coincidence that he chose as his confessor a priest who was the son of a famous perpetrator. Two aspects of this confession are important:

1. There was a "double wall" between the perpetrators and their social surroundings that helped the former to maintain a conspiracy of silence about the atrocities they had committed in postwar Germany.

2. The perpetrators developed a kind of "paradoxical morality" after the war. Most of them did not become postwar criminals and were even attentive to the moral upbringing of their own children. With regard to any atrocities they committed, however, they usually only maintained a vivid memory of a single act about which they felt guilt and shame. With the help of this single memory they established a sense of their own humanity and repressed

the memory of all the other atrocities in which they had been involved. Had they recalled more, they would have faced the danger of moral disintegration and collapse.

SEE ALSO Explanation; Political Theory; Sociology of Perpetrators

BIBLIOGRAPHY

Arendt, Hannah (1963). *Eichmann in Jerusalem: Report on the Banality of Evil.* New York: Viking.

Bar-On, Dan (1989a). *Legacy of Silence: Encounters with Children of the Third Reich.* Cambridge, Mass.: Harvard University Press.

Bar-On, Dan (1989b). "Holocaust Perpetrators and Their Children: A Paradoxical Morality." *Journal of Humanistic Psychology* 29 (4):424–443.

Bar-On, Dan (1990). "The Use of a Limited Morality to Rationalize Horrendous Evil: Interviews with an Auschwitz Doctor and His Son." *Journal of Traumatic Stress* 3:415-427.

Bauman, Z. (1989). *Modernity and the Holocaust.* Ithaca, N.Y.: Cornell University Press.

Browning, Charles (1992). *Ordinary Men.* New York: HarperCollins.

Charny, I. W. and C. Rappaport (1982). *How Can We Commit the Unthinkable? Genocide: The Human Cancer.* Boulder, Colo.: Westview Press.

Darley, J. M. (1992). "Social Organization for the Production of Evil." *Psychological Inquiry* 3:199–218.

Dicks, H. V. (1972). *Licensed Mass Murder: A Social Psychological Study of Some SS Killers.* New York: Basic Books.

Gilbert, G. M. (1948). "Hermann Goering: Amiable Psychopath." *Journal of Abnormal and Social Psychology* 43:211–229.

Goldhagen, D. J. (1996). *Hitler's Willing Executioners: Ordinary Germans and the Holocaust.* New York: Knopf.

Klee, E., W. Dressen, and V. Riess (1991). *"The Good Old Days": The Holocaust as Seen by Its Perpetrators and Bystanders.* New York: Free Press.

Lifton, R. J. (1986). *The Nazi Doctors: Medical Killing and the Psychology of Genocide.* New York: Basic Books.

Milgram, S. (1974). *Obedience to Authority: An Experimental View.* New York: Harper & Row.

Reichart, E. (1995). *February Shadows.* Salzburg, Austria: Otto Mueller.

Staub, E. (1989). *The Roots of Evil: The Origins of Genocide and Other Group Violence.* New York: Cambridge University Press.

Waller, J. (2002). *Becoming Evil: How Ordinary People Commit Genocide and Mass Killing.* New York: Oxford University Press.

Zimbardo, P. G. (1972). "Pathology of Imprisonment." *Society* 6:4–8.

Dan Bar-On

Psychology of Survivors

Jewish survivors of the Holocaust were the first group of genocide victims to be systematically examined. Having an opportunity to follow their postwar adjustment for sixty years has enabled the rest of humanity to clearly understand the lifelong effects of such personal and group trauma.

Survivors of genocide are forever transformed. They speak of having lived three lives: their life before the genocide, their life during the genocide, and their life after the genocide. These individuals have experienced a shattering of basic human assumptions—that the world is safe, and that others will extend care and protection.

Memories of their terrifying experiences may involuntarily intrude on a daily basis. The sights, smells, and sensations associated with past trauma can be vividly recalled. At the same time survivors of genocide wish to move on with their life as rapidly and fully as possible. With many tragic exceptions they are successful at gathering the shattered remnants of their pregenocidal self, grafting them onto a postgenocidal self, and leading a relatively normal existence. However, unlike other victims of emotional traumas who wish to bury their past encounters with evil, survivors of genocide are committed to memory and the remembrance of all those who were lost.

Individuals who undergo extreme stress are often more psychologically vulnerable to future blows than nontraumatized persons. Furthermore, with increasing age survivors of genocide have more time to ruminate about past horrors, and this may diminish an already fragile sense of safety. On the other hand, many survivors of genocide develop an extraordinary life-long confidence in their ability to persevere through any adversity ("I survived *that*, I can survive anything!").

The most striking aftereffect of genocidal trauma is an ongoing, perennial sense of vulnerability. When asked "How did you survive?" most survivors answer, "Luck." Such a response acknowledges that many stronger and craftier people did not last, and that those who experienced countless close calls made split-second decisions based on little information, and witnessed the death of others who were less fortunate. The attribution of luck, may, however, have subtle implications. If one believes one is alive simply or mostly because of luck, one may live with considerable uneasiness. Just as life was given by chance, capriciousness may snatch it away.

Early reports on the impact of massive psychic trauma experienced by Holocaust survivors offered an extremely bleak picture. In 1964, after years of clinical experience in diagnosing and treating concentration camp survivors, William Niederland, a psychiatrist and a refugee from Nazi Germany, published a landmark study proclaiming the existence of a survivor syndrome. He listed a host of symptoms manifest in individuals who had survived Nazi persecution. They included chronic anxiety, fear of renewed persecution, depression, recurring nightmares, psychosomatic disorders, anhedonia (an inability to experience pleasure), social withdrawal, fatigue, hypochondria, an inability to concentrate, irritability, a hostile and mistrustful attitude toward the world, and a profound alteration of personal identity.

Other mental health professionals reported that survivors were overwhelmed by indelible and grotesque images of death. Survivors often isolated themselves because they believed no one could understand the horrors they had endured. They had been immersed in a different reality, the world of the *Lager* (camp), a world that would be absolutely incomprehensible to others. A sense of alienation naturally ensued.

The bleakest psychological snapshots of survivors of genocide are often taken soon after their ordeal, when the imprints of previous blows are most palpable, and when the individual has not yet accepted and adapted to a new life bereft of all those who were lost forever. However, most survivors suppress their posttrauma symptoms as they desperately want to get on with life once again, to look forward, not back. Indeed, the story of survivors of genocide is an example of human resilience and the primal desire to live as fully as possible.

It is important to note that, even when available, the great majority of genocide survivors never seek psychiatric treatment. Some survivors fear the transformation of a self-image predicated on a feeling of the uniqueness of one who has survived and conquered death to one who is mentally ill, from one who is unusually strong to one who is damaged. In addition, survivors do not wish to closely examine the compartmentalization of their past for fear of it spilling over uncontrollably onto their present reality. While fear, rage, and grief lurk in the background, the survivor attempts to keep him- or herself in the foreground, moving ahead to life and farther away from death. Survivors may unconsciously fear being blamed by a psychotherapist or other mental health professional for particular actions, or for their inactions during the genocide. Survivors are also convinced that no one who did not live in the midst of the genocide can possibly understand the motivation for their situational behavior or the psychological effects of those experiences.

Many victims of genocide suffer from what clinicians refer to as post-traumatic stress disorder. Having experienced intense fear, helplessness, and horror, these individuals live with recurrent, distressing recollections of the events, nightmares, flashbacks to past events that are felt so keenly it is as if they are occurring in the present, an oversensitivity to environmental cues reminiscent of the trauma, profound feelings of being different and subsequent estrangement from those who have not undergone savage cruelty, and a hypervigilence about new assaults on their person. Indeed, because their view of fellow human beings has become such a pessimistic one, victims of genocide assume that further brutalization is only a matter of time.

In order to truly understand the innocent victim of heinous crimes, one must know and appreciate the details of their experiences. Not all victims of a particular genocide endured the same brutalities or witnessed the same horrors. For example, during the reign of the Khmer Rouge in Cambodia, children were sometimes forced to kill their parents. In general, those parents whose children are genocidally murdered are often deeply impacted as well. The relationship of the perpetrator to the victim is important in determining the victim's reaction. In Rwanda the assaults were more devastating because they often came from neighbors and colleagues, people known to the sufferers.

Young children may be particularly vulnerable to the effects of violence because their coping mechanisms are undeveloped and their slight stature increases their sense of vulnerability. Traumatic effects may include anxiety, nightmares, fears of being alone, aggressive behavior, regression in toilet training and language, in addition to an inhibition of their natural drives for autonomy and the exploration of their environment. Very young children, in particular, require secure, sensitive, responsive caregivers in order to establish a basic sense of security and trust in the world. Without that foundation they may find it difficult to establish meaningful attachments later in life. If their parents were victims of genocide, these mothers and fathers may be too preoccupied with their own losses to provide these psychological essentials. During the genocide adolescent victims may psychologically fare somewhat better than adults because they do not fully appreciate the gravity of the situation and succeed in denying the improbability of survival. Even in perilous times teenagers are prone to feeling invincible and anticipate an unending life.

In addition to their permanently changed sense of self, survivors of genocide may have other experiences of uprootedness as well. Physical dislocation from their communal roots creates an additional loss of familiarity, continuity, and sense of security. Many of those who were religiously devout before the trauma lose a critical anchor and source of strength, namely their faith in God and that higher power's ability to protect and provide justice. On the other hand certain spiritual precepts may soften the blow. For example, a belief in karma may induce the calming sensation of inevitability.

Finally, one need not be personally brutalized in order to be traumatized. Witnessing violence perpetrated against another innocent may arouse intense fear and helplessness. One assumes, "If it could happen to that person, it could happen to me."

Survivor Guilt

Survivor guilt is the term used to describe the feelings of those who fortunately emerge from a disaster that mortally engulfs others. On an irrational level these individuals wince at their privileged escape from death's clutches. Guilt is the penance they pay for survival. Moreover, this penance contributes to them remaining mired in their hellish past.

Survivor guilt is most marked soon after the traumatic event. It is difficult to maintain an awareness of guilt feelings for a protracted period, particularly when one is keenly motivated to move forward with one's life. Most likely to feel the protracted discomfit of survivor guilt are those whose children were murdered while they felt powerless to intervene. Survivors not only torture themselves with memories of what they did in order to survive, but also what they failed to do in order to help others.

Survivors are haunted by the question: Why me? Often they are convinced that the best did not survive, and, they, therefore, are less deserving of life. Sole surviving members of a family are more likely to experience survivor guilt than those who were left with a parent or sibling.

Innocent human beings crave acknowledgment of the unwarranted pain induced by others. However, those survivors of genocide who did not experience the worst genocidal brutalities often inhibit themselves from speaking of their ordeals. This deference to those who survived worse circumstances prevents them from receiving any recognition of their suffering.

Transmission of Trauma

The traumatic impact of genocide extends beyond the victim to at least one succeeding generation. All children of survivors of genocide are affected in some manner, although the effects widely vary in their form and intensity. The debilitating effects of genocide on the second generation are clearly not as consuming as they may be for those who had direct contact with persecution. There is, moreover, a relationship between the severity of traumatic aftereffects on the parent (particularly the mother) and the child. The greater the pain evidenced by the parent, the more likely it is to infect the child.

Expectations of further assault are communicated by survivors to their children. The irrational, frightened reactions of survivors to seemingly benign stimuli may produce a generalized uneasiness in their offspring. Survivors' pessimistic view of humanity often induces mistrust and exaggerated fears in their children, particularly their daughters. Moreover, survivors' attempts to shield their children from anticipated harm can lead to an unhealthy overprotectiveness and interfere with the normal separation process that must occur between parent and child.

Survivors of genocide may look to their children to compensate for their losses. Survivor mothers, in particular, may live vicariously through their daughters. In an attempt to psychologically move away from the catastrophe as quickly as possible and begin a new life, survivors may enter poorly matched marriages, thereby increasing the pressures on their children to provide gratification to their parents. Preoccupied with their tragic past, survivors may have little empathy for the everyday, normal tribulations of their children ("You think that's a problem?"). For some survivors their depression, emotional numbness, and fear of future losses may prevent them from forging a deep, loving bond with anyone, including their own sons and daughters.

Survivors may inhibit the normal rebelliousness of their children by explicitly referring to their past ("How could you do this to me after all I have been through?") or using the implicit plea of their ongoing symptoms. Children of survivors may despair at not being able to relieve the pain of their parents or compensate for their losses. Not surprisingly, many children of survivors display an ambivalence when relating to their parent's traumatic past. Depression may result from an overidentification with the parent. On the other hand, in an attempt to shield themselves from the pain and vulnerability of a survivor, children may be prone to guilt feelings if they attempt to sever themselves from any psychological connection to the genocide.

It is of singular importance to the survivors of genocide that their losses and the cruelty to which they were subjected be recognized. When the perpetrators of genocide are brought to justice, the profound sense of injustice experienced by the survivor may be somewhat attenuated. Conversely, when there is no retribu-

tion, the psychic wounds of survivors fester even more. Unfortunately, the traumatic effects of genocide clearly extend even beyond the individual and the family. They infect group identity and perpetuate an ongoing sense of grievance and defensiveness as further assaults are expected. For survivors of genocide the world will never feel safe again.

SEE ALSO Collaboration; Psychology of Perpetrators

BIBLIOGRAPHY

Améry, Jean (1986). *At the Mind's Limit.* New York: Schocken.

Hass, Aaron (1990). *In the Shadow of the Holocaust: The Second Generation.* Ithaca, N.Y.: Cornell University Press.

Hass, Aaron (1995). *The Aftermath: Living with the Holocaust.* New York: Cambridge University Press.

Kertész, Imre (1996). *Fateless.* Evanston, Ill.: Hydra Books.

Krystal, Henry, ed. (1968). *Massive Psychic Trauma.* New York: International Universities Press.

Niederland, William (1964). "Psychiatric Disorders among Persecution Victims: A Contribution to the Understanding of the Concentration Camp Pathology and Its Aftereffects." *Journal of Nervous and Mental Diseases* 139:458–474.

Aaron Hass

Psychology of Victims

When one enters a new situation, one looks for familiar signposts to provide direction for the appropriate adaptive behavior. However, the concentration camp was a universe that had never before been encountered or imagined. Because of the camp's incomparable nature, the inmate's initial reaction on arrival was generally one of disorientation. The Nazis' deliberate strategy of having transports arrive in the middle of the night, clubbing prisoners out of the cattle cars into the blinding glare of spotlights, and terrorizing them by the sounds and sight of vicious barking dogs added to this disorientation.

Those who were not selected for death on arrival were immediately stripped of their individual identity. All inmates had their body hair shaved, were handed striped uniforms, and given a number to replace a name. Chronic starvation and hard labor soon contributed to a similar appearance. Daily humiliations due to unsanitary conditions, overcrowding, and beatings by the guards defined the inmate's existence. This degradation was purposeful as it reduced prisoners to an animal-like state, reinforcing the belief in their captors that they were, indeed, subhuman and deserving of such treatment. In general, Jews from Eastern European locations who had already endured a prolonged period of extreme deprivation were able to adapt more quickly and effectively to the camp's hardships than those arriving from Western Europe, where persecution had not been as severe prior to their deportation.

Inmates were subjected to recurrent episodes of terror. At the *appel* (roll call) each morning, selections were made to determine who would be killed and who would be spared. Inmates were continually exposed to the beatings and torture of other prisoners, thereby enhancing their sense of personal vulnerability. The senselessness and arbitrariness of these attacks provoked further feelings of powerlessness and dread. Bizarre and contradictory demands by their captors fueled the inmate's fear and impotence. For example, one had to appear as clean and healthy as possible in order to be allowed to live and provide slave labor for another day, and, yet, the means to achieve that appearance were absent. Inmates frequently resorted to washing themselves with their own urine.

Inmates seized any opportunity to increase their chance of survival. They had to find an edge. Procuring a job indoors might shield one from harsh weather conditions. It became imperative to find some way to augment one's daily rations as the limited amounts of food allotted could not sustain an individual over a prolonged period, particularly in such arduous circumstances. Although some survivors have described an utterly selfish, "every man for himself" mentality in the camps, others have emphasized that they would not have emerged alive had it not been for a relationship they forged with another inmate, which provided physical and emotional sustenance.

The inmate had to remain hyper-alert, in order to both avoid further difficulty and pounce on any possible advantage. Emotional numbing was also adaptive. Allowing oneself to feel sadness or terror would have produced internal weakness and the possibility of paralysis in an environment that required quick thinking and nimble behavior. The expression of rage might have resulted in mortal punishment.

In order to escape the continuous onslaught of humiliation and terror, the prisoner sought succor, and even pleasure, in fantasy. Pleasant fantasies of prewar family life were common. Due to the fact that prisoners were often abruptly separated from family members either during round-ups, deportations, or selections on arrival at the camps, they clung to the hope and fantasy of being reunited with them. Some inmates seized restful moments and retreated into a spiritual frame of mind.

In an environment in which death was omnipresent and life hung by a tenuous thread, the inmates found ways to bolster some sense of control over their fate. Small decisions (e.g., "Should I eat my ration now or save it for later?") took on exaggerated psychological significance. Petty victories (e.g., securing an extra piece of bread) over the concentration camp system were inordinately relished. Small pleasures became magnified.

In order to tolerate their dreadful ongoing condition, inmates had to find powerful reasons to continue. They hoped to reunite with family. They committed themselves to bear witness for all those who could not. They refused to allow the extinction of the Jewish people. A few dreamt of revenge. Some of those who could not find a powerful enough reason to endure the continuous assaults on their person impaled themselves on the camp's electrified fence. Others simply became passive, and this stance doomed them. Fatalism was fatal. The profound apathy of this group could be seen in the familiar, vacant stare of the prisoner who was referred to as a *musselman*. Inmates immediately recognized such an individual as not long for this world.

Human beings can endure much pain and suffering if they know that a reasonable end point is in sight. For the concentration camp inmate, unfortunately, a Thousand Year Reich seemed increasingly evident. (Indeed, toward the end of the war rumors of the approaching Russian army immediately buoyed spirits in the camp.) To combat this demoralizing factor of indefiniteness, inmates adopted a short perspective of daily survival. To assess the possibility of survival for months or years would have produced demoralization. They also utilized the powerful psychological defense mechanism of denial. Inmates had to deny the overwhelming odds against their survival. "If I keep working and do not bring attention to myself, I will survive," the inmate repeatedly intoned.

Even after one survived the initial life-or-death selection on arrival, the concentration camp system of hard labor, meager rations, and horrific conditions was designed to kill that same inmate within a relatively brief period of time. In the end certain personal qualities—resourcefulness, flexibility, vigilance, the ability to make split-second decisions based on little information, physical hardiness—were necessary in order to outlast the tormentors until the day of liberation. Having (or pretending to have) a useful skill helped make one seem momentarily indispensable. But, because opportunities for effecting the environment were so limited, one had to rely, to a great extent, on intra-psychic coping mechanisms such as denial and retreating into fantasy to diminish the horrific impact of one's world. Yet, despite all these necessary personal qualities and coping strategies, survivors will say that the overwhelming, critical factor in determining whether one inmate would die and another would live until liberation was luck: not being in the wrong place at the wrong time, not being capriciously assaulted by a sadistic guard, not being subjected to the mortal whim of your captor, or not being confined to conditions akin to the worst in hell. This realization of the capriciousness of life and death remained with survivors after liberation and, understandably, impacted their post-Holocaust approach to life and view of humanity.

SEE ALSO Psychology of Perpetrators; Psychology of Survivors

BIBLIOGRAPHY

Améry, Jean (1986). *At the Mind's Limit*. New York: Schocken.

Hass, Aaron (1995). *The Aftermath: Living with the Holocaust*. New York: Cambridge University Press.

Levi, Primo (1959). *Survival in Auschwitz*. New York: Macmillan.

Levi, Primo (1988). *The Drowned and the Saved*. New York: Summit.

Wiesel, Elie (1958). *Night*. New York: Bantam.

Aaron Hass

Punishment

Although nations speak out strongly against the crime of genocide and crimes against humanity, these same nations have done very little to punish individuals accused of committing such heinous acts. Prosecution and the subsequent penalties imposed for genocide and crimes against humanity, while gaining momentum through international support, remain rare. Practice is sparse, but a significant shift is evident in attitudes toward the applicable penalties for genocide and crimes against humanity since these acts were first punished in 1946.

Purposes of Punishment
Scholars and criminologists describe two main purposes of punishment—utilitarian and retributive. The first includes attempts at deterrence and incapacitation, whereas the second focuses more on the notion of just deserts or the ancient pronouncement of "an eye for an eye." Theoretical approaches to punishment have been studied and advanced by such renowned scholars as Hugo Grotius, Cesare Beccaria, Immanuel Kant, Jeremy Bentham, Michael Foucault, and John Rawls.

Beccaria believed that the certainty of some punishment, in whatever form, was more likely to deter future criminal acts than the imposition of a severe pun-

ishment. The key to deterrence under Beccaria's view was assurance that a swift punishment would follow the criminal act. Beccaria, a utilitarian, advocated immediate and proportionate sentences. Punishment, to be just and effective, could be only as severe as necessary to ensure that others would not commit similar offenses. Bentham and Grotius were also advocates of the utilitarian approach.

In contrast to Beccaria's philosophy, Immanuel Kant adhered to retribution as a basis for punishment. Under Kant's theory, those who committed crimes deserved to be punished. In fact, Kant believed that those who committed crimes needed to be punished. One of the more common justifications for the death penalty is retribution. Retributivists believe that those who murder deserve to die. A modern disciple of the retributive theory is Andrew von Hirsch. And, in modern application, the International Criminal Tribunal for the Former Yugoslavia (ICTY) quoted Kant during the sentencing proceedings for General Radislav Krstic, reminding spectators that, as Kant believed, if justice is ignored, life on this earth has no value.

In truth many punishments reflect more than one approach. Some punishments even adopt a rehabilitative component recognizing that convicts are often reintegrated into society on completion of their sentence. The most recent example, the Rome Statute establishing the International Criminal Court (ICC), combines the utilitarian and retributive approaches to punishment. At least one punishment theory scholar, Nigel Walker, has noted that consideration of mitigating and aggravating factors in sentencing suggests a retributive theory of punishment. Both current United Nations (UN) tribunals, the ICTY and the International Criminal Tribunal for Rwanda (ICTR), embrace the notion of aggravating and mitigating factors in determining sentence. The ICC likewise envisions a penalty scheme that assesses both aggravating and mitigating factors for sentencing purposes.

Prohibitions and Penalties in Law
Throughout recorded history, there have been many pronouncements and declarations calling for prosecution and punishment of acts constituting genocide and crimes against humanity. These pronouncements, however, have not always had the force of law or the agreement of all nation-states. In the seventeenth century Hugo Grotius, considered by many to be the father of international law, published *The Law of War and Peace*. In this major work Grotius discussed the nature of punishment as it relates to crimes committed during war and devoted an entire chapter to those penalties that might be appropriate for punishing individual war

criminals. Although many describe Grotius's approach as utilitarian, he defined punishment generally as signifying "the pain of suffering which is inflicted for evil actions." Grotius dedicated a great deal of his penalty chapter to comparing the divine right to punish with human law and the laws of nature. He clearly disfavored revenge as a motive for punishment, underscoring that such a basis is "condemned by both Christian teachers and heathen philosophers." However, Grotius emphasized the proportionality component of utilitarian punishment, reminding his readers that "[i]t is undoubtedly one of the first principles of justice to establish an equality between the penalty and offense."

The first national code defining crimes of war and applicable penalties was a direct by-product of the American Civil War. Upon witnessing the atrocities committed on the battlefield during that conflict, Professor Charles Lieber was inspired to draft a code of conduct for soldiers during warfare. This code was officially adopted as General Orders 100: Instructions for the Government of Armies of the United States in the Field and unofficially became known simply as the Lieber Code. The Lieber Code presented an extensive list of prohibited behavior during war—including applicable penalties—and was adopted by President Abraham Lincoln in 1863. Thereafter copies of the Lieber Code were distributed to the American military and it became the governing law for all U.S. soldiers. Under the code soldiers who committed atrocities on the battlefield or against an enemy civilian population could be subjected to severe penalty, including death.

Crimes against humanity and genocide have been clearly outlawed in treaties and many domestic legal systems since the late 1940s. The 1948 UN Convention on the Prevention and Punishment of the Crime of Genocide (the Genocide Convention), which entered into force on January 12, 1951, does not specify what measure of punishment is appropriate for crimes defined under the Convention. Rather, the Convention outlaws genocidal acts, conspiracy to commit genocide, incitement to commit genocide, and attempts to commit genocide. Article V specifies that contracting parties shall provide the "necessary legislation to give effect to the provisions of [the Convention], and in particular, to provide effective penalties for persons guilty of genocide." No definition of "effective penalties" is given.

Similarly, the four Geneva Conventions of 1949 do not identify any penalties for violations arising under these treaties but merely outlaw acts that qualify as "grave breaches," that is, war crimes. These early attempts at proscribing international crimes did not explicitly provide a clear list of possible penalties or prof-

fer any guidance regarding what penalty scheme would be acceptable. Instead, tribunals and courts could resort to any penalty scheme deemed just—including, frequently, penalties of death.

Modern international law illustrates a change in approach regarding punishment for international crimes. In 1993 and 1994 the UN created two ad hoc international tribunals to punish crimes committed in Yugoslavia and Rwanda. The statutes creating the two tribunals strictly limit punishment to terms of imprisonment. This modern approach was followed in the Rome Statute creating the ICC. Article 77 of the Rome Statute limits penalties for violations committed under the statute to prison terms and possible fines.

Although the death penalty has been discarded by most nation-states and is a prohibited penalty before the modern international tribunals, including the ICTY, ICTR, and ICC, certain domestic statutory schemes still permit resort to capital punishment for crimes of genocide and crimes against humanity. Thus, the question of whether the death penalty is an available option for the punishment of genocide or crimes against humanity depends on the character of the tribunal involved. The most stark example of this distinction can be seen in the disparity of punishment between the ICTR and the domestic Rwandan courts. Defendants facing justice before the ICTR are protected from capital punishment by the ICTR statute. In contrast, individual defendants tried domestically by Rwandan courts have been sentenced to death. The Rome Statute prohibits resort to capital punishment and, thus, no ICC defendant will be, or can be, sentenced to death.

Historical Punishment
The first recorded international adjudication for war crimes, including allegations of rape and murder, involved Sir Peter von Hagenbach. Von Hagenbach was tried and found guilty by what many scholars believe was the first international tribunal established to address atrocities committed during war. In 1474 a panel of international judges convicted von Hagenbach. In sentencing, the court not only condemned von Hagenbach to death, but also stripped him of his title as knight and took from him all the privileges attendant to his rank. Thus, the first international tribunal for war crimes imposed the first international death sentence and a penalty that focused on the shameful nature of the crimes, by depriving von Hagenbach and his family of the privileges to which they had been previously entitled by virtue of his title.

Nearly four hundred years later humanity witnessed the second major punishment imposed for crimes committed during war. In 1865 Captain Henry

Russian guards in formation outside Berlin's Spandau Prison, where former Nazis Rudolf Hess, Albert Speer, and Baldur von Shirach were incarcerated after their 1946 conviction by the International Military Tribunal at Nuremberg. Spandau was demolished following Hess's death. [HULTON-DEUTSCH COLLECTION/CORBIS]

Wirz, a Swiss-born doctor and solider in the Confederate Army, was prosecuted and convicted by a controversial military commission following the U.S. Civil War. Wirz was held responsible for overseeing the operations of the Andersonville Prison, officially known as Camp Sumter, in Andersonville, Georgia. Under his command many prisoners perished as a result of extremely poor conditions. The indictment also charged that Wirz was directly responsible for the murder of thirteen individuals at Andersonville. Upon conviction for murder in violation of the laws and customs of war, Wirz was sentenced to hang for his crimes and was later executed.

The evolving doctrine relating to punishment for war crimes and crimes against humanity appeared to take a very severe and unyielding approach, but few individuals faced prosecution or punishment. This sporadic approach toward prosecution and punishment is most clearly illustrated in the aftermath of World War I. The Treaty of Versailles signed on June 28, 1919, officially brought the war to an end. It reserved an entire section, Section VII, and four distinct articles, Articles

227 through 230, for the issue of "penalties." Furthermore, Article 227 explicitly provided that the former German Emperor, Kaiser Wilhelm II of Hohenzollern, was to be publicly arraigned "for a supreme offense against international morality and the sanctity of treaties." The treaty envisioned the creation of an international tribunal to prosecute the Kaiser and military commissions for the prosecution of "persons accused of having committed acts in violation of the laws and customs of war." No specific penalties were set forth or identified in the section on penalties. Rather, the treaty simply called for penalties "laid down by law."

Kaiser Wilhelm II would never be punished for his alleged crimes. The lesser defendants covered by Article 228 of the Treaty of Versailles were effectively protected from punishment when the Allied forces delegated the responsibility for trying these individuals to the defeated nation of Germany. The Allied forces initially demanded that 896 Germans face trial for their crimes and misdeeds committed during World War I. Germany balked at the extensive list and ultimately agreed to prosecute a mere twelve individuals.

The Supreme Court of Germany at Leipzig tried the twelve persons accused of committing crimes during war. Three of them were convicted, while the remaining nine were acquitted of all charges. The three convicted war criminals received the following sentences: six months, ten months, and two years in prison. It is doubtful that these sparse convictions and equally terse penalties embodied the criminal solution proposed in the Treaty of Versailles.

The most renowned international tribunal to prosecute war crimes, crimes against humanity, and crimes against peace was undoubtedly the Nuremberg Tribunal. Nuremberg, officially known as the International Military Tribunal (IMT), was established to assess the criminal responsibility of the main architects of World War II. Created and governed by the Charter of the International Military Tribunal, which was annexed to the London agreement on August 8, 1945, the Nuremberg Tribunal prosecuted only twenty-three individuals—including one defendant in absentia.

Of the twenty-two defendants physically present and facing justice at Nuremberg, eighteen individuals were indicted for crimes against humanity and sixteen were found guilty. The IMT took a very stern approach toward penalizing the convicted, as twelve of the sixteen were sentenced to death by hanging. Despite cries of "victor's justice," many scholars note that Nuremberg represented an improvement over Joseph Stalin and Winston Churchill's unsuccessful pleas for summary execution. The remaining four convicts received prison sentences ranging from life imprisonment (one defendant) to twenty years (two defendants) to a sentence of fifteen years in prison (one defendant). When one compares the gravity of sentences handed down at Nuremberg, it is notable that those who were not convicted of crimes against humanity were all spared the death penalty, with two individuals receiving life sentences (Rudolf Hess and Erich Raeder) and one (Karl Dönitz) receiving a sentence of ten years.

The Allied forces undertook additional prosecutions of Germans for crimes against humanity and other offenses of war pursuant to Control Council Law No. 10. Of 185 defendants in seven cases alleging crimes against humanity, seventy-eight individuals were convicted. The sentences imposed ranged from death (twenty-four defendants) to life imprisonment (eighteen defendants) to various prison terms between twenty-five and five years. Not all the death sentences were carried out. Furthermore, although numerous prison sentences were also imposed (eighteen life sentences, two sentences of twenty-five years, nine sentences of twenty years, nine sentences of fifteen years, twelve sentences of ten years, one sentence of eight years, two sentences of seven years, and one sentence of five years), most defendants were released well before their sentences had been fully served. Historian Peter Maguire reported that the majority of sentences imposed under Control Council Law No. 10 were paroled between 1949 and 1958—barely a decade after the end of World War II.

War crimes committed by the Japanese in the Pacific theater also resulted in the creation of an international military tribunal—the International Military Tribunal for the Far East, more commonly referred to as the Tokyo Tribunal. The Charter of the Tokyo Tribunal was proclaimed by U.S. General Douglas MacArthur without major deviation from the Nuremberg Charter. Similar to the punishments imposed at Nuremberg, the Tokyo Tribunal meted out seven death sentences (General Doihara Kenji, Baron Hirota Koki, General Seishrio Itagaki, General Kimura Heitaro, General Matsui Iwane, General Muto Akira, and General Tojo Hideki) and eighteen prison sentences. The main dispute at Tokyo was not the guilt of the defendants, as all were convicted on at least one count, but rather, the nature of the punishment handed down to each defendant.

At Tokyo, unless a defendant was found guilty of committing a crime against humanity, the tribunal only imposed a punishment involving prison. It assessed sixteen life sentences and two lesser sentences of twenty and seven years, respectively. The seven death sentences imposed were carried out on December 23, 1948, at Sugamo Prison. Those who were not sentenced to die remained at Sugamo until their paroles

between 1949 and 1955. Here, just as at Nuremberg, the defendants were initially punished with relatively severe sentences. But also as with the individuals convicted at Nuremberg, those punished were often not required to serve their entire sentence. Of the eighteen individuals sentenced to imprisonment, all, except the six who died in prison, were released prior to the expiration of their respective sentences.

There were secondary prosecutions in Japan following the Tokyo Tribunal just like those conducted under Control Council Law No. 10 in Europe. Although the statistics for these tribunals are more difficult to catalogue, penalties imposed did not differ markedly from either those meted out at Tokyo or those imposed under Control Council Law No. 10. The two most common penalties included death sentences and prison sentences. And, as occurred with the other World War II tribunals, very few individuals were required to serve out their initial sentence and, if not executed quickly, either received a reprieve or were paroled from prison early.

Thus, the historical approaches to punishment can best be summarized by the sentences imposed at Nuremberg and Tokyo. Of those individuals who were convicted of crimes against humanity committed during World War II, most were given a sentence of death. Of those whose crimes were of a lesser character, however, most defendants were burdened with a prison sentence of some length that was partially served out at either Landsberg or Spandau Prison in Germany or Sugamo Prison in Japan. In both instances most prison terms were paroled within a decade after prosecution, well before the sentence would otherwise have expired.

The Modern Approach Toward Punishment

Two notable domestic prosecutions of Nazi defendants involved Klaus Barbie and Adolf Eichmann. Both were tried by domestic courts for crimes against humanity. A French court convicted Barbie of crimes against humanity and sentenced him to life in prison. He remained in a French prison until his death in 1991.

The trial of Eichmann is one of the most renowned in history. Eichmann fled Germany after escaping from an American prisoner-of-war camp. He was later kidnapped by Israeli officials while living in Argentina under a false name. Once the fervor regarding Eichmann's abduction diminished, he was tried under a 1950 Israeli law for crimes he committed during World War II. The Israeli law permitted prosecution for crimes against humanity and crimes against the Jews despite the fact that such acts had been committed several years prior to the creation of the state of Israel. Under many punishment schemes the application of a law to acts that occurred prior to its adoption constitutes an impermissible ex post facto application of law. Israel, however, did not interpret its law in this fashion. In December 1961, Eichmann was found guilty of all counts against him and sentenced to the same fate suffered by many at Nuremberg—death by hanging. Less than one year later his sentence was carried out by Israel.

In contrast to the spectrum of penalties available under domestic sentencing schemes, neither the death penalty nor any other form of corporeal punishment is available under any of the modern international tribunals—the ICTY, ICTR, or ICC. This limit represents a clear deviation from the historical efforts to punish crimes against humanity, where the death penalty was a common feature. Rather, both the ICTY and ICTR penalty schemes are specifically limited to terms of imprisonment. The language governing penalties is virtually identical under the ICTY and ICTR statutes. Both statutes provide initially that "[t]he penalty imposed by the Trial Chamber shall be limited to imprisonment." Thereafter, both statutes admonish that "[i]n determining the terms of imprisonment, the Trial Chambers shall have recourse to the general practice regarding prison sentences in the [domestic] courts [of Yugoslavia and Rwanda, respectively]." The second paragraph under these penalty provisions, Article 24 of the ICTY statute and Article 23 of the ICTR statute, provides that "[i]n imposing the sentences, the Trial Chamber should take into account such factors as the gravity of the offense and the individual circumstances of the convicted person." The Rules of Procedure and Evidence for both tribunals permit terms of imprisonment up to and including a life sentence. Rules 100 through 106 are related directly to penalties but provide very little additional guidance in relation to sentencing. Rule 101 provides only generally that the Trial Chambers should take into account both aggravating and mitigating circumstances in pronouncing sentence. Although the governing articles on punishment prohibit the imposition of fines or resort to corporeal punishment as a penalty, an explicit provision is made for the return of wrongfully obtained property or proceeds occurring as a result of the criminal conduct.

Another interesting distinction between the World War II tribunals, domestic prosecutions, and the modern-day UN tribunals is that there are no prearranged or permanent prison facilities for individuals convicted by the ICTY, ICTR, or the ICC. Rather, under the governing statutes, individuals convicted of crimes before these tribunals will be transferred to a cooperating state that has signed an agreement with the respective tribunal for the purpose of enforcing sen-

tences. During its first ten years, eight Western European nations signed sentence enforcement agreements with the ICTY: Italy (1997), Finland (1997), Norway (1998), Sweden (1999), Austria (1999), France (2000), Spain (2000), and Denmark (2002). In addition, Germany has entered into two ad hoc agreements with the ICTY to accept particular prisoners (Dusko Tadic and Dragoljub Kunarac). No North American, South American, Eastern European, Middle Eastern, Asian, or African country has agreed to accept prisoners sentenced by the ICTY.

The ICTR has an identical protocol for placing convicted individuals in the domestic prisons of cooperating states. Much like the paradigm at the ICTY, the countries that have agreed to accept ICTR prisoners are regionally restricted and include only African nations. For socio-cultural reasons the ICTR has specifically stated a preference for placing ICTR convicts with African states. During the ICTR's first ten years only three African nations (Mali, Benin, and the Kingdom of Swaziland) have agreed to accept its prisoners. Thus far only Mali has actually received ICTR convicts and, as of 2003, just a total of six prisoners.

The sentencing range for those finally convicted of genocide, crimes against humanity, and war crimes by the ICTY is between three and forty-six years in prison. Six individuals have received sentences of less than ten years, including Zlatko Aleksovski (seven years in prison—sent to Finland to serve his sentence), Damir Dosen (five years in prison—sent to Norway to serve his sentence), Drazen Erdemovic (five years in prison—sent to Norway to serve his sentence), Dragan Kolundzija (three years), Milokica Kos (six years in prison), and Zdravko Mucic (nine years in prison—released early after serving two-thirds of his sentence). All individuals whose sentences were less than ten years were released from custody on or before the ICTY's tenth anniversary.

In contrast three individuals have received a sentence of forty years or longer (General Tihomir Blaskic, Goran Jelisic, and Radislav Krstic). Only one individual, Milomar Stakic, has received a life sentence from the ICTY. Three individuals have received sentences of twenty years or longer: Radomir Kovac (twenty years), Dragoljub Kunarac (twenty-eight years), and Dusko Tadic (twenty years). Two individuals have received eighteen year sentences from the ICTY: Hazim Delic and Vladimir Santic. Two individuals have received sentences of fifteen years: Esad Landzo and Dusko Dikirica. The remaining five prisoners have been sentenced to terms ranging from twelve years (Drago Josipovic and Zoran Vukovic) to eleven years (Biljana Plavsic, the only female convicted by the ICTY) to ten years (Anto Furundzija and Stevan Todorovic). In many respects these sentences are similar to, although slightly less severe, than those meted out by the judges enforcing Control Council Law No. 10 in postwar Europe. The main distinction between the ICTY and the World War II tribunals is that no one appearing before the ICTY will receive the death penalty because this practice is not permitted under modern international tribunals. However, much like the World War II tribunals, individuals convicted by the ICTY stand a very solid chance of actually serving less time than the punishment initially imposed against them. In fact, several have already been granted early release by the tribunal.

From this small sampling before the ICTY, there is little information that can be gleaned about international sentencing policies. The ICTY and ICTR statutes both suggest that "[i]n imposing sentences, the Trial Chambers should take into account such factors as the gravity of the offense and the individual circumstances of the convicted person." This vague statement has not yielded any consistent pattern in actual sentencing practices. Rather, the tribunal must grapple with some of the most heinous crimes ever committed and carefully delineate a punishment meriting three years as opposed to ten as opposed to eighteen as opposed to forty. Because none of the main architects or perpetrators of the Yugoslavian genocide have yet been convicted, it may be entirely reasonable that only one ICTY defendant has received the most lasting punishment, life in prison. This sentence remains on appeal and may be changed.

In comparison, the ICTR, which is nearing its tenth anniversary, has issued eight final convictions against individuals for genocide, crimes against humanity, and war crimes. The sentencing range for persons convicted before the ICTR is between life in prison and twelve years' imprisonment. ICTR penalties seem more severe than those imposed by the ICTY. For example, five of the eight individuals convicted have been sentenced to life in prison: Jean-Paul Akayesu, Jean Kambanda, Clement Kayishema, Alfred Musema, and George Rutaganda. In contrast to the ICTY with its minimum sentence of three years, the minimum punishment imposed by the ICTR has been twelve years in prison. Furthermore, while the ICTY has sentenced six individuals to prison terms of less than ten years, the three ICTR defendants not receiving life sentences have been sentenced to twelve (George Ruggiu), fifteen (Omar Serushago), and twenty-five (Obed Ruzindana) years in prison. One possible explanation for the deviation between the ICTY and ICTR is that both statutes permit the Trial Chamber to consider the domestic sentencing practices in the applicable nations—the former

Yugoslavia and Rwanda. Although the Balkan nations have been reluctant to pursue any consistent course for domestic prosecutions, Rwanda has aggressively prosecuted and punished individual defendants for the country's 1994 genocide. Of the domestic Rwandan convictions occurring between December 1996 and January 2000, 15 percent of all defendants (roughly 370 individuals) have been sentenced to death, 32 percent of defendants (approximately 800 individuals) have been sentenced to life in prison, and 33 percent of defendants (approximately 830 individuals) have been sentenced to prison terms of varying lengths. The remaining 20 percent of domestic defendants (approximately 500 individuals) have been acquitted and, thus, received no sentence.

It is difficult in studying both the ICTY and ICTR to discern a clear mandate regarding international punishment for genocide and crimes against humanity. If the crimes committed in these regions were similar, one would expect some similarity in the courts' sentencing practices. A clear omission before both tribunals is any reference to gradations of punishment—penalties that become increasingly severe based on the crime committed and its underlying circumstances. There is not always a readily defensible or easily explainable reason why one individual received twelve years for participating in genocide while another defendant received life in prison. Both tribunals are permitted by their governing statutes to consider mitigating and aggravating factors in pronouncing sentence. The tribunals have considered a defendant's role in the crime, the defendant's position of leadership or authority (if any), the depravity of the crime, and the status of the victim (such as women, children, the elderly, or other vulnerable victims) as aggravating factors in determining sentence. Likewise, the tribunals have accepted the following as mitigating factors: the defendant's cooperation with the prosecutor, the defendant's lack of authority or position, the defendant's plea of guilty in saving tribunal resources, the defendant's family and personal circumstances, any acceptance of responsibility, and any expression of remorse.

Contemporary international tribunals have not, by either custom or statute, placed any consistent sentencing range on crimes falling within their jurisdiction. Rather, because there is no set range for crimes against humanity or genocide, despite the fact that such gradations or sentencing ranges appear in nearly every domestic punishment scheme, sentencing remains a discretionary exercise delimited only by the tribunals' governing statutes. Because the international community has not definitively placed any one crime, such as genocide, at the top of the hierarchy for sentencing purposes, tribunals have often pronounced their punishment without reference to any standard international penalty scheme. In certain instances judges could provide a more severe sentence for crimes against humanity than might be imposed for genocide despite the much greater intent that is required to secure a prosecution for genocide. Thus, it is difficult to project with any certainty what sentence lengths will be imposed by either tribunal as they assess the guilt of the numerous individuals still awaiting prosecution.

The Future
The penalty scheme embraced by the ICC underscores the movement toward more standardized punishment—prison and fines only. Although the Rome Statute does not create gradations for crimes committed or provide any solid guidance relating to punishment, the law established by its predecessor institutions (the IMT at Nuremberg, the Tokyo Tribunal, the ICTY, and the ICTR) should shed some light on the punishment of future atrocities. As prosecutions for these heinous acts increase, there is a greater likelihood that the penalties will become more certain and the bases for punishments more consistently articulated and applied. However, until these international tribunals establish a more structured approach to punishment, future defendants can be sure of only one thing—an international conviction for genocide or crimes against humanity will, at most, result in a prison term to be determined by an international court. A fine or the opportunity for reparations may follow, but international law only allows for penalties that begin with imprisonment.

Rule 145 of the ICC Rules of Procedure and Evidence provides some measure of guidance in determining sentences. First, Rule 145 states that the court shall "[b]ear in mind that the totality of any sentence of imprisonment and fine, as the case may be, imposed under Article 77 must reflect the culpability of the convicted person." Next, Rule 145 mandates that the court "[b]alance all the relevant factors, including any mitigating and aggravating factors and consider the circumstances both of the convicted person and of the crime." The court is further admonished to consider the following factors, although they are not specifically labeled as either mitigating or aggravating factors: the extent of damage caused—especially in relation to the victims and their families; the nature of the unlawful behavior and the means employed to execute the crime; the degree of participation of the convicted person; the degree of intent; the circumstances of time, manner, and location of the crime; and the individual circumstances of the offender, especially as they relate to the individual's age, education, and socioeconomic status.

In addition to the litany of variables listed for consideration in punishment, Rule 145 further requires that the Court shall take into account, as appropriate:

(a) Mitigating circumstances such as:
  (i) The circumstances falling short of constituting grounds for exclusion of criminal responsibility, such as substantially diminished mental capacity or duress;
  (ii) The convicted person's conduct after the act, including any efforts by the person to compensate the victims and any cooperation with the Court;

(b) As aggravating circumstances:
  (i) Any relevant prior criminal convictions for crimes under the jurisdiction of the Court or of a similar nature;
  (ii) Abuse of power or official capacity;
  (iii) Commission of the crime where the victim is particularly defenseless;
  (iv) Commission of the crime with particular cruelty or where there were multiple victims;
  (v) Commission of the crime for any motive involving discrimination on any of the grounds referred to in article 21, paragraph 3; [and],
  (vi) Other circumstances which, although not enumerated above, by virtue of their nature are similar to those mentioned.

Under the ICC sentencing paradigm in Article 77(b), a life sentence may only be imposed when justified by the extreme gravity of the crime and the individual circumstances of the convicted person, as evidenced by the existence of one or more aggravating factors.

The ICC provides hope that punishment for crimes against humanity and genocide will serve one of the underlying purposes of punishment—deterrence. It would be a welcome advancement if humanity no longer needed a tribunal to evaluate the guilt of individuals accused of committing acts of genocide or crimes against humanity. However, for those future cases in which a just punishment must be meted out, there now exists a permanent international body capable of rendering justice. And, for sentencing purposes, there increasingly exists a body of comparable cases and maturing, although still rudimentary, statutory guidance for judges to rely on in assessing proper penalties.

SEE ALSO International Criminal Tribunal for Rwanda; International Criminal Tribunal for the Former Yugoslavia; Prosecution; War Crimes

BIBLIOGRAPHY

Appleman, John Allen (1954). *Military Tribunals and International Crimes*. Westport, Conn.: Greensswood Press.

Beccaria, Cesare (1973). *Essays on Crimes and Punishments*. Philadelphia: Temple University Press.

Cassese, Antonio, ed. (2002). *The Rome Statute of the International Criminal Court: A Commentary*. Oxford: Oxford University Press.

Earle, Alice Morse (1896). *Curious Punishments of Bygone Days*. Detroit, Mich.: Singing Tree Press.

Ginn, John L. (1992). *Sugamo Prison, Tokyo*. Jefferson, N.C.: McFarland & Co.

Grotius, Hugo (1901). *The Rights of War and Peace*, trans. A.C. Campbell, London: M. Walter Dunne.

Grupp, Stanley E., ed. (1971). *Theories of Punishment* Bloomington: Indiana University Press.

Henkin, Louis (1979). *How Nations Behave: Law and Foreign Policy*, 2nd edition. New York: Columbia University Press.

Minear, Richard H. (1971). *Victor's Justice: The Tokyo War Crimes Trial*. Princeton, N.J.: Princeton University Press.

Morris, Virginia, and Michael P. Scharf (1994). *An Insider's Guide to the International Criminal Tribunal for the Former Yugoslavia*. Irvington-on-Hudson, N.Y.: Transnational Publishers.

Persico, Joseph E. (1994). *Nuremberg: Infamy on Trial*. New York: Viking.

Schabas, William A. (2001). *An Introduction to the International Criminal Court* Cambridge: Cambridge University Press.

Schabas, William A. (2002). *The Abolition of the Death Penalty in International Law* Cambridge: Cambridge University Press.

Shaw, George Bernard (1946). *The Crime of Imprisonment*. New York: The Philosophical Library, Inc.

Taylor, Telford (1992). *The Anatomy of the Nuremberg Trials*. New York: Knopf

Von Hirsch, Andrew (1978). *Doing Justice: The Choice of Punishments*. New York: Hill and Wang.

Walker, Nigel (1980). *Punishment, Danger and Stigma: The Morality of Criminal Justice* Totowa, N.J.: Barnes and Noble Books.

Walker, Nigel (1991). *Why Punish?* Oxford, U.K.: Oxford University Press.

Wells, Donald A. (1984). *War Crimes and Laws of War*. Lanham, Md.: University Press of America.

Willis, James F. (1982). *Prologue to Nuremberg: The Politics and Diplomacy of Punishing War Criminals of the First World War*. Westport, Conn.: Greenwood Press.

Meg Penrose

Racial Groups

Even if from a medical and biological point of view, all of humankind belongs to one race, namely the human race (as the UNESCO Declaration on Race and Racial Prejudice [1978] emphasized), all human beings belong to a single species and are descended from a common stock. Legal and political language use the term *races* in the plural sense in order to cover different ethnicities or geographically characterizable subgroups, such as Caucasians, Africans, Mongoloids. Because of the well-established (but erroneous) custom, political and legal language is still using this term.

Racism

Racism as a policy is more than the affirmation or the recognition of special human characteristics linked to color, facial characteristics, or other visible specificities. Racism as a policy attributes a distinct legal status to certain members of a society. Racism can be manifested *inter alia* in the postulation of an alleged "superior race," having more rights than others, but also as the complete or partial denial of rights to special human subgroups.

Different religions have different approaches to the diversity of humankind: Certain religions recognize the distinct legal status of certain human groups; other religions, like Judaism and Christianity, are rooted in the divine unity of humankind. According to the Bible, God said, "Let us make man in our image, after our likeness" (Gen. 1:26). Nevertheless, racism occured in several Christian states during their history.

For the common perception of the term *racism*, one can refer to the United Nations (UN) International Convention on the Elimination of All Forms of Racial Discrimination (1965) which states that "any doctrine of superiority based on racial differentiation is scientifically false, morally condemnable, socially unjust and dangerous" and that "there is no justification for racial discrimination, in theory or in practice, anywhere."

Racism can be manifested in several forms, from the violation of minority rights to segregation and apartheid to genocide, with genocide being the most extreme form of racial hatred. Genocide aims not only to oppress a people group, but to achieve the complete destruction of distinct human communities.

Apartheid policy in South Africa aimed to perpetuate the white minority's power over black masses by denying blacks' political rights. When Afrikaans recognized that they could not maintain this policy which was condemned by the international community, they sought escape through the bantustan policy, which created "homelands" according to tribal appartenance. The alleged citizens of these homelands were considered immigrant workers in the key cities and plantations of South Africa. The United Nations appealed at that time with the strongest terms against the recognition of the bantustans as sovereign states. When apartheid was abolished, Nelson Mandela established a well-functioning compromise that involved cooperation between blacks and whites and between the different black communities.

Racism often has deep roots. The persecution of racial groups in some African states is partly due to their colonial heritage. The colonial powers often used enthic groups as the local administrative staff and as the auxiliary force of the police and the army. The life of these tribal communities became very threatened once sovereinty had been granted to the country. In Rwanda, the Tutsis were considered traitors by the formerly more oppressed Hutus, who formed the ruling majority of the new country. Until the 1990s, harassment, intimidation campaigns, and pogroms were organized by the Hutu elite. In Nigeria in the 1960s, the Ibos unsuccessfully attempted to secede by creating Biafra, a decision which ended in genocide-like bloodshed. During the same period even the anticolonialist freedom fighters were organized, despite the official name of their organization in Angola or Zimbabwe. After the country was liberated from colonial oppression, the organizations entered into armed conflicts between themselves, especially when governmental power was monopolized by one of them. Inherited artificial boundaries have generally nothing to do with ethnic and linguistic realities, and the imported and imitated nation-state concept contributed to the maintenance of the animosity in Africa. Religious differences between Christians, Muslims, and Animists often contribute to wounds remaining unhealed.

Fighting Racism

Several documents related to the fight against racism have been adopted by the United Nations, and some of them are of binding nature. Two examples are the International Convention on the Elimination of All Forms of Racial Discrimination (1965) and the International Convention on the Suppression and Punishment of the Crime of Apartheid (1973). Other documents are recommendations of the UN General Assembly (i.e., the Declaration on the Elimination of All Forms of Racial Discrimination [1963]) or of the United Nations Educational, Scientific, and Cultural Organization (UNESCO), such as the Declaration on Race and Racial Prejudice (1978); the Declaration on Fundamental Principles Concerning the Contribution of the Mass Media to Strengthening Peace and International Understanding to the Promotion of Human Rights and to Countering Racialism, Apartheid and Incitement to War (1978).

The United Nations has defined its focus on fighting racism: the fight against apartheid and institutional segregation, the promotion of the media in the destruction of sometimes deeply rooted stereotypes, and the reduction of economic and social differences. Therefore, these documents proclaim not only the resolute fight for the eradication of racism, but they also emphasize the importance of affirmative action in order to enhance the standing of the disadvantaged group and achieve genuine equality among all people.

Since the time that apartheid became abolished, the attention of the United Nations and other international organizations turned to the fight against anti-Semitism and racial intolerance, the victims of which are often immigrant workers. They have also sought to fight against racism against the Roma community in Europe, as well as the indigenous peoples all over the world, but especially in America and Asia.

The importance of good education and career motivations are emphasized by the international organizations, with the aim of diminishing the dependence of these communities on per capita subsidies, which is an underlying cause of overpopulation in underdeveloped countries in the Third World.

The need to correct the failures of the nation-state concept in Africa is of utmost importance. In the 1990s and 2000s, so-called "transitional justice" programs have been introduced in several African (and South American) states—traditional battlefields of genocide—to show them how they were manipulated and to teach them how to prevent the renewal of racial hatred and of ethnic conflict. In the transitional justice programs, truth-seeking seems to be more important to victims than the penalization of petty offenders. However, this does not negate the necessity for the trial and punishment of the instigators of crimes, including those members of the government or armed forces who may have been responsible.

SEE ALSO Ethnic Groups; Minorities; Racism

BIBLIOGRAPHY

Anderson, Pauline, and Jenny Williams, eds. (2001). *Identity and Difference in Higher Education: Outsiders Within.* Aldershot, U.K.: Ashgate.

Anthias, Floya, and Nira Yuval Davis (1995). *Racialized Boundaries: Race, Nation, Gender, Color, and Class and the Anti-Racist Struggle.* New York: Routledge.

Barndt, Joseph (1991). *Dismantling Racism: The Continuing Challenge to White America.* Minneapolis, Minn.: Augsburg Fortress.

Fine, Michelle, Lois Weis, Linda C. Powell, and L. Mun Wong, eds. (1997). *Off White: Readings on Race, Power, and Society.* New York: Routledge.

Jones, James M. (1972). *Prejudice and Racism.* Reading, Mass.: Addison-Wesley.

Kivel, Paul (1996). *Uprooting Racism: How White People Can Work for Racial Justice.* Philadelphia, Pa.: New Society Publishers.

Law, Ian (1996). *Racism, Ethnicity and Social Policy.* London: Prentice Hall.

Solomos, John, and Les Back (1996). *Racism and Society.* New York: St. Martin's Press.

Tischler, Henry L., ed. (2000). *Debating Points: Race and Ethnic Relations*. Upper Saddle River, N.J.: Prentice Hall.

United Nations. "Fact Sheet No. 12, the Committee on the Elimination of Racial Discrimination." Available from http://www.unhchr.ch/html/menu6/2/fs12.htm.

Péter Kovács

Racism

Once considered an objective scientific theory of difference within human populations, racism has become regarded as an ideology of social domination and exclusion on the basis of biological and genetic variation. The scientific basis of racism has been largely discredited, but the ideas that human populations can be divided into distinct groups based on phenotype, that the culture and behavior of these groups is determined by genetic differences, and that biological difference justifies the dominance of certain races over others remain widely influential.

Racism often figures prominently in the ideologies that justify and promote genocide and other crimes against humanity. Dominant social groups commonly use racial categorizations to differentiate other social groups and justify their exclusion and marginalization. The belief that personality and social behavior are linked to biology and therefore are unalterable makes physical removal or annihilation the only possible means of solving the perceived problem of undesirable social groups.

Scientific Racism

The idea that human populations can be divided into distinct racial groups based on physical differences dates back many centuries. Modern racism, however, is distinguished by the assumptions that racial categorizations are scientifically valid and objective, and that personality, mental ability, and social behavior of individuals within racial groups are biologically determined. Racial prejudice and discrimination may be based on various factors, but racism focuses explicitly on the hereditary and immutable nature of social difference. Racism blames the subordinate and exploited status of certain racial groups on genetic inferiority.

The roots of modern racism lie in the late Medieval period, when Jewishness came to be regarded as an issue of ancestry rather than belief and black skin was seen as a curse that doomed Africans to mental and cultural inferiority. Because racism regarded Jewishness and blackness as unalterable biological facts, it followed that Jews and blacks could never be reformed and integrated into civilized society. Racism thus justified the expulsion and massacre of Jews in Spain beginning in 1492, and the subsequent persecution of Jews in other countries. It also justified the enslavement of millions of Africans in the trans-Atlantic slave trade. The British came to excuse their domination of Ireland, in part, by depicting the Irish as an inferior race who would benefit from British rule.

During the Enlightenment, race became a focus of scientific analysis, as biologists and anthropologists sought to develop objective measures for differentiating between peoples. Yet the study of race was never truly objective, because race scientists were deeply influenced by the assumption that Caucasians were more evolved than other races and that Western civilization was superior to all others. The measurement of physical attributes of various racial groups, phrenology, the quantification of intelligence, and other supposedly objective tools were used to explain the biological sources of the preconceived inferiority of non-white groups and to justify their colonization and domination by Europeans.

Comte Arthur de Gobineau's 1855 "Essay on the Inequality of the Human Races" popularized the idea that social differences were linked to biology, and inspired extensive scientific study of the biological roots of social distinction and identity. Francis Galton, adapting Darwin's ideas on evolution to the study of human development, argued in 1869 that selective breeding could be used to create a superior race of human beings. He coined the term *eugenics* for this idea, which later influenced the development of Nazism and other genocidal ideologies.

Racism and Genocide

The idea that group identities are fixed and that group characteristics are rooted in biology has often been used to justify crimes against humanity. Minority groups have commonly faced exclusion and discrimination on the basis of their language, religion, or other cultural factors, but when cultural differences are regarded as natural and therefore immutable, more drastic and violent responses become more defensible. Viewing other racial groups as not simply different but inferior effectively dehumanizes them, making violence against them more acceptable.

Racism influenced the development of the institution of slavery in the Americas in the sixteenth and seventeenth centuries, shaping an emerging distinction between indentured laborers from Europe and and those who came from Africa. The status of European indentured servants gradually improved, while Africans lost rights and benefits, until slavery became an institution uniquely imposed upon those of African ancestry.

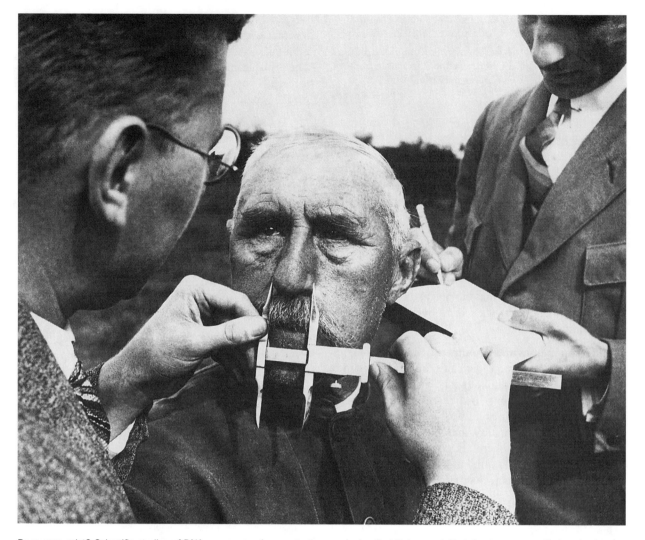

Does race exist? Scientific studies of DNA sequences give way to the conclusion that it does not (that the term, as applied to the human species, has no concrete meaning). Here, in 1941, German officials use calipers to take measurements of a man's nose, which will then be used to calculate his race. [**HULTON-DEUTSCH COLLECTION/CORBIS**]

The assumption that black people were inferior, even subhuman, justified the extreme brutality of the slave trade, in which Africans were captured and shipped across the Atlantic in terrible conditions, leading to the deaths of millions. Even after the elimination of slavery, ideas of racial superiority continued to justify the social, political, and economic dominance of whites or those with more European ancestry in the United States, Brazil, the Caribbean, and South Africa, the denial of rights to black people, and atrocities such as lynching.

Racism also justified colonialism and the massacre and subjugation of native populations by colonial powers throughout much of the world. Viewing Native Americans as a different, sub-human race allowed Spanish colonizers to feel justified in enslaving and slaughtering them in Central and South America, wiping out entire native peoples. The belief in racial inferiority likewise allowed colonists in North America to displace, subjugate, and kill Native Americans. Colonial conquest of Asia and Africa was promoted as a moral obligation for Europeans, the "white man's burden" to bring civilization to supposedly inferior races. When indigenous populations resisted conquest, these same ideas of their inferiority were used to justify the use of brutal force against them, as in the German extermination of the Herero in Southwest Africa from 1904 to 1907. Africa was colonized after ideas of scientific racism had become widely accepted, and this powerfully shaped colonial policy on the continent. In particular, the British and Belgians understood ethnic group differences in racial terms, and discriminated

encyclopedia of GENOCIDE *and* CRIMES AGAINST HUMANITY

among their colonial subjects on the assumption that certain "tribes" were better at ruling, others at fighting, and others at laboring.

Within Europe, scientific racism transformed the nature of anti-Semitism, providing scientific justification for the exclusion and persecution of Jews. These ideas reached their peak in the ideology adopted by the National Socialist Party in Germany. The idea that Jews were not simply believers in a different faith but were a different race whose supposed negative characteristics, such as greed and cunning, were biologically programmed excluded the possibility of conversion, assimilation, or reform. Because Nazis regarded the Jewish race as inherently dangerous to Aryan civilization, their complete extermination was posited as the only possible "final solution" to the "Jewish problem," ultimately justifying the massacre of six million Jews. Ideas of racial inferiority and the need to preserve Aryan racial purity were also used to justify the Nazi extermination of an estimated 400,000 Roma people, pejoratively known as Gypsies.

Racism has served as a factor in more recent genocides as well. In the early 1990s, Serbian and Croatian leaders in the states of the former Yugoslavia depicted Muslims not simply as a religious minority but as a non-Slavic racial group, related to the much-hated Turks, who had to be eliminated from the territory in order to purify it. Such beliefs were used to justify ethnic cleansing and ethnic massacres in Croatia and Bosnia and Herzegovina. In Rwanda, German and Belgian colonizers understood the Hutu, Tutsi, and Twa as three distinct racial groups, an artificial interpretation of ethnic differences that Rwandans themselves came to internalize. Colonial policies regarded the minority Tutsi as a superior Hammitic race and gave them control over the rest of the population. A Hutu uprising just prior to independence transferred power to Hutu hands, transforming the Tutsi into a persecuted minority. Hutu extremists ultimately used the idea that the Tutsi were a separate race whose origins lay outside Rwanda to dehumanize the Tutsi and justify the mass slaughter of more than 500,000.

SEE ALSO Anti-Semitism; Eugenics; Genocide; Holocaust; Nationalism

BIBLIOGRAPHY
Balibar, Etienne, and Immanuel Walerstein (1991). *Race, Nation, and Class: Ambiguous Identities*. London: Verso.
Bauman, Zygmunt (1989). *Modernity and the Holocaust*, Ithaca, N.Y.: Cornell University Press.
Fein, Helen (1993). *Genocide: A Sociological Perspective*. London: Sage Publications.
Fredrickson, George (2002). *Racism: A Short History*. Princeton, N.J.: Princeton University Press.
Marx, Anthony W. (1998). *Making Race and Nation: A Comparison of South Africa, the United States, and Brazil*. Cambridge: Cambridge University Press.
Memmi, Albert (2000). *Racism*. Minneapolis: University of Minnesota Press.
Sanders, Edith R. (1969). "The Hamitic Hypothesis: Its Origins and Functions in Time Perspective." *Journal of African History* 10(4).

Timothy Longman

Radio

Radio was one of the great forces behind social and political mobilization in the twentieth century. Joseph Goebbels, one of Adolf Hitler's earliest and most enthusiastic supporters, understood the potential power of this media. When Hitler rose to power in 1933, he appointed Goebbels as his minister of propaganda; in this role, the latter displayed his talents, particularly where radio broadcasts were concerned. Under Goebbels's leadership the Nazis subsidized the production and distribution of millions of cheap radios in order to strengthen their grip on the population. Goebbels's first radios were deliberately designed with a limited range so that they would not pick up foreign transmissions. At the beginning of World War II over 70 percent of all German households owned a radio, the highest percentage in the world.

The extent to which Nazi radio broadcasts played a clear role in preparing and then swaying German public opinion toward the extermination of the Jews is hard to evaluate. Like the press or cinema, radio was one of the media used to diffuse anti-Semitic themes. In the early years of the Nazi regime the radio called for a boycott of Jewish shops. However, not a single radio program with a specific theme of anti-Semitism was designed. Entertainment programs did not include such messages. Of course, speeches given by Hitler and other Nazi leaders containing angry passages condemning the Jews were routinely broadcast on the radio. On the eve of Kristallnacht (Night of broken glass) on November 9, 1938, Goebbels used the radio to urge the German public to pillage Jewish shops and burn down synagogues. During World War II the Nazi media repetitively depicted Jews as devilish characters responsible for the soon worldwide conflict but they continued to keep their extermination a secret.

Some fifty years later the radio was used in a much more direct way to set the stage for and then perpetrate genocide in Rwanda. Within the context of civil war, initiated in October 1990 by the Tutsi-dominated Rwanda Patriotic Front (RPF), Hutu extremists decided to create their own radio station. Their intention had been to counteract the RPF broadcasts (Radio Muhabura) and those of the official national station (Radio Rwanda) the latter was indeed considered too moderate and had simply become an outlet for the new multiparty government by 1992. This project, driven by the historian Ferdinand Nahimana who had been dismissed from the Rwandan Office of Information (ORINFOR) that supervised Radio Rwanda, commenced in April 1993 with the creation of Radio Télévision Libre Mille-Collines. This new station was formally independent, but in fact influential politicians belonging to the president's entourage, some of them related by marriage, supported it. As in Nazi Germany, many cheap radio receivers were distributed to the population in different regions of the country. Starting in August 1993 the station broadcast rousing Zairian music popular among Rwandans, and the station became rapidly renowned. RTLM presented itself as an interactive radio station, giving listeners the opportunity to speak to the Hutu people by calling into the station.

This broadcasting format was new to Rwanda at that time. RTLM attracted the populace with its candor and humor, but its ideological message was clear: It was the voice of the Hutu people, victims of the profiteering elites, of calculating Tutsis and those who betrayed the Hutu cause. After the Hutu president of Burundi, Melchior Ndadaye, was killed on October 21, 1993, RTLM programming became still more aggressive. All day long the station repeated a political jingle that prompted its audience to wait: "We have hot news," the broadcasters would proclaim, and when the news was finally diffused, listeners would hear a series of vicious anti-Tutsi slogans. Several times a day the station also broadcast songs written by the Hutu extremist Simon Bikindi.

Immediately after the assassination of the Rwandan president, Juvenal Habyarimana, on April 6, 1994, RTLM openly called for the massacre of Tutsis, Hutu opponents, and even Belgian peacekeepers. Hutu extremists used their radio station to ridicule those in the local administration who called for calm. From April to June 1994 RTLM helped mobilize the Hutu population in support of the killing of the Tutsi minority. The radio station even dared to name the Tutsis who remained to be killed. For the first time in history radio was used to directly perpetrate genocide.

The role of radio in the killings must not be overestimated, however. Numerous massacres were committed without the direct influence of RTLM. Military officers, militia leaders, and mayors who supervised Hutu peasants on the ground played a crucial role in organizing the population to kill. Nevertheless, it is evident that radio, the main media in a country where newspapers are hardly read and television remains in short supply, played an important role in the diffusion of racist anti-Tutsi ideology. RTLM provided Hutu extremists with a useful communications tool that reinforced their political influence over the people. Radio can be a most formidable weapon, in particular when introduced to a population already weakened by fear. Words conveyed over the radio may thus turn deadly.

SEE ALSO Incitement; Propaganda; Radio Télévision Libre Mille-Collines; Rwanda; Television

BIBLIOGRAPHY

Chalk, Frank (1999). "Hate Radio in Rwanda." In *The Path of a Genocide,* ed. Howard Adelman and Astri Suhrke. New Brunswick, N.J.: Transaction Publishers.

Chrétien, Jean-Pierre, ed. (1995). *Rwanda. Les médias du génocide.* Paris: Karthala.

Marszolek, Inge (1998). *Zuhoeren und Gehoertwerden. Vol. 1: Radio im Nationalsozialismus,* ed. Adelheid von Saldern. Tuebingen: Diskord.

Jacques Semelin

Radio Télévision Libre Mille-Collines

The anti-Tutsi newspaper *Kangura* and Radio Télévision Libre Mille-Collines (RTLMC), known as the Hate Radio in Rwanda, are recent examples of hate propaganda that paved the way to genocide. The role of both media was examined by the International Criminal Tribunal for Rwanda (ICTR) in the trial of Ferdinand Nahimana, Jean-Bosco Barayagwiza, and Hassan Ngeze, better known as the *Media* trial.

In Rwanda, the ratio of illiterate people was significantly high. Radio, therefore, was the medium with the broadest reach. During the Rwandan genocide, the radio became the sole source of news, but it was also the voice of authority for most people. Rwandans listened to RTLMC (also known as "Radio Machete") everywhere, including at roadblocks during the killings. Messages transmitted by radio were readily taken at face value and orders issued during the broadcasts were followed.

RTLMC was created in June 1993. Ferdinand Nahimana was its founder and director, and Jean-Bosco Barayagwiza was his second in command. RTLMC was owned predominantly by members of the party of the president of the Republic, Juvenal Habyarimana. They were surrounded by influential Hutus, including the close entourage of the president and his wife. Simon Bikindi, a famous anti-Tutsi singer, and Kantano Habimana were the radio's most famous presenters. Officially, RTLMC was an independent radio station, but its tight ties to the government made that independence little more than a cosmetic claim. Ironically, the incorporation document of the radio states that the purpose of RTLMC was to create harmonious development within the Rwandan society.

RTLMC broadcasts accused the Tutsis of being plotters and parasites, and it used the Tutsis' historical domination over the Hutus, as well as the fear of an armed Tutsi insurrection to mobilize the Hutu population. RTLMC broadcasting was like a drumbeat, calling on listeners to take action against the *Inkotanyi* enemy ("infiltrators," a name often given to the Front Patriotique Rwandais, or FPR) and their *Inyenzi* accomplices (*inyezi*, which means "cockroach," was an epithet often hurled at Tutsis). A call by the radio to take up arms against "infiltrators" was clearly intended to be understood as a call to take up arms against all Tutsis. RTLMC sometimes used a more direct approach, naming individuals that it falsely accused of being FPR members, which led to their being killed. RTLMC once broadcast a false claim that the FPR planned to assassinate Hutu leaders. This announcement triggered the killing of hundreds of Tutsi civilians in the Bugesera region. RTLMC was also instrumental in the negative perception of the United Nations among Rwandans, and issued a direct call to attack and kill the UN peacekeepers, including General Dallaire.

RTLMC advised its listeners to identify Tutsis by examining their physical appearance, to "look at their small noses, and then break them." After April 6, 1994, RTLMC broadcast more and more virulent calls for violence and explicitly urged its listeners to exterminate the Tutsi from the surface of the earth. Listeners were encouraged to kill so that future generations would only be able to guess what Tutsis looked like. The on-air personalities advised their audience that they should kill Tutsis even if they were already fleeing. The Militias followed these orders.

Before and during the genocide, all inside Rwanda, as well as many who lived abroad, were aware of RTLMC's direct incitement to violence against Tustis. It nonetheless pursued its broadcasting without much interference.

Kangura

Kangura was an anti-Tutsi publication, and one of the most virulent media voices promulgating ethnic hatred. Hassan Ngeze was *Kangura*'s founder, owner, and editor in chief. He was also in charge of the overall management of the paper and thus controlled its content. *Kangura* promoted the fear of Tutsis among its Hutu readership. *Kangura* contributed to the climate that led to the genocide by publishing numerous explicit

threats and messages inciting people to exterminate the Tutsis.

Direct incitement to violence and extermination of the Tutsis were frequent themes in *Kangura* articles. The paper warned readers to wake up, to be firm and vigilant against the Tutsi scourge. *Kangura* described the Tutsis as "bloodthirsty" and exhorted the Hutu to have no pity for the Tutsis, simply to kill them. *Kangura* frequently used its articles to imply Tutsi complicity with the FPR, which was another of its common targets. A *Kangura* article even incited the Hutu population to kill UN peacekeeping soldiers, prophecying that this would cause the UN to pull out of Rwanda. The prophecy went on to predict that Tutsi blood would then flow freely, and that all Tutsis would be tortured to death and exterminated. This scenario would later become reality.

A central piece of *Kangura*'s propaganda was the Hutus' Ten Commandments, a compendium of discriminatory behaviour against Tutsis. Tutsis were invariably portrayed as the enemy, as evil and dishonest, and Tutsi women were said to be enemy agents. The imperative style employed in *Kangura*'s articles unequivocally called upon the Hutus to take action against the Tutsis.

In one of its issues, *Kangura* rhetorically asked which weapons Hutus should use to conquer the *Inyenzi* once and for all. Accompanying the article was a drawing of a machete. This was perhaps the most graphic expression of the paper's genocidal intent. Many Tutsis were killed when *Kangura* published lists of people whom it referred to as *Inkotanyi*, asking readers to send information on those mentioned in the lists.

The ICTR Judgement and Direct and Public Incitement to Commit Genocide

The *Media* trial before the International Criminal Tribunal for Rwanda (ICTR) raised important legal principles regarding the role of the media, which had not been addressed at the level of international criminal justice since Nuremberg. The ICTR investigated the accountability of those who directly and publicly incited Rwanda's Hutu population to commit genocide, but it also looked at those who controlled such media.

The ICTR found that *Kangura* and RTLMC made the same propaganda endeavor, conveyed the same message, and publicly promoted each other. *Kangura* openly identified itself with RTLMC and worked with the radio to acquaint the station's listeners with its ideas. Barayagwiza served as the link between the two media outlets. The accused once made a public appearance together at a stadium in Kigali. There they urged the crowd to listen to RTLMC and pleaded that the radio should be used to disseminate the Hutus' empowerment ideas and to fight against the *Inyenzi*. RTLMC broadcast many of the speeches given during that public appearance. The ICTR found that the meeting and the RTLMC report on it generated an atmosphere of hostility toward the Tutsis.

The power of the media to create and destroy human rights implies a very high degree of responsibility. For the ICTR, those who control media such as *Kangura* and RTLMC are accountable for the consequences of their programs. As two of the RTLMC Steering Committee's most active members, Nahimana and Barayagwiza were deemed responsible for the radio's overall management. Nahimana and Barayagwiza had the power to stop transmissions and change the content of the programs, but they did not exercise that power. In fact, Nahimana was happy that RTLMC had been instrumental in "raising awareness," that it was effective in the incitement to violence.

In the *Media* trial, Nahimana and Barayagwiza were indicted for their role at RTLMC, whereas Ngeze's indictment was mainly with his work at *Kangura*. All were found guilty of genocide and of direct and public incitement to commit genocide. The ICTR found that the writings of *Kangura* and the broadcasts of RTLMC constituted conclusive evidence of the genocidal intent of the accused. For the tribunal, genocide is a crime so serious that direct and public incitement to engage in it must be punished, even in cases where such incitement fails to produce the desired result. The mere potential of the communications media to cause genocide is enough to turn it into incitement. The ICTR recognized that the death of President Habyarimana was the trigger that precipitated the killings, but it viewed the work of the RTLMC and *Kangura* as the bullets in the gun. The ICTR also held that there was a causal connection between the broadcast of the names of Tutsis who were subsequently killed.

The ICTR also found Barayagwiza and Nahimana guilty of superior responsibility. This was an historic development in international criminal justice. The ICTR found that their roles in controlling RTLMC's programming, and their failure to take the necessary measures to prevent the killings instigated by RTLMC, as further elements of their guilt. The tribunal thus recognised a positive obligation to prevent direct and public incitement to commit genocide.

SEE ALSO Incitement; International Criminal Tribunal for Rwanda; Propaganda; Radio

BIBLIOGRAPHY

Des Forges, Alison (1999). *Leave None to Tell the Story*. New York: Human Rights Watch.

Hatzfeld, Jean (2003). *Une Saison de Machettes*. Paris: Seuil.

Schabas, William A. (2000). *Genocide in International Law*. Cambridge: Cambridge University Press.

Martin Imbleau

Rape

In the period immediately following World War II, when the London and Tokyo Charters attempted to establish a list of crimes against humanity, rape was not explicitly mentioned. In contrast, the underlying crimes of extermination, persecution, and enslavement were expressly included as part of the unlawful acts committed against a civilian population. Whether sexual assaults, in particular rape, could be manifestations of crimes against humanity under the Nuremberg and Tokyo Charters is usually answered in hesitant or dumfounded terms. International criminal scholars, however, such as Cheriff Bassiouni, contend that rape was indeed subsumed in the explicit, residual crime of "other inhumane acts." the last category of crimes against humanity as listed in both the London and Tokyo Charters. International lawyers, such as Patricia Sellers and Kelly Askin, assert that rape not only could constitute at least a part of a crime against humanity, but that the Nuremberg Tribunal accepted evidence of sexual violence as valid in the prosecution of crimes against humanity.

Although the fact is frequently ignored, evidence of rapes and other sexual abuse was introduced by the French and Russian Allied prosecutors at the Nuremberg Tribunal. Witnesses testified about rapes committed by German soldiers in occupied France and on the Russian front. Testimony also informed the judges about sexual abuse, male and female, including sterilization experiments, in Nazi concentration camps. The Nuremberg Judgment specifically addressed crimes such as the killing of prisoners of war, the persecution of Jews, and the deportation of individuals to serve in slave labor programs but, unfortunately, did not refer even once to the crime of rape or other sexual violence. In an apparent effort to explain their decision, the judges observed that, in the section of the judgement that dealt with wars crimes and crimes against humanity, "the evidence was overwhelming in its volume and detail." They proposed, therefore, to deal with the multitude of atrocities quite generally, noting that "every conceivable circumstance of cruelty and horror" had been perpetrated. The judges distinguished, rather hastily, the difference between war crimes and crimes against humanity in their analysis of the "overwhelming" evidence, and they found that:

[I]nsofar as inhumane acts charged in the indictment and committed at the beginning of the war,

In an overgrown field in Djakovica, Kosovo, the discovery of the remains of an Albanian girl believed to have been raped and then killed by Serbian troops. July 1993. [TEUN VOETEN]

did not constitute War Crimes, they were all committed in execution of, or in connection with, the aggressive war, and therefore constituted Crimes Against Humanity.

To the extent that the rapes and other forms of sexual violence inflicted upon German civilians, or civilians of other nationalities, were not judged to be traditional war crimes, the Tribunal condemned such conduct as inhumane acts under crimes against humanity. The failure to expressly include rape among the listed crimes against humanity, together with the paucity of clearer judicial explanation on how sexual assault evidence was characterized, has contributed to the continuing myth that rapes and other sexual violence evidence were not pursued at Nuremberg.

At the Tokyo Tribunal, prosecutors submitted harrowing evidence of rapes committed by the Japanese forces in Nanking and other Chinese cities. The evidence also confirmed that rapes, sexual mutilations, and forced sexual intercourse between prisoners oc-

curred frequently. Even though the Tokyo Charter provided for crimes against humanity, the Tokyo Tribunal judges held that all the atrocities committed by the Japanese forces, including the rapes, constituted war crimes. The crimes against humanity provision was not relied upon, probably because initially, crimes against humanity were thought to apply to acts committed against one's own civilian population. The Japanese, unlike the Nazis, were not accused of committing crimes against Japanese citizens. Moreover, crimes committed by the Japanese against peoples they subjugated in Korea and Taiwan were not prosecuted at all, even though they fit the criteria of crimes against humanity. Hence, the Tokyo Tribunal judges employed traditional theories of war crimes in their legal analysis of rapes and other sexual violence.

Control Council Law No. 10 and the Subsequent Nuremberg/Tokyo Trials

After the major Axis criminals were prosecuted at Nuremberg and Tokyo, the minor Axis war criminals, in

Alice, a 20-year-old Liberian woman and rape victim, in 2003. In August 2003 media outlets around the world reported that Liberian rebels and government soldiers were assaulting thousands of girls and women under the cover of war. Victims said that, as Charles Taylor's regime was crumbling, fighters on both sides regarded the female civilian population as the spoils of war—and wished to exploit the general anarchy before peacekeepers arrived.[AP/WIDE WORLD PHOTOS]

both Europe and the Pacific theatre, were tried by military courts set up by the Allies in their respective occupations zones. In what is commonly referred to as the "subsequent trials," minor criminals faced charges in the British, Polish, French, and American military courts. Within the U.S. Army occupation zone, these proceedings were established and governed by Control Council Law No. 10. Its provisions proscribed crimes against peace, war crimes, and, importantly, crimes against humanity. For this latter criminal category, the definition reads as follows:

> Crimes Against Humanity. Atrocities and offenses, including but not limited to murder, extermination, deportation, imprisonment, torture, rape, or other inhumane acts committed against the civilian population, or persecutions on political, racial or religious grounds whether or not in violation of the domestic laws of the country where perpetrated.

Control Council Law No. 10, unlike the Nuremberg and Tokyo Charters, expressly names rape as a type of crime against humanity. In its strictest sense, however, the law was national military law, decreed to aid in the administration of foreign occupied lands. It was not international law per se, and differed to some extent from the law applied at the International Military Tribunals.

These subsequent trials, held in the occupied sector governed by Control Council No. 10, did not produce as great a wealth of jurisprudence as was generated during the trial of Nazi doctors who performed medical experiments or the trial of the industrial producers of the Zyklon B gas that was used in the concentration camps. There was little jurisprudence on rape, although several cases did roundly condemn other forms of sexual abuse, such as forced sterilization, as inhumane acts prosecutable under the heading of crimes against humanity. The significance of Control

Council No. 10 in regard to rape, therefore, lay not in straightforward jurisprudence on the subject, but rather in its clear acknowledgement, so soon after the Nuremberg and Tokyo Charters, that acts of rape could be considered a crime against humanity.

In the Far East, the trails were held to prosecute minor war criminals. In one of these, the U.S. military court charged Japanese General Yamashita for multiple crimes, including rapes committed in the occupied Philippines. In the Dutch Batavia trials in Indonesia, other defendants were prosecuted for forced prostitution. Consistent with the factual and legal holdings of the Tokyo Tribunal, these subsequent trials condemned the rampant commission of rape as a category of war crimes.

In 1950, at the direction of the General Assembly Resolution 95, the International Law Commission produced the Nuremberg Principles to codify the offenses contained in the Nuremberg Charter. The Commission set forth the verbatim text of crimes against humanity as drafted into the Nuremberg Charter. Unfortunately, rape was omitted from this list, even though Control Council No. 10 was still in force. As a result, the legacy of World War II regarding the classification of rape as a war crime remained ambiguous.

The Modern Recognition of Rape as a Crime Against Humanity

The concept of crimes against humanity is one of the few international crimes that has never been grounded in a treaty. Unlike the crimes of apartheid, torture, or genocide, all of which are replete with conventions devoted to their legal terms, there existed no convention establishing internationally agreed upon terms of crimes against humanity, until the adoption of the Rome Statute of the International Criminal Court in 1998. As a result, the modern understanding of crimes against humanity derives from its incorporation into national laws and, more recently, its ubiquitous insertion into the statutes of international courts and tribunals. A notable example of a domestic provision which includes rape among its list of crimes against humanity is found in the law of Bangladesh.

In 1971, East and West Pakistan fought a bloody war of secession, which resulted in the creation of an independent Bangladesh. During that armed conflict, tens of thousands of women were reportedly raped. In 1973, the newly formed Bangladesh legislature published Act XIX to set forth the legal basis upon which to prosecute Pakistani prisoners. Its provision on crimes against humanity read:

> Crimes Against Humanity: namely; murder, extermination, enslavement, deportation, impris-

> onment, abduction, confinement, torture, rape, or other inhumane acts committed against any civilian population or persecution on political, racial, ethnic or religious grounds, whether or not in violation of the domestic law of the country where perpetrated.

This legislation exemplifies the ongoing evolution of the legal concept of crimes against humanity. Like Control Council Law No. 10, the law includes rape and torture among recognized crimes against humanity, along with additional proscriptions outlawing abduction and confinement.

The aftermath of Pakistan's 1971 war did not, however, include the prosecution of rape as a crime against humanity. Instead, an eventual political agreement was reached whereby Pakistan recognized Bangladeshi independence in exchange for the return of its prisoners of war. This agreement derailed any hope of prosecution. A pervasive lack of political will to prosecute international crimes in general, and rapes in particular, created a dearth of jurisprudence on rape as a crime against humanity during the latter half of the twentieth century. Only with the establishment of the ad hoc tribunals for the former Yugoslavia and Rwanda did rape as a crime against humanity receive diligent international attention and concerted enforcement.

In 1991 the disintegration of Yugoslavia devolved in to an armed conflict during which thousands of acts of sexual violence were committed, most notably the rape of detained Bosnian Muslim and Bosnian Serb women. The worldwide media and women's rights and other human rights movements vociferously urged the United Nations to condemn the rapes. Without hesitation, the UN Security Council issued Resolution 820, condemning "the massive, organized and systematic detention and rape of women and reaffirmed that those who commit . . . or order . . . the commission of such acts will be held individually responsible." In 1993, the Security Council established the ad hoc International Criminal Tribunal for the Former Yugoslavia to investigate, prosecute, and judge criminals from all sides of the conflict. The Secretary-General's Report to the Security Council detailed the nature of rapes and sexual violence that occurred during the armed conflict and explained its rationale for placing crimes against humanity within the Yugoslav Tribunal's jurisdiction.

> Crimes against humanity refer to inhumane acts of a very serious nature, such as wilful killing, torture, or rape, committed as part of a widespread or systematic attack against the civilian population . . . such inhumane acts have taken the form of so-called "ethnic cleansing" and widespread and systematic rape and other forms

of sexual assault, including enforced prostitution.

The ensuing Article 5 of the Yugoslav Statute explicitly enumerated in subsection (g) rape as a crime against humanity.

In 1994, Rwandan ethnic tensions devolved into genocide. The Secretary-General of the United Nations drafted the Statute of the Rwanda Tribunal and included an express provision for rape as a crime against humanity under Article 3(g). The inclusion of rape in the Article 5 of the Yugoslav Statute, and in Article 3 of the Rwanda Statute highlighted the international community's acceptance that the crime formed a part of the customary law that binds all states, even though it had no basis in any formal treaties. The UN's inclusion of rape as a crime against humanity within both statutes signaled the Security Council's intent to ensure that the perpetrators of rape in Rwanda and Yugoslavia would be prosecuted under international law.

Since 1950, the International Law Commission, the body that penned the Nuremberg Principles, had been tasked by the United Nations General Assembly to draw up a Draft Code of Crimes Against Mankind. In 1996, as a result of the Yugoslav and Rwanda Statues, the Commission inserted rape into the crimes against humanity provision of the Draft Code and finally redressed its omission in the Nuremberg Principles.

By the late 1990s, the universal acceptance of the legal concept of crimes against humanity spurred its incorporation into several other statutes of international tribunals. The Rome Statute, which governs the jurisdiction of the International Criminal Court, was signed in 1998 and ratified in 2003. It is the first truly international treaty, drafted to prosecute international crimes (even when they were not generated by a war) or genocide. Article 7(g) of the Rome Statute proscribes a panoply of violent sexual offenses under the heading of crimes against humanity. Included among these offenses are "rape, sexual slavery, enforced prostitution, forced pregnancy, enforced sterilization, or any other from of sexual violence of comparable gravity." The International Criminal Court, a permanent body with prospective jurisdiction (the ability to judge international crimes committed in the future), included several explicitly described forms of sexual violence under the heading of crimes against humanity. Prosecutors and judges will eventually be able to rely upon these provisions when prosecuting a widespread or systematic attack against civilians.

The ad hoc tribunals constituted under the Sierra Leone Special Court, the Panels of East Timor, and the anticipated Extraordinary Chambers in Cambodia,

have also revisited the concept of sexual assault as a crime against humanity. As a direct outgrowth of the Rome Statute's broader definition of sexual violence, two of the courts have incorporated rape and a selection of other sex-based crimes into their crimes against humanity provision. For instance, Article 2 of the Sierra Leone Special Court includes rape, sexual slavery, enforced prostitution, forced pregnancy, and any other form of sexual violence as crimes against humanity. Section 5 of the United Nations Transitional Administration in East Timor Regulation 2000/11 incorporated the Rome Statute's list of crimes against humanity verbatim, thus including sexual offenses as prosecutable by the East Timor Special Panel. The proposed Extraordinary Chambers of Cambodia, the subject of tense political negotiations between the national leaders and the United Nations, includes rape as the only sex-based conduct explicitly listed under crimes against humanity.

Jurisprudence of Rape as a Crime Against Humanity

In 1998, the Rwanda Tribunal delivered its first judgment, in the case against Jean-Paul Akayesu. Mr. Akayesu was the highest-ranking political official in a commune where about 2,000 Tutsis were slaughtered by a Hutu political militia group called the Interhamwe. During the killings, many Tutsi women fled their homes and sought sanctuary at the communal headquarters where Akayesu presided. The women pleaded with Akayesu to protect them from the oncoming massacre. Testimony revealed that the women were subjected to rapes, gang rapes, and sexual humiliation. The acts often preceded their deaths.

The *Akayesu* Trial Chamber pronounced a detailed opinion based on the rape testimony it heard. The judges cited the testimony of a Tutsi witness identified as JJ, who asserted that

she was taken by force from near the [municipal office] into the cultural centre . . . in a group of approximately fifteen girls and women. In the cultural center, they were raped. She was raped twice. Then another man came to where she was lying and he also raped her. A third man then raped her, she said, at which point she described herself as near dead.

The Trial Chamber also heard from a Hutu woman, identified as PP, who observed the rape of Alexia, a Tutsi. Witness PP testified that "one person held her neck, others took her by the shoulders, and others held her thighs apart as numerous Interhamwe continued to rape her—Bongo after Pierre, and Habarunena after Bongo."

The Trial Chamber concluded that the sexual assault described in the testimony constituted rape under Article 3, the crimes against humanity provision of the Rwanda Statute. It also found these incidents of sexual violence to constitute an act of genocide, under the prohibition of "causing serious bodily or mental harm to members of the group." In finding Mr. Akayesu guilty, the Trial Chamber, for the first time in international law, undertook to define rape:

> The Chamber must define rape, as there is no commonly accepted definition of this term in international law. While rape has been defined in certain national jurisdictions as non-consensual intercourse, variations on the act of rape may include acts which involve the insertion of objects and/or the use of bodily orifices not considered to be intrinsically sexual.

> The Chamber defines rape as a physical invasion of a sexual nature, committed on a person under circumstances which are coercive.

Mr. Akayesu was sentenced to life imprisonment for genocide and crimes against humanity, including the relentless rapes committed upon Tutsi women by the Interhamwe.

The jurisprudence of the Yugoslav Tribunal developed along parallel lines with that of its sister tribunal in Rwanda, yet its conception of rape was distinctly different. In a 1998 case, against an individual named Furundzija, the Yugoslav Tribunal employed a more mechanical definition of rape, treating it as a war crime.

In 2000 a Trial Chamber heard a case against Kunarac et al., in which three Bosnian Serbs were charged with rapes, torture, and enslavement. During the trial it was revealed that hundreds of Bosnian Muslim women and girls had been caught up in the military takeover of the town of Foca, in eastern Bosnia. The women were held in a series of Serb-run detention centers. Some were eventually expelled, but others were held by individual Serb soldiers and forced to serve as their personal, sexual slaves.

Each of the accused was found guilty of rape as a crime against humanity under Article 5 of the Yugolsav Statute. They were all sentenced to terms of imprisonment, ranging from sixteen to twenty-eight years. In rendering its decision, this time the Trial Chamber set forth a definition of rape that placed it within the category of crimes against humanity:

> The actus reus of the crime of rape in international law is constituted by: the sexual penetration, however slight: (a) of the vagina or anus of the victim by the penis of the perpetrator or any other object used by the perpetrator; or (b) the mouth of the victim by the penis of the perpetra-

tor, where such sexual penetration occurs without the consent of the victim. Consent for this purpose must be consent given voluntarily, as a result of the victim's free will, assessed in the context of the surrounding circumstances. The mens rea is the intention to effect this sexual penetration, and the knowledge that it occurs without the consent of the victim.

This definition combines the mechanical terms employed in the Furundzija case with new considerations. Specifically, the Kunarac definition adds the requirement that the sexual intercourse occur without the victim's consent, and that the perpetrator be aware of the absence of consent.

In the Kunarac Appeals Decision, the Appeals Chamber offered extensive clarification on the meaning of lack of consent as an element of rape as a crime against humanity. It stipulated that the conditions of the rape must be such that true consent is not possible. Moreover, it rejected the ground of appeal put forth by the defendant, who argued that resistance to rape had to be "continuous" or "genuine." The appellate court concluded that:

> the Appellants were convicted of raping women held in de facto military headquarters, detention centres and apartments maintained as soldiers residences. As the most egregious aspect of the conditions, the victims were considered the legitimate sexual prey of their captors. Typically, the women were raped by more than one perpetrator and with a regularity that is nearly inconceivable. (Those who initially sought help or resisted were treated to an extra level of brutality). Such detention amounted to circumstances that were so coercive as to negate any possibility of consent.

Even though the Furundzija/Kunarac definition of rape resembles the definition used in many national laws, it is designed for application in periods of armed conflict or in the context of crimes against humanity. Accordingly, any allegation of the possibility of consent must take into account the military, social, and political upheaval that prevail in such circumstances. In order to prove that a victim-survivor of rape did not consent, it is crucial to introduce evidence of the actual circumstances of the offense. Elements such as abduction and detention of civilians can be invoked to show the perpetrator's awareness of inherently coercive circumstances. This broad approach to evidence of consent also reflects the original intent of procedural Rule 96, which is in force at both tribunals. Rule 96 discounts consent as a defense against the charge of sexual assault and rape if a victim has been subjected to or threatened with violence, duress, detention, or psychological oppression.

The definition of rape as a crime against humanity at the Rwanda Tribunal has incorporated the Furundzija/Kunarac approach since 2003. In the Rwandan case of *Prosecutor v. Kajelijeli*, the Trial Chamber noted that, "given the evolution of the law in this area . . . the Chamber finds the [Furundzija/Kunarac] approach of persuasive authority."

Another important stage in the evolution of rape as a crime against humanity is exemplified by findings of the Yugoslav Tribunal. This is the development of a gender-neutral orientation, which acknowledges that men and boys can be subjugated to rapes. In 2004, in the *Prosecutor v. Cesic*, the Trial Chamber sentenced Bosnian Serb Ranko Cesic to eighteen years in prison for committing ten camp killings and for committing rape upon two brothers. The Trial Chamber found the following:

Regarding the sexual assaults, the factual basis indicates that the victims were brothers, who were forced to act at gunpoint and were watched by others. . . . [t]he assault was preceded by threats and that several guards were watching and laughing while the act was performed. The family relationship and the fact that they were watched by others make the humiliating and degrading treatment particularly serious. The violation of the moral and physical integrity of the victims justifies that the rape be considered particularly serious as well.

Until recently, the recognition of rape as a crime against humanity that protects both males and females has not been clearly articulated in international jurisprudence. Rapes involving male victims will notably require a different development of the factual basis for rapes. For example, the forced sexual penetration commonly performed in the rape of males was often not physically committed by the accused. Instead, such rapes usually involve two male victims who were directed by the accused to assault one another. Another common element of male rapes in this context is the public nature of the assault. It may be the case that the prosecution of male rape will entail the use of different standards to demonstrate lack of consent than that employed in cases of female rapes.

Future Trends

The initial concept of crimes "repugnant to the principles of humanity" gradually stimulated the development of crimes against humanity. From rape's rather hesitant debut within the crimes against humanity provision after the World War II International Military Tribunals to its uniform acceptance by the beginning of the twenty-first century, many men, women, and children have endured rapes committed as part of attacks on civilian populations. The body of judgments that condemn rape as a crime against humanity have helped to close a legal loophole that resulted from earlier understandings of the offense, which consigned it to the category of war crimes. As the concept evolves, the prohibition of rape under crimes against humanity may become more readily enforcible.

The establishment of the permanent International Criminal Court, the mixed national and international courts, and the ongoing issuance of judgements from the ad hoc tribunals raise valid expectations that the interpretation of rape as a crime against humanity will constantly evolve. Under the International Criminal Court, rape is presently defined as an act in which:

The perpetrator invaded the body of a person by conduct resulting in penetration, however slight, of any part of the body of the victim or of the perpetrator with a sexual organ, or of the anal or genital opening of the victim with any object or any other part of the body.

The invasion was committed by force, or by threat of force or coercion, such as that caused by fear of violence, duress, detention, psychological oppression or abuse of power, against such person or another person, or by taking advantage of a coercive environment, or the invasion was committed against a person incapable of giving genuine consent.

The definition borrows from the substantive jurisprudence of the Yugoslav and Rwanda Tribunals and certain aspects of the procedural safeguards of Rule 96, but it still leaves room for further challenges and development. Issues still to be addressed include the concept of genuine consent, and determining when, other than the presence of force or coercion, a person may be deemed incapable of giving that consent. It might be argued, for instance, that incapacity may be due to age. A further issue lies in the clinical specificity of the definition currently in use, which singles out penetration by a sexual organ of the anal or genital opening. It might be argued that other parts of the body are subject to rape or capable of being an instrument of rape. The answers will be shaped by the horrible conduct of future perpetrators, as well as by the legal deliberations of judges.

SEE ALSO Crimes Against Humanity; International Criminal Court; International Criminal Tribunal for Rwanda; International Criminal Tribunal for the Former Yugoslavia; War Crimes

BIBLIOGRAPHY
Bassiouni, M. Cherif (1992). *Crimes Against Humanity in International Criminal Law*. Dordrecht, Netherlands: Martinus Nijhoff Publishers:.

Sellers, Patricia Viseur (2000). "The Context of Sexual Violence: Sexual Violence as Violations of Humanitarian Law." In *Substantive and Procedural Aspects of International Criminal Law: The Experience of International and National Courts*, eds. Gabrielle Kirk-McDonald and Olivia Swaak-Goldman. The Hague, Netherlands: Kluwer Law International.

Swaak-Goldman, Olivia (2000). "Crimes Against Humanity." In *Substantive and Procedural Aspects of International Criminal Law: The Experience of International and National Courts*, eds. Gabrielle Kirk-McDonald and Olivia Swaak-Goldman. The Hague, Netherlands: Kluwer Law International.

Patricia Viseur Sellers
I am setting forth the above in my personal capacity. This article represents neither the policies of the Office of the Prosecutor of the International Criminal Tribunal for the Former Yugoslavia nor the United Nations.

Ratification see International Law; Proxmire, William.

Reconciliation

Reconciliation can refer to a condition in which there is a restoration of wholeness—a bringing together of that which has been torn apart. However, the term reconciliation may also be applied to a process: Those that have been divided by destructive conflict and enmity begin to forge new relationships that hold the promise and seeds of a shared future. The first dimension of a reconciliation process addresses the painful trauma of the past; the second focuses on those that have been divided acquiring the hope necessary to anticipate some kind of shared future. In all instances different circumstances will result in different types and degrees of reconciliation.

The bereaved and dispossessed can never recover that which they have lost, but they can learn to live with their sense of personal and collective loss. For the sake of future peace, this is particularly vital for societies emerging from terrible experiences such as genocide.

The relative success of community efforts to deal constructively with the legacy of fear and hatred that divides it appears to depend in the first instance on three factors:

1. Truth: The perpetrators are prepared to acknowledge their guilt and publicly validate the historical experience of the victims' pain and suffering.

2. Security: The degree to which survivors can orientate themselves toward the future is crucially dependent on their sense of security and corresponding freedom from fear of a return of violence and abuse.

3. Justice: Individual and collective culprits must move beyond acknowledging their guilt and show evidence of being prepared to suffer punishment and/or make reparations.

To these three factors three contextual variables should be added:

- Time enables people to learn how to live with the scars that remain from past events.

- A moral culture of the victims-survivors, which emphasises the interdependency linking all together as part of a common humanity, better equips them to become reconciled to their losses and orientated toward some kind of future coexistence.

- Sustainable reconciliation processes require complementary changes in those political, economic, and social institutions that provided the structures within which the crimes of the past were perpetrated.

Reconciliation after Genocide?
A brief review of some of the postgenocide processes of the last century indicates that there is no common pattern to reconciliation efforts.

Armenian Genocide
Armenians throughout the world agree that there can be no reconciliation with Turkey or the Turkish people until they acknowledge their culpability in the campaign of extermination against the Ottoman Empire's Armenian population during World War I. Various states around the world have acknowledged the crime committed against the Armenians, but there has been no indication that the Turkish authorities are prepared to make the gesture necessary to initiate some kind of reconciliation process.

Cambodian Genocide
Since the overthrow of the Khmer Rouge regime in 1979 Cambodians have struggled to come to terms with their legacy of autogenocide. The challenge Cambodians face is to become reconciled with each other and their own history. For many the principal response to the horrors of the past has been an attempt to simply forget them; some justify such an approach by referring to the beliefs of Buddhism and the moral imperative to avoid "the spirit of revenge," while others are driven by the fear of a return of violence should efforts be made to bring the main perpetrators to trial. This social amnesia was initially facilitated by agreements and amnesties proffered by the Cambodian political elite to the surviving Khmer Rouge leadership in order to preserve a fragile peace within the country. However, with the passage of time and in the face of internal and external

pressure the Cambodian regime eventually reached an agreement with the United Nations in 2003 for the establishment of a tribunal to try the surviving senior Khmer Rouge leaders. Many Cambodians continue to ask, though, "Why did we do this to ourselves?"

Rwandan Genocide

Since the Rwandan genocide of 1994 a range of initiatives has attempted to address its legacy and build a new future. Some of the main organizers of the slaughter have been brought before the International Criminal Tribunal for Rwanda. By 2001, however, there were still some 120,000 people in Rwanda's prisons awaiting trial for genocide-related offenses. In response the new Rwandan regime began to introduce a form of community-based justice by adapting the traditional conflict resolution process of *gacaca*. The aim was to promote reconciliation. It is too early to pass judgment on this initiative. However, as historian Mahmood Mamdani has so clearly pointed out, Rwanda's key dilemma remains one of building a democracy that can incorporate a guilty majority alongside a bitter and fearful minority in a single political community. At present to be a Hutu is to be a presumed perpetrator to whom the pursuit of justice seems like victors' revenge. According to Mamdani, the prime prerequisite for reconciliation and a common future in Rwanda is a form of political justice whereby Tutsis relinquish their monopolization of political power rather than continue to hold on to it out of fear of the majority.

Germany and the Holocaust

Following the mass murder of European Jewry and the displacement of the majority of those that survived at the outset, little was done to acknowledge the horror of the slaughter or to create the spaces necessary for survivors to tell their stories. Justice was confined to military trials, internal purges of collaborators in formerly occupied countries, and a de-Nazification program in Germany. Monetary reparations were made to Israel, but the dominant concern seemed to be ensuring that such crimes against humanity would never reoccur. In time, however, interest in the Holocaust grew. In Germany and beyond there are museums, national days of remembrance, educational programs, and many other forms of memorializing the Holocaust. The result has been an expansion of the space available for dialogue within and between the communities that were once so divided. Thus, two generations after the genocide the acknowledgment of the historic crime and the suffering of its victims and survivors, along with efforts at restitution, have helped Jewish communities around the world make a distinction between the culpability of past perpetrators and contemporary generations—a

perception necessary for the creation of a shared future in postgenocide societies.

SEE ALSO Armenians in Ottoman Turkey and the Armenian Genocide; Cambodia; International Criminal Tribunal for Rwanda; Reparations

BIBLIOGRAPHY

Abu-Nimer, M., ed. (2001). *Reconciliation, Justice and Coexistence.* Lanham, Md.: Lexington Books.

Bloomfield, D. et al., eds. (2003). *Reconciliation after Violent Conflict: A Handbook.* Stockholm, Sweden: International Institute for Democracy and Electoral Assistance.

du Toit, F., ed. (2003). *Learning to Live Together: Practices of Social Reconciliation.* Cape Town, South Africa: Institute for Justice and Reconciliation.

Mamdani, Mahmood (2001). *When Victims become Killers: Colonialism, Nativism and the Genocide in Rwanda.* Oxford, U.K.: James Currey.

Minow, M. (1998). *Between Vengeance and Forgiveness.* Boston: Beacon Press.

Rigby, A. (2001). *Justice and Reconciliation: After the Violence.* Boulder, Colo.: Lynne Rienner.

Andrew Rigby

Refugee Camps

A refugee camp is a place where people who flee their country to escape persecution, armed conflict, or political violence, can (in principle) live in safety. Over thirty-nine million people worldwide live as refugees or internally displaced persons (IDP). Not all of them gather in camps. Some are settled among the local population, and some try to seek asylum in other countries. However, the majority of the world's refugee population finds an immediate, if temporary, protection in camps.

Refugee camps are usually close to borders of the country in which the refugees originate and are established by host countries or an international organization, such as the United Nations High Commissioner for Refugees (UNHCR) or the International Committee of the Red Cross (ICRC). Some camps are carefully planned, but others emerge spontaneously, out of necessity, despair, and destitution, without taking fundamental considerations such as geography, resources, policy, or economy into account.

Camps are an essential element of the humanitarian response to refugees. They are a temporary solution to a crisis, and they allow most refugees to remain in safety until it is possible for them to go back to their homes or move on to more permanent resettlement. Unfortunately, certain camps take on a permanent

Children are often the largest group displaced by conflict. At this refugee camp in Khoja Bahauddin, Northern Afghanistan, they look to an uncertain future. October 2001. [TEUN VOETEN]

character, and some refugee populations are born, live out their lives, and die in their camp. This is the case of Palestinian refugees.

The creation of a refugee camp frequently results from an armed conflict in which the civilian populations suffered and feared for their lives. It is not rare that such persecutions constitute crimes against humanity or crimes of genocide. Refugee camps give rise to complex situations, especially when their residents are still confronted with danger. Because of the coexistence of enemy combatants, or of people from different ethnic groups who have a stake in the conflict, violence is a frequent occurrence in the camps. The conditions of containment are also favorable to the development of organized crime.

Furthermore, camps are not always protected from external attacks, which may constitute the continuation of the crimes against humanity or the genocide they were fleeing. Because refugee camps are temporary in nature, host countries are often eager to close them as quickly as possible. This raises the possibility that refugees may be forced to repatriate to places where

they are still in danger and where they fear falling victim to crimes against humanity or of genocide.

Camps May Protect Against Crimes Against Humanity and Genocide

The causes of refugee flows are as diverse as they are numerous. At times, however, those causes may, in themselves, constitute a crime of genocide or a crime against humanity. In such cases, the establishment of a camp presents new and complex challenges. Such camps tend to be quantitatively larger and are likely to result in a dangerous exposure for the residents. The post–cold war era has given many tragic examples of this.

Between 1988 and 1996, nearly three million Iraqi Shiites and Kurds streamed toward the borders of Iran and Turkey, piling up in camps. Hundreds of thousands of ex-Yugoslavs were expelled from their homes and persecuted as a result of ethnic cleansing conducted in the region between 1992 and 1995. The phenomena repeated itself with the Albanian Kosovars in 1999. In 1994 more than two million Rwandans also fled a genocide that killed over 800,000 people, seeking shelter in camps in Zaire, Tanzania, and Burundi. Protracted political situations have led to the creation of permanent refugee residents in other countries: the Palestinians, for example, make up half of Jordan's population.

Camps and Insecurity

Camps are often cities built of mud, wood, corrugated iron, and plastic sheeting. The weak, poor, sick, old, young, or female are often very vulnerable to stronger, more predatory camp residents. Host countries are reluctant to police the camps, so protection is rarely available. Refugees who are already fragile, or who become weak because of the living conditions of the camp, may easily be targeted. Rape, assassination, forced prostitution, beatings, and overall intimidation inside the camp are commonplace, as is hunger.

International aid is very much a part of the camps' organization. Despite the hard work of relief agencies, however, the people living in a camp often lack nearly everything they need to create a semblance of normal life. Sometimes, when camps become permanent, they no longer receive a full share of international emergency relief. Food shortages and water deficiencies put refugees' survival into question. Because there are no employment program or agricultural opportunities, camp residents are often forced into complete idleness, which can have devastating consequences on their mental health.

Often refugees bring the seeds of the conflict they are fleeing with them into the camps. When camps contain combatants, they have been targeted by enemy forces, who believe the camp is providing their foes with assistance and protection. In addition, local populations may resent the foreign aid offered to refugees, who often receive more than they ever will. Almost everywhere, refugee camps are likely to be run by resistance factions, which can forcibly recruit refugees into guerrilla armed forces, as well as for sex or labor purposes. Furthermore, they often divert international assistance, including food, water, and medical supplies, to their own uses.

Enrollment in armed militias or organized crime, as well as random crime and violence, are easily increased by the circumstances of the refugee camps. People living in the camp are uprooted and destabilized. The majority of them are women and children, many have little education, and most have lost all their possessions. Many have lost family members, and they frequently suffer psychological ailments due to stress and grief. These conditions are extremely favorable to clashes, abuse, wrongdoings, and violent and criminal behaviors.

In Afghanistan, warlords began arming refugee camps as soon as the international peacekeepers arrived in Kabul in 2001, in order to fill the power vacuum and keep their profits from drug trafficking and smuggling. In Morocco, the Polisario (a political movement) has used a refugee camp in southwest Algeria—fully equipped and supplied by international assistance—as military headquarters and a detention center for their prisoners of war. Sometimes, though not always, host countries, assisted by international agencies, will relocate camps farther away from their borderlands, in order to separate genuine refugees from combatants.

Attacks on the Camps

Given the right circumstances, military attacks on refugee camps are very easy to mount. Target populations are all gathered in one place and are in an extremely vulnerable situation because the camps are generally not protected by police or military forces. In September 1982, for instance, the Palestinian refugee camps of Sabra and Chatila were destroyed, and more than 2,000 Palestinians, including children and women, were tortured, raped, and killed by the Lebanese Phalangist militia allied to Israel, after Lebanon had been invaded by Israel.

In 1995 and 1996, in eastern Zaire, the Rwandan Patriotic Front and President Kabila's forces mounted successive attacks on Hutu refugee camps. Hutu militias were using their own camps as a staging ground for attacks against nearby Tutsi communities. The attacks on the Hutu refugee camps resulted in their dismantling. As many as 700,000 Rwandese returned from their camps to Rwanda; others went west into the forest and often died of disease or hunger.

After the Camps: The Issue of Return

Among the durable solutions promoted by UNHCR, repatriation is often considered best. According to UN policy, refugees are uprooted people whose ties to their birthplace, culture or identity, have been broken, so whenever it is possible to do so in safety and dignity, they should be repatriated. Despite the voluntary repatriation standard set by UNHCR, humanitarian agencies and refugees often have to deal with forced repatriations, as occurred in the camps that harbored Rwandan refugees. The UNHCR participating in the dismantlement of the Rwanda refugee camps, which constituted a forced repatriation. It has been severely criticized for its role in this action.

The Russian intervention in Chechnya caused human rights violations of an exceptional gravity. The ensuing destruction of villages, military attacks on marketplaces, and the bombing of refugee corridors probably amount to crimes against humanity. Strong pressures were applied to force Chechens out of their refugee camps, including beatings, aggressions, murders, vanishing bodies, arrests, repeated military interventions, blocked humanitarian aid, and degrading living conditions. Since April 2002, the stress has grown and some of the camps are being closed. One such camp is called Bart, which is one of three tented camps for Chechens in Ingushetia, and which was officially closed on March 1, 2004. The residents have no choice but to return to their home communities, where they still fear persecution and where no protection is available. The UNHCR does not operate in Chechnya, as Russian authorities consider this conflict to be a domestic matter.

Most of the time, refugee camps provide at least a basic degree of protection against crimes against humanity and genocide. However, their residents are extremely vulnerable, due to their location, their overcrowding, the scarcity of resources available, and the continuing political troubles of their country of origin, not to mention those of the host country. They also are essentially a temporary emergency measure that must lead to more permanent solutions, such as voluntary repatriation, integration in the host country, or resettlement in a new country. If the residents are forced to wait too long, the refugee camps may come to represent the worst of the political situation that the refugees were fleeing. Protracted refugee situations result in camps remaining in place for years or even decades. Sometimes, when repatriation becomes possible, refugees return to a place that is very different from the one they once left.

SEE ALSO Refugees

BIBLIOGRAPHY

Black, Richard, and Khalid Koser (1999). *The End of the Refugee Cycle? Refugee Repatriation and Reconstruction.* Oxford: Berghahn Books.

Indra, Doreen (1998). *Engendering Forced Migration: Theory and Practice.* Oxford: Berghahn Books.

Kourula, Pirrko (1997). *Broadening the Edges: Refugee Definition and International Protection Revisited.* Boston: Martinus Nijhoff Publishers.

Loescher, Gil (1993). *Beyond Charity: International Cooperation and the Global Refugee Crisis.* Oxford: Oxford University Press.

Médecins Sans Frontières (1995). *Deadlock in the Rwandan Refugee Crisis: Repatriation Virtually at a Standstill.* Available at http://www.doctorswithoutborders.org/publications/reports/before1999/deadlock_1995.shtml.

Mtango, Elly-Elikunda (1989). "Military and Armed Attacks on Refugee Camps." In *Refugees and International Relations,* ed. Gill Loescher and Leila Monahan. New York: Oxford University Press.

Prunier, Gérard (1995). *The Rwanda Crisis: History of a Genocide.* London: Hurst.

François Crépeau
Caroline Lantero

Refugees

Refugees have always existed, but the establishment of the international community's responsibility to provide protection to and solutions for refugees only dates back to the League of Nations. After the Armenian Genocide of 1915 and the Russian Revolution of 1917, refugees became, for the first time in modern history, an issue for the world community. In 1921 the League of Nations created the Office of the High Commissioner for Refugees, headed by Fridtjof Nansen. He established the "Nansen passport," which provided refugees with an official identity and recognizable status, and enabled them to start afresh. Nansen's mandate was subsequently extended to other groups of refugees, including the Armenians in 1924, and Assyrian, Assyro-Chaldean, and Turkish refugees in 1928. Nansen's successor, the American James McDonald, resigned late in 1935: He believed that a large-scale human tragedy was unfolding in Nazi Germany, one that the Office of the High Commissioner for Refugees was ill-equipped to stop because the international community remained unwilling to help fleeing Jews. Despite international conferences (in Evian, Switzerland, in 1938 and Bermuda in 1943) and the creation of an Intergovernmental Committee on Refugees to address the growing problem, only limited numbers of Jews were saved from the Holocaust. The fact of thirty million persons uprooted by war and the world community's comprehension of the full scale of Nazi atrocities did, however, lead to the development of institutions with more authority to deal with the plight of refugees (Kushner and Knox, 1999).

The United Nations Relief and Rehabilitation Administration (UNRRA), founded in 1943 to provide relief to areas liberated from Axis powers, returned some seven million displaced persons to their countries of origin and provided camps for approximately one million refugees unwilling to be repatriated. UNRRA was replaced by the International Refugee Organization (IRO) in 1946. Conceived as a temporary agency, the IRO attempted to find permanent solutions for the 1.5 million refugees remaining on the European continent, but was quickly hampered by the cold war, unable to operate in the Soviet-occupied zone in Germany. IRO terminated its work in 1952 and was succeeded by another temporary organization to aid the remaining refu-

Afghanistan has been a war zone for twenty-four years. In the 1990s, owing to near-constant fighting between the Taliban and the Northern Alliance and the proliferation of landmines, many citizens of rural Afghanistan (mostly nomads) fled the countryside and took shelter in Kabul. In this photo, refugees with blankets sit against a wall that had been part of the former Soviet embassy there. [TEUN VOETEN]

gees in Europe, the Office of the United Nations High Commissioner for Refugees (UNHCR). The UNHCR was created in January 1951 and has remained in existence ever since, with its mandate renewed every five years.

Evolution of the Definition of *Refugee*

In the period between World War I and World War II the League of Nations defined refugees according to group affiliation, specifically in relation to their country of origin. For instance, the definition of a Russian refugee adopted by the Office of the High Commissioner for Refugees in May 1926 included "any person of Russian origin who does not enjoy, or who no longer enjoys the protection of the government of the Soviet Union and who has not acquired another nationality" (Kushner and Knox, 1999). This group definition inspired much dissension over which refugee groups should be assisted. Germany opposed the notion of aid to Jews and dissidents fleeing the Third Reich and deliberately hindered responses to their exodus in the 1930s. After

World War II pressure for a universal definition of refugee gathered momentum, leading to the definition included in the 1951 UN Convention Relating to the Status of Refugees (the so-called Refugee Convention), which emphasized the causes of flight. The Refugee Convention, still the standard benchmark for establishing refugee status, defines a refugee as "a person who, . . . owing to a well-founded fear of being persecuted for reasons of race, religion, nationality, membership of a particular social group or political opinion, is outside the country of his nationality and is unable or, owing to such fear, is unwilling to avail himself of the protection of that country" (Article 1A[2]). The defining event is one's physical presence in a foreign land in order to secure protection from persecution in another country.

The Refugee Convention was modified by the 1967 Bellagio Protocol that removed the limitations that restricted the scope of the refugees in time and geography (in Europe who had fled as a result of events occurring before 1951). The Refugee Convention delineates the content and conditions of refugee rights that must be respected by a host state. The cornerstone of refugee protection is the principle of "nonrefoulement," stating that "no Contracting State shall expel or return ('refouler') a refugee in any manner whatsoever to the frontiers of territories where his life or freedom would be threatened on account of his race, religion, nationality, membership of a particular social group or political opinion." This principle applies to all refugees, whether or not they have been recognized as such by a host state, and, indeed, many historians have concluded that Article 33 has achieved the status of customary international law in that it is a reflection of state practice and recognized by states as legally binding.

Challenges to the Definition of *Refugee*

The Refugee Convention has not gone unchallenged since its adoption. First, it has often been regarded as irrelevant. For example, falling outside the mandate of the UNHCR are "internally displaced persons" (IDPs), people who flee for the same reasons as refugees, but do not cross an international border. By not actually leaving their country of origin and therefore remaining at the mercy of their persecutors, IDPs are generally more vulnerable than refugees outside their homelands who are the beneficiaries of international protection and assistance. The principle of territorial sovereignty prevents "humanitarian interventions" to assist and protect them.

Second, the word *persecution* is not a precise legal term and many countries have tried to evade their international obligations by narrowly interpreting the

Chechnyan women depart from the ruins of Grozny, their capital. April 1995. [TEUN VOETEN]

definition of refugee. It should be noted that the Refugee Convention does not prescribe any obligation with respect to the means for determining refugee status. In practical terms a state that refuses to determine the status of refugees will be in breach of its obligations to protect refugees under international agreements concerning refugees, but it remains free to decide, on a discretionary basis, how it will fulfill its substantive obligations (although international human rights law also limits a state's freedom of action in certain areas; see Goodwin-Gill, 1989). This has resulted, on the one hand, in some European states excluding individuals who flee situations of generalized violence and civil war, such as in Sri Lanka, or persecution by nonstate actors, such as guerrilla groups in Colombia, or situations of state breakdown, such as in Somalia or Afghanistan.

During the 1990s, Germany, for example, refused to recognize as refugees the almost 400,000 Bosnians living there, in spite of their clear need for protection, as they were deemed to be victims of civil war, not of persecution per se. The UNHCR did not officially protest, as Germany was providing the Bosnians with a measure of protection. At the same time France refused to recognize as refugees the numerous Algerians who fled the civil war in their homeland, declaring that persecution meant victims of government-sponsored violence. The Algerians were, in fact, mainly victims of violence committed by Islamist fundamentalists against whom the government was fighting. French authorities very often provided them with no protection whatsoever, save not returning them to Algeria.

On the other hand, some countries, such as Canada, have recognized this new climate and suggested a teleological interpretation of the refugee definition, by focusing on not only individualized persecution by the infrastructure of state authorities, but also situations of generalized violence and persecution by nonstate actors. As such, they follow the lead of two important regional legal instruments that updated the international definition of refugee by expressly extending it to victims of generalized conflict and violence, when the state is unwilling or unable to protect them: the 1969 Organization of African Unity (OAU) Convention Governing the Specific Aspects of Refugee Problems in Africa (the so-called OAU Convention) and the 1984 Latin American Cartegena Declaration on Refugees (the so-called Cartagena Declaration). The OAU Convention notes that "the term *refugee* shall also apply to every person who, owing to external aggression, occupation, foreign domination or events seriously disturbing public order in either part or the whole of his country of origin or nationality, is compelled to leave his place of habitual residence in order to seek refuge in another place outside his country of origin or nationality." The Cartegena Declaration includes "persons who have fled their country because their lives, safety or freedom have been threatened by generalized violence, foreign aggression, internal conflicts, massive violation of human rights or other circumstances which have seriously disturbed public order."

Third, in spite of its numbers, the persecution of women has often been viewed as falling outside the purview of international protection. The UNHCR and other humanitarian organizations agree that 80 percent of refugees and displaced persons are women and children, many of whom have experienced rape and sexual violence in their countries of origin before fleeing. In spite of the high levels of abuse, persecution, and vulnerability for women and children, according to Nahla more than 75 percent of the refugees seeking asylum in industrialized countries are men. Indeed until recently, a woman's ability to seek protection from her own state was tenuous. One writer has characterized the use of violence against women in developing states as a "global holocaust," a situation tantamount to "the systematic genocide of Third World women" (Wali, 1995, p. 339). In international criminal case law and the 1998 Rome Statute of the International Criminal Court (ICC), systematic rape gained the status of a war crime and crime against humanity. This should help justify refugee status for women victims of violence, as Canada has already recognized (Immigration and Refugee Board, 1993).

The debate surrounding the complexity of determining refugee status has to be understood in light of the overall objective of all modern-day industrialized states to reduce the number of asylum claims to be processed by any refugee determination system. Several mechanisms aimed at better controlling and preventing migratory flows now coalesce to achieve a clear cumulative effect. Either they aim at the return as soon as possible of the maximum number of persons who have entered the territory and made a claim of asylum (maximization of removal mechanisms, accelerated procedures in the refugee status determination system, alternative national protection regimes of more limited duration and scope than that of the Refugee Convention, reduction of lawyers' assistance, suppression of appeal procedures, safe third-country agreements, readmission and asylum-sharing agreements, etc.), or

they attempt to prevent asylum-seekers from even reaching a state's borders (visa requirements, reinforced border controls, carrier sanctions, training of carrier and airport personnel, short-stop operations, police cooperation, readmission agreements, immigration intelligence gathering, etc.).

A concrete example of this phenomenon is the Bosnian refugee crisis brought on by that country's civil war and Germany's protection of the Bosnians residing there through the establishment of an alternate protection regime. The 1995 Bosnia peace plan turned the spotlight on the Bosnians living in Germany in identifying them as *geduldet* ("tolerated" foreigners) allowed to remain in Germany at least until March 1996. The German government granted these Bosnians only temporary protection status and expressly disallowed their application for refugee status: The purpose of this policy decision was for Germany to avoid the restrictions of any international obligations and secure the freedom to treat the Bosnians as it saw fit. This precarious status, in turn, facilitates their return to Bosnia as soon as materially possible and spares Germany the somewhat permanent nature of refugee status generally associated with the Refugee Convention. It results in unequal levels of protection: Several years after fleeing Bosnia, on the expiration of their temporary protected status (decided by the host country's authorities at will), it will be difficult for individuals to provide evidence of their well-founded fear of persecution were they to return, and to demonstrate that they should be awarded refugee status. Most Bosnians would therefore be returned quickly (forcibly if necessary), and this was the ultimate objective of German policy.

Refugees are to be protected even if they have committed certain crimes in their country of origin. However, some crimes are so horrendous that they justify the exclusion of the perpetrators from the benefits of refugee status, as stated in Article 1F(a) of the Refugee Convention: genocide, war crimes, and crimes against humanity. In this sense the perpetrators are considered "undeserving of refugee protection" (Lisbon Expert Roundtable, 2001, p. 1). Other reasons for exclusion clauses include the need to ensure that fugitives from justice do not avoid prosecution by resorting to the protection provided by the Refugee Convention, and to protect the host community from serious criminals. The purpose of exclusion clauses is therefore to deny refugee protection to certain individuals, while leaving law enforcement to other legal processes. The tension between the need to avoid impunity and the need for protection has been sometimes questioned: The refugee crisis following the Rwandan genocide dramatically illustrated the international community's lack of pre-

In the shadows of the border between Tanzania and Rwanda, those who escaped their death at the hands of the Tutsi gather at this makeshift refugee camp. [TEUN VOETEN]

paredness in establishing procedures to deal with refugees who had committed international crimes in their country and later taken control of refugee camps abroad through intimidation and access to international assistance.

Conflicts in Liberia and Sierra Leone in the late 1990s sparked another exodus of civilians. Failure to implement exclusion again compromised the civilian nature of refugee camps, put refugees at risk, and fostered impunity. The crisis in West Africa confirmed the findings from Rwanda and revealed tensions between the rights of refugees and security of countries at war. It was clear, in all these situations, that if the refugees were to be protected effectively in instances of mass influx, exclusion of war criminals and perpetrators of massive human rights violations or crimes against humanity would have to be approached in a consistent manner. At the same time, at the other end of the spectrum, the rights of refugees in other parts of the world were also being threatened by the way in which exclusion was applied within individualized refugee determination procedures. In those contexts an overly broad

interpretation of exclusion constituted a convenient "one-size fits-all" approach to unwanted applications.

An urgent need exists for benchmarks to steer decision makers between these two extremes, as well as a growing recognition of the need to interpret Article 1F(a) within the context of different, rapidly evolving sources of international criminal law (the Rome Statute, the statutes of the two ad hoc international criminal tribunals for the former Yugoslavia and Rwanda, and other instruments of international humanitarian law), refugee law, and human rights law. Specific avenues and complementary security strategies for refugees, from camp size and location to military intervention, must be taken into account.

The search for solutions, such as excluding some people from refugee camps, is a clear sign of the overwhelming complexity of the modern world. Given the new emphasis placed on civilian populations as instruments in warfare and the flow of displaced persons generated by contemporary conflicts, the definition of refugee within the Refugee Convention remains continuously challenged. The experience in the Great Lakes region of Central Africa (Burundi, Congo, Uganda, Rwanda) also raised a host of questions related to the role of humanitarian actors in complex emergencies, in particular those having to do with the relationship between humanitarian action and political/security interests. For example, can humanitarian action increase insecurity? How do humanitarian actors reconcile the different parts of their mandate that may come into conflict?

Controversial Role of the UNHCR during the Rwanda Genocide

The mass movements of population linked to widespread human rights abuse are not a new phenomenon in the Great Lakes region, but they have reached unprecedented proportions since the 1994 genocide in Rwanda, which claimed as many as one million lives. In its aftermath two million Rwandese fled their country for Zaire, Tanzania, and Burundi, and set up refugee camps. These, however, were the scene of widespread violence, which provoked fear and instability in host countries and compromised humanitarian assistance efforts. In the worst moments of the Rwandan genocide, thousands of refugees were slaughtered, settlements were destroyed, and refugees were again compelled to flee, into the Zairian forests or toward Rwanda. The presence in the refugee camps of soldiers who had actively participated in the genocide, and who were in a position of authority over the population, was one of the main obstacles preventing the safe and voluntary return of refugees to Rwanda. Indeed, those who wished to return home were often threatened by camp leaders and pressured into changing their minds.

Faced with this terrible situation, the UNHCR organized, in 1996, forced repatriations and the dismantling of camp facilities. A key issue was the applicability of the principle of nonrefoulement: Refugees were frequently sent back to their country of origin against their will and were, for a number of reasons, unable to actually make a decision whether to return or not. Furthermore, there were no reliable mechanisms to ensure that human rights were protected in the event of a mass return. The role played by the UNHCR has come under great criticism by humanitarian organizations that contend it was not appropriate for a protection agency to provide a political solution to the crisis. Others still believe that it was the best course of action, given the exceedingly complex and insecure situation and the international community's overall lack of support.

SEE ALSO Humanitarian Law; War Crimes

BIBLIOGRAPHY

Crépeau, François (1998). "International Cooperation on Interdiction of Asylum Seekers: A Global Perspective." In *Interdicting Refugees*, ed. Canadian Council for Refugees. Montreal: Canadian Council for Refugees. May 1998. pp. 7-20.

Goodwin-Gill, G. S (1989). "International Law and Human Rights: Trends Concerning International Migrants and Refugees." *International Migration Review* 23:526–546.

Helton, Arthur C. (1996). "The Legal Dimensions of Preventing Forced Migration." In *Cooperation and Conflict in the Former Soviet Union: Implications for Migration*, ed. J. R. Azrael, E. A. Payin, K. F. McCarthy, and G. Vernez. Santa Monica, Calif.: Rand Corporation.

Immigration and Refugee Board (1993). *Women Refugee Claimants Fearing Gender-Related Persecution*. Guidelines Issued by the Chairperson Pursuant to Section 65(3) of the Immigration Act. Ottawa, Canada: Immigration and Refugee Board.

Immigration and Refugee Board (1996). *Civilian Non-Combatants Fearing Persecution in Civil War Situations*. Guidelines Issued by the Chairperson Pursuant to Section 65(3) of the Immigration Act. Ottawa, Canada: Immigration and Refugee Board.

Kushner, Tony, and Katharine Knox (1999). *Refugees in an Age of Genocide: Global, National and Local Perspectives during the Twentieth Century*. London: F. Cass.

Lawyers Committee for Human Rights (2002). *Refugees, Rebels and The Quest for Justice*. New York: The Lawyers Committee for Human Rights.

Lisbon Expert Roundtable (2001). *Exclusion from Refugee Status*. Global Consultations on International Protection. UN Document EC/GC/01/2Track/130.

Médecins du Monde (1999). "A Case by Case Study Analysis of Recent Crises Assessing 20 Years of Humanitarian Action: Iraq, Somalia, the Former Yugoslavia, Rwanda, Burundi, the Former Zaire, Chechnya and Kosovo." In *Proceedings of Protecting People in Times of War International Conference*. Paris: Arche de la Défense

Mills, Kurt (2003). "Refugee Return from Zaire to Rwanda: The Role of UNHCR." In *Analyzing and Evaluating Intervention in Zaire*, 1996–97, ed. Howard Adelman. Lawrencevill, N.J.: Africa World Press/The Red Sea Press.

Nahla, Valji (2001). "Women and the 1951 Refugee Convention: 50 Years of Seeking Visibility." Available from http://www.isanet.org/archive/valji.html.

Wali, Sima (1995). "Women in Conditions of War and Peace." In *From Basic Needs to Basic Rights: Women's Claim to Human Rights*, ed. M. Schuler. Washington, D.C.: Women, Law and Development International.

François Crépeau
Delphine Nakache

Rehabilitation

Victims/survivors of genocide, crimes against humanity, and other serious violations of human rights and international humanitarian law often suffer physical and psychological effects, sometimes long after the traumatic events. Massive trauma causes such diverse and complex destruction that only a multidimensional, multidisciplinary integrative framework can adequately describe it, and only such an approach can optimally treat its effects. Typical reactions may be powerful negative feelings, painful physical sensations, or horrific imagery of the events. Many studies document the serious, chronic, sometimes life-long, and even multigenerational effects of massive trauma, including fear, paranoia, depression, anxiety, and personality changes. Starvation, untreated disease, experiences of persecution, psychological shock (or numbing), and head injury may interfere with the recall and verbal description of traumatic experiences.

Although ordinary stressful life events tend to release a strong need for sharing, victims/survivors of extreme traumatic events often encounter a societal imposed silence and thus share neither their experiences nor the aftermath. One study of torture victims by Weisaeth and Lind found that fewer than one out of ten victims disclosed details of their experiences to their close relatives. Even when released from captivity, victims continue to suffer stress over, for example, possible recapture or reprisals from agents of the state who had violated their human rights in the first place. The pervasive conspiracy of silence following trauma is detrimental to survivors' familial and sociocultural (re)integration and healing. It intensifies their already profound sense of isolation and mistrust of society, and makes the task of mourning their losses impossible. Further, survivors' rehabilitation can never be fully achieved if the society in which they live continues to tolerate serious or systematic human rights violations.

However, the needs of victims will require understanding more than their perceptible symptoms. Understanding their specific experience of physical and psychological trauma, the nature of the crime, and their cultural, economic, personal, and group historical backgrounds is also necessary.

Medical and trauma practitioners recognize that approaches to treatment must reflect the victim's personal experience of physical and psychological trauma. Experts, many of whom are vicariously traumatized by survivors' experiences, emphasize a holistic approach in which trust and the doctor/patient relationship are critical. Treatment strategies are most effective when they utilize local sources of social, cultural, and organizational support. Rehabilitation following egregious violations of human rights must not only address the traumatized individual, but also the family, local community, society, nation, and the international community. The individual needs to know that society as a whole acknowledges and understands what has happened. A true healing process includes apology, reparations, education, commemorations, and other ways of acknowledging what has taken place.

Genuine rehabilitation must include redress and justice as well as the restoration of dignity to the victim/survivor, and must be established in a sociopolitical context in which the experience and pain are shared by the larger society. The story must be told accurately, the public records secured, and mechanisms for monitoring and preventive intervention established to ensure nonrepetition and break the intergenerational chain of transmission.

It is increasingly recognized that impunity for perpetrators contributes to social and psychological problems and impedes healing by adversely affecting bereavement, inducing self-blame, and eroding society's moral codes. Justice denied exacerbates the victim/survivor's psychic wounds. Impunity for the wrongdoers becomes an additional traumatic factor that renders closure impossible and leads to a loss of respect for law and government, and an increase in crime. Further systematic exploration of how survivors experience efforts to bring perpetrators to justice and provide compensation, and how these efforts impact healing, is needed.

Despite the widespread recognition of the importance of physical and psychological treatment to aid the recovery process and restore the dignity of victims, their number far exceeds the available services, even in the most developed countries. Often services that do exist come too late. In many of the countries emerging from mass conflict, the few available programs are usually transitory, have not been well integrated into the health and social services sectors of the countries, and are often externally financed. As a result, many laudable initiatives are not sustainable and may not be able to address the long-term and often multigenerational needs of victims of mass trauma. In other cases the special needs of trauma victims have not been dealt with separately and what general services exist are not tailored to meet their needs.

The plight of victims of the worst crimes has created an international impetus to develop a legal framework to guarantee respect for their rights. In 1985 the United Nations (UN) General Assembly unanimously adopted "the Victims' Charter," the UN Declaration of Basic Principles of Justice for Victims of Crime and Abuse of Power. It galvanized support for the recognition of the rights of victims, in particular their rights of access to justice and redress, restitution, compensation, and assistance. This led to the UN Commission on Human Rights' appointment of an independent expert to further study the issue of victim redress. As of 2004 the draft of the basic principles and guidelines on the right to remedy and reparation for victims of violations of international human rights and humanitarian law is under discussion for adoption by the Commission. Most recently the Rome Statute of the International Criminal Court has recognized that justice serves not only a retributive but also a reparative function; it enshrines victims' rights to restitution, compensation, and rehabilitation and provides the Court with a mandate to give effect to these rights.

Significant strides have been made in recognizing the rights of victims of the worst crimes, and there is an increasing appreciation of the complexity of their needs. However, much remains to be done to realize these rights and provide those who have suffered the most abominable crimes with the critical multidimensional and multidisciplinary help they need.

SEE ALSO Compensation; Reparations; Restitution

BIBLIOGRAPHY

Danieli, Yael (1985). "The Treatment and Prevention of Long-Term Effects and Intergenerational Transmission of Victimization: A Lesson from Holocaust Survivors and Their Children." In *Trauma and Its Wake*, ed. C. R. Figley. New York: Brunner/Mazel.

Danieli, Yael (1988a). "Confronting the Unimaginable: Psychotherapists' Reactions to Victims of the Nazi Holocaust." In *Human Adaptation to Extreme Stress*, ed. J. P. Wilson, Z. Harel, and B. Kahana. New York: Plenum.

Danieli, Yael (1988b). "The Use of Mutual Support Approaches in the Treatment of Victims." In *Grief and Bereavement in Contemporary Society. Vol. 3: Support Systems*, ed. E. Chigier. London: Freund Publishing House.

Danieli, Yael (1988c). *Remembering for the Future, Theme II: The Impact of the Holocaust on the Contemporary World*. Oxford: Pergamon Press.

Danieli, Yael (1992). "Preliminary Reflections from a Psychological Perspective." In *The Right to Restitution, Compensation and Rehabilitation for Victims of Gross Violations of Human Rights and Fundamental Freedoms*, ed. T. C. van Boven, C. Flinterman, F. Grunfeld, and I. Westendorp. Netherlands Institute of Human Rights Special Issue No. 12:196–213.

Danieli, Yael (1994). "As Survivors Age—Parts I and II." *National Center for Post Traumatic Stress Disorder Clinical Quarterly* 4(1):1–7; 4(2):20–24.

Danieli, Yael (1998a). "Justice and Reparation: Steps in the Process of Healing." *International Review of Penal Law* 14:303–312.

Danieli, Yael, ed. (1998b). *International Handbook of Multigenerational Legacies of Trauma*. New York: Kluwer Academic/ Plenum.

Danieli, Yael, ed. (2002). *Sharing the Front Line and the Back Hills: International Protectors and Providers, Peacekeepers, Humanitarian Aid Workers and the Media in the Midst of Crisis*. Amityville, N.Y.: Baywood Publishing Company.

Danieli, Yael, Elsa Stamatopoulou, and Clarence J. Dias, eds. (1999). *The Universal Declaration of Human Rights: Fifty Years and Beyond*. Amityville, N.Y.: Baywood Publishing Company.

Ochberg, F. M., ed. (1988). *Post-Traumatic Therapy and Victims of Violence*. New York: Brunner/Mazel.

Weine, S., Y. Danieli, D. Silove, M. Van Ommeren, J. A. Fairbank, and J. Saul (2002). "Guidelines for International Training in Mental Health and Psychosocial Interventions for Trauma Exposed Populations in Clinical and Community Settings." Psychiatry 65(2):156–164.

Weisaeth, L., and I. Lind (1990). "A Follow-up Study of a Tortured Norwegian Ship's Crew." In *Proceeding of the 2nd International Wartime Medical Services Conference*, ed. J. E. Lundeberg, U. Otto, and B. Rybeck. Stockholm, Sweden: Swedish Defense Research Institute (FOA).

Yael Danieli

Religion

Religious people are not only the victims of mass killings, they also can be the perpetrators of violence. Although it would be much too simplistic to suggest that religion causes genocide and crimes against humanity, it nevertheless is true that religious people, prompted by religious motivations and employing religious symbols, have committed mass atrocities. A long tradition of this exists in Europe, with early examples being the Crusades, the destruction of Jewish communities and the Inquisition's bloody assaults on the Cathars of Montsegur and Montaillou.

Although religion has been implicated in mass killings, there is often a reluctance to acknowledge its role; indeed, religions themselves typically deny their complicity. In fact, it is even controversial to suggest the role that religion and religious communities may have played in atrocities. For example, the Nazi state is typically portrayed as atheist; religious people of the period are often considered either as heroes, such as Dietrich Bonhoeffer and the clergy who spoke out against Adolf Hitler, or as victims, such as the Jews and Jehovah's Witnesses. Generally, accounts do not emphasize the fact that the vast majority of those who committed the crimes against humanity were Protestants and Catholics. Thus, the Holocaust is depicted in terms of Nazi crimes and not crimes committed by Christians. In the twenty-first century, however, the historical literature has increasingly focused on the role of Christian anti-Semitism underlying the Third Reich and the role of military chaplains providing spiritual comfort to the perpetrators of crimes. (Simultaneously, as allies of

[WITCH-HUNTS]

The persecution and often murder of persons reputed to be "witches" is a phenomenon found in many less advanced societies. The witch-hunt was relatively widespread in Europe from about the sixteenth century. In more modern times, the term has been used to describe attacks on and purges of persons identified with certain political views. A link between the historic witch-hunts of unconventional women in seventeenth-century America and the post–World War II attacks upon public figures with left-wing views for alleged communist sympathies is the theme of a classic work of modern theater, *The Crucible* (1953), by Arthur Miller.

European witch-hunts were associated with the religious turmoil of the fifteenth through seventeenth centuries that brought the Reformation. They were no doubt also influenced by the social and economic transformations of those times. European witch-hunts appear to have begun to decline with the Peace of Westfalia, signed in 1648 after thirty years of war—probably because of the climate of religious tolerance that the treaty encouraged. Nor could such primitive views broadly survive in the intellectual ferment of the Enlightenment.

Many Christian denominations, both Catholic and Protestant, encouraged belief in the existence of witches and witchcraft. A widely circulated publication, *Malleus Maleficarum,* which appeared in 1486, promoted the fear of witches, who were usually poor, rural, and single women. Two years earlier, Pope Innocent VIII issued a bill titled *Summis desiderantes,* which allowed the Inquisition to pursue witches and witchcraft as enemies of Christianity. According to the *Malleus Maleficarum,* "[A]ll wickedness is but little to the wickedness of a woman . . . What else is woman but a foe to friendship, an unescapable punishment, a necessary evil, a natural temptation, a desirable calamity, domestic danger, a delectable detriment, an evil nature, painted with fair colours. . . .

Women are by nature instruments of Satan—they are by nature carnal, a structural defect rooted in the original creation" (Accessed at http://www.malleusmaleficarum.org/index.html).

Victims were portrayed as being evil and unclean. Subsequent feminist analysis of witch-hunts explains them as campaigns to challenge rebellious role models for women. Some men were also victims of these witch-hunts, sometimes because they attempted to protect the women who had been targeted. Nevertheless, because most alleged victims were women, some have described these witch-hunts as "gendercide."

The witch-hunts were generally provoked by campaigns of denunciation often initiated by children or nuns. Those who were accused were then tortured until they confessed, although some died in the process. Show trials were often held, and convictions generally resulted in capital punishment. Historians believe that anywhere between 50,000 and 200,000 people were killed in the European witch-hunts.

The most famous witch-hunts in America took place in the Puritan community of Salem, Massachusetts, in 1692. The Salem witch-hunt began when two Puritan women, Abigail Williams and Betty Parris, accused the slave of Samuel Parris of the practice. The slave girl was named Tituba, and was either of aboriginal American or African origin. Quickly, the campaign became hysterical, and for many in the community the only way to avoid an accusation was to become an accuser.

Although the European witch-hunts are the best documented, many societies have engaged in similar campaigns of persecution directed against women and men believed to have supernatural powers. In a famous judgment on capital punishment in June 1995, South African judge Albie Sachs described how the death penalty, though not generally employed in pre-colonial southern Africa, was practiced in the case of alleged witchcraft.

The contemporary usage of the term *witch-hunt* describes the purges of communists, communist sympathizers, and persons with left-wing views, principally in the United States, in the early years of the cold war. Academics, film producers, diplomats, and journalists often lost their jobs as a result of the anti-communist witch-hunts of the 1950s led by Senator Joseph McCarthy of Wisconsin. At the height of the witch-hunt, in 1953, Communist Party members Julius and Ethel Rosenberg were executed for espionage, the only time that capital punishment has been used for that crime during peacetime. For further reading, see Farrington, Karen (1996). *Dark Justice: A History of Punishment and Torture.* New York: Smithmark; Gragg, Larry (1992). *The Salem Witch Crisis.* New York: Praeger; Klaits, Joseph (1985). *Servants of Satan: The Age of the Witch Hunts.* Bloomington: Indiana University Press; and Levack, Brian P. (1995). *The Witch-Hunt in Early Modern Europe,* 2nd edition. New York: Longman. **WILLIAM A. SCHABAS**

Nazi Germany, many Catholic clergy in Croatia during World War II bore responsibility for supporting the Ustashe in the killing of Muslims, a circumstance that the Roman Catholic Church continues to deny or downplay.)

The Bosnian genocide provides a different type of example. In Bosnia, unlike Nazi Germany, state political and military leaders intentionally employed Christian religious language and symbols to stimulate popular violence and justify military slaughter. Although studies of Bosnia may suggest, for example, that the ethnic cleansing of Muslims was a "result of the political contest behind the wars, not ethnic or religious hatreds," (Woodward, 1993, p. 243), it is far more likely that political leaders deliberately manipulated religious imagery from Serbian history to suggest Orthodox Serbs were innocent victims of Muslim atrocities. (Sells, 1996, 2001). Many within the Slavic Orthodox churches continue to insist that the Serbs were the real victims and deny their complicity other than some understandable but limited overreactions in a "civil war."

As yet another example, the Rwandan genocide did not break out along religious lines, but religious institutions and personnel were used to promote the massive killing of Tutsi by Hutu. There have been many reports of Hutu religious leaders urging Tutsi to seek sanctuary in churches against rampaging Hutu mobs, only to learn that the supposed sanctuary was simply a planned gathering place to make the slaughter of the Tutsi more convenient for the perpetrators. Further, high officials in the Catholic Church of Rwanda allegedly participated in the organization of the genocide, in this case against other Catholics who were Tutsi. As in the other examples given here, the Protestant and Catholic churches have been reluctant to acknowledge the roles of their local leaders in the violence.

Although religious beliefs certainly are not necessary to prompt mass killings, as the history of Stalinist Russia, Maoist China, and Pol Pot's Khmer Rouge demonstrate, religion can play an important role in providing perpetrators with a sense of a God-ordained mission to cleanse the world of evil, offering solace to those who commit violence, or justifying actions taken by others. In this way, when religion provides a rationale for zealotry, religious people can be seduced into becoming murderers—just as in cases of religiously inspired terrorism and other forms of religiously inspired violence.

Religion does not, of course, play only a negative role in atrocities. Many courageous religious leaders have found spiritual inspiration that has moved them to sacrifice their lives in defense of others. Though less known than the stories of killings, devout and committed religious believers have risked and lost their lives sheltering Armenians in Turkey, Jews in France, Belgium, and the Netherlands, and Muslims in Bosnia and Serbia. Religion also can play a valuable—and sometimes decisive—role in reconstruction and reconciliation after the atrocities end.

SEE ALSO Catholic Church; Religious Groups

BIBLIOGRAPHY

Bergen, Doris L. (2001). "Between God and Hitler: German Military Chaplains and the Crimes of the Third Reich." In *God's Name: Genocide and Religion in the Twentieth Century*, ed. Omer Bartov and Phyllis Mack. New York: Berghahn Books.

Gellately, Robert, and Ben Kiernan, eds. (2003). *The Specter of Genocide: Mass Murder in Historical Perspective*. Cambridge: Cambridge University Press.

Neier, Aryeh (1998). *War Crimes: Brutality, Genocide, Terror, and the Struggle for Justice*. New York: Random House.

Sells, Michael A. (1996). *The Bridge Betrayed: Religion and Genocide in Bosnia*. Berkeley: University of California Press.

Steigmann-Gall, Richard (2003). *The Holy Reich: Nazi Conceptions of Christianity, 1919–1945*. Cambridge: Cambridge University Press.

Woodward, Susan L. (1993). *Balkan Tragedy: Chaos and Dissolution after the Cold War*. Washington, D.C.: The Brookings Institution.

T. Jeremy Gunn

Religious Groups

Religious groups are one of the four groups identified for protection by the 1948 United Nations (UN) Convention on the Prevention and Punishment of the Crime of Genocide. In order to convict an individual of genocide, according to the Genocide Convention, it must be proved that the accused committed one or more of the specific acts prohibited (such as killing or causing serious bodily harm) and that the act was "committed with intent to destroy, in whole or in part, a national, ethnical, racial or religious group, as such" (Article 2). The same components of "intent" and "religious group" mentioned in the Genocide Convention also appear in the Statute of the International Criminal Tribunal for the Former Yugoslavia (ICTY; Article 4.2), the Statute of the International Criminal Tribunal for Rwanda (ICTR; Article 2.2), and the Elements of Crimes of the International Criminal Court (ICC; Article 6). The elements of crimes section additionally provides that the targeting of persons on the basis of their belonging to a religious group constitutes the "crime against humanity of persecution" (Article 7[1][h]), and that the humiliation or degradation of "religious personnel" is a violation of the "war crime of outrages upon personal dignity" (Article 8[2][c][ii]).

The meaning of "religious group" and "religion" within international law and the Genocide Convention is more complicated than might at first be imagined. In fact, the difficulty of identifying when the intent to destroy a religious group, either in whole or in part, has occurred illustrates some of the underlying difficulties of interpreting the meaning of the Genocide Convention, whether in strictly legal terms or within the context of public language where the word "genocide" is often used rhetorically to describe an atrocity.

For example, did the massive killings by the Khmer Rouge in Cambodia constitute genocide? The strict legal application of the Genocide Convention aside, the killing of between 2 and 3.5 million Cambodians would certainly qualify as an egregious case of genocide in ordinary human discourse. But when subjected to legal analysis, can it be questioned which "national, ethnical, racial or religious *group* [emphasis added], as such" the perpetrators intended to destroy in whole or in part? The vast majority of those killed were the Khmer people—the same national and ethnic group that perpetrated the killings. Most observers would identify the clearest case of genocide within Cambodia as the annihilation of the Cham Muslims, a religious group, who were targeted with particular vengeance. However, does it make sense to conclude that the millions of Khmer people killed were not victims of genocide and that only the Cham were because they experienced a higher percentage of victims (although numerically smaller)? Although Buddhists were not targeted per se, the Buddhist clergy was. Should the Buddhist clergy then be considered a "religious group" within the meaning of the Genocide Convention?

It is also complicated, and sometimes controversial, to suggest that a particular people were marked for extinction in whole or in part because of their religion. For example, approximately two million southern Sudanese died in the last fifteen years of the twentieth century as a result of the policies and actions of the government in Khartoum. Were the southern Sudanese victimized by northern Muslims because of their religious affiliation (principally indigenous religions and Christianity), racial and ethnic differences, or historical and economic reasons? Did Saddam Hussein, modern-day Iraq's former leader, target Kurds and Marsh Arabs (*Mad'am*) for reasons of religion, politics, or economics?

Although the answers to the Cambodian, Sudanese, and Iraq questions trigger (or not) a discussion of the applicability of the Genocide Convention, such questions are purely academic to the victims of executions, rampages, and starvation.

Regardless of the applicability of the Genocide Convention, the religious divide between perpetrators and victims is frequently a salient characteristic of mass killings. Principally Muslim Turks either killed, forcibly converted, or exiled Christian Armenians. Although the Nazi state was officially atheist, the vast majority of those responsible for operating the death camps and exterminating Jews were born, raised, and died Christians. Orthodox Christian Serbs killed Bosnian and Albanian Muslims. The atheist Chinese state executed Tibetan Buddhists. In each of these cases, of course, there were other victims. Muslim Turks who tried to rescue Armenians also were executed as sympathizers. Romani, homosexuals, political dissidents, Christian clergy, and the physically and mentally handicapped also were victims of the Nazi death camps. In other cases of mass violence, though not typically identified as cases of genocide, similar hostilities are often provoked by government officials and executed by crowds, as in Gujarat, India. Thus, in many cases of genocide and mass killings, religion serves as a marker of differences.

Despite the importance of religion in many (though certainly not all) cases of genocide and crimes against humanity, historians and other commentators often have the tendency to emphasize the ethnic characteristics of the victims, as opposed to their religious characteristics. This reluctance may in some cases result from misapprehension about the meaning of the victim's religion to the perpetrators. It is important to understand that with regard to religious discrimination, persecution, and violence, there are three aspects of religion which should be differentiated: religion as belief, religion as identity, and religion as way of life. The first of these pertains to spiritual beliefs or theological opinions, and adherence to doctrines and teachings. Religion as "identity" refers to the community into which one is born regardless of one's individual beliefs or observance of sacred rituals. According to this view, people might believe that all Turks are Muslim, all Poles are Catholic, and all Russians are Orthodox. "Way of life" refers to religion and its manifestations in rituals, diet, and social activities. Although these three aspects are not mutually exclusive, and they can be interrelated in the minds of the religious person and the persecutor alike, genocide and crimes against humanity emerge most commonly within the context of religion as identity. Victims are targeted most directly because of who they are rather than what they believe or what they do. In Nazi Germany a Jew could not escape brutalization by simply renouncing his or her beliefs, or maintaining a secular lifestyle. While a religious group is likely targeted because of its despised identity, its beliefs and way of life may well serve as the signals that inflame the hostility initially aroused because of identity.

SEE ALSO Minorities; Persecution; Religion

BIBLIOGRAPHY

Gellately, Robert, and Ben Kiernan, eds. (2003). *The Specter of Genocide: Mass Murder in Historical Perspective.* Cambridge: Cambridge University Press.

Gunn, T. Jeremy (2003). "The Complexity of Religion and the Definition of 'Religion' in International Law." *Harvard Human Rights Journal* 16:189–215.

Mojzes, Paul, ed. (1998). *Religion and the War in Bosnia.* Atlanta, Ga.: Scholars Press.

Neier, Aryeh (1998). *War Crimes: Brutality, Genocide, Terror, and the Struggle for Justice.* New York: Random House.

Sells, Michael A. (1996). *The Bridge Betrayed: Religion and Genocide in Bosnia.* Berkeley: University of California Press.

Suny, Ronald Grigor (2001). "Religion, Ethnicity, and Nationalism: Armenians, Turks, and the End of the Ottoman Empire." In *God's Name: Genocide and Religion in the Twentieth Century,* ed. Omer Bartov and Phyllis Mack. New York: Berghahn Books.

T. Jeremy Gunn

Reparations

The term *reparations* usually refers to the measures that a state must take after it violates a rule of international law. Reparations can also apply more generally to remedying all wrongs, whether committed by a state and its agents or by private parties. Reparations for genocide and crimes against humanity will usually require remedial action by both individual perpetrators and the state involved because such acts are illegal under international and national law. Human rights law and humanitarian law also impose a duty on states to take reasonable measures, or in legal terminology to "exercise due diligence," to prevent violations of human rights by private persons. If the state fails to do so, it will be responsible for providing reparations.

In an early international court case, the Permanent Court of International Justice called the obligation to make reparations for an unlawful act "a general principle of international law" and part of "a general conception of law" (Factory at Chorzów [*Germany v. Poland*], 1928 P.C.I.J. [ser. A], no. 17 at 29 [September 13]). This reflects the fact that all legal systems require those who cause harm through illegal or wrongful acts to take action to repair the harm they have caused.

In addition, human rights treaties and declarations adopted by the United Nations guarantee individual victims the right to a remedy, that is, access to justice and reparations in national proceedings. The Universal Declaration of Human Rights, Article 8, proclaims that "[e]veryone has the right to an effective remedy by the competent national tribunals for acts violating the fundamental rights granted him by the constitution or laws." This guarantee would, of course, include remedies for criminal acts that violate guaranteed rights. The International Covenant on Civil and Political Rights contains a similar guarantee in its Article 2(3). The UN Human Rights Committee overseeing compliance with the covenant has stated that when acts of torture occur, for example, a government is

> under a duty to . . . conduct an inquiry into the circumstances of [the victim's] torture, to punish those found guilty of torture and to take steps to ensure that similar violations do not occur in the future. The committee also has called for investigation and prosecution in cases involving arbitrary executions and disappearances. All these acts constitute types of reparations for the wrong done.

The aim of reparation is, where possible, to restore the situation that would have existed had there been no wrongful act. This means to wipe out all of the consequences of the act and try to reestablish the situation that in all probability would have existed if the act had not been committed. Restitution means to restore exactly the preinjury status. If this is not possible, full compensation equivalent to restitution may be required. Satisfaction is an additional set of remedies designed for noneconomic losses, such as harm to dignity. Most important, the wrongful act must cease.

One widely accepted purpose of reparations is remedial justice, to undo the wrong done to an injured party. Reparation is thus designed to put the injured party in the same position as if no wrongful act occurred, without respect to the cost or consequences it may have for the wrongdoer. Reparations may also serve to punish and deter wrongdoing or aim at reconciliation and inducing positive future behavior.

Procedures for Claiming Reparations

The issue of reparations for genocide and crimes against humanity is complex because the acts usually involve simultaneous breaches of national and international law by individuals and states. Reparations may be owed by both the state and the individuals responsible, and claims may be made by survivors at either the national or international level. Taking together the traditional law of state responsibility, human rights law, and international criminal law, claims for reparations can be presented in one of five ways: (1) The state of nationality of the victims could bring a claim on their behalf against the state responsible for the wrong; (2) the victims may be able to bring a claim against the responsible state in an international human rights tribunal; (3) victims may bring claims against the responsible state in national judicial or administrative bodies; (4) victims may present their claims against the individual perpetrators in an international criminal court; and (5) the victims may make a claim against the individual perpetrators in a national civil or criminal proceeding.

In nearly all instances, reparations are first claimed through administrative or judicial procedures within a state. International law requires that such procedures be followed before a case can come to an international body. This is known as the *doctrine of exhaustion of local remedies*. Those who have been wronged may sue the wrongdoer for civil remedies or seek to have the perpetrator prosecuted according to criminal law. If the wrongdoer is an agent of the state, a special law and/or process may govern or restrict the right to sue. Many government officials have immunity from lawsuit for their official acts. In such instances, the state itself may have an obligation to make reparations to the injured party.

At the international level, reparations may be sought either by one state bringing a claim against another or by individuals filing a petition against the state committing the wrong. There are presently no international courts in which an individual can sue another individual for reparations, although it may be possible for victims of abuse to seek reparations from perpetrators convicted by the International Criminal Court (ICC).

Interstate claims for reparations on behalf of their nationals have a long tradition, especially at the conclusion of a war. Most of the experience with reparations in international law concerns postwar agreements to settle claims, whereby one state may pay large amounts of compensation to another state. The recipient then should use the funds to redress the injuries to its nationals. A provision of the Treaty of Sèvres concluded between the Allies from World War I and Turkey in 1920 provided for the restitution of property of Armenians killed by the Turks. At the conclusion of World War II, Article 14 of the September 8, 1951, peace treaty between the Allies and Japan "recognized that Japan should pay reparations to the Allied Powers for damage and suffering caused by it during the war."

Once local remedies have concluded, individuals who do not obtain redress may be able to bring claims directly against their own governments or another state in a human rights tribunal. It is necessary that the state

In the twentieth century Menominee feared that, without federal protection, their tribal lands would pass into the hands of non–Native Americans. On December 22, 1973, U.S. President Richard Nixon signed the Menominee Restoration Bill, and in April 1975 the lands of Menominee County (Wisconsin) reverted back to reservation status. In this photo from the same time period, U.S. Secretary of the Interior Rogers Morton shakes hands with Ernest Neconish, elder statesman of the Menominee. [AP/WIDE WORLD PHOTOS]

involved be a party to the human rights treaty establishing the tribunal to which the individual seeks access and in some instances the state must separately accept the jurisdiction of the tribunal. Each human rights treaty usually specifies the rights that are protected and the types of reparations that the tribunal can award the individual whose rights have been violated.

Types of Reparation

Restitution is intended to restore the victim to the situation that existed before the violations occurred. In many cases of international crimes, particularly genocide, this will not be possible. Even if restitution is possible in theory, the individual perpetrator may not be able to provide it and the state will have to take on responsibility for the crime. Restitution may include restoration of liberty, legal rights, social status, family life and citizenship, return to the place of residence, resto-

Demonstrator at the United Nations World Conference Against Racism, August 31, 2001. Some 6,000 delegates gathered in the coastal city of Durban, South Africa, where a diverse range of human rights issues, including reparations for past atrocities, were discussed. [REUTERS/CORBIS]

ration of employment, and return of property. When restitution cannot be provided, compensation and/or satisfaction must substitute to remedy the harm that has been done.

Compensation is often inadequate, and the more serious the harm, the more compensation as a remedy becomes a problem. Criminal conduct harms not only the victim, it also undermines the rule of law and societal norms. For this reason, compensation is inevitably a second-best response when prosecution and restitution prove impossible to achieve. However, for many crime victims, damages are important. Compensation supplies the means for whatever part of the former life and projects remains possible and may allow for new projects. In cases where the perpetrator is made to pay, compensation also reflects a moral judgment of wrongdoing. Clearly, for survivors of genocide and crimes against humanity, large amounts of money may be necessary to place victims in the same position of relative

satisfaction that they occupied before certain events took place.

Compensation should be provided for any economically assessable damage resulting from the wrongful acts. Widely acceptable compensable losses include physical or mental harm, including pain, suffering, and emotional distress; lost opportunities, including education; material damages and loss of earnings, including loss of earning potential; harm to reputation or dignity; and costs required for legal or expert assistance, medicines and medical services, and psychological and social services. Rehabilitation costs are also normally provided, including future medical and psychological care as well as legal and social services. Full reparations should include attorneys' fees and costs incurred in bringing a claim. If not, individuals will not be fully restored to their preinjury state.

As part of satisfaction, appropriate mechanisms also are needed to confront and process trauma and abuse, facilitating closure rather than repression. Dealing with grief, anger, and rehabilitation takes time. Victims may harbor deep resentments that if not dealt with could result in vigilante justice and retribution. The long-term mental health of individual victims and society as a whole may be threatened if adequate treatment and rehabilitation are not provided. States and international organizations have introduced a variety of nonmonetary measures to respond to these needs in redressing genocide and crimes against humanity.

International and National Claims
Some victims of genocide and crimes against humanity committed during wars have received restitution or compensation negotiated between states. Germany created a system of compensation for Nazi genocide and crimes against humanity. From 1939 onward, those who had escaped from countries overrun by the Germans demanded compensation for property and monies taken from them. Some argued that in addition to individual compensation, a collective claim must be presented for reparations to the Jewish people for the property whose owners were unknown or dead, for institutions and communities that had been destroyed or had vanished, and for damage done to the very fabric of the Jewish people's existence. On September 29, 1945, Chaim Weizmann presented the four Allied powers (France, Great Britain, United States, USSR) with the first postwar Jewish claims, which later became the basis of the claim for the state of Israel (of which Weizmann served as its first president): (1) restitution of property; (2) restoration of heirless property to representatives of the Jewish people to finance the rehabilitation of victims of Nazi persecution; (3) transfer of a

percentage of all reparation to be paid by Germany for rehabilitation and resettlement in Palestine; and (4) inclusion of all assets of Germans formerly residing in Palestine as part of the reparations.

The first Allied statement on restitution and reparation (January 5, 1943) announced that the governments reserved all their rights to declare invalid any transfers of property or title of property in territory under German or Italian control, whether the transfers were effected by force or by quasilegal means. The Paris Reparations Conference (November 9–December 21, 1945) accepted the principle that individual and group compensation should be paid to the victims of Nazi persecution in need of rehabilitation and not in a position to secure assistance from governments in receipt of reparations from Germany. Receipt of rehabilitation funds would not prejudice a later claim for compensation. Restitution would apply to identifiable property that had been seized during the period of conquest with or without payment. Indemnification was to be paid for objects of an artistic, educational, or religious value that had been seized by the Germans, but that could no longer be restored to their rightful owners.

The Paris Reparations Conference agreed on several points concerning individual claims, including priority to claims of the elderly and indemnification for damage to vocational and professional training. Claimants who could prove they had been held in concentration camps would receive an overall sum of 3,000 deutsche marks as compensation for deprivation of liberty. The conference set a cap of 25,000 deutsche marks for damage that occurred before June 1, 1945. Another 450 million deutsche marks were paid to the Conference on Jewish Material Claims against Germany, a common holding for twenty-three Jewish organizations, for the settlement of Jewish victims living outside Israel. Finally, a special fund of 50 million deutsche marks was created for nonpracticing Jews.

Successive German compensation laws and agreements were enacted and concluded between 1948 and 1965, including a 1952 treaty between the Federal Republic of Germany (FRG) and Israel. The preamble to the 1952 agreement noted that "unspeakable criminal acts were perpetrated against the Jewish people" and that Germany agreed "within the limits of their capacity to make good the material damage caused by these acts." It also mentioned that Israel had assumed the burden of resettling many destitute Jewish refugees. Article I stated that "the Federal Republic of Germany shall, in view of the considerations herein before recited, pay to the State of Israel the sum of 3,000 million Deutsche Marks."

Between 1959 and 1964 Germany concluded treaties with thirteen European states providing for the payment of 977 million deutsche marks for injury to the life, health, and liberty of their nationals. It also agreed to further contributions: with states in Eastern Europe for the victims of pseudo-medical experiments (122 million deutsche marks) and to the UN High Commissioner for Refugees (57 million deutsche marks). In terms of domestic law, the culmination of German reparations can be found in the Federal Law on Reparation (the *Bundesentschaedigungsgesetz*). Under this law, various categories of damage are provided for anyone who was oppressed because of political opposition to National Socialism, or because of race, religion, or ideology, or who suffered in consequence loss of life, damage to limb or health, loss of liberty, property, or possessions, or harm to professional or economic prospects.

In 1990 the former East Germany, in a unilateral declaration, offered the World Jewish Congress the sum of $100 million. The total sums paid by Germany in reparations for the actions of the Nazi regime during World War II amount to some 103 billion deutsche marks.

Other persons and groups who have suffered from crimes against humanity, including those used as slave laborers during World War II, have attempted to sue governments or companies to obtain reparations. Japanese Canadians have asked the Canadian government for redress, apology, and the revision of history books with regard to their World War II relocation and detention. Italian Canadians have done the same. Asian women who were forcibly detained as sex slaves by the Japanese military have demanded redress. Former prisoners of war and civilians also seek compensation for the forced labor they performed in Germany and Japan. The lawsuits have generally been unsuccessful, either because they are barred by World War II peace treaties or because the governments involved have immunity from lawsuits. In contrast, banks, museums, art dealers, and governments in several countries have faced claims from victims and their heirs for the restitution of money and works of art stolen during World War II. Problems of proof and conflicting local laws make it difficult to resolve the claims, but many have proven successful or have led to negotiated settlements.

In contrast to the extensive international law and practice on state reparations, there is very little in law or practice on obtaining reparations from individual perpetrators in international proceedings. Before the Rome Statute of the ICC, no international criminal tribunal was expressly authorized to award victims reparations other than restitution. The Security Council resolution establishing the ad hoc International Criminal Tribunal for Rwanda (ICTR) promised to ensure that violations would be "effectively redressed," but the statute of the ICTR limits redress to restitution as a punishment additional to, but not as a substitute for, imprisonment. Neither it nor the statute for the ad hoc Tribunal for the Former Yugoslavia empowers the courts to award compensation or measures of rehabilitation to victims of the crimes being prosecuted, but both statutes foresee the possibility of compensation to victims by national courts in national proceedings.

In contrast to the limited mandates of the ad hoc tribunals, the statute of the ICC expressly includes the possibility for victims to obtain reparations from convicted criminals (Rome Statute, Article 75). The court has discretion to order the perpetrator to provide the victim "restitution, compensation, rehabilitation and other forms of remedy." Nonmonetary awards such as an apology also could be involved. Recognizing that many of those convicted of international crimes may be poor or without any assets, Article 79 of the Rome Statute establishes a trust fund "for the benefit of the victims of crimes within the jurisdiction of the Court" and "of the families of such victims."

Apart from international criminal courts, international tribunals for the protection of human rights may hear cases, judge violations, and afford reparations. Such human rights cases cannot be brought against individuals, but only against the state responsible for the violations. The European Convention for the Protection of Human Rights and Fundamental Freedoms, which went into effect on September 3, 1953, was the first to create an international court for the protection of human rights and a procedure for individual denunciations of human rights violations. The European Court of Human Rights renders judgments in which it may afford "just satisfaction" to the injured party, including compensation for both monetary losses and nonmonetary (moral) damages. In the European Court of Justice of the European Union, individual claimants may plead for an award of damages or other remedies for the violation of fundamental rights. Such rights form an integral part of the general principles of law the court is required to apply. In the Western Hemisphere, the American Convention on Human Rights adopted by the Organization of American States establishes an Inter-American Court of Human Rights that has broad power to order reparations on behalf of victims of human rights violations.

Satisfaction and guarantees of nonrepetition are the most problematic forms of reparations in the context of international crimes and individual responsibility, although some types of satisfaction are inherent in

the criminal process: Cessation normally results from the arrest, trial, and conviction of the perpetrator. Disclosure of the truth should occur during the trial. More difficult is the question of locating killed or missing persons and obtaining an official declaration or judicial decision restoring the dignity, reputation, and legal and social rights of the victim and close associates. These forms of redress may not be possible through the criminal prosecution of individual perpetrators. Commemorations of and tributes to the victims also are matters for state action rather than for individual perpetrators.

The prosecution of those committing international crimes is a form of reparation. The obligation on states to prosecute or extradite those accused of genocide, crimes against humanity, and war crimes exists in several international agreements, including the Genocide Convention, the Geneva Conventions of 1949, and the 1977 Protocol I to the Geneva Conventions. Global and regional conventions against torture impose a similar duty. These agreements require states to cooperate with each other in the investigation, prosecution, and adjudication of those charged with the crimes covered under the agreements and the punishment of those convicted. In 1971 the UN General Assembly affirmed that a state's refusal to cooperate in the arrest, extradition, trial, and punishment of persons accused or convicted of war crimes and crimes against humanity is "contrary to the United Nations Charter and to generally recognized norms of international law." The commentary to the Geneva Conventions also confirms that the obligation to prosecute is "absolute" for grave breaches committed within the context of international armed conflicts.

A key role of prosecution is to establish an authoritative record of abuses that will withstand later revisionist efforts. The emphasis in criminal trials on full and reliable evidence in accordance with due process usually makes the results more credible than those of other, more political proceedings, including truth commissions. The chief prosecutor at Nuremberg said that the documentation of Nazi atrocities was one of the most important legacies of the trials. The Nazi actions were documented "with such authenticity and in such detail that there can be no responsible denial of these crimes in the future and no tradition of martyrdom of the Nazi leaders can arise among informed people."

Right to Reparations

UN human rights bodies have considered the issue of ensuring remedies to victims of atrocities, including genocide and crimes against humanity. In resolution 1988/11 of September 1, 1988, the Sub-Commission on Prevention of Discrimination and Protection of Minorities recognized that all victims of gross violations of human rights and fundamental freedoms should be entitled to restitution, fair and just compensation, and the means for as full a rehabilitation as possible for any damage suffered. In draft principles submitted to the UN, one study proposed that states must act "to prevent violations, to investigate violations, to take appropriate action against the violators, and to afford remedies and reparation to victims. Particular attention must be paid to the prevention of gross violations of human rights and international humanitarian law and to the duty to prosecute and punish perpetrators of crimes under international law" (Van Boven, 1996, p. 1). Principle 4 calls on every state to ensure that adequate legal or other appropriate remedies are available to all persons claiming that their rights have been violated.

In 1985 members of the UN adopted the Declaration of Basic Principles of Justice for Victims of Crime and Abuse of Power. The declaration details the types of reparations due to crime victims in national law. Principle 8 states that, when appropriate, restitution should be made to victims, their families, or dependents by offenders or the third parties responsible for their behavior. This includes the return of property and may include compensation for harm or loss suffered. Restitution may be considered as a sentencing option in criminal cases in addition to other sanctions. Because cases often involve state agents or officials acting in an official or quasi-official capacity, paragraph 11 provides that victims should also receive redress from the state. Paragraph 12 requires states to endeavor to provide financial compensation to victims who have sustained significant injury as a result of serious crimes, when compensation is not fully available from the offender or other sources. When persons have died or become incapacitated as a result of such victimization, their families or dependents should be compensated financially. For this purpose, states should establish or strengthen national funds to compensate victims. In addition, victims should receive the necessary material, medical, psychological, and social assistance through governmental, voluntary, community, and indigenous means. Finally, attention must be given to victims who have special needs because of the nature of the harm inflicted or other factors that may disadvantage them in some way.

In practice, reparations may be difficult to obtain. The UN has thus created a voluntary fund for victims of torture and a voluntary fund for victims of slavery and slavelike practices. These funds finance programs that provide medical, psychological, social, or legal assistance to victims and their relatives. Examples of this include the establishment of treatment centers, meetings of experts, aid to child victims, publications, legal assistance, and economical and social rehabilitation. Although these funds do not serve the purpose of making the perpetrators redress the harm they have caused, the money collected is used with the aim of ensuring some relief for those who are victims of the acts specified.

SEE ALSO Compensation; Restitution

BIBLIOGRAPHY

Hayner, Priscilla B. (2001). *Unspeakable Truths: Confronting State Terror and Atrocity*. New York: Routledge.

Minow, Martha (1998). *Between Vengeance and Forgiveness: Facing History after Genocide and Mass Violence*. Boston: Beacon Press.

Rosenberg, Tina (1995). *The Haunted Land: Facing Europe's Ghosts after Communism*. New York: Random House.

Shelton, Dinah (1999). *Remedies in International Human Rights Law*. New York: Oxford University Press.

Van Boven, Theo (1996). *Revised Set of Basic Principles and Guidelines on the Right to Reparation for Victims of [Gross] Violations of Human Rights and International Humanitarian Law*. UN Document E/CN.4/1997/104 (month, day, year?), Appendix. Available from http://www.unhchr.ch/huridocda/huridoca.nsf/Documents?OpenFrameset.

Dinah L. Shelton

Reproduction

The widely accepted belief that genocide only entails killing members of a racial, religious, national, or ethnic group misconstrues the multiple ways that genocide is perpetuated. Article II of the 1948 United Nations (UN) Convention on the Prevention and Punishment of the Crime of Genocide (hereafter referred to as the Genocide Convention) underscores the reality that genocide can be accomplished by other acts, independent of or along with killings. The infliction of serious physical or mental harm to members of a group, or the transfer of children from one group to another, suffices, under certain conditions, as an act of genocide. Likewise, Article II(d) of the Genocide Convention seeks to prevent, suppress, and punish those who would "impose measures intended to prevent birth within the group." This provision verifies that by impeding a group's ability to reproduce and thus denying the physical existence of its members, even prior to their birth, a group can be destroyed in whole or part.

German Laws on Racial Purity
In the mid-1930s Germany enacted a series of laws, ostensibly to ensure the physical health of its citizens, but

in reality, to oversee the purity of "the German race." The idea that the political state should be composed of a single race or unique people intertwined several political and pseudo-scientific theories. The Enlightenment philosophy of the 1700s exalted the natural rights of man. Eighteenth-century European revolts against the monarchy and American revolts against colonialism were heavily influenced by Enlightenment philosophers who advocated the restructuring of political states according to the true nature of the democratic individual.

In the mid-nineteenth century ethnologists, influenced by Charles Darwin's theories on the biological origin of the species, tried to determine the historical origins of the races. In the 1850s Arthur de Gobineau, horrified by the decline of French society, proposed a racial theory to explain the evolution of human societies. In his *Essay on the Inequality of the Human Race*, Gobineau maintained the existence of three unequal races: white, yellow, and black. The white race was superior to the others, while the black race was inferior to the white and yellow races. Each race also possessed inherent intellectual abilities. A race's physiological traits, such as prominent noses among the white race, supposedly revealed immutable values. Gobineau concluded that the major threat to human society and the harbinger of a civilization's degeneration was mixed-race procreation.

In the late nineteenth century Houston Stewart Chamberlain, an Englishman residing in Germany, disseminated the "scientific" idea that among the white races, only the Teutons stood at the pinnacle of racial evolution. Chamberlain touted the Teutons, also called Aryans, as an ancient, noble, pure-blooded race. He believed that Teutons had, over the centuries, developed a "race-soul" that biologically rendered them morally, spiritually, and creatively superior. Chamberlain's findings nourished a genre of romantic-political myth about the Aryan race and prompted some Germans to believe that they were pure descendants of the Teutons. Inspired by Chamberlain's race-based premises, ethnologists eagerly unearthed certain linguistic and semiotic proof of the longevity and original purity of the Aryan race.

By the 1930s, when the Nazi Party assumed power in Germany, eugenics, the science of selective biological breeding, became a political goal under the guise of health regulations, euphemistically termed racial hygiene. Consequently, the state regulated reproductive capacity with the aim of preserving national purity by suppressing racial impurity. Initially, German racial hygiene laws affected persons who were racially recognized as German, but who comprised part of the less desirable segments of German society.

In July 1933 the Law for the Prevention of Genetically Diseased Offspring provided for the sterilization of an individual if he or she suffered from genetically determined illnesses, including feeblemindedness, schizophrenia, manic depression, epilepsy, Huntington's chorea, genetic blindness or deafness, and severe alcoholism. Commonly known as the Sterilization Law, it signalled a direct reversal of German policy that, until the 1930s, had strictly forbidden sterilization procedures. Germany justified its reversal, in part, by citing the example of other civilized countries such as Denmark, Norway, Czechoslovakia, Hungary, and the United States that permitted sterilization of the criminally insane or feebleminded.

In the first year after the Sterilizations Law was promulgated, genetic health courts, staffed by physicians, secretly administered and authorized over 56,000 sterilization procedures. In November 1933 the German state passed the Law Against Dangerous Career Criminals that required the castration of sex offenders. On July 26, 1935, a supplemental ordinance, authorizing forced abortions for women who were genetically unfit but who had already conceived and thus fell outside of the scope of the original sterilization edict, became law.

By the mid-1930s Germany asserted that only a subsection of Germans could be recognized as racially pure or Aryan. As a result in 1937, the genetic health courts, together with the Gestapo and state police, began to enforce the restrictive birth policy against mix-raced individuals. Under the *Rheinlandbastarde* policy, they secretly authorized the sterilization of some five hundred persons of mixed German and African ancestry. Reference to non-Aryans increasingly meant all Jews, even those who were German citizens. In 1938 a law provided for Jewish women to abort their pregnancies solely based on their new racial status.

By 1939 these sterilization policies ensured that over 400,000 Germans, either mixed-raced, Jewish, non-Aryan, or mentally or physically infirm underwent forced sterilization. The sterilization procedures included tubal ligation, vasectomy, x-ray exposure, or hysterectomy. The policies were a precursor to the Nazi euthanasia laws, which became law at the start of World War II. The euthanasia laws decreed that the outright killing of potential parents of undesirable offspring was preferable to regulating their ability to reproduce. Euthanasia was regarded as the ultimate means of ensuring racial and national purity.

The Nazi sterilization policies complemented another set of reproductive edicts that were collectively referred to as the Nuremberg Laws. In September 1935 the Reich Citizenship Law mandated that only full-blooded Germans were entitled to citizenship, whereas Jews would only be considered residents of Germany. Also in September of that same year the Law for the Protection of German Blood and German Honor proscribed marriages and sexual relations between Jews and non-Jews illegal. In October 1935 the Law for the Protection of the Genetic Health of the German People required couples to submit to premarital medical examinations to check for any of the illnesses sanctioned in the 1933 Sterilization Law; when deemed necessary, these marriages were prevented.

Whereas the sterilization policies mandated surgical interventions to stop reproduction, the Nuremberg Laws racially "declassified" individuals in declaring that they were not of German blood. They outlawed sexual contact between racially superior Germans and those termed racially denigrated. It is thus easy to understand why these measures, namely sterilization or compulsory abortions, segregation of the sexes, or obstacles to marriage, concerned the drafters of Article II(d) of the Genocide Convention.

A third set of reproductive policies introduced in the mid-1930s compelled German women considered to be racially Aryan to procreate, by offering pro-birth incentives. The German state awarded mothers of four or more children bronze, silver, or gold medals. It also provided loans of up to one year's salary to persuade women to leave the workforce and return home. Aryan women were encouraged to bear children out of wedlock. Infertility became recognized as grounds for divorce. A system of disincentives discouraged Aryan types from remaining childless. A penalty tax was levied on Aryans who had married and not procreated within five years. Stiff fines and prison sentences were meted out to physicians or others who performed abortions on Aryan women.

These birth incentive policies purported to rectify "the disproportionate breeding of inferiors, decrease the rampant celibacy of the German upper classes and control the threat posed by working women, liberated from the household" that the state viewed as detrimental "to the reproductive performance of the family." Although Article II(d) of the Genocide Convention refers to measures that prevent births, these countermeasures, to stimulate births among the Aryan population, unambiguously illustrate the fact that the Nazi sterilization policies and Nuremberg Laws did function as measures imposed to regulate all births.

This complex system of reproduction policies, based on the state's concepts of race and nation, must be grasped to understand the potential scope of Article

II(d). Incongruously, when Japan, India, and Iraq became German allies in arms during World War II, the non-Aryan racial and political treatise was not directed against them.

Eric Weitz, in *A Century of Genocide Utopias of Race and Nation*, observed that "slippage from the nation as a political community to the nation as a racial community became more prevalent when culture, not political rights was made the defining element in the formation of a nation" (2003). In the early twenty-first century ethnic, national, or religious identity might fall prey to subjectivity, as did racial groupings under the Nazi government. One need only reflect on white Australian immigration policies between the 1940s and 1970s, the former apartheid regime of South Africa, or the expulsion of Asian-descended Ugandans from their homes in the 1970s to comprehend the twentieth-century's malleable concepts of race and nation.

Article II(d) and World War II Cases

The potential breadth of Article II(d)'s prohibition is also rooted in the egregious forced labor programs and concentration camp experiments of World War II. Germany invaded Eastern Europe in 1939 and established forced labor programs, using Polish and Russian workers of both sexes. The Allied military trials of minor Nazi officials made clear that the Third Reich built into its forced labor policies measures intended to prevent birth among non-Aryan workers. In the *United States v. Greifelt et al.*, the defendants were leading officials in the SS Main Race and Settlement Office and the Repatriation Office for Ethnic Germans. The SS Main Race and Settlement Office devised the following measures for foreign workers:

> Comprehensive sterilization of such men and women of alien blood in German agriculture who, on the basis of our race laws—to be applied even more strictly in these cases—have been declared inferior with regard to their physical, spiritual and character traits.

> A ruthless but skillful propaganda among farmworkers of alien blood, to the effect that neither they nor their children, produced on the soil of German people, could expect much good; in other words, immediate separation of parents and children, eventually complete estrangement; sterilization of children afflicted with hereditary disease.

Charged with crimes against humanity and war crimes for "compelling abortions on Eastern workers" and "preventing marriages and hampering reproduction of enemy nationals" Griefelt and all but one of the defendants were pronounced guilty and sentenced to imprisonment of up to twenty-five years.

In *Poland v. Höss*, the defendant, commandant of the Auschwitz concentration camp, was charged with the persecution of Poles and Jews, a crime against humanity, as well as war crimes against Soviet prisoners of war. Under the command of Höss, camp personnel performed medical experiments on the male and female prisoners. Data were collected to quantify the most effective means to castrate men, sterilize women, or terminate pregnancies. The castration experiments employed high dosages of x-rays that caused infertility together with severe burns on prisoners' genitalia, physical debilitation, mental stress, and often the death of the victims. The pregnancy experiments involved the premature terminations of pregnancy, including injecting pregnant women with typhus-infected blood and then artificially provoking labor. The Polish tribunal found Höss guilty and sentenced him to death.

In 1961 Israel prosecuted former Nazi Adolf Eichmann for devising measures intended to prevent childbearing among Jews in the Theresienstadt (in Czech Terezín) ghetto. The court found, however, that Eichmann was not involved in the imposition of measures to prevent births as an act of genocide. It held that the primary intent of forbidding births and interrupting the pregnancies of Jewish women in the Theresienstadt ghetto was to exterminate Jews and not prevent births. The court drew a distinction between the intent of cruel medical procedures and that of measures intended to prevent births as proscribed in Article II(d).

The three cases are instructive. The *Greifelt* case demonstrated the actual measures executed by Nazi racist ideology to prevent births among foreign forced laborers. The *Höss* and *Eichmann* cases revealed the gruesome nature of medical procedures performed on camp inmates who were already condemned to death. The experiments conducted at Auschwitz were not performed to prevent births among the inmates, but rather, they served to perfect any future measures to restrict births. The medical procedures cited in the Eichmann case were a first step in the extermination of Jewish inmates. Even though the medical experiments and other acts did not represent the imposition or execution of measures to prevent births among inmates, a frighteningly direct ideological link exists between Nazi sterilization policies, the Nuremberg Laws, and the camp experiments. Auschwitz and Theresienstadt were precursors of what would have become even more draconian measures to prevent births among non-Aryans had the Third Reich triumphed.

Legal Background of Article II(d)

On December 11, 1946, the General Assembly passed Resolution 96(I). It defined genocide as a denial of the right of existence of entire human groups and "[a]ffirmed that genocide is a crime under international law which the civilized world condemns." Resolution 96(I) was a declaration of principles that guided the drafting of the Genocide Convention. Another historical forerunner to the Genocide Convention was the Draft Convention for Genocide prepared by the UN Secretariat. The Draft Convention divided genocidal acts into three subcategories: the physical, biological, and cultural. Article I(2) of the Draft Convention characterized biological genocide as "measures aimed at extinction of a group of human beings by systematic restrictions on births, without which the group cannot survive." Methods cited to accomplish this form of genocide were sterilization or compulsory abortions, segregation of the sexes, or obstacles to marriage.

An ad hoc committee revised the Draft Convention and proposed language for Article II(4) that proscribed "imposing measures intended to prevent births within the group." The eventual Genocide Convention adopted the ad hoc committee's language. The final wording abandoned the terms "biological genocide" and "restricting births" and made no direct references to measures such as sterilization, compulsory abortions, or obstacles to marriage, or to the systematic allocation of work to men and women in different locations. Still, the drafters' objective in crafting Article II(d) was to shield groups from these very acts. The essential aspect of Article II(d) is that it condemns, as an act of genocide, measures intended to prevent births within a racial, national, religious, or racial group.

Commentary on Article II(d)

In 1949 Nehemiah Robinson wrote an early noteworthy commentary on the Genocide Convention. He focused on two aspects of Article II(d): the number of births that must be prevented and the range of acknowledged measures to prevent births. He addressed the first aspect as follows:

> Subparagraph (d) may in practice give rise to the problem whether the intention must be to prevent *all* births within the group or is it sufficient that it relates to *some* births only [emphases in original]. Although this subparagraph speaks not of restriction but prevention, it must be admitted that the intent of partial prevention suffices since the requirement of total prevention would conflict with the definition of Genocide as relating not only to the group as a whole, but also to a part of it.

> [T]he factual extent of prevention should be of no import once it is established that it was imposed on members of the protected groups only (1949).

Robinson observed that the number of actual births prevented is relevant only in terms of whether the intention was to prevent, even partially, the births within a group.

In Robinson's second commentary on the Genocide Convention, written in 1960, he reiterated the view that the "the actual extent of prevention may not be decisive once it is established that it was imposed . . . with the intent of destruction." Among contemporary historians, William A. Schabas writes that "Article II(d) of the Convention does not make a *result* [emphasis in original] a material element of the offence. The *actus reus* consist of the imposition of measures; it need not be proven that they have actually succeeded" (2000). Hence, a common interpretation of Article II(d) is that quantity or actual numbers of unborn members of a group is not required to establish an act of genocide. Such statistics could, however, demonstrate that the measures imposed were intended to prevent births and that they were effective.

Robinson's other observation in the 1949 commentary expressed the view that the Genocide Convention purposely implied a nonexhaustive range of measures which could satisfy Article II(d), noting that "the measures imposed need not be the classic actions of sterilization; separation of the sexes, prohibition of marriages and the like may achieve the same results" (p. ?). In his second commentary, written in 1960, Robinson added that other measures could be "equally restrictive." Schabas and Otto Triffterer agree with Robinson's remarks that Article II(d) does not limit the types of measures which can be imposed to prevent births within a group.

The language of the treaty leaves open for debate the scope of what could be considered "measures imposed with the intent to prevent births." During the prolonged period before the United States ratified the Genocide Convention, the phrase "intent of measures imposed" provoked controversy and remains polemical. The modern debate is linked to the historical circumstances that prodded the writing of Article II(d).

U.S. Ratification and Article II(d)
The United States was one of the original signatories of the Genocide Convention in 1948, but the U.S. Senate only gave advice and consent to ratification in 1987, after bouts of indifference, defiance, and finally adherence. The acceptance of Article II(d) was contentious. Some senators questioned whether government-sponsored birth control programs used overwhelmingly by African Americans, Hispanic Americans, or Native Americans might be construed as an act of genocide within the context of Article II(d). They pointed to a

thesis of African American genocide that questioned the motives behind proposed legislative bills to authorize involuntary or punitive sterilizations, or the real objectives of legalized family-planning programs and abortion laws as acts of genocide. Black Brazilians voiced similar concerns in the 1970s about state policies that favored a reduction in the number of Black Brazilian births. U.S. proponents of ratification countered such arguments by emphasizing that government-sponsored birth control and family planning programs are voluntary, not compulsory, and they do not aim to destroy any group within the United States.

Another issue of concern for lawmakers considering the ratification of Article II(d) was the history of medical experiments in the United States, notably the Tuskegee syphilis experiment. Between 1930 and 1950 U.S. government officials intentionally withheld the diagnosis of syphilis from a sampling of African American men, all the while diligently but silently recorded the progression of their disease, including the inevitable side-effect of sterility. The officials did not medically treat the men to alleviate or stop the disease. Some senators raised concerns that such acts would constitute violations under Article II(d). Proponents of the Genocide Convention insisted that such medical experiment policies had come to a halt by the 1960s.

Qualms about the United States' racist past and its vulnerability to charges under the Genocide Convention had been voiced from the outset of the Convention's existence. Raphael Lemkin, in the 1950s, had attempted to quell these American fears by observing that "in the Negro problem the intent is to preserve the group on a different level of existence, . . . but not to destroy it."

In 1986 the United States officially ratified Article II(d) as well as other provisions of the Genocide Convention. The Senate, however, expressed general reservation about the terms of the Convention, indicating that the United States could refuse the compulsory jurisdiction of the International Court of Justice (ICJ) if another state accused it of violating the Genocide Convention.

Article II(d) and International Criminal Tribunals
Several international tribunals have included Article II(d) of the Genocide Convention verbatim in their statutes. The ad hoc International Criminal Tribunals for the Former Yugoslavia (ICTY) and Rwanda (ICTR), as well as the Special Panels of East Timor, have jurisdiction over alleged acts of genocide that involve the imposition of certain measures to prevent births. As of 2003 cases tried before these international tribunals have not included prosecutions fort measures intended

to prevent births. The *Akayesu* judgment, issued by the ICTR in 1998, however, held that measures under Article II(d) "should be construed as sexual mutilation, the practice of sterilization, forced birth control, separation of the sexes and prohibition of marriages."

On another matter, the *Akayesu* judgment abruptly departed from Robinson's list of measures, which argued that forced births could not be viewed as a measure to prevent births. The ICTR stated that in patriarchal societies, the rape of women during times of war could be construed as the enemy's attempt to impose their ethnic identity on any newborn children. The Trial Chamber opined that:

> [A] measure intended to prevent births within a group is a case where during a rape, a woman of the said group is deliberately impregnated by a man of another group, with the intent to have her give birth to a child who will not consequently belong to the mother's group.

Similarly, in 1996, the ICTY had held, in a preliminary proceeding against former Bosnian Serb president Radovan Karadzic, that the "systematic rape of women in some cases is intended to transmit a new ethnic identity." The *Akayesu* judgment also observed that a psychological component to the prevention of birth could operate to violate Article II(d) safeguards:

> [T]he Chamber notes that measures intended to prevent births within a group may be physical, but can also be mental. For instance, rape can be a measure intended to prevent births when the person raped refuses subsequently to procreate, in the same way that members of a group can be led, through threats or trauma, not to procreate.

The ICTR *Akayesu* judgment is considered obiter dicta, meaning that its interpretation lay outside of the relevant factual and legal issues in the actual case before the judges. In *Kayishema and Rutaganda*, the second judgment issued by the ICTR, the Trial Chamber concurred, again in obiter dicta, with the interpretation of Article II(d) that had been voiced in the *Akayesu* case. Schabas acknowledged the potential absurdity of the judicial views that classify rape as a measure to prevent births; however, he also recognized that a sober reading of Article II(d) lends itself to the contemplation of any measures as long as the intent to prevent births is present. Infliction of rapes, sexual mutilations, and any other actions that transfer the ethnic identity of the child to a group other than the mother's, or that intentionally discourage or restrict future procreation feasibly, lies within Article II(d). Triffterer noted the potential judicial relevance of these ICTR findings and the influence they might exert on the interpretation of the Rome Statute of the International Criminal Court (ICC).

Biological Weapons and Article II(d)

Speculation about other potential "measures imposed to prevent births within a group" remains lively. Several propositions, related to wartime scenarios, are repeatedly raised, such as biological or chemical warfare or rape-induced AIDS as acts that could contravene Article II(d).

The Genocide Convention does not explicitly cite military weapons as a type of measure intended to prevent births within a group. Even though the Draft Genocide Convention employed the term "biological genocide," its use was unrelated to biological or chemical warfare, as those terms were utilized in World War I to denote the deployment of mustard gas against enemy soldiers. Modern armed conflicts have employed biological or chemical agents against enemy soldiers, civilian populations, or the environment to defoliate jungle terrain. Scientific research acknowledges the existence of the short- and long-term affects of these chemical or biological agents on male and female reproductive abilities. Exposed female populations exhibit higher rates of spontaneous abortions or miscarriages and the birth of terminally ill or severely disabled children. Exposure to chemical and biological weapons has prompted some men and women to forego childbearing, due to their fear of conceiving mentally or physically disabled offspring. Could the use of biological or chemical weapons be a means to prevent births within a group, or similar to the medical experiments performed in concentration camps during World War II, if the primary intent is to kill the population and not to prevent their reproductive capacity?

Analogous observations have been raised in regard to women raped by AIDS-infected soldiers during wartime. Sexually transmitted diseases that eventually kill the offspring of women who were raped could be seen as measures intended to prevent births. Women may make an anguished decision not to reproduce in order to refrain from bearing terminally ill children. The mental trauma that the ICTR cases refer to, which could cause victims of rape to forsake procreation, might apply to individuals exposed to chemical or biological agents, or sexually transmitted diseases. Either act could lead to the decision not to give birth. If the intent behind deploying biological weapons or ensuring the transmission of fatal sexually transmitted diseases, such as AIDS, includes destroying a religious, racial, ethnic, or national group, in whole or part, by preventing births, such measures clearly run afoul of Article II(d).

Conclusion

Genocide, the denial of the right of existence of entire groups of human beings, often erupts during vast political or military upheavals. Certain acts of genocide, however, can exist and flourish when—ostensibly non-wartime—policies are aimed at eliminating racial, religious, national, or ethnic groups. Policies supporting racial purity or nationhood, as when transformed into measures to determine who should live and procreate, are acts of genocide. Whether prompted by legislation, or overseen by politicians, doctors, lawyers, or cruel camp commanders, these are acts of genocide. Like massive extermination or killings, the intent to suppress a group prior to its birth and reduce or decimate the membership to a designated purpose is a fundamental crime, one that the Genocide Convention, as recognized in Article II(d), seeks to prevent or punish.

SEE ALSO Nuremberg Laws; Rape

BIBLIOGRAPHY

Abdias do Nascimento (1978). *O Genocidio Do Negro Brasileiro-Processo de um Racismo Mascarada*. Rio de Janiero, Brazil: Paz e Terra.

Ad Hoc Advisory Panel (1973). *Tuskeegee Syphilis Study*. Washington, D.C.

Annas, George, and Michael Grodin (1992). *The Nazi Doctors and the Nuremberg Code*. New York: Oxford University Press.

Poland v. Hoess. Case No. 7 LRTWC II, Supreme National Tribunal of Poland (1948).

Power, Samantha (2002). *A Problem from Hell–America and the Age of Genocide*. Hammersmith, U.K.: Flamingo/ HarperCollins.

Proctor, Robert N. (1988). *Racial Hygiene Medicine under the Nazis*. Cambridge, Mass.: Harvard University Press.

Schabas, William A. (2000). *Genocide in International Law: The Crime of Crimes*. Cambridge: Cambridge University Press.

United States of America v. Geifelt et al. Case No. 13 LRTWC, United States Military Tribunal (1948).

Weitz, Eric D. (2003). *A Century of Genocide Utopias of Race and Nation*. Princeton, N.J.: Princeton University Press.

Patricia Viseur Sellers
I am setting forth the above in my personal capacity. This article represents neither the policies of the Office of the Prosecutor of the International Criminal Tribunal for the Former Yugoslavia nor the United Nations.

Rescuers, Holocaust

In wartime Europe, the appearance of gentiles who rescued Jews signaled an opposition to German policies of Jewish annihilation. Saving Jews violated German laws, endangering the rescuers' lives and the lives of their families. Because anti-Jewish measures were intro-

duced in different places at different times, with varying degrees of ruthlessness, the presence of gentile rescuers also varied with time and place. Yet, each country under the German occupation had some people who risked their lives to protect Jews.

Importance of Rescuers to Jewish Survival
Practically all of the Jews who survived the war by living in the forbidden Christian world had benefited from some kind of aid. Exact figures of those who risked their lives to save Jews are elusive. Most researchers agree that those who protected Jews were but a small minority. They also agree that the number of these rescuers by far exceeds the 20,205 gentiles who were recognized as Righteous Among the Nations according to the January 1, 2004 compilation put together by Yad Vashem, the Holocaust Martyrs and Heroes Remembrance Authority.

Yad Vashem was established in Israel in 1953 as a memorial to European Jewry who perished during World War II, and as a tribute to those non-Jews who selflessly risked their lives for them. Most Holocaust publications about gentile rescuers concentrate on those whose aid was based on altruistic motives and those who received recognition from Yad Vashem. In Nechama Tec's 1986 study, *When Light Pierced the Darkness*, which considered the cases of more than three hundred Jews who survived on the Aryan side and almost two hundred altruistic gentile protectors, more than 80 percent of the Jewish survivors were found to have benefited from altruistic gentile aid.

According to Tec, most gentiles had to overcome a variety of barriers before they were able to rescue Jews. The outer and most serious obstacles to Jewish rescue were the German legal prohibitions against such aid, and a corresponding legal obligation to report all known efforts to save. In Eastern Europe, particularly in Poland, helping Jews was a crime punishable by death. By contrast, in Western Europe, German punishments for the protection of Jews, was vague. However, if a rescue attempt was discovered, it often led to the incarceration of the rescuers in a concentration camp, or even to the rescuer's murder.

Additional barriers to the rescuing of Jews grew out of anti-Semitism. Most anti-Semites objected to providing aid to Jews. This hostility extended to gentile protectors, as well. Finally, in depth interviews with gentile rescuers has revealed that many of them had to overcome their own, often unconscious, internalized anti-Semitism.

The Story of Two Rescuers
Given these obstacles, who within the gentile population was most likely to stand up for the persecuted

Visitors regard a 1994 museum exhibit on German businessman Oskar Schindler. Owner of enamel works outside the Krakow ghetto, Schindler saved the lives of approximately 1,200 Polish Jews by falsifying factory records, listing the trades of his workers as those deemed essential to the Nazi war effort. [TODD A. GIPSTEIN/CORBIS]

Jews, who traditionally were perceived as "Christ killers" and who, for many still unexplained reasons, were routinely blamed for every conceivable ill? What propelled these altruistic rescuers toward such life-threatening activities?

Attempts to apply conventional classifications to the individual gentiles who became altruistic rescuers yield heterogeneous results. Two examples illustrate this diversity. In wartime Warsaw, a young Polish factory laborer named Stanislawa Dawidziuk, who had not completed elementary school, shared a one-room apartment with her husband (a waiter) and her teenage brother. In 1942, at her husband's request, Stanislawa agreed to add to their cramped quarters Irena, a woman whose looks betrayed her Jewish background. A Polish policeman named Laminski brought Irena to the Dawidziuks' household. At the outset, Irena was only expected to stay overnight, but Laminski could find no other place for her to go. One day stretched into weeks, and Stanislawa's husband objected to Irena's continued presence in the apartment. He refused to endanger his life for a Jew, but Stanislawa could not turn away their uninvited guest. She knew that Irena's appearance in the street would lead to her arrest and murder. After a stormy quarrel, the husband left, never to return, not even when his wife gave birth to their son.

In contrast, Laminski continued his visits to Stanislawa and Irena, supplying them with food and protection. Despite many close calls, Stanislawa never even considered sending Irena away. They became devoted friends, comforting each other. After the Warsaw Uprising in 1944, the Germans evacuated almost the entire locale population. The rumor was that mothers with small children would be spared. Because Stanislawa was worried about Irena's "Jewish looks," she insisted that Irena should claim the baby as her own, and thus avoid deportation. In the end, however, both she and Irena stayed in the apartment.

After the war, Irena left for Israel, where she died in 1975. Stanislawa remarried, gave birth to another son, and worked in the factory until her retirement. In 1981, Stanislawa was honored with a Yad Vashem distinction that named her a "Righteous Among the Nations." She died in 1991.

Another non-Jewish rescuer, Sempo Sugihara, was the Japanese consul at Kovno (present-day Kaunas, in Lithuania). When the city fell to German expansion and was made part of Poland, Sugihara became aware of the Jewish plight in the summer of 1940. For humanitarian reasons, Sugihara issued Japanese transit visas to Jewish refugees without checking the validity of their supporting documents. The holders of such visas could travel to Japan through the Soviet Union if they were able to pay the fare in U.S. dollars for the trip across Siberia. When the Japanese foreign ministry learned about Sugihatra's aid to Jews, they ordered him to stop, but Sugihara continued to issue visas. He worked non-stop for twelve consecutive days, enlisting the help of Jewish refugees, and he was still issuing visas while boarding his train for Berlin, on August 31. Sugihara estimated that he had distributed 3,500 transit visas.

In Tokyo, Sugihara was fired. He had a hard time finding work, and was forced to move from one job to another. Only in 1985, old and bedridden, when Sugihara was officially designated by Yad Vashem as a "Righteous Among the Nations," did the Japanese press give extensive coverage to his selfless wartime aid to Jews.

Altruistic Rescuers: Characteristics and Motivations

In *When Light Pierced the Darkness*, Tec compared a large group of gentile protectors in terms of their social class, amount of education, political involvement, degree of anti-Semitism, extent of religious commitment, and friendship with Jews. None of these characteristics served as predictors of rescue. These gentile rescuers came from all walks of life, and varied greatly in terms of their education, politics, religion, friendship with Jews, involvement with anti-Semitism, and most other conventional ways of classifying individuals. However, when these rescuers' life styles and pastimes were examined at a close range, the results yield a cluster of six shared characteristics and motivations. These characteristics and motivations can be viewed as a set of interrelated explanations or hypotheses.

One of these shared characteristics can be characterized as individuality or separateness. It shows that these gentile altruistic rescuers did not fit into their social environments. Those who are on the periphery of their community, regardless of whether they are or are not aware of their separateness, are less likely to adhere to the community's expectations and values than those who are well integrated into their environments.

With individuality comes a higher level of independence, which is another of the significant characteristics shared by altruistic rescuers. In turn, freedom from social constraints and a high level of independence creates opportunities to act in accordance with personal values and moral precepts, even when these are in opposition to societal expectations. This is the third characteristic that altruistic rescuers have in common.

In Tec's study, some gentile altruistic rescuers were unaware of their individuality. Nonetheless, they spoke readily about their self-reliance and the need to follow their personal inclinations. Thus, nearly all of the altruistic gentile rescuers (98%) saw themselves as independent. Additional support for this finding comes from Jewish survivors, most of whom described their protectors as independent and as being motivated by special personal values. Another quality often mentioned in the testimonies and memoirs of survivors, one that comes close to independence, was the rescuers' courage. An overwhelming majority (85%) described their helpers as courageous.

With the rescuers' view of themselves as independent came the idea that they were propelled by moral values that do not depend on the support and approval of others but rather on their own self-approval. Again and again, they would repeat that they had to be at peace with themselves and with their own ideas of what was right and wrong. Closely related to their moral convictions were their long-standing commitments to the protection of the needy. This commitment was expressed in a wide range of charitable acts that extended over long periods of time. Evidence about their selfless aid also came from survivors, who describe their rescues as good-natured, whose help to the needy was a long-established character trait.

There is some continuity between the rescuers' history of charitable actions and their protection of Jews. That is, risking their lives for Jews fit into a system of values and behaviors that included helping the weak and the dependent in general. This analogy, however, has its limitations. Most disinterested actions that benefit others may involve inconvenience, even extreme inconvenience. Only rarely would such acts demand from others the ultimate sacrifice of his or her own life. In fact, for these altruistic rescuers, in wartime there was a convergence between historical events demanding ultimate selflessness and their already established predisposition to help.

For example, Marie Baluszko an outspoken peasant who protected many Jews, said: "I do what I think is right, not what others think is right." At first she did not see that her aid to Jews was an extension of a tradition that involved helping the poor and the destitute. When questioned further about her reasons for aiding

Jews, Baluszko was somewhat at a loss for answers. Instead, she asked: "What would you do in my place, if someone comes at night and asks for help?. . . One has to be an animal without a conscience not to help." After a pause, she continued: "In our area there were many large families with small farms; they were very poor. I used to help them; they called me mother. . . . When I was leaving the place people cried. I helped all the poor, all that needed help" (Tec, 1986, p. 165).

Baluszko's reactions suggest that we tend to take our repetitive actions for granted. What we take for granted we accept. What we accept, we rarely analyze or wonder about. In fact, the more firmly established patterns of behavior are, the less likely are these to be examined and analyzed. In a sense, the constant pressure of, or familiarity with, ideas and actions does not mean that we know or understand them. On the contrary, when habitual patterns are accepted and taken for granted, this may impede, rather than promote, understanding.

Closely related to this tendency is another one. Namely, what we are accustomed to repeat we don't see as extraordinary, no matter how exceptional it may seem to others. Thus, the rescuers' past history of helping the needy may explain, at least in part, their modest appraisal of their own life-threatening actions. This modesty was expressed in a variety of ways. In Tec's study, most of the rescuers (66%) perceived their protection of Jews as a natural reaction to human suffering, and almost a third (31%), insisted that saving lives was nothing exceptional. In contrast, only three percent described the saving of Jews as extraordinary. This kind of an attitude, shared by the majority of gentile rescuers, was often expressed as follows: "All of us looked at this help as a natural thing. None of us were heroes; at times we were afraid, but none of us could act differently" (Tec, 1986, p. 169).

The six characteristics and conditions shared by gentile altruistic rescuers can be summarized as follows:

1. Individuality or separateness, an inability to blend into their social environments;

2. Independence or self-reliance, a willingness to act in accordance with personal convictions, regardless of how these are viewed by others;

3. An enduring commitment to stand up for the helpless and needy reflected in a long history of doing good deeds;

4. A tendency to perceive aid to Jews in a matter-of-fact, unassuming way, as neither heroic nor extraordinary;

5. An unplanned, unpremeditated beginning of Jewish rescue, a beginning that happened gradually or suddenly, even impulsively; and

6. Universalistic perceptions of Jews that defined them, not as Jews, but as helpless beings and as totally dependent on the protection of others.

Additional Kinds of Gentile Rescuers

Historical evidence shows that most Jews who survived the Holocaust by living illegally on the Aryan side had benefited from the protection by altruistic gentile rescuers. History shows that, in addition to the altruistic rescuers, there were gentiles who rescued Jews for other reasons.

One of these groups can be called "paid helpers." These were gentiles for whom the protection of Jews was a commercial undertaking. Without payment, such rescues would not have happened. The other group consisted of gentiles who had previously been open, avid anti-Semites. This group of rescuers felt that their hostility to the Jews was partly responsible for German destruction of Jews. They felt that their anti-Semitism contributed to the systematic murder of the Jewish people. Most of these anti-Semitic rescuers were also devout Catholics who, by saving Jews, hoped to atone for their sins.

Jewish Holocaust Rescuers

This category is distinctive in that the rescuers were not gentile. There is scattered evidence of Jews who, although they were targeted for annihilation, had selflessly helped others. An emergent interest in Jews as rescuers has not yet yielded systematic research. Nonetheless, there are some questions that can be profitably asked. How do Jewish rescuers compare to their non-Jewish counterparts? Did the kind of help offered by Gentile and Jewish rescuers vary? If so, how?

During World War II, among the variously persecuted groups, the Germans specifically targeted the Jews for humiliation, followed by annihilation. The realization that all Jews were slated for murder probably affected people's perceptions about them. Deprived of all rights, reduced to the most dependent and degrading position, the Jews were easily perceived as helpless victims, even before they were sent to their deaths. For many people, the belief in the supremacy of the drive for self-preservation, leads us to assume that, when faced with a death sentence, people will concentrate on their own survival rather than on the survival of others.

Closely connected to this expectation is the fact that, during the Nazi era, the perception of Jewish helplessness and humiliation overshadowed all of the victims' other attributes. Certainly, gentile rescuers saw in their Jewish charges only haunted and persecuted human beings. It was, in fact, just this perception of Jewish suffering that prompted the rescuers to give aid.

However, overlooking Jews as rescuers reinforces the perception that those who face overpowering threats are incapable of helping themselves and, by extension, of offering protection to others. Common sense and some available facts seem, at first, to justify such conclusions. When exposed to extreme dangers, people are often paralyzed into inaction. Whether this occurs is, in part, contingent on the extent to which people define a situation as hopeless. Fighting for oneself and for others requires hope. Hope wanes with grave dangers. Danger and no hope often add up to no struggle. Some individuals who have been sentenced to death give up hope. Even heroic revolutionaries, when captured, have usually gone to their executions without opposition.

However, even the slimmest of hopes can inflame the desire to live, making it an all-engrossing preoccupation. Still, a strong personal desire to live need not be translated into a willingness to protect others from becoming victims. Yet, despite all these arguments, there is concrete historical evidence of persecuted Jews who took on additional perilous duties to save others.

In *In the Lion's Den* and *Defiance*, Nechama Tec examines the question of Jewish rescuers. Her work is guided by the hypothesis that the more threatening a situation is, the greater is the need for compassion, mutual help, and cooperation. Mutual help and cooperation appear under a variety of guises.

In extremis, distinct forms of mutual help and cooperation appear to be intricately connected to the quality of life and survival. These complex associations, however, await future explorations. Even partial answers to questions pursued through this future research promise fresh insights, insights reaching beyond specific times, places, and circumstances.

SEE ALSO Altruism, Ethical; Holocaust; Wallenberg, Raoul

BIBLIOGRAPHY
Fogelman, Eva (1994). *Conscience and Courage: Rescuers of Jews during the Holocaust*. New York: Anchor Books/Doubleday.

Friedman, Philip (1957). *Their Brothers' Keepers*. New York: Crown.

Gilbert, Martin (2003). *The Righteous: The Unsung Heroes of the Holocaust*. New York: Henry Holt.

Hallie, Philip Paul (1979). *Lest Innocent Blood be Shed*. New York: Harper & Row.

Oliner, Samuel P., and Pearl M. Oliner (1988). *The Altruistic Personality: Rescuers of Jews in Nazi Europe*. New York: Free Press.

Paldiel, Mordecai (1993). *The Path of the Righteous: Gentile Rescuers of Jews during the Holocaust*. New Jersey: KTAV Publishing House.

Phayer, Michael, and Eva Fleischner (1997). *Cries in the Night: Women Who Challenged the Holocaust*. Kansas City: Sheed & Ward.

Tec, Nechama (1986). *When Light Pierced the Darkness*. New York: Oxford University Press.

Tec, Nechama (1990). *In the Lion's Den*. New York: Oxford University Press.

Tec, Nechama (1993). *Defiance*. New York: Oxford University Press.

Tec, Nechama (2003). *Resilience and Courage: Women, Men, and the Holocaust*. New Haven, Conn.: Yale University Press.

Nechama Tec

Residential Schools

Residential schools in Canada were based on the Carlisle Indian Industrial School model founded in 1879 by Lieutenant Richard Henry Pratt in Carlisle, Pennsylvania. The aim of such a schooling system was the forced assimilation of aboriginal people into the colonial society. This was to be achieved by wiping out their past ethnic and cultural associations and replacing them with European ones. Driven by a kind of missionary zeal, Pratt believed it was important to remove all aspects of being aboriginal from the child and to immerse that child, as a kind of baptism, into white socialization. The duty to "civilize" lay on the shoulders of the white man. This was rationalized as a viable alternative to war and the slaughter of people. In spite of this rationalization, however, economic considerations were their actual driving force. Trade with the aboriginal peoples in the United States had begun to diminish, and was replaced with a scramble by white settlers to lay claim to aboriginal lands. To facilitate this, aborigines were herded onto reservations, enabling the white settler community to claim the "new" territories. It was thought that residential schools would assist this process, because assimilation would make the taking of lands easier, at little or no financial cost to the settler communities.

The Rationale

In the nineteenth century, Canada adopted a policy of assimilation of all aborigines into the Christian culture of the white settlers. Church organizations were enlisted in the effort, and became enthusiastic and active participants in this system. Children were taken from their homes on the reservations and compelled to attend residential schools because "the influence of the wigwam was stronger than that of the [day] school," in the words of the Davin Report of 1879 which is contained in the report to the Royal Commission on Aboriginal People in 1991.

As was true in the United States, the Canadian plan was actually motivated by economic considerations, specifically, by the prospect of creating a hard-working labor force. Aborigines were often stereotyped as lazy drunkards. The residential schools were to be cure these deficiencies by teaching aboriginal children industrial or domestic skills. Boys were taught such subjects as agriculture, carpentry, shoemaking, printing, blacksmithing, and tinsmithing. Girls were taught general household chores such as sewing, shirt making, knitting, cooking, laundry, ironing, as well as dairy farming. In addition, students were expected to engage in practical work in many of these areas of instruction, providing yet another source of free labor.

Implementation

In order to ensure that there were sufficient numbers enrolled in all the residential schools, the Minister for Indian Affairs determined which school each student would attend. However, the children of Protestant and Roman Catholic parents could insist that their children attend a school run by representatives of their own faith.

Upon entering the schools, children were stripped of all aspects of their traditional way of life. For instance, their long hair was cut to conform to European styles, and their traditional dress was replaced by European-style clothing. They were taught to view the world through the prism of European values and beliefs. They were expected to abandon their native language and speak only in English (or French, in the schools established in Quebec). All of this was considered essential to the "civilizing" process, by which aboriginal children would ultimately be assimilated into Canadian society.

The Results

After education was completed, the plan called for the integration of residential school graduates into the broader Canadian society, so as to prevent any return to the reservation and further backsliding. Most attempts at placing the graduates of this system were a failure, however, because the system made no effort to eradicate the widespread anti-aboriginal prejudice of white Canadians. Unwelcome among white Canadians, most of the aboriginal graduates of the residential schools did return to the reserves, only to find that their European-style education had rendered them misfits in that society, too.

The industrial school model was eventually replaced by a new type of boarding school, the model for

which attempted to overcome the problem of student placement in society after graduation. Graduates were sent to model settlements where they were supplied with land, farming equipment, and housing materials, and were expected to create a new community for themselves. That scheme was soon abandoned as a failure, however, and the failure was blamed on allegations that the graduates lacked sufficient motivation. The model settlements were replaced by a new scheme which granted residential school graduates a loan and limited agricultural materials for individual use.

By the time residential schools were finally abandoned, it was apparent that this type of social engineering was unlikely to succeed. At its peak in 1931, the residential system had grown to 80 residential schools, located throughout Canada. While it is unclear how many children passed through the residential school system, one estimate suggests that one-third of all aboriginal children between the ages of six and fifteen were in residential schools during the 1930s. Other estimates place the figure closer to fifty percent.

The Royal Commission Report

In 1991 the Royal Commission on Aboriginal Peoples was assigned the task of examining the social, economic, and cultural situation of the aboriginal peoples of Canada. This included a full examination of residential schools through oral testimonies from inmates and employees, as well as archival research.

The findings of the Royal Commission were published in 1996. The report documented widespread physical, sexual, and emotional abuse within the residential school system. It also reported that the schools routinely disparaged the traditional culture of their students, and that children were punished for speaking their own language or for practicing their own religion and culture. The Royal Commission's report went on to confirm that the system's goal of forced assimilation had "an inherent element of savagery," at its core, expressed in such phrases as "kill the Indian in the child."

The Royal Commission's report dealt with the traumatic effects that the residential schools had on the children, their communities, and on succeeding generations. Aboriginal people and professional consultants alike testified that the schools bred social maladjustment, family breakdowns, suicide, alcoholism, domestic violence, and the loss of parenting skills. This last item is significant, for without parenting skills, the schools' graduates had severe difficulty in raising their own children. In the residential schools, children learned that adults often exerted power and control through physical abuse. When they became parents they had no other parenting model to fall back upon, and so inflicted abuse on their own children. This ultimately set up a vicious cycle, which continued in succeeding generations.

The Canadian Government's Response

The Royal Commission further demonstrated that the churches and the Canadian government had been aware of some of the documented abuses for some time. Many reports from school inspectors corroborated the pattern of abuse. The Commission went so far as to find the department guilty of neglecting the children and breaching its duty of care. It noted that, although church organizations assumed responsibility for actual instruction, the department of Indian Affairs was charged with administering the schools and funding their construction and maintenance. However, the residential schools were always under-funded and badly administered. Because each school's funding was determined by the number of students enrolled, there was a strong incentive to take in more students than the school could properly hold. This resulted in severe overcrowding, which in turn led to high rates in death from diseases like tuberculosis.

In response to the Royal Commission Report, the Canadian government issued a Statement of Reconciliation in 1998. In it the government acknowledged that the Canadian residential school system separated many children from their families and communities and prevented them from speaking their own languages and from learning about their own heritage and cultures. The government further accepted the key role it had played in the development and administration of the schools. Children who were the victims of sexual and physical abuse were singled out for special mention. The statement included the Canadian government's explicit apology to all the victims of the residential school system. In addition, the Minister of Indian Affairs announced the availability of $350 million for community-based healing, earmarked for those who suffered the effects of physical and sexual abuse.

No monetary compensation was offered for individual victims, however. In reaction, victims of the residential school system turned to the Canadian courts. By June 1998, approximately 1,000 lawsuits were filed. It is estimated that by early 2004, more than 5,000 people may have entered into litigation for damages against the Canadian government. It has also been reported that by March 1999, some $20 million had been spent by the Canadian government in settling residential school claims. It is not clear how the state is likely to deal with these cases in the future, however. It may opt for out-of-court settlements in order to avoid setting legal precedent for the concept of monetary reparations.

Residential Schools and the Crime of Genocide

Although the term *genocide* was raised during the hearings of the Royal Commission, the remark was dismissed as a "rhetorical flourish," It can be argued, however, that this dismissal was at least premature. Article III of the Convention on the Prevention and Punishment of the Crime of Genocide defines genocide to include the causing of serious bodily or mental harm to members of a national, racial, or religious group, and the deliberate infliction on the group of conditions of life calculated to bring about its physical destruction in whole or in part.

Using this definition, most of the criteria can be substantiated from the testimony presented before the Royal Commission. The difficulty lies in establishing the element of intent. It can be argued that residential schools were not calculated to bring about the physical destruction of the aboriginal people, but might instead have been a well-intentioned plan for the good of the people that went awry through inept administration and implementation. The Royal Commission appears to lean to this view. Nonetheless, the Commission's report does call for further public inquiry, the establishment of a university for aboriginal peoples that would be dedicated to researching and documenting the residential schools, and compensation for community-based healing programs. These recommendations appear to aim at arriving at some kind of truth surrounding the residential schools with a view to implementing a program of action.

Some, however, charge that the Royal Commission's recommendations are dilatory tactics intended to frustrate those who seek to resolve the damage done by the residential schools. In this view, the aims and objectives of the residential school plan were clearly calculated to destroy the cultural and physical life of Canada's aboriginal peoples and to replace the traditional way of life with a new set of values that were more acceptable to the white people. As a direct consequence of this policy, the residential schools brought about the physical destruction of most of Canada's aboriginal peoples, and, according to this perspective, the actions of the Canadian government did, in fact, constitute genocide.

The Australian Experience:

In her article "Squaring the Circle: How Canada is Dealing with the Legacy if its Indian Residential Schools Experiment," Pamela O'Connor draws attention to the striking similarity between the Australian aboriginal "stolen children" experience with Canada's residential school system. The assimilation of indigenous children in Australia was undertaken under child welfare laws supposedly to protect aborigines. It called for the permanent separation of aboriginal children from their families and communities, placing them in the care of foster homes, church missions, state- or church-run children's homes, boarding schools, and workplaces. Many of the children who were removed were brought up in complete ignorance of their aboriginal identity, parentage, or community affiliations.

In 1995 the Australian government asked the Human Rights and Equal Opportunities Commission to conduct a national inquiry into this situation. After conducting hearings around the country, the Commission reported in 1997 that the policy of assimilation through the forced removal of aboriginal children had given rise to gross violations of human rights law. The Commission's recommendations included reparations through a government cash-compensation scheme and an apology to Australia's aboriginal peoples.

The Australian government, however, has refused to apologize or to pay compensation. Instead, it proposed to spend $63 million on the preservation of records, language and cultural maintenance programs, family reunification services, counselling, therapy, and vocational training for victims of its policy of forced removal. It is thought that the refusal to pay reparation may be based on the fear of opening a torrent of claims against the state. The Australian response, like that of the Canadian government, is defensive and appears to be aimed at minimizing future claims of liability. Neither government, however, has effectively denied the legitimacy of the complaints of their respective aboriginal victims.

SEE ALSO Canada; Indigenous Peoples

BIBLIOGRAPHY

Indian and Northern Affairs Canada (2002). "Looking Forward Looking Back, Part Two: False Assumptions and a Failed Relationship." Available from http://www.ainc.gc.ca/2002-templates/ssi/print_e.asp.

O'Connor, Pamela (2000). "Squaring the Circle: How Canada Is Dealing with the Legacy of Its Indian Residential Schools Experiment." *International Journal of Legal Information* 28:232–265.

Schabas, William. A (2000). *Genocide in International Law*, Cambridge: Cambridge University Press.

Vinodh Jaichand

Resistance

Resistance is one of the most controversial and emotional issues associated with the Holocaust and other genocides. The overwhelming scope of the Holocaust raised the question, How could so many people be mur-

dered? Initially, writers proposed that it could only happen if the victims allowed it to happen through their own powerlessness. The phrase, "Jews went like sheep to the slaughter," as described most famously in the writings of Hannah Arendt, and later adopted by Raul Hilberg, summed up the early opinion that Jews offered little or no resistance. Later research, however, demonstrated that the issue was perhaps not the lack of resistance but how resistance was defined and, equally important, not why there was so little but how there was so much resistance that actually occurred.

Jewish Resistance during the Holocaust

The overwhelming might of the Nazi machine, together with local collaborators, made large-scale armed resistance impossible. Jews were isolated, with little arms or training, often disoriented by the progressive stages of the Final Solution and physically beaten down and systematically starved. Furthermore, most were primarily burdened by communal or familial responsibility and feared to act in the face of brutal Nazi reprisals. This limited the options of the more settled and older members of the community. Thus, in the ghettos, younger Jews—often those who had been members of the pre-war Zionist youth movements—usually carried out armed resistance. The most famous resistance was the uprising in the Warsaw ghetto, where a small number of Jews held out for almost a month. Other ghettos where Jews fought back included Vilna and Kovno in Lithuania and Bialystok, Kracow, and Czestochowa in Poland. According to some estimates, there were more than sixty ghettos in the Baltic areas that had underground resistance groups.

Jewish resistance was eventually found in the midst of the death camps, under the worst possible conditions. In camps such as Sobibor (August 1943) and Treblinka (October 1943) armed revolts caused both camps to stop functioning (Sobibor immediately and Treblinka after a few months). In Auschwitz-Birkenau another revolt (October 1944) resulted in the destruction of at least one gas chamber. This revolt was carried out by the Sonderkommando, the Jewish prisoners who were forced to work in the gas chambers and crematoria and who were supplied with gunpowder smuggled by women inmates from their slave labor in munitions factories.

Outside of the camps and ghettos Jewish resistance appeared as a form of partisan or resistance movements. However, in many cases, particularly in Eastern Europe, the Jewish units were not only forced to operate separately but also hunted and targeted by local resistance units, such as the Armia Krajowa in Poland. These Jewish units were often denied arms by both the

Jewish fighters lie dead. The fiercest resistance to the Nazis occurred in the Warsaw ghetto, where members of the Jewish Fighting Organization (*Zydowska Organizacja Bojowa*) pelted the tanks of entering German troops with hand grenades. It took the Nazis twenty-seven days to destroy the ghetto and snuff out resistance. [**USHMM**]

national underground movements and the Allies, and they often had to protect themselves from these national units as well as the Nazis. Nonetheless, there was resistance, which usually took two forms. The first was offensive and consisted of attacks against Nazi forces and installations, or against places that could harm the Nazi war effort (such as trains, bridges, and telephone wires). The second was defensive and consisted especially in the formation of "family camps"; Jews who had succeeded in escaping the Nazis and had fled into the dense woods of Eastern Europe could find refuge in these camps, which were run and defended by Jews. The most famous of these camps was the Bielski otriad, which saved more than 1,100 Jews in Belorussia. An estimate of the number of these partisans in the East puts the figure at about 30,000.

In Western Europe, such as in France and Belgium, some separate Jewish groups did operate, but many of the Jews who were active in the resistance contributed in the context of the national underground. This was

also the pattern with other lands, such as Slovakia, Yugoslavia, Italy, and Greece.

Whether resistance only involves fighting and violence is another question. While some scholars dismiss all forms of nonviolent or spiritual resistance, others such as Tzvetan Todorov have pointed out that nonviolence does not mean nonresistance to evil. In contrast to Hilberg and his followers, they advance the idea that as Yehuda Bauer put it, "one resists without using force" (2001, p. 120). Scholars are still exploring the precise definition of the term *resistance*, but various actions that fit into the definition might include smuggling food in opposition to Nazi decrees, establishing medical efforts to provide for the community, and continuing religious, educational, and cultural activities. Forms of these activities all took place in the ghettos and camps, and all were based on the idea of working to attempt to survive until liberation, thus depriving the Nazis of their goal of creating a Europe that was *Judenrein* ("free of Jews"). These actions also defied the

Nazi attempt to define Jews as *Untermenschen* ("subhuman"), by affirming Jewish self-definition. In religious terms, in a reversal of the traditional term *Kiddush Ha-Shem* (literally "Sanctification of the Name" in Hebrew, referring to the obligation to accept martyrdom in certain conditions), a rabbi in the Warsaw ghetto put forward the commandment of *Kiddush Ha-Hayyim,* the "Sanctification of Life," as a religious obligation.

Resistance during Other Genocides

While resistance during the Holocaust is the best documented and most discussed example of resistance to genocide, it is not the only example. And as each example of genocide in history has its own unique features, so too do the other examples of resistance. But the lack of specific studies and detailed documentation hampers the discussion of other examples of resistance. For example, Soviet archives have only become accessible since the end of the cold war. Their availability gives historians the opportunity to compare Joseph Stalin's gulags to the Nazi concentration camp system, but significant differences do exist. While even in the midst of the gulag, at the height of Stalin's terror (and immediately after his death in 1953), there existed a network of anti-Stalinist and anti-Soviet activities that included strikes, protests, underground newspapers, and, ultimately, armed revolts in 1942, 1953, and 1954 that involved thousands of inmates. Resistance by refusal to work would have been futile in a Nazi system that existed to provide death, not products.

Also, while the myth of the impossibility of escape from the Gulag was one that was popularized by many, including survivors such as Alexander Solzhenitsyn, others, such as the scholar Anne Applebaum, have pointed out that thousands did escape, especially in the early years of the Gulag. For example, Applebaum cites official Soviet statistics: in one year alone (1947), 10,440 prisoners escaped and only 2,894 were recaptured.

While there is not a specific account of Tutsi resistance to the Hutu genocide, reports of resistance have surfaced. Philip Gourevitch described Bisesero as being "the only place in Rwanda where thousands of Tutsi civilians mounted a defense against the Hutus who were trying to kill them" (1998), and he also described nonviolent rescues by individuals. As the war crimes tribunals continue their prosecutions in 2004, more evidence of both resistance and rescue are being documented.

Ultimately, resistance to genocide on a large scale can only succeed with assistance either from significant segments of the local populations or with international assistance. Failing that, resistance can save some, but its more lasting value might exist in giving the threatened group a sense of pride and self-determination, even in the sense of choosing the time, place, and method of their death, and in leaving a lasting legacy both to the survivors and to those who will come later. And, it is this sense of self-determination that can be a basis for rebuilding the family and community with a sense of group self-worth and shared humanity, both of which are necessary for the ability to not forget and to stand as equals among others.

SEE ALSO Bystanders; Perpetrators; Rescuers, Holocaust

BIBLIOGRAPHY

Applebaum, Anne (2003). *Gulag: A History.* New York: Doubleday.

Bauer, Yehuda (2001). *Rethinking the Holocaust.* New Haven, Conn.: Yale University Press.

Gourevitch, Philip (1998). *We Wish to Inform You That Tomorrow We Will Be Killed with Our Families: Stories from Rwanda.* New York: Picador.

Hilberg, Raul (1992). *Perpetrators, Victims, Bystanders.* New York: Aaron Asher.

Todorov, Tzvetan (1996). *Facing the Extreme: Moral Life in the Concentration Camps.* New York: Metropolitan Books.

Mark Weitzman

Responsibility, State

The law of State responsibility is the chapter of international law that concerns the breach by a State of one or more of its international obligations. In international law, responsibility is the corollary of obligation; every breach by a subject of international law of its international obligations entails its international responsibility. The law of State responsibility defines when an international obligation is to be held to have been breached, as well as the consequences of that breach, including which States are entitled to react, and the permissible means of that reaction.

Unlike national laws, wherein different rules often apply according to the source of the obligation breached (e.g., contract law, tort law, criminal law), international law does not concern itself with the source of the obligation that is breached; in principle (and unless otherwise specifically provided) the same rules apply to the breach of an obligation whether the source of the obligation is a treaty, customary international law, a unilateral declaration, or the judgment of an international court.

In August 2001 the International Law Commission (ILC, a body of legal experts set up by the United Nations [UN] General Assembly in 1949 to codify and progressively develop international law) completed its Articles on the Responsibility of States for Internationally Wrongful Acts (ARSIWA), a project on which it had been working for more than forty years. The aim of the articles is to codify the generally applicable rules of State responsibility.

It should be noted that the ARSIWA are envisaged as laying down general rules that apply in default of any more specific rule applicable to the obligation in question. In some cases, special rules may apply to an obligation (either as a result of the formulation of the rule itself, or because the obligation in question forms part of a special regime); for instance, it is possible that a particular obligation may be subject to a special rule requiring fault or damage before there is held to be a breach, or it may be that the category of States entitled to react is wider than the default position under the ARSIWA. This is the principle of *lex specialis* (to the extent that special rules are applicable and inconsistent with the rules contained in the ARSIWA, the special rules will prevail and displace the more general rules).

The Elements of State Responsibility

The starting point of the articles is that "every internationally wrongful act of a State entails the international responsibility of that State" (Article 1, ARSIWA). The act or omission of a State will qualify as an "internationally wrongful act" if two conditions are met. First, the act or omission must constitute a breach of an international obligation, or, as the articles put it, must be "not in conformity with what is required" by the international obligation (Article 12, ARSIWA). This implies that the obligation in question must be binding on the State at the time of the conduct, which is said to constitute a breach. Second, the act or omission must be "attributable" to the State.

The general rule is that a State is not responsible for the acts of private individuals. The State is of course an abstract entity, unable to accomplish any physical act itself. Just as in domestic law corporations act through their officers and agents, so in international law the State normally acts through its organs and officials. The first, and clearest, case of attribution is that of the organs of the State (e.g., police officers, the army) whose acts are attributable to the State even in instances where they contravene their instructions, or exceed their authority as a matter of national law (Article 7, ARSIWA). No distinction is made based on the level of the particular organ in the organizational hierarchy of the State; State responsibility can arise from the actions of a local policeman, just as it can from the actions of the highest officials, for instance a head of state

or a foreign minister. Nor is any distinction made upon the basis of the separation of powers; State responsibility may arise from acts or omissions of the legislature and the judiciary, although by the nature of things it is more common that an internationally wrongful act is the consequence of an act or acts of the executive. Second, the rules of attribution cover situations in which individuals, not otherwise State organs, are exercising "elements of governmental authority" at the time that they act (Article 5, ARSIWA). Third, acts of private individuals are attributable to the State if those individuals are acting on the instructions of the State, or under its effective direction or control (Article 8, ARSIWA). Fourth, in exceptional circumstances in which there is an absence or default of governmental authority, the acts of private individuals may be attributable to the State if those individuals, in effect, step into the breach and perform necessary governmental functions (Article 9, ARSIWA).

With regard to certain obligations, a State may incur responsibility even though actions have been carried out by private individuals, because the essence of the obligation was to ensure that a given result occurred. For instance, if a foreign embassy is overrun by a mob, or harm is done to diplomatic staff by private individuals, as occurred with the U.S. embassy in Tehran during the Iranian revolution of 1979 to 1980, a State may incur responsibility, even if those individuals act on their own initiative. Equally, under Article V of the 1948 Convention on the Prevention and Punishment of the Crime of Genocide, the obligation of a State to punish those responsible for genocide earlier on related to genocide may be breached in instances in which a State fails to punish any person responsible for the genocide, "whether they are constitutionally responsible rulers, public officials, or private individuals." There is probably a similar rule in general international law in relation to crimes against humanity. In both cases, the basis of responsibility here is not the attribution to the State of the acts of the individuals; it is the failure by the State as an entity to comply with the obligations of prevention and prosecution incumbent on it.

A somewhat anomalous instance of attribution is that covered by Article 10 of the ARWISA. As was noted above, in the normal course of events, a State is not responsible for the acts of private individuals; *a fortiori*, it is not responsible for the acts of insurrectional movements, because, by definition, an insurrectional group acts in opposition to the established state structures and its organization is distinct from the government of the State to which it is opposed. However, Article 10(1) ARSIWA provides that "the conduct of an insurrectional movement which becomes the new government of a State shall be considered an act of that State under international law." Article 10(2) provides for a similar rule with respect to an insurrectional movement that succeeds in establishing a new State within the territory of a pre-existing State. The effect of the rule is to attribute retrospectively the conduct of the movement in question to the State. In the case of a successful insurrectional movement, the acts of the movement are attributed to the State as if the movement had been the government at the time of its acts, even though, if the insurrection had failed, no attribution would be possible. In the case of the establishment of a new State, the effect is even more drastic because acts are attributed to the State retrospectively to a time when it did not yet definitively exist.

Except in this case, there is no established machinery for attributing collective responsibility (e.g., for war crimes, genocide, or crimes against humanity) to an armed opposition group. In such circumstances individual responsibility is the only possibility at the international level of ensuring a degree of responsibility for criminal acts.

Certain circumstances may serve to preclude the wrongfulness of a breach of international law by a State, in much the same way that defenses and excuses work in national criminal law. In international law these are termed "circumstances precluding wrongfulness" (Part One, Chapter V, Articles 20–27, ARSIWA). For instance, the consent of the state to which the obligation was owed will prevent the breach being wrongful, as will, under certain restrictively defined conditions, force majeure, distress, and necessity. The fact that a State acts in legitimate self-defense in accordance with the Charter of the United Nations may preclude the wrongfulness of an act. Finally, a State taking countermeasures (defined as the nonperformance of an obligation in response to a prior wrongful act of another State, in order to induce that State to comply with its obligations) may mean that what would otherwise be a breach of an international obligation is not in fact wrongful. However, quite apart from the strict procedural conditions with which the taking of countermeasures is hedged, it should be noted that certain obligations may not be the object of countermeasures. Among these are the obligation to refrain from the threat or use of force, obligations for the protection of fundamental human rights, obligations of a humanitarian character prohibiting reprisals under peremptory norms of general international law (*jus cogens*). This last limitation in fact applies generally to circumstances precluding wrongfulness: it is never possible to plead that a breach of a peremptory norm was justified.

The Content of International Responsibility

Upon the commission of an internationally wrongful act, new legal obligations come into existence for the State responsible for that act. First, that State is under an obligation to make full reparation for the injury caused by the internationally wrongful act. Reparation may take one of three forms: restitution, compensation, or satisfaction (or some combination of them). Traditionally, restitution has played the primary role, although in instances in which restitution is materially impossible, the injured State may have to content itself with compensation or satisfaction. Second, the responsible State is under an obligation to conclude the internationally wrongful act if it is continuing, and in an appropriate case, may be required to make assurances and guarantees of non-repetition.

The ARSIWA mark a decisive step away from the traditional bilateralism of international law and toward what has been called "community interest" in the provisions dealing with the States that are entitled to react to the breach of an internationally wrongful act. Traditionally, only the State that was directly injured, or in some way "targeted," by the breach of an international obligation could demand reparation. In addition, although any state could take unfriendly measures that did not constitute the breach of an international obligation owed to the State at which they were directed (retorsion), the taking of countermeasures was commonly understood as being limited to these "injured States."

The first major move away from the strict bilateralism of international law was the judgment of the International Court of Justice in the *Barcelona Traction, Light and Power Company Limited (Belgium v. Spain)* case. In that case, the court stated:

[A]n essential distinction should be drawn between the obligations of a State towards the international community as a whole, and those arising vis-à-vis another State in the field of diplomatic protection. By their very nature the former are the concern of all States. In view of the importance of the rights involved, all States can be held to have a legal interest in their protection; they are obligations *erga omnes* (*ICJ Reports 1966*, p. 3 at 32 [para. 33]).

In the next paragraph, the court went on to state that "such obligations derive, for example, in contemporary international law, from the outlawing of acts of aggression, and of genocide, as also from the principles and rules concerning the basic rights of the human person, including protection from slavery and racial discrimination." This distinction between obligations of which only the injured State may complain, and those in the observance of which a wider community of States have an interest, is reflected in Articles 42 and 48 ARSIWA, although it should be stressed that the latter provision is undoubtedly one of the clearest examples of progressive development to be found within the articles. It seems indisputable that all other States have an interest in the observance by other States (and individuals) of the prohibitions of genocide and crimes against humanity. However, the exact implications of this interest require further working out in the light of State practice.

The Rise and Fall of the Notion of State Crimes

The ILC proposal, as adopted on first reading in 1996, sought to introduce the notion of "international crimes" of States. However, there were major flaws with the proposal, despite the strong support they received from some writers and from some groups of States. Their major deficiency was that they did not envisage anything even approaching a form of sanction in keeping with the normal domestic conception of crime; this was crime without punishment.

In addition, there were none of the other trappings that one would expect with a penal form of responsibility. For instance, there was no adequate definition of the internationally wrongful acts that constituted State crimes (in order to comply with the principle *nullum crimen sine lege*), nor was there any system for objective and impartial investigation on behalf of the international community of the facts alleged to constitute a State crime. Perhaps most tellingly, there was no system of due process in relation to the trial of State crimes, nor was there envisaged the establishment of a forum having compulsory jurisdiction over the crimes and the States alleged to have committed them. Rather the notion of crime was to be grafted onto the existing decentralized system of enforcement, with all of the possibilities of abuse and misuse that this implied.

On the other hand, certain limited consequences above the normal regime of responsibility attached to the concept of crime. For instance, in the case of State crimes, all other States were to be regarded as injured and could thus invoke responsibility, and it was generally accepted that there was an obligation incumbent on all other States not to recognize the consequences of a crime.

The notion of State crimes, and its consequences, caused a great amount of controversy, and created deep differences of opinion within the ILC. Some members took the view that the label crime was merely a pejorative way of describing the category of very serious breaches of obligations of concern to the international community as a whole, and that the solution was to remove the language of crime, while retaining the conse-

quences that were accepted as constituting part of contemporary law. In the end it was this approach that prevailed; in 1998, the concept of "international crimes of States" was set aside, and was ultimately dropped from the text that was adopted on second reading. The excision of the language of crime was one of the major factors contributing to the unopposed adoption of the ILC articles in 2001.

The Relationship between State Responsibility and Individual Responsibility

The relationship between State responsibility and individual responsibility has until recently been a neglected issue, principally due to the late development of international individual criminal responsibility.

In 1947 the International Military Tribunal at Nuremberg stated that "crimes against international law are committed by men, not by abstract entities, and only by punishing individuals who commit such crimes can the provisions of international law be enforced" (*Trial of the Major War Criminals before the International Military Tribunal*, Vol. 1, p. 223). This statement says much about perceptions of the international legal system in the immediate aftermath of World War II; however, insofar as it seems to assert that observance of the rules of international law prohibiting atrocities can only be achieved through the prosecution of individuals, the assertion no longer holds true.

During the 1990s a number of inter-State cases alleging *State* responsibility for violations of the international rules concerned with the outlawing of atrocities were brought before the International Court of Justice. Some of these cases, in particular those between the States that had emerged after the disintegration of the Socialist Federal Republic of Yugoslavia (*Bosnia and Herzegovina v. Yugoslavia* [Serbia and Montenegro], 1993 onward; *Croatia v. Yugoslavia*, 1999 onward), concerned situations involving allegations of genocide and crimes against humanity that were concurrently the subject of investigation and prosecution of individuals before the International Criminal Tribunal for the Former Yugoslavia (ICTY). Other cases (*Democratic Republic of the Congo* [D.R.C.] v. *Rwanda* [1999–2001; New Application: 2002–ongoing]; *D.R.C. v. Uganda* [1999 onward]; *D.R.C. v. Burundi* [1999–2001]) alleged, among other things, violations of the 1948 UN Genocide Convention, serious violations of human rights, and war crimes that had not been the subject of international prosecution, although one should note the issuance by a magistrate in Belgium of an international arrest warrant for the foreign minister of the D.R.C. in relation to a charge of "serious violations of international humanitarian law"; the International

Court of Justice held that under international law a sitting foreign minister enjoys absolute personal immunity and inviolability, and that therefore Belgium was in breach of its international obligations (UN International Court of Justice, *ICJ Reports 2002, D.R.C. v. Belgium, Arrest Warrant of 11 April 2000*, p. 3).

At the preliminary objections stage of the case (mentioned above) between Bosnia and Serbia-Montenegro, the respondents argued for a restrictive interpretation of the jurisdictional provision contained in Article IX of the 1948 UN Genocide Convention. Article IX provides as follows:

> Disputes between the Contracting Parties relating to the interpretation, application or fulfillment of the present Convention, including those relating to the responsibility of a State for genocide or for any of the other acts enumerated in Article III, shall be submitted to the International Court of Justice at the request of any of the parties to the dispute.

Serbia-Montenegro argued that the provision only conferred jurisdiction on the court in relation to responsibility for failure to comply with the obligations to *prevent* and *punish* genocide, as contained in Articles V, VI, and VII of the convention, and not to State responsibility for violations of the substantive prohibition of genocide contained in Article III. Accordingly, it was argued, as the jurisdiction of the court is based on consent, the court had no jurisdiction in relation to the allegations made by Bosnia and Herzegovina of violations of the prohibition of genocide by individuals whose acts were attributable to Serbia-Montenegro.

The court dealt with the point briefly, observing:

> [T]he reference in Article IX to "the responsibility of a State for genocide or for any of the other acts enumerated in Article III," does not exclude any form of State responsibility. Nor is the responsibility of a State for acts of its organs excluded by Article IV of the Convention, which contemplates the commission of an act of genocide by "rulers" or "public officials" (*ICJ Reports 1996*, p. 595, at p. 616, para. 32).

Accordingly, it held, a dispute existed between the parties on this point, as well as on the "the facts of the case, their imputability, and the applicability to them of the provisions of the Genocide Convention," and was sufficient to its jurisdiction (*ICJ Reports 1996*, p. 595, at p. 616, para. 33). Two points bear emphasizing. First, the argument of Serbia-Montenegro did not have as a necessary premise that State responsibility for actual acts of genocide attributable to a State does not exist; rather, the argument was that State responsibility of this type did not fall within Article IX. Second, the decision of

the court at the preliminary objections stage of the case did not definitively decide whether breach of the 1948 UN Genocide Convention by an individual necessarily involves State responsibility if the relevant acts are attributable to a State, as the only hurdle that had to be surmounted was whether there was a dispute between the parties as to the interpretation or application of the convention. However, the tone of the court's judgment seems to suggest that State responsibility does arise in these circumstances, and this would be consistent with general principle.

Conversely, the ICTY has made reference to State responsibility in elucidating the law relevant to the international criminal responsibility of individuals. In the *Furundzija* case the Trial Chamber held that the international legal norms prohibiting torture arising from human rights law and international humanitarian law "impose obligations upon States and other entities in an armed conflict, but first and foremost address themselves to the acts of individuals, in particular to State officials or more generally, to officials of a party to the conflict or else to individuals acting at the instigation or with the consent or acquiescence of a party to the conflict" (para. 140). As a consequence,

> Under current international humanitarian law, in addition to individual criminal liability, State responsibility may ensue as a result of State officials engaging in torture or failing to prevent torture or to punish torturers. If carried out as an extensive practice of State officials, torture amounts to a serious breach on a widespread scale of an international obligation of essential importance for safeguarding the human being, thus constituting a particularly grave wrongful act generating State responsibility (para. 142).

It is therefore now generally accepted that a single act can give rise to "two distinct types of responsibility coming under mutually autonomous legal regimes" (Dupuy, 2002, p. 1098). The ILC intentionally left the question of the interplay of the two bodies of law open for future development, inserting a saving clause as Article 58, ARSIWA, which reads, "These articles are without prejudice to any question of the individual responsibility under international law of any person acting on behalf of a State." Similarly, the Rome Statute of the International Criminal Court (ICC) provides in its Article 25(4) that "[n]o provision in this Statute relating to individual criminal responsibility shall affect the responsibility of States under international law."

However, although the rules constituting the general framework of State responsibility and international criminal responsibility may constitute distinct bodies of law, there are inevitably certain overlaps or points of contact between the two systems due to the fact that at the root of both are the same norms of substantive international law, that is, those prohibiting anyone from committing genocide, crimes against humanity, and so on.

Most obviously, for instance, it is clear that an individual cannot be found guilty of genocide if he did not have the "specific intent" to "destroy in whole or part, a national, ethnical, racial, or religious group, as such," required by Article II of the 1948 Genocide Convention. Equally, in seeking to establish State responsibility for genocide, it seems clear that at least one person, if not more, whose acts are attributable to the State should have the requisite specific intent. In this sense, the 1948 Genocide Convention operates as a *lex specialis* in relation to the generally applicable rules of international law, in which *culpa* or intention is not generally required.

Second, although the definition of genocide is not expressed in such terms, the logistical and organizational structures necessary for the commission of the crime inevitably involve State or para-statal structures. A person who murders a single person on the basis of the national, ethnic, racial, or religious group to which that person belongs does not commit genocide, even though it may be that he would murder all of the members of the group if he could, and thus arguably has the required specific intent. A certain amount of concertation is necessary, and there is a certain threshold of scale both for genocide and crimes against humanity (of which, ultimately, genocide is a species).

In relation to crimes against humanity, Article 3 of the Statute of the International Criminal Tribunal for Rwanda (ICTR) requires that the acts have been committed as part of "a widespread or systematic attack against any civilian population on national, political, ethnic, racial, or religious grounds," whereas Article 5 of the Statute of the ICTY, which only requires that the acts have been committed "in armed conflict, whether international or internal in character, and directed against any civilian population" has been interpreted by the ICTY as requiring that there be a widespread or systematic attack. In similar fashion, Article 7 of the Rome Statute of the ICC imposes the slightly different requirement of "a widespread and systematic attack directed against any civilian population" in its definition of crimes against humanity. As with genocide, the requirement of "a widespread or systematic attack" implies an element of scale or of planning, and will in most cases involve structures and apparatus that will normally only be disposed of by a State or by an armed opposition group, although proof of a plan or policy is not a necessary part of the definition of the crime.

It was for reasons of this kind that the ILC included in its articles a provision dealing specifically with the issue of responsibility for what are termed *composite acts*—that is, acts wherein the gist of the wrong is the combination of individual acts that are not in themselves necessarily wrongful or criminal as a matter of international law. Article 15 of ARSIWA provides as follows:

1. The breach of an international obligation by a State, through a series of actions or omissions defined in aggregate as wrongful, occurs when the action or omission occurs which, taken with the other actions or omissions, is sufficient to constitute the wrongful act.

2. In such a case, the breach extends over the entire period starting with the first of the actions or omissions of the series and lasts for as long as these actions or omissions are repeated and remain not in conformity with the international obligation.

According to the commentary, this has specific application to crimes against humanity and genocide.

Even though it has special features, the prohibition of genocide, formulated in identical terms in the 1948 Convention and in later instruments, may be taken as an illustration of a composite obligation. It implies that the responsible entity (including a State) will have adopted a systematic policy or practice. According to Article II(a) of the Convention, the prime case of genocide is "killing members of [a national, ethnical, racial or religious group]" with the intent to destroy that group as such, in whole or in part. Both limbs of the definition contain systematic elements. Genocide also has to be carried out with the relevant intention, aimed at physically eliminating the group "as such." Genocide is not committed until there has been an accumulation of acts of killing, causing harm, etc., committed with the relevant intent, so as to satisfy the definition in Article II. Once that threshold is crossed, the time of commission extends over the whole period during which any of the acts was committed, and any individual responsible for any of them with the relevant intent will have committed genocide (Crawford, 2000, pp. 141–142).

The Distinction between Commission and Failure to Prevent or Punish

The 1948 UN Genocide Convention distinguishes between the basic prohibition of genocide and conduct ancillary to genocide—incitement, conspiracy, and so on (defined in Articles II and III), and the question of prevention and punishment (addressed in Articles I, IV, V, and VI). Persons committing genocide (whether or not State officials) are to be punished. The State is under an obligation not merely to enact laws prohibiting genocide (Article V), but also to prevent and punish actual violations occurring within its territory. Thus, there is a distinction between the criminal act, which is committed by individuals and is punishable accordingly, and the State's obligation to prevent and punish—failure to do which is not as such criminal, but amounts to a breach of an international obligation. In the *Application of the Genocide Convention* case, as noted already, Yugoslavia (Serbia and Montenegro) argued that the only obligation that had been incumbent upon it under the convention was to prevent genocide and punish acts of genocide occurring on its territory; the court rejected this argument, affirming that the jurisdictional provision did not exclude "any form of State responsibility" (*ICJ Reports* 1996, pp. 595, 616). The court left to the merits phase of the case the question of the scope of the obligations under the convention, and accordingly the extent of State responsibility falling within the jurisdictional provision. However, leaving aside the technicalities of jurisdiction, the better view is that—whether under the convention or as a matter of general international law—a State is responsible for any act of genocide committed by one of its organs or by other persons whose conduct in the relevant respect is attributable to the State.

As indicated by the *Bosnia* case, it is arguable that, in these as in other respects, there may be a distinction between on the one hand the scope of responsibility (and accordingly of jurisdiction) under the convention, and on the other the scope of the obligations, and of responsibility under general international law. For example, national jurisdiction to try persons suspected of genocide is limited by Article VI to genocide committed on the territory of the implicated State. It is inconceivable that jurisdiction is so limited under general international law, given such developments as the extension of national jurisdiction over international crimes in general (including crimes less serious than genocide).

SEE ALSO International Court of Justice; International Law; Reparations; Restitution

BIBLIOGRAPHY

Cassese, A. (2003). *International Criminal Law*. Oxford, U.K.: Oxford University Press.

Crawford, J. R. (2002). *The International Law Commission's Articles on State Responsibility: Introduction, Text and Commentaries*. Cambridge: Cambridge University Press.

Crawford, J. R., and S. Olleson (2003). "The Nature and Forms of International Responsibility." In *International Law*, ed. M. Evans. Oxford, U.K.: Oxford University Press.

Dominicé, C. (1999). "La question de la double responsabilité de l'Etat et de son agent." In *Liber Amicorum Judge Mohammed Bedjaoui*, ed. E. Yakpo and T. Boumedra. The Hague, Netherlands: Kluwer Law International.

Dupuy, P.-M. (2002). "International Criminal Responsibility of the Individual and International Responsibility of the State." In *The Rome Statute of the International Criminal Court: A Commentary*, ed. A. Cassese, P. Gaeta, and J. R. W. D. Jones. Oxford, U.K.: Oxford University Press.

Nollkaemper, A. (2003). "Concurrence between Individual Responsibility and State Responsibility in International Law." *International and Comparative Law Quarterly* 52:615–640.

Sassòli, M. (2002). "State Responsibility for Violations of International Humanitarian Law." *International Review of the Red Cross* 84:401–434.

Schabas, W. A. (2000). *Genocide in International Law*. Cambridge: Cambridge University Press.

Shaw, M. N. (1989). "Genocide and International Law." In *International Law at a Time of Perplexity; Essays in Honour of Shabtai Rosenne*, ed. Y. Dinstein and M. Tabory. Dordrecht, Netherlands: Martinus Nijhoff.

Verdirame, G. (2000). "The Genocide Definition in the Jurisprudence of the Ad Hoc Tribunals." *International and Comparative Law Quarterly* 49:578–598.

Zegveld, E. (2002). *The Accountability of Armed Opposition Groups in International Law*. Cambridge: Cambridge University Press.

James Crawford
Simon Olleson

Restitution

Restitution is generally associated with the idea of returning something lost or stolen to its legitimate owner. In international law, however, the notion of restitution is linked with the issue of state responsibility. In this sense, restitution is one of the forms through which a state may discharge its obligation to provide reparation for the harm caused by its wrongful acts. More precisely, the term is used, in international practice, in at least two senses. In the strict sense, it signifies the return of unlawfully taken property to the original owner. In the broad sense, restitution (or, in its Latin version, *restitutio in integrum*) is the re-establishment, as far as possible, of the situation that existed before a wrongful act was committed.

Restitution as a Form of Reparation under International Law

A broad consensus exists among the international community preferring restitution over other forms of reparation under international law. This view is in line with the essential goal of reparation, which, according to the

Permanent Court of International Justice's holding in its famous *Chorzów Factory* decision (1928), "must, so far as possible, wipe out all the consequences of the illegal act and re-establish the situation which would, in all probability, have existed if that act had not been committed."

It follows that restitution—which most closely conforms to that goal—is to be preferred over compensation and other forms of reparation whenever possible, unless the injured party renounces it. This primacy of restitution has been embedded in the articles on the responsibility of states for internationally wrongful acts, adopted on second reading by the United Nations International Law Commission (2001). Even advocates of this primacy, however, recognize that it is not unconditional, and they accept that compensation should be preferred at least when providing restitution would, in a situation involving two states, put a burden on the responsible state that is out of all proportion to the corresponding benefit for the injured state.

Restitution for Gross Human Rights Violations Amounting to Genocide and Crimes Against Humanity

The principles of restitution have been developed in the context of interstate relations. With the development of international human rights law and humanitarian law, however, some have come to believe that if individuals are the direct and ultimate holders of substantive rights under international law, they must also enjoy international remedial rights for obtaining redress when their rights have been infringed. The issue of reparation, including that of restitution, plays a prominent role in this context.

Although there is no reason for excluding the primacy of restitution with regard to gross violations of human rights, its usefulness may be limited, in practice, by the specific type of harm caused by these kinds of wrongs. In effect, genocide and crimes against humanity cause harm, first and foremost, to immaterial and unique interests, such as dignity, personal integrity, and liberty. These cannot be restored to their original status once they are impaired.

Restitution is most suitable and appropriate with regard to violations of property rights, such as illegal or arbitrary expropriations. However, this does not mean that the role of restitution with regard to crimes against humanity is only marginal. In fact, the most invasive attacks on property are often linked with gross human rights violations. Genocide, for instance, may be accompanied by the destruction of houses and the pillage of goods. Furthermore, the destruction, plundering, and pillage of private property can by themselves amount to crimes against humanity or war crimes. This may occur, for example, when the dispossession or destruction is achieved through blatant discriminatory measures, or with the intent of persecuting a group or a collectivity, or when it is "committed by pressure of mass terror." However, a number of practical and political factors may hinder the concrete possibility for the victims to get their property back. This is particularly true with regard to two types of highly politicized restitution claims: those related to historical injustices and those connected with armed conflicts.

The former type of claim relates to serious impairments of human rights committed in a distant past, at a time when they possibly did not even constitute a breach of the existing law. The specificity of these claims lies in the fact that they are arguably based on moral grounds, rather than on the legal responsibility of the state involved. This is one of the reasons why this type of claim is generally dealt with in the framework of political settlements, rather than in the courts. The huge lapse of time passed since the occurrence of the injury poses an additional major obstacle for restitution in these cases. Properties are often destroyed or no longer identifiable, their economical destination may be irreversibly changed, or they may have been transferred to third parties acting in good faith. Under these circumstances, restitution of full ownership is often a virtually impossible option. This situation is well illustrated by land restitution claims put forward by indigenous communities for historical dispossessions.

Restitution claims connected with armed conflicts are complicated by the fact that the dispossessions often take place in conjunction with ethnic cleansing and land occupation with a view to annexation. Here, restitution may still be materially possible but politically unrealistic, particularly when it would mean the return of huge numbers of forcibly displaced persons to territories that have passed under the control of the same group who forced them to flee. In this context, property restitution can hardly be seen as an absolute goal but needs to be reconciled with other, concurring goals, to be settled in the framework of political negotiation.

Restitution in the Framework of International, Treaty-Based Judicial Mechanisms for the Protection of Human Rights

The substantive duty to provide reparations is reinforced in the context of judicial mechanisms of protection, where international courts are vested with the power to adjudicate both on the merits of allegations and on remedies. The potential of remedies, however, may be partly frustrated by the courts themselves if—on the basis of a restrictive interpretation of their remedial powers—a timid, low-profile approach to reparation is taken. A quite restrictive approach is adopted, for instance, by the European Court of Human Rights, which is generally reluctant to order specific remedies. However, it seems to be more audacious when it comes to infringements of property rights. The court has occasionally ordered states to return unlawfully seized properties to the former owners, thus affirming the primacy of restitution. The fact remains, however, that even in property cases, the court is not always prepared to order reparation to take place on the basis of restitution.

The Inter-American Court of Human Rights, enjoying broader remedial powers than its European counterpart, handed down a landmark judgment in 2001 in the *Awas Tingni* case. The Court found that Nicaragua had violated the rights to property and judicial protection of the members of the Mayagna (Sumo) community of Awas Tingni, an indigenous community located on the forested area of Nicaragua's Caribbean coastal region. For reparation, the Court ordered the government to take various measures to recognize, protect, and enforce the community's historical title on its ancestral land and resources. Although restitution was not an issue as such, the decision shows the potential of human rights mechanisms in cases of large-scale operations of dispossession that affect whole communities.

Unlike international state responsibility, the international responsibility of individuals has traditionally been conceived as being criminal in nature. Accordingly, the focus of international justice, as administered by international criminal tribunals, has centered on imposing penalties to the perpetrator, rather than on affording redress to the victims. Over the years, however, the view has gradually emerged that the international responsibility of individuals must include some obligations of a civil nature in respect of the victims.

The Rome Statute of the International Criminal Court (1998) recognizes the right of the victims to reparation in general and to restitution in particular. Article 75 of the statute enables the ICC to "make an order directly against a convicted person specifying appropriate reparations to, or in respect of, victims, including restitution, compensation and rehabilitation." It remains to be seen whether the ICC will, in practice, be able to make an effective use of the power thus granted to it.

Restitution outside the Framework of International Adjudication

Most reparation claims relating to gross human rights violations have been dealt with through political agreements reached outside of the typically adversarial procedures of judicial litigation. These agreements often include the setting up of specific procedures and ad hoc bodies to process individual claims.

In the late 1990s groups of Holocaust survivors have provided the impetus for establishing important reparations programs in Germany, Austria, Switzerland, and other European countries, to provide comprehensive solutions to the quest for reparation for damages incurred as a consequence of or in relation to events that happened during the Nazi era. Because of the legal and material hurdles accompanying restitution, however, most of these reparation programs have been designed to provide financial compensation rather than the restitution of the original property. A notable exception is the General Settlement Fund, established in Austria in 2001. This program comprises a specific procedure for the return of property wrongfully taken in Austria during the Nazi period. Restitution, however, is only possible under the condition that the property concerned was owned by the Austrian federal government at the moment when the fund was established.

Another example of Holocaust-related restitution is provided by the Claims Resolution Tribunal. The tribunal was established through a class action settlement in the United States, by an agreement between two Jewish associations and the Swiss Bankers Association. The tribunal is tasked with providing restitution to the legitimate owners of the assets they deposited with Swiss banks before World War II and which have remained dormant since then.

Restitution of property has also been a key element of the South African democratic transition. Individuals and collective entities that were dispossessed of property during the apartheid regime on the basis of racially discriminatory laws or practices, have the right to receive restitution of that property or equitable redress. Various organs and procedure, including a Land Claims Court and a Commission on Restitution of Land Rights, have been established to give effect to the victims' right to restitution.

Finally, the Dayton Peace Agreement of 1995, dealing with the situation in Bosnia and Herzegovina, paid special attention to the issue of restitution. It established a Commission for Displaced Persons and Refugees (subsequently renamed Commission for Real Property Claims of Displaced Persons and Refugees), which was mandated to receive and decide reparation claims relating to forcible dispossessions in Bosnia and Herzegovina during the war. Under the terms of the agreement, claimants had the right to choose between a return of the property they lost or to accept "just compensation in lieu of return." Similarly, some years later, the Housing and Property Directorate and Claims Commission were established in Kosovo (1999) for dealing with claims of individuals who had lost property as a result of discriminatory laws enacted under the Slobodan Milosevic regime or in connection with the conflict of 1999.

SEE ALSO Compensation; Rehabilitation; Reparations

BIBLIOGRAPHY

Alford, Roger P. (2002). "The Claims Resolution Tribunal and Holocaust Claims against Swiss Banks." *Berkeley Journal of International Law* 20:250–281.

Barkan, Elazar (2000). *The Guilt of Nations: Restitution and Negotiating Historical Injustices.* New York: Norton.

Bazyler, Michael J. (2002). "The Holocaust Restitution Movement in Comparative Perspective." *Berkeley Journal of International Law* 20:11–44.

Das, Hans (2004). "Restoring Property Rights in the Aftermath of War." *International and Comparative Law Quarterly* 53:429–444.

Ellis, Mark S., and Elizabeth Hutton (2002). "Policy Implications of World War II Reparations and Restitution as Applied to the Former Yugoslavia." *Berkeley Journal of International Law* 20:342–354.

Gray, Christine (1999). "The Choice between Restitution and Compensation." *European Journal of International Law* 10:413–423.

Kirgis, Frederic L. (2001). "Restitution as a Remedy in U.S. Courts for Violations of International Law." *American Journal of International Law* 95:341–348.

Kriebaum, U. (2003). "Restitution Claims for Massive Violations of Human Rights during the Nazi Regime: The Austrian Case." In *Reparations: Redressing Past Wrongs. Human Rights in Development Yearbook 2001,* ed. George Ulrich and Louise Krabbe Boserup. The Hague: Kluwer Law International.

Leckie, Scott, ed. (2003). *Returning Home: Housing and Property Restitution Rights for Refugees and Displaced Persons.* Ardsley, N.Y.: Transnational Publishers.

McBride, J. (2000). "Compensation, Restitution, and Human Rights in Post-Communist Europe." In *Property and Protection: Essays in Honour of Brian W. Harvey,* ed. Brian W. Harvey, Franklin Meisel, and P. J. Cook. Oxford: Hart Publishing.

Mostert, Hanri (2002). "Land Restitution, Social Justice and Development in South Africa." *South African Law Journal* 119:400–428.

Nowak, M. (2003). "The Right to Reparation of Victims of Gross Human Rights Violations." In *Reparations: Redressing Past Wrongs. Human Rights in Development Yearbook 2001,* ed. George Ulrich and Louise Krabbe Boserup. The Hague: Kluwer Law International.

Ratner, Morris A. (2002). "The Settlement of Nazi-Era Litigation through the Executive and Judicial Branches." *Berkeley Journal of International Law* 20:212–232.

Thomsen, S. (2000). "Restitution." In *Encyclopedia of Public International Law,* ed. Rudolf Bernhardt. New York: North-Holland.

Wassgren, Hans (1995). "Some Reflections on Restitutio in Integrum Especially in the Practice of the European Court of Human Rights." *Finnish Yearbook of International Law* 6:575–595.

Pietro Sardaro
Paul Lemmens

Ríos Montt, Efraín
[JUNE 16, 1926–]
Former dictator of Guatemala

On March 23, 1982 a coup of the Guatemalan Army set the stage for the massacre of over 75,000 people between 1982 and 1983. General José Efraín Ríos Montt was president of the military junta established by the coup, and in 2004 he and five other commanding officers remain charged with crimes against humanity and crimes of war.

Ríos Montt began his career in 1946, quickly rising through the military ranks to oversee the counterinsurgency campaign of the late 1960s and peasant insurgency in the eastern provinces, in which an estimated 10,000 people were killed by the army. After serving as Army Chief of Staff (1970–1974), he ran for office as the presidential candidate of the Christian Democratic Party in 1974. On March 23, 1982, a movement led by young officers within the military asked Ríos Montt to rid the country of corruption, this while he was being paid by the extreme right to prepare a revolt and head a military junta to fight a prolonged war against the guerrillas. With a new National Plan of Security and Development, referred to as "a process of national reconstruction," a state of siege was declared, all constitutional rights suspended, special secret tribunals established to try a variety of crimes, congress and all political parties banned. The massacre, to last some eighteen months, commenced in April 1982.

The 1999 UN-directed Historical Clarification Commission (CEH) Report found that the Guatemalan state and its agents (i.e., the army high command) was institutionally responsible for "acts of genocide." It distinguishes between a policy of genocide intended to exterminate a group in whole or in part and acts of genocide when "the goal is political, economic, military or whatever other such type, and the method that is utilized to achieve the end goal is the extermination of a group in whole or in part" (Vol. 2, p. 315). This distinction is based on two facts: in the epoch of greatest repression, 1)13 percent of those killed in the violence were non-Mayan (*ladino*), and 2) it was believed the Maya served as a social base for the guerrilla in certain

Former Guatemalan dictator Efraín Ríos Montt presides over a session of Guatemalan congress on March 20, 2001, in Guatemala City. The next day, Rios Montt said he would not step down from his position, despite orders from Guatemala's highest court. Court members issued the order after Rios Montt and several other lawmakers modified a law on liquor. [AP/WIDE WORLD PHOTOS]

areas; hence, those killed suffered not for their membership in an ethnic group but for being stigmatized as guerrillas.

This finding for institutional responsibility is highly significant as it focuses on the structures and apparatuses of repression and not just on the offenses of individual officers, as occurred in the eventual prosecutions in Argentina, among other countries.

Moreover, on August 9, 2000, President Alfonso Portillo acknowledged the institutional responsibility of the Guatemalan state arising from a "breach of the obligation imposed by Article 1 of the American Convention to respect and ensure the rights enshrined in the Convention" in ten cases before the Inter-American Commission on Human Rights. This acknowledgment prompted the commission to take up a petition submitted by the Human Rights Office of the Archdiocese of Guatemala and the International Human Rights Law

Group that held the Guatemalan state responsible for not respecting and ensuring basic human rights.

Criminal cases brought before the Guatemalan Supreme Court have charged Ríos Montt and his high command (1982–1983), as well as Lucas Garcia and his high command (1978–1981), with genocidal acts on behalf of survivors and families of massacre victims. These cases are based on witness testimonies as well as numerous documents, including the 1997 Guatemalan Archdiocese REMHI Report as well as the CEH Report.

Not only has Rios Montt violated massive human rights, but he has also debilitated the structures that seek to uphold them. For example, the Guatemalan constitution clearly states that no one involved in a coup d'etat may run for president; however, in August 1990 Ríos Montt attempted to do just that, asserting that the law did not apply to him. On March 4, 1991, Ríos Montt filed a complaint against the Guatemalan government with the Inter-American Human Rights Commission, alleging that in declaring his candidacy for the presidency unconstitutional, judicial, legislative, and executive officials had in their resolutions and actions violated the American Convention on Human Rights. Ríos Montt further argued that a provision in one of the early Guatemalan peace agreements of Esquipulas in 1987 states that all who had participated in the conflict would be declared free of political crimes.

The Guatemalan Supreme Court again ruled against Ríos Montt's candidacy in 1995. In 2003, as President of the National Congress, he was permitted to register as a presidential candidate by the Constitutional Court, packed with his political supporters. When the Supreme Court upheld the constitutional ban, mobs of the general's Guatemalan Republican Front Party rampaged through the center of Guatemala City, attacking judges and journalists who had opposed Ríos Montt's candidacy. The Constitutional Court overturned the Supreme Court decision a week after the riots—further debilitating Guatemala's democratic institutions.

By only placing third in the November 2003 presidential elections, Ríos Montt lost his parliamentary immunity and became the centerpiece of the campaign against impunity, headed by families of the victims of the massacre. The Popular Social Movement, which comprises dozens of organizations in Guatemala, asked the two remaining presidential candidates in the 2003 elections to pledge to bring the former general to trial for genocide, and not grant him immunity in exchange for votes, which they agreed to do.

SEE ALSO Argentina; Guatemala

BIBLIOGRAPHY

Center for Human Rights Legal Action (CALDH) website. Available from http://www.caldh.org.

Menchu, Rigoberta (1984). *I, Rigoberta Menchu.* Ed. Elizabeth Burgos Debray. London: Verso Press.

Oficina de Derechos Humanos del Arzobispado de Guatemala (ODHAG) (1997). *REMHI Project for the Recuperation of Historic memory Guatemala.* Guatemala: ODHAG.

Schirmer, Jennifer (1998). *The Guatemalan Military Project: A Violence Called Democracy,* 1st edition. Philadelphia: University of Pennsylvania Press.

United Nations (1999). *Guatemala: Memoria del Silencio,* 1st ed. Historical Clarification Commission Report. New York: United Nations. Also available from http://www.hrdata.aaas.org/ceh/report/english/toc.html.

Jennifer Schirmer

Romania

After the coup of August 23, 1944, in which King Michael ordered the arrest of Romania's pro-German dictator, Ion Antonescu, Soviet troops entered Bucharest and found an interim Romanian government ready to negotiate peace. From the armistice Joseph Stalin fashioned a legal framework for the Soviet Union's political and economic domination of Romania; he secured this through the imposition of rule by the Romanian Communist Party (RCP). On March 5, 1945, a pro-Soviet government came to power and used the country's political structure, trade unions, and educational system to make Romania completely subservient to the Soviet Union. A vital step was the dissolution of the major democratic parties in the summer of 1947, and the indictment and imprisonment of their elderly leaders, Iuliu Maniu and Constantin Bratianu, as "agents of Britain and the United States." Both died in communist prisons, along with many of their associates. Their trial was followed by the enforced abdication of King Michael on December 30, 1947.

The RCP moved swiftly to transform Romania, following the Soviet model and employing Stalinist norms and practices. All private enterprises were nationalized in June 1948, and in March 1949 the ownership of land was completely removed from private hands without compensation. The confiscated land was used to create state farms or organized into collectives. Peasant resistance to collectivization resulted in some 80,000 imprisonments, with 30,000 peasants tried in public. Collectivization was finally completed in 1962.

Police terror is an intrinsic feature of totalitarianism, and communist rule in Romania confirmed this. The destruction of an existing society and the creation of a new one were achieved by a single mass party com-

On December 17, 1989, Nicolae Ceausescu, shown here, ordered his security forces to fire on antigovernment demonstrators in the city of Timisoara. The demonstrations soon spread to Bucharest, and on December 22 Ceausescu and his wife fled the capital in a helicopter, but were captured and taken into custody by army officers. Ceausescu and his wife were hurriedly tried (for mass murder and other crimes) in a special military tribunal, and shortly thereafter went before a firing squad. **[AP/WIDE WORLD PHOTOS]**

posed of an elite and dedicated membership whose objectives were central control and direction of the economy, a technologically perfected monopoly of the media, and complete direction of the armed forces. The Communist Party assigned to the secret police (Securitate) the task of removing the so-called enemies of the regime and those classes of the population who were considered an obstacle to centralized control of the economy. Communist leader Gheorghe Gheorghiu-Dej initiated this program in 1945. Nicolae Ceausescu inherited it in 1965.

The Securitate's most potent weapon was fear, and the depth of its inculcation in the Romanian population was the principal reason for its success. In Romania police terror was used in two stages: first, to eliminate opponents in the drive to consolidate power and, second, to ensure compliance once revolutionary change had been effected. The first stage, broadly speaking, encompassed the years from 1945 until 1964, when there was a period of general amnesty for political prisoners, and the second ran from 1964 until December 1989, the date of Ceausescu's overthrow. There was a noticeable relaxation in the degree of repression exercised by the regime after 1964, which resulted from Gheorghiu-Dej's need for internal support following his political rift with the Soviet Union. Until the final year of the Gheorghiu-Dej era terror was inflicted on the whole of Romanian society, in the search for actual or potential opponents of totalitarian conformity, and many citizens began to feel as if they were being personally hunted down. After 1964 Romanians were marked by a deep-rooted fear of the government, rather than the terror exercised by the Securitate, and the Ceausescu regime, for all its appalling abuses of human dignity and disrespect for human rights, never repeated the tactics of mass arrests and wholesale deportations that were a feature of most of Gheorghiu-Dej's rule.

Repression under Gheorghiu-Dej

The Securitate was the blunt tool of repression of the Communist Party. It was established according to a Soviet blueprint and under Soviet direction. In the building of a people's democracy, the Securitate were called on to eradicate existing political institutions and social structures. Police coercion and intrusion became part of everyday life and a feature of existence that generated pervasive fear, a state of mind which revolutionized not just society's structures, but also personal behavior. In public places the furtive whisper became second nature. Fear induces compliance and is therefore a tremendous labor-saving device. Records indicate that in 1950, two years after its creation, the number of officers and other personnel in the Securitate totaled almost 5,000. In 1989 this number had risen to 14,259, according to figures published after the revolution in December of that year. These numbers do not include the army of informers whom the Securitate, by exploiting fear, was able to recruit. By the same token, it was a mark of the Securitate's success in instilling fear that Romanians came to widely view so many of their fellow citizens as active collaborators with the Securitate, and but a small part of the larger network of officers and informers. The Securitate became as much a state of mind as the instrument of national terror. At the time of the 1989 revolution there were alleged to be more than 400,000 informers (out of a population of 21 million) on the Securitate's books.

The Communist Party set the machinery of terror in motion to carry out the mass deportations of Serbs and Germans living in the area of the Banat adjacent to Yugoslavia. These groups were considered a security risk when tension between Yugoslavia and Romania grew following Marshal Tito's rift with Stalin in June 1948. The deportations began in the summer of 1951: 40,320 persons were targeted, more than half being former landowning peasants. They were moved by train and truck to the southeastern part of Romania. The deportees were only allowed to take what belongings they could carry, and on arrival they were allocated makeshift clay-walled huts with straw roofs in special settlements. Others, even on the Securitate's own admission, were literally deposited in the middle of nowhere. The same reports talk of a lack of drinking water, but despite such deprivations, the deportees erected simple houses of clay and wood, and coaxed the soil into producing crops.

Romania's principal ethnic minority, the Hungarians of Transylvania (numbering approximately 1.6 million in 2002), escaped the fate of the Serbians and Germans of the Banat. The contiguity of Hungary coupled with the size of the Hungarian minority made, and continues to make, the treatment of the Hungarian minority a sensitive issue for both states. During the communist period integration or, as Ceausescu often termed it, *homogenization*—an extension of the strategy of consolidation of the newly enlarged state pursued by Romanian governments in the interwar period—was accelerated by the drive for industrialization undertaken by the communist regime after 1948. It increased the urbanization of the population as a whole and led to the massive migrations of workers, usually from Romanian areas into those with a Hungarian population, thus diluting the proportion of Hungarians and changing the cultural aspect of traditionally Hungarian-dominated towns.

The depths of terror under communism were plumbed in the prison at Pitesti, situated some 75 miles northwest of Bucharest. It became notorious for an experiment of a grotesque nature that originated there on December 6, 1949. Termed *re-education,* the experiment employed techinques of psychiatric abuse designed not only to instill terror in opponents of the regime, but also to destroy their individual personalities. The experiment lasted until August 1952 and was conducted in other prisons as well, albeit on a smaller scale. The victims, estimated at one thousand, were mainly anticommunist students arrested in 1948.

Nothing illustrated more graphically the coercive nature of the centralizing policies pursed by the communist regime than its use of forced labor. Just as Beria was, at Stalin's death in 1953, the second largest employer in the Soviet Union, so too the Ministry of the Interior in Romania was effectively charged with managing part of the economy. Forced labor was formally introduced in June 1950 although it had been practiced for more than a year in a prestige project involving the construction of a canal shortening the passage of the river Danube to the Black Sea. By the spring of 1952, 19,000 political prisoners—including many peasants and students—were used on the canal. In addition, 20,000 voluntary civilians workers were employed together with 18,000 conscripted soldiers. Many of the prisoners endured appalling conditions in Romania's fourteen labor camps. The shortage of water and medicine, and primitive sanitary conditions, led to disease and death. An official report of the Securitate admitted that "many prisoners were beaten without justification with iron bars, shovels, spades and whip. . . . Many died as a result of the blows received." The project was abandoned in 1954. A 1967 Securitate investigation into deaths at the camps put their number at 1,304.

This highlights the problem of compiling accurate statistics on the number of persons arrested during the communist period, and the number of those in detention who died, either as a result of execution, abuse, neglect, or natural causes. First, no Securitate statistics on the number of prisoners who died while in detention are available. Second, the Securitate statistics on the numbers arrested are themselves contradictory. Third, the only independent statistical studies are fragmentary. One Securitate report states the following: In the 10 years from 1948 to 1958, 58,733 persons were convicted of a multitude of crimes, all of which were of a political nature. They included conspiring against social order, belonging to subversive or terrorist organizations (including the former democratic political parties and extreme right-wing Iron Guard), illegally crossing the frontier, failing to report a crime against the state, crimes against humanity and "activity against the working class," treason, espionage, distributing forbidden leaflets, sabotage, and "hostile religious activity." Most of those convicted received sentences ranging from one to ten years imprisonment. A total of 73,310 persons were sentenced to imprisonment during the period from 1945 to 1964; of these, 335 received the death penalty (for several the sentence was commuted). An additional 24,905 were acquitted or had the cases against them dropped. Another 21,068 were sent to labor camps during this same period. The number of those who died while in detention is estimated at 3,847; of these 2,851 died while serving their sentence, 203 under interrogation, 137 as a result of execution, and 656 in the labor camps. Independent sources have produced quite a different set of figures; an examination of court records from the period indicates that from 1949 to 1960, 134,150 political trials took place involving at least 549,400 accused.

Ceausescu Era: 1965 to 1989

Gheorghiu-Dej's successful harnessing of Romanian ambitions of autonomy from the Soviet Union and development of internal support for the RCP in the early 1960s were further developed by Ceausescu who claimed for himself and the Party legitimacy as defender of the national interest. The corollary of this was that any criticism of the Party or its leader from Romanians, whether inside or outside the country, could be branded as treachery against the nation, a charge that was to be leveled in the early 1970s against dissenting voices, in particular, Paul Goma. In the 1980s a small number of Romanians displayed remarkable courage in defying the regime by publicly calling for a measure of democracy, among them Doina Cornea, Ionel Cana, Vasile Paraschiv, and Radu Filipescu. They were all rounded up by the Securitate and detained or imprisoned for varying lengths of time.

In Romania the brutality of some of the beatings administered to opponents of the regime was evident from the fate of Gheorghe Ursu, an engineer from Bucharest, who was arrested on September 21, 1985, for keeping a diary and writing correspondence critical of Ceausescus. He was held at Securitate headquarters on Calea Rahovei, where he was beaten by two criminals, acting on orders from senior officers in the interrogation directorate of the Securitate. As a result of his injuries, Ursu was moved to the hospital at the Jilava jail. He died there on November 17th. An official inquiry in March 1990 revealed that Ursu had died as a result of repeated blows with a heavy object to his abdomen. As of 2003 the Securitate officers involved have still not been brought to justice.

The degree of Ceausescu's interference with the lives of his citizens was most potently illustrated within the realm of family planning. To increase the declining birthrate, he introduced punitive additional taxation for all childless couples over the age of twenty-five. In 1986 he raised the minimum age for women allowed an abortion (from forty to forty-five) and lowered the age at which girls could marry (from sixteen to fifteen). As a result, there was a dramatic increase in "backstreet" and self-induced abortions, especially among young working women, despite the harsh penalties. The statistics for deaths among Romanian women resulting from the antiabortion law are the single most powerful indictment of the inhumanity of Ceausescu's regime. In the twenty-three years of its enforcement, the law is estimated to have resulted in the death of over nine thousand women from unsafe abortions. The majority died from postabortion hemorrhage and blood poisoning.

That Ceausescu would not stop short of murder to maintain his grip on power became evident during the

December 1989 revolution. When anti-Ceausescu protests were mounted in Timosoara on December 17th, Ceausescu issued orders to the army to open fire on the demonstrators. Those orders were relayed by General Ion Coman to the senior officer in Timosoara, General Victor Stanculescu, who instructed units under the command of General Mihai Chitac to carry them out. At the time the rumor spread that some 60,000 people had been shot dead in Timosoara, but subsequent investigations showed that the true casualty figures were 72 people killed and 253 wounded on December 17th and 18th. In the Transylvanian city of Cluj, 26 demonstrators were shot dead by army units on December 21st. That same evening Securitate troops and army units in Bucharest killed scores of anti-Ceausescu demonstrators. On the following day Ceausescu and his wife Elena fled the capital city, but were arrested outside the town of Târgoviste. After a summary trial on Christmas Day before a tribunal selected in part by Stanculescu, one in which due process was patently lacking, they were found guilty of the genocide of 60,000 Romanians—the alleged number of dead in Timosoara—and immediately executed by a firing squad. A parliamentary commission concluded in 1995 that 1,104 died in the revolution throughout the country (162 between December 16th and December 22nd, and 942 in the days following Ceausescu's flight). In Bucharest alone 543 persons were killed and 1,879 injured.

After Ceausescu's overthrow Romania's transition to democracy was checkered. The constitution of 1991 defined Romania as a republic with a multiparty, bicameral parliamentary system. Economically speaking, the country was a middle-income, developing nation in transition from a centrally planned economy to a market economy. But the vestiges of the communist mentality were evident in the attempts by former communists—many of whom dominated the political and economic arena—to oppose transparency in public affairs. This attitude also colored attempts to shed more light on the abuses of the communist past. The unreliability of witnesses, bureaucratic inertia, and the desire to protect vested interests—the post-1989 presidential bodyguard, the Serviciul de Paza Protectie (SPP), contained former Securitate officers—explains why the investigations into the deaths of the revolution's victims were not completed, and why relatively few charges were ever brought. Nevertheless, some senior Securitate officers were prosecuted. The first was Iulian Vlad, the last head of the security force, who was arrested on December 28, 1989, on the charge of "complicity to genocide," which carried a maximum penalty of life imprisonment. A military court later reduced the charge to "favoring genocide," and Vlad's sentence was subsequently reduced to nine years, which was to run con-

currently with two other lesser terms. Both Stanculescu and Chitac were charged in January 1998 with "incitement to commit murder" for their part in events in Timosoara. They were each sentenced by the Romanian Supreme Court on July 15, 1999, to fifteen years in jail. Both generals lodged an appeal against their conviction. The Supreme Court upheld their sentences on February 25, 2000. After Ion Iliescu was elected president in December 2000, they appealed once again and on this occasion their appeal was upheld by a reconfigured court.

SEE ALSO Nationalism

BIBLIOGRAPHY

Bacu, D. (1977). *The Anti-Humans*. Monticello, Ill.: TLC.

Constante, L. (1995). *The Silent Escape. Three Thousand Days in Romanian Prisons*. Berkeley: University of California Press.

Courtois, S., and N. Werth, eds. (1999). *The Black Book of Communism: Crimes, Terror, Repression*. Cambridge, Mass.: Harvard University Press.

Deletant, D. (1995). *Ceausescu and the Securitate: Coercion and Dissent in Romania, 1965–89*. White Plains, N.Y.: M.E. Sharpe.

Deletant, D. (1999). *Communist Terror in Romania: Gheorghiu-Dej and the Police State, 1948–65*. New York: St. Martin's Press.

Eyal, J. (1990). "Why Romania Could Not Avoid Bloodshed." In *Spring in Winter: The 1989 Revolutions*, ed. G. Prins. Manchester, U.K.: Manchester University Press.

Fischer, M. E. (1989). *Nicolae Ceausescu: A Study in Political Leadership*. Boulder, Colo.: Lynne Rienner.

Georgescu, V. (1991). *The Romanians: A History*. Columbus: Ohio State University Press.

Giurescu, D. (1989). *The Razing of Romania's Past*. Washington, D.C.: US/ICOMOS.

Ionescu, G. (1964). *Communism in Rumania, 1944–1962*. Oxford, U.K.: Oxford University Press.

Kligman, G. (1998). *The Politics of Duplicity. Controlling Reproduction in Ceausescu's Romania*. Berkeley: University of California Press.

Levy, R. (2001). *Ana Pauker: The Rise and Fall of a Jewish Communist*. Berkeley: University of California Press.

Pacepa, I. (1988). *Red Horizons*. London: Heinemann.

Ratesh, Nestor (1991). *Romania: The Entangled Revolution*. New York: Praeger.

Shafir, M. (1985). *Romania. Politics, Economics and Society*. London: Frances Pinter.

Tismaneanu, V. (1989). "The Tragicomedy of Romanian Communism." *East European Politics and Societies* (Spring):329–376.

Tismaneanu, V. (2003). *Stalinsim for All Seasons: A Political History of Romanian Communism*. Berkeley: University of California Press.

Tokes, L. (1990). *With God, for the People.* As told to David Porter. London: Hodder and Stoughton.

Dennis Deletant

Romanis

Although for centuries the Romanis have been referred to by a score of exonyms, such as gypsies, *Tsiganes, Zigeuner, Gitanos,* and others, the preferred self-ascriptions—Romani, Romanies, or Roma—are being used more frequently as media attention focusing on the Romanis has multiplied in recent years. This has been the result of social changes brought about by the collapse of communism in Europe, which then led to the emergence of previously suppressed ethnic nationalism with such extreme measures as ethnic cleansing in the early 1990s, and the expulsion or even destruction of non-co-ethnics from historically claimed ethnolinguistic territories. Lacking a country of their own into which to retreat, the Romanis have suffered a particularly harsh existence as a consequence.

Almost the entire experience of the Romanis has, in fact, been one of conflict, highlighted by two major episodes in their millennium-long history: enslavement and the Holocaust. Their plight does not seem to be improving; at the beginning of the twenty-first century the magazine *The Economist* reported that throughout Europe, the Romanis were "at the bottom of every socioeconomic indicator: the poorest, the most unemployed, the least educated, the shortest-lived, the most welfare dependent, the most imprisoned and the most segregated" (2001, p. 29). In the early 2000s there were between nine and twelve million Romanis worldwide, with the majority residing in Central and Eastern Europe, and about a third of that number living throughout North and South America.

Origins

The original homeland of the Romanis was India. Knowledge of this fact was not retained by the population itself, nor was it recognized by Western scholars until the mid-eighteenth century. Before that time many other places of origin, some quite imaginative, were proposed, including Atlantis, Nubia, and the Moon. Since the Indian connection was first established (through the Romanis language), scholars have attempted to piece together the historical details. The prevalent hypothesis is that the ancestors of the contemporary Romanis population were a conglomerate of diverse ethnolinguistic peoples assembled into a military force together with their camp-followers in order to resist the incursion of Islam in northwestern India during the early eleventh century. Many thousands were taken prisoner by the Muslim Ghaznavids; these

An elderly Romani tinkers with scrap metal outside his motor home in Corkes Meadow (near Kent in the United Kingdom). According to a 2001 report published by *The Economist,* Europe's Romani population remains "at the bottom of every socioeconomic indicator." [HULTON-DEUTSCH COLLECTION/CORBIS]

captives were then subsequently co-opted by the Seljuqs for use as a militia when they defeated the Ghaznavids in 1038 CE.

The Seljuqs, in turn, brought their captive Indian troops to Anatolia when they occupied Armenia in 1071. It was here that this population, of various Indian origins, gradually melded into a single ethnic one, and where the Romanis language took shape within the linguistic and social environment of the Byzantine variety of the Greek language. It has been suggested that the very name *Rom* may derive from the Seljuqs' then newly established Sultanate of Rum, although an Indian etymology is more likely. The Byzantine Empire conquered the Sultanate in 1099, but the entire area was gradually infiltrated by the Ottoman Turks, who took control of Constantinople in 1453 and extended their territory across into Europe, using the Romanis as military personnel and manufacturers of weaponry. A Romanis presence in Byzantine and Venetian territory in the Balkans was documented as early as the thirteenth century.

Expansion into Europe and the World

Once in Ottoman-controlled Europe, the Romanis found themselves in an economy in decline. The Crusades had failed, and the trade routes to the East were blocked—resulting in the shift of economic strength to

Romani have often been the target of "ethnic cleansing" and expulsion. Here, they flee Kosovo, where they were considered Serb collaborators during the hostilities of the 1990s. [CHIN ALLAN/CORBIS SYGMA]

Western Europe and the beginnings of colonial expansion overseas. One repercussion of this in the Balkans was the transition from an agriculture based to a market-based economy, with an increased reliance on artisan labor. In the area of present-day Romania, the Romanis population was used to supply this need, quickly becoming indispensable to the economy. To keep this source of manpower from leaving, laws defining Romanis as property (and referring to them as *sclavii*, or slaves) began to be written into the civil code by the early 1500s; slavery was not completely abolished until 1864. Nevertheless, some Romanis were able to avoid this condition of servitude by continuing their journey to other parts of Europe. Their presence in almost every European country was recorded by about 1500. It is because of this late medieval diaspora that there are many different present-day Romanis populations, distinct from each other in their dialect of the Romanis language and the extent of Asian vs. European elements in their respective cultures and genetic makeup.

Antigypsyism

As early as 1416 the first anti-Romanis law was issued, in Germany, with fifty more to be enacted during the course of the next four centuries. Romanis in Spain were persecuted during the Inquisition, and in 1498 they were ordered to be expelled from all German-speaking territories of the Holy Roman Empire. The following year the Romanis were banished from Spain by order of the Catholic Church, and in 1504 France expelled them. Many other governments followed suit. Western European nations found an easy way to accomplish this: by shipping Romanis to their overseas colonies. Portugal transported them to Angola, India, and Brazil; Spain, France, England, and Scotland relocated them to the Americas. In 1568 Pope Pius V ordered the expulsion of the Romanis throughout the realm of the Holy Roman Church. In 1659 their mass round-up and murder took place outside of Dresden; in 1721 King Charles VI ordered the extermination of all Romanis throughout Germany. A year later Friedrich Wilhelm of Prussia made it an offense, punishable by hanging, to be born a Romani, and in 1727 the mass public torture of this group took place in Giessen. The roster of atrocities seems endless.

If the identity of the Romanis as a distinct ethnic population only dates from the Byzantine period then, their Asian roots notwithstanding, they are in one sense a Western people who came into being in a Christian, Greek-speaking land. Certainly, their entire experience since that time has occurred exclusively in the Western world. The Asian component of their heritage, however, which manifests itself in language, culture, and often appearance, must be acknowledged as an overriding factor in the pervasive discrimination against them. Regarded as Christians by the Ottoman Muslims, although considered as heretics by the Christian establishment, they were probably already slaves of the Turks even before that condition was instituted in Europe.

The Islamic presence along the eastern routes out of Europe threatened not only trade but also the religious establishment; Muslims, who had also occupied Spain, were viewed as the enemy of the Christian Church. Romanis were perceived to be Muslims, and even Turks in countries where the Ottomans were only known by reputation. *Turks* is still a name applied to Romanis in some locales. This perception of the newly arriving Romanis as a non-European invading force is evident in yet another label applied to them: *Tatars*. In twentieth-century newspapers one can find numerous references to the arrival of Romanis in an area as an "invasion."

In addition to their foreign appearance and language, the Romani's lack of a country has added to their "outsider" reputation; their nonterritoriality remains a major characteristic, especially in countries where nationality is judged more by one's ethnicity than passport. Over the centuries these factors have created a situation that stigmatizes the overwhelming majority of Romanis in Europe as illiterate, unemployed, criminal, and impoverished, locked in a self-perpetuating cycle for which the means of escape simply do not exist without intervention from various human rights and other non-Romanis bodies. This image of "dependency," whether on philanthropic organizations or public sympathy, only fuels the overall distaste and hostility that segments of the non-Romanis population harbor.

The details of Romanis history are not generally known, and this was especially true during the decades of communism, whose ideology placed little emphasis on history in the classroom. The fact that for centuries Romanis have routinely been refused access to shops, schools, and churches is never taken into account as an underlying reason for their contemporary plight. Even the fact of their centuries of enslavement finds no discussion in modern history books, and only in the early twenty-first century is their targeting during the Holocaust receiving acknowledgment. Their present-day situation alone forms the basis for growing negative attitudes about them. Furthermore, countries in which such thinking predominates have traditionally regarded themselves as single-nation states, not egalitarian multiethnic societies, and the tolerance of ethnolinguistic minorities within their borders has been—and remains—minimal. Many Romanis would welcome a return to communism if only for the protection from interethnic conflict it afforded, in addition to the greater chances of employment.

External circumstantial factors contributing to antigypsyism, such as the historical association of Romanis with Islam, their nonterritoriality, and their fragmentation into numerous distinct and widely separate subgroups lacking any central representation, have only been reinforced by the overriding internal factor of exclusionism. Undoubtedly traceable to the Indian caste system, the self-imposed separateness of Romanis has been strengthened by centuries of slavery and other kinds of social distancing practiced by the European host societies. From group to group, and to a greater or lesser extent, the different Romanis populations maintain cultural behaviors that curtail intimate interaction with the non-Romanis world. From the Romanis perspective, one's luck and health depend on spiritual balance, which can only be acquired by interacting circumspectly with *gadj* (non-Romani; singular, *gadjo,* feminine, *gadji*), as well as with members of the opposite sex within the group, with animals, with the preparation of food, and so on. Because non-Romanis do not maintain the same behaviors, they are regarded as polluting, in a ritualistic sense, to Romanis individuals with whom they might come in contact in too intimate a manner (e.g. by sharing food, clothing, or bedding, etc.). Thus, the extent to which a Romanis would create a permanent business relationship with a non-Romani, eat food prepared by a non-Romani, allow his or her children to attend public school, or condone intermarriage seriously impacts on the achievement of an integrated society.

Porrajmos—The Romanis Holocaust

The Holocaust is undeniably another major factor in explaining the poor living conditions of the Romanis in the early twenty-first century. That "it was the will of the all-powerful Reichsführer Adolf Hitler to have the Gypsies disappear from the face of the earth," (Broad, 1966, p. 41), because they were considered a genetic contaminant threatening the gene-pool of his envisioned "master race," has been well documented. The first document referring to "the total solution to the Gypsy problem on either a national or an international level" was drafted by the Reich Ministry of the Interior in March 1936. In March 1938 Heinrich Himmler issued a statement entitled "The Final Solution of the Gypsy Question," and on December 16, 1942, he put this proposed policy into effect along with an order that "all Gypsies . . . be deported to the *Zigeunerlager* at Auschwitz concentration camp with no regard to their degree of racial impurity." Although Romanis losses amounted to between a half and three-quarters of their total population in Nazi-occupied Europe, no reparations were made to survivors, nor indeed were any Romanis called to testify on their own behalf at the Nuremberg Trial. Indeed, pre-Nazi anti-Romanis laws were still in effect after World War II, and numerous Romanis survivors were arrested for not possessing documents of citizenship. Some remained in hiding in abandoned concentration camps because of this until as late as 1947. The files of the Washington, D.C.–based War Crimes Tribunal from 1946 state plainly that of all the groups victimized by the Nazis, only Jews and Romanis were to be exterminated "unconditionally." Despite this, no reparations were set aside for the latter, funds that would have been of immense help to the surviving population in the areas of health, education, and assimilation, and that, one might assume, would have yielded a more positive present-day reality.

Both the targeting of Romanis by the Nazis and the failure of the world to respond to their plight after the Holocaust are the result of the extremely marginalized and fragmented nature of the Romanis people. Following World War II there were no international Romanis bodies to speak out and demand reparations, and pervasive Antigypsyism ensured that few non-Romanis organizations were moved to come forth on their behalf. The targeting of the Romanis was the culmination of centuries of German Antigypsyism, which only mirrored similar attitudes evident throughout Europe.

Solutions

Romanis issues are given higher or lower priority from country to country, and Romanis populations regard themselves—and are regarded—as functioning nationally, not internationally. In practical terms, a pan-Romanis global identity, an attractive ideal for the growing number of Romanis nationalists, although a threat to the leaders of some European governments, is not likely to be achieved in the short term, if ever.

In 1993 the president of the new Czech Republic, Václav Havel, stated that how the plight of the Romanis was addressed throughout Europe following the demise of communism would be "a litmus test not of democracy but of a civil society" (Crowe, 1996, p. 1). One can count since then hundreds of racially motivated Romanis deaths, document flagrantly discriminatory statements made by spokespersons for several different

governments, and evidence of the forced sterilization of Romanis women, and permanent removal of Romanis children from their homes and parents in different parts of Europe well into the 1970s and 1980s. Some of the new European democracies continue to fall short of Havel's civil ideal. In the United States too, the last of many local laws (at the state and county level) against so-called gypsies were only removed from the books in 1989, and racial profiling, in the form of "gypsy" crime units, remains a reality.

In addition to the historical and cultural factors, the institutionalized attitudes toward, and beliefs about, Romanis have been overwhelmingly reinforced by the creation of a fictional gypsy persona, which portrays Romanis as romantic, wandering thieves, and as possessing magical powers. The word *Romanis* is still not widely recognized, and if asked what a gypsy is, most people will offer the literary stereotype instead of an accurate description. If Romanis continue to be perceived as fantasy figures, then the serious consideration of their problems will never occur. Clearly, education is fundamentally key to positive change. For non-Romani, ethnic diversity programs in the public schools is a place to start, as well as required sensitivity training for employers, educators, and hospital staff; it is neither difficult nor expensive to accommodate the cultural requirements of Romanis in a non-Romanis environment, but they first have to be recognized. For the Romanis themselves it is recommended that externally funded teacher-training programs be instituted, or that instruction in business and artisan skills, and legal rights be available. Harsh penalties for discrimination in housing, education, and healthcare should be enforced, and compliance closely monitored. What is essential is that the cycle of dependency and exclusion be broken, and the Romanis develop the wherewithal to determine their own destinies.

SEE ALSO Holocaust; Minorities

BIBLIOGRAPHY

Crowe, David (1994). *A History of the Gypsies of Eastern Europe and Russia.* New York: St. Martins Press.

Economist (2001). May 12, p. 29.

Fraser, Angus (1992). *The Gypsies.* Oxford: Blackwell.

Guy, Will (2001). *Between Past and Future: The Roma of Central and Eastern Europe.* Hatfield, U.K.: Hertfordshire University Press.

Hancock, Ian (1987). *The Pariah Syndrome: An Account of Gypsy Slavery and Persecution.* Ann Arbor, Mich.: Karoma.

Hancock, Ian (2002). *We Are the Romanis People.* Hatfield, U.K.: Hertfordshire University Press.

Ian Hancock

Roosevelt, Eleanor

[OCTOBER 11, 1884–NOVEMBER 7, 1962]
American first lady, humanitarian, and diplomat

No issue was more important to Eleanor Roosevelt than the question of how nations should respond to the refugee crisis after World War II, and her appointment by President Harry Truman to the U.S. delegation to the United Nations (UN) put her at the center of the discussion. Roosevelt's first major achievement as a delegate was to defeat Andrei Vishinsky, the leader of the Soviet delegation, in a debate in the General Assembly on the issue of whether European displaced persons should be forced to return to their countries of origin or be free to seek asylum. As the U.S. representative on the Committee for Social, Humanitarian, and Cultural Affairs, Roosevelt participated vigorously in the debates on the creation of the International Refugee Organization (IRO), which was established to resettle or repatriate the refugees. Vishinsky argued that those who did not wish to return were traitors, war criminals, or collaborators. Roosevelt replied that many displaced persons feared returning because they disagreed with the new regimes in their home countries and insisted that refugees decide for themselves under what form of government they wanted to live.

As chair of the UN Commission on Human Rights (CHR), Roosevelt guided her colleagues in the creation of the Universal Declaration of Human Rights (1948). She insisted that the Declaration be written in clear, nonlegal language that the average person could understand. Under her leadership, the majority of the CHR thwarted the efforts of the Soviets and their allies to qualify the protection of individual rights in the Declaration by asserting the rights of the state. On the other hand, Roosevelt believed strongly that the Declaration should include economic and social rights as well as civil and political rights, and she persuaded a skeptical U.S. State Department to accept their inclusion. The majority of the CHR wanted to make the rights in the Declaration a part of international law. Once again bucking resistance in the State Department, Roosevelt sided with the majority but supported the drafting of two documents, a nonbinding statement of principles (the Declaration) and a covenant. She pushed for the drafting of the Declaration first, recognizing that drafting the covenant would take longer and that the Declaration would not require ratification by the U.S. Senate. When the Declaration came to a vote in the General Assembly in December 1948, the vote was 48 in favor, 0 against, 8 abstentions, and 2 absent. Although the CHR did not complete the covenants on civil and political rights and economic and social rights until 1966, Roo-

A member of the initial U.S. delegation to the United Nations, Eleanor Roosevelt served as chair of the organization's Commission on Human Rights. Here, she exchanges thoughts with René Cassin, French human rights scholar and vice-chair of the Commission, at a session in Geneva, Switzerland, December 9, 1947. [BETTMANN/CORBIS]

sevelt's years as chairperson prepared the way for the CHR's later accomplishments.

Although successful in defending the rights of refugees at the UN, Roosevelt was less successful in persuading Americans to admit more displaced persons. In her newspaper column, "My Day," and speeches, she urged Congress to fund the United Nations Relief and Rehabilitation Administration (UNRRA) and the IRO and argued that more refugees should be admitted to the United States. Her 1946 visit to displaced persons camps in Germany fueled the urgency of her appeal and made her "more conscious than ever of what complete human misery there is in the world" (Roosevelt, February 20, 1946). When the Daughters of the American Revolution opposed President Truman's modest 1946 proposal to fill the unfilled immigration quotas with displaced persons from Europe, Roosevelt asked, "Why should other countries make any sacrifices" when America refused to act accordingly? (Roosevelt, November 20, 1946).

In 1948 she supported a bill aimed at assisting the IRO in resettling thousands of European refugees by admitting 200,000 persons to the United States. She helped raise funds for refugee groups, such as the United Jewish Appeal. She supported the immigration of Jewish refugees to Palestine and, frustrated by the refusal of the United States and other nations to accept more Jewish immigrants, became a strong supporter of the establishment of the state of Israel. When war broke out in 1948 over the creation of the Jewish state, creating thousands of Palestinian refugees, Roosevelt supported a UN resolution granting $29 million in aid to them, although she blamed the problem on the Arab leaders for urging the Palestinians to leave their homes. When she visited the Middle East in 1952, she toured Palestinian refugee camps in Jordan. Upset by the conditions she observed, she urged continued international assistance, but she remained blind to Israel's share of responsibility for the situation. Throughout the 1940s and 1950s Roosevelt was frustrated by the unwillingness of the U.S. Congress to make it easier for refugees to immigrate to the United States. In 1955 she criticized the Refugee Relief Act of 1953 for placing obstacles in the way of European refugees seeking entry into the United States. She also responded to hundreds of pleas from refugees around the world.

SEE ALSO United Nations Sub-Commission on Human Rights

BIBLIOGRAPHY

Glendon, Mary Ann (2001). *A World Made New: Eleanor Roosevelt and the Universal Declaration of Human Rights.* New York: Random House.

Lash, Joseph P. (1972). *Eleanor: The Years Alone.* New York: W. W. Norton.

Roosevelt, Eleanor. "Address by Mrs. Franklin D. Roosevelt at the Opening Campaign Rally of the Women's Division." United Jewish Appeal of Greater New York, at the Hotel Waldorf-Astoria, Wednesday, February 20, 1946.

Roosevelt, Eleanor. "My Day." November 20, 1946.

Roosevelt, Eleanor. "My Day." June 5, 1948.

John F. Sears
Allida M. Black

Rosewood

During the 1920s racial violence exploded in Florida, including Rosewood, a predominantly black community destroyed in 1923. Located in North Central Florida approximately 9 miles east of Cedar Key, Rosewood was home to several black families, many of whom were related. They were property owners and small-time entrepreneurs, and looked forward to passing on a better life to their children. Some were self-employed, others labored at the Cummer Lumber Mill in nearby Sumner, and a number of the women worked as domestics for white families in the surrounding area.

The beginning of 1923 changed the lives of Rosewood residents forever. Several people were killed or injured, and those who survived the terror were scarred for life by the week-long outbreak of racial violence that began on January 1. On that morning, a white Sumner resident, Fannie Taylor, reported an attack by an unidentified black man. The search for Taylor's alleged attacker led to Rosewood and the death of six African Americans. Two local whites were killed when blacks fought back. African-American residents were forced to hide in the neighboring woods and swamps, while whites looted their possessions and burned their homes.

On Saturday, January 6, many of the women and children hiding in the swamps were evacuated to Gainesville by train. And on Sunday, January 7, approximately 150 whites returned to Rosewood to burn the remaining structures. Rosewood ceased to exist. A grand jury convened to investigate the Rosewood incident in February of that same year found "insufficient evidence" to indict anyone from the local white community. No one was ever prosecuted for the death and destruction that occurred in Rosewood, Florida, during the week of January 1 to 7, 1923.

Seventy-one years later, in 1993, Rosewood survivors and their descendants sought redress and filed a claim seeking $7.2 million in compensation. Representative Miguel De Grandy and Senator Al Lawson subsequently initiated legislation on their behalf. The Florida House of Representatives commissioned a thorough, objective, and scholarly study of the Rosewood incident. Based on the research conducted by an academic team, testimony from survivors and other witnesses, Special Master Richard Hixson ruled that the state had a "moral obligation" to compensate survivors for the loss of property, violation of constitutional rights, and mental anguish. On May 4, 1994, Florida Governor Lawton Chiles signed a $2.1 compensation bill into law. Nine survivors received $150,000 each for mental anguish, a state university scholarship fund was created for the families and descendants of Rosewood, and a separate fund was established to compensate those Rosewood families who could demonstrate property loss. Florida thus became one of the first U.S. states to admit that it had failed to offer protection to its black citizens during a time of racial strife. Before signing the controversial measure, Governor Chiles asserted in the *Tallahassee Democrat,* "Ignorance and racial hatred can lead to death and destruction. Let us use the lesson of Rosewood to promote healing" (pp. 1b, 3b).

SEE ALSO Massacres; Reparations

BIBLIOGRAPHY

D'Orso, Michael (1996). *Like Judgment Day: The Ruin and Redemption of a Town Called Rosewood.* New York: Grosset/Putnam.

Jones, Maxine D., with David Colburn, Tom Dye, Larry E. Rivers, and William W. Rogers (1993). "A Documented History of the Incident Which Occurred at Rosewood, Florida, January 1923." Commissioned by the Florida State Legislature.

Jones, Maxine D. (1997). "The Rosewood Massacre and the Women Who Survived It." *Florida Historical Quarterly* (Fall):193–208.

Tallahassee Democrat (1995). May 5: 1B, 3B.

Maxine D. Jones

Rwanda

The 1994 genocide in Rwanda represents one of the clearest cases of genocide in modern history. From early April 1994 through mid-July 1994, members of the small Central African state's majority Hutu ethnic group systematically slaughtered members of the Tutsi ethnic minority. An extremist Hutu regime, fearing the loss of its power in the face of a democracy movement and a civil war, made plans for the elimination of all those—moderate Hutu as well as Tutsi—it perceived as threats to its authority. The genocide ended only when a mostly Tutsi rebel army occupied the country and drove the genocidal regime into exile. Over a period of only one hundred days, as many as one million people lost their lives in the genocide and war—making the Rwandan slaughter one of the most intense waves of killing in recorded history.

Competing Theories of Ethnicity

The origins of ethnic identity in Rwanda remain a subject of considerable controversy. Nearly all scholars agree that populations having the designations Hutu, Tutsi, and Twa existed in the pre-colonial Rwandan state (prior to 1895); however, the exact historic and demographic meanings of these designations remain contested. A theory—developed during the colonial period—that Rwanda's ethnic groups emerged out of successive waves of conquest and immigration has now been largely discredited among scholars, but it dominated understandings of Rwanda's past for several decades. According to this theory, the hunting and gathering Twa were the original inhabitants of the territory. They were subsequently overrun and dominated by

Hutu agriculturalists who arrived in the region approximately two thousand years ago from more western regions of Africa. Tutsi cattle herders are alleged to have conquered the territory around five hundred years ago, and to have established their authority over the two groups despite their inferior numbers. Accordingly, the Rwandan genocide was the final outcome of the resentment that was generated by this occupation and subjugation.

Two other theories now dominate discussions of ethnic origins in Rwanda. Both theories maintain that ethnicity is a social construct, that it is fluid, and that ascriptions of ethnicity cannot be made on the basis of physical characteristics, but they diverge with respect to the question of when ethnicity in Rwanda is supposed to have gained its modern form. Many current politicians in Rwanda, as well as some scholars, hold the theory that, in pre-colonial Rwanda, Tutsi, Hutu, and Twa were categories that derived from work-related activity and possessed little social significance—citing that the groups shared a common language and culture and lived among one another throughout the territory. According to this theory, colonial policies and ideologies subsequently transformed these categories into ethnic identities.

Proponents of the second theory believe that the terms Tutsi, Hutu, and Twa conferred status and were freighted with status difference even in pre-colonial Rwanda. Beginning in the mid-1800s, the central court of the kingdom of Rwanda used the categorization of population by ethnicity as a means of extending its control, installing an elite Tutsi class in marginal areas of the kingdom to represent the court. According to this theory, the development of Tutsi dominance that had begun in the late pre-colonial period was accelerated by colonial rule. Colonization transformed group identities via the introduction of Western ideas of race and discrimination on the basis of ethnicity that endowed those identities with greater meaning than they had held previously.

Early Instances of Ethnic Violence

Rwanda was colonized by Germany, which ceded the region to the Belgians during World War I. Supporters of the two theories of the origins of Rwandan ethnic identity agree that violent conflict along ethnic lines rarely, if ever, occurred in pre-colonial Rwanda, and that German and Belgian colonial policies exacerbated the already existing divisions among Hutu, Tutsi, and Twa. Catholic missionaries, who arrived in Rwanda in 1900, influenced the development of ethnic identity in Rwanda. They believed that Rwanda had three distinct racial groups. The Tutsi were supposedly a Hamitic

Rwandan children view a mass grave near Goma. [TEUN VOETEN]

group—tall, thin, of aristocratic demeanor, and more closely related to Europeans (and therefore destined to rule over inferior races). The Hutu were supposedly a Bantu group—shorter and stronger and (purportedly) fit for manual labor. The Twa were considered a Pygmy group—very small and dark and inferior to other peoples.

These interpretations ultimately shaped how Rwandans saw themselves and understood their group identities; moreover, they had become a basis for policies. German and Belgian colonial administrators practiced ethnic group-based indirect rule. They put power in the hands of Tutsi and gave administrative and political positions to Tutsi, and at the same time eliminated the power of Hutu kings and chiefs. The Belgian colonial administration issued identity cards to all Rwandans that named their ethnicity. In addition the Belgian colonial law of Rwanda dictated that one's ethnicity was the ethnicity of one's father—which effectively eliminated the prior fluid nature of ethnic identities. Occupational and educational opportunities were reserved for Tutsi, whereas Hutu were required to provide forced labor for the Tutsi chiefs. As a result of these and other policies, the Hutu population of Rwanda became increasingly impoverished and embittered. In the 1950s a Hutu elite, supported by progressive

Catholic missionaries, emerged to challenge the inequality of Rwandan society. In 1959 a Hutu uprising drove Tutsi chiefs from their positions and thousands of Tutsi citizens of Rwanda into exile. The uprising marked the beginning of the transfer of political power to the majority Hutu. Rwanda gained its independence in 1962. The Hutu-dominated post-independence governments referred to the 1959 uprising as a social revolution. (The current Rwandan government refers to the turbulent events of 1959 as Rwanda's first instance of genocide—though in fact few Tutsi were killed at that time.)

In 1962 Grégoire Kayibanda, the leader of the Party of the Movement for the Emancipation of Hutu (Parmehutu), became Rwanda's president. Kayibanda used ethnic appeals to build his support—thereby creating a tense social environment. When rebel groups that had taken form among the exiled Tutsi attacked the country several times in the early 1960s, Rwandan troops responded by massacring thousands of Tutsi. Thousands more were driven into exile. Ethnic violence erupted in Rwanda again in 1973, partially in response to the 1972 genocide of educated Hutu in neighboring Burundi (which had an ethnic composition similar to that of Rwanda), where Tutsi had retained control. The resulting social disruption in Rwanda was a factor that contributed to the July 1973 coup d'etat that installed army chief Juvenal Habyarimana as the president of Rwanda.

Under Habyarimana, ethnic tensions in Rwanda initially diminished, as the regime focused on attracting international assistance for economic development. The establishment of ethnic quotas in education and employment (which shrank opportunities for Tutsi) appeased Hutu, and the creation of a single political party, the National Revolutionary Movement for Development (MRND), sharply constrained potentially inflammatory political activity. Tutsi were still required to carry identity cards and faced discrimination, but active ethnic tensions diminished. The resulting political calm attracted both internal and international support for Habyarimana, and allowed a decade of steady economic growth.

By the mid-1980s, however, among Rwandans, frustration with the Habyarimana regime was on the rise. A collapse in the price of coffee, Rwanda's main export, caused a sharp economic downturn and a massive increase in youth unemployment. In the context of economic decline and a growing gap between rich and poor, increasingly apparent corruption among officials in the Habyarimana regime became a growing source of criticism. Preferential treatment for Hutu from Habyarimana's home region of northern Rwanda angered both southern Hutu and Tutsi from throughout the country. In 1990 public frustration manifested itself in a democracy movement that called for expanded civil rights, a legalization of multi-party politics, and free and fair elections. Facing growing unrest, President Habyarimana announced that he would consent to limited political reforms.

The October 1990 invasion of Rwanda by the Rwandan Patriotic Front (RPF) changed the political equation in the country, as it both further compromised the security of the regime and provided an opportunity for Habyarimana and his cohorts to regain popular support by playing the ethnic card. The RPF was a rebel group composed primarily of Tutsi refugees seeking the right to return to Rwanda. Since the beginnings of anti-Tutsi violence in Rwanda in 1959, tens of thousands of Tutsi had been living as refugees, primarily in the neighboring states of Zaire (present-day Democratic Republic of Congo), Burundi, and Uganda—countries in which their safety was precarious. In 1982 persecution of Tutsi by the regime of President Milton Obote in Uganda led thousands of Tutsi to try to return to Rwanda. They were turned away at the border: the Habyarimana regime claimed that there was no room for them in Rwanda. In Uganda, a number of Rwandan Tutsi joined the rebel movement that carried Yoweri

Museveni to power in 1986, which afforded them political influence even as they remained vulnerable in that country. It was Tutsi within Museveni's National Resistance Army that had founded the RPF, which received clandestine support from the Museveni regime.

The initial RPF attack on Rwanda's northeastern frontier, on October 1, 1990, was easily quelled by troops of the Habyarimana regime, with the support of troops from Zaire, Belgium, and France. Nevertheless, Habyarimana used the invasion to retake the political lead. On the night of October 4, his supporters in the military staged what appeared to be an attack by the RPF on Kigali. This bogus attack was used to justify the arrest of thousands of prominent Tutsi and moderate Hutu, under the accusation of their being RPF accomplices. At the same time, regime officials organized massacres of Tutsi in several communities in the north of the country, which they portrayed as spontaneous popular revenge killings in response to the RPF attack. These assaults served to fan the flames of the ethnic tensions in the country.

Over the next several years, Habyarimana and his supporters used a cunning two-pronged strategy to improve their political position. On the one hand, they appeased critics by entering into negotiations with the RPF and offering political concessions, including the legalization of opposition parties and the creation of a government of (ostensible) national unity. Yet on the other hand they actively undermined these concessions. They denied opposition politicians real political power as they simultaneously blamed them for any problems that the country faced, such as the economic decline and the growing unemployment resulting from the civil war and an International Monetary Fund (IMF)–imposed austerity program and currency devaluation. Habyarimana's supporters encouraged acts of violence between the members of opposing political parties and were complacent toward an increase in overall criminal violence, then blamed the growing insecurity on the shift to multi-party politics. They appealed to anti-Tutsi sentiments (which had been intensified by the RPF invasion), and characterized all members of the anti-government opposition as RPF sympathizers. Each time negotiations with the RPF were on the verge of a breakthrough; Habyarimana's allies instigated small-scale massacres of Tutsi in various parts of the country and in general used ethnic violence to further inflame ethnic tensions. These massacres ultimately served as dress rehearsals for the eventual genocide, and were part of a strategy of mobilizing the population and motivating it further in the direction of violence. Throughout this period, Habyarimana's supporters increased their coercive power through a massive expansion of the Armed Forces of Rwanda (FAR).

The Road to Genocide

Within the powerful clique close to Habyarimana known as the *akazu*, the idea of retaking broad political control via the setting off of large-scale massacres of any and all persons they regarded as threats to the Habyarimana regime was apparently first proposed sometime in 1992. The akazu was composed primarily of individuals from Habyarimana's home region in the north of Rwanda, and included descendants of Hutu chiefs who had been displaced by Tutsi during the colonial period—such as some of the relatives of Habyarimana's wife Agathe Kazinga, who for this reason had retained great personal animosity toward Tutsi. Members of the akazu had acquired significant personal wealth and power under Habyarimana's rule, and they were feeling increasingly threatened by political reforms and negotiations with the RPF. Some in the akazu—allegedly by mid-1993—had devised a plan to eliminate both Tutsi and moderate Hutu, as a final solution to the threats against themselves.

A series of events in 1993 shifted popular support in favor of the Habyarimana regime, supplying the popular base that would make the genocide possible. Massacres of Tutsi in the prefectures of Gisenyi and Kibuye in January triggered a major RPF offensive in February, which captured a large swath of territory in northern Rwanda and displaced a million people (mostly Hutu) from the Ruhengeri and Byumba prefectures. With so many people having been displaced and rumors of civilian massacres in areas controlled by the RPF beginning to swirl, public opinion in Rwanda shifted sharply against the RPF. Even as the Habyarimana regime feigned participation in peace negotiations with the RPF and other opposition parties, it sought to undermine the negotiations by fostering anti-Tutsi and anti-RPF sentiments and attributing any concessions it made to the participation of opposition politicians. This strategy effectively split each of the opposition parties, thereby preventing the installation of a new unity government of transition and realigning many southern Hutu with Habyarimana. The final peace agreement, known as the Arusha Accords, signed in August 1993, was widely perceived within Rwanda as having ceded too much to the RPF and having solidified the division of political parties into pro-Arusha Accords and anti-Arusha Accords wings. The anti-Arusha Accords party factions joined with Habyarimana's MRND and the extreme anti-Tutsi party named the Coalition for the Defense of the Republic (CDR) in a loose pro-regime coalition that called itself "Hutu Power."

Hutu Power promoted an ideology that revived much of the anti-Tutsi rhetoric of the Kayibanda period. According to this ideology, Hutu had the right to rule Rwanda because they constituted a majority and because Hutu had a long history in Rwanda (whereas Tutsi had supposedly arrived more recently to conquer and dominate the country). Proponents of the Hutu Power ideology sought to promote a collective memory of Tutsi exploitation of Hutu during the colonial period, and warned that the RPF sought to annul the social revolution of the early 1960s and reassert Tutsi dominance and Hutu subservience. They claimed that all Tutsi within the territory of Rwanda were RPF sympathizers who could not be trusted, and that Hutu who opposed Habyarimana and supported the Arusha Accords were either traitors to the Hutu cause or secretly Tutsi. Associates of Habyarimana established a new quasi-independent radio station in late 1993, Radio Télévision Libre Mille-Collines (RTLM), which broadcast Hutu Power's anti-Tutsi, anti-opposition, and anti-Arusha Accords rhetoric.

The October 1993 assassination of Melchior Ndadaye, Burundi's first popularly elected Hutu president, had a major impact within Rwanda. Hutu Power leaders claimed that the failure of a transition to majority rule in Burundi demonstrated that Tutsi could not be trusted. Inter-ethnic violence that swept through Burundi over the several weeks that followed drove thousands of Hutu refugees into Rwanda, where they helped to further radicalize the political climate. Rwandan military personnel began to provide paramilitary training for the youth wings of the Hutu Power parties, such as the MRND's *Interahamwe*—expanding the membership of these youth groups and transforming them into civilian militia. In November the Catholic bishop of Nyundo parish near the city of Gisenyi warned that arms were being distributed to these civilian militias.

Both political and ethnic tensions continued to rise in Rwanda in early 1994. Even as provisions of the Arusha Accords were being implemented, Hutu Power forces sought to scuttle the final transfer of power to a new unity government. The United Nations (UN) Assistance Mission in Rwanda (UNAMIR) stationed international troops in the country to oversee the transition; a battalion of six hundred RPF troops was stationed in Kigali. Rather than reduce its forces, the FAR continued to expand in size and acquire arms—receiving weaponry from France, Egypt, and South Africa. In February Faustin Twagiramungu, the transitional prime minister named in the Arusha Accords, narrowly escaped an assassination attempt, while Félicien Gatabazi, the executive secretary of the moderate Social Democratic Party, was assassinated. In response, a crowd that had assembled in Gatabazi's home commune lynched the national chairman of the CDR, Martin Bucyana. These political assassinations intensified the sense of crisis in the country and set the stage for the genocide. Intelligence reports coming out of the United States, France, and Belgium in early 1994 all warned that ethnic and political massacres were an imminent possibility in Rwanda. The commander of UNAMIR forces, General Roméo Dallaire, sent a memo to UN headquarters informing them that he had been informed of the existence of the secret plans of Hutu extremists to carry out genocide. None of these warnings were headed.

The Genocide

On April 6, 1994, the plane carrying President Habyarimana and Cyprien Ntaryamira, the president of Burundi, who were returning from a meeting in Tanzania that had focused on the implementation of the Arusha Accords, was shot down by surface-to-air missiles as it approached the airport in Kigali, and all on board were killed. The downing of the plane remains shrouded in mystery, since the Rwandan military restricted access to the area of the crash and blocked all serious investigation. Although associates of Habyarimana initially blamed the RPF for the assassination, many other observers believed that troops close to the president had carried out the attack—possibly because of an awareness of Habyarimana's reluctance to permit the plans for genocide (of which he was alleged to have been aware) to move forward, or the perception that he had been too moderate in his attitude toward the RPF. In part because of evidence that was eventually presented before the International Criminal Tribunal for Rwanda (ICTR), many political experts now believe that the RPF, frustrated at the president's resistance toward implementing the Arusha Accords, did in fact fire the rockets that brought down Habyarimana's plane.

Whoever was responsible for the crash, the assassination of Habyarimana served as the spark that set the plans for genocide in motion. Within hours of the crash, members of the presidential guard and other elite troops—carrying hit lists composed of the names of persons perceived to be RPF sympathizers, including prominent Tutsi and Hutu opposition politicians and civil society activists—were spreading throughout the capital. On the morning of April 7, the presidential guard assassinated the Prime Minister, Agathe Uwilingiyimana, a moderate Hutu, along with ten Belgian UNAMIR troops who had been guarding her. On the first day of the genocide, death squads also killed leaders of the predominantly Tutsi Liberal Party and the multiethnic Social Democratic Party, several cabinet ministers, justices of the constitutional court, journalists, human rights activists, and progressive priests.

For the first several days, the murderous attacks took place primarily in Kigali and were focused on prominent individuals, both Hutu and Tutsi, perceived to be opponents of the regime. The international community, at this initial stage of the genocide, construed the violence in Rwanda as an ethnic uprising, a spontaneous popular reaction to the death of the president. Without clearly condemning the political and ethnic violence that was taking place, foreign governments moved to evacuate their nationals from Rwanda. Despite calls from UNAMIR Commander Dallaire to have troop strength increased, the member states of the UN Security Council voted to cut the UNAMIR presence from around 2,500 to a token force of 270, largely because countries such as the United States feared becoming entangled in an intractable conflict that would be reminiscent of the then recent disastrous intervention by the United States in Somalia. Belgium quickly withdrew its forces, and was followed by most other participating countries. From the beginning of the violence, the international community thus promulgated a clear message that it was disinterested and would not act to stop the massacres in Rwanda.

Far from being a spontaneous popular uprising, the 1994 genocide had been carefully planned and coordinated by a small group of government and military officials who used the administrative structure and coercive force of the state to invigorate the genocide and extend it across the country. Following Habyarimana's death, a new interim government composed entirely of Hutu Power supporters had seized control. Once it became clear that the international community was not going to intervene, the death squads moved the genocide into a second phase, expanding the violence until it engulfed the entire country and focusing it more specifically on Tutsi. Using the language of self-defense, the interim government called upon the population to help protect Rwanda from the invading RPF and to root out collaborators and infiltrators within the country. It sent word to regional and local leaders of the *Interahamwe* and other militias to move forward with existing "civil self-defense" plans that entailed the elimination of all "threats to security" (understood to mean all Tutsi and, to a lesser extent, moderate Hutu). Political officials had to support the "security" efforts or relinquish their government positions.

Following Habyarimana's death and the start of the civilian massacres, the RPF ended the ceasefire that had been in effect since the previous year and renewed its assault on the country. The RPF troops stationed in Kigali as part of the terms of the Arusha Accords quickly occupied a section of the capital, which became a safe zone for Tutsi and others threatened by the genocidal regime. Other RPF troops advanced on the capital from the north, overtaking the prefecture of Byumba and

Genocide requires no advanced technology. Here, countless machetes line the border between Rwanda and Tanzania. The machete, originally devised for cutting sugarcane and underbrush, was the weapon of choice during the 1994 rampage. [TEUN VOETEN]

moving east and south through the prefecture of Kibungo and into the Bugesera region. As RPF leaders were claiming that their offensive was necessary to protect the Tutsi from extermination, their advance across Rwanda provided ideological support for those promoting the genocide. As Rwandans fled in advance of the RPF onslaught, Radio Rwanda and RTLM widely disseminated reports of civilian massacres by the RPF, fueling popular fears of the rebel army.

The genocide in each community followed a pattern. First, the civilian militias raided Tutsi homes and businesses. Fleeing Tutsi were forced to seek refuge in central locations, such as schools, public offices, and churches, where they had been protected during previous waves of violence. Coordinators of the genocide actively exploited the concept of sanctuary and encouraged Tutsi to gather at these places, offering promises of protection when in fact they were calling Tutsi together for their more efficient elimination. In some communities, a limited number of moderate Hutu were killed early in the violence—as a way of sending a message to other Hutu that they needed to cooperate. Once Tutsi had been gathered, soldiers or police joined with the militia in attacking them: first firing on the crowd and throwing grenades, then systematically finishing off survivors with machetes, axes, and knives. In some cases, buildings teeming with victims were set on fire or demolished. In instances in which communities initially resisted the genocide, militias from neighboring areas arrived on the scene and participated in the attacks until local Hutu joined in the killing. Generally armed only with stones, Tutsi were able to pose effective resistance in only a few locations.

By early May the large-scale massacres were complete, and the genocide in each community moved into a second stage of seeking out survivors. The organizers of the genocide clearly sought in this stage to lessen their own responsibility by implicating a larger segment of society in the killing. Although the massacres were carried out by relatively limited groups of militia members and members of the armed forces, all adult men were expected to participate in roadblocks and nightly patrols. People passing through roadblocks were required to show their identity cards. If a person's card stated that his or her ethnicity was Tutsi, he or she was killed on the spot. If a person had no card, he or she was assumed to be Tutsi. Persons who looked stereotypically Tutsi were almost certainly killed. The military patrols ostensibly searched for perpetrators, but they actually looked for surviving Tutsi who were hiding in communities. Many Hutu risked their own lives to protect Tutsi friends and family. The patrols searched homes where Tutsi were believed to be hiding, and if Tutsi were found, the patrols sometimes killed both Tutsi and the Hutu who were harboring them. Twa, who were a minuscule minority of the Rwandan population, were rarely targets of the genocide and in many communities participated in the killing in an effort to improve their social status.

Post-Genocide Reconstruction and Reconciliation
From the vantage point of the Hutu Power elite, the genocide, although effective at eliminating internal dissent, proved to be a terrible military strategy, as it drained resources and diverted attention from the RPF assault. Better armed and better organized, the RPF swiftly subdued FAR troops. It advanced across eastern Rwanda, then marched west, capturing the former royal capital Nyanza, on May 29; the provisional capital Gitarama, on June 13; and Kigali, on July 4. As it advanced, the RPF liberated Tutsi still being harbored in large numbers in places such as Nyanza and Kabgayi, but they also carried out civilian massacres in many communities they occupied, sometimes after gathering victims for supposed public meetings. Much of the population fled the RPF advance. As the RPF occupied eastern Rwanda, nearly one million refugees fled into Tanzania, while in July, over one million fled into Zaire.

After initially refusing to intervene in Rwanda and to stop the genocide, the UN Security Council, on May 17, authorized the creation of an expanded international force, UNAMIR II—but by the time the force was ready to deploy, the genocide was over. The RPF, angry at international neglect and believing that it could win an outright victory, rejected the idea of a new international intervention. In mid-June France, which had

encyclopedia of GENOCIDE *and* CRIMES AGAINST HUMANITY

Corpses of victims of the 1994 Rwandan genocide that have been thrown into the Akagera River, which traverses the border between Rwanda and Tanzania. The corpses floated downstream to Lake Victoria. [TEUN VOETEN]

been a close ally of the regime that turned genocidal, intervened in Rwanda, supposedly to stop the massacres—but it also wished to prevent an absolute RPF victory. French forces established the "Zone Turquoise" in southeastern Rwanda, which they administered for over a month after the RPF had occupied the rest of Rwanda. Nearly two million people gathered in camps for the internally displaced and came under French protection. The French presence also enabled many of the organizers of the genocide, as well as the armed forces, to flee safely into Zaire with their weapons.

On July 17, 1994, the RPF declared victory and named a new interim government. The post-genocide Rwandan government faced the inordinately daunting task of rebuilding a country that had been devastated by violence. The exact number of people killed in the

genocide and war remains disputed, and ranges from 500,000 to over a million, with serious disagreement over the portion killed by the RPF and the portion killed by the genocidal regime. Whatever the exact number of dead, the loss of life was massive and the impact on society immeasurable. The RPF, seeking wider popular support, based the new government loosely on the Arusha Accords and appointed a multiethnic slate of ministers from the former opposition parties that included a Hutu president and prime minister. Real power, however, remained firmly in RPF hands, with Defense Minister and Vice President Paul Kagame widely acknowledged as the ultimate authority in the country.

The RPF, which became Rwanda's new national army, took as its first main task the taking of control over the territory, which it did with considerable brutality. The RPF summarily executed hundreds of people who were suspected of involvement in the genocide, and arrested thousands more. Following the late August departure of French forces, the RPF sought to close the camps for the internally displaced. It used force in some cases, such as in its attack on the Kibeho camp in April 1995, in which several thousand civilians died. The refugee camps just across the border in Zaire continued to pose a security threat for the new government, as members of the former FAR and citizen militias living in the camps used the camps as a base from which to launch raids on Rwanda. In mid-1996 the RPF sponsored an antigovernment rebellion in eastern Zaire by the Alliance of Democratic Forces for the Liberation of Congo-Zaire (ADFL). The RPF itself attacked the refugee camps. The RPF killed thousands of refugees who sought to go deeper into Zaire rather than return to Rwanda. With support from the RPF and troops from Uganda and Burundi, the ADFL swiftly advanced across Zaire, driving President Mobutu Sese-Sekou from power in early 1997.

After taking power, the new government of Rwanda set about rebuilding the country's physical infrastructure, but it also committed itself to reconstructing the society. The establishment of the principle of accountability for the genocide and a repudiation of the principle of impunity were primary goals. By the late 1990s the government had imprisoned 120,000 people under the accusation of participation in the genocide. Although considerable effort was put into rebuilding the judicial system, trials of persons accused of genocide proceeded very slowly—beginning only in December 1996 and with fewer than five thousand cases tried by 2000. Responding to the need to expedite trials, but also hoping more effectively to promote accountability and reconciliation, the government decided in 2000 to implement a new judicial process, called *gacaca,* based loosely on a traditional Rwandan dispute resolution mechanism. The new gacaca courts, the first of which began to operate in June 2002, consist of panels of popularly elected lay judges from every community in the country. The panels preside at public meetings, at which all but the most serious genocidal crimes are tried. Beginning in 2003, the government began to release provisionally thousands of people who had had no formal charges brought against them or who had confessed to participation in the genocide (and would therefore be given reduced sentences). In addition to judicial strategies, the government has sought to promote reconciliation by promulgating a revised understanding of Rwandan history that emphasizes a unified national identity; creating reeducation camps for returning refugees, released prisoners, entering university students, and newly elected government officials; establishing memorials and annual commemorations of the genocide; changing the national anthem, flag, and seal; decentralizing the political structure; and adopting a new constitution.

Efforts to promote reconciliation have been undermined by the RPF's continuing mistrust of the population and its desire to retain control. The government has been highly intolerant of dissent, accusing critics of supporting the ideology of division and genocide. The government has harassed, outlawed, and co-opted human rights organizations, religious groups, and other segments of civil society. Journalists have been harassed and arrested. All political parties but the RPF have been tightly controlled. Power has become increasingly concentrated in the hands of the RPF and of Tutsi, and Paul Kagame has amassed and continues to amass increasing personal power. Kagame assumed the presidency in 2000. A putative "democratic transition" in 2003 actually served to consolidate RPF control over Rwanda.

The international community, plagued by guilt over its failure to stop the genocide, has been highly forgiving of the human rights abuses of the RPF, generally treating the abuses as an understandable or even necessary occurrence in the aftermath of genocide. It has given backing and assistance to both to the camps in Zaire and the reconstruction of Rwanda. The main outcome of the international reaction to the Rwandan genocide was the creation of the ICTR, based in Arusha, Tanzania. Created by the UN Security Council in late 1994, the ICTR is entrusted with trying the chief organizers of the 1994 genocide as well as RPF officials responsible for war crimes. Despite a slow start, the ICTR has tried or at least holds in its custody many of the most prominent officials of the former Rwandan regime. No RPF officials have yet come into ICTR custody.

Ten years after the 1994 genocide, ethnic relations in Rwanda remain tense. The government has become increasingly intolerant of dissent, and a steady flow of individuals has sought political asylum outside Rwanda. Although initially these exiles were mostly Hutu, they now include many Tutsi, including genocide survivors as well as RPF members who have fallen afoul of Kagame. These exiles could eventually become a basis for a serious challenge to the present regime. The constraints that have been put on open communication within Rwanda have hampered discussions about the genocide and its causes, but political reforms and an emphasis on national unity, as well as the active use of security forces, have helped to maintain peace in the country.

SEE ALSO Altruism, Biological; Altruism, Ethical; Burundi; Comics; Ethnicity; Genocide; Humanitarian Intervention; Identification; Incitement; Memorials and Monuments; Racism; Radio; Radio Télévision Libre Mille-Collines; Refugee Camps; Refugees; Safe Zones; United Nations

BIBLIOGRAPHY

Adelman, Howard, and Astri Suhrke, eds. (1999). *The Path of a Genocide: The Rwanda Crisis from Uganda to Zaire.* New Brunswick, N.J.: Transaction Publishers.

African Rights (1995). *Rwanda: Death, Despair and Defiance,* revised edition. London: African Rights.

Article 19 (1996). *Broadcasting Genocide: Censorship, Propaganda, and State-Sponsored Violence in Rwanda, 1990–1994.* London: Author.

Barnett, Michael (2002). *Eyewitness to Genocide: The United Nations and Rwanda.* Ithaca, N.Y.: Cornell University Press.

Chrétien, Jean-Pierre (1995). *Rwanda: Les médias du génocide.* Paris: Karthala.

Chrétien, Jean-Pierre (1997). *Le defi de l'ethnisme: Rwanda et Burundi, 1990-1996.* Paris: Karthala.

Dallaire, Roméo (2003). *Shake Hands with the Devil: The Failure of Humanity in Rwanda.* Toronto: Random House Canada.

des Forges, Alison (1999). *Leave None to Tell the Story: Genocide in Rwanda.* New York: Human Rights Watch.

Guichaoua, André (1995). *Les Crises Politiques au Burundi et au Rwanda.* Paris: Diffusion Karthala.

Lemarchand, René (1970). *Rwanda and Burundi.* New York: Praeger.

Linden, Ian (1977). *Church and Revolution in Rwanda.* Manchester, U.K.: Manchester University Press.

Mamdani, Mahmood (2001). *When Victims become Killers: Colonialism, Nationalism, and the Genocide in Rwanda.* Princeton, N.J.: Princeton University Press.

Melvern, Linda (2000). *A People Betrayed: The Role of the West in Rwanda's Genocide.* London: Zed Press.

Melvern, Linda (2004). *Conspiracy to Murder: The Rwandan Genocide.* London: Zed Press.

Neuffer, Elizabeth (2001). *The Key to My Neighbor's House: Seeking Justice in Bosnia and Rwanda.* New York: Picador.

Newbury, Catharine (1988). *The Cohesion of Oppression: Clientship and Ethnicity in Rwanda, 1860–1960.* New York: Columbia University Press.

Pottier, Johan (2002). *Re-Imagining Rwanda: Conflict, Survival and Disinformation in the Late Twentieth Century.* Cambridge: Cambridge University Press.

Prunier, Gerard (1995) *The Rwanda Crisis: History of a Genocide.* New York: Columbia University Press.

Reyntjens, Filip (1985). *Pouvoir et Droit au Rwanda.* Butare, Rwanda: Institut National de Recherche Scientifique.

Reyntjens, Filip (1994). *L'Afrique des Grands Lacs en Crise.* Paris: Karthala.

Sibomana, André (1999). *Hope for Rwanda.* Sterling, Va.: Pluto Press.

Uvin, Peter (1998) *Aiding Violence: The Development Enterprise in Rwanda.* West Hartford: Kumarian Press.

Vansina, Jan (2001) *Le Rwanda ancien: le royaume nyiginya.* Paris: Karthala.

Timothy Longman

S

Sabra and Shatila

On September 16 and 17, 1982, members of the LF (the "Lebanese Forces"), a Christian-Maronite militia, carried out a massacre targeting civilians at the Palestinian refugee camps Sabra and Shatila, located in the southern part of Beirut, the capital of Lebanon. Nearly a thousand people lost their lives in this massacre and many other were wounded.

The Lebanese Forces were established by Bashir al-Jumayyil in 1976 as the military wing of the Lebanese front. Their aim was to unite all Maronite forces in Lebanon. However, most members of the LF also belonged to a second Maronite party called the Lebanese Phalanges, which had been established by Bashir al-Jumayyil's father, Pierre, in 1936. This is why some sources refer to the Phalanges as those who had carried out the massacre, while other sources refer to the LF.

The Lebanese Forces entered the refugee camps two days after the assassination of their leader and their founder, Bashir al-Jumayyil. They did so in coordination with and at the request of the Israeli Defense Force (IDF), which was in full control of Beirut at that time.

The IDF had invaded Lebanon on June 5, 1982. After a few days, the Israeli forces reached the outskirts of Beirut. The IDF's mission was named by the Israeli government "the Peace for the Galilee Operation." Its ostensible aim was to remove the threat of attack by the Palestinian Liberation Organization (PLO) against the Israeli settlements along the Israeli-Lebanese border. It soon became clear, however, that the operation had more far-reaching targets. One such goal was to bring

to power in Beirut an element friendly to Israel that would sign a peace agreement with it. This element was, in the eyes of the Israelis, the Lebanese Forces under the leadership of Bashir al-Jumayyil, who at that time maintained close ties with Israel.

The IDF reached Beirut within a week of the start of the war. They were joined by the LF and sealed off the Western part of the city, where Sunnis, Shi'ites and Palestinians lived. On August 13, the PLO and Syrian forces, which were deployed in Western Beirut, started leaving the city, and on August 23, 1982, Bashir al-Jumayyil was elected President of Lebanon. But on September 14, 1982, Bashir al-Jumayyil was killed in an explosion—a bomb had been planted in his headquarters by a member of the Syrian Socialist Nationalist Party (SSNP), a radical Lebanese party known for its close ties with Syria. Israel's illusions of being able to dictate a new Lebanese order were dashed.

After Jumayyil's death, the Israeli government, on the initiative of the then Defense Minister Ariel Sharon and Chief of the General Staff Refael Eytan, decided to take control of the western part of Beirut. The reason given for this move was the need to ensure peace and stability in the city for all its citizens. In fact, it was a clear effort to save at least a part of the massive investment Israel had made in Lebanon. On September 15, 1982, the IDF entered West Beirut. The Israeli commanders feared that members of the PLO who remained in the refugee camps would shoot at their soldiers, so they sent in their Lebanese allies, the LF, to take control.

On September 16 and 17, 1982, members of the Lebanese Forces, a Christian-Maronite militia, stormed the Sabra and Shatila Palestinian refugee camps in the southern part of Beirut, the capital of Lebanon. Here, two women inspect the bodies of some of the massacre's estimated 2,000 victims, possibly searching for missing relatives. [REUTERS/CORBIS]

On the evening of September 16, 1982, LF units under the command of Elie Hubayka entered the refugee camps. Hubayka served in the capacity of intelligence and security officer. Upon entering the Palestinian camps the LF unit began killing Palestinian civilians.

One reason for the killing was, no doubt, a desire to take revenge on the Palestinians for the assassination of Bashir al-Jumayyil. Another compelling reason, however, may have been the belief, commonly held within the hard core of the Maronite community, that the best way to deal with the Palestinians in Lebanon was through drastic measures that would cause them to flee the country. The massacre that ensued in Sabra and Shatila was but one of many civilian massacres to take place during the civil war in Lebanon. These further acts included the massacre of Christians in January 1976, after the Palestinians captured the Maronite town of Damur, and the massacre of Palestinian civilians in the refugee camp Tal al-Za'tar, which fell into the hands of the LF in August 1976.

First reports of sporadic killings among civilians in the refugee camps Sabra and Shatila reached the Israeli forces surrounding the camps throughout the evening of September 16, and more reports were received throughout the following day. The IDF commanders, however, responded to these reports with indifference, and preferred to treat them as exaggerations or as exceptions that did not represent the general activity of the Lebanese Forces in these camps. The IDF even provided some technical assistance to the Lebanese Forces, such as projectors and a bulldozer that was brought in to clear away the rubble. Only after the reports could no longer be ignored or dismissed did the IDF order the LF to pull out of the camps.

There is some dispute regarding the number of the casualties in the massacre. The Lebanese investigation committee, established to inquire into the massacre, reported 460 dead. Of these, 15 were women and 20 were children. The remaining 425, all adult males, included 328 Palestinians, 109 Lebanese, 7 Syrians, 3 Pakistanis, 2 Algerians, and 2 Iranians. The Kahan Committee, organized by the Israelis, reported between 700 and 800 dead. The Palestinian Red Cross estimated that the number of the dead was 2,000 and reported that it issued death certificates for 1,200 people.

The Lebanese investigation, headed by the Military Attorney General, Asa'd Jaramnus, cleared the LF of any responsibility for the massacre, but failed to place responsibility on anyone else. However, it did mention reports alleging that some of the dead were killed by PLO activists before they left Beirut, or by members of Sa'd Haddad's militia. Sa'd Haddad was the commander of an Israeli-supported Maronite militia that had been deployed along the Israel-Lebanese border.

The Kahan committee, established in Israel as a result of public pressure to investigate the massacre, came to a different conclusion. The committee determined that members of the LF were responsible for the massacre. It also concluded that the Israeli military and the political leadership in Israel took no part in the planning or conduct of the massacre in the refugee camps but that, nonetheless, Israel did bear indirect responsibility. The committee argued that Israel's leaders and the army commanders failed to seriously consider the possibility that its LF proxies would carry out such a massacre when they were allowed into the camps. In addition, the committee pointed out that the Israeli commanders in the field did not react quickly enough when they first heard reports about the massacre while it was still ongoing. As a result of the committee's conclusions, Ariel Sharon was forced to resign his office as Israeli Minister of Defense, as was Yehushua Shagi, then Israel's Chief of Military Intelligence. The Chief of the General Staff, Refael Eytan, was permitted to finish out his term of office.

The findings of the Lebanese investigators reflected the public desire to bury the memory of the massacre so it would not disturb the process of conciliation among the various communities within Lebanese society. The fact that the dead were mainly Palestinian, a rejected element within the Lebanese society, made it easier to downplay the extent and significance of the massacre. Those who were directly responsible for the Sabra and Shatila killings were never brought to trial. The most prominent among them, Elie Hubayka, defected to Lebanon's pro-Syrian political camp and became an ally of Damascus. Under Syrian patronage he served as a minister in various Lebanese governments during the 1990s. He was assassinated in 2002, and some believe that his assassination was linked to his involvement in the massacre.

In Israel, in contrast, the massacre led to a public debate about Israel's moral responsibility for the massacre. Nevertheless, the indirect responsibility that the Kahan committee placed on some Israeli figures, such

as Ariel Sharon, did not cause any lasting damage to their public standing. Indeed, in January 2001, Ariel Sharon was elected Prime Minister of Israel.

SEE ALSO Massacres; Refugee Camps

BIBLIOGRAPHY
Benziman, Uzi (1985). *Sharon, an Israeli Ceaser*. New York: Adama Books.

Hanf, Theodor (1993). *Coexistence in Wartime Lebanon, Decline of a State and Rise of a Nation*. London: I. B. Tauris.

Rabil, Robert G. (2003). *Embattled Neighbors, Syria, Israel and Lebanon*. Boulder, Colo.: Lynne Rienner Publishers.

Sayigh, Rosemary (1994). *Too Many Enemies, the Palestinian Experience in Lebanon.* London: Zed Books.

Schiff, Ze'ev, and Ehud Ya'ari (1994). *Israel's Lebanon War*. New York: Simon and Schuster.

Eyal Zisser

Saddam Hussein
[APRIL 28, 1937–]
Late-twentieth-century dictator of Iraq

Saddam Hussein (also, Husayn and Husain) al-Majid was born to a poor Sunni Muslim Arab family from al-Awja, a village in north-central Iraq. Sources vary as to whether Saddam was actually born in al-Awja, or in the nearby town of Tikrit. Saddam's father left (some sources say he died) prior to his birth. His stepfather, Ibrahim al-Hasan, was physically and psychologically abusive to young Saddam, forcing him to steal for him and refusing to allow him to go to school. Saddam ended up being raised in Tikrit by his maternal uncle, Khayrallah Talfa. He moved to Baghdad in 1956, and reportedly joined the pan-Arab nationalist Arab Socialist Renaissance Party (also called Ba'th Party) the following year. He quickly became a hired gun for the party, liquidating, for example, a relative who was a communist rival to the Ba'th.

Saddam continued as a Ba'th Party enforcer by taking part in a failed attempt to assassinate Iraqi president Abd al-Karim Qasim (1941–1963) in October 1959. He was wounded in the attack, and fled to Egypt via Syria. He returned to Iraq after the February 1963 Ba'th coup against Qasim, but was imprisoned from 1963 to 1967 along with other Ba'thists after another coup deposed the Ba'th several months later. Saddam rose in the ranks of the party's international, pan-Arab leadership known as the Ba'th "National Command," as well as of its local Iraqi "Regional Command." He was appointed to the leadership of the National Command of the party in 1965 while still in prison, and became deputy secre-

A loyal, often fanatical, military were key to Saddam Hussein's continued rule and murderous campaigns in Iraq. Here, the dictator honors his officers, Baghdad, January 2000. [AFP/ CORBIS]

tary-general of the Iraqi Regional Command in September 1966. Saddam helped carry out the final Ba'thist coup of July 17, 1968. Although he only assumed the title of vice-chairman of the new state executive committee, the Revolutionary Command Council, Saddam was the real force behind politics in Iraq thereafter.

Rise to Power

On July 16, 1979, Saddam pushed aside ailing Iraqi president Hasan al-Bakr (1914–1982), to become the undisputed leader of Iraqi Ba'th and state apparati. He assumed the titles of secretary-general of the Iraqi Ba'th Regional Command, chair of the state Revolutionary Command Council, and president of the republic. For ceremonial purposes, he also became deputy secretary-general of the pan-Arab National Command of the Ba'th in October 1979 (the titular secretary-general of the National Command, aging Ba'th Party co-founder Michel Aflaq (1910–1989), was merely a figurehead kept in place for ideological reasons).

Saddam's ruthlessness continued unabated after 1979. A symbol of things to come was the infamous purge he carried out shortly after shuffling al-Bakr out of office. Saddam announced at a party meeting that twenty-one senior Ba'thists present at the meeting were part of an alleged Syrian conspiracy against him. One by one, he called out the names of the "traitors" while smoking his trademark cigar, filming them as they were led out of the conference hall to be shot. He later en-

sured that copies of the film were circulated throughout the country. Thereafter, Saddam took great pains to eliminate any possible rivals. He presided over a totalitarian regime in Iraq from 1979 to 2003, the cruelty and brutality of which were matched only by the fear it inspired. Saddam succeeded in using this fear to stay in power, which he did longer than any ruler in modern Iraqi history. An expert in the bureaucracy of terror, Saddam oversaw five overlapping intelligence agencies plus the Ba'th Party's own security service. These agencies not only spied on the populace, but on each other, so that Saddam could foil any plots from within the regime. To protect himself, Saddam also created two Praetorian Guard organizations. He presided over one of the twentieth century's most pervasive cults of personality as well. Photos and statues of the dictator were ubiquitous, and constituted a visible reminder throughout the country of his seeming omnipresence.

The Ba'th regime also persecuted entire groups of people. The large-scale deportations, destruction of villages, and executions Saddam ordered against the country's non-Arab Kurdish population during the 1988 "Anfal" campaign rose to the level of genocide. He is responsible for war crimes and/or crimes against humanity during the 1980–1988 Iran-Iraq War, when Iraqi forces used chemical weapons against Iranian troops. During the 1990–1991 Iraqi invasion and occupation of Kuwait, such crimes went beyond the torture, execution, and disappearances mounted against Kuwaiti individuals to include large-scale looting of museums and archives.

U.S. Invasion of Iraq

Saddam's reign of terror ended in April 2003 when American troops entered Baghdad and put Saddam to flight. He was eventually captured in the village of Dura, near al-Awja, on December 14, 2003. The Americans held him until June 28, 2004, when the United States "returned sovereignty" to a provisional Iraqi government. That government immediately submitted papers to the Americans requesting the formal transfer of legal custody, whereupon Saddam ceased being a prisoner of war protected by the Geneva Conventions, and became a criminal suspect under Iraqi jurisdiction. He remained physically in U.S. custody in Baghdad, however.

In April 2003, U.S. Ambassador-at-Large for War Crimes Issues Pierre-Richard Prosper announced that Iraqis charged with genocide, crimes against humanity, and war crimes would be tried by Iraqi courts. International human rights advocates urged that an international court try Saddam instead. The International Criminal Court (ICC) would not be an option in that

CenCom (the U.S. military's Central Command stationed in Kuwait) released this photo of a disheveled Saddam Hussein shortly after his capture on December 13, 2003. When tracked down by U.S. troops, the former Iraqi president was huddled in the cellar of a farmhouse south of his hometown, Tikrit.
[HANDOUT/CORBIS]

regard; neither Iraq nor the United States are signatories to the Rome Statute that created the ICC, and the crimes were committed before July 1, 2002, the date the statute took effect. However, the United Nations (UN) Security Council could have created a special international tribunal like that for the former Yugoslavia. On December 11, 2003, however, the American-appointed Iraqi Governing Council enacted the Statute of the Iraqi Special Tribunal for Crimes Against Humanity for future trials instead.

This domestic, Iraqi tribunal was empowered to investigate crimes committed between July 17, 1968 and May 1, 2003, the period of Ba'thist rule. The tribunal's jurisdiction covered acts of genocide, as defined by the 1948 Convention on the Prevention and Punishment of the Crime of Genocide; war crimes, defined as grave breaches of the 1949 Geneva Conventions; and crimes against humanity, defined as a number of acts spelled out in the law that are committed as part of a widespread or systematic attack directed against any civilian population, with knowledge of the attack. Saddam was arraigned before an Iraqi investigative judge of the tri-

bunal on July 1, 2004, and faced seven preliminary charges. By mid-2004, the Kuwaiti government had prepared 200 major indictments against Saddam as well. Iran also indicated that it would bring charges against Saddam for war crimes.

Saddam's trial could well play a crucial role, both for the sociopolitical rehabilitation of Iraq and for the growing international legal consensus on prosecuting crimes against humanity, by exposing the breadth and scope of his crimes. The tribunal can avail itself of more than 6 million Iraqi military, intelligence, and Ba'th Party documents that were captured in 1991 and 2003. These offer an excruciatingly detailed view into the bureaucracy of terror employed by Saddam's regime, as well as devastating evidence in the hands of prosecutors. The trial could well become the most significant trial dealing with genocide, war crimes, and crimes against humanity since the trial of Nazi war criminal Adolf Eichmann in 1961.

SEE ALSO Eichmann Trials; Iraq

BIBLIOGRAPHY
Aburish, Said K. (1999). *Saddam Hussein: The Politics of Revenge.* London: Bloomsbury.
Cockburn, Andrew, and Patrick Cockburn (2000). *Out of the Ashes: The Resurrection of Saddam Hussein.* New York: Perennial.
Makiya, Kanan (1998). *Republic of Fear: The Politics of Modern Iraq,* updated edition. Berkeley: University of California Press.
Makiya, Kanan (2004). *The Monument: Art and Vulgarity in Saddam Hussein's Iraq.* London: I.B. Tauris.

Michael R. Fischbach

Safe Zones

During periods of armed conflict or strife places are set aside where people who are not involved in the fighting may find a degree of refuge. Such places have at times been referred to as safe zones; however, this is not a technical term. Comparable terms include *safe havens, safe areas, corridors of tranquility, humanitarian corridors, neutral zones, protected areas, secure humanitarian areas, security corridors,* and *security zones.*

Treaty-Based Safe Zones

Some treaties allow countries to establish specific types of safe zones. For example, the 1949 Geneva Conventions provide for the establishment of hospitals and safe zones or localities to protect the wounded, the sick, the elderly, children, and pregnant women from the effects of war (First Geneva Convention, Article 23; Fourth Geneva Convention, Article 14).

Under the Fourth Geneva Convention a country may set up safety and hospital zones by itself, for exam-

Although the United Nations had declared Srebrenica a safe zone in the 1990s, Bosnian Serb forces eventually overran it. Here, Nazira Efendic, a Muslim woman who lost most of her relatives in the ensuing ethnic cleansing, peers through the window of her devastated house in the village of Gornji Potocari, March 26, 2002. [REUTERS/CORBIS]

ple, in peacetime as a matter of defense planning. After a war starts the country may ask its enemy to recognize the hospital or safety zone as such, or it may work with another country to establish such zones. Ordinarily, the establishment of a safety zone is without legal effect until a country's enemy recognizes the hospital or locality as a safety zone. An official agreement on safety zones provides exactly this kind of recognition. Such agreements may extend protection to other categories of civilians, and the International Committee of the Red Cross may facilitate their conclusion.

United Nations Safe Zones

Pursuant to its mandate to maintain or restore international peace and security, the United Nations (UN) Security Council has recently designated safe zones and otherwise urged the protection of innocent persons in certain places. Although such safe zones purport to protect all civilians from attack and otherwise serve as places of refuge and aid, the precise legal meaning of the phrase has never been delineated. The creation of safe zones has sometimes been accompanied by the im-

position of *no-fly zones*, which may be employed to provide a degree of enforcement.

Common Element: Nonmilitary Use

A key aspect common to all types of safe zones is that they are nonmilitary in use. Essentially, a bargain is struck—the zone is protected so long as it does not serve a military purpose, such as housing soldiers or storing munitions. Further, safe zones and military assets must not be situated near one another, particularly when the intent is to protect military assets from attack.

If a safe area is in fact used for military purposes, the zone may be attacked. However, the attack must follow the laws and customs of war. Specifically, the attacker must direct an attack only against legitimate military objectives, and no attack is allowed where harm to civilians and civilian property would be excessive in relation to the tangible and direct military advantage anticipated. In other words, the presence of a few soldiers might warrant a small and carefully controlled raid, but not a full-scale attack.

encyclopedia of GENOCIDE *and* CRIMES AGAINST HUMANITY

Practice

The notion of setting aside refuges is not new. In 1870 Henry Dunant, founder of the International Committee of the Red Cross, suggested the designation of towns as safe places during the Franco-Prussian War, and later suggested that parts of Paris be established as refuges. Temporary zones were set up during the Spanish Civil War in Madrid in 1936 and during the conflict in Shanghai, China, in 1937. Governments were cool to proposals to establish safe zones during World War II, but three neutral zones were established during the conflict in Palestine in 1948. These zones were successful enough that the drafters of the 1949 Geneva Conventions firmly established the concept of safe zones in international law. More recently, safe zones have been set up to protect civilians not only from the dangers of war, but also from the prospect of suffering crimes against humanity, such as extermination or deportation.

Nonetheless, safe zones have not always provided the envisioned protection. A handful of safe zones established in the 1970s in Bangladesh, Cyprus, and Vietnam were to some degree successful, but a hospital and safety zone attempted in Phnom Pen, Cambodia, quickly fell apart. An armed conflict in the Falklands/Malvinas ended before proposed safe zones could be established. In 1992 the parties to the conflict in Croatia, with the assistance of the International Committee of the Red Cross, established two neutral zones centered on Dubrovnik.

Recent safe zones have been designated in Iraq and Bosnia and Herzegovina. The UN Security Council demanded in 1991 that Iraq end its repression of Kurds in the north of Iraq and Shi'a in the south. The United States, United Kingdom, and France used this resolution to set up safe zones and impose no-fly zones over the northern and southern parts of the country. Occasionally, the United States and United Kingdom fired on the Iraqi military, but this generally happened either in response to the use of air defenses or to attacks on Kurds in the north. Because the Security Council resolution did not grant explicit authority for no-fly zones and air combat operations, the right to resort to such measures was disputed.

The UN Security Council declared six safe zones in Bosnia and Herzegovina early in the 1991 to 1995 war, specifically in Srebrenica, Sarajevo, Tuzla, Zepa, Gorazde, and Bihac. The UN also imposed a no-fly zone over all of Bosnia and authorized the use of air power by the North American Treaty Organization (NATO) to protect every safe zone in Bosnia. In addition the area in and around Srebrenica was declared a *demilitarized zone* by agreement between the warring parties, and the UN guaranteed the safety of all people within it.

However, both Bosnian Serb and Muslim forces violated the safe area agreement to keep Srebrenica "free from armed attack or any other hostile act." Sarajevo was also fired upon from surrounding hills for most of the war, and Bosnian Serb forces eventually overran Gorazde, Zepa, and Srebrenica. Some seven thousand Muslim men and boys were killed in and around Srebrenica alone. NATO eventually responded with an air campaign against Serb positions, notably those around Sarajevo. Bosnia was relatively quiet thereafter.

In 1994 the UN authorized France to establish a safe area in Rwanda in response to the genocide of Tutsis and moderate Hutus. This was a belated response, occurring after the worst of the genocide there was over, and in practice it protected more Hutus than Tutsis.

The term *safe zone* has other uses as well. During the Second Persian Gulf War the United States and its allies declared the area around Basra, Iraq, to be a safe zone in the sense that it was safe for humanitarian relief efforts. In the mass media, safe zone means a place where there is no fighting, as used in West African conflicts of the past few years. It is unlikely that either meaning will displace treaty law and practice denoting a safe zone as a place officially set aside for the protection of war victims.

SEE ALSO Early Warning; Prevention

BIBLIOGRAPHY

Akashi, Yasushi (1995). "The Use of Force in a United Nations Peace-Keeping Operation: Lessons Learnt from the Safe Areas Mandate." *Fordham International Law Journal* 19:312.

Geneva Convention for the Amelioration of the Condition of the Wounded and Sick in the Armed Forces in the Field (August 12, 1949). *United States Treaties,* vol. 6; *United Nations Treaties Series,* vol. 75 (also known as the First Geneva Convention of 1949).

Geneva Convention Relative to the Protection of Civilian Persons in Time of War (August 12, 1949). *United States Treaties,* vol. 6; *United Nations Treaties Series,* vol. 75, p. 287 (also known as the Fourth Geneva Convention of 1949).

Pictet, Jean S. (1952). *Commentary: I Geneva Convention for the Amelioration of the Condition of the Wounded and Sick in the Armed Forces in the Field.* Geneva: International Committee of the Red Cross, 1995.

Protocol Additional to the Geneva Conventions of 12 August 1949, and Relating to the Protection of Victims of International Armed Conflicts (adopted June 8, 1977, entered into force December 7, 1978). *United Nations Treaty Series,* vol. 1125 (also known as Protocol I).

Roberts, Adam (1999). "Safety Zones." In *Crimes of War: What the Public Should Know,* ed. Roy Gutman and David Rief. New York: W. W. Norton.

Sandoz, Yves et al., eds. (1958, 1995). *Commentary on the Additional Protocols of 8 June 1977 to the Geneva Conventions of 12 August 1949.* Geneva: International Committee of the Red Cross.

Silliman, Scott L. (2002). "Responding to Rogue Regimes; from Smart Bombs to Smart Sanctions; the Iraqi Quagmire: Enforcing the No-Fly Zones." *New England Law Review* 36:767–773.

Uhler, Oscar M. and Henri Coursier, eds.; Pictet, Jean S., general ed. (1958). *Commentary: IV Geneva Convention for the Amelioration of the Condition of the Wounded and Sick in the Armed Forces in the Field.* Geneva: International Committee of the Red Cross, 1995.

John Cerone
Ewen Allison

Sand Creek Massacre

During the summer of 1864 an Indian war erupted over the plains of Kansas, Nebraska, and the Colorado Territory following the murder of Cheyenne Chief Lean Bear. Lean Bear, a leading peacemaker who had previously met with President Abraham Lincoln in Washington, D.C., was shot from his horse without warning by U.S. troops during a Kansas buffalo hunt. The troops were acting under orders from Colonel John M. Chivington who commanded the military district of Colorado: "Find Indians wherever you can and kill them" (*The War of the Rebellion,* 1880–1881, pp. 403–404).

In September 1864 the principal chief of the Cheyenne, Black Kettle, and other Cheyenne and Arapaho leaders hazarded a visit to Denver to hold peace talks with Chivington and Governor John Evans. The chiefs were assured that they would be safe from attack if they made the trip to Fort Lyon on the Arkansas River. When Black Kettle arrived there, however, post commander Major Scott J. Anthony turned him away, ordering the Cheyenne leader to remain in camp on Sand Creek, forty miles north of the fort (Hoig, 1961, p.125).

In Denver, meanwhile, Chivington gathered his military forces for a strike against the Cheyenne. He and his command arrived at Fort Lyon at noon on November 28 and prepared for an assault on the Indian camp. With his Colorado First Cavalry, Anthony joined Chivington. But other officers, who had helped escort Black Kettle to Denver, attempted to dissuade Chivington from such an attack. Chivington, a former Methodist minister, threatened to put them in chains, ranting, "Damn any man who is in sympathy with an Indian!" (U.S. Senate, 1867, p. 47).

Chivington's army of nearly seven hundred men with four mule-drawn mountain howitzers arrived at the bend of Sand Creek at the break of dawn, November 29. Even as the cavalry began its charge and howit-zers shelled the village, Black Kettle hoisted a U.S. flag over his lodge. Chief White Antelope, who had visited Washington, D.C., in 1851, pressed forward to meet the soldiers, insisting that the village was peaceful and posed no threat. He was cut down midstream.

Indian villagers fled from their lodges only to be pursued in every direction and killed by the mounted troops. A number of women and children took refuge in a cattail pond. Soldiers surrounded it and began shooting them at will. The atrocities did not end when the battle was over. Witnesses described the horrific aftermath. John Simpson Smith, a long-time Cheyenne associate who was in the camp and whose half-blood son was murdered by Chivington's men, with his body dragged behind a horse, testified as follows: "They [the Indians] were terribly mutilated, lying there in the water and sand, dead and dying, making many struggles. They were badly mutilated" (U.S. House of Representatives, 1865, p. 8).

Chivington and his Colorado Third troops returned to Denver and proudly displayed Cheyenne scalps and other body parts they had removed from men, women, and even children. Newspapers and citizens exulted in the soldiers' victory. The intensity of hatred became apparent when Senator Benjamin Doolittle later addressed a Denver crowd regarding Indian policy. His audience shouted, "Exterminate them! Exterminate them!" (Scott, 1994, p. 168).

Chivington's massacre at Sand Creek raised a firestorm of protest nationally and led to investigations by both the U.S. Army and Congress. The embattled Indian tribes of the Plains saw the U.S. military action as strong evidence of the white man's perfidy. Black Kettle, who had somehow survived, felt he had betrayed his people in trying to make peace. "My shame is as big as the earth," he said. "I once thought that I was the only man that persevered to be the friend of the white man, but it is hard for me to believe the white man any more" (*Annual Report,* 1865, p. 704).

SEE ALSO Indigenous Peoples; Massacres; Native Americans; Trail of Tears

BIBLIOGRAPHY

Annual Report of the Commissioner of Indian Affairs (to the U.S. Secretary of the Interior) (1865). Washington, D.C.

Hoig, Stan (1961). *The Sand Creek Massacre.* Norman: University of Oklahoma Press.

Scott, Bob (1994). *Blood at Sand Creek, the Massacre Revisited.* Caldwell, Idaho: Caxton Publishers.

U.S. House of Representatives (1865). "Massacre of Cheyenne Indians." *Report on the Conduct of the War.* 38th Cong., 2d sess.

U.S. Senate (1867). "Sand Creek Massacre." *Senate Document 26.* 39th Cong., 2d sess.

A July 18, 1864, telegram to Colonel John M. Chivington requesting troop reinforcements in the Colorado Territory. Within months Chivington ordered the brutal massacre of several hundred unsuspecting Cheyenne at Sand Creek. [CORBIS]

The War of the Rebellion: A Compilation of the Official Records of the Union and Confederate Armies (1880–1881). Washington, D.C.: Government Printing Office.

Stan Hoig

Satire and Humor

The 1997 Academy Award-winning movie by the Italian filmmaker Roberto Benigni, *La Vita è Bella* (Life Is Beautiful), raised the fundamental question of whether it is permissible to use satire and humor in confronting the Holocaust. Many critics and general audiences, particularly those not immediately affected by the events of the Holocaust, expressed great delight with Benigni's film. Others registered their deep disgust.

The literary form of satire has a long tradition and is closely associated with writers such as Jonathan Swift, Voltaire, Heinrich Heine, Kurt Tucholsky, and Erich Kästner. Similarly, artists such as William Hogarth, Honoré Daumier, George Grosz, and John Heartfield used their drawings to ridicule social events.

With the advent of fascism in Germany in 1933, many writers and visual artists emulated their pre-

decessors and even stepped up their attempts to use satire as a weapon in the fight against fascism. Their plays, sketches, poems, and caricatures were meant to undermine the power of the Nazis and provide encouragement to those directly affected by fascism. As early as October 1933 the prominent Austrian writer and satirist Karl Kraus had voiced sincere doubt on the ability of words to truly combat the imminent evil.

Kraus's reservations were, in fact, contradicted by the course of action taken by the Nazis from the moment they assumed power. The writer Carl von Ossiezky and journalist Fritz Gerlich were among the first to be arrested, tortured, and killed. In 1932 Gerlich had published a biting essay questioning whether the dark-haired Adolf Hitler might not be of "Mongolian" lineage. Kurt Tucholsky had mocked German militarism and blind obedience for years. In his 1930 publication, *Herr Wendriner steht unter der Diktatur* (Mr. Wendriner under the Dictatorship), Tucholsky made fun of Nazi stormtroopers and even predicted the requirement of yellow identification papers for Jews. His clever witticisms delighted many audiences and, not surprisingly, on May 10, 1933, the Nazis burned his books throughout Germany for their "impertinence" and "lack of respect." Tucholsky went into exile in Sweden, where he committed suicide in 1935. In addition, Erich Kästner, a beloved author of children's books, wrote entertaining and sarcastic poems warning about the dangers of fascism. His books were also burned in May 1933.

From the onset writers and journalists found the Nazis' overblown seriousness, lack of humor, pomposity, and constant obsession with uniforms an easy target for mockery. They ridiculed the hyperbolic language of Hitler's *Mein Kampf*, and the book's title quickly became known as *Mein Krampf* (My Cramp). In 1940 the British poet R. F. Patterson escalated the attack on Hitler's tome. In *Mein Rant: A Summary in Light Verse*, the author claims his own version of the oeuvre to be far more acceptable than the original. In 1941 playwright Bertolt Brecht, by that time already living in exile in Finland, wrote *Der aufhaltsame Aufstieg des Arturo Ui* (The Resistible Rise of Arturo Ui). The drama is a "gangster parable" and satirizes Hitler's rise to power supported by terror and backed by financial support from big industry. Brecht ridicules Hitler's frugal and petty-bourgeois lifestyle as well. Brecht's expectations for this play remained unfulfilled. By 1941 it was too late to show his audiences how Hitler's ascent to power could have been stopped. In 1936 Lion Feuchtwanger used the genre of the historical novel to shed light on the true nature of National Socialism. His satirical novel *Der falsche Nero* (The Pretender) also fell short of what the author had intended.

The influence of exiled writers was restricted because they were cut off from their usual audiences. In addition, scholarly literary forms such as novels and plays only reached a limited audience. On the other hand, poems, ballads, and songs performed in cabarets reached a wider audience. Political cabarets were a staple in the cultural landscape of pre-Hitler Germany and existed in virtually every large city. Erika Mann's *Die Pfeffermühle* (The Peppermill) continued to delight audiences from late 1932 through 1937, even though most of the cabaret's later years of existence coincided with the Mann family's forced exile in Switzerland. The ensemble also gave guest performances in countries not yet occupied by Nazi Germany.

A close cousin of the cabaret was the Kleinkunst Theater. Whenever its actors, writers, or performers were no longer permitted to perform in public, many turned to the newest technical medium, the radio. The Austrian refugee actor and writer Robert Ehrenzweig (in England he became known as Robert Lucas) originated the "Hirnschal Letters," broadcast in 1941 by the German language division of the BBC. The main character is Adolf Hirnschal, a German private, who writes to his wife admiring letters about Hitler and the Third Reich. But as his name Hirnschal (literally meaning cerebral cavity) suggests, the protagonist is quite clever. In talking about every-day events, the "Hirnschal Letters" undermined the authority of official propaganda and raised the morale of radio listeners. Other popular radio programs were "Blockleiter Braunmüller" (Blockleader Brownmiller) and "Frau Wernicke" (Mrs. Wernicke). These radio spoofs were created by Bruno Adler, another German writer in exile working for the BBC.

John Heartfield perfected the genre of the photomontage, creating hundreds of images that appeared in popular German newspapers and magazines, and on book covers. Heartfield juxtaposed fragments of photographs with snippets of newsprint. With his montages he intended to create new images yielding original points of view. Heartfield's work referred to particular current events in an insolent, funny, and biting manner. After his escape from Germany in 1933, Heartfield continued his work in Czechoslovakia. A photomontage of December 1935 derides the food shortages as a result of Germany's remilitarization. Entitled "Hurray, the Butter Is All Gone," it shows a family seated around the dinner table gnawing on metal chains, handlebars, screws, bicycle parts, and shovels.

Photomontages and caricatures published in the popular print media had a more decisive influence on audiences than elite literary forms—even though their practitioners were no longer able to work from within Germany. The graphic artist Carl Meffert published early caricatures of the Nazi elite, which resulted in an expulsion order from Germany. He fled to Argentina, where he assumed the name of Clement Moreau. In exile Moreau published some of the most ferocious and poignant anti-Hitler caricatures in daily newspapers.

Humor, comedy, and laughter also existed under extreme conditions of incarceration and confinement. During the latter part of 1943 and through the summer of 1944, various cabaret performances were staged in the Dutch camp of Westerbork. The melodies for these cabaret pieces about lack of food and cramped living conditions derived from the heydays of cabaret life in Berlin and Vienna. Most of the performers were murdered in extermination camps in the East.

Survivors of the Kraków ghetto recount how in 1942 a Nazi slogan was transfomed into its opposite meaning by the substitution of a single letter. As a consequence of this witty action, the propaganda catchphrase *Deutschland siegt an allen Fronten* (Germany Is Victorious on All Fronts) became *Deutschland liegt an allen Fronten* (Germany Is Defeated on All Fronts). This subversive prank provided the ghetto inhabitants with a sense of joyful empowerment.

SEE ALSO Comics; Drama, Holocaust; Film,
Dramatizations in

BIBLIOGRAPHY

Heartfield, John (1992). *John Heartfield*. Exhibition
Catalogue. New York: Harry N. Abrams.

Lareau, Alan (1995). *The Wild Stage: Literary Cabarets of
the Weimar Republic*. Columbia, S.C: Camden House.

Lipman, Steve (1991). *Laughter in Hell. The Use of Humor
During the Holocaust*. London: Jason Aronson.

Nauman, Uwe (1983). *Zwischen Tränen und Gelächter.
Satirische Faschismuskritik 1933–1945* (Between Tears
and Laughter. Satirical critique of fascism 1933–1945).
Cologne: Pahl-Rugenstein.

Tauscher, Rolf (1992). *Literarische Satire des Exils gegen
Nationalsozialismus und Hitlerdeutschland* (Literary Satire
against National Socialism during Exile). Hamburg:
Verlag Dr. Kovac.

Wiener, Ralph (1994). *Gefährliches Lachen: Schwarzer
Humor im Dritten Reich* (Dangerous Laughter: Black
Humor during the Third Reich). Reinbek: Rowohlt.

Viktoria Hertling

Shaka Zulu
[c. 1787–SEPTEMBER 24, 1828]
Founder of the Zulu Empire

Between the end of the eighteenth century and 1825,
societies on the eastern coastal seaboard of southern
Africa underwent a radical and violent political transformation. The cause of this upheaval remains obscure,
but an established order of independent chiefdoms collapsed, to be replaced by a number of much larger,
more militarily robust kingdoms. The most powerful of
these was the Zulu state, which emerged under the
leadership of King Shaka kaSenzangakhona. Shaka remains one of the most complex and controversial figures in southern African history, a man still revered as
the founding father of his nation, a conqueror of extraordinary vision and political ability whose methods
have nonetheless earned him the reputation of a brutal
tyrant. A minor—and possibly illegitimate—son of
Chief Senzangakhona of the small Zulu clan, Shaka
grew up amid escalating social conflict and displayed
an early talent for warfare. In 1816, following the death
of his father, he assumed control of the Zulu and began
a program of expansion. A charismatic and innovative
military commander, Shaka introduced new forms of
warfare that relied on close-quarter (hand-to-hand)
combat and were highly destructive. By an astute mixture of extreme force and political acumen, Shaka had
come, by 1824, to dominate most of the African groups
in the present-day South African province of KwaZulu-
Natal.

Beyond the immediate Zulu borders, groups dislo-
cated by the violence spread the disruption across

Shaka believed in the total annihilation of his tribal war enemies.
When he became Zulu chief, he replaced the javelin (as weapon
of choice) with the heavy-bladed thrusting spear. He holds such a
spear in this lithograph. [THE GRANGER COLLECTION, NEW YORK]

southern Africa. In the areas under his control, Shaka
imposed new political structures in which the conquered chiefdoms became subordinate to a Zulu elite.
Central to his authority was the army, in which young
men from across the kingdom were required to serve
in regiments under the direct control of Shaka himself.
By carefully cultivating a warrior ethos, Shaka deliberately created a climate of discipline and obedience. The
army was used both as a means of enlarging the kingdom and suppressing internal opposition. To enhance
his base of support within the army, Shaka rewarded
individuals who displayed conspicuous courage, but
executed those accused of cowardice. Shaka himself
presided over the military reviews that routinely followed successful campaigns, in which regimental commanders identified so-called cowards who were then
publicly stabbed to death. King Shaka's reputation has
undoubtedly suffered at the hands of the European colonial and apartheid regimes that displaced Zulu authority—and for whom Shaka became an emblem of
savagery justifying white intervention. He certainly was

autocratic and ruthless; however, the popular image of Shaka as personally bloodthirsty and psychotic is not supported by contemporary evidence, even though he made extensive use of terror as a political tool.

Executions for infringements of etiquette were a feature of daily life in Shaka's court. He condemned individuals on the spur of the moment and with a calculated insouciance for offenses such as sneezing when he was talking, or making him laugh when he wanted to be serious. Victims were usually clubbed to death and their bodies left in the veldt for the vultures, who became known throughout Zululand as "the king's birds." Although the number of individuals killed in this manner was probably small, it served not only to intimidate the opposition but also to invest the new Zulu monarchy with a terrifying aura of power. Political dissidents were isolated by accusations of witchcraft and executed, together with their families who were viewed as being tainted by association. The use of torture was still unknown at this time.

Nevertheless, so great were the political and social changes inherent in Shaka's revolution that it proved impossible to eliminate opposition entirely, and from 1824—when he survived an assassination attempt—Shaka became increasingly preoccupied with efforts to hold the kingdom together. When, in 1827, his mother Nandi died, he used his personal grief to mask the true motives behind an extensive political purge. Those who stood accused of breaking mourning taboos prescribed by Shaka himself were attacked and killed. One contemporary British observer estimated that, during the mass hysteria of the funeral ceremonies alone, as many as seven thousand people died from dehydration and exhaustion; although this statistic is probably an exaggeration, the loss of life was undoubtedly severe, and it fell heaviest on those groups who had remained unreconciled to Shaka's rule.

Shaka's attempts to secure his position were ultimately unsuccessful, however, for in September 1828 he fell victim to a coup orchestrated by members of his own family and was stabbed to death. He had ruled for just ten years, but helped to reshape the political geography of the region and left behind a complex and ambiguous legacy that associated political power with violence.

SEE ALSO South Africa; Zulu Empire

BIBLIOGRAPHY

Fynn, H. F. (1950). *The Diary of Henry Francis Fynn*. Ed. J. Stuart and D. M. Malcolm. Pietermaritzburg, South Africa: Shuter and Shooter.

Hamilton, Carolyn (1998). *Terrific Majesty: The Powers of Shaka Zulu and the Limits of Historical Invention*. Cape Town, South Africa: David Philip.

Knight, Ian (1994). *The Anatomy of the Zulu Army, from Shaka to Cetshwayo*. London: Greenhill Books.

Laband, John (1995). *Rope of Sand: The Rise and Fall of the Zulu Kingdom in the Nineteenth Century*. Johannesburg, South Africa: Jonathan Ball.

Taylor, Stephen (1994). *Shaka's Children*. London: HarperCollins.

Ian Knight

Sierra Leone

In eleven years of civil war, an estimated 150,000 people died, more than half the country was rendered homeless, 600,000 refugees (12% of the population) fled to neighbouring countries, more than 200,000 women were raped, and about 1,000 civilians suffered the amputation of one or more limbs. Fighting began on March 23, 1991, when the (student-led) Revolutionary United Front (RUF) crossed the eastern border of Sierra Leone from Liberia. The RUF was formed, with Libyan backing, to overthrow the government of the All People's Congress (APC). The APC was a one-party regime under the presidencies of Siaka Stevens (1968–1985) and Joseph Momoh (1985–1992) that maintained itself through thuggery and corruption to the point where the economy all but collapsed. The RUF also received support from the Libyan-backed forces of Charles Taylor, leader of the National Patriotic Front of Liberia (NPFL). The RUF appealed to disaffected local sentiment in the border region, and expanded its ranks largely by capturing and training young people from dysfunctional rural primary schools in eastern and southern Sierra Leone. A small cohort of radicals from the teacher training college at Bunumbu, adjacent to the Liberian border, also rallied to the movement. President Momoh created immediate conditions for the war by defaulting on the terms of an IMF loan agreement and thereafter being unable to pay for basic government services. He alienated many young people by declaring education a privilege, not a right.

The inefficient and politicized national army, riddled by corruption and nepotism, had little interest in fighting the war from its outset. The APC, appealing for international intervention, sought to deny the independent existence of the RUF, making the rebellion appear solely the work of Charles Taylor. Guinean and Nigerian troops took up key defensive positions in Daru and Gondama (near Bo) in April and August 1991, and slowed the advance of the RUF, which depended mainly on raiding opposing forces for its weapons and other supplies. Thereafter, successive governments claimed to be engaged in peace processes, while mainly concentrating on ways to manage a small war to consolidate the political advantage of the elite.

A military coup in 1992 brought a faction of young army officers to power, but they were opposed by a larger group within the army that was still loyal to the previous regime. The National Provisional Ruling Council (1992–1996), under its chairman, Captain Valentine Strasser, offered to negotiate with the RUF, but also recruited and armed large numbers of unemployed young people. Poorly trained and ill disciplined, these new recruits were resented by the APC elements in the army. A small group of NPRC officers—some from the eastern border regions—pressed the war against the RUF, and by the end of 1993 they had forced the movement's leadership out of its temporary headquarters in northern Kailahun (Sandeyalu). The movement scattered, and various members built a number of secure forest camps in different parts of the country. Some of these were in the forest reserves along the Liberian border, others towards the center of the country, approaching Freetown. From these green fortresses, cadres raided villages to capture recruits and spread panic among local populations. Government depots and convoys were attacked to acquire supplies. The RUF was denied the opportunity for peace negotiations, largely because the NPRC continued to maintain that the organization was a front for Charles Taylor and not an indigenous Sierra Leonean movement. Facing troops that were untrained and ill-equipped for jungle warfare, the RUF began to exploit the divisions in the national army.

The RUF conducted raids wearing stolen army fatigues and carrying fake identification, creating an impression in the minds of civilians that the army was the main cause of the violence, and thus turning civilians against their own security forces. Disgruntled army units added to the impression by carrying out extensive looting in areas that had been emptied by RUF hit-and-run raids. Widespread civilian protest was directed against the military regime, to which was added international pressure for democratic reform. The NPRC agreed to elections in early 1996, thinking it would be able to manipulate the election of its own candidate. Instead, the victory went to the opposition party (the Sierra Leone Peoples Party, SLPP), even though it had been banned under a one-party constitution in 1978. The new civilian government, under President Ahmad Tejan-Kabba, a retired UN bureaucrat, had no confidence in the army of the previous government, and turned instead to an ethnically based civil defence force (CDF). This military organization was trained by Nigerian peacekeepers and a South Africa–British merce-

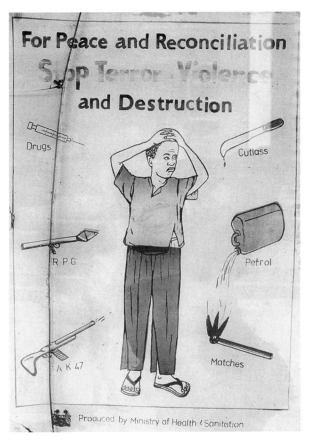

In a war-weary Sierra Leone, government-released posters, similar to this one, sought to promote peace and reconciliation. May 2000. [TEUN VOETEN]

nary company that had originally been contracted to protect kimberlite (hard-rock) diamond mining concessions in Sierra Leone.

Despite a cease-fire agreement, civil defence forces destroyed several of the main forest camps of the RUF prior to the RUF leadership agreeing to a peace treaty in Abidjan, Ivory Coast, on November 30, 1996. Having signed under duress, the civilian leadership of the RUF was unable to get its fighters to accept the deal, and the war continued. Although a failure, the Abidjan agreement remains significant, because it marks the date from which the Sierra Leone Special Court indicts participants in the war for war crimes.

The RUF believed that the peace process was no more than a pretext to wipe it out and consolidate (with international support) the results of a democratic transition from which the movement was excluded. RUF fighters escaping the sack of their camps regrouped in the north and center of the country. They began again to gather new recruits by force, vowing revenge on a society that had rejected the revolutionary message. It was from this time that some of the worst

A determined Foday Sankoh, rebel leader of the Revolutionary United Front, rallying his troops at Port Loko. [TEUN VOETEN]

raids and massacres occurred, especially in villages from which the civil defence fighters had been recruited. There seems no doubt that counterinsurgency activities by the CDF broke the 1996 cease-fire accords to which the RUF had mainly adhered. The Kabba government argued that civil defence was a civilian movement over which it had no control. The point is crucial to understanding why the RUF became so unstable, seeking the destruction of communities it once hoped would offer it welcome. Demobilized cadres spoke openly about a link between heightened violence and the rejection of their movement by a majority of the rural population. Amputations and massacres imposed random destruction on the countryside and were brutally expressive of the feelings of embittered RUF cadres that their own lives became, under the movement, no more than a lottery of poverty, capture, and ostracism.

In May 1997 the army was faced with the cancellation of food subsidies at the insistence of the IMF. Soldiers mounted a mutiny, forcing the civilian regime into exile in Guinea. A Momoh loyalist in the army, Major Johnny Paul Koroma, accused of collaboration with the enemy in acts of sabotage, and later jailed by

the Kabba government, emerged to become leader of a new regime (the Armed Forces Revolutionary Council, AFRC). The AFRC sought to end the war by enticing the RUF into a power-sharing regime, but the junta was shunned internationally, and the alliance between former enemies soon fell apart. The RUF used its time in government to stockpile weapons in its rear bases, convinced by its charismatic leader, a cashiered former army corporal named Foday Sankoh, that one day, despite all hardships, it was destined to rule. Negotiations over the return of the legitimate government proved inconclusive. Although the deadlines had not yet expired, Nigerian General Sanni Abacha ordered Nigerian troops in the regional peacekeeping force, ECOMOG, to take Freetown and restore the deposed government in February 1998. The irony of a military dictator fighting for democracy in a foreign country was not lost on the international community, despite general relief that the way was open for the legitimate government to return (which it did in March 1998). The army was disbanded, but army loyalists calling themselves the West Side Boys went to ground in villages behind the Ocra Hills, only about forty miles from Freetown. The RUF resumed its positions on the forested Liberian border. It offered refuge to elements in the former junta leadership, although some say it held them hostage—Koroma was held in virtual captivity by his erstwhile comrades-in-arms. The RUF also strengthened its links with the Taylor regime and its allies in Burkina Faso and Libya.

In exile in Conakry, Guinea, the Kabba government engaged another branch of the South African–British security and mining company that had helped undermine the RUF. It directed these allies to support loyalist fighters in southern Sierra Leone and mount a counter-coup. Alleged involvement of U.K. officials and military intelligence in this arrangement, contrary to UN sanctions, caused a storm in British politics, leading to a parliamentary investigation by Sir David Legg into the shipment of arms to Sierra Leone. The kimberlite concession held by the main mining associate of the security company in question (valued at around $450 million on resumption of operations in 2002) stimulated business rivalry in the murky world of African minerals capitalism. Competitors, mainly from the former Soivet Union, ventured to re-arm and retrain remnant junta forces, hoping once again to topple the Kabba government and thus overturn the kimberlite concession granted in return for security services. The RUF had its own political reasons for going along with this scheme. In October 1998, RUF forces led by Samuel Bockarie, a Libyan-backed Sankoh loyalist, battled Nigerian troops to seize the main diamond-mining district of Kono. It was widely reported that the Nigerian peacekeepers were lax due to their own involvement in alluvial diamond mining. RUF and junta forces soon took control of the Makeni-Magburaka axis, giving them control of the main approach roads to Kono and much of the north of the country, where former government troops had their greatest support. In December, an audacious attempt to take Freetown began.

Junta fighters entered eastern Freetown on January 6, 1999, forcing sections of the government to flee. For a period of time, the president slept in Conakry, the Guinean capital, and by day he administered his country from Freetown's international airport at Lungi, protected by Nigerian troops. The civilian casualty rate from the attack amounted to some 7,000 to 8,000 deaths. Many terrible atrocities were committed, including random amputations and burning alive entire households. These acts were committed especially by units of the West Side Boys, which by then included former army recruits and their irregular associates.

The RUF tended to occupy rear positions, such as at Waterloo, on the road out of Freetown, and close to the forest in which they felt most at home. Some RUF units were at the forefront, however, focusing in particular on Pademba Road Prison. These forces were hoping to find and release their leader, Foday Sankoh, who had been detained in the aftermath of the Abidjan peace negotiation, in February 1997. Sankoh had been tried for treason in October 1998, as the junta revival began, and was awaiting confirmation of his death sentence. The government quickly moved him to another location when the attack on Freetown began. The peacekeepers were also guilty of abuses, carrying out summary executions of young people suspected of RUF membership. Civilians manipulated the excited Nigerian troops to settle old scores, at times pointing the finger at young neighbors suspected of thieving or adultery. Under the rules of the Sierra Leone Special Court, war crimes by troops invited into the country by the legitimate government can only be tried in the sending country.

Nigerian troops ousted the junta from Freetown after three weeks of fighting, but suffered heavy casualties—as many as 1,000 Nigerian soldiers may have been killed. A scaling back of Nigerian peacekeepers was underway before the attack. Abacha had died, and Nigeria was about to return to democracy. The president-elect, Olusegun Obasanjo, had made it clear, even while campaigning, that he had reservations about Nigeria's peace-enforcement role in Sierra Leone. The days of the Nigerian-dominated ECOMOG were numbered. President Kabba, with no army of his own, had little option but to sue for peace.

The Lomè Peace Agreement offered the RUF a better deal than it had been offered at Abidjan. The death sentence on Sankoh was lifted, and the movement was offered three senior government posts in a power-sharing agreement. Fighters were amnestied, although the UN entered a reservation concerning amnesties for indictable war crimes. Sankoh became the national commissioner for minerals, with vice-presidential status. The RUF hoped this would lead to controls on the cancerous corruption that had blighted politics in Sierra Leone for more than forty years. Some assumed that the diamonds were all Sankoh ever wanted, and that he and his cronies would become the new national mineral-rich elite. Former army elements were marginalized in the agreement. The West Side Boys took up a life of banditry and hostage-taking on the main road leading into Freetown, later clashing with the British army.

British intervention in Sierra Leone in May 2000 was occasioned by the near collapse of the Lomè agreement. ECOMOG finally withdrew in April 2000, to be replaced by a UN force, UNAMSIL, as had been envisaged in the Lome agreement. UNAMSIL was ill prepared for its task, however. In particular, it knew little about the identities, backgrounds, and factions within the fighting groups controlling the RUF. Political leaders of the RUF had never gone back to the movement in the bush when the Abidjan agreement foundered. Not many military commanders in the field had passed through the RUF ideological training program, which was based on the *Green Book* and other Libyan writings, teachings of Kim Il Sung, and Sandanista sources on guerrilla warfare, as well as various manuals on community leadership and cooperative development. Those without political training made up disciplinary rules in very harsh operational conditions, and with little or no effective supervision from Sankoh or other movement intellectuals. Violent and sometimes bizarre punishments were their main tools for subjugating unwilling civilian populations, at times reflecting the codes and norms of adolescent gang culture.

UN peacekeepers (familiarly known as Blue Helmets) attempted forcibly to disarm the RUF. Oblivious of the international consequences, nervy teenage fighters hit back at the Blue Helmet forces, killing some and taking large numbers hostage. Meanwhile, rumors swept Freetown that the RUF was once again on the march. These were given currency by UN sources and only later corrected. Some members of the RUF political leadership in Freetown were rounded up and jailed on Sunday, May 7, 2000, and a peace demonstration at Foday Sankoh's house on Spur Road on the next day turned violent; it was described by one of the organizers as a "riot cum lynch-mob." Sankoh's panicky guards opened fire after the security forces lost control of the crowd, killing over twenty demonstrators. Sankoh and his supporters escaped into the hills above Freetown. Some made it through bush tracks to the movement's safe haven in Makeni. A group of women fighters saved their lives by claiming to be out collecting firewood when they were attacked by the escaping RUF party. Sankoh himself spent several days in the forests above Freetown before deciding to surrender himself to the authorities. Detained by the government for many months, he was eventually handed over to the jurisdiction of the special court, and died in captivity in August 2003, before he could stand trial for his alleged war crimes.

The objective of the British intervention in Sierra Leone was to stabilize the situation, encourage resolution of the UN hostage crisis, enable the full deployment of UNAMSIL, and (over the longer term) train a new Sierra Leonean army. The British government, under prime minister Tony Blair, had been uneasy about Sierra Leone ever since the Legg report revealed collusion between the private security company assisting the exiled government of Sierra Leone and middle level officials of the British Foreign Office acting without proper political authorization. The Legg enquiry and subsequent parliamentary debate exposed an agent of British overseas military intelligence, earlier based in Namibia, who had become, after retirement in 1993, a representative of the mining company seeking a kimberlite concession in Sierra Leone. It also disclosed the role played by the British ambassador, who had offered advice to the Kabba government on certain security options "in a private capacity." Sources in the Sierra Leonean Ministry of Defence have indicated that they were advised to maintain military pressure on the RUF during the Abidjan negotiations and were promised international military assistance should the policy backfire; but it may not have been clear that some of the advisors came wearing two hats, and that military assistance would come from private sources. The scandal made a mockery of New Labour's boast of an ethical foreign policy, and the Blair cabinet was persuaded that a properly authorized military intervention in Sierra Leone might make amends.

British forces were deployed to secure a road linking the airport at Lungi, the main junctions controlling road connections from Freetown to the provinces, and Freetown itself. This calmed the city and sobered the RUF. Having offered support to groups seeking to destabilize the regime in neighboring Guinea, the RUF was further constrained by decisive cross-border action by the Guinean army. Careful negotiations were begun with the RUF to release the UN hostages. In August the

West Side Boys, marginalized from the peace process and anxious to advertize their own plight, seized a British security patrol. They were met with a sharp military response. The hostages were freed and the group rounded up, lifting the threat of bandit raids on the Freetown road.

The deployment of the Bangladesh Battalion of UNAMSIL along the Makeni-Magburaka axis was also an important step in consolidating the peace. Some of the RUF commanders had encountered texts on postwar cooperative development in Bangladesh during their ideological training, and these welcomed the arrival of the UNAMSIL forces. The battalion has since encouraged community reconstruction activities led by demobilized RUF commanders. Foday Sankoh came from a village in the vicinity of Magburaka, and his movement began to show signs of developing a permanent presence in the area, deploying in particular into community reconstruction and agricultural development.

With little scope for further RUF offensives after the British and Guinean interventions, the government and the RUF, under Issa Sesay, a commander trusted by Sankoh, negotiated a permanent cease-fire agreement—the Abuja Accord—in November 2000. Other RUF commanders, including a Green Book die-hard named Samuel Bockarie, removed to Liberia, where they worked for Charles Taylor. They later shifted operations to the war in Cote d'Ivoire. Bockarie was indicted by the Sierra Leone Special Court in absentia. He was killed in May 2003 on the Liberian-Ivoirian border, allegedly in a shoot-out with his own forces. He may, however, have been killed on the orders of Charles Taylor, who was no doubt anxious to prevent Bockarie from testifying against him should he be brought before the court. Johnny Paul Koroma escaped from the RUF in Kailahun, and was reinstated in Freetown in negotiations with junta elements subsequent to the signing of the Lome accord. Pledging loyalty to Kabba, he helped defend Freetown in May 2000, but was subsequently accused of a further coup attempt and escaped the country. He was sought by the special court for war crimes. It was rumored that he had been killed in Liberia, but other sources suggest Koroma escaped to Ghana. The RUF, CDF, and elements from the former government army submitted to disarmament, demobilization, and reintegration, a process effectively completed by the end of 2001. President Kabba declared the war at an end on January 18, 2002.

The war in Sierra Leone is complex and fits no prevailing stereotype. It is not the aftermath of a cold war proxy struggle (unlike wars in Angola or Somalia). Nor is it a war of ethnic animosity (as in Rwanda). The RUF

Charles Ghankay MacArthur Dakpana Taylor was born in Arthington, Monrovia, on January 29, 1948. He became the leader of the armed National Patriotic Front of Liberia (NPFL) and later became president of that country from 1997 to 2003. On June 4, 2003, Taylor was indicted by the Special Court in Sierra Leone, accused of crimes against humanity in the civil war in Sierra Leone. The charges relate to a broad range of atrocities, indictees being not necessarily actual perpetrators, but those who "bear the greatest responsibility" for the commission of the acts. The case against Taylor alleges his material support for and encouragement of the Revolutionary United Front of Sierra Leone (RUF) after the collapse of the Abidjan peace accords signed in November 1996.

The UN Security Council's panel of experts on Liberia established in 2000 that Liberia was at the heart of a shadowy international network of support for the RUF, involving Israeli, South African, Kenyan, and Ukrainian arms suppliers and diamond mining interests. The Abidjan peace accords were still in the process of implementation when army mutineers overthrew the elected government of Sierra Leone and invited the RUF to take part in a military regime (May 1997). This junta was, in turn, deposed by Nigerian-led peacekeeping troops in February 1998, and the RUF was forced into the bush once more.

Charles Taylor helped the movement to revive. Arms were flown in from Eastern Europe via Burkina Faso. Training of RUF fighters was undertaken in Liberia by a former colonel of the South African Defence Forces, recruited in 1998 to develop an anti-terrorist unit from fighters formerly associated with Taylor's guerrilla forces. This group included Sierra Leonean, Burkinabe, and Gambian nationals. The RUF took over the rich Kono diamond fields in eastern Sierra Leone in October 1998, paying its materiel suppliers in diamonds. Liberia briefly became a major exporter of rough diamonds from Sierra Leone. In effect, these "blood diamonds" paid for the revival of the war.

This was the period when many of the worst atrocities occurred, and Charles Taylor was indicted as one of those "most responsible." The Liberian leader first encountered the leaders of the RUF at the "World Revolutionary Headquarters" (al-Mathabh al-Thauriya al-Amaniya), a facility run by the Libyan secret services in Benghazi, Libya. Colonel Gaddafi was at the time encouraging a pan-Africanist movement that included the leaderships of various West African revolutionary groups. Taylor had reached Libya by a tortuous route. Having first worked for and then falling out with the Doe government in Liberia, he fled to the United States, pursued by a Liberian arrest warrant for embezzlement. He was taken into custody and held in the Plymouth County House of Correction, Plymouth, Massachussets, to await extradition, but he escaped and eventually joined a group of Liberian dissidents who had helped Blaise Compaore overthrow Thomas Sankara to become President of Burkina Faso. It was Compaore who introduced Taylor to Gaddafi. The Libyan leader initially accepted the Liberian economist as a true convert to the Green Book cause (the *Green Book* was Gaddafi's version of *Mao Zedong*), but later decided that Taylor was a fake.

RUF fighters helped Taylor in his struggle for political predominance in Liberia—a result finally achieved not through the gun but through the ballot box in a war-weary country. Taylor's support for the RUF was based not only on long-term loyalties among Green Book comrades-in-arms, but also designed to secure a flow of resources from the rich diamond fields and forest of eastern Sierra Leone to sustain his own political hegemony in Liberia. As a result of Security Council scrutiny of his support for the Sierra Leone rebels, Taylor was made the subject of a UN travel ban in 2001, and the Swiss government later froze his overseas assets. Wounded economically, Taylor could no longer hold armed dissident groups at bay. War again flared in Liberia. To end fighting that threatened large numbers of civilians, Nigeria offered Taylor conditional asylum, an offer that Taylor accepted on July 11, 2003. He stepped down as president one month later and departed for Calabar in Nigeria, beyond the jurisdiction of the Special Court.

For further reading, see Ellis, S. (1999). *The Mask of Anarchy: The Destruction of Liberia and the Religious Dimension of an African Civil War.* London: Christopher Hurst; and UN Experts (December 2000). *Report of the Panel of Experts Appointed Pursuant to the UN Security Council Resolution 1306 para. 19, in Relation to Sierra Leone.* New York: United Nations Organization.

was founded by and recruited young people from all ethnic backgrounds suffering educational marginalization and social exclusion. More recently, the war has been assimilated to a thesis fashionable in the World Bank that all recent civil wars are better understood in economic rather than in political terms. Because the economy of Sierra Leone is dominated by alluvial diamonds, the war—it is reasoned—must have been

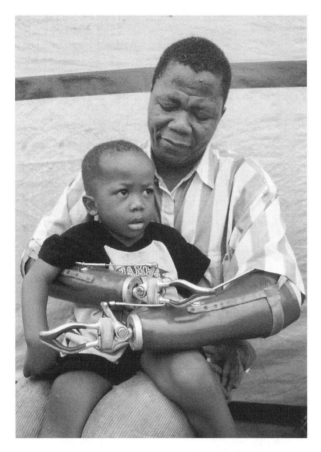

During the ten-year civil war in Sierra Leone, the Revolutionary United Front routinely perpetrated mutilation as a form of punishment or coercion. [LOUISE GUBB/CORBIS]

caused by the struggle for diamond wealth. The diamond thesis is useful in explaining how all factions (government troops, international peacekeepers, and the RUF) succumbed to diamonds, either to pay for weapons or as a diversion from fighting, thereby compromising operations and prolonging conflict. But the RUF did not prioritize control of diamond districts. In 1991, its sights were set on capturing Bo and Kenema, key provincial towns, and in 1995 it was hammering on the gates of Freetown. The movement itself argues that it was dragged into the diamond districts by its enemies, who preferred skirmishing around diamond pits rather than being ambushed in the forests of the Liberian border. Greed for diamonds is thus, at best, only a partial explanation for the war in Sierra Leone.

The conflict might be better regarded as a reflection upon poverty and globalization, resting on an awareness (created by videos, satellite broadcasting, and mobile phones, available even in remote mining camps) of the huge gap in life chances between the world's richest and poorest countries. Many RUF cadres state frankly that their personal ambition is to reach

America or Europe, perhaps to obtain a technical education, for which mastery of an AK47 is a poor substitute. Many senior fighters in the RUF, women included, have opted for computer training as part of their demobilization package, believing this will put them in contact with a wider technological world. In the bush, the movement offered able children technical training in its signals unit, and Sankoh, a signaller in the army, supervised the examination procedures.

Two key statistics are germane to understanding the crisis in Sierra Leone. According to the UN Development Program (UNDP), Sierra Leone has hovered for a number of years at or near the bottom of the Human Development Index, which measures not just per capita income, but aspects of social development such as gender equality, educational opportunity, and life expectancy. Additionally, Sierra Leone has now surpassed Brazil as the most unequal country in the world. In such a small, compact, and tightly intermarried nation, this is a staggering fact. It means that all the contrasts of wealth and poverty in the world can be found even at the family level.

In a reflective mood, villagers sometimes openly state that the greater part of the destruction was done by their own kith and kin. A political figure confessed that an RUF raiding party that burned several family houses was led by his own half-brother. A leading advisor to the president wrote in a newspaper about how, under the junta, he was humiliated by learning that an RUF killer, renowned for his atrocity, turned out to be his own nephew. What sense of humiliation fuels desire for bloody vengeance against even family members? A major factor seems to be that, underneath the veneer of local social and family solidarity, there lurks a huge inequality. Some members, through the unaccountable wealth from diamonds, are able to access modern education and live fulfilling and successful professional lives, often in international employment, whereas others, barely able to complete primary education, are condemned to an impoverished existence on farms, regulated by elders who operate legal procedures bequeathed by colonialism in which some of the social disadvantages of domestic slavery remain encoded.

Young RUF recruits rallied to the movement because of the fines, beatings, and (at times arbitrary and illegal) punishments of village elders and chiefs. Village marriage continues to reflect conditions of production and reproduction associated with the days of domestic slavery. Most girls are married in their teenage years to older polygynists, and young men cannot afford to marry. Those who set up informal unions risk being fined for "woman damage." Much farm labor still goes to elders and in-laws in the form of bride service. Sierra

Leone was founded in 1787 as a home for former slaves, and later for those who were rescued on the high seas by the Freetown-based British anti-slavery squadron but, ironically, domestic slavery was abolished there only in 1928, after prodding by the League of Nations. The British were anxious not to provoke the rural chiefs, who were stirred to revolt in 1898 by the threat that colonial law would free their tied labor force. Even in the early twenty-first century, the government seems at times more concerned to placate rural tradition than to address the needs of disenchanted youth, confusing the causes of the war of 1898 with the causes of the war of 1991.

If there was any ethnic component to the war, it is found in Kailahun, and especially among the Kissi, an ethnic group that straddles the borders of three countries by the artificial borders established during colonialism. Anthropologist Claude Meillassoux has written that "Kissi" derives from a name given by a savannah merchant group, the Fula of Futa Jallon, to the forest peoples they raided for slaves. In some respects the civil war, and its extremes of brutalizing, dehumanizing violence, can be regarded as a long-delayed slave revolt, at least in this region. Slave revolts are especially notorious for atrocities when the denial of human potential exists side-by-side with freedoms enjoyed by others, in short, when slaves live as part of a domestic group. The horribly violent Turner Revolt in Virginia in 1834 is an example of this. Similarly apocalyptic and brutal ideas about the need to destroy society itself, in conditions where only some are free, can be detected in aspects of the war Sierra Leone.

More routine explanations may serve to account for much of the violence, however. A depressing law of tit-for-tat escalation seems all too apparent. The thuggery of the APC regime under Stevens deadened political nerves and consciences. From its involvement in the Liberian war, the RUF imported knowledge that civilians can be controlled by terror. The army's summary execution of rebels in the early days of the war locked up captives in the RUF, turning them into loyalists. Double-dealing in peace negotiations resulted in a further cycles of revenge attacks. Few prisoners were taken by peacekeepers, private security, or civil defence militia forces. Fear of summary executions turned embattled RUF cadres against communities that had clubbed together to pay for the initiation of CDF volunteers. Civilian lynchings of rebel suspects laid the foundations for the massacres and mass amputations that followed. Atrocities mounted as militias were forced into retreat.

All this violence was illegal, and none of it is excusable. But the world's media only notice a country as apparently insignificant as Sierra Leone when the level of violence passes a certain threshold. The search for justice and accountability has to dig deeper. Here the UN-funded Special Court for Sierra Leone has been, in some eyes, something of an expensive disappointment. It took so long to arrange the court that some of its key defendants were lost. It is a very expensive process, in the world's poorest country, where most citizens agree that grinding poverty was a main cause of the war. Sankoh and Bockarie have taken their testimony to the grave. Taylor and Koroma remain fugitives. Hinga Norman (the leader of the CDF) is a national hero to many. Several of the RUF military command lack insight into the movement's origins and political aims, and even if condemned, are unlikely to expose the political issues at the heart of the conflict. The indictments are too general—referring not to specific involvement in war crimes and atrocities, but to the general responsibility for mayhem borne by the senior military commanders of RUF and CDF alike.

The Truth and Reconciliation Commission (TRC) is, perhaps, in some respects even less satisfactory. Most testimony appears to have been regulated by adherence to a well-known local proverb: "talk half, leave half." All sides have things to hide, and listeners to the sessions that have been broadcast on the radio suck their teeth at the omissions and half-truths. The TRC seems, to some, more a ritual of reconciliation than an attempt to get at the truth. Opinions are divided about whether this is a good or bad thing. Some think that the truth shall make you free, and others—aware that local culture often deploys ritual in order to forget—believe that in a conflict as complex as Sierra Leone, it is better to look only to the future. Until the world is ready to admit that its own failure to abolish extreme poverty or to uphold the right to social and economic development has contributed to this war of globalization, it is perhaps unfair to expect Sierra Leoneans to expose the secrets of a violent family quarrel.

SEE ALSO Liberia; Mercenaries; Peacekeeping; Sierra Leone Special Court; Truth Commissions

BIBLIOGRAPHY

Abdullah, I., and P. K. Muana (1998). "The Revolutionary United Front of Sierra Leone (RUF/SL)." In *African Guerrillas*, ed. C. Clapham. Oxford: James Currey.

Abdullah, I., and Y. Bangura, Y. eds. (1997). *Lumpen Culture and Political Violence: The Sierra Leone Civil War*. Special Issue of *Africa Development* 22(3–4).

Amnesty International (1992): *The Extrajudicial Execution of Suspected Rebels and Collaborators*. London: International Secretariat of Amnesty International, Index AFR 51/02/92.

Archibald, S., and P. Richards (2002). "Conversion to Human Rights? Popular Debate about War and Justice in Rural Central Sierra Leone." *Africa* 72(3):339–367.

Keen, D. (2004). *Conflict and Collusion in Sierra Leone.* Oxford: James Currey.

Muana, P. K. (1997). "The Kamajoi Militia: Civil War, Internal Displacement and the Politics of Counter-Insurgency." *Africa Development* 22(3–4):77–100.

Peters, K., and P. Richards (1998). "Why We Fight: Voices of Youth Ex-Combatants in Sierra Leone." *Africa* 68(1):183–210.

Richards, P. (1996). *Fighting for the Rain Forest: War, Youth, and Resources in Sierra Leone.* Oxford: James Currey.

Paul Richards

Sierra Leone Special Court

The eight and one-half year armed conflict between the government of Sierra Leone and rebel groups (in effect a civil war), which officially ended on July 7, 1999, with the signing of the Lomè Peace Agreement, is unrivalled in its particularly mindless violence, directed mainly against the civilian population. The signature of the Revolutionary United Front (RUF) rebel group was the amputation of the hands, arms, and other body parts of civilians, including those of children and babies—a grimly ironic reference to the election slogan of the President of Sierra Leone, Ahmad Tejan Kabbah: "The future is in your hands." Other favored practices of the rebels included burning civilians alive; gouging out eyes; attacking civilians with machetes and/or shooting them; the forced recruitment of child soldiers; and the kidnapping of girls (who would be coerced into sexual slavery).

It would be difficult to be categoric about the war aims of the RUF and other armed opposition groups. The RUF was established and originally funded by former Liberian President Charles Taylor, who had the intention of grabbing power in Sierra Leone. But the real driving force of the conflict was control over natural resources, especially the country's diamonds. This war was the continuation of business by other means, to paraphrase the famous military tactician, Karl von Clausewitz.

The extreme nature of the violence, and the fact that the victimization of the civilian population was not the "collateral damage" of a conflict otherwise fought between two armies but the modus operandi of the rebels, brought the conflict in Sierra Leone to international attention. However, while expressing concern, the international community would make no commitments to armed intervention or the type of help that could have turned the tide of the civil war. Two peace agreements were signed and quickly collapsed. The regional peacekeeping force, ECOMOG, which is the armed force of the Economic Community of West African States (ECOWAS), was deployed to assist the government of Sierra Leone in defeating the rebels. The government even resorted to hiring mercenaries to help it win the war, but to no avail. With the rebels controlling two-thirds of the national territory (containing one-half of the population), and seemingly no way to defeat the rebels militarily, the government—under pressure from the international community, particularly the United States and the United Kingdom—decided once again to sue for peace.

The Lomé Peace Agreement, signed on July 9, 1999, in the capital city of Togo, was a highly compromising document in which the government of Sierra Leone, in its desperate bid to end the conflict, offered a blanket amnesty to all the rebels, as well as government troops that might have committed serious crimes, and agreed to bring the RUF into the government. It also placed the RUF's notorious leader, Foday Sankoh, at the head of a commission known as the Strategic Minerals Commission, which would oversee the country's mineral resources and postwar reconstruction, with responsibility for "securing and monitoring the legitimate exploitation of Sierra Leone's gold and diamonds" and reviewing all mining licenses in the country. What were in effect rewards for brutality outraged many international observers, and the amnesties were considered to violate international law. In an oral disclaimer to the Peace Agreement, made at the time of the signing of the agreement, the United Nations (UN) Special Representative for Sierra Leone, Francis Okelo, said that the amnesty did not apply to genocide, crimes against humanity, and other serious violations of international humanitarian law. Backed into a corner, the government of Sierra Leone felt that it had no alternative.

The government's willingness to offer the best possible terms to the rebels in order to persuade them to renounce violence did not produce the hoped for peace and stability. By May 2000 the Lomé Peace Agreement was on the verge of collapse, as the RUF and other rebel groups, who had refused to disarm or demobilize, attacked the UN peacekeepers who had been sent to police the shaky "peace."

Establishment of the Special Court for Sierra Leone

With the spirit of reconciliation fading fast in Sierra Leone, the government called for the creation of an international criminal tribunal that would try the rebels who had committed war crimes and crimes against humanity.

In response, on August 14, 2000, the UN Security Council unanimously adopted Resolution 1315, setting in motion a process intended to culminate in the establishment of a body to be called the Special Court for Sierra Leone. The resolution expressed the Security Council's distress over the "very serious crimes committed within the territory of Sierra Leone against the people of Sierra Leone and the United Nations and associated personnel, and at the prevailing situation of impunity." It declared that persons who commit such crimes are individually criminally responsible, and that "the international community would exert every effort to bring those responsible to justice in accordance with international standards of justice, fairness, and due process of law." The resolution went on to say: "[I]n the particular circumstances of Sierra Leone, a credible system of justice and accountability for the very serious crimes committed there would end impunity and would contribute to the process of national reconciliation and to the restoration and maintenance of peace."

UN Resolution 1315, consisting of nine paragraphs, entrusted to the UN Secretary-General the task of negotiating an agreement to create an independent special court with the government of Sierra Leone. It recommended that the Special Court have subject matter jurisdiction over crimes against humanity, war crimes, and other serious violations of international humanitarian law. In contrast to the already existing ad hoc International Criminal Tribunals for the Former Yugoslavia (ICTY) and Rwanda (ICTR), the Special Court was to have a mixed character, with both international and national elements.

There were several reasons for the decision by the UN to propose a court of mixed character rather than a "pure" international one such as the ICTY or ICTR. In the first place, the government of Sierra Leone itself favored the establishment of a court that would have both international and national features. Second, there was no support at the international level for the creation of yet another very expensive ad hoc international criminal tribunal modeled on the ICTY or ICTR, which by the year 2000 were as a pair costing the UN approximately $200 million per year. Although the Statute of the International Criminal Court (ICC, located in The Hague, Netherlands) was adopted in July 1998, it could not hear cases concerning the war in Sierra Leone, as under Article 11(1) of the Statute: "The Court has jurisdiction only with respect to crimes committed after the entry into force [of the Statute], on July 1, 2002."

Following the adoption of Resolution 1315, the next step in the creation of the Court was the issuance by the Secretary-General, on October 4, 2000, of a Report on the Establishment of a Special Court for Sierra Leone. Annexed to the report were a draft agreement between the UN and Sierra Leone concerning the establishment of the Court and a draft statute for the Court, which were the starting points for the subsequent bilateral negotiations. The final versions of both the Statute and the Agreement were signed sixteen months later, in January 2002. In the interim letters were exchanged among the Security Council, the Secretary-General, and the government of Sierra Leone in an effort to resolve the main issues in contention, which were the size of the Court, its jurisdiction over persons, and funding for the Court. Final agreement on these issues was reached in February 2001. Delays thereafter were attributable to difficulties having to do with the acquisition of sufficient funding to establish and operate the Court. When the funding was secured, work began on the actual establishment of the Court, the hiring of staff, and the preparation of the first indictments.

The Agreement and the Statute
Although the Special Court for Sierra Leone has much in common with its antecedents (the ICTY and ICTR), it differs from them in several key respects. One fundamental distinction is that the legal basis of the Court is the bilateral agreement between the UN and Sierra Leone, and not a resolution of the Security Council.

The establishment of the Special Court by an agreement rather than a Security Council resolution offered both advantages and disadvantages. On the plus side, it meant that Sierra Leone was able to put the stamp of its own personality on the Court—to a far greater extent than the former Yugoslavia or Rwanda had been able to put theirs on the international tribunals. On the minus side, the Special Court, not having been established pursuant to the Security Council's Chapter VII powers, lacks the authority to issue binding orders to states. Although the Secretary-General had recommended to the Security Council that it endow the Special Court with binding powers, the Security Council declined to do so. This means that the Court cannot, for example, order a state to surrender a person for trial, and must depend on states' good will when it comes to cooperation.

Although the Agreement and the Statute each has its own purpose, there is some overlap between them and they should be read together. Apart from establishing the legal basis of the Special Court, the Agreement lays out the composition of the Court and the procedure for the appointment of its judges, prosecutor, and registrar. It establishes that the Special Court shall be located in Sierra Leone. There are provisions in the Agreement that deal with administrative and other technical matters, including the legal status of the

Court itself; the privileges and immunities of the judges, prosecutor, and registrar; and the privileges and immunities of international and Sierra Leonean court personnel. Immunity of counsel, witnesses, and experts, as well as the security, safety, and protection of these persons, are guaranteed. Practical arrangements regarding the establishment of the Court, the settlement of disputes, and the entry into force of the Agreement are also spelled out.

Structure and Size of the Special Court

The Special Court for Sierra Leone has a tripartite structure, consisting of a Registry, an Office of the Prosecutor, and Chambers of the judges.

The UN Secretary-General had originally proposed a Chambers consisting of two trial chambers, both composed of three judges, and one Appeals Chamber, in which five judges would serve. However, the Security Council rejected this, primarily on the basis of financial constraints, stating that "the Special Court should begin its work with a single Trial Chamber with the possibility of adding a second Chamber should the developing caseload warrant its creation." The Security Council also rejected the Secretary-General's suggestion of alternate judges.

Although the Security Council had asked the Secretary-General to consider the possibility of the Special Court's sharing the judges of the Appeals Chamber of the ICTY and ICTR, the Secretary-General rejected this proposal as unworkable. While the Secretary-General recognized the advantages of having a single Appeals Chamber that, as the ultimate judicial authority in matters of interpretation and application of international humanitarian law, would offer the guarantee of a coherent development of the law, he found that this goal might also be achieved by linking the jurisprudence of the Special Court to that of the international tribunals. Article 20(3) of the Statute provides that the Court shall be guided by the decisions of the Appeals Chamber of the ad hoc international criminal tribunals (for Rwanda and the former Yugoslavia), whereas Article 14(1) references the Rules of Procedure and Evidence of the ICTR.

As the Special Court has jurisdiction over domestic as well as international crimes, it was necessary that at least some of the Court's judges have knowledge of Sierra Leonean law or at least have a common law background. The Agreement and Statute thus provide that one of the three judges of the Trial Chamber and two of the five Appeals Chamber judges shall be appointed by the government of Sierra Leone. The Agreement further provides that the Secretary-General should particularly seek nominations for the remaining Trial and Appeals Chambers judges from member states of the ECOWAS and the British Commonwealth. Judges serve four-year terms and are eligible for reappointment.

The chief prosecutor, who works only for the Special Court, is chosen by the UN Secretary-General; the Deputy must be a Sierra Leonean national. The prosecutor is appointed for a four-year term and is eligible for reappointment. The prosecutor acts as an independent and separate organ of the Court and is prohibited from receiving any instructions from any government.

The Registry is responsible for the day-to-day running of the Court. It includes the Victims and Witnesses Unit, which is responsible for establishing security measures for the protection of witnesses who testify before the Special Court.

The Jurisdiction of the Special Court

The Statute stipulates that the Special Court shares jurisdiction with the national courts of Sierra Leone, but enjoys primacy over those courts and, at any stage of its proceedings, may formally request a national court of Sierra Leone to defer to its competence. Defendants are not vulnerable to the risk of double jeopardy. Article 9 of the Statute makes clear that no person who has been tried before the national courts can later be tried by the Special Court in respect of the same acts. But there are exceptions. Retrial is possible if: (1) the acts for which the defendant was tried in a national court were characterized as ordinary crimes; (2) the national proceedings were not impartial or independent; or (3) the national proceedings were designed to shield the accused from international criminal responsibility or were not diligently prosecuted.

Time Limits

Given the Special Court's limited budget, there existed a need to limit its caseload. This was partly achieved by restricting the Court's temporal jurisdiction. Although the Secretary-General recognized in his Report on the Establishment of a Special Court for Sierra Leone that the armed conflict in Sierra Leone officially began on March 23, 1991, when the RUF invaded Sierra Leone from Liberia, the Court was given temporal jurisdiction that extended only as far back as November 30, 1996, the date of the signing of the Abidjan Peace Agreement. This latter date meant that the Court's jurisdiction would encompass the period during which the most serious crimes were committed. The Court's jurisdiction is open-ended.

A further issue that might have impacted on temporal jurisdiction was the amnesty granted in the Lomé Peace Agreement. If the amnesty were considered to be legal and in force, the Special Court's jurisdiction would then extend only to crimes committed after July 7, 1999—whereas if that amnesty were illegal, the Court would also enjoy jurisdiction over crimes committed before that date. In his October 2000 report, the Secretary-General stated: "[T]he United Nations has consistently maintained the position that amnesty cannot be granted in respect of international crimes, such as genocide, crimes against humanity, or other serious violations of international humanitarian law." Scholars agreed. Article 10 of the Statue of the Special Court therefore rejects amnesty in respect of international crimes, but leaves open the question of whether national crimes can be prosecuted by the Special Court in instances in which an amnesty has been granted. It can be argued that the Court's temporal jurisdiction concerning national crimes begins only on July 7, 1999.

Jurisdiction over Persons

Discussion of the Special Court's personal jurisdiction focused on two issues: (1) defendants' position in the chain of command and level of personnel responsibility; and (2) whether the Court should have jurisdiction over children who were suspected of having committed atrocities.

Concerning the first issue, the parties to the Statute had to decide whether the Statute itself should place restrictions on who was and was not a prosecutable defendant, or whether this should be left to the discretion of the prosecutor. From the outset it was agreed that only those most responsible for the crimes committed in Sierra Leone should be prosecuted before the Special Court. However, some time elapsed before there was agreement as to the exact wording of the Statute's Article 1, concerning the Court's personnel jurisdiction over persons. The Secretary-General's original draft statute provided that the Special Court should have jurisdiction over "persons most responsible for serious violations of international humanitarian law and Sierra Leone law." Subsequently, the Security Council changed this to "persons who bear the greatest responsibility." The Security Council added to the Secretary-General's draft Article 1 the words: "including those leaders who, in committing such crimes, have threatened the establishment of and implementation of the peace process in Sierra Leone." This removes any ambiguity as to whether the Court has jurisdiction over crimes that were committed after the signing of the Lomé Peace Agreement.

Responding to these adjustments, the Secretary-General stated that "the words [of the Security Council]. . .provide guidance to the prosecutor in determining his or her prosecutorial strategy." He also stated that although he agreed that the Special Court should prosecute only those most responsible for serious violations of international humanitarian law, such a restriction "does not mean that the personal jurisdiction is limited to the political and military leaders only. Therefore, the determination of the meaning of the term *persons who bear the greatest responsibility* in any given case falls initially to the prosecutor and ultimately to the Special Court itself."

At the same time, the inclusion of this wording (having to do with the Court's ultimate discretion in respect of jurisdiction over persons) in the final version of the Statute of the Special Court in combination with the Court's limited financial resources suggested that the Court's main focus would be rebel leaders. The initial indictments filed by the Chief Prosecutor David Crane supported this assumption. Although violations of international humanitarian law by persons other than rebel leaders were documented, the Security Council indicated that they should be tried in other forums. The Security Council specified that the primary responsibility for prosecuting members of peacekeeping forces, for example, fell to the sending state.

The other aspect of the Special Court's jurisdiction over persons that was in contention concerned the politically sensitive question of whether the Court should be able to prosecute child soldiers—and if so, what should be the age of criminal responsibility.

The involvement of minors (some not yet teenagers) in the commission of atrocities during the armed conflict in Sierra Leone has been well-documented. These children were mostly abducted and forcibly recruited into rebel groups, and were compelled to carry out atrocities, sometimes against members of their own families.

The Secretary-General's Report of October 2000 made reference to the "terrible dilemma" of jurisdiction in relation to these minors. Although it was widely recognized that the crimes in question were committed by youths who had been under some form of duress and intoxication, there was considerable popular support within the country for prosecuting at least those minors suspected of having committed the very worst crimes.

The agreed upon solution left open the possibility of their being tried, and built into the Statute a number of safeguards in the event that they would be tried. Article 7 of the Statute provides that the Special Court has jurisdiction over persons who were fifteen years of age or older at the time of the alleged commission of the crime. It allows the Court to prosecute minors if they are judged by the Court to be among those persons who bore the greatest responsibility for alleged crimes, in accordance with Article 1. The judicial safeguards include separate trials from adults, protective measures, and provisional release pending trial.

Article 7(2) stipulates that any juvenile who is tried and found guilty by the Special Court should not be subject to imprisonment. It further provides that the Court may order any of the following as an alternative to imprisonment: "care guidance and supervision orders; community service orders; counseling; foster care; correctional, educational, and vocational training programs; approved schools; and, as appropriate, any programs of disarmament, demobilization, and reintegration or programs of child protection agencies." Moreover, several articles stipulate that judges, prosecutors, investigators, and registry staff shall be experienced in juvenile justice. Article 15 also provides that, in the prosecution of juvenile offenders, the prosecutor shall ensure that the child-rehabilitation programs are not endangered, and that, where appropriate, resort shall be made to the Truth and Reconciliation Commission.

Although the age of criminal responsibility, fifteen years, is considerably less than the eighteen years stipulated in the Statute of the International Criminal Court, criminal responsibility at age fifteen is arguably not contrary to customary international law. The UN Convention on the Rights of the Child (1989) has provisions in respect of the prosecution of children and the legitimate detention of children, but does not specify a minimum age of criminal responsibility—although it stipulates that capital punishment should not be imposed on anyone younger than eighteen years at the time of the alleged offense. In relation to this, the criminal codes of many states allow prosecutions of even very young children. In fact, the age of criminal responsibility under Sierra Leonean law is ten years of age, and persons over seventeen years can be given the death penalty.

Jurisdiction over Subject Matter

The Special Court has subject matter jurisdiction over four categories of crimes: crimes against humanity; violations of Article 3 (of the Statute), which provides for the protection of civilians in wartime (essentially a recapitulation of portions of the 1949 Geneva Conventions and their Additional Protocol II of 1977); other serious violations of international humanitarian law; and crimes under Sierra Leonean law. The last category of crime in particular contributes to the individual character of the Special Court and distinguishes it from the earlier ICTY, ICTR, and ICC, all of which have jurisdiction only over international crimes. Yet all of the provisions that specify the Special Court's subject matter jurisdiction to some degree depart from similar provisions that regulate those other tribunals.

Article 2 of the Statute of the Special Court offers another definition of crimes against humanity, or at least one whose common elements diverge slightly from those of earlier definitions contained in the ICTY, ICTR, and ICC Statutes, as well as the Charter of the Nuremberg Tribunal. Of all the definitions, the one contained in Article 2 of the Statute of the Special Court is the most pared down and essential definition, but at the same time it contains elements of each of the earlier definitions. It provides: "The Special Court shall have the power to prosecute persons who committed the following crimes as part of a widespread or systematic attack against any civilian population: [the list follows]." By contrast, each of the definitions in the ICTY, ICTR, and ICC Statutes required additional common elements, which were added in order to limit the jurisdiction of those particular tribunals. In particular, unlike the statute of the ICTY, the Statute of the Special Court in contrast does not require that crimes against humanity be linked with an armed conflict. As for the specific acts listed in Article 2 of the Statute of the Special Court, most are taken almost verbatim from the Statutes of the ICTY and ICTR. The list is not as comprehensive as that contained in the crimes against humanity provision of the ICC Statute. The most significant variation (from the ICTY and ICTR delineations of crimes against humanity) is found in paragraph (g) of Article 2 of the Statute of the Special Court, which has provisions related to sexual crimes, and which was borrowed from the ICC Statute. Whereas the ICTY and ICTR Statutes simply list "rape" as a crime against humanity, the Statute of the Special Court mentions "rape, sexual slavery, enforced prostitution, forced pregnancy, and any other form of sexual violence." The other crimes designated as crimes against humanity in Article 2 include: murder; extermination; enslavement; deportation; imprisonment; torture; and persecution. The only distinction between this list and analogous lists in the ICTY and ICTR Statutes (excluding the sexual crime distinction) concerns the crime of persecution. Whereas the Statutes of the ad hoc tribunals refer to "persecutions on political, racial, and religious grounds," the Statute of the Special Court adds the designation "ethnic." Proof of malevolent intent is a required element of conviction for the crime of persecution, but not for the other crimes against humanity.

Article 3 of the Special Court Statute, which concerns war crimes committed during internal armed conflicts, is based on the equivalent Article 4 of the ICTR Statute. Article 3 identifies as war crimes: (1) violence to life, health, and physical or mental well-being of persons, in particular murder, as well as cruel treatment such as torture, mutilation, or any form of corporal punishment; (2) collective punishments; (3) the

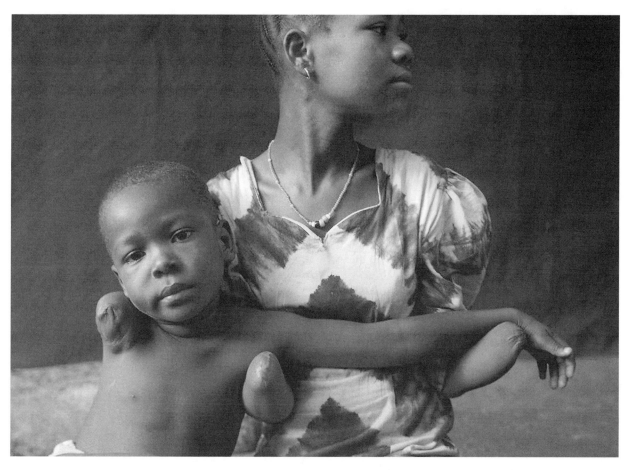

Sierra Leone victims of rebel attacks sit in front of a tent at the Camp for War Wounded and Amputees in Freetown, October 11, 1999.
[AP/WIDE WORLD PHOTOS]

taking of hostages; (4) acts of terrorism; (5) outrages upon personal dignity, in particular humiliating and degrading treatment, rape, enforced prostitution, and any form of indecent assault; (6) pillage; (7) the passing of sentences and the carrying out of executions without previous judgement pronounced by a regularly constituted court, affording all the judicial guarantees which are recognized as indispensable by civilized people; and (8) threats to commit any of the foregoing acts. The list is not exclusive and other war crimes may be prosecuted.

Like the ICTR (but unlike the ICTY and ICC), the Special Court does not have jurisdiction over war crimes committed in international armed conflicts. Although the armed conflict in Sierra Leone was generally a noninternational armed conflict (between the armed forces of Sierra Leone and armed opposition groups), the involvement of non-Sierra Leonean parties has been documented. The opposition groups are known to have received financial and military assistance from Liberia and Guinea. Whether or not that assistance was suffi-

cient to require the reclassification of the conflict is an open legal question.

Article 4 of the Statute of the Special Court deals with other serious violations of international humanitarian law and has no equivalent in the ICTY or ICTR Statutes. It mentions three separate and distinct war crimes, only one of which is concerned with the conduct of hostilities. Its paragraph (a) gives the Special Court the power to prosecute persons for "intentionally directing attacks against the civilian population as such or against individual civilians not taking direct part in hostilities." Paragraph (b) gives the court jurisdiction with respect to the crime of "intentionally directing attacks against personnel, installations, material, units, or vehicles involved in a humanitarian assistance or peacekeeping mission in accordance with the Charter of the United Nations." Finally, paragraph (c) allows the Court to prosecute a crime (mentioned previously) that was common during the conflict in Sierra Leone, that is: "abduction and forced recruitment of children under the age of fifteen years into armed forces or groups for the purpose of using them to participate actively in hostilities." This crime is not mentioned in the ICTY or ICTR Statutes, although it appears in another form in the ICC Statute. Article 5 allows the Special Court to prosecute some crimes under Sierra Leonean law. The crimes are: (1) offenses relating to the abuse of girls, which are prosecuted under the Prevention of Cruelty to Children Act (1926); and (2) offenses relating to the wanton destruction of property, prosecuted under the Malicious Damage Act.

The Special Court lacks jurisdiction over the crime of genocide, in contrast to what is provided in the Statutes of the ICTY, ICTR, and ICC.

The Truth and Reconciliation Commission and Its Relationship to the Special Court

Following the adoption of the Truth and Reconciliation Commission Act on February 22, 2000, Sierra Leone took steps to establish a Truth and Reconciliation Commission (TRC). Although there is no formal relationship between the Special Court and the TRC, and although they are meant to operate completely independently from one another, their roles are designed to be complementary. Whereas the Special Court focuses on prosecuting the most serious perpetrators of offenses related to the Sierra Leonean armed conflict and should only gather information relevant to that purpose, the TRC's role is to provide the bigger picture in relation to the conflict, and to assist in the process of reconciliation. In particular, it gives a voice to the victims, and especially those who cannot appear before the Special Court. This is especially important considering that the Special Court allows victims only a very limited role. The TRC also provides a mechanism for dealing with child soldiers, and for allowing other former combatants to express remorse and ask for forgiveness.

The Commission is composed of seven members, four Sierra Leoneans and three non-nationals. It has a one-year mandate, to be preceded by a preparatory period of three months. The Commission's purpose is clearly set out in Article 6(1) of the Truth and Reconciliation Commission Act:

> The object for which the Commission is established is to create an impartial historical record of violations and abuses of human rights and international humanitarian law related to the armed conflict in Sierra Leone, from the beginning of the conflict in 1991 to the signing of the Lomé Peace Agreement; to address impunity; to respond to the needs of the victims; to promote healing and reconciliation; and to prevent a repetition of the violations and abuses suffered.

What this means in practice is that the Commission's functions are:

> (a) to investigate and report on the causes, nature, and extent of the violations and abuses . . . to the fullest degree possible, including their antecedents, the context in which the violations and abuses occurred, the question of whether those violations and abuses were the result of deliberate planning, policy, or authorization by any government, group, or individual, and the role of both internal and external factors in the conflict; and (b) to work to restore the human dignity of victims and promote reconciliation by providing an opportunity for victims to give an account of the violations and abuses suffered and for perpetrators to relate their experiences, and by creating a climate which fosters constructive interchange between victims and perpetrators, giving special attention to the subject of sexual abuse, and to the experiences of children within the armed conflict.

The Commission is instructed to carry out its work by means of undertaking research and investigations; holding sessions (some of which are public); listening to the stories of victims, perpetrators, and other interested parties; and taking individual statements and gathering additional information. It is to submit a report to the president at the end of its work. The TRC was formally inaugurated on July 5, 2002, began taking statements from victims and witnesses in December 2002, and is expected to complete its work sometime in 2004.

SEE ALSO International Criminal Court; International Criminal Tribunal for Rwanda; International Criminal Tribunal for the Former Yugoslavia; National Prosecutions; War Crimes

BIBLIOGRAPHY

Cryer, Robert (2001). "A Special Court for Sierra Leone?" *International and Comparative Law Quarterly* 50:443.

Frulli, Micaela (2000). "The Special Court for Sierra Leone: Some Preliminary Comments." *European Journal of International Law* 11:859.

McDonald, Avril (2000). "The Amnesties in the Lomé Peace Agreement and the UN's Dilemma." *Humanitäres Völkerrecht* 1:11.

McDonald, Avril (2002). "Sierra Leone's Shoestring Special Court." *International Review of the Red Cross* 84:121.

National Commission for Democracy and Human Rights Sierra Leone (2001). *The TRC at a Glance*. Series No. 7.

Statute of the Special Court for Sierra Leone and the Agreement between the United Nations and the Government of Sierra Leone. Available from http://www.icrc.org/ihl.nsf/WebFULL?OpenView&Start=98.

Truth and Reconciliation Commission Act (2000). Sierra Leone Gazette CXXXI (9), supplement. Also available from http://www.sierra-leone.org/trcbook-TRCAct.html.

United Nations (2000). *Letter Dated 22 December 2000 from the President of the Security Council Addressed to the Secretary-General.* UN Document S/2000/1234.

United Nations (2000). *Report on the Establishment of a Special Court for Sierra Leone.* UN Document S/2000/915.

United Nations (2001). *Letter Dated 12 January 2001 from the Secretary-General to the President of the Security Council.* UN Document S/2001/40.

United Nations (2001). *Letter Dated 31 January 2001 from the President of the Security Council Addressed to the Secretary-General.* UN Document S/2001/95.

United Nations Mission in Sierra Leone. "Truth and Reconciliation in Sierra Leone." Available from http://www.sierra-leone.org/trcbook-contents.html.

UN News Center (2002). "Sierra Leone: UN, Government Sign Historic Accord to Set Up Special War Crimes Court."

Avril McDonald

Slavery, Historical

The growing concern with achieving freedom and social equality focuses attention on the inequity of slavery in the past, and poses continuing questions. Was large-scale slavery a necessary and inevitable stage of human development? Or was it an accident of history that might have been avoided? What is the nature and extent of slavery's legacy?

Slavery before Modern Times

Slavery existed in most societies for which we have historical records, but became extensive only where there were strong states or systems of commerce, and not in all of these. Of the populous regions of the pre-modern world, one belt of territories saw a particular development of slavery: the lands adjoining the Mediterranean, the Black Sea, and the Persian Gulf. From the time of the Babylonians through the classical era of the Greeks and Romans, the medieval societies of Muslims and Christians, and the rise of the Ottoman Empire, slavery waxed and waned with greater intensity in this region than elsewhere.

Captives were drawn from the region's peripheries: from the Nile Valley, the Caucasus, Slavic populations, and others. While the occupations of male slaves ranged widely—including miners, galley slaves, and soldiers—most slaves were female, working as domestics. In medieval times, the cultivation of sugar spread from the eastern Mediterranean to the west, with much of the work done by slaves. In time, the cultivation of sugar spread to islands of the Atlantic, and eventually to the Americas.

Distinctiveness of Modern African Slavery

The capture and enslavement of Africans by fifteenth-century Portuguese voyagers was initially little different from earlier Mediterranean slavery, of which it formed a small portion. By the late seventeenth century, however, the transatlantic shipment of African captives exceeded all the rest of slave trade, and the majority of the world's slaves were located in the Americas.

From then until the twentieth century, what distinguished African enslavement by Europeans from earlier systems of slavery was its magnitude, its incidence primarily on Africans, the development of racial categories, and the imposition of racialized social inferiority on Africans. Transatlantic slavery stimulated a more widespread system of slavery during the eighteenth and nineteenth centuries, including the expansion of slavery in Africa and the rise of slavery on all the shores of the Indian Ocean.

Rise and Fall of Atlantic Slavery and Slave Trade

The Atlantic slave trade began with the fifteenth-century capture of Africans who were sent to work in Iberian farms and households and who became laborers on sugar plantations from São Thomé to Madeira and the Canaries. With the discovery of the Americas, Africans were taken first to the Caribbean, then to the centers of Spanish colonies in Mexico and Peru. Portuguese settlers in Brazil relied first on enslaved Amerindians for labor, but in the late sixteenth century began sending slaves from West and Central Africa to Brazil. Slaves in this era came mainly from Senegambia, Upper Guinea, Congo, and Angola, with the total of slave cargoes ranging from 1,000 to 4,000 per year.

Early in the seventeenth century, the emerging Dutch Republic set a plan of displacing the Portuguese from the Atlantic, and began seizing Portuguese slave entrepôts in Africa and plantations in Brazil. Once Portuguese resistance had largely repulsed the attacks by 1650, the Dutch turned to using their new African and Caribbean bases for introducing the system of sugar plantations to the Caribbean. The English and French joined them in expanding Caribbean and continental American slavery. From this time forth, the Atlantic slave trade exceeded the trans-Saharan trade in volume.

European purchasers of captives set up diplomatic and commercial relations with African leaders. Wherever warfare emerged, purchasers appeared to buy captives. As the slave trade continued from generation to generation, regular systems of supply developed. These ensured the transport and nutrition of captives in Africa, the paying of duties and fees to authorities along the trade routes, the sale and loading of captives aboard ship, and the Middle Passage of several weeks at sea.

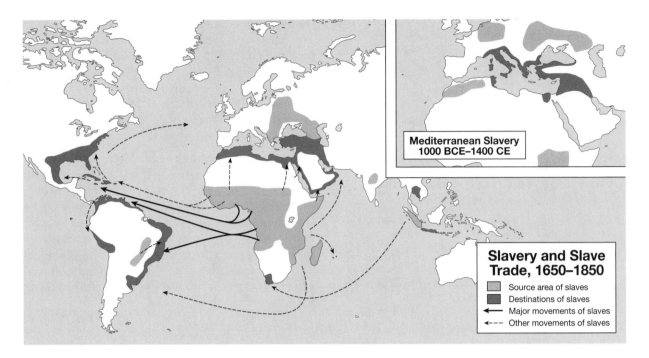

Map showing historical slavery routes across globe. [MAP BY XNR PRODUCTIONS. THE GALE GROUP.]

Once in the Americas, captives underwent seasoning and socialization, further transport to their final destination, and assignment to their work.

With the turn of the eighteenth century, the demand for slaves rose rapidly. In the period from 1790 to 1830, the volume of slave exports nearly doubled and the prices of slaves purchased in Africa rose by a factor of four or more. The processes of enslavement included warfare (notably in the Gold Coast and Bight of Benin), raids (especially in the upper Niger Valley), kidnapping (in the Bight of Biafra), and enslavement through judicial process (in the Bight of Biafra and Angola). The West African ports of Ouidah and Bonny and the Central African ports of Luanda and Loango accounted for about two thirds of all slave exports, but slave merchants bargained for portions of their cargoes at almost every port along the African littoral. In contrast to the West African system of slave trade, in which Europeans remained offshore or in small coastal enclaves, in Angola the Portuguese controlled a sizable colony. There Portuguese officials and their allies oversaw the conduct of warfare and the collection and dispatch of captives to Brazil, in the largest segment of the eighteenth-century Atlantic trade. The Bight of Benin was the most intensively harvested region, followed by the Bight of Biafra and Central Africa, but every region adjoining the western coast of Africa suffered significant disruption. Slave cargoes rose to a peak of some 60,000 per year transported across the Atlantic in the 1790s. The eighteenth-century Atlantic slave trade comprised the largest-ever human migration, to that point.

The nineteenth-century Atlantic slave trade was contested. It became illegal for British and Americans from 1808, but substantial shipments to Brazil and Cuba continued up to 1850. These shipments drew especially from the port of Luanda in Central Africa, but also from Lagos in the Bight of Benin. Meanwhile, as the Atlantic slave trade reached its peak and then began to decline, expanding demand caused slave shipments across the Sahara, the Red Sea, and the Indian Ocean to rise in the late eighteenth century and to continue until the end of the nineteenth century.

From the sixteenth through the nineteenth centuries, some eleven million captives were dispatched from the western coast of Africa across the Atlantic, another five million were sent across the Sahara and the Red Sea, and two million were carried off from the eastern coast of Africa in the nineteenth century. Somewhere between five and ten million inhabitants of sub-Saharan Africa lived in slave status at the end of the nineteenth century.

Modern Slavery to 1880: Causes and Effects
The demand for labor by European-based colonizers in the Americas was the single greatest cause for this system of slavery. Yet this demand, to be effective, required the concomitant supply of laborers who could be purchased at a sufficiently low price because they

N. B. FOREST,
DEALER IN SLAVES,
No. 87 Adams-st, Memphis, Ten.,

HAS just received from North Carolina, twenty-five likely young negroes, to which he desires to call the attention of purchasers. He will be in the regular receipt of negroes from North and South Carolina every month. His Negro Depot is one of the most complete and commodious establishments of the kind in the Southern country, and his regulations exact and systematic, cleanliness, neatness and comfort being strictly observed and enforced. His aim is to furnish to customers A. 1 servants 'and field hands, sound and perfect in body and mind. Negroes taken on commission.   jan21

Nineteenth-century public notice advertising slaves for sale. [BETTMANN/CORBIS]

had been stolen, and perhaps because the productivity of African hoe agriculture was lower than that of European plow agriculture. The wealth generated in the Americas and the political disarray fomented in Africa by enslavement each served to reinforce the system. Ideologies of racial hierarchy grew up to rationalize this thriving but exploitative system, based on Christian doctrines of God's will and the curse of Ham or on secular doctrines of natural law and evolutionary hierarchy. The growth of the system and rebelliousness of the enslaved led to increasing violence from the masters. Although prejudice against foreigners existed in many societies, the history of the Atlantic slave trade shows that explicit racial discrimination was a result rather than a cause of the expansion of slavery.

Global effects of slavery and the slave trade included the creation of the African diaspora, that dispersal of persons of African origin all around the Atlantic, with smaller numbers as well at the shores of the Mediterranean and Indian Ocean. Slavery brought the development of racist practice and ultimately of its formulation in scientific terms. In response, however, slavery brought religious and secular movements for liberation

and a movement for emancipation that went beyond slavery itself to address oppression by gender, nation, and religion.

In Africa, the effects of slavery were pervasive. Slavery expanded throughout Africa in association with the export slave trade. The population of West and Central Africa declined in the eighteenth and nineteenth centuries, and the population of East Africa declined in the nineteenth century in response to the captures and mortality of the slave trade. European conquests in Africa after 1880 brought an end to slave raiding, but generally did not bring emancipation to slaves until the passage of two or three decades.

The societies of the Americas all became racialized in one form or another. The Caribbean became dominantly African in ancestry, but with a hierarchy of color gradations. Brazil brought in nearly as many Africans as the Caribbean and became a racialized society, with overlapping subgroups. Racialization in the United States took the form of sharp white-black distinctions. Former Spanish territories of the mainland have significant African heritage, but this heritage has been minimized with time through the expansion of the category

Mestizo. Africans on the continent lived under racialized colonial rule for much of the twentieth century. Meanwhile, communities of African ancestry subsisted throughout the Mediterranean and Indian Ocean regions.

Heritage of Slavery since 1880
The end of slavery as a major social institution was a slow process. The major episodes of legal emancipation or gradual manumission of slaves took place across a century and a half. Slaves gained freedom in Haiti in the 1790s, in former Spanish America from the 1820s, in British territories in 1838, in French territories in 1848, in the southern United States in 1865, in Brazil in 1888—and the final absorption of millions of African slaves into other categories of subordination took place in the 1920s and 1930s.

Nonetheless, from the mid-nineteenth century, post-emancipation societies emerged in region after region as the slave trade and then slavery ended. The heritage of slavery in post-emancipation societies included the efforts of ex-slaves to achieve full social equality: reuniting and creating families, schooling at both basic and advanced levels, gaining entry to new occupations, and emphasizing development of a public culture, especially in the arts. Yet the moves of freed persons to advance themselves met with the elaboration of new ideologies and techniques to maintain the subordination of former slaves. Scientific racism, articulated progressively throughout the nineteenth century, was followed by social movements of racial discrimination and segregation at the turn of the twentieth century. Segregation and lynching in the American South were paralleled by occupational hierarchies elsewhere in the Americas and by residential segregation and colonial hierarchies in Africa. In the same era and through analogous rationale, anti-Jewish sentiment became reformulated in racial terms, and grew to its peak.

In the post–World War II era of civil rights, decolonization, and response to the Holocaust, slavery itself seemed clearly a thing of the past, yet the heritage of slavery continued to be debated. In the 1980s and 1990s some public figures began to use the terms *genocide* and *Holocaust* to refer to the Atlantic slave trade and its impact. While this use of these terms died down after some debate, the call for defining and assessing reparations for the inequities of the slave trade gained a more permanent place in the discussion of the heritage of slavery. In this and other ways, the heritage of slavery brings a continual concern with the meaning of this past of oppression.

SEE ALSO France in Tropical Africa; King Leopold II and the Congo; Slavery, Legal Aspects of

BIBLIOGRAPHY
Finley, Moses I. (1998). *Ancient Slavery and Modern Ideology*, ed. Brent D. Shaw. Princeton: Markus Wiener Publishers.
Klein, Herbert S. *African Slavery in Latin America and the Caribbean*. New York: Oxford University Press, (1986).
Lewis, Bernard. *Race and Slavery in the Middle East: An Historical Enquiry*. New York: Oxford University Press, 1990.
Lovejoy, Paul E., and Jan. S. Hogendorn. *Slow Death for Slavery: The Course of Abolition in Northern Nigeria, 1897–1936*. Cambridge: Cambridge University Press, 1993.
Manning, Patrick. *Slavery and African Life: Occidental, Oriental, and African Slave Trades*. Cambridge: Cambridge University Press, 1990.

Patrick Manning

Slavery, Legal Aspects of

Slavery's evolution from an accepted worldwide practice to its present status as an international crime, took place over the course of only a century and a half—from about the beginning of the nineteenth century to the middle of the twentieth century. Slavery has existed since ancient times, dating back to at least the times of the Old Testament. The practice was deeply engrained in ancient Rome, Greece, and the cultures of the ancient near east. The Bible contains numerous references to the practice of slavery, and Roman law had elaborate statutes and precedents for the regulation of slaves. Well before the Europeans went to the New World, there was an elaborate slave trade between the Baltic and Mediterranean regions, and slavery was legal almost everywhere in medieval and early modern Europe. Throughout the Islamic world, slavery was a fixture of society. Long before Europeans went to Africa or the New World, Arab traders were crossing the Sahara to bring slaves from south of the desert for sale in the Arab world. Some of these African slaves eventually ended up in Sardinia, Sicily, and southern Europe.

Direct European involvement in the African slave trade to Europe began in 1434, when the Portuguese began transporting Africans to Portugal for labor. The practice was institutionalized in Europe by the sixteenth century. For the next two centuries, slavery and slave-trading in Africa were not only permitted by Western governments, but were actively protected and encouraged as a lucrative branch of international commerce. During the seventeenth and eighteenth centuries, slavery was considered legal under the law of nations if not the laws of nature. In 1772, in the case of *Somerset v. Stewart,* Lord Mansfield of the King's Bench stated that in England

> [t]he state of slavery is of such a nature, that it is incapable of being introduced on any reasons,

moral or political; but only positive law, which preserves its force long after the reasons, occasion, and time itself from whence it was created, is erased from memory: It's so odious, that nothing can be suffered to support it but positive law.

But this attitude did not hold true for the American colonies. Nor was it the dominant philosophy in the many European nations, including Holland, Spain, France, and Portugal, that inherited a Roman legal tradition that included slavery.

Slave Laws in the New World

At the beginning of the American Revolution slavery was legal everywhere in the New World, and every Old World country involved in colonization accepted the legitimacy of the practice. England and France had some case law, such as *Somerset*, that undermined slavery in the home country, but neither of them found anything wrong with permitting slavery to continue in their colonies, nor did they interfere with the African slave trade.

During the Revolution, all of the new American states banned the African slave trade, basing their decision, in part, on economic necessity. After the war, the states continued the ban for a combination of reasons, including economics, prudence (the fear of newly imported Africans), and humanitarian concerns. Between 1780 and 1804, all the New England states, as well as Pennsylvania, New York, and New Jersey, either ended slavery outright, or passed gradual emancipation acts. With gradual emancipation, the children of all slave mothers would be born free, and thus it was expected that slavery would literally die out.

The result of these laws was that, in one section of the nation, slavery was either completely illegal, or legal only for a small and diminishing class of existing slaves. The U.S. Constitution nevertheless continued to recognized slavery in a variety of ways, and it remained an ongoing practice in much of the new nation. Until the Civil War, the Supreme Court consistently protected the rights of slave masters to their property. Although some northern state courts held that slavery was contrary to natural law and state law, at no time in this period did the American federal courts find that slavery was illegal under either domestic law or international law.

Banning the Slave Trade

In 1807 and 1808 the governments of Great Britain and the United States banned the African slave trade and declared all who continued to practice it to be pirates. This piracy, however, was limited to those who violated British and American law by attempting to sell their slaves in U.S. or American markets. If the slaves were destined for countries where the practice was legal, both U.S. and British courts upheld its legality. Thus, for example, in the famous 1841 case of *The Amistad*, the U.S. Supreme Court freed a group of Africans who had been illegally imported to Cuba, because their importation violated international treaties and agreements. However, had the slaves on *The Amistad* been legally held as slaves in Cuba, the U.S. Supreme Court would have been prepared to return them to Cuba.

Illustrative of this is the case of *The Antelope* (1825), which involved a Spanish ship seized by pirates and eventually taken into a U.S. port by the American Navy. Chief Justice John Marshall ordered that some of the slaves on that unlucky ship be returned to the Spanish government, because their slave status was legally recognized under Spanish law. Others on board the ship, however, were deemed to be free, because they had been illegally taken from Africa. The court ordered that lots be drawn to determine which of the 280 Africans on the ship would be considered slaves, and which would become free. In reaching this result, Chief Justice Marshall noted that the African slave trade was "contrary to the law of nature" but that it was "consistent with the law of nations" and "cannot in itself be piracy." This analysis led Marshall to uphold the right of foreigners to engage in the slave trade, if their own nations allowed them to do so. Marshall wrote: "It if be neither repugnant to the law of nations, nor piracy, it is almost superfluous to say in this Court, that the right of bringing in for adjudication in time of peace, even where the vessel belongs to a nation which has prohibited the trade, cannot exist."

Indeed, throughout the first half of the nineteenth century, Anglo-American judges and diplomats resisted finding that slavery and the slave trade were against the laws of nations or international law. Meanwhile, most of the nations of Western Europe banned the trade for their nationals and in their colonies, and prohibited their ships to engage in the trade. In 1792, Denmark declared that the slave trade would be illegal as of 1803. The United States and Great Britain followed suit in 1807, as did France in 1815. Britain freed all slaves within its jurisdiction in 1833. At the same time, many of the European peace treaties contained statements condemning the slave trade as repugnant to the principles of justice and humanity, and called upon each other for its eradication. In 1815 the Declaration at the Congress of Vienna declared:

The commerce, known by the name of Slave Trade (*Traite des Nègres d'Afrique*) has been considered, by just and enlightened men in all ages, as repugnant to the principles of humanity and universal morality; . . . [so that] . . . at length the public voice, in all civilized countries, calls aloud for its prompt suppression . . . [and] several European Governments have virtually come to the resolution of putting a stop to it.

However, none of these treaties contained concrete measures for stopping the slave trade. Nations did not consider the transport of slaves on the high seas a violation of the law of nations that justified encroaching upon another nation's sovereignty. Under the doctrine of state sovereignty, a nation had the right to adhere to its own laws within its own borders and on ships flying its flag. Thus, nations did not have the right to stop and search another nation's vessels on the high seas. The one recognized exception to this rule was for acts committed on the high seas that were condemned as acts of piracy and thus outlawed by the law of nations. In those cases, every nation had the right to punish certain offenses committed onboard ships, regardless of the flag under which the offending ship sailed. By declaring that slavery was not a crime against the law of nations, the offense did not meet the criteria for this exception, however.

As late as 1928, James Brierly, the British publicist, wrote that it was a rule of law of the sea, as established by nineteenth century slave trading cases, that the jurisdiction of each nation was limited to its own ships and nationals. Although he recognized the exceptions of "hot pursuit" and piracy, slavery and slave trading were still not included in either exception. However, in the early nineteenth century, Britain entered into a series of bilateral agreements with Portugal, France, the Netherlands, Spain, Brazil, Haiti, Uruguay, Venezuela, Ecuador, Bolivia, Chile, the Persian Gulf states, Mexico, Texas, and Sweden. According to these agreements, the signatories declared the slave trade to be an act of piracy and thus granted each other the right to search or visit ships flying the other's flag, if those ships were suspected of transporting slaves.

In 1841 Austria, Great Britain, Prussia, Russia, and France signed the Treaty for the Suppression of the African Slave Trade, commonly known as the Treaty of London. This was the first multilateral treaty to proclaim the trade in slaves an act of piracy. It provided that each party had the power to stop merchant ships flying the others' flags in prescribed zones, but was weakened by the fact that France never ratified it. In 1862, after the outbreak of the U.S. Civil War, the United States and Great Britain signed a new Treaty for Suppression of African Slave Trade, commonly known as the Treaty of Washington. This was the first time the United States granted another nation the right to board

and search any of its ships if they were suspected of engaging in the slave trade, albeit such searches could be undertaken only in a narrowly prescribed zone. The treaty provided for the special courts made up of equal numbers of individuals from each nation, with one established in Sierra Leone, one at the Cape of Good Hope, and one in New York. However, these courts only functioned until 1870, when they were replaced by the more traditional trial process carried out by the nation to whom the captured ship belonged.

By the end of the nineteenth century, the market for African slaves in the United States and Europe was nonexistent, but continued to flourish in Africa and the Middle East. Toward the end of the century, many European nations sought to not only prevent the importation of slaves into their own countries, but into other nations as well. The General Act of the Conference at Berlin Respecting the Congo, February 26, 1885, was the first multilateral trade agreement to address this traffic. The act provided that the entire Congo Basin, that region of Africa from the Atlantic to the Indian Ocean, would be an area of free trade without import duties. It also provided that, within this region, "trading in slaves is forbidden in conformity with the principles of international law as recognized by the signatory powers," but contained no enforcement provisions.

In 1889 representatives from seventeen countries met at a conference in Brussels with the goal of finally putting an end to the slave trade and the crimes it engendered. The comprehensive General Act for the Repression of the African Slave Trade, July 2, 1890, commonly known as the Brussels Act, contained several articles obligating the parties to undertake economic, legislative, and military measures towards the eradication of slavery in Africa. It provided for the establishment of military stations in the interior of Africa to prevent the capture of slaves, to provide for the interception of caravans, and to organize expeditions. It also contained a comprehensive system to eradicate the slave trade at sea. The act applied to a maritime zone that included the Red Sea and the Indian Ocean, where most of the slave trading was taking place. There were rules concerning the use of signatories' flags by "native" vessels, the embarkation of African passengers, and stopping and examining ships believed to be engaged in the slave trade. The officer in command could stop any ship under 500 tons that was operating within the prescribed zone. He could board the ship and examine the list of passengers and crew. However, cargo could be searched only on those ships flying the flag of a signatory to the treaty. If the investigating officer believed that the ship was engaged in the slave trade, he had the right to bring it to the nearest port of the nation whose flag the ship was flying. The act outlined rules for the trial of the seized ship. This act was still in force at the outbreak of World War I.

Efforts to Eliminate Slavery

At the end of World War I, a new convention was achieved between nations with the goal of revising earlier treaties and newly addressing the elimination of slavery. This formal title of this new agreement was the Convention Revising the General Act of Berlin of February 26, 1885, and the General Act and Declaration of Brussels, July 2, 1890. It is more familiarly known as the St. Germain-en-Laye Convention, and it was signed on September 10, 1919, by Belgium, Great Britain, France, Italy, Japan, Portugal, and the United States. It was subsequently ratified by all the other signatories to the Treaty of Versailles as well. The general purpose of the convention was to restore the previous system of free trade within a prescribed zone in Africa, as well as the Indian Ocean and Red Sea regions. With regard to slavery and slave trading, the parties merely agreed to "endeavor to secure the complete suppression of slavery in all its forms, and of the slave trade by land and sea." The right to stop and search vessels on the high seas, a feature of both the older treaties, no longer existed.

Following World War I, slavery was one of the first issues addressed by the League of Nations. In 1924, it established a Temporary Slavery Commission charged with studying the existence of slavery throughout the world. The commission reported that the status of slavery was recognized in Abyssinia (Ethiopia), Tibet, Nepal, and most "Mohammedan States," including Afghanistan, the Hedjaz, and other Arab nations. It reported that slave trading was openly practiced in the Arabian Peninsula, and that most of the slaves were originally from African territories. The study led the League to adopt the Slavery Convention of September 25, 1926, which was immediately signed by twenty-five League of Nations members. The convention entered into force on March 9, 1927, but remained open for signature until April of that year, by which time eleven more members had signed.

The Slavery Convention was the first time international legislation sought the abolition of slavery and the slave trade. It defined slavery as the "status or condition of a person over whom any or all of the powers attaching to the right of ownership are exercised." The slave trade was defined to include all acts involved in the capture, acquisition, or disposal of a person with the intent to reduce him or her to slavery; all acts involved in the acquisition slaves with a view to selling or exchanging them; all acts of disposal by sale or exchange

of a slave acquired with a view to being sold or exchanged and, in general, every act of trade or transport in slaves. Due to disagreements over whether forced labor was analogous to slavery, the provisions regarding the two institutions were treated separately. Article 5b of the convention stated, "compulsory or forced labor may only be exacted for public purposes," and sought to prevent forced labor from "developing into conditions analogous to slavery."

The signatories agreed to prevent and suppress the slave trade, and to work progressively towards the complete abolition of slavery within their jurisdictions. The word "progressively" was inserted because many nations were concerned about the hardships and social upheavals that would be created if all slaves were suddenly liberated. The convention did not outlaw slave trading as an act of piracy. Instead, it provided that each nation would take appropriate measures to prevent the embarkation, disembarkation, and transport of slaves within their territorial waters and upon vessels flying their respective flags. Its signatories also agreed to promulgate a convention providing for rights to stop and search vessels suspected of slave trading outside of their territorial waters, as provided in the Convention on Supervision of International Trade in Arms and Ammunition and in Implements of War of June 17, 1925. However, such an agreement was never promulgated. The only enforcement provisions in the convention were that each signatory would forward to the League of Nations the laws and regulations they enacted pursuant to the convention, and that each nation had the right to bring any dispute regarding implementation of the convention to the Permanent Court of International Justice.

As of 1937, only twenty-nine nations had ratified the Slavery Convention and were therefore affirmatively bound by its terms. The United Nations adopted the convention in 1953, and adopted a Supplementary Convention on the Abolition of Slavery, The Slave Trade, and Institutions and Practices Similar to Slavery in 1956. The Supplementary Convention, which remains in force, applies the Slavery Convention to debt bondage, serfdom, the sale of women, and child labor practices.

Slavery and Human Rights

Freedom from enslavement did not become a fundamental human right solely as a result of states ratifying and acceding to the Slavery Convention. The convention is not framed in terms of preserving a fundamental right. Instead, it outlines the duties of nations to eradicate slavery and the slave trade without declaring that every human being has the right to be free from enslavement. In fact, the signatories to the Convention did not even agree to completely eradicate slavery; they only agreed to "progressively work for its abolition." However, the League of Nations did establish first a temporary and later a permanent Advisory Committee of Experts on Slavery, which was authorized to receive, organize, and publish information furnished by the signatories to the convention, and to make recommendations regarding the eradication of slavery in particular nations. The committee was formed to study possible means of eradicating slavery and to examine the feasibility for the League of Nations to provide financial assistance to nations needing help in solving their slavery problems. It was specifically not intended to deal with forced labor. Its proceedings were confidential, and it could communicate its findings only through governments. It could not communicate directly with non-governmental persons or organizations. By 1937 the committee reported that the League of Nations had been largely successful in eliminating the traffic in slaves by encouraging members to outlaw slavery within territories under their control. However, it found it more difficult to convince independent members and nonmembers to follow suit. At the outbreak of World War II, slavery continued to be practiced in some form in Liberia, Ethiopia, and parts of the Middle East.

In the early twenty-first century, the world continues to grapple with slavery and abuses resembling slavery. In the United States, sexual and labor exploitation are often considered forms of slavery and are outlawed. Nevertheless, tens of thousands of people are held against their will in the United States. Slavery is not a crime in some European Nations. However, trafficking in human begins as defined by the European Union law is firmly established as a crime and a violation of human rights. Moreover, every general international human rights instrument proclaims the right of every person to be free from slavery and slavelike practices: the Universal Declaration of Human Rights (art. 4), the International Covenant on Civil and Political Rights (art. 8), the European Convention on Human Rights (art. 4), the American Convention on Human Rights (art. 6) and the African Charter on Human and Peoples' Rights (art. 5). Most recently, the Rome Statute of the International Criminal Court included slavery as a crime against humanity (art. 7) and when committed during war time, declared it to be a war crime (art. 8).

SEE ALSO African Americans; Rosewood; Slavery, Historical

BIBLIOGRAPHY

DuBois, W. E. B. (1898). *The Suppression of the African Slave Trade to the United States, 1638–1870.* Cambridge, Mass.: Harvard University Press.

Finkelman, Paul (2001). *Slavery and the Founders: Race and Liberty in the Age of Jefferson,* 2nd edition. Armonk, N.Y.: M.E. Sharpe.

Miers, Suzanne (2003). *Slavery in the Twentieth Century: The Evolution of a Global Problem.* Walnut Creek, Calif.: AltaMira Press.

Morris, Thomas D. (1996). *Southern Slavery and the Law, 1619–1860.* Chapel Hill: University of North Carolina Press.

Noonan, John T., Jr. (1977). *The Antelope: The Ordeal of the Recaptured Africans in the Administrations of James Monroe and John Quincy Adams.* Berkeley: University of California Press.

Redman, Renee C. (1994). "The League of Nations and the Right to be Free from Enslavement: The First Human Right to be Recognized as Customary International Law." *Chicago-Kent Law Review* 70:759–802.

Watson, Alan (1989). *Slave Law in the Americas.* Athens: University of Georgia Press.

                                    Renee C. Redman
                                    Paul Finkelman

Social Darwinism

Social Darwinism can be defined either strictly, with reference to theories of social and cultural change implied by the theory of natural selection developed by Darwin, or loosely, as that distinct family of historical theories that claim to be theories of social and cultural change logically entailed by Darwinian theory. Historical social Darwinism, which emerged in the late nineteenth century and continues in some forms today, exploited ambiguities in Darwinian concepts such as struggle and development in advancing social theories that defended ethnic, racial, class, and gender inequality as necessary aspects of a wider conflict from which a technically and morally advanced humanity would emerge. It mattered little to social Darwinists like Herbert Spencer and William Graham Sumner that Darwin himself used the phrase "struggle for survival" metaphorically to describe all that organisms do in order to reproduce successfully. He utilized terms such as development and evolution in ways that resisted the imputation of progress or improvement. Nevertheless, in the United States, social Darwinist theories and an associated eugenics movement grew steadily in the deteriorating racial environment that characterized the final decades of the 1800s and the early 1900s.

The meaning of Darwin for social theory has been a matter of controversy from its earliest days, as can be seen in the debates between figures like Thomas Huxley and Peter Kropotkin. Huxley argued that biology implied a Hobbesian, atomistic conception of individuals in society. Kropotkin posited to the contrary—the central implication of Darwinism was that sociality, trust, and mutual aid are the sustaining characteristics of humankind's behavioral repertoire. One can easily find in such controversy the echoes of previous lasting debates in Western political and social theory. Nonetheless, feeding off justifications for conquest that long predated Darwin, social Darwinists claimed to extend Darwin's theories into the realm of politics and society, as if such issues had been settled. In the early twenty-first century, however, no reputable school of evolutionary biology or psychology maintains that a theory of social Darwinism in the strict sense would endorse the conclusions of historical social Darwinism, especially its tendency to rationalize conflict and conquest. It is not too much to say as a historical matter that social Darwinism was neither Darwinist, nor particularly social. Its point was never to promote scientific discussion of the complex implications natural selection offers in providing resources for social and political thought. Instead, it has tended merely to use Darwinism as a rationale for existing forms of exploitation and their extension, especially but not exclusively in support of racism and genocide.

The list of atrocities defended on supposedly Darwinian grounds might fill several pages. Social Darwinist theories have been invoked in the United States in support of everything from laissez faire policies of tariff and trade to African slavery and genocide against the indigenous inhabitants of the Americas. Richard Hofstadter has suggested that such rationalizations have been effective in the United States in part because of the fatalism and scientism they promote. By teaching children that other lifestyles are destined to vanish, atrocity is rendered palatable and elevated from obvious injustice to high historical tragedy. This scientization of history at the center of social Darwinism is most obvious in the eugenics movement, which was much more popular in the United States in the early 1900s than in Germany. A line connects interpreters of Spencer, like the sociologist Ludwig Gumplowicz (1838-1909), with the rise of Anglo-Saxonism in the United States and the global eugenics movement. Nazi eugenics drew on an already well-established and well-rooted phenomena. But social Darwinism and similar theories have reportedly been used by apologists to defend genocidal Japanese actions in China, Italian actions in in Ethiopia, and Australian policies toward Native peoples.

SEE ALSO Eugenics; Racism

BIBLIOGRAPHY
Friedlander, Henry (1997). *The Origins of Nazi Genocide: From Euthanasia to the Final Solution.* Chapel Hill: University of North Carolina Press.
Gould, Stephen Jay (1980). *Ever since Darwin.* New York: Penguin.
Hofstadter, Richard (1964). *Social Darwinism in American Thought,* revised edition. Boston: Beacon Press.
Singer, Peter (2000). *A Darwinian Left: Politics, Evolution, and Cooperation.* New Haven, Conn.: Yale University Press.

Peter Amato

Sociology of Perpetrators

There are many approaches that sociology can take in the explanation of genocide; in fact, every field of sociology may contribute, from the study of social deviance (of Nazi leaders, e.g.) to the sociology of knowledge (how knowledge is gained and promulgated, and how definitions and explanations are socially structured and defined).

Sociology has been underutilized in the study of genocide; its many perspectives could add significantly to the field. A standard textbook such as *Sociology in Our Times* by Diana Kendall (2000) reveals how sociology can contribute:

- The social structure and interaction of everyday life during genocide;
- The racial, class, and stratification systems of genocide;
- The impact of genocide on families and kinship patterns;
- The relationship and impact of education and religion on genocide;
- The diverse cultural reactions to genocide and mass killings;
- The politics and economic impact of genocide;
- Health and medical aspects of genocide;
- Population, migration, and refugees after genocide;
- Social change, technology, and social movements.

Sociological Applications

The first dilemma studies of genocide have had to address involves definition, application, and intention, that is, questions related to the sociology of knowledge. Jack Nusan Porter posed these questions more than twenty years ago when he suggested that genocide had been applied to all of the following: race-mixing, drug distribution, methadone programs, birth control, abortions, the medical treatment of Catholics in Northern

Ireland, the closing of synagogues in the former Soviet Union, and the treatment of Palestinians under Israeli occupation. All have been labeled as forms of genocide. In other words, when one needs a catchall phrase to describe oppression or mistreatment, the more electric term *genocide* is often invoked in order to gain media attention and international political intervention.

A second area to which sociology can contribute is in defining the social, structural, and ideological components of genocide. Again, Porter has described a three-point triangulation of racist ideology, technology, and state bureaucracy as major elements. These elements range from sophisticated to crude, but all are vital to any process of genocide.

A third sociological perspective is a predictive one. What are the social conditions that increase the likelihood of genocide, and conversely, what are the conditions that make genocide less likely and lead to peaceful societies?

Furthermore, at what point does genocide occur? There are three distinct times. One is during wartime conditions. Another is during colonialization and decolonialization, that is, when a society is conquered and subdued, or later when it vanquishes a colonizer. Both periods are problematic for minorities. Both instances pose extreme danger. And finally, during tribal, ethnic, and racial conflicts, such as those that occurred in Kosova, Burundi, and Rwanda.

Comparative Sociological Approaches

Sociology's comparative approach is quite valuable in conjunction with political, historical, and economic perspectives in widening human understanding of genocide. Comparative analysis does not diminish the uniqueness of any one genocide, but instead recognizes the basic commonalities of all genocides and genocidal acts, namely that people at various times in history and throughout various parts of the world, regardless of race, religion, or national origin, behave quite similarly when confronted with genocide. If and when there is an exception, it may prove the rule, as the saying goes, and it should prompt further investigation.

Most research has focused on a two-case analysis, usually the Holocaust and another, such as the genocide of Armenians or Native Americans. The best and earliest examples appear in the work of Vahakn Dadrian (1974), who analyzed the common features of Armenian and Jewish genocides from a victimological perspective, and Helen Fein (1978), who compared the Turkish genocide of 1915 to the German Holocaust that occurred from 1939 to 1945. Some areas require more in-depth analysis, in particular:

- Stigma, that is, the methods by which victims are demonized and placed outside the realm of the moral universe, to use Fein's felicitous phrase, and also the presentation of self in various genocides. This concerns not only the way victims respond— with acquiescence, retreat, depression, or resistance—but how one internalizes the threat to one's self posed by genocide.

- Reaction of victims, from passivity (a common reaction of victims, not just during the Holocaust or the Turkish genocide of Armenians, but among later genocides) to resistance (rare yet important in most genocides) to going into hiding (which may in fact be an example of passivity or resistance.)

- Rescuers, bystanders, and perpetrators.

- Factors leading to genocide: societal, political, economic, military (wartime conditions), colonization and decolonization, tribal conflict, to name just some.

- The aftermath, including post-traumatic stress, compensation, tribunals, legacies, and remembrance/memorialization.

As this list suggests, any attempt to characterize an act of genocide as entirely unique limits the scope of one's findings. Much more important is research of a comparative nature. Such research is essential not only for theory-building, but also in order to prevent future genocides.

Postmodern Theories of Genocide

Last but not least, sociology can help scholars develop new theories. Sociology was late to study genocide, but it has attempted to make up for lost time. Several postmodern sociological approaches have given new life to the field. A new emphasis on sex and gender illuminates how genocide affects diverse people. For example, does genocide impact women, gays, and other outsiders differently than heterosexual men? Postmodern theories reject an androcentric, male-centered viewpoint.

Theories that reject a strictly Eurocentric or Western perspective and embrace a more global viewpoint might prove useful if one does not swing too far in observing political correctness. Finally, some recent postmodern theories, with their emphasis on media interpretation, argot, texts, and cultural studies, could open up new vistas for scholars and students in the study of genocide.

SEE ALSO Explanation; Political Theory;
    Psychology of Survivors; Psychology of Victims

BIBLIOGRAPHY

Chalk, Frank, and Kurt Jonassohn (1990). *The History and Sociology of Genocide: Analyses and Case Studies.* New Haven, Conn.: Yale University Press.

Dadrian, Vahakn (1974). "The Common Features of the Armenian and Jewish Cases of Genocide: A Comparative Victimological Approach." In *Victimology: A New Focus: Violence and Its Victims*, ed. Israel Drabkin and Emilio Viano. Lexington, Mass.: D.C. Heath.

Fein, Helen (1978). "A Formula for Genocide: Comparison of the Turkish Genocide (1915) and the German Holocaust (1939–1945)." *Comparative Studies in Sociology* 1:271–293.

Fein, Helen (1996). *Genocide: A Sociological Perspective.* Sherman Oaks, Calif.: Sage.

Kendall, Diana (2000). *Sociology in Our Times.* Belmont, Calif.: Wadsworth/Thomson Learning.

Porter, Jack Nusan (1982). *Genocide and Human Rights: A Global Anthology.* Lanham, Md.: University Press of America. Newton, Mass.: Spencer Press, 2002.

Porter, Jack Nusan (2003). *The Genocidal Mind: Toward a Sociological Construct.* Newton, Mass.: Spencer Press.

Jack Nusan Porter

Sociology of Victims

Under what circumstances and by what methods is a group identified as a distinctive "other," an alien "other," and an inferior "other" to be excluded from membership in that society and then exterminated? How and why are certain people placed "outside the universe of moral obligation" to paraphrase sociologist Helen Fein's aphorism? Several sociological theories help explain such victimization.

In the 1940s, Hans Von Hentig, a German criminologist, launched the study of the relationship between criminals and their victims. Hentig argued that much of what victims do or who they are leads to their victimization; crime is a product of an interaction between offender and victims, he said. The field of victimization was thus born. The earliest victimization studies were heavily influenced by Freudian psychology, which argued that victims yearned, and were in some way responsible, for their victimization. A good example of such an approach was scholar Bruno Bettelheim's analysis of Holocaust victim Anne Frank. However, the concept of "blaming the victim" for horrific acts at the hand of a perpetrator has been rejected by most scholars.

In his 1976 book *Blaming the Victim*, William Ryan also discussed this contention. According to sociologist Erich Goode, contemporary criminologists are much more careful to make a distinction between the terms *blame* and *cause*. Victims may be selected by offenders in part because of what they do or who they are, but they should not be blamed for their victimization. *Blame* is a heavily value-laden term, whereas *cause* denotes a much more objective, determinable sequence of events, according to Goode.

For example, young women are more likely to be raped or sexually assaulted than older women—this is a causal, not a moral statement—but younger women must not be blamed for being raped. The same is true with poorer households. They are more likely to be burglarized than more affluent households, but to assign blame to poor people for these statistics would be incorrect

The same reasoning is true with regard to victims of genocide and mass violence. They are victimized based on who they are and what they have done or become, but they should never be blamed. Surprisingly, several prominent Holocaust scholars have "blamed" the Jews themselves for their plight during World War II. Bettelheim blamed Anne Frank and her family's passivity and naivety for their fate. Raul Hilberg blamed Jewish lack of resistance on their historically passive and nonviolent nature. Younger scholars and more militant members of such victim groups as Armenians and Native Americans point out that such passivity will not happen again. They tend to emphasize resistance and revenge.

Stigma and Social Identity

Sociologist Erving Goffman in his classic *Stigma: Notes on the Management of Spoiled Identity* (1963) applied the term *stigma,* a Greek word (*stigmata*) with heavily religious overtones to physical, racial, or sociological categories. According to Goffman, stigma refers to "bodily signs designed to expose something unusual and bad about the moral status of the signifier. The signs were cut or burnt into the body and advertised that the bearer was a slave, a criminal, or a traitor—a blemished person, ritually polluted, to be avoided, especially in public places" (Goffman, 1963, p. 1).

While Goffman does not specifically relate this "stigma" to genocide or the Holocaust, the conclusion is obvious: he could easily be talking about Jews who were branded in Auschwitz with numbers or told to wear the "Yellow Star"; Armenians who were branded by the Turks; Cambodians who were distinguished by blue or yellow kerchiefs or by dark tans (implying those who worked in the sun as opposed to intellectuals and bureaucrats); Hutus and Tutsis who were distinguished by their identity papers; and numerous other marks of distinction of victims of genocide.

The stigma marks the discredited with a visible sign that the bearer must be avoided; that he or she is polluted; and that death will result from physical or sexual contact. Often, these "deviants" are members of racial or religious minorities that have historically been isolated and marginalized as well.

Theories of Victimization

There are many theories to explain victimization. A few of the most salient include Marxist-economic theories; radical conflict theory; and labeling theory.

Marxist-Economic Theories

The targeted group is seen as an economic threat, such as with the Jews and the Armenians. In both the Holocaust and the Armenian Genocide, persecution took place in two phases. First, contact was limited. For example, Jewish doctors and lawyers could no longer represent or treat German clients or patients; Jewish physicians and managers were terminated from their jobs. Second, small businesses and factories were taken by force and given to non-Jewish "Aryan" owners. Such pauperization was rationalized as "payback" for all "offenses," real or imagined that the victim group had instigated. For example, during *Kristallnacht,* on November 9, 1937, not only were hundreds of Jewish synagogues, shops, and factories destroyed, but the insurance policies that should have covered such crimes were paid by the Jews as well.

Radical Conflict Theory

The victim group may not perceived as wealthy or powerful—such as the Jews, Armenians, or city-dwelling Cambodians—but the opposite, as weak. The genocide of the natives in Central and South America, the Aborigines in Australia, or the Maoris in New Zealand are examples of a class struggle of the strong defeating and exterminating the weak and defenseless victims of colonial and imperial conflict.

Labeling Theory

Sometimes called interactionist or symbolic interactionist theory, this theoretical approach is based on three premises. First, people act on the basis of meaning that things have for them. Second, this meaning grows out of interaction with others, especially intimate others. Third, meanings are continually modified by constant interpretation.

Labeling theory emphasizes target audiences, "moral entrepreneurs" (people such as ministers and politicians) who promulgate moral "panics," and promote the stigmatization of victim groups. Major proponents of this theory include not only Goffman but Howard S. Becker, John Kitsuse, and Kai Erikson.

Attitudes toward the Victims: The Contribution of Erich Goldhagen

Scientists are constantly amazed on how ingenious humans are in marginalizing, labeling, and victimizing others. The reactions toward the victims are also worth noting. Former Harvard University professor Erich Goldhagen has delved into the many ways that perpetrators have reacted to their victims throughout history. The various reactions ranged from indifference to amused gawking to deep involvement with murderous intent. There were a vast array of reactions, both ideological and social.

Conclusions: A Two-Step Solution

Why are people victimized? Some feel it is due to ideological concepts such as racism and anti-Semitism; others believe it is due to social pressure and conformity. In *Becoming Evil,* James Waller undertakes a wide-ranging analysis of these various theories. Other social scientists have embraced a "two-step solution," combining both ideology and obedience to orders.

According to this theory, ideology is the animus that starts genocide but then second elements kick in, such as obedience to orders, peer pressure, careerism, and conformity. All the myriad sociological, organizational, bureaucratic, and psychological motivators take over, under what Goldhagen calls the "foot in the door" theory: Once the killing starts, it takes on a momentum of its own and is difficult to stop.

In short, ordinary human beings become extraordinary killers in a very short time. People can live together peacefully for decades, even centuries, and then suddenly become lethal killers, such as with the events that took place in Bosnia in the early 1990s. Scholars may never uncover a satisfactory answer to this kind of victimization.

SEE ALSO Explanation; Political Theory; Psychology of Survivors; Psychology of Victims

BIBLIOGRAPHY

Blumer, Herbert (1969). *Symbolic Interactionism.* Englewood Cliffs, N.J.: Prentice-Hall.

Charny, Israel W., ed. (1999). *Encyclopedia of Genocide.* 2 vols. Santa Barbara, Calif.: ABC-Clio.

Goffman, Erving (1963). *Stigma: Notes on the Management of Spoiled Identity.* Englewood Cliffs, N.J.: Prentice-Hall.

Goode, Erich (2001). *Deviant Behavior,* 6th edition. Upper Saddle River, N.J.: Prentice-Hall.

Porter, Jack Nusan, ed. (1982). "Introduction." *Genocide and Human Rights: A Global Anthology.* Lanham, Md.: University Press of America.

Porter, Jack Nusan (1999). "Genocide Prediction." In *Encyclopedia of Genocide,* vol. 1., ed. Israel W. Charny. Santa Barbara, Calif.: ABC-Clio.

Porter, Jack Nusan, and Steve Hoffman (1994). *The Sociology of the Holocaust/Genocide: A Curriculum Guide.* Washington, D.C.: American Sociological Association.

Rosenbaum, Ron (1999). *Explaining Hitler: The Search for the Origins of His Evil.* New York: Harper Perennial.

Von Hentig, Hans (1948). *The Criminal and His Victim.* New Haven, Conn.: Yale University Press.

Waller, James (2002). *Becoming Evil: How Ordinary People Commit Genocide and Mass Killing.* New York: Oxford University Press.

Jack Nusan Porter

Somalia, Intervention in

When genocidal violence exploded in Rwanda in May 1994, the United States sounded a particularly strident, even obstructionist, voice of caution against intervention by any outside forces to stop the atrocities. Although the United Nations Assistance Mission in Rwanda (UNAMIR) already had a small contingent on the ground at the time of the crisis, the United States quickly moved to oppose an expanded UN presence.

As events unfolded in Rwanda, American policy makers were strongly influenced by the specter of the Somalia "disaster" of less than a year earlier as they deliberated possible options. In December 1992 American forces entered Somalia as part of a UN mission to feed starving people in a nation wracked by internal chaos. With CNN broadcasting images of the soldiers coming ashore to rescue the at-risk population, this gesture of international goodwill seemed destined for success. Over the next year the mission expanded from humanitarian relief to include elements of "nation building," which translated into helping Somalia establish some sort of stable, workable, democratic polity that would ultimately prevent the need for future outside interventions. As a result of this expanded mandate (soon thereafter referred to as "mission creep"), American forces found themselves at odds with local warlords in the capital city of Mogadishu. This conflict culminated on October 3, 1993, with a firefight between U.S. Army Rangers, members of the elite Delta Force, and forces loyal to Somali leader Mohammed Aideed. After hours of intense fighting eighteen Americans lay dead and seventy-three wounded.

The loss of American lives was difficult and dramatic enough, but the Battle of Mogadishu earned its lasting legacy when triumphant Somalis dragged the body of an American helicopter pilot through the city streets. Covered in the news, complete with graphic video footage, the episode seared powerful images into the memories of most Americans—policy makers, politicians, the public, and military personnel alike. And while a majority of Americans continued to support an American presence there, Somalia sent shockwaves of caution and reflexive anti-interventionism through the Pentagon and the White House. Intervention in Africa then appeared to involve a maximum of risk with limited returns at best.

Within the military establishment, an angry belief developed that the administration of President Bill Clinton had failed to provide it with requested equipment; there was also irritation within the military at the United States' subsequent hasty withdrawal from Somalia following the Battle of Mogadishu. Both factors contributed to the administration's reluctance to commit U.S. forces to another UN mission, especially one in Africa. At the same time American domestic politics suggested that few, if any, constituencies supported risky U.S. involvement in Africa, no matter what the cause, following the debacle in Somalia. To put it simply, the president feared a decline in public support in opinion polls and losing more votes in a reelection bid than he would gain by authorizing any African intervention, even if just or successful.

Despite the episode in Somalia it is important to note that policy makers did not share a monolithic view of the appropriate and necessary response to the Rwandan crisis. The State Department's Africa Bureau, headed by George Moose, urged an expanded and more vigorous UN military presence. Deputy Assistant Secretary Prudence Bushnell and Central Africa Office Director Arlene Render "argued fiercely at interagency meetings within the executive branch for a stronger mandate and a troop increase for UNAMIR as well as for a number of diplomatic measures to isolate and stigmatize the rump regime" (Burkhalter, 1994/1995, p. 47). Secretary of State Madeleine Albright also reportedly opposed a bystander role for the United States. However, proponents of stronger action faced an uphill battle within the administration in the post-Somalia era, particularly with the Pentagon.

The Pentagon based much of its position on the crisis in Rwanda on an analogy with Somalia, arguing that an all-too fine line existed between sending in UN forces and eventually having to follow up with American soldiers. Pentagon officials were wary of the possible eventual need to bail out a floundering UNAMIR and, therefore, opposed even multilateral involvement at any level. This was an understandable concern, but one born of selective memory—the costly Battle of Mogadishu had been a U.S., not UN, operation. Proponents of intervention in any form were outranked in discussions within the Clinton administration. For a lower-level official such as Bushnell, a difficult argument became even more challenging because it in-

U.S. military troops upon their December 1992 arrival in the capital city of Mogadishu. They entered Somalia as part of a UN mission to feed starving people in a nation wracked by internal chaos. [PETER TURNLEY/CORBIS]

volved having to go head-to-head with more senior officials from the Pentagon, including Undersecretary of Defense John Deutch who staunchly opposed intervention.

Compounding this was an apparent lack of interest or support among higher-level officials at the State Department. Peter Tarnoff, the undersecretary of state for political affairs and the overseer of the Africa bureau and other regional departments, "apparently had no interest in Rwanda," whereas Tim Wirth, undersecretary of state for global affairs, "seemingly played no role at all in the question of U.S. policy during the genocide, even though his brief included human rights" (Burkhalter 1994/1995, p. 47). Meanwhile, at the National Security Council, senior officials demonstrated their disinclination toward any sort of action. Throughout the administration policy makers viewed Rwanda through the prism of Somalia. As a consequence, they thought in terms of a failed state and quickly assumed that any intervention would have to be large-scale and costly, and would probably result in no measurable improvement.

The United States also operated under a significantly flawed understanding and interpretation of events. In large part the Clinton administration mistakenly identified and therefore addressed the Rwandan issue as a "peacekeeping" matter, as a more or less "traditional" civil war between two armed forces—not as large-scale genocidal violence directed against helpless civilians. Therefore, any proposed action to alleviate the situation in Rwanda fell under the rubric of peacekeeping and was far more likely to fall victim to flawed analogies born of the experience in Somalia. It also made more likely—and perhaps more understandable and defensible—extreme caution and trepidation at the thought of interposing any foreign force between the warring parties no matter what the reported loss of life was. As former U.S. envoy to Somalia, Robert Oakley, explained at the time of the Rwandan genocide, "Somalia showed just how difficult and dangerous the mission of saving a country can be. The international community is not disposed to deploying 20, 40, 60,000 military forces each time there is an internal crisis in a failed state."

As the focus of the Clinton administration's foreign policy shifted to altering Somalia's political leadership, tensions mounted between American forces stationed in Mogadishu and local warlords. In this photo dated March 3, 1993, Somalians—possibly fleeing the city—file past U.S. soldiers. [PETER TURNLEY/CORBIS]

This peacekeeping frame of mind and its outgrowth from the events that had transpired in Somalia became manifest with the public release on May 5, 1994 (concurrent with the genocide in Rwanda) of Presidential Decision Directive 25 (PDD-25). PDD-25 marked a determined effort to redefine the conditions and contexts for U.S. participation in UN peacekeeping operations. Although President Clinton came into office trumpeting support and enthusiasm for multinational operations on issues ranging from nonproliferation to international crime, the events that occurred in Somalia chastened his administration. As a presidential candidate, Clinton had even spoken openly of the need to establish a UN rapid reaction force to intervene on humanitarian grounds.

Post-Somalia, Clinton's vision of assertive multilateralism dissipated, giving way to extreme caution and calculation, despite the fact that the mission in Somalia likely saved upwards of a quarter-million people. With new-found "prudence" and the haunting "precedent" of Somalia in the background, the Clinton administration formulated an official reassessment of U.S.

support for UN peacekeeping initiatives. Termed "the first comprehensive U.S. policy on multilateral peace operations suited to the post–Cold War era," PDD-25 responded to some hard questions: when, where, and how to intervene. The document defined the U.S. national interest in terms of limited involvement and low cost. Furthermore, it declared that U.S. involvement in UN missions would occur only if it had a "direct bearing on U.S. national interests," which represented a fairly limited rather than expansive point of view, and one that would more than likely exclude places such as Somalia and Rwanda in the future.

At the press briefing introducing the directive, National Security Advisor Tony Lake stated that "the central conclusion of the study is that properly conceived and well-executed, peacekeeping can be a very important tool of American foreign policy." Shortly thereafter, though, Lake added a qualification echoing back to Somalia: He noted that although the United States can sometimes help other countries in times of need, "we can never build their nations for them."

PDD-25 addressed six major issues: (1) making disciplined and coherent choices about which peace operations to support; (2) reducing U.S. costs for UN peace operations; (3) clearly defining policy on the command and control of U.S. forces; (4) reforming and improving the UN's ability to manage peace operations; (5) reforming and improving U.S. ability to manage peace operations; and (6) improving cooperation between the Executive, the Congress, and the American public on peace operations. Among a variety of factors PDD-25 stressed that the United States would participate in a UN peace mission when the mission (1) responds to a threat to or breach of international peace and security; (2) advances U.S. interests (with unique and general risks weighed appropriately); (3) includes acceptable command and control arrangements; and (4) includes clearly defined objectives with realistic criteria for ending the operation (i.e., an exit strategy). At the policy unveiling Lake discussed each of these six imperatives and highlighted the notion that "peacekeeping is a part of our national security policy, but it is not the centerpiece. The primary purpose of our military force is to fight and win wars."

The public announcement of PDD-25 and comments like those made by a senior foreign policy official such as Lake did not bode well for American support of a strengthened UN response to the crisis in Rwanda, and certainly not for any intervention by American forces. The thrust of PDD-25 and its post-Somalia release during the crisis in Rwanda suggested that some policy makers mistakenly viewed any mission to Central Africa as a traditional peacekeeping expedition to maintain a cessation of hostilities between two fighting parties. In an operational sense the directive essentially rendered nearly impossible any significant initiatives to help Rwanda because next to none could realistically succeed or even be implemented without U.S. support.

PDD-25 was a potential catch-22 for the future deployment of UN forces: "The United States would refuse any new deployment of UN Blue Helmets unless all the necessary conditions (logistical, financial, troop deployments, etc.) were fulfilled—yet they could never be fulfilled *without* [italics in original] the active support of the superpower" (Destexhe, 1995, p. 50). Commenting on PDD-25 and its application to Rwanda, Richard Dowden of Britain's *Independent* newspaper referred to the policy statement as the result of a "poker mentality: Problem: Somalia. Response: Intervention. Result: Failure. Conclusion: No More Intervention" (Ronayne, 2001, p. 167). In Congress Representative David Obey (Democrat from Wisconsin) explained the policy as a fulfillment of the American public's desire for "zero degree of involvement and zero degree of risk

and zero degree of pain and confusion" (Ronayne, 2001, p. 167). Born of Somalia, the PDD-25 mindset significantly influenced administration thinking and policy even prior to its public announcement and had striking implications for America's determination not to become involved in Rwanda during the spring of 1994.

SEE ALSO Rwanda; United States Foreign Policy Toward Genocide and Crimes Against Humanity

BIBLIOGRAPHY

Allard, Kenneth (1995). *Somalia Operation: Lessons Learned*. Washington, D.C: National Defense University Press. Available from http://www.theinteragency.org/index.cfm?state=resource.4#9.

Bowden, Mark (2000). *Black Hawk Down: A Story of Modern War*. New York: Penguin USA.

Burkhalter, Holly (1994/1995). "The Question of Genocide: The Clinton Administration and Rwanda." *World Policy Journal* 11(4):44–54.

Crocker, Chester A. (May/June 1995). "The Lessons of Somalia: Not Everything Went Wrong." *Foreign Affairs* 74(3).

Destexhe, Alain (1995). *Rwanda and Genocide in the Twentieth Century*. New York: New York University Press.

Leitenberg, Milton (November/December 1994). "Rwanda 1994: International Incompetence Produces Genocide." *Peacekeeping & International Relations* 23(6).

Power, Samantha (2002). *A Problem from Hell: America and the Age of Genocide*. New York: Basic Books.

Ronayne, Peter (2001). *Never Again? The United States and the Prevention and Punishment of Genocide Since the Holocaust*. Lanham, Md.: Rowman & Littlefield.

Sciolino, Elaine (1994). "For West, Rwanda is Not Worth the Political Candle." *New York Times* (April 15):A3.

U.S. Department of State (1994). "Presidential Decision Directive 25." Washington, D.C: Bureau of International Organizations, U.S. Department of State. Available from http://www.fas.org/irp/offdocs/pdd25.htm.

Peter Ronayne

South Africa

Old South African history books date the beginning of the country to the arrival of the first Europeans at the tip of the African continent in 1652. The Dutch East India Company needed a refreshment station for its ships while sailing around Africa to trade with its empire in Batavia (Indonesia). However, when Jan Van Riebeek founded the settlement that was called the Cape of Good Hope, the first three dozen company employees did not raise cattle and grow fruits and vegetables on empty territory. Like European colonialists ev-

Until the early twenty-first century, the gold fields of Johannesburg were the largest gold resources in the world. The gold-bearing stone is mined at considerable depth. Mining at deep levels is highly problematic, in part owing to the high temperatures and high humidity. This 1948 photo shows two South African gold miners in their living quarters, with the individual spaces for sleeping visible. [**BETTMANN/ CORBIS**]

erywhere else, they encountered indigenous people who had lived on the land from time immemorial. The story of South Africa is the dispossession, resistance, liberation, and ultimate reconciliation of foreign intruders with indigenous inhabitants. When and how the colonialists themselves became indigenous—in short, whether there can be white Africans with equal rights and privileges, despite the colonial legacy—is still a matter of debate in the twenty-first century.

In this analysis the common label of "African" for the black majority does not preclude members of other groups from being African in the political sense of citizens belonging to the African continent as it is their only home and place of origin. In contrast to the Middle East, all parties in South Africa have accepted this status of original "settlers." Therefore, not all Africans are black, and not all blacks are Africans. It should also

be noted that since the rise of the black consciousness movement in the late 1960s, "black" has become a proud political term, comprising politically conscious members of all three disenfranchised groups, including South Africans of Indian descent and those of mixed origin (the coloreds).

In the Western Cape there were two distinct aboriginal groups: (1) the Khoikhoi, seminomadic herders and (2) San-speakers, hunting and gathering people, whom the Europeans derogatively referred to as Bushmen. A hundred years later and 500 kilometers further east, the expanding settlers clashed with a third indigenous people, who spoke yet another language and practiced a different way of life: (3) agriculturalists who made their living from subsistence farming and were called Bantu, or in modern times blacks or Africans.

Because Africans were more numerous and better organized in rudimentary states with chiefs and kings, they offered the stiffest and longest resistance to the European colonization of all three indigenous groups. However, they were also weakened by their own infighting, superstition, technological underdevelopment, and the colonial policy of divide and rule. Yet, unlike the Xhosa subgroup in the Eastern Cape (from which Nelson Mandela originates), the related Zulus in Natal were only subdued by the British colonial army in protracted battles as recently as 1900. The first democratic election in 1994 reversed this colonial conquest, by replacing 350 years of minority racial domination with majority political rule. In 2004, 76 percent of South African voters belonged to the African group, whereas 11 percent were classified as white.

The weakest San-speakers befell the worst fate of near-genocide. Like wild game, they were often shot on sight by special raiding parties who claimed they were habitual cattle thieves. In the early twenty-first century only about thirty thousand San people survive in the whole of Southern Africa, mainly in neighboring Botswana and Namibia, where they are still treated as second-class citizens in state parks or reservations. Were it not for the manufactured tourist attraction they provide or the tracking services they offered to the South African army during the war, most of these survivors from a different age would have vanished altogether.

The Cape settlers initially established an uneasy bartering relationship with the Khoikhoi; their rebellious chiefs were incarcerated at Robben Island, but most of the people gradually became absorbed into the feudal Cape economy as farm laborers or domestic servants. Missionaries converted the majority of Khoikhoi to Calvinism, and many Khoikhoi women intermarried with Europeans or had children out of wedlock or as a result of rape. Descendants of this group are known as coloreds in the contemporary world; the overwhelming majority speak Afrikaans as their mother tongue and make up approximately 9 percent of the total South African population of 44 million.

The ethnic mix of South Africa was further complicated by the importation of slaves from Angola, Indonesia, Malaysia, Madagascar, and elsewhere, a mere ten years after the Cape colony was founded. During the first hundred years the Cape colony barely grew through additional immigration from Europe, yet the outpost needed a dependent labor force. The huge gender imbalance among the Europeans—three men to one woman—encouraged sexual liaisons across the groups. The leading South African historian Hermann Giliomee probably understates the sexual violence and exploitation in the colonial status hierarchy when he

points out: "There was also large-scale miscegenation in the form of casual sex, especially in the slave lodge frequented by European men as well as sailors and soldiers" (2003, p. 18). Because most children born from such encounters were absorbed into the Afrikaner community, the racial consciousness and assertions of racial purity during the later apartheid period appear particularly absurd. Social science research across cultures has revealed that insistence on exclusive racial or ethnic identity is particularly strong among people who have an insecure self-concept and are not sure of their own identity. Sigmund Freud has called this phenomenon the narcicissm of small difference. Ironically, early Cape society seemed to be more color-blind and free of racially defined opportunities than the frozen twentieth-century legislated race classifications of apartheid.

Among the European colonial powers, South Africa became a desired possession and the Cape colony changed hands several times between the Dutch and British who feared the French under Napoleon. Unlike the earlier immigration by Dutch and German unemployed adventurers and a few hundred religiously prosecuted French Hugenots, large-scale immigration from Britain started only in the early nineteenth century. These were largely government-selected immigrants with crafts and skills who came with their families. Most settled on the Eastern seaboard, particularly in Natal. British control of the Cape and the abolition of slavery are usually mentioned as the reasons for the Great Trek of Afrikaner farmers beyond the Cape frontier into the interior in the second quarter of the nineteenth century. Giliomee sees the diverse causes in "a lack of land, labor and security, coupled with a pervasive sense of being marginalized" (2003, p. 142). The trek left Afrikaners dispersed throughout the country. The Orange Free State and Transvaal emerged as the two new independent Boer republics.

The British influence and influx were also supplemented after 1860 by immigrants from British India on five-year contracts as indentured laborers for the sugar plantations and market gardens around Durban. Most of these poor labor migrants stayed in South Africa after the expiration of their contracts, brought their families over, and gradually prospered on the basis of solidarity with their kin and emphasis on education for their children, despite severe discrimination. This middle minority faced animosity from the dominant whites as well as the subordinate blacks. During the 1949 Durban riots 150 Indians were killed until the army restored order belatedly. Unlike the wealthy Indian trading minorities in East Africa, the Indian community in Natal consists mostly of working-class people. This did not prevent them from becoming a scapegoat and target of resentment for the Zulu population, who competed with them for jobs and scarce resources.

About 75 percent of the 1.3 million Indian population are Hindus from various Indian linguistic groups and 20 percent are Muslims. Together with the so-called Malay coloreds, 800,000 Muslims comprise approximately 2 percent of the South African population. The majority of the South African population profess to belong to various mainstream Christian denominations, whereas about 30 percent claim membership in independent (Zionist) churches.

Rise of Afrikaner Nationalism

The discovery of diamonds in Kimberley and rich gold reserves around Johannesburg in the second half of the nineteenth century again changed the course of South African history. It established the foundations for the only industrialized country in Africa. Deep level mining required long-term capital investments that only British imperialists were prepared to supply. Unlike colonies of exploitation where a few temporary colonists export their profits to the European metropole, the permanent settler colony of South Africa reinvested its profit inside the colony for further economic expansion. That presupposed political control over the territory which Cecil Rhodes and other British rubber barons needed to wrest from the Boer republics.

Imperialist greed was the simple reason for the Boer war at the turn of the century. The Boers outgunned in their guerrilla war against superior English forces enjoyed widespread global support, including that of Lenin, in what was considered the first anti-colonial war of Africa. The Boers lost this war and about 10 percent of the Afrikaner population was killed. In the bitter struggle the ruthless British army practiced a scorched earth policy against the rural civilian population and established for the first time concentration camps in which many women and children died from starvation and disease.

The trauma of the conflict resulted in a quest for revenge and the emergence of Afrikaner nationalism. British colonial policy everywhere aimed at the anglicization of culturally different groups. The public use of the Afrikaans language was discouraged, outlawed in public, and penalized in schools. British cultural arrogance denigrated different cultural practices. Very much like the situation in Quebec until 1960, English-speakers dominated the economy and only English-speakers could hope for a substantial business career. This forced assimilation triggered a counternationalism that clamored for the equality of an impoverished people with their English overlords. The Afrikaner intellectual ethnic mobilizers stressed pride in the then fully developed Afrikaans language. They encouraged Afrikaners to accumulate capital in their own insurance companies. About 90 percent of Afrikaners in the 1920s and 1930s lived in rural areas; many drifted as landless, unskilled *bywoners* into the cities in search of work. They competed with African workers who were largely preferred by employers, because they were cheaper and considered less rebellious and more malleable. Approximately 25 percent of Afrikaners were classified as poor whites at the time.

The government at the time consisted of an English-Afrikaner United Party under the leadership of the highly reputed General Jan (Christiaan) Smuts. In 1940 it joined the war against Nazi Germany on the British side. A minority of nationalist Afrikaners strongly opposed this, mainly because of anti-British sentiments but also because of residual sympathies for German racist ideologies and anti-Semitic sentiments. The many alienated Afrikaners considered Jewish owners (*Hoggenheimer*) of the large Anglo-American gold and diamond corporation the local oppressors and exploiters.

Being that Afrikaners constituted 60 percent of the white voting population (as compared with 40% English-speakers) and only a few Cape nonwhites were enfranchised, the Afrikaner National Party not surprisingly won the 1948 general election. Capturing state control marked the triumph of Afrikaner nationalism. It now could use the state apparatus for patronage of Afrikaner interests and keeping black competitors at bay. The English United Party also practiced racist segregation, but less openly than Afrikaners. The National Party replaced segregation with apartheid, an unprecedented policy of statutory racial reordering. Its main architect was the new charismatic leader of the National Party, Hendrik Verwoerd.

In short, Afrikaner nationalism, with exclusive control of the South African state, institutionalized the Anglo informal segregation policy into formal, legalized apartheid. This grand experiment of race-based social engineering eschewed any assimilation and instead fostered ethnic difference among the black population. *Separate development,* as the ideology of divide and rule was euphemistically labeled, attempted to ethnisize the black majority and racialize the white minority of different cultural origins. It thereby tried to unify Europeans (particularly the Afrikaans and English-speakers of the white minority) into a white nation, but fragment Africans into nine tribal national groups. The imagined white nation was built on race and biology. The envisaged black nations were based on partially invented ethnic and cultural differences. The fate of the two middle groups (colored and Indians) was left undecided

The movement of black South Africans into and out of urban and employment centers was regulated by the Blacks Consolidation Act of 1945. These citizens of South Africa were required to carry special pass books at almost all times. In the photo, Africans queue up to get their new pass books at a government office in Johannesburg, April 7, 1960. [AP/WORLD WIDE PHOTOS]

initially, but this changed in the early 1980s when open cooptation strategies were adopted. Coloreds and Indians were enfranchised on separate voter's rolls for separate parliaments with limited powers that could not threaten overall white domination. The attempt backfired because of the exclusion of the majority black African population. Apartheid imposed a state-decreed identity on different groups and disallowed people to define their own identity. In all other ethnic conflicts around the world, people belong to and identify with a group because of self-association.

Many Faces of Apartheid

The American sociologist Pierre van den Berghe has distinguished three forms of apartheid:

1. *Micro-apartheid,* or petty apartheid, segregated people from birth to death in daily life. Whites and nonwhites had to use separate facilities, from hospitals to cemeteries, elevators to toilets, restaurants to park benches, buses to beaches, post-office counters to railway coaches. All facilities were of superior quality for whites and, if provided at all, of inferior quality for blacks, Indians, and coloreds.

2. *Meso-apartheid* denotes the residential segregation enforced under the Group Areas Act. Cities that had once been integrated were forcibly segregated during the 1960s and nonwhites deported to outlying areas. In the contemporary world this is referred to as *ethnic cleansing.* The four racial groups were allocated different residential areas of their own. Whites could generally remain in the better parts of the city, while houses and shops were expropriated (particularly from Indians and coloreds) and the owners forced to relocate far from city centers. This eliminated competition for white traders and amounted to the confiscation of valuable real estate. The policy was justified under the banner of "slum clearing." However, once a slum was cleared, its residents or shop- or home-owners were not allowed back to rebuild.

3. *Macro-apartheid* refers to the division of South Africa into nine tribal homelands on 13 percent of the land, while the rest was declared white territory. Blacks could live in white South Africa only with special permission, if they were needed as laborers. Slightly more than half of the total black population fell into this category. Some of the

black homelands, which were also called Bantustans, declared themselves politically independent with their own flags and border controls, but their alleged sovereignty was recognized only by white South Africa. The government in Pretoria heavily subsidized its homeland creations, because they were the supposed answer to the anticolonial independence movements on the rest of the African continent.

Apartheid constituted domestic or internal colonialism. Generally corrupt and unpopular black appointees of the white government in the capital of Pretoria were designated to administer their own poverty and police themselves. The minority Afrikaner central government wanted to shed territory and responsibility for people considered useless, costly, and politically undesirable. Since all blacks would have acquired citizenship in their own independent states, there would be no need to grant them a vote in the white state. They would have been legally denationalized in the country of their birth. Only a few black Bantustan leaders, the Zulu chief Mangosutho Buthelezi being the most prominent, refused to go along with this charade. His Inkatha movement had broken away from the African National Congress (ANC) in 1979 and decided to oppose apartheid legally from within.

Economically, a small aristocracy of whites benefited from job reservation, differential salaries for work of the same variety, or preferential promotion in a system that officially referred to itself as a "civilized labor policy." Poor Afrikaner whites enjoyed the most successful affirmative action policy. They found jobs on the railways, in the post office, or with state corporations, whether they were qualified or not. Forty-five percent of economically active Afrikaners were employed in the civil service, in what comprised a unique nation of bureaucrats. Better qualified professionals were looked after by the secret *Broederbond,* an ethnic male employment agency which ensured that Afrikaners and not English competitors filled the most influential positions in the universities, media, or senior civil service. The 12.000 member elitist organization simultaneously functioned as a think tank and clearinghouse for strategies of Afrikaner nationalism. Together with the founding of several new Afrikaner universities and the expansion of several older ones, such patronage activities ensured that Afrikaners gradually closed the wide educational and income gap with their English counterparts. Especially after Harry Oppenheimer's giant Anglo-American corporation allowed Afrikaner entry into the mining sector in the 1960s, the traditional ethnic divisions within the boardrooms of the nation faded. Beyond continuing ethnic particularities, Afrikaner and English capitalists shared basic common interests in defending their country against sanctions, perceived ANC communists abroad, and increasingly militant trade unions at home.

The majority of rural blacks were deprived of the right to seek work in urban areas through pass laws. These restrictions banned the elderly, women, and children to the desolate countryside, in order to save the system the social costs of education, unemployment, and old age. Eventually, all black South Africans were supposed to become foreigners in the country of their birth by acquiring citizenship in one of nine ethnic homelands. They would be "guest workers" without rights in 87 percent of the land, unable to own property or acquire a sense of a permanent home and belonging.

Colonialism everywhere operated on the distinction between citizens and subjects (Mamdani, 1997). Just as women in Europe were variously disenfranchised until the first half of the twentieth century, so indigenous subject populations (both in Africa and North America) were treated as so-called wards of the state, unworthy or incapable of participating in public affairs as equal citizens. A condescending paternalism confronted the allegedly childlike underlings when they demanded their rights: These had first to be earned, they were told, and their abilities demonstrated during a slow process toward equality. Colonial ideologues declared this the "burden of the white man" who had assumed the mission of "civilizing" primitive Natives in Africa.

Segregated education with different curricula and characterized by the differential allocation of resources was one of the main tools by which this policy was achieved. Bantu education was shaped by essentialized notions of what the black mind was capable of and the kind of corresponding lower skills needed in an industrialized economy. Depoliticized compliance, acquiescence, and acceptance of the status quo as the natural order were the expected attitudes. More open and progressive missionary schools were brought under state control. The few nonwhite students who attended the liberal white universities were channeled into new tribal colleges of students from the same ethnic group, all located in remote rural areas with the exception of the Coloured University of the Western Cape and the Indian University of Durban-Westville. Most faculty at these ethnic institutions were initially conservative Afrikaner civil servants. Little did the apartheid planners envisage that these colleges would gradually evolve into hotbeds of black nationalism and anti-apartheid resistance.

Ethnically based apartheid education, although imposed and resented, nevertheless built on entrenched traditions and linguistic backgrounds that are alive and relevant among the African rural population. Even in the cities, every black South African speaks an African language and more often is polyglot, although the medium of public discourse is almost exclusively English, despite eleven official languages. But English, poorly taught as a second language, severely disadvantages many African learners in the competition for good grades and jobs.

Even in the early twenty-first century those living in the rural areas under the authority of traditional chiefs are handicapped by customary law. Officially recognized as a concession to powerful traditional leaders, customary law does not sit well with liberal notions of equality and individual freedom. An unresolved contradiction exists between individualistic notions of citizenship and community-based rights and customs. The authority of chiefs does not rest on democratic legitimacy. Traditional leaders insist on inherited, dynastic rights. Women, in particular, suffer under communal obligations and status inequalities. Mamphela Ramphele speaks of a "dual citizenship that creates tensions between loyalty to the nation and to one's own group, however defined" (2000, p. 7). The tensions remain unresolved, and glaring discrepancies exist between the constitution and customary law. For example, the post-apartheid constitution insists on gender equality, but under customary law women cannot inherit property. Precolonial African society tends to be romanticized as communal decision making by consensus, but the monopoly of power in the hands of male elders and chiefs can hardly be called democratic.

Resistance and Liberation

European penetration of the African hinterland destroyed most of the traditional African subsistence economy. Squeezed into ever more overcrowded reserves, its inhabitants increasingly relied on the remittances of migrant workers in the cities. At the beginning of industrialization Africans had to be forced into poorly paid work on the mines through "head and hut" taxes that British administrators first introduced in the Eastern Cape. Later it was sheer rural poverty that drove blacks into the city slums, dormitories, and compounds. Migrant labor not only destroyed the African peasantry but also undermined the traditional family. The competition among ethnically housed migrants in insecure urban settings encouraged tribalism as a form of solidarity and the protection of one's own group in a tough struggle for survival.

In 1910 the ANC was founded. Among its first goals was the battle for African unity against tribalism. Under the influence of supportive white and Indian liberals and communists, this priority was later extended to color-blind nonracialism. A moderate black elite, educated at Christian missionary schools, repeatedly pleaded with the government for recognition. The much celebrated Freedom Charter of 1955 claimed the right of all South Africans to the land of their birth. A campaign of civil disobedience against new pass laws, inspired by the earlier campaigns led by Mahatma Gandhi, who lived as a British-trained lawyer in the Transvaal and experienced racial discrimination firsthand, was tried in Natal, but failed when the government simply imprisoned its peaceful protesters. The National Party government responded with ever more repressive legislation. The 1960 Sharpeville massacre of more than sixty protesters marked a turning point. The ANC and its rival, the more radical Pan African Congress (PAC), decided to go underground, revert to sabotage without hurting civilians, and establish an in-exile presence for the anti-apartheid struggle after both organizations were outlawed inside the country. After a few years in hiding Mandela and his comrades were caught and sentenced to life imprisonment, to be freed in 1990 only after serving twenty-seven years on Robben Island.

In 1983 the National Party split and shed its conservative wing. In 1989 its hard-line president, Pierre Willem Botha, was replaced with Frederik Wilhelm de Klerk, who had finally realized that apartheid did not work. Its costs outweighed its benefits. Attempts to control the influx of blacks into the cities had failed; businesses needed more skilled employees who were also politically satisfied; a powerful union movement had assumed the role of banned political organizations starting in the late 1970s; restless townships could not be stabilized, despite an essentially permanent state of emergency; demographic ratios had changed in favor of blacks, with more whites emigrating and draining the country of skills and investments; the costs of global sanctions, particularly loan refusals, and moral ostracism of the pariah South African state were felt. The collapse of communism and the end of the cold war in 1989 provided the final straw for the normalization of South Africa. The National Party decided to negotiate a historic compromise from a position of relative strength while whites were still dominant. With the loss of Eastern European support, the ANC also had to turn away from an armed struggle and seek a political solution. A perception of stalemate on both sides prepared the ground for a constitutionally mandated agreement to share power for five years. The first free democratic elections in 1994 and 1999 provided the ANC with a two-thirds majority.

Assessing the Post-Apartheid State and Future Trends

The compromise for whites involved handing over political power to the black majority, but in return leaving the economic order essentially intact. The ANC abandoned its socialist platform of "capturing the commanding heights of the economy" and turned into a right-of-center social democratic party with neoconservative fiscal and privatization policies that suited the powerful business community. A rapidly growing patriotic bourgeoisie has happily joined its white counterpart in defending nonracial capitalism (see Adam et al., 1997). Although the white–black income gap has narrowed, the inequality within each racial group has widened. Black empowerment programs and affirmative action policies have mainly favored an already privileged elite, but barely addressed mass unemployment and poverty.

The ANC has to ask itself what happens when the euphoria of liberation wears off? Black frustration has turned inward: A spiraling crime rate, sexual violence, and escalating rates of HIV infection, due to inexplicable government stalling on available counterstrategies, affect the physical well-being of the post-apartheid generation even more than what their parents experienced under apartheid. Despite holding one-third of the seats in the South African parliament, African women are not yet empowered in the private sphere in a highly patriarchal system. Although the government has made significant progress in supplying new housing, electricity, water, health, and educational services to the needy, it has also wasted precious resources on unnecessary arms purchases. Several high-profile corruption scandals have raised eyebrows. Quiet ANC support for the tyrannical Mugabe regime in Zimbabwe has not reassured jittery minorities that their long-term interests are safe in South Africa.

The cherished South African constitutionalism has not yet been tested in a real crisis of good governance, although the democratic record of the post-apartheid government cannot be faulted. Trends toward authoritarianism and highly centralized decision making in the president's office undermine democratic grassroots participation. Authoritarianism originates not from overwhelming governance as in the former order, but on the contrary, from the widespread crisis of authority and the inability to enforce order. The country lacks the institutional capacity for effective governance in many realms. An admirable human rights culture but fledgling democracy, it faces its most severe challenge both from cynical withdrawal into the private realm and support for a strong hand to impose order and economic progress without debate. A fragile, colonized civil society in South Africa is no guarantee that democracy will prevail in a crisis when even black and white businesses might side with the stability and predictability that a more authoritarian order promises.

The celebrated Truth and Reconciliation Commission (TRC) has affirmed the past sufferings of victims and made some perpetrators confess, because of its unique reward of amnesty after full disclosure of past crimes. The commission has, however, only achieved symbolic reconciliation. The TRC is more admired abroad than within South Africa. By focusing only on perpetrators and a few thousand individual victims of gross human rights violations, the TRC ignored the millions of ordinary people who suffered under apartheid. It also let white beneficiaries off the hook. Claims for reparations are still being debated.

Was apartheid genocide, or a crime against humanity? If one defines genocide as the planned and premeditated physical elimination of a people on the basis of their group membership, apartheid did not constitute genocide. Whites depended on blacks for cheap labor. However, depriving a people of fundamental human rights on the basis of their race and origin, stifling and wasting untold talents through arbitrary restrictions of advancement and differential resource allocation, or systematically insulting the dignity and equal recognition of citizens because of their descent, certainly constitutes a crime against humanity. That atrocities also occurred in countries who were among the harshest critics of apartheid South Africa should not be used to excuse the crimes of apartheid. While the perpetrators should not be labeled the Nazis of Africa, their different motivations and actions do not exonerate them. Although guilt cannot be collectively ascribed and there were also many brave dissidents and human rights activists among the dominant group, the white community bears responsibility for the continuing legacy of crimes committed in its name. All South African whites benefited, willingly or unwillingly, from a horrendous legalized racial system whether they supported it or not. Many victims of apartheid continue to bear visible and invisible scars. That those historical legacies must be acknowledged by all sides and serious efforts made to redress such wounds should be self-evident for all politically literate South Africans.

SEE ALSO Apartheid; Goldstone, Richard; Identification; Mandela, Nelson; Nationalism; Racism; Reparations; Shaka Zulu; Truth Commissions; Zulu Empire

BIBLIOGRAPHY

Adam, Heribert, and Hermann Giliomee (1979). *Ethnic Power Mobilized.* New Haven, Conn.: Yale University Press.

Adam, Heribert, and Kogila Moodley (1986). *South Africa without Apartheid.* Berkeley: University of California Press.

Adam, Heribert, and Kogila Moodley (1993). *The Opening of the Apartheid Mind.* Berkeley: University of California Press.

Adam, Heribert, Frederik Van Zyl Slabbert, and Kogila Moodley (1997). *Comrades in Business: Post-Liberation Politics in South Africa.* Cape Town, South Africa: Tafelberg.

Alexander, Neville (2002). *An Ordinary Country.* Pietermaritzburg: University of Natal Press.

Dubow, Saul (1989). *Racial Segregation and the Origins of Apartheid in South Africa.* London: Macmillan.

Giliomee, Hermann (2003). *The Afrikaners.* Cape Town, South Africa: Tafelberg.

Greenberg, Stanley (1980). *Race and State in Capitalist Devlopment.* New Haven, Conn.: Yale University Press.

Horowitz, Donald L. (1991). *A Democratic South Africa? Constitutional Engineering in a Divided Society.* Berkeley: University of California Press.

Lipron, Merle (1986). *Capitalism and Apartheid.* London: Gower Press.

Mamdani, Mahmood (1997). *Citizens and Subject: Contemporary Africa and the Legacy of Colonialism.* London: James Curry.

Mattes, Robert (2002). "Democracy without the People?" *Journal of Democracy* 13(1):22–36.

Moodley, Kogila (2000). "African Renaissance and Language Policies in Comparative Perspective." *Politikon* 27(1):103–115.

Moodley, Kogila, and Heribert Adam (2000). "Race and Nation in Post-Apartheid South Africa." *Current Sociology* 48(3):51–69.

Ramphele, Mamphela (2001). "Citizenship Challenges for South Africa's Young Democracy." *Daedalus* 130(1):1–17.

Sparks, Allister (2003). *Beyond the Miracle.* Johannesburg, South Africa: Jonathan Ball.

Waldmeir, Patti (1997). *Anatomy of a Miracle.* New York: Norton.

Kanya Adam
Heribert Adam

Soviet Prisoners of War, 1941 to 1945

Soviet prisoners of war (POWs) constitute one of the major groups that fell victim to Nazi German mass violence. For territories under German military occupa-tion, the Department of Military Administration, Quartermaster General in the Supreme Command of Ground Troops (OKH) was in charge of Soviet POWs, whereas in Germany and areas under German civil administration, responsibility lay with the General Administration of the Armed Forces under the Supreme Command of the Armed Forces (OKW). Prior to the attack on the USSR on June 22, 1941, German military authorities had decided that international law would not apply to Soviet POWs (unlike Polish, French, or British prisoners), with minimal provisions made for their shelter, food, transport, and medical supplies. Later Soviet proposals that both sides act in accordance with the Hague and Geneva Conventions were refused by Germany. On OKW instructions, most Soviet POWs were not registered by name in the camps in Soviet areas under German military occupation (Durchgangs-lager, or *Dulags*), and consequently no lists were passed on from these camps to the International Committee of the Red Cross (ICRC).

Following the German invasion, huge numbers of Red Army soldiers were captured, especially in July, September, and October 1941. Crammed into camps of up to 100,000 men, poorly fed, often without housing or sanitary provisions, the prisoners soon suffered from debilitation. Certain groups of military personnel were denied POW status: On Adolf Hitler's instruction, the OKW issued its "commissar order" on June 6, 1941, according to which political officers in the Red Army were shot in 1941 and 1942. Other groups killed by German troops included Soviet soldiers shot on the battlefield although they had surrendered, alleged Jews, in many camps so-called Asians, women in the Red Army, and in some camps Soviet officers. Orders for these killings originated from platoon to army command levels. More than 100,000 prisoners were handed over to the SS and police in 1941 and 1942; very few survived. In addition, an undetermined number of Soviet POWs, believed to be in the six-digit range, were shot by military guards because of their fatigue during marches or when unloading trains that had transported POWs. In certain German-occupied Soviet areas, Soviet military stragglers were killed instead of being taken prisoner, as were most Soviet partisan fighters. The Germans arbitrarily interned Soviet civilians in several POW camps in 1941.

The German capture of large numbers of prisoners in similarly short time periods had not led to mass deaths in the German campaign against France in 1940. The majority of Soviet POWs died as a result of the deliberate undersupply of food, consequent starvation, frost, and hunger-related diseases. Prior to attacking the USSR, German authorities had planned the killing

During Germany's invasion of the USSR, countless Red Army soldiers were captured, like those shown in this c. 1941 photograph. It is estimated that hundreds of thousands were shot on capture; an equally large number were transported to Nazi prisoner-of-war camps that few survived. [CORBIS]

of tens of millions of Soviet citizens in "food-deficient" regions and in urban areas through starvation and a policy of brutal occupation. Racist and anticommunist, that scheme was to make good the overall German food deficit and to relieve the critical shortage of supplies for troops at the Eastern Front, perceived as crucial for the success of the giant military campaign. Thus, the plan was backed and coinitiated by the military. As military supplies always took priority, Soviet POWs became one of the specific groups targeted for extinction.

In October 1941 food rations particularly for Soviet POWs considered "unfit for labor" were significantly reduced. On November 13 the German Quartermaster-General Eduard Wagner stated, "Soviet POWs unfit for labor in the camps have to die of starvation" (Notes of the Chief of Staff of the 18th Army, quoted in Streit, 1997, p. 157). In many camps those "fit for labor" were separated from those deemed unfit. Yet as guards often mistreated both groups equally and prisoners were worked to exhaustion with insufficient food, this intended distinction scarcely made any difference and

initially fit prisoners perished, too. Death figures shot up to 2 percent daily, especially in the German-occupied Soviet and Polish territories. Nearly two out of three million Soviet POWs had died by the end of 1941. Measures to reduce the mortality rate, adopted from December on, only succeeded in the spring of 1942. However, hard labor, poor rations, and bad treatment continued to take their toll until 1945. Orders by the German leadership were countered with brutality, violence, or gross neglect on the ground. Military and economic considerations, racism against Slavs, Jews, and so-called Asians, and anticommunism were at the core of interrelated motives.

In total, out of 5.7 million Soviet POWs, about three million died in German captivity, almost exclusively at the hands of the German military. Serious calculations, based on the interpretation of fragmentary German documents, range from "at least" 2.53 million to 3.3 million (Streit, 1997), with death figures revised downward for camps inside Germany on the basis of German records discovered in Russia and Germany in the late 1990s. Adding to their suffering, Soviet POWs returning to the USSR encountered collective suspicion and many were imprisoned without proper trial, as about a million had been forced or agreed under pressure to work for the German army, with hundreds of thousands fighting for the German army or SS under arms.

SEE ALSO Hitler, Adolf; Stalin, Joseph; Union of Soviet Socialist Republics

BIBLIOGRAPHY

Streim, A. (1981). *Die Behandlung sowjetischer Kriegsgefangener im "Fall Barbarossa."* Heidelberg, Germany: C. F. Müller.

Streit, C. (1978/1997). *Keine Kameraden: Die Wehrmacht und die sowjetischen Kriegsgefangenen, 1941–1945,* 4th edition. Bonn, Germany: Dietz.

Streit, C. (2000). "Soviet Prisoners of War in the Hands of the Wehrmacht." *War of Extermination: The German Military in World War II, 1941-44,* eds. Hannes Heer and Klaus Naumann. New York: Berghahn.

Christian Gerlach

Sparta

A precursor of genocidal regimes, ancient Sparta shared some characteristics with modern cases. Relevant features of its classical history include territorial expansion, war crimes, ethnic conflict, a tyrannical domestic hierarchy, and an agrarian, anti-urban ideology.

Territorial Expansion

Sparta was an expansionist militaristic state in what is present-day Greece. Historian Paul Cartledge called it a "workshop of war" (Cartledge, 2001, p. 89). In the eighth century BCE, Sparta destroyed Aigys in its own region of Lakonia. Next, the conquest of neighboring Messenia doubled Lakonia's population and made Sparta the wealthiest Greek state, facing no invasions of its territory for more than three centuries. Sparta exploited Messenia from 735 to 370 BCE, crushing revolts in the seventh and fifth centuries. Messenians comprised most of Sparta's serflike labor force, the Helots.

In the sixth century, Sparta expanded across southern Greece, conquering Tegea, controlling Arcadia, defeating Argos, seizing Cythera; as Herodotus wrote, "subjugating" most of the Peloponnese (Cartledge, 2001, p. 119). Cartledge described Sparta as "a leader of the Greek world" by the year 500, when it directed the Peloponnesian League (Cartledge, 2001, p. 124). It played key roles in the Greek victories over Persia in 490 and 480, and its defeat of Athens in the Peloponnesian War (431–403) brought Sparta to its zenith. Eventually, however, a Theban invasion liberated Messenia in 370 and 369. Sparta lost its independence in 195, before Rome conquered all of Greece.

Ethnic Conflict and Expansion

Sparta's expansion exacerbated ethnic conflicts. Its ruling Ephors ritually declared war on the Helots, in what Cartledge called "politically calculated religiosity designed to absolve in advance from ritual pollution any Spartan who killed a Helot."

Early Athenian politician Thucydides described a Helot revolt at Mt. Ithome in the 460s, which produced "the first open quarrel" between Sparta and Athens. The Spartans had called on Athenian aid against the Helots. However, disheartened by failure of their combined assault on Mt. Ithome, "apprehensive of the enterprising and revolutionary character of the Athenians, and further *looking upon them as of alien extraction,*" Sparta sent the Athenians home. The offended Athenians "allied themselves with Sparta's enemy Argos." The Messenian rebels surrendered to Sparta's conditions: "That they should depart from the Peloponnese under safe conduct, and should never set foot in it again; any one who might hereafter be found there was to be the slave of his captor" (Thucydides, I.102–3).

The warfare fostered increased brutality. According to Thucydides, on the outbreak of the Peloponnesian War, "the Lacedaemonians butchered as enemies all whom they took on the sea, whether allies of Athens or neutrals." Spartan troops took Plataea and coldbloodedly "massacred . . . not less than two hundred" of its men, "with twenty-five Athenians who had shared in the siege. The women were taken as slaves." In 419, Spartans captured Hysiae, "killing all the freemen that fell into their hands" (Thucidides II.67.3, III.68.2, V.83). Spartan massacres ranged from what historians define as war crimes to racial murder and brutal domestic repression.

Domestic Tyranny

At the bottom of the social ladder, the Helots' agricultural servitude released every Spartan from productive labor. Bound to a plot of land, Helots worked "under pain of instant death"; even the local Lakonian Helots were often expendable (Cartledge, 2001, pp. 89, 24). Scholar G. E. M. de Ste. Croix wrote that Spartans could "cut the throats of their Helots at will, provided only that they had gone through the legal formality of declaring them 'enemies of the state'" (de Ste. Croix, 1972, p. 92). According to Thucydides, the Spartans had "raised up some Helot suppliants from the temple of Poseidon at Taenarus [in Lakonia], led them away and slain them" (Thucydides I.128). Cartledge noted that Helots were "culled" by Spartan youth as part of their training: the *Krypteia,* or "Secret Service Brigade" of select eighteen-year-olds, had to forage for themselves across the countryside, commissioned "to kill, after dark, any of the Spartans' enslaved Greek population of Helots whom they should accidentally-on-purpose come upon" (Cartledge, 2001, pp. 88–89). In the eighth year of the Peloponnesian War, Spartan forces massacred 2,000 Helots who had served in their army. Under a pretext, they were invited to request emancipation, "as it was thought that the first to claim their freedom would be the most high-spirited and the most apt to rebel" (Thucydides IV.80).

Above Helots on the social ladder were about eighty communities of skilled townsmen or *Perioikoi.* Free but under Sparta's suzerainty, they lacked Spartan citizenship rights, even though the Lakonian Perioikoi were "indistinguishable ethnically, linguistically and culturally from the Spartans" (Cartledge, 2002, p. 84); others were Messenian.

One-tenth of the polity's population, fewer than 10,000 people, were full citizens. These *Spartiates,* the male inhabitants of Sparta's five villages, trained there, barred from agricultural labor. Their occupation was warfare. The Spartiates paid common mess-dues out of the produce delivered to them individually by the Helots tied to working their private plots. Though their land was unequally distributed, Spartiates adopted simple, uniform dress.

Agrarian Ideology
From its beginnings, Sparta's system was almost totally agricultural, conservative, and land oriented. Thucydides reported four centuries later that Sparta was not "brought together in a single town . . . but composed of villages after the old fashion of Greece" (Thucydides I.10.2). Its closed system contrasted with the Greek city-states. Sparta favored autarchy over both trade and towns, carefully controlling commerce. Spartiates could not trade nor purchase a range of consumption goods. Cartledge wrote that Lakonia "was extraordinarily autarchic in essential foodstuffs, and its possession of abundant deposits of iron ore within its own frontiers may have been a contributory factor in its decision not to import silver to coin," a policy dating from c.550 BCE (Cartledge, 2002, p. 134). Until the early third century, Sparta coined no silver, unlike other Greek states in their prime. Iron spits apparently figured in Spartan exchanges. Plutarch asserted that the early Spartan lawgiver Lycurgus "introduced a large iron coin too bulky to carry off in any great quantity." Seneca said Spartans paid debts "in gold or in leather bearing an official stamp" (Bondanella and Bondanella, 1997, p. 387). Archaeologists have found few coins at Perioikic sites. Sparta, like Pol Pot's Democratic Kampuchea, seems to have been one of history's few states without a currency.

It was a demanding state. Rich or poor, the Spartiates or *homoioi* ("peers"), were subject to collective interests and obliged to undergo "an austere public upbringing (the *agoge*) followed by a common lifestyle of participation in the messes and in military training and service in the army" (*Oxford Classical Dictionary online*). The state, not individual landowners, owned the Helots who worked the Spartiates' private landholdings. The state alone could emancipate Helots. And it not only enforced communal eating and uniformity of attire, but according to Thucydides, "did most to assimilate the life of the rich to that of the common people" (Cartledge, 2002, p. 134; Thucydides I.6.4). The state prohibited individual names on tombstones (Cartledge, 2001, p. 117).

Ancient Greek historian Xenophon noted that Lycurgus had arranged for the Spartans to eat their meals in common, "because he knew that when people are at home they behave in their most relaxed manner" (Whitby, 2002, p. 98). Communal living facilitated state supervision. Spartan boys left home at age seven for a rigorous state upbringing. A Spartiate who married before age thirty was not allowed to live with his wife beyond infrequent secret visits. Fathers who had married after thirty lived most of their lives communally, with male peers. In Cartledge's view, Spartan women enjoyed "certain freedoms, including legal freedoms, that were denied to their Athenian counterparts, but they were not, to put it mildly, as liberated as all that" (Cartledge, 2001, p. 106).

Classical Sparta's fusion of the rhetoric of freedom with expansionist violence, racial xenophobia, domestic repression, and agrarian ideology recurred in the twentieth century. Praising Sparta for its "abandonment of sick, frail, deformed children," Adolf Hitler called it "the first racialist state" (Weinberg, 2003, p. 21). Pol Pot's communist Cambodia reproduced many ideological features of ancient Sparta, including expansionist militarism and war crimes, ethnic brutality, egalitarian rhetoric with a harshly exploitative tripartite social pyramid, an austere communal barracks lifestyle, and repression of the family unit.

SEE ALSO Ancient World; Athens and Melos; Carthage

BIBLIOGRAPHY
Cartledge, Paul (2001). *Spartan Reflections.* Berkeley: University of California Press.

Cartledge, Paul (2002). *Sparta and Lakonia: A Regional History 1300 to 362 B.C.,* 2nd edition. London: Routledge.

de Ste. Croix, G. E. M. (1972). *The Origins of the Peloponnesian War.* London: Duckworth.

Kagan, Donald (1969). *The Outbreak of the Peloponnesian War.* Ithaca, N.Y.: Cornell University Press.

Kiernan, Ben (2004). "External and Indigenous Sources of Khmer Rouge Ideology." In *The Road to the Third Indochina War,* ed. Odd Arne Westad and Sophie Quinn-Judge. London: Frank Cass.

Kiernan, Ben (2004). "The First Genocide: Carthage 146 BC." *Diogenes* 203:27–39.

Pomeroy, Sarah B. (2002). *Spartan Women.* New York: Oxford University Press.

Rawson, Elizabeth (1969). *The Spartan Tradition in European Thought.* New York: Oxford University Press.

Thucydides. *History of the Peloponnesian War.*

Weinberg, Gerhard L., ed. (2003). *Hitler's Second Book: The Unpublished Sequel to Mein Kampf.* New York: Enigma.

Whitby, Michael, ed. (2002). *Sparta.* New York: Routledge.

Ben Kiernan

Srebrenica

The Srebrenica massacre, in which some seven thousand Bosnian Muslim males were executed by Bosnian Serb forces in July 1995 in the Yugoslav War, is widely recognized as the worst single war crime committed in Europe since World War II. The International Criminal Tribunal for the Former Yugoslavia (ICTY) has condemned the crime as an act of genocide. Srebrenica has also become synonymous with a great failure of the international community. Neither the protection of United Nations (UN) Security Council Resolutions nor the presence of a Dutch peacekeeping battalion deterred the Bosnian Serb attack on the "safe area" or prevented the subsequent massacre. Not until June 11, 2004, did the Bosnian Serb government, responding to strong international pressure, release a forty-two-page report admitting that police and army units under its control had "participated" in the massacre, and that government forces had undertaken extensive measures to "hide the crime by removing bodies."

The Massacre

Srebrenica is a little town in eastern Bosnia and Herzegovina that was bypassed in the Serb offensive in the opening stages of the war in March and April 1992. A renewed offensive in 1993 led to UN Security Council Resolution 819 (April 16, 1993), which declared the town and its surroundings a "safe area." Some 40,000 Muslim refugees from all over eastern Bosnia were surrounded in the isolated enclave. On July 6, 1995, as part of the attempt to "clean up the map" in preparation for ending the war, Bosnian Serb forces launched a carefully prepared attack, which led to the fall of the enclave on July 11. Approximately 15,000 Muslim men tried to break out and reach Bosnian government–held

territory in central Bosnia. Thousands were captured and executed in a well-organized operation, lasting slightly more than a week. Some 25,000 people sought refuge around the main UN compound. Males were separated from women and children. While the 23,000 women and children were deported, approximately 2,000 men were taken away and executed.

The massacre reveals a pattern that was common to Serb strategy and tactics in the war. Srebrenica is a clear instance of the strategy of ethnic cleansing practiced by the Serbs since 1991. This strategy aimed to create an ethnically homogenous Serb state by forcing non-Serbs to flee as the result of acts of demonstrative atrocity against civilians. In the atrocities, men were objects of special attention. Their removal in particular was deemed to render communities incapable of further resistance and prevent the return of the surviving population to their original homes.

Nonetheless, the scale of the massacre was uncommon. Why did the Bosnian Serbs attempt to kill all the men from Srebrenica? The official Dutch investigation concluded that it was a combination of anger and frustration at the surprise escape attempt by the men, as well as of a desire to revenge the vicious attacks by Bosnian Muslims from the enclave in the previous years. A more convincing explanation, also accepted by the Appeals Chamber in the Krstic trial, is that the genocide would remove a cross-section of men from all over eastern Bosnia and thereby secure the whole region from effective Muslim irredentism. A related contentious issue is the timing of the decision to massacre the men. The official Dutch investigation claims that the decision was taken after the fall of the enclave and hence the genocide was a largely improvised action. Others argue that the decision was taken much earlier and thus the genocide was a premeditated act.

The Aftermath

Soon after the event, the ICTY indicted prominent Bosnian Serb leaders for their crimes. In November 1995 the first individuals to be indicted were Bosnian Serb president Radovan Karadzic and the Bosnian Serb Army commander, General Ratko Mladic. Although as of mid-2004 they had avoided capture, the former Yugoslav leader, Slobodan Milosevic, appeared before the Tribunal and was accused of complicity in the genocide (although the evidence linking him with Srebrenica was slight). Many of the "second echelon" of lesser military figures with direct involvement were also tried. A member of one of the execution squads, Drazen Erdemovic, was convicted in 1996. More importantly, the commander of the Bosnian Serb Army Corps that controlled the area, General Radislav Krstic, was sentenced to forty-six years in 2001 (a sentence that was reduced to thirty-five years on appeal in 2004). A number of his subordinate officers were convicted in late 2003. The massacre was committed by relatively small numbers of troops and guided primarily by Security and Special Police personnel. The most senior officers were Colonels Ljubisa Beara and Ljubomir Borovcanin. They, like their commanding officer General Mladic, remained at large as of mid-2004.

The evidence in the trials was based on forensic proof, witness statements, and documents. This has led to the judgment that the Srebrenica massacre constituted genocide. The exhumation of bodies reveals that many thousands of Muslim men died not as the result of combat, but of large-scale executions. Moreover, the victims were not exclusively of military age, but included boys, old men, and invalids. Finding witnesses has posed a problem. Very few Muslims survived the massacres and few Serb suspects have admitted guilt. Controversially, the prosecution reverted to plea-bargaining. Trial judges, however, have expressed great reservations about this practice as it suggests that individual punishment for some of the most heinous crimes possible can be avoided by testifying against others.

Documentary evidence has been critical in all trials. A key part is formed by the military archive of the Bosnian Serb armed forces that was captured by North American Treaty Organization (NATO) troops after the war ended. This archive included, for example, the plan of attack and much administrative material that revealed which units and personnel were involved in the Srebrenica operation. A second important documentary trail involved intercepts of radio communications of Bosnian Serb forces made by Bosnian Muslim military intelligence. These intercepts played a major role in the Krstic trial as they tended to be more explicit about what actually took place than the written documents. On appeal, however, many intercepts were judged sufficiently ambiguous to allow for weaker interpretations benefiting the defendant. Hence, General Krstic's conviction for being a "principal perpetrator" of genocide was reduced to one of an "aider and abettor."

Unsucccessful Humanitarian Intervention
Srebrenica is often regarded as the emblematic failure of the humanitarian intervention in the former Yugoslavia. The Dutch UN battalion that was there to protect the "safe area" has become a particular focus of criticism. The unit appeared to have consciously allowed itself to be reduced to the role of impotent bystander while the genocide was committed. Despite undoubted shortcomings, much of the criticism is

misplaced. In the end, Srebrenica fell because of a lack of will on the part of the international community to use force in defense of human rights. The weak and ambiguous mandate of the 1993 UN Security Council Resolution that made Srebrenica a "safe area" already exemplified this. It was confirmed by a string of other actions, ranging from the unwillingness to back up the implementation of peace plans by force, if necessary, to the half-hearted attempt to use NATO air power in May and June 1995 (which resulted in extensive hostage taking by the Bosnian Serbs and a swift capitulation by the international community). Within this political context, the behavior of the Dutch troops and, more broadly, the UNPROFOR mission in the former Yugoslavia, becomes understandable. They were expected to avoid actions that led to UN casualties and might involve the international community in a shooting war. Added into this mix was a persistent disbelief that the Bosnian Serbs would dare take the whole safe area and commit genocide. The shock of Srebrenica did directly lead to the armed intervention of August and September 1995 that resulted in the Dayton Peace Agreements being signed the following November. It also led to a much firmer stance, and ultimately armed intervention, over Kosovo in 1999.

SEE ALSO Bosnia and Herzegovina; Bystanders; Genocide; Humanitarian Intervention; Massacres

BIBLIOGRAPHY
Gow, James (2003). *The Serbian Project and Its Adversaries: A Strategy of War Crimes* London: Hurst.
Honig, Jan Willem, and Norbert Both (1997). *Srebrenica: Record of a War Crime,* revised edition. New York: Penguin.
Netherlands Institute for War Documentation. (April 2002). "Srebrenica, a 'Safe' Area: Reconstruction, Background, Consequences and Analyses of the Fall of a Safe Area." Available from http://www.srebrenica.nl.
Report of the Secretary-General Pursuant to General Assembly Resolution 53/55. (November 15, 1999). *The Fall of Srebrenica.* Available from: http://www.un.org/peace/srebrenica.pdf.
Wood, Nicholas (June 12, 2004). "Bosnian Serbs Admit Responsibility for the Massacre of 7,000." *The New York Times.*

Jan Willem Honig

Sri Lanka

Ethnic groups in Sri Lanka have been at war since 1983. The war is dominantly ethnic in its construction but not genocidal in a strict sense of the definition of the term, in that the conflict or war is not directed toward the elimination of a population on ethnic or racial grounds. However, the passions of the war are fueled in an ideology of nationalism, given greater impetus through religious values that are one major basis for ethnic distinction. This ethnic distinction took on a destruction of genocidal quality not dissimilar from other conflicts of a genocidal character, in Kosovo, Bosnia, Rwanda, and increasingly in other parts of Africa.

The war in Sri Lanka has affected the lives of all communities in Sri Lanka. These include the major parties to the conflict, the dominant Sinhala-speaking largely Buddhist population (some two-thirds of the island's population) located mainly in the fertile central, western, and southern coastal zones of the island, and the Tamil-speaking, mainly Hindu, population (less than one-third of the total population) who live in the dry northern and eastern parts of the island. Both populations have significant minorities of Christians (mainly Catholic, but also Protestants). There is an important minority of Muslims who are mainly Tamil-speaking and these are found in communities throughout the island. They have been caught up in the fighting, sometimes the victims of violence from both Buddhist Sinhala and Hindu Tamils.

All of these populations have a history in the island stretching far back into precolonial times. Both Sinhala Buddhists and Hindu Tamils make claim to the island as their indigenous heritage and the often furious debate involving archaeological and other evidence is very much a part of the enduring crisis, legitimating the rival claims of the warring parties. However, the grounds for the war were largely established in recent colonial history starting with the arrival of the Portuguese in the early fifteenth century and ending with Dutch occupation, and from the late eighteenth century through to the mid-twentieth century, with the British. The political and economic changes that occurred in the island in these colonial periods and in the postcolonial aftermath created the structures within which the ethnic crisis and war of the early twenty-first century took form.

In the course of twenty years of open ethnic hostilities in Sri Lanka official statistics indicate that some sixty thousand individuals have lost their lives on both sides of the Sinhala/Tamil ethnic divide. Many of the deaths have been among Sri Lanka military and among combatants in various Tamil guerrilla groups, but especially the commanding Liberation Tigers of Tamil Eelam (LTTE). Civilian populations and particularly Tamil Hindus (but also Tamil Christians and Muslims sometimes as a result of LTTE attacks) have suffered the greatest number of casualties and despair resulting from social, economic, and territorial dislocation and from the deprivations and rigors of confinement and restriction imposed by the ebb and flow of combat.

Sinhalese populations both directly and indirectly have also suffered. A serious spin-off from the intensification of ethnic hostilities and the changing fortunes and uncertainties of the war has been growing civilian unrest among the Sinhala population. A major insurrection organized in the late 1980s by the Janatha Vimukthi Peramuna (JVP), also known as the Peoples Liberation Movement, and largely supported by unemployed rural and urban Sinhala youth, activated repressive military and paramilitary organizations of the Sri Lanka state. These, which had assumed much of their character because of the larger ethnic conflict, focused their acutely destructive capacities on the Sinhala civilian population (and not merely JVP supporters). Various clandestine operations by military and paramilitary forces resulted in an extremely high loss of life, which, as of the early 2000s, has received little in the way of open or serious investigation. Although tensions run high in the early twenty-first century, there are indications that the war is drawing to a close.

Ethnic Diversity

The ethnic/religious shape of the conflict and war has a long history of development. Undoubtedly, other forces of a nonethnic or religious character—often of a social class kind—also gave impetus to the struggle. Social-class issues have sustained the war even when ethnic and religious factors have declined in importance.

The hostility of mainly ethnic Sinhala majority toward the Tamil ethnic minority has its roots in colonial and postcolonial history. The ethnic categories and their political significance arose during the course of Western imperial intrusions into the island, known as Ceylon from the colonial era and until 1972, and especially under the British who subdued the entire island with their conquest of Kandy in 1815. Ethnic identity became a marker of cultural and social distinction in a colonial political order whose rigidity that was not typical of Ceylon's past. As various scholars have stressed, terms like "Sinhala" and "Tamil" used in ancient precolonial sources often described ruling lineages and structures of political allegiance that were often very fluid. The kings who defended largely Sinhala-speaking populations during the Western invasions (Portuguese, Dutch, and finally the British) were of Tamil lineage from South India. With colonial rule, ethnic distinctions served bureaucratic and governing interests and the social boundaries described ethnically became far less porous and situationally relative than before. Such ethnic boundaries informed the formation of constituencies of political interest and nationalist resistance leading to Independence in 1947 and the burgeoning of postcolonial nationalism.

Ethnically based political rhetoric of a powerfully nationalist kind further bolstered by appeals to common language and religious affiliation was integral in the formation of political communalism. Moreover, political parties in the postcolonial period expressed a variety of socioeconomic concerns and felt inequalities under cover of debates over ethnicity. The language issue was of supreme importance in the years following independence, when Sinhala (*swabasha*) became the main language of the state. The policy of Sinhala-only was promulgated by Prime Minister Solomon West Ridgeway Dias (SWRD) Bandaranaike in order to appeal to a largely Sinhalese-speaking peasantry and the lower middle class and working class in the central, western, and southern regions of the island. English, the language of colonialism, was generally seen as a means of exclusion, only available to educated elites and inhibiting the opportunities for employment and upward social mobility of hitherto depressed groups. Tamils were widely perceived as advantaged in the job market (especially in access to the professions and highly prized positions in government bureaucracies) because they were seen as better qualified in their English-speaking abilities (to some degree a legacy of missionary activity in the Tamil north). The postcolonial politics of language intensified ethnic division. Ethnically motivated restrictions on Tamil access to university places (especially in medicine) and to positions in the civil service were a major source of discontent among Tamils from the 1970s.

Anti-Tamil feeling was also apparent in a series of attempts to repatriate to India Tamils who had been brought as indentured laborers to work on the British and later largely Sinhala-owned tea estates in the highland areas of the island. These highly exploited estate workers attracted little help from the larger Tamil population on the island who, as with the dominant Sinhala population, saw themselves as indigenous to the island and distinct in certain cultural and linguistic ways from Tamils in India. A closer feeling of identity between tea-estate Tamils (who were also discriminated against in terms of caste) and the larger Tamil community in Sri Lanka is a late 1990s development and, perhaps, one positive outcome of the ethnic war.

Religious Factors

The misconception among Sinhalese that Sri Lanka was the last refuge of Buddhism was a further factor in the growth of ethnic hostility especially by Sinhala toward Tamils. British rule was regarded as instrumental in the reduction of the preeminence of the Buddhist religion. Sinhala nationalism from the late nineteenth century to the 2000s was largely motivated by a movement of Buddhist revitalization (linked to a reassertion of the value of Sinhala custom) against the effects of colonial domination. This was keenly supported by members of the urban merchant classes situated along the western and southern coasts. The various caste-based communities that formed around members of these classes were and continue to be forceful in the pursuit of Sinhala interests defined in opposition to Tamils. The engagement of religion (specifically Buddhism) to nationalist ethnic allegiance is a key factor in generating the passions of the conflict. It politicized the Buddha clergy, making them central to ethnically defined communal political and economic interest (a legacy of the revitalization movement that paradoxically made a doctrinally other worldly religion acutely this worldly). The assassination in 1959 of Prime Minister Bandaranaike, the chief architect of Sinhala ethnic nationalism, by a member of the Buddha clergy, is significant in this regard. In 1972 Bandaranaike's widow, Sirimavo Bandaranaike, the then-elected prime minister, declared Buddhism to be the national religion.

Communalist rioting and killing of an ethnic kind was gathering force in Sri Lanka through to the early 1980s. Major attacks against ethnic Tamils occurred in 1947 soon after its independence, in 1956 and 1958, and there were incidents throughout the 1960s. The 1970s were full of ethnic tension and the capital, Colombo, as well as other urban centers became increasingly subject to curfews in order to dampen any ethnic disturbances. Ethnic tensions, especially in the south (a powerful region of Sinhala nationalism), precipitated a form of ethnic cleansing. Minority Tamil populations went to Tamil areas in the large urban centers such as Colombo. The participation of Sinhala in Tamil Hindu festival events—a feature of religious life in some centers in the south (and also in the Colombo areas)—declined and eventually stopped. The increasingly greater divisions of ethnicity that appeared in everyday social life heightened communal divisions.

All came to a head in August 1983 when a unit of Sinhalese soldiers was ambushed near the sacred Buddhist city of Anuradhapura. Anti-Tamil riots spread through major urban centers but were the most fierce in Colombo. There were attacks on middle-class Tamil residential areas but perhaps the strongest were in the abject shanty communities of the poor. Sinhalese attacked their Tamil neighbors, many of them refugees from the tea estates. Sinhalese thugs roamed the streets. Government authorities were slow to react and there were many stories of Sinhalese police standing by as

Since 1948 the struggle between majority Sinhala-speaking Buddhists and minority Tamils (mostly Hindu) has been a feature of political life in Sri Lanka. There has been on-and-off civil war in Sri Lanka since 1983, with village-scale slaughters on both sides. In this photo taken in April 2004, Tamil women stand in line to vote at a polling station in the district of Batticaloa, in Eastern Sri Lanka. [**AP/WORLD WIDE PHOTOS**]

atrocities were committed. Suggestions of government complicity were strong, as were rumors that President Jayawardena's conservative United National Party government had instigated the rioting as a type of pogrom. There is some evidence that gangs of thugs were bussed to Tamil zones (violence having a long history in political party rivalry). Indeed, prior to the rioting, serious threats urging Tamil independence had been directed at the then relatively small LTTE guerrilla movement and the Tamil population as a whole. The riots blazed for four days. Official estimates of Tamil deaths are in the vicinity of 300, although other estimates are far greater. There is only one recorded instance of a Sinhala death, a person fleeing rioters. Approximately 300,000 Tamils living in Sinhala-dominated areas fled their homes. The start of the ethnic war that has consumed Sri Lanka and in which Tamil civilians have

been the greatest victims can be traced to these events of 1983.

Socioeconomic Factors

Violent nationalism of a genocidal kind can generally be shown to have its roots in socioeconomic crises. There was growing unemployment in Sri Lanka partly as a consequence of the liberalizing and opening up of a hitherto relatively closed economy. Sri Lanka was one of the first countries to apply structural adjustment policies recommended by the World Bank and the IMF. Liberalization of the economy was accompanied by a paring down of state-supported welfare services, the laying off of staff in state bureaucracies (a major employer), and the winding down of state industries and their privatization. These changes seemed to coincide with the increase in ethnic tensions that were further exacerbated by the Jayawardena government's intensifi-

encyclopedia of GENOCIDE *and* CRIMES AGAINST HUMANITY

cation of a populist rhetoric promoting Sinhala Buddhist nationalism.

The Role of Nationalist Rhetoric

Much of the discussion regarding the violence toward Tamils by ethnic Sinhalese populations has rightly emphasized its similarity with ethnic nationalism elsewhere, especially in Europe. Scholars discovered parallels with Nazi Germany and blamed the invention of a tradition of postcolonial government-sponsored Sinhala history narratives (which drew on Western constructions of the colonial period). Powerful criticisms were made of those nationalist arguments that asserted a continuity of ancient historical experience into the present; for example, that contemporary violence was a modern manifestation of ancient enmity between Sinhala and Tamil or was the latest instance of a long cycle of revenge. The essentialism and primordialism of such arguments were attacked not only because they were empirically inaccurate but also because they displaced responsibility for the destruction and suffering away from the contemporary state and its ruling interests. The hatred that was unleashed was the result of the constructions and falsehoods of modernity. The inventions of ethnic nationalism on both sides (for the rhetoric of Tamil nationalists paralleled, if in distinct ways, those of the Sinhala) encouraged sentiments that gave emotional force to the destruction.

Perhaps the politics of ethnic hatred and exclusion and extermination in modern times carries a potent hierarchical force. But in Sri Lanka this potential gathered much energy through the mythologies of nationalist rhetoric as this found a degree of acceptance in everyday religious and ritual practices. In other words, a nationalist argument of hierarchy—that the Tamil others should exist in a generally subordinate relation to Sinhala—was more evident given the nature of the mythological sources of Sinhala nationalism. The ethnic violence during the rioting in 1983, as well as the violence of the ensuing war involving attacks on Tamil civilian populations, often took a marked hierarchical form. Incidents were recorded of victims being forced to submit their bodies after the manner of Tamil victims before Sinhala heroes of the past. Some of the fury of the destruction, the radical disordering, often dismemberment of victims and fragmentation of their possessions, carried the disordering passion of a ritual process restructuring of person and world. In many respects the direction of the ethnic war as it developed in terms of strategy and in the control and occupation of territory assumed symbolic values appropriate to the nationalist mythologies that gave it impetus. Leading politicians, including the president, and military commanders not only appealed to the ideas conveyed in an-

cient mythology but to a degree came to live and act them out.

The symbolic values born of nationalist discourse that have framed both ethnic conflict and war continue to have force into the 2000s. To some extent Sinhala often appear to be imprisoned in their dialectic even though there is an urgency among many sections of the population to break free. There is clear evidence that the urban and rural poor who have borne the greatest brunt of the tragedies of the war have grown tired of nationalist rhetoric. But it is still engaged by elites and this has complicated efforts by international groups (the Norwegians especially) to broker a settlement. Such an observation demands a stress on the social and economic lineaments underpinning the conflict, the almost total lack of trust that has developed between the warring parties notwithstanding.

There have been numerous shifts in elite formation, especially in relation to liberalization and contemporary globalization. To some extent this has driven an anxiety to achieve a settlement to the war, and was evident in the political tussle, given wide global media coverage, between the recently defeated prime minister and the elected president, Chandrika Kumaratunga, the daughter of Bandaranaike whose family is from the upper echelons of the still largely Kandyan-based ruling groups. The prime minister was closely associated with urban business and merchant groups with substantial local and international interests in peace. The general mood for peace was for a limited time encouraged by the U.S.–driven war on terrorism. This also produced a climate necessary for the highly successful guerrilla movement of the LTTE to come to the negotiating table. But this impetus to peace started to slow and became further hampered by the concern of powerful Sinhala elite groups to maintain a political and economic grip on the island, which the nationalist discourse they encouraged initially facilitated. It is the social dynamics of this elite (Sinhala and Tamil), many members of which have their roots in the colonial past and have spread their influence internationally (as a function of migration, some forced as a consequence of the war), that holds the much of the key to understanding the durability of the war and the persistence of suffering for all communities.

Conclusions

As the dominant population and in control of the machinery of power of the Sri Lanka government, much of the responsibility for reconciliation rests with Sinhala leaders. They, perhaps, have become weakened in responsibility with the growth in power of the LTTE. Overall, all sectors of Sri Lanka society have become subordinated to the logic of war in itself and this has driven other nationalist discourses among Tamil Hindus and the minority Muslim population alike. These paradigms in their own particular histories enlivened by the horrors of war, are making moves toward a peaceful solution.

The result of the conflict has had enormous polarizing effects on the society of Sri Lanka, creating a degree of division that was more imagined than real in the years leading to the war. The war has caused much death and suffering, which sometimes appeared to have genocidal ingredients. However, to label the events "genocidal" would be to indulge in a discourse that is part of the inflammatory rhetoric often used by members of the warring parties to justify the perpetration of violent acts.

SEE ALSO Death Squads; Ethnic Cleansing; Ethnic Groups; India, Modern; Nationalism; Refugees; Religion

BIBLIOGRAPHY

Ali, Ameer (2001). *Plural Identities and Political Choices of the Muslim Community.* Colombo, Sri Lanka: Marga Institute.

Bastin, Rohan (2001). *Globalization and Conflict.* Colombo, Sri Lanka: Marga Institute.

Daniel, E. Valentine (1997). *Charred Lullabies: Chapters in an Anthropography of Violence.* Princeton, N.J.: Princeton University Press.

Dumont, Louis (1974). *Homo Hierarchicus: The Caste System and Its Implications.* Chicago: University of Chicago Press.

Gunasinghe, Newton (1984). "Open Economy and Its Impact on Ethnic relations in Sri Lanka." In *Sri Lanka: The Ethnic Conflict,* ed. Committee for Rational Development. New Delhi, India: Navrang.

Gunatilleke, Godfrey (1984). "People of the Lion: Sinhala Consciousness in History and Historiography." In *Ethnicity and Social Change in Sri Lanka.* Colombo, Sri Lanka: Karunaratne for Social Sciences Association.

Hoole, Ranjan (2002). *Sri Lanka: The Arrogance of Power.* Jaffna, Sri Lanka: UTHR.

Kapferer, Bruce (1996). "Remythologizing Discourses: State and Insurrectionary Violence in Sri Lanka." In *Legitimization of Violence,* ed. David E. Apter. London: Macmillan.

Kapferer, Bruce (1997). *The Feast of the Sorcerer: Practices of Consciousness and Power.* Chicago: Chicago University Press.

Kapferer, Bruce (1998). *Legends of People, Myths of State: Violence, Intolerance, and Political Culture in Sri Lanka and Australia.* Washington, D.C.: Smithsonian Institution Press.

Moore, Mick (1993). "Thoroughly Modern Revolutionaries: The JVP in Sri Lanka." *Modern Asian Studies* 27(3): 593–642.

Ondaatjie, Michael (2001). *Anil's Ghost.* London: Picado.

Roberts, Michael, ed. (1979). *Collective Identities, Nationalism, and Protest in Modern Sri Lanka.* Colombo, Sri Lanka: Marga Publications.

Roberts, Michael (1982). *Caste Conflict and Elite Formation: The Rise of the Karava Elite in Sri Lanka 1500–1931.* New York: Cambridge University Press.

Roberts, Michael (1993). "Nationalism, the Past and the Present: The Case of Sri Lanka." *Ethnic and Racial Studies* 16(1):133–166.

Tambiah, Stanley J. (1986). *Sri Lanka: Ethnic Fratricide and the Dismantling of Democracy.* Chicago: Chicago University Press.

Tambiah, Stanley J. (1992). *Buddhism Betrayed? Religion, Politics, and Violence in Sri Lanka.* Chicago: Chicago University Press.

Wilson, Jayaratnam (1988). *The Break-Up of Sri Lanka: The Sinhala-Tamil Conflict.* Honolulu: University of Hawaii Press.

Bruce Kapferer

SS

Schutzstaffel, abbreviated as SS, literally means "protective guard." The roots of the SS go back to 1923, when Hitler designated fifty men to serve as his personal bodyguards. After Hitler and the Nazi Party came to power in January 1933, the tasks of the SS expanded, eventually resulting in the SS serving as instruments of murder, terror, repression, and intimidation under the direction of Heinrich Himmler, who held the office of Reichsführer-SS (Reich leader of the SS) through 1945.

After Hitler's failed attempt to overthrow the government of Weimar Germany in November 1923, the Nazi Party and all its organizations were temporarily declared illegal. When the Nazi Party was allowed to participate again in the political life of Germany in 1925, Hitler created the SS, a small force of some two hundred men, to provide protection for himself and other Party members.

In 1929, Hitler appointed the former Bavarian chicken farmer, Heinrich Himmler, to the post of Reichsführer-SS, and charged him with forming the SS into "an elite troop of the Party." In addition to protection for the Führer, it performed a number of different tasks, including carrying out functions previously reserved for the police. By this time, the SS had grown into a 52,000-man strong organization. As early as the spring of 1933, Himmler assigned members of the SS Death's Head Division (*Totenkopf*) to stand guard over the growing number of political opponents of the regime who were incarcerated in the first concentration camps in Nazi Germany. The SS also played a prominent role in cooperation with the German armed forces

Here, SS General Jurgen Stroop and German soldiers prepare to quell the Warsaw uprising, August 1943. One of many photos that Stroop later included in his report to the Nazi high command detailing his success in liquidating the Jewish ghetto. [SNARK/ART RESOURCE]

(*Wehrmacht*) in the June 1934 plot to murder Ernst Röhm and the leadership of the Brown Shirts (*Sturmabteilung* [SA]), which had begun to threaten the supremacy of the army.

As a reward for its role as assassins in the Röhm purge (also known as "The Night of the Long Knives"), Hitler established the SS as an independent organization within the Nazi Party. In 1936, Himmler, newly appointed Chief of Police in the Ministry of the Interior in addition to his title of Reichsführer-SS, consolidated the entire German police force, bringing the regular uniformed police (*Orpo*) and the Criminal Police (*Kripo*) together with the SS. This resulted in a single Party organ having jurisdiction over all of the police forces in Germany.

Once the Germans attacked Poland in September 1939 to start World War II, the infrastructure of the SS, now 240,000-strong, changed again. Himmler created the Reich Security Main Office (RSHA) as both a departmental agency of government and the SS. He ap-

pointed Reinhard Heydrich, head of the Security Service (*Sicherheitsdienst* [SD]) of the SS to lead the RSHA. Under Heydrich, the RSHA developed plans for the destruction of enemies of the State. These included the implementation of Nazi racial policies against targeted groups such as Jews, gypsies (Roma and Sinti), and Red Army and civilian political commissars through the deployment of mobile killing units (the *Einsatzgruppen*) of the SS (SD) and Security Police, which followed the German Army into the Soviet Union beginning in the summer of 1941, as well as the work of the Gestapo (secret police) in arranging deportations of millions of Jews to extermination camps or execution sites in occupied territories of Europe from 1941 to 1945.

The SS was also involved in the administration of concentration camps and extermination camps. By 1942 the Economics and Administration Main Office (WVHA) of the SS, under the direction of Oswald Pohl, had a firm hold on the exploitation of slave labor throughout the camp system. At its peak, it controlled more than six million prisoners, serving the economic interests of the Reich to replace the shortage of labor due to mounting casualties on all fronts.

In addition, the SS played an active role in the German armed forces. Originally intended as an elite group of "political soldiers," the Waffen-SS expanded its recruitment outside the Reich, and had over 900,000 men under arms by 1942. Known to have taken part in numerous violations of the laws of land warfare throughout the war, including the massacre of American POWs at Malmédy during the Battle of the Bulge in December 1944, members of the Waffen-SS earned a notorious reputation for brutal behavior. However, units of the Waffen-SS were some of the most highly decorated soldiers in the German armed forces.

The tribunal at the Nuremberg War Crimes Trials in 1946 declared that the SS as a whole, distinguished by their black uniforms (the Black Corps) with the signature markings of the SS written as twin lightning bolts in imitation runic script, was a criminal organization.

SEE ALSO Barbie, Klaus; Einsatzgruppen; Germany; Goebbels, Joseph; Heydrich, Reinhardt; Himmler, Heinrich; Streicher, Julius

BIBLIOGRAPHY

Breitman, Richard (1991). *The Architect of Genocide: Himmler and the Final Solution.* Hanover, N.H.: Brandeis University Press/University Press of New England.

Browder, George C. (1996). *Hitler's Enforcers: The Gestapo and the SS Security Service in the Nazi Revolution.* New York: Oxford University Press.

Hoffmann, Peter (2000). *Hitler's Personal Security: Protecting the Führer, 1921–1945.* New York: Da Capo Press.

Höhne, Heinz (1969). *The Order of the Death's Head: The Story of Hitler's SS.* New York: Penguin Books.

Krausnick, Helmut, Hans Buchheim, Martin Broszat, and Hans-Adolf Jacobsen, eds. (1968). *Anatomy of the SS State,* trans. Elizabeth Wiskemann. New York: Walker and Company.

Stein, George H. (1966). *The Waffen-SS: Hitler's Elite Guard at War.* Ithaca, NY: Cornell University Press.

Robert B. Bernheim

Stalin, Joseph

[DECEMBER 21, 1879–MARCH 5, 1953]
Russian revolutionary and politician; successor to Lenin as ruler of the Soviet Union and head of the Communist Party (1929 to 1953)

One of the bloodiest despots in modern history, Joseph Stalin helped transform the Soviet Union into a military and industrial superpower, but at a staggering cost in human lives and suffering. In the words of scholar Stephen Cohen, Stalin's rule was a "holocaust by terror" that "victimized tens of millions of people for twenty-five years."

Stalin was born Iosif Vissioronovich Djugashvili on December 21, 1879, in the Georgian village of Gori. The son of a poor shoemaker, Iosif became a professional revolutionary and at age thirty-four adopted the political name of Stalin, meaning "man of steel." A member of the Bolshevik faction of the Russian Social-Democratic Party, Stalin played a minor role in the 1917 October Revolution and entered the new Soviet government as Commissar of Nationalities. In 1922 he became General Secretary of the Communist Party, a position he subsequently transformed into the major base of power in the Soviet state. A gifted politician, Stalin outmaneuvered his rivals to become the sole leader of the party and the state by 1929.

Human life had little value for Stalin, who viewed people largely as instruments for serving the needs of the state. In the late 1920s, Stalin launched a massive drive to transform Soviet industry and agriculture. To support industrialization, he ordered the collectivization of agriculture and the creation of large-scale communal farms. But collectivization soon turned into a bloody civil war that raged across the countryside, resulting in the death and deportation of five to eight million people. Those who resisted faced either execution or exile to "special settlements" in remote northern regions, where up to a third of them died from the harsh conditions. Collectivization proved even more deadly during the famine years of 1932 and 1933 when an estimated five to eight million peasants died in Ukraine and Central Asia. Some scholars view this famine as a deliberate act of genocide, whereas others blame it on bureaucratic incompetence and poor planning.

Repression was central to Stalin's leadership from the beginning. Throughout the period from 1929 to 1953 the regime employed tactics of terror, arresting people on false charges of conspiracy and espionage, then either executing them or sentencing them to labor camps, where they toiled in harsh, debilitating conditions. Chronic absenteeism at work or picking up grain husks from a harvested field could bring a ten-year sentence. According to one scholar, over twenty-eight million Soviet citizens passed through the forced labor camps and colonies between 1929 and 1953. Located all across the Soviet Union, in every time zone, the camps were filthy, brutal, and dehumanizing. Death rates were high, averaging about 6 percent per year. One archival source states that over two million inmates died in the camps between 1929 and 1953, but this does not include all categories of prisoners.

The height of the Stalinist repression, known as the Great Terror, lasted from 1936 to 1939. The majority of victims during this period were from the Communist Party, the economic ministries, the military, the Communist International, and minority nationalities. No precise figures exist. Official KGB figures for 1937–1938 claim that just under 700,000 were executed and that at the beginning of the 1940s there were about 3.6 million in labor camps and prisons. Stephen Wheatcroft and R. W. Davies have calculated that the total number of excess deaths from 1927 to 1938 may have amounted to some ten million persons, 8.5 million killed between 1927 and 1936 and about 1 to 1.5 million between 1937 and 1938.

Historians disagree over the motives behind the terror. Some focus on Stalin's paranoia and thirst for power, while others cite fears of an internal "fifth column" in the face of pending war and the Nazi threat. Still others argue that the process moved in part from below, due to party in-fighting, the desire to settle personal scores, and anti-elitist sentiments among the rank and file. Stalin's role as author of the terror, however, is clear: He formulated the majority of the directives and personally commanded and supervised arrests, show trials, and executions.

During World War II, the Stalinist regime carried out ethnic cleansing, though the exact motives remain unclear. It deported 400,000 Volga Germans to Central Asia and Siberia out of fear that they would support the invading enemy. Between 1943 and 1944, Stalin ordered the deportation of about a million Chechens, Crimean Tatars, Balkars, Kalmiks, and Turks from their homelands to Central Asia, alleging that they had collaborated with the Germans. Transported in sealed boxcars, with no fresh air, proper food, sanitation, or medical care, as many as 40 percent died along the way from hunger, cold, and disease. Those who resisted the deportation were shot. Prior to the war, in 1940, Stalin had ordered the execution of 21,857 Poles. Of these, over 4,000 were officers who were shot and buried in mass graves in the Katyn Forest (Smolensk region). This crime was denied by the Soviet regime for fifty years.

After the war, smaller-scale repressions continued to fill the camps. The number of prisoners rose from 1,460,676 in 1945 to 2,468,524 in 1953. The postwar period was marked by fierce attacks on creative artists, deportations of Balt, Moldavian, and Ukrainian populations, and a virulent anti-Semitic campaign that culminated in the arrests in 1953 of nine Kremlin doctors on charges of murder and treason. In addition, there were

A portrait of Joseph Stalin to commemorate his seventieth birthday, on December 21, 1949. Communists around the world sent gifts to Stalin in 1949. During his lifetime he was often admired as a great world leaderusually by those living outside the Soviet Union (where little was known about its Gulags, mass executions, and state terrorism). [AP/WORLD WIDE PHOTOS]

over four million foreign POWs in the camp system, many of whom either died in captivity or had to wait up to ten years for repatriation.

Tragically, even Stalin's death in 1953 came at a price. On the day of his funeral, tens of thousands of people crowded in the streets to view the body, and many were crushed to death in the ensuing panic. Despite the magnitude of his crimes, Stalin's legacy remains complex. Some see him as the worst monster who ever ruled, a modern Genghis Khan who devoured his own children. Yet others consider him a resolute and even heroic leader who did what was necessary in order to modernize Russia and defeat its enemies. Some who lived through the Stalin years later remembered them as a time of vibrant idealism and energy. But no evaluation of Stalin's leadership can ignore the horrific price paid in human lives, and the incalculable physical, moral, and psychological destruction he left behind.

SEE ALSO Gulag; Katyn; Lenin, Vladimir; Ukraine (Famine); Union of Soviet Socialist Republics

BIBLIOGRAPHY

Applebaum, Anne (2003). *Gulag. A History*. New York: Doubleday.

Cohen, Stephen F. (1999). "Bolshevism and Stalinism." In *Stalinism: Essays in Historical Interpretation*, ed. Robert C. Tucker. New York: Transaction Publishers.

Davies, R. W., Mark Harrison, and Stephen Wheatcroft, eds. (1994). *The Economic Transformation of the Soviet Union*. Cambridge: Cambridge University Press.

Naimark, Norman M. (2001). *Fires of Hatred. Ethnic Cleansing in Twentieth-Century Europe*. Cambridge, Mass.: Harvard University Press.

Read, Christopher, ed. (2003). *The Stalin Years. A Reader*. New York: Palgrave Macmillan.

Elaine MacKinnon

Statistical Analysis

Throughout conflicts, apologists for the side in power often excuse atrocities committed by their side with the claim that "violations are being committed on all sides of the conflict." The objective of such a statement is to render the parties morally equivalent, thereby relieving observers of the responsibility or duty to make a judgment about whether one side is the aggressor and the other is acting in self-defense. Even when the greater historical narrative involves more than these labels imply, in situations of massive human rights violations the perpetrators are rarely balanced in power. Although it may be literally true that all parties to a conflict have committed at least one violation, often the number of violations each party commits differs by a factor of ten or more relative to their opponents. In some cases quantitative analysis may offer a method for assessing claims about moral responsibility for crimes against humanity, including genocide. Statistics provide a way to measure crimes of policy—massive crimes that result from institutional or political decisions.

Although all parties may be guilty, they are rarely guilty in equal measure. Only with quantitative arguments can the true proportions of responsibility be understood. In this way one can transcend facile claims about "violations on all sides" in favor of an empirically rich view of responsibility for atrocities. Did the monthly number of killings increase or decrease in the first quarter of 1999? Were there more violations in Province A or in Province B? Were men more affected than women, or adults relative to children? These simple quantitative evaluations may be important questions when linked to political processes. Perhaps a new government took power and one needs to assess its im-

pact on the state's respect for human rights. Or a military officer may move from Province A to Province B, and one may wish to determine if he is repeating the crimes he committed in Province A. Simple descriptive statistics based on properly gathered data can address these questions more precisely than the kinds of casual assessments that nonquantitative observers often make.

There are three areas in which nonquantitative analysts most often make statistical mistakes: estimating the total magnitude of violations; understanding how bias may have affected the data collection or interpretation; and comparing the relative proportions of responsibility among perpetrators. Poor information management and inappropriate statistical analysis can lead to embarrassing reversals of findings once proper methods are applied.

The use of statistical methods that demonstrably control biases and enable estimates of total magnitude can give analysts a rigorous basis for drawing conclusions about politically important questions. One such method, multiple systems estimation, uses three or more overlapping lists of some event (such as killings) to make a statistical estimate of the total number of events, including those events excluded from all three lists. "Overlapping" in this sense means events that are documented on two or more lists. The estimate made by this technique can control for several biases that might affect the original reporting which led to the lists of events.

For example, among the most important questions the Guatemalan Commission for Historical Clarification (CEH is the Spanish acronym) had to answer was whether the army had committed acts of genocide against the Maya. Using qualitative sources and field investigation, the CEH identified six regions in which genocide might have occurred. Data were collated from testimonies given to three sources: nongovernmental organizations (NGOs), the Catholic Church, and the CEH.

If genocide has been committed, then at least two statistical indicators should be clear. First, the absolute magnitude of the violations should be large. Second, there should be a big difference in the rate of killing between those who are in the victim group versus those people in the same region who are not in the victim group. It is inadequate to argue that some large number of people of specific ethnicities have been killed, because it might have been that they were simply unfortunate enough to live in very violent areas. Killing in an indiscriminate pattern might be evidence of some other crime, but if genocide occurred, a substantial difference in killing rates between targeted and nontargeted groups should exist. Thus, to find statistical evidence consistent with genocide, it is not enough that certain people were killed at high rate, but also that other nearby people were killed at much lower rates.

The CEH analysts conducted a multiple systems estimate of the total deaths of indigenous people and nonindigenous people between 1981 and 1983 in the six regions identified. For each group in each region, the estimated total number of deaths was divided into the Guatemalan government's census figures for indigenous and nonindigenous people in 1981. The CEH showed that resulting proportions were consistent with the genocide hypothesis. In each region indigenous people were killed at a rate five to eight times greater than nonindigenous people. This statistical finding was one of the bases of the CEH's final conclusion that the Guatemalan army committed acts of genocide against the Maya.

Other human rights projects have incorporated statistical reasoning. Sociologists and demographers have testified at the trial of Slobodan Milosevic and others tried before the International Criminal Tribunal for the Former Yugoslavia. They have provided quantitative insights on ethnic cleansing, forced migration, and the evaluation of explanatory hypotheses.

In the early twenty-first century, the statistical analysis of human rights violations is just beginning, and much work remains. New techniques should be developed, including easier methods for conducting random probability sampling in the field, richer demographic analysis of forced migration, and more flexible techniques for rapidly creating lots of graphical views of data. Human rights advocacy and analysis have benefited tremendously from the introduction of better statistical methods. The international community needs to continue to find new ways to employ existing methods, and to further research on new methods, so that human rights reporting becomes more rigorous. Statistics help establish the evidentiary basis of human rights allegations about crimes of policy.

SEE ALSO Forensics; Genocide; Massacres

BIBLIOGRAPHY

Ball, Patrick (2000). "The Guatemalan Commission for Historical Clarification: Inter-Sample Analysis." In *Making the Case: Investigating Large Scale Human Rights Violations Using Information Systems and Data Analysis*, ed. Patrick Ball, Herbert F. Spirer, and Louise Spirer. Washington, D.C.: AAAS.

Ball, P., W. Betts, F. Scheuren, J. Dudukovic, and J. Asher (2002). *Killings and Refugee Flow in Kosovo March–June 1999*. Washington, D.C.: AAAS.

Brunborg, H., H. Urdal, and T. Lyngstad (2001). "Accounting for Genocide: How Many Were Killed in Srebrenica?" Paper presented at the Uppsala Conference on Conflict Data, Uppsala, June 8–9, 2001. Available from http://www.pcr.uu.se/conferenses/Euroconference/paperbrunborg.doc.

Ward, K. (2000). "The United Nations Mission for the Verification of Human Rights in Guatemala." In *Making the Case: Investigating Large Scale Human Rights Violations Using Information Systems and Data Analysis*, ed. Patrick Ball, Herbert F. Spirer, and Louise Spirer. Washington, D.C.: AAAS.

Patrick Ball

Statutory Limitations

Statutory limitations (also known as prescriptions or prescriptibility) bar state authorities from investigating and prosecuting a crime after a certain length of time. These limitations are based, in part, on the premise that a fair trial becomes increasingly difficult as time passes following the alleged act. Evidence may be lost or destroyed, memories may become faulty, and proof that might otherwise support a valid defense may become inaccessible. After a certain amount of time has passed, the risk of irremediable harm to the rights of the accused is seen to outweigh the state's interest in prosecuting a crime. Thus, statutory limitations require prosecutors either to start proceedings within a set time or to free a potential accused from the threat of prosecution.

Statutes of limitations are frequently found in civil law or continental legal systems. In common law countries a long delay is more likely to lead to questions about abuse of process, the right to be tried within a reasonable time, or the public interest in addressing a matter long after the suspected crime took place. When limitations exist, exceptions or extensions are increasingly recognized for certain crimes (e.g., the sexual abuse of children, where for various reasons the crime may be reported only many years later). The nature of the crime and the state's interest in its punishment are seen to strike a different balance with respect to the fair trial concerns that underlie the principle of prescription.

The same concerns arise with genocide and crimes against humanity. The high-profile trials at Nuremberg and subsequent proceedings following World War II did not lead to the widespread prosecution that some sought of the many suspected Nazi and other war criminals who lived either openly or in hiding around the world. In addition, neither the founding instruments of the military tribunals that sat at Nuremberg and Tokyo, the 1948 United Nations (UN) Convention on the Prevention and Punishment of the Crime of Genocide, nor the four Geneva Conventions of 1949 mentioned statutory limitations (one exception is Control Council Law No. 10, which adapted the norms of the Nuremberg Charter for use by the Allies' military courts in Europe, and which made clear that statutes of limitations were suspended for the entire period of Nazi rule, 1933–1945). As time passed, concerns arose that statutory limitations might forever block the possibility of holding the perpetrators of World War II's crimes accountable. Israel's prosecution of Nazi functionary Adolf Eichmann in 1961 focused international attention on the problem of the unredressed crimes of World War II and gave impetus to efforts to ensure that prescription would not bar later prosecutions.

In response, the UN General Assembly on November 26, 1968, adopted the Convention on the Non-Applicability of Statutory Limitations to War Crimes and Crimes Against Humanity, which specifically included genocide within the definition of crimes against humanity, and entered into force on November 11, 1970. It declares that "[n]o statutory limitation shall apply [to these crimes] . . . irrespective of the date of their commission" (Article 1). States ratifying the Convention "undertake to adopt, in accordance with their respective constitutional processes, any legislative or other measures necessary to ensure that statutory or other limitations shall not apply to the prosecution and punishment of the crimes referred to. . .and that, where they exist, such limitations shall be abolished" (Article 4). The Convention's preamble expresses the conviction that the potential application of statutory limitations to these crimes is "a matter of serious concern to world public opinion" and that their effective punishment "is an important element in the prevention of such crimes, the protection of human rights and fundamental freedoms . . . and the promotion of international peace and security."

The words "irrespective of the date of their commission" in Article 1 make clear the potential for retroactive application of the 1968 Convention to crimes taking place before its ratification. This has been controversial and is part of the reason that states have been slow to adhere to the Convention (Argentina became the forty-eighth state party in August 2003). Some states have filed declarations upon ratification, stating that the Convention applies only with respect to crimes committed after its entry into force for their country (e.g., Mexico and Peru). Moreover, concern about the retroactive abolition of limitation periods led the Council of Europe (CoE) to adopt an otherwise almost identical regional instrument, the 1974 European Convention on the Non-Application of Statutory Limitations to Crimes Against Humanity and War Crimes, which declares in Article 2 that it applies only to offenses com-

mitted after its entry into force or to those that, if committed previously, have not yet been prescribed by statutory limitations. Similarly, the 1994 Inter-American Convention on Forced Disappearance of Persons, in Article 8, affirms the imprescriptibility of forced disappearance, but only provided that there is no "norm of fundamental character preventing application" of this principle. When such a fundamental norm exists, prescription is allowed, provided that any limitation period is "equal to that which applies to the gravest crime in the domestic laws of the corresponding State Party."

Such concerns with retrospectivity are not universal, however, and other states have deliberately embraced this dimension of the 1968 Convention in support of their countries' reckoning with past undemocratic regimes. Hungary's Constitutional Court, for example, in 1993 upheld a law revoking statutes of limitations with respect to crimes against humanity committed in the suppression of the 1956 uprising, and Argentina in 2003 approved and constitutionally incorporated the 1968 Convention even as it annulled two laws that provided amnesties in relation to the military dictatorship that ruled from 1976 to 1983. In addition, the norm of imprescriptibility has gained support beyond the confines of state parties, if sometimes imperfectly. For example, the Court of Cassation in France, notably through its 1984 and 1985 decisions in the case against Klaus Barbie, has affirmed that, in accordance with a 1964 French law, crimes against humanity cannot be subject to statutory limitations, although (and contrary to the 1968 Convention) war crimes can.

With the end of the cold war and the beginning of the 1990s, the movement for international justice gained momentum with the establishment of the International Criminal Tribunals for the Former Yugoslavia (ICTY, 1993) as well as Rwanda (ICTR, 1994), and renewed work toward a permanent International Criminal Court (ICC). In addition, the International Law Commission's Draft Code of Crimes Against the Peace and Security of Mankind, in its 1991 version, states that "[n]o statutory limitation shall apply to crimes against the peace and security of mankind" (Article 7). The principle was omitted from the much abbreviated 1996 Draft Code (which was not approved by the General Assembly), apparently out of concern that the nonapplicability of statutory limitations was a principle which could be applied only to the "core crimes" (such as genocide and crimes against humanity) but not all international crimes.

The crowning achievement in the development of international criminal law during the 1990s was the 1998 adoption of the Rome Statute of the International

Criminal Court. In Article 29 the Rome Statute declares that "the crimes within the jurisdiction of the Court shall not be subject to any statutes of limitations." Thus, any statutory limitations in national law will have no bearing on the ICC's investigation and prosecution of genocide, crimes against humanity, and war crimes (as well as the crime of aggression, should a definition ever be adopted). States that ratify the Rome Statute are obliged to cooperate with the Court, including the arrest and transfer of suspects sought by it. Given the clear wording of Article 29, this should mean regardless of whether a statutory limitation has expired under national law. Of course, the principle of complementarity underlying the Rome Statute ensures that governments will always have the right to investigate and prosecute these crimes first. Moreover, it can be expected that in most or all cases the ICC will investigate and, where appropriate, prosecute crimes before any statute of limitations applicable at the national level expires. In principle, however, if such limitations do obstruct domestic prosecution, the ICC will be able to act, provided of course that other criteria of its jurisdiction are met (including that the crime occurred after the entry into force of the Statute). Thus, if governments wish to prevent the ICC from acting on their behalf in such circumstances, they have a further incentive to eliminate any statutory limitations applicable to crimes covered by the Rome Statute.

Taken together with the 1968 Convention, other international instruments, case law, and national legislative measures, the ICC Statute reinforces the progressive movement of customary international law toward the imprescriptibility of the core crimes and, in particular, of genocide and crimes against humanity.

SEE ALSO Barbie, Klaus; Crimes Against Humanity; International Criminal Court; Prosecution; War Crimes

BIBLIOGRAPHY

Kritz, Neil J., ed. (1995). *Transitional Justice: How Emerging Democracies Reckon with Former Regimes.* 3 vols. Washington, D.C.: United States Institute of Peace.

Schabas, William A. (1999). "Commentary on Article 29." In *Commentary on the Rome Statute of the International Criminal Court: Observers' Notes, Article by Article,* ed. Otto Triffterer. Baden-Baden: Nomos.

United Nations General Assembly (1968). *Convention on the Non-Applicability of Statutory Limitations to War Crimes and Crimes Against Humanity.* Adopted by Resolution 2391 (XXIII). United Nations Treaty Series.

Van den Wyngaert, Christine and John Dugard (2002). "Non-Applicability of Statute of Limitations." In *The Rome Statute of the International Criminal Court: A Commentary,* ed. Antonio Cassese, Paola Gaeta, and John R. W. D. Jones, 2 volumes. Oxford: Oxford University Press.

Bruce Broomhall

Streicher, Julius
[FEBRUARY 12, 1885–OCTOBER 16, 1946]
Nazi Party's primary anti-Semitic propagandist

Julius Streicher was the most visible and prolific anti-Semitic propagandist for the Nazi Party. Unlike Adolf Hitler, Heinrich Himmler, and Joseph Goebbels, who focused on a number of policy issues besides anti-Semitism, Streicher's career was single-minded in its devotion to rousing hatred against the Jews. From the founding of his weekly newspaper *Der Stürmer* (The Stormer) in 1923 to its final issue in February 1945, his slogan remained, "The Jews are our misfortune."

Streicher served with distinction in World War I. Like many others, he found it hard to accept the fact that Germany lost the war despite the country's enormous efforts. The Jews became his scapegoat. After joining several anti-Semitic organizations, Streicher brought his personal following of approximately five thousand to the Nazi Party in 1922, nearly doubling the membership of the party and earning Hitler's lasting gratitude. Streicher became the Nazi leader in the Nuremberg area, maintaining that position until he was deposed in 1938 for financial and personal irregularities.

Der Stürmer's circulation increased dramatically after 1933, reaching about 500,000 by the mid-1930s. Special editions on topics such as the alleged Jewish world conspiracy or ritual murder had print runs as high as two million. Many of Streicher's readers even proudly posted copies of each issue in display cases. He also owned a publishing house that produced three anti-Semitic children's books, an anti-Semitic teacher's guide, and several pseudo-scholarly works on the Jews.

Streicher chaired the April 1, 1933, Nazi boycott of Jewish shops and professionals. He had no other official role in Nazi anti-Jewish policy. However, *Der Stürmer* constantly attacked the Jews. It accused thousands of Jews, by name, of various crimes ranging from embezzlement to rape. Streicher took particular interest in sensational sexual accusations, earning the mocking title of "the national pornographer of the Third Reich." He also attacked any non-Jews who had contact with Jews. Between 1934 and 1938 *Der Stürmer* named more than 6,500 Germans for offenses such as buying from Jewish firms or attending Jewish funerals. These accusations often had unpleasant consequences, so Streicher made a major contribution to the climate of intimidation that made Germans who did not share Nazi views reluctant to protest.

Although Streicher called for the annihilation of the Jews as early as the 1920s, such calls increased dramatically once the war began. One of his children's books, published in 1940, stated: "[T]he Jewish question will only be solved when Jewry is destroyed" (Hiemer, 1940, p. 74). He made many similar comments in *Der Stürmer*.

Many Germans found Streicher's material and style repellent, but he was widely appreciated by the worst anti-Semitic elements. More than that, he provided a convenient excuse for others, who could justify their anti-Jewish attitudes by thinking that they were less crude than Streicher's.

Streicher was tried by the Nuremberg International Military Tribunal after the war, along with other such leading Nazis as Hermann Göring and Albert Speer, and sentenced to death by hanging for the widespread effects of his anti-Semitic propaganda. Although the court concluded that Streicher played no direct role in the Holocaust, it found that his propaganda was a crime against humanity that set the stage for Nazi genocide.

SEE ALSO Anti-Semitism; Derstürmer; Nuremberg Trials; Propaganda

BIBLIOGRAPHY

Bytwerk, Randy L. (2001). *Julius Streicher*. New York: Cooper Square Press.

German Propaganda Archive. Translations of Streicher's writing available from http://www.calvin.edu/academic/cas/gpa.

Hiemer, E. (1940). *Der Pudelmopsdackelspinscher*. Nuremberg, Germany: Der Stürmer Buchverlag.

Schowalter, D. E. (1982). *Little Man, What Now?: Der Stürmer in the Weimar Republic*. Hamden, Conn.: Archon Books.

Randall L. Bywerk

Sudan

Although the first recorded account of the acquisition of slaves from the Sudan was inscribed in stone near the second cataract of the Nile during the reign of Egypt's First Dynasty Pharaoh Djer (c. 2900 BCE), the modern history of slavery in the Nile basin begins with the conquest of the Sudan by Muhammad Ali of Egypt in 1821 and the enslavement of Africans in the southern Sudan by Muslim Arabs from the north. Thereafter and throughout the nineteenth century, a well-organized slave trade provided thousands of African slaves for Egypt and the Middle East until the Sudanese revolution by the Mahdi in 1881. After the conquest of the Sudan by Anglo-Egyptian forces in 1898 British administrators curtailed the slave trade, but slavery in a variety of forms continued. The independence of the Sudan in 1956 brought to a head the deep tensions between the African traditionalist and Christian southern Sudanese and the northern Sudanese oriented to the Arab world and Islam. Their irreconcilable differences in culture, religion, and race precipitated a fifty-year spiral of violence that had revived the slave trade and slavery, killed more than two million southern Sudanese, and produced another four million refugees by ethnic cleansing, war, famine, and accusations of genocide.

The Turkiyya, 1821 to 1881

After his imperial conquests in the Levant and Arabia, the Turkish Viceroy of Egypt, Muhammad Ali Pasha (1769–1849), conquered the Sudan in 1821 to seek gold for his treasury, and territory to enlarge his personal empire, but primarily to acquire slaves for his army. He made this quite clear to his commander. "You are aware that the end of all out effort and this expense is to procure Negroes. Please show zeal in carrying out our wishes in this capital manner" (Hill, 1959, p. 13).

The Turco-Egyptian administration (known as the *Turkiyya*) immediately organized the systematic acquisition of slaves demanded by the viceroy. When the number of slaves that were remitted in place of taxes by the northern Muslim Sudanese proved insufficient, the government resorted to the slave raid, the infamous *razzia*, to seize non-Muslim Africans on the Kordofan and Ethiopian borderlands.

The razzia soon became an annual event, yielding thousands of slaves to be sent to Egypt by the officials who often subjected them to sadistic abuses and brutal atrocities similar to those that have been reported by the Human Rights Watch and Amnesty International in the contemporary Sudan. In Kordofan at Taqali alone, five thousand slaves were seized in 1839. In 1854 the Egyptian viceroy, Muhammad Sa'id, succumbed to European pressure and abolished the government slave raids, but his decree was studiously ignored by private traders in the Sudan. In the early twenty-first century the government of Umar Hasan Ahmad al-Bashir in the Sudan has issued similar declarations that are disregarded by those over whom his administration exercises little or no authority, but who benefit from so-called abductions, the trade in slaves. In the mid-nineteenth century the demand from the Ottoman world for Sudanese slaves became inexhaustible and soon focused the attention of European abolitionists on the Nilotic slave trade in the southern Sudan.

The great swamps of the Nile (*sudd*) had first been penetrated in 1841, and thereafter the whole of the

Upper Nile basin was opened to Sudanese from the north. The isolated African southern Sudanese then became exposed to the designs of private entrepreneurs of every ethnicity—Turk, Arab, European, Sudanese. Known as Khartoumers, these adventurers flocked to the Sudan to organize the corporate ivory and slave trade. These were well-financed companies equipped with a fleet of boats on the Nile and forts (*zariba*) throughout the southern Sudan from which their armed retainers (*bazinqir*) sallied forth to raid for slaves. By the 1860s regular contingents of slaves were exported annually from the Bahr al-Ghazal and Upper Nile.

This dynamic intervention by the Khartoumers created a spiral of violence that overwhelmed the southern Sudanese 150 years before the same destructive process devastated them at the end of the twentieth century. The merchant princes were accompanied by the *jallaba*, petty traders, who seized the few who fled from the razzia to engage in small trades that increased the volume and profits of their trade to the annoyance of the principal merchants. Like past and present governments in the Sudan, the Khartoumers played the internal rivalries of the southern Sudanese to their advantage. The African allies of the Khartoumers would acquire cattle and grain from a troublesome neighbor; the merchants would obtain ivory and captives as slaves. This expedient and mutually profitable association during the reign of the *Turkiyya* established the fundamental relationship between the interlopers—Turks, Egyptians, British, Sudanese—and the southern Sudanese characterized by the exploitation of historic, local animosities to achieve economic and political control in return for ivory and slaves. The historic pattern continued into the twenty-first century with the 2004 government of the Sudan unabashedly manipulating rival factions in the southern Sudanese liberation movements. In 1868 the Khartoumers exported an estimated 15,000 slaves down the Nile and another 2,000 overland through Kordofan: the 30,000 transported in 1876 were more of an anomaly than the average. Within the Sudan a quarter of the population in the nineteenth century is estimated to have been of slave origins.

When Ismail Pasha became the Khedive of Egypt in 1863, he was determined to modernize Egypt and borrowed heavily from European bankers to build railways, hospitals, palaces, and the Suez Canal. He was soon deeply in debt while at the same time under intense pressure from the European abolitionist movements and their governments to end the Nilotic slave trade, but he could not realistically expect officials in the Sudan or the powerful Khartoumers to abandon a

Map of Sudan. [COURTESY OF BRILL ACADEMIC PUBLISHERS]

highly profitable slave trade. He, therefore, turned to Christian administrators with no ethnic or cultural ties to the Turco-Egyptian officials, merchant princes, or Muslim Sudanese. He appointed as governor-general of the Sudan Charles "Chinese" Gordon (1833–1885), the British military leader of the victorious army in China. Gordon recruited Christian Italian, German, and British adventurers as provincial administrators. By 1879 they had crushed the corporate slave trade, but not before the khedive himself was forced to abdicate because of his profligate spending. The administration of the Sudan was then controlled by Christians, the prosperous slave trade had collapsed, and in their despair over these developments the Sudanese surmised that Islam as practiced by their Turco-Egyptian rulers was as corrupt as their secular involvement in the slave trade.

The *Mahdiyya*: 1881 to 1898

In 1881 Muhammad Ahmad (1848–1885) declared himself to be the long-awaited Mahdi whose revolutionary cause was to dispel the religious practices of the Turks and their Christian surrogates and inaugurate a new age of Islamic righteousness. The Mahdi's divine mission was to return Sudanese Islam to the fundamental Principles of the Prophet that included strong elements of *Sufishm*, Islamic mysticism. The Sudanese enthusiastically rallied behind Ahmad's message and became his devoted followers (*Ansar*). They defeated the Turco-Egyptian military expeditions dispatched to fight them, culminating in victories in January 1885 when the Mahdi's forces stormed Khartoum and killed Governor-General Gordon, making him one of Britain's most famous military martyrs.

When the Mahdi died six months after his triumph at Khartoum, his successor, the Khalifa 'Abd Allahi Muhammad Turshain (1846–1899), refused to restore the power of the great slavers that was disrupted by the Mahdi's messianic revolution. The slave trade was continued by the jallaba, who conducted their still thriving exchange of slaves in village markets (*suqs*). The primary interest of the khalifa in slavery, like that of Muhammad Ali, was not commercial but military—slaves for his loyal pretorian guard (*mulazimiyya*), ten thousand strong; it consisted of slaves from the jihadiyya troops of the Turks and the bazinqir irregular mercenaries of the Khartoumers. Two expeditions were sent into the southern Sudan for slaves, but the first was recalled immediately after the death of the Mahdi and the second, dispatched to the Upper Nile in 1888, limited its operations to occasional razzia. The British then controlled Egypt and the Red Sea, so the means to organize and transport slaves to the markets of the Middle East no longer existed. Compared to the raids for slaves during the reign of the *Turkiyya*, the brief decades of *Mahdiyya* rule were halcyon years for the southern Sudanese.

The Anglo-Egyptian Condominium: 1898 to 1956

On September 2, 1898, the Mahdist state came to an end after the disastrous defeat of the Sudanese army of the Khalifa 'Abd Allahi by Anglo-Egyptian forces under the command of General Sir H. H. Kitchener. The abolition of the slave trade and slavery in the Sudan received overwhelming support from the British people, parliament, and abolitionists. It became one of the most powerful arguments for committing British forces to the conquest of Sudan. Article 11 of the 1899 agreement with Egypt that established the Anglo-Egyptian Condominium made the distinction, however, between the institution of slavery and the slave trade in the Sudan. British officials were not about to disrupt the social order of the Sudan by prohibiting slavery, but they were determined to eliminate the slave trade. From 1899 until its dissolution in 1922, the Department for the Repression of the Slave Trade (the Slavery Department) effectively eliminated any open practice of the trade. This was followed by the legal end of slavery when the Sudanese government signed the Slavery Convention at the League of Nations (1926), an action acknowledged and supported by all governments of the independent Sudan.

Independent Sudan: Since 1956

The declaration of an independent Sudan on January 1, 1956, and the departure of British officials did not result in any resurgence of slavery, which had been contained but not completely eliminated. The peaceful transfer of power, however, was marred by the mutiny of the Equatorial Corps of the Sudan Defense Force in the southern Sudan. The mutiny was suppressed, but it ignited the longest civil war in any country in the twentieth century, one that has continued into the twenty-first century. From its beginnings in 1955 the southern insurgency has became a symbol of the antagonism created by the nineteenth-century reality of slavery and the twentieth-century perceptions of racism among Arabs from the north who regarded the southern Sudanese as slaves (*'abid*) or property (*malkiyya*). Reports issued by the United Nations (UN) and in the international media of vulnerable African southern Sudanese being forced into involuntary servitude have been vehemently denied by the Sudanese government, but the government's incompetence in governing its vast hinterland and its ideology, combined with famine, war, and racism, have provided the opportunity for the revival of customary practices of slavery, euphemistically referred to as abductions, and its trade. In the violence of civil war human rights have been ignored and innocent African civilians slaughtered by the thousands. Although the southern Sudan is the conspicuous scene of this terrible conflict, no government of the Sudan at Khartoum has effectively governed the marginalized Sudanese people on the periphery in the south, west, or east.

So long as Sudanese government officials cannot control the country, whatever may be their ideologies, political persuasion, or religious beliefs regarding human relationships, slavery, and the indiscriminate slaughter associated with the seizure of slaves will continue in the Sudan. The northern Sudanese have done little to disguise their contempt for the African Sudanese from the non-Arab regions because of their color, culture, and religion. In the half-century of independence in the Sudan, the ill-defined concept of race has complicated the confusion of identity in the Sudan and reinforced historic perceptions of inferiority that may no longer be legal, yet confirm convictions of superiority that are more pervasive and powerful than the law. The persistence of this doleful inheritance has been a central cause of a rationale justifying, the killing fields in the southern Sudan.

The First Civil War: 1955 to 1972

The southern disturbances of August 1955 marked the beginning of resistance by the African Sudanese practicing traditional religions or Christianity against the government in Khartoum, dominated by the northern Arab, Muslim Sudanese. In 1964 Christian missionaries were expelled from the Sudan. They had been the teachers of the small southern Sudanese elite who soon organized rudimentary associations to mobilize political dissent and to create the African, non-Muslim southern guerrilla forces, known as *Anya Nya* (snake venom). After eighteen years of fighting President Ja'Far Numayri, the *Anya Nya* signed an agreement at Addis Ababa in 1972 that conferred on the southern provinces a modest degree of autonomy which brought an end to the fighting but not the political turmoil between the northern and southern Sudan. Within ten years Numayri unilaterally abrogated the Addis Ababa Accords in a futile attempt to secure the support of the Islamists, Muslim fundamentalists in the Sudan, who sought to impose Islam and its laws (*Shari'a*) on non-Muslim African Sudanese. The southern Sudanese resumed their fighting in 1983, led by Colonel John Garang who reorganized former guerrilla *Anya Nya* fighters into the Sudan People's Liberation Movement/Army (SPLM/SPLA).

The First Civil War, 1955 through 1972, ended with a litany of brutality and terrorism in remote places where accountability was of little concern and the media absent. The fighting was unremitting for the civilians and debilitating for the army of the Sudan. The conflict displaced thousands of southern Sudanese, resulting in a massive number of refugees. It created a coterie of exiled southern elite. It destroyed the fragile infrastructure left by the British. It produced Christian martyrs. It convinced many southern Sudanese that there could be no compromise with the northern Sudanese.

Second Civil War: Since 1983

By 1984 Garang had consolidated the SPLM/A and forced the termination of the exploration for oil and the construction of the Jonglei Canal to supply additional water for irrigation in the northern Sudan and Egypt. Meanwhile, the SPLA, supplemented by substantial defections from the security forces, had occupied extensive areas in the rural south and driven the Sudan army onto the defensive in the major towns of Juba, Wau, and Malakal. To add to the disastrous consequences produced by war, African drought and the decision by the Sudan government in 1984 to distribute automatic weapons to the Baggara tribesmen of Darfur and Kordofan, members of the Arab militia or *murahileen*, combined to escalate war-related deaths of the southern Sudanese into the hundreds of thousands. The great African drought of the 1980s devastated the plains of the Sahil from Senegal across Africa through Darfur, Kordofan, and into southern Sudan. Here the popula-

[DARFUR]

The conflict in Darfur began in 2003, when black African rebel groups began an uprising over a number of long-standing grievances, including ongoing slave-trading and discrimination. The government retaliated by unleashing a militia known as the janjaweed on the civilian population. By the middle of August 2004 some 300 Darfur villages had been burned and the population displaced through ethnic cleansing. The United Nations estimated that if humanitarian aid reached the area quickly some 300,000 people would die, but if it were delayed, more than a million lives would be at stake. The U.S. Congress labeled the situation a genocide.

In response to the crisis, the UN Security Council passed a resolution on July 30, 2003, threatening Sudan's government with sanctions if the government of Sudan does not, within 30 days, disarm the Arab militia, known as the janjaweed, that has been killing, raping, and terrorizing black African civilians in the Darfur region of Sudan. The resolution passed by 13-0 with two abstentions (China and Pakistan). The resolution came three days after the African Union's decision to consider expanding its observer mission in Darfur into a full-scale peacekeeping mission; it would be the AU's first military intervention in a member state. Sudan's authoritarian regime, led by president Omar Hassan al-Bashir, denied arming and backing the janjaweed, although human rights groups and other observers showed evidence to the contrary. **DINAH SHELTON**

tion had been increasing more rapidly than the production of food and livestock. Customary exchange in times of hardship collapsed. Crops failed to germinate without water, and the cattle died without grass. During the winter of 1984 and 1985 tens of thousands of southern Sudanese, Nilotes, and Equatorians began to flee into southern towns and then to the north and to Ethiopia seeking food. By January 1987 hundreds of thousands of southern Sudanese were dead or in flight to the anonymity of towns and the camps for the displaced from Kordofan to Khartoum and from the Bahr al-Ghazal to Ethiopia to avoid death from starvation and war, with disease often accompanying starvation.

In 1984 Numayri's Minister of Defense, General Suwar al-Dhahab, equipped the Arab militia with automatic weapons and unleashed these *murahileen* into the southern Sudan in a desperate attempt to stem the spread of the rebellion among the Dinka who were allied with Garang, a Dinka from Bor. The raiders were mostly young Rizayqat and Messiriya Baggara tribesmen who, imbued with the folklore of their forefathers, raided the Dinka for cattle, pastures, and *'abid* (slaves), and felt they had a license to kill in order to replenish their own herds decimated by drought. With their superiority over a traditional enemy guaranteed by the AK-47, the tenuous equilibrium that had existed for more than a half-century on the Baggara-Dinka frontier dissolved into a *razzia* of indiscriminate plunder and wanton killing. A somnolent village would be surrounded before dawn and attacked at first light. The women, children, and teenage males that had not escaped were collected with the cattle. The men were indiscriminately killed, often accompanied by mutilation, and the village and cultivations were then methodically destroyed and the Dinka cattle, women, and children divided among the Baggara to serve or to be sold.

By 1987 the SPLA had established its military presence in the Bahr al-Ghazal, inflicting heavy casualties on the Baggara militia and the officers and men of the army, the Sudan People's Armed Forces (SPAF). On the night of March 27, 1987, more than a thousand Dinka were immolated and slaughtered at Ed Diein in southern Darfur in a vengeful race riot. In November the SPLA captured Kurmuk, producing a hysteria in Khartoum that culminated in the successful coup d'état of Umar Hasan Ahmad al-Bashir on June 30, 1989. He installed the first theocratic Islamist government in the Sudan. His supporters, the National Islamic Front (NIF), were more determined than ever to defeat the southern Sudanese insurgents in order to impose Islam and Arab culture on the Africans of the southern Sudan.

Islamist government of the Sudan: Since 1989

Unlike many coup d'état that are motivated by discontent, the officers who seized control of the Sudan government on June 30th were determined to construct a new Sudan defined by Islam, with the laws of the Q'uran (*Shari'a*) interpreted and regulated by the doctrines of the National Islamic Front (NIF) and promulgated by the Revolutionary Government of National Salvation led by Umar al-Bashir. To be Sudanese was to conform to the rigid ideology of the Islamists. Whoever refused to conform to its creed would be excluded for not being Sudanese. To produce the new Sudan, the Islamists introduced a complete ideology that affected all aspects of life in the Sudan. It was an attempt to indoctrinate, shape, and thereby control the Sudanese to produce a homogeneous Islamic society even if it required the destruction of the *kafirin*, unbelieving Africans in the southern Sudan, by jihad (holy war). By

1991 the *Shari'a* had been embodied in the Sudan penal code; in 1992 Islamic legal traditions were employed to justify the jihad against apostates and heathens; after 1993 Islamic principles were invoked as the guide for all agencies of government, civilian and military. The creation of the new Sudan as a monolithic and homogeneous society reduced the non-Muslim African Sudanese before the law and in society to less than equal status. The legal and religious definition of non-Muslim Sudanese Africans as second-class citizens provided welcome relief, if not justification by the Islamists in Khartoum to carry on total war with greater intensity. During the decade of drought and the *razzia* (1983–1993) more than 1 million southern Sudanese died and another 4 million became refugees in foreign countries, or internally displaced within the Sudan.

Having little confidence in the SPAF to pursue a jihad aggressively, the NIF-controlled government introduced universal conscription to create the People's Defense Forces (PDF) composed of raw recruits and government-supported militias. In 1990 the air force began indiscriminate aerial bombing of civilians in the southern Sudan; its only targets were villages, cattle, churches, schools, and hospitals. An estimated eleven thousand Sudanese were either killed or wounded. The offensive was symbolic of more demonstrable efforts by the SPAF, supported by the PDF, to eliminate the presence of the SPLA by premeditated ethnic cleansing. Between 1990 and 2000 the jihad in the Nuba Mountains had killed more than an estimated 100,000 and resettled another 170,000 Nuba in so-called peace villages on the Sahilean plains of Kordofan where they labored in fields and towns for northern Sudanese entrepreneurs.

During the same decade military offensives by the SPAF and the *razzia* of the Baggara *murahileen* and the Dinka militia of Kerubino Kwanjin Bol, who had defected from the SPLA to join the government forces, resulted in the death of another estimated 200,000 Dinka and Nuer in the Bahr al-Ghazal by killing and famine. Others were displaced by the hundreds of thousands. During the drought of 1993 and 1994 the Sudan government deliberately intervened in the distribution of humanitarian food aid by Operation Lifeline, a Western organization. The Sudan effectively utilized famine as a weapon of war to depopulate large areas of the Bahr al-Ghazal by starvation, forcing its inhabitants to become internally displaced persons (IDP).

In the Upper Nile in 1991 the SPLA commanders Riak Machar, Lam Akol, and Gordon Kong Cuol formed a rival South Sudan Independence Movement/Army (SSIM/A) to overthrow Garang. The SSIM/A was dominated by the Nuer. In a formal alliance with the

Sudan government, they received large numbers of automatic weapons that they promptly used to kill many thousand of their traditional Dinka enemies who were supporters of the SPLA and their kinsman, Garang. The ensuing local Nilotic civil war within the larger Sudan civil war killed more southerners than the SPAF. The southern Sudanese casualties from 1991 to 2000 are estimated at approximately 250,000, and an equal number of southerners were displaced. In Equatoria, the heartland of the SPLA, the fighting intensified throughout the decade as the SPAF sought to capitalize on the bitter feud within the SPLA to recapture strategic towns they had previously lost. During this same tragic decade in Equatoria war-related deaths averaged ten thousand per year.

Although oil had been discovered on the northern borders of the southern Sudan in 1976, the renewal of the civil war in 1983 delayed its export by pipeline to Port Sudan until August 1999. At this time further exploration demonstrated that large Sudanese oil reserves were located in the sudd and surrounding grassland plains of the Upper Nile and Bahr al-Ghazal. These oil-rich regions could obviously not be exploited if controlled by southern insurgents, whether the militias of southern warlords or the SPLA that had frustrated the development of Sudanese oil for twenty years. In order to secure the oil fields, the government launched military offensives to clear the land of southern Sudanese by killing its inhabitants and their cattle and forcing the survivors to seek refuge in the southern Bahr al-Ghazal as internally displaced persons. The government then had at its disposal millions of dollars from oil revenues. Over half of this money was used to purchase sophisticated weapons and the especially feared helicopter gun ships, which are more effective at driving people off the land than the indiscriminate high-level bombing of the past. Better equipped, the regular army, the PDF, and the southern Sudanese militias were initially successful in their campaigns of ethnic cleansing to secure the flat pasture lands of the western Upper Nile and eastern Bahr al-Ghazal. The war-related deaths of the southern Sudanese continued to grow.

Quantifying War-Related Deaths of Southern Sudanese

The southern Sudan has been one of the most remote regions of the earth—it was not opened to the outside world until the mid-nineteenth century. This isolation continued through the half-century of the Anglo-Egyptian Condominium (1899–1956) and during the First Civil War (1955–1972). There are no reliable statistics and only unreliable estimates of the southern Sudanese losses during the seventeen years of this conflict. In contrast, the Second Civil War (1983–present)

has been well recorded by the international media, in massive reports by human rights and relief agencies, and through the writings of Sudanese and foreign participants. Unlike the First Civil War, advances in technology have now made it possible to transmit visually and through the media the disastrous consequences of the vicious fighting in the forests, plains, and swamps of the southern Sudan on the civilian population. Despite the plethora of information about this tragic conflict, there has been only one serious study attempting to quantify the number of war-related deaths, *Quantifying Genocide in Southern Sudan and the Nuba Mountains, 1983–1998*, authored by J. Millard Burr.

Burr estimates that more than 1.3 million southern Sudanese perished in the conflict between 1983 and 1993 in a population, according to the 1983 national census, of some 5 million in the southern provinces of Equatoria, the Bahr al-Ghazal, and Upper Nile; the victims constitute one-fourth to one-third of the Sudan's total population. There has been no further census, but ten years later, if one accepts the folk figure of 3.2 million residing in the south and another 1.8 million IDP living in the north, and assumes a generous 3 percent population growth, the number of southern Sudanese has not increased because of war-related losses. During the next five years, 1993 through 1998, Burr estimates that another 600,000 southern Sudanese perished in the war. This represents an annual average of 120,000, a number close to the 130,000 who died each year from 1983 to 1993. Because the intensity of fighting in the southern Sudan has escalated since the acquisition of arms for oil revenues, the annual losses from 1998 to 2003 have certainly not diminished from the 120,000 each year during 1993 through 1998. Consequently, the total war-related deaths of southern Sudanese during the twenty years from 1983 to 2003 numbers more than 2.5 million. Although precise figure for these war-related deaths in the southern Sudan will never be available, Burr's estimates speak to the enormity of the consequences of this continuing conflict.

There is no way to distinguish between military and civilian casualties, but given the size of the government forces and those of the SPLA, their casualties can only be numbered in the tens of thousands, whereas those of the civilians must be counted in the hundreds of thousands. Many more southern Sudanese have undoubtedly died from disease and starvation as a direct result of the policies of the Sudan government than have died by the bullets of their armed forces. The stark conclusion remains that during the period of 1983 to 2003 the death of at least one in five southern Sudanese can be attributed to this terrible civil conflict.

After a half-century of civil war punctuated by a decade of peace (1972–1983) and infrequent ceasefires during which a host of international mediators have sought to broker a peace between the Sudan government and the SPLM/A, the question of genocide on the part of the Sudan government was first raised by the international non-governmental organizations (NGOs) working in the Sudan, and then discussed at the UN and in the international media. After 1989 the determination of the Islamist government of Umar al-Bashir to defeat the southern insurgents and impose by jihad Islam, Arabization, and the Shari'a throughout the southern Sudan leaves little doubt that the government in Khartoum actively participated or quietly condoned the death by famine or slaughter of hundreds of thousands of civilian African Sudanese. There are numerous definitions of genocide, but the standard definition is contained in the 1948 UN Convention on the Prevention and Punishment of the Crime of Genocide. *Genocide* means the intent to destroy, in whole or part, any national, ethic, racial, or religious group by killing, bodily harm, preventing birth, or transferring children from that group to another one.

Although there is no evidence that the Sudan government officially adopted a policy to eliminate any particular ethnic group in the southern Sudan or the southern Sudanese as a whole, their policies involved the indiscriminate aerial bombing of civilians and their installations, the withholding of humanitarian aid to cause death by starvation, and silent indifference to the activities by government-supported militias to loot, kidnap, and enslave. The Islamist government has worked assiduously to deny these charges by defending its actions as a necessary military response to defeat the southern Sudanese insurgents, the SPLA, preserve the unity of the Sudan, and incorporate the African Sudanese into an Islamic, Arab Sudan. Under international pressure the government of Umar al-Bashir has sought to dispel the accusations of genocide by greater cooperation with the West and a willingness to discuss peace with the SPLA. Without peace in the Sudan there is no prospect of resolving whether the massive loss of southern Sudanese lives was, in fact, a deliberate policy of genocide by the government of the Sudan.

SEE ALSO Ethiopia; Ethnic Cleansing; Famine; Refugees; Religion; Slavery, Historical; Uganda

BIBLIOGRAPHY
Africa Rights (1995). *Facing Genocide in the Nuba Mountains.* London: Author.
Africa Watch (1990). *Denying "The Honor of Living." Sudan. A Human Rights Disaster.* Washington, D.C.: Author.
Amnesty International (2000). *Sudan: The Human Price of Oil.* New York: Amnesty International.
An-Na'im, A. A., and Peter N. Kok (1991). *Fundamentalism and Militarism: A Report on the Root Causes of Human Rights Violations in the Sudan.* Fund for Peace.
Beshir, M. O. (1968). *The Southern Sudan, Background to Conflict.* London: C. Hurst.
Burr, J. M. (1998). *Quantifying Genocide in Southern Sudan and the Nuba Mountains, 1983–1998.* Washington, D.C.: United States Committee for Refugees.
Burr, J. M., and R. O. Collins (1995). *Requiem for the Sudan: War, Drought and Disaster Relief on the Nile.* Boulder, Colo.: Westview Press.
Collins, R. O. (1962). *The Southern Sudan, 1883–1898: A Struggle for Control.* New Haven, Conn.: Yale University Press.
Collins, R. O. (1971). *Land beyond the Rivers: The Southern Sudan, 1898–1918.* New Haven, Conn.: Yale University Press.
Collins, R. O. (1999). "Slavery in the Sudan in History." *Slavery and Abolition* 20:3, 69–95.
de Waal, A. (1990). *Famine Crimes: Politics and the Disaster Relief Industry in Africa.* Bloomington: Indiana University Press.
Gray, R. (1959). *A History of the Southern Sudan, 1839–1889.* London: Oxford University Press.
Harirm, S., and Terje Tvedt (1994). *Short Cut to Decay: The Case of the Sudan.* Uppsala: Nordiska Afircainistitutet.
Hill, R. L. (1959). *Egypt in the Sudan, 1820–1881.* London: Oxford University Press.
Holt, P. M. (1970). *The Mahdist State in the Sudan, 1881–1898,* 2nd edition. Oxford: Clarendon Press.
Human Rights Watch (1999). *Famine in the Sudan, 1998: The Human Rights Causes.* Washington, D.C.: Human Rights Watch.
Johnson, D. H. (1988). "Sudanese Military Slavery from the Eighteenth to the Twentieth Century." In *Slavery and Other Forms of Unfree Labour,* ed. L. Archer. London: Routledge.
Johnson, D. H. (1992). "Recruitment and Entrapment in Private Slave Armies: The Structure of the Zara'ib in the Southern Sudan." In *The Human Commodity. Perspectives on the Trans-Saharan Slave Trade,* ed. E. Savage. London: Frank Cass.
Johnson, D. H. (2003). *The Root Causes of Sudan's Civil Wars.* Bloomington: Indiana University Press.
Jok, J. M. (2001). *War and Slavery in the Sudan.* Philadelphia: University of Pennsylvania Press.
Keen, D. (1994). *The Benefits of Famine: A Political Economy of Famine and Relief in Southwestern Sudan, 1983–1989.* Princeton, N.J.: Princeton University Press.
Report of the Commission of Enquiry (1956). Southern Sudan Disturbances, August 1955. Khartoum: McCorquedale.
Ushari, A. M. and Suleyman Ali Baldo (1987). *Al Diein Massacre—Slavery in the Sudan.* Khartoum: Khartoum University Press.
Verney, Peter (1995). *Sudan: Conflict and Minorities.* London: Minority Rights Group International.

Verney, Peter (2000). *Raising the Stakes: Oil and Conflict in Sudan.* Hebden Bridge: Sudan Update.

Robert O. Collins

Superior (or Command) Responsibility

International law provides two primary modes of liability for holding an individual criminally responsible: (1) individual or personal criminal responsibility and (2) superior or command responsibility. The latter concept is reflected in the statutes of international criminal courts and tribunals that hear cases arising under international humanitarian law (such as Article 28 of the Statute of the International Criminal Court, Article 6[3] of the Statute of the International Criminal Tribunal for Rwanda and Article 7[3] of the Statute of the International Criminal Tribunal for the Former Yugoslavia), as well as in many nations' military and civilian criminal codes. The doctrine of superior or command responsibility (the terms will be used interchangeably in this entry) differs from other forms of criminal liability in that it is based on omissions rather than affirmative actions. Under the doctrine of superior responsibility, the accused may be convicted based on his or her failure to prevent the crime from occurring in the first place (or to punish the perpetrator) after having learned that the offense was committed. It is important to stress that superior responsibility does not cover situations where a superior (or military commander) orders persons under his or her control to commit crimes. (Under such a scenario, the superior would be responsible under a theory of individual or personal criminal responsibility.) After a brief historical discussion, the doctrine of command responsibility will be analyzed here, with particular emphasis on its application as reflected in the jurisprudence of the International Criminal Tribunal for the Former Yugoslavia (ICTY) and the International Criminal Tribunal for Rwanda (ICTR).

Historically, this doctrine was used exclusively as a basis to prosecute superior military officers for offenses committed by their subordinates. More recently the statutes of the ICTY, ICTR, and the International Criminal Court (ICC) refer to "superior responsibility," reflecting the fact that the doctrine also applies to paramilitary or irregular commanders and civilian leaders, in addition to traditional military commanders. The doctrine of command responsibility, as reflected in these statutory instruments, expresses a well-established rule of international customary law, as reflected in numerous treaties.

History and Background

Prior to World War II there are few recorded cases involving prosecutions on the basis of command responsibility, reflecting the fact that this doctrine rarely formed the basis for criminal prosecution. Although the roots of the modern doctrine of command responsibility may be found in the 1907 Hague Conventions (such as Hague Convention IV, Annex, Article 1, or Hague Convention X, Article 19), it was not until immediately after World War I that the notion of prosecuting military commanders before international tribunals on the basis of command responsibility was developed. Thus, the International Commission on the Responsibility of the Authors of the War and on Enforcement of Penalties presented a report to the 1919 Preliminary Peace Conference, in which they recommended that an international tribunal be established to prosecute, among other matters, individuals who, "with knowledge . . . and with power to intervene, abstained from preventing or taking measures to prevent, putting an end to or repressing violations of the laws or customs of war." Similarly, Article 227 of the Treaty of Versailles envisioned the trial of Kaiser Wilhelm by an international tribunal.

After World War II several important trials involving Japanese and German war criminals were conducted, in which the doctrine of command responsibility was invoked as the grounds for establishing criminal liability, were conducted. The Charters governing both the Nuremberg and Tokyo trials were silent as to criminal liability under the doctrine of command responsibility. Likewise, Control Council Law No. 10, the basis for trials of war criminals by the Allies in Germany, did not specifically provide for this form of criminal liability. Nevertheless, command responsibility issues were raised in several post–World War II cases, including the Yamashita trial and *United States v. Wilhelm von Leeb, et al.*, known as the *High Command* case and *Hostages case* (*United States v. Wilhelm List et al.*)—cases prosecuted under Control Council Law No. 10, the law governing the trials of war criminals in Germany other than those prosecuted in the large Nuremberg trial.

The trial of General Tomoyuki Yamashita stands for the proposition that military superiors may be found guilty if it can be established that they must have known offenses were being committed and failed to either halt such crimes or punish the perpetrators. The *High Command* and *Hostages* cases further developed this area of the law. Thirteen senior German officers were tried in the *High Command* case (reported in Volumes 10 and 11 of *Trials of War Criminals before the Nuremberg Military Tribunals under Control Council Law No. 10,* hereafter referred to as TWC), for a variety of offenses, including murder and mistreatment of prisoners of war (POWs), refusal of quarter, and other inhumane acts and violations of the laws or customs of war. The prosecution argued a form of strict liability should apply to commanders. The tribunal rejected this theory and held that for a commander to be criminally responsible for the acts of subordinates, the commander must breach a rule of international law and such a breach must have occurred voluntarily and with the knowledge that the act was criminal under international law. Other command responsibility issues raised during the course of the trial included: (1) the liability of a commander for actions committed by subordinates pursuant to criminal orders passed down independent of his or her command; (2) the liability of commanders for criminal orders issued by members of their staffs; and (3) the duties and responsibilities of the military commander of an occupied territory whose authority is limited.

Like the *High Command Case*, the *Hostages Case* (reported in TWC, Vol. 11, starting on p. 759) dealt with multiple accused and was prosecuted by authorities of the United States under Control Council Law No. 10. The judges dismissed the contentions of the accused that reports and orders transmitted to them were not brought to their attention by members of their staffs and addressed the issue of notice to the commander, making several important observations:

> An army commander will not ordinarily be permitted to deny knowledge of reports received at his headquarters, they being sent there for his special benefit. Neither will he ordinarily be permitted to deny knowledge of happenings within the area of his command while he is present therein. It would strain the credulity of the Tribunal to believe that a high ranking military commander would permit himself to get out of touch with current happenings in the area of his command during wartime. No doubt occurrences result occasionally because of unexpected contingencies, but they are unusual (TWC, Vol. 11, p. 1260).

With respect to information contained in such reports, the tribunal went on to state that "[a]ny failure to acquaint themselves with the contents of such reports, or a failure to require additional reports where inadequacy appears on their face, constitutes a dereliction of duty which he cannot use in his own behalf" (TWC, Vol. 11, p. 1271).

Considered together, these three cases stand for the proposition that commanders could not be held to a strict liability standard with respect to offenses committed by their subordinates, although the law did impose on them a duty to stay informed with respect to the acts of such subordinates. Based on the rulings handed down on these cases at the end of World War II, the scope of the international law of command responsibility could be summed up as follows:

- There was a presumption that orders were legal, and that commanders could pass orders from higher headquarters to lower-level commands with minimal scrutiny.
- There was a presumption that commanders would be aware of the contents of reports received at their headquarters.
- In the event such reports were inadequate or unclear, commanders had a duty to request that additional reports be prepared.
- There was a presumption that commanders were aware of events (including crimes) that occurred within the geographic scope of their areas of responsibility.
- To be criminally responsible, commanders must have known that patently criminal acts were committed and they acquiesced to, participated in, or criminally neglected to interfere in their commission.
- Commanders could delegate authority, but responsibility for the conduct of the troops remained with the commander.
- In examining the alleged criminal conduct of commanders, a variety of factors could be relevant for determining whether the commander was on notice, including the scale and geographic scope of the alleged criminal acts.

Notwithstanding these cases, the four 1949 Geneva Conventions were silent as to command responsibility, with the exception of Article 39 of the third Geneva Convention, which requires POW camps to be "under the immediate authority of a responsible commissioned officer." This situation was not rectified until the adoption of Additional Protocol I Relating to the Protection of Victims of International Armed Conflicts in 1977. Consequently, state practice played an important role in the development of the concept of superior responsibility during this period. Both during and immediately after World War II many states incorporated superior responsibility provisions in their national legislation. On the basis of these statutory provisions, some states prosecuted individuals, among the most well-known are the cases of Lieutenant William Calley and Captain Ernest Medina of the United States Army for their role in the 1967 My Lai massacre in Vietnam.

The Jurisprudence of the ICTY and ICTR

The ICTY was established in 1993 and was vested with jurisdiction to prosecute superiors for offenses committed by their subordinates, as the following paragraph from the Secretary-General's Report to the Security Council on the establishment of the ICTY indicates:

A person in a position of superior authority should, therefore, be held individually responsible for giving the unlawful order to commit a crime under the present statute. But he should also be held responsible for failure to prevent a crime or to deter the unlawful behavior of his subordinates. This imputed responsibility or criminal negligence is engaged if the person in superior authority knew, or had reason to know, that his subordinates were about to commit or had committed crimes and yet failed to take the necessary and reasonable steps to prevent or repress the commission of such crimes or to punish those who had committed them (1993, para. 56).

The doctrine of superior responsibility has been applied by ICTY and ICTR trial chambers in numerous cases and has also been the subject of several Appeals Chamber decisions and judgments. These decisions have elaborated on the legal elements constituting this form of criminal liability.

The Elements
In order to prevail on a command responsibility theory of criminal liability, the prosecution must establish, beyond reasonable doubt, each of the following elements:

- An offense was committed.
- There was a superior-subordinate relationship.
- The superior knew or had reason to know that the subordinate was about to commit the offense or had done so.
- The superior failed to take the necessary and reasonable measures to prevent the offense or to punish the principal offenders.

With the exception of the first element, which simply requires proof that a certain perpetrator or group(s) of perpetrators committed an offense for which the tribunal has jurisdiction, each of these elements will be analyzed.

The first requirement is the existence of a superior-subordinate relationship between the accused superior or commander and the subordinate perpetrator at the time the offense was committed. This form of liability does not apply in the event the accused and the perpetrator(s) are of the same rank; there must be a hierarchical relationship for superior responsibility to apply. This raises several issues: the test to be used in determining this relationship; whether the commander must have de jure or de facto control; whether this liability also extends to civilian superiors; and whether more than one superior in the chain of command may be held liable for acts committed by subordinates.

"Effective Control"
The term *superior* is not necessarily restricted to military commanders senior to the actual perpetrator in the chain of command. As long as the superior exercises effective control over subordinate(s), superior responsibility may attach. Thus, a commander may incur criminal responsibility for offenses committed by persons who are not formally his or her subordinates, provided that he or she exercises effective control over them (*Prosecutor v. Zejnil Delalic et al., Čelebići* Appeal Judgment, para. 196). Moreover, in the *Prosecutor v. Dragoljub Kunarac et al.* case, the Trial Chamber stated that there is no requirement that the person committing the offense be in a permanent or fixed relationship with the commander, so long as the commander exercised the prerequisite effective control (*Kunarac* Trial Judgment, para. 399).

Effective control is a prerequisite in establishing that the superior had the material ability to prevent or punish the commission of violations of international humanitarian law committed by subordinates. The conflicts in both the former Yugoslavia and Rwanda saw instances where offenses were committed by paramilitary and irregular militia forces, who often lacked de jure authority over the actual perpetrators. On the basis of their de facto control over the offenders and applying the effective control test, the leaders of such groups may be found criminally responsible for the crimes committed by subordinates.

Military and/or Civilian Leaders
Under customary international law, the doctrine of command responsibility extends to both civilian and military superiors, as well as to individuals exercising both types of functions. Article 7(3) of the ICTY Statute is consistent with this customary law, in that it does not qualify the term superior by explicitly limiting the theory to military superiors. Moreover, Article 7(2), which provides that the official position of a person "shall not relieve such person of criminal responsibility nor mitigate punishment," supports the proposition that civilian superiors may fall within the bounds of Article 7(3). This issue was dealt with by the ICTY Appeals Chamber in the *Prosecutor v. Zlatko Aleksovski* case, when the Court stated that "[t]he Appeals Chamber takes the view that it does not matter whether he was a civilian or a military superior, if it can be proved that within the Kaonik prison, he had the powers to prevent or to punish in terms of Article 7(3)" (*Aleksovski* Appeal Judgment, para. 76).

The ICC Statute takes a slightly different approach with respect to the distinctions between civilian and military superiors. Article 28(a) applies to military commanders and those "effectively acting as a military commander," while Article 28(b) limits civilian responsibility to those instances where the subordinates were under the "effective authority and control" of the civilian superior and:

1. The superior either knew, or consciously disregarded information which clearly indicated, that the subordinates were committing or about to commit such crimes.

2. The crimes concerned activities that were within the effective responsibility and control of the superior.

3. The superior failed to take all necessary and reasonable measures within his or her power to prevent or repress their commission or to submit the matter to the appropriate authorities for investigation and prosecution.

Until the ICC has the opportunity to address this issue in an on-going case, it is unclear whether these provisions reflect newly emerging customary law.

Multiple Commanders in the Chain of Command

Because the military laws of every state require all soldiers to comply with international humanitarian law, every person in the chain of command who exercises effective control over subordinates is responsible for crimes committed by such persons, if we assume all the elements of Article 7(3) are met. This means that more than one superior may be responsible for crimes committed by the same subordinates, as long as each superior in the chain of command exercises effective control.

The Knowledge Requirement

The knowledge (or mens rea) element of superior responsibility entails two distinct components: The accused "knew" or "had reason to know" that a subordinate was about to commit a crime or had done so. The term *knew* means actual knowledge, which may not be presumed and may be established either through: (1) direct evidence of actual knowledge or (2) circumstantial evidence, from which it can be inferred that the commander must have had actual knowledge. Proof of actual knowledge can be established, among other things, by introducing evidence that the accused commander acknowledged receiving reports that subordinates committed crimes. In most cases, however, the prosecution will rely on circumstantial evidence to prove that a superior had actual knowledge and the following factors may constitute such evidence:

- Number of illegal acts
- Type of illegal acts
- Scope of illegal acts
- Time during which the illegal acts occurred
- Number and type of troops involved
- Logistics involved, if any
- Geographical location of the acts
- Widespread occurrence of the acts
- Tactical tempo of operations
- Modus operandi of similar illegal acts
- Officers and staff involved
- Location of the commander at the time
- Nature and scope of the particular position held by the superior
- Character traits of subordinates
- Events taking place during any temporary absences of the superior
- Level of training and instruction provided by the commander to the subordinates

The phrase "had reason to know" has proven more difficult to interpret and apply, with different courts coming to different conclusions on this issue. The fact that the ICC Statute has adopted different mens rea standards for military and nonmilitary superiors only tends to complicate this area of the law.

In the *Čelebići* case, the appeals chamber discussed what must be established to prove that the accused had reason to know. The judges concluded that the prosecution must demonstrate that "information of a general nature was available to the superior that would have put him or her on notice of offenses committed by subordinates" (*Čelebići* Appeal Judgment, para. 241). This information does not have to be conclusive that crimes were committed, but it must be specific enough to indicate the need for additional investigation to determine if crimes had been, or were about to be, committed. This places a duty on commanders to investigate once they are notified of the possibility that offenses may have been committed.

As noted above, the ICC Statute sets forth different standards for military and civilian superiors, and these differences also include different mens rea requirements. Pursuant to Article 28(a) of the ICC Statute, the mens rea for military superiors is that the accused "knew or, owing to the circumstances at the time, should have known that the forces were committing or about to commit such crimes." With respect to civilian superiors, it must be proven that the civilian superior "knew or consciously disregarded information that clearly indicated, that the subordinates were committing or about to commit such crimes."

Necessary and Reasonable Measures to Prevent or Punish

The requirement that superiors take necessary and reasonable measures to prevent or punish is the third element of superior responsibility, and overlaps with the first element, because commanders who lack effective control will not be able to satisfy this requirement. The obligation of the superior to act is triggered once he becomes aware that crimes have been or are about to be committed. In the *Prosecutor v. Tihomir Blaskic* case, the trial chamber concluded that the two components of this obligation must be considered together, stating, "Obviously, where the accused knew or had reason to know that subordinates were about to commit crimes and failed to prevent them, he cannot make up for the failure to act by punishing the subordinates afterwards" (*Blaskic* Judgment, para. 336).

However, as the judges noted in the *Čelebići* case, the first instance in which the ICTY dealt with superior responsibility, there are limits as to what may be expected of superiors:

> International law cannot oblige a superior to perform the impossible. Hence, a superior may only be held criminally responsible for failing to take such measures that are within his powers. The question then arises of what actions are to be considered to be within the superior's powers in this sense. As the corollary to the standard adopted by the Trial Chamber with respect to the concept of superior, we conclude that a superior should be held responsible for failing to take such measures that are within his material possibility (*Čelebići* Trial Judgment, para. 395).

The determination of whether a superior has fulfilled this obligation is thus highly fact-specific and consequently a practical approach is required. Subsequent cases, for example, have demonstrated that a commander may meet this obligation by reporting the matter to his or her superior officer.

Responsibility for Crimes Committed before the Superior-Subordinate Relationship Exists

Until a recent decision of the ICTY Appeals Chamber in the *Prosecutor v. Enver Hadzihasanovic et al.* case (Decision on Interlocutory Appeal Challenging Jurisdiction in Relation to Command Responsibility), it was unclear whether such responsibility included obligations on commanders stemming from crimes committed prior to the establishment of the superior-subordinate relationship. The following hypothetical demonstrates this point. Assume that Soldier A, who is under the command of Commander A, commits an offense on January 1. On January 3, Commander A is informed of this crime, but the following day Commander A is reassigned and Commander B assumes command of the unit that includes Soldier A. May Commander B be held criminally liable for the failure to punish Soldier A for crimes committed prior to Commander B's assumption of command, assuming Commander B is aware of the allegations? The Appeals Chamber of the ICTY has held that he or she may not, based on customary international law. Two of the five judges on the appeals chamber dissented, arguing that customary international law supported the notion that commanders could be held liable for such crimes, provided that the commander had reason to know of the crimes.

Internal Armed Conflict

Historically, the doctrine of command responsibility has been applied in international armed conflicts only, as is clear from a reading of Articles 86 and 87 of Additional Protocol I and by the fact that Additional Protocol II Relating to the Protection of Victims of Non-International Armed Conflicts has no corresponding provisions. This reflects the hesitation that most states have traditionally demonstrated in entering into treaties with specific provisions governing internal armed conflict (civil wars). Nevertheless, recent developments, as illustrated in the jurisprudence of the ad hoc international criminal tribunals, indicate that the characterization of a conflict is irrelevant for purposes of holding a superior responsible for offenses committed by subordinates. It is well-established that command responsibility is part of the customary international law relating to internal armed conflict.

Relationship between Article 7(1) and Article 7(3)

An accused who exercises effective control over subordinates who commit crimes may also be held responsible as a direct participant, depending on the facts of the case, although the recent trend has been to convict the accused under only one form of liability, the one that most accurately describes his or her participation. As a result, it is not uncommon for the ICTY prosecutor, for example, to allege simultaneously that an accused is liable under both ICTY Statute Article 7(1), on a theory of joint criminal enterprise, and under Article 7(3) of the same statute, on the basis that the accused was a superior.

When used together, these forms of liability provide the prosecutor with a variety of theories on which to charge an accused in command of or exercising authority over the perpetrators of serious violations of international humanitarian law. Perhaps the best example of this practice occurred in the *Prosecutor v. Radislav Krstic* case, in which General Radislav Krstic was charged under both Article 7(1), including joint criminal enterprise, and Article 7(3) for his role in the genocide at Srebrenica. The judges held that a joint criminal enterprise existed in the Srebrenica enclave and the object of this common plan was, among other things, the forcible transfer of the Muslim civilian population out of Srebrenica and killing of military-aged Bosnian Muslim men. These acts were committed with the awareness that theys would lead to the annihilation of the entire Bosnian Muslim community in Srebrenica.

Before the killings many of the Bosnian Muslims living in Srebrenica had fled to Potocari, a few miles from the town of Srebrenica, but within the Srebrenica "enclave." A significant number of those who fled to Potocari were the victims of murder, rape, beatings, and other abuse. The trial chamber made the following findings:

> The Trial Chamber is not, however, convinced beyond reasonable doubt that the murders, rapes, beatings and abuses committed against the refugees at Potocari were also an agreed upon objective among the members of the joint criminal enterprise. However, there is no doubt that these crimes were natural and foreseeable consequences of the ethnic cleansing campaign (*Krstic* Judgment, para. 616).

Thus, the crimes committed at Potocari were not part of the joint criminal enterprise "as agreed upon" by the members of that group. Although Krstic did not personally commit these crimes, he was convicted for the "incidental murders, rapes, beatings and abuses committed in the execution of this criminal enterprise at Potocari" (*Krstic* Judgment, para. 617).

Moreover, in light of the knowledge requirement under Article 7(3) of the ICTY Statute, it is interesting that the trial chamber stated the following in support of its conclusions:

> Given the circumstances at the time the plan was formed, General Krstic must have been aware that an outbreak of these crimes would be inevitable given the lack of shelter, the density of the crowds, the vulnerable condition of the refugees, the presence of many regular and irregular military and paramilitary units in the area and the sheer lack of sufficient numbers of UN soldiers to provide protection (*Krstic* Judgment, para. 616).

The "must have been aware" standard should be compared with the interpretation of the "had reason to know" standard rendered in the Čelebići appeal. It seems to be the case that if it can be established that a superior was part of a joint criminal enterprise, it may be easier to convict that superior under Article 7(1) than Article 7(3). Because offenses alleged under Article 7(1) typically result in a harsher penalty on conviction than similar crimes alleged under Article 7(3), it is clear that the joint criminal enterprise theory, and superior responsibility as either complementary or alternative bases of liability, play important roles in terms of prosecutorial charging policy.

In the *Prosecutor v. Milorad Krnojelac* case, however, a different trial chamber focused on the relationship between joint criminal enterprise liability and aiding and abetting liability under Article 7(1) on the one hand, and criminal liability as a superior under Article 7(3) on the other hand. The prosecution established that the accused was aware both of the illegality of the detention of non-Serbs in a camp where he was the warden and that his acts and omissions contributed to this unlawful system. Nonetheless, the trial chamber concluded that it was possible that the accused was "merely carrying out the orders given to him by those who appointed him to the position of [the camp] without sharing their intent" (*Krnojelac*, Trial Judgment, para. 12). Consequently, the judges determined that

> [T]he criminal conduct of the accused is most appropriately characterized as that of an aider and abettor to the principal offenders of the joint criminal enterprise to illegally imprison the non-Serb detainees pursuant to Article 7(1) of the Statute. As to the accused's superior responsibility for illegal imprisonment of non-Serb detainees pursuant to Article 7(3), the most which could have been done by the accused as a superior would have been to report the illegal conduct to the very persons who had ordered it. Accordingly, the Trial Chamber considers that it would not be appropriate to find him responsible as a superior (Krnojelac, Trial Judgment, paras. 127 and 173).

Conclusion

The theory of superior responsibility is a well-established principle of customary international law and has been developed through a variety of sources, including treaties, Security Council resolutions, and domestic and international case law. Moreover, command responsibility plays an important role in ongoing cases at the ad hoc international criminal tribunals and is likely to play a similarly important role at trials conducted before the ICC. Several important conclusions may be drawn concerning command or superior responsibility. First, the doctrine applies only to those commanders who exercise effective control over their subordinates. Second, this theory applies equally to all superiors who exercise effective control, whether military or civilian, provided that civilians exercise the type and scope of control normally associated with military commanders. Third, formal characterization of the relationship is not required and either de jure or de facto superiors may be held liable for the conduct of subordinates. Fourth, actual knowledge is difficult to establish in most cases, but there are several indicators from which inferences may be drawn that a commander had knowledge, and such circumstantial evidence may be sufficient to establish this point. Fifth, the mens rea requirement of either "knew" or "had reason to know" has not developed in a linear fashion and is likely to be influenced by developments emanating from the ICC, based on Article 28 of that court's statute. Sixth, the superior may not be held responsible for offenses committed by subordinates prior to the assumption of command by the superior. Finally, commanders must take action when they receive information that suggests a subordinate may have violated a provision of international humanitarian law.

SEE ALSO Complicity; Geneva Conventions on the Protection of Victims of War; International Criminal Tribunal for Rwanda; International Criminal Tribunal for the Former Yugolsavia; War Crimes

BIBLIOGRAPHY

Bantekas, Ilias (1999). "The Contemporary Law of Superior Responsibility." *American Journal of International Law* 93:573. Also available from http://www.asil.org/ajil/bantekas.htm.

Boelaert-Suominen, Sonja (2001). "Prosecuting Superiors for Crimes Committed by Subordinates: A Discussion of the First Significant Case Law Since the Second World War." Virginia Journal of International Law 41:747.

Jia, Bing Bing (2000). "The Doctrine of Command Responsibility: Current Problems." In *Yearbook of International Humanitarian Law*, Vol. 3. The Hague: T.M.C. Asser Press.

Mundis, Daryl A. (2003). "Crimes of the Commander." In *International Criminal Law Developments in the Case Law of the ICTY*, ed. Gideon Boas and William A. Schabas. Leiden: Martinus Nijhoff Press.

Parks, William H. (1973). "Command Responsibility for War Crimes." *Military Law Review* 62:1.

Report of the Secretary-General Pursuant to Paragraph 2 of Security Council Resolution 808 (1993). UN Document S/25704.

NUREMBERG CASES

United States v. Wilhelm List et al. (1948). In *Trials of War Criminals Before the Nuremberg Military Tribunals Under Control Council Law No. 10*, Vol. 11. Washington, D.C.: U.S. Government Printing Office.

ICTY CASES

Prosecutor v. Dragoljub Kunarac et al. Trial Chamber, Kunarac Judgment, Case No's. IT-96-23 and IT-96-23/1 (February 22, 2001). Available from http://www.un.org/icty/foca/trialc2/judgement/index.htm.

Prosecutor v. Enver Hadzihasanovic et al. Appeals Chamber, Decision on Interlocutory Appeal Challenging Jurisdiction in Relation to Command Responsibility, Case No. IT-01-47 (July 16, 2003). Available from http://www.un.org/icty/ind-e.htm.

Prosecutor v. Milorad Krnojelac. Trial Chamber, *Krnojelac* Judgment, Case No. IT-97-25 (March 15, 2002). Available from http://www.un.org/icty/krnojelac/trialc2/judgement/index.htm.

Prosecutor v. Radislav Krstic. Trial Chamber, *Krstic* Judgment, Case No. IT-98-33 (August 2, 2001). Available from http://www.un.org/icty/krstic/TrialC1/judgement/index.htm.

Prosecutor v. Tihomir Blaskic. Trial Chamber, *Blaskic* Judgment, Case No. IT-95-14 (March 3, 2000). Available from http://www.un.org/icty/blaskic/trialc1/judgement/index.htm.

Prosecutor v. Zejnil Delalic et al. Appeals Chamber, *Čelebići* Appeal Judgment, Case No. IT-96-21 (February 20, 2001). Available from http://www.un.org/icty/celebici/appeal/judgement/index.htm.

Prosecutor v. Zejnil Delalic et al. Trial Chamber, *Čelebići* Trial Judgment, Case No. IT-96-21 (November 16, 1998). Available from http://www.un.org/icty/celebici/trialc2/judgement/index.htm

Prosecutor v. Zlatko Aleksovski. Appeals Chamber, *Aleksovski* Appeal Judgment, Case No. IT-95-14/1 (March 24, 2000). Available from http://www.un.org/icty/aleksovski/appeal/judgement/index.htm.

Daryl A. Mundis
I am setting forth the above in my personal capacity. This article represents neither the policies of the Office of the Prosecutor of the International Criminal Tribunal for the Former Yugoslavia nor the United Nations.